Agriculture in the United States

A Documentary History

WAYNE D. RASMUSSEN is an Agricultural Historian in the Economic Research Service, United States Department of Agriculture, Washington, D.C. He received his Ph.D. in 1950 from George Washington University. In 1973, Dr. Rasmussen was awarded the Distinguished Service award of the United States Department of Agriculture. He is the editor of *Readings in the History of American Agriculture* (1960), and co-author of *Century of Service: The First 100 Years of the United States Department of Agriculture* (1963), and *The Department of Agriculture* (1972).

Agriculture in the United States

A Documentary History

Edited by

Wayne D. Rasmussen

National Economic Analysis Division
United States Department of Agriculture

Volume 2

Random House New York

Reference Series Editors:

William P. Hansen
Fred L. Israel

FIRST EDITION

9 8 7 6 5 4 3 2 1

MANUFACTURED IN THE UNITED STATES OF AMERICA

Library of Congress Cataloging in Publication Data

Rasmussen, Wayne David, 1915-   comp.
  Agriculture in the United States.

1. Agriculture — United States — History — Sources.
I.   Title.
S441.R33   **630′**.973   74–9643
ISBN 0-394-49977-8   Vol. 2

Contents

Changes in Farming (Continued)

Farming in 1869

From Joseph C. G. Kennedy (Superintendent of the Census), *Agriculture of the United States in 1860; Compiled from the Original Returns of the 8th Census*, (Washington, 1864), pp. iii–iv, viii–xxix, xli–xliv, cxxxvi, clxiv–clxix.

Preface

The importance of agriculture as a recourse for wealth, and as supplying the means of subsistence to all classes of community, is so well understood, and its relation to manufactures, so many of the products whereof it consumes, and which it supplies with so many of its most important elements, is so generally appreciated, as to render superfluous any argument to prove its value. It is an interest which, better than any other, may be expected to flourish as manufactures and the arts prosper, and it is of more importance to those interested in its advancement to understand its progress from time to time than to secure any special legislative acts with the view to stimulate its productions. Agriculture will prosper in proportion to the progress of population, and its employment in other productive pursuits. In the early history of all countries prior to the period when manufactures flourish, and the arts are cherished, foreign demand is relied on for the surplus products of the earth, and the ease with which they are supplied enables the producer to incur the cost of their transportation to market to procure certain necessaries and luxuries in exchange; but as a country becomes peopled, the relation of the producer to a foreign market insensibly becomes less, until at last it ceases, except upon peculiar emergency, or for articles restricted to climate. With an intelligent people, where land is abundant, the direct application of laws is of but little consequence in invigorating a pursuit which will be prosecuted with greater activity only with the ratio of increased home consumption, as foreign demand, with the exception of that for strictly climatic productions, is too precarious to justify any great expenditure of labor and means solely with a view to exportation; and that country of any great extent which never fails to produce a full supply of the necessaries of life for the wants of its own population, will be sure of ability to spare whatever may be necessary to fill any casual extraordinary demand abroad. Many persons are impressed with the belief that it is in the power of the government to promote the interests of the farmer, and that great and direct efforts should be put forth by the state to advance the science of husbandry. In our opinion, however, the surest way in which the power of the government can effectually promote agriculture, is by a steady and consistent policy adapted to encourage the arts and give confidence to the stability of our manufactures; population will then rapidly increase, commerce be promoted, internal improvements multiply, and the power of the state will augment as a natural consequence. Political laws will not modify climate, change the nature of plants, nor fertilize land; they may occasion the distribution of cotton-seeds north and west, but cannot insure the growth of cotton north of thirty-eight degrees, while private enterprise produces 8,000,000 pounds of tobacco in Connecticut, and will produce it wherever the conditions are favorable. The enlightened wisdom of the world, if applied directly to the improvement of agriculture, would not be productive of any sensible increase of crops, while any contingency tending to a greater consumption of the earth's products would be certain to stimulate the efforts of the husbandman, and insure enlarged production. That which renders the pursuit of agriculture honorable and remunerative, and therefore attractive and popular, is a certain home market; and wherever such exists there prevails a better system of culture, a more refined population, higher energy, a better morality, and in all things a happier condition both for the permanent welfare of the people and good of the state. It is under such circumstances that the merit and adaptation of every new plant deemed useful for food, or in the arts, will not only be cheerfully and intelligently tested, but its value will be made available. Under such circumstances the crops seldom fail, nor do the lands grow poor; the people are not addicted to efforts in short roads to fortune by impositions of marvellous productions at fabulous prices, and it is but seldom they are the victims of such. They never find abundant crops ruinous, nor realize the fertility of their fields only with chargin. Home demand for many products stimulates variety in cultivation, and increases the capacity of the soil, and as in this country scarcity seldom attends more than one staple production in a season, and then only to a limited extent, the nation is protected from all danger of want or famine so paralyzing to every interest, and so much feared in countries of more dense population, and of smaller area. The state or kingdom, therefore, which pursues a policy best adapted to consume as food, or in manufactures, the products of the soil, confers the greatest possible benefit, not only on that portion of its people engaged in agriculture, but upon all classes of population; and the most enlightened farmers only desire that the general government abstain from all legislation tending to make precarious a sure remunerative demand for its products, and observation proves that those who depend much for direct aid from government are not of that numerous class in our country who by their industry, energy, and success, present noble examples for imitation, and elevate and distinguish the pursuit of husbandry. There is not anything but confidence in certain adequate remuneration that will insure heavy crops of grain and grass, choice breeds of live-stock, produce good fruits, good wine, and develop an improved agricultural literature, and without such inducement we would no sooner expect the farmer to raise supplies of either, if the government should devote all its revenues to the free distribution of seeds and plants, than we would expect the mechanic arts to flourish without a demand for their products, should the government distrubute gratuitously the tools of trade; and there rests no more obligation upon the state to legislate specially for the one interest than for the other. By the anomalous policy at present pursued to promote agriculture, the government is sure to incur a large outlay of funds, often resulting in loss of time and disappointment to individuals, and it is an inevitable consequence of failure to equal cherished expectations, to perceive recourse to some novel fallacious expedients to blunt the edge of disappointment, or raise new hopes — at the same time charging iniquity or folly upon former administrators, rather than admit the impracticability of the resort and confess its failure. It was a remark of Buffon, that in "agriculture, as in all other arts, the model which performs best in small, oftentimes will not execute in great;" but our people have been too much tempted by highly colored representations, to build hopes on something new, which, although procured at much outlay, has not so much as been previously tested as to its adaption to our climate or soil by the most limited trial. . . .

Agriculture in the United States

In 1860, the agricultural area of the country embraced 163,110,720 acres of Improved Land and 244,101,818 acres of Land Unimproved. In other words, for every two acres of improved land there are three acres of land connected therewith not yet under cultivation; while the gross aggregate of uncultivated territory, fertile and waste, swells to 1,466,969,862 acres.

This fact gives color to the agriculture of the country. Land is abundant and cheap, while labor is scarce and dear. Even in the older-settled States there is much land that can be purchased at extremely low rates; and, by a recent act of Congress known as the Free Homestead law, every citizen of the United States, or any foreigner who shall declare his intention of becoming a citizen, can have a farm of 160 acres without charge. As good land as any in the world is offered to actual settlers on these easy terms.

Under such circumstances it is evident that the *intensive* system of agriculture which is practiced in some older and more densely populated countries, where labor is abundant and the land mostly under cultivation, cannot, as a general rule, be profitably adopted at present in this country. It has been said that American agriculture is half a century behind that of Great Britain. In one sense this is, perhaps, true. Our land is not as thoroughly under-drained, manured, and cultivated as that of England, Scotland, or Belgium; but we can, and do now, produce a bushel of wheat at much less cost than the most scientific farmer of England can by the best approved method of cultivation, *even if he paid nothing for the use of his land.*

We do not contend for a superficial system of agriculture. All that we ask is, that those who censure our farmers for not cultivating and enriching their land more thoroughly, should take into consideration the circumstances which have surrounded us. High farming involves high prices. The system of cultivation and manuring which is profitable in Great Britain would not be remunerative in the State of New York, because labor is higher and produce lower; and the system which is profitable in New York might not be advantageous in Iowa. An artificial manure that could be profitably used on wheat which brings $2 per bushel, might prove a very unprofitable application where wheat is worth only $1.50 or $1 per bushel. In the State of New York, where land is comparatively high and prices good, there are many instances where $20 to $30 per acre have been expended in under-draining, with great profit. But it does not follow that the same expenditure would be advisable in a section where the best of land can be purchased in fee simple for $10 per acre. The same is true of all other improved processes of agriculture. Their adoption is simply a question of profit and loss. Where land is cheap and rich, it will not pay to expend much labor and money in making or in purchasing manure.

But, it may be asked, "Will not the practice of raising crops without manure impoverish the land?" Certainly it will; but our hardy pioneers, having enjoyed the cream of the soil as a reward of their enterprise, go into a yet newer country, cut down the original forests, clear up the land, and raise all the grain they can. The money thus obtained is expended in the construction of roads, houses, barns, schoolhouses, churches, and colleges. Smiling villages and populous cities spring up, and in a few years the comforts, convenience, and even luxury of civilization are enjoyed — all the result of wealth which has been dug from the soil. Admitting that after all this is effected, the land is not so rich as when first cleared, and that more labor has to be expended in its cultivation, nevertheless much good has been accomplished. The fact is, this question of impoverishing the soil is not clearly understood. Much has been written on this subject, both in Europe and America; and a leading English agricultural journal, the Mark Lane Express, says: "It has long been our opinion that the grain-exporting power of the United States was likely rather to diminish than to increase under the ordinary circumstances of the country. This opinion was derived from the statistical notices of the census and of the Patent Office, and confirmed by the statements of Jay, Wells, and other American writers on the subject. These authorities have warned the agriculturists that if an alteration did not take place in the mode of cultivation, the United States would, in a few years, require a large importation of wheat, instead of being able to export to Europe."

This was written in 1861. Since then we have *exported more grain to Europe than during any former period.* The reason assigned for the opinion thus expressed, that the United States would soon become a wheat-importing instead of a wheat-exporting country, is "the scourging and exhaustive system of husbandry now practiced." There is *some* truth in these remarks. Our system of cultivation has been, and is now to some extent, a scourging and an exhaustive one. *It takes more from the soil than it returns;* and the time will come, as it already has in some sections, when wheat cannot be as easily or as cheaply raised as it was when the country was new. But it does not at all follow from this that the United States will cease to grow all the wheat it requires. We will have to manure our land and cultivate it better; but this is nothing more than has been experienced in other countries. We shall farm better as soon as such improvement is perceived to be profitable and necessary.

But what are we to understand by an "exhausted soil?" No phrase is more common in agricultural literature, and none more vague and indefinite. JOHN BEN-NETT LAWES, than whom there is no higher authority, speaking of his field on which his celebrated wheat experiments were made, says, it was purposely *"exhausted"* before the commencement of the experiments, and in another of his able papers in the *Journal of the Royal Agricultural Society,* he says: "All the experimental fields were selected when they were in a state of agricultural exhaustion." And he tells us what he understands by the term. He says: "The wheat-field after having been manured in the usual way for turnips at the commencement of the previous rotation, had then grown barley, peas, wheat, and oats, without any further manuring, so that when taken for experiment in 1844, it was, as a grain-producer, considerably more exhausted than would ordinarily be the case."

Here we have the highest English agricultural authority speaking of land as "exhausted" after having grown four crops without manure, the previous crop having been manured; and if this is all that is meant by exhaustion of the soil, we must admit that much of the cultivated land in the older parts of the United States has been exhausted. But one plat in Mr. Lawes's wheat-field has produced a crop of wheat *every year* since 1844, averaging about fifteen bushels per acre, and this without one particle of manure. It is clear, therefore, that the land itself was not exhausted, and in speaking of this as an agriculturally exhausted soil, Mr. Lawes simply intended to say that the *manure* which had previously been used was exhausted.

In this sense our farmers are rapidly exhausting their soil. The English farmer manures his land, grows three or four grain crops, and then considers his land exhausted. The American farmer cuts down the forest, burns more or less of the timber on the land, and scatters the ashes on the surface, then turns up the soil as best he may among the stumps, sows his grain and gets good crops. Why? Because the land has *been heavily manured by nature*. The trees and underwood have through their deep roots been drawing up mineral matter from the earth, and the leaves absorbi carbonic acid and ammonia from the atmosphere.

Shall he avail himself of this manure, or shall he let it lie dormant? What would be said of the farmer who should give his land a heavy coat of manure and then neglect to raise crops? If it will produce good wheat and other cereals that command the ready cash, is he to be accused of adopting a "scourging and exhaustive system of agriculture" for growing these crops? And yet this is what the American farmer has done. His land was rich, but he was poor and raised those crops which afforded the most immediate profit. We would not be understood as advocating the continued growth of grain crops without manure; our only object is to show the erroneous conclusions to which a misuse of statistical facts may lead, and to vindicate the American farmers from the charge so frequently preferred against them, of recklessly exhausting their soil. We think they have simply exhausted the manure which nature has spread upon their recently cleared fields, and that in doing so to a prudent degree, they were not wise.

But when this natural manure begins to fail, we must manure the land and vary our system of agriculture. That any of our so-called exhausted land can be speedily restored to its original fertility, we have abundant evidence. All that is necessary, is to cultivate the soil more thoroughly, under-drain where it is wet, sow less grain and more clover and grass, keep more stock, and make more and richer manure, and the farmer is wise who makes the transition from natural to artificial fertility easy and gradual, so as to avoid all sterility.

American agriculture is in a transition state. In the older-settled sections of the country there is much land that has been exhausted of its original fertility. Here the old system of farming, which was simply to raise all the grain that the land would produce, is no longer profitable. But yet some farmers, with that aversion to change for which they are everywhere proverbial, are slow to adopt an intelligent system of rotation and manuring, and cling to their old ways.

One of the ablest agricultural writers of England remarked some time since, that his only hope of seeing any great improvement in agriculture lay in the rising generation. This remark is quite as applicable to American as to English agriculture. We must look to the intelligent young men of our country for any great improvement in its agriculture, and it is a matter on which we may well congratulate ourselves, that even during the present terrible struggle, agricultural education is not neglected. We have two agricultural colleges in active operation, and others in process of organization. Our young men are beginning to realize that agriculture is worthy their highest ambition, and that in no other pursuit will intelligent labor meet with a surer reward.

Farming implements and machinery in use, value of.

STATES.	1860.	STATES.	1860.
Alabama......................	$7,433,178	Rhode Island	$586,791
Arkansas	4,175,326	South Carolina	6,151,657
California	2,558,506	Tennessee	8,465,792
Connecticut................	2,339,481	Texàs	6,259,452
Delaware	817,883	Vermont....................	3,665,955
Florida.....................	900,669	Virginia	9,392,296
Georgia.....................	6,844,387	Wisconsin..................	5,758,847
Illinois	17,235,472		
Indiana.....................	10,457,897		
Iowa........................	5,327,033	Total States	245,205,206
Kansas......................	727,694		
Kentucky	7,474,573		
Louisiana...................	18,648,225	TERRITORIES.	
Maine.......................	3,298,327		
Maryland	4,010,529	District of Columbia	54,408
Massachusetts	3,894,998	Dakota......................	15,574
Michigan	5,819,832	Nebraska	205,664
Minnesota...................	1,018,183	Nevada	11,081
Mississippi.................	8,826,512	New Mexico.................	192,917
Missouri....................	8,711,508	Utah........................	242,889
New Hampshire............	2,683,012	Washington	190,402
New Jersey	5,746,567		
New York...................	29,166,695		
North Carolina	5,873,942	Total Territories......	912,935
Ohio........................	17,538,832		
Oregon......................	952,313		
Pennsylvania...............	22,442,842	Aggregate	$246,118,141

Statistics of agricultural implements produced in the United States during the year ending June 1, 1860.

	No. of establishments.	Capital employed.	Raw material. value of.	Number of hands. Male.	Number of hands. Female.	Cost of labor.	Value of product.	Value of product in 1850.
New England States......	213	$1,021,800	$749,530	1,577	1	$ 534,837	$ 1,934,924	$1,662,426
Middle States.............	678	3,972,116	2,026,233	5,113	1	1,634,496	5,791,224	2,471,806
Western States	840	5,807,358	2,526,578	7,006	....	2,529,809	8,707,194	1,923,927
Southern States	241	664,265	310,569	1,095	2	356,232	1,018,913	784,452
Pacific States	10	11,700	12,259	19	....	15,300	35,705	....
Total	1,982	11,477,239	5,625,169	14,810	4	5,070,674	17,487,960	6,842,611
Scythes*..................	22	667,025	214,037	474	....	174,948	552,753	....
Shovels, spades, hoes, and forks*	53	961,000	865,068	1,183	1	413,540	1,635,676	....
Cotton-gins*..............	57	758,825	287,488	614	2	266,168	1,152,315	....
Total	132	2,386,850	1,366,593	2,271	3	854,656	3,340,744	....
Aggregate............	2,114	13,864,089	6,991,762	17,081	7	5,925,330	20,828,704	....

*Value of, not represented in 1850.

Agricultural Implements

Probably no exhibition of our national statistics is more important or satisfactory, than the foregoing tables showing the great increase and present extent of the construction and employment of agricultural implements and machinery.

The high price of labor has stimulated mechanical invention. In no other country are there so many cheap and efficient implements and machines for facilitating the labors of the farm. In older and richer countries we find more expensive machinery, but, as a general rule, it is too complicated and cumbersome for our use. We have been thrown on our own resources, and have no reason to regret it.

Whatever augments the productive capacities of the soil, or increases the profits of labor and capital employed on so large a scale, either in the first production or the subsequent handling of crops, becomes a practical element in the general prosperity. The vast power resident in machinery, even the more simple applications of the mechanical powers, with their modern perfection of detail, gives this creative force, which may be increased almost beyond computation by the use of steam as a prime mover. Thus, every machine or tool which enables one farm-hand to do the work of two, cheapens the product of his labor to every consumer, and relieves one in every two of the population from the duty of providing subsistence, enabling him to engage in other pursuits, either laborious, literary, professional or scientific, practically duplicating at the same time the active capital or the purchasing power of the producer, thus enhancing the comfort of all and stimulating the common enterprise.

When the utility of labor-saving appliances in agriculture shall come to be fully apprehended, and made generally available in the clearing, draining, and tilling of the soil; in the planting, irrigating, cultivating and harvesting of crops, and in their speedy preparation for market, we may regard the occurrence of famine, either from deficiency of labor, as in time of war, or from the contingencies of soil and climate, as practically impossible. Already has the use of improved implements, aided by scientific and practical knowledge in all the processes of the farm, resulted — like the use of machinery in other departments of industry — in such a diversification and increase of the forms of labor, and such a cheapening of its products under ordinary circumstances, that we rarely hear of the unreasoning and jealous violence of farm laborers, who in England, a generation since, wantonly destroyed all the agricultural machinery of a neighborhood, even to the common drills, in the mistaken opinion that its use was an infringement of their rights to labor. Its palpable advantages has disarmed the traditional prejudice of the husbandman himself, who is fast becoming as progressive as his neighbor. It has lifted much of the drudgery from the shoulders of the country-bred youth, who no longer loses his elastic step and suppleness of limb in the moil of the farm, which he once instinctively shunned as degrading, while he sought the lighter and more or less intellectual pursuits of the city. It has thus tended to elevate the pursuit of agriculture to its proper position in the social scale, as one of dignity and independence, and not one of mere physical toil, to be shared in common with the brute.

It is in the United States especially, where vast areas of improvable and fertile lands invite the labor of a sparse population, that agricultural machinery is capable of effecting its greatest triumphs. Far back in our colonial days the stream of emigration bore the young and adventurous of the Atlantic settlements toward the richer bottoms and prairies of the west. A gradual deterioration of the fertility of the soil of the older States from constant cropping, and the consequent increased labor required with the imperfect implements formerly in use, were sufficient to maintain the yearly exodus. Columns of hardy laborers from Europe have annually sought our shores, and for the most part have as promptly filed off in the same direction in quest of cheap farms, or in the more alluring search for the precious metals. As a consequence, civilization smiles upon the shores of either ocean, and looks down from the mountain summits which separate them. A prosperous and expanding agriculture, with most of the arts which it demands and fosters, has been rapidly extended over a territory of enormous breadth and fertility, which lacks only the labor of adequate cultivation to develope its vast resources in a wealth of cereal production as yet scarcely imagined. The very causes, however, which have opened up this territory to agriculture and the arts have produced and maintained a continued scarcity of labor, and kept its wages at a permanently high price. It is this enormous area of farm lands, and this great dearth of manual labor throughout the Union, that our inventors and mechanics have from an early period been invited to supply with labor-saving contrivances.

Fortunately the people of this country have not been slow to adopt the most efficient substitutes for animal power, and the inventive talent of the nation has found an ample and remunerating field for its exercise in originating and perfecting instruments adapted to all the wants of the farmer and planter. The great staple products of cotton, grain, and hay, have especially demanded the substitution of mechanical for muscular labor, and some of the happiest products of American skill have been the result.

Scarcely less valuable in the aggregate, however, are the numerous minor inventions whereby the labors of the farm and the household have been saved. Implements of this kind make up a large portion of the stock in trade of the makers and venders of agricultural wares. This successful application of the mechanics of agriculture has happily supplemented the rapid displacement of a large amount of rural labor called off by the war, manufactures, and the mines, and has itself in turn been stimulated by the high prices of produce consequent upon increased demand both for home and foreign consumption.

Evidence that this scarcity of labor in the United States has been a principal incitement to the invention and manufacture of agricultural implements is found in a late report of the Commissioner of Patents, who states that "the most striking fact connected with this class is the rapid increase of applications filed. Notwithstanding half a million of our agriculturists have been withdrawn from the farm to engage in military service, still the number of applications for patents on agricultural implements, (exclusive of reapers, bee-hives, horse hay-forks, and horse hay-rakes,) has increased from three hundred and fifty in 1861, to five hundred and two in 1863." The number of patented inventions belonging to the class of agriculture, previous to 1848, was 2,043, since which time the number has been vastly augmented. In the United States, as in Europe, the principal improvements in agricultural and horticultural implements have been made within the present century. As a branch of manufacture, this class of machinery has been wonderfully extended within the last ten or fifteen years, having received a great impetus from the exhibition in London in 1851 — where our own progress in this respect created so much surprise among foreigners — and the several international fairs which have taken place since that time. Throughout Europe and America, until a comparatively recent date, the implements of the farm remained extremely rude, primitive, and inefficient in form. Attention appears to have been first strongly awakened to the value of mechanical aids in farming about the period of the first introduction of agricultural societies.

The Royal Society, established in England in 1660, encouraged improvements in agriculture. But in the transactions of the Society for the Encouragement of Arts, Manufactures, and Commerce, instituted in London in 1753, we trace a still more liberal promotion, and a general interest in agricultural progress. These societies prepared the way for the establishment of purely agricultural associations. The first associated effort made in England to encourage agriculture by specific rewards was in the premiums annually offered by the Society of Arts after the year 1758, for experiments in husbandry, and for improved implements of the farm. The first agricultural society in Great Britain, the Society of Improvers in Scotland, established in 1723, encouraged improvements in tillage, and in farm implements, with such effect that "more corn was grown yearly where corn never grew before than a sixth of all that the kingdom used to produce at any previous time." About the same time Jethro Tull introduced — along with his system of deep tillage and thorough pulverization of the soil — the use of the horse-hoe, the drill, and other improved utensils, and became the greatest practical improver of agriculture in the last century. He even attempted an automatic threshing-machine, and incurred the usual charge of being a visionary innovator. The profit of drill husbandry was also demonstrated by John Wynn Baker, of Kildare, in Ireland, who in 1766 commenced a series of experiments with a view of systematizing agricultural knowledge by establishing fixed principles of rural economy, and showed by actual experiment that the saving effected by the drill and horse-hoe amounted in fifteen years to the fee-simple of all the tillage lands of the kingdom. He established as a part of his project a manufactory of farm implements, and issued a catalogue of seventy different machines and tools, all new to the agriculturist at that time. Agricultural machines were thenceforth made with more regard to scientific principles.

The earliest agricultural associations in the United States were established in 1785, in South Carolina and Pennsylvania. In the first-mentioned State, indeed, nearly a century before, the assembly passed "an act for the better encouragement of the making of engines for the propagating the staples of the colony," which was followed by legislative encouragement to various individuals who improved the machines for pounding and cleaning rice. In 1784 the assembly enacted a regular patent and copyright law, giving to the authors of books and the inventors of useful machinery the exclusive benefit of their productions for fourteen years. The Philadelphia Society for Promoting Agriculture, established in March, 1785, and after a period of inaction revived and incorporated in 1809, through the exertions of the Hon. Richard Peters, awakened much attention to the subject of improved implements and machinery, by means of a judicious system of premiums, and of practical essays. In July, 1809, Mr. Peters proposed to the society "a plan for establishing a manufactory of agricultural instruments, and a warehouse and repository for receiving and vending them." In that paper he states that no manufactory of agricultural implements in general existed in the United States, although the demand was prodigiously great. The proposed manufactory was to produce, under the patronage of the society, every implement of husbandry, both common and extraordinary, in use at home or abroad, if approved on trial; none to be sold without inspection and the stamp of the society's agent. His plan also embraced a collection of models in the manner of the Conservatory of Arts and Trades, established at Paris a few years before. The Massachusetts Society for Promoting Agriculture, incorporated in 1792, labored successfully to promote like improvements. The first statistics of the national industry collected in the following year embraced one small manufactory of hand-rakes, in Berkshire county, Massachusetts, which made annually 1,100 rakes, valued at $1,870. The census of 1820 gave very meagre information respecting this branch of production. Several small manufactories of ploughs, scythes, axes, shovels, hoes, &c., existed in different States, and one of patent steel pitchforks, in New Haven, Connecticut, turned out about $5,000 worth annually. During the next thirty years the business increased more rapidly, the traditional prejudices of farmers gradually giving way before the established utility of labor-saving appliances in the cultivation of the vast domain of our national agriculture. The form and finish of ordinary farm tools were much improved, and a few grand inventions were brought forward. In 1833 rice was successfully threshed out in the southern States by animal and steam power. The harvesting of grain by machinery, which had been several times essayed at an earlier period, was the same year attempted at Cincinnati, where the late Obed Hussey cradled wheat as fast as eight persons could bind it.

State and county agricultural societies were, during the same time, organized in nearly every section of the Union where they did not already exist. The system of annual fairs and exhibitions of farm products and machinery instituted by them, and encouraged by public awards of premiums, powerfully stimulated invention, and made our farmers familiar with the best forms of agricultural implements in use at home or abroad. Of like influence, but wider scope, was the American Institute in New York, which has made its influence felt in every department of industry.

The exhibition of the industry of all nations held in London in the year 1851 exerted a vast influence upon the progress of ideas on the subject of mechanical agriculture, as it did upon all other branches of art. The contrasts there presented between the highest results of modern skill and ingenuity exercised upon the implements of husbandry, and the rude models of the plough and other tools to be seen in the Indian department, little improved since the days of the Hebrew prophets, forcibly illustrated the agency of the mechanic and the engineer in the art of subduing nature to the will and service of mankind.

Although the number of implements of each kind exhibited by the United States on that occasion was small, the variety shown was considerable. The general excellence of American ploughs, reapers, churns, scythes, axes, forks and other implements, was acknowledged by the public admission of disinterested judges from all parts of the world, and the particular merits of many by the medals awarded, and by the number of orders received at the time by the manufacturers. The triumph of the American reapers marked a new era in agriculture, and gave a strong impulse to the inventive genius of Europe and America. The emulation awakened among manufacturers by the London exhibition was still further stimulated by the Crystal Palace exhibition, which took place in New York in 1853–'4, when more than one hundred American manufacturers competed for honorable distinction in this department of mechanics.

The influence of these exhibitions of the collective ingenuity of the world upon our own countrymen, in furnishing our mechanics with a standard of comparison by which to measure their own contributions to the world's progress with the most improved implements of the civilized world, and our agriculturists — already familiar with American instruments through our State and local fairs — with a view of the appliances of agriculture in other lands, can scarcely be overrated.

Credit is also due to the United States Agricultural Society for instituting a great national field trial of reapers, mowers, and other implements, held at Syracuse, New York, in 1857, for the purpose of testing practically the relative merits of different machines and rewarding special excellence.

The magnitude of the interests involved in the successful production of a new labor-saving implement for husbandry should alone prove a sufficient spur to inventors and manufacturers. A slight improvement in straw-cutters has enabled its inventor in a western tour of eight months with a model to realize forty thousand dollars. Another has been known to sell a machine to thresh and clean grain, after fifteen months use, for sixty thousand dollars. The McCormick reaper is believed to have yielded its inventor annually a princely income. A single manufacturer has paid the legal representatives of a patentee $117,000 in a single year for the use of a patent-right on an agricultural machine which others were making at the same time by contract with the owner.

From an article upon agricultural implements, published in the annual report of the Department of Agriculture, by the Hon. M. L. Dunlap, of Illinois, we are pleased to see that invention in this branch has not been stationary during the war. Among the principal competitors for public favor in prairie farming, to which his remarks chiefly relate, are the rotary spader with horse-power, which promises to be more effective than the steam-plough with traction engines, the latter having thus far proved a failure in moist or cultivated soils; the steel-clipper plough, with polished cast-steel mold-board; the two-horse cultivator or plough; the iron roller; the hand sowing-machine; reaping and mowing-machines, separate or uncombined; the sulky, wire-tooth horse hay-rake; the horse hay-fork or patent pitchfork; the horse-power thresher with straw-carrier and bagging apparatus attached; the drain-plough; the portable farm mill and the sorghum mill. But the statistics of the eighth census will measure the public appreciation of these and other new productions of American skill, and their influence upon the rural economy of the nation.

The cash value of farms under actual cultivation in the United States in 1850 was $3,271,575,426. Their value had risen in 1860 to $6,645,045,007, an increase of 103 per cent. in ten years. The amount of capital invested in implements and machinery for their cultivation in 1860 was $246,118,141, having in ten years increased $94,530,503, or more than sixty-three per cent. Thus, the fixed capital of the agriculturists in farms, and in farm tools and machinery, both increased in a ratio much more accelerated than that of the population, which during the same time augmented at the rate of only thirty-five and one half per centum. If we suppose the rural population to have increased in the same proportion with the whole, and the productiveness of the soil to have remained unchanged, we shall perceive that an immense increment of productive force accrued to the nation within ten years in the mechanical appliances of agriculture alone. Taking the aggregate number of acres of improved lands in the United States to be, in round numbers, one hundred and sixty-three millions, as shown by the returns, it would thus appear that the average value of farm implements and machinery for each farm of one hundred acres is only about $150, which is probably less than one third the sum that could be so invested with profit, at least in the older settled States. The greatest deficiency in this respect is found in New England, where it is only $1.34 per acre, probably due to the ruggedness of the country. In the middle States the value of machinery employed is $2.07 per acre; in the western States $1.56, and in the southern $1.48 per acre. Notwithstanding the evidence, therefore, of an improvement in the quantity and quality of implements, and inferentially of a better system of farming, there is manifestly room for further improvements in this respect, and ample encouragement to our agricultural machinists to supply the growing demand.

The production of labor-saving machinery, as will be shown by the tables of manufactures, was still going on to the amount of $17,487,960 in 1860, which was likewise an increase of nearly 156 per cent. over the value made in 1850, when it reached the sum of $6,842,611. This was exclusive of all articles made on the farm, which was formerly considerable, but is yearly decreasing as regular manufactories and depots for the sale of farm implements are multiplied, and their cost diminished. It also excludes cotton-gins, scythes, hoes, shovels, spades, forks, and some other articles of hardware, wagons, carts, and wheelbarrows, the value of which amounted to $11,796,941, and might appropriately be added to the above table.

Of the total product in 1860, nearly two millions in value was made in New England, being an increase of about sixteen per cent. upon the returns of 1850.

The middle States increased their production from less than two and a quarter to upward of five and three-quarter millions, or 134.2 per cent. The great States of New York and Pennsylvania returned, the one 333, and the other 260 establishments devoted to this branch of manufacture, and the increase in their product was 172.7 and 85.5 per cent., respectively, over the business of 1850.

In the western States the increase was most extraordinary, the value having augmented from $1,923,927 to $8,707,194, or 352.5 per cent. Their total production was nearly one-half that of the whole Union. Its increase alone was nearly thirty-nine per cent. of the whole, and nearly equalled the total manufacture of the United States in 1850. The States of Ohio and Illinois, together, manufactured to a greater amount than any other two States in the Union, the value amounting in the former to $2,820,626, and in the latter to $2,379,362, and the increase to 405.5 and 212.2 per cent., respectively. Iowa increased its manufacture 1,208.6 and Kentucky 755.4 per cent. over the product of 1850.

In the southern States the aggregate was but little over one million, and the rate of increase nearly thirty per cent. Virginia was the largest manufacturer, but in several there was a falling off from the product of 1850, after excluding cotton-gins, &c., as before mentioned.

The largest amount manufactured in any one county in 1860 was in Stark county, Ohio, in which fifteen establishments produced $900,480, the larger part of which consisted of mowers and reapers, and of threshing-machines and separators, in each of which three factories were employed. The next largest county production in this branch was in Cook county, Illinois, which made to the value of $529,000, chiefly in the city of Chicago. Of that sum, $414,000 was the value of 4,131 reapers and mowers made by a single establishment, the largest in the country. Rensselaer and Cayuga counties, in New York, each produced upward of $400,000 worth of agricultural implements, and a single firm in Canton, Stark county, Ohio, made reapers, mowers, and threshers to the value of $399,000.

From the New England States there is a considerable exportation of agricultural implements to the British provinces, the southern States, and other parts of the world.

That the large rates of increase in this branch indicated by the foregoing figures are not due simply to the increase of population, is shown by the fact that in Illinois, whose rate of increase with so large a population is without a parallel, the increase in value of agricultural implements manufactured in 1860, as compared with 1850, was 212 per cent., while the increase of population during the same period was only 101 per cent. In Ohio the population increased only 18.14 per cent., while its production of agricultural implements was augmented 417.6 per cent.

We subjoin a summary of the progress of invention in relation to a few of the more important instruments of this class, having given in the preliminary report an account of the progress in threshing implements.

THE PLOUGH. — Could the history of this machine, the type and pioneer of all other implements of husbandry, be traced from its origin, it would probably be found that few agricultural utensils have undergone greater modifications, or been more slowly improved than the plough. Originally, nothing more than the rude branch of a tree, with its cleft and curved end sharpened to scratch a furrow for the seed, possibly, as suggested by the ingenious Tull, in imitation of the tillage effected by swine, the instrument appears at this time to have been brought as nearly to perfection as it is possible to attain. The primitive plough, a ''mere wedge with a short beam and crooked handle,'' became in time fitted with a movable share of wood, stone, copper, or iron, wrought to suitable shape, as we find it in the hands of our Saxon ancestors. To this a rude wooden mould-board to turn the furrow was afterward added, and with various improvements in shape, continued in use until near the present time.

What was its form or efficiency in the days when Elisha was summoned from ploughing with twelve yoke of oxen, to assume the mantle and functions of the Hebrew prophet, may not be quite apparent, but the plough was certainly hundreds of years in reaching the imperfect state above described, and was several hundred more in approximating its present improved condition. In the middle of the last century the ploughs of southern Europe had been little improved, and were still destitute of a coulter, as in the old Roman plough of the days of Virgil and Columella. It has received few modifications there down to this time. Even in England, at that period, the plough was an exceedingly rude and cumbersome affair compared with the best now in use. It was no uncommon thing in parts of the island thirty years ago to see from three to five horses in light soils, and in heavy ones sometimes, as many as seven attached to a plough, which turned about three-quarters of an acre per diem. The old Scotch plough was still worse, and in Scotland, where agricultural machinery is now most perfect, no instance was known of ploughing with less than four horses. The usual number was six horses, or four horses and two oxen, and sometimes as many as ten or twelve were yoked to it, each requiring a driver. William Dawson, soon after 1760, introduced the custom of ploughing with two horses abreast with lines.

Although the swing-plough is believed to have been the earliest used in Great Britain, one and two wheel ploughs — long used on the continent — were most in favor. Turn-wrest ploughs, drill, drain, and trenching ploughs, and others adapted to different uses, were employed in considerable variety.

A capital improvement in the plough was the invention of the iron mould-board and landside. An approach to this was made by Joseph Foljambre, of Rotherham, England, who in 1720 took out the first patent of the kind recorded. It was for a mould-board and landside of wood sheathed with iron plates, the share and coulter being made of wrought iron with steel edges. One of these patent or Rotherham ploughs — as all similar ones were called for many years — was imported and used for some time with much satisfaction by General Washington, but, becoming worn, our ploughwrights were unable to repair it. The ploughs used in New England early in this century, and more recently in the south, were of similar construction. About the year 1740 James Small, of Berwickshire, in Scotland, first introduced the cast-iron mould-board, still using wrought-iron shares. During fifty years he continued to manufacture and improve the Scotch swing-plough, which, since made wholly of iron, has long been regarded as the best in use in England. In 1785 Robert Ransome, of Ipswich, introduced cast-iron shares, and about 1803 made improvements still in use, by making the cutting edges of chilled iron harder than steel, by casting them in moulds upon bars of cold iron. The making of the first iron plough has been attributed to William Allan, a farmer of Lanarkshire, in Scotland, in 1804, but an iron plough was presented to the Society of Arts in London as early as 1773, by a Mr. Brand. The cast-iron plough was introduced soon after. Like most other improvements in rustic machinery, the iron ploughs, though doing much superior work at less than half the expense of the clumsy wooden plough of that date, came tardily into use. It is said that Sir Robert Peel, in 1835, having presented a farmers' club with two iron ploughs of the best construction, found on his next visit the old ploughs with wooden mould-boards again at work; "Sir," said a member, "we tried the iron, and be all of one mind, *that they made the weeds grow.*" A similar prejudice opposed the introduction of the first cast-iron plough in America, patented in 1797 by Charles Newbold, of New Jersey, who, after spending, as he alleges, $30,000 in trying to get it into use, abandoned the attempt, the farmers declaring that iron ploughs poisoned the soil and prevented the growth of crops.

The plough has received many improvements at the hands of Americans, and has become an article of frequent exportation, while even in Great Britain the ploughs now used are generally made after American models. The year 1617 is mentioned by an early annalist as the "remarkable period of the first introduction of the labor of the plough" in Virginia. In 1625 we find the Dutch colony on the Hudson supplied with "all sorts of seeds, ploughs, and agricultural implements," to which in 1662 was added a first-class wheel-plough, with its pulleys, &c., at a cost of sixty florins. In 1637 the colony of Massachusetts contained but thirty ploughs, and Connecticut probably less than one-third the number. Nevertheless, the same year a resident of Salem was promised an addition of twenty acres to his original grant if he would "set up ploughing." We involuntarily think of the steam-plough when we read that another citizen of that town in the following year was allowed more land because he had "not sufficient ground to maintain a plough" on his farm of 300 acres. Owing to the scarcity of mechanical labor, most of the ploughs and other farm utensils were for a long time made on the farm, with the aid of the nearest smith. The casting of plough-irons was done at nearly every small foundry. Their make was, of course, clumsy and inefficient. Among the kinds still remembered by many was the Cary plough, with clumsy wrought-iron share, wooden landside and standard, and wooden mould-board plated over with sheet-iron or tin, and with short upright handles, requiring a strong man to guide it. The bar-share plough was another form still remembered by many for its rudely fitted wooden mould-board and coulter, and immense friction from the rough iron bar which formed the landside. The Bull-plough was similar in form, but without a coulter. Even the shovel-plough, not unlike the rude instrument still used by the Chinese, may be remembered by some, and was in common use in the cotton States a few years since. As early as 1765 the London Society of Arts awarded a gold medal to Benjamin Gale, of Killingworth, Connecticut, for a drill-plough, the invention of which was claimed by Benoni Hilliard, of the same place. The first patent taken out after the organization of the United States Patent Office was in June, 1797, by Charles Newbold, of Burlington, New Jersey, for the cast-iron plough already mentioned, which combined the mould-board, share and landside, all in one casting. He afterwards substituted wrought-iron shares, objections having been made to the cast iron probably because not chill-hardened. He did not succeed in getting them into permanent favor, although cast-iron ploughs were advertised for sale in New York in the year 1800, by Peter J. Curtenius, a large iron founder of the city. Newbold was paid one thousand dollars by David Peacock, a fellow-townsman, who, in April, 1807, patented a modification of the iron plough, having the mould-board and landside cast separate, with a wrought-iron steel-edged share attached.

As early as 1798 Mr. Jefferson also exercised his mechanical tastes in improving the mould-board of ploughs, which he afterwards adapted to an improved plough sent him by the Agricultural Society of the Department of the Seine, in France. His son-in-law, Mr. Randolph, whom Mr. Jefferson thought probably the best farmer in Virginia, invented a side-hill plough, adapted for the hilly regions of that State, and designed to turn horizontally, in the same direction, the sides of steep hills, which, in northern Europe, was effected by a shifting mould-board, constituting the variety called turn-wrest ploughs. Colonel Randolph's plough was made with two wings welded to the same bar, with their planes at right angles to each other, so that by turning the bar, adjusted as an axis, either wing could be laid flat on the ground, while the other, standing vertically, served as a mould-board. Mr. Jefferson advocated an adherence to scientific principles in the construction of the plough. Perhaps the first attempt to carry out these suggestions was made by Robert Smith, of Pennsylvania, who, in May, 1800, took out the first patent for the mould-board alone of a plough. It was of cast iron, and of improved form, the principles of which were published by him. In July, 1814, Jethro Wood, of Scipio, New York, was granted a patent for a cast-iron plough having the mould-plate, share, and landside cast in three parts. The mould-plate combined the mechanical principles of the wedge and screw in raising and inverting the furrow-slice. It became the foundation of many patented improvements of later date, and of a handsome competence to the inventor, who, in 1819, received a second patent, which was renewed by act of Congress in 1832.

A series of improvements in the cast-iron ploughs was commenced about 1810 by Josiah Ducher, of New York, which were patented in 1822. Some of them are still retained in use. Two improvements in the cast-iron plough, designed to make it easier of draught, were covered by letters patent issued in April, 1821, to A. L. & E. A. Stevens, of Hoboken, New Jersey. One of these was for hardening the cutting-edges and parts exposed to wear by cold-chilling them. Four other patents on the cast-iron plough were granted the same year. Much credit is also due to Joel Nourse, of Massachusetts, and his partners, for improving and perfecting the cast-iron plough, which was comparatively a rude instrument, in limited demand, as late as 1836, when they commenced the manufacture of agricultural implements at Worcester. The sale of twenty thousand ploughs in a single year by this firm, within twenty years after they commenced business, indicated the increased demand for ploughs, which they were able to supply, of one hundred and fifty different forms and sizes. Among these were *subsoil* ploughs adapted to teams of from one to six horses, the first implement of that kind in the United States having been imported by them in 1840 from Scotland, and subsequently improved by making it more simple, light, and cheap in construction. American hill-side ploughs are now exported to Great Britain. The number of patents granted for ploughs previous to 1830 was 124, and up to 1848 had reached between three and four hundred.

A distinctive feature in American ploughs is their great simplicity, lightness of draught, neatness, and cheapness, which is often in striking contrast with those of foreign make. This economy of power attracted attention to two ploughs sent, in 1815, to Robert Barclay, of Bury Hill, near Dorking, in England, by Judge Peters, president of the Philadelphia Society of Agriculture, the seal of which society, by the way, bears as a device a representation of the plough of the date of 1785. The ploughs referred to were made by order of Mr. Peters, to combine the best principles and forms of American ploughs, and when tested in August of that year against the best English ploughs, were found to do the work quite as well and as easily with two horses as the other did with four. American ploughs obtained favor with English farmers for substantially the same characteristics, namely, "extraordinary cheapness and lightness of draught," at the trial of ploughs at Hounslow during the great exhibition in 1851.

In the early part of this century the manufactories of ploughs in the United States were few and small in size. It has since become an important branch of the agricultural implement business. Ploughs were made and exported in considerable quantity at Enfield, Connecticut, previous to 1819. One of the largest establishments in this or any country, devoted chiefly to plough-making, was established in Pittsburg, Pennsylvania, in 1829. In 1836 it made by steam-power one hundred ploughs daily, of patterns adapted largely for the lower Mississippi, and cotton and prairie lands of the south and west. The iron-centre plough, and hill-side revolving beam-plough, were among the valuable modifications originated by the concern which now makes also the steel-ploughs so valued in prairie farming. Another steam-plough factory in Pittsburg made in 1836 about 4,000 ploughs annually, including wood and cast-iron ploughs, and a great variety of other kinds. These two factories, together, made 34,000 ploughs yearly, of the value of $174,000. There are several other extensive and numerous smaller manufactories throughout the country, particularly in the western States, in which plough-making is carried on as a specialty. It forms, however, a branch of the general manufacture of agricultural implements. In the best conducted of these, machinery is extensively employed, and such a division of labor as to secure great speed and perfection of workmanship, as well as a great reduction of the cost. For each size and pattern of plough, the several parts subject to wear are made all alike, so as to fit any plough of that class, and allow it to be readily replaced without the aid of the plough-right. Sulky-ploughs, with a seat for the driver, and gang-ploughs, cutting several furrows at a time, have been introduced, but have not proved generally satisfactory. Rolling or wheel coulters have, in many cases, taken the place of the old standing coulter. Many ploughs now have a hook attached for turning the weeds under the furrow, an important improvement for prairie farms, where weeds, like other vegetation, are luxuriant.

Several attempts were made in 1858, and the following years to introduce steam-ploughs, for which the Illinois Central Railroad Company offered a premium of $3,000. They have been employed with success for several years in Great Britain. English steam-ploughs are operated by stationary engines placed at one side of the field, and draw the plough from one side to the other by means of wire-chains. At other seasons the engines are used in driving threshing-machines and performing other farm labor. Our inventors have employed traction engines of several tons weight, which on hard ground worked satisfactorily, but on cultivated or moist soil were found to bury themselves inextricably in the ground. They appear to have been abandoned for the present.

A more recent machine, which promises to be a valuable one, is the rotary-spader, which, with the power of four horses, spades the ground eight inches deep and three feet wide, at the rate of five or six acres a day. It is rather too costly for small farms, but on large ones may prove valuable, and in time may be adapted to steam-power.

Many improvements have been made in implements for cultivating corn and other hoed crops, among which the horse-hoe or cultivator is exceedingly popular, and in corn-growing districts has nearly supplied the loss of manual labor by the war. The importance of frequently stirring the soil is becoming better understood, and in our dry climate the effects of severe drought may be almost entirely obviated by the use of the cultivator on rich, well-prepared lands.

Mowers and Reapers

These implements, making so large an item in the manufacture, deserve a brief notice. The great breadth of land devoted to grain in the western country has rendered mechanical appliances for gathering the crop altogether indispensable to the farmer. But contrivances for that purpose have long been in use. Pliny the elder, in the first century of our era, gives us the earliest description of such an instrument in use among the Gauls. It was a large van, or cart, driven through the standing corn by an ox yoked with his head to the machine, which was fitted with projecting teeth upon its edge for tearing off the heads, which dropped into the van. It is supposed to have been in use for several centuries. . . .

The first American patent for cutting grain was issued in May, 1803, to Richard French and J. T. Hawkins, of New Jersey. Their machine was propelled on three wheels, one of which extended into the grain. Samuel Adams, of the same State, followed in 1805; J. Comfort, of Bucks county, Pennsylvania, and William P. Claiborne, of King William county, Virginia, in 1811; Peter Gaillard, of Lancaster, Pennsylvania, in 1812, and Peter Baker, of Long Island, New York, in 1814. The next was the machine of Jer. Bailey, of Chester county, Pennsylvania, patented in February, 1822, which was a rotary mowing-machine, having six scythes attached to a shaft. Four other patents were registered previous to 1828, when Samuel Lane, of Hallowell, Maine, patented a machine for cutting, gathering, and threshing grain all at one operation. It does not appear, however, to have been successful. Only one other machine, that of William Manning, of Plainfield, New Jersey, registered in 1831, and having several points of resemblance to some now in use, was patented previous to that of Obed Hussey, of Cincinnati, Ohio, in December, 1833. The first public trial with this instrument was made before the Hamilton County Agricultural Society, near Carthage, July 2, of that year. During the next it was introduced into Illinois and New York; in 1835 into Missouri; in 1837 into Pennsylvania; and in 1838 the inventor established his manufactory at Baltimore. In June, 1834, Cyrus H. McCormick, of Rockbridge county, Virginia, received his first patent for cutting grain of all kinds, by machinery, which was worked in 1831, improved since, proving a source of large profit to the proprietor, as well as a great boon to this country and foreign lands. From that time to the present nearly every year has produced one or more modifications of harvesting-machinery, among which may be mentioned that of Moore & Haskell, of Michigan, patented in June, 1836, which cuts, threshes, and winnows grain at the same time. From the date of this patent to the issue of McCormick's second patent, in 1845, fifteen other machines were registered, including that of W. F. Ketchum, of New York, in 1844, which has since obtained a high reputation. Since 1851, the new machines brought forward have been numerous. In June, 1852, twelve different reaping-machines and several mowers were entered for trial before the Ohio State Board as contestants for the premium, all of them — including McCormick's and Hussey's — possessing nearly equal merits.

The United States Agricultural Society, in 1857, instituted an elaborate trial of reapers, mowers, and implements, which took place at Syracuse, New York, in July of that year, when fifteen mowing-machines, nine reapers, and fourteen combined mowing and reaping machines were entered. Medals and diplomas were awarded to several. Among those entered were Pell's, Manny's, Haines's (Illinois Harvester,) W. A. Woods's, (J. H. Manny's improved,) Seymour & Morgan's, Burrall's, Warder, Brokaw & Childs's, Atkins's, (automaton self-raker,) Moore & Patch's, and C. H. McCormick's, for reaping alone. Mowing-machines were entered by several of the same inventors, and also by Heath, Ketchum, Ball, Aultman & Miller, Hallenbeck, Kirby, Hovey, Allen, and Newcomb, and combined machines by some of the same parties, and by A. H. Caryl, Obed Hussey, J. H. Wright, and Dietz and Dunham.

The whole number of harvesting-machines produced in England and the United States up to that time amounted to 160 different kinds, about 100 of which were American; and in October, 1854, it had reached about 200.

The progress of ideas, or the different channels in which they have run in regard to the mode of action of the cutters of reaping-machines, has been shown by Bennett Woodcroft, esq., of England, in a patent office publication containing illustrations of sixty-nine examples of reapers, including nine American machines. In thirty-one of the number the motion of the knives was rectilinear, and in thirty-three it was circular, while in five the knives were moved by hand. Previous to the introduction of American reapers, the tendency in England was toward a circular action of the cutters; since that time reciprocating motion has been more employed. Although reciprocating and rectilinear motion was used by Salmon, in 1807, only two of the English machines introduced previous to 1862, viz: Ogle's and Bell's, were examples of that kind of motion, and three American, namely, Manning's, Hussey's, and McCormick's, while there were twenty-one of the other kind. Of later examples there were seventeen with reciprocating motion, to eleven with circular.

Diversities have also existed as to the mode of gearing the horse. Pitt's, Boyce's, Plucknett's, and Gladstone's machines were drawn behind the horses; Salmon's, Kerr's, Harke's, and other early English machines, were pushed before the horses, after the manner of the Romans and Gauls. In America both plans have been used, but since 1833 they have usually been placed behind the horses. By recently proposed improvements, horse-power harvesting-machines with four horses will cut twenty acres of grain in a day, at a net cost — including eight dollars for the use of the machine, a driver, two binders, and two hands to shock up — of ninety cents an acre, which harvested by hand would cost $1.90 per acre. The binding is now done with wire on the large grain-fields of the west, and a machine has lately been invented for performing that part of the labor. There can be little doubt that we shall soon have machines that will cut, gather, and bind up the grain at one operation. American reaping and mowing machines have now been introduced into every civilized country. Their usefulness has been universally acknowledged. In our own land, where labor is so high, and the season so short, they are indispensable. In many sections the labors of sowing and planting the spring crops are quickly followed by haying and harvesting. Corn, beans, potatoes, and other crops require the use of the hoe and cultivator. Summer fallows, for wheat claim attention at this time; and no sooner is the labor of harvesting over, than the American farmer is under the necessity of sowing his winter wheat, which in the northern and western States is sown from one to two months earlier than in England.

The nature of our climate, the character of our crops, the scarcity of labor, and the extent of our agricultural operations, all conspire to increase the introduction and use of these and all other implements and machines that will expedite the labors of the farm.

It is difficult to conceive that American agriculture could have attained its present condition had the invention of reaping and mowing machines been delayed thirty years. The extent to which they are already used is enormous.

The editor of the Genesee Farmer, Rochester, N.Y., has collected directly from the manufacturers the following statistics of the number of reaping and mowing machines made by a few of the leading firms engaged in this important branch subsequent to the returns of the census in 1860.

C. Aultman & Co., Canton, Ohio, made last year (1863) 3,100 "Buckeye" mowing and reaping machines, and this year (1864) 6,000 of the same machines.

Bomberger, Wight & Co., of Dayton, Ohio, have made 1,250 "Ohio Chief" reapers; and Rufus Dutton, who formerly manufactured the same machine, has made 3,156, making 4,306 in all.

Of the "Manny" reaping and mowing machine there have been manufactured in the State of Illinois, up to 1863, about *forty thousand*. In 1864 there have been made of the same machines in Rockford, Illinois, 10,500.

Messrs. Adriance, Platt & Co., of Poughkeepsie, New York, have also made 2,500 "Manny" machines for the New England States. The same parties have also manufactured 1,100 "Buckeye" machines for the New England States, New Jersey, &c.

S. M. Osborne & Co., of Auburn, New York, have made 15,000 of "Kirby's" mower and reaper. The Buffalo Agricultural Machine Works have also made 7,000, and other parties have made 5,000, making 27,000 of these machines that have been manufactured in the United States.

Messrs. Seymour, Morgan & Allen, of Brockport, New York, have made 7,200 of their "New Yorker" and other machines. Messrs. Warder & Childs, of Springfield, Ohio, also manufacture the same machine, and have made about 9,000.

The Messrs. McCormick Brothers have manufactured at their establishment in Chicago over 55,000 of their celebrated reaper — 6,000 in 1864.

The establishment of Mr. R. L. Howard, of Buffalo, New York, has manufactured 20,000 of the "Ketchum" mowing-machines, and 5,000 reapers and mowers combined, and 3,500 of the "Howard harvesters."

Mr. Walter A. Wood, of Hoosick Falls, New York, has made over 30,000 reaping and mowing machines. In 1858 Mr. Wood sent an agent to England with fifty; the next year he sent two hundred and fifty machines, and since then his sales in great Britain and on the continent of Europe have averaged over 1,000 per annum.

It thus appears that the manufacturers we have named have made two hundred and fourteen thousand and ninety-four mowers and reapers.

We present these facts, obtained directly from the manufacturers, that our readers may form some idea of the magnitude of the reaper and mower business. There are other machines manufactured of which we have not ascertained the number, but we may safely conclude that there have been two hundred and fifty thousand reaping and mowing machines manufactured and in use in the United States; the importance of which may be estimated, when it is considered that a common reaper will cut from ten to twelve acres in a day of twelve hours, and a mower eight to ten acres in the same time.

Another valuable implement for facilitating harvesting operations is the hay-unloading fork, with which, by the aid of a horse, a load of hay can be elevated to the stack or mow in a few minutes. Several varieties of these useful little machines are manufactured, and tens of thousands are already in successful use.

The wooden revolving hay-rake, (invented by Moses Pennock, of Pennsylvania, in 1824, and now well known in all parts of the country,) also greatly lessens the labor of haying. Fine steel-toothed rakes leave less hay on the ground, but for general use on American farms this wooden revolving hay-rake is one of the most simple, useful, and efficient machines yet invented. On large farms, the sulky wire-tooth rake is fast superseding all others. They throw the windrow into heaps or bundles of eighty or one hundred pounds each, ready for cocking or loading. A boy and horse can thus rake and bunch twenty acres a day. The hay-fork, or patent pitch-fork, is another recent improvement of value.

FOR THRESHING AND CLEANING GRAIN, we have machines which are confessedly unsurpassed. In our preliminary report we gave an outline of the progress of invention in this class of implements.

Nearly all threshing-machines now in use have an apparatus for separating the grain from the straw and chaff, and carrying the straw up on to the stack. This simple apparatus is now so common that it attracts no notice, except from the English or continental visitor, to whom it is a novelty. Many machines have also an apparatus for bagging the grain when clean.

The English threshing-machines, especially those drawn by steam, have a much more finished appearance, but for simplicity and efficiency they are in no way superior to those of American manufacture. In fact, wherever the American threshing-machines have come into direct competition with those of British and European construction, the American machines have proved superior.

Scythes

Although the genius of modern improvement promises ere long to rob haymaking of one element of the picturesque, it has not yet wholly succeeded in banishing the hand-scythe and mower from modern scenery. Tedious and laborious as its use appears, compared with that of the mowing-machine, it is wonderfully effective in comparison with the rude practice of the Mexican of our day, who cuts his grain and hay by handfulls with a common knife. It may not be generally known that the most valuable improvement made upon this implement for centuries was by one of the first iron-workers of Massachusetts, more than two hundred years ago, in the very infancy of the colony. In the year 1646 the general assembly of that province granted to Joseph Jenckes, of Lynn, a native of Hammersmith, in England, and connected with the first iron-works in that colony, the exclusive privilege for fourteen years "to make experience of his abillityes and inventions for making," among other things, of "mills for the making of sithes and other edge-tooles." His patent "for ye more speedy cutting of grasse" was renewed for seven years in May, 1655. The improvement consisted in making the blade longer and thinner, and in strengthening it at the same time, by welding a square bar of iron to the back, as in the modern scythe, thus materially improving upon the old English scythe then in use, which was short, thick, and heavy, like a bush-scythe.

The introduction of the scythe and axe manufacture into Massachusetts, Connecticut, and Rhode Island, is to be in a great measure ascribed to Hugh Orr, a Scotchman by birth, who came to Massachusetts about 1737, and a year or two after erected at Bridgewater the first trip-hammer probably in the colony. He engaged in the manufacture of scythes and other edge-tools, in which he acquired a wide reputation. His son, Robert Orr, by successful experiments, established the improved manufacture of scythes by the trip-hammer, and also introduced the iron shovel manufacture into the State. As early as 1766, samples of home-made scythes, shovels, spades, hoes, &c., were laid before the Society of Arts, in New York, and approved. They were probably from the manufactory of Keen & Payson, of that neighborhood, whose improved scythes, often called Salem scythes, then claimed to be superior in quality and form to any others. The non-importation and non-intercourse of the revolutionary period, and during the last war with England, encouraged the domestic manufacture of scythes and other articles of hardware, which, before the end of the last century, were made in different parts of New England in considerable quantity. Scythes were made in Plymouth county, Massachusetts, and to the number of two or three hundred dozens annually, at Canton, in Norfolk county, and also at Sutton, in Worcester county, which town had in 1793 seven trip-hammers and five scythe and axe factories. In 1810 there were nine factories in Sutton, and two in Oxford, and in 1814 seven others had been erected in the county, some of which could make 1,000 dozens annually. Scythes were at the same time made in Boston, and in 1803 the manufacture was commenced at Orange, by Levi Thurston, who employed in it the first tilt-hammer in the town. A few years later there were two scythe factories at Colebrook, in Litchfield county, Connecticut, which county in 1820 returned the largest manufacture of scythes of any in the Union. At Southfield, Rhode Island, large numbers of scythes were made at that time for exportation. As early as 1812, the scythe factory of S. & A. Waters, at Amsterdam, in Montgomery county, New York, turned out about 6,000 scythes annually. They were made at many small establishments throughout the Union, along with axes, sickles, and other edge-tools and cutlery, shovels, &c., by the aid of the trip-hammer, and were in good demand. The price in 1820 ranged from twelve dollars to eighteen dollars per dozen.

About the latter date was commenced, at West Fitchburg, Massachusetts, one of the oldest scythe factories now in the country, then owned by F. T. Farwell & Co., which in the hands of its original and later proprietors has originated many improvements in the manufacture, and given reputation to its well-known brand. At a later period, Harris's scythes, extensively manufactured at Pine Plains, in Dutchess county, New York, obtained a high repute, and are said to have been counterfeited in England. The mammoth scythe factory of R. B. Dunn, at North Wayne, in Maine, was a few years ago considered the largest in the world. In 1849 it turned out 12,000 dozens, requiring 450,000 pounds of iron, 75,000 pounds of steel, 1,200 tons of hard coal, 10,000 bushels of charcoal, 100 tons of grindstones, and half a ton of borax. About the same time, the scythe and cast-steel fork manufactory of D. G. Millard, near the village of Clayville, New York, made about 13,000 dozens of scythes and forks annually, by water-power. In 1860 Massachusetts was the largest producer of scythes, returning $168,550 as the aggregate value of the product of ten establishments. Maine ranked second in the value of its scythe manufacture — $129,363 by three factories. In New York, four establishments turned out scythes worth $117,440, and one factory in Rhode Island employed 100 hands, producing to the value of $100,000. The total value of scythes made in 1860 was $552,753, which was the product of twenty-two factories and 474 hands.

Shovels, Spades, Hoes, and Forks

These articles, intimately but not all so directly connected as the foregoing with agriculture, in 1860 gave employment, in five States, to forty-three establishments, the value of whose manufacture was $1,452,226. The hands engaged in them numbered 1,015. Upward of one-half the whole value was made in eleven factories in Massachusetts, which, together, employed 578 workmen, and produced an annual value of $777,048, being relatively much the largest concerns in the country. In New York there were twenty-three manufactories, whose product was $307,428, and the number of hands employed 233. Six factories in Pennsylvania employed 177 men, and produced wares to the value of $312,450.

The manufacture of these articles has long been an established industry in Massachusetts and some other States, having been commenced before the Revolution. The shovel manufacture was successfully introduced at an early period at Easton and Bridgewater, in Massachusetts, where the Messrs. Orr, before mentioned, were instrumental in establishing it by the use of the tilt-hammer. In 1788 the iron-plate shovels made at Bridgewater were deemed superior in workmanship to the foreign article which they undersold. The Easton shovel manufactory — commenced on a small scale nearly sixty years ago by the late Oliver Ames — made in 1822 about 2,500 dozen annually. The proprietor in 1827 took out a patent for improvements in the manufacture, which contributed to give his wares a high reputation, and greatly to extend and perfect the business of his establishment. In 1835, Oliver Ames & Sons had large manufactories at Easton, Braintree, and West Bridgewater, which employed nine tilt-hammers, and were capable of making forty dozen spades and shovels per diem, each shovel passing through the hands of twenty different workmen. They now run twenty-six tilt-hammers, and produce two hundred and fifty dozen per diem. In 1822 three factories in Plymouth county, Massachusetts, made from one to two thousand dozens each per annum. In 1831, it was estimated that about 5,000 dozens of shovels, worth $35,000, were made in New York State annually. It was computed that Litchfield county, Connecticut, at the same date made shovels and spades to the value of $6,500, hoes worth $7,150, pitchforks to the value of $20,000, and scythes valued at $56,000. A steel shovel and spade factory in Philadelphia consumed annually about fifty tons of American steel. The sheet-iron shovel was patented in 1819, and cast-steel shovels in 1828. The first American patent for improvement in hoes was registered in 1819, and for cast-steel hoes in 1827, by C. Bulkley, of Colchester, Connecticut. But cast-steel hoes were made in Philadelphia by at least two manufacturers in 1823. In Pittsburg, Pennsylvania, where scythes, sickles, hoes, shovels, and other hardware was made in considerable amount previous to 1803, Messrs. Foster & Murray carried on the manufacture by steam-power in 1813. On account of the fall in the price of iron and steel, superior steel hoes were made in Pittsburgh in 1831 for about $4.50 per dozen, or one-half the price of iron hoes ten years before. Socket-shovels were made at nearly the same price, which was about one-third their former price. Two large establishments in that place in 1836 made annually about 1,600 dozen steel hoes, 8,000, dozen of shovels and spades, 950 dozen steel and other hay and manure forks, and 600 dozen saws. Four establishments in 1857, in addition to nearly half a million dollars' worth of axes, made 32,000 dozen of hoes, worth $208,000, and 11,000 dozen of planters' hoes, worth $94,000, besides picks, mattocks, vices, saws, &c. The Globe Sickle Factory, in the same place, produced a superior article of sickles to a greater value than all the other factories in the United States. The Steel spring pitchfork was introduced by the late Charles Goodyear, by whom it was patented in September, 1831, at which time, and for several years previous, he was engaged with his father, Amasa Goodyear, in the manufacture and sale of hay and manure forks, and other hardware. Their store in Philadelphia is believed to have been the first in the United States for the sale of American hardware exclusively; but the failure of the business during the commercial troubles of that period led the junior Goodyear to abandon it for the new manufacture of India-rubber goods, with which his name will be ever associated in the annals of industry.

A firm in Philadelphia now manufactures eyeless or solid axes, hoes, picks, shovels, &c. The instrument is made solid, while the handle with which it is to be worked has upon the end an iron socket through which the pick, &c., is put, and kept in its place by an iron wedge. The handle does not become loose, and will answer for any number of tools of the same size, and the blow is rendered more effectual. Many of these tools have been exported to California, where they are prized by the miners.

There can be no doubt that our agricultural tools, such as hoes, forks, rakes, &c., are in most respects superior to those in common use in Europe. An English gentleman, who has spent some time in this country, says: "For lightness and finish, combined with strength and durability, American forks and hoes are superior to all others."

Dr. Hoyt, alluding to the great international exhibition in London, in 1861, says: "Among the minor implements of agriculture, we were both surprised and gratified to find a collection of American forks and hoes. The exhibitor was a sensible English dealer, who, discovering the superiority of this class of American implements as compared with articles of the same description manufactured in his own country, has for years been importing and selling them to his customers. On being asked why English manufacturers did not make them, he replied: 'We can't do it; have been trying ever since the great exhibition of 1851, but somehow don't succeed. It is a mortifying admission to make, but it is nevertheless true, that you Yankees have a knack of doing some things which we have not the skill to imitate.'"

Cotton-Gins

Although cotton-gins are made by a few establishments in the northern States, their manufacture is principally a southern one, and amounted in 1860 to the value of $1,077,315, which was the product of fifty-five establishments, all but three of them southern. Alabama is the largest manufacturer of machinery for cleaning cotton, having sixteen factories, employing 178 hands, and producing gins to the value of $434,805. Georgia ranks next, having twelve establishments, whose product exceeded a quarter of a million. The manufactories of cotton-gins in Mississippi are relatively the largest, three factories employing seventy hands, and returning an aggregate product of $131,900. In Texas, where the first cotton-gin was erected about 1823, there are four manufactories of gins. Many of these machines are made in northern machine-shops, along with other cotton machinery, from which they are inseparable in the general estimate of value.

The history of the cotton-gin furnishes one of the most remarkable examples on record of the power of a single labor-saving machine to influence the social and industrial interests, not merely of a single nation, but in a great measure of the civilized world. The simple mechanism of the saw-gin invented by Whitney enabled one farm-hand to separate the seed from 300 pounds of cotton fibre in a day, instead of one pound, as he had been able to do by hand. Its introduction at the particular period when the completion of the brilliant series of inventions for carding, spinning, and weaving cotton had created a demand for the raw material, at once directed into a new and profitable channel the agriculture of the south, and at the same time furnished the manufacturing industry of Europe and America with one of the most valuable staples, and the shipping and commercial interests of the world with an enormous trade in its raw and manufactured products. The increase in the growth and exportation of raw cotton which followed has no parallel in the annals of industry, save in the wonderful development of its manufacture in England and the United States. The effects of this growth of the husbandry and manufacture of cotton in increasing national wealth, in furnishing employment to labor and capital, and in increasing the comfort of all classes, can scarcely be conceived in all its magnitude.

In 1792, the year preceding the introduction of the saw-gin, the amount of cotton exported from the United States was only 138,328 pounds, and the total domestic consumption was about five and a half millions of pounds. During the next year there were exported nearly half a million pounds; in 1794, 1,601,700 pounds; in 1795, 5,276,300 pounds; and in 1800, 17,789,803 pounds. In 1860 the production of ginned cotton in the southern States amounted to 5,198,077 bales of 400 pounds each, or 2,079,230,800 pounds, which was more than seven-eighths of the total production of cotton throughout the world. The quantity exported in that year was 1,765,115,735 pounds, equivalent to 4,412,789 bales of 400 pounds each. To prepare this large amount of cotton for market by the primitive methods would have been utterly impracticable. Not only is the labor of the planter facilitated and cheapened by the use of the machine, but the cotton is much better cleaned than by the old methods, which left it unsuitable for the finer fabrics.

Although the earliest mode of separating cotton from the seed, and the one chiefly practiced in the cotton States previous to the invention of the saw-gin, was to separate the seed with the fingers; yet mechanical contrivances for that purpose have been long in use, having been chiefly borrowed from India, the cradle of the cotton culture and manufacture. In that country the practice of beating out the seed was long in use. A more effectual modification of the same method, employed for centuries in eastern countries, and very early introduced into Georgia, which took the lead in cotton husbandry, was the bow-string operation. It consisted in the employment of a long bow fitted with a multitude of strings, which being vibrated by the blows of a wooden mallet while in contact with a bunch of cotton, shook the seed and dust from the mass. Hence upland or short staple cotton became known in commerce as "bowed cotton." A form of the roller-gin appears also to have been used in India in early times, as mentioned by Nearchus, and consisted of two rollers of teak-wood fluted longitudinally, and revolving nearly in contact. In 1728 we find mention of "little machines, which being played by the motion of a wheel, the cotton falls on one side, and the seed on the other, and thus they are separated."

About the year 1742, M. Dubreuil, a wealthy planter of New Orleans, invented a cotton-gin which was so far successful as to give quite an impulse to the cotton culture in Louisiana, but nearly forty years later the colonial authorities in Paris recommended the importation of machinery from India for cleaning the seed.

Early in the Revolution, Kinzey Borden, of St. Paul's Parish, South Carolina, constructed a roller-gin, believed to have been the first ever used in that State for cleaning the long staple and silky cotton, of which he was one of the first cultivators. It consisted of pieces of burnished iron gun-barrels secured by screws to wooden rollers turned by wooden cranks, like a steel corn-mill. A Mr. Bisset, of Georgia, in 1788, contrived a gin having two rollers revolving in opposite directions, operated by a boy or girl at each, by which five pounds of cleaned cotton was made per diem. Nothing but hand-gins, resembling the cotton hand-mills of India, were yet known in the south, although foot or treadle gins appear to have been in use at this date in Philadelphia and vicinity, some cotton being then raised in New Jersey, Maryland, and Delaware. A great improvement in the treadle gin was made about the year 1790, by Joseph Eve, of Providence, Rhode Island, then residing in the Bahamas, and was patented by him in 1803. It was a double gin, with two pairs of rollers placed obliquely one above the other, and by adding iron teeth and pulleys, was made by a little assistance to feed itself. It could be worked either by horse or water power. Mr. Pottle, of Georgia, substituted two single rollers for the double ones, and produced a gin very popular in that State for some time. The present form of foot or treadle gin was first introduced into Georgia from the Bahamas, in 1796. It was improved in 1820 by Mr. Harvie, of Berbice, who obtained a patent, and afterwards by another person, who obtained a patent in the United States for making the rollers hollow, to prevent them from becoming hot while revolving. Other improvements on the roller-gin were patented in 1823, and subsequent years by Eleazer Carver, of Bridgewater, Massachusetts, who in 1807 commenced the manufacture of saw and roller gins in Mississippi and Louisiana, then a new country without saw-mills — of which he erected one of the first in these territories — or any machinery for manufacturing the several parts. The Whittemores, of West Cambridge, also secured patents for improvements on the roller-gin, which was in some respects superior to all others, but was found to injure the staple, and was abandoned. Other modifications of these machines were introduced by Birney, Simpson, Nicholson, Farris, Logan, Stevens, McCarthy, and others, several of which were popular in their day, and preferred in certain sections of the cotton States. The machines of Farris and Logan were improvements upon Eve's mechanism, and at a recent period were still used to some extent with steam-power. Jesse Reed, of Massachusetts, inventor of the tack-machine, patented cotton-gins in 1826 and 1827, the latter for cleaning Sea Island cotton, and the eminent American inventors, Jacob Perkins and Isaiah Jennings, each labored in this field. The roller-gin is especially adapted for cleaning the long staple or Sea Island cotton, the long, silky, delicate fibre of which is injured by the saw-gin. In the original machines, a pair of rollers worked by one hand would make about twenty-five pounds of clean cotton in a day. A recent improvement by Mr. Chichester, of New York, consisting of a fluted roller of polished steel, and one of vulcanized rubber, &c., is said to clean 300 pounds per diem, without crushing a seed. The Parkhurst roller-gin, though costly, is deemed a superior machine in Alabama and other cotton districts. The Louisiana cylinder-gin for short staple cotton, made by Jenks, of Bridesburg, Philadelphia, is also much esteemed for completely removing all extraneous matters without injury to the fibre. But as the Upland short staple, or black-seed cotton, was the first variety cultivated in the south, a means of removing the seed from its tenacious envelope was early sought, and happily supplied by the genius of Eli Whitney, a native of Worcester county, Massachusetts, under the patronage of the widow of General Greene, of Georgia, and her husband, Mr. Miller. Whitney's saw-gin, patented in March, 1794, was the first cotton-cleaning machine recorded in the United States Patent Office. Its appearance produced intense excitement, and numerous infringements of his patent rights, which involved him in expensive and vexatious lawsuits, and finally drove him into other enterprises, in which his ingenuity achieved reputation and success. In 1796 Whitney and partner had thirty machines in operation in Georgia by animal or water power, and in December, 1801, the legislature of South Carolina purchased the right for that State at a cost of $50,000, and threw it open to the public. One of the early invasions of the patent was by Hogden Holmes, of Georgia, who also patented a saw-gin in 1796. Two other Georgians the same year took out patents for saw-gins, and in 1803 another was taken for a saw-gin by G. F. Saltonstall, of North Carolina. Among other improvements on gins made by Mr. Carver, before mentioned, who had long experience in their manufacture, was the grate patented by him in 1823, which being placed where the seed is arrested and the fibre taken from it by the saw, prevented clogging, and the delay of cleaning the saw, &c. In 1837 he patented an improvement in ribs for saw-gins. Mr. McCarthy in 1840 connected a vibrating saw to the roller-gin, adapting it for cleaning both green and black seed cotton. This machine it was thought would supersede Whitney's, the fibre cleaned by it having brought three cents per pound more in the Mobile market than that cleaned by the latter.

The manufacture of cotton-gins has long formed a branch of business in the machine-shops of the northern and middle States, and an independent business in several southern cities. One of the earliest and most extensive of these concerns was that of Samuel Griswold, at Clinton, Georgia. In 1833 the business was commenced in Autauga county, Alabama, by Daniel Pratt, a native of New Hampshire, who had learned the business with Mr. Griswold. He there manufactured cotton-gins of superior quality for the neighboring southwestern States, including many for Texas, and even New Mexico, and acquired reputation and fortune in supplying the great demand, which required a branch house in New Orleans. His large accumulations were employed in erecting saw and planing mills, one of the first flouring-mills in Alabama, grist-mills, large cotton and cotton-gin factories, and other factories and tenements, forming the flourishing village of Prattville, where in 1851 he employed 200 hands, and made annually about 600 gins. He had manufactured since 1833 upwards of 8,000 cotton-gins. In 1846 he received from the University of Alabama the honorary degree of *master in the mechanic arts,* for the intelligent and benevolent exercise of his mechanical ingenuity and ample means.

We have thus very briefly, as compared with the importance of the subject, given a sketch of the rise and progress of the manufacture and introduction of some of the most important implements connected with husbandry. To some it might seem a subject better discussed in the volume on manufactures; but believing it to be one of special interest to agriculturists, we have not hesitated respecting the propriety of incorporating the facts in a volume prepared especially for the farmers of the country, with whose tastes and progress we feel a deep interest, and whose advantages in late years we can appreciate from experience. We hope we may be pardoned for referring in a public work to our personal experience in stating that, as recently as 1849, when we relieved ourselves of the cultivation of a farm in Pennsylvania to take charge of the census, nearly all the operations of agriculture, except that of threshing the grain, were performed by manual labor; and the number of workmen to be provided for, especially during the period of harvest, rendered several months of the year a season of family solicitude and drudgery. On the same farm the crops of the past year were sown and gathered in a much shorter time, in better condition, with one-fourth the number of laborers — the grain being cut by machinery, and the grass mown, loaded on the wagon, and transferred therefrom to mow by means of mechanical appliances. The effects of such changes upon the character of the rural population of our country will soon manifest themselves by their elevating influences.

Wheat

Bushels of wheat produced in 1860.

States.	Bushels.	States.	Bushels.
Alabama	1,218,444	Oregon	826,776
Arkansas	957,601	Pennsylvania	13,042,165
California	5,928,470	Rhode Island	1,131
Connecticut	52,401	South Carolina	1,285,631
Delaware	912,941	Tennessee	5,459,268
Florida	2,808	Texas	1,478,345
Georgia	2,544,913	Vermont	437,037
Illinois	23,837,023	Virginia	13,130,977
Indiana	16,848,267	Wisconsin	15,657,458
Iowa	8,449,403		
Kansas	194,173	Total, States	172,034,301
Kentucky	7,394,809		
Louisiana	32,208	*Territories.*	
Maine	233,876		
Maryland	6,103,480	District of Columbia	12,760
Massachusetts	119,783	Dakota	945
Michigan	8,336,368	Nebraska	147,867
Minnesota	2,186,993	Nevada	3,631
Mississippi	587,925	New Mexico	434,309
Missouri	4,227,586	Utah	384,892
New Hampshire	238,965	Washington	86,219
New Jersey	1,763,218		
New York	8,681,105	Total, Territories	1,070,623
North Carolina	4,743,706		
Ohio	15,119,047	Aggregate	173,104,924

States in the Order of Their Wheat Product in 1850 and in 1860

The census of 1850 showed that Pennslyvania produced more wheat in 1849 than any other State in the Union, 15,367,691 bushels. Ohio ranked second, producing 14,487,351; New York stood third on the list, 13,121,498; Virginia came next, 11,212,616; Illinois stood fifth, 9,414,575; Indiana, sixth, 6,214,458; Michigan, seventh, 4,925,889; Maryland, eighth, 4,494,680; Wisconsin, ninth, 4,286,131; Missouri, tenth, 2,981,652; Kentucky, eleventh, 2,142,822; North Carolina, twelfth, 2,130,102; Tennessee, thirteenth, 1,619,386; New Jersey, fourteenth, 1,601,190; Iowa, fifteenth, 1,530,581; Georgia, sixteenth, 1,088,534; South Carolina, seventeenth, 1,066,277; Vermont, eighteenth, 535,955; Delaware, nineteenth, 482,511; Maine, twentieth, 296,259; Alabama, twenty-first, 294,044; Oregon, twenty-second, 211,943, Arkansas, twenty-third, 199,639; New Hampshire, twenty-fourth, 185,658; Mississippi, twenty-fifth, 137,990; Connecticut, twenty-sixth, 41,762; Texas, twenty-seventh, 41,729; Massachusetts, twenty-eighth, 31,211; California, twenty-ninth, 17,228; Minnesota, thirtieth, 1,401; Florida, thirty-first, 1,027; Louisiana, thirty-second, 417; Rhode Island, thirty-third, 49 bushels; Kansas, no report.

The census of 1860 (crop of 1859) placed Illinois, which was fifth in 1850, at the head of the list in 1860 — 23,837,023 bushels.

Wheat-growing in the west. — The increased production of wheat in the western States in proportion to population has been most gratifying. Greatly as the means of transportation have increased, they have not kept pace with the increase in production. The navigation of the Mississippi becoming closed as a result of the present civil war, it was impossible to transport the large crops of the west to the Atlantic markets. Freight rose to such an extent that it cost more than *five times* as much to transport a bushel of wheat from Iowa to New York as the farmer received for it. The crops were sold at prices ruinous to the producer.

As the war continued, however, and as our western army advanced south, a demand for agricultural produce was created which gave buoyancy to prices, and at the present time (1864) the western farmer obtains nearly as much for his produce as the farmers of the middle States.

The effect on wheat, however, has been less marked than on oats, corn, hay, and other articles largely consumed by the army. The price of wheat is relatively lower than that of any other produce. So long as we continue to export wheat to Europe, the price will be regulated by the foreign markets, and the cost of sending it there. The bountiful wheat-harvest of 1863 in Great Britain and France, reduced prices so low that English farmers found wheat one of the cheapest grains they could feed to their stock. Had it not been for the high premium on gold, the price of wheat in this country, and especially at the west, would have been less than the cost of production; as it is, the advance in gold has served to increase prices in the west much more in proportion than in the eastern and middle States. For instance, if a bushel of American wheat sells at $1.25 in London, and the cost of sending it from Iowa is $1, the Iowa farmer, with gold at par, receives only twenty-five cents a bushel for the wheat.

Should gold continue at $2.50, (the price at the present writing,) though the wheat still brings only $1.25 per bushel in London, and the cost of sending it there should be $1 a bushel, as before, the Iowa farmer would receive $2.12 per bushel for his wheat, instead of twenty-five cents, as would be the case if gold was at par. The wheat is sold for gold, and $1.25 in gold sells for $3.12 in legal money. Deduct $1 as the expense of sending it to London, and we have $2.12 as the price which wheat should bring in Iowa. In other words, the premium on gold increases the price of wheat in Iowa *eight-fold*.

On the same basis, the farmer in New York, whose wheat costs only twenty-five cents a bushel to ship to London, would receive, with gold at par, $1 a bushel; and with gold at $2.50, as before, he would receive $2.87.

The premium on gold, which advances the price of wheat eight-fold in Iowa, increases it less than three-fold in New York. In other words, the *increase* in the price of wheat caused by the premium on gold is more than twice as great in the west as in the eastern and middle States.

These figures are not intended to represent the actual cost of sending wheat to Europe, but are used merely to illustrate the effect on prices of the present premium on gold. There can be no doubt that the western farmer obtains a relatively higher price for his produce, owing to the premium on gold, than the eastern farmer.

Of course any conclusions based on the present anomalous condition of affairs will be unsatisfactory. When we return to a specie basis, it would seem that the present high prices of produce in the west, being caused by the premium on gold, must rapidly fall.

For some time before the war our western farmers were beginning to complain that wheat-growing was not profitable — that the cost of transportation left them barely enough to meet the cost of production — and it was argued wisely, as we think, that it would be more profitable to grow less wheat, and raise more cattle, pork, wool, &c., the cost of transporting which, in proportion to value, is much less than that of a more bulky produce.

When things return to their natural channel, there can be little doubt that the west will find it more profitable to produce meat and wool, than to grow wheat. It was so for some years previous to the war, and will be so again when the war ends.

In the mean time the demand for wheat and other grain, induced partly by the increased consumption caused by the war, and the decreased production caused by the abstraction of labor employed in the mechanic arts and the military service, will for some years, probably, keep prices high enough to make wheat-growing at the west exceedingly profitable. The time must be expected, however, when the western farmer will again find the cost of sending wheat to the eastern cities and to Europe, so high as to leave him barely margin enough to pay the cost of production.

The western farmer for a year or two has been receiving high prices for his produce. He would do well fully to understand the causes which have led to this result. They are by no means permanent, and as long as we continue to export breadstuffs to Europe, and prices remain there as they are at present, nothing but a high premium on gold would enable us to command high prices for breadstuffs. When we return to specie payments, if we have a large surplus of wheat to export, it is vain to expect, as a general rule, anything like present prices in the west.

The rapidity with which manufactures have increased in the west, as well as at the east, render it highly probable that in future there will be a much greater home demand for agricultural products of all kinds, than existed for a few years previous to the war. Some of the largest coal-fields in the world exist in the western States, while iron and other metals are found there in great abundance. Everything is favorable for building up a great manufacturing interest. Whatever may be the result of the war in other respects, it seems certain that the price of manufactured articles must also continue high. The interest on our national debt, and the increased yearly expenses of the government, will require heavy duties on foreign manufactures; and this, in addition to the heavy expenses of transportation, will give the manufacturers in the west all the protection that can be desired. The discovery and development of the immense mineral resources of our western Territories, and their astonishing richness in gold, silver, and other metals, also favor the idea that in a few years the centre of population will be found in the west, whither it has been marching with steady progress, rather than in the Atlantic States. Most of the produce which is now sent east at such a great expense will be consumed at home, and the farmers of the interior will thus obtain a more equable market at fair remunerative prices.

There is, perhaps, no one fact which gives a clearer idea of the great growth of the west, and the increase of its products, than the amount of grain which is shipped each year from Chicago. In 1838 seventy-eight bushels of wheat comprised the total exports from what has since become the greatest grain market in the world. In 1839 it was 3,678 bushels; in 1840, 10,000 bushels; in 1841, 40,000 bushels; in 1842, 586,907 bushels; in 1845 it first reached a million bushels; in 1847 over 2,000,000 bushels. In 1851 and 1852 it again fell off to less than a million bushels; but in 1853 again rose to 1,680,998 bushels. In 1854 it was 2,744,860 bushels. In 1855, 7,110,270 bushels; in 1856, 9,419,365 bushels; in 1857, 10,783,292 bushels; in 1858, 10,759,359 bushels; in 1860, 16,054,379 bushels; in 1861, 22,913,830 bushels; in 1862, 22,902,765 bushels; and in 1863, 17,925,336 bushels of wheat.

Our official tables show that there were 173,104,924 bushels of wheat raised in the United States in the year 1859. In that year we exported to Great Britain only 295,248 bushels of wheat. In other words, out of every thousand bushels produced, we exported to Great Britain less than one and three-fourths bushels. In 1860 our exports of wheat amounted to 11,995,080 bushels, or, assuming that no more was raised that year than in 1859, over seventy bushels in each one thousand produced. In 1861 and 1862 the exports were even still greater — greater by far than ever before known, being 20,061,952 and 29,798,160 respectively — falling down in 1863 to 16,069,664. The closing of the Mississippi, and the loss of the southern trade, caused by the rebellion, together with the comparative failure of the wheat crop in Great Britain, accounts for this large increase in our foreign exports.

There can be no doubt that the west, directly or indirectly, is the source of all the wheat that is exported from the United States, and this in addition to supplying New England with breadstuffs. Under these circumstances, or such as are likely to exist, shall we continue to export wheat?

This question has been raised both in Europe and in this country. The question is not whether the western States can raise more than enough for home consumption. There can be no doubt on this point. But New England and the middle States are increasing in population, while their production of wheat is declining. Can the west supply this increased demand and growing deficiency of the New England and middle States, besides supplying the rapidly increasing home demand, and have a surplus left to export to foreign countries? Had the country continued united and prosperous, had the west continued to develop her rich agricultural resources with the rapidity of the last ten years, there can be little doubt that we should have continued for a considerable time at least to export wheat; but, with the increased demand caused by the war, with the abstraction of labor from agricultural pursuits, and the stimulus given to manufactures, it is a question not so easily answered, whether we shall, for a few years to come, continue to produce a surplus. Much depends on the middle States, to the productiveness whereof very slight improvement in our system of agriculture would add greatly.

There is no reason why the middle States should not raise wheat as abundantly as in past years. While the aggregate production of wheat has greatly decreased, there are farmers in every county who, by a judicious system of cultivation, raise as much wheat as at any former period. Let this improved system of farming become general, and the middle States would soon become large exporters of wheat, unless the stimulus given to manufactures shall greatly increase the home demand. Farmers are now receiving better prices for their produce than at any former period, and this is favorable to the introduction of improved systems of cultivation. With prices as low as they have ruled from 1850 to 1860, it was not clear whether farmers in the middle States could afford to underdrain, manure, and cultivate their land to that extent which is necessary for the production of large crops. This has been done in individual cases with much profit, but still the great majority of farmers could not see their way clear in expending so much capital, and, indeed, it must be confessed that it is not easy to show how *high farming* can be made profitable with low prices. All this for the present, however, is now changed. Prices have increased to a figure never before reached in this country. Everything that the farmer can raise, is in demand at rates which are highly remunerative. This demand and high prices cannot fail to stimulate farmers to put forth every energy to increase their crops. A higher system of culture will be introduced, and, when once adopted and found profitable, will be continued, even though prices should fall to the old standard.

There can be little doubt that the war is destined to make great changes in our agriculture. Farming never was so remunerative as at the present time. Hitherto, while the profits have been generally steady and sure, they have not been large, and the best talent of the country found greater attraction in other pursuits.

As a people we have been distinguished for our material prosperity. ''Labor is wealth,'' and this has poured in upon us from every country in Europe. This labor, directed by men of superior education and enterprise, has developed the vast resources of the country to an extent without a parallel in history. We had enjoyed a long period of peace. The expenses of the government were but little, people were active, industrious, intelligent, and enterprising. No wonder we became wealthy. But did our gains favor agricultural improvement? We think not, materially. Being rich, with none of those social distinctions which in Europe are kept up at such great cost, our wealth has been expended in luxuries. The result was, that those who contributed to our pleasures and the gratification of our tastes were more in demand and received a higher compensation than those who furnished the mere necessaries of life. The war will, in the end, make us poorer and more economical, and the time must sooner or later arrive when we shall have less to spend in mere luxuries; and those who furnish the necessaries of life will receive a higher consideration and better compensation. The importance of agriculture will be realized, and will attract the best minds of the country, and vast improvements rapidly follow, succeeded by enlarged production. This great change, however, will not be brought about at once.

It will require time to introduce an improved system of agriculture and to materially increase the productiveness of our farms.

In the mean time, it is highly probable that our exportation of breadstuffs to Europe will be materially lessened, unless a European war should greatly enhance prices. It is, however, to an increased home consumption that we look for those higher prices that will give that stimulus to American agriculture it has hitherto needed. As long as we continue to export wheat, no matter to how small an extent, the price in Europe will regulate the price in this country.

The price obtained in England for the 295,241 bushels of wheat which we exported in 1859 determined the price of our whole crop of over 173,000,000 of bushels raised that year. The price of the one and three-fourths bushel exported fixed the price of the thousand bushels consumed at home. If, for a few years, the price of grain in this country is determined not by what it will bring when shipped to Europe, but by the price at which Europe can furnish it to us here, and if we are compelled to forego some of the European luxuries which have of late years absorbed such a large proportion of our wealth, it will be no great misfortune to us as a people.

For the following remarks on wheat culture in California we are indebted to ex-Governor Downey to whom we are under great obligations for other important statements:

"Thus far in our history the wheat crop is next in importance to our product of the precious metals; yielding an abundant supply for home consumption, and a large surplus for exportation. All of our valleys north of the Salinas plains, in Monterey county, are admirably adapted to the production of this great staple, yielding from 30 to 60 bushels to the acre, and generally exempt from all diseases that affect and annoy the farmer in the Atlantic and Mississippi States. Our virgin soil as yet requires neither fallowing nor manuring, but year after year yields from the same field its heaps of golden grain. From the bay of Monterey to the head of Russian river, an extent of 250 miles, is one vast wheat field. Barley and oats are produced in great abundance, but their export demand is limited. The wild oats, which is fully as luxuriant as the cultivated, is one of our most important grasses, and, cut while the grain is in its lactescent condition, is considered the best hay in the world. From the 10th of May until the 1st of November the farmer expects no rain. He therefore cuts, threshes, and sacks on the same field, and houses in a sound and perfect condition, rendering it perfectly safe for the mill or the longest voyage."

Cattle and Cattle Trade of the West

It was not long after the first settlement of the interior of Ohio before the earlier pioneers perceived the absolute necessity for a market for the product of the soil. They had cast their lot in the midst of an extensive new country, where the land was eminently fertile; and the question, how could the product of that soil be advantageously disposed of, received their early and earnest consideration. The early great immigration would furnish a market for the time being, but the rapidly increasing production would soon outstrip this consumption, and to attempt to transport the surplus grain in its primitive bulky state was out of the question. The great distance from market would require it to be condensed to its smallest possible compass. The article of wheat might be made into flour, and by the means of flatboats or barges floated out of the tributaries of the Ohio river, thence down that stream and the Mississippi to New Orleans. This was the only practical way open, and that only, to any great extent, for the one product — flour; and notwithstanding the hazards and hardships to be encountered in that trade at an early day, the extreme scarcity of money, combined with the restless and daring character of the young men of that period, it was entered into with a will, and for a time the enterprise was generally remunerative, and oftentimes highly so. The trials and hardships of a flatboat voyage to New Orleans before the days of steamboats are but little appreciated by the present generation. To float a boat down to New Orleans was easy enough, provided they got safely out of the smaller streams; but the return-trip of nearly one thousand miles by land, the greater part of the way through an uninhabited and almost unbroken forest, was generally made on foot, and if the freshets in the smaller streams did not occur until middle or late spring, these trips were oftentimes attended with great mortality. Nevertheless, the trade flourished, and rapidly increased, until at length, some years after the close of the war of 1812, the supply so far outran the demand that the business became very precarious, oftentimes resulting in a loss to the shipper of almost the entire cargo. The consequence was the price of wheat was reduced so low as no longer to be regarded as the staple product of the western farmer, and indeed it finally ceased for a time to be a cash article; and it was no uncommon sight to see stacks of wheat rotting down in the field — twenty-five cents per bushel in store-goods or trade being the highest price obtainable by the farmer.

The large bodies of rich bottom-land lying on the borders of the tributary streams of the Ohio were not adapted to wheat-culture, and on the Scioto river much of the land was owned by immigrants from the south branch of the Potomac river, Virginia, where the feeding of cattle had been carried on for many years in a manner peculiar to that locality, and which materially differed from the mode practiced in Pennsylvania or further north. The cattle were not housed nor sheltered, but simply fed twice a day in open lots of eight or ten or more acres each, with unhusked corn with the fodder, and followed by hogs to clean up the neglected grains and ears; which practice was adopted here, and is still the almost universal method throughout the west, having undergone but little or no material change in fifty years. It may be worthy of remark here, that the method of securing the corn after maturity by cutting off the stalks near the ground, and stacking it in the field where it was grown in stacks of from twelve to sixteen hills square, also originated with the feeders of cattle of the south branch, the convenience and utility of which mode is made manifest by its general prevalence at the present day.

Although the business of fattening cattle was well understood by many of the earlier pioneers, and to find a market for corn was an anxious thought, yet they hesitated to engage in it. By many it was considered that the great distance from market would render that mode of disposing of their surplus corn impracticable; the long drive to an eastern market would so reduce the cattle in flesh as to render them unfit for beef; but some thought otherwise, and among the latter was George Renick, lately deceased, an enterprising and intelligent merchant, who, owning a considerable landed estate, concluded, himself, to try the experiment. Accordingly in the winter of 1804–'05, he fed a lot of cattle and sent them to Baltimore the following spring — (the first fat cattle that ever crossed the Alleghany mountains;) the result was a complete success. Thus was another avenue of trade practically opened, which for half a century contributed largely to the wealth of the Scioto valley; and from this small beginning the trade increased gradually, but not rapidly, until some years after the close of the war, when the failure of wheat to command cash gave a great impetus to the raising and feeding of cattle and hogs; for, although the selling price of such stock was very low, they were the only remaining cash articles of the farmer, and the cost of production was not very carefully considered. There was no alternative, as he was obliged to have some money wherewith to procure the necessaries of life, pay taxes, &c., and the business continued to increase rapidly until about the year 1850, notwithstanding the opening of the New York and Ohio canals in the mean time, had added greatly to the resources of the Ohio farmer by giving him access to a better and more reliable market, enabling him to sell for cash, not only his wheat, but every other product of the soil, at much more remunerating prices than formerly. The completion of the great through railroads added still further to the farmer's resources, enabling him to diversify his pursuits, and assisted in bringing the corn-feeding of cattle, so far as Ohio was concerned, to its culminating point. From his personal knowledge of the business, it is the conviction of the present Mr. Renick, that since then it has been on the decline. The whole number of cattle corn-fattened in Ohio may not have perceptibly decreased, but the home consumption, including the extensive barrelling, has greatly increased; but the excess or the number sent to an eastern market from that region has evidently, during the last decade, fallen off, and the cattle of late years are not so heavy nor made so fat as formerly. Mr. Renick gives it as his opinion that cattle can no longer be corn-fed in Ohio for the great length of time and in the profuse manner as formerly, with profit; indeed, in some of the largest feeding districts of twenty years ago the business has entirely ceased; and he very much questions whether the business can be profitably carried on as a leading one with the farmer in any locality possessing other ordinary modern resources, when the population of that locality exceeds fifty inhabitants to the square mile, exclusive of populous towns, and can then only be done profitably in a limited way, as a secondary or attendant on other pursuits of the farmer, and then in a different manner from that now generally pursued. The construction of the great through railroads, which tended to diminish the feeding of cattle in Ohio, contributed largely to its wonderful increase in Illinois and other western States, affording them facilities for reaching an eastern market of which they had hitherto been almost deprived — the distance the cattle had to travel *proving actually* too great, as the pioneers at first *supposed* it would, from Ohio; and though the railroads also facilitated the transportation of fat cattle from Ohio, adding but little to the cost, and saving to the drover near or quite one hundred pounds of flesh, on an average, to each animal, yet, by affording quicker and at all times a more certain conveyance for other things as well, particularly the article of whiskey, and the manufacturers of that article being able to pay more for corn than the cattle-feeders could possibly afford to do, they more than counterbalanced the advantages derived therefrom to stock-raising. Hence, in localities favorably situated for the sale of corn, the business of feeding it to cattle has become a comparatively unimportant one.

Before the era of railroads, to break the long drive, large numbers of stock or store-cattle were annually driven from Illinois and the west into Ohio to be fed there, and when made fat were sent to an eastern market; but that trade has now become almost obsolete. Formerly, too, the driving of stock-cattle from Ohio to

Pennsylvania and the east was conducted on an extensive scale, and indeed that trade, during the State's gloomiest pecuniary period, ranked as one among her chief resources, always commanding money in hand, however low the price might be; but that trade has also ceased, except to a comparatively limited extent from the northern part of the State into that of New York.

To avoid misapprehension, let us here say, that our remarks thus far with reference to beef-cattle in Ohio apply only to those made fat, or mostly so, on corn, as doubtless the number of *grass-fattened,* or those that have been but slightly fed on corn, has somewhat increased. Indeed, the whole business of fattening cattle has undergone a great change since the era of railroads. Formerly the great bulk of the corn-fed cattle of the west, nine-tenths of which were from Ohio and Kentucky, chiefly from Ohio, sent to the eastern markets, arrived there between the middle of April and 1st of August, and the markets of New York in particular were chiefly supplied from those sources during that time, and grass-fattened cattle were sent in the fall from Ohio in limited numbers, and no cattle arrived in those markets from the west during the winter or first month of spring; but now they are sent at all seasons of the year, and but few of those are so heavily corn-fed or made so fat as formerly. In a word, there is not near so much consumed in fattening cattle in Ohio now as there was twelve or fifteen years ago; yet there are, doubtless, more cattle partially fed now than then, but grass is more relied upon to prepare the cattle for market. Now is there the same *occasion* to make them so solidly fat as formerly, for the conveyance to market by railroad is a great saving of flesh over the former method of driving.

It is not to be understood that cattle are better or longer grazed than formerly, for the contrary is the fact; but formerly, when the business of feeding cattle on the Scioto river was at its height, say from 1840 to 1850, to make an A No. 1 lot of fat cattle, the best grades were fed some ten to twenty bushels of corn in March and April when they were three years old, and other cattle at the age of four years; they were then grazed throughout the whole summer and fall in the best manner, then fed from four to five and a half months all the corn they would eat — say full half bushel per day each before starting to market; cattle that had no corn the previous spring were well grazed and fed from five to six months. Now, cattle handled as the former would begin to go to market by the 1st of July, and all or nearly all would be in market before the 1st day of January. Quite a common way of prosecuting the business now is to commence feeding the cattle in January or February, *when less than three years old,* on corn in limited quantities, substituting more fodder or other rough feed, but increasing the quantity of corn in March or April, often to full feeding, say from twenty-five to forty bushels in the aggregate, per head, and these cattle will commence to be sent to market by the 1st of June, and by the 1st of October by far the greater portion will have gone; comparatively few of them, perhaps, having been detained to be fed on corn for a month or two before starting them. Of course the quality of the beef of cattle so young, and handled after this fashion, can bear no comparison with that as made by the former method.

The first introduction into the west of English cattle was made by Matthew Patton, (hence the name given to that celebrated stock,) who removed from Hardy county, Virginia, to Kentucky, about the year 1794, and brought the cattle with him. Patton had obtained the ancestors of this stock of Mr. Goff, of Maryland, in

1783, who had then recently imported them from England. John Patton, a son of Matthew, removed in 1800 from Kentucky to Chillicothe, Ohio, bringing a part of the same stock with him. Between that time and 1817, occasionally a few other animals were introduced, mostly of the same breed, but including some of an importation made by a Mr. Miller, of Maryland, between 1790 and 1795. These cattle, both Goff and Miller importations, were of very large size, and the cows generally good milkers, and when first introduced were a fine quality of beef-cattle — bone not large for the size of the animal — but on account of their great growth were longer maturing than the common stock of the country; but in the course of time their defects grew upon them. They became larger, coarser, and longer maturing, and of course harder to fatten. This change was attributed to the rich feed, which was probably the fact. We know that poor feed will degenerate, and it was probably this latter fact that led Count Buffon, the great European naturalist, to assert that all animals when translated from Europe to America would degenerate. The finest animal of the cow kind I have ever seen was of this breed; in the fall of 1819 this was six and one-half years old, and was estimated to weigh over 2,000 pounds, net beef. His head, neck, and limbs were remarkably neat, his brisket very deep and broad, and he girted immediately behind the shoulders the extraordinary measure of ten feet ten inches, and his back and loin I certainly never have seen excelled, if equalled. I have been thus minute in this description, because I have seen several treatises, or rather communications on the comparative excellence of the different breeds of cattle imported into this country, and all of them disparaging in a greater or less degree this breed of cattle. This breed proved an admirable one for crossing with the *common* stock of the country better, perhaps, than any following importation. In 1817 Messrs. Saunders, Zugarden, and ——, of Kentucky, imported from England five bulls — three short horns and two long horns — and eight or nine cows of the two breeds. The long horns being the most sightly animals, took the fancy of the people at first, and some of those having good stock of former importations wellnigh ruined them for the shambles by introducing the long horns among them. Their flesh was very dark and tough, without any admixture of fat, as a butcher's animal should have, and withal the cows were poor milkers. The short horns proved a valuable acquisition to the existing stock of the country, though the quality of their beef was perhaps no better than the Patton or Miller stock, nor were the cows better milkers, but their early maturity, and aptitude to fatten were qualities peculiarly desirable at the time, had they been properly appreciated and improved upon by the breeders generally. But unfortunately, in Kentucky in particular, the long horns got a pretty general dissemination before they were entirely discarded, and a practice of somewhat indiscriminate breeding followed, producing about as undesirable a stock for the shambles as could well be imagined. They were very large, but very unsaleable, and nick-named by the butchers of the eastern cities, "red horses." There never was enough of the short horned breed clear of admixture in the eastern markets for their shamble qualities to be clearly established by the butchers there, though in the west it was known to be at least not inferior to any breed then existing.

But it was not until about 1832 to 1836 that a general interest for the improvement of the stock of cattle began to be manifested by the farmers and cattle men at large. Hitherto it had been confined chiefly to a few individuals in different localities in Kentucky, Ohio, and other western States, though more general in the former. But the beautiful display at the county fairs (then recently revived) and elsewhere of the many beautiful animals of the English improved Durhams, imported by the different associations into Kentucky and Ohio about that period, combined with the almost fabulous prices which they would command, contributed in no small degree towards creating the general interest on the subject that followed, and which resulted within a few years thereafter in a great improvement in the quality of the stock throughout the whole west, greater, perhaps, than would have otherwise taken place within a quarter of a century. Nor were the people misled by appearances this time; for, after thirty years' trial, this breed, when well cared for, still maintains its English reputation of possessing, in a greater degree than any other stock, all the essential qualities, such as size, neatness of form, early maturity, aptitude to fatten, and the marbled admixture of fat with the lean in the beef requisite to make both the raising and feeding more profitable, as well as furnishing to the consumer a superior quality of beef. But the present management of these cattle, and their crosses, called "grades," is nowise calculated to sustain the hitherto high character of their beef among consumers. Apparently both feeders and drovers, not willing to be behindhand with the railroads, nor any other fast thing in this fast age, make haste to realize and hurry off their *half-fatted* stock to market at the early age of three years, thereby involving an absolute waste of "raw material;" whereas, if those same cattle were kept one year longer, and made ripe for the shambles, there would not only be a gain of full one-third in weight but they would produce a quality of beef not excelled in any country or clime.

The wonderful increase of late years both in the production and consumption of beef cattle in the United States, the one obviously keeping pace with the rapid strides of the other, has developed in part the capabilities of the vast western prairies, providentially provided beforehand to meet the wants of a great nation increasing in population and advancing in wealth and power with a rapidity wholly unprecedented in history.

The original or common cattle of the west were introduced into the country from various quarters, the earlier immigrants from Pennsylvania, Virginia, and other States bringing a greater or less number of cows with them, and the Indians furnished a part. Of course they were a heterogeneous collection; yet, in the process of time, in each considerable district of country of similar formation and resources; where there was no effort made at improvement, the stock assimilated or acquired characteristic qualities peculiar to itself, and so dissimilar from other sections as to enable the experienced cattle dealer to readily determine, by the general appearance of the stock, the region of country in which the cattle were raised. In the more hilly and timbered localities the cattle were smaller, of compact build, hardy, healthy, and easily fatted; whereas, in the more open portions of the country, where the feed was abundant, the stock became larger, looser made, coarser, more subject to disease, and harder to fatten; but the general effort made of late years to improve the stock by the introduction of improved breeds has rendered these local characteristics less distinguishable than formerly.

The manner of raising or breeding of cattle has undergone considerable change of late years. Formerly, when the price of land was very low, and the range extensive, it was the general custom of farmers and cattle men to keep more cows than were actually necessary to supply the wants of the family; indeed, many of them kept large herds of cows for the sole purpose of raising cattle. But that business has now, at least so far as Ohio and Kentucky are concerned, almost entirely ceased, though it is still carried on to a limited extent further west and south, more particularly in Texas, where, before the war, many individuals could count their herds by the thousand. Yet, even in Ohio and Kentucky, the number of cows has not decreased, but, on the contrary, doubtless has largely increased, more especially in Ohio, where, in addition to the largely increased home consumption, the extensive cheese manufactories and large export of butter of late years have rendered a largely increased number of cows necessary. The calves of these cows are, to a considerable extent, bought up by dealers in the fall who, perhaps, keep them a year, and then they pass into other hands, who, in turn, keep them another year, when the stock in large numbers passes into the hands of the feeders. This cannot be said to be the universal custom, but its practice is sufficiently prevalent to be designated as general. A very limited proportion of this stock is housed or sheltered during the winter, at least south of forty-one degrees of north latitude, unless it be the calves the first winter to some extent; nor is it the custom to house any cattle even while preparing for market. They are generally fed in open lots, though positions sheltered from wind and storms by timber or other natural obstructions are taken advantage of.

In communicating his experience with Texas cattle, Mr. Renick writes as follows:

"In the winter of 1853–'54 I had purchased for use about 1,200 head of cattle in the northern part of Texas, which section of country had been to a considerable extent settled by immigrants from Illinois and Missouri, and who had brought their stock with them; and this stock had not yet been sufficiently intermixed with the Spanish or Opelousas cattle further south to materially deteriorate their original qualities; consequently they were a much better and larger stock than I expected to see, though they had in some measure acquired the wild nature of the more southern stock. These cattle were brought to Illinois in the spring and summer of 1854 — the first, I believe, that ever came from Texas, at least in large numbers. This enterprise created quite an excitement in the northern part of Texas, and all my correspondents there manifested a strong desire to have this new trade continued and extended, freely offering their best efforts to encourage it, as they believed it would result advantageously to all concerned, and promising, if successful, to send north for a better breed of cattle, as they said, and with truth, that they could raise cattle and deliver them in Illinois, with satisfactory profits to themselves, for less, by one-half, than they could be raised in that State. In anticipation of this trade being continued the following season, quite a large number of cattle were brought up from points further south, and, as was expected, the trade opened lively; but an unforeseen difficulty exploded the whole business within the next two years. It was found that the southern or Spanish cattle were subject to an epidemic or contagious disease somewhat resembling the yellow fever in the human race, and so contagious did it prove that all along the track those cattle were driven the farmers lost large numbers of their cattle from that disease, many losing almost their entire stock within a few days. So serious was the loss occasioned by each drove of Texas cattle passing through, that the inhabitants of southwestern Missouri held conventions in divers places, and resolved that no more Texas cattle should pass through the country, and, by order of these conventions, armed bands or patrols were appointed, whose duty it was to turn back all Texas droves that might attempt to pass, which they did effectually. Thus ended what at one time seemed a promising trade. From the short trial, however, it became evident that, from the inferiority of the Texas stock as beef cattle, the trade would not have resulted as satisfactorily as was anticipated; the cattle were very light weighers for their size of frame, with but little room for improvement, and so wild as to be almost unmanageable. For oxen for the Santa Fe trade, or long drives over flinty roads, their hardness of hoof, their agility and endurance render them unrivalled; and, though they never lose entirely their wild nature, yet, when judiciously trained, they become quite tractable.''

The Pork Trade

The first general violations of the levitical law prohibiting the use of swine flesh must have occurred in comparatively modern times, inasmuch as that article has only recently become sufficiently well esteemed to be introduced largely into commerce. Since, however, it has been discovered to be one of the most easily produced, and about the most easily preserved of all meats, but few articles of food have come into more general use among civilized nations.

The raising of the hog has proved to be so well adapted to the varied systems or phases of agriculture in the United States, that in nearly all parts of the country it is carried on, and the animal made to serve as a popular and cheap article of food. The preparation of the meat, however, for commerce on a large scale, is confined mainly to those districts where Indian corn is most profitably raised, and where the winters admit of the process of cure with least expense and greatest certainty. This trade can only flourish where the extremes of heat or cold do not prevail, and is comprised principally within the region of country between the 35th and 45th degrees of latitude, and within the Mississippi valley. Farmers within this region have found the hog to be the best animal into which to condense for market a portion of the products of their farms; the quickest to come to maturity, besides requiring the least skill and labor to handle, hence best adapted particularly to the use of the pioneer, and is that most universally relied upon for domestic consumption and profit.

In quest of articles of cheap food, Europeans, gradually at first, more rapidly of late, have formed an appreciation of provisions of American cure. With increasing demand, necessarily came enlarged competition, both amongst producers and packers, resulting in marked improvements in breeds of hogs, in their preparation for market, and in the reduction of the business of packing to a nearly perfect system, as well as to fixed scientific principles. Within twenty years, especially within the last decade, the whole packing trade has undergone improvements as marked as has been its growth. The relations of supply and demand, though very irregular in a country so large and of such wonderful resources, have come to be more nearly comprehended and adjusted, so that much less risk is now incurred by the packer than in former years. Scarcely a particle of the animal is now wasted in the process of transformation into articles of food or commercial use, and the collateral trade in bristles, lard-oil, stearine, grease, skins, &c., has grown to be scarcely less important than the original one in food was twenty years ago.

The number of hogs which are used in the regular commercial packing business of the country can only, under the present system of statistics, be approximated. For the western States, through the efforts of private enterprise inaugurated in Cincinnati, it has become a matter of quite close calculation; but for the eastern States there are no reliable data on which to base a close computation. Of marketable hogs, such as would average 200 pounds net, it may be fair to estimate that the number packed in the entire country in 1859–'60, and entering into the commerce of the country, was 3,000,000 head, at an aggregate prime cost of $35,000,000. The cost of packing, transportation, &c., would add to this a value of near $15,000,000, making a total of about $50,000,000 capital employed. So many circumstances transpire to cause a variation in one season as compared with another, in the prime cost of the hog and in the expense of packing, that fair averages are difficult to arrive at, and those who engage in the business find that the most extensive experience furnishes but few data for reliable precedents. In great part the business has to be prosecuted each season in the lights of intuition rather than of positive information as to what may be the best policy to pursue. These intuitions, however, have given those engaged in the trade as much stability of position, perhaps, as merchants engaged in any other line of commerce, and causes the very large capital invested in the business to fluctuate now comparatively little.

The greatly increased use of lard for manufacturing oil, has made for it a relatively higher price than for other parts of the hog, in which the discovery of petroleum and its rapid adoption as a luminating and lubricating material seems to have produced no essential change. This fact can only be accounted for by the well-sustained demand for candles made from stearine, enabling manufacturers to keep lard-oil in constant competition with all similar articles, and to find their profit in the stearine. The future of the trade promises a growth rapid as the past. An increasing manufacturing population and constant large augmentation of laboring force from foreign emigration, the yearly increasing acceptability of American packed provisions as articles of cheap food in foreign countries, all unite in assuring a consumption that will grow in equal pace with the production, and maintain for the pork trade its prominent position among the great commercial interests of the country.

The Grain Trade of the United States

The grain trade of the United States, viewed in all its features, is one of the chief marvels of modern commercial history. To trace its rise and progress would be almost to complete a record of the development of this entire continent, for it has been the leading agency in the opening up of seven-eighths of our settled territory. First, in the march of civilization, came the pioneer husbandman, and following close on his footsteps was the merchant; and after him were created in rapid succession our ocean and lake fleets, our canals, our wonderful network of railroads, and, in fact, our whole commercial system.

The grain merchant has been in all countries, but more particularly in this, the pioneer of commerce, whether we refer to the ocean or the inland trade, and not till he was established could other commercial adventurers find a foothold. The commercial history of the United States is based mainly on breadstuffs — staples always marketable at some quotation wherever the human family dwells.

The exportation of American products to foreign countries continues to form one of the chief characteristics of our national commerce. The development of our agricultural resources, and the increasing demands of Europe, particularly England, for foreign breadstuffs, seem to have continued at pretty regular pace. As the production of the United States increased, new and more extensive markets were thrown open — illustrating a grand design of Providence in thus developing a New World to feed the rapidly increasing populations of the Old, and supply homes for their redundant numbers. For upwards of a quarter of a century the extension of the manufacturing interests of Great Britain has been gradually but surely rendering that country more and more dependent upon other nations for the breadstuffs with which to feed her people; and from a grain-exporting country, as she was only half a century since, she now finds herself in a position in which she has to import annually from nine to fifteen millions of quarters of grain. Had that country twenty-five years ago been as dependent as she is now upon other nations, with the grain resources of that period, there would have been much suffering among the poorer classes everywhere; while on the other hand, without this European demand for the grain produced in the United States, the same inducements for opening up the fertile lands of the western States would not have existed. Capitalists would not have been encouraged to construct our immense canals, and lines of railroads, nor to have built our fleets of grain-carrying vessels to traverse the lakes and seas. The steady and increasing demand for American breadstuffs in Europe, however, greatly stimulated the production — made the unbroken and wild, yet fertile wilderness and prairie attractive to the agriculturists of all countries, and created a commerce for which history has few parallels. At the same time it has enriched our country beyond all calculation, enabled us to pay our European debts, given us an enterprising population, drawn from the industrious classes of every nationality, state, or kingdom in the Old World, and has endowed millions of human beings with wealth and the rights and privileges of free institutions.

Commencing at an early period with the scant products of the Atlantic States, the grain trade was gradually pushed up the Hudson river as far as navigation would permit; and where that ceased, the Erie canal commenced and carried it to the great lakes. It was on the completion of this great achievement that the real history of the grain trade of the United States began. Then it was that our "inland seas" became the highway of a commerce which has already attained a magnitude surpassing that of many of the oldest European nations. Then it was that the vast territory west of the lakes, hitherto the home of the "red man," and range for the buffalo, became the attractive field for the enterprising pioneers of industry and civilization, who laid the foundations of what are now seven large and flourishing States of the Union, peopled by a population vigorous and hardy, and well calculated to succeed either in the arts of peace or war.

At the same time, the grain trade was steadily progressing up the Mississippi river into the heart of the west, and on whose banks were built large and flourishing cities, the great depots for nearly a quarter of a century for the products of the rich valley of that river.

The grain trade has progressed, year after year, from small beginnings, till now it has become one of the leading interests of the country, and among the most important in its influence on the world, as on it depends much of the peace, happiness, and prosperity, not only of the people of the United States, but also of many of the kingdoms of Europe.

Influence of Railroads Upon Agriculture

The first impression made on the popular mind by any great improvement in machinery or locomotion, after the admission of their beneficial effect, is that they will, in some way or other, diminish the demand for labor or for other machinery. Hence it was that in Europe the introduction of printing was denounced on account of its supposed tendency to diminish the employment of writers or copyists, and the associations of individuals against its employment, similar to the opposition subsequently manifested to the use of labor-saving machinery in manufactures. It was long before this prejudice could be overthrown, but the subject is now much better understood. It is now established, as a general principle, that machines facilitating labor increase the amount of labor required. This is done chiefly by cheapening the products of labor so that more can be consumed, and ultimately more labor employed. The introduction of cotton and wool machinery was followed by outbreaks of workmen against machinery; yet nothing is more certain than that hundreds of thousands of men and women are employed in the manufacture of cotton who would not have been if machinery had not cheapened cotton cloth so that it could be introduced into general use. So it might be assumed that the introduction of sewing-machines would at once throw many sewing women out of employment; but such is not the fact. Many more sewing women are now employed than there were before the sewing-machine was introduced. In the same way the influence of railroads was at first very much misconceived; even among civil engineers the vast power of steam and of cohesion on the tracks were not understood. On the completion of the Liverpool and Manchester railway, some of the ablest engineers laid it down as a settled principle that railroads would not be able to carry heavy freights, and their business must be confined to the carriage of passengers. It was also considered impracticable to ascend over fifty feet per mile with ordinary locomotives; as a consequence of this theory *inclined planes* were for several years made wherever the grade was over fifty feet. If this practice had continued, it must obviously have proved a great obstruction to the carriage of heavy freight. Time and inventive genius have happily overcome all these difficulties; but still, in this, as in other cases, there was an idea that the transportation of agricultural products would result in diminishing the number of horses, wagoners, and steamboats. Indeed, this would seem a natural, if not a necessary, effect of transporting immense quantities of agricultural produce by a machinery which did not before exist. The result, however, proves precisely the contrary. Horses have multiplied more rapidly since the introduction of locomotives than they did before; and even steamboats, on such rivers as the Ohio and the Mississippi, where the recently constructed railroads have been in direct competition with them, have continued to increase almost without interruption. Before we look at the general results of railroads on the agricultural interests, we will glance at their incidental connexion with the other means of transportation. Take, for example, the increase of horses in connexion with the increase of railroads.

The following is the number and increase of horses in the last twenty years, including mules and asses:

	No. of horses.	Increase.
In 1840	4,335,669	
In 1850	4,896,050	12 per cent.
In 1860	7,400,322	51 per cent.

Three-fourths of all the miles of railroad have been made since 1850; and we see that since then the increase of horses has been the greatest. If we pursue this inquiry a little further, we shall find that horses have increased the most in those States in which the greatest extent of railroads has been made since 1850. Take, for example, the number of horses employed in agriculture and for other purposes in the five great States of the west:

Number of horses employed in agriculture and for other purposes in the five great States of the west:

States.	1850.	1860.	Increase, per cent.
Ohio	466,820	753,881	61
Indiana	320,898	592,069	84
Illinois	278,626	724,138	160
Michigan	58,576	167,999	186
Wisconsin	30,335	145,584	380
Aggregate	1,155,255	2,383,671	106

In these five States there have been constructed since 1850 nearly nine thousand miles of railroad; and yet there we find this extraordinary increase in the number of horses. We do not present this as evidence that the construction of railroads necessarily augments the demand therefor, and therefore increases the number of horses, although we have no doubt that such is the case; but simply to show that railroads have not diminished one of the great elements in competing means of transportation. It must be recollected that only forty years ago the only means of transporting goods and products between the eastern and western States was by wagons, and that the business of transportation in this way was as much a business, on relatively as large a scale, as that of transportation by canal and railway is now. The first great change in this mode of transportation was by the New York and Pennsylvania canal; but the whole business of the canals in the first years of their introduction was small in comparison with that of the railroads now. Hence it seemed that railroads must diminish the number and importance of horses, but such was not the fact; and we shall see in this, as in the case of all animals, that railroads tend to increase their number and value. This is now an established principle, which we shall illustrate in regard to other domestic animals.

Although but slightly connected with the interests of agriculture, we may here state another fact, that since the introduction of railroads, the building and employment of steamboats on our interior rivers have also increased largely, so that, even where railroads have competed directly with them, the steamboat interest has continued to increase in value and importance. This has not been always, we admit, in direct proportion to the growth of the country, but enough to show that, even where competition was greatest, this interest has not been injuriously affected. More than double the number of steamers were built on the waters of the interior west in 1861 than were in 1850.

We advance these facts, not so much to show the direct and positive influence of railroads on agriculture, as to show that there is no interest of agriculture and commerce that railroads have injured, even, when upon the most plausible theories, such results were anticipated.

We now proceed to show the positive advantages which all departments of agriculture have derived from the construction of railroads. So great are their benefits that, if the entire cost of railroads between the Atlantic and western States had been levied on the farmers of the central west, their proprietors could have paid it and been immensely the gainers. This proposition will become evident if we look at the modes in which railroads have been beneficial, especially in the grain-growing States. These modes are, first, in doing what could not have been effected without them; second, in securing to the producer very nearly the prices of the Atlantic markets, which is greatly in advance of what could have been had on his farm; and, third, by thus enabling the producer to dispose of his products at the best prices at all times, and to increase rapidly both the settlement and the annual production of the interior States. A moment's reference to the statistics of internal commerce will illustrate these effects so that we can see the vast results which railroads have produced on the wealth and production of the country.

1. If we examine the routes and tonnage of the trade between the Atlantic cities and the central western States, we shall find some general results which will prove the utter incapacity of all other modes of conveyance to carry on that trade without the aid of railroads. Between Lake Erie on one side and the Potomac on the other, the commerce between the east and west is altogether carried on by way of several great arteries, which are these, viz; the Erie canal, the Oswego canal, the Champlain canal, the Centeral railroad, the Erie railroad, the Pennsylvania railroad, and the Baltimore and Ohio railroad. There are no other great channels of conveyance between the east and the west, and in fact no other routes appear practicable. However large an amount of product or merchandise may be carried by the lakes, it must be shipped to or from Buffalo, Oswego, or Ogdensburg. However multiplied may be the routes by rail or canal, by which products may arrive at Buffalo, Pittsburg, Wheeling, or Parkersburg, all the freights carried over them going east must pass over these great routes. We have, therefore, the means of determining accurately the relative transportation by different routes and modes. The different modes are all reduced to two — canals and railroads. The proportion of tonnage on these several lines of conveyance, as reported in 1862, was as follows:

Canals.

Tons.

Erie Canal	2,500,762
Oswego canal	852,920
Champlain canal	650,000
Aggregate	4,003,682

But we must observe that the Oswego canal joins to the Erie canal, and its tonnage, arriving at or leaving Albany, is included in that of the Erie canal. In fact, the tonnage of the canals, which is counted at Albany, is only that of the Erie and the Champlain, and of the latter but a small portion goes to or from the west. We have at the utmost, then the carriage on canals between the Atlantic cities and the west of 3,150,000 tons.

Railroads.

Tons in 1862.

Pennsylvania railroad	1,792,064
Erie railroad	1,632,955
New York Central railroad	1,387,433
Baltimore and Ohio (estimated)	1,200,000
Aggregate tonnage of these lines	6,018,452

We observe that in 1862 the tonnage of the six great arterial lines of transportation between the east and west amounted to over nine millions of tons, of which only one-third were carried by water. We must recollect that this was the case when the Erie canal of New York had been enlarged and refitted with the express purpose of transporting the products of the west, and was supplied with five thousand canal-boats. It is evident, therefore, that railroads not only carry two-thirds of the freights to and from the west at the present time, but that such is the rapid increase of western products, and the surplus carried to Atlantic or foreign markets, that the time is near when all that can be carried by water will be but a small proportion of the whole. The transportation by wagons is no longer possible to carry the surplus products of the interior States to either foreign or domestic markets. In fine, in the absence of railways the cultivation of grain beyond the immediate wants of the people must cease, or the surplus perish in the fields. Such was exactly the state of things in the west before the general introduction of railroads. The great grain-fields of Ohio, Indiana, Illinois, and beyond the Mississippi, have been mainly cultivated because railroads made their products marketable and profitable. In one word, railroads did what could not have been done without them.

2. Railroads secured to the producer very nearly the prices of that Atlantic markets, which was greatly in advance of any price which could possibly be obtained in western markets. It might be supposed that if the carriage of a bushel of grain from Sandusky to New York was reduced from forty cents a bushel to twenty cents, the gain of twenty cents would inure, in part at least, to the consumer; but experience shows this is not the fact. This gain of twenty cents inures to the producer. In proof of this it will be sufficient to adduce two or three well-known facts. The prices of flour and meat at New York (estimating them at the gold standard) have not been reduced in the least, notwithstanding the immense quantities of the products of grain imported into that city. On the other hand, the prices at Cincinnati, on the Ohio, have doubled, and in some articles, such as pork, have trebled. The great bulk of the gain caused by the cheapness of transportation has gone to the producer. This depends on a general principle, which must continue to operate for many years. The older a country is, the more civic and the less rural it becomes; that is, the greater will be the demand for food, and the less the production. The competition of the consumer for food is greater than that of the producer for price. Hence it is that Europe, an old country, filled with cities makes a con-

tinual demand on this country for food. Hence it is that New England and New York, continually filling up with manufacturers, artisans, and cities, must be supplied with increased quantities of food from the interior west; and hence, while this is the case, prices cannot fall in the great markets. Hence it is that the cheapening of transportation inures to the benefit of the agricultural producer. New England consumes more than a million barrels of western flour. The transportation is cheapened a dollar per barrel; and thus, in New England alone, in the single item of flour, a million of dollars, net profit, is put into the pockets of the western farmer by the competition of railroads; for a large portion of this flour is carried over the Massachusetts Western railroad. It is entirely true that the manufacturer of New England shares, on his side, in the gain of cheap transportation; but we are here considering simply the influence of railroads on agriculture.

In the western markets the gain to the farmer is palpable in the enhanced prices of every article. At Cincinnati, in 1848 and 1849, (which was the beginning of the greatest railroad enterprises,) the average price of hogs was $3 per hundred. In 1860 and 1861 it was double that, and has continued to increase. This was a net gain to the farmers of Ohio alone of from three to four millions of dollars. In the entire west it was a profit of more than twenty millions on this single animal; for, if there were now no railroads, this product could not be carried to market except on foot, which would take away half the value. No further illustration of this point need be made. Take the market prices of New York and Boston, on the Atlantic, and of St. Louis and Cincinnati, in the west, at an interval of twenty years, and it will be seen that the cheap prices of the west have gradually approximated to the high prices of the east, and this solely in consequence of cheapening the cost of transportation, which inures to the benefit of the farmer.

3. By thus giving the farmer the benefit of the best markets and the highest prices, railroads have increased the agricultural productions of the interior States beyond anything heretofore known in the world. We have already shown that this increased production, or rather its surplus, could not have been carried to market without the aid of railroads, more than two-thirds of the whole being carried off by that means. Let us now reverse this operation, and we find, on the other hand, that railroads have stimulated and increased production. The northwestern States are those in which the influence of railroads on agriculture is most obvious. In the five States of Ohio, Indiana, Illinois, Michigan, and Wisconsin there were comparatively few miles of railroad prior to 1850; but from 1850 to 1860 the construction of roads was most rapid. In 1850 there were only 1,275 miles of railroad in those States, but in 1860 there were 9,616 miles. Let us now examine the products of those States in 1850 and 1860, and see how the progress of railroads has sustained and stimulated agricultural production. The following table shows the increase of the principal vegetable and animal production in the five States of Ohio, Indiana, Illinois, Michigan, and Wisconsin in the ten years from 1850 to 1860:

	In 1850.	In 1860.	Increase per cent.
Wheat	39,348,495 bushels.	79,798,163 bushels.	100
Corn	177,320,251 "	280,268,862 "	58
Oats	32,660,251 "	51,043,334 "	50
Potatoes	13,417,896 "	27,181,692 "	100
Cattle	3,438,000 "	5,371,000 "	59

This increase is decidedly beyond that of the population; showing that the products of agriculture are, in those States, profitable. The aggregate of grain products in those States was:

In 1850..255,240,444 bushels.
In 1860..422,369,719 "

What part railroads have had in carrying this product to market we small see by ascertaining the surplus, and the manner in which it was transported. The commissioner of statistics for the State of Ohio, in his report to the legislature of Ohio, estimates (in the actual carriage of railroads and canals) that *three-fifths* of the value of agricultural products of Ohio are exported, excepting, of course, pasturage, fruits, garden products, &c. In 1859–'60, twelve millions of bushels of wheat were exported from that State, and an equal proportion of corn, reduced into other forms, such as fat cattle, hogs, pork, lard, whiskey, cheese, &c. Three-fifths of the aggregate grain production of these five States (1860) will give two hundred and fifty millions of bushels of grain. This is vastly greater than the whole tonnage of canals and railroads, and would, therefore, seem incorrect. This, however, is not so. The heaviest article (corn) is reduced to a fourth, perhaps, less weight by being changed into whiskey, pork, and cattle. The same is true of oats, and thus the ten millions of tons represented by the canals and railroads may cover all the surplus which finds the extreme eastern markets. A large quantity of the surplus products of these States is consumed in way-markets. We see now, that, since railroads carry two-thirds of this immense export, they represent nearly or quite the same proportion of the capacity of those States to raise any surplus, and therefore two-thirds of the profit made upon it. If we now consider the question of the profits of agriculture, the case becomes still stronger. The actual cash value of the products carried to market from these five States (that is, the surplus) is two hundred millions of dollars, and it is safe to say that one-half this sum is due to the influence of railroads. There are some interesting facts on this subject, to some of which we will briefly allude. Take, for example, the prices of both products and lands in the interior States, and compare them at different periods. Forty years ago (1824–'25) the surplus products of Ohio had already accumulated beyond the means of transportation. In consequence of this fact, wheat was sold in the interior counties, for 37 cents per bushel, and corn at 10 cents. After the New York canal (Erie) was finished, in 1825, and the Ohio canals several years later, these prices were raised more than fifty per cent.; but when two or three of the main railroad lines were finished in 1852–'53, the rise in prices and the amount carried forward to the eastern markets were even more increased. To show, in some measure, the effect of the improved means of transportation on the value of produce in the interior, we make the following table of prices at Cincinnati at several periods:

	In 1826.	In 1835.	In 1853.	In 1860.
Flour	$3 00 per barrel.	$6 00	$5 50	$5 60
Corn	0 12 per bushel.	0 32	0 37	0 48
Hogs	2 00 per cwt.	3 12	4 00	6 20
Lard	0 05 per pound.	0 08	0 08½	0 11

We find that in 1860 the price of flour was nearly double that of 1826; the price of corn nearly four times as much; the price of hogs three times as much, and the price of lard double. From 1835 to 1860, (when the railroads were completed,) under the influence of railroad competition with canals the price of corn advanced 50 per cent., and that of hogs 100 per cent. Perhaps no articles can be selected which furnish a more complete test of the value and profits of farming in the States of the northwest than that of these staples, corn and hogs.

But there is another respect in which the influence of railroads is almost as favorable to agriculture as that of cheapening the transportation of produce. It is that of cheapening the transportation, and therefore reducing the prices of foreign articles and eastern manufactures consumed by the farmers of the interior. We need not adduce tables to illustrate this; for it is quite obvious and well known that this has been the effect, though perhaps not to so great an extent as the reverse, in the case of produce. In 1839–'40 sugar was just the same price as in 1857 and 1858; but the average price of coffee from 1833 to 1838 was three cents higher than it was from 1853 to 1860. On the whole, the prices of articles carried from the east to the west were diminished, while those from the west to the east were increased. Again, the influence of railroads on the value of farming lands is too great and striking not to have been noticed by all intelligent persons. We have, however, some remarkable instances of the specific effect of certain railroads; we have, for example, the immediate effect produced on the lands of Illinois by the Illinois Central railroad. That company received from the government a large body of land at a time when the government could not sell it at a dollar and a quarter ($1.25) per acre. Since then the company has constructed its road and sold a large part of those lands at an average of $11 per acre, and the greater part of the lands of Illinois is fully worth that. Notwithstanding the rapid growth of population, the larger part of this advance is due to railroads. The following table shows the advance (by the census tables) of the cash value of farms in the five States mentioned in the ten years from 1850 to 1860:

	1850.	*1860.*
Ohio	$358,758,602	$666,564,171
Illinois	96,133,290	432,531,072
Indiana	136,385,173	344,902,776
Michigan	51,872,446	163,279,087
Wisconsin	28,528,563	131,117,082
Aggregate	671,678,075	1,738,394,188
Increase in ten (10) years		$1,066,716,113

It is not too much to say that one-half this increase has been caused by railroads, for we experience already the impossibility of conveying off the surplus products of the interior with our railroads. Putting the increase of value due to railroads at a little more than one-third, we have four hundred millions of dollars added to the cash value of farms in these five States by the construction of railroads. This fact will be manifest if it is considered that the best lands of Illinois were worth but a dollar and a quarter per acre prior to the construction of railroads, and are now worth twenty dollars.

We need not pursue this subject further. If the effect on the central western States has been so great, it is still greater in the new States which lie beyond the Mississippi. They are still further from market, and will be enriched in a greater ratio by the facilities of transportation. Indeed, railroads are the only means by which the distant parts of this country could have been commercially united, and thus the railroad has become a mighty means of WEALTH, UNITY, and STABILITY.

On Cattle Disease, 1860

From *New England Farmer*, June 1860, pp. 289–290; July 1861, pp. 321, 329.

GENTLEMEN: — In obedience to a call from the State Board of Agriculture, I turned out this morning at three o'clock, and in company with Dr. JOSEPH REYNOLDS, as a delegate from the Middlesex County Society, came to this place to examine some of the sick cattle, both dead and alive, and to inquire into the present condition of matters in regard to the disease, and the efforts already made, as well as those in contemplation, to stay its further progress.

In order to meet the six o'clock train from Boston, at Framingham, we came across the country fifteen miles by horse power, and in season to get breakfast before the train came along. Arriving at East Brookfield, we took stage, six miles, to North Brookfield, over one of the finest roads I ever saw. At the latter place I found gentlemen from various sections of the State, ready to proceed to an examination, and we were conducted about three miles, to the farm of Mr. B. W. Dean, whose herd consisted of twenty-eight head, every animal of which was pronounced to be infected. Two weeks ago, this herd was examined by the Commissioners, and by skilful medical men who had given special attention to the symptoms and character of the disease, and it was then thought to be free from it.

After inquiring of Mr. Commissioner WALKER what the leading indications of the disease were, I examined the herd, and felt quite confident that I could select every case where it had made some progress by the appearance of the eye alone, without reference to percussion, or rapidity of breathing.

I found Dr. DADD of Boston, acting with the Commissioners, aided by Dr. TYLERherds of North Brookfield. A cow was driven from the barn, led alongside a deep pit, dispatched, and examined. One lung was found enlarged to double its healthy size, and both had the plainest evidence of disease. A heifer, and then an ox were killed and examined, and in each, the evidence of deeply-seated disease was unmistakable. The Commissioners and visitors then proceeded to other herds that had been condemned, to witness their destruction, and to exhibit the disease in its more advanced stages. But futher details on this pointare unnecessary.

It is hardly possible that the calves sold by Mr. Chenery could have gone into hands better calculated to spread the disease indefinitely than into those of Mr. Stoddard, as he not only deals in cattle largely, but has teams continually on the road. In removing a building, twenty-three yoke of oxen were used, one yoke of which was diseased, and infected every other ox in the string, and those communicated it to thirteen other herds. While teaming on the road, a pair of Mr. Stoddard's oxen were put up two or three times in the barn of Mr. A. B. Woodis, and his whole herd has been swept away. A Mr. Gilbert had a heifer of Mr. Stoddard, last September, which has quite recently proved a decided case.

The disease presents some singular aspects. In one animal the lungs are greatly enlarged; in another assuming the appearance of liver, or highly discolored, or hardened so as to be nearly solid. In one, a tumor was found weighing more than twenty pounds! In some instances the Commissioners have allowed persons to keep their oxen a week or two, in order to help them out with their spring work. Some of these cattle gained appetite and flesh, but upon opening them, presented tumors on the lungs as large as cocoa-nuts! Up to this time 574 animals have been condemned, and about 400 killed. All trading in cattle has ceased — on many farms no herds graze on the hills, or low in the stalls, and the farmers stand aghast at the spectacle and the prospect. Their farm work is behind, because they have not yet had time to provide themselves with horses; the manure heaps are not accumulating to stimulate future crops; the dairy room will be desolate, and many families must go half amile, at least, for the milk for their coffee and tea! The scene is truly a sad one. Fifty head have died of the disease, beside what have been destroyed by order. With the exception of a single case in New Braintree, the Commissioners think the disease is confined within the limits of North Brookfield. But as Mr. C. Stoddard, 2d, sold a portion of his stock by auction, last November, it may break out from those at some new point.

The appropriation by the Legislature was only $10,000; the Commissioners have already expended $20,000, and the work is not completed. What is to be done? It must be this. The people all over the State must subscribe a guarantee fund, and this must be done so generally that if the Legislature refuses to cancel the debt — which it will *not* refuse to do — the assessment will fall upon so many as not to become a burden. Without such a fund, the Commissioners will not feel justified in going much further, and thus all that has been done will be lost. We suggest, also, to the several county societies to pledge their bounty to the cause for one year, and to omit the show of neat stock in the next autumnal exhibitions. Decided and substantial measures must be at once adopted, or a calamity will befall the Commonwealth such as it has never yet experienced.

I should be glad to make some further suggestions were not my letter already long, and my heart pained with the sad details of the day. If any entertain doubts or lack sympathy for those suffering, let them witness the scenes we have seen to-day and they will no longer be indifferent or doubting. The Commissioners have gained a high reputation for the energy and fairness they have exhibited.   Truly yours,

SIMON BROWN.

* * *

No person who has bestowed any consideration upon this subject will wonder at the prominence which we have given it in our paper, or think the space unprofitably occupied in which we have endeavored to arouse the community to a sense of the imminent danger that is threatening one of the most important interests of the Commonwealth. In this State, in the year 1855, the number of milch cows (we copy from the *Advertiser,* not having the documents at hand) was 148,569, and of heifers 35,441; valued together at ($4,892,291) a little short of five millions of dollars. Of oxen there were 50,225, and of steers 27,286, valued together at ($3,246,341) more than three millions of dollars; an aggregate exceeding eight millions altogether. Of these 33,917 milch cows, 9444 heifers and 18,561 oxen and steers valued together at $2,022,921, or more than one-quarter of the whole, were returned from Worcester County, in the very heart of which is raging a disease affecting those animals, as novel in this State, as it is dangerous and destructive. Nor is this all; 8,116,009 pounds of butter, valued at $1,678,557, and 5,762,776 pounds of cheese, valued at $464,250, are returned as the annual product derivable directly from the useful animals that are now threatened with extermination by a disease more destructive than any thing that has ever affected neat stock in this country.

Could the disease be confined to this State alone, it would be bad enough, but it threatens to spread over the whole country. Cases are reported in New Hampshire and Connecticut, which can be traced to exposure from the infected districts, and the proper precautions are being taken, we trust, in time, to prevent its spread. . . .

The Extra Session

The Massachusetts Legislature rose on Wednesday morning, June 13th, after a session of fourteen days. The subject which called them together was one of grave moment to the Commonwealth, and they have acted quite as promptly, and probably as wisely, as could be desired or expected. The bills relating to the cattle disease, as they finally passed, we present below, and those who peruse them will get some idea of the extent and novel intricacy of the subject, and the necessity of consistent, fair and efficient, as well as speedy action. "For our part," says the *Journal,* and we copy their remarks as expressing our own opinion in the matter, "we think the State deserves great credit for the manner in which it has dealt with this mysterious visitation upon our herds. The course of the Commissioners is now generally approved. The Governor did well to summon the Legislature as soon as the extent of the evil became clearly apparent; and the members of the two Houses have met their duties in a becoming spirit. The appropriations have been liberal; and as to these two bills, time and experience only can disclose wherein they are defective. They seem to us tobe the best, on the whole, that can be devised in the present state of information on the subject matter. We trust now that the towns and all public officers will see that the provisions are rigorously carried out."

An Act

Concerning Contagious Diseases among Cattle.

Be it enacted by the Senate and House of Representatives, in General Court assembled, and by the authority of the same, as follows:

Sect. 1. The Selectmen of towns and the Mayor and Aldermen of cities, in case of the existence in this Commonwealth of the disease called pleuro-pneumonia, or any other contagious disease among cattle, shall cause the cattle in their respective towns and cities, which are infected, or which have been exposed to infection, to be secured or collected in some suitable place or places within such city or town, and kept isolated; and, when taken from the possession of their owners, to be maintained, one-fifth of the expense thereof to be paid by the town or city wherein the animal is kept, and four-fifths at the expense of the Commonwealth, such isolation to continue so long as the existence of such disease, or other circumstances, renders the same necessary.

Sect. 2. Said Selectmen or Mayor and Aldermen, when any such animal is adjudged by a veterinary surgeon or physician, by them selected, to be infected with pleuro-pneumonia, or any other contagious disease, may, in their discretion, order such diseased animal to be forthwith killed and buried at the expense of such town or city.

Sect. 3. Said Selectmen and Mayor and Aldermen shall cause all cattle which, in their opinion, should be killed, to be appraised by three competent and disinterested men, under oath, at the value thereof at the time of the appraisal, and the amount of the appraisal shall be paid, as provided in the first section.

Sect. 4. Said Selectmen, and Mayor and Aldermen within their respective towns and cities, are hereby authorized to prohibit the departure of cattle from any enclosure, or to exclude cattle therefrom.

Sect. 5. Said Selectmen and Mayor and Aldermen may make regulations in writing to regulate or prohibit the passage from, to, or through their respective cities, or towns, or from place to place within the same, of any neat cattle, and may arrest and detain at the cost of the owners thereof all cattle found passing in violation of such regulations, and may take all other necessary measures for the enforcement of such prohibition, and, also, for preventing the spread of any such disease among the cattle in their respective towns and cities, and the immediate vicinity thereof.

Sect. 6. The regulations made by Selectmen and Mayors and Aldermen, in pursuance of the foregoing section, shall be recorded upon the records of their towns and cities respectively, and shall be published in such towns and cities in such manner as may be provided in such regulations.

Sect. 7. Said Selectmen, and Mayor and Aldermen, are authorized to cause all cattle infected with such disease, or which have been exposed thereto, to be forthwith branded upon the rump with the letter P, so as to distinguish the animal from other healthy cattle; and no cattle so branded shall be sold or disposed of except with the knowledge and consent of such Selectmen and Mayor and Alderman. Any person, without such knowledge or consent, selling or disposing of an animal so branded, or selling or disposing of an animal known to be affected with such disease, or known to have been exposed thereto within one year previous to such sale, or disposal, shall be punished by a fine not exceeding five hundred dollars, or by imprisonment not exceeding one year.

Sect. 8. Any person disobeying the orders of the Selectmen or Mayor and Aldermen, made in conformity with the fourth section, or driving or transporting any neat cattle contrary to the regulations made, recorded and published as aforesaid, shall be punished by fine not exceeding five hundred dollars, or by imprisonment not exceeding one year.

Sect. 9. Whoever knows or has reason to suspect the existence of any such disease among the cattle in his possession, or under his care, shall forthwith give notice to the Selectmen of the town, or Mayor and Aldermen of the city where such cattle may be kept, and for failure to do so shall be punished by fine not exceeding five hundred dollars, or by imprisonment not exceeding one year.

Sect. 10. Any town or city whose officers shall neglect or refuse to carry into effect the provisions of sections one, two, three, four, five, six and seven, shall forfeit a sum not exceeding five hundred dollars for each day's neglect.

Sect. 11. All appraisals made under the provisions of this act shall be in writing, and signed by the appraisers, and the same shall be certified to the Governor and Council, to the treasurer of the several cities and towns wherein the cattle appraised were kept by the Selectmen and Mayors and Aldermen respectively.

Sect. 12. The Selectmen of towns and Mayor and Aldermen of cities are hereby authorized, when in their judgment it shall be necessary to carry into effect the purposes of this act, to take and hold possession, for a term not exceeding one year, within their respective towns and cities, of any land, without buildings other than barns thereon, upon which it may be necessary to inclose and isolate any cattle, and they shall cause the damages sustained by the owner in consequence of such taking and holding to be appraised by the assessors of the town or city wherein the lands so taken are situated, and they shall further cause a description of such land, setting forth the boundaries thereof, and the area as nearly as may be estimated, together with said appraisal by the assessors, to be entered on the records of the town or city. The amount of said appraisal shall be paid as provided in the first section, in such sums and at such times as the Selectmen or Mayor and Aldermen respectively may order. If the owner of any land so taken shall be dissatisfied with the appraisal of said assessors, he may by action of contract recover of the town or city wherein the lands lie a fair compensation for the damages sustained by him; but no costs shall be taxed, unless the damages recovered in such action, exclusive of interest, exceed the appraisal of the assessors. And the Commonwealth shall reimburse any town or city four-fifths of any sum recovered of such town or city in any such action.

    Sect. 13. This act shall take effect from its passage.

    Approved, June 12, 1860.

Farming in Iowa, 1860

From Iowa State Agricultural Society, *Report, 1861* (Des Moines, 1863), pp. 3–13.

If the advancement of agricultural interests be measured according to the abundance of the crops, we may say the past year has been one of average prosperity; but if it be determined by our ability to convert these crops at remunerative prices into means whereby to supply the comforts and meet the necessities of life, it is far below an average. Still, although the products of the soil do not bring more than half the price they did a year or two ago, there have been several seasons in our history when the husbandman received no better prices than he does to-day. Hard and discouraging though the times be, we have been able to contribute more than our share of muscle, and there is no doubt by economy and thrift, we will be able to contribute our full share of money also to the support of the Constitution and the Union. Although thousands of brave hearts and stout arms have left the plow standing in the furrow and seized the musket and the sword, our energies have not been crippled, nor our resources exhausted. With what devout thankfulness we should contemplate that good Providence that has preserved our own borders from the horrors and devastations of war — that has kept us "from the pestilence that walketh in darkness and the destruction that wasteth at noonday."

The last Exhibition of this Society was held at Iowa City, Sept. 24th–27, and failed be as successful as some of its predecessors. From some "military necessity" the grounds were taken possession of by the 10th Regiment of Volunteers some time in the summer, and not vacated till three days before the Fair, having in the meantime destroyed many fixtures and derange the balance. Until just a week previous great uncertainty existed as to whether these troops could be removed in time for the Exhibition. This state of things, taken together with the fact that for the first time in our history the weather was extremely stormy, wet and disagreeable, may account for the slim attendance on that occasion. Notwithstanding all this, the entries were more numerous than any previous year, except 1860, and many of the leading departments were well represented, from which data it is fair to infer that if the weather had been favorable the exhibition would have been fully up to a progressive average. But by the continuous storm and rain the people were kept away and consequently the treasury was kept low. After the premiums had been awarded all those interested were assembled around the stand and addressed by the President, who faithfully recited the causes and announced the fact that our receipts would not enable us to pay in full at that time the premiums awarded, and submitted for their action what should be done. It was moved and seconded by several winners that they take fifty per cent., receipt in full, and be thankful for that much. Remarks were called for and made by several individuals who had a pecuniary interest in the question, all expressing themselves unqualifiedly in favor of the plan. Upon the vote being taken there was not found a single dissenting voice. The premiums were accordingly paid at this rate — receipts in full were taken and every person went home in good humor. Although this instance of a promiscuous assembly voting money out of their own pockets, may be justly considered an anomaly in this selfish age, it is not here related because it is so, but to show the attachment and confidence of the friends of the Society in it, as an institution of great public importance, and their desires and even sacrifices, in order to keep its usefulness free from a crushing weight of debt. . . .

Trusting that out of the vast amount of trash that is distributed through the agency of the Patent Office in the shape of seeds — that out of a thousand some one thing might prove valuable — the system has been adopted of furnishing that office annually with a list of the Presidents and Secretaries of the different County Societies, with the request that whatever may be intended for those Societies be forwarded directly to them. . . .

The Wheat Crop

The cultivation of Fall Wheat has been substantially abandoned in all parts of the State. In the south-eastern counties, a little is still raised, and the past year it did well, which will probably restore it to higher favor for a time. The crop of Spring Wheat has fallen materially short of the year 1860; the average being fourteen bushels per acre. In some parts of the State it has been preyed upon by insects to a limited extent, but the principal drawback reported, has been unfavorable weather as a general cause, and as a special rust has injured it more or less in most localities. The Canada Club in the central and northern counties, and the Wild Goose in the southern, have been the leading varieties for several years, and complaints have come up from several quarters that they have ceased to yield as formerly. The China Tea, a very valuable variety introduced by the Patent Office, is growing rapidly in favor and is being very generally spread. Some other new varieties have been recently introduced, but without results sufficiently promising to enumerate them. The fact established in manh the older States, proves itself equally true here — that the seed of all our cereals needs to be frequently changed.

The Corn Crop

Among all the varieties of our food promising products, Corn occupies pre-eminently the first place. But, notwithstanding it is a hardy and vigorous feeder, and peculiarly adapted to our rich, new soil, it is not always free from the viscissitudes of climate. The past season has not been a favorable one for this crop, any more than it has been for wheat, and the consequence is, that we have to record it below an average. From the counties reported, the average yield has been 39 bushels per acre. If we take into consideration the large portion of the old crop that has been kept over, in connection with the one just gathered, we will find that we never had so vast an amount of a good thing that we did not know what to do with it.

The Markets

Although, in many foreign countries, short allowance is chronic, and this year the starving point has been reached, yet our overflowing graneries are to their mouths inaccessible, and to our pockets unavailable; and this state of things must remain so long as our great natural channel of access to the ocean is closed up by a hostile armament. Upon the closing of the Mississippi River all our products had to seek a market by Railroad to the eastern sea-board; and every cent of advance in the Atlantic cities upon the products of the North-west, was at once covered by increased tariff of charges on these roads, until now, freights are from 30 to 40 per cent. higher than ever before.

More than this, these roads have been found utterly inadequate, at any price, to carry our marketable surplus. Not only in itself, then, but as a corrector of railroad monopolies, the free navigation of our Great River is indispensable to our very existence as a grain producing State. If that river were unobstructed, our wheat and pork would bring nearly, or quite, twice the price they do to-day. Its loss would fall upon some of our sister States, although situated in its valley, comparatively lightly: but under no possible state of things can the destiny of this State be severed from this great high-way which God has made for our use. Owing to our geographical position, and the fact that we are strictly an agricultural people, the burthens of the war have already, and will continue to weigh heavily upon us. While many great communities, if not States are growing rich out of the war, we have been permitted to furnish a few hundred horses at from ten to forty per cent less than the government paid for no better animals in the older States. More than this, by the system under which the war tax has been levied, it is practically true, that the young farmer just beginning on our prairies, has to pay just as much as the wealthy citizen in his luxurious New England home. Still our patriotic, Union-loving, western people will not grumble at any sacrifice nor succomb to any burthen, if, thereby, the Union and the Constitution can be restored and perpetuated.

Sorghum

At the annual fair, at Muscatine, in 1856, Mr. F.S. Dumont of Jones county, exhibited specimens of this plant, and syrup made from it. This was the first occasion on which it was brought to public attention, and although it attracted a good deal of interest, it was looked upon merely as a curiosity, and Mr. Dumont's statements concerning it were received with very marked incredulity. In 1857 there were two or three specimens of syrup on exhibition by other parties in the vicinity of Muscatine.

In 1858, about one farmer in twenty, in the older portions of the State experimented with a few hills in his garden, and in response to premiums offered by this Society, the results of several experiments were presented to the public in that year. In 1859 and 1860, this Society held out greater inducements to its introduction; offering large premiums, not only for syrup, but also for sugar made from this plant. The result was that last year several samples of beautifully granulated and lively sugar were in competition from different parts of the State for the Society's premium. Demonrating beyond doubt, that in our saccharine stores we can be independent of all other countries and climates. From the few stalks exhibited as a curiosity, in 1856, it is now grown as a staple in every county, and almost in every field, in larger or smaller quantities throughout the length and breadth of the State. From every County Society in the State we have the uniform reply to interrogatories on the subject, that its cultivation is increasing, and that it fully and more than meets the expectations of all who try it. It does well in the southern part of the State, and appears to do just as well in the northern. One county in the north — Cerro Gordo — reports having produced more than enough syrup for home consumption; Wright and Humboldt — enough, and Webster and Kossuth seventy five per cent. of the consumption. Counties in the interior have generally produced a larger per centum than those on the eastern border, with the exception of Lee and Henry, each of which claims to have produced sufficient to supply the home demand. Mahaska claims to have produced enough for two years. Taking the counties altogether, it is found that the product is equal to 76½ per cent. of the demand, and that the cost has been nearly 33 cents per gallon.

Considering the universal success in making molasses, and the occasional, in making sugar, in connection with the recent high tariff that has been imposed upon the importation of these articles, it is fair to conclude that if a kind Providence should bless us with a favorable season, another year we will not be compelled, as a State to contribute to the expenses of the war in the shape of high prices for sugar and molasses, but may let our patriotism exercise itself in some other channel. It is also said that the seed of this plant is altogether a better substitute for coffee than any of the cereals we have heretofore used for that purpose. If this be so, we may be able, still further, to retrench at the expense of the National customs.

But, whilst we have been successful as to quantity of syrup produced, and established the fact that sugar may be made beyond doubt, it must be admitted that the quality of neither article is all that may be desired. It all has more or less of that extraneous vegetable taste that is anything but agreeable to the palate. Some experiments have recently been made by the Chicago Sugar Refinery which have been entirely successful in removing that disagreeable quality. This refined molasses is said to rank with the best refined "golden syrup" of Eastern refineries, and can be put through the process at a cost not exceeding six cents per gallon. There is, as yet, no refinery in this state, and although the establishment of such a concern involves quite a large capital, we know that according to the laws of trade, the want will be speedily supplied. In the making of sugar, it must be admitted that the year just closed has not shown any marked advancement over the one which preceded it; but in order to stimulate effort in this direction, it is proposed to offer a premium of one hundred dollars for the best sugar from the crop of 1862, under such requirements as may be determined upon.

Hungarian Grass

This plant which doubtless had its American origin in Monroe County in this State, has been the object of many hopes and the subject of a vast amount of controversy among agricultural jouranals. It has spread with unprecedented rapidity, not only upon the prairies of the west, but also in the older States. It is but four or five years since its introduction — its cultivation had become almost universal — but after the experience of a few crops it is now very generally discarded. Aside from the fact of its being considered by many a dangerous feed for horses, it has been found exceedingly exhaustive to the soil and troublesome when followed by hoed crops.

Wool Growing

This is the only branch of stock raising to which our interrogatories to County Societies the past year have been specifically directed, and the replies which are hereunto appended contain a vast amount of most valuable experience and information on this much neglected interest. It is known to the "old settlers" that from 12 to 18 years ago many large flocks of sheep were brought into different parts of the State, and it is believed they ran down and failed in every instance. Many of these flocks were sent here on the shares as a speculation; others were brought in by residents who had more means to buy them, than experience to manage their flocks successfully. Thus in the too great haste to get rich these early flocks universally fell into the hands of either careless or inexperienced men, and when taken in large numbers, either disqualification must eventuate in failure. For the last four or five years sheep husbandry has been again looking up. There are now many instances in the State, which with the experience of that number of years have proved unqualifiedly successful. There is no longer any question about our dry rolling prairies being adapted to wool-growing, especially the heavier qualities, and as to climate, there is none better. What then is necessary to success? This may be answered in two words — a reasonable amount of *experience* and *care*. There has been no instance of failure in the State, in either earlier or later years, when the flock-master was possessed of these two qualifications. Our most successful flock-masters, indeed, our only successful ones have commenced in a small way, and their experience and observations have grown up with their flocks. A half hour's conversation with such men, or a few pages from their pen, are worth whole volumes of nicely systematized theory. They make no complaint of soil or climate, but there is one point on which they are unanimous and persistent in their complaints, and that is, that at the last regular session of your honorable body, when they appealed to you for some just and equitable assistance in the protection of their flocks from the ravages of dogs, the measures they proposed did not meet that consideration they were entitled to. Notwithstanding this neglect this branch of industry has increased, and now, in a state of war, considering that the supplies of cotton are cut off, and that wool, of all our products, is most easily carried to market, at expensive rates its growth has become a question of the most vital and prominent importance, not only in an interested, but in a patriotic point of view. Numerous petitions and numerously signed by the most intelligent and enterprising farmers of the State will again be presented at the present session, praying that in your wisdom you will devise some measures by which wool-growers may have their flocks protected from the ravages of the myriads of worthless curs that infest the State, especially the neighborhoods of towns and villages. To these petitions the several members of this Board would add whatever of influence they possess and urge upon you to provide that dogs may be taxed, slain, destroyed, or got rid of in any way, so that their shiftless owners may be relieved of a burthen, the flock-masters of a scourge, and the community at large of a pest.

The Fence Question

In the last decade the population of this State has increased from 192,000 to 675,000, but it must be confessed that for the last three or four years we have but little more than held our own. In every light from which it can be viewed, it is the interests of our people and the duty of the legislators, by just and equitable enactments, to encourage the increase of our population as fast as possible. In this time of bearing of burthens, he will be looked upon as a benefactor, who will devise some plan by which the tide of immigration may be again set in motion and attracted to our own State. Double, triple or quadruple our population, and just in that proportion the load of every individual will be lightened from the highest to the lowest, and every individual will be lightened from the highest to the lowest, and every interest will be promoted. Now it is claimed by many of the best farmers and thinkers of the State that this much desired object can be secured, fully, without injustice to any, and with inconvenience to but few, while the great mass of the people would be directly and greatly benefited. The plan is simply *to require every man to take care of his own stock,* and the immediate effect would be that our pastures would be fenced and our grain fields left out of doors. Without committing the different members of the Board to an endorsement of this theory, or to a recommendation of *immediate* legislative action upon it, as it must involve a revolution to a greater or less extent in our modes of conducting farm operations — which should be approached with great caution; yet it embraces questions of such grave importance and interests of such great magnitude, that its careful consideration is demanded of all who wish to see our State rich and populous. It would be out of place in a report of this kind to discuss this question, but it may be permitted to state in general terms the basis on which the advocates of this measure rest their arguments.

In this State we have an area of over thirty-three millions of acres, of which only three millions and a quarter are under cultivation; and after leaving a very large margin for timber and water lands, we must have twenty-five millions of arable acres — unsurpassed in fertility — that have never been touched by the plow share. The question then arises, will this vast territory ever be cultivated? To this question any one familiar with the geography of the State, must return the answer, that so long as a fence is the first requisite of a farm, but little can be done towards subduing these 24,000,000 acres. In most of the settled counties, it must be admitted that the present growth of timber, can do but little, if anything more than support the farms already opened. Under the present system then it is claimed that we are shut up to the necessity of admitting that any considerable enlargement is impossible. Shall we then plod along in the steps of our fathers who never dreamed of a prairie country, or shall we rather look upon our surroundings and as wise men adapt ourselves to the circumstances in which we are placed, giving due heed to the voice of necessity which tells us if we would have these prairies all dotted over with farms, we must adopt a different method of making farms.

Again, if an array of figures were drawn up showing truthfully the original cost of the fences in the State, and the annual cost of interest and wear and tear, it would astonish the most credulous. Our taxes have been high and it may be expected they will be increased; but no difference how normous they may become, they will scarcely be a tithing to the tax we have all along been paying from year to year in the shape of interest on the cost and repairs of our fences. Without any *necessity* whatever but on the grounds of *cost* alone, it is urged by the leading farmers of some of the older wooded States — Ohio for instance — that their true policy is to adopt this system. If the argument of *cost* is good there, it must be overwhelming when you add to it the *necessity* which exists here.

As stated before, our population in ten years has increased from 192,000 to 675,000. Now let it be supposed that in 1850 it had been known to the world, that in Iowa farms could be made without fences, and what would have been our population to-day? There can be no doubt, it would have been nearer two millions than what it is.

The State has been at very considerable expense in keeping an immigrant agent at New York to direct those seeking a home in the new world to the fruitful prairies of Iowa. He doubtless was able to do something towards sending some of his countrymen among us. But a hundred immigrant agents located at a hundred ports like New York, can do nothing towards populating the State when compared with the effects of a simple enactment, restoring the old common law rule, that every man must take care of his own animals, and restrain them from committing depredations on his neighbor. This alone would control and secure an unprecedented stream of immigration, such as has never been witnessed on this continent.

Farm Living in 1861

From *American Agriculturist* (New York, April, 1861) XX, p. 112.

It is no small tribute to Agriculture that it has inspired the most successful efforts of both painters and poets. It shows that therein are the elements which appeal to the higher and better nature, and it needs only that the cultivator shall open his mind and heart to the influences around him, to become the highest style of man. The noblest men that have lived, Cincinnatus, Washington, Garibaldi, have proved that in such labors may be found enjoyment to satisfy the most exalted powers. And this is not strange. Nature will ever excel art, for it is the work of the Master Artist. While intercourse with men in the strifes of business, or for pre-eminence, continually reveals selfishness and heartlessness which make the heart grow weary, intercourse with nature brings only lessons of beneficence and love. In this connection we may appropriately introduce the following well conceived lines written for the *American Agriculturist,* by George W. Bungay, in which poetry adorns the truths conveyed.

Bronzed Agriculture, with his hand has spread
The board, at which our hungry world is fed —
And should he cast his shining coulter by,
The famished nations must lie down and die.
Not armies of brave hunters in the chase,
Could feed the wants of this omniverous race.
We have no land of Bulah, where 'tis said,
The trees are loaded down with loaves of bread,
And pigs already roasted run the street,
Squealing for customers to cut and eat;
Where fishes cooked, come swimming in to shore,
And turtle soups, in streamlets pass the door.
This world is practical, and he, in brief,
Must work, who would have daily bread and beef.
We have two hands to earn our daily bread,
And one mouth only to be daily fed;
Teaching a lesson, even fools might learn,
We have no right to eat, what others earn.
The ancient patriarchs toiled in days of old,
Abram was rich in cattle, sheep, and gold;
In times unknown to iron steeds and steam,
Job had three thousand camels in his team,
Five hundred yoke of oxen in his stalls,
And flocks of sheep, to fleck the mountain walls
He had five hundred asses, and I fear,
They have descendants, in this hemisphere.
The workers are the uncrowned kings of earth,
Lords of the land, without the badge of birth:
They need no coat of arms, no scroll of fame,
No trumpeter, to blow abroad their name,
They swing the ax, where the great forests bow,
And golden harvests smile behind their plow.
But he, who never cultivates his lands,
Like Hermes, has more mouth than heart or hands.
Yonder, the youthful farmer walks in pride,
Before his steps, both clods and cliques divide,
Though times be harder than the frozen ground,
His bank, amid the shocks on 'change, issound,
The more it *breaks* the more his *dividends.*
He toils among ancestral oaks and pines
Where wood-birds sing, and the wild blossom shines;
He learns a lesson from each living thing
That folds a blossom or unfolds a wing;

For vines and corn and tesselated grass
Show what has been and what will come to pass.
O glorious world afloat in crystal air,
The sky bows with its sun to kiss the fair
Prairies of grass and flowers of every hue,
Sunshine and starlight left on petals blue,
As though the beauties of the Summer skies
Had been repeated in the wild flowers' eyes.

Massachusetts Wheat, 1861

From Massachusetts Board of Agriculture, *Annual Report,* 1861, pp. 117–33.

Massachusetts is within the limits of the wheat-growing regions of the world; yet wheat is not one of our staple crops. And though Canada, on the north, raises on the average between sixty and seventy millions of bushels annually, and New York, on the west, and Pennsylvania, on the south, raise large quantities for exportation, we, in Massachusetts, do not produce enough for our own bread. With a climate and soil essentially the same as that of countries where this cereal is successfully cultivated, producing not only enough for home consumption, but also for large exportation, we yet fail to raise it in any considerable quantity, and purchase in other States nearly all we consume.

In Great Britain, six bushels of wheat are allowed for the usual consumption of each inhabitant. In this State, we undoubtedly consume more. But taking this as the data, our population yearly require six million eight hundred thousand bushels for their sustenance. Of this quantity, there is raised on our own soil, according to the returns of 1855, but forty thousand three hundred bushels. We are therefore obled yearly to purchase abroad six million seven hundred and fifty-eight thousand four hundred and ninety bushels, at a cost of more than ten millions of dollars. According to the returns of the last industrial statistics, we cultivate, on the average, two thousand six hundred acres of wheat. But to produce enough for our bread, would require four hundred and twenty-two thousand four hundred acres. At first thought, these items are apalling; yet it is believed that by proper modes of cultivation and effort, the farmers of the State can produce everything necessary for the sustenance of its people. And agricultural and State pride should spur them persistently to the work.

It may be said by some doubter that our soil and climate are such that we had better engage in manufacturing and mechanical pursuits, and exchange the products of our labor in these branches of industry, for our bread stuffs. This question it is not proposed to argue to any length here. But it is extremely humiliating to our feeling of pride and independence to know that we are indebted to any body for the staff of life. It is true of States and Nations, as of individuals, that those are most truly prosperous and powerful which rely solely on their own exertions and skill to produce a supply for all their varied wants. Colman justly remarks, that "An agricultural community should, as far as possible, produce every article of first necessity, which they require for consumption. There may be products utterly unsuited to their soil and climate, but in all cases, and always, when there is no obstacle absolutely insurmountable to persevering labor, success is a moral gain. In a pecuniary view, however, there can be no doubt that Massachusetts won't find her account in producing her bread from her own soil. Vast sums of money are now sent out of the State for bread. This capital, applied to the improvement and cultivation of her own soil, would immensely increase its productiveness. Labor, judiciously and liberally applied to agriculture, produces not merely the immediate and particular crop sought for, but has a cumulative influence in preparing the same land for other and larger crops. The value of the land thus cultivated is often doubled, quadrupled, and increased ten-fold, by being thus rendered more productive."

Another important consideration is the fact that the native qualities of the great wheat regions of the West, for growing wheat, are becoming exhausted by constant cropping, and unless some new modes of cultivation are adopted, will soon fail in their ability to furnish our supply. A few years ago, Delaware, Maryland and Virginia were great wheat-growing States. Now it is cultivated there to a unlimited extent, and with indifferent success. Sections of New York, which formerly produced thirty bushels per acre, have been so reduced by this process, that they do not now produce more than eight. Ohio does not average over thirteen bushels per acre, and Illinois but seven. If this process continues, the time is not far distant when all the wheat they can raise will be consumed at home, and we shall, from necessity, be compelled to produce our own, or use other grain as a substitute. Would it not be wise, then, while we foster industry in mechanics and manufactures, to engage with spirit and enterprise in the raising of our bread stuffs, and by the light of science and experience learn to do it with success.

The facts abundantly warrant us in the opinion, that wheat can be successfully and profitably cultivated in this State. A little more than a century ago it was one of the common, ordinary crops. Sufficient was raised for home consumption, and it was an article of export. A history of the commencement, progress and decline of its cultivation, might be interesting and profitable, but necessity compels us to pass over it in a cursory manner.

The first wheat planted in the soil of Massachusetts, and probably of the continent, was by Gosnold, in 1602, when he first explored the New England coast. He landed on the Elisabeth Islands, and to prove the soil, planted pease and beans, and sowed wheat, barley and other grain. This was eighteen years before the arrival of the Mayflower. The first settlers of the Plymouth Colony brought no seed of wheat with them for sowing; and their crops for several years were Indian corn, barley, and pease.

The settlers of the Massachusetts Colony, who arrived in 1628, among other grains, seeds and plants, brought over a hogshead of wheat in the ear for sowing, and as soon as the first rude preparations of the settlement were completed, its cultivation was commenced. The new grain seems to have taken kindly to the soil and climate. No mention is made for many years of any want of success in its cultivation. On the contrary, its growth was so successful that it soon became an important article of export from the colony, and laws were passed to regulate the trade in wheat. At a "Generall Court held at Boston the 7th day of the 9th M[o]. 1641, it was voted that a deuty of every towne should send in writing to Capt. Gibons the 21st p'sent. what wheate wilbee adventured to bee ready by the first of the first month, and who will undertake for the towne." At the same was passed: — "Forasmuch as it appeareth to this court, that wheate is like to bee a staple comedity, and that a ship is with all speed to bee set forth and fraited with wheate, for fetching in of such ferraine commodities as wee stand in need of, it is Therefore Ordered; that after the last day of this p'sent 8th month, no baker or ordinary keeper, or other p'son, shall bake to sell, or set for sale, any bread or cakes made of wheate meal, or wherein any wheate meal shall bee put, upon paine to forfeit double the valewe thereof. And the Cunstables of every towne are hereby required to see that this order be observed and that they make seizure of all such bread so set to sale and distribute the same to the poor."

In October, 1648, a law was passed making wheat legal tender, and ordering it to be received in payment for taxes at five shillings per bushel. This law remained in force, with occasional changes in price to correspond with the supply, for about a century. It is a significant fact that the price of wheat thus fixed by law, was often the same as that of Indian corn, the native grain of the country, and rarely more than two shillings per bushel higher. And that price was generally from three shillings to five shillings sixpence. The "Great and General Court," from year to year, determined the price at which it should be bought and sold, and as it was a staple article of food, watched with Argus eyes, the yearly crops and supplies, that if possible, enough should be on hand for the sustenance of the colonists, and new emigrants who were continually arriving. At times, it was permitted to be exported, and again its exportation was interdicted. Occasionally, it might be brought in, in foreign ships; then, "taking into their serious consideration the great necessitye of upholding the staple comodityes of this countrye for the support of the inhabitants thereof," it was forbidden to import it.

In May, 1662, the Court passed an order in the following words: "The Court being informed by the deputyes of the seueral townes that bread corn is scarce amongst the people, and that seueral ships and passengers out of England are arived and more dayly expected, wth the consideration of supplying the fishing trade and others, doe therefore order and declare, that no person or persons shall export out of this jurisdiction any wheate or wheate-flower, after the 25th of this instant m[o]. upon penalty of confiscation thereof unto the country, one fowerth part whereof shalbee to the informer. This order to continue in force untill the Gen'll Court or Council shall take further order."

In November, 1675, it was enacted as follows: "The Court, considering the present state of affairs amongst us in respecting the Indian warr, and what hindrance the same may bee to the raysing supplyes of prouissions amongst ourselwes, Judge meete that the law prohibiting importation of wheate, biskeet and flower, be suspended as to the particulars above mentioned until this Court take further order." Notwithstanding the interruption to husbandry this year (1675,) by King Philip's war, the records speak of large crops of wheat in the State, especially on the "Quenecticott;" and it was when on their return from threshing the crop in the town of Deerfield, that "eighty young men, the flower of the county of Essex," were slaughtered by the savages at Bloody Brook.

No mention is made in the Court Acts or Records of those early times, of any failure of the wheat crop, from disease, or unsuitableness of soil and climate for its cultivation. It grew luxuriantly on the newly cleared lands; and was often sown for several successive years on the same field, after taking off the forest; and continued to be the chief crop, until by constant cropping without manuring, the lands failed to bear this grain.

Jared Elliott, in his "Essays on Field Husbandry in New England," published about 1760, speaks of the complaints made by farmers of the failure of their wheat crops, and imputes it to thriftless husbandry. He very frankly tells them that if they would spend less time in complaining, running about, and moving to find new and unexhausted lands, and more in manuring, and thoroughly cultivating the farms they now have, they would have no cause to complain of their crops. He says': "We find land will yield wheat best, when it is ploughed three times. An old and experienced farmer recommended deep ploughing, even on thin, shallow lands. Thereupon I ordered a piece of land to be ploughed so deep that our farmers thought I had spoiled our land. I have had wheat twice on that land, and think the deep ploughing did no hurt, but good."

Passing over a period of nearly three-fourths of a century, during which it cultivation was pursued with indifferent success, not withstanding the efforts of the older agricultural societies, especially of the Massachusetts Society for the Promotion of Agriculture, to promote its cultivation by the almost yearly offer of large premiums, its cultivation grew less and less, until we find, that about 1830, it had ceased to be a common crop. A field of wheat was rarely seen in any part of the State; in fact it had become quite a curiosity, and we were, as a State, entirely dependent on other countries for our breadstuffs, except the coarse kinds. This disgraceful fact was urged upon the attention of the legislature from year to year, until, in order to ascertain the cause of the failure, and if possible to find out new modes by which it might be successfully and profitably cultivated, an Act was passed in March,1838, as follows: "That there be allowed, and paid as a bounty, to the person who shall raise fifteen bushels of well-cleaned wheat, the sum of two dollars; and for every additional bushel above fifteen bushels, five cents, from the treasury of the city or town where such person shall reside. Also, the sum of one hundred dollars to the person who shall raise the greatest quantity in one year of not less than five hundred bushels, on one farm."

The passage of this law called the attention of farmers to its cultivation in good earnest, in all parts of the State. There were applicants for the bounty in nearly or quite every town; and the number of persons to whom the bounty was paid, the first year of the law, was 3,642; the amount of money drawn from the treasury of the Commonwealth was $9,280. There were cultivated that year 6,846 acres, yielding 108,570 bushels of wheat. The highest average yield in any county was in Worcester, of sixteen bushels per acre. The smallest average yield, in Nantucket, of ten bushels. As a fact showing the universality of its cultivation that year, it may be stated that in the town of Pittsfield, Berkshire County, there were two hundred and twenty-one farms, on one hundred and nineteen of which wheat was raised. During the second year of the law, $8,999 were paid in bounties, and $4,277 the third year. The law expired on the 3d of March, 1841. The experiment, as this result proves, was a failure. And although each claimant for the bounty was obliged to make a minute statement of his process of culture, no new light was obtained of practical importance. There was much complaint of injury to the crop by drought, grain insect, smut, &c., and but little enterprise and perseverance shown in continuing its cultivation. As a consequence, from 1838 to 1845, the crop fell off forty thousand bushels, and its general cultivation soon after ceased.

From this glance at the history of wheat culture in our State, notwithstanding the many discouraging aspects of the case, it is evident, first, that a large share of our soil, when uninjured by cropping and exhausting cultivation, is capable of bearing highly remunerative crops of this grain. Second, that the enemies of the plant are no more numerous or destructive here than elsewhere. Third, that our climate is not unsuitable. It has not changed perceptibly in the last two hundred years, and is nearly identical with that of wheat-growing sections. In further proof of this position, it may be adducedhat it is the universal testimony of the present and past generations of farmers, that wheat will grow finely on all new lands not subject to inundations and great structural changes by frost. Also, that there have always been farmers in nearly every part of the State who have judiciously pursued its cultivation with unvarying success.

In 1838, a farmer in Essex County says: "I have raised wheat on my farm every year since 1812, and with uniform good success. Have always sown spring wheat, and on land in good condition." The same statements are made by farmers of that time, in Middlesex, Hampden, Hampshire and Franklin Counties. It is true, that wheat is not one of the hardier kind of plants. It is badly injured by drought, by the early and later frost. Insects prey on it, and disease destroys it. Like the rest of the vegetable kingdom, it has enemies to be guarded against, and laws of life and growth to be obeyed, or it ceases to flourish. These facts sometimes caused the loss of a crop and had their influence, but in our opinion the great controlling reason why wheat was so little cultivated here during the latter part of the last century, and the first half of the present was, that the native fertility of our older fields, necessary for wheat-growing, had become exhausted; and the few attempts made to renovate them for its culture, were, by methods and manures, injurious to the full and healthy development of the plant. The mere fact of its liability to disease, to destruction occasionally or frequently by enemies, will not account for its non-cultivation. The rot has occasionally turned our potato fields into a nuisance, that were giving promise of a bountiful harvest, and thus blasted the farmer's hope. The frost frequently, at one fell swoop, cuts off nearly all our fruits, when the trees are growing luxuriantly. Our corn fields are injured by frost, blast and smut, when their growth gives indication of abundant crops. And drought often causes all our productions to give us but a scanty supply. And yet no one thinks it best to cease the cultivation of these products, so long as the power of the earth to produce them has not failed. These causes and results are transient as the various changes of the seasons, and may occur only at long intervals. But if the soil, as is found in the survey of our wheat culture, refuses for a long series of years to bring forth its product, an effectual stop is put to all success, until it is renovated.

Since 1855, unceasing efforts have been made in all parts of the State, to increase its cultivation by new methods of culture and fertilization. The agricultural societies have, most of them, offered yearly premiums to encourage farmers to engage in this branch of husbandry, and with success. The following is the sum paid by each society in 1861: — Hampden East, four dollars; Hoosac Valley, seven dollars; Hampshire, six dollars; Worcester South-East, six dollars; Plymouth, thirteen dollars; Franklin, five dollars; Hampshire, Franklin and Hampden, one dollar; Middlesex, five dollars; Martha's Vineyard, seven dollars; Worcester West, four dollars; Norfolk, six dollars; Worcester North, ten dollars; Middlesex North, six dollars; Nantucket, eight dollars; Housatonic, nineteen dollars; Worcester, four dollars; Essex, eight dollars; Bristol, six dollars. The societies that offered no premiums were the Highland, Hampden, Barnstable, Berkshire, Massachusetts, and Worcester South. Most of the gentlemen who answered our circulars say, "A large portion of the farms raise wheat." That "the farmers raise enough for their own consumption and some to spare." From the most reliable information obtained, it is believed, that the crop of last year, though not so good as that of 1860, cannot be less than two hundred and fifty thousand bushels. No complaint is made of any obstacles to its cultivation in the least formidable, where the soil is sufficiently fertile. Most say, "wheat is as sure as any other grain." "Can raise more bushels of it to the acre on the same land than we can of rye." Smut, rust, blast and insects do not injure it if the general management is correct, and land well cared for.

These facts appear to be unimpeachable, and should stimulate and encourage us to engage more largely in its culture. There is but little variation of opinion respecting the soil best adapted to the growth of wheat. A writer in an agricultural journal in New York, as long ago as 1820, says: "Wheat will grow best on land which contains just as much clay as can be combined with it, without subjecting the wheat to being frozen out; and the point can be ascertained by washing a little of the soil in a tumbler of water, and seeing how long it will take it to become clear. If it takes it more than three hours, it is liable to be injured by frost." Any warm, friable soil, of moderate tenacity, whether it be sandy or gravelly loam, will bear wheat. But a light per cent. of clay with it is preferable. If intended for winter wheat the per cent. of clay should be small, as it increases its liability to winter-killing. Be the soil what it may, the surface should be so undulating, that no water will stand on it during the thaws of winter and spring, or the heavy showers of summer. This is essential to complete success; and also that the soil should be brought to a perfect tilth; be made mellow and permeable to a depth as great as the roots of the plants penetrate, and if the subsoil is hard, and water-bearing, it should be broken up or brought to the surface, that the superabundant water may drain off quickly and without injuring the plants.

The best manure for this crop, and what crop it should succeed, are questions about which there is more doubt. It is the common practice to sow wheat after Indian corn, clover, or tobacco, and as it succeeds well thus, no change is sought or desired. Fine crops have been grown after potatoes. If sown after corn it should be in the spring, as winter wheat on old land should be sown before corn is ready to harvest, to avoid winter-killing. Nearly all substances, mineral, vegetable, and animal, have been used at various times, with judgment and without, with gain and with loss, as manures and fertilizers for this crop. No one of them all, however, can be recommended as the special manure which under all circumstances and on all soils is particularly adapted to it. It is certain that all strong unfermented animal manures should be always avoided, as they almost invariably produce injury by stimulating the straw to an unnatural, sickly growth, which causes it to fall, producing shrunken berries, and flour of inferior quality.

But all wheat lands should be rich in well-decomposed organic substances, and they may be applied from the yard, the woods, muck-heap or roadside, (and just here, in our opinion, lies the secret of success or failure in wheat growing,) and heavy clay soils will be much improved by dressings of sand. Lime as a special manure for this crop has many advocates. But the farmer who expects to realize large crops on old fields by simply applying a dressing of lime, will most likely meet with disappointment. On clay soils and those rich in vegetable mould, lime is undoubtedly highly beneficial; but it will not supply the place of these substances in the soil, or produce good crops where they are wanting. It is the concurrent testimony of all wheat-growers, that on lands long cultivated, wood ashes are the very best fertilizer for wheat, producing a strong, clean, healthy straw, and well-filled grain. On much worn, sandy soils, heavy dressings of ashes have been known to produce great crops without any other manure. Guano has been long used as a special manure for the wheat fields of Maryland and Virginia. But being too much relied on, as the cheapest, best, and in fact as the only manure, those fields have deteriorated, until the harvest is of little worth. In this State, good success has attended its use, especially on the lighter soils; but it would be unwise to depend on it, to bring our lands into proper condition for wheat bearing, or to preserve their fertility through a course of cropping. The experiment has been tried and found faulty, and we can but be the loser by any attempt of the kind. But if used in connection with those substances that form mould, and give permanent fertility, it may increase our crops and profits.

The varieties of wheat, though undoubtedly springing from a common stock, are almost numberless, and their varying qualities are probably owing to soil, climate, and modes of cultivation. Of the kinds cultivated in this State the principal are, the White Flint, Blue Stem, White Kentucky, Black Sea, Mediterranean, Java, Wisconsin Club, and Bearded Spring; all of which are good, but neither of which can be recommended in all respects as superior to any other. Wheat, like other grains and vegetables, if long cultivated in any locality, is prone to deteriorate in quality and yield, and therefore requires changing. By this a change of variety alone is not intended, but also a change of locality. The Mediterranean of Plymouth County, would be improved by transferring to Berkshire County, and *vice versa*. Each in its new home would produce finely for several years, and then gradually decline, requiring another removal. The various winter varieties are generally preferred by *millers* for flouring. They produce more flour from a given quantity, and it is whiter, but its bread is no sweeter or more nutritious than from spring wheat, and their greater uncertainty on account of winter-killing, leads our *farmers* generally to prefer the spring varieties.

The destruction of wheat, by what is termed winter-killing, may be accomplished in either of three ways: First, by "heating or smothering." The wheat field is sometimes covered deeply with a solid, impervious body of snow, when the earth is not frozen. The active vitality of the roots continues, but all air and light being excluded from the leaves, and consequently all action necessary to preserve the equilibrium of the plant, together with the heat at the surface of the ground, disposing vegetation to decomposition, it is destroyed. The same thing is accomplished, and on the same principle, when vegetation is covered with boards, or stocks of grain or corn. Second, by absolute freezing, in open winters. The ground being bare of snow, and the weather very severe, it becomes frozen to great depth, and very hard. The plant also is exposed to the fierce winter blasts and extreme cold, and not being sufficiently hardy for such treatment, it dies. Third, by the changes of spring, or the freezing and thawing process the soil goes through in the change from winter, to the settled warm weather. The roots of the plant are often drawn from the soil, or broken, and thus ruined. For the first of these evils, we know of no way of escape or remedy; but experience proves that injury by the two last, if not prevented, is very much ameliorated by sowing early, (on or before the first of September,) and covering the seed deep. The young plants thus become strong and hardy, and the roots well and firmly set in the ground, and it is thus enabled the better to withstand the rigors and changes of the season.

The time of sowing, quantity of seed, and its preparation, have each more or less influence on the crop. The time of sowing the winter variety has been alluded to above, but this is a matter of so much importance, that it is well to call attention to it again, as the reasons for sowing at certain times are good for both the spring and winter varieties. The desideratum in sowing is, if possible, to place the seed in the earth at such a time of the season, that it may be sufficiently late to escape the frosts of May and June, early enough to be out of its bloom and milk, at the time its numerous insect enemies are depositing their eggs, (for it is only when in this state that most of them can do it any injury,) and to be well advanced towards ripening, before the hot, dry weather of late July and early August. In the greater part of the State there is but little danger of the frosts of May and June, therefore sow early as possible. In April, if it can be done, but under no circumstances, until the soil is sufficiently dry and warm to work up fine and mellow. In elevated mountainous localities, where the springs are late, and the earth not in condition to receive the seed until after the middle of May, defer sowing until the first or second week in June. Its flowering season will then come after the insects have disappeared, and early September will bring in the grain in perfection.

The quantity of seed per acre should be of the winter variety, one bushel and a half, as the rule; but if sown early, it may be diminished a peck; if late, increased by that amount. The question of the influence of soil of different degrees of fertility on the plants, as affecting their tillering, and consequently the quantity of seed, is of but little practical importance, as the life-long experience of intelligent wheat-growers has led them to adopt nearly this rule. Of spring wheat, two bushels, increased or diminished according to the same circumstances. Should wheat receive any preparation before sowing? Yes, answers Mr. A, I raise fine crops of wheat, and I invariably soak my seed in strong brine, and roll it in lime, plaster or ashes. But, replies Mr. B, my average crop is twenty-five bushels to the acre, and I neither soak nor roll my seed, lest its germinating power should be destroyed. Here are two undisputable facts. Good crops are grown from both prepared and unprepared seed, and occasionally with each there is a failure.

The diseases of the plant show themselves alike whether the seed be prepared or not. In the growth of the plant, and at the harvest, there is apparently neither gain nor loss by the operation. He that sows, without preparation, does well; and he that prepares his seed does no better. How strongly soever we may cling to supposed ntirt laws, and theorize on the idea, that by soaking the seed in certain preparations, we are filling it with a fertilizing matter that increases its vital power, and makes it stronger and more prolific, yet the fact is patent, and cannot be impeached, that wheat succeeds equally well if the seed receives no preparation. It is highly important to sow well-developed, healthy seed; therefore, if it is of doubtful character, or is supposed to contain foul seed, there is great benefit in putting it into brine, and taking off every thing that rises to the surface.

Some farmers, influenced apparently by the idea that wheat needs constant nursing and feeding, are accustomed to top-dress their fields, when the plants are young, with some such preparation as lime, plaster, ashes, or guano. Now, while each of these substances may be a good fertilizer for wheat, yet close observation and experience teaches that this mode of application is not economical, and is often injurious. Such substances, by their pungent, acrid properties, are likely to injure to some extent, tender vegetation, if applied directly to its leaves and tissues, and there is great loss of the substances themselves, when left on the surface, exposed to the full action of sun, wind and rain. To receive the full benefit of these fertilizers, they should be applied at the time of sowing, and thoroughly incorporated with the soil.

So far as known, drill-sowing is not practiced in this State. A few farmers cover their seed with a cultivator, or a light horse-plough, but the almost universal practice is, to cover with the common harrow. Seed sown in this manner, we must admit, ''is at the mercy of the harrow, the winds, the birds, the insects, and the clouds.'' The practice of the best English and Western wheat-growers is, to plant with the drilling machine. The advantages claimed for this method, over broad-cast sowing, are, that time and labor are economized, seed is saved, and a larger yield secured. It is estimated that other things being equal, drill-sown grain will yield one-fifth more than that sown broad-cast. We trust the time is not distant, when the extent of our wheat fields will justify our farmers in the expense of using this instrument of cultivation.

The proper time and manner of harvesting wheat are items of great importance. The general practice is believed to be far from correct. Klippart, an able writer on the wheat plant, makes the following judicious remarks on this topic: ''The most judicious millers and grain dealers are decidedly in favor of early harvesting, and certainly their opinion is worth something. In New York, and indeed in all the great grain-growing States, the practice of cutting grain before it is dead ripe, universally prevails. With them, the exact time when it should be cut is no longer a matter of doubt, all being perfectly convinced that the right period is indicated by that change which the grain experiences when passing from a milky state, to that of complete hardness; or, in other words when it is in the dough, and when the kernels without being sticky are not sufficiently hard to resist the pressure of the thumb and finger. The proper maturity for cutting may be judged of more accurately, perhaps, if described as that when the stalk immediately below the head, for two or three inches, becomes yellow and dry, consequently cutting off the circulation — and the grain, though soft and doughy, ceases to yield any milk on pressure. This occurs about a fortnight before the seed becomes dead ripe.''

In early harvesting, greater care and attention must of course be given to the curing of the crop. It should be allowed to lay in the swarth but a few hours, especially if the sun be shining clear and warm at the time, but be bound in small bundles, lest the grain should dry too quickly, and immediately place the bundles in stacks, of a circular form, six or eight bundles in a stack, and cover them with a cap sheaf, or hay caps, where it may be allowed to remain without further labor, until sufficiently cured to take to the barn.

A light, straw-colored worm, resembling in its structure the common wire worm, but much smaller, has infested the wheat fields in some localities, and of which we can find no description by writers on the enemies of the wheat plant. Its ravages are usually committed when the plants are young, and not more than five or six inches in height. The worm burrows in the ground, sometimes cutting off the plants just beneath the surface, and again eats its way into the stalk and up through the centre or beneath the outer leaf, killing every plant it touches, and making the grain too thin and scattering for great crops. Of its nature and habits, length of life or manner of propagation, we know little or nothing, though its works are very manifest. To guard against injury by it, we would suggest the ploughing of those fields in the fall, that are intended for spring wheat. If done immediately before the ground freezes, they might be destroyed by the frost, if in their incipient state, and before they could burrow below its reach, if they are then in maturity.

The past season has witnessed the advent upon our wheat fields, of an insect, identical in every respect, with what is known as the Indian corn plant louse, though that insect is not supposed to prey upon wheat. Its presence has not been noticed in all localities. It causes injury by extracting the juices of the straw and head, while yet quite green, and causing the berries to be less plump and heavy. Whether this insect is to continue its work, and become a pest to our fields, time alone will determine. The past season, early fields almost universally escaped injury from it. And in the future, the early sown may be safe from its depredations. We have thus finished all we deem it desirable to say respecting the modes of wheat culture suitable for our State. We entertain the idea, and have made it sufficiently evident throughout the report, that wheat can, with proper cultivation, be successfully grown here. But the vital point is, will it pay? Of itself, is there any direct profit in it? Can we not make more money by raising other crops, and purchasing our wheat? Leaving out the indirect profit of wheat culture by the increased value of our lands caused by the cultivation necessary to produce it, and the social and political independence resulting from producing this article of prime necessity, we will answer these questions by presenting the following table, showing the probable average cost per acre of its cultivation in this State: —

Cost of ploughing, per acre,	$ 1 50
Harrowing,	75
Seed and sowing,	3 75
Interest on land at $50, and taxes at $1 per hundred,	$3 50
Manure,	10 00
Total cost,	$19 50

The average yield is supposed to be twenty bushels per acre, and the average price $1.50 per bushel, making the value of an acre of wheat, ...$30 00

Profit on an acre, ...$10 50

In this no estimate is made of the value of the straw, or the cost of harvesting the crop. This estimate pays for all the labor, manure, taxes, and twenty-six per cent. on the capital invested in the land.

It cannot be objected to this estimate that the profit of raising wheat should be very much less, in consequence of its liability to failure, because it is a more certain crop than potatoes, equally sure as oats or rye, and nearly so as corn. And besides, an item of much importance which has not been brought into the account is the fact that wheat is the best crop with which to stock down to grass, (unless it be barley.) With the farmer who is pursuing a system of rotation, or whose crop of hay enters largely into his account of profit or loss, this fact is one which under no circumstances should be overlooked. Some writer has said that the cultivation of the wheat plant is the distinctive mark showing that a people have passed from the nomadic into the civilized state. And that in countries where its cultivation has fallen into disuse, there has civilization also retrograded; and were it not for commerce with enlightened and refined nations, they would speedily relapse into all the horrors of absolute barbarism. "Truly," he says, "the wheat plant is the corner stone of civilization, and its destruction would overwhelm society with darkness blacker than the storm cloud at midnight." We trust the future history of our beloved Commonwealth will in this respect, as in all others, give us a right to the name, and to every blessing of enlightened civilization.

LEVI STOCKBRIDGE,
MOSES STEBBINS,
NATHAN DURFEE,
Committee.

Hog Cholera, 1856–61

From Edwin M. Snow, "Hog Cholera," U.S. Patent Office, *Annual Report, Agriculture, 1861* (Washington, 1862), pp. 147–49, 152–54.

The disease to which the name of "Hog Cholera" has been generally but improperly applied has prevailed more extensively in this country than most persons are aware of. The first appearance of the disease, of which I have been able to find any notice, was in Indiana, in the summer of 1856. It has continued, to a greater or less extent, since that time in our western and southern States, in nearly all of which it has at some period attained the character of a wide-spread and fatal epidemic. Its victims in those States are numbered by hundreds of thousands, if not by millions.

During the last five years this disease has been seen, from time to time, in portions of the more eastern States, sometimes, as in western New York in 1856, proving quite severe and fatal in comparatively limited localities. But in the eastern States it has, to a great extent, originated with and has generally been confined to hogs imported from the west. I think that in no State east of Ohio has the disease prevailed extensively, or attained the character of a wide-spread epidemic.

In the vicinity of Providence, Rhode Island, it has prevailed to some extent, more particularly among large herds of swine, during each of the last five winters, but has been mostly confined to hogs brought from the west, and has usually disappeared with the approach of warm weather. During the last winter it was more severe than in any preceding, and was not confined to western hogs. Neither did the disease, as heretofore, cease with the cold weather, but it continued until August, having destroyed more than five hundred hogs in Providence and in the adjoining towns during the first seven months of the present year, 1861. I have also heard of its prevalence in various towns in Massachusetts during the same period.

It is evident that a subject of so great importance to the agricultural interests of the community deserves attention. It is also interesting to all classes of the community on account of the relations of this disease to epidemic diseases which afflict the human race, and on account of its effects upon the supply of animal food for cities. For these reasons I have, in connexion with Dr. Collins and other physicians of this city, made some investigations upon the subject. We have visited and examined many sick hogs, and have examined the bodies of some of them after death. I have also made inquiries of those who have had the care of the hogs in relation to the symptoms, and have obtained information so far as possible from those who have seen the disease at the west, where it has prevailed so extensively. The results of these investigations I propose to give briefly in the following pages.

Symptoms

The symptoms, as described by persons unaccustomed to such observations, are extremely various. By combining the information obtained from others with the results of our own observations, the symptoms, as seen during the life of the animal, are nearly as follows:

1. *Refusal of food.* — This is the first symptom usually noticed by those who have the care of the animals, though, as will be seen hereafter, this symptom by no means indicates the beginning of the disease. The refusal of food, after it is first noticed, generally continues through the whole sickness, and food of every description is mostly refused.

2. *Great thirst.* — This is constant, and large quantities of cold water will be swallowed if it can be obtained. Even after the animal is unable to stand alone it will drink cold water with eagerness.

3. After a time, the length of which varies very much, the animal begins to show signs of weakness; reels, staggers, and, in attempting to walk, often falls down.

4. In most cases there is a diarrhoea, with copious fluid discharges of dark, bilious, and very offensive matters. In a few cases there is no diarrhoea, but evacuations of hard, black balls; but in some of these cases the fluid offensive matter is found in the intestines after death.

5. In a few cases there is vomiting; but this is not often severe, nor is it continuous for any length of time.

6. The external appearance of the animal is at first paler than usual; but towards the last of the sickness purple spots appear, first on the nose and sides of the head. These extend along the sides and belly, and between the hind legs, after which the animal soon dies.

7. In many cases, perhaps a majority, ulcers are found on the different parts of the body. These were particularly noticed on the inside of the lips and gums, and on the feet, and were often quite deep and excavated. In some cases these ulcers were seen in the nostrils, and in one case there were extensive ulcerations in the back part of the mouth, on the tonsils.

8. In some cases the legs are swelled, and the animal is lame; sometimes the ears and sides of the head are swelled and red; sometimes the eyes are sore and inflamed; sometimes swellings like carbuncles are seen; and, generally, the glands near the surface seem to be enlarged.

9. In most cases the pulse is quickened, the breathing is hurried and difficult, and there is much cough. But in some genuine cases there is no perceptible trouble with the lungs, and no important signs of disease are found in them after death.

10. The duration of the disease in fatal cases, after the first symptoms are noticed, is extremely variable. We have seen some which have died within two or three hours; others have lived many days. It is difficult, however, to fix the time of the appearance of the first symptoms. The first noticed is usually the refusal of food; but it is probable, indeed it is certain, that the sickness is in progress for a considerable period before the animal refuses food. Cases like the following are sometimes seen: A hog refuses to eat; it soon grows weak; staggers in walking; turns purple on the sides and belly, and dies within two or three hours after the first symptom is noticed. But, on examination after death, extensive disease is found in the intestines, or in the lungs, or in both, at a stage of development which must have required many days to reach. . . .

Causes

In this and other similar diseases among animals, as well as in epidemic diseases in the human race, the universal tendency of the public mind is to ascribe their propagation to *contagion*. Dr. Sutton, whom I have already quoted, says: "Although this disease must occasionally have a spontaneous origin, yet, when once produced, it will spread rapidly by contagion."

The investigations of the cattle disease in Massachusetts in 1860, and the action of the legislature in regard to it, seem to have been based upon the theory that the disease was a "pleuro-pneumonia" only, and that it was contagious.

It is comparatively but a few years since the belief was universal that yellow fever and cholera were contagious, and the most oppressive and inhuman quarantine restrictions, based upon this belief, were enforced to prevent these diseases in every port of the civilized world. But the enlightened opinion of the medical profession and of sanitarians of the present day has formally decided that yellow fever is not contagious; while the idea that cholera is contagious is abandoned, so far as I know, by all intelligent physicians at the present time.

So I firmly believe it will soon be with reference to this and other similar diseases among animals. They are not contagious, and the belief that they are so is productive of great injury in the adoption of measures for their prevention. But this disease among swine is an epizoötic disease, or perhaps we shall be better understood by saying that it is an epidemic disease among animals.

If, then, this be an epidemic or epizoötic disease, its causes are similar in their nature and operation to those of other epidemics. The following, then, as I understand the subject, *are the causes* not only of this disease among swine, but also of the disease referred to among cattle, as well as of epidemics in the human race, viz:

1. *An epidemic atmospherical poison.*

2. *The local conditions or circumstances adapted to receive and propagate the poison existing in the atmosphere.*

With regard to the first cause, the atmospherical poison, very little is certainly known. It may be an animal or vegetable existence, or a chemical or electrical change in the atmosphere. Nor do we know anything of the differences in the condition of the atmosphere by which such dissimilar epidemic and epizoötic diseases are produced at different times. But, judging from their effects, we conclude that these primary causes of epidemics probably exist in the atmosphere; that they progress over a greater or less extent of country, in accordance with laws with which we are not acquainted, and alighting upon the earth produce their effects wherever they find the local conditions adapted to their propagation.

The local conditions, or causes of this disease among swine, are more obvious and much better understood. They are, briefly, impure air arising from the filth with which the animals are surrounded, the location and want of ventilation of the pens in which they are kept, the use of improper and unhealthy food, and the want of pure water. Common sense shows that cleanliness, good food, pure air, and pure water are as important to prevent disease in hogs as in men, though the fact is generally ignored by those who have the care of these animals. Another condition, though not absolutely essential to produce the disease, has a very great influence in increasing its severity and fatality. It is the crowding of large numbers of animals together. It is a well-established fact that the severity and fatality of cholera, and of other epidemics in the human family, is in direct proportion to the density of the population.

The coexistence of both the causes given, viz: the atmospherical poison and the local conditions, is necessary for the extensive development of the disease. When both these causes are present in any locality, and healthy animals are brought into the locality, a portion of them, and sometimes all, will contract the disease. But this important fact is to be remembered, that both these causes may exist in a locality whether any animals are present or not.

Perhaps I have said more than some might think necessary in relation to the causes of the disease; but the subject is of the utmost importance in its relations to preventive measures. If this and other similar diseases are not contagious, but arise from causes which may, and do, originate and exist wholly independent of the presence of animals, it is manifestly absurd to attempt, as has been done in some cases, to prevent and eradicate them by the wholesale destruction of the animals.

Prevention

Keeping in mind the causes of the disease as I have given them, the measures necessary for prevention are obvious, and may be stated in a very few words. They are, to remove as far as possible the causes. The general cause existing in the atmosphere cannot be removed, nor can it be avoided, except by the removal of the animals beyond the limits of its existence, and this is not usually practicable. But the local causes can, to a very great extent, be removed, and without these the general cause cannot produce any very serious results.

The hogs can be removed from their filthy pens and can be kept clean; they can be removed from low ground to more elevated places; they can be separated and isolated as far as possible; they can be allowed an abundance of pure air and of pure cold water; and they can be supplied with nourishing, healthy food. In a word, they can be placed in the conditions which common sense shows to be essential to health, whether of hogs or of other animals. When this is done, everything is done that is necessary or possible for the prevention of this as well as of other similar diseases.

Treatment

In the treatment of a disease of this character we have little to expect from the specific or direct action of medicine of any kind. The most that we can hope to do is to support the system so as to enable nature to overcome the disease.

In a human being, with a disease of a similar character, we should first remove the patient to a healthy locality, and provide for an ample supply of pure air and good nursing. This, faithfully done, would be the most important step towards recovery. We should then give, as the symptoms might require, beef tea or broths, milk, wine-whey, brandy, quinine, and other similar preparations; always remembering that the object is to sustain the animal powers so as to enable the system to withstand the depressing effects of the poison and free itself from its presence.

The treatment of hogs with this disease must be of a similar character. Stimulants and tonics of some description, with plenty of pure air, pure water, and suitable nourishment must be given. Chlorate of potash, in full doses, from its known effects on the human subject, has been proposed as a remedy, but of its value I am unable to speak. Powdered charcoal is undoubtedly of some value when scattered freely about the pens and given to some extent in the food.

But, in the severer cases, treatment of any kind is generally unsuccessful, and if successful would cost more than the animal is worth. We might succeed, by the use of the remedies named, and by careful nursing, in prolonging the life of the diseased hog; but success of this kind would hardly compensate the trouble and expense necessary to secure it.

But a large number of the milder cases will recover without treatment of any kind, and in this, as in other epidemics of a similar nature, it will be found that the first cases that occur will be very severe, and will nearly all prove fatal; while after the epidemic has existed for a time, the disease will seem to become more mild, and a much larger proportion will recover.

The important fact to be remembered is, that it is for the interest of the owner of these animals to use every possible means *to prevent the disease, as prevention is of infinitely more importance to him than treatment;* but if the disease becomes established, it should be treated in a rational manner, not forgetting that Nature, when properly aided, will do infinitely more than medicine for the cure.

Colorado — Its Soil, Climate, and Resources, 1861

From Edward Bliss, "Territory of Colorado," U.S. Patent Office, *Annual Report, Agriculture*, 1861, pp. 154–157. Washington: Government Printing Office, 1862.

THE act of organization of the Territory of Colorado describes its boundaries as follows: "Commencing on the thirty-seventh paralell of north latitude where the twenty-fifth meridian of longitude west from Washington crosses the same; thence north on said meridian to the forty-first parallel of north latitude; thence along said parallel west to the thirty-second meridian of longitude west from Washington; thence south on said meridian to the northern line of New Mexico; thence along the thirty-seventh parallel of north latitude to the place of beginning."

The Great American Desert

An examination of the map, and a careful tracing of the limits above described, will convey some general idea of the topography of Colorado Territory. The Rocky Mountain range — the great backbone of the North American continent — runs through the Territory from north to south, dividing the vast plains of the eastern slope from the extensive parks and savannas which stretch away towards the Sierra Nevada. The eastern portions of Colorado embrace that mythical region laid down on all the old maps as the "Great American Desert." It is almost needless to add that the discovery and development of the mineral resources of the Rocky Mountain region has furnished the evidence of over one hundred thousand witnesses against the existence of the "Desert." The commerce of the plains, involving the necessity for the employment of immense herds of beasts of burden, has effectually dissipated the fabulous belief that a vast desert existed in the basin east of the mountains, where nothing to sustain animal life could be obtained. The writer of this has often seen herds of several hundred cattle feeding in various portions of the "Desert" district. On all the watercourses, and especially in bottom lands, the grasses thrive most luxuriantly. It is, nevertheless, true that on some of the uplands there is a tendency to barrenness, caused not only by the aridity of the climate, but by extended strata of sand. Yet even upon these wastes there are frequent patches of thrifty vegetation, while the cactus covers the earth with its brilliant and beautiful rosettes of flowers.

The Pastoral Region

Near the base of the Rocky range, and along the valleys of the streams which have their origin in the mountains, vegetation is more prolific and the soil more arable. The grasses here are not only abundant, but grow to immense size, and contain more nutriment than the cultivated species of the most prosperous agricultural districts of the Mississippi valley. These grasses cure standing, and cattle feed and thrive upon them throughout the entire winter months. As a great grazing and stock-raising region, Colorado possesses advantages over Texas. The latter is subject not only to terrible storms, but long-continued rains, which to unsheltered stock are so fatal; while in Colorado no bleaching rains, no tornadoes, destroy the standing grasses or waste their nutriment. It is rarely that unworked cattle in Colorado require winter fodder. For three winters past there has not been twenty days in each that loose stock required feeding, and it is a remarkable fact that they will not eat cured hay so long as they can have access to ungrazed pasture lands. Beef cattle are driven in the months of January and February direct from the fields to the shambles, and nowhere in the world can finer or more tender beef be found than in the markets of Denver.

Agricultural Resources of Colorado

These facts furnish incontestable proof that the soil of that region is highly productive. But a serious apprehension exists in the minds of many that the capabilities of the country for extended agricultural purposes are limited. This opinion is based upon the fact that rains throughout that entire region are unfrequent, and occur at seasons when their grateful influences are not beneficial. Candor compels the admission that there is some truth in this statement. Throughout nine months of the year — from October to July — not an inch of rain falls; and even in July and August, when showers are common, they are of such short duration that the parched earth is seldom satisfied. The observation and experience of three years has demonstrated that the cereal grains cannot be extensively and profitably cultivated in Colorado by the same system generally followed in the grain-growing districts of the States. Ploughing, sowing and harvesting, even though prosecuted with the same skill, will never produce the satisfactory results which reward similar efforts in the western States. Nature withholds her rains from the plains of Colorado, and admonishes her people that they must strive to overcome this deficiency by artificial appliances.

Irrigation

Thanks to the record of history, to the necessity and experience of various portions of the world, and to the actual successful efforts of the people of Colorado, they are not to be deprived of the inestimable blessings which flow from agricultural enterprise. Throughout the entire length of the mountain range the rocky barrier is rent with canōns, through whose beds copious volumes of pure water rush forth into the valleys beneath, and stretch their limped arms far out into the plains. The sturdy farmer has but to check the dashing torrent in its course, and divert a portion of its grateful element, through artificial channels, across his thirsty and arid fields. A combination of interests, and a general and well-directed system of *irrigation,* will soon relieve the Territory of Colorado from the difficulties which now limit agricultural labors. Indeed, the results of numerous irrigating enterprises during the past season, for gardening purposes solely, were not only most gratifying, but immensely profitable. It was ascertained that in the wide bottom lands of the Platte river, and other streams near the base of the mountains, there was a rich alluvial deposit which only required water at long intervals to promote an astonishing vegetable growth. All the succulent varieties of plants attained to an enormous size, retaining the tenderness, juiciness, and sweetness which almost everywhere else belong only to the smaller varieties. The wild fruits of Colorado are also various and abundant. Of these, cherries and currants are most numerous, while raspberries, grapes, and plums are in some sections quite plenty.

The Climate

The climate of Colorado, especially that portion lying at the base and east of the mountains, is not only most delightful, but remarkably healthy. The frosts come early in the autumn and continue far into the spring months, but they are not severe. Throughout the winter months the sun blazes down with almost a tropical glow; little or no snow falls, and although the nights are sometimes sharp and frosty, there is no steady intensity of cold. In the mountains there is, of course, a lower temperature. The nights are much colder; there is more snow, and the rigors of winter are not only protracted, but severe. But this is the characteristic of all high mountain regions; and as the residents of the sierra in Colorado can, by riding from six to ten hours, reach the genial atmosphere of the valley, they are never "winter-bound." Some idea of the climate may be gathered from the following extract from the *"Rocky Mountain News,"* published at Denver. The article from which the extract is made appeared in the *News* of the 21st of *December:* "The office in which we write has not had a fire in it, nor the need of one, this winter." These facts ought certainly to establish the claim of Colorado to mildness and salubrity of climate. The record of mortality, as seen by reference to the obituary heads of the newspapers of the Territory, affords gratifying evidence of the healthiness of that region. When it is remembered that the principal occupation of the inhabitants — mining — involves the most tedious, laborious effort, great exposure, and oftentimes imminent danger, and that many are there who have never before experienced the hardships and privations incidental to frontier life, the sanitary condition of Colorado is truly remarkable.

Mineral Products, Improvements, etc.

The Rocky Mountain ranges are evidently of Plutonic origin, and consequently abound in rich and valuable minerals. Gold, silver, iron, copper, lead, and coal, have been discovered, and a variety of sulphurets, carbonates and oxyds. The principal resource of Colorado Territory thus far has been its auriferous product. Public attention was first attracted in this direction in the fall of 1858, at which time good "prospects" were found on Cherry creek, near its confluence with the Platte. Since then prospecting and exploration has rapidly developed the existence of gold throughout a wide extent of territory along the mountain ranges, and encouraged the investment of a large amount of capital. It is estimated that there are not less than two hundred quartz mills and rastras already erected in different portions of the Colorado gold region, involving in their transportation and fitting up not less than one million of dollars. In addition to the cost of this machinery, vast sums of money have been expended in opening and working quartz veins, in river and bar mining, and in various other enterprises indispensably attendant upon mining operations. Fine coach roads have been constructed over and through the mountain ranges, where three years ago the most sure-footed animal could not have safely ventured. Ditches of many miles in length now convey water around mountain sides and across deep valleys for the use of miners, and away up under the very shadows of the Snowy range are busy towns teeming with all the life and enterprise which characterize thrift and progress in the old settlements of New England. Night and day, and in all seasons, may be heard the clanking of heavy stamps, and shrill scream of the steam whistle, the roar of exploding blasts away down in the bowels of the earth, and the rush of waters over ponderous wheels, and yet scarce three years have passed since the solitude of that region was only broken by the scream of the panther, the howling of the wolf, and occasional death struggles between hostile savage tribes.

The results of mining operations in the Colorado gold region during the past year are encouraging. It is estimated that the gold product will not fall much short of four millions of dollars, and it is confidently believed that the current year will close with an exhibit of three times that amount as the yield of 1862. Time which has heretofore been expended in erecting machinery, opening claims, and *preparing* for business, will this year be devoted to actual gold mining efforts. The experiments of the past will give place to the successes of the future, and even those who have toiled long and gained nothing may, with some degree of confidence, look forward to a more prosperous period.

Life of an Overseer

From *Southern Cultivator* (Augusta, Ga., July–August, 1862) xx. p. 136.

EDITOR SOUTHERN CULTIVATOR — If there ever was, or ever will be a calling in life as mean and as contemptible as that of an Overseer — I would be right down glad to know what it is, and where to be found. I am just tired of it, and I will quit it, as soon as I can find a better business.

If there be good seasons, a favorable crop year, the *master* makes a splendid crop; if any circumstances be unpropitious and an inferior crop be made, it is the overseer. If the hands are runabouts, it is the overseer's fault; and if he flogs them to keep them at home, or locks up, or puts them in stocks, he is a brute and a tyrant. If no meat is made, the overseer *would* plant too much cotton, and of course 'tis his fault. If hogs are taken good care of, the overseer is wasting corn, and "the most careless and thriftless creature alive." If he does not "turn out" hands in time, he is lazy; if he "rousts" them out as your dad and mine had to do, and to make us do, why he is a brute.

Thus is it from No. 1 to No. 144, all through the multiplication table. I care not in what way you examine it, it is all the same. Complaining, complaining from beginning to end. Can't you give a word of advice to planters, not to listen to negro news; and particularly not to ask for news. I admit the master is the negro's protector, and he ought to do it at all hazards. But, we are on questionable ground, and had well move circumspectly. An overseer worth a fip, will govern the negroes placed under him and if the master or mistress, picks up news or inquires for it, whether through first or second-hand, they will as certainly hear things unpleasant and cause the overseer double trouble to get negroes in a bee-line of duty. Every one conversant with negro character, knows well their proclivity for lying and stealing.

Make inquiry of them, and the owner can soon get a budget of news, sufficient to hang any overseer. A man's character is precious, even if he is an

OVERSEER.

American Agriculture in 1863

From U.S. Department of Agriculture, *Report of the Commissioner*, 1862, pp. 4–25.

DEPARTMENT OF AGRICULTURE,
Washington, January 1, 1863.

IN compliance with the foregoing law organizing the Department of Agriculture, I have the honor to submit my first annual report. In so doing, I have deemed it not inappropriate to offer some observations on the magnitude of the interests intimately connected with, or growing out of agriculture, the most ancient, the most honorable, and the most indispensable of all the occupations of man, and to give a rapid glance at the improvements which successive ages have wrought in this department of knowledge, and the progress made in our country in later years, as well as the special operations of this department since its organization.

Agriculture in its first inception could scarcely be considered as an art, or even occupation. The ancients, deriving their food chiefly from the spontaneous productions of the soil, styled the earth their mother; but we, in the light of a higher philosophy, are reminded by our own harvest home and finished year, of our obligations to one common Father, who gives "rain from heaven and fruitful seasons, filling our hearts with food and gladness." Health has everywhere prevailed; and notwithstanding the temporary transfer of large numbers of our patriotic countrymen from their farms to the ranks of the army and navy, yet the great interests of agriculture in the loyal States have not materially suffered. Abundant crops of the cereals and other grains, of grasses, of roots and fruits, have been garnered. Besides feeding the settled and increasing population of the country and our immense land and naval forces, we have exceeded the exportation of any previous year by over 17,000,000 of bushels of grain.

Agriculture, whether viewed as an art or science, presents a history as marked and important as that of any other great civilizer in the world's progress. In its rudest state men subsist, for the most part, upon the chase, or such roots, fruits, and grains as are easily gathered. In its second stage men follow the pastoral life, wherein as nomadic tribes, inhabiting hilly countries or table-lands, they depend chiefly upon flocks and herds for food, raiment, and locomotion. In Central Asia — that mysterious source of languages, religions, and races — this condition of agriculture has ever prevailed. Next, increase of population, demand for food, richness of soil, and the spirit of adventure, have forced or attracted men to the now celebrated alluvial plains of the world. Finally, from the great centres of modern population the same migrations of races are taking place as of old; planting new empires in the wilderness, and making a superior agriculture — whether in hilly countries, table-lands, or alluvial plains — the great and essential art of life.

As history is philosophy teaching by example, it would be highly instructive to discuss the condition of influence of agriculture as exhibited in the life of the two great nations of classical antiquity. For want of space, let us select for instruction the one which in magnitude, soils, wealth, power, energy, enterprize, and institutions resembled most our own republic. After a splendid career of prosperity, filling the world with her fame, Rome culminated and declined. No historical proposition is more susceptible of proof than that the great causes of that decline were the laws enacted affecting real estate and the condition, skill, and products of labor. For many years after Rome had grown to greatness, the cultivation of the soil was not only deemed honorable, but was regulated by law, in order that agriculture might yield the largest return to labor, and be, in reality, the great conservator of the empire. Not only were flocks and herds kept for food and raiment, and alluvial lands tilled, but the soils in more unfavorable regions were carefully and skilfully cultivated. At first the allotment of land to each citizen was but six acres. It was not ploughed, but spaded, and the yield was very great. Virgil, Cato, and Columella, Rome's chief agricultural writers, invariably urge the cultivation of small farms, in order that the tillage may be thorough. The subdivision of estates, the limitation of their extent, and the habit of personal attention to farming, were excellent conditions for success. "The Romans," says Frederick Von Schlegel, referring to the last days of the republic, "were a thoroughly agricultural people." Changing this splendid basis of prosperity, permanency, and power, whereby, resting in the soil, Rome pierced the heavens by the force of thought, she grew proud and oppressive; the reins of power slipped from the hands of the middle classes; labor became disreputable; the soil a monopoly, and the masses of the people reckless, unpatriotic, and degraded. A few proprietors held the land and owned the labor. The poverty of the many, with its evils of want, of ignorance, and dependence, existed by the side of the excessive wealth and culture of the few. The lands in Italy and in the conquered provinces were apportioned among the families of the great, instead of being given or sold as free homesteads to the poor. By this unequal distribution of property, and by forcing the husbandman into the army and buying up or taking his land, much of the soil was cultivated by servile labor. This monopoly of the land and condition of labor operated unfavorably to agriculture, and thus to the prosperity and permanency of the empire. These two causes were destructive to intelligent, interested, and really productive agriculture. Certain staples, it is true, were raised in vast quantities; but these required little skill, and prevented the cultivation of a variety of crops. Old and exhausted lands were abandoned without any attempt to renew their fertility. The laborer felt no moneyed interest, no personal pride, in the result of his toil, and all generous progress in agriculture was retarded. The voice of history proclaims, in the clearest manner, that free labor and ownership of the soil by the laborer, if possible, are necessary conditions to the highest success in agriculture and national prosperity. Give the laborer no interest, prospective or otherwise, in the soil he tills, and he cannot be otherwise than wasteful and inefficient.

In the earlier days of the empire the maximum limitation of freeholds to 500 acres, in connexion with the old Roman love of agriculture, led to a careful and exact mode of culture. But in the later days of the empire, says Hallam, "the laboring husbandman, a menial slave of some wealthy senator, had not even the qualified interest in the soil which the tenure of villanage afforded to the peasant of feudal ages." At this period, notwithstanding Rome's matchless soil and climate, she was compelled to import food from her conquered provinces. Rome remained free while her middling classes retained a controlling influence; but when the tenure of the soil passed into the hands of the few, the incentives to industry, to order, and to a quiet life were gone. Her young men sought the excitement of the camp, the city, or foreign lands. Cut loose from the ties of home, and maddened by the bad example of the landed aristocracy, the poorer classes lost their old love of country and liberty. The mad prodigality which prevails in the confusion of a shipwreck may serve to explain the progress of luxury amid the misfortunes and terrors of a sinking nation. Some of the landed proprietors, at the period of which we speak, owned estates of such magnitude that, though tilled by slaves, the annual revenue of each amounted to nearly $3,000,000, which was squandered by the nobles in every excess of luxury. "Rivers," says Seneca, "which had divided hostile nations flowed, during this period, through the vast estates of private citizens." Read but the following graphic descriptions from the pen of Ammianus, the Roman, after the lands had been monopolized by the few, and agriculture degraded by servile labor, and say if here was not cause enough for Rome's ruin and warning to America! "A secure and profound peace succeeded the tumults of the republic. Distant nations revered the name of the people and the majesty of the Roman senate. But this native splendor was degraded and sullied by the conduct of those who displayed the rent-rolls of their estates, and provoked the just resentment of every man who recollected that their poor and invincible ancestors were not distinguished one above another. Whenever these rich land owners visited public places they assumed a tone of loud and insolent command towards their equals, and appropriated to their own use the conveniences designed for the Roman people."

"Owing to the degradation of labor," says Gibbon, "the plebeians disdained to work with their hands, and the husbandman, being obliged to abandon his farm during the term of his military service, soon lost his zest for work. The lands of Italy, which had been originally divided among the families of free and indigent proprietors, were insensibly purchased or usurped by the avarice of the nobles. In the age which preceded the fall of the republic it was computed that only 2,000 citizens were possessed of any independent subsistence. When the prodigal, thoughtless commons had imprudently alienated not only the *use* but the *inheritance* of power — to wit, their own homesteads and free life — they sank into a vile and wretched populace!"

Such is one of the great lessons of history; and any nation that desires permanent prosperity and power should learn it well, wisely protecting labor and capital, and encouraging the division and cultivation of the soil.

There has been no *great and general* advance in agriculture in modern times till within the last thirty years. In particular localities, it is true, there was earlier improvement. In the Low Countries roots were cultivated with success, and the Dutch became celebrated for the products of the dairy. In portions of France, Germany, and Spain, the vine was extensively cultivated. But a writer who had observed extensively himself, and had access to the best information, says, in 1828, that the agriculture of continental Europe at that time was not very different from that of Britain during the middle ages.

Great Britain is indebted in a large measure to Lord Bacon for her early attention to progressive agriculture. That great thinker gave to the world inductive philosophy, which teaches man to experiment, to question, and test nature by her great alphabet of soils, gases, elements, and phenomena — a philosophy which is at once positive, progressive, and eternal, making man the "minister and interpreter of nature." It would be highly interesting and instructive to notice at length, were there space, the successive English writers on agriculture, themselves practical farmers, who accepted Bacon's philosophy, from their first publications, early in the 17th century, down to our own day. A gradual but positive improvement appears in their works and in their noble calling. Increased attention was paid to rural pursuits and the other arts, science meanwhile developing the importance of agriculture, and foreshadowing its ultimate triumph.

Early in the 18th century Jethro Tull, one of England's earliest and best writers on agriculture, recorded and published his experiments in new modes of culture. Some of his theories were erroneous, but his experiments were invaluable. Farmers are indebted to him for the horse-hoe and for drill husbandry. He also invented, but failed to perfect, the threshing machine, which, by the improvements of our own countrymen in our day, is rendered a most effective auxiliary to the labor of man. Arthur Young, who wrote in the latter part of the 18th century, was another zealous contributor to agricultural progress. He wrote and edited nearly one hundred volumes on subjects more or less directly connected with farming. He travelled extensively, both in England and on the Continent, to observe the modes of culture which prevailed. He made numerous experiments on soils to ascertain the causes of fertility, and thus prepare the way for the more scientific researches of a later period.

Many writers in Scotland, among whom Lord Kames is conspicuous, aimed to awaken a deeper interest in agriculture; but to no one is the farmer more deeply indebted than to Sir John Sinclair. At his suggestion, and under his personal supervision, a statistical account of Scotland was undertaken, embracing a complete agricultural survey of that country. It was completed and published in forty volumes, and forms a noble monument to his perseverance and energy of character. It was followed by most important results, for it led to the establishment of the board of agriculture by Mr. Pitt, in 1793. This association brought farmers together, promoted an interchange of thought, made them acquainted with each other's mode of culture, and produced throughout the United Kingdom the stimulus which intelligent, associated effort always produces. More than all, the board was instrumental in employing Sir Humphrey Davy to make those experiments, which are not only an honor to intellect, but which established agricultural chemistry as a department of science, and of inestimable value. He delivered his lectures on this subject in 1802. The fundamental principle which he developed, and demonstrated, was this: That the productions of the soil derive their component elements which, for the most part, are hydrogen, carbon, oxygen, and nitrogen, either from the atmosphere by which they are surrounded, or from the soil in which they grow. He showed that the process of vegetation depends upon the perpetual assimilation of various substances to the organs of the plants, in consequence of the exertion of their living powers and their chemical affinities, stimulated chiefly by moisture, light, and heat. The discoveries in chemical science before Davy's time had, undoubtedly, prepared the way for his triumph, but he is none the less entitled to praise. He first recognized a plant as a living thing, the laws of whose existence were to be studied in order to develop a perfect growth. He showed, by analysis of soils and plants, what properties and conditions would best furnish the elements needed in cultivation. The success of Mr. Coke, afterwards Earl of Leicester, in the cultivation of his estate at Holkham, is a memorable instance of what scientific farming will do. When he succeeded to the estate, in 1776, large parts of it were so sterile that they were let on long leases at about seventy-five cents per acre per annum. Wheat was not grown upon it. One part of the soil was a "blowing sand" and the other a flinty gravel; yet on these strata, aided by the skill, the capital, and the enterprize of the proprietor, the estate became fertile — the pride of the country! In 1816 Mr. Coke estimated the yield of wheat alone at forty to forty-eight bushels per acre. Such were the men who wrought that marvellous change of which Macauley speaks. "At the close of the seventeenth century," says the historian, "agriculture in Great Britain was in a rude and imperfect state. The arable and pasture lands were not supposed to amount to more than half the area of the kingdom. The remainder was believed to consist of moor, forest, and fen. In the course of little more than a century, a fourth part of England had been turned from a wild into a garden." After the introduction of drill husbandry, the total value of agricultural products in the United Kingdom has more than doubled. Fifty years ago, even, there was much land in Great Britain in the condition of some lands in our older States at present — either left in their wild state or exhausted of fertility. This has been entirely changed. An hundred acres which, under the old system, produced annually, as food for cattle and manures, not more than forty tons, now produces 577 tons.

Prior to the commencement of the present century, there was but little agricultural progress in the United States. The first settlers had many and great difficulties to encounter in clearing the land, in bringing it under cultivation, and in defending themselves against the Indians. Besides, the French and revolutionary wars very much interfered with the peaceful pursuits of agriculture. Nor could the people, after the peace of 1783, burdened with debt, without money to pay their taxes, with no manufactures, and no foreign demand for breadstuffs, be expected to make much progress in tilling the soil. Washington was unquestionably one of the most enlightened and successful farmers of his day. His correspondence with Sir John Sinclair, and his constant supervision of his estate, even during the stormy period of the revolution, and amidst the pressing cares and anxieties of the presidency, afford conclusive evidence that he was first in the arts of *peace* as he was "first in war and first in the hearts of his countrymen."

But notwithstanding our early difficulties in planting an empire in the wilderness, our wars, our want of a market, our vast territory, sparse population, cheap land, and ruinous system of exhausting a virgin soil, yet great and manifold progress has been made in agriculture. The cast-iron plough, first patented in New Jersey in 1797, has undergone various modifications, until it has reached a high degree of perfection. The spade, the hoe, the hay fork, and the other common implements, tools, and vehicles of husbandry, are lighter, of better material and temper, and more adapted to the use of the farmer. A large number of our farmers now use mowers for cutting their grasses, and the vast wheat fields of the west and northwest could not be harvested without the use of the reaper, nor the wheat separated from the straw, and the corn from the cob, without threshing and shelling machines. So great is the demand for farm labor, so great the spirit of enterprise which urges our young men and adopted citizens to become freeholders, and so sure, so near, and so vast the market, that without mechanical appliances, and the use of horse and steam power in the cultivation of the soil, our vast fields of grain could not be harvested and made ready for food and shipment. At present the United States are somewhat behind England in substituting steam for human muscle; but many years cannot elapse ere steam will be made by our enterprising farmers to plough and plant, to dig, haul, and grind, and to pump, saw, and thresh, and thus allow them to devote more attention to those branches of agriculture requiring special study, time, and taste. In all portions of our country, but particularly in the older States, a great improvement is noticed in tillage. Lands are being extensively under-drained, deep and subsoil ploughing practiced, and great care and considerable skill exercised in the preparation and application of manures. In the use of improved agricultural implements a great change has everywhere taken place. It is common to see the best plough, rollers, cultivators, reapers, threshers, fanners, hay and cotton presses, sugar mills, horse and steam powers, and a thousand other labor-saving machines, the results of skill and science.

This imperfect sketch of agricultural improvement in England and the United States is given in order to show that *progress* has not been the result of mere routine farming, but of *practically applied science* — of classified knowledge. The great channels, for the most part, through which this knowledge has been widely and authoritatively diffused, are agricultural societies and publications. Wherever they have been established, either in England, on the Continent, or in America, the spirit of inquiry and emulation is awakened, prejudices are removed, and the results of a wide and varied experience, both of individuals and associations, in every branch of agriculture, are classified and published for the benefit of every farmer.

Notwithstanding the relation which the mass of farmers in England and on the Continent hold to the soil, enjoying neither ownership nor hope of wealth, yet these societies and publications have awakened a genuine, wide-spread enthusiasm and desire for further information. They have been the means of rousing American farmers, especially, to the importance of artificial manures, to the necessity of under-drainage, to the most successful modes of culture, and to the best farm implements and machinery. It is an auspicious indication of the progress made in agriculture in our country that already a thousand associations exist in the various States, and that most of our farmers read one or more agricultural papers.

But, however encouraging these noble aids to intelligent and successful farming may be, yet the surest evidence of our progress is furnished by the Preliminary Report of the Census Bureau for 1860. The facts there published have been carefully collected, and the comparisons or results which they afford are exceedingly important.

The total value of agricultural implements manufactured in the United States for 1860, not including, of course, those made on the farm, was $17,802,514 — being an advance of 160 per cent. on the amount manufactured in 1850. Among these implements are some of the highest importance to the farmer.

The threshing machine referred to before has been brought to a high degree of perfection, there having been issued, during the last fifty years, nearly three hundred patents for improvements. Being moved by horse or steam power, and furnished at a moderate cost, they are now in extensive use, greatly abridging the amount of manual labor, and enabling the wheat-growers to prepare their crops seasonably for the market.

In grain the census report gives the following results:

Wheat. — The quantity grown in 1859 was 171,183,381 bushels, being an advance, in ten years, of seventy per cent.; yet during the decade the ravages of the wheat midge in some of the older states have been very extensive. It is stated, however, that the midge is disappearing where, formerly, most destructive, and that wheat-growing will be resumed in many localities where, for a time, it was almost abandoned.

Indian corn. — The quantity grown in 1859 was 830,451,707 bushels, being an increase of over forty per cent. Drill planting, the horse-hoe, and improved corn-shellers, have greatly reduced the amount of manual labor necessary to the production of this crop, while the increased facilities for transportation to market have enhanced its value.

Dairy products. — The butter produced in 1859 was 460,509,854 pounds — an increase of forty-six per cent. The amount of cheese made, and the amount of milk and cream furnished to cities and towns, presents the same increase.

Cotton. — In the beginning of the present century the annual exportation was less than 5,000 bales; in 1859 production had increased to 5,198,077 bales. What is to be the future yield of this great staple time alone can reveal.

The value of animals slaughtered in 1859 was $212,871,653 — an increase of nearly 100 per cent. We have no tables to show the increase of imported stock. There is evidence, however, that various improved breeds of cattle and sheep have been largely introduced into the United States during the last decade, and that better cattle and sheep of finer wool and heavier fleeces are now becoming common throughout the country. Sheep we have imported from France and Germany, and while the quality of the wool has been maintained we have increased the quantity.

When the census of 1860 is published in full the inexorable logic of its statistics will astonish the world, and prove to every intelligent mind that agriculture is the grand element of our progress in wealth, stability, and power. All the new States, during the early periods of their settlement, have rapidly advanced in population and agricultural wealth. This has, of course, been owing chiefly to the rapid influx of residents from the older States and Europe, and to the fact that large tracts of land have been rapidly brought under cultivation. Let Minnesota, during the last decade, be selected as a specimen of progress.

In 1850 the number of acres of ploughed land was 1,900; in 1860, 433,267. In 1850 the number of bushels of wheat raised was 1,401; in 1860, 5,001,432. This rapid agricultural development in ten years is not only an encouraging agency of future progress, but a most remarkable fact of American history.

Various other facts, which cannot now be stated in detail, strengthen the conclusion that American agriculture, especially during the last ten years, has made great progress. Farms throughout the country are more thoroughly cleared of stumps and stones, fences are neater and more durable, farm-houses are more conveniently and tastefully built and adorned, barns are constructed with more reference to the comfort of stock, to the housing of produce, and to the preparation and preservation of manures. A more ready access to markets is afforded by good roads, railways, and canals, improved implements are in general use, while a salubrious climate, a prolific soil, a broad and quiet land, and a beneficent Providence have crowned with abundant success the labors of the husbandman.

Having reached this agricultural vantage ground by honest toil, guided by the lights of experience and science, it is an interesting question, to every American, What are the conditions of a still grander progress and prosperity?

The essential conditions, it seems to me, are — *peace; a continued and increasing demand for agricultural products, both at home and abroad; an increased respect for labor; a more thorough knowledge and practice of agriculture as an art and science;* and, finally, *a more thorough education of our farmers in the physical sciences, in political economy, in taste, and general reading.* Let us consider, briefly, these conditions. A state of war, whether civil or foreign, always reduces the productive industry of a country, and disturbs nearly all the great interests of society. Thus far, it is true, agriculture in the loyal States has been but little embarrassed by the march of armies and the devastations of battle; but this immunity cannot always be enjoyed should the war continue. We must return, therefore, to our normal condition, which is *peace,* if agriculture is to prosper.

With all its wide-spread evils, the rebellion offers, nevertheless, some compensations, and these will plainly appear should the government finally triumph. In order to preserve the unity of our soil and nation, a noble patriotism has withdrawn, for the time being, a large number of citizens from the peaceful employments of agriculture. Some sleeping on blood-stained fields of glory, or beneath the sea, will never more return to the farms which they have tilled; others will come home with broken health, while the many with strong frames will remain, or return to the regions where the storm of war has passed, to make them again blossom as the rose, and to rear new homes for themselves and their children.

The transfer of labor is one of the results of war in every age. In our own case the gain will be considerable, as free labor, smaller homesteads, a greater variety of products, and higher skill and energy in agriculture will take the place of the old system. There must be for a time, in many portions of our country, a scarcity of labor. Men enough, however, for the ordinary requirements of agriculture will be found in every community until labor flows in from Europe, equalizing, somewhat, the demand and supply. Besides, the increased value and labor, and the great demand for breadstuffs at home and abroad, will bring more extensively into use the drill, the horse-hoe, the mower, reaper, thresher, and other labor-saving machines, driven either by steam or horse-power.

If our present unhappy war soon terminates, and the knowledge of our homestead law and increased demand for labor is disseminated throughout Europe, the tide of emigration must speedily set toward America with increased power. Without any special stimulant there has been, hitherto, a steady and large increase in this class of our population. In the decade ending 1840 the number of passengers of foreign birth who arrived in this country was 552,000; in that ending 1850 the number was 2,707,624. The proportion of males to females for the three decades was as 60 to 39. Almost one-half of the whole number was between fifteen and thirty years of age. Of this total of 4,817,924 immigrants, 2,044,678 — nearly all the males — were classed in the official returns as farmers, laborers, and mechanics. I believe this vast influx of labor will continue as heretofore, stimulated by the character of our institutions, the fertility and cheapness of our lands, the demand and remuneration of labor, the increased facilities for immigration, and the noble homestead law, which at once goes into effect. "Every acre of our fertile soil," says a great political economist, "is a mine which only waits the contact of labor to yield its treasures, and every acre is opened to that fruitful contact by the homestead act. When the opportunity, thus afforded to industry, shall be understood by the working millions of Europe, it cannot be doubted that great numbers will seek American homes in order to avail themselves of the great advantages tendered to their acceptance by American law. Every working man who comes betters the condition of the country as well as his own. He adds in many ways, seen and unseen, to its wealth, its intelligence, and its power." It is difficult to estimate the contribution which immigration, properly encouraged by legislation and administration, will make to the revenue, and therefore to the prosperity of the Union, under the guarantee and inspiration of this magnificent law.

The second condition, on which depends our agricultural progress, *is the continued and increased demand for our products, both at home and abroad.* If our country increases in population in the ratio of the last decade, 100,000,000 of inhabitants will be under American law in the year 1900. Besides supplying this rapidly-growing population, Europe and portions of South America will continue to be our customers. Some of the great southern staples, it is true, are temporarily withheld from Europe; but, unless the war continues long enough to create new fields of culture elsewhere, the demand will continue as of old. The statistics of our commerce, even in a time of war, prove that corn is king, and that it can always be made, as it is now, the great conservator of peace between England and the United States. The parliamentary returns of Great Britain for the calendar year 1861 exhibit the following important fact in regard to the amount, in bushels, of breadstuffs imported for that year:

Wheat and flour, 86,552,097 bushels; of which the United States furnished 38,361,675 bushels, or forty-four per cent.

Indian corn, 20,360,004 bushels; of which the United States furnished 11,705,034 bushels, or fifty-seven per cent.

Total, 106,912,101 bushels, or forty-eight per cent.

The New York trade tables show that the United States exported to Great Britain and the continent, for the year ending September 1, 1861, wheat, flour, and Indian corn, 42,524,816 bushels; for the year ending September 1, 1862, wheat, flour, and Indian corn, 52,112,225 bushels. Finally, the report of the British board of trade, for the ten months ending October 31, 1862, shows that Great Britain received from the United States during that time produce amounting to $87,412,325, against $81,728,035 in 1861. This vast amount has been imported while all the southern ports have been blockaded, showing that we furnish, even in a time of war, about one-half of all the food imported into Great Britain, and that the amount is steadily increasing.

The third condition on which depends our agricultural progress is, *increased respect for labor.* In many portions of the United States this condition is amply fulfilled, and the healthful results are plainly seen in finely cultivated farms, in improved homes, in education, thrift, and all the pursuits of an honest, intelligent, and respected industry.

The two prominent causes which have tended to degrade labor in the United States are, first, *the many avenues to wealth, respectability, and position open to young men, independent of manual labor;* and, secondly, *the condition of a large portion of our laboring population.* A great point will be gained for agricultural purposes when farmers shall cherish not only a high respect for their employment themselves, but instil their convictions into the minds of their children. It is not only a great mistake but a great misfortune that young men should feel dissatisfied with the comparatively slow gains of agriculture, or that they should regard the farmer's life as one of tameness and drudgery. They notice the rapid growth of the property of the merchant, the trader, or the professional man, and see him in situations of apparent comfort and ease, limiting, however, their observations to the few who are successful, and not noticing the many who fail of ultimate success. Independent of the unrest, the disappointed ambition, the wear and tear, and mean rewards of public life, it is said that of one thousand merchants who had kept an account at one of the Boston banks, only *six died rich*. The number of successful merchants in New York is even less than this. On the other hand, the farmer, if not absolutely rich, is, at least, independent. He has a home which his labor and his taste have adorned; he has broad acres, not held by lease, as in many countries, but as a freehold. In the Old World land is generally divided into large estates, and owned by few proprietors. In England, for instance, the number of acres is 32,342,400; the number of proprietors about 44,000; in Scotland, 19,738,930 acres and 4,000 proprietors. Such is not the case in our country. No law of entail or primogeniture fosters the accumulation of large estates. It is one of the blessings of the American farmer that he owns in fee simple the land which he cultivates. He has not to stoop and cringe and stand in awe in the presence of those whom he calls masters. He has no master — no favors to beg of man. He has a sturdy independence of character, adorned, perhaps, by culture and refinement. He belongs to a class of citizens who hold in their hands five-sixths of the wealth of the country and its entire political power; and the hands which have wrought this wealth are able to defend the Constitution which makes us one people.

In speaking of the other influence which tends to degrade labor in the United States I do not propose to discuss the vexed question of the relation between capital and labor, but to state a fact as patent as any other on the surface of American society. Slavery always and everywhere degrades labor. This degradation is positive at the south, while its reflex influence is felt throughout the north, in spite of the teaching of the press, the pulpit, the platform, and the example of millions of honest, noble, hard-working men. Had labor been respected at the south — had the soil, divided into moderate farms, been owned by those who tilled it, as at the west — no rebellion would have been desirable or possible. In Brazil the same influences are at work as in our own country. Servile labor has so degraded agricultural industry that a plough was unknown there thirty years ago, and an empire capable of feeding all Europe has never been able to raise food sufficient for its own 7,000,000 of inhabitants, but depends for its breadstuffs upon the United States and the neighboring republics. Though the greatest inducements have been held out by the government, immigrants, owing to the condition of labor, have hitherto been slow in settling in Brazil. Those who have gone, however, are forcing, by superior skill, intelligence, and public sentiment, slave labor towards the equator, and winning the victory which free labor ever gains.

Labor, for a fair remuneration, whether of the brain or hand, should be the glory of America; besides, there is true dignity in labor, especially in cultivating the soil. The object which the farmer has in view is to subdue the earth; to eradicate its briars and thorns, and to plant in their stead what is useful and beautiful to man. It is to fulfil the original appointment of the Creator, that man "shall eat bread in the sweat of his face." "Labor," says a noble worker, "has been made by Providence the law of man's condition. It is the price at which whatever is valuable in life must be earned. Whatever, therefore, degrades labor as the business of life, or renders it distasteful or dishonorable, does violence to our social laws no less than to a wise economy." All improvement — all progress of the race in civilization — has been the result of intelligent labor. It has built our cities, dug our canals, constructed our railways, developed our mines, built our steamers and ships, given life and energy to the industrial arts, and, above all, is feeding and clothing our people and providing for their happiness. "The nation," swys Dr. Sam. Johnson, "that can furnish food and raiment, those universal commodities, may have her ships welcomed at a thousand ports, or sit at home and receive the tribute of foreign countries, enjoy their arts, or treasure up their gold." Let labor, therefore, be crowned with honor — that labor, especially, which contributes so much to the welfare of man, and allows him to approach nearest, through Nature, to Nature's God.

The fourth condition on which depends our agricultural progress is *a more thorough knowledge and practice of agriculture as a science and as an art;* and by this is meant a knowledge of the principles — the *whys* and the *wherefores* — which lie at the foundation of successful farming, and of the practical application of those principles, combining skill, economy, and all the appliances of art. The great difficulty with the American farmer has been, and still is, that he has been nurtured and educated in the habit of cultivating a *primitive soil.* The labor and expense attending the accumulation and application of manures, with the necessity of *unlearning* old habits and theories, have made him tempt nature to the verge of exhaustion, and degrade a noble profession to one of mere routine. While Americans are ever disposed to boast of their inventive skill and teachable disposition, the elder nations, which we affect to despise, offer us some valuable lessons in agriculture. The Chinese, by minute and careful culture, by rotation of crops, and by the use of *every possible kind* of manure, have made their lands yield undiminished products for thousands of years. The northern provinces of China produce two annual crops, and towards the south five are usually obtained every two years. This prodigious yield has continued for ages, and yet the soil is rich and productive, teeming with nearly four hundred millions of human beings. The spade is extensively used; every inch of ground is thoroughly tilled; the hills are terraced, and the soil irrigated wherever possible. Agriculture is everywhere honored and encouraged. The Emperor himself goes annually to the field and turns the first vernal furrow. If China or Japan were to follow our methods of tillage, famine and death would soon sweep millions into their graves.

There is still in our country, strange to say, a large amount of what may be styled *routine* farming. The soil is tilled, the same seed sown, and the crops succeed each other year after year. In some cases, when the soil is inexhaustible, this may be the best method of farming for the present owners; besides, the example of father to son is invaluable, provided that example be good. Practical knowledge is certainly superior to mere theory; but to persist in the same succession of crops, in replanting the same and often the poorest seed, in pursuing the same methods of culture, in rearing the same common breeds of stock, in using the same poor implements of husbandry, is to deny the value of the aggregate experience of men of similar pursuits, and to ignore the progress of the age in science and the useful arts. It should be the aim of every young farmer to do not only as *well* as his father, but to do his best; "to make two blades of grass grow where but one grew before."

"Agriculture," says an ingenious writer, "is an art — man the artist. The soil is his laboratory; manures and seeds his raw material; animal strength and machinery his power; air, heat, and moisture his agents; and grain, roots, fruits, and forage his products. Agriculture is also a science, teaching the artist the best modes of improving and fitting up his laboratory; instructing him in the properties and economical use of his raw material; teaching him how best to apply his power and profit by his agents, thereby enabling him greatly to abridge his labors and multiply his products." Art teaches the hand to do — science, *what* and *how* to do. Art belongs to the individual — science is the concentrated experience of ages and the labor of nations. It is, in short, classified knowledge illustrated in practice and confirmed by experience, and as certain and eternal as truth itself.

The great object of agriculture, as a result, is to develop from the soil as large a quantity and as excellent a quality of useful vegetable, or, indirectly, of animal, products as possible. In order to do this, the farmer should aim to preserve and increase the fertility of the soil; to free it from moisture when superfluous, or add to it when insufficient; to cultivate it thoroughly by the most approved methods, sowing the best seeds according to soils, climate, localities, and markets; to economize labor and expense by using the best implements and power; to select the finest breeds of animals, feeding and sheltering them in the most judicious manner; to secure most perfectly the several harvests, and prepare all farm products for the market in the best manner.

In order to make the farmer most successful, and thus to advance agriculture, the great interest of the republic, he should study chemistry as applied to soils, plants, grains, animals, manures, climates, localities, and tillage. This science, applied to agriculture, teaches him that of the sixty-four simple substances some thirteen go to form vegetation. It cannot be said that any one of these elements is more important, absolutely, than another, except that some of them are scarcer in some soils than in others, and more difficult to procure, and therefore, agriculturally, more valuable. Chemistry, by its powers of analysis, reveals the nature and composition of soils; teaches the proper kind, value, and application of manures; the mode and means of nutrition; and the knowledge of supplying wants and of correcting deficiencies and excesses, wherever noticed, in cultivation. Agriculture is a growth, like the plant it cultivates; and like the mind, also, the more it is developed the more it yields. It can be easily shown that there is no occupation of life where extensive knowledge is more necessary than in the proper cultivation of the soil. There is no occupation so intimately blended with all the branches of the natural sciences; to which geology, chemistry, botany, and entomology are such valuable auxiliaries. Of all human pursuits agriculture is first in order, in necessity, and importance. The best farmer is always the most intelligent man, and a community of knowledge is one of the strongest ties that can bind and bless society. The simple argument, therefore, is this: increased scientific and practical knowledge in any occupation increases man's power in a tenfold ratio; agricultural knowledge, therefore, begets *productiveness,* and in the same proportion develops the wealth, the prosperity, and the progress of our country. Sir Humphrey Davy once remarked, when speaking of the future influence of agricultural chemistry, that "nothing is impossible to labor aided by science. The objects of the skilful agriculturist are like those of the thoughtful patriot. Men value most what they have gained with effort, and a just confidence in their own powers results from success. They love their country better, because they have seen it improved by their own talents and industry, and they identify with their own interests the existence of those institutions and pursuits which have afforded them security, independence, and the multiplied enjoyments of civilized life.'' How strongly do these noble words from the father of agricultural chemistry appeal to the judgment and pride of every farmer to excel in his calling!

Another essential condition to agricultural progress, and following naturally the last named, *is a more thorough education of the farmer in physical science, in political economy, in taste, and general reading.* In fulfilling the condition of a thorough agricultural knowledge, the farmer will have advanced considerably towards an honorable education, and the greatest efficiency and success in his special calling. Still, there is a certain general culture which should characterize every intelligent citizen of a free country, fitting him to think and act wisely and well in all the relations of life. As our government, laws, institutions, and administration spring from the people, and as nine-tenths of our people are tillers of the soil, how important that, as a class, they should have broad and just views of whatever affects the common weal! Though far away from the great centres of political and commercial influence, yet they have the power to make all public servants respect and study their interests, which are eminently those of the whole country. Every farmer, therefore, should aim to be instructed, not only in his special calling, but to know something of general science, of political economy, of taste, and current and general reading.

First, then, in regard to those sciences which are the handmaids of agriculture — what a field of study! These are meteorology and electricity, explaining atmospheric phenomena, upon the changes of which nearly all the operations of farming depend; hydraulics, suggesting plans for the recovery of swamps and submerged lands; botany and vegetable physiology, teaching the relations between natural plants and their soils, in order to establish artificial soils and the highest cultivation; exhibiting, also, the structure of the different orders of cultivated plants, and explaining their nature, and the use of the healthy, and the injurious effects of diseased secretions of plants; geology, explaining the formation of the earth's crust in reference to drainage, and the effects of subsoils on the growth of trees and plants; mechanics, teaching the principles of machinery; anatomy and animal physiology, explaining the structure and functions of animal economy, with a view to perfect development and the prevention of disease; and many other cognate branches, a knowledge of which tends to make man the master of nature. The farmer should also be educated in political economy and those kindred studies which aim to make him a thoughtful and intelligent citizen. Being the vast majority in numbers and wealth, and sustaining the wheels of finance, of trade, manufactures, and commerce, the agriculturist has too much at stake to be behind any in education and influence. Finally, the farmer should breathe that general atmosphere of thought, which, coming to us from distant ages and across the sea, is fanned by pulpit, press, and printed book. Our fathers endured many hardships and privations; but the young farmer of to-day possesses a wealth of advantages for general culture enjoyed by no other people. In some portions of our country these advantages are being improved, and the yield of cultivated mind, like that of the earth, is, indeed, wonderful; but as there is no royal road to agriculture, neither is there to knowledge. The latter must be acquired by long mental husbandry, but, like that of the soil, it yields many solid pleasures during the period of hardest toil, while old age is full of health, wealth, ripeness, and joy, like the rich harvest of autumn. There are, really, but two great sources of national wealth — the *soil* and the *mind* of a nation. Where do we find the most prosperous individuals, communities, and nations? Where the mind and the soil are most cultivated. If, then, the cultivation of these adds wealth, power, and prosperity to a nation, the lack of either, where it might abound, is so much waste of national capital. Why is it, let me ask, that the annual earnings and products of Massachusetts — a State unfavored in soil and climate — exceed, *per capita,* not only those of every other State in our Union, but of the world? Why is it that the labor of a single man in Massachusetts is equal, in profit, as has been conclusively shown by the census, to the labor of five men in South Carolina? It is because her people believe, most thoroughly, that "knowledge is power," and that it is the highest wisdom of political economy to invest largely in schools, colleges, books, a free press, and the highest culture of the individual, to the end that labor may be more productive because more skilled and better directed. But this culture of the mind in science, taste, and general reading, should be based on a higher consideration than that of mere moneyed profit. It should be sought for its own sake, and the pleasures which it brings. The farmer should have taste to appreciate and enjoy the beautiful in nature and in art; taste to adorn his home and his lawns with shrubbery, flowers, and works of art; taste to admire the ripening fruits, the glowing landscape, the processes of nature, and the living groups of animals which he has reared — more attractive to the eye than any painting, though drawn by the genius of Landseer.

Let the farmer, therefore, as a cultivated man, magnify his occupation. In all ages wise, learned, and good men have gladly turned away from the employments of public life to the pleasures, the consolations, and the quietude of rural pursuits. Without citing the men of other countries and ages, who can forget how eagerly Washington laid aside his robes of office and sought the repose of Mount Vernon; how gladly Clay returned to the shades of Ashland after the excitement and honors of congressional life; and how Webster hastened from the cares of state to his herds and fields, and the sight and sounds of the ocean, all endeared to him by the sweet memories of rural life? Men who have chosen to follow other avocations of life, and who pursue them with success, still long for the pleasures and employments of the farm. All their plans of life have a kind of natural culmination in the determination to retire into the country and share with the farmer the healthful and dignified occupation of husbandry.

I have dwelt thus at length on the history of agriculture, and on the conditions of agricultural progress in the United States, in order to show that a great national department of agriculture, enjoying the sympathy and co-operation of the government, of agricultural societies and publications, and of individual farmers, will most rapidly and certainly develop and strengthen these conditions, and thus augment the wealth, the prosperity, the permanency, and the glory of the republic. I hardly deem it necessary to attempt to convince our intelligent countrymen of the vast importance of such a department, inasmuch as whatever improves the condition and the character of the farmer feeds the life-springs of national character, wealth, and power. What agricultural societies and publications have done for single counties and States, this department should do for the whole country, but with a liberality, wisdom, and catholicity commensurate with the resources of the nation, the importance of agriculture, and the co-operation of individuals both at home and abroad.

The objects of a great national department of agriculture were well stated by Judge Buell over twenty years ago, and they are chiefly these:

1. Collecting, arranging, publishing, and disseminating, for the benefit of the nation, statistical and other useful information in regard to agriculture in its widest acceptation, embracing, not only the usual cultivation of the soil, but orcharding, plain and ornamental gardening, rural embellishment, the veterinary art, and household economy. In this connexion the department should aim to teach or recommend authoritatively, by concentrating the ripest agricultural experience and scholarship, the best methods of culture, the choicest plants, vegetables, and fruits, the most valuable grains, grasses, and animals, domestic and otherwise, and the most improved implements of husbandry.

2. Collecting, from different parts of our own and foreign lands, such valuable animals, cereals, seeds, plants, slips, and cuttings as may be obtained by exchange, purchase, or gift, with information as to their modes of propagation, culture, preservation, and preparation for market, and distributing the same throughout the country. Through our postal franking privilege at home, and our foreign ministers, consuls, merchants, missionaries, travellers, and the officers of our naval and merchant fleet, the government enjoys unusual facilities for carrying out this object.

3. Answering the inquiries of farmers and others on all matters relating to agriculture, at the same time stimulating inquiry, inviting discussion, and rewarding research by publishing agricultural statistics of the various States and sections of States in order to guard against the excess or diminution of given products, thereby saving much time, labor, and capital to farmers. And as this department has been created and is sustained for their benefit, they are earnestly invited to correspond with it in order that a proper selection of subjects may be afforded for publication.

4. Testing, by experiment, the value of different agricultural implements and their adaptation to the purposes intended, as well as testing the value of cereals, seeds, and plants, and their adaptation to our soil and climate, before transmitting them to our farmers. In order to carry out this object the department should have under its control a model farm.

5. Analysis, by means of a chemical laboratory, of various soils, grains, fruits, plants, vegetables, and manures, and publishing the results for the guidance and benefit of agriculturists.

6. Establishing a professorship of botany and entomology. It is well known that insects are annually destroying a vast amount of the products of our soil, and that their ravages appear to be on the increase. If the damage done to our wheat crop alone could be prevented, millions of money would be saved to the country.

7. Establishing an agricultural library and museum. In this library the most valuable works would gradually accumulate by exchange, gift, and purchase, for-

ming a rich mine of knowledge. The museum would embrace models of all the most approved implements of husbandry; specimens of soils, rocks, &c.; samples of the various productions of the garden, field, and forest; varieties of grain in straw, and in sample, now generally cultivated or recently introduced into the country, with explanations respecting their soils, climates, weight, yield per acre, and their value as food. Here should be arranged specimens of the component parts of soils, manures, and all the products of agriculture, showing especially the values of different kinds of food. On the walls of this museum should hang the portraits of animals of the most celebrated breeds, and under its roof should be gathered whatever would tend to attract and instruct persons of the highest taste and education.

In regard to the actual condition, workings, and plans of the department, as at present constituted, a few remarks are submitted.

The Department of Agriculture entered into operation on the 1st of July, 1862. The sum expended under its direction, for all purposes, to the 1st of January, 1863, amounts to $34,342 27, leaving an unexpended balance of the appropriation (act of March 1, 1862, chapter 34) for agricultural purposes, for the fiscal year ending June 30, 1863, of $25,657 73. I have asked Congress for an appropriation of $130,000 to meet the expenses of this department for the fiscal year ending June 30, 1864, which is deemed a low estimate. That amount has been approved of and passed by the House of Representatives with almost unanimous consent, and I cannot but believe that it will meet with the concurrence of the Senate of the United States.

Up to January 1, 1863, there have been distributed to members of Congress and other persons throughout the Union 306,304 packages of seeds and cereals, and a much larger number will be sent out between this and the 1st of April next. A large quantity of cotton and choice tobacco seeds, not included in the above enumeration, besides cuttings, bulbs, and plants, have been widely distributed.

A vast amount of labor has been performed in the department since its organization, and its business operations have increased and are daily increasing beyond my most sanguine expectations. Information from every available source, both at home and abroad, has been laboriously sought for, and is now being obtained, which, in due time, when properly classified, will be disseminated, like the seeds, cereals, and plants, gratuitously. The mighty and growing west, especially, has been foremost in this generous rivalry of agricultural exchange, both of products and knowledge.

While the farmer and planter are thus encouraged in their experiments, this department becomes a means of communication with the governments and peoples of all lands. It aims to provide samples of whatever American seeds, plants, &c., may be best suited to foreign climates and soils. It strengthens our friendly relations abroad and at the same time uses its official power and influence to obtain whatever may advance the agricultural interests of our own country.

The third section of the act referred to above, stipulates that the Commissioner of Agriculture "shall receive and have charge of all property of the agricultural division of the Patent Office in the Department of the Interior, including the fixtures and property of the propagating garden, &c." I regret to have to state that, up to this time, no official transfer in compliance with said act has been made to this department; nor has any official report or statement been submitted to me, (although the attention of the Secretary of the Interior was called to the subject early in July last,) setting forth the true condition of the affairs of the said Agricultural Division on the 30th of June, 1862. Fortunately the chemist to the department was in possession of an extensive scientific library and apparatus which he kindly placed at my disposal at the commencement of my duties as Commissioner. The season had so far advanced, however, that but few tests could be made. The chemist has, nevertheless, analyzed some twenty-two varieties of grapes, and is at present engaged in the examination of ten or twelve varieties of American wine; also sorghum, from eight or ten different localities, in order to determine the relative value of the sirup and its capabilities for producing sugar and molasses when compared with sugar cane. The department expects samples of the sorghum from all the States where it is grown, and also from the different sections of each, with samples of the soils from which each specimen of sorghum was produced, in order to determine what composition of soil will produce the best sugar or the largest quantity of sirup. The simple facts in regard to the introduction of the sorghum into the United States afford the strongest argument in favor of testing the value of other foreign products. This plant was first introduced in 1835, through the agency of the Agricultural Bureau of the Patent Office. The yield of sirup, in 1862, in the western States has exceeded 40,000,000 of gallons, an amount in cash value more than sufficient to compensate the government an hundred fold for every dollar ever expended in this bureau. Another interesting fact in regard to the sorghum is, that from its fibre two mills in Illinois are already manufacturing a good article of paper.

As soon as arrangements now being made in the laboratory are completed, the chemist will enter into the analysis of the various grasses and grains of the United States, in order to learn which will produce the greatest amount of fat, flesh, muscle and bone; also of soils, manures, and the constituents of plants, with special reference to restoring fertility to exhausted farms.

The culture of cotton has lately attracted much attention in the free States — especially in Illinois — owing to the rebellion and the consequent scarcity of the staple. Last summer, as a matter of experiment, 500 to 1,000 pounds of cotton were raised per acre by many farmers of Illinois. This department will take early and active measures to induce farmers in Kentucky, Missouri, Southern Illinois, Indiana, and Kansas — all of which States will undoubtedly produce cotton — to turn their attention to the culture of this important staple.

Special interest is felt by the department in the propagation and culture of the ailanthus silk worm of China. This insect has been successfully bred in this country during the last season. It will live and grow and spin its silk in the open air in most of the States of the Union, feeding upon the leaves of the ailanthus, hitherto regarded among us as a worthless, if not a noxious, tree. The worm has recently been introduced into France, and has excited an extraordinary interest. The silk of this worm lasts twice as long as that of the mulberry worm, and can be washed like linen. Indeed, in China the garments made from it are often worn by the second generation.

The attention of the department has been particularly directed, by an act of Congress, to the mode of preparing flax and hemp as a substitute for cotton. Persons engaged in experimenting on these fibres feel sanguine of success. The department has already been put in possession of some fine specimens of the flax-cotton, as well as several samples of fabrics woven from the thread of that material. The investigation will be continued.

The introduction and naturalization of the alpacca should also receive the attention of the government. Although found under the equator, it lives and thrives in the highest inhabited districts of the Andes, where the cold is more severe than in most parts of our country. The animal is hardy, and can subsist on the coarsest and scantiest food, where common sheep would die. While its flesh is excellent, its fleeces are fine, and used for many purposes, to which our Saxon or merino wools, owing to the shortness of their staple, and the difficulty of making them perfectly white, are inapplicable. The British government has expended large sums of money in introducing, (and successfully,) the Alpaca to Australia, and our government should follow at once the same wise policy.

The *papaver somniferum,* or true opium poppy, can, no doubt, be successfully and profitably cultivated in some parts of the United States. It is notorious that no drug is so generally adulterated as opium when received from abroad. As in the case of wines, a native cultivation would supply a pure article, and certainly such a result would be desirable, when the object is a medicinal agent so important and invaluable.

The Department of Agriculture cannot, of course, carry out the general or particular objects indicated in this report, unless it receives, in a liberal measure, the aid of the government and the co-operation of the friends of progressive agriculture. Without entering upon an elaborate discussion, let the vast interest which the department proposes to foster and develop be the high argument in its favor. However much I have shown, indirectly, from history and statistics, the importance of agriculture, I now urge it, directly, as the great element of national unity and prosperity.

Agricultural pursuits tend to moderate and tranquillize the false ambition of nations, to heal sectional animosities, and afford a noble arena for honorable rivalry. The acquisition of comparatively slow, but sure, wealth, drawn from and reinvested in the soil, develops health of body, independence and simplicity of life, and love of country; while the rapid accumulation of wealth, not by production, but by trade and speculation, is unnatural and unhealthful. It attracts men to cities and tempts to wild investments. It too often unsettles moral principle, and substitutes selfishness for patriotism. Men of the country, living in calm content, and forming almost the entire wealth and population of the Union, constitute the truly conservative element in our politics. The men of the city, living in the midst of excitements, political, social, monetary, and moral, too often feed those baneful causes of national ruin, to wit: speculation, luxury, effeminacy, political corruption, and personal ambition. Never was truer or more comprehensive line of poetry penned than that which declares that

"God made the country — man made the town."

Next after moral and intellectual forces, home and foreign commerce, manufactures, lines of intercommunication and agriculture, form the great arch of our national prosperity — agriculture being the keystone as well as the foundation of all. Agriculture furnishes the food of the nation, the raw materials of manufactures, and the cargoes of domestic and foreign commerce. It is the cause and the evidence of true civilization; for, when tillage begins barbarism ends, and the various arts commence. When agriculture prospers, all other interests prosper. When this fails, depression, panic, ruin, ensue. The surplus of agriculture not only allows the farmer to pay his debts and accumulate wealth, but also does the same for the nation. To increase this surplus, therefore, to develop and bring out the vast resources of our soil, and thus create new additional capital, should be the great object of the Department of Agriculture and of legislation. Wise governments, with limited, available territory, so shape their political economy as to reap the advantages of agricultural nations. Thus the United States, agriculturally, form a part of England's prosperity. It has come to pass that her capitalists, her operatives, and her poor, are in nearer sympathy with, and more dependent upon, our broad acres than are our own people. Food, therefore, and next raiment, is the great central interest, around which all other interests revolve. "Grain," says Adam Smith, "is the regulating commodity by which all other commodities are finally measured and determined;" and on this account grain-growing nations will ever command the precious metals and the respect, if not the fear, of mankind.

The United States are, and must always remain, an agricultural nation. For this the soil, the climate, the institutions of the country, and the age of the world, have peculiarly fitted them, and it is the duty of the government to take all possible measures to secure to the agriculturists of America the fullest benefits of its ample resources.

It is hard to realize, and yet as true as Holy Writ, that some who shall read, to-day, these lines, will live to see one hundred millions of freemen dwelling in this dear land of ours. With peace and union restored, based on equity and freedom; with all the conditions of agricultural and mental progress fulfilled; with iron bands stretching from the pines of Maine to the Golden Gate; with the hum of factories on ten thousand streams, and swift-winged commerce flying to distant lands, what pen can sketch the possibility of this young giant of the west?

Old Rome, with all her elements of decay constantly at work, lasted nearly one thousand years, and carried her culture, civilization, and arms to a wondrous pitch of glory. May we not hope and devoutly pray that, taking warning from history and the signs of the times, our republic may so learn lessons of wisdom, that, eradicating all destructive tendencies, she will fortify herself against decay, and become, what Rome was not — eternal?

ISAAC NEWTON,
Commissioner of Agriculture.

His Excellency ABRAHAM LINCOLN,
President of the United States of America.

Health of Farmers' Families, 1862

Source: U. S. Department of Agriculture, *Annual Report*, 1862, pp. 453–70

The impression pervades all classes of society that the cultivation of the soil is the most healthful mode of life, and gives the highest promise of a peaceful, quiet, and happy old age. Dwellers amid brick and mortar, looking on from a distance, have visions in which it is a luxury to indulge, of independence, of comfort, of repose, and of overflowing abundance, as inseparable from a farmhouse; and under the influence of these, with the bewitching and sweetly sad memories of blossoms and budding trees, of green pastures and waving meadows and birds of spring, of fishing and hunting, of shady woods and cool, clear waters dashing briskly over pebbled bottoms, they pine for the country with deep and abiding longings. It may, therefore, be practically useful to inquire as to the correctness of these views, whether they are not materially modified by incidental circumstances which do not necessarily exist, and if so, what may be the best remedy for their prevention or removal. To do this properly, we must look whole facts full in the face, and take our de-parture from what is, and not from what we may think ought to be.

In passing through a lunatic asylum the visitor is sometimes surprised to learn that the most numerous class of unfortunates are from the farm; yet in England, in 1860, but about one-fifth of the population was agricultural. Persons who have taken pains to inquire report that the number of farmers is much less than is generally supposed, in comparison with those engaged otherwise, in the mechanic arts, professional life, the army and navy, &c. The census of 1840 shows that for Eastern Pennsylvania there were eighty thousand farmers, and seventy-four thousand engaged in trade and commerce. While looking at a list of occupations,

The professions number... 32
Farmers 60
Commerce 65
Mechanic arts 147

Adding to these the number who have "no occupation," the proportion of farmers to the whole will be considerably less than one farmer to four of all others.

Dr. Kirkbride, of the Pennsylvania Hospital for the Insane, in his report to the legislature, says one-seventh of the male patients had no regular occupation at the time of attack, while for 1850 the most numerous class were those who had been in some way engaged in agriculture, either as farmers, farmers' wives or daughters. This proportion is not invariable, for in 1862 the same gentleman reports that of 3,947 insane there were 297 farmers, 170 of their wives, and 95 of their daughters — a little less than one-seventh of the whole were from the farm. Of the 4,014 patients in the Central Lunatic Asylum of Ohio, as reported to the legislature for 1862, 1,108 were from the farm. The statistics of the insane in Massachusetts show that the largest number of cases were of farmers' wives.

Nor do farmers live the longest. Travellers and natural philosophers average a greater age. The clergyman, who devotes his life to study and late hours, who spends three-fourths of his existence in-doors, who does not average two hours' daily exercise in twenty-four, who is compelled to an inactivity of body which would seem enough to undermine any constitution, to say nothing of the many depressing influences connected with his office, in listening to the troubled, in counselling the sick, and in waiting upon the dying and the dead — even he often survives the farmer, who rises with the lark to breathe the pure out-door air, whose undisturbed nights, whose supposed independence of the world tend to health, whose table is thought to be spread every day with the freshest butter from the dairy and the new-laid eggs, with pure, rich milk from the spring-house, all cool and sweet, vegetables just dug from the ground or pulled from the vine, and melons taken from the garden, berries from the bending bushes, and fruits, luscious, perfect, and ripe, from the orchard, within the hour; in short, a class of persons whose whole surroundings are universally believed to be the synonyms of quiet, plenty, and independence, and which would seem to be a full guarantee of a healthful and happy old age, does not attain it as often as some other classes whose habits and modes of life are not, other things being equal, as favorable to longevity. In the light of these statements it is proposed to inquire —

First. Why is the farmer more liable to insanity than the citizen? Second. Why does he not average a longer life?

Incessant thinking on any one subject tends to craze the brain, and it does unhinge the intellect of multitudes, as witness the fate of men of "one idea;" of inventors; of inveterate students of prophecy; of those who abandon themselves to thinking of the loved and lost; of the victims of remorse or mortified pride; or of those who feed on sharp-pointed memories. Learned physicians of all civilized countries agree that, in cases like these, it is best to divert the mind, by travel, to a new class of thoughts, to a greater variety of objects of contemplation. It is known that within a short time the attention of the French government has been officially drawn to the fact that one in ten of the young gentlemen who are educated for the army, in the mathematical department, becomes deranged; this is because the mind will not bear exclusive action on one subject. This is the key to the so frequent cases of insanity and suicide among farmers; their subjects of thought are to few; their life is a ruinous routine; there is a sameness and a tameness about it, a paucity of subjects for contemplation, most dangerous to mental integrity.

It is too much the case with our farming population that they have no breadth of view; they cannot sustain a conversation beyond a few comments on the weather, the crops, the markets, and the neighborhood news. And it is worthy of note that their remarks on these subjects are uniformly of the complaining and uphopeful kind, as if their occupation and their thoughts were on the same low and depressing level. This is because the mind is not used enough; is not waked up by a lively interest in a sufficient variety of subjects to promote a healthful tone.

The proper and the all-powerful remedy against the sad effects of a plodding routine existence is a higher standard of general intelligence and a livelier attention to what is too often derisively styled "book-farming." The highest form of human health is found in those who exercise the brain and the body in something like equal proportions. If the greater share of the nervous energies is sent out through the muscles, they will be largely, even preternaturally, developed; but then the brain languishes for want of its due amount of aliment, vigorous thought, while that same body, having been unduly worked, wears out before its time and prematurely decays. It is even better for the mind and body both, that if either has the larger share of exercise it should be the brain, for thereby the chances of longer life are increased, since statistics clearly show that, as a general rule, the most intellectual live the longest. Professor Pierce, of Cambridge, after having examined the subject closely in reference to the young gentlemen pursuing their studies at Harvard University, remarks, as the result of his observations, that, "taking classes in the average, those are the first to die who are the dullest and most stupid, while, as a general rule, those who exercise their brains most constantly, thoroughly, and faithfully, are the longest lived."

The lamented President Felton was accustomed to urge upon the young gentlemen of his classes, with great earnestness, as a means of high health, that they should "use the mind;" use it actively, and on a variety of subjects, so as to avoid any dull routine.

It is an observed fact that many of those sent to penitentiaries for long terms, or for life, become idiotic; but that among the number there is seldom found one who had even small pretensions to a liberal education or to mental culture in any direction. The gifted and unfortunate Mary Queen of Scotts, after lingering eighteen years in prison, came forth to the block with that vigor of mind and clearness of intellect and composure of manner which bespoke a healthful brain. Multitudes of distinguished men have passed a large portion of their lives in prisons, yet maintained their mental integrity, and lived long enough afterwards to accomplish great deeds. Count Confalioneri, having rendered himself obnoxious to the Austrian government, was confined in a dungeon ten feet square for six years, with so dim a light that he could not distinguish the features of the solitary companion of his misfortunes; after which time he remained nine years longer, entirely alone. He writes of himself: "Only one event broke in upon my nine years' vacancy. One day — it must have been a year or two after my companion left me — my dungeon door was opened, and a voice, I knew not whence, uttered these words: 'By order of his Imperial Majesty, I intimate to you that one year ago your wife died.' Then the door was shut. I heard no more. They had but flung this great agony in upon me, and left me alone with it again." Without a book, without a companion, without any intelligence from the outer world, confined in a dark dungeon, living on the coarsest food, having those inward resources which a superior education gave, he fed upon them, and thus maintained both mental and bodily health; while the uninstructed farmer, who can feed on the fat of the land, who passes near three-fourths of his existence in the blessed sunlight, greedily drinking in the luscious out-door air in all its purity, with no restraints of bodily liberty, so abandons himself to the dull routine which comprises almost nothing but to work and eat and sleep, often finds in a less time than fifteen years that vigor of mind and health of body are both on the wane. But a better time is coming, through the influence of our glorious public school system, when it shall no longer be considered an all-sufficient qualification for a farmer that he have a vigorous frame and intelligence enough to skillfully wield an ax or turn a furrow or drive a team. Men are already beginning to perceive that encouragingly remunerative farming is the reward of those who have made themselves familiar with the analysis of soils, who have some knowledge of botany and vegetable chemistry, who have given some study to ascertain the surest way of obtaining the best seeds and the best breeds, and who have "method in their" book "madness," in the selection of cions and grafts and roots and plants. Such men not only make money by farming, but have a positive delight in their labor, and in waiting for results; for one of the sweetest sensations possible to the human mind is the development of useful practical facts as the result of trials and experiments. If the young farmer then begins life with a better literary education, and every farmhouse is regularly visited by some well conducted agricultural periodical, the mental horizon of the hard working tiller of the soil will soon become so extended that a demented farmer will become the rarest of sights. There is another item in reference to the farming population of this country, which certainly adds to the number of its lunatics: it is that grim specter DEBT, which is voluntarily set up in the households of three farmers out of four, whether in the cabin of the thriftless squatter or in the mansion of the princely planter. It is generally a very grave mistake, in the hope of making money by the rise of land, to purchase more than can be conveniently paid for on the spot, or more than can be advantageously cultivated with the force at command. This demon of debt, with its "interest" eating out the farmer's substance ceaselessly and remorselessly, day and night, summer and winter, in sunshine and in shade, is in multitudes of cases a vain sacrifice to the Moloch of gain, a yawning maelstrom, pitiless and unappeasable; it eats out half the joys of many families by reason of the self-denials, the always losing "make-shifts," the working to disadvantage and consequent extra labor, with those anxieties and solicitudes which are necessarily imposed, and which, in their turn, induce irritation of mind, irascibility of temper, and that forgetfulness of those domestic amenities which many times convert a trouble into a pleasure and alleviate or take entirely away half the burdens of life. These acerbities of temper grow by what they feed upon, and seldom fail in the end to leave an evil impress on the character of those upon whom the disturbing consciousness of debt presses with the weight of the nether millstone, impelling too often to the razor, the river, or the halter; for it is not an unknown thing, by any means, that the hard working farmer becomes a suicide. To make this article more specifically practical, the attention of farmers' families is invited to the chief and direct causes of nine-tenths of the diseases which cloud their happiness, which interfere with their prosperity, and often largely add to discouraging expenditures of the means which it caused so much labor to acquire; and first to

Eating

The stomach has two doors, one for the entrance of the food, on the left side, the other for its exit after it has been properly prepared for another process. As soon as the food is swallowed, it begins to go round and round the stomach, so as to facilitate dissolution, just as the melting of a number of small bits of ice is expedited by being stirred in a glass of water; the food, like the ice, dissolving from without, inwards, until all is a liquid mass.

When food is unnaturally detained in the stomach, it produces wind, eructations, fullness, acidity, or a feeling often described as a "weight," or "load," or "heavy." But nature is never cheated. Her regulations are never infringed with impunity; and although an indigestible article may be allowed to pass out of the stomach, it enters the bowels as an intruder, is an unwelcome stranger, the parts are unused to it, like a crumb of bread which has gone the wrong way by passing into the lungs, and nature sets up a violent coughing to eject the intruder. As to the bowels, another plan is taken, but the object is the same — a speedy riddance. As soon as this unwelcome thing touches the lining of the bowels nature becomes alarmed, and, as when a bit of sand is in the eye, she throws out water, as if with the intention of washing it out of the body; hence the sudden diarrhoeas with which persons are sometimes surprised. It was a desperate effort of nature to save the body, for if undigested food remains too long, either in the stomach or bowels, fits, convulsions, epilepsics, apoplexies, and death, are very frequent results.

As a universal rule in health, and, with very rare exceptions, in disease, that is best to be eaten which the appetite craves or the taste relishes.

Persons rarely err in the quality of the food eaten; nature's instincts are the wise regulators in this respect.

The great sources of mischief from eating are three: Quantity, frequency, rapidity; and from these come the horrible dyspepsias which make of human life a burden, a torture, a living death.

By eating fast the stomach, like a bottle being filled through a funnel, is full and overflowing before we know it. But the most important reason is, the food is swallowed before time has been allowed to divide it in sufficiently small pieces with the teeth; for, like ice in a tumbler of water, the smaller the bits are, the sooner are they dissolved. It has been seen with the naked eye, that if solid food is cut up in pieces small as half a pea, it digests almost as soon, without being chewed at all, as if it had been well masticated. The best plan, therefore, is for all persons to thus comminute their food, for even if it is well chewed the comminution is no injury, while it is of very great importance in case of hurry, forgetfulness, or bad teeth. Cheerful conversation prevents rapid eating.

It requires about five hours for a common meal to be dissolved and pass out of the stomach, during which time this organ is incessantly at work, when it must have repose, as any other muscle or set of muscles after such a length of effort. Hence persons should not eat within less than a five hours' interval. The heart itself is at rest more than one-third of its time. The brain perishes without repose.

All are tired when night comes; every muscle of the body is weary and looks to the bed; but just as we lie down to rest every other part of the body, if we, by a hearty meal, give the stomach five hours' work, which, in its weak state, requires a much longer time to perform than at an earlier hour of the day, it is like imposing upon a servant a full day's labor just at the close of a hard day's work; hence the imprudence of eating heartily late in the day or evening; and no wonder it has cost many a man his life.

No laborers or active persons should eat later than sun-down, and then it should not be over half the midday meal. Persons of sedentary habits or who are at all ailing should take absolutely nothing for supper beyond a single piece of cold stale bread and butter or a ship-biscuit, with a single cup of warm drink. Such a supper will always give better sleep and prepare for a heartier breakfast, with the advantage of having the exercise of the whole day to grind it up and extract its nutriment.

It is variety which oftenest tempts to excess. Many a man has been about to push himself back from the table with a feeling as if he did not want any more, when the unexpected appearance of some favorite dish has waked up a new appetite, and he "disposes" of an amount almost equal to that already taken. To prevent over-eating take food deliberately, keep up a lively conversation on pleasurable subjects during the entire repast, and avoid a variety of dishes. For ordinary purposes, there should be on the family table but one kind of bread, one kind of meat, one kind of vegetable, one kind of drink, and one kind of fruit or berries, as dessert; butter, olive-oil, salads, cream, salt, and pepper not being counted, but to be used as desired.

The most ruinous practice in reference to this subject is eating in a hurry, or under the influence of any disagreeable mental excitement, whether of anxiety, passion, or grief, for many have died within an hour by so doing.

Multitudes bring on themselves the horrors of a life-long dyspepsia by drinking large quantities of cold water at their meals, because by cooling the contents of the stomach, which maintains a heat of ninety-eight degrees, to that of the water drank at forty — ice-water being about thirty-two — digestion is as instantly arrested as a burning coal is extinguished by a dash of cold water; and this process is not resumed until heat enough has been drawn from the other parts of the body to raise the whole mass to its natural temperature; but this leaves the other parts of the system so cold that those who have not robust health sometimes rise from the table in a chill; at other times the general system, from want of vigor, has not been able to furnish the amount of heat necessary, digestion is not resumed, and diarrhoea endangers life or convulsions destroy it within a few hours. Large quantities of hot drinks at regular meals will, with equal certainty, destroy the tone of the stomach and lay the foundation for tedious and painful diseases. Invalids should never take any cold drink at meals; and whether hot or cold, they are wise and safe who never allow themselves over a quarter of a pint of any liquid at a regular meal, or within an hour afterwards. A good position for the first half hour after eating is either to stand or sit erect; better still, walk leisurely in the open air, if not too cold, or across the room with hands behind, chin a little elevated, maintaining an agreeable frame of mind. Particularly avoid a stooping position in sewing or reading for the first hour or two after meals, and also heavy lifting, hard study, or any intense mental emotion; these are all destructive of health; and although a single slight error may do no appreciable injury, it never fails to make an impress for ill, until at last there is one repetition too much, and a painful sickness, a life-long torture, or a speedy death from heart disease, hemorrhage, or apoplexy winds up the sad history.

Never force food on the stomach. Never eat without an appetite. Never eat between meals.

Always take breakfast before leaving the house in the morning. This will prevent an easy and early tiring, while the testimony of observant farmers of education corroborates the teachings of the best medical minds, that by strengthening the stomach and sending invigorating nutriment to the whole system, weakened by the long fast of the night, there is generated a power of resistance against the onsets of disease from the cold of winter and from the malarias and miasms of summer, especially in all flat, damp, and luxuriant soils, which can not be adequately expressed in language; while both experience and experiment have combined to show that, by the simple expedient of an early breakfast, individuals and families and neighborhoods have exempted themselves from that scourge of all new countries, "fever and ague," especially if followed by a supper a little before sundown from May to November.

Catching Cold

Experienced physicians in all countries very well know that the immediate cause of a vast number of cases of disease and death is a "cold;" it is that which fires a magazine of human ills; it is the spark to gunpowder. It was to a cold taken on a raw December day that the great Washington owed his death. It was a common cold, aggravated by the injudicious advice of a friend, which ushered in the final illness of Washington Irving. Almost any reader can trace the death of some dear friend to a "little cold."

The chief causes of colds are two: first, cooling off too soon after exercise; second, getting thoroughly chilled while in a state of rest without having been overheated. This latter originates dangerous pleurisies, fatal pneumonias (inflammation of the lungs) and deadly fevers of the typhoid type.

Persons in vigorous health do not take cold easily. They can do with impunity what would be fatal to the feeble and infirm. Dyspeptic persons take cold readily, but they are not aware of it, because its force does not fall on the lungs but on the liver through the skin, giving sick headache, and close questioning will soon develop the fact of some unusual bodily effort followed by cooling off rapidly.

A person wakes up some sunny morning and feels as if he had been "pounded in a bag." Every joint is stiff, every muscle sore, and a single step cannot be taken without difficulty or actual pain. Reflection will bring out some unwonted exercise, and a subsequent cooling off before knowing it — as working in the garden in the spring-time; over exertion about the house-work; showing new servants "how to do;" in going a "shopping," an expedition which taxes the mind and body to the utmost — these and similar "little nothings" rouse women's minds to a pitch of interest and excitement scarcely excelled by that of counsellors of state in determining the boundaries of empires or the fate of nations, to return home exhausted in body, depressed in mind, and thoroughly heated. The first thing done is to toss down a glass of water to cool off, next to lay aside bonnet, shawl, and "best dress," and lastly, to put on a cold dress, lie down on a bed in a fireless room and fall asleep, to wake up almost certainly with a bad cold, which is to confine to the chamber for days and weeks together, and not unseldom carries them to the grave!

A lady was about getting into a small boat to cross the Delaware; but wishing first to get an orange at a fruit stand, she ran up the bank of the river, and on her return to the boat found herself much heated, for it was summer, but there was a little wind on the water, and the clothing soon felt cold to her. The next morning she had a severe cold, which settled on her lungs, and within the year she died of consumption.

A stout, strong man was working in a garden in May. Feeling a little tired about noon, he sat down in the shade of the house and fell asleep; he waked up chilly; inflammation of the lungs followed, ending, after two years of great suffering, in consumption.

A Boston ship-owner, while on the deck of one of his vessels, thought he would "lend a hand" in some emergency, and pulling off his coat, worked with a will until he perspired freely, when he sat down to rest awhile, enjoying the delicious breeze from the sea. On attempting to rise he found himself unable, and was so stiff in his joints that he had to be carried home and put to bed, which he did not leave until the end of two years, when he was barely able to hobble down to the wharf on crutches.

A lady, after being unusually busy all day, found herself heated and tired toward sundown of a summer's day. She concluded she would rest herself by taking a drive to town in an open vehicle. The ride made her uncomfortably cool, but she warmed herself up by an hour's shopping, when she turned homeward; it being late in the evening, she found herself more decidedly chilly than before. At midnight she had *pneumonia,* (inflammation of the lungs,) and in three months had the ordinary symptoms of confirmed consumption.

A lady of great energy of character lost her cook, and had to take her place for four days; the kitchen was warm, and there was a draught of air through it. When the work was done, warm and weary, she went to her chamber, and lay down on the bed to rest herself. This operation was repeated several times a day. On the fifth day she had an attack of lung fever; at the end of six months she was barely able to leave her chamber, only to find herself suffering with all the more prominent symptoms of confirmed consumption; such as quick pulse, night and morning cough, night-sweats, debility, short breath, and falling away.

A young lady rose from her bed on a November night, and leaned her arm on the cold window-sill to listen to a serenade. Next morning she had *pneumonia,* and suffered the horrors of asthma for the remainder of a long life.

Farmers' wives lose health and life every year in one of two ways: by busying themselves in a warm kitchen until weary, and then throwing themselves on a bed or sofa without covering, and perhaps in a room without fire; or by removing the outer clothing, and perhaps changing the dress for a more common one, as soon as they enter the house after walking or working. The rule should be invariable to go at once to a warm room and keep on all the clothing at least for five or ten minutes, until the forehead is perfectly dry. In all weathers, if you have to walk and ride on any occasion do the riding first.

An engineer, in the vigor of manhood, brought upon himself an incurable disease through a cold taken by standing on a zinc floor as soon as he left his bed in the morning, while he washed himself. Many a farmer's wife or daughter has lost her life by standing on a damp floor for hours together on washing days.

A young lady, the only daughter of a rich citizen, stood an hour on the damp grass, while listening to the music in the Central Park; the next day she was attacked with inflammation of the lungs, of which she died within a week.

An estimable lady, a farmer's wife, busied herself in household affairs on a summer's day; late in the afternoon, having perspired a good deal and being weary, she rode to town in an open vehicle to do some shopping; finding herself a little chilly, she walked rapidly on leaving her carriage, and soon became comfortably warm again. While shopping it rained. After the shower she started homeward in a cool wind; this checked the perspiration the second time, and with all available precaution she reached home chilled through and through, and died the victim of consumption within the year.

A farmer's daughter "went a berrying;" the ground was flat and a little marshy; her shoes were thin, and by the excitement of company she remained several hours. She was ill next day. Four years later she stated to her physician that she had not seen a well hour since. She was then in the last stages of a hopeless decline, and died soon after.

A little attention would avert a vast amount of human suffering in these regards. Sedentary persons, invalids, and those in feeble health, should go directly to a fire after all forms of exercise, and keep all the garments on for a few minutes; or, if in warm weather, to a closed apartment, and, if anything, throw on an additional covering. When no appreciable moisture is found on the forehead the out-door garments may be removed. The great rule is, cool off very slowly always after the body has in any manner been heated beyond its ordinary temperature.

The moment a man is satisfied he has taken cold let him do three things: First, eat nothing; second, go to bed, cover up warm in a warm room; third, drink as much cold water as he can, or as he wants, or as much hot herb tea as he can; and in three cases out of four he will be almost well in thirty-six hours; if not, send for an educated and experienced physician at once, for any "cold" which does not "get better" within forty-eight hours is neither to be trifled with nor experimented upon.

Dress

The main object of dress is not to impart warmth, but to keep the natural warmth about the body, and thus prevent those sudden and fatal changes from heat to cold which occur in passing from an in-door temperature of sixty-five degrees to that of zero or lower without, as in mid-winter. The temperature of the northern States varies over a hundred degrees during the year, sometimes nearly half that within twenty-four hours. Dress provides against these destructive sudden changes, by maintaining the warmth of the skin at its natural state, which is ninety-eight degrees, whether a man is on an iceberg in Greenland or on a sand island in a tropical sea. The materials of clothing which best keep the heat about the body are called *non*-conductors, such as furs and woollens, while the conductors are such as cool the body, by conveying the natural heat from it with great rapidity; the greater conducting ability is measured by the greater coldness which an article causes on the first instant of its application. In the very coldest weather fur and woollen flannel appear but a little cool, and that but for an instant, and the next there is a sensation of increasing, comfortable warmth; cotton flannel feels colder than woollen, silk colder than cotton, Irish linen colder than silk, and damp Irish linen greatly colder than either. A damp woollen shirt feels but a little cold, and begins to get warm and dry in an instant, even if the person is in a profuse perspiration; while an Irish linen or silk shirt, if damp with perspiration or otherwise, feels cold and clammy and sepulchral on the instant of its touching the skin, and will remain so for hours without getting dry, never failing to leave a cold in some troublesome or even dangerous form; hence, as persons perspire easily and profusely in summer, Irish linen cannot be worn in warm weather with impunity by the working classes and those liable to perspiration from a little walking or exercise. Thus it is that British sailors in the navy are compelled to wear woollen flannel shirts all the year and in all latitudes — in the north, because it keeps the natural warmth from escaping from the body, thus maintaining a temperature of ninety-eight degrees about the skin; and in hot climates in summer because, although woollen is a bad conductor of heat, it is a good conductor of water; for, if a woollen blanket is thrown over a sweating horse, in a very short time his hair and the inner side of the blanket will be dry, while the microscope will discover the whole outside surface spangled with millions of tiny drops of water. For these reasons woollen flannel should be worn next the skin by all our people from one year's end to another — a gauze material in summer; in winter a more substantial article. White flannel fulls up, and becomes hard and stiff unless about a fifth of it is cotton. Colored flannel, especially the red, always remains soft and pliable. These things are indisputably true, and a practical attention to them, on the part of all hard-working people, would prevent an amount of pain and sickness every year which figures cannot express. This would be especially true if, in warm weather, when fires are not needed in the house, farmers and other laborers would wear a moderately stout article of red woollen flannel as a shirt, with nothing over it while at work, but at other times a thin coat over that. Any flannel garment worn during the day should be hung up to air at night, while the night-gown all the year round should be of stout cotton shirting, for if woollen is worn next the skin all the time it makes it callous, and is otherwise injurious. The best, safest, and most healthful head-dress for farmers and workmen all the year round is a common, easy-fitting wool or felt hat; in winter it keeps the head warm; in summer it is a great protection against sun-stroke, especially if a silk hankerchief or a few leaves of a tree are worn in the crown. Such a hat is a great preventive of baldness, if worn from early youth, because it allows the blood to flow freely to and from the scalp; but if the vessels are compressed, as is done by the common unyielding silk hat, the free circulation of the blood is obstructed, and the nourishment of the hair-roots or bulbs being cut off, the hair perishes irretrievably, causing all the discomforts and inconveniences of baldness.

Death often comes to the honest laborer, as well as to others, through the feet, either by tightly-fitting shoes, which, by obstructing the circulation, keep the feet cold, thus laying the foundation for troublesome diseases, or by shoes which do not keep out the dampness. In purchasing new shoes, or having the measure taken, put on two pairs of woollen socks, without the knowledge of Crispin, and the new pair will feel from the first "as easy as an old shoe."

A piece of tarred or pitch cloth sewed between the layers of the shoe-sole is a great protection against dampness from without; or take pitch, not hot enough to burn the leather, and apply it to the bottom and edges of the sole with a rag, let it dry thoroughly, and repeat the application thus three or four times; it is contended that a sole thus treated will not only be impervious to water and dampness, but will wear nearly twice as long as a sole not thus treated. It is an excellent plan to have two pairs of shoes, to be worn on alternate days, so as to have a perfectly dry pair to put on every morning, allowing the unworn ones to remain in a warm, dry place. Washing the feet every night in warm weather, and soaking them in warm water for ten minutes three times a week in winter, admirably promotes that warmth, pliability, and softness of the skin of the feet, so indispensable to health and comfort, saying nothing of the cleanliness of the practice, and its tendency both to prevent and to cure corns. But after all washings of the feet it is of the first importance, after wiping them well, to hold them to the fire and rub them with the hands until perfectly dry and warm in every part.

It will be useful to add here, in reference to corns, that they are caused by pressure and by friction also; hence they may be the result of a shoe that is either too tight or too loose. They can be always either permanently cured or kept within bounds by simply soaking the corn in hot water twenty minutes every night, and then patiently rub a few drops of sweet oil on the top of the corn; repeat the oil in the morning, and continue these until the core of the corn can be picked out with the finger-nail: nothing harder or sharper should ever touch a corn.

Part II

Hardships of Farmers' Wives

A sad record is it, and short! but its details would fill whole shelves of a library, more intensely interesting than any tale fancy every told, as found in an official report for 1862, made to the legislature of an agricultural State, that of six hundred and seven patients in an insane asylum thirty-nine were farmers' wives, sixteen farmers' daughters; no other class of wives or daughters was half as numerous! and this in spite of all that has been said and sung of the dairy-maid, so ruddy of cheek, where the roses and the lily vie, so lithe of limb, whose breath as pure as the air of the morning, whose laugh as merry as the voices of the birds in the wood, and whose step as springy and elastic as the new-made bow; all these bright fancies vanish like mists of the morning before a summer's sun, in face of the hard, dry, and statistical line written above; and there comes up another vision, not of youth and beauty and innocence and exuberant health, but that of the pale and wan and haggard face, half covered with long black hair, and coal black eyes peering hotly on you from behind the bars and grates of a dark prison-house! True, happily true is it, that this state of things is not part and parcel, necessarily, of the farmhouse; it is not an inherent calamity; it is only an accidental circumstance, which can be remedied promptly and forever; and it is because of this delightful truth these pages are written. Fortunately, it cannot be denied that there is scarcely any lot in life, in this country, which promises so much quiet enjoyment, such uniform health and uninterrupted prosperity, as that of a gentleman farmer's wife; of a man who has a well-improved, well-stocked plantation, all paid for, with no indebtedness, and a sufficient surplus of money always at command to meet emergencies and to take advantage of those circumstances of times and seasons and changing conditions which are constantly presenting themselves. Such a woman is incomparably more certain of living in quiet comfort to a good old age than the wife of a merchant-prince, or one of the money-kings of Wall street; who, although they may clear thousands in a day, do, nevertheless, in multitudes of cases, die in poverty, leaving their wives and daughters to the sad heritage of being slighted and forgotten by those who once were made happy by their smiles; and to pine away in tears and destitution. On the other hand, it is often a sad lot indeed to be the wife of a farmer who begins married life by renting a piece of land or buying a "place" on credit, with the moth of "interest" feeding on the sweat of his face every moment of his existence.

The affectionate and steady interest, the laudable pride, and the self-denying devotion which wives have for the comfort, prosperity, and respectability of their husbands and children, is a proverb and a wonder in all civilized lands. There is an abnegation of self in this direction as constant as the flow of time; so loving, so uncomplaining, so heroic, that if angels make note of mortal things they may well look down in smiling admiration. But it is a melancholy and undeniable fact that, in millions of cases, that which challenges angelic admiration fails to be recognized or appreciated by the very men who are the incessant objects of these high, heroic virtues. In plain language, in the civilization of the latter half of the nineteenth century, a farmer's wife, as a too general rule, is a laboring drudge; not of necessity by design, but for want of that consideration, the very absence of which, in reference to the wife of a man's youth, is a crime. It is perhaps safe to say, that on three farms out of four the wife works harder, endures more, than any other on the place; more than the husband, more than the "farm-hand," more than the "hired help" of the kitchen. Many a farmer speaks to his wife habitually in terms more imperious, impatient, and petulant than he would use to the scullion of the kitchen or to his hired man.

2. In another way a farmer inadvertently increases the hardships of his wife; that is, by speaking to her or treating her disrespectfully in the presence of the servants or children. The man is naturally the ruling spirit of the household, and if he fails to show to his wife, on all occasions, that tenderness, affection, and respect, which is her just due, it is instantly noted on the part of menials, and children too, and they very easily glide into the same vice, and interpret it as an encouragement to slight her authority, to undervalue her judgment, and to lower that high standard of respect which of right belongs to her. And as the wife has the servants and children always about her, and is under the necessity of giving hourly instructions, the want of fidelity and promptness to these is sufficient to derange the whole household, and utterly thwart that regularity and system, without which there is no domestic enjoyment, and but little thrift on the farm.

The indisputable truth is, that there is no other item of superior, or perhaps equal, importance, in the happy and profitable management of any farm, great or small, than that every person on it should be made to understand that deference and respect and prompt and faithful obedience should be paid, under all circumstances, to the wife, the mother, and the mistress; the larger the farm, the greater interests there are at stake. If poor, then the less ability is there to run the risk of losses which are certain to occur in the failure of proper obedience. An illustration: a tardy meal infallibly ruffles the temper of the workmen, and too often of the husband; yet all the wife's orders were given in time; but the boy has lagged in bringing wood; or the girl failed to put her loaf to bake in season, because they did not fear the mistress, and the master was known not to be very particular to enforce his wife's authority. If by these causes a dinner is thrown back half an hour, it means on a good-sized farm a loss of time equivalent to the work of one hand a whole day; it means the very considerable difference between working pleasantly and grumblingly the remainder of the day; it means, in harvest time, in showery weather, the loss of loads of hay or grain.

3. Time and money and health, and even life itself, are not unfrequently lost by want of promptitude on the part of the farmer in making repairs about the house, in procuring needed things in time, and in failing to have those little conveniences which, although their cost is even contemptible, are in a measure practically invaluable. The writer was in a farmer's house one night, where the wife and two

daughters were plying their needles industriously by the dim light of a candle, the wick of which was frequently clipped off by a pair of scissors. And yet this man owned six hundred acres of fine grazing lands, and every inch paid for. I once called on an old friend, a man of education, and of a family loved and honored all over his native State. His buildings were of brick, in the centre of an inherited farm of several hundred acres. The house was supplied with the purest, coldest, and best water from a well in the yard; the facilities for obtaining which were a rope, one end of which was tied to a post, the other to an old tin pan, literally. The discomfort and unnecessary labor involved in these two cases may be estimated by the reader at his leisure.

I know it to be the case, and have seen it on many western farms, when firewood was wanted, a tree was cut down and hauled bodily to the door of the kitchen; and when it was all gone another was drawn up to supply its place, giving the servant and the wife green wood with which to kindle and keep up their fires.

There are thousands of farms in this country where the spring which supplies all the water for drink and cooking is from a quarter to half a mile distant from the house, and a "pailful" is brought at a time, involving five or ten miles' walking in a day, for months or years together, when a little mechanical ingenuity or a few dollars expense would bring the water to the door. How many weeks of painful and expensive sickness; how many lives have been lost of wives and daughters and servants, by being caught in a shower between the house and the spring, while in a state of perspiration or weakness from working over the fire, cannot be known, but that they may be numbered by thousands will not be intelligently denied.

Many a time a pane of glass has been broken out, or a shingle has been blown from the roof, and the repair has not been made for weeks or many months together; and for want of it have come agonizing neuralgias; or a child has waked up in the night with the croup, to get well only with a doctor's bill, which would have paid twenty times for the repair, even if a first-born has not died, to agonize a mother's heart to the latest hour of life; or the leak in the roof has remained, requiring the placing of a bucket or the washing of the floor at every rain.

4. Cruelties are thoughtlessly sometimes, and sometimes recklessly, perpetrated by farmers of their wives, as follows: a child or other member of the family is taken sick in the night; the necessary attention almost invariably falls on the wife, to be extended through a greater part, if not the whole night. Wearied with the previous day's duties, with those solicitudes which always attend sickness; with the responsibilities of the occasion, and a loss of requisite rest, the wife is many times expected to "see to breakfast" in the morning, as if nothing had happened. The husband goes to his work, soon becomes absorbed in it, and forgets all about the previous night's disturbance; meets his wife at the dinner-table; notices not the worn-out expression on her face; makes no inquiry as to her feelings; and if anything on or about the table is not just exactly as it ought to be, it is noticed with a harshness which would be scarcely excusable if it had been brought about with a deliberate calculation.

The same thing occurs multitudes of times during the nursing periods of mothers; how many nights a mother's rest is broken half a dozen times by a restless, crying, or ailing infant, every mother and observant man knows. In such cases the farmer goes into another room, and sleeps soundly until the morning; and yet, in too many cases, although this may be, and is repeated several nights in succession, the husband does not hesitate to wake his wife up with the information that it is nearly sunrise, the meaning of which is, that he expects her to get up and attend to her duties. No wonder that in many of our lunatic asylums there are more farmers' wives than any other class; for there is no fact in medical science more positively ascertained than that insufficient sleep is the most speedy and certain road to the madhouse. Let no farmer, then, let no mechanic, let no man, who has any human sympathy still left, allow his wife to be waked up in the morning except from very urgent causes; and, further, let them give every member of the household to understand that quietude about the premises is to be secured always until the wife leaves her chamber; thus having all the sleep which nature will take, the subsequent energy, cheerfulness, and activity which will follow will more than compensate for the time required to "get her sleep out," not only as to her own efficiency, but as to that of every other member of the household; for let it be remembered that a merry industry is contagious.

There are not a few farmers whose imperious wills will not brook the very slightest dereliction of duty on the part of any hand in their employ, and whose force of character is such that everything on the farm, outside the house, goes on like clockwork. They look to their wives to have similar management indoors, and are so swift to notice even slight shortcomings, that at length their appearance at the family table has become inseparable from scenes of jarring, fault-finding, sneering, depreciating comparisons, if not of coarse vituperation; and all this simply from the failure to remember that they have done nothing to make the wife's authority in her domain as imperative as their own. They make no account of the possible accidents of green wood to cook with; of an adverse wind which destroys the draught of the chimney; of the breaking down of the butcher's cart, or of their own failure to procure some necessary material. They never inquire if the grocer has not sent an inferior article, or an accident has befallen the stove or some cooking utensil. It is in such ways as these, and many more like them, that the farmer's wife has her whole existence poisoned by those daily tortures which come from her husband's thoughtlessness, his inconsideration, his hard nature, or his downright stupidity. A wife naturally craves her husband's approbation. "Thy desire shall be to thy husband" is the language of Scripture, which, whatever may be the specific meaning of the quotation, certainly carries the idea that she looks up to him with a yearning inexpressible, for comfort, for support, for smiles and sympathy; and when she does not get these, the whole world else is a waste of waters, or life a desert, as barren of sustenance as the great Sahara. But this is only half the sorrow. When, in addition to this want of approbation and sympathy, there comes the thoughtless complaint; the remorseless and repeated fault-finding and the contemptuous gesture, when all was done that was possible under the circumstances — in the light of treatment like this, it is not a wonder that settled sadness and hopelessness is impressed on the face of many a farmer's wife, which is considered by the thoughtful physician as the prelude to that early wasting away which is the lot of many a virtuous and faithful and conscientious woman.

The attentive reader will not fail to have observed that the derelictions adverted to on the part of farmer husbands are not regarded necessarily as the result of a perverse nature, but rather in the main from inconsideration or ignorance; but, from whatever cause, the effect is an unmixed evil, and it is to be hoped that our religious papers and all agricultural publications will persistently draw attention to these things, so as to excite a higher sentiment in this direction. It can be done and ought to be done; and it is highly creditable to the Department of Agriculture to have expressly desired that an article should be written on the subject of the hardships and the unnecessary exposures of farmers' wives, to the end that information and instruction should be imparted in this direction.

There are some suggestions to be made with a view to lightening the load of farmers' wives, the propriety, the wisdom, and advantages of which cannot fail to be impressed on every intelligent mind.

1. A timely supply of all that is needed about a farmer's house and family is of incalculable importance; and when it is considered that most of these things will cost less to get them in season, and also that a great deal of unnecessary labor can be avoided by so doing, it would seem only necessary to bring the fact distinctly before the farmer's mind to secure an immediate, an habitual, and a life-long attention. The work necessary to keep a whole household in easily running order is very largely curtailed by having everything provided in time, and by taking advantage of those little domestic improvements devised by busy brains, and which are brought to public notice weekly in the columns of our agricultural papers.

2. It requires less time and less labor to have the winter's wood for house-heating and cooking brought into the yard and piled up cozily under a shed or placed in a wood-house in the fall, than to put it off until the last moment, when perhaps it is saturated with water, or, still worse, to compel the women to use green wood, and perhaps to cut and split it at that.

3. It is incalculably better to have the potatos and other vegetables gathered and placed in the cellar or in an outhouse near by in the early fall, so that the cook may get at them under cover, than to put it off week after week, until near Christmas, compelling the wife and servants, once or twice every day, to leave a heated kitchen, and most likely with thin shoes, go to the garden with a tin pan and a hoe, to dig them out of the wet ground and bring them home in slosh or rain. The truth is, it perils the life of the hardiest persons, while working over the fire in cooking or washing, to go outside the door of the kitchen for an instant; a damp, raw wind may be blowing, which, coming upon an inner garment, throws a chill or the clamminess of the grave over the whole body in an instant of time, to be followed by the reaction of fever or fatal congestion of the lungs; or by making a single step in the mud, which is in thousands of cases allowed to accumulate at the very door-sill for want of a board or two, or a few flat stones, not a rod away.

4. No farmer's wife who is a mother ought to be allowed to do the washing of the family; it is perilous to any woman who has not a vigorous constitution. The farmer, if too poor to afford help for that purpose, had better exchange a day's work himself. There are several dangers to be avoided while at the tub. It requires a person to stand for hours at a time. This is a strain upon the young wife or mother, which is especially perilous; besides, the evaporation of heat from the arms, by being put in warm water and then raised in the air alternately, so rapidly cools the system that inflammation of the lungs is a very possible result. Then the labor of washing excites perspiration and induces fatigue; in this condition the body is so susceptible to taking cold that a few moments' rest in a chair, or exposure to a

draught of air, especially in hanging out clothes, is quite enough to cause a chill, with results painful or even dangerous, according to the particular condition of the system at the time. No man, however poor, has a right to risk his wife's health in this way, if he has vigorous health himself; and, if poor, he cannot afford, for the three to six shillings which would pay for a day's washing, to risk his wife's health, her time for two or three weeks, and the incurring of a doctor's bill, which it may require painful economies for months to liquidate.

5. Every farmer owes it to himself, in a pecuniary point of view, and to his wife and children, as a matter of policy and affection, to provide the means early for clothing his household according to the seasons, so as to enable them to prepare against winter especially. Every winter garment should be completed by the first of November, ready to be put on when the first winter day comes. In multitudes of cases valuable lives have been lost to farmers' families by improvidence as to this point. Most special attention should be given to the under clothing; that should be prepared first, and enough of it to have a change in case of an emergency or accident. Many farmers act even niggardly in furnishing their wives the means for such things. It is far wiser and safer to stint the members of his family in their food than in the timely and abundant supply of substantial under clothing for winter wear. It would save an incalculable amount of hurry and its attendant vexations, and also of wearing anxiety, if farmers were to supply their wives with the necessary material for winter clothing as early as midsummer. In this connexion it would be well for farmers to learn a lesson of thrift from some of our long-headed city housewives. It is particularly the habit of the well-to-do, the forehanded, and the rich — by which they legally and rightfully get at least twenty per cent. for their money — to purchase the main articles of clothing at the close of any season, to be made up and worn the corresponding season of the next year. Merchants uniformly aim, especially in cities, to "close out" their stocks, for example, for the winter, at the end of winter or beginning of spring. They consider it profitable to sell out the remnant of their winter stock in March at even less than cost, for on what they get for these remnants they make three profits — on the spring, the summer, and the fall goods — whereas had they laid by their winter stock they would have had but one profit, from which would have to be deducted the yearly interest, storage, and insurance. Thus by purchasing clothing materials six or eight months beforehand, the farmer not only saves from twenty to forty per cent. of the first cost, but gives his wife the opportunity of working upon them at such odds and ends of time as would otherwise be unemployed in a measure, and would enable her also to have everything done in a better manner, simply by having abundant time, thus avoiding haste, vexation, solicitude, and disappointment, for nothing so clouds a household as a sense of being behindhand and of the necessity of painful hurry and effort.

6. Few things will bring a more certain and happy reward to a farmer than for him to remember his wife is a social being; that she is not a machine, and therefore needs rest, and recreation, and change. No farmer will lose in the long run, either in money, health, or domestic comfort, enjoyment and downright happiness, by allotting an occasional afternoon, from mid-day until bedtime, to visiting purposes. Let him, with the utmost cheerfulness and heartiness, leave his work, dress himself up, and take his wife to some pleasant neighbor's, friend's, or kinsman's house, for the express purpose of relaxation from the cares and toils of

home, and for the interchange of friendly feelings and sentiments, and also as a means of securing that change of association, air, and food, and mode of preparation, which always wakes up the appetite, invigorates digestion, and imparts a new physical energy, at once delightful to see and to experience; all of which, in turn, tend to cultivate the mind, to nourish the affections, and to promote that breadth of view in relation to men and things which elevates, and expands, and ennobles, and without which the whole nature becomes so narrow, so contracted, so barren and uninteresting, that both man and woman become but a shadow of what they ought to be.

7. Let the farmer never forget that his wife is his best friend, the most steadfast on earth; would do more for him in calamity, in misfortune, and sickness than any other human being, and on this account, to say nothing of the marriage vow, made before high Heaven and before men, he owes to the wife of his bosom a consideration, a tenderness, a support, and a sympathy, which should put out of sight every feeling of profit and loss the very instant they come in collision with his wife's welfare as to her body, her mind, and her affections. No man will ever lose in the long run by so doing; he will not lose in time, will not lose in a dying hour, nor in that great and mysterious future which lies before all.

8. There are "seasons" in the life of women which, as to some of them, so affect the general system, and the mind also, as to commend them to our warmest sympathies, and which imperatively demand from the sterner sex the same patience, and forbearance, and tenderness which they themselves would want meted out to them if they were not of sound mind. At these times some women, whose uniform good sense, propriety of deportment, and amiability of character command our admiration, become so irritable, fretful, complaining, quarrelsome, and unlovely as to almost drive their husbands mad. Their conduct is so inexplicable, so changed, so perfectly causeless that they are almost overcome with desperation, with discouragement, or indignant defiance of all rules of justice, of right, or of humanity. The ancients, noticing this to occur to some women for a few days in every month, gave it the appellation of "lunacy," *luna* being the Latin name for moon or monthly. Some women, at such times, are literally insane, without their right mind, and, as it is an infliction of nature, far be it from any husband, with the feelings of a man, to fail at such times to treat his wife with the same kind care, and extra tenderness, and pitying love that he would show to a demented only child. The skillful physician counsels in such cases the scrupulous avoidance of every word, or action, or even look which by any possibility could irritate the mind, excite the brain, or wound the sensibilities, and, as far as possible, to yield gracefully and good-naturedly to every whim and every caprice; to seem to control in nothing, to yield in all things. Under these calming influences the mind sooner resumes its wonted rule; the heart gushes out in new loves and wakes up to a warmer affection than was ever known before. A misunderstanding of the case and an impatient resistance at all points has before now driven women to desperation, to a life-long hate, to suicide, or to a fate worse than all — to peer through the iron bars of a lunatic's cell for a long and miserable lifetime. Let every husband who has a human heart consider the subject well.

9. In these and other peculiar states of the system, arising from nervous derangement, women are sometimes childish, and various curious phenomena take place. There is an inability to speak for a moment or a month, the heart seems to

"jump up in the mouth," or there is a terrible feeling of impending suffocation. At other times there are actual convulsions, or an uncontrollable bursting out into tears. These and other disagreeable phenomena are derisively and unfeelingly called "hysterics" or "nervousness," but they are no more unreal to the sufferer than are the pains of extraction for "nothing but the toothache." These symptoms are not unfrequently set down to the account of perverseness when it should no more be done than to call it perversity to break out in uncontrollable grief at the sudden information of the death of the dearest friend on earth. The course of conduct to be pursued in cases of this kind is at once the dictate of science, of humanity, and of common sense; it is to sympathize with and soothe the patient in all ways possible, until the excess of perturbation has passed away, and the system calms down to its natural, even action.

10. Unless made otherwise by a vicious training a woman is as naturally tasteful, tidy, and neat in herself, and as to all her surroundings, as the beautiful canary, which bathes itself every morning, and will not be satisfied until each rebellious feather is compelled to take the shape and place which nature designed. It is nothing short of brutality to war against those pure elevating and refining instincts of a woman's better nature, and it is a husband's highest duty, his interest, and should be his pleasure and his pride, to sympathize with his wife in the cultivation of these instincts, and to cheerfully afford her the necessary means, as far as he can do so consistently. No money is better spent on a farm, or anywhere else, than that which enables the wife to make herself, her children, her husband, and her house appear fully up to their circumstances. The consciousness of a torn or buttonless jacket or soiled dress worn at school degrades a boy or girl in their own estimation, and who that is a man does not hate to feel that he is wearing a ragged or dirty shirt? The wife who is worthy of the name will never allow these things if she is provided with means for their prevention, and it is in the noble endeavor to maintain for herself and family a respectability of appearance which their station demands, with means and help far too limited, which so irritates and chafes and annoys her proper pride that many a time the wife's heart and constitution and health are all broken together. This is the history of multitudes of farmers' wives, and the niggardly natures which allow it, after taking an intelligent view of the subject, are simply beneath contempt. What adds to the better appearance of the person elevates; what adds to the better appearance of a farm increases its value and the respectability of the occupant; so that it is always a good investment, morally and pecuniarily, for a farmer to suppy his wife generously and cheerfully, according to his ability, with the means of making her family and home neat, tasteful, and tidy. A bunch of flowers or a shilling ribbon for the dress, or a few pennies' worth of lime or a dollar's worth of paint for the house, may be so used as to give an impression of life, of cheerfulness, and of thrift about a home altogether beyond the value of the means employed for the purpose.

Many a farmer's wife is literally worked to death in an inadvertent manner from want of reflection or consideration on the part of her husband. None can understand better than he, in ploughing, or sowing, or harvest time, that if a horse gets sick, or runs away, or is stolen, another must be procured that very day or the work will inevitably go behindhand. He does not carry the same practical sense into the kitchen when the hired help leaves without warning or becomes disabled, although he knows as well as any man can know that "the hands" will expect their meals with the same regularity, with the same promptness, and with the same proper mode of preparation; but, instead of procuring other "help" on the instant, he allows himself to be persuaded, if the "help" is sick, she will get well in a day or two, or in a week at furthest, and that it is hardly worth while to get another for so short a time. If the "help" has taken "French leave" his mind fixes on the fact that it is a very busy time, and neither he nor a single hand can be spared, or that, in the course of a week, some one will have to go to town for some other purpose, and both these matters can be attended to at the same time. Meanwhile the wife is expected not only to attend to her ordinary duties as usual, but somehow or other to spare the time to do all that the cook or washerwoman was accustomed to, that is, to do the full work of two persons, each one of whom had already quite as much labor to perform as she could possibly attend to. The wife attempts it. By herculean efforts all goes on well. The farmer perceives no jar, no hitch in the working of the machinery, and, because no complaint is uttered, thinks that everything is going on without an effort. Meanwhile time passes, and (infinite shame on some of them) they begin to calculate how much has been saved from servants' wages, and how much less food has been eaten, and, because still no complaint is made, the resolution quietly forms in the mind to do nothing until she does complain; but, before that takes place, she falls a victim to her over-exertions, in having laid the foundation for weeks and months of illness, if not of a premature decline and death. Sincerely it is believed that these statements ought to be written in large letters above the mantels of half the farmers of the country, and, if over the other half also, it would not be labor lost in favor of many a heroic and uncomplaining but outraged farmer's wife and daughter.

Let all, especially the young, who look to farming as the future pursuit of life, and who desire to avoid a large share of the ordinary discomforts, privations, unhappiness, and want of health which too often befall so worthy and so large a class of society as farmers' families are, remember these two cardinal suggestions:

First. Never purchase more land for farming purposes than can be paid for without borrowing.

Second. Never attempt to cultivate more than can be thoroughly done with the help which can be readily commanded; for one acre will yield more with a given amount of well-expended labor than two acres will yield with the same.

Finally, let the farmer always remember that his wife's cheerful and hearty co-operation is essential to his success, and is really of as much value in attaining it, all things considered, as anything that he can do; and, as she is very certainly his superior in her moral nature, it legitimately follows that he should not only regard her as his equal in material matters, but should habitually accord to her that deference, that consideration, and that high respect which is of right her due, and which can never fail to impress on the children and servants, who daily witness it, a dignity and an elevation of manner, and thought, and feeling, and deportment which will prove to all who see them that the wife is a lady, and the husband a man and a gentleman, and large pecuniary success, with a high moral position and wide social influence will be the almost certain results.

The remedy for the startling evil, which the official statement made in the beginning brings to light, is in the husband and mother. Let the farmer feel that his wife is an equal partner on the farm, and as such is entitled to as high consideration as he claims for himself. He should have a jealous care for the "good name of the house." Let him feel that what degrades his wife degrades himself, that whatever weakens her authority weakens his own power of success, and that in the great struggle of life they must of necessity rise or fall together. But while he cherishes these views as a business matter, as a practical thing of profit and loss, let him make an effort in another direction, not considering his wife merely as his partner in business, but as the love of his youth, who having, in a perfect abandon of trustfulness, thrown herself into his strong arms to be guided, protected, and sustained through life's long journey, has claims on him for these stronger than any tie other than that which binds man to Divinity; so strong, indeed, that inspiration has declared, that in heaven was it made, and by Heaven only can it be unloosed; and feeling thus, let him see in the wife of his bosom, though she may be all wrinkled with age, only the fair and loving and the fondly trusting girl as she appeared at the moment of saying "I will" many years agone. Let the mother also busy herself in teaching her daughters what they ought to do, what they have a right to expect in the marriage relation; and above this even, ler her inculcate on her sons, day by day, with wisdom and tenderness, charging them lovingly to remember when she is dead and gone, by all the respect and reverence and affection which they may have for her memory, to treat, for her sake, the wives of their bosoms with all that affection and tenderness and consideration and sympathy which they would have their father show her if she could but be brought back again, or which they themselves would gladly show her if they had the opportunity.

Utah Territory, 1862

From **Richard F. Burton**, *The City of the Saints, and Across the Rocky Mountains to California* (New York, 1862), pp. 282–87.

Utah Territory is pronounced by immigrants from the Old Country to be a "mean land," hard, dry, and fit only for the steady, sober, and hard-working Mormon. Scarcely one fiftieth part is fit for tillage; farming must be confined to rare spots, in which, however, an exceptional fertility appears. Even in the arable lands there is a great variety: some do not exceed 8–10 bushels per acre, while Captain Stansbury mentions 180 bushels of wheat being raised upon 350 acres of ground from one bushel of seed, and estimates the average yield of properly-cultivated land at 40 bushels, whereas rich Pennsylvania rarely gives 30 per acre. I have heard of lands near the fresh-water lake which bear from 60 to 105 bushels per acre.

The cultivable tracts are of two kinds, bench-land and bottom-land.

The soil of the bench-lands is fertile, a mixture of the highland feldspath with the débris of decomposed limestone. It is comparatively free from alkalines, the bane of the valleys; but as rain is wanting, it depends, like the Basses-Pyrénées, upon irrigation, and must be fertilized by the mountain torrents that issue from the kanyons. As a rule, the creeks dwindle to rivulets and sink in the porous alluvium before they have run a mile from the hill-foot, and reappear in the arid plains at a level too low for navigation: in such places artesian wells are wanted. The soil, though fertile, is thin, requiring compost: manure is here allowed to waste, the labor of the people sufficing barely for essentials. I am informed that two bushels of semence are required for each acre, and that the colonists sow too scantily: a judicious rotation of crops is also yet to come. The benches are sometimes extensive: a strip, for instance, runs along the western base of the Wasach Mountains, with a varying breadth of 1–3, miles from 80 miles north of Great Salt Lake City to Utah Lake and Valley, the southern terminus of cultivation, a total length of 120 miles. These lands produce various cereals, especially wheat and buckwheat, oats, barley, and a little Indian corn, all the fruits and vegetables of a temperate zone, and flax, hemp, and linseed in abundance. The wild fruits are the service berry, chokecherry, buffalo berry, gooseberry, an excellent strawberry, and black, white, red, and yellow mountain currants, some as large as ounce bullets.

The bottom-lands, where the creeks extend, are better watered than the uplands, but they are colder and salter. The refrigerated air seeks the lowest levels; hence in Utah Territory the benches are warmer than the valleys, and the spring vegetation is about a fortnight later on the banks of Jordan than above them. Another cause of cold is the presence of saleratus or alkaline salts, the natural effect of the rain being insufficient to wash them out. Experiment proved in Sindh that nothing is more difficult than to eradicate this evil from the soil: the sweetest earth brought from afar becomes tainted by it: sometimes the disease appears when the crop is half grown; at other times it attacks irregularly — one year, for instance, will see a fine field of wheat, and the next none. When inveterate, it breaks out in leprous eruptions, and pieces of efflorescence can be picked up for use: a milder form induces a baldness of growth, with an occasional birth of chenopodiaceæ. Many of the streams are dangerous to cattle, and often in the lower parts of the valleys there are ponds and pools of water colored and flavored like common ley. According to the people, a small admixture is beneficial to vegetation; the grass is rendered equal for pasturage to the far-famed salt-marshes of Essex and of the Atlantic coast; potatoes, squashes, and melons become sweeter, and the pie-plant loses its acidity. On the other hand, the beet has been found to deteriorate, no small misfortune at such a distance from the sugar-cane.

Besides salt-drought and frost, the land has to contend against an Asiatic scourge. The cricket *(Anabrus simplex?)* is compared by the Mormons to a "cross between the spider and the buffalo:" it is dark, ungainly, wingless, and exceedingly harmful. The five red-legged grasshopper *(Œdipoda corallipes),* about the size of the English migratory locust, assists these "black Philistines," and, but for a curious provision of nature, would render the land well-nigh uninhabitable. A small species of gull flocks from its resting-place in the Great Salt Lake to feed upon the advancing host; the "glossy bird of the valley, with light red beak and feet, delicate in form and motion, with plumage of downy texture and softness," stayed in 1848 the advance of the "frightful bug," whose onward march nor fires, nor hot trenches, nor the cries of the frantic farmer could arrest. We can hardly wonder that the Mormons, whose minds, so soon after the exodus, were excited to the highest pitch, should have seen in this natural phenomenon a miracle, a special departure from the normal course of events, made by Providence in their favor, or accuse them, as anti-Mormons have done, of forging signs and portents.

But, while many evils beset agriculture in Utah Territory, grazing is comparatively safe, and may be extended almost *ad libitum*. The valleys of this land of Goshen supply plentiful pasturage in the winter; as spring advances cattle will find gamma and other grasses on the benches, and as, under the influence of the melting sun, the snow-line creeps up the hills, flocks and herds, like the wild graminivorants, will follow the bunch-grass, which, vivified by the autumnal rains, breeds under the snow, and bears its seed in summer. In the basin of the Green River, fifty miles south of Fillmore City, is a fine wool-producing country 7000 square miles in area. Even the ubiquitous sage will serve for camels. As has been mentioned, Durhams, Devons, and Merino tups have found their way to Great Salt Lake City, and the terrible milk-sickness of the Western States has not.

In 1860 the Valley of the Great Salt Lake alone produced 306,000 bushels of grain, of which about 17,000 were oats. Lieutenant Gunnison, estimating the average yield of each plowed acre at 2000 lbs. (33½ bushels), a fair estimate, and "drawing the meat part of the ration, or one half," from the herds fed elsewhere, fixes the maximum of population in Utah Territory at 4000 souls to a square mile, and opines that it will maintain with ease one million of inhabitants.

Timber, I have said, is a growing want throughout the country; the "hair of the earth-animal" is by no means luxuriant. Great Cotton-wood Kanyon is supposed to contain supplies for twenty years, but it is chiefly used for building purposes. The Mormons, unlike the Hibernians, of whom it was said in the last century that no man ever planted an orchard, have applied themselves manfully to remedying the deficiency, and the next generation will probably be safe. At present, "hard woods," elm, hackberry, pecan or button-wood, hickory, mulberry, basswood, locust, black and English walnut, are wanted, and must be imported from the Eastern States. The lower kanyons and bottoms are clothed with wild willow, scrub maple, both hard and soft, box elder, aspen, birch, cotton-wood, and other amentaciæ, and in the south with spruce and dwarf ash. The higher grounds bear stunted cedars white and red, balsam and other pines, the dwarf oak, which, like the maple, is a mere scrub, and the mountain mahogany, a tough, hard, and strong, but grainless wood, seldom exceeding eight inches in diameter. Hawthorn (a *Cratæ-gus*) also exists, and in the southern and western latitudes the piñon *(P. monophyllus)*, varying from the size of an umbrella to twenty feet in height, feeds the Indians with its oily nut, which not a little resembles the seed of the pinaster and the Mediterranean *P. Pinea*, and supplies a rich gum for strengthening plasters. . . .

Wheat thrives better than maize, which in the northern parts suffers from the late frosts, and requires a longer summer. Until oats and barley can be grown in sufficient quantities, horses are fed upon heating wheat, which only the hardest riding enables them to digest. *Holcus saccharatum*, or Chinese millet, succeeds where insufficient humidity is an obstacle to the sugar-cane. The fault of the vegetables here, as in California, is excessive size, which often renders them insipid; the Irish potato, however, is superior to that of Nova Scotia and Charleston; the onions are large and mild as those of Spain. The white carrot, the French bean, and the cucumber grow well, and the "multicaulis mania" has borne good fruit in the shape of cabbage. The size of the beets suggested in 1853 the project originated in

France by Napoleon the Great: $100,000 were expended upon sugar-making machinery; the experiment, however, though directed by a Frenchman, failed, it is said, on account of the alkali contained in the root, and the Saints are accused of having distilled for sale bad spirit from the useless substance. The deserts skirting the Western Holy Land have also their manna; the leaves of poplars and other trees on the banks of streams distill, at divers seasons of the year, globules of honey-dew, resembling in color gum Arabic, but of softer consistence and less adhesiveness: the people collect it with spoons into saucers. Cotton thrives in the southern and southwestern part of Utah Territory when the winter is mild: at the meeting-place of waters near the Green and Grand Rivers that unite to form the Colorado, the shrub has been grown with great success.

The War and Farm Machinery, 1863

From *Country Gentleman* (Albany, September 10, 1863), XXII, no. 11, p. 169.

Every year increases the necessity for substituting horse for hand labor. The superior cheapness of the former is shown by the simple estimate, that while the strength of an active man is only one-fifth that of a horse, the cost of the latter, as usually kept by farmers, is but a little more than one-third; in other words, a horse will accomplish any heavy labor that he can perform at about one-twelfth the cost of employing men to do the same. This estimate will, of course, vary with localities and circumstances, but is a fair, approximate average, and shows the importance of applying this cheap strength by means of farm machinery to every possible operation.

The present war has withdrawn from the farms of the North nearly a million of laborers. The inquiry occurs, what part of this loss is supplied by agricultural machines? We have no statistics to show the actual number of mowing machines, reapers, horse-rakes, horse-forks, thrashing machines, planting machines, &c., in present use. But it is not difficult to make an estimate of the advantages to be derived from their general introduction to all the farms of considerable size in the North. There are at least one million farmers in the Northern and Western States, whose tillage lands are sufficiently extensive to render their use eminently economical. The meadow lands of each of these farmers will average, say, twenty acres; to cut these acres by hand would cost twenty dollars, more or less, and only about ten dollars if performed by mowing machines, that is, a saving of ten dollars to each of these million farmers. This estimate does not take into account the impossibility of securing enough hands, at the critical period of haying, to perform all this labor at present wages. The advantages which the rapid execution of this work by machinery would give in the way of hastening its progress, in preventing over-ripening, or in escaping storms, would perhaps be as much more. In other words, twenty million dollars would be saved annually by the general introduction of mowing machines. Reapers would doubtless accomplish as much more; although they do not lessen the amount of hand labor actually employed so much as mowers, they prevent a greater loss, which would result if the crop were not gathered at precisely the right time. We may, therefore, put these down at twenty millions more. The various other improved machines and implements would probably, if all taken together, swell the amount to at least one hundred millions yearly. This vast amount would go far towards supplying the labor withdrawn by the war; and when we take into the account the fact that some of this machinery, and more especially the harvesters, supply a place and accomplish a service, at a critical period, which the million laborers could not do, it may be questioned whether the machinery, on the whole, is not the more important of the two.

This estimate may be corrected in its details — the object being to show the vast importance of every improvement in farm implements and machines, in a national point of view. English political economists predicted ruin in the Northern States by the withdrawal of farm laborers to carry on the war; the London Mark Lane Express annually publishes its stereotyped prediction, that no more wheat can come from America; and without machinery this prediction would doubtless prove true.

There are two individuals who hold prominent places among their countrymen — the inventor, and the political office-seeker and speech-maker. The latter makes himself prominent in the crowd, and often receives adulation at great assemblies and through daily newspapers. The former is found alone in his study or workshop, and excites no attention at the time, but like a Watt, an Arkwright, or a Fulton, to the commercial world; or a Hussey, or Ketchum, to the agricultural interest, their unostentatious productions have proved far more essential to the safety of the country, and saved it from desolation in the hour of peril.

Nothing has contributed more to disseminate correct information on the merits of machines than agricultural fairs, aided by agricultural periodicals. We trust that the officers having charge of these exhibitions will continue to give a prominent place to the machinery department, and to offer increased inducements to exhibitors; and that whenever practicable, these machines shall be seen in operation on the ground, or provision be made for their special trial.

Farm Life, 1863

From Donald Grant Mitchell, *My Farm of Edgewood* (New York, 1863), pp. 73–81.

Laborers

Having decided upon a plan, the next thing to be considered is the personal agency for its administration.

There was once a time, if we may believe a great many tender pastorals and madrigals such as Kit Marlowe sang, when there were milkmaids: and the sweetest of Overbury's "Characters" is his little sketch of the 'faire damsel,' who hath such fingers "that in milking a cow, it seemes that so sweet a milk-presse makes the milk the whiter or sweeter." But milkmaids now-a-days are mostly Connaught men, in cowhide boots and black satin waistcoats, who say "begorra," and beat the cows with the milking stool.

Overbury says of the ancient British type — "Her breath is her own, which sents all the yeare long of June, like a newmade haycock."

And I may say of the present representative — His breath is his own, which 'sents all the yeare long' of proof spirits, like a newmade still.

Overbury tenderly says — "Thus lives she, and all her care is she may die in the spring time, to have store of flowers stucke upon her winding sheet."

And I, as pathetically: — Thus fares he, and all his care is he may get his full wage, and a good jollification 'nixt St. Parthrick's day.'

This is only my way of introducing the labor question, which, in every aspect, is a serious one to a party entering upon the management of country property. If such party is anticipating the employment of one of Sir Thomas Overbury's milk-maydes, or of the pretty damsel who sang Marlowe's song to Izaak Walton, let him disabuse his mind. In place of it all, he will sniff boots that remind of a damp cattle yard, and listen to sharp brogue that will be a souvenir of Donnybrook Fair. In briefest possible terms, the inferior but necessary labor of a farm must be performed now, in the majority of cases, by the most inefficient of Americans, or by the rawest and most uncouth of Irish or Germans.

There lived some twenty or thirty years ago in New England, a race of men, American born, and who, having gone through a two winters' course of district school ciphering and reading, with cropped tow heads, became the most indefatigable and ingenious of farm workers. Their hoeing was a sleight of hand; they could make an ox yoke, or an axe helve on rainy days; by adroit manipulation, they could relieve a choking cow, or as deftly, hive a swarm of bees. Their furrows indeed were not of the straightest, but their control of a long team of oxen was a miracle of guidance. They may have carried a bit of Cavendish twist in their waistcoat pockets; they certainly did not waste time at lavations; but as farm workers they had rare aptitude; no tool came amiss to them; they cradled; they churned, if need were; they chopped and piled their three cords of wood between sun and sun. With bare feet, and a keen-whetted six-pound Blanchard, they laid such clean and broad swaths through the fields of dewy herdsgrass, as made "old-country-men" stare. By a kind of intuition, they knew the locality of every tree, and of every medicinal herb that grew in the woods. Rarest of all which they possessed, was an acuteness of understanding, which enabled them to comprehend an order before it was half uttered, and to meet occasional and unforeseen difficulties, with a steady assurance, as if they had been an accepted part of the problem. It was possible to send such a man into a wood with his team, to select a stick of timber, of chestnut or oak, that should measure a given amount; he could be trusted to find such, — to cut it, to score it, to load it; if the gearing broke, he could be trusted to mend it; if the tree lodged, he could be trusted to devise some artifice for bringing it down; and finally, — for its sure and prompt delivery at the point indicated. Your Irishman, on the other hand, balks at the first turn; he must have a multitude of chains; he needs a boy to aid him with the team, and another to carry a bar; he spends an hour in his doubtful estimate of dimensions; but "begorra, its a lumpish tree," and he thwacks into the rind a foot or two from the ground, so as to leave a 'nate' Irish stump. Half through the bole, he begins to doubt if it be indeed a chestnut or a poplar; and casting his eye aloft to measure it anew, an ancient woodpecker drops something smarting in his eye; and his howl starts the ruminating team into a confused entanglement among the young wood. Having eased his pain, and extricated his cattle, he pushes on with his axe, and presently, with a light crash of pliant boughs, his timber is lodged in the top of an adjoining tree. He tugs, and strains, and swears, and splits the helve of his axe in adapting it for a lever, and presently, near to noon, comes back for three or four hands to give him a boost with the tree. You return — to find the team strayed through a gate left open, into a thriving cornfield, and one of your pet tulip trees lodged in a lithe young hickory.

"Och! and it's a toolip — it is! and I was thinkin' 'twas niver a chistnut; begorra, it's lucky thin, it didn't come down intirely."

These and other such, replace the New-Englander born, who long ago was paid off, wrapped his savings in a dingy piece of sheepskin, scratched his head reflectingly, and disappeared from the stage. He has become the father of a race that is hewing its way in Oregon, or he is a dignitary in Wisconsin, or thwacking terribly among the foremost fighters of the war.

Here and there remains an aged representative of the class, with all his nasal twang and his aptitude for a score of different services; but the chances are, if he has failed of placing himself in the legislative chambers of the West, or of holding ownership of some rough farm of his own, that he has some moral obliquity which makes him an outcast.

Certain it is, that very few native Americans of activity and of energy are to be decoyed into the traces of farm labor, unless they can assume the full direction. American blood is fast, and fast blood is impatient with a hoe among small carrots. It is well, perhaps, that blood is so fast, and hopes so tall. These tell grandly in certain directions, but they are not available for working over a heap of compost. The American eagle is (or was) a fine bird, but he does not consume grasshoppers like a turkey.

In view of the fact that dexterous labor is not now available, there is a satisfaction in knowing that the necessity for it is year by year diminishing. Upon the old system of growing all that a man might need within his own grounds, a proper farm education embraced a considerable knowledge of a score of different crops and avocations. The tendency is now, however, to centralize attention upon that line of cropping which is best suited to the land; this limits the range of labor, while the improved mechanical appliances fill a thousand wants, which were once only to be met by a dexterous handicraft at home. None but a few weazen-faced old gentlemen of a very ancient school, think now-a-days of making their own ox yokes or their own cheese presses; or, if their crop be large, of pounding out their grain with a flail. And it is noticeable in this connection, that the implements in the use of which the native workers were most unmatchable, are precisely the ones which in practical farming are growing less and less important every year; to wit, the axe and the scythe: the first being now confined mostly to clearings of timber, and the second is fast becoming merely a garden implement for the dressing of lawns.

I perceive, very clearly, from all this, that I am not to be brought in contact with a race of Arcadians. Meliboeus will not do the milking, nor Tityrus, — though there shall be plenty of snoozing under the beech trees. It is also lamentably true that the uncouth and unkempt Irish or Germans, whom it becomes necessary to employ, place no pride or love in their calling like the English farm laborers, or like that gone-by stock of New England farm workers at whom I have hinted.

Your Irish friend may be a good reaper, he may possibly be a respectable ploughman (though it is quite doubtful); but in no event will he cherish any engrossing attachment to country labors; nor will he come to have any pride in the successes that may grow out of them.

Every month he is ready to drift away toward any employment which will bring increase of pay. He is your factotum to-day, and to-morrow may be shouldering a hod, or scraping hides for a soap boiler. The German, too, however accomplished a worker he may become, falls straightway into the same American passion of unrest, and becomes presently the dispenser of lager bier, or a forager "mit Sigel."

There is then no American class of farm workers in the market — certainly not in the Eastern markets. The native, if he possess rural instincts, is engrossed, as I have said, with some homestead of his own, or is trying his seed-cast among the Mormons, or on the prairies. All other parties bring only a divided allegiance, and a kind of makeshift adhesion to the business; in addition to which, they bring an innocency that demands the supervision of a good farm teacher.

Such a teacher your foreman may be, or he may not be; if the latter, and he have no capacity to convert into available workers, such motley materials, the sooner you discharge him the better; but if he have this capacity, and is, besides, so far cognizant of your ownership, as not to take offence at your presence, and to permit of your suggestions — cherish him; he has rare virtues.

From the hints I have already dropped in regard to the qualities and characteristics of the available "milkmaids" and ploughmen, it will naturally be inferred that I would not be anxious to entertain a large squad of such, under the low-browed ceilings of the country home I have described.

And here comes under observation that romanticism about equality of condition and of tastes, which many kindly and poetically-disposed persons are inclined to engraft upon their ideal of the farm life. There is, indeed, a current misjudgment on this head, which is quite common, and which the exaggerated tone of rural literature generally, from Virgil down, has greatly encouraged. The rural writers dodge all the dirty work of the farm, and regale us with the odors of the new-mown hay. The plain truth is, however, that if a man perspires largely in a cornfield of a dusty day, and washes hastily in the horse trough, and eats in shirt sleeves that date their cleanliness three days back, and loves fat pork and cabbage "neat," he will not prove the Arcadian companion at dinner, which readers of Somerville imagine, — neither on the score of conversation, or of transpiration. Active, every-day farm labor is certainly not congruous with a great many of those cleanly prejudices which grow out of the refinements of civilization. We must face the bald truth in this matter; a man who has only an hour to his nooning, will not squander it upon toilet labors; and a long day of close field-work leaves one in very unfit mood for appreciative study of either poetry or the natural sciences.

The pastoral idea, — set off with fancies of earthen bowls, tables under trees, and appetites that are sated with bread and milk, or crushed berries and sugar, and with the kindred fancies of rural swains, who can do a good day's work and keep their linen clean, — is all a most wretched phantasm. Pork, and cabbage, and dirty wristbands, are the facts.

Good Farming

From Hugh M. Thompson, "Experiences," in Iowa State Agricultural Society, *Transactions*, 1863 (Des Moines, 1864), pp. 122–25.

DR. SHAFFER — Dear Sir: In giving you a brief outline of my experience as a farmee on the prairies of Iowa, it will be proper to give my location, and the period over which that experience extends. First, then, my home is on the open prairie, a mile and a half from natural timber, in the north part of Scott county, or in a direct line 12 miles due north of Davenport, and my experience commenced with the summer of 1844. At the commencement of my career as a prairie farmer, the country was almost wholly in a state of nature. Pasturage around us was almost as boundless as the ocean itself, and the fertility of our soil was such that if we could only get the surface sod torn up during the summer, and loosened to the depth of a couple of inches, so as to have soil enough to cover the seed, we could look forward to a luxuriant crop of grain, if put in any time between the opening of the following spring and the first of May, and the winter food for stock was so easily procured that fat cattle could be bought readily at from 12 to 15 dollars each, and other stock in proportion; but gradually, almost imperceptibly, a change has come over the whole, both the country and the people in it. Good crops, produced with little labor, and sold for a proportionably small price, had, as was naturally to be expected, a tendency to produce in many an indolent disposition, and the result was that many of the original settlers sold out and moved back, back, back, where new land, &c., could be had, as was the case in this county during the territorial condition of our own beautiful Iowa. About the period that Iowa emerged from her territorial condition, and for several years thereafter, the influx of immigration into this part of our State was so great that very soon every spare lot of prairie fit for the plow passed into private hands. Then those who had chosen to remain in their first Iowa homes, made the discovery first that cutting grass from Uncle Sam's domain could no longer be resorted to with profit, and land had to be converted into meadows, and here begins the first part of my experience, which may be of benefit to others.

Our first attempt to cultivate grasses for hay were confined to timothy, without any mixture of clover. Well, the first and second year, (and probably the third, if the season was favorable, we had good crops; but after that, unless we had frequent rains during May and June, our timothy was often so light as to be hardly worth cutting. This led to an investigation, and in the first place, a top dressing with well rotted manure in the fall was resorted, and the hay crop was for a time good; but another fact began to dawn upon us, and it was this: We found we needed manure for our other crops as well, and clover was resorted to to bring out our hay crops. The reader will here most likely enquire, how was clover to make timothy grow? Well, we found that the roots of the timothy were all so near the surface of the ground, that unless we topdressed about every two years or so, the surface soil became so impoverished, and what is called hide-bound, that except in a very rainy season, the roots could not reach sufficient nourishment to grow a good crop, and by mixing a small quantity of clover with the timothy, the long, carrot-shaped roots of the clover kept the soil loose and porous, and by that and other means so benefited the timothy that (where the meadows are not pastured too late in the spring,) the hay crop seems to improve year after year, and when the land is again plowed up for other crops, it seems to be fully equal to new broke up prairie. One of my nearest neighbors has mown the same field with the result as above, for, I think, somewhere about ten years, and I believe his last crop was the heaviest one. The sod was ploughed up last spring, and I think as fine a crop of oats as I ever saw was raised on it.

We (and in using the word "we" I speak for myself and several of my immediate neighbors,) were, by resorting to the clover, (which, bye-the-bye, seems to be well adapted to our soil,) enabled to reserve what manure we could make for other crops, and we find it so necessary to the raising of good crops, that we use all we can conveniently make on our farms. Our general mode of using it is as follows: After the wheat and small grains are put in, we have our manure hauled out and spread over that portion of our land that is intended for corn, and immediately plowed in so as to prevent evaporation. One decent manuring will tell on every crop for 4 or 5 years, and one important advantage, now that the country is so overrun with insect enemies, a wheat crop will be ready fully a week earlier than one not manured, soil and crop, (except the manure), being treated in every respect alike. I have also found the roller a great advantage; when the ground is dry, roll immediately after sowing, and my experience is, that the crop will stand thicker on the ground, also ear out and ripen earlier, thus further enabling us to head off the chinch-bugs.

Now for a word in respect to the mode of croping, many of our farmers continue to raise, or attempt to raise, wheat year after year on the same soil, and because the crops gradually get poorer they lay the blame on the soil, say it is worn out &c., while all the time the fault lies in their own want of a proper consideration of the nature and wants of the plants under cultivation. Take a piece of land that has been sown with wheat for 4 or 5 years in succession and give it a thorough deep plowing in the fall and soon as the ground is in good order after the first of May run a cultivator over it, and plant it with corn and if sufficient attention is paid to cultivation so as to keep down the weeds, it will produce as good a crop of corn as ever it would have done, but it will require a great deal more labor to keep down the weeds which the injudicious system of wheat cropping had suffered to become incorporated with the soil. I don't mean to convey the idea that the soil will not become poorer in time, but I mean to say that with the aid of manure and a proper rotation of crop, clover and pasturing, we can continue to produce as good crops (the seasons being alike favorable) as ever have been produced from the same soil. Are the farmers of Europe enabled to step off to a piece of new land whenever the crops begin to become defective? On the contrary I have seen fields in England that were said to be in cultivation before the Mayflower left the shores of our Fatherland, but necessity has taught the farmers there that to keep their lands in a paying condition it is necessary to return to the soil an equivalent for what is taken from it. Now it is not absolutely necessary that all this should be done by hauling into and over our fields the amount in fertilizers of all that has ever been taken from them. A large part of what we call a crop is derived from the atmosphere and we must keep our sod in a condition to admit of the different fertilizing gases continually afloat to permeate the soil to a sufficient depth to get at the roots, consequently we require to plow deep and whenever it can be done it is better to do it in the fall so that the frost and snow may be admitted into closer contact with the newly turned up soil. If farmers would only study the nature of the soil they cultivate they would find that (for all clay soils at least) the action of the atmosphere during winter is of great value to the crop of the following year; and in addition to all this the spring work can be accomplished in most seasons much sooner and more satifactorily.

Therefore, I would say to all our farmers plow in the fall, plow deep, adopt a steady rotatory system of croping and pasturing. Never let your soil become so reduced as to produce only half a crop, plow in every spadefull of manure you can collect on your farms, it will pay much better than letting it lie rotting in your barn yards breeding flies in summer to anoy yourself and every living thing near you, and in spring and fall causing foot rot to your sheep and cattle and damp feet and rheumatism to yourself and family. Hauling out and plowing in manure will pay all the time, and stacking the straw so as to convert it into manure will pay much better than burning it, although it may be a little more trouble at first. Facts daily before me have convinced me that poor farming is an unprofitable occupation, but that with careful management of what the poor farmer throws away the industrious, prudent one will become rich.

Farming in Iowa, 1864

From Iowa State Agricultural Society, *Report,* 1864 (Des Moines, 1865) pp. 3–4, 7–9, 11–12, 14–15.

A benificent Providence has smiled upon the labors of the husbandman. The varied changes of the season conspired to fill the land with plenty. Blast, or mildew, or tempest, "has not visited the fields, nor retarded the growing crops, nor prevented the golden gatherings of harvest." The "early and latter rains" refreshed the greater portion of the land, and abundant blessings crown the year with joy and fill the land with fatness. Despite the unusual drought that afflicted a small part of the land, the crops of all kinds are more plentiful, and the farmer has met a more remunerative reward for his labor than for several years past. For these gifts and mercies, and marks of favor, our people should be devoutly thankful to Almighty God.

Fifty thousand of our citizens are absent from their accustomed field of labor, engaged in the holy work of maintaining and preserving the government of Washington and his compeers against the assaults of the treason of our own people. Many, who less than four years ago left the farm for the tented field, sleep in honored graves, the victims of a causeless rebellion, the martyrs to the shrine of liberty and independence. All over this land the sons of Iowa have left the impress of their courage, skill, devotion and endurance; and the hearts of a grateful people will swell with pride for generations to come, upon the remembrance of their heroic virtue. And the end is not yet. Rebellion is not yet subdued. Armed resistance is not yet crushed out. Vast armies of brave, but misguided men, well equipped, under the leadership of skillful generals, still confront the hosts of freedom, and defiantly talk of peace upon the sole basis of independence and separation. More men will be needed to finish up the work, brought to so comforting and hopeful a point as it is now, by our brave people. And Iowa will still pour out her blood, and will still prosper in her agricultural development. It cannot fail to be the surprise of the reader of history, that this war called forth so many thousands of men from the ranks of productive industry, and still the land enjoyed a prosperity that is of itself unparalleled. No such instance can be found among the records of the past.

With so many of our fellow citizens in the field, and a prospect that more will soon be called to "fill the broken ranks of our brothers gone before," it might be supposed that there would be some waning in the vast interest of agriculture — some abatement of the prosperity which marked our progress before the war. But the actual result is wholly different. At no time has there been so great attention paid to the importation of improved breeds of stock — especially sheep; to the purchase of labor-saving machinery, and to the improvement of the home, and farm, and orchard, as during the past few years. The accompanying documents show an interest in all branches of agriculture, that cannot fail to gratify every one proud of our advancement.

We should especially be grateful in considering the fact that our borders have been saved from the horrible devastation and destruction of war. Peace has triumphed throughout the land. Neither hordes of hostile savages, nor emissaries from the rebellious south, nor internecine war has ravaged any portion of our State. Outlaws and villians, taking advantage of the general unrest of the country, made several futile attempts to over-ride the civil authority, but they were met by such swift measures, that though the surface presented signs of ebullition, the depths below remained undisturbed. . . .

Sorghum

In 1860 the product of this crop was but a little less than two millions of gallons of syrup, furnishing a large proportion of that required for home consumption, and even enabling the producer in some instances to export large quantities. In 1863 the census returns report the product of syrup at 3,012,396 gallons, and of sugar at 21,469 pounds. It was hoped some years ago, and the Board declared in 1861, that "it is fair to conclude that if a kind Providence should bless us with a favorable season another year, we will not be compelled as a State to contribute to the expenses of the war, in the shape of high prices for sugar and molasses, but may let our patriotism exercise itself in some other channel." But the prices of sugars and syrups were never so high, and the consumption is enormous in spite of this fact. From 28 to 37 cents per pound for common and refined sugar, and the price of imported syrup is not greatly above that of sorghum; the history disappoints the hope and dispels the delusion. An enterprising gentleman of Jefferson County, where the production of cane is very extensive, fitted out at an expense of $25,000 machinery for refining sorghum syrup. In 1863 the mill did not make a beginning, the drought and early frost having cut short the crop. This year, with all conditions, except too great drought, apparently favorable to a large yield, the machinery is compelled to be idle, and the gentleman has concluded to abandon the enterprise. The local societies organized in the interest of this product have disbanded, or at least given no outward signs of vitality, and the reports of the different County Societies scarcely mention it as an important branch of husbandry. Had the rate of increase from 1856 to 1860 in the growth of this plant obtained from 1860 to 1864, enough syrup would have been manufactured for home demand, and a large margin would have been afforded for exportation, and all this without making any appreciable difference in the products of other departments of agriculture. Whether the belief in the general fitness of this soil and climate for the production of sugar and syrup has been staggered, whether other interests have usurped its place, whether the people wearied in the process of manufacture, and were disgusted with the failure to make a good merchantable sugar, whether the scarcity of labor deterred from planting, or whether all these causes combined to bring the plant into disfavor, it is patent that the bright hopes engendered by its first success have been but very imperfectly realized. Yet no one should be so discouraged as to abandon this crop. It has been very remunerative. A profit has been realized when syrup sold at twenty cents. Let it be remembered that it requires an unusual amount of help to take care of the crop, and reduce the cane to syrup, that help is scarce and labor high, that men expected too much from it, and above all that it requires great care to prevent deterioration, by the proper selection of seed, and then let the producer take courage and try again. It is believed that the day is not distant when it will take rank as one of the chief sources of our wealth, and these occasional disappointments should only stimulate to greater exertion.

Honey

There is another source from which much saccharine matter is derived, that is absolute, never-failing. The reports of this Society present evidence that Iowa is the paradise of the bee, and the literal land that "flows with honey." Within our border are accomplished Apiarians that can teach the teachers of other localities. Accompanying this report are statistics that show clearly that it is a very remunerative branch of industry. The famed Italian Bee has been introduced and has fully met the expectations of the followers of bee culture; and we are not behind any country in the skilled management of bees. An Apiarian Association is one of the fixed institutions of Iowa. Bee keeping is spoken of as a labor both light, pleasant and lucrative, and the rules of conducting an Apiary are so plain that any one of ordinary capacity can comprehend them, the expense of establishing it so comparatively trifling that it will not fail to bring a handsome return for the investment. In 1850 Iowa produced 321,711 pounds of honey; in 1860, 919,750 pounds; and in 1863, 1,052,685 pounds, a steady, regular, gratifying increase of a product of utility and luxury, that is by no means to be despised. . . .

Sheep

In 1850 sheep numbered 149,960. At that period and for some years previous, thousands of sheep were imported from the older States, but disaster, misfortune and loss to the individual, were the general consequences. Large flocks brought by men who had no knowledge of their management, and who had no adequate preparation for them, dwindled away and greatly disheartened the pioneer. Sheep were exported from Eastern States where there were shelter, tame grasses, highly cultivated and well sub-divided fields of pasturage, and every appliance known to skill and experience for their successful management. They found here insufficient protection from the elements, the tall, waving grass of the boundless prairies, and what is worse than all, found themselves in the hands of inexperienced or careless owners, that had no knowledge of their wants and no skill in their rearing. The pioneer found a farm almost ready prepared for him by the hand of a prodigal nature; corn grew almost spontaneously, and he shed few regretful tears to see his flock dwindle and perish from neglect, because forsooth his cribs of golden grain fattened hogs and cattle and brought a speedy return for his labor. He sacrificed this interest which required skill and care for one which became a source of wealth almost without effort.

Those farmers who in 1850 succeeded with large flocks were the rare exceptions to the general rule. Hence the interest of wool-growing for some years waned; men settled down in the belief that sheep would not flourish here, and there was a virtual abandonment of the flock. The old Spanish proverb, "Wherever the foot of the sheep touches, the land is turned into gold," was almost reversed, and the owner of sheep was commiserated upon his investment of capital in unproductive stock. In 1860, the next decade, a period of unexampled prosperity in all departments of our agriculture, sheep only increased to 258,228. The renewal of the old idea that "this was no country for sheep," operated unfavorably upon the minds of hundreds of our people, even at this date. But soon thereafter an unparalleled impetus was given to the importation of sheep, and the interest in this branch of husbandry forms an epoch in our history. So great and wide-spread was the mania for sheep, that the faint-hearted stood back in alarm, and referred with emotion to the Morus Multicaulus, and the days of Shanghai chickens.

In 1863 the census returns place the number of sheep on hand at shearing time at but sixty-two less than six hundred thousand; estimating the increase at but one-fourth, and the importation at 150,000, it would give the number at shearing time in 1864, at 900,000.

Taking a national view of this subject, Dr. Randall, the very highest authority on all questions that pertain to sheep, says in his address to the Ohio Wool Growers' Association one year ago: "Let us assume that the war will close by the end of 1864. If we then have 32,000,000 of people, and they again commence increasing in the usual compound ratio of three per cent. per annum, we shall have at the close of 1874, a population of 43,005,321, requiring 194,613,944 pounds of wool. If the 25,000,000 sheep now in the loyal States, should continue to increase through the same ten years, as rapidly as they have done for the last four years, viz: at the rate of ten per cent. per annum, they will be just doubled in 1874; and the 50,000,000 of them, then in the United States, will have to yield nearly four pounds of wool per head to meet the requirements of that year — supposing the supply to be drawn wholly from domestic sources.'' And what is true of the nation, may be said with equal force of Iowa.

Intimately connected with this subject is the question of tame grasses. These flourish luxuriantly. In the older settled portions of the State, the wild grass of the prairie has disappeared, and waving blue grass and white clover on the commons, have usurped its place. Evidence is before us that an unusual degree of attention has been paid to the cultivation of grasses, and the success has been uniform. The reward from the well set and well cultivated meadow is sure; and while crops of cereals tend to exhaust the soil, the meadow being pastured by the flock, constantly increases in richness and productiveness. As the breadth of meadow increases, there will be still greater profit in the rearing of sheep; for pasturage invariably improves the crop, and returns to the soil more than it receives.

In the accompanying papers will be found some suggestions of very great value — the results of long practical experience in the rearing of sheep in Iowa. The large importation of sheep, and the exportation of wool; the fact that Iowa already helps supply the eastern market with mutton; that men everywhere speak encouragingly of their efforts to rear sheep; that at least one local organization in this interest is in active operation, doing much good, and diffusing much useful information — all these signs indicate that sheep are fast becoming a most important source of our wealth.

Corn is the principal element of our wealth. In 1863, there were 63,883,916 bushels harvested, being an average of about 36 bushels per acre. It will be remembered that the frost of August, and the drought during the growing season, cut off many acres and shortened the crop. Reports from the different County Societies speak encouragingly of the yield, and it may be safely estimated at 40 bushels per acre.

Brigham Young On Manufactures, 1863

From Brigham Young, "Home Manufactures — The Necessity of Greater Attention to Them," *Journal of Discourses* (Liverpool, 1865), X, pp. 200–02.

HOME MANUFACTURES. — THE NECESSITY OF GREATER ATTENTION TO THEM. — TITHING

Discourse by President Brigham Young, delivered in the Bowery, Great Salt Lake City, June 7, 1863

Reported by G. D. Watt

I have a few things to say to the Latter-day Saints with regard to ourselves. From the first of our coming into these valleys we have instructed the people concerning the facts that are now so visible and manifest in the nation to which we are attached. It was then understood by us and was as plainly before our minds as are the facts that are now in their progress.

We also have a warfare to engage in, and, as the Apostle says, "The weapons of our warfare are not carnal, but mighty through God to the pulling down of strongholds; casting down imaginations and every high thing that exalteth itself against the knowledge of God, and bringing into captivity every thought to the obedience of Christ; and having in a readiness to revenge all disobedience, when your obedience is fulfilled."

The warfare that I wish particularly to speak of to-day is that which wars against all opposition to economy and to the obtaining of the knowledge of God and that wisdom which comes from him pertaining to self-preservation. My warfare is, and has been for years, to get the people to understand that if they do not take care of themselves they will not be taken care of; that if we do not lay the foundation to feed and clothe and shelter ourselves we shall perish with hunger and with cold; we might also suffer in the summer season from the direct rays of the sun upon our naked and unprotected bodies. We have striven for years to convince the Latter-day Saints that rags and ruffles will cease being brought to us from a foreign market, though a struggle is still made to bring them here. We have warred against the principle of promoting and making wealthy those who wish us no good, and we have found it hard to convince our brethren and sisters that the saying of the Savior is really as true when applied to us as it was when applied to his followers in his day, "He that is not with me, is against me; and he that gathereth not with me, scattereth abroad." Thousands of this people this day will not believe that saying. We have this to war against, and the warfare should be engaged in by every Latter-day Saint. The same responsibility, the same influence, the same power and the same objects to be attained should rest upon every person who is a member of the Church, as much as upon me and my brethren who are contending with me constantly for the permanent good of Israel. We have contended long to convince this people that they must become self-sustaining.

I can, notwithstanding this, endorse all that brother George A. Smith said this morning concerning the great improvement of this people and the good feeling they manifested to us on our southern trip. The people who have settled in that country are certainly contented. Many of them said to me, "We love to live in Great Salt Lake City, love to go to meeting there, but we should very much dislike now to be counseled to return there again to make our permanent abode. We like the country and climate here, we like our calling and situation, and we are happy and contented." I am ready to endorse all the goodness and good-feeling that were manifested, and I can truly say that love, union, faith, fervency of spirit and faithfulness to our religion are greatly on the increase among the Latter-day Saints, or I am much mistaken; still the warfare is not ended in regard to our being self-sustaining.

We have evidence now before us which sufficiently proves that the ruffles and the rags will not continue to come here for a great length of time, and we shall have to do without them or make them ourselves. Sixteen years ago, when we were camped upon this temple block, I told the people that there existed, in the elements around us in these mountain regions, wheat, corn, rye, oats, barley, flax, hemp, silk and every element for producing the necessary articles used by man for food, raiment and shelter. We breathe it in the atmosphere, drink it in the water, dig it when we dig in the earth, and walk over it when we walk. Here are the elements for every cereal, vegetable and fruit, and for every textile material that grows in the same latitude and altitude in any part of the world. No country in the world will yield more and a greater variety of the products of life than will portions of this mountain country. We have proven all this to be true. There is not a better wheat country than this, and we can raise as good rye and corn as can be produced in any part of the earth; we can also raise as good vegetables as I ever saw, and in as great a variety as need be asked for. We have raised hemp, flax, cotton and silk, all of the best quality. We can make ropes and sacking, and cotton, silk and woollen goods in abundance; we have the elements and skill to combine them.

There is no better sheep country than this. Some farmers suppose that their failure to raise wool is owing to ill luck; this is a mistake. I have expended more, in the early settlement of this country, to produce wool than any one man. I have bought sheep by hundreds, but I never saw the time that I could go out and herd them myself, consequently had to depend upon others. The treatment that sheep receive from most of those having them in care is by no means conducive to their thrift. The lambs are too often left for the wolves and dogs to herd or to the care of an inexperienced boy or girl. Large numbers of sheep are often huddled into little, filthy pens and kept sixteen hours out of the twenty-four in their own filth and stench. For this you will be called to judgment, and if there is no one else to charge you with the wrongs I will. There is not a better country in the world to produce wool than this mountain country, if the sheep are properly taken care of.

"American Dairying: Its Rise, Progress, and National Importance"

From U.S. Department of Agriculture, *Annual Report*, 1865, pp. 431–33.

The dairy has become an important branch of national industry. It is rapidly spreading over new fields, and is engaging the attention of farmers in the western, northwestern, and middle States, wherever the lands are adapted to grazing and there are springs and streams of living water. The dairy districts, though comparatively limited, embrace a larger area than has been commonly supposed.

It is true, there are extensive plains at the south and southwest where the business of dairying cannot be carried on, but broad belts and isolated patches of land are scattered over our vast domain, well adapted to grazing, and such lands, when taken in the aggregate, cover a wide extent of territory.

There are two causes that have been operating the past few years to stimulate the development of this branch of industry, and have caused it to assume proportions that give it a distinctive feature of nationality. The first is a large and increasing foreign demand for dairy products; the second is the American system of "associated dairies," now brought to such wonderful perfection that the business can be readily introduced into new sections with all the ease and certainty of success in producing the qualities attained in old dairy districts.

The foreign demand for cheese, it is believed, will be permanent, and exportations from year to year must largely increase, since the finest American grades are acknowledged to be equal to the best manufactured abroad, while the cost of production is so much less as to render competition with European dairies an easy matter on our part. This fact alone gives confidence to those about entering upon the business of dairy farming — that it will be remunerative and enduring.

In addition, as the texture and flavor of cheese have been improved, a large home demand has sprung up, which requires large quantities to meet its wants. It is believed by many that the home demand, for years to come, will more than keep pace with increased production; and home sales for the last two years would seem to prove that this view is not without foundation.

With a constantly increasing home trade and a reliable market abroad, no branch of farming to-day offers prospects of better or more permanent remuneration than the dairy.

Commencement of Cheese Dairying as a Specialty — Its History, Etc.

The history of American cheese dairying has never been written, and perhaps a brief glance at its rise and progress will not be out of place.

Cheese making began in Herkimer county, New York, more than fifty years ago. For upwards of twenty years its progress was slow, and the business was deemed hazardous by the majority of farmers, who believed that over-production was to be the result of those making a venture upon this specialty. The fact, however, gradually became apparent that the cheese makers were rapidly bettering their condition, and outstripping in wealth those who were engaged in grain raising and a mixed husbandry.

About the year 1830 dairying became pretty general in the towns of Herkimer county north of the Mohawk, and some years later spread through the southern district of the county, gradually extending into Oneida and adjoining counties. Up to this period, and for several years later, little or no cheese was shipped to Europe. It was not considered fit for market till fall or winter. It was packed in rough casks and peddled in the home market at from five to eight cents per pound. All the operations of the dairy were rude and undeveloped; the herds were milked in the open yard; the curds were worked in tubs and pressed in log presses. Everything was done by guess, and there was no order, no system, and no science in conducting operations.

In 1840 the value of the dairy products of New York — butter, cheese, and milk — was estimated by the United States census returns at $10,496,021, and in all the States at $33,787,008. Some idea of the comparative increase will be found when it is known that the value of the butter products of New York alone, in 1865, was more than $60,000,000.

From 1840 to 1850 cheese began to be shipped abroad, the first shipments being inaugurated under the auspices of Herkimer county dealers.

In 1848–'49 the exports of American cheese to Great Britain were 15,386,836 pounds. Much of the cheese manufactured this year was of poor quality, and British shippers claimed to have sustained heavy losses. There was a more moderate demand the following year, and prices fell off a penny a pound, varying, from fair to strictly prime, from 6 to 6¼ cents for Ohio, and 6 to 6¾ for New York State. The exports in 1849–'50 were 12,000,000 pounds, and continued to vary, without important increase, for several years. From September, 1858, to September, 1859, the exports of cheese to Great Britain and Ireland were only 2,599 tons, and in the following year, for the same corresponding period, they were increased to 7,542 tons.

During the early part of the year 1860, Samuel Perry, of New York city, a native of Herkimer, and one of the earliest operators in the cheese trade, endeavored to control the market, purchasing the great bulk of cheese manufactured in the country. He was possessed of great wealth, and had for years enjoyed the confidence of dairymen, and being liberal and straightforward in his dealings, he was enabled to secure the dairies by contract, making his purchases at from 9 to 10 cents per pound. Then commenced the exportation of American cheese on a scale hitherto unknown in the history of the trade; and to him belongs the credit of opening up a foreign market for this "class of goods." The exportation of cheese from New York to Europe during 1860 was 23,252,000 pounds, which was increased on the following year to 40,041,000 pounds.

About this time (1860) the associated dairy system began to attract attention. Several factories were in operation in Oneida county, and were turning out a superior article of cheese. The system had been first inaugurated by Jesse Williams, a farmer living near Rome, in that county, and was suggested from mere accidental circumstances. Mr. Williams was an experienced and skillful cheese maker, and at a time when the bulk of American cheese was poor. His dairy, therefore, enjoyed a high reputation, and was eagerly sought for by dealers. In the spring of 1851, one of his sons, having married, entered upon farming on his own account, and the father contracted the cheese made on both farms at seven cents per pound, a figure considerably higher than was being offered for other dairies in that vicinity. When the contract was made known to the son, he expressed great doubt as to whether he should be able to manufacture the character of cheese that would be acceptable under the contract. He had never taken charge of the manufacture of cheese while at home, and never having given the subject that close attention which it necessarily requires, he felt that his success in coming up to the required standard would be a mere matter of chance. His father therefore proposed coming daily upon the farm and giving the cheese making a portion of his immediate supervision. But this would be very inconvenient, and while devising means to meet the difficulties and secure the benefits of the contract, which was more than ordinarily good, the idea was suggested that the son should deliver the milk from his herd daily at the father's milkhouse. From this thought sprung the idea of uniting the milk from several neighboring dairies and manufacturing it at one place. Buildings were speedily erected and fitted up with apparatus, which, proving a success, thus gave birth to the associated system of dairying now widely extended throughout the northern States.

The system of associated dairies, during the last eight years, has been carried into the New England States and into the Canadas. It is largely adopted in Ohio, and has obtained a foothold in Wisconsin, Illinois, Iowa, Kansas, and other States. It is known abroad as the "American system of dairying," and its peculiarities are so well adapted to the genius of our people as to give it a distinctive character of nationality.

Missouri Farming, 1865

From Missouri State Board of Agriculture, *Annual Report*, 1865, pp. 7–8, 11–13, 15.

The Missouri State Board of Agriculture was organized on the 13th of March last, (1865) pursuant to an act of the Legislature. At a subsequent meeting held on the 28th following, the board adopted by-laws for its government, and at that time the office of Corresponding Secretary was created.

The seventh section of the act of incorporation requires the annual report of the Board of Agriculture to embrace, among other matters specified, *"a general view of the condition of agriculture throughout the State."* Owing to the facts that the board was organized but a few months since, and with no means to prosecute the work thoroughly; that nearly all the county agricultural societies were broken up during the war by the ravages of contending armies in our State; and that the great majority of the counties have failed to respond properly to the circulars which were sent to them asking for the necessary information, it will be impossible to give such a full and correct view of the condition of agriculture throughout the State as the law undoubtedly contemplates and as would be interesting and useful. . . .

Under the circumstances, little more can be done than to allude to some of the more prominent features of the past. Probably it is quite as well that it is so, for indeed, with the exception of some of the more important counties, very little of a creditable character can be said of the past agriculture of the State. It has been chiefly of the pioneer style, and not the best phase of that. The present is full of encouragement and bright prospects, promising a rich harvest and a glorious future. . . .

The agriculture of Missouri may be said to be in a transition state, although not the kind of transition which has been observed in some of the older States eastward of us. There the transition has been made, or is going on, from a system of depletion, a constant drawing of wealth from the soil with little or no effort to secure continued fertility, to a system of "improved agriculture," which recognizes the great law of nature that the soil cannot continue to *give* without being replenished with the material. The former system prevails in all new countries where labor is scarce and manures not plenty, and where the virgin soil produces abundantly without manure and with comparatively little labor. And again, the class of pioneers are not generally men of the most advanced ideas of farming. They lead the way, open up the country, make improvements, establish schools and churches, do a vast deal of good and flourish like a "green bay tree," until population thickens around them and their lands begin to fail to yield remunerative crops with the same skill and labor formerly required, and then they seem to know no resource but to sell out and go further west, get new land and repeat the same system. A useful class of people they are, and if they are satisfied with their system it is not easy to see why any one else should find fault with it. Among the great mass of immigrants now flocking to Missouri, it remains to be seen what proportion belong to the class of pioneers who have worn out the soil elsewhere. In all older settled countries an improved system of agriculture is adopted *per force* as it were, because without it the land would not sustain the increased population.

In a large proportion of Missouri, agriculture has been nearly or entirely prostrated during the war; buildings and fences demolished and the inhabitants obliged to flee from their homes for safety. From that prostration we are now recovering with astonishing rapidity under the benign influences of peace, and doubtless by the energy and enterprise inspired by the new *regime*. We have been undergoing the transition from a slave labor system to one of free labor. The effect upon many of our farmers has been discouragement and prostration. Having a large amount of property in slaves, which they have suddenly found to be *not property,* they have felt very much as a man does who has been robbed. Having all their lives long depended greatly upon slaves, and having lived comparatively *"free and easy"* lives, they have lacked the enterprise and mental resources which seem to be generated by the more energetic life of the free States, and which was so much needed to enable them to meet successfully the great change. Some instances of the kind referred to could but have been expected. Agriculture probably suffers little in consequence, rather gains ultimately, because such men sell or rent at the first opportunity to men of more enterprise. The great majority of our slaveholding farmers, however, it is believed, met the change in a different spirit, welcomed it, in fact, and gained by it. Not a few rejoiced at it. A new and lively interest has been manifest in agriculture; many of the old county societies have been revived and fairs held, and these social reunions of the farmers have been enjoyed with all the zest of former days.

Some of the evils and defects of the past it may be well to consider, because these evils must be rooted out in order to insure prosperity in the future. This subject we must present briefly, leaving the more important considerations of the kind to a future time, when an opportunity shall have been afforded for becoming better acquainted with the wants and necessities of agriculture in the State. The few remarks submitted should be received with due allowance for the circumstances, namely, that the work undertaken is new, and the means were not provided for visiting the various parts of the State to obtain the facts in regard to the condition of agriculture.

Too Large Farms

Our farms are too large. This is one of the evils accompanying slavery. Slaveholders have evidently regarded it necessary to have large farms, in order to keep their increasing forces employed, and in case their old fields became exhausted to turn their attention to new ones. In this respect they were undoubtedly right, for slavery is certainly incompatible with "improved agriculture," in the modern acceptation of this term. Improved agriculture requires the application of a degree of intelligence, even in the laborer, that has not been considered consistent with slavery. How often have improved implements been laid by for years, because there was not intelligence enough in the slaves to use them, and often not enough in the masters to put them together properly so that they would work? It is not pleasant to tell unwelcome truths, but it is better sometimes that they should be told.

As the country becomes older, and with the change in our labor system, if we would farm profitably we must farm well. There must be a radical change in the mode of culture hitherto generally practiced. We must avail ourselves, to a greater extent, of the advantages of labor-saving machinery. We must adopt such a system of thorough culture as will produce the best results with the least proportionate expenditure, and at the same time preserve and increase the fertility of our soils, and such a system is inconsistent with the too common practice of "skim culture" of a large number of acres.

A writer in the *Missouri Republican,* in treating of this subject recently, says:

"The superior advantages of cultivating small parcels of land well, over large quantities poorly taken care of, is patent to any one who has given the subject proper consideration, and it needs no new ideas upon the subject to prove it, but it should be impressed upon our farmers as often as possible, many of whom, brought up to work slaves, found them as much as they could attend to, and thought it necessary to have large quantities of land to keep them at work, and raise food to support them, and many, no doubt, who had good land and negroes, made money easy enough — but that day is past, and a quite different and better system will now have to be adopted to make farming profitable. I know it is not profitable to farm here in the same manner as in England, Lombardy or the Netherlands, in consequence of the difference in price of labor and amount of capital used, but a medium course should and must be pursued to make farming pay well in this State. . . .

Farmers own too much land, cultivate too much land, and pay too little attention to improvement in cultivation. A few years ago it was not difficult to raise one hundred bushels of wheat from three acres of land. Now it can scarcely be done in the older settled localities from six acres. Consequently, the farmer generally increases the number of acres in cultivation in order to make up the deficiency in product. There is a downward tendency in this that should be arrested. The same amount of labor and capital, with more judicious cultivation, would produce as large results from at least one third less land, and prevent deterioration of the soil.

The general complaint among the thousands who have recently been in the State to buy land, is that the farms offered for sale are too large. It is believed to be the true policy of our large landholders to sell off portions of their lands in small tracts, even at low rates, to thrifty farmers, who will improve them, thereby increasing the value of the remainder. We think it the duty of many of our farmers, to themselves and to the State, to sell off portions of their large estates. They will thus benefit the State by aiding to populate it with industrious and thrifty citizens. They will benefit themselves by the increased prosperity they will bring around them, and by having more means to employ in improving more thoroughly their smaller farms.

Deep Plowing

Our culture is almost invariably too shallow. This is one of the natural evils of cultivating too much land. Farmers generally do not plow as deeply as they suppose. They will find by measuring accurately on the land side, that four inches will appear to be quite a deep furrow. When land is plowed only two or three inches deep, as stated in some county reports, if the land is rolling and the sub-soil compact, the rains will soon wash what little loose soil there is off into the stream, and by the time such land is fairly subdued it will be nearly worn out; whereas, if the land is deeply tilled, it will absorb the water and gain in fertilizing materials which are brought down from the atmosphere by the rains.

Horticulture in Illinois, 1866

From M. L. Dunlap, "The Status of Horticulture," in Illinois State Agricultural Society, *Transactions,* 1865–66 (Springfield, Ill. 1868), pp. 376–84, 386–87.

And just here we may stop to consider the use and value of an agricultural college, and see if its educational advantages can in any way benefit horticulture; to examine if we have such an interest in it that we may not lay a claim to a share in its management, to give it direction and derive benefit from its usefulness.

Agriculture begins with the matter of soil; in this, as agriculturists, we also have a deep interest; its texture, porosity, color, and mechanical condition, all interest us. We have many things yet to learn in regard to soils, as adapted to specific plants and fruits. This involves a study of chemistry, mineralogy, and geology, for soil is but the debris of rocks and minerals. We must study manures, and know when and in what quantity to apply them to each particular crop, of their economy of cost and comparative value. While the farmer on the rich prairies may not require large amounts of manure to grow the grains and grasses, yet horticulture can not be successful without their aid, and will make large demands in this direction, both for the orchard and garden; hence we have a special interest in insuring proper attention to this subject.

Plants, both for their seed and fibre, must be considered, and have space and attention and be considered in regard to their commercial value. The place that grain holds in the markets of the world, admonishes us that a small percentage saved in its production would more than pay the annual cost of the proposed college. In this, horticulture has but a common interest with others.

When we take a view of the great variety of agricultural products, we can come to no other conclusion than that it must needs have a division of labor similar to that of the mechanic arts. The farmer may raise grain and cattle and fruits and garden vegetables for market, but when he attempts them all on an even scale, he will make a signal failure. He must choose one of these as the main business, and make the others only secondary, to be pursued as convenient. This is becoming a well settled principle in rural economy, and the true one. We have grain farmers, dairymen, stock-growers, hog-raisers, orchardists, and market-gardeners; connected with these are the architect, the landscape gardener, and the land drainer. To this must be added arboriculture, or forest tree-planting.

In all new countries husbandry is the first business, and the others follow as towns and cities are built up, while horticulture is a fair index to the mechanical and commercial resources of the State. We have reached that point in our progress that the demand for horticultural products is of such a nature that a large part of our rural population and capital can be most profitably employed in it. The demands from our manufacturing cities and marts of commerce must be supplied. But we now have new demands upon us — the railways have opened up to us new markets, and we can send the products of the orchard to the miners of the Rocky Mountains, and the regions of the more inhospitable North. This new field of demand will tax our energies and stimulate us to a more thorough study of the capacity of our resources; hence, this agricultural college grant is just in time to give us the much needed aid.

It is time that we began to beautify and to adorn our homes, to put a cheerful aspect to the outside, to shelter it alike from the burning heats of summer and the keen blasts of winter. A garden needs buildings, and so does the farm; and hence we have architecture as a closely allied branch, for buildings and grounds must harmonize to give a pleasing effect; therefore, architecture should be taught in the agricultural college; or, at least, rural architecture, that will give useful and symmetrical houses and other buildings. We want the solid and useful, not the gaudy, showy style with which the city architect has so often marred the beauty of the suburban homestead. This style of building has been a great drawback on the country, for the real value has borne no comparison to the outlay, and has too often disgusted sensible business men with the country.

We have another thing that all cultivators are interested in; for, besides seeds and plants that are useful, we have weeds that are pernicious, and that draw largely on the labor of both field and garden; we must then have a class in botany for the study of these.

Horticulture has use for animals for motive power, for food and for clothing, in common with agriculture; we must learn how to feed them in the most economical way, to manage their labor, increase their fleeces, and to improve them for food. To do this, we must keep them in good health, and hence we have use for the veterinary art; and this, too, must be taught in our proposed school.

But we are not through with our demands; for after we have the soil, the seeds, the plants, the animals, and the buildings, we must have implements, not only for the farm, but the garden, the orchard, and the lawn. Plows, harrows, rollers, and cultivators; hoes, seed-sowers, drills, weed-cutters, garden-lines, trowels, pruning-shears, grafting tools, wheel-barrows, spades, tools to dig, to stir, to level, and to drain the soil. Hence, we must call to our aid the mechanic; and for him there must be a department, in which he may be taught the science of his profession.

And yet we have further use for our school. The insect tribes that prey upon our crops, although small in themselves, are a formidable army, and must be overcome by constant war on their approaching column; and yet, among them we have valuable friends — the cannibal insects. These we must learn to distinguish from our enemies, and protect them. We shall, therefore, need an entomologist to assist us in this intricate and perplexing warfare.

Yet, there are other demands before our list of needs is complete. The prairies are so destitute of timber, that, for domestic use, a large part of what we use must be purchased in distant States, and shipped to us at great expense of transportation.

Railroad ties by the hundreds of thousands are required annually, and will be for all time. Hence, we must make the culture of forest trees a part of our study, so that we may determine what to plant, and what will best supply our needs in that department of our local demand.

For railroad ties, shall we plant European Larch, or our own Red Cedar, Black Walnut, Chestnut, or the hardy Oak? To enable us to do this in a satisfactory manner, we shall need not less than twenty acres of land for each variety of forest trees. This will make a forest of one hundred acres, to be carved out of the prairies, and set like a gem in a kingly crown. We must have an exact record of the cost of the soil, its preparations, planting, culture, and marketing of the forest growth, that we may know how its profits may compare with other branches of farming.

No individual has as yet entered upon so valuable an experiment, and one so promising in good results. There is no good reason why the State of Illinois should not delegate this new feature to our agricultural college. Such a tree-planting would be followed by thousands on a smaller scale, for it would furnish the requisite knowledge to prosecute the business with success, and these practical lessons would be the teacher that would rapidly enrich the timber resources of our State, and our now almost treeless plains be robed with the leafy treasures of the forest to give us fuel, timber for domestic use, and to so change the climate that all crops would be made to produce with greater certainty.

We want no model farm, and yet in all of its departments there must be order and good management, whether the experiments prove successful or a failure. It must, to a great extent, be an experimental farm, not only for new products, new implements, but for new modes of culture.

The publication of all these in detail will be alike useful, whether they herald a success, or point out a failure. Ocean charts point out hidden rocks, and the river pilot must know where the sandbars are located, so as to enable him to guide the vessel in safety past them.

There is no product of the old world that we may not grow, but we must know in what soil and what location they will thrive the best, and this involves the study of soil and climate.

Can you tell me why the rich soil of the prairie will not grow canary seed, a grain so natural to all the maritime nations of Europe? I answer, for just the same reason that Sea Island cotton is not produced on the uplands of Georgia — the climate is not adapted to it. The farmers of Ohio failed in the culture of mustard and rape seed from the same cause. But this does not argue that canary seed, mustard, rape, and Sea Island cotton can not be profitably grown in the United States.

Another important interest, in which horticulture makes a demand, is the testing of all new fruits, plants, trees, and vegetables, that may be presented from time to time, and to furnish seeds, scions, cuttings, and roots of those that prove useful to those who wish to enter more largely into their culture, and to condemn those that prove of no value, that cultivators may not spend either time or money on them. This would do away with the whole race of plant charlatans that now infest the rural population.

The money spent on Morus multicaulis, China Tree Corn, Rohan potatoes, Bokara clover, sugar millet, sugar producing sorghum, Chinese potatoes, wonderful strawberries, and Brobdignag grapes, would have endowed an agricultural college in every State in the Union.

To teach the science of farming we need practical men, professors who can manage a practical department, and can actually demonstrate what they teach by tangible results.

We do not ask them to hold the plow, to plant, to reap, to mow or to thresh, but that they give directions how these things shall be done, and prepare all the crops for market.

They shall test different grains and grasses, and give us the result of their investigations in actual facts and figures. The orchard shall be for the testing of all new varieties of fruit, and the garden in like manner for vegetables. We must therefore have a large farm, divided into departments, and these under the supervision of the persons who are to teach the students in that particular branch of the art. In no other way can we educate a class of teachers that will be of any practical value to the State.

From what college shall we select our professor of husbandry? Who will teach the art of the dairy? Who will give us lessons in orcharding? Who shall be our market gardener, and who shall take charge of our forests? The schools have not the men ready for this work, and they must yet be taught. A man may study Choptel, Johnston and Liebig, and yet know little of practical husbandry; he must learn this before he can succeed.

In this day of progress, a cultivator of the soil must keep up with the requirements of the age. The changing demands of the markets, and the competition in every branch of business, do not permit of laggards in the onward march of new ideas. We have a soil and climate, in many respects different from other parts of the world, and while there are certain modes of culture common to all, yet we must adopt many new ones that apply particularly to our own soil and climate. Nor are these cultural rules so well understood and so plainly laid down that we have no need of further improvement. On the contrary, it is so progressive that the professor of horticulture of this year would, the next, be behind the age.

For six months the professor might teach, and for six months study new truths or verify old ones. The students could return home in summer to practice and fix upon their minds what they had been taught in winter. If a part of them choose to remain on the college farm and work as laborers, under the direction of teachers, let them do so, but at liberal wages. Let the farm pay, as far as possible, the cost of its management, and only the failures or the experimental part be a charge upon the State.

After we have made a farmer, a gardener, an orchardist, a dairyman, an architect, an arboriculturist or a mechanic out of a student, we have yet another duty to perform: we must make him a business man. He must know how to keep books and manage the routine of business, and to do this he must have also a commercial education.

We do not expect any one will acquire all these branches, but only so far as they are applicable to the particular calling that he may choose to follow. To expect that all the sons of those engaged in rural pursuits can or will be educated at this one school is out of question; but it will be the normal school from which will go out teachers, who may give lessons of practical value. It will require a year to found such a school, for at present we are almost without teachers, and must wait patiently for their education; and that education, to be of value, must be practical.

The new implements and new modes of culture that have within the past twenty-five years given such value to the State, have not been as yet laid down in text-books, but must be gathered and reduced to a system, ready for new additions.

I think that it is plainly demonstrated that the horticulturist has a deep interest in the founding of this new school, and that he is entitled to a large share in its direction. We therefore need a school that shall be to the horticulturist what the normal school is to the common school; a place for the education of practical and scientific teachers in the several departments of industry, as more directly connected with the culture of the soil. Wherever it may be located, let us see to it that our rights are not frittered away, either by dreamy philosophers or political demagogues. We want no division of its funds among the colleges, but one great central institution, from which the influence shall go out to all parts of the State.

We, as members of this great State Horticultural Society, are midway between the great commercial cities of the Northwest — Chicago, St. Louis and Cincinnati — that ask us for the products of the orchard and the garden, and which in return give us the comforts and the elegancies of life.

Before the day of railroads, we were simply herdsmen, producing cattle, horses and swine; these were driven on foot through the great forests of Indiana and Ohio, over the mountains of Pennsylvania, and down their long slopes to the markets of the seaboard. Then we had no cities to supply with horticultural products, and the few villages were but straggling hamlets, half village and half cultivators of the soil; we had no manufacturers then, and none but the rudest of farm implements were at hand to aid in the culture of the field. Horticulture was then comprised within the limits of a few cabbages, beets and onions in the garden, a score or two of apple trees, a few of the peach and an occasional seedling pear in the orchard.

Seeding machines, horse and hand hoes, weeding knives mounted on wheels, that cut down the noxious growth like magic, trowels and dibbles for transplanting, garden lines, rakes and grafting tools, had either not been invented or had not found their way to the gardens of the West. These great plains, so rich in the elements of fertility, were given up to the red man and to ignorance. But this state of things was destined to a change. The genius of Fulton invaded our rivers and introduced new music to their solitudes. The cloud that went up from the steamer's deck, bore in its folds the smoke from the alembic of the alchemist that should, out of the crude element, bring forth refined gold; the wild places should be made useful, and the solitudes henceforth yield to the dominion of man.

The strictly pastoral character of the sparse population no longer remained intact, and a mixed husbandry gradually appeared; the spinning wheel and the hand loom, whose music had become a part of the household, grew less and less as the eastern factories supplied the clothing of the people; the gardens became enlarged, and floral treasures were sought after; but it was not until the iron horse sounded his clarion notes, as he thundered over the vast towns that lay smiling in the summer sun, that great changes came. The spirit of progress was fully aroused, and from that time may be dated a new era in the history of the West. Not only were the cities of the East brought near to us, but great marts of commerce and of manufacturing grew up in our midst; villages were planted along the iron way, and stood like mile-stones to count its progress. The shop of the artisan, the house of worship, the district school, and all the appliances of the most civilized nations of the world have become accustomed to our use.

The inventive genius of man has wrought all this change. A thousand years ago the prairies were just as rich in the elements of fertility as now, the vernal and summer flora made the same obeisance to the winds that came ladened with whispers from the southwest, as to-day; the birds had the same gay plumage, and sang the same cheerful songs; the wild bison, the fallow deer and the elk, cropped the grasses of the plain with the same relish as do the herds that are now subservient to our use; the prairie fires lapped up that which summer had turned over to the frosts of autumn with the same greed as now; the water of our streams run as lazily to the sea as when the light canoe skimmed its surface; and the keen frosts of winter swept down from the north with the same icy breath as we have seen it within the last decade.

Steam, the giant power, more wonderful than the genii that attended the bidding of Aladdin, has passed within our borders, and given us a new condition of things. The pastoral age is passed and we are just beginning a new system; in fact, a new era is opened up to the hand of industry, at once genial, moral, and healthful. Twenty-five years ago a meeting like this, to discuss the subject of horticulture in its relation to commerce and its social advantages, would have been Utopian and the time spent in its pursuit of no value.

Now, horticulture has become a business of vast importance, requiring large outlay of capital, and no small amount of talent and muscular energy in its pursuit. It supplies a large amount of food to all classes of our population. A large share, both of garden and orchard products, formerly claimed by the rich as luxuries, have become necessities on the tables of all classes of society. It is therefore a pursuit in which we are all interested, and we are stimulated thereto both by profit and pleasure.

The loss of the apple crop for a single season may be considered a public calamity only second to that of the small grains, and to a certain extent we may say the same of all the whole range of pomonal products. The potato has passed from the garden to the field, and only that portion of the crop which we denominate early potatoes are allowed a place in the garden. Fifty years ago the potato was only grown in a small way, the farmer supplying the village mechanic and the tradesman an occasional load. Now they have become an important article of commerce, and whole farms almost exclusively devoted to their culture. Fifty, aye thirty years ago, and the strawberry was not found in our markets; horticulture had not then taken it into its keeping, and it nestled in the meadow, only sought after by the school-girl, the vagrant boy, or, occasionally, by the careful housewife. The best of our farmers seldom enjoyed the taste of this delicious fruit more than once or twice during the season, and even then, while the farmer was regaling himself on the dainty, his thoughts went back to the tangled grass, that was the price of the luxury. Who then dare say, when he sees the farmer's wagon piled high with boxes and crates filled with this rich fruit, that horticulture is not one of the useful pursuits of rural life.

The fruit and vegetable garden are now indispensable adjuncts to the farm, and no farmer can safely neglect their demands. They furnish not only a health-giving, but a substantial food for all classes of our population. The pork diet of the pioneer has given place to better food, and scrofula no longer baffles the village doctor. The gay ribbon grass of the farmer's daughter have given place to roses, verbenas, dahlias and carnations, while the living room is odorous with flowers.

The comparative cheapness of transportation, over the old modes of transit, the rapidity with which transfers are made, and the increased demand for horticultural products, permit us to send distant cities their daily supplies of horticultural dainties. This is particularly the case with all points to the north. The season follows the line of road from south to north in spring, and closes the autumn from north to south. For a time, therefore, in the season of fruits and vegetables, we can have no competition from any other point, for we then command the market.

Scarcely a decade back on the record of time, an orchard of a hundred apple trees was looked upon as a large outlay of capital, that would make but feeble returns; now, fifty to a hundred acres cease to excite our wonder, and he who sells a hundred bushels of apples from his winter store, is but an amateur, hardly worthy of having his name written in the list of the votaries of pomona. The orchard that flanked the cabbage garden, and sent a load or two of seedling peaches to market, was not long ago highly esteemed; but now whole car loads pass our doors, grown in a more genial clime. But horticulture will soon take this fruit in her keeping, and girt it around with shelter belts, and make annual plantings that shall load our tables with its delicious fruit.

Commerce, the great distributor and equalizer, can send the products of our orchards and gardens hundreds of miles, north or south, to meet the demands of the season and the climate. The south needs our late keeping apples, our potatoes and onions, while the north demands the early vegetables and the summer fruits; and from this central point we can send the useful in horticulture to make glad the more exacting regions of the north, and to give health and vigor to the sun-browned sons of toil of the sunny south. . . .

Manufacturers are swelling our cities into vast proportions, that have given new energy and life to horticulture, and placed it among the leading pursuits of the day, and now a large part of our rural population can make it their especial business.

We must have to do with commerce, and to this end, in our commercial orchards and gardens we must grow early fruits and vegetables for the north, and late, long keeping ones for those of the south.

Cider and cider vinegar, not the cider vinegar of the cities, sold under the trade mark of "pure cider vinegar," made of the washings of the liquor saloons and of breweries, or of a gallon of molasses and four pounds of tartaric acid to forty gallons of rain water, filtered through cobs saturated with acids, but the pure juice of the apple fermented and changed to a healthful condiment.

Thus far we have considered the business of horticulture, in what we should do; but there are things that we may not do. We should not plant a tree or shrub, a vegetable or flower, if it has no recommendation but its novelty or commended to us by some itinerent vender. Let nurserymen and amateurs first test these things before we plant them in our gardens or orchards.

Thousands of dollars have been worse than wasted on new things, thus palmed off on the public. Out of a thousand varieties of the apple, less than fifty will be found eminently profitable; out of the whole list of cherries, not three are worthy of a place in your grounds; out of nearly two thousand varieties of the pear, twenty will cover the very best for the orchard; out of the vast list of peaches, not a dozen have been proved; out of the almost endless list of new grapes, the really profitable thus far proved do not number a score; out of the list of plums, I ask you to name three that give you fruit; out of the hundreds of new strawberries, what have you for market but the Wilson; out of the endless list of the raspberries, that fill your gardens like worthless weeds, what have you beyond the purple cane and black cap of any commercial value; out of the list of blackberries, are you fully satisfied with any in the open ground? Have you a better currant than the Red Dutch, a more profitable gooseberry than the Houghton, a better rhubarb than Myatt's Victoria and Linæus? Why then run after new things for their novelty, or take the word of some interested party? The rage for novelties among horticulturists is one of the great drawbacks.

Prove all things and hold fast that which is good, was never intended to convey the idea that we should purchase every new thing for the purpose of proving its want or value. No doubt that new fruits of great value will be discovered, but it is not our duty to become experimenters on a large scale. Let all these be thoroughly tested before they are put upon the market. Some day we hope the agricultural college will form the crucible through which these will pass.

And just here is the great value of this association, that gives us the combined experience and skill of the many.

Cotton Industry, 1866

From N. B. Cloud, "Cotton Culture in 1866," U.S. Department of Agriculture, *Annual Report*, 1866, pp. 190–93.

In accordance with the request of the Commissioner of Agriculture, I propose to embody some suggestions relative to the culture of cotton in 1866, the peculiar difficulties attending it, and "the necessity and advantage of the general introduction of labor-saving machinery to reduce the cost of culture, and to neutralize the embarrassments arising from the existing and prospective scarcity of labor."

I may premise that the natural history and true philosophy of the culture of the cotton plant have been my constant study for more than a quarter of a century; therefore I shall write not merely what I think, but what I know from personal observation and practical experience, for a series of years, on the cotton field.

It was but reasonable to calculate upon a comparatively short crop of cotton the present year. The plantations of the country were in a rough and dilapidated condition generally; stock, mules, and horses for plough-teams were scarce, as was also grain to feed them during the ploughing season, and in very many localities extremely difficult to procure, which, of course, measurably prevented the proper preparation of the land for planting. Then, again, most of the seed was old and imperfect from neglect during the war. From this cause few plantations obtained even a tolerable stand, and on many not until after planting over two or three times.

These discouragements at the very beginning of the crop started the cotton plant very late. Then again, to meet and encounter these serious disadvantages, the planters found themselves in the use of a new and untried system of labor, and the laborers generally disinclined to do full work. Superadded to this already frightful array of difficulties attending the commencement of the crop, we had the most unprecedented amount of spring rain through the early summer that has ever been known in the cotton States, culminating in the great flood of June 10, which almost entirely drowned out the cotton plant on the rich river and creek bottom lands.

This long-continued, extremely wet weather not only injured the plant by a surcharge of water in the soil, thereby retarding its growth and rendering the plant more liable to succumb to the ravages of the *aphis,* (plant louse,) but promoted the rank growth of grass and weeds that proved seriously injurious to the crop in the acreage *"turned out"* to grass. This long spell of rainy weather was succeeded by sunny and dry weather, enabling the planters, by *unseasonable work,* to clear their crops — such as were not lost and given over — of the grass and weeds.

But this open dry weather, promising so propitiously in June, continued through July into August, and in many sections of the country to September, proving almost as destructive to the plant as did the rainy weather. In the beginning of September, the heavy rains commenced, and with them both the boll worm and the cotton caterpillar; the former destroying the bolls even half grown, while the latter stripped the plant of its foliage, blooms and all young fruit, (bolls.)

Such is a brief statement of the "difficulties" attending the culture and production of the present very short cotton crop of the United States, which cannot much exceed the crop of 1836 — thirty years ago, when Alabama and Florida produced comparatively little, and nearly ten years before Texas was a State of the Union. In a paper of this character, I cannot go into the minutiæ of these difficulties attending the operations of the past season.

In regard to these difficulties, an important question arises: Are they likely to continue to embarrass the culture of cotton for the future? To this question I answer emphatically that most of them will not; the plantations have received and are still receiving repairs for the next crop; the horse and mule force is being largely increased, and the planters have an abundant supply of good seed for the crop of 1867. Of the labor as much cannot be said; it is deficient in quantity, and in quality uncertain and unreliable.

Here we have a very serious embarrassment, that will not only continue, but will probably increase so long as we depend upon the freedmen in the culture of cotton. The other difficulties, of seasons, boll-worm, and cotton caterpillar, are natural, and not therefore entirely within the control of the planter; yet we may reasonably hope that Providence will in the future dispose them as in former years.

I now come to the proposition that labor-saving machinery is essential to future improvement in cotton culture; and I am gratified to be able to bring to its discussion an experience and practical observation, on the field, of more than twenty-five years.

As early as 1840 I saw the fallacy and destructive effect on the soil of the country of the common system of cotton culture; and at that time I instituted and commenced putting in practical operation a series of experiments founded upon philosophical principles: first, in the preparation and artificial fertilization of the soil; and secondly, in the subsequent culture of the cotton plant. In 1842, with the disadvantages of slave labor, while this system was yet crude and not fully perfected, I grew upon a single acre of thin or poor (naturally) sandy pine land nearly 6,000 pounds of seed cotton. This crop was grown by first applying a heavy dressing of good compost manure (barn-yard) broad-cast on the land, which was then laid off in five feet rows and bedded out with a good turning plough very deep.

The position of each plant in these rows or beds was spaced exactly three feet apart, and a half gallon, or spade full, of good compost manure deposited in each hill or position to be occupied by the plant. On the 10th day of April the seed was planted, after being first rolled in ashes, by dropping half a dozen in each place. The only difficulty here, and it was a serious one, the seed being placed in immediate contact with the manure, was the destruction of the vitality of many seeds while vegetating, and I obtained a bad stand at first; but by a quick perception of the difficulty and determined perseverance, I very soon obtained a perfect stand. The culture consisted of one light ploughing, while the plants were yet young, with a common shovel plough, and afterwards entirely with the weed hoe and a sweep running very shallow. Subsequently, and in the perfection of the system, I have abandoned placing any manure in the hill, but apply it broadcast entirely, which secures a good stand at first planting.

Here you have a brief yet plain and simple statement in detail of the mechanical and operative manual labor process by which this new and improved system of cotton culture is conducted in the field. The philosophy and science upon which the system is based, I shall show to be equally plain and simple, and easily to be comprehended by any laborer of good judgment and ordinary intelligence.

This may be first stated in brief previous to illustration. A farmer desires to produce upon a given area of ordinary common cotton land, say one or more acres, two or more bales of cotton to the acre. It is first necessary to incorporate with the soil a sufficient quantity of phosphoric acid in a soluble form, which the cotton plants may take up from the soil and assimilate into cotton seed, bearing the proportionate quantity of lint (cotton) for the desired bale or bales. This is conveniently had in good barn-yard compost or a good and genuine article of superphosphate of lime.

The illustration here is more satisfactory by taking a practical example. For instance, an intelligent farmer or planter, with his family located on his own little farm, or on a leased one, proposes to raise five bales of cotton, weighing 500 pounds each, the next year; this he intends to do on five acres of ordinary cotton land. His intelligence and judgment prompt him fist to lay his level on this little field and bring his cotton rows to a horizontal. That same intelligence teaches him that the elements of plant food for five bales of cotton do not exist in a soluble form in the soil of his five acre field. What then? He has already prepared, in and from his stock yards and stables, 500 bushels of good compost manure for each acre, which any planter may do at two cents per bushel; if he has it now already prepared he purchases one ton of superphosphate, pure and genuine, which he uses instead of the home-made compost. This is hauled out and spread uniformly over the soil, and then with a two horse "Brinley Eagle," or some other good turning plough, he beds out his rows deep and thoroughly, intimately incorporating this fertilization or plant food with the soil, at the same time effecting the proper and necessary pulverization. This beautiful process accomplished, his five acres of ordinary cotton land become the repository of the available elements of five bales of cotton. At the proper time, between the first and fifteenth of April, he plants his cotton seed; it now becomes necessary that the planter exercise his mechanical skill and judgment in the operation of planting; he is satisfied that he has stored in the soil of this field the crude elements of five bales of cotton, which field, before being fertilized, under the ordinary system of culture, might have produced but 250 to 300 pounds of seed cotton per acre. Now to secure five bales of cotton from it, a certain number of plants must be had standing on it in an even and uniform relation to each other; in other words, this being the first year of the shift or rotation, (this system embracing a beautiful and most profitable method of rotation of crops, as was successfully practiced by myself,) a bale of cotton only is intended to be had from each acre. For this end his rows are laid four feet wide, and the seed planted by spacer (compass) or seed planter thirty inches apart on the row. This gives him 4,368 cotton plants to each acre, taking seventy yards square as the acre. Thus he has on each superficial square of ten feet throughout each acre a cotton plant, thereby securing to each plant its natural (pyramidal) form and continuous healthy growth to perfect maturity; hence there is here no crowding of the plants, nor is there any space unoccupied. And here allow me to remark, emphatically, that this natural (pyramidal) form of the plant is absolutely essential to its perfect maturity. It is not possible for this unformity and perfect stand of plants to be had by any other mode or system of culture yet devised.

Another short paragraph will simplify this illustration. Take, for instance, an acre of common cotton land anywhere in the cotton region proper, seeding it with wheat, and give it the necessary fertilization and culture for the production of 1,800 pounds of grain, (30 bushels;) a result easily attainable. Then take an adjoining acre of the same character of land, with the same fertilization, and plant it with cotton seed, cultivated in all respects according to this improved system, and it will produce the first year 1,500 to 1,800 pounds of cotton seed; with this important addition, that from the atmosphere the cotton plant clothes the seed by assimilating its carbonic acid with 500 pounds of snow-white lint or cotton.

Here we have an improved system of cotton culture, practical and certain in its results, entirely adapted in every operation to "labor-saving implements and machinery." The land may be thoroughly ploughed with "gang ploughs," the seed dropped and covered at regular distances apart in the rows by seed planters, when all the subsequent work in its culture is just such as the intelligent gardener applies to his enriched soil in growing his superior vegetables. This system of cotton culture commends itself to intelligent laborers and their families; its various operations are comparatively light, (five acres to the hand.) Then again its highest recommendation consists in its permanent improvement of the soil and the bountiful crops of grain it secures to the planter. This five acres, after the cotton is picked off, has returned to the soil the leaves of the cotton plant, the burrs, the stalks, and the seed, except three to four bushels for planting other five acres the next year.

The rows being laid level, neither the enriched soil, nor the debris of the cotton plant returned as above to the field, can be washed off by the rains. This five acres the second year is planted in corn, which yields readily, or an ordinary season, 40 bushels of corn per acre, or 200 bushels to the hand.

The third year it is seeded to wheat, rye, oats, or any small grain crop the farmer may desire. With a light dressing of plaster or superphosphate, (the latter preferable,) an entirely remunerating yield is obtained.

The fourth year it lies in grass fallow, to be disposed of through the season as the interest of the farmer may require.

Texas Fever Among Cattle, 1866

From Missouri State Board of Agriculture, *Annual Report*, 1866 (Jefferson City, Mo., 1867), pp. 16–19.

Another pest which has made its appearance in the state within the past season is the "Texas fever," "Spanish fever," or "Texas murrain," as it is variously known. This is not a new pest in the state, as the statutes show. There was, however, almost an entire immunity from the disease during the war, when the driving in of Texas cattle was entirely suspended, with the exception, perhaps, of a very few isolated cases, which gave rise to the only cases occurring during the war.

The subject is an interesting one, and one which will demand legislation. The existing law in the case seems to be entirely inadequate for protection, and the people have frequently been obliged to resort to other means.

Mr. William Montgomery, of Stockton, Missouri, writes: "We are at a loss as to how the disease is communicated, as there is no apparent disease among the Texas cattle, but wherever they are herding any length of time, our cattle take some disease similar to dry murrain, and the actions of the animal with the disease are similar to a horse with the botts or colic. They seem to suffer severely with inward fever. When dissected, they appear to be dry and scorched with inward fever. Nearly all that take the disease die, unless treated immediately. Our remedy is to drench them with lard, or slugs of fat bacon. It does not look reasonable that the Texas cattle could communicate disease when they have no disease themselves, but the general opinion is that the disease is communicated by the breath.

"As to an amendment of the laws, we think it would be well to have them so amended as to prohibit Texas cattle from passing through the state, except during the cool season of the year, as we have noticed no disease similar to Texas or Spanish fever, except during warm weather — mostly contracted near ranches and watering places."

Another gentleman of southwest Missouri writes as follows: "I have lost very heavily this season by the, Texas fever,' and although it is very strange to me how an animal that is healthy itself can impart so dangerous a disease to other healthy cattle, I am nevertheless satisfied it can be done, as I have lost about one hundred and fifty head by the disease. They show the first symptoms by standing perfectly still in the position that they take to hold back, head down, fore feet thrust a little forward, ears dropped down, and are neither hungry nor thirsty. Their bowels become very costive; in fact, it seems as if their intestines became entirely dry, and unless an operation can be obtained, they die. Our most successful mode of treatment was to make them swallow a piece of fat meat (bacon), and force another one up their posterior (rectum) with the arm, as large as admissable and as far as possible. We saved about sixty after we adopted this mode of treatment, but the hair came off in spots from one to five inches in diameter. I doubt whether it can be cured in every case. I have heard a great many theories about it, but I understand you want facts, and I have written them.

"There is another fact that cannot be gainsaid; that is, since 1861 there has not been a single case of Texas fever in southwest Missouri, neither has there been any Texas cattle. Until the past spring and summer we have had Texas cattle and Texas fever. I have been dealing in cattle all the time since 1861, and in the time did not lose a brute until the past summer; so I say it is the southern cattle, and they ought not to be allowed to enter the state from the 15th of April to the 1st of October. Kansas learned this, and has legislated accordingly." . . .

The Spanish or Texas fever is well known to the older residents of this county.

This disease was first recognized as having been propagated by cattle driven from Texas some twelve or thirteen years ago; the disease having been in the county some two seasons previous to its having been traced to the Texas cattle.

From the first breaking out of this fever it was found to be confined to the large roads or highways running through the county from south to north, and, finally, was centered on the Texas cattle, I believe, in the year 1853, by its being confined to one highway through the county over which these cattle passed in that year. On this road the disease was quite fatal, killing about fifty per cent. of all the cattle on the road, and persons living near the water courses over which the road crossed lost as high as ninety per cent. Captain Freeman Barrows and Peter Colley, the one living at the ford of the Osage river, the other near by, lost the latter per cent. — one of them owing about one hundred head, while the former had considerably above that number, Mr. Collins, living at the ford of Clear creek, south of the above, lost an equal proportion.

The disease being in no other part of the county that year, satisfied the people, on this road at least, that they had found the true origin as it had been among the cattle in the country for two summers past. In a season or two after, almost every settler of the county was convinced that the Texas cattle in some way communicated this fever to our stock, although a few persons living secluded from the great highways were unbelievers, and still remain so. In fact, the way this disease is propagated, the obscurity surrounding it for want of a defined cause, together with the different conflicting opinions of almost every citizen familiar with it, gives them at least a reasonable excuse for believing no one's opinion. Two things only, the symptoms of the fever and its fatality, are agreed to by every one, the latter being much greater in a warm dry summer than in a cold wet one; the disease always ceasing when the frosts and freezes have killed the vegetation. . . .

Discourse by Apostle Orson Hyde, 1867

From Orson Hyde, "Instructions," *Journal of Discourses* (Liverpool, 1867), XI, pp. 148–51.

There is a good deal of ambition among our people to cultivate a great quantity of ground, the result of which is, that we cultivate our lands poorly in comparison to what we would if we were contented with a smaller area, and would confine our labors to it. We have found some difficulty with regard to water, and complaints have been made about a scarcity of water in many places, when, indeed,

I suppose the Lord has apportioned the water to the amount of land he intended should be cultivated. I do not think that these things are passed over unnoticed by Him without some kind of arrangement or calculation. He understands perfectly well what the elements are capable of producing, and how many of His people may be established here or there with profit and with advantage. I have labored most industriously since I have acquired a little experience myself, to induce my brethren to direct their energies upon smaller tracts of land; for I have noticed where men would attempt to raise a crop off forty acres of land, that they could not get their crops in in season, and frequently the frost came early and destroyed a great portion of them. This is bestowing our labor for that which does not profit. Now, would it not be better to confine our energies to a small tract of land, put in our crops in due season, have ample time to do it, do it well, and then it would only require one-half or one-third the amount of water to mature them, and they would mature in advance of the frost?

I do not know how it is in other sections of the country, but I presume it is more or less with them like the circumstances I will relate. I have known men, single handed, attempt to raise twenty-five and thirty acres of grain, when it is more than any one man can well do; the result is, they find themselves troubled to get the water; they run from break of day until dark at night, wearing themselves out, and with all they can do they cannot bestow that attention upon their fields which they need, and they only get from eighteen to twenty bushels of wheat to the acre. When men have confined themselves to ten acres of land, having plowed it well the season before, all the foul weeds killed out and the soil left clean, the seed sown at an early day in the Spring, and put in in good order, I have known such fields to produce from forty to sixty bushels of good plump wheat to the acre. Besides, when fields are so cultivated, less water is used; the necessary labor can be performed without being hurried, and a plentiful harvest of golden sheaves reward the toil of the laborer.

This season, in all probability, our crops will fall short of other years some thirty thousand bushels of wheat, by reason of the early frosts. While I regret this loss, I am happy to say that there is plenty of good wheat in the granary, or in the Egypt of Utah; and I think the loss this year, through early frosts, will aid very much in enforcing the principles which I have endeavored to advance, namely, to confine our labors to smaller tracts of land and put in our crops in good time; that while they are growing luxuriantly and yielding bountifully, filling our bins with golden grain, we are not worn out with toil before the days allotted to us to live are expired; but we still have our strength, time to build comfortable houses for our families to live in, barns and sheds, and to prepare shelter for our stock.

I find the longer we live in these valleys that the range is becoming more and more destitute of grass; the grass is not only eaten up by the great amount of stock that feed upon it, but they tramp it out by the very roots; and where grass once grew luxuriantly, there is now nothing but the desert weed, and hardly a spear of grass is to be seen.

Between here and the mouth of Emigration kanyon, when our brethren, the Pioneers, first landed here in '47, there was an abundance of grass over all those benches; they were covered with it like a meadow. There is now nothing but the desert weed, the sage, the rabbit-bush, and such like plants, that make very poor feed for stock. Being cut short of our range in the way we have been, and accumulating stock as we are, we have nothing to feed them with in the winter and they perish. There is no profit in this, neither is it pleasing in the sight of God our Heavenly Father that we should continue a course of life like unto this. Hence, in my labors I have exerted an influence, as far as I have been able, to cultivate less land in grain and secure to ourselves meadows that we might have our hay in the time and in the season thereof, shades for our stock, barns, and stables for our horses, and good houses for our families, where they may be made comfortable and happy, and that we may not be everlasting slaves, running, as it were, after an *ignus fatuus,* or jack in the lantern, following a false light, but that we may confine ourselves to a proper and profitable course of life. I do say, that a man's life consisteth not in the abundance of the things that he possesses, nor upon the vast amount he extends his jurisdiction over, but it consists in a little well cared for, and everything in order. When we confine ourselves and our labors to small tracts of land, we shall then find time to do everything that is necessary to be done; but if we branch out so largely in plowing, sowing and reaping, we have no time to make necessary improvements around our homes and in our cities; in fact, we have so much to do that we can do nothing at all.

Now I speak of these things, my brethren, not because I think that they are the most edifying to you, but I speak of them because I consider that a temporal salvation is as important as a spiritual one. It is salvation in every respect that we are laboring to obtain, not only to make ourselves comfortable and happy, so far as the physical energies of the body are concerned, but, also, that the mind should not constantly be on the strain day and night. There should be a little time for relaxation and rest to both body and mind, that while our bodies are resting the mind may be fresh to plan and arrange for our personal comfort and how to make everything snug and tidy around us. How much more agreeable is life when everything is in order and good regulation is maintained in and around our homes and cities. This is what I have endeavored, in my weak way, to instil into the minds of the Saints. In some instances I have been successful, and where men have adopted the course I have suggested, they have invariably borne testimony in its favor. I would rather have half a dozen cows in the winter, and have them well taken care of, than to have twenty and have fourteen of them die for want of feed and proper attention, which would leave me only six. I would rather only have the six to begin with, then I would not have the mortification of seeing so many suffer and die. In the present condition of the ranges, we cannot indulge in the hope of raising such large herds of stock as we have done heretofore; but we have got to keep about what will serve us, and take care of them well; then we can enjoy ourselves, and we are not the authors of misery to any part of creation.

We are trying to get into this way; it is a slow operation, and it seems that men's inordinate desire for wealth and extensive possessions is hard to overcome. They hate to be limited; they think their fields are not large enough for their strength; but it is a good thing to have a little strength on hand all the time, and not let out the very last link, because there might be an emergency that would really require it. If we drive a pair of horses all the time at their utmost speed they are soon worn out; and if you want to make a trip very speedily, you cannot do it, your animals are run down, you have not husbanded their strength, and they are not capable of performing the journey you wish; whereas, if they are properly driven, judiciously fed, and their strength properly husbanded, when you want to make a sudden dash you have the power to do it. We are not unlike, in this respect, to other portions of the animal creation. Perhaps I have said enough upon this subject.

We have had our difficulties to encounter in the south; it has not all sunshine and fair weather with us, but we have got along as well as we could. Perhaps that is saying too much, it is saying a good deal; I do not know that I dare say it. I look back frequently upon my past life and find many places that I think I could have bettered; but were I to live my life over again I do not know that I could do any differently. I will, however, let the past take care of itself, and for the future seek to do the will of God and keep myself in subjection to it.

I have no objections to men obtaining wisdom and learning from books, whether old or new; that is all right and good enough; but I consider it is better to have the Spirit of God in our hearts, that we may know the truth when we hear it; and not only know it when we hear it, but be capable by that Spirit of bringing forth things that we never heard. I feel that it is our privilege, brethren and sisters, to have this principle dwelling within us; and when I see men laboring through books, ancient and modern, to find but little that is good, I am reminded of those who run over forty acres of land in a superficial manner, and only reap a little, when a small quantity of land, well watered and well cultivated, would be sure to yield a rich harvest.

Wages of Farm Laborers, 1867

From U.S. Department of Agriculture, *Monthly Report,* January, 1867 (Washington, 1867) pp. 4–15.

In a single hundred years a change has been wrought in this country which may well challenge the admiration of the civilized world, and all that has been accomplished is the direct result of labor, and of that labor the largest portion, if not the most productive of net profits, is the labor of agriculture.

Only one branch of agricultural industry is to be considered at this time. Farm workers are here farm proprietors. Scarcely more than one-fourth of those who obtain their living by agriculture, in this country, hire out their service to farmers for a monthly or other consideration. It is of this class that a systematic course of inquiry in every State and Territory has been made, and it is, as is believed, the first attempt of the kind ever made here.

The result shows an increase of the rates of wages in five years amounting to about fifty per cent. This is less than the increase of the cost of living; still the purchasing power of a month's wages is probably greater than in any other country in the world. Farm laborers, especially in the west, can enjoy more of the comforts of life, and attain a higher rank in the social scale, than those of any other country. They do not obtain the wages conceded to mechanics and other classes, perhaps better entitled to be considered skilled laborers, yet they enjoy an advantage, which is a partial compensation, in lower rents and cheaper subsistence supplies, and fewer temptations to extravagance and waste.

In view of the superior condition of the class, in comparison with rural laborers in other countries, it is not strange that the European peasant should covet such advantages, and seek them even at the expense of exile from the fatherland.

Table showing the average rate of wages of agricultural labor per month, when employed for the year, from returns from statistical correspondents, county clerks, and county auditors, made in December, 1866.

States and Territories.	Per month, for the year, (without board.)	Per month, for the year, (with board.)	Per month, for the season, (without board.)	Per month, for the season (with board.)
Maine	$27 00	$17 44	$31 76	$23 07
New Hampshire	32 74	22 48	39 12	28 43
Vermont	32 84	21 00	37 44	25 72
Massachusetts	38 94	22 36	41 61	27 83
Rhode Island	34 40	20 50	40 00	26 33
Connecticut	34 25	21 54	39 66	28 30
New York	29 57	19 32	34 88	24 26
New Jersey	32 27	18 98	33 13	23 78
Pennsylvania	29 91	18 84	34 10	22 87
Delaware	24 93	13 25	26 25	15 25
Maryland	20 36	12 76	23 83	15 58
Virginia	14 82	9 36	17 20	12 09
North Carolina	13 46	8 15	15 18	10 00
South Carolina	12 00	7 66	14 00	9 46
Georgia	15 51	9 67	18 45	12 07
Florida	18 00	12 12	20 55	14 46
Alabama	13 40	9 80	16 38	11 00
Mississippi	16 72	11 58	22 58	16 80
Louisiana	20 50	12 42	22 25	18 34
Texas	19 00	12 72	23 73	16 76
Arkansas	24 21	15 80	29 61	19 46
Tennessee	19 00	12 58	22 00	16 61
West Virginia	25 35	16 47	29 34	21 20
Kentucky	20 23	13 65	23 80	17 06
Missouri	26 75	18 08	30 84	21 66
Illinois	28 54	18 72	33 09	23 30
Indiana	27 71	18 72	31 50	22 50
Ohio	28 46	18 96	32 45	23 15
Michigan	31 26	20 48	34 95	24 15
Wisconsin	30 84	19 87	35 65	24 60
Minnesota	31 65	21 10	38 40	27 17
Iowa	28 34	18 87	33 24	23 82
Kansas	31 03	19 81	36 40	25 46
Nebraska Territory ..	38 37	24 64	46 42	31 36
Utah Territory	44 71	26 32	58 22	38 41
Colorado Territory ...	67 50	42 12	79 16	50 00
New Mexico	25 00	16 50	30 00	25 00
California	45 71	30 35	50 00	34 39
Nevada	75 00	60 00	85 00	70 00
Washington Territory	52 25	36 25	60 50	44 50
Dakota	30 20	20 00	32 00	22 00
Oregon	35 75	22 53	41 60	29 00

Immigration

It is a suggestive fact that the immigration of millions of foreigners has not, as native laborers once feared, proved a serious competition, reducing the rate of wages. On the contrary, it has advanced great public works which have opened new and wider fields of industry, and has pushed the native laborer into the artisan ranks and the sphere of skilled labor, with higher wages, more exercise of mind and less of muscle than before. When it is remembered that in 1860 there were 4,136,175 foreign residents, and at least 5,000,000 at the present time, or one-seventh of the population, and a still larger proportion of the actual labor of the country, this result must be acknowledged to be convincing evidence of the great resources and vast power of labor absorption possessed by the United States.

Increase of Rate of Wages

More than thirty years ago Mr. H. C. Carey made the following estimate of the average of agricultural labor in this country: "Agricultural labor has not varied materially in these forty years in its money price; but the variation that has taken place has been in its favor — the wages of men having been very steadily about nine dollars per month and their board; but higher wages are now not very unusual." The average for white labor at the present time, as presented in the accompanying tables, is fairly stated at $28 per month, or nearly $15 50 and board. This indicates an advance of seventy per cent. In the lapse of a generation, mostly in the last six years, or fifty per cent. since 1861.

Accuracy of the statement

The returns from which this table is prepared were remarkably full, numerous, and satisfactory. It was deemed best not to load the circular with too many inquiries, or those difficult of prompt and universal answer. It embraced fifteen separate inquiries relative to farm labor, by hand or machine. A deep interest in the subject, with a proper appreciation of its importance, was manifested by correspondents, who replied with promptness and intelligence, after consultation with the best judgments in their vicinity. In a very few cases where any misunderstanding of a single point apparently existed, the difficulty was cleared up by correspondence. The extent and completeness of the work may be inferred from the number of returns, mostly representing counties, though occasionally subdivisions of counties; and each one of these returns compiled in accordance with the combined judgment of several local correspondents, or other individuals. Ohio, for instance, is represented by 114 returns; Indiana by 110; Illinois by 103; Iowa by 104; New York by 109; Pennsylvania by 75; smaller States by a less number; in all, 1,510 formal statements, each made up of several others, usually representing a defined territory or district.

As an example of uniformity in a populous, central, prosperous belt, interlaced with railroads and traversed or skirted with navigable water, let the reader note the figures for the States on the fortieth parallel. The monthly rate of wages, without board, is placed at $29 91 in Pennsylvania, $28 46 in Ohio, $27 71 in Indiana, $28 54 in Illinois, $28 34 in Iowa. The east is subject to a somewhat higher cost of living, while in the west the scarcity of labor has the same tendency to advance prices. This scarcity in Nebraska pushes the rate to $38 37. The rate of wages, with board, is still more uniform: Pennsylvania, $18 84; Ohio, $18 96; Indiana, $18 72; Illinois, $18 72; Iowa, $18 87; showing an entire range of variation in the net price of labor of only twenty-four cents!

Very general returns were received from the southern States, yet fewer than from the northern. These States rest under the disadvantage of a disturbed condition of labor relations, resulting from the war and manumission of slaves. Assuming as a truth the proposition of Mr. Amasa Walker, that involuntary servitude is not labor, it might be declared that labor in the south has scarcely progressed beyond the period of helpless infancy. Low rates of wages are, therefore, returned from this section. The multiplicity of modes of contracting for service of freedmen, involving, in some cases, semi-partnerships or shares in the products of labor, and in others total or partial supplies of food or implements of labor, renders it difficult to report with accuracy its actual market value. Yet, the result of the inquiry has been, upon the whole, quite satisfactory.

The average rate of wages, viz: $28 for labor of whites, and $16 per month for that of freedmen, was obtained by careful and laborious calculation. First, the average monthly wages in a State was multiplied by the number of farm laborers in such State, and so with each member of the Union. Then the sum of the aggregate monthly wages was divided by the aggregate number of laborers, giving as a quotient the proper average monthly pay of the farm laborer. An average of the several State averages, it will readily be seen, would by no means answer the purpose of approximate accuracy, as such a mode of *miscalculation* would give to a State with few laborers as much influence as one with many.

Causes and Results of High Rates

In those States in which regular labor is most general among the inhabitants, and where it is prosecuted in greatest variety, there will wealth abound and prosperity be most generally enjoyed. And another fact relative to such States will also be noted — their laborers receive the highest rate of wages.

Massachusetts has a poor soil, and cannot be considered a farming State. In 1860 the United States census returned 45,204 farmers, and 17,430 farm laborers, while the total return of all occupations was 454,632. The State census of 1865 makes the number engaged in agricultural pursuits 68,636, and those employed in manufacturing 271,241. The employment of all this labor in commerce, in fisheries, in manufactures, in the mechanic arts, and in trade, requires a consumption of farm products far greater than the home supply. This enables farmers to select those branches of their business most profitable under the circumstances, and least affected by foreign competition, as the milk trade, the fruit supply, and production of perishable vegetables. The facility of obtaining employment in other occupations gives the farm laborer a material advantage, and enforces his demand for higher rates of labor. The result is, at the present time, higher monthly pay than any other State in the Union, except California, viz: $38 94 per month for farm labor, without board. And while the necessaries of life are also high, there is no State in which the agricultural laborer enjoys the comforts of life to a greater extent, or is better fitted to act a creditable part in his sphere in society.

The advantages of great variety in industry are manifold, one of the highest of which is the fact that all classes and capacities, young and old, male and female, are furnished with something to do, and with a motive for doing it, and thus labor in some form becomes the rule, to which there are few exceptions. Consumers and producers are at each other's doors, or commingled in the same household, and carriers and go-between absorb but a small portion of the profits of industry. There is no glut of the markets from excess of production or the deficiency or great expense of transportation. There is no occasion to sell corn for ten cents per bushel, or eggs at six cents per dozen, or cattle, as in Texas, at five dollars per head.

It is fashionable in communities with but one prominent industry to decry the promoters of these industrial enterprises as monopolists and heartless oppressors. Thirty-eight dollars per month for farm labor, and twenty to thirty for light employments of females, are sufficient answers to such ill-natured charges. Tidy and well-furnished houses, and evidences of refinement in humble life, are not the concomitants of the oppression and tyranny of capital. These same communities must adopt the same variety in industry which they might have done and should have done many years ago, or the compulsive idleness and resultant poverty of large masses of their people will continue, and become intensified and chronic, until their whinings over the prosperity of more industrious communities shall become an envious wail of misery.

This path of progress has been equally open to all; laws supposed to favor a diversified industry have been applicable to all States alike; the best waterpower and the cheapest coal are in States that make no extensive use of either; milder climates and superior facilities for cheap transportation have furnished advantages that have not been transmuted into net profits; and yet such communities, daily inflicting irreparable injury upon themselves, by neglecting the gifts of God and spurning the labor of man, are wont to deem themselves injured by the prosperity flowing from superior industry and a practical political economy.

Will States that are almost deserts from a suicidal policy of growing agricultural products for exportation, and importing everything, learn wisdom from poverty, and grow prosperous and wealthy, with laboring classes comfortable and intelligent, and advancing in moral and mental culture?

The rate of wages in the several States differs just in proportion to the multiplication of separate industries, modified in new States in process of settlement by the increased demand for consumption occasioned temporarily by in-coming settlers who are as yet non-producers, or in the mining States and Territories by the employment of the majority in mining. The following is a table of average wages per month of farm laborers employed for the year, in the different sections of the country:

Eastern States $33 30
Middle States 30 07
Western States...28 91
Southern States 16 00
Oregon..35 75
California...45 71

One cause of high rates of labor in this country is the superior intelligence and activity of the laborers. Nowhere else is so much agricultural labor done by machinery requiring skill and knowledge in its management, and accomplishing marvellous results in its swift and efficient action. An English writer on political economy recognized this element of increase in labor rates when he said: "The average annual wages in England are three times as high as in Ireland; but as the laborer in Ireland is said not to do more than one-third of what is done by the laborer in England, the price of labor may in both countries be about equal." There is a tendency to a just equilibrium in the labor markets as in all other markets; and if laborers by superior skill and celerity of movement may do double work, they will obtain, other things being equal, a double price. Agricultural machinery has done more in this country than anything else towards the elevation of labor.

Local Variation of Rates

The "Panhandle" of West Virginia is a notable example of high local rates of wages as compared with the State average. Its circumstances have been peculiar. Hemmed in between Ohio and Pennsylvania, and with fair facilities for getting to market, it has developed higher skill and a better style of farming than other sections of the State. The influence of slave labor in depressing rates of wages has aided in widening this difference and reducing the State average below that of the Panhandle. Sheep husbandry, which has here been successfully and very extensively conducted, (placing a sheep upon each acre of improved land,) has contributed to the high prices here prevailing. The comparison is as follows:

	Question 1.	Question 2.	Question 3.	Question 4.
Panhandle........................	$31 75	$18 50	$37 00	$25 50
State of West Virginia...........	25 35	16 47	29 34	21 20

The rates with and without board also differ widely — $13 25 and $8 88.

Dairying. — The dairy and fruit-producing interests of northern Ohio have been of late unusually prosperous. Labor has been in demand at comparatively high rates, as will be seen from a comparison of the averages for the western reserve, the Miami valley, and the entire State:

	Question 1.	Question 2.	Question 3.	Question 4.
Western reserve..................	$30 43	$20 72	$36 24	$26 22
Miami valley	28 79	18 75	32 71	23 08
State of Ohio	28 46	18 96	32 45	23 15

The difference in wages with board is not very material. The board allowance is slightly greater in the western reserve than the average for the State, and more for the "season" than for the entire year. The reverse is true of the Miami valley.

Wages in Indiana

The average rate of wages of Indiana, south of thirty-nine degrees north latitude, and the average for the whole State, are as follows:

	Question 1.	Question 2.	Question 3.	Question 4.
Southern Indiana..................	$26 25	$18 56	$29 24	$21 77
State of Indiana...................	27 71	18 72	31 50	22 50

The average differences in board allowances are respectively $7 61 and $8 99.

This average for southern Indiana, a region having in the past a reputation for comparative inferiority in agricultural improvements, indicates increasing skill in farm processes and general industrial progess, and shows a close appproximation to the average of the entire State.

Southern Illinois

Southern Illinois, too, with its rolling surface covered with forests, and less desirable soils than those of the northern prairies, has failed to secure hitherto so rapid settlement, or such an increment of improvement. Yet this region has its peculiar advantages, which have recently been seized upon by eager immigrants; and the results have been eminently satisfactory.

The following exhibit of wages is shown:

	Question 1.	Question 2.	Question 3.	Question 4.
Southern Illinois	$26 06	$16 83	$30 36	$21 41
State of Illinois...................	28 54	18 72	33 09	23 30

Nearness to Cities

The influence of diversification of industry, and the consequent withdrawal of labor from farms to manufactures and trade, increasing the price of farm labor, as well as of farm products, is shown in the average for St. Clair county, opposite St. Louis.

	Question 1.	Question 2.	Question 3.	Question 4.
St. Clair county...................	$40 00	$20 00	$50 00	$35 00

Omitting from the table the vicinity of St. Louis, the showing for southern Illinois is as follows:

	Question 1.	Question 2.	Question 3.	Question 4.
Southern Illinois	$24 83	$16 62	$28 85	$20 06

Easy Transportation and Skilled Labor

The advantage of facilities for transportation are shown by the increased rates of wages near navigable rivers and lines of railroad. This is conspicuously seen in a comparison of the river counties of Kentucky with those of other portions of the State. Other elements of difference appear in a comparison of the river counties of the Kentucky side with those of the Ohio shore. A more diversified industry in Ohio, and the employment of free instead of slave labor, enter into the calculation and make a material advance in the rate. The following table exhibits nearly as great a difference between the river counties of Ohio and those of Kentucky as exists between the latter and those of the entire State:

	Question 1.	Question 2.	Question 3.	Question 4.
State of Kentucky	$20 23	$13 65	23 80	$17 06
River counties, Kentucky	24 23	16 36	28 79	20 36
River counties, Ohio	28 27	17 36	32 81	22 33

Free Labor Influence

The influence of changing the system of labor in a State from slave to free is illustrated very conspicuously in the belt of States from Virginia to Missouri. Virginia has been divided for several years, and that portion west of the mountains, formerly in comparative discredit as an agricultural region, shows a much higher rate of wages than Virginia proper. Slave labor, for several years, has scarcely been known in a large portion of Missouri. The following is a showing of the rate of wages for these States:

	Question 1.	Question 2.	Question 3.	Question 4.
Virginia	$14 82	$ 9 36	$17 21	$12 09
West Virginia	25 35	16 47	29 34	21 20
Kentucky	20 23	13 65	23 80	17 06
Missouri	26 75	18 08	30 84	21 56

Board of Farm Laborers

The difference between wages without board and the rate allowed when board is furnished by the employer is naturally found to vary quite regularly with the cost of food products, the rate being higher in the east than in the west, and higher still in the Territories of the Rocky mountains, but less in California than in Massachusetts. In the south the board of freedmen, consisting mainly of corn meal and bacon, is, of course, very low. Possibly in Alabama the difference between labor with and without board may be too small. The mode of hiring and supplying these laborers varies so much with circumstances that our correspondents found it difficult to reduce their information to the system required.

The following is a statement of these differences in monthly pay on account of board, averaging $6 26 in the southern States, and $12 51 for the other States:

Maine	$ 9 56		New York	$10 25
New Hampshire	10 76		New Jersey	13 29
Vermont	11 84		Pennsylvania	11 07
Massachusetts	16 58		Delaware	11 68
Rhode Island	13 90		Maryland	7 60
Connecticut	12 71		Virginia	5 46
North Carolina	5 31		Ohio	9 50
South Carolina	4 34		Michigan	10 78
Georgia	5 84		Wisconsin	10 97
Florida	5 88		Minnesota	10 55
Alabama	3 60		Iowa	9 47
Mississippi	5 14		Kansas	11 22
Louisiana	8 08		Nebraska Territory	13 73
Texas	6 28		Utah Territory	18 39
Arkansas	8 41		Colorado Territory	25 38
Tennessee	6 42		New Mexico Territory	8 50
West Virginia	8 88		California	15 36
Kentucky	6 58		Nevada	15 00
Missouri	8 67		Washington Territory	20 00
Illinois	9 82		Dakota Territory	10 20
Indiana	8 99		Oregon	13 22

The average, as above, for white laborers, is $12 51 per month; in the south, with reference mainly to freedmen, $6 26.

The following questions were fully answered, but, owing to the great diversity in the mode and conditions of such operations, no average could fairly be drawn:

" 0. Price, per bushel, of threshing and separating wheat?

"11. Price, per bushel, of threshing and separating oats?

"12. Price, per bushel, of husking and cribbing corn?

"13. Price, per bushel, of shelling corn?

"14. Price, per acre, of cutting and stacking hay?"

In some localities the machine and its manager only are furnished, at a low price per bushel; in others, additional men or horses; in others still, all labor, board, or other expense. The prices, therefore, vary, as in Illinois, for instance, from three to seventeen cents per bushel. And so in other States. The actual returns from Illinois would average $8^7/_9$ cents; question 11th, average $5^1/_{10}$ cents. In cutting and stacking hay, in Illinois, the returns ranged from $1 50 to $4 per acre.

The following extracts from correspondence will show further the impossibility of obtaining uniformity in returns relative to machine labor, and, to some extent, freedmen's labor:

A Pennsylvania correspondent says of harvesting wheat: "Men are either hired by the day and furnished with horses and wagon, or receive a portion of the crops, (threshed,) to be agreed upon. In out lots, adjoining towns, it is customary to get a neighboring farmer to do the work, and to deliver to the owner of the soil one-half the threshed grain. This includes ploughing and sowing, each party furnishing half the seed.

"As to your 12th question, men are hired by the day, and the corn is cribbed or otherwise disposed of at the expense of the owner. The shelling of corn is done by the farmers themselves, with such hired assistance as the mode of operation requires. Large lots are tramped out with horses. It is generally sold in the ear, however. Cutting, curing, and stacking hay is done for one-half the crop, the cropper finding all."

Table showing the rate of wages of agricultural labor, per day, in transient service, from returns from statistical correspondents, county clerks and county auditors, made in December, 1866.

States.	Per day, for transient service in harvest, (without board.)	Per day, for transient service, in harvest, (with board.)	Per day, for transient service other than in harvest, (without board.)	Per day, for transient service other than in harvest, (with board.)
Maine......................	$2 02	$1 56	$1 49	$1 13
New Hampshire...........	1 98	1 52	1 67	1 26
Vermont...................	2 32	1 85	1 76	1 32
Massachusetts	2 41	1 92	1 83	1 38
Rhode Island	2 23	1 71	1 83	1 33
Connecticut................	2 43	1 90	1 75	1 29
New York..................	2 41	1 92	1 75	1 23
New Jersey	2 68	2 38	1 68	1 20
Pennsylvania...............	2 32	1 80	1 59	1 00
Delaware	2 09	1 62	1 31	94
Maryland...................	2 00	1 68	1 31	96
Virginia...................	1 46	1 21	82	57
North Carolina	1 53	1 17	72	50
South Carolina	1 25	93	69	45
Georgia.....................	1 48	1 06	99	70
Florida.....................	1 12	83	1 00	74
Alabama....................	1 27	1 04	78	55
Mississippi.................	1 65	1 14	1 34	89
Louisiana...................	1 66	1 20	1 08	70
Texas	1 65	1 32	1 31	98
Arkansas	2 07	1 52	1 34	88
Tennessee	2 01	1 54	1 15	83
West Virginia	1 78	1 31	1 31	92
Kentucky...................	2 10	1 70	1 21	86
Missouri....................	2 15	1 72	1 44	1 07
Illinois	2 41	1 91	1 62	1 21
Indiana.....................	2 23	1 76	1 45	1 06
Ohio........................	2 20	1 73	1 54	1 13
Michigan	2 62	2 14	1 78	1 30
Wisconsin..................	2 68	2 15	1 78	1 28
Minnesota..................	2 68	2 27	1 75	1 35
Iowa........................	2 38	1 88	1 62	1 19
Kansas.....................	2 31	1 82	1 65	1 19
Nebraska Territory	2 65	2 15	1 93	1 43
Utah Territory.............	3 42	2 49	2 27	1 63
Colorado Territory........	4 17	2 87	3 29	1 93
New Mexico Territory	1 50	1 12	1 00	90
California	2 56	2 06	2 26	1 72
Nevada	3 50	3 00	3 00	2 50
Washington Territory	3 00	2 25	2 25	1 75
Dakota Territory	2 50	2 00	2 00	1 50
Oregon.....................	2 40	1 80	1 75	1 40

Table showing the average prices of harvesting and stacking wheat and cutting and stacking hay.

States.	Price per acre of harvesting and stacking wheat including all the labor of men and horses.	Price per acre of cutting, curing, and stacking hay.	Price per acre of cutting hay only.
Maine	$4 37	$3 54	$1 16
New Hampshire	5 75	3 77	1 33
Vermont	4 33	3 48	1 19
Massachusetts	4 72	5 19	1 75
Rhode Island	6 00	6 12	1 71
Connecticut	3 70	4 75	1 81
New York	3 88	3 28	1 11
New Jersey	4 36	4 04	1 52
Pennsylvania	4 36	4 10	1 38
Delaware	3 25	3 87	1 50
Maryland	4 21	4 83	1 57
Virginia	2 07	1 98	1 05
North Carolina	1 84	2 67	1 59
South Carolina	1 56	3 37	1 50
Georgia	2 41	2 82	1 81
Florida			
Alabama	2 17	3 66	1 75
Mississippi	2 66	3 31	1 50
Louisiana			
Texas	2 65	4 06	1 70
Arkansas	3 00	4 37	1 96
Tennessee	2 36	3 49	1 86
West Virginia	2 75	2 74	1 07
Kentucky	3 03	3 51	1 60
Missouri	3 59	3 25	1 12
Illinois	3 32	2 69	90
Indiana	3 33	3 09	1 07
Ohio	3 18	3 10	1 00
Michigan	3 41	3 14	1 09
Wisconsin	3 28	2 73	1 05
Minnesota	3 33	3 34	1 26
Iowa	2 95	2 58	81
Kanas	3 73	3 90	1 03
Nebraska Territory	4 28	3 53	98
Utah Territory	9 32	8 91	3 37
Colorado Territory	9 56	7 79	3 85
New Mexico Territory	6 50		
California	2 76	3 00	1 25
Nevada		8 00	3 00
Washington Territory	3 00	5 50	2 00
Dakato Territory	2 50	4 00	1 50
Oregon	3 75	3 00	94

Charleston, Kanawha County, West Virginia

"I have had some difficulty in getting the price per acre for harvesting — no two agreeing as to the exact price; for some machines require more labor than others, and no one, it appears, has kept regular account as to the real cost. I have, however, taken the medium. The greatest portion of this county is harvested by manual labor, except hauling."

Ottawa County, Michigan

"The person owning the threshing machine charges six cents per bushel for wheat, and three cents for oats, but his employer furnishes about seven men and two teams in addition, which would make the whole cost as reported. In consequence of the lumbering business, labor is no cheaper for the whole year than for six or eight months in summer."

Pineville, McDonald County, Missouri

"This county is just recovering from the effects of the war, and it would be impossible to give a correct list of prices and wages, or anything near it."

Mt. Olive, North Carolina

"As to the price of harvesting and stacking wheat, husking and cribbing corn, shelling corn, &c., it is impossible for me to give an answer, as such work is never let out here."

Thomasville, North Carolina

"There is no machinery used in this county for harvesting wheat. Corn is still husked by means of the old-fashioned 'husking,' called by us 'shucking,' when the neighbors in turn assist each other in husking their corn at night."

Paris, Texas

"The harvest labor mentioned in the report is the old style of harvesting by hand; we having but few machines in the county, not more than one-tenth of our grain being harvested by machinery."

Oceana, West Virginia

"We have no machines in this county for cutting wheat; hence I am unable to give a price, as it is always performed by day laborers with cradles."

Cornersville, Giles County, Tennessee

"The answers to the wages of hands are given from actual contracts. It is proper to remark that it costs more to feed a white laborer than a black one. The whites require flour, sugar, coffee, &c., whereas the blacks, in the main, have their thirteen bushels meal and one hundred and eighty-seven and a half pounds bacon per hand, together with milk, potatoes, and vegetables, given to them for a year's allowance, and they do their own cooking. White men without families eat at our family table. Negroes are less in the way, and it don't cost as much to feed them. Whites are more reliable, have better judgment, and a higher regard for their obligations.''

Sanilac County, Michigan

"It is the universal custom here to board hired men, so I have included board in the within estimate, except the price of threshing wheat and oats, which would double if board is to be included.''

Summit, Mississippi

"As in this State all agricultural pursuits are subordinate to the cultivation of cotton, but few of the questions are applicable to the system of agriculture in the cotton region. The planter regulates the area of land planted by the labor he can command for the whole year, and it is only in a wet spring or a productive season that extra labor is wanted. Should the spring be wet the cotton cannot be worked, and the grass will get such a hold that extra labor is required or a portion of the crop has to be abandoned. In productive seasons it is often necessary to employ extra labor to pick the cotton. Except in one or the other of these contingencies, extra labor is rarely employed on a cotton farm. During the past season the cotton farms were worked but upon two principles: One to hire labor, and the prices then assimilated to those appended to the questions; the other to give the laborer a share of the crop. The apportionment of the laborer's interest depended much on his ability to labor, and the size of his family. Generally where the landed proprietor furnishes the working stock and the plantation tools, and the laborer supports himself and family, they are equal partners in the crop. Where the proprietor furnishes the above and supports the laborer, the laborer gets from one-quarter to one-sixth of the crop, depending on his family. The experience of the last year is, that the freedman works well for a few months, but becomes restless and desires to change, and this season many have abandoned half a year's work and gone off without saying a word. I think there is a growing disposition on the part of freedmen to work on shares, and a large number of planters have abandoned the idea of working their places with hired labor, and will rent their places out. My own experience is, that the only way to benefit the freedman and make his labor available is to make him rely upon himself for his support.''

Madison County, Virginia

"In some instances it has been found difficult to ascertain the true cost of labor, owing to the diversity of contracts entered into with colored laborers; for instance, a man with a wife and three or four children, boarded and clothed, receives no additional pay, while others, with families of same size, would command, without clothes, from thirty dollars to sixty dollars per annum. It is believed, from present indications, that for the ensuing year but few, if any, colored laborers will enter into any sort of contract for a year, evincing a total aversion to regular work. Many of them are now busily engaged in building shanties, with a view to setting up for themselves, without a dollar to begin. In my estimate of cost for cutting, curing, and stacking hay the aid of machinery has not been taken into account; in shelling corn, however, it has been.''

Union County, South Carolina

''All laborers are included, from the best to those who are only able to earn their rations and clothing. Negroes constitute about nineteen-twentieths of the hired labor of the county.''

Farm Machinery, 1867

From *American Agriculturist* (New York, August, 1867), VI, p. 284.

One of the most cheering indications of the times is the rapid introduction of improved implements in husbandry, especially of those that are moved by horse-power. In this matter the West is far ahead of the East, and the grain growing districts greatly excel the dairy regions. Corn, where it is grown upon a large scale, is now very generally cultivated by horse-power, without the use of the hand hoe. Five times cultivating is much better than three times hoeing, and much cheaper. Some drill in their corn, one kernel in a place and one foot apart, by a horse drill, and claim that they not only do the work at much less expense, but get a much larger crop. There is no hand labor about it until you come to the harvesting, and even this, we anticipate, will soon be done by machinery. Potatoes are cut, dropped, and covered, cultivated and dug by horse-power, and, we think, will soon be bagged and binned in the same way. Wheat is put in by the horse drill, and cut by the horse reaper. The hay harvest is now all secured by horse power. These machines are not indeed universally introduced, but their economy is so apparent, and they put the hay and grain harvests so completely into the power of the farmer, that no man can long afford to do without them. The manufacture of these machines has become a vast business, giving employment to tens of thousands of men, and the demand for them is constantly increasing. They are a powerful argument for the clearing out of stumps and boulders, and for making the rough ways smooth. The man who clings to the time-honored tools, and the good old ways, will be badly beaten in the market.

Improvement of Native Cattle

From Lewis F. Allen, "Improvement of Native Cattle," U.S. Department of Agriculture, *Annual Report*, 1866, pp. 294–302.

To properly understand the subject in its several bearings, it is necessary that the past history and present status of our American cattle should be explained to some extent.

The first cattle introduced into North America were brought to the coast of what is now Mexico by the Spaniards. They came from Spain and the Spanish West Indies, and were landed probably at Vera Cruz, as early as the year 1525. In the mild climate and on the abundant pasturage of that country they thrived and spread with the increase of the population, and in the course of years ranged over the country, in both domestic and semi-wild condition. They have so lived and increased to the present time. Of what particular kind or breed the cattle were it is now impossible to say, but they were no doubt of the same race as those long bred and kept by the Moors in Andalusia and the south of Spain, and, after the expulsion of the Moors from the country, retained by the Castilians, and continued by them till after the discovery of America, and probably to the present day.

The same race of cattle still exists in Mexico and its several provinces, and is now the chief stock of New Mexico, Texas, and California. . . .

In the year 1608 Quebec, in Lower Canada, was first settled, and the surrounding country was peopled by emigrants from western France, who brought over with them cattle from Normandy, a small race, and noted for their kind domestic qualities. In that cold climate they received care and protection, and proved a highly useful breed.

In the year 1607 Virginia was first settled, on the James river, by a colony from England. Again, in 1609, another colony came over, and in 1610 and 1611 cattle were brought there from the West Indies. The colony was nearly destroyed by the Indians in 1622, but whether their cattle shared the fate of the colony is not accurately known. The survivors, however, received accessions from England soon afterwards, with cattle of the same stocks, probably, as those subsequently brought into the New England colonies. Of what care they received, or how rapidly they multiplied, we have no account; but, in all probability, by natural increase and frequent importations, the wants of the settlers were tolerably supplied. The climate was mild, wild forage abundant, and we may presume they thrived apace and spread with the necessities of the population.

The Dutch emigrants first settled New York in the year 1614, and brought with them cattle from Holland, of a different race from either of the others above mentioned. They were noted as good milkers, and black and white, and red and white, in colors. They also multiplied by natural increase and continued importations until the further supply from Holland was unnecessary.

In the year 1624 the English colonies, then settled at Plymouth and Boston, in Massachusetts, made their first importations of cattle from England. The mother country, at that day as now, possessed several different breeds. Of what breeds these early importations were we have no distinct knowledge. It may be supposed that they were gathered from near the localities whence they were shipped, and of the breeds then prevailing in the countries from which the emigrants proceeded to this country.

New Jersey was settled in 1624 by the Dutch, and Delaware about the same time by the Swedes, the settlers bringing cattle with them. The early records of New Hampshire show that cattle were imported into that colony in the years 1631, 1632, and 1633, from Denmark, with many Danish emigrants, who settled on the Piscataqua river. These Danish cattle were large, coarse in shape, and of a yellowish or dun color.

In 1633 Maryland was settled by English, and with Catholics under Lord Baltimore, who brought cattle from England and Ireland. North Carolina and South Carolina were settled in 1660 and 1670 by the English, and Pennsylvania in 1680, the settlers bringing their cattle from England.

It thus appears that the original stocks of cattle brought into the colonies were mainly English, with the few exceptions made by the Dutch, Danish, and Swedish importations, and perhaps a few French cattle introduced by the Huguenots into South Carolina, and possibly by some of the Huguenots who early came into New York. These cattle spread along the coast and into the interior, with the colonists, and as the latter intermixed their settlements, their herds became intermixed also, and in time made up that *conglomerate* race which has since spread throughout the United States, and is now known as "native cattle."

Ingenious efforts have been made by occasional American writers on cattle to identify some of the present native stocks with the original breeds of England, by their resemblance, more or less, to them, and thus claim them as direct descendants of such breeds; but that descent has been too remote, and the originals too uncertain in *legitimate* breed, to prove any certainty in the matter. We may well suppose, however, that Devons, the Herefords, the Long-horns, the Short-horns, the Alderneys, and the polled or hornless cattle of Sussex and Norfolk, all of England, as well as black and white belted cattle of Holland, and others less distinct in breed, came over; and as these emigrating cattle were confined to the localities near which they were first landed, they doubtless perpetuated their qualities and appearance among their descendants more strongly than in other districts where they were miscellaneously bred, and without regard to distinction in appearance or race. Some of the colonists were more painstaking then others, having a fancy for shape, color, size, and dairy qualities, and hence bred in their stock with care, to perpetuate their desirable qualities through their descendants. The New England people were rather famous for this. They worked oxen largely on their rough and strong land, and those colonies and States for nearly two centuries were the chief cheese-producing localities of the country. The "red cattle" of New England were sometimes claimed by their advocates as of a distinct breed, but without sufficient evidence that they were entitled to such merit; their superior qualities only showing that good husbandry had developed them to a higher degree than that attained by others of the same original stock, which had been neglected, or in the breeding and rearing of which less discriminating care had been used.

Bred through every possible degree of intermixture from Maine to Georgia, and far into the interior, so far as the extending settlements progressed, our native cattle have ranged, better in some States and worse in others, according to the care and keeping received, and they are now found an indefinitely mixed race, without blood or pedigree other than that which may be traced to a source common with all.

As the colonists increased in prosperity, history gives us some vague information, and local tradition supplies other accounts, of individual importations in the last century of cattle of some particular breeds for the purpose of improving our domestic stock.

But *these* breeds were not preserved in their purity, and after some years of trial they were lost in the *grade* blood of their descendants, and only recognized as an occasional resemblance to the original blood would "crop out" in a subsequent generation.

Our cattle history, thus vague and indefinite, brings us down through the last two centuries to the year 1793, at which time it was not known that a single herd of any distinct, improved foreign breed existed in the United States.

The Introduction of Pure Foreign Breeds of Cattle

In the year 1793, as near as can be ascertained, a Mr. Miller, of Virginia, and a Mr. Gough, of Baltimore, imported some cattle from England, which, from all the accounts we have had of them, were pure short-horns. Into what particular part of the country they went we are not advised, but our inference is that some of the blood was soon taken to the south branch of the Potomac river, in Virginia, a fine grazing region, which for many of the early years of the present century was noted for its superior cattle. As early as 1797 a Mr. Patton, from Virginia, took some of these short-horns into the blue-grass region of Kentucky, where they were afterwards known as the "Patton stock." They were there bred, and became decided favorites with the breeders and graziers of that young State.

In 1815 or 1816 a few short-horns were imported into — county, New York. In 1818, and down to 1824, several importations of short-horns were made into Massachusetts, New York, Pennsylvania, and Maryland, and it was then that these various importations began to be separately and distinctly bred. For more than a century they had maintained a distinguished character of superiority over some of the old breeds in England, and were owned and bred by men of enterprise, who had bestowed great care in their selection, with a view to developing the valuable properties, both in flesh and for the dairy, which they possessed in an eminent degree. They had been cultivated for several centuries in three of the northeastern counties of England — Northumberland, Durham, and York — and the most sedulous care taken to transmit their blood in its greatest purity. These facts being known to the American importers, impressed them with a necessity, hitherto unappreciated here, of preserving the purity of blood, and, as evidence of it, the pedigree of their herds.

In the year 1817, an importation of three bulls and three heifers of the short horn breed was made by Col. Lewis Sanders, of Lexington, Kentucky, followed soon after by a bull and heifer, imported by a Captain Smith, of the same place. These were interbred among themselves, also into the Patton stock, and so laid the foundation of many valuable Kentucky breeds. After the year 1824 but few importations of short-horns were made, although those which had been previously brought out were carefully bred, and made their way successfully into various parts of the country. The States west of the Alleghanies, particularly Kentucky and Ohio, had then become largely engaged in cattle-breeding, and their fat cattle had been driven over the mountains in great numbers to the eastern markets; the attention of the breeders and graziers had become aroused to the importance of cultivating a better stock than they had previously possessed, but they could find no immediate means at home to meet the necessity. Hence, in 1834, the fist combined and vigorous effort was made (in the Scioto valley of Ohio) to secure an importation that would supply the long-sought material for the improvement of the blood of their native breeds. In that year an agent was sent out by an organized association, and nineteen head of the best short-horns that could be obtained in England were brought over. In the immediately succeeding years, two other importations were made by the same company. These were followed by other importations, by individuals and associations in Kentucky, Pennsylvania, New York, and other States, down to the year 1860; so that, in these forty odd years, several hundreds of the best short-horns to be found in England have been brought into the United States — all of approved blood, and with distinct pedigrees, showing their lineage for generations, even centuries back.

It may appear invidious to thus distinguish the short-horns as the only approved foreign race of cattle to which the attention of our enterprising cattle-breeders had been aroused. But the object of this paper precludes any extended or particular notice of other breeds. In common justice, however, to the great cattle interests of the country, I must briefly allude to them. About the year 1816 two pairs of Hereford cattle were imported by the distinguished Kentucky statesman, Henry Clay, and taken to his farm at Lexington. A year or two afterwards, a pair of long-horn cattle were imported into the same State. But no particular results followed this introduction, and they were soon afterwards lost in the more absorbing blood of the short-horns. Many Devons were soon after imported into Maryland, New York, and New England, some Herefords into Massachusetts, and two considerable herds of the latter into New York and some into Canada; scattering along in time, also, Ayrshires for dairy purposes, together with the Dutch or Holsteins, Alderneys for their rich, yellow milk, cream, and butter; and last of all, the black Galloways from Scotland (famous for their excellent beef) into Canada. These are all good breeds, celebrated for their various qualities for both flesh and dairy use, and by their crosses on our native cattle the quality and value of the latter have been greatly improved.

The short-horns, however, in their superior size, compactness of frame, symmetry of form, rapid growth, early maturity, and imposing appearance, have acquired a wider popularity for their great beef-producing qualities than all the others put together, although the possessors of some of the other breeds challenge a rivalry of their own favorites as beef-producing animals, on equal *economical* grounds, and proportionate expenditure of food. The question of their comparative merits, however, forms no part of the present discussion. It is simply the value of the *short-horns* in benefiting, by their crosses, the native cattle of our country, particularly in the great stock-producing States and Territories of the west.

The Value and Importance of Our Neat Cattle

This subject is most important in view of the vast interest connected with it, and its extent will now be considered. According to the census of the year 1860, the neat cattle of the United States and their Territories were: cows, 8,728,862; of working oxen, 2,240,675; of other cattle, 14,671,400; in all, 25,640,937. The value of these cattle may be estimated, at present prices, as follows:

Cows, at $40 each..	$349,154,480
Oxen, at $50 each	112,033,750
Other cattle, at $25..	366,785,000
Total	$827,973,230

"Other cattle" includes all under three or four years old, and as many of them are steers, intended for beef, the average price is not too high.

As I am not now estimating any quality in these cattle, except for the production of beef, and as the beef-producing States and Territories lie at the west, where it can be more cheaply and readily grown that in the middle and eastern States, I give a table of those States and Territories, with the cattle of the census of 1850 and 1860, to show the relative increase in their neat stock in ten years:

States.	Milch cows.		Working oxen.		Other cattle.	
	1850.	1860.	1850.	1860.	1850.	1860.
Arkansas	93,151	158,873	34,239	70,944	165,320	318,355
California	4,280	198,859	4,780	31,527	253,599	952,048
Illinois*.........................	294,671	532,731	76,156	90,973	541,209	881,977
Indiana*	284,544	490,033	40,221	95,982	389,891	582,990
Iowa*	45,704	188,546	21,892	56,563	69,025	281,145
Kansas*		26,726		20,133		41,000
Kentucky*	284,475	269,215	62,274	108,999	442,763	457,845
Michigan*......................	99,676	200,635	55,350	65,940	119,471	267,683
Minnesota*	607	40,386	27,574	740	51,043	
Missouri*	230,169	345,243	112,168	166,588	449,173	657,153
Ohio*	544,499	696,309	65,381	61,760	749,067	901,781
Oregon*	9,427	53,072	8,114	7,426	24,188	93,001
Tennessee*......................	250,456	247,105	86,255	104,495	414,051	408,574
Texas*	217,811	598,086	51,285	172,243	661,018	2,733,267
West Virginia	106,000	110,210	30,000	33,000	223,000	200,000
Wisconsin......................	64,339	193,996	42,801	93,660	76,293	225,210
Nebraska		7,125		12,720		8,870
New Mexico Territory........	10,635	34,461	12,557	26,104	10,085	29,228
Utah Territory.................	4,861	13,052	5,266	9,903	2,489	17,369
Washington Territory		10,034		2,777		16,072
Total	2,508,305	4,414,697	1,259,320	4,591,320	7,134,611	

*Estimated at one-third of the original State.

I have not taken the middle, eastern, or planting States into account, as they show little increase in cattle, and as there is much more consumption than increase in them, beef-making is only incidental, in fattening such as are no longer fit for the dairy, or for work. Arkansas, Tennessee, and Texas have been placed in the list of cattle-growing States, although they are, to some extent, planting States; but large portions of their lands are stock-growing, for export as well, and may be classed with the others.

The large percentage of increase in the new States and Territories within the last ten years, will be observed, and a considerable, indeed the main part of it, in the newest of them, has been made by emigration from the older States. The average increase in the whole number, in 1860, is over sixty per cent. of the returns of 1850. The enormous increase of the Texas returns of "other cattle," if correct, cannot be accounted for by natural, production, and could only arrive by emigration from the Mexican border. I think there must be some error in the return, if there has been no emigration of stock, although the figures are *possible* in a country enjoying so mild a climate and such abundant pasturage. The fair basis on which to calculate an increase is the number of cows, and in a stock-growing country, allowing the cows to produce eighty per cent. of their number annually — a moderate calculation — and two-thirds of these calves to be reared, the annual increase may be thus stated:

Increase of Our Neat Cattle

Discarding fractions, there were, in 1840, in the States and Territories named, 4,000,000 cows, which, at eighty per cent. annual increase in calves, (leaving off fractions for casualties,) would make 3,000,000. Two-thirds of these, reared, would be 2,000,000; so it will be readily seen that the increase in ten years, in a country where the husbandry is so largely devoted to cattle as in these western prairie States, would be enormous, as is shown in the newer States and Territories set down in the foregoing table; and as the new country beyond the Mississippi and Missouri rivers is chiefly prairie, with abundant herbage, where cattle can range for a great portion of the year without winter forage, their increase will probably be greater than in any of the older States east of the Mississippi. In fact, the capacity of our whole country for producing cattle has not yet been tested fully, and the year 1860 is about the time when the production may be said to have fairly commenced in a largely increased ratio. Since then, Kansas, Minnesota, Nebraska, Utah, Colorado, Dakota, Oregon, and Washington, have really begun to be settled, and cattle have not yet been taken there in numbers at all commensurate with the wants of the people for domestic use, to say nothing of a surplus for breeding.

It may be said that the late war has stopped the increase of our neat stock. This may be so in the States over which the hostile armies ranged; but I hazard the opinion that the other States and Territories named will show an increase, in 1870, equal to that of 1860 over 1850. We are, in fact, just beginning to get a glimpse of the vast resources of the West for cattle-production. Those broad savannas beyond the Missouri river, until recently supposed to be nothing but arid plains destitute of water and nutritious grasses, are found, to a considerable extent, to abound in the best grasses, with streams running over the surface and water accessible by boring to no great depth, and capable of supporting herds innumerable.

The great buffalo ranges contain untold millions of acres where the nutritive qualities of the grasses are not injured by frost, and are capable of supporting cattle, as well as the buffalo, the year round. That this wide region must be mainly a cattle-growing country is evident, owing to its great altitude, which does not permit Indian corn to grow to any extent; and of other grains, only wheat, oats, and barley, and then only in certain favored spots, by means of irrigation, always an expensive and laborious process.

It is true that hostile Indians and the buffalo may retard the settlement of those vast plains, but these obstacles will rapidly disappear before the grand march of civilized industry. The telegraph poles are already planted there; emigrant, passenger, and traffic trains have taken permanent possession of the route over the plains; the great Pacific railway, tapping it on both sides, is making rapid progress in construction, and in less than five years its locomotives and trains will be daily thundering over the line; and at no distant day, its various branches will be threading every mountain valley and considerable water-course between the Rocky mountains and the Sierra Nevada, reaching the innumerable mines, and the hundreds of towns and cities scattered among them.

Our national territory is now measured on so vast a scale that any intelligent mind, looking over the map from one ocean to the other, and considering the diversities of climate, will see at a glance that important subdivisions of labor must ultimately take place in prosecuting our agricultural industry. East of a line drawn north and south five hundred miles west of the Mississippi, will be the land of cultivated crops, cotton, grains, and grasses, in a mixed agriculture. The great plain thence to the Rocky mountains will mostly be devoted to stock growing, as will also the great basin west to the Sierra Nevada. California will be devoted to mixed farming; as the hill and mountain lands of Scotland grow their cattle, which are annually driven to the lowlands and to England, on a diminutive scale compared to our extended capabilities, so, in time, will these plains grow their herds, to be transported to the richer grain regions east and west for feeding and consumption. Cheap and ready intercourse will promote this division of industry and aid its prosperity. The States east of the Rocky mountains, after supplying their own wants in beef and dairy products, will send their surplus abroad. The extreme western States will export their beef surplus by the way of California and the Pacific ocean to China, and the furthest Indies.

The rural population of the great western plains and the central basin will be composed chiefly of herdsmen, and their main occupation that of grazing cattle. We have seen that the soil and climate are better fitted for that pursuit than any other. The mining population which is to exist among them will, for many years, consume all other products which the farmers may have to spare, besides taking a great many of their cattle. Let there be peace throughout our borders and no foreign war to disturb our industry, and it is safe to predict that the census of 1870 will give the United States and Territories forty millions, and that of 1880 sixty millions of neat cattle within their limits.

Present Consumption of Beef Cattle in the United States

It is impossible to arrive at anything like accurate data in this matter. The census returns give no account of the number of beeves slaughtered in the United States. The city of New York, and its immediate suburbs, averaging a population of, say 1,200,000, with its shipping and various accessories, received for the year 1866, according to its market reports, about 6,000 beef cattle per week, amounting in round numbers to 312,000 head for the year. Supposing the present population of the United States to be thirty-eight millions, (as, according to the *estimated* census of 1870, it will then be rising of forty-two millions,) and allowing that the population of New York and its environs consume double the average quantity of beef required for other portions of the country, by reason of so much more *fresh* meat being consumed in the city than by the country population generally, the annual number of beef cattle slaughtered would be 4,940,000 — say five millions in round numbers. This is probably not far out of the way, as the whole number of neat cattle now in the country (1867) may be estimated at thirty-six millions. One-seventh of the number may be slaughtered annually for consumption, and another million go for casualties, accidental deaths, disease, &c., giving an average life of seven years to the stock, which is also not far out of the way, as beef cattle are generally slaughtered at from three to five years old, and cows and working oxen may average full ten years before fed off for the shambles.

The New York Tribune allows the average weight of the beef — the four quarters only being estimated as weight in that market — at 750 pounds to each animal, worth, in 1866, 15 cents per pound. This would make the value of the 312,000 cattle in New York thirty-five millions of dollars, the hides and tallow being thrown in or not estimated outside of the price paid for the meat, giving an average value to the cattle of about $112. From this deduct, say $23, average cost of getting them to market, and it leaves $90 as the average value of each beast at home.

It will not do, however, to place so high a value per head, individually, on all the cattle annually slaughtered. It must be recollected that *most* of the heaviest, as well as some of the lightest, cattle go to New York and other seaboard markets, and the *very* lightest, poorest, and youngest are mostly slaughtered at home, or in the immediate neighborhood where grazed and fed. The rule generally applied to fair beef cattle in the seaboard markets is to estimate the weight of the *five* quarters, as they call them, in beef animals, at three-fifths the live weight. Thus, if the four quarters, as estimated in the Tribune reports, be 750 pounds, the hide and tallow, or fifth quarter, added would swell the live weight to 1,250 pounds, which would be 10 cents a pound all round for meat, hide, and tallow.

Now taking the 5,000,000 cattle annually slaughtered throughout the country at 1,000 pounds each, *live weight,* and allowing three-fifths of that weight to make the five quarters of beef, hide, and tallow, it would give 600 pounds each; estimating this 600 pounds at eight cents *home* value, we have $240,000,000 as the annual product of our stock in beef alone. It may be said that these are war prices, arising from an inflated currency, and so on, but they are the *current* prices of the day, and although they may fall when other commodities do, the estimate is fair, with other things.

If I were going into an estimate of the *entire* annual production from our neat stock, the dairy products and labor of the working oxen would come in for a share of credit, but as their *flesh* production is the only subject of the present discussion, attention will be confined to that alone.

We have seen that as our herds are now constituted they are made up of all qualities, good, bad, and indifferent, some very good, others execrably bad, almost worthless so far as any *profit* is connected with their breeding or rearing. All this may be improved by the use of bulls of better breed. It has been so done, and too long practiced by good stock-growers to admit of doubt or argument, and our stock-growers will never arrive at the maximum of profit in their business until a radical change in this regard is adopted.

Increase of Weight in Our Cattle

It is estimated by the most experienced stock-growers of our country — men who have been engaged in the vocation for forty years of their lives, and handled and kept cattle of every description — that *at least* 200 pounds can be added to the profitable or consumable weight of every steer or bullock at three and a half to four years old, when fairly fitted for slaughter. In other words, if the average weight now of a fair beef animal be 600 pounds, it may just as easily be made 800, and with no more expenditure of food, and but a small increased expense to the producer. This is asserted as *a fact*. I believe it, and so believing, shall proceed to its demonstration.

I desire to start fair, not as the champion of the *exclusive* value of one breed of improved cattle over all others, for I consider them all to have their peculiar values or merits, according to circumstances; but as the short-horns are the breed selected for this discussion, they only will be considered in explaining the present mode of improving our native cattle for *beef* purposes. We have seen that the short-horns have been in the United States for fifty years. They have been imported in much greater numbers than all the other foreign breeds put together, and are more widely known, and have acquired a greater popularity, than the others.

Southern Agriculture, 1867

From U.S. Department of Agriculture, *Annual Report*, 1867, pp. 412–48.

The whole country is desirous of knowing the present and prospective condition of agriculture in the States which were directly involved in the rebellion and resultant emancipation. The people of those States are presumed to be still more anxious for a speedy return of agricultural and general prosperity. The more intelligent and progressive are fully aware that such prosperity must come through means and agencies adapted to the changed circumstances surrounding southern industry. From the first moment permitting the slightest action of this department, unremitting efforts have been made, so far as means and facilities were at hand for the work, to ascertain the pressing wants of this section, to furnish information and advice suited to the exigencies of the case and to initiate a new era in the history of its productive industry.

In the hope of obtaining facts of importance, and learning the views of the most practical men of the south, the following queries were directed to our regular corps of reporters and agricultural editors, and planters distinguished in their vocation:

1. Prior to 1860, what percentage of acreage actually cultivated in your State was annually planted in cotton? Please make this an average for a series of years.

2. What percentage was in corn?

3. What was the prevailing mode of culture, product of ginned cotton per acre and per hand, and profit of the crop?

4. What were the prices of labor per annum, in 1860, of men; of women; of youth of 14 years?

5. What were the prices for the same classes in January, 1867?

6. What are the contract prices of the same classes for the present year?

7. What changes in modes of culture, size of plantations, and contracts for labor, have been made since 1860, with comparative production and profit? Please give an accurate idea of the terms of different contracts, and indicate the comparative prevalency of each.

8. Please give individual cases of improved modes of culture, with successful results, including the name of proprietor, number of acres, mode and amount of culture, kind and quantity of fertilizers, and product of ginned cotton, with cost per pound.

9. Give instances of cotton planting by colored men, with results.

10. What circumstances affect the comparative profit of large and small plantations, and what number of hands would be likely to prove most profitable?

11. Give name and description of different agricultural implements now in use.

12. What facts have you tending to illustrate practically the saving of labor, reduction of cost of culture, or increase of production and profit, by the use of improved implements of husbandry?

13. The culture of what crops promises to pay better than cotton planting; and the reason why?

14. What are the inducements to stock-growing, and improvement of breeds of stock?

15. What suggestions would you commend to your neighboring planters as to the enrichment of their fields, the variety and proportion of crops to be cultivated, the improvement of their neighborhood, and advance in values of lands? What home resources for fertilization are available, as marls, lime, gypsum, &c.?

The responses to these inquiries afford the most gratifying evidences of a strong desire for improvement in agricultural processes, and the dissemination of just views of true agricultural economy. They are generally full, and often elaborate in the expression of individual views. While their hints towards improvement are locally suggested and various, there is less divergence in spirit, and an actually nearer approach to unity than could have been expected in the chaotic state in which all social and industrial elements of the south now exist. In the brief space allotted to this article it will be impossible to make many extracts from correspondence. The returns are necessarily so nearly alike that repetition can only be avoided by giving, in condensed form, an average expression of the statements and recommendations of all. The department is under great obligations for the care and fidelity with which its inquiries were met, and has filed for special and local reference all matter connected with the subject.

Acreage in Cotton and Corn

The twin crops of the south, cotton and corn, have monopolized its tilled land, crowded out the grasses which are essential to permanent success in agriculture, and left 100,000,000 acres of "old fields" to the greed of hungry broom sedge and insatiable pines. In a small section of South Carolina and Georgia 170,000,000 pounds of rice have been grown; in Louisiana 220,000 hogsheads of sugar were made upon a narrow margin of river land in a few of the lower parishes of the State; and a moiety of wheat was harvested, two or three bushels only to each inhabitant of the cotton States. A beggarly list of other products might be specified, all occupying a percentage of the cultivated area scarcely computable. Cotton and corn have been planted in four-fifths of the tilled lands of the cotton States, and a large portion of the other fifth, assigned to other crops, has been found in the mountain sections of Tennessee, the Carolinas, and Georgia. The best soils of the Gulf region have been so exclusively given up to these favorite crops that in plantations of hundreds of acres scarcely a single acre has been permitted to produce anything else,

An effort was made to ascertain approximately the proportion which these crops have respectively borne in former years to the total acreage actually tilled each year, and from the county returns the following averages are calculated:

States.	Cotton.	Corn.
	Percent.	*Per cent.*
North Carolina	20	46
South Carolina	37	40
Georgia	43	40
Alabama	47	37
Mississippi	53	36
Louisiana	56	30
Texas	44	36
Arkansas	45	37
Tennessee	16	48
Average	44	38

The great fertility of Louisiana lands, mainly Mississippi bottoms, places that State at the head of the list, as to excessive cotton acreage, after making full allowance for cane culture. It is lowest on the corn list on account of the facility of obtaining corn from the western States; Mississippi stands next, both in excess of cotton and deficiency of corn. A verification of this estimate may be obtained from the census figures, which give 21 bushels of corn for each bale of cotton in Louisiana, and 24 bushels for one bale in Mississippi. The difference in acreage is still more apparent in view of the larger average yield of corn in Louisiana. As appears from the table the relative positions of the States are as follows: cotton, Louisiana, Mississippi, Alabama, Arkansas, Texas, Georgia, South Carolina, North Carolina, Tennessee; corn, Tennessee, North Carolina, South Carolina, Georgia, Arkansas, Alabama, Texas, Mississippi, Louisiana. The last is first; Tennessee, once the first corn State in the Union, heads the list, and it is curious to observe that the others follow in order exactly the reverse of that of the cotton list, except in the displacement of Texas.

Mode of Culture and Product

The mode of culture before the war is too well known to require extended description. It consisted of ploughing in beds of four to six furrows each, more or less, in accordance with the size of the ploughs and the desired distance between the rows, sowing thickly in a drill opened in the centre of the bed, at the rate of two or more bushels of seed per acre, covering with a strip of board (screwed to the foot of a common shovel or scooter plough) made concave on the under surface, to fit the crest of the ridge, with sharp bevelled edges, a device which leaves a slight elevation to prevent saturation with water and dresses neatly the surface of the ridge; chopping out the surplus plants and all weeds on the appearance of the third or fourth leaf, with the hoe, followed by a plough to round up the ridge and cover weeds, or preceded by it when the field is so rough as to expose the plants to the liability of being covered and smothered; ploughing again, and bringing to "a stand" with the hoe by leaving two plants (where but one is eventually allowed to remain;) and at the intervals of 20 days continuing to plough less deeply and closely to the plants each time, cleaning up with the hoe any remaining patches of grass, and keeping the surface of the ridge clean, mellow, and smoothly rounded.

The minor details of the culture vary with the circumstances of soil or season and the peculiar views of the planter, but its main features are nearly invariable, and are founded on the practice of the best cultivators.

No radical change in the order of this culture, or in the general character of its processes, is looked for, though positive or marked changes are highly desirable in thoroughness and economy of culture; nor are persons hitherto unacquainted with cotton-planting expected to succeed best in it. The wisest of the old planters are the most successful cotton-growers; they are borrowing suggestions from other branches of agriculture, accepting hints of economy, and adopting labor-saving appliances, and they are reaping substantial benefits from their efforts in perfecting and improving the old practices; but the masses are not following except in squads, slowly and far behind. Many new-comers, after a season or two of trial, and sometimes sad experience, learn the business and infuse into it new energy and elements of success.

There are other questions involving the management and economy of labor, improvement in farm machinery and enrichment of soils, upon the solution of which depends the profit of cotton production, to a far greater extent than upon the order and peculiar mode of planting and cultivating; yet, small changes in these particulars will eventually facilitate and cheapen the processes of cotton culture. The practice of sowing by hand, now in so general use, will give place to seed planters, and the covering will be accomplished simultaneously. The present modes of covering are various, some of them rude; they include the concave board, the notched block, a forked plough or arrangement of two scooters, the harrow, and a plough followed by a block, to obviate the effects of deep covering. The improvements needed in ploughs will be considered in another chapter.

Yield

The average yield of cotton per acre has never been ascertained by an actual census. As with corn and wheat, the real average is not half the product commonly realized by the best cultivators, and not one-fourth the quantity a good soil, rightly managed, is capable of producing. The local returns upon this point are quite full, and doubtless nearly correct, though probably too high rather than under statement. Averaging them, with due regard to prominence of States and sections of States in this production,* the following table is obtained, showing the estimated average product per acre, and the average product per "hand," or laborer:

States.	Product per acre.	Product per hand.
	Pounds	*Pounds*
North Carolina	160	1,475
South Carolina	145	1,400
Georgia	170	1,550
Florida	165	1,525
Alabama	175	1,620
Mississippi	195	1,825
Louisiana	250	2,200
Texas	225	2,150
Arkansas	240	2,175
Tennessee	165	1,640
Average	190	1,750

This exhibit places the States in the following order, as to yield per acre: Louisiana, Arkansas, Texas, Mississippi, Alabama, Georgia, Florida, Tennessee, North Carolina, South Carolina. The plantations in the first two States are mostly Mississippi bottoms, unsurpassed for fitness in the world. The Texas cotton fields are on the Red River bottoms, and alluvial soils of other river valleys of southern Texas. Mississippi has cotton lands on the Mississippi, Big Black, and Yazoo rivers, as good as the best of Louisiana or Texas, and also has thousands of acres in the eastern and southern parts of the State, of moderate fertility, which tend to reduce her average. Alabama naturally comes next in order, and the Carolinas, with the most depleted, ravaged, and depopulated cotton plantations of the country, close the list. The highest average is but half a modern bale, the lowest less than a third, and the general average, 190 pounds, is quite as large a figure as the truth will warrant.

Some of the most productive counties on the Mississippi river report 10 bales per hand, or 4,800 pounds, or almost three times as much as the general average; and the same localities cultivate additionally to the hand, five acres in corn, yielding 35 bushels each.

The order of the average product per hand in the several States corresponds with the products per acre of each, except Tennessee. The general average per hand, 1,750 pounds, makes the average cotton area per hand between nine and ten acres.

Price of Labor

The returns relative to the prices of labor in 1860, and for the last two years, are of much interest, showing the effect of fluctuations in value of products, the

*For instance, of 86 counties in Tennessee, scarcely one-third have ever produced cotton as a market crop, and the largest portion of the yield of any year is obtained from half a dozen counties.

difference in productive value of soils, the result of local competition for labor, and other causes.

In the following table of wages per annum, rations and clothing are included with the money in 1860, rations without clothing in 1867. The rations consist principally of bacon and meal; three and a half pounds of the former, and a peck of the latter. The clothing comprised two suits of summer clothes, two pairs of shoes or one of boots, and sometimes a pair of blankets. In the term "youth" are included children of both sexes, of not less than fourteen years. There is difficulty in obtaining strictly true averages, from the differing conditions in employment of labor, and the uncertainty that a return fully represents all such peculiarities, but the result suffices to show the feverish excitment in cotton-planting in the beginning of 1867, along the Mississippi river, in Tennessee, Texas, and Georgia, and the collapse of a year later, when prices ruled low, a burdensome tax was imposed, loss and bankruptcy were rife, and gloom overspread the planting community. The table is as follows:

States.	1860.			1867.			1868.		
	Men.	Women.	Youth.	Men.	Women.	Youth.	Men.	Women.	Youth.
Virginia	105	46	39	102	43	46	102	41	45
North Carolina ...	110	49	50	104	45	47	89	41	39
South Carolina ...	103	55	43	100	55	43	93	52	42
Georgia...........	124	75	57	125	65	46	83	55	47
Florida...........	139	80	65	139	85	52	97	50	44
Alabama..........	138	89	66	117	71	52	87	50	49
Mississippi........	166	100	71	149	93	61	90	66	40
Louisiana.........	171	120	72	150	104	65	104	75	60
Texas	166	109	80	139	84	67	130	72	65
Arkansas	170	108	80	158	94	78	115	75	67
Tennessee	121	63	60	136	67	65	109	51	43

Wages

The payment of wages — a plan tried extensively in 1866 — generally proved unprofitable, the freedmen being inclined to use too freely their newly-found liberty, and planters were generally quite as little at home in the management of free labor. Much of the labor was inefficient; idleness became contagious, of a more malignant type in proportion to increase of numbers working together, crops were neglected, upbraidings and threats sometimes followed, and the cotton fields were in many cases left in the lurch at the critical season of picking. Other plans had been followed, and promised to be more extensively adopted. One of these was

Renting

The rent is sometimes agreed to be paid in money, but generally in a stipulated portion of the crop, usually one-third. In parts of Texas, one-fourth of cotton and one-third of grain crops, is a common rent. In some parts of Tennessee, as in Polk county, more farms are taken for rent than on shares. It is asserted that persons renting good lands "at halves," often do better than to get two-thirds of the produce of poor farms.

The most prevalent and popular mode of contracting proprietors and laborers is —

Working upon shares

Great diversity has existed in the form and character of contracts. Few freedmen have means to provision themselves, and exceedingly rare are the cases in which they can obtain credit for any supplies whatever. Therefore, whether they engage to furnish rations with their labor, or half of the feed for horses or mules, these supplies are all charged, the aggregate to be deducted from their share of gross returns. The mode of contracting preferred in 1867, in South Carolina, required the payment of one-third of the crop to the laborer, who furnished his own rations. A similar arrangement was common in Georgia, where, also, many plantations were rented for half, all expenses to be borne equally by planter and laborers. In some parts of Florida, labor was furnished with all supplies except clothing, and paid one-fourth of the crop, or one-third of the crop without rations. In Marengo county, Alabama, a region of fine plantations, one-fourth for labor is the rule, or one-third without rations; and similar rates are offered for the cultivation of other rich soils in Alabama, Mississippi, and further west, while somewhat better terms are given to labor in less productive locations. In Amite, Mississippi, labor and board are made equivalent to farm and stock; in Greenville, Mississippi, one-fourth is paid for labor, one-third for labor furnishing its own supplies, and one-half if the expense of forage is shared by the laborer; in the vicinity of Louisville, three-tenths of the crop is given for labor; on the Yazoo river, one-fourth of the gross product is paid for labor furnished with rations; in Tippah, Mississippi, the farm tools and stock are an equivalent for labor, rations, and feed.

Profits of labor

The results of planting in 1866 and 1867 were, in most cases, disastrous to planters, and disappointing to laborers working on shares. In some sections, the entire crop, as is asserted of the majority of plantations, did not suffice to pay laborers and their food and clothing, yet the price of labor might be lower than in 1860, though it would have been higher, but for its comparative inefficiency. The general complaint is, that labor has proved unreliable, unprofitable, and vexatious. There is no doubt that freedmen's labor, in this transition period, has yielded lower results than the compulsory labor of 1860. This was to be expected. To presume that ignorant slaves, herded in masses, released from all control except the restraints of statute law, should at once become models of industry, frugality, and foresight, is to accredit to them a higher wisdom than could be expected of their masters in their new relations.

Both parties have much to learn, many errors of policy or practice to renounce, and success to win, by a better understanding of the means for attaining it. This correspondence has proved such success attainable, and already attained by a few persons, who not only had the confidence of their laborers, but directed and supervised their labor, with a full understanding of the altered conditions of cotton-planting, and a high appreciation of the required changes in its economy.

It has been declared by representative southern men that negro labor is the best on the continent. It is best in the south at present, because, rude as it may be, it is almost the only skilled labor for cotton culture. When white men, in any considerable numbers, become practically acquainted with the processes of cotton-growing, their labor will probably prove superior. A very few white men in the cotton section are engaged in the labors of agriculture. When the absurd prejudice of the poor man against the labor necessary to raise him to comfort and competency no longer finds a place in the bosom of the white man, there will be no lack of production for home supply, or for export, and the waste places will be built up, and prosperity and abundance will bless the land.

Changes in Culture and Management

It would be gratifying to be able to say that better culture, greater economy in agricultural processes, a general practice of fertilization, and a thorough adaptation to changed conditions have already obtained; yet it would be absurd to expect it at once or under existing circumstances. It is enough to know that an unusual spirit of energy is awakened, which has already begun to yield valuable fruits, here and there, at isolated points throughout the southern States. The agricultural mind is wakeful and active. Intelligent and practical writers enrich the agricultural press with advanced ideas. In the Carolinas and Georgia commercial and artificial fertilizers are used to a very great and increasing extent, and their comparative value, mode of application, and results upon different soils, are more eagerly canvassed than ever before. It is but fair to say that pecuniary inability has proved a bar to improvement dictated by the deliberate judgment of many planters.

An instance or two of successful planting will serve as an example of progress, to which the most conservative are compelled to look. The gentleman mentioned by Benjamin T. Harris, our correspondent in Hancock county, Georgia, in the following extract, has long been known as an exponent of high culture:

David Dickson, of this county, has produced the most successful results in growing corn, cotton, wheat, oats, potatoes, &c., on a large scale, for the last 20 years, of any one in this vicinity. He originated the mode which he has so successfully pursued and which is now generally followed. It is peculiar only in the fact that he gives more distance, both to corn and cotton, than was formerly given; that he has used more commercial manures, ploughed deeper in the preparation of the ground, cultivated shallower, and with more care for the young plant, especially, and more land per hand and per horse, than our planters generally have done. It is but just to him to add that these results were obtained with more satisfaction to himself and laborers than is often found on other plantations. He uses Peruvian guano, bone-dust, plaster and salt, combined or mixed, under his own watchful eye, with such domestic manures as can be economically raised and applied. He made, in former years, from 3,000 to 5,000 pounds of ginned cotton to the hand, with a superabundance of corn, pork, beef, wheat, oats, potatoes, cheese, watermelons, &c., &c., for his own use and for the use of his negroes, and to sell to others who were not so fortunate. Like all others in the country, he cannot now produce the same results with the same number of laborers.

Mr. Dickson pulverizes the soil thoroughly in preparation for cotton, and manures an acre (when expecting the best results) with 160 pounds guano, 240 pounds dissolved bones, 100 pounds salt, and 160 pounds plaster, thoroughly mixed, costing about $16, the mixture deposited in an eight-inch furrow, which is covered with a long scooter running deeply on each side, leaving a rich and mellow seed-bed. He cultivates cleanly with sweeps and uses the hoes once or twice. His crops are remarkably reliable, the most destructive casualties causing only partial failures; and though he often suffers from worms or drought, he rarely gets less than a bale per acre, and oftener obtains nearly two. Mr. Dickson purchased, in 1867, Peruvian guano to the amount of $12,000, and found the investment a profitable one. Whether this profit might not have been more cheaply obtained by making at least a portion of these fertilizers upon the farm is a question pregnant with meaning to southern farmers.

James Davison, of Greene county, Georgia, experimented quite extensively last year with stable manure and several of the commercial fertilizers. The experiment with Peruvian guano increased the yield 140 per cent. when compared with the yield from the same quantity of land without fertilizers. Common wood ashes and salt gave an increase of 200 per cent.

Large results have been obtained upon poor soils by fertilizers. An instance is reported from Onslow county, North Carolina, of a product of 2,700 pounds of seed cotton, or about 800 pounds of lint from one acre. The cotton was cultivated in the usual way, the land highly manured with a compost manure containing a large percentage of stable manure. Other cases are reported from "the old north State." A. B. Davis, of Carteret county, produced in 1867, from an acre of land, 2,300 pounds of seed-cotton, using for manure fish only, which he caught himself. Calvin Tucker, of Pitt county, also produced from one acre 2,300 pounds of seed cotton, using barn-yard manure, shell lime, and leached ashes. J. T. Pearson, of Wayne county, produced from one acre 2,200 pounds of seed cotton, using with barn-yard manure, cotton-seed and Baugh's superphosphate of lime. R. W. Pelletier, of Lenoir county, produced from one acre 2,061 pounds seed cotton. The mode of cultivation in these cases was not unusual, the increased yield being mainly due to the fertilizers used. The season was an unfavorable one, and the yield would have been much larger in a good season. Instances are given of similar increase of production in other farm crops, as the cereals and roots.

B. F. Ward, of Butts county, Georgia, gives his experience in the management of freedmen as follows:

In 1866 I gave my laborers, all negroes, $120 as wages to men, and $75 to women and boys, and fed them. Some worked as well as I wished; about one-third would not work unless I was present, and then not cheerfully or well. I lost my provisions of corn and meat, and made about enough cotton to pay them their wages in full. I settled with them fairly; all were satisfied, and wanted to stay another year. They were all worked together. I selected for the next crop those with families who worked well, and turned off the drones. I kept married men altogether. I had a great many applications to hire, which gave me choice of the laborers around, and got as many as I wanted to work my land. I then divided them into squads and families, or let them make selections of their own co-workers. I measured off to each squad a portion of land, and gave a mule to each two workers. I gave them one-half the corn and fodder, peas, potatoes, sorghum, melons, and half the dried peaches, and one-third of the cotton. I fed the plough stock, and they fed themselves and found their own clothing. They went to work very earnestly. The heads of squads were good practical farmers. I had rented a portion of the land to white laborers, and I was soon enabled to get up a good state of excitement and ambition to excel in the quantity of crops to be made. The negroes worked well, and made good crops. Some made 300 or 400 bushels of corn to the hand, and some from three to five bales of cotton per capita, besides large quantities of potatoes, and about 250 gallons of sirup in all. We sold over 700 pounds of dried peaches, besides what was kept for home consumption. They were to furnish their own provisions, but by about the middle of June all except two had applied to me for meat, and some for corn, and some for both. I referred them to our contract; they acknowledged its terms, but said it took more to feed them than they thought for; they had "eat up all their meat, and their money was all gone too." I had to supply them or lose the crop; I furnished them, of course. They did very little after the crop was laid by until time to gather it. They finished gathering before Christmas.

The following from R. H. Springer, of Carroll county, Georgia, furnishes another illustration of the benefits derived from judicious management of operative freedmen:

In 1866 I employed freedmen and gave them one-third of all that was made. I furnished everything — land, tools, horses, seed, &c., but I found that was hardly enough, although they worked well. In 1867 I gave them one-half, and only furnished the land and stock, and fed the stock, they being at all other expense. They repair my fences, clean out my ditches, and keep the plantation in good order. This plan worked well. My plantation looks better than ever before; the freedmen work better, and make an abundance to supply themselves and families. I am at but little trouble, and, if anything, they are working better this year than ever. They repair and keep up the plantation at times when they would do nothing else; therefore it is no expense to them but labor, and a great saving to me. I will add that this plan is being rapidly adopted by the farmers of this county. Freedmen would do much better if there were not so many villians prowling over the country seeking to swindle the negroes out of their hard-earned wages.

Mr. Springer cultivates cotton at the cost of 10 cents per pound, getting four bales per hand, besides grain, peas, potatoes, and other crops.

Dr. Tanner, in the same county, obtained 500 pounds per acre on very poor land by the use of stable manure.

A planter of Johnson county, Georgia, cultivates 1,500 acres, with fertilizers made by supplying his own stables with pine straw. His cotton is estimated to cost but six cents per pound.

Dr. S. P. Burnett, of Fort Gaines, Georgia, manured 25 acres of poor pine land, and obtained 18 bales of 500 pounds each, costing six cents per pound.

In Tatnall county, Georgia, an experiment with guano resulted as follows: 7 rows, with guano under the ridge, 331 pounds; 7 rows, with an equal quantity on the surface, 246 pounds; 7 rows, without guano, 104 pounds.

The product of the soil has been increased one-third in Clarke county, Alabama, by the use of superphosphate of lime.

Albert Crumpler, near Childersburg, Talladega county, Alabama, cultivates 15 acres per hand, 10 in cotton and 5 in corn, bedding high, manuring in the drill with a compost of stable manure and muck. He obtains an increase of one-third by the use of guano. His cotton is estimated to cost 11 to 12½ cents per pound.

Instances of intensive culture are reported in Mississippi and other States. Fertilizing is little practiced except in the Atlantic States. The alluvial soils of Alabama, Mississippi, Arkansas, and Texas, are practically regarded as inexhaustible, and are cropped continuously, with little fear of exhaustion. It has not been discovered, however, that manures occasion any injury in such locations.

There is not only an expressed intention of diversifying agriculture, but a few are making efforts in that direction, neglecting cotton, or wholly discarding it.

Thomas R. Tennison, of Clark county, Arkansas, illustrates the views and practice of this class:

> I cultivate about 80 acres, one-half bottom land, the other rolling, sandy land; about 40 acres in fruit — apples, pears, peaches, plums, cherries, and a general variety of small fruits, all of which do extremely well here. I have a barn, cotton-gin, mill, wood-saw, (cut-off,) sugar mill, and evaporator, sulky plough, double shovels, Collins and Co.'s cut steel ploughs, Geddes' harrow, cotton planter, corn planter, one Avery, No. 8, and, perhaps, one bull tongue.
>
> I use barn-yard and stable manures, incorporated with swamp muck. I have, also, a bank of shell marl, which is abundant in all parts of this country, on which I draw occasionally. We use all our spare cotton seed, also, as a fertilizer. I find by experience that a corn crop can be doubled by using rotted seed, a handful to the hill. The above is the only farm I know of where an improved implement is used, or has a barn or shelter for stock, or uses a level on hillsides. As I have no disposition to gamble, or invest in lotteries, I do not raise cotton.
>
> Every variety of farm product for use and for sale, fat stock, no debts, and money in pocket, are indications of my way of striking a balance in favor of the improved mode and implements.

Planting by Colored Men

The general tenor of information upon this point is that such efforts have usually resulted in failure. It should also be remembered that failures have been more numerous than successes among whites, as shown by the same returns. The difficulties to be encountered have been not only worms, excessive rains, droughts, floods, and fields overrun with pernicious growths of neglected years, but inexperience in business calculations, a proverbial lack of foresight in the uneducated plantation negro, a prodigal hospitality while a pound of bacon or a bushel of sweet potatoes remains, and an inability to appreciate the economic value of passing time. There are instances enough of thrift and foresight to refute the proposition that the race is and must be incapable of business management, when time and opportunity for such practical education shall be enjoyed; at the same time it is shown to be unwise, in view of the overwhelming evidence of their present unfitness to manage plantations, to advocate the undertaking of cotton planting or general farming by the freedmen generally. If there are any ambitious enough to brave the risk, with money enough to make a commencement, they should be permitted the trial; but the "hands" generally should be encouraged to work for wages until they can test their ability to manage for themselves, at least to the extent of economizing their earnings, and saving a surplus for the contingency of the future in a life of freedom.

A sufficient number of the various classes of reported experiments to give an accurate idea of the import of the returns will be briefly presented. A repugnance to cotton culture was early evinced, which rendered it difficult at first to contract for their labor, and prevented engaging in it on their own account. They knew it meant work from January to Christmas, and work was not the idea of freedom which they had received from the inculcation of example or the teaching of observation; to be free was to hunt and fish, and lounge about the county town; to the women it was to desert out-door employment, and ape, in a slight degree, the fashions and habits of the more fortunate white race. Those having the disposition to labor were encumbered and impeded by gossiping idlers.

Failures

Among the many cases of unsuccessful planting reported, is one of a black man in Mississippi, who lost $10,000 in an attempt to cultivate cotton. Another in Amite county, Mississippi, hired five or six hands, obtained credit for farm stock and utensils, and in two years was left in debt between $1,000 and $2,000. Another in the same county who had formerly managed successfully 18 hands for his master, and who was deemed an intelligent and excellent manager, went to work with a force of 17, four being women, and three youths; rented fertile bottom land, agreeing to pay one-third of the product as rent. He bought of his landlord two mules, four horses, eight cows, and borrowed four yoke of oxen, a wagon, 1,200 pounds of bacon, 40 bushels of corn, 3,000 pounds of fodder, and obtained credit for $1,000. He obtained four bales of cotton, raised no corn, fodder or vegetables; both mules were dead at the end of the year, two horses were run off and sold, two yoke of oxen reported dead, one yoke of oxen and two horses turned over to the landlord so poor they could scarcely stand, and no rent or debts were paid, and $500 debt was further incurred.

Such an occurrence as the following has been common: A planter who had furnished a yoke of oxen and a cart to a freedman, who had four children to help him in the field, seeing him on his way to a neighboring village with a small load of wood, and knowing that his little cotton farm was rapidly going to grass, asked him, "How is this?" "Oh! I an out of tobaccy, and am gwine to town to sell a load of wood." His wife was housekeeping, and his four children had gone fishing. His cows brought him two calves, but he lost both because he was too indolent to mow a small quantity of hay and pea vines. The veteran agricultural editor, Dr. M. W. Phillips, of Mississippi, gives the result of extensive observation, declaring that the freedman may have a third, a half, or even an entire interest in a crop he is cultivating, and if any one will give for a week, or for a single day, more than usual rates in cash, he will leave the crop in the grass, and earn a few dollars to spend "for some trifle that would only please a child." In portions of Arkansas, it is asserted, only the poorest hands who cannot get situations set up for themselves.

From Alabama come reports that their management of farms has proved 33 per cent. less effective than that of whites; and one correspondent says they do not produce a bale to the hand.

Reports of farming by freedmen in Avoyelles, Louisiana, represent the colored managers as "the choice of the ex-slaves;" that "they work steadily, but lack foresight, as in their race generally." A correspondent in the parish of East Feliciana, Louisiana, writes:

> In every instance within my knowledge where colored men have attempted to raise cotton, or to cultivate any other product whatever, on their own account, they have entirely failed, and those furnishing them with supplies have invariably lost money. The restraint of former times being removed they are not yet adapted to the new state of things, and cannot bear to be confined to regular labor. Their disposition is to be content with the most precarious subsistence; where left to themselves they reside in huts, and live upon small game and corn meal.

A correspondent in Washington county, Mississippi, where the soil is as fertile as the valley of the Nile, says he had four squads of freedmen at work, each squad consisting of ten hands. One party raised 31 bales of cotton; a second 25; a third 22, and the fourth 12, all averaging 430 pounds each. The net proceeds of the cotton would not pay the expenses. In every case within his knowledge the planter having his work done for a share of the crop lost money and the freedmen were unable to pay for what was furnished; and all independent attempts at planting by freedmen brought them into debt. Many cases are mentioned of industrious men, successful managers for years, under direction of the masters, who had failed to produce enough to pay expenses. Many writers concur in stating that they do not know of an instance in which a freedman would have anything left after paying his debts. The following statement concerns a region in which farming is more diversified. The writer, of Stanley county, North Carolina, gives both unpromising and favorable data upon the subject:

A neighbor was keeping, in 1860, six male hands, with two women, and three or four children, on a plantation containing 80 acres of bottom land, and as much upland. These hands and their overseer, with the help of six head of mules or horses, were in the habit of making yearly 20 bales of cotton, 150 barrels of corn, 50 bushels of rye, besides roots, hay, and garden vegetables. Last year he divided his farm into three lots, gave charge of one lot to one of his former slaves, the most intelligent among them, who has a wife and four children able to do good work. The landlord found two mules, their feed, and all the necessary implements. The freedman found himself and family, and was at no other expense. The whole management of the crop was left to him. A second lot was intrusted to two good hands, with their wives — also two mules, as with the first. The third lot was left to the owner's son, who hired a black man for a part of the crop. The three lots were tolerably well laid off as to equality of fitness for the crops to be made. One-half of the crop was the stipulated rent. All went to work, each left to his own judgment. They made corn, wheat, oats, and cotton. I went through the crop several times while it was growing. A worse condition of things had never been seen on the premises on the part left to the management of the freedmen. The small grain in many places was choked with bushes and briars; the grass and weeds gained and kept the upper hand everywhere. At the close of the year the two families of colored people had made less than 20 barrels of corn each, 30 bushels of wheat, 50 bushels of oats, and two bales of cotton each. The owner's son, with one helper, made as much corn, wheat, oats, and cotton as the other two sets of tenants put together. The whole crop was not worth more than half the value of the crop of 1860. The colored men went into debt so largely for provisions and otherwise, that but a few bushels of the corn and wheat falling to their share was left them; the price of the cotton was nearly all absorbed by the advances made during the year, and there was nothing left whereon to make another crop. The result was that of their own accord the colored men entreated the son of the landlord to take everything under his control. On that condition they are farming this year on the same premises.

On the contrary, two families of colored people, composed of six hands, two women and two children, undertook to make a crop on a plantation where some 75 acres of middling bottom land alternate with 50 acres of upland. They worked bravely, listened with docility to advice in regard to their work, and the result, in spite of adverse seasons, was 100 barrels of corn, 200 bushels of wheat, 100 bushels of oats, 25 bushels of peas, 75 bushels of potatoes, and 4,000 pounds of ginned cotton. The value of that crop in 1860 would have been $1,200, but is now equal to $1,800, the half of which falls to the share of the freedmen, as per contract. They farm this year on the same premises, with their own horses and feed, and pay the landlord such rent only as any white man would have to pay under the same circumstances.

Successes

Comparatively few cases are mentioned. Among them are the following: A freedman in Johnson county, Georgia, cultivated with his own hands 25 acres of cotton, and made 15 bales averaging 480 pounds each.

In Lauderdale county, Mississippi, an intelligent man procured two horses in 1866 and made six bales of cotton on rented land, coming out $100 in debt. He retained the same hands in 1867 and made nine bales cotton and was $200 in arrears, but has paid off old scores and says he will try it again. He had corn and forage sufficient for the season, and is getting a stock of hogs and cattle. The reporter believes he will eventually succeed.

An Alabama freedman produced 500 pounds of cotton on a small farm of his own by working in leisure hours at intervals of regular service.

A correspondent in Ellis county, Texas, writes:

I have had 10 or 20 negro families cultivating land — generally on the shares. All planted cotton. Only one made a respectable crop. He was a very old man, formerly a foreman, and off three acres he raised three bales, and nicely picked it so as to class a strictly "low middling" in market. I know of another who did justice to his cotton crop. He is a neat farmer and is respected by all who know him. My other hands hardly averaged 700 pounds of seed cotton per acre.

A freedman in Georgia cultivated seven acres in cotton and 23 in corn, and three in other crops, with his own labor and that of one horse. The work was accomplished with ease. The corn and cotton he kept clean, and no help was required or delay suffered.

All these facts show many difficulties to be encountered, valuable capabilities to be improved, and a splendid opportunity for the exercise of patience, humanity, tact, wisdom, and a genius for reducing order out of chaos. The task is difficult — the prospect of ultimate success hopeful.

Size of Plantation

The views of correspondents as to the numer of hands most profitably employed on a plantation generally hinges on the reliability of freedmen's labor. If planters could obtain and profitably manage large numbers, most of them would now, in obedience to the prevailing custom of the country, hire as many as their means would provide for or their land would keep employed. While many intelligent planters deprecate the insane pursuit of one object, tending to decrease the value of one product and enhance the price of all others, the great desire for immediate returns, and the general ignorance of all cropping, except that which brings cotton and corn, combined to make cotton, if not so much a specialty as formerly, the great resource still for ready money. Yet all are compelled to yield to the fiat of inexcrable circumstances. Large planting operations have been tried and failed. Smaller undertakings have generally succeeded; and small farms, cultivated with the constant supervision of an intelligent and industrious owner, have always as a rule brought comfort and prosperity, and always will. It must be admitted, however, that this superior profit of small farms depends on the greater economy of labor under the eye of the farmer. If it is possible, as it may not now be generally in the south, to secure actual performance of service in full proportion to the number employed, the larger the farm the greater the profit. As in the case of a large hotel or manufactory, where perfection of system is attained, the profit would be increased in greater proportion than the increase of acres or capital. As one writing remarks "an engine will grind the meal, gin the cotton, and do the sawing'' on a large farm as well as a small one. The answer to this question, therfore, depends not only on the comparative reliability of different families or groups of freedmen, but on the farmer's working capital and his capacity.

The estimates of the proper number of hands, under present circumstances, are quite various, as might be anticipated. Each correspondent, from his own standpoint, reasons plausibly, and perhaps judges accurately. One deems 30 a profitable number, because he has seen 30 managed with profit. Another in his vicinity has witnessed failure on large plantations, and success with a single family or two of freedmen, and he suggests three or four unhesitatingly; others think 10 a judicious medium, or perhaps 15 or 20. The reasoning on this point is copioius and interesting. An extract or two only can be given:

> The congregating of a large number of freedmen on large plantations, solely with a view to obtaning their labor, and as much of it as possible, with the least outlay, without affording opportunity of education and moral improvement, has resulted in disagreement, insubordination and loss to all parties concerned. A few colored people employed by a white family or in a neighborhood where there are but few freedmen, educate themselves rapidly, and adopt the habits and morals of the whites around them.

Where jealousies or quarrels do not spring from associating large numbers, many complain of the very common evil of shirking, as in the following homely but unequivocal terms:

> With a large number of hands, one does bad work, another follows suit, until all get to cheating — so many the boss can't tell who does the bad work.

A correspondent says: "The less the better — better if none at all."
Another would employ a large number upon the following plan:

> I would state that my hands this season are working in squads of from three to nine, and if I was able I would divide land into small lots, and put a comfortable house on each lot, have a school house and church in the most central part, and I would compel all children to go to school and pay for the same by working in the crop. And I would force them to go to school and to work.

Improved Farm Implements

The instruments used in cotton culture have been exceedingly rude. Until within a few years, most of them have been made in neighborhood blacksmith shops, and often by the blacksmith of the plantation, in a style which was the excess of bungling. Some of the implements were of peculiar form, not in use in other sections of the country, as the scooter, or bull-tongue, a straight strip of four-inch bar iron, pointed and bent; and the sweep, cleaning and stirring from 18 to 32 inches of surface, is universally popular. These implements are, doubtless, susceptible of great improvement; if of the best form, they can be far more regular in curves and smoother in surface, and of better material, working with less power, and lasting longer. Then there is the "scraper," the "half-shovel," "shovel," "gopher," and other peculiar forms of implements. The turning plough, used in bedding-up, has already been greatly improved, though the improvement has not been sufficiently disseminated. Steel ploughs are beginning to come into use. One correspondent says he would assoon think of using an iron axe as a plough all iron. A great variety of ploughs is reported, of local or general popularity, as the "Collins," "Brinly," "Avery," "Dodge," "Livingston," "Taylor," "Allen," "Calhoun," "Duvall,""Miller," "Mohawk Clipper," "Carey," "Watt," "Brooks" sub-soiler, and others. Gang ploughs and sulky cultivators have recently been introduced, but have not become popular. The complaint is made that they "do not kill the crab-grass" and thoroughly clean the rows.

The opinion is expressed by some correspondents that greater care in breaking up and laying off the land would facilitate the use of these implements, and greatly reduce the cost of cultivation. Knox's horse-hoe is popular where introduced. The Scovil hoe is frequently mentioned very favorably.

Dr. M. W. Phillips, of Mississippi, in discussing the economy of "cotton planters," says he can open the furrows, and drop and cover as many acres by the use of this implement as can be planted by double the force in the old way; and also, that with a horse-hoe he can cultivate as well and nearly twice as much as with a turning-plough. He believes that a large field can be kept cleaner with the sulky cultivator than with any other implement, but that two horses cannot properly prepare land enough to keep it going. This is a subject of great importance, demanding separate and full discussion. It is evident that a great impetus has recently been given to the use of improved forms of implements; that many of them may require particular adaptation for use in cotton fields; that there is much prejudice yet to overcome in securing their general introduction; and that they are destined to cheapen the cost and enhance the profit of southern agricultural production.

Is Cotton the Most Profitable Crop?

In districts where cotton has long been produced exclusively, the predominating opinion is that it is the most profitable crop. In localities in which failure has marked the record of the last two years, doubts are expressed of its superiority in this respect. Some assert that "anything is more profitable." Want of experience with other crops has evidently influenced the opinions of many in favor of this staple product.

There is a growing tendency to enlarge and extend into new districts the area of sugar-cane planting. Florida and southern Georgia are regarded as promising sections for this purpose. In Conecuh county, Alabama, the following comparison is made:

J. M. McIntire planted one acre in sugar-cane, and 20 in cotton. The one acre in cane made seven barrels of molasses, at $1 25 per gallon, and 1,000 stalks for seed, altogether worth $400. The 20 acres in cotton made six bales, which sold at 12½ cents per pound, and netted $375. The cane did not require any more labor than one acre of cotton.

Returns from Louisiana indicate a revival of the sugar interest, and point to an increase of 100 per cent. in 1868 over the crop of 1867. In the parish of Avoyelles, last year's area of 150 acres of canes will be increased to 600 acres, all the canes being reserved for planting.

A correspondent enthusiastically claims north Louisiana as "the best grape and peach region of the world," and that fruit culture will displace cotton-growing there. Strawberries begin to ripen by the 23d of March; the Scuppernong family of grapes never fails, and figs are prolific and hardy.

The *Palma Christi* (castor-oil bean) is very profitable in Texas. It grows spontaneously in some parts of the State. The Cameron county correspondent deems it the crop that will ultimately enrich the Rio Grande valley. Stock-growing is also mentioned as promising better profit than the prevailing culture.

The average product per acre — 190 pounds — as deduced from these returns, is not a very remunerative exhibit. At 15 cents per pound, an acre would produce $28 50, and each laborer, at an average of 1,750 pounds, would "make" a gross earning of $262 50. An acre of wheat, at the average for 1867, throughout the United States, is worth $23. If the estimate given in the statistician's report of $33 per acre, based upon a somewhat higher price of cotton for the past year, be taken for this comparison, the advantage will still be largely on the side of wheat, in view of the wide difference in the labor required in the culture of these crops.

A wide field is opened for comparison, which may profitably be entered in the future. It is safe to assert, without further investigation, that cotton will always constitute a profitable element in the future system of farm rotation of the south.

Stock-growing

The testimony to the value of this part of the country for stock-growing is voluminous and convincing. Little has been done in this direction; the predatory character of a portion of the population has, in many places, reduced the stock of hogs and sheep to a minimum. The climate and products of this region are, in many respects, admirably suited to the cheap production of meat and wool. Swine can be profitably fattened on such luxuries as peaches and sweet potatoes. Of the entire stock of domestic animals, in certain sections of the cotton States, less than one pound in every hundred is produced by feed furnished by the care of man. In the area between the Yazoo and Mississippi rivers, inhabited in 1860 by less than 9,000 whites, in which 428,000 acres were in cultivation, there were then 87,000 hogs, 10,980 sheep, and 69,260 cattle, all raised without care, with no reference to a market, entirely for home consumption. Fortunes are made in Texas by rearing cattle for sale at $5 to $10 per head. That the business of stock-growing will be greatly extended within ten years and be found very remunerative, may be considered certain. (Allowing) for protection against the ravages of dogs, the south can easily supply the *entire* country with wool, and furnish an equal amount for exportation at a better profit than has ever been obtained in the culture of cotton.

Suggestions Towards Improvement

Every intelligent correspondent presents some judicious suggestions of improvement, in accordance with his own practical education, and the peculiar circumstances of his neighborhood. There is abundant evidence of a change of views, more or less wisely suited to changed circumstances; and with all the diversity of climates, soils, and other elements of production in agriculture, which influence individual opinions, there is a degree of unanimity in views of what shall constitute a reformed system of culture, that proves unerringly their truth and wisdom. Adopting them so far as they appear reasonable, and in accordance with the true principles of culture, as recognized in the practice of scientific farmers of this and other nations, the following hints for the agricultural reconstruction of this section are presented:

Reduction in Size of Farms

In all countries where land is cheap, there is a tendency to attempt the cultivation of too large an area in proportion to capital and labor — a course which leads to impoverishment and ruin. A working capital of $50 to $100 per acre is required in England, aside from the value of the land, which is seldom owned by the farmer. In the south the landholder should have at least a sum equal to the average value of the farms of that section, for expenses of stocking and working. Failing either in sufficiency of money or labor, he should sell land enough to obtain it, whether it be a fourth, half, or even three-fourths of his present farm. Land without labor is worthless; and if the coming of laborers is awaited, in the expectation of accruing wealth in real estate, while the owner refuses to sell, his ultimate loss will exceed by far a present sacrifice of half his estate.

Diversity in Production

While cotton may ever be a prominent crop, it should only be cultivated as *one* of several products for exportation, and an ample sufficiency of everything consumed upon the farm should be grown at home. The idea that southern horses should be obtained from Kentucky, flour from Missouri, and part of the corn supply from Illinois, has been a curse to the cotton States. Specious and false with the theory of reciprocity of material interests; it never can be profitable to carry bulky agricultural products a thousand miles, to be used on soils as rich and cheap as any in the world, at an expense for transportation far exceeding the cost of production at the place of consumption. The variety of which this region is capable is truly wonderful; embracing all the cereals, grasses, vegetables, and fruits of the temperate zone, with many of the productions of the tropics. A belt extending from 25° to 39° north latitude, including a range of elevations amounting to 6,000 feet, and geological formations from the primitive granite to alluvion now in process of deposition, cannot become a wealthy region, rich by persistence in the culture of a single product.

Sugar production, though a special industry, must become, from the necessities of our people, as also from the adaptation of soil and climate to the growth of cane, a prominent, growing, and profitable interest, which should not be neglected. It promises at present to become, within three years, a business of greater magnitude than in 1860.

The Ramie, *(Boehmeria tenacissima,)* a fibre of superior strength and beauty, is upon trial, and hopes are entertained that it may eventually add to the productive resources of this region.

The production of cotton-seed, castor and other oils should be largely extended.

The culture of grapes, peaches, olives, figs, oranges, lemons, bananas, and a great variety of other fruits of the semi-tropical and temperate climates is destined to afford pleasant and profitable occupation to a large number of people.

Rotation

With variety of crops there may be system and recuperation in place of the present waste and exhaustion. Ruin follows continuous planting of hoed crops; the soil must be shaded with the luxuriance of green crops; grasses must be furnished to stock for supplies, both of meat and fertilizers. Heretofore, as exhaustion was threatened, "rest" has been the remedy — such *rest* as attends the growing of weeds and broom sedge, filling the soil with seeds of pernicious growth and roots of tenacious grasses to plague the future cultivator.

The rotation should include but one year of cotton, with corn and peas and clover and other crops, varying the order and variety according to soil and other circumstances, the course extending four or five years, and so arranged as to cover the surface with green crops at least half the time. A correspondent says:

> The whole of eastern Virginia could be renovated in six years if farmers had energy and means to persevere in a proper system of rotation. Instead of two and three field shifts, they should adopt and adhere to a six-field rotation, somewhat as follows: First, corn; second, oats, seeded with clover; third, clover, pastured by sheep and hogs; Fourth, wheat, seeded with clover and orchard grass; fifth hay; sixth, pasture.

Two years of clover to one each of corn and wheat, are suggested as a proper rotation by correspondents in western Carolina. Dr. Phillips, of the Southern Farmer, would place three-fourths of the land in pasture, grow roots and vegetables for stock, and three acres of corn for every one of cotton.

For feeding stock and fertilizing the soil, the cultivation of peas promises better than that of corn. Peas, sweet potatoes, and clover should occupy a prominent place in the rotation.

Improved Culture

In former years culture has been equivalent to careless scratching of the surface to the depth of two and a half inches, more or less. Deep thorough culture has proved as beneficial, in the few instances in which it has been practiced, as in other climates and soils. The case of David Dickson, of Georgia, is a representative one upon this point.

Horizontal culture and hill-side ditching are requisite on hilly lands. It is probable that uplands are deteriorated much more rapidly by washing than by the abstraction of the elements of crops. The best soils are of a texture so fine as to yield readily to the force of the surface currents, and the rains are so heavy that the utmost care only suffices to prevent destruction of the soil of hillsides.

Farm Economy and Improvement

Winter shelters for stock should be provided. Barns for protection of farm animals, for economy in their management, and the preservation of farm products and implements, should be erected, with cellars adapted to the collection and preservation of manures. No farm is in its highest condition of efficiency without these improvements, and no climate sufficiently mild to dispense with them.

Fertilizers

With "full garners, good pasture, and fat stock," as a correspondent suggests, there is no lack of abundant means of fertilization. To force a single crop, or to obtain a stand of clover or other resources for feeding animals or for green manuring, guano often gives marked and profitable results; in combination with other fertilizers, to supply a deficiency of ammonia, it is often highly advantageous; where more bulky manures, furnishing similar elements of fertilization, are difficult to obtain or expensive in transportation, it is sometimes admissible; but as a regular resource for the annual crop, the use of guano will ultimately impoverish the soil and its owner. Every farmer should rely mainly upon his stock for manures; hogs should be fattened upon field peas; cattle and horses should be penned at night in deeply littered yards. Accretions to the manure pile may be made from a great variety of sources, including all decaying vegetable and animal matter, waste and wash from the kitchen, muck from the swamps, and pine straw or leaves from the forest.

There are many special fertilizers in this section, ample for a perpetual supply of all possible drain upon the resources of the soil. The coast line from Virginia to Texas, including all the sounds, inlets, bays, and estuaries, has an aggregate extent of thousands of miles, and every mile can furnish abundant stores of fish and sea-weed for manuring adjacent fields. Oyster-shell lime is also plenty and cheap in the tide-water region.

No mineral manure is more abundant than marl, which is found in the whole tide-water section of the Atlantic coast, in the Mississippi valley, and in Texas. It underlies wide belts of various depths, often very near the surface; it is in many localities easily obtained in large quantities; and its value, though variable, is undoubted for application to soils needing lime. Gypsum can be obtained from native beds, at no great distance from any locality in the South. Lime is abundant in the mountain valleys, from Virginia to northern Alabama; and the "rotten lime-stone" formations of Alabama and Mississippi are unsurpassed for fertility.

All these home resources should be used in bringing up the average cotton yield from 190 to 500 pounds per acre, and obtaining, from half of the present acreage, all of the fibre needed, leaving free a sufficient area to produce the bread, the fruits and vegetables, the beef and mutton necessary for the home population, and a surplus of the lighter products for exportation.

Farm Implements

When half a million men were withdrawn from the agriculture of the northern States, by the exigencies of war, their place was supplied by farm implements and machinery. The scarcity of labor in the south, resulting from a like cause, must be remedied in the same way. It is probable, that of every $3,000 spent for farm labor, $1,000 at least might be saved by the introduction and effective use of the most approved labor-saving appliances. Corn has been cultivated, on certain prairie farms of large size, on which labor-saving machinery has wrought with the minimum of human aid, at a cost of scarcely more than a dollar per acre; and it is probable that southern crops will soon be cultivated at half the average cost of the past three years, in part through the economy of farm implements. Improved ploughs, cultivators, capable of cleaning daily greatly enlarged areas, steam engines for driving gins and threshing grain, and perhaps steam ploughs for breaking the soil, with many other forms of applied mechanical science, will ere long save annually $100,000,000 otherwise payable for animal or human muscle. This is the labor that is reliable, controllable, ever ready, never failing, and cheap withal. It is the labor that has given wealth to the north, and it is destined to perform an equal service for the south.

Miscellaneous Desiderata

One of the most essential needs of the South, attainable only with improvements already suggested and with the increase of population, is a better quality of roads and greater care in keeping them in good condition. A saving of transportation and breakage amounting to tens of millions annually would ensue from the accomplishment of this item of advancement.

An increase of laborers, especially of intelligent and skilled workers in every branch of agriculture and horticulture, are necessary to rapid progress. A portion of this increase should be obtained at home, and the remainder should be drawn by special inducements from other States and other countries.

Our correspondents very properly suggest, as aids to agricultural advancement, the dissemination of agricultural newspapers and books, the increase of schools, workshops, grist and saw-mills, manufactories, and railroad facilities.

A new career is opened to the South; a new system of agriculture is beginning to be adopted which promises, even while emerging from the chaos of abrupt change and the shock of grievous disappointment, to bless her people with a higher prosperity, within a single decade, than they have ever previously enjoyed.

Patrons of Husbandry, 1867

From Kelley, O. H. *Origin and Progress of the Order of the Patrons of Husbandry in the United States* (Philadelphia, 1875), pp. 13, 17–20.

DEPARTMENT OF AGRICULTURE,
WASHINGTON, D.C., *January 1st,* 1866.

To O. H. KELLEY, ESQ.:

SIR: — The relations of the Southern States with the Government for several years past having prevented this Department from obtaining the usual statistical and other information from those States, and a prevailing desire for reliable information being manifested on the part of the people, I have determined, with the advice and authority of his Excellency, the President of the United States, to appoint you an

Agent of this Department, to proceed immediately through the States lately in hostility against the Government, to procure such information, and report the same to this Department for publication. Having reference to the enclosed instructions, you will immediately enter upon the discharge of your duties as such Agent.

ISAAC NEWTON, *Commissioner.*

My instructions required me to communicate at regular intervals with the Commissioner, which was done promptly, also taking the precaution to keep for myself a daily record of my trip and observations.

I made a short stay in Virginia and North Carolina, and reached Charleston, S. C., January 29th. Here and in the vicinity I remained until the 15th of March, visiting rice and cotton plantations, and obtaining much valuable information. In my intercourse with the planters it was evidently no disadvantage to be a member of the Masonic fraternity, and as such I was cordially received. . . .

I afterwards suggested to Ireland that Mr. Saunders might be a valuable aid to us, owing to his position in the Department of Agriculture. He acquiesced, and we talked over our project more fully with him. Mr. Saunders informed us of his intended visit to St. Louis, to attend the meeting of the United States Pomological Society, and said if we would give him in writing an outline of the proposed society, he would submit it to some of those he should meet, and see how it would take.

I gave him the following

OUTLINE OF THE ORDER:

August, 1867.

WILLIAM SAUNDERS, ESQ., — DEAR SIR:

Notwithstanding a large majority of the people of this country are directly engaged in Agriculture, I regret to say in my travels North and South, East and West, I find there is a great lack of interest on the part of farmers, — a visible want of energy on their part to favor progressive agriculture. Where we find one who reads agricultural books and papers, there are ten or more who consider "book farming," as they term it, nonsense. This average is too small. In one of our Western States, after making a general investigation, I found the circulation of *purely* agricultural papers was but one to every two hundred and thirty inhabitants; and libraries of fifty bound volumes were exceptions, yet but very few who could not read and write. Their system of farming was the same as that handed down by generations gone by, with the exception that economy prompted them to use reaping and threshing machines. Of the science of agriculture, the natural laws that govern the growth of plants and kindred subjects of pleasing and vital interest to farmers, when once they turn their attention to them, there was ninety per cent. who were totally ignorant.

Agricultural editors have worked faithfully for years, to induce our rural population to read and think — their increasing circulation (that of older papers) indicates that they have made some progress, but we see there is something wanted to produce an excitement which, when once created, we can throw on fuel and increase the flame.

Agricultural societies have done much good by establishing fairs; yet these are generally the work of a few right-minded, enthusiastic men, aided oftentimes by aspiring politicians. At these fairs the great attractions generally are implements and works of art, while the products of the soil offer the least attractions, and to bring the farmers out in any numbers, it is actually necessary to introduce, as a prominent feature, horse-races and numerous side-shows.

I think we can revolutionize all this, and I suggest the project of organizing an Order to embrace in its membership only those persons directly interested in cultivating the soil. I should make it a secret order, with several degrees, and signs and passwords. The lectures in each degree should be practical, appertaining to agricultural work, at the same time convey a moral lesson. While the order would aim to advance agriculture to a higher rank, by encouraging education, it would at the same time naturally embrace the benefits to its members guaranteed by Masonry. Every tool used by farmers and gardeners could be emblems of the Order in some degree, and each convey a practical and moral illustration. Being a rural organization, lodge furniture need not be extravagant, yet appropriate.

Of membership, I should advocate both sexes being admitted, having separate degrees for the ladies, yet all meet in common. Making the expense of each degree but one dollar, would place it within the means of all. The secrecy would lend an interest and peculiar fascination, while the material for manufacturing new degrees to keep up an interest, would be inexhaustible; and here I can safely say no Order could surpass this in sublimity of the degrees that can be introduced.

My plan of work is this: Having a complete, but temporary organization of an United States lodge, dispensations are to be granted to lecturers to organize in several counties in each State; these county organizations to elect one delegate each to the State organization, and the State organization one each to the United States. As soon as the majority of the States shall be represented, the temporary organization shall be permanently organized by the United States delegates. A small fee from each membership shall be annually paid to the united organization, and this will defray its expenses.

The grand head of the organizations will be an auxiliary to the department of agriculture; and as soon as this shall become a permanent department, with its Secretary in the Cabinet, it seems to me Government can aid materially in advancing the agricultural interests of the entire country. I should object to any State, or United States delegate, holding any Government or State political appointment, while serving in that capacity, and thus keep it free from contamination. I should advocate the department sending out agents, men of known ability, for the collection of statistical information, who should be versed as botanists, horticulturists, entomologists, etc., who should deliver free lectures for the organizations, and to which the Order should invite the public. In this way, by practical lectures properly illustrated, a vast amount of good could be effected through appropriations of Congress, and hardly any member of Congress would wish to vote against appropriations that would be called for by the department.

There is nothing now that binds the farmers together, and I think such an Order would, with the most cheerful results. Its tendency would be to encourage the circulation of our agricultural newspapers, which insure the co-operation of the editors. It will increase the demand for fruit trees and nursery products, securing the support of horticulturists, etc. We only need to secure the approval of our leading agriculturists. If such gentlemen as Col. Wilder, Barry, yourself and others, besides the editors of the agricultural press, will endorse the movement, it can possibly be inaugurated by the middle of September.

Trusting these views will meet with your hearty approval, I remain

Your sincere your friend,

Fraternally,

O. H. KELLEY.

P.S. — I venture to enclose the initiatory degree for your perusal.

Wisconsin Farming, 1868

From Wisconsin State Agricultural Society, *Transactions*, 1861–68 (Madison, 1868), pp. 30–40.

During the war, when husbandry was necessarily somewhat retarded by the withdrawal of so large a proportion of the working force, it is not surprising that many who had formed, or were forming, habits of more thorough and systematic management should have relaxed their efforts in that direction and made immediate advantage the chief object of their labors; nor that, under this plan of operations, broader areas were devoted to the best paying crops than could be cultivated in.the most approved manner. Nor is it strange, though none the less *reprehensible* on that account, that even during the years since the close of the war, under the stimulation of high prices, wheat, the great staple crop of Wisconsin, has, over and over again, been inflicted upon lands long since impoverished by the unchanging, *land-skinning* practices of former years. It is nevertheless a just ground of encouragement that, on the whole, there has been a steady progress in the direction of systematic farming.

Our farmers have been steadily learning that Science — that great bugbear of earlier times — is simply organized *knowledge,* and, therefore, in no possible sense justly obnoxious to the contempt or prejudices of him whose success in his business must, of necessity, be proportioned, other things being equal, to the amount of real agricultural science he may be able to master. And accordingly, it is more common — though, as yet, by no means universal — to find on their tables, and in their usually scanty libraries, some one or more of the many excellent agricultural journals and a more or less liberal supply of the hundreds of valuable, practical books that now treat on almost every branch of hubandry. In propotion as this foolish prejudice against all knowledge that has once found its way between the lids of a book, or into the columns of an agricultural journal, dies away, our farmers will become more successful as individuals and respected as a class.

The time has been when no Wisconsin farmer thought of draining his land, either by open or under drains, unless they were marsh or damaged by permanent ponds of stagnant water. Now there are many who not only drain lands of this class but such as hitherto have borne orchards of fruit or been cultivated for years as being dry enough for all practical purposes. They do not in all cases fully understand the philosophy of drainage as applied to lands not over-burdened with water, but they have learned by observation or experience that it *pays* in many cases where formerly deemed useless, and they require no further argument.

When they come more fully to understand that it not only removes stagnant water from the surface and surplus water from under the surface, but that it likewise warms the subsoil; equalizes the temperature of the soil throughout the season of growth, which is also by these means prolonged; deepens the soil; supplies a greater amount of mineral food to the crops by the oxidation of valuable substances otherwise incapable of assimilation; carried down soluble substances to the roots of plants — thus increasing the efficacy of manures; bring up from the depths below moisture and with it soluble food which else could not rise sufficiently near the surface — thus at once opening new store-houses of food and preventing the disastrous effects of drouth, starvation, rust and rot; diminishes the liability to heaving and winter-killing; and that thus in all these and other ways it tends to improve both the quantity and quality of crops; — then drainage will be more common, and, in the case of particular locations, soils and crops, so far as means and circumstances shall warrant, become the general rule.

It is also a ground of congratulation that the farmers of Wisconsin are beginning to realize the importance of studying more carefully the adaptation of grain crops to particular soils and conditions; to appreciate the deteriorating effects of some crops and the ameliorating influence of others; and to understand that, inasmuch as the plant feeds largely on elements contained in the soil, it cannot flourish either if these elements, or any one of them, be not found in the soil where planted, or, if, being present, they are not in an available form — in short, that rotation of crops and proper manuring of lands are based on science and common sense, and are, therefore, not to be disregarded.

The old rule of wheat, wheat, wheat, is giving way to a more rational practice. Clover, that invaluable ameliorator of soils, so seldom seen as late as 1860, now rejoices the hearts of thousands of weary, half exhausted fields with the promise of a better day; and the disposition to cultivate a variety of crops has been growing stronger with advancing years.

Fewer of the old barns lie inaccessible and useless in the steaming, stenchy craters of surrounding manure heaps; and a less number of those newly built are found standing on the brow of a hill or on the brink of some stream, with a view to an easy riddance of such "miserable offal" as, somehow, will accumulate in and about every stable and cow-yard!

Burning straw-stacks, kindled for a like reason, or for the sake of a cheap pyrotechnic display, are less frequently seen scattering the precious food of succeeding crops to the four winds of heaven.

Some very radical farmers, after keeping as much stock as their farms would warrant, with an express view to an increased amount of manure, and taking great pains to convert all unfed straw and other material, into fertilizers, have gone so far as to work up great quantities of muck in stall, yard and piggery, and still not content, have dug into neighboring marlbeds, and as a delicacy for certain favorite crops, even ordered bone-dust and plaster from other states! It is proper to state, however, that the number of such is not sufficiently large, as yet, to be an occasion of well-founded anxiety on the part of the great body of our more staid and conservative farmers.

Wheat, during all the past years since 1860, has scarcely lost prestige with our farmers; who, because of the scarcity of labor essential to the cultivation of all hoed crops, the increase of mechanical facilities for harvesting, and a steady increase in price, have even cultivated it with more than former zeal and energy.

The greatest crops of the period were raised in 1861 and 1863; in which years, respectively, the yield is believed to have been as high as twenty to twenty-five million, and twenty-five to thirty million bushels.

In 1864 to 1866, inclusive, the chinch bug *(Micropus leucopterus, of Say,)* committed such ravages as greatly to diminish, and in some cases almost entirely destroy, the crop. All attempted remedies, except the very manifest but rather slow and laborious one of stamping them under foot, or beating them to death with billets of wood — both of which were nearly as destructive to the wheat as to the bug — failed; so that an utter abandonment of the cultivation of this crop for a time seemed inevitable. But, happily, the intensely cold winters that succeeded, or some other natural cause or causes, so crippled the energies of the enemy that from that time forward his attacks were less and less serious, until the farmer again held undisputed possession of the field.

In 1863, just before harvest, the wheat aphis *(Aphis avenœ, of Fab.)* also made its appearance, and occasioned much alarm, though it did not prove so destructive as was feared.

As to varieties, the Canada Club, which for some years pretty much occupied the ground, has, in part, given place to others.

So long as present high prices ($1.75 to $2.00, and over, per bushel) continue, there is certainly profit in the business for such as understand and regard the conditions of its successful production, and less prospect than ever of getting the great mass of our farmers out of the old beaten track.

Of the other cereal crops nothing special need be said, as their cultivation has been in no very remarkable manner disturbed, and they each relatively hold their accustomed places in the agriculture of the State.

The potato has not been so fortunate. For, although it has pretty well escaped the *rot,* early in the summer of 1866 (and perhaps during the year previous, in some sections), there appeared great numbers of the *Doryphora dicemlineata,* now familiarly known as the "potato-bug," and commenced so vigorous a destruction of the vines as to occasion serious alarm. This insect is familiarly known to our people as of a dark-brown, when young, but handsomely striped with yellowish-white when full grown, and as preying upon the leaves of the potato with so much vigor as, in a few days, if unmolested, to leave the crop above ground a shrivelled, blackened remnant of half consumed stalks. Of course the young and tender tuber, though untouched by the insect, is about as effectually disposed of as if literally eaten up.

Which commenced in Wisconsin, as an experiment, in the year 1857, grew rapidly in favor for a time and became so general during the period of the war and the two years succeeding as even to awaken in the minds of the more sanguine the belief that it was to become an important staple crop. According to the very incomplete returns made to the Secretary of State for the years 1860, 1865 and 1866, respectively, the acreage and product were as follows:

	1860.	1865.	1866.
Acres planted	314	1,736	3,486
Gallons of Syrup	51,085	138,607	403,952
Value of product	$21,000	$151,345	$331,334

. . . But the war ended, and with it the hope of making sorghum always successfully compete with the sugar-cane of the South. Slowly the conviction crept over the State, as crop after crop of seed failed to ripen, that the real habitat of the plant was in lower latitudes; the promised refineries never came to the relief of the disappointed palates of fastidious consumers; and the "ten pounds" of nice, dry, genuine sorghum sugar, for which this Society, through so many years, persistently offered a handsome premium, never gladdened our eyes.

Still, Sorghum has by no means been a *multicaulis* inovation. It came, as it were, providentially, just before all saccharine supplies from the south were cut off by the rebellion, and during that protracted struggle furnished our people with a very fair substitute. . . .

Hop culture, the extent to which it is now being carried, is another innovation upon the old routine of Wisconsin farming that dates back but a few years and is of such importance as to require notice in this general review.

Its introduction and extraordinary run in this State are mainly due to three circumstances — the failure of the crop, or rather repeated and utter failures of it, owing to ravages of its insect foes, in New York and other portions of the East, whence Western supplies even had been largely drawn; to the fact that some of the largest establishments in the country — and a good many of them — were located in our own metropolitan city; and to the further reason that the climate and soils of Wisconsin were found to be admirably adapted to its healthy growth.

The crop in 1860 was so trifling as scarcely to deserve mention. But in the year 1864 it amounted to 385,538 pounds, as shown by the incomplete returns to the Secretary of State, with a value of $135,127; and in 1865 to 829,377 pounds, with a total value of $347,587. But even this was only the beginning. In 1866 the business of planting and poling began in earnest, and before the season was over the fever raged like an epidemic. Gathering renewed force with every new acre planted in the county of Sauk, where it may be said to have originated, and where the crop of 1865 was over half a million of pounds, it spread from neighborhood to neighborhood, and from county to county, until by 1867 it had hopped the whole State over; so completely revolutionizing the agriculture of some sections that one in passing through them found some difficulty in convincing himself that he was not really in old Kent, of England. Even many of our old-fashioned wheat farmers caught the infection, and for once have disturbed the routine of their operations. In 1867 the crop in Sauk county alone, which still has the honor of being foremost among the forty or more counties that have enthusiastically followed, is believed to have been over four million of pounds, with a cash valuation of but little if anything short of $2,500,000! Cases are numerous in which the first crop has paid for the land and all the improvements; leaving subsequent crops a clear profit, minus the cost of cultivation and harvesting. The crop of the present year, throughout the State, will be so great that we dare not venture an estimate.

The yield in various parts of the State often equals one ton to the acre, and the Wisconsin hop commands the highest price in the Eastern markets.

It is hardly the business of a review to anticipate the future; but we cannot forbear a few words of warning to the farming public, whose permanent interests are endangered by the strong hold this mania has taken upon them. They who were quick to discover the deficiency of the supply, and prompt to act, have undoubtedly reaped rich harvest of profit, and will still continue for a time to make it a paying business. But it is certainly questionable whether it be policy at this late day to make a beginning. There will probably be no immediate end to the drinking of beer and the consequent demand for hops in large and perhaps increasing quantities, but there is certainly a *limit* to the demand; and it is equally certain that Wisconsin is not the only portion of the country in which hops can or will be grown. Already the hop-louse, that great enemy of the plant, has discovered our magnificent crop of the present year, and sent out his skirmishers to preapre the way, doubtless, for a general attack. Moreover the price seems sure to decline before any newly planted yard or field can possibly yield its first marketable crop. Fifty-five cents, the price of last year's crop, paid magnificently; but twenty-five would hardly warrant the sacrifice of every other interest to go into this particular business.

As to the mechanical branch of agriculture, we may safely assert that it has made more progress during the years embraced in this Report than ever before within the same length of time. The number of original inventions may not have been greater, but under the stimulus of necessity during the war, very great improvements have been made in nearly every class of machines and implements, until now there seems but little more wanting to give the farmer comparative independence of the slow manual labor on which but one or two decades since he was compelled to rely altogether. For the incalculable service they have rendered during our national struggle, and for the yet greater service they will render the future by means of still further improvement and indefinite multiplication, the American inventor, manufacturer, and we may even add vendor of agricultural implements and machines, are entitled to rich material reward and the gratitude of the nation and the world.

No matter how great the industry and patriotism of the people, it is universally conceded that the success of our Government in bringing the late war to a favorable issue in so short a time and without serious financial distress or disturbance of social order; is very largely due to the numberless labor-saving inventions with which American industry has been so pre-eminently blessed.

Our farmers are, nevertheless, all the more in need of warning, lest the ease with which crops may be grown and harvested should tempt them to cover even larger areas than heretofore, without the possibility of proper manuring, and then aggravate and perpetuate that old mania for large present profits, though at the cost of ruin to their lands, which thus far has been the characteristic curse of our agriculture in the Western States.

The number of reapers and mowers annually sold in Wisconsin, during the period under review is really marvellous; compelling the conviction that at present there must be very few farmers unsupplied. One single firm in the city of Madison is this year selling no less than six thousand machines of a particular patent. And judging from the equal activity and large income returns, of other agents, not only at this one point, but in various portions of the State, this number will be many times multiplied.

The number of farmers in the State is no criterion, however, by which to judge of the number of implements or machines of a given class that may be sold. For many of our farmers are raising such large cereal crops as to be forced, from motives of economy, to throw aside their old implements the moment an unmistakably improved one comes to their knowledge.

Grain drills, "sulky " cultivators, revolving steel-toothed rakes, horse hay-forks, and numerous other inventions of great value are also being sold in most incredible numbers; thus further demonstrating the enterprise of our farming population, as well as the incalculable benefits conferred upon agriculture by the mechanic arts.

Maine Farming, 1868

From Maine Board of Agriculture, *Annual Report,* 1868, (Augusta, Me. 1868), pp. 8–13.

Mr. Holmes of Oxford, submitted a paper being a report on a topic committed to him for investigation at the previous session:

On the Comparative Profit of Cattle and Sheep Husbandry

"Which is the more profitable, the raising of sheep or cattle?"

When I proposed this question to the Board, I had no doubt but the raising of sheep was much more profitable than that of cattle, and probably this would be the case should we have no reference to the profits of the dairy. If the farmer should calculate nothing but the amount arising from the sales of cattle, throwing out of the account the benefit or profit of the milk from his cows, which is converted into butter and cheese or consumed as food for his children and other uses in his family, and helps to raise and fatten his pork, and should set aside the advantages of the labor of his steers and oxen, and making no account of the greater quantity of manure produced by his cattle, no doubt he would find the raising of sheep more profitable than the raising of cattle. What I shall say on this subject will be mostly from my own experience during the past six or eight years.

I have kept good cows of the breeds common in my vicinity, but no fancy breeds. My sheep are of the common breed also. I have generally selected the largest and strongest sheep to keep, such as would be good breeders, having much regard to their capacity for raising lambs; for I have realized more from the sales of my lambs than I have from wool. On an average my sheep have produced four pounds per head. Some years they have averaged four and a quarter pounds.

In comparing the profits of raising cattle and sheep, I shall estimate the keeping of eight sheep to be equal to the keeping of one cow; or the keeping of forty sheep as equal to the keeping of five cows. We will now call the expense in stocking a farm either with cows or sheep equal, that is, that five cows will cost the same as forty sheep. Forty dollars for a good cow, in the fall of the year, would be as much as the average price has been for the last eight years; and five dollars per head would buy the best of our common sheep in the same years. We know this comparison of prices will not exactly suit the present state of things, the price of sheep having diminished beyond that of cattle, but I propose to answer this question agreeably to the state of affairs as they existed when the inquiry was made, presuming they may compare for the next decade about the same as in that which has passed. We will next consider the profits of forty sheep. We will calculate the sheep to bring up one good lamb each, which will sell in the fall for three dollars, amounting to one hundred and twenty dollars; and that the sheep will average four pounds of wool per head, giving a yield of one hundred and sixty pounds of wool. I have sold my wool for the last eight years at the average price of fifty-six and one-fourth cents per pound. At this price the wool will bring ninety dollars, which makes two hundred and ten dollars income from the forty sheep. The sheep must be well kept and cared for to produce the above result, and it must be admitted that I have allowed for more than ordinary success in raising lambs.

We will now see what will be the income of five cows. It has been ascertained by actual experiment that one gallon of milk will make a pound of cheese. I think that calculating two and a half gallons of milk per day from each cow for four months, reckoning from the middle of May to the middle of September, would not be too high an estimate. This would give fifteen hundred gallons of milk, which will make fifteen hundred pounds of cheese. I think the average price of good cheese, for the last eight years, has been about sixteen and two-thirds cents per pound. At this price fifteen hundred pounds of cheese would bring two hundred and fifty dollars. One gallon and a half of milk per day for each cow, would not, I think, be a high estimate, from the middle of September to the middle of December, by which we get from the five cows six hundred and seventy-five gallons. Allowing three gallons of milk to make a pound of butter, we get two hundred and twenty-five pounds of butter, after suspending cheese-making. I believe the average price of good butter for the last eight years has been about thirty cents per pound. At this price we get sixty-seven dollars and fifty cents for the butter. Now we will suppose the cows to have a calf each in the month of March, and we will keep them until the middle of May, when they will be from six to eight weeks old, and will sell as per average of past prices for eight dollars each, making forty dollars for the calves. We now have the following results as the gross income of the five cows: Calves, $40; cheese, $250; butter, $67.50 — total income, $357.50. We made the income of the sheep, $210, showing a difference in favor of the cows of $147.50.

It may be said that it requires much more labor to take care of the cows, and to manufacture the cheese and butter, than it does to take care of the sheep. This I admit; but sheep need a good deal of care and attention, especially in the spring of the year when they are bringing their lambs, and it requires some labor to wash and shear them, besides more care and pains in fencing, as a general thing, than for cows. From the cows while manufacturing the butter and cheese, we get sour milk and whey, which will do much towards compensating for the labor of attending the dairy. The whey and skim milk will aid much in keeping and fattening hogs, and the hogs will make much valuable manure if properly attended to, by being well supplied with muck, loam, weeds, leaves, &c., so that with the cows and hogs we have a greater quantity of manure than we can obtain from the sheep; enough perhaps, with the pork from the hogs, to fully compensate for the extra labor of the dairy. It will be seen that by keeping cows we can obtain more manure to enrich our soil, we can raise more corn, potatoes and hay, &c., and keep our farms in a higher state of cultivation.

But we will say nothing of the profits of pork and manure as connected with the dairy, and confine ourselves to the more immediate and direct profit of the two species of stock under consideration. We will suppose it would take a woman one-half of the time for twenty-eight weeks to manufacture and take care of the butter and cheese, and that her labor and board would cost six dollars a week; half this expense would be three dollars a week for twenty-eight weeks, which would be eighty-four dollars. We take this from our former balance of one hundred and forty-seven dollars and fifty cents, and there is still left in favor of cows, a balance of sixty-three dollars and fifty cents. Many farmers believe that a farm stocked wholly with sheep will deteriorate or "run out" sooner than if stocked with cattle. This idea I believe correct. It is certain that we obtain much less manure from them and that they crop the feed much closer than cattle, especially on the high land where the feed is the sweetest, and will not feed on low, swampy land, if they can find green roots of grass on high land.

As to the raising of cattle — steers or heifers, to sell while young for beef or other purposes, I am of the opinion that though the profit may preponderate in favor of sheep, the advantage is not so great as many people suppose, when taking into consideration the extra labor of caring for and attending to the sheep, with the benefit resulting to the farm by keeping cattle instead. The labor of the ox is almost indispensable, and with many farmers the steer, after he becomes two years old, nearly or quite pays for his keeping if properly fed and well treated, without materially injuring his growth. Many do not fully appreciate the useful labor of the ox, and do not sufficiently consider that much of the income of the farm, and even the means to rear and provide for their sheep, is due to the usefulness of this valuable animal, and should be set down as part of the profit of raising him.

I believe the reason why sheep are considered by many the more profitable stock to keep, is because the income of the flock comes in at stated seasons in whole sums, or solid parcels, while that of cows is frittered away in family use, and the ox is only credited for what the butcher may pay for him after his service is rendered. It is the opinion of many of the farmers of Oxford County, that it would be well for them to give more attention to dairy products and the raising of cattle, and less to the raising of sheep, especially to fine wooled sheep, as it is thought we shall be likely to have more competition from the Western States in wool than in dairy products, and in this opinion, after giving the subject some thought and attention, I am led to coincide, and believe that the raising of cattle is more profitable than the raising of sheep.

Mr. Moore next presented a report on the topic committed to him at the last session, as follows:

Sheep Husbandry in Somerset County

In treating upon this subject, it is assumed, first, that the best interests of the farmers of Maine demand a system of mixed husbandry — not only of the immediate productions of the soil, but of the live stock raised upon the farm. And second, the consumption, on the farm, of all the crops produced. Any other system would fail of success, under the exhaustive process of taking from, without replenishing the fertility of the soil, except near good markets, where products could be exchanged for fertilizers.

Starting from these premises, the advantages of sheep raising, in connection with other agricultural pursuits, would seem to be the practical question to solve to be of value to the farmers of Maine. Not whether wool and mutton can be produced in Maine cheaper than in Ohio, Texas or California, but does it pay to raise sheep in Maine? for if this point is negatived, further discussion is useless and better be abandoned. On this point, a late number of the *Wool Grower* well says, that "everywhere and anywhere the sheep will live and thrive, and with proper care, pay more for the labor and capital invested, than any other animal or any other system of farming. It is one of the most useful and economical modes which have been given us to convert the vegetation of the farm to money. There is no animal in which there is so little waste or so little loss. For at least seven years of its life, it will give an annual fleece of the value of the carcass, and the yearly increase will be nearly or quite equal to the cost of keeping." The farmers of Maine are coming to appreciate advantages of wool-growing, so tersely stated in this extract, and we find the flocks increasing on the thousand hills of our rough and mountainous State, from 374,000 in 1860, to 1,041,724 in 1866, as reported in the February number of the report of the Commissioner of agriculture — an increase of 667,724 in six years, and an annual increase of 111,287.

In my county, the county of Somerset, the statistics for the year 1862, show 81,599 sheep, and 1863, 93,119. I have been able to find no county statistics reported since 1863; but taking the statistics of the town of Anson, to which alone I have had access, I find it had in 1862, 8,616 sheep; in 1863, 11,944; 1865, 13,098; 1866, 13,199; 1867, 13,592 — an increase in five years of 4,976 average annual increase, 995. The same ratio of increase would give Somerset county in 1867, 128,725, an increase in five years of 47,126, an average annual increase of 9,425 — equal now to about one-eight of the whole State. These evidences of the thrift and prosperity of this branch of agriculture seem to furnish an answer to the question, does sheep husbandry pay? But it may be asked, will the figures, which it is said never lie, show a corresponding result? The following statements, of some of the most intelligent and practical sheep-growers in Somerset county, in answer to questions propounded, are to this point:

W. W. Pease of Anson, states: "My sheep number about three hundred; are Spanish Merino, pure and grade; use the best buck I can obtain; lambs come in April and May; flock will produce one-third its number of lambs, besides loss and waste; one hundred sheep will consume eighteen or twenty tons of hay or its equivalent in other feed — my sheep averaged the last year, six pounds of wool a head; think that the flocks through the town will average five pounds per head; one hundred sheep will consume about the same amount of hay as ten cows — average time of feeding, five months."

Major Samuel W. Tinkham of Anson, states: "My flock numbers two hundred and twenty, consisting of grade and pure-blood Merinos; breed from pure American Merino bucks, always obtaining the best I can; my lambs are dropped in May, after the sheep are put to grass, I therefore feed no grain; flock averages six pounds per head; average price of sheep now about $5, though they have been much higher; lambs average $5; twenty tons of hay to one hundred sheep is a fair estimate of feed; consider that ten cows will consume the same amount of hay as one hundred sheep; sold my wool in 1863 for 75 cents; in 1864, for $1; 1865, for 74 cents; 1866, for 70 cents; 1867, for 46 cents per pound; I think as long as the present tariff exists, wool will bring at least 50 cents per pound. The following is about an average of expenditures and receipts on my flock, per hundred, for the past five years'':

EXPENDITURES.

Sheep, valued at $5. each,	$500 00	
20 tons of Hay, average price $12,	240 00	
Pasturing,	40 00	
Washing and Shearing,	15 00	
	———	$795 00

RECEIPTS.

600 lbs. of Wool, average 70 cents per lb.,	$420 00	
40 Lambs, more than waste,	200 00	
Flock worth now,	500 00	
	———	$1,20 00

Profit,	$325 00

On Plows, 1869

From *Southern Cultivator* (Athens, Ga. April, 1869), XXVII, pp. 126–27.

Every farmer knows that by change in the ''set'' or shape of a plow, the labor of a horse may be increased, although the furrow made is no deeper or wider. The plows put on the market by different manufacturers, varying much in shape, &c., &c., we may be assured will not all accomplish the same amount of work, with the same power applied. To arrive at clearer and more precise knowledge on this subject, suppose we interpose a strong spring balance between the end of plow beam and the ''single tree,'' and observe how much the spring is drawn out in cutting a furrow of certain depth and width — repeating the operation for each kind of plow. Numerous trials of this character, repeated often enough to eliminate accidental variations, would prove of great value to the agricultural community. We have before us the accounts of four trials of this kind — two made in Great Britain and two in the United States. We are indebted for these, to the Report on Trial of Plows, at Utica, in September, 1867, and at Brattleboro, Vt., June 1868, by the New York State Agricultural Society. The reports are too long to be transferred to our columns, but some of the results may interest our readers.

In place of the ordinary spring balance, an instrument called the Dynamometer (acting on the same principle) is used, and the draught of plow is given in terms of pounds — thus, if when the horses are pulling the plow, the Dynamometer index stands at the same point which it would do if a 500 lb. weight were hung to it, the draught of the plow is said to be equal to 500 lbs. The first point we notice, is the conclusion that increasing the *speed* of the plow, has little or no effect upon the power required to move it. We quote:

"It has been generally supposed that the power required to draw a plow increased as the square of the velocity, but experiments show that this is not the case.

"Mr. Pusey made repeated trials in order to settle this point under a great variety of circumstances. The first trial was in the moory ground mentioned in preceding tables, and with Clark's plow. The horses were made to walk as slowly as possible, and the draught was found to be 336 pounds in a five inch furrow. The horses were now urged forward at their highest rate of speed, and the draught was 350 pounds, which is only fourteen pounds more than when they were walking slowly.

"A second trial was had in an adhesive loam, in so bad a condition, that the polished mould board was completely encrusted with earth. Hart's plow was selected for the experiment, and one hundred and ten yards, or one sixteenth of a mile, were accurately measured off. At the first trial the horses traveled the distance in two minutes and forty seconds, being at the rate of one and a half miles in an hour. The dynamometer showed a draft of 322 pounds, the furrow being four by nine inches. At the second trial the distance was done in two minutes and twenty-five seconds, being at the rate of one and three-quarter miles in an hour. The furrow was of the same size, and the draught was still 322 pounds as before. At the next trial the rate was one minute and forty seconds, which was at the rate of two and three-quarter miles in an hour; the draught, from some cause, was reduced instead of being increased, and stood at 308 pounds. Finally the distance was accomplished in one minute and five seconds, or at the rate of three and a half miles in an hour. The draft was increased, but the increase was only fourteen pounds, which might very probably be due to an increased tenacity of the soil.

"The following table shows the time which would be required for plowing an acre, with a furrow nine inches wide, at the different rates of motion, exclusive of stoppages:

Rate of going per hour	Time required to plow an acre.	Draught of plow.
1½ miles	7 hours, 20m.	322 pounds.
1⁸/₄ miles	6 hours, 30m.	322 pounds.
2⁸/₄ miles	4 hours, 00m.	308 pounds.
3½ miles	3 hours, 08m.	336 pounds.

"Mr. Morton's experiments were first with a speed equivalent to two and a half miles in an hour. The furrow was four by nine inches, and the draught was 378 pounds. At five miles an hour the draught was 392 pounds. His experiments were made with a self recording dynamometer, in which the pencil described the extent of every oscillation. It is worthy of remark that these oscillations were very greatly increased at the higher rate of speed, ranging between the extremes of 210 and 744 pounds, while at the lower rate the oscillations ranged from 280 to 504 pounds.

"This result might have been reasonably expected, as when the plow strikes a stone or other obstruction, the horses will naturally exert all their strength, and by so doing cause a wide sweep of oscillation.

"We can say in conclusion that the results obtained upon this point by Messrs. Morton and Pusey are fully corroborated by our own observations. We could detect no difference between the draught at high or low speeds, except such as are within the limit usually allowed for errors of observation. In fact, the dynamometer sometimes showed a less draught at a high speed than it did at a low one.

"It will be seen at once by every farmer, that the conclusion we have come to, in view of the experiments, is one of very great practical value. It shows, as Mr. Morton remarks, "the importance of employing draught animals which *naturally* walk at a rapid pace. Such animals, with *same effort*, get through double the work of those of a more sluggish movement — *with the same effort*, and therefore at no greater expense to the farmer. — The employment of active animals is obviously one of the most influential methods of diminishing the expense of horse labor."

As illustrating what portion of the draught is due to weight, what to width of share, what to mould board, &c., &c., the following will probably surprise most readers:

"The third question which we have proposed is, "What proportion of the power required by a plow is used by the sole? What by the land side? What by the coulter? What by the mould-board?"

"The question is answered by Mr. Pusey's experiments, as follows:

PLOWS.	Surface draught	Weight of plow.
	lbs.	lbs.
Fergusson's Swing	168	180
Clark's Swing	168	180
Hart's Wheel	42	168
F F Wheel	112	179
F F Swing	140	147
King's Swing	112	122
King's Wheel	84	140
Old Berk's Wheel	112	. . . .
Rutland Wheel	112	210
Average	117	164

"The average draught of these plows working in strong loam, and with a furrow of five by nine inches, was, as we have seen, 440 pounds. Hence the ratio of the power consumed by the friction of the sole to the whole power is as 1:3.76.

"We have met with no experiments having for their object the determination of the friction of the land side separately from the other portions of the plow.

"The only experiments known to us on the influence of the share on draught are those of Mr. Morton, which, although they do not give a complete answer to our question, are sufficient to show that this part of the plow exercises a very important influence upon the action of it. — The draught of Fergusson's Swing plow, with a share ten inches wide, was 630 pounds. In the former case the whole of the lower portion of the furrow was cut off; in the latter case four inches on the right side of the furrow were uncut, and were *torn* off by the wedge of the share and mould board. The experiment shows that the cutting of these four inches and the increased friction of the wider share increased the power required to the extent of twelve per cent.

"According to Mr. Morton's experiments the whole draught of the plow is 476 lbs.; the removal of the mould board diminishes this only to 434 pounds; in other words, only ten per cent of the whole draught is caused by the turning of the furrow slice. The draught of the plow running along the open furrow was 168 pounds, which, being subtracted from 434 pounds, the draught without the mould board, leaves 226 pounds as the draught required for the *cutting* of the furrow slice. Should this division of the draught hold generally true, we may infer that the labor of plowing may be distributed as follows: Thirty-five per cent for the weight of the implement; fifty-five per cent to cutting of the furrow slice, and only ten per cent to the action.

"This conclusion, if correct, will change the former current of opinion to a very great extent. Great labor has been expended upon the mould board, upon the hypothesis that the draught depends to a very great extent upon its shape, but it will be seen that the share, the coulter, and the weight of the plow are far more promising points for its improvement than the mould board."

As showing the effects of different soils, and of different shaped plows upon the draught, we extract the following:

"What power is required to plow a furrow of a given size, with the same plow, in soils differing in their cohesive properties?" Fergusson's swing plow, taking a furrow five inches wide and nine inches deep, showed a draught in a sandy loam 266 pounds; a loamy sand, 266 pounds; a moory soil, 322 pounds — increase, twenty one per cent; a strong loam, 490 pounds — increase, 84 per cent; a blue clay, 700 pounds — increase, 163 per cent.

"In our trials, Collins and Co.'s steel plows, with a furrow twelve inches wide and twelve inches deep, showed a draught in an indurated clay soil, mixed with coarse gravel, or 513 pounds; an unctuous tough clay of 705 pounds, the increase being 15 per cent. Holbrock's plow, taking the same furrow, and in the same clay of 671 pounds; difference 9 per cent.

"From these data it is obvious that the draught of plows taken in *different* soils cannot be compared with each other since the difference in the power required to overcome their cohesion has, by actual trial, been found to extend to one hundred and sixty-three per cent, and it is quite probable that future trials may disclose even wider differences than this.

"In answer to our second question, 'What is the power required to draw different plows through the same soil, with furrows of equal size, we have the following experiments by Mr. Pusey. The furrow was five inches by nine inches:

PLOWS	Sandy loam lbs	Blue clay, lbs	Loamy sand lbs	Strong loam lbs	Moory soil. lbs	Average. lbs
Fergusson's Swing	266	700	266	490	322	406
Clark's Swing	280	728	238	462	322	406
Hart's one-wheel	196	602	168	322	224	201
Ransom's two-wheel	196	602	182	462	196	320

(Continued)

PLOWS	Sandy loam lbs	Blue clay, lbs	Loamy sand lbs	Strong loam lbs	Moory soil. lbs	Average. lbs
Ransom's Swing..................	252	616	224	420	294	364
King's Swing......................	252	672	210	378	266	350
King's one-wheel.................	238	602	238	420	252	350
Rutland R. two-wheel	238	700	224	504	294	392
Old Berkshire wheel	322	728	294	504	350	441
Holkham two wheels.............	252	....	....	....	....	....
Averages	250	661	227	440	280	271

"We learn from this table that there is a difference between plows in the same soil, and with equal furrows of forty-six per cent in the extreme case of the Old Berkshire as compared with Hart's one wheel Berkshire, while the average difference in the draught of nine plows was twenty-three per cent."

The Decline of Fruits, 1870

From *Southern Cultivator* (Athens, Ga., Jan., 1870) XXVIII, pp. 22–23

One of the great difficulties we have to encounter, is the deterioration of varieties. However we may theorize in regard to this matter, it must be admitted, from the practical point of view, that some fruits have so declined, as to render it absolutely necessary, to replace them with new varieties. And what has been true in the past, will be so in the future. Witness certain kinds of pears in our own day — the St. Germain, Crassane, Brown Beurre, White Doyenne and others — once so excellent; where are they now? Some of them are occasionally to be seen on the virgin soils of the West and South; yet for the great majority of locations, they will continue to be worthless.

Within less than a generation the pears alluded to flourished throughout western New York, as well as in their early history, on the propitious soil of France. And even among the more modern pears we notice — as for instance, in the Beurre Diel and Flemish Beauty — signs of the same decay. And so with the grape. Where the Catawba and Isabella grapes once succeeded perfectly, they seem now to be failing, and in many sections of our country, are no more to be relied on. Even the Concord, now so popular, indicates that in time, it may follow in the same degenerate strain. While we indulge in these forebodings, we cannot but express the deep regret we feel for the loss of such fine fruits. Other fine fruits are following in the course. This should not discourage us, but rather increase our enterprise, for the production of new sorts to counteract the deterioration, which seems incident to cultivation.

Already we have ascertained that some kinds, flourish throughout a wide range of territory. For instance, the red Astrachan apple and Bartlett pear, seem to prosper everywhere. Who can estimate the importance and value of a new variety of fruit, which shall be adapted to the wide range, of our rapidly extending cultivation? He who shall originate a new apple, pear or grape, which shall be worthy of being handed down to posterity; should be held in remembrance as a benefactor of mankind. He who shall discover a remedy for the pear blight, and other diseases incident to vegetation, which now affect our trees, or an easy method for the destruction of the horde of insects, so alarmingly injurious to our fruit crops; shall have his name transmitted to future time, as second only to those who discover methods, for the alleviation and cure of diseases, which affect the human system. — MARSHALL P. WILDER.

Hog Breeding, 1870

From *Southern Cultivator* (Athens, Ga., Feb., 1870,) XXVII, pp. 38–39.

EDITORS SOUTHERN CULTIVATOR — This question has been asked me so often, that I desire to give some reply through your popular journal; and as concisely as so comprehensive a subject will admit.

It may be safely said, that *no particular breed is best for all situations and circumstances.* Every farmer therefore must select for himself, that breed which has the traits and qualities which best adapt it to his peculiar purposes and advantages. The very extensive hog family has almost infinite varieties in it, which have been produced, somewhat spontaneously, by climate and diet, and also by the skill and care of man, in crossing and breeding them. The *depression or swaying of the spinal column* or the elevation of it into an arch, is the feature which will most commonly distinguish the family, and designate the traits of the different varieties of it. The former generally have round bodies, short legs, wide shoulders, small bones, delicate skins, thin hair; they mature early, and fatten kindly to medium size, if well provided for. They are to a great extent artificial by the skill of man, and their defects must be supplied by the same skill and care which made them. The large predominance of muscle and fat over their bony structures, necessarily makes them indisposed to activity, and the food which they cannot seek for themselves must be supplied to them. Their skins and hair are delicate and thin, and the care of man must protect them from the causes of cutaneous diseases; and from the sun in summer, and the cold in winter. Though they are of prolific character they will overlay their young, on account of the indolence of their natures, if they are fat at the time of parturition. The cavities of their bodies being small in proportion, they necessarily have when fatted, an over-proportion of outside fat, and less leaf fat. The Chinese, Calcutta, Guinea, and Thin-Rhind are the oldest types of this class; while many others have been produced by crossing with them.

The class with elevated backs is in many respects the opposite of the last. The less improved animals of this class, have too much bone in proportion to the amount of muscle and fat, which gives them greater industry of habit, and activity of character. They can consume not only what may be supplied to them, but can also seek their food and water in larger fields and pastures; and even range the hills, bottoms, and woodlands, in quest of food supplied by nature.

Their skin is thicker and coarser, enabling them to resist injury and repel disease, especially such as is in induced by sleeping in dust, mud, straw or leaves. Their hair is thicker and longer, sometimes being woolly and bristly, thereby giving protection from sun or snow, in turn. The great depth from the tops of their arched backs to the bottoms of their bellies, and the large natural cavities of their bodies, gives them larger middlings when fatted and killed, and a larger proportion of leaf and other inside fat, and a smaller proportion of out side fat. *The native hogs of Berkshire, Essex, Yorkshire, and Suffolk counties of England* were chiefly of this class. Their general qualities were good, and they afford the best basis for improvement, by the skill of man. The English breeders, while they place a high estimate on the value of blood, know also the importance of a fresh infusion of it, to give tone and vigor to the constitution; and they knew the greater value of crossing the different breeds through the male animals of each; thereby transfering the good qualities of one breed to the form and constitution of another, thus removing defects, and increasing excellences. The Berkshire hog of England was thus produced, by breeding the larger, coarser and more active old native sows of that country, to the Neapolitan (Italian) boar; and so of the Essex.

The Middlesex was produced by crossing with the Chinese; and the Suffolk by the Chinese and Berkshire. *The Duke of Bedford* improved two families of hogs in this mode also, by crossing mainly with the Chinese boar; one of which families he called White Bedford after himself, and which retained the white color of their progenitor; and the other he called Woburn, after his castle, and which retained the color chiefly of their native female ancestry being dark gray, or dark and white spotted. Hogs of this last variety were presented by the Duke of Bedford to Gen. Washington. They were adapted to Virginia; multiplied and became common; were brought to Kentucky by the earliest settlers, and have been diffused over the vast West; and their form, color and character are even yet seen to predominate in the general stock of the West, thereby showing their better adaptation to all the requirements of the country; while many other varieties have, in turn, become fashionable, and then have disappeared. A fresh infusion of this blood was afforded to Kentucky about thirty years since, by the importation to Kentucky of some Woburn hogs from Belmont county Pa., by Dr. S. D. Martin of Clake county, Kentucky; and they were for many years the most common and popular and practical family and pork house hog in the State; and their blood yet shows its prevailing excellence in many stocks.

Let the American breeders do as did the English; and in each great section of the country produce a variety of hogs, which shall be specially adapted to it, in all of its requirements and circumstances. They have intelligence skill and science, and practical advantages not inferior to any other people; and the whole country should discard the old fogy idea, derived from our forefathers, that what is *native* is therefore inferior, and what is *imported* is of consequence superior. Let us remember that the basis and secret of improvement, lies in the inherent procreative power of the male to transmit his qualities and attributes, be they good or bad, and that whatever quality or excellence we desire our stock to possess, may be derived by breeding to a male which possesses it in a high degree; and in whose constitution it is deeply and indelibly improved by propagation through many generations. And while we attach all due importance to purity of blood, let us not pay it a blind adoration, which will bar still further improvement; but let us remember, that all of these popular and valuable breeds of hogs have been made by *crossing;* and that Hubbac, the great progenitor of the improved Short Horn Durham cattle of England and the United States was a bull of unknown blood, picked up in the commons, by Mr. Collins.

The English breeders are progressive. The Berkshires recently imported from England are greatly superior to the Berkshires of thirty years since. Then they required so much care, that they were commony called "the gentleman hog." Now they are larger, have more hair, and more bone in proportion, are more active, higher over the kidneys, and more elevated in the spine, showing they have been crossed with the Woburn, or with some other breed.

But crosses should not be made blindly, or at random; but rather to engraft or to impress some good point of form or character, in which the male is superior and the female is inferior; or else to infuse fresh blood, and thereby give new and greater tone and vigor to the constitution, and thereby greater power to digest food, and to repel diseases.

Too much consequence should not be attached to color. It rather indicates the particular breed, than the character of the animal. It does not make blood, bone or muscle for the animal, and is palpable to one only of our senses. Nor does it fully indicate breed. The Chinese are either black or white, and so of the Berkshires. — The Woburns, and Bedfords (essentially the same hog) are either white, or spotted. Some white hogs will *sun burn,* others will not; and those which are spotted, will not sunburn in the white spots and repel it in the black; and so of the mange and other cutaneous diseases, showing that the virtue lies not in the color of the hair or the skin, but rather in its character.

With these considerations hog raisers will be able to judge what breed, or variety, or character of hogs will suit them best, climate, food and uses being considered. If the dairyman, the farmer, the planter, or the distiller, or the hotel keeper does not find a breed to suit him exactly, the raw material is close at hand, in a male of some other breed, which will supply what he requires — avoiding however, bringing very diverse animals into juxtaposition, as such do not blend harmoniously.

Of the two great divisions of the hog family, the China, the Berkshire, the Essex and the Chester, are the leading, and most popular breeds of the first division; while the Irish Grazier, the Woburn, the White Bedford and the Yorkshire are the most prominent in the other division — the former being depressed, and the latter being elevated in the spine; and each class having similar characteristics in other respects. These are all valuable varieties, and are more or less so to the owner, in proportion to their adaptation to his advantages and uses. Let each one study, and choose what suits him best.

ROBERT W. SCOTT.

Near Frankfort, Ky., Nov. 30, 1869.

The Labor Question, 1870

From *Southern Cultivator* (Athens, Ga., April, 1870), XXVIII, pp. 108–09.

EDITORS SOUTHERN CULTIVATOR: — Your valuable work comes regularly, and is always a welcome visitor. The suggestion I made you in a former number, to urge upon the people in every community the formation of agricultural associations has not been adopted by you. I still think such a course made universal, would do more good, than any one thing — to cost no more — could do.

The people in Mississippi are taking a lively interest in encouraging immigrants from Europe, and so far, the experiment bids fair to succeed. The only error committed, is in not sending reliable agents to Norway, Sweden, Scotland, Ireland, Austria, Poland, Hungary, Prussia, and taking the immigrants from the rural districts, free from the vice and corruption which, a few months schooling in the haunts of vice and villainy in Northern and Western cities readily imparts, gendering habits unsuitable to laborers. Taking them second handed from Northern and Western cities — the jail birds of those localities, always ready for a change of home at another's expense, to fleece communities unaccustomed to such characters — will not add popularity to the step, but create at home and abroad unwarrantable prejudice. A few hundred Swedes, Norwegians, Danes and Germans have arrived here, and were readily distributed, and I am pleased to say women as cooks, girls as house-servants, and men as choppers, rail splitters and farm-laborers, are giving entire satisfaction. — Men of capacity and honesty to judge, pronounce them not only equal, but far superior to the darkey. Some go so far as to pronounce one of these men equal to two negroes, but you know a new broom sweeps clean. They are hired for wages and part of the crop, as negroes are hired. The desire to get these laborers is increasing daily, and many are writing and sending directly to Europe for them — a right step in the right direction. I admit filling the country with such valuable labor, is calculated, if exclusively appropriated to the production of cotton, to lower the price of it. Behold the immense fields of the South, now a desert waste, once rich and productive, now grown up in sedge-grass, briars and cotton wood, brought about by lack of labor. How many widows, orphans and men are now in want, from lack of labor to fence in and cultivate their once beautiful estates? And shall we not lend a helping hand, from fear the price of cotton is to be lessened by over-production? Let gentlemen lend their talents and a portion of their money to introduce these laborers, for the good of our country. Put a portion to spinning into yarn the raw material, and part to making cloth of the yarn, and never let a pound of the raw material be exported, when there is labor to prevent it. Plant out vineyards, cultivate tobacco and manufacture it as it now comes to us. An acre of Cuba tobacco two years ago, paid me more than 10 in cotton, had I availed myself of its profits to the fullest extent. These laborers are needed for a thousand purposes.

But, say some, the religion of the Chinaman is dangerous. Is there any danger of a spurious coin being substituted for that which is genuine — a gold dollar for pewter, tin or brass? Is the Christian of the 19th century afraid he will become an idolator, because he employs an idolatrous laborer? Is he afraid to let Christianity come in contact with that of the Pagan? If so, a poor argument against Paganism and worse for Christianity. I wish to see the broom-sedge and briars in our deserted fields extirpated, and I care not what religion the man has that does it. Leave the taking care of other people's consciences to New England puritans.

I prefer laborers from Europe, but if we cant get enough there, let us have John Chinaman. Nearly every man familiar with the history of slave labor, admits its rapid degeneracy and approach to worthlessness. I think white labor in a fourth of a century will be almost entirely substituted for that of the black race. The black man is rapidly throwing aside the influence of the white man. This completed, he is immediately enfeebled, and becomes childish. God in His wisdom, in the formation of the races, gave to each a different organism, and neither Mr. Sumner nor anybody else can change it. Between the two races in immediate contact, there will always be an antagonism unconquerable. In 1844, the Northern people ran wild with the theory of Robert J. Walker, that Mexico would swallow up the black race of this continent, and that the Mexican nation being of negro descent, would readily accept them, when the question of slavery was solved, and this country asked to give them a home. It this is still practicable, would not the African race be far better off, to have a country he could call his own; and if this race cannot be happy and free as they desire, as tenants and laborers among the whites here, does not humanity demand of the Government means adequate to the attainment of that object? Let Congress divest itself of false sympathy, and carry out the decrees of Almighty God, that the white and black races shall be distinct and separate. Such a course would promote the welfare of both races, and meet with the universal approval of all true philanthropists. The vacuum created in our labor system would soon be filled by laborers from Europe. — Enough was developed in our last election in Mississippi to prove there can be no safety to the white race, where a majority of the black race exists.

C. M. VAIDEN.
Vaiden, Miss., Feb. 25, 1870.

The Opium Poppy

From U.S. Department of Agriculture, *Annual Report*, 1870, pp. 206–10.

From experiments which have been made in the cultivation of the poppy in several of the States, it is evident that opium of good quality can be produced in this country. Good Turkey opium is worth at wholesale $10 50 to $11 per pound, and $20 to $22 at retail. The importations into the United States during the year ending June 30, 1870, amounted to 254,609 pounds, valued at $1,776,908. There has been a gradual increase in the importation from year to year, corresponding to the increase of population. If a portion of the opium employed by the medical profession could be produced in our own country it would afford a pleasant and, doubtless, profitable employment to persons of small means, as no capital is required in outlay for machinery in the ordinary mode of collecting it. The aim should be to produce a prime unadulterated article by scarification, and in this way to establish a reputation for the production of opium of the best quality. Reckoning thirty pounds to an acre, at $8 a pound, the income would be $240, a sum which is far above the value of most cultivated crops.

Species and Culture

All species of the poppy yield opium, but not in equal quantity, nor of the same quality. The common garden poppy *(Papaver somniferum)* is the species cultivated in Turkey, India, and in this country for medicinal purposes. There are two principal varieties of this species, one with white seeds and usually with white flowers, and the other with black seeds and violet or red flowers. The former is generally cultivated for opium, and the latter for oil, although both products may be obtained from each variety. The poppy thrives best on a light sandy loam, and is not an exhausting crop. In the commencement the ground should be prepared as for garden culture, and enriched with a liberal supply of nitrogenous manures. When the plant has arrived at full maturity at the end of the season it decomposes very quickly; and, if plowed under, is said to furnish, after the first year, a very large proportion of the manure necessary to keep the ground in good condition.

The mode of culture usually adopted in this country differs in some particulars from that pursued in Turkey and India, where the seeds are sown broadcast, and thinned out to such distances as best suit the convenience or the taste of the cultivator. It has been found with us most convenient to sow the seeds in drills about eighteen inches apart, and to thin out to six or eight inches between the plants. In order to get as many plants as possible on a given area, some prefer to make the first two rows a foot apart, and then to leave a space of eighteen inches, thus alternating throughout the field. Three or four ounces of seed are said to be sufficient to sow an acre, but in order to insure a "good stand" a much larger quantity is generally used. The covering should be very slight, not exceeding one-fourth of an inch. The time for sowing should be such that the plant may mature its blossoms and the opium be gathered in the dry season of the year; for, if the soil is wet at the time of blossoming, opium will not be formed in large quantity, nor will it be of good quality. The plant matures sufficiently for gathering its opium in ninety to one hundred days. In Jefferson County, New York, the time of sowing is from the 5th to the 20th of May; at Benares, in Hindostan, in November. In the former place the flowers mature in July; in the latter in February, before the rainy season commences; therefore a favorable season is secured for maturing and gathering the opium.

Collecting the Opium

No other process yet devised for collecting opium has proved equal to that of scarifying the capsules. A knife has been invented which is said to be well adapted to this purpose. It has four lancet-points fixed in the end of a wooden handle, the end being curved in such a manner as to conform to the spherical shape of the capsule, and the blades of such length as to penetrate only through the epidermis, or outer skin. A deeper incision would be injurious. The capsule is held in the left hand, and the knife applied at the bottom and drawn upward, making four incisions at once. Some make three incisions and others one, horizontally around the capsule, and think more opium can be obtained in this way than by making them in a vertical direction. Some practical culturists say that the most favorable results can be obtained by making one spiral incision around the capsule, from the top to the bottom. When the incisions are made vertically the operation may be performed from two to six times during the season on each capsule, according to its size and yield; but, when they are made horizontally or spirally, one operation on each capsule is usually found sufficient to extract all the opium; and it is asserted that the experience of European culturists have proved that one incision is as effectual as three or four. The process of scarifying the capsules must commence in a few days after the petals of the flowers have fallen. The first part or middle of the afternoon is usually selected for scarifying, on the supposition that the dampness of the night is more favorable to the exudation of the opium than the dry atmosphere of the day. The opium exudes in the form of white tears, and hardens into a brown substance around the incisions. It is scraped off the next morning as soon as the dew is off, with the crooked blade of a small knife, and placed in a vessel prepared to receive it. This is the best quality of opium. When it has hardened to a convenient consistency itis worked into balls, and may be ready for market in forty-eight hours after being collected.

Another mode of extracting the opium is by grinding or pounding the capsules, a little water being added, and then expressing and straining the juice, and evaporating it by a gentle heat. The watery portion will pass off, and the inspissated opium will be left in the vessel. A more detailed account of this process is taken from the Scientific Press, as follows:

In collecting opium by expression the capsules are cut from the stems and ground or mashed to a pomace. The vat for holding it should be lined with tin or brass. Before putting the pomace into the press, half a pint of alcohol is added to every forty or fifty pounds of pomace, the whole being well stirred together and allowed to stand for about an hour. The mass is then ready for the press. The alcohol used unites with the juice and renders it limpid and more easy to be taken away from the pomace by the action of the press. The liquid, as it comes from the pomace, is received into a "settler," in which it should be allowed to stand about one hour; during which time the green matter of the plant will settle to the bottom, so that the opium liquid may be drawn off from the surface by faucets properly arranged for the purpose. This should be immediately placed in shallow tin pans, so as to stand about half an inch deep, and the pans arranged on suitable racks in a drying or evaporating room. This room should be tight, and so arranged that the heat and moisture may escape from a single opening at or near the top. The temperature should never be allowed to fall below 130°F., nor to exceed 160°. If the heat gets too low the juice will become sour and spoiled; if too high it will scald. The evaporating process must be carefully watched day and night until completed, and it should be continued until the opium is dry enough to be scraped from the plates, care being taken not to allow it to get too dry for that operation. When taken from the pans it should be molded into balls of about one pound weight, when it is ready for market. In cutting the capsules for grinding, care should be taken that they be as ripe as is required for collecting opium by scarification.

Sometimes, when the scarifying process has been continued till the juice ceases to exude, the capsules are then cut from their stems and the remaining opium extracted by the foregoing process, but the produce is inferior, and is often used for the extraction of morphia, or sometimes fraudulently for adulterating opium of good quality. Although a larger quantity of opium can be obtained by the evaporating process than by scarification, in all cases the quality is inferior and the seeds are lost, which are worth about one-third as much for oil as the opium obtained.

Quality and Climate

The quality of opium is generally estimated by the quantity of morphia which it contains. A certain amount of heat is necessary in the cultivation of the poppy in order to produce opium of the best quality and in the largest quantity. This requisite is commonly supposed to be found only in what may be called warm climates. The poppy is extensively cultivated for opium in Asiatic Turkey, India, Egypt, and France. Turkey opium, most of which is obtained from Smyrna, has the highest reputation for medicinal purposes, and is that which is principally used by physicians in this country. It is declared, however, on the best authority, that opium is produced in France fully equal to the best quality from Smyrna, and is less frequently adulterated than that obtained from the latter place. The mean annual temperature of the opium districts of the foregoing countries, named in their order, is respectively 65°, 80°, 75°, and 50°. There are doubtless other conditions besides temperature which are essential to the production of opium of the first quality, as soil, equability of climate, and a proper proportion of wet and dry weather — things which can be accurately determined only by actual trial in the different localities in which it is proposed to cultivate it. We give the results of analyses of dried specimens of opium from the countries named, recently made by M. Guibourt, in which he gives the percentage of morphia found in each, as follows: Turkey opium, from Smyrna, highest percentage, 21.46; lowest, 11.70; mean, 14.78. India, from Patna, highest 7.72; lowest, 5.27; mean, 6.45. Egypt, from Alexandria, highest, 12.21; lowest, 5.81; mean, 9.01. France, from Amiens, highest, 22.28; lowest, 14.83; mean, 17.69. The mean percentage here given of each kind of opium is the mean of all the specimens analyzed, and therefore does not in every case correspond with the mean of the highest and lowest. From an examination of the mean temperature of the climates of the countries named, it will be seen that the opium of India and Africa, which have the hottest climates, is of the poorest quality; while that of Turkey and France, which have the coldest, is the best. In India the average yield of opium per acre is said, by good authority, to be from twenty-five to forty pounds avoirdupois. In the department of Somme, in France, 40,000 acres are cultivated annually with the poppy, and the good opium sells at wholesale for $8 to $10 per pound, according to the quality. At a standard of 10 per cent. of morphia it will sell for $7 to $7 50 per pound. Besides the opium extracted from the capsules of the plants cultivated on this large area of land, the seeds have some years been sold for about $896,000 for the oil which they contained. The average yield of oil from the seeds of capsules which have not been scarified is 25 to 27 per cent., and it is considered better for salad oil than most olive oils sold in the market. Seeds from scarified capsules should not be used for planting, as their vitality has been much weakened by this process, and the plants which they produce are correspondingly feeble. They yield only about two-thirds as much oil as other seeds. The poppy is also cultivated in Germany on a large scale, both for opium and for oil. Its culture commenced only a few years ago, but so great has been its success that the opium produced there has nearly supplanted the use of the foreign article. From Germany it passed over to France, and there are now 60,000 to 70,000 acres under profitable cultivation in the latter country.

Experiments

In Jefferson County, New York, one-fourth of an acre, planted with the poppy, produced twenty-seven pounds of opium in four years, equal to one crop of twenty-seven pounds per acre, which, at $10 per pound, would amount to $270, as the income of one acre of land for one year. Specimens were sent to New York for analysis, and the percentage of morphia was found to be equal to the average of the best imported. The grower thinks it will pay to cultivate the poppy in this country, if the work is conducted with proper skill; and that he can get more money from one acre of land planted with poppy than from three acres with any other crop which he has ever seen. A man of small means, who will cultivate it with skill and perseverance, can make it profitable. A capable boy can cultivate a quarter of an acre easily. It requires no more weeding and hoeing than any garden crop. Good, rich land is required, which should be pulverized and leveled as for onions. He sows in drills as given in our second method, and thins out to six inches between the plants. The young plants which are thinned out make excellent greens, fully equal to the beet or the spinach.

Dr. E. Lewis, of Topeka, Kansas, cultivated the poppy in York County, Pennsylvania, and gives it as his opinion that opium can be profitably produced in the latter State. He makes one incision horizontally around the capsules soon after the petals of the flowers have fallen, and usually performs the operation only once upon the same capsule; but if it is large he would perform it twice at different times.

Mr. W. H. White, of South Windsor, Connecticut, has cultivated the poppy, on a small scale, in the garden. After the petals have fallen he makes five, six, or more slight cuts in the capsules from top to bottom a little before noon. A few hours after the incisions have been made the opium is scrapped off and allowed to stand for a short time, when it is worked into balls. Families in that State sometimes collect it in this way for their own use as a medicine for their children, and find that it answers all the purposes of the opium of the shops. A ball as large as a small pea is frequently obtained from the heads of a single plant.

The cultivation of the poppy is becoming an important industry in Vermont, especially in Addison County, on Lake Champlain. Mr. Robbins, of Hancock, has cultivated it for some years, and specimens of his opium have yielded 15.75 per cent. of morphia. Two years ago Mr. Monkton, who resides near the village of Middlebury, raised $3,000 worth of opium. Mr. W. C. Wilson, of Monkton Ridge, has been cultivating it for five years, and has derived a handsome profit from the sales. On one farm in East Middlebury there are several acres under cultivation, and the business is gradually extending throughout that part of the State.

Mr. Baudrye, of Nevato, Marin County, California, has just commenced the culture of the poppy in that town. Specimens of opium analyzed yielded 5.75 per cent. of morphia, which, though small, is nearly equal to the average of opium from India. Mr. Baudrye sold his opium in California for $7 per pound. Mr. Guillardon, of Lower Lake, Lake County, has thirteen acres planted with the poppy, which he is cultivating both for opium and oil. A gentleman who is familiar with opium culture in India and Germany thinks the middle and southern portions of California are unsurpassed in soil and climate by any country for the production of opium, and that with a little irrigation two crops might be raised yearly.

The Beet-Sugar Industry, 1870

From U.S. Department of Agriculture, *Annual Report*, 1870, pp. 210–215.

After a series of preliminary disappointments and failures, such as embarrass almost every improvement, the economic difficulties of the beet-sugar industry seem to have been measurably overcome. Much still remains to be done, but from the results already attained capital finds fair inducements for more extended investment, both in the culture and the manufacture. Three establishments — one at Chatsworth, Illinois, one at Alvarado, California, and the third in Sauk County, Wisconsin — are manufacturing a good quality of sugar with sufficient success to render future efforts promising. Other manufacturing enterprises have been projected, while in many places the experimental culture of the beet has been inaugurated with a view to manufacture. At Chatsworth, Illinois, in 1864, Messrs. Gennert purchased two thousand acres of land and erected a manufactory. They subsequently sold out to an association called "The Germania Sugar-Beet Company. This establishment has motive power and machinery sufficient to work up fifty tons of beets per day. In 1866 they raised four thousand tons of sugar-beets on four hundred acres, at an estimated cost of $4 per ton. Since that time, however, the cost of production is said to have been reduced to $2.70 per ton, through the introduction of machinery. The crop of 1870 covered only three hundred and thirty acres, of which one hundred and thirty proved an entire failure through the drought, leaving but two hundred productive acres. The seed used is known as the "White Imperial," and was imported specially for this enterprise. In order to decrease the size of the beets, and thus obtain a larger percentage of sugar, the seed is sown quite thickly, and the roots in ordinary seasons do not exceed one and a half or two pounds each. By allowing the beets to grow large the crops may be raised to an average of twenty-five tons per acre, but the decline of saccharine properties counterbalances the increase in quantity. The average crop of the two hundred productive acres in 1870 was about nine tons, but the beets were much richer in sugar than in wet seasons. Much labor is saved in harvesting the beets, by a simple contrivance admitting the application of horse-power. The roots are preserved in pits, and protected from the frost until the manufacturing season approaches. Hand labor in cultivation is almost entirely confined to thinning out the beets. The full success of the enterprise, however, can be secured only by the extension of sugar-beet culture among the farmers, to whom it recommends itself by several economic advantages. Its beneficial influence upon the soil, and the cheap stock-feed which it furnishes, will doubtless attract the attention of the meat producers of Illinois.

The sugar already produced at Chatsworth is highly recommended. The first yield was placed in the Chicago market without brand, and was pronounced by experts to be equal to A 1 New York sugar, readily bringing the price of that article. From the beginning, a fair article of sugar was made by this establishment, but in the earlier efforts the expense of the process overbalanced the market value of the product. This has been attributed to injudicious management of the enterprise in its earlier stages, and to a too rigid adherence to the ideas and formulae of European industry. The present superintendent, Mr. Jonathan Perriam, is a native American and a Western farmer. He seems to have overcome, to a great extent, the practical obstacles in the way of the economic success of the enterprise. In a letter to this Department, dated January 2, 1871, he states: "The continued lack of water puts us to the most serious disadvantages in the manufacture." He further complains of the necessity of depending "upon foreign laborers who do not understand our language, nor appreciate the necessity of economizing." He hopes by the extension of machinery to overcome this latter difficulty, and expresses his decided opinion that "beet-sugar, upon favorable soils, with plenty of good water for manufacturing, will be a success, in a business point of view, if economically managed." It is proposed to remove this establishment to a location having a soil better adapted to the growth of the sugar-beet, and one with a more abundant supply of water.

Great confidence is felt upon the Pacific coast in the final success of the beet-sugar industry in that region. Ten years ago Mr. George Gordon, since deceased, exhibited at the fair of the Mechanics' Institute, in San Francisco, a superior article of beet-sugar. Still later, Mr. Claus Sprechman, of the California sugar refinery, imported beet seeds from Germany and France, and made a liberal distribution of them among the farmers of California, stipulating for a specific quantity of beets in return, with information as to locality, modes of culture, &c. With these beets critical and scientific experiments were made by machinery. It was found that alkaline elements in the soil deteriorated the practical value of the roots. This result so discouraged Mr. Sprechman that he abandoned the enterprise. Mr. Gordon proposed to resuscitate it, but prior to commencing operations he associated with him Mr. Sprechman and a Mr. Wentworth, with whom he visited Europe to observe the beet culture and sugar manufacture on that continent. They never renewed their efforts in this country.

In the spring of 1870 Messrs. Bonesteel, Otto & Co., who had been engaged in the beet-sugar enterprise at Fond du Lac, Wisconsin, were induced to remove to California, where they organized the Alvarado Beet-Sugar Manufactory, at Alvarado, in Alameda County, under the auspices of a company of capitalists, who had invested $250,000 in the enterprise. The initial results of this movement were so flattering as to give rise to some extravagant anticipations. One enthusiastic journalist predicted that in five years California would be a sugar-exporting State. The Alvarado company now occupy a three-story building, 150 feet long by 50 feet wide, with a boiler-house 59 feet by 50, and a bone-coal house 75 feet by 40. The machinery is sufficient to work up fifty tons of beets per day. The motive power is furnished by four tubular steam-boilers, each 16 feet long and 54 inches in diameter. These drive the three steam-engines, of which two are 14 by 30, (first-class finish,) and one 16 by 12. The apparatus embraces vacuum pans, saturation pans, air-pumps, filters, filter-pumps, beet-grater, beet-washing machine, beet-breaking machine, tanks for elevating sirup and sugar from one floor to another, and a number of sheet-iron tanks for various purposes. An abundant supply of shafting, pulleys, pipes, pumps, and other fittings incidental to a complete sugar manufactory and refinery have been provided, enabling the company to transform the beets into fine granulated sugar within twenty-four hours after their reception.

Through delay in receiving that portion of the machinery which had been ordered from Germany, the manufactory did not commence operations until Tuesday, November 15, 1870. On the following Thursday many friends of the enterprise assembled to witness the first turn-out of sugar. Anxiety and unbelief were the prevailing expression, both of voice and of countenance, as, at 10 o'clock a.m., the contents of one of the large pans were emptied into one of the sugar centrifugals and set in revolution. In less than three minutes the white sugar began to crystallize, doubt gave way to enthusiasm, and all present pronounced the sugar superior to cane sugar. Some allowance, however, must be made for the excitement of the occasion.

In this establishment the beets are first thoroughly washed in a cylinder composed of slats, one end of which is depressed in a tank of water. By revolution upon its axis, the beets, rubbing constantly upon each other in the water, are thoroughly cleansed by the time they reach the lower end. They are then elevated to the grater, a formidable piece of machinery upon the third floor, furnished with a rasp which revolves 1,500 times per minute. Against this rasp the bright, clean roots are pressed, and in a very short time are reduced to a fine watery pulp, which is then drawn off into the centrifugals below. Of these there are ten, each revolving 1,200 times per minute, and thoroughly separating, by their rapid movement, the juice from the pulp. The former passes through large troughs into defecating pans; the latter is removed through a spout into the dried-pulp room below. In the defecating pans the inpurities of the juice are absorbed by a preparation of lime; thence it runs into two close upright boilers, called by the French *montejus*. These are located on the lower floor, and by steam pressure elevate the juice to large filter-presses in the second story. It then passes into the saturating pans, where the lime, previously absorbed in the clarifying process, is eliminated by an infusion of carbonic acid gas. It is then filtered through animal charcoal, whence it passes into two evaporating pans, and is subjected to a boiling heat till it reaches the proper consistency. It is then drawn off into iron tanks to cool and crystallize; after which it is placed in an open upright cylinder, in which an iron axle with projecting arms slowly revolves, mingling the entire mass into a sort of heavy molasses. The sirup is then expelled by a rapid revolution in four sugar centrifugals, the residuum being "first-class" sugar, ready for market. The ejected sirup is again placed in the centrifugal and "second-class" sugar is produced. The process is repeated for the third and sometimes for the fourth time.

The heavy-lifting operations of this establishment are all done by steam raised from the screenings of the Monte Diable coal mines, about nine tons of which are consumed daily. The working force embraces about thirty white men, and as many Chinese. The greatest economy of material is strictly observed in all parts of the process. The scum of the defecating pans is removed, and subjected to a separate filtering process, when its residuum is allowed to mingle with the defecated juice. The machinery, so far, has worked remarkably well.

The success of this enterprise being greatly dependent upon an abundant supply of raw material, the company have engaged extensively in the culture of the beet. About eight hundred acres of their land will be planted in beets during the season of 1871, for which a full supply of seed has been imported from Germany. This arrangement is provisional, and will be superseded when a sufficient number of farmers can be found competent and willing to engage in the culture. Allowing an average of twenty tons of beets per acre, and an average yield of 8 per cent. of sugar, the company will have a sufficient supply of raw material to enable them to operate at least three hundred days in the year, and nearly two and a half millions of pounds of sugar to produce.

This union of diverse processes of production, embracing both raw material and finished product, is not in accordance with that principle of division of labor which has enabled modern industry to achieve its splendid results. It is to be hoped that the agricultural part of the enterprise will soon be assumed by agricultural men. The Mitchell nursery, near San José, has produced fifty tons of good beets per acre. The present price of roots at the Alvarado factory is $3 50 per ton. A product of twenty tons will realize $70 per acre.

The Alvarado Company has hitherto confined its attention exclusively to the German beet. Experiments will be made with other seeds to discover the variety best adapted to the soil.

An establishment has been in operation at Sacramento, and during the past year a considerable quantity of sugar has been produced, but expenses have not been realized, and an assessment of $2 per share has been made upon the stockholders. This company has been paying $5 per ton for beets; $1 50 more than was paid by the Alvarado Company. The difficulties that embarrass the enterprise seem to be in the beet culture of the neighborhood, and in the low percentage of sugar secured. The experience of the proprietors leads them to conclusions very different from those of European beet-growers. The latter obtain the maximum of saccharine matter in the latest growth prior to autumnal frosts. The beets grown here lost half their sugar during the last six weeks of their growth. Perhaps in the adjustment of this difficulty the beet culture here may find its final opening to success.

Under date of December 29, 1870, Tyler Beach, secretary of the Santa Clara Valley Agricultural Society, informs this Department that, under the auspices of that society, a beet-sugar company has been formed, with a capital of $200,000 for the manufacture of beet sugar at San José, California. He solicits from this Department a variety of beet seeds, in order to test by actual experiment the adaptability of each to the soil and climate of that locality. In answer to this request four varieties of seeds were sent. This enterprise is prosecuted by intelligent and careful business men, who, with the experience of the Alvarado Company before them, entertain strong hopes of success.

Sugar-beet culture has been commenced in Colorado with very promising initial results. Reports of enormous yields are received, two cultivators having secured over seventy tons per acre. Farmers were sanguine as to their ability to raise an average of fifty tons. Their quality is now being tested at Chatsworth, Illinois. Efforts are being made to establish a manufactory in Colorado.

The value of success in industry may be partly estimated from our enormous importation of foreign sugar. During the fiscal year ending June 30, 1870, we imported 1,160,460,114 pounds of brown sugar, 151,520 pounds of refined sugar, 36,161,935 pounds of melado and sirup of sugarcane, 55,820 pounds of candy and confectionery, and 56,373,537 gallons of molasses. The total declared value of these imports was $69,827,884. Our domestic sugar-cane, beet, maple, and sorghum did not amount to one-eighth of this aggregate. Europe, from the expansion of her beet-sugar production, now supplies one-half of her home demand, and the industry is extending into England upon a scale which promises to rival that of the continent. We see no reason to doubt that we, with our abundant natural resources, may be able to do fully as well as Europe. Estimates by French statisticians prior to the insurrection in Cuba place the world's aggregate sugar production at 2,300,000 tons, one-third of the whole amount being assigned to Cuba. The industry of the cane-producing countries of the world, from which the great mass of our import is derived, is mostly in a rudimentary or in a disorganized condition. Slave labor still exists in Brazil and the Spanish West Indies, while the emancipated labor of other regions as yet works at a disadvantage, not having been systematized or adapted to the conditions of a progressive civilization. The reorganization of this free labor has been in progress for many years, yet it is not so far advanced as in our Southern States after an interval of only five years of peace; nor does it present any prospect of a more rapid reconstruction in the future. Hence, though enjoying the exuberant natural resources of a tropical soil and climate, these foreign sugar industries will work at an essential disadvantage with our own. The insurrection in Cuba has desolated the finest portions of the island, and the financial condition of the sugar interests is critical. Of 1,800 plantations it is reported that scarcely 1 per cent. is free from mortgages, and that operations are prosecuted at such a disadvantage as to return not over 4 per cent. on the capital, while money loans cost 9 per cent. Into this breach, then, the beet-sugar industry of the United States should at once be thrown, and the best use be made of its excellent opportunity.

The value of the beet-sugar manufacture, as an aid to stock fattening and to intensive culture, has frequently been mentioned. Both leaves and pulp furnish valuable food for stock. Dr. Voelcker, in the Journal of the Royal Agricultural Society of England, gives the following analysis of beet-root pulp, from Mr. Duncan's experimental crops at Lavenham:

Water	70.11
Flesh-forming substances, (containing nitrogen)	2.25
Sugar	3.39
Mucilage	1.93
Digestible vegetable fiber	15.13
Wood fiber	5.32
Ash	1.87
	100.00

The best root contains 15½ per cent. of solid matter, while, from the above analysis, it appears that the pulp yields nearly 30 per cent. This is accounted for by the fact that in the process of manufacture the residuary product has lost a large proportion of its water. The pulp obtained from 20 tons of beets would amount to about 72 cwt. yielding about 21.6 cwt. of solid matter. According to the same authority mangel-wurzel contains but 11 per cent. of solid matter, and a crop of 20 tons would yield but 44 cwt. Hence the pulp alone of an acre of sugar beets would be nearly equivalent in solid material to a half crop or 10 tons of mangel-wurzel. Dr.

Voelcker estimates that in availibility for stock feeding a ton of pulp equals 1½ tons of sugar beets, or 2 tons of common beets. Another English agricultural writer estimates the value of 20 tons of sugar beet, as stock feed, as equal to that of 30 tons of mangolds. The agricultural branch of the sugar industry has many elements of prospective profit. The skill of our manufacturers will keep pace with our agricultural production in simplifying, cheapening, and extending the processes of extraction. From all present indications no reason appears why our beet-sugar production should not at least equal that of Europe, if not greatly surpass it.

The Texas Cattle Trade, 1870

From U. S. Department of Agriculture, *Annual Report*, 1870, pp. 346–52.

Among the important developments of our domestic commerce, following closely upon the construction of the Pacific Railroads, is the Texas cattle trade, which has attained gigantic proportions, within the past three years. Previously, with greater obstructions to travel and longer distances to market, it had a slow growth. In all the more densely populated communities of the civilized world, the question of the continued supply of animal food long since assumed an important phase. Even on our own new continent, especially in the older settled portions on the Atlantic slope, the upward tendency of the meat market has long been remarked. If prices should continue to increase, as in the past few years, it requires no prophetic gift to foretell the transfer of animal food from the list of necessaries to that of the luxuries of life, attainable only by the middle or wealthier classes of society. The movements of population, the conditions of agriculture, and the developments of mechanical industry have been unfavorable to cheap meat production in the older States. In the Southern States population has tended hitherto to settle in the river bottoms, leaving immense plateau and mountain regions available to cattle-raising, but the system of agriculture prevalent in that section previous to the war was not favorable to this branch of industry. Its capacities in this direction have not yet been developed, and consequently no relief from the pressure can be expected from that quarter. The irruption of cheap beef from the Southwest is, therefore, very timely and acceptable.

Texas has been aptly designated the great cattle-hive of North America. More than half a century ago, under inducements offered by the Spanish colonial authorities in Mexico, the coast region from the Sabine to the Rio Grande, a level and fertile belt from thirty to sixty miles broad, was settled by Spanish and American emigrants, who brought with them their native breeds of cattle, which, under remarkably favorable circumstances of climate and pasturage, amalgamated into a common stock, combining in a larger degree the better points of the constituent breeds. Up to the struggle for Texas independence the increase of these herds was remarkably rapid. In the disturbances and social dislocations which then ensued, the western portion of this cattle region became almost depopulated, and the cattle, for lack of owners, relapsed into a state of wildness. Social order was not finally reëstablished till after the annexation of Texas to the United States, and the treaty of peace with Mexico, in 1848. The cattle-raising industry then revived. The wild herds were either reclaimed by their former owners or appropriated by others. Large numbers were driven to eastern markets, but enough remained to stock immense ranches, on which a class of men of enterprise and resolute character have since organized a very thrifty pastoral industry. During the late rebellion the Texas cattle regions were but very slightly devastated by the ravages of war, which, on the contrary, greatly enhanced their prosperity by increasing the price of Texas beef. Its very large production has of late been rendered available to the public interest through the various lines of the Pacific Railroad system.

In the coast regions of Texas are found cattle lords whose animated treasures surpass, in number and value, even the flocks and herds of the great man of Uz. The Santa Cabrutas ranch, on the Santa Cabrutas River, owned by Colonel Richard King, embraces 84,132 acres of land, stocked with 65,000 cattle, 10,000 horses, 7,000 sheep, and 8,000 goats. For the management of these immense herds, 300 Mexican herdsmen and 1,000 saddle-horses are held in constant requisition. Colonel King each year brands 12,000 calves, and sells 10,000 fat cattle, constantly investing the surplus proceeds in stock cattle. O'Conner's ranch, twenty miles below Goliad, on the San Antonio River, in 1862 contained over 40,000 cattle; during that year on this estate 12,000 calves were branded, and $80,000 realized by the sale of cattle. This enterprise was inaugurated ten years previously, with 1,500 cattle. The Rolideaux ranch, between the Nueces and Rio Grande Rivers, owned by Mr. Kennedy, is a fertile peninsula of 142,840 acres, jutting out into the Gulf of Mexico, the isthmus being secured by thirty miles of plank fence, guarded at intervals of three miles by herdsmen's ranches. It already contains 30,000 beef cattle, besides large numbers of other stock. Other magnificent cattle-herds might be enumerated.

The net increase of cattle in this region has been estimated as high as 25 per cent. per annum prior to the opening of the Texas cattle trade. Turning his animals loose to graze at will over a range of country often fifty miles square, covered with nutritious grasses, in a genial climate, in which shelter is unnecessary, the Texas stock-raiser confines his care to the identification and marketing of his animals. For the former purpose the stockmen of the neighboring ranches assemble semi-annually in considerable force, to scour the country for the purpose of branding the calves, the ownership of which is determined by the brand borne by the cows they follow or suck.

This stock business, which has thus grown up from small beginnings, now amounts to a magnificent industry, the product of which reaches our most distant markets. Its conditions, both economical and productive, have been gradually changing with the growth of our resources. For several years after the annexation of Texas to the United States, the domestic market ruled very low. Stock cattle brought not over $4 or $5 per head, while beeves fattened for market did not command more than double these prices. These rates, however, were abundantly remunerative under the conditions of cheap production then subsisting. When steamers began to touch at different points on the coast, and to ship beeves on the hoof to New Orleans and to other eastern and northern markets, the stock-raisers near the seaboard were soon able to realize double the rates above named. During the later years of the rebellion, the blockade of the coast and of the Mississippi River, by the Union forces, cut off nearly all access to markets; but since the return of peace, and especially since the opening of the so-called Texas cattletrade, prices have been constantly advancing. At a convention of Texas cattle-raisers, held in Live Oak County during the last autumn, the following tariff of prices was fixed, viz: For first-class animals, $18 per head; second class, $15; third class, $11.

The extension of crop-raising agricultural settlements in the coast regions seriously deranged the conditions of cheap production of cattle, by raising the value of land and by restricting the range of free pasture. The stock business was then extended northward to the central region of high rolling prairies and even to the plateaus of Northern Texas, localities scarcely less congenial to this attractive industry than even the rich plains of the coast. They present large areas tolerably well watered, and sufficiently well timbered for the wants of the stock-raiser. The climate is mild and salubrious. The soil is a rich black mold, yielding, to a very imperfect culture, large crops of cereals and fruits. In their wild state the prairies are covered with excellent grasses, and already feed large herds of cattle, bearing the brands of different owners. Immense quantities of beef are annually lost, like the waste wood of the forest, for lack of means of preserving it. Hides rot on the ground for lack of tanneries, and because of the great cost of transportation to market, while imported leather is scarce and dear. Industry and trade are still in a very rudimentary condition, society being yet in a formative state.

The number of cattle in Texas in 1870 is estimated at about 4 to 1 of the population; whereas, in the three great States of Ohio, Pennsylvania, and New York, the proportion is reversed. Texas is supposed to contain at least 3,000,000 beef cattle, besides 600,000 cows. There are annually raised and branded about 750,000 calves. From this basis of production, it is a question how long the demands of the present cattle-market can be met. The impression is beginning to prevail that the enormous exportation both of stock cattle and of fat beeves has measurably curtailed production. To such an extent has this movement increased, that even yearlings are now driven to the pastures of Colorado and Kansas to fatten for eastern markets. The great demand for stock has also induced the occupancy of ill-watered districts, resulting in a large loss of animals by thirst. It seems probable that the capacities of the system hitherto pursued are about exhausted, and that more careful and economical methods and more scientific principles must be introduced into the business to enable it to meet the growing demand upon it. The ideas of the present race of stock-raisers, it is charged, are ultra-conservative and hostile to the introduction of improvements; but the rapid extension of railroad facilities into Texas will enforce an entire reorganization of this industry. The great primary depot of the Texas cattle trade is now at the Abilene Station, on the Kansas River, one hundred and sixty miles west of the Missouri River, four hundred and forty from St. Louis, and six hundred and seventy from Chicago. The special advantages of this locality were found in its admirable facilities for pasturing large herds of cattle beyond the settled portion of Kansas, upon a leading railroad route. The herds from Texas, however carefully driven, must necessarily arrive, after a march of seven hundred miles, in a very impoverished condition, while very many herds are driven without intelligent regard to the condition of the animals. From six to nine months' feeding in the genial climate, and abundant, well-watered pastures of this locality, where the plague of insects is unknown, is required to fit the stock for market. The shipments of cattle on the Kansas Pacific Railroad for the four years past are stated by Mr. A. Anderson, the general superintendent, in a letter to this Department dated December 17, 1870, as follows: In 1867, 30,000 head; 1868, 57,000; 1869, 47,000; 1870, 125,000. Of these aggregates he estimates that 97 to 98 per cent. were Texas cattle. The decline of shipments in 1869, as compared with 1868, was due to the statute of Illinois prohibiting the introduction of Texas cattle into that State during certain seasons of the year. The arrivals of cattle of all grades at the various stock-yards along the line of this road, during 1870, probably amounted to about 150,000.

The Union Pacific Railroad has made strong efforts to attract a portion of this trade by establishing at Schuyler, twenty-five miles west of Omaha, special facilities for the shipment of cattle, and by lowering the tariff of transportation charges. Notwithstanding the two hundred miles additional drive, as compared with Abilene, the business at this point has attained unexpected dimensions. Under date of December 16, 1870, Mr. T. E. Sickels, general superintendent Union Pacific Railroad, reports to this Department the shipment of 10,234 Texas cattle in 1870, besides 9,110 western cattle. The total shipment of any previous year was less than 500. It is thought that the local demands of Nebraska, Iowa, Minnesota, and Dakota will greatly enlarge this trade.

Baxter Springs, in Southeastern Kansas, on the Missouri River, Fort Scott and Gulf Railroad, promises to become a formidable rival to Abilene in this Texas cattle trade. Mr. B. S. Henning, superintendent, under date of December 15, 1870, reports to this Department the shipment of 85,000 head subsequent to June 1, 1870, the date at which the road was opened to Baxter Springs. This point is located one hundred and fifty-nine miles from Kansas City, and four hundred and forty-one from St. Louis, by the Missouri Pacific Railroad. The extension of the Atlantic and Pacific Railroad, now completed to Pierce City, two hundred and ninety-one miles from St. Louis, and at no great distance from Baxter Springs, will soon open a much shorter route to this traffic. In fact, this latter route, according to the statement to this Department of Mr. W. H. Paniarche, superintendent, dated December 16, 1870, gave transportation to 7,520 head of cattle in 1869, and to 40,960 head in 1870, of which latter aggregate 20,000 were known as Texas and Indian cattle. Mr. W. H. Downes, general superintendent of the central branch Union Pacific Railroad, reports the shipments of cattle over that line, in 1870, at 112 car-loads, or, at an average of 20 head per car-load, 2,240 head. This road is completed from Atchison to Waterville, Kansas, one hundred miles.

The general northward movement of Texas cattle during 1870 is variously estimated between 100,000 and 200,000 head. The aggregate shipments of the five railroad lines above mentioned were 232,000. How large a portion of these cattle were from the Indian Territory there is no means of determining, inasmuch as these are consolidated with the Texas cattle in all the reports. The estimates quoted do not appear to be extravagant. The cattle brought to market by these lines of transportation are from Northern or Central Texas, those of the coast regions finding a more eligible market by sea. They were bought by the herd in Texas during 1870 at about the following prices, viz: Beef cattle, $11 per head; milch cows, $6; three-year olds,

$7; two-year olds, $4; yearlings, $2.50. When only beef cattle were bought, the prices ranged higher, averaging from $12 to $14 per head. The average drive to Abilene, seven hundred miles, occupies about two months, and costs about $2 per head, besides a margin of 20 per cent. for stampeding, stealing, &c. Arriving at Abilene in tolerable order, a mixed drove will command about the following prices, viz: Beef cattle, $20 per head; milch cows, $12; three-year olds, $10; two-year olds, $8; yearlings, $5. After grazing through the summer, their market value is advanced 20 to 25 per cent. Beef cattle, well matured for market, readily command $25 per head.

Chicago has largely controlled the Texas cattle trade since its inauguration, but St. Louis is organizing a formidable competition, with the advantage of shorter lines of communication with the cattle regions. It is evident that the present arrangements of the traffic are mostly provisional and temporary. This great mass of production cannot remain dependent upon the present imperfect outlets to market. The monopoly of transportation, now enjoyed by the Kansas Pacific Railroad and its connections, will be broken up when the southwestern lines, now in progress, shall have been completed. Cattle shipments to eastern markets, over these shorter lines, will be preferable to those over the long elbow-routes through Chicago and St. Louis.

The prices of beef on the hoof in the New York market during the first ten months of 1870 averaged about 8 cents per pound, or about double the rates ruling in Chicago and St. Louis. The animals average about 900 pounds, representing a valuation of $72, and costing the importer about $55 per head — a profit of about 30 per cent., counting all incidental and unavoidable risks. In the St. Louis and Chicago markets the Texas steer represents a value of about $31.50 per head, at 3½ per pound. The expense of bringing him to the abattoir of those cities is about $23, leaving a profit of $8.50, or nearly 40 per cent. Chicago livestock reports mention the fact that Texas cattle lose less weight in dressing than Illinois cattle, and can, therefore, be sold at finer margins to carcass-butchers. Beef-packers assert their superiority for packing to the rough, coarse stock previously imported from west of the Missouri River, being finer-grained, richer, and more tender. Their hides are also worth from 15 to 20 per cent. more, and their yield of tallow is larger.

The Chicago live-stock reports, during the latter half of 1870, represent a continued and increasing pressure of Texas cattle upon the market. The extreme range of prices has been between $2 and $7 per hundred pounds, for thin stock cattle and for well-matured fat beeves, respectively. In the lower grades Texas cattle have mainly monopolized the market. The low prices caused by this abundant supply have influenced all the markets in the country. In the opinion of intelligent cattle dealers in Chicago, the immense cattle irruption from the Southwest has alone prevented the average price of beef, live weight, from ruling as high as 12 cents per pound in the eastern markets. Complaints have been heard from even New England farmers of their being compelled to accept lower prices than had been anticipated. There is scarcely room to doubt that the Texas cattle trade has been overdone, and that the late abundant supply has been secured at the cost of a crippled production in the future.

The farmers of the Northwest must secure more valuable breeds of stock.

They must select animals which, with the same acreage of summer pasture and the same amount of winter feeding, will yield beef in greater quantity, of finer quality, and of higher market value.

The more intelligent cattle-raisers in the older States have already anticipated this necessity by supplanting their common stocks with improved breeds of cattle. The pressure of circumstances will drive the farming interest generally in the wake of these pioneers, and a speedy demand for superior animals may be expected. In the next ten years we may anticipate an immense improvement in the stocks of the Northwest. For such there is no danger of a failing market. While wealth, under our free civilization, is accumulating and diffusing itself through more numerous classes of society, the demand for better food will keep pace with any improvement in production that may be made. In this branch of the business, Texas cattle-raisers, under their present conditions of production, can offer but slight competition. To raise the finer breeds of cattle will involve a revolution in their whole system. It is one thing to send out, from time to time, gangs of Mexican vaqueros to lasso and drive in the spontaneous products of wide, unoccupied wastes of rich pasture, but entirely another thing to operate within narrower limits, and to develop the latent resources of nature by a scientific application of her higher laws. It is unreasonable to expect a sudden change in the loose methods of production now employed in the Southwest; but the time is coming when such a change will be a necessity. The pressure of population and the rise in the value of land will soon demand greater economy of resources. Wide-spread pastures will be restricted by farming inclosures, and the ability to produce coarse beef at low prices, without any of the expenses of the Northern and Western stock-grower, and with less scientific intelligence, will no longer exist.

The Texas cattle trade has its evils, which should be ameliorated. The transportation of cattle for great distances by rail involves many abuses. Healthy animals suddenly removed from the free range of pasture and crowded into cattle-cars, kept standing for days and nights in an uncomfortable posture, deprived of food and rest, worried and confused by the constant roar of machinery, cannot long preserve their healthful condition. In the hot summer months, bodily exhalations create an intensely mephitic atmosphere; the jarring, unequal movements of the cars jostle the animals against each other, injuring their limbs, abrading their flesh, and adding cutaneous and muscular inflamations to the other evils of this "middle passage."

Different State legislatures have attempted to relieve these difficulties by special enactments. New York forbids the confinement of live-stock for longer consecutive periods than twenty-eight hours, without intervals of ten hours for rest. Inventive genius is also devising more comfortable cattle-cars. It can render the most effective service in the perfection of refrigerator cars, whereby the animal may be slaughtered on his native soil, and the meat sent to distant markets, preserved by artificial refrigeration perfectly fresh and untainted. This method has already been successfully inaugurated in some portions of the country, and there is but little doubt of its general introduction when the requisite machinery shall have been devised and constructed.

Colonization in 1870

From U.S. Department of Agriculture, *Annual Report*, 1870, pp. 569–72.

The settlement of countries by colonies is by no means new. The children of Israel went to the land of Canaan as a colony. Athens and Rome were founded as colonies, and it is well known that much of New England was settled in this manner. Of late years few colonies have been founded, and settlements have been by individual effort. The laws relating to Government land require that titles pass directly to an individual, and no combined effort, no coöperation is recognized. Hence, when a colony undertakes to acquire a title to Government land, there are great difficulties; for, as soon as the location is made, squatters and land speculators rush in, and appropriate whatever lands they can seize, not in good faith, but that they may realize more or less on the rise in the price of land, caused by those who do come in good faith. Where there are railroad grants covering one-half of the region, the difficulties are proportionally diminished.

The objects to be secured in organizing a colony may be definitely stated: First, to secure choice and cheap land; second, to divide such land equitably among the members; third, to build a town, centrally located, that each may have a share in the increased value of town and of country property, and that there may be the advantages of schools, churches, and good society at an early day; fourth, to obtain reduced rates on freight and passage; and fifth, to prohibit the sale of intoxicating liquors and the introduction of gambling establishments. Theoretical ideas are of little value unless enforced by practical examples. The most noticeable recent example is that of the Union colony, the center of which is the town of Greeley, in Weld County, Territory of Colorado.

A visit was made to Colorado, late in the fall of 1869, by a gentleman interested in the formation of a colony, when the remarkably fine climate, the fertile soil, the abundance of minerals, and the majestic scenery attracted his attention. Almost every part of the United States had been previously visited with a view to impart information on the best localities for those seeking new homes on cheap lands, and it was seen that Colorado offered many inducements, an important one being its freedom from malarious diseases. But it was seen that to remove so far, in the common isolated method, would entail hazards of no ordinary character, and at the best it would be many years before the settler would have schools and churches near him, while the expense required to prepare for emigration presented a formidable obstacle. The only plan promising much success was to organize a colony of several hundred families that a large body of land might be acquired, and that the schools and churches might be built by a common fund.

Hon. Horace Greeley, having been consulted, entertained the proposition, and a call was made, December 7, through the columns of the New York Tribune. The plan of organization was substantially as set forth above, and the responses were numerous. December 23, a public meeting was held, and Mr. Greeley was appointed treasurer. A locating committee was sent out in February, 1870, various parts of the Territory were visited, and a selection was finally made, April 5, on the Cache à la Poudre, five miles above where it empties into the South Platte, twenty miles from the Rocky Mountains, and on the line of the Denver Pacific Railroad, midway between Denver and Cheyenne, fifty-fiive miles from each.

About twelve thousand acres of land were bought of the railroad company, and two thousand from preëmptors and squatters. The alternate sections, belonging to the Government, were to be homesteaded and preëmpted. In addition, a contract was made with the railroad for fifty thousand acres more, running for three years. The Commissioner of the General Land Office, at Washington, had been visited for the purpose of obtaining the privilege of having the Government land kept out of market until the colonists could go on from the States, and application was made to several members of Congress, but nothing seemed likely to be done, and the attempt was abandoned. However, a remedy was found, which was not at first fully recognized. As soon as the location was definitely made, a charter was taken out, under the territorial law of Colorado, for a series of irrigating ditches, which practically gave not only control of all the alternate Government sections adjoining those held in fee, but also of all the land, whether belonging to the railroad or Government, which the ditches might cover; for the company were empowered to charge such a sum per acre for the use of water as made them masters of the situation, and this has been made manifest by the fact that they are not troubled with squatters or speculators. Had the country been one where irrigation is not required, they would undoubtedly have met with great difficulties. The sum fixed upon for membership was $150, and $5 in addition for expenses. The number of members paying the full fee was about six hundred and thirty, and the total receipts by the treasurer, about $100,000. The land purchased was divided as follows: A section of six hundred and forty acres, a mile square, was laid off for a town, and divided into lots ranging from 25 to 200 feet front. Adjoining the town came, first, lots of five, next ten, next twenty, and next forty acres, each of which was appraised as being worth $150, and members were to choose which they would take. A member could homestead a Government half-quarter section, the fees on which would be paid, and have the use of water for his share, or he could preëmpt the same amount and have water. Thus far the smaller parcels have been considered preferable to the larger ones; but all are held in esteem, and plowing and improvements have progressed above equally over the whole domain. The lots within the town are sold to the members at $25 for inside, and $50 for corners lots, and the sums received are to be devoted to school purposes and general improvements. About one hundred lots are held in reserve, to be sold hereafter at an advanced price, for the use of schools.

Arrangements had been made with railroad companies at New York, Boston, Buffalo, Cleveland, and Chicago, for the transportation of the colonists at a reduction in rates of about one-third, and early in May they began to arrive. The weather was cold, there were no houses, and, although a contract had been made for 70,000 feet of lumber, it was not fulfilled, and there was considerable suffering. The first relief was obtained in buying houses at a town five miles distant, and in hauling them to the ground with ox-teams; and a large building was bought at Cheyenne, and transported in sections on the cars. It was several weeks before any considerable quantity of lumber could be obtained, but finally there were large arrivals from Chicago and other points. For some time there was considerable dissatisfaction. All were strangers to each other, some were suspicious, and the officers were charged with inefficiency, neglect, and even with dishonesty. Much of the discontent was bred by those who expected to get a better chance than others, and much by the forbidding appearance of the country. Where irrigation is a necessity the grass has a brown appearance at all seasons of the year; and, as the ditch contracted for was not completed, many thought it doubtful whether life could be sustained. A visit to several ranches, a few miles distant, always dispelled the illusion. Water came into the town about the 1st of June, gardens and small fields were planted, and by the 1st of July vegetation grew with remarkable rapidity. Experience has demonstrated that the soil is remarkably fertile, and that if there should be any difficulty it will be in disposing of surplus crops; but of this there need be little fear, as the hundreds of mines and mining towns near by will always afford a good market.

The working of the official machinery of the colony has been reasonably harmonious. There have been jealousies, unkind remarks, ungrateful expressions, and some aspirations for position, but, in the main, matters have been kept well in hand. The locating committee received fair wages for their services; the superintendent was paid $7 a day until the middle of July. The president refused to receive any reward after the first week in May, and the only office to which any salary is now attached is that of secretary. The property is held in trust by a board of trustees, who grant deeds to members in fee whenever they make improvements on the land they have selected, either within the town or on their outlying land, and the charter for the irrigating ditches is held by them in trust. When members receive their deeds they are entirely independent of the colony, although they are members, inasmuch as each holds a certificate which entitles him to the use of water for all time: and in the election of officers he has one vote. No member can hold more than one share, and he can buy of the colony no more than one hundred and sixty acres of land; but few have bought so much. The sons and daughters of a member, if of age, can hold shares. The plan under which this colony was organized has worked extremely well, and in the formation of other colonies which are about to join it, without any charge above cost of land or charter privileges, only a few unimportant changes have been thought desirable. At the close of the year, that is, when the town was nine months old, there were nearly four hundred and fifty houses, many of them large and well finished; about twenty stores of all kinds, some of them first-class, both in regard to appearance of buildings and stock of goods; mechanics of all kinds, a weekly newspaper, three schools, and a population of at least one thousand souls. No liquor is sold in the place, nor is there a gambling establishment of any kind. Perhaps three-fourths of the members belong to some religious denomination. The navigation of the river on which the town is situated is to be improved for the purpose of floating timber from the mountains, and extensive saw-mills, as well as other mills are to be erected.

The experience of the colony in irrigation is favorable. It makes farming a scientific pursuit. The expense and labor are by no means formidable, and the colonists are found to adapt themselves to their requirements without any difficulty whatever. The incentive is, large crops; thirty bushels of wheat, fifty of oats, forty of barley, and two hundred and fifty of potatoes being a probable average. Finally, its success seems to arise mainly from adopting an organization that gives to the producer those profits which, under other conditions, are appropriated by speculators and capitalists.

Agriculture in the United States in 1870

From U.S. Census Bureau, *Ninth Census of the United States, 1870, Agriculture, pp. 81–85.*

| STATES AND TERRITORIES. | ACRES OF LAND IN FARMS | | | PRESENT CASH VALUE. | | Total amount of wages paid during the year, including value of board. | Total (estimated) value of all farm productions, including betterments and additions to stock. | Orchard products. | Produce of market gardens. |
| | Improved. | UNIMPROVED | | Of farms. | Of farming implements and machinery. | | | | |
		Woodland.	Other unimproved.						
	Number.	*Number.*	*Number.*	*Dollars.*	*Dollars.*	*Dollars.*	*Dollars.*	*Dollars.*	*Dollars.*
Total United States	188,921,099	159,310,177	59,503,765	9,262,803,861	336,878,429	310,286,285	2,447,538,658	47,335,189	20,719,229
Alabama	5,062,204	8,380,332	1,518,642	67,739,036	3,286,924	11,851,870	67,522,335	37,590	139,636
Arizona	14,585	....	7,222	161,340	20,105	104,620	277,998	....	2,850
Arkansas	1,859,821	3,910,325	1,827,150	40,029,698	2,237,409	4,061,952	40,701,699	157,219	55,697
California	6,218,133	477,880	4,731,092	141,240,028	5,316,690	10,369,247	49,856,024	1,384,480	1,059,779
Colorado	95,594	11,504	213,248	3,385,748	272,604	416,236	2,335,106	9	55,020
Connecticut	1,646,752	577,333	140,331	124,241,382	3,246,599	4,405,064	26,482,150	535,954	599,718
Dakota	42,645	22,605	237,126	2,085,265	142,612	71,156	495,657	....	500
Delaware	698,115	295,162	59,045	46,712,870	1,201,644	1,696,571	8,171,667	1,226,893	198,075
District of Columbia	8,266	2,428	983	3,800,230	39,450	124,338	319,517	6,781	112,034
Florida	736,172	1,425,786	211,583	9,947,920	505,074	1,537,060	8,909,746	53,639	31,983
Georgia	6,831,856	12,928,084	3,888,001	94,559,468	4,614,701	19,787,086	80,390,228	352,926	193,266
Idaho	26,603	7,476	43,660	492,860	59,295	153,007	637,797	725	24,577
Illinois	19,329,952	5,061,578	1,491,331	920,506,346	34,576,587	22,338,767	210,860,585	3,571,789	765,992

Indiana	10,104,279	7,189,334	826,035	634,804,189	17,676,591	9,675,348	122,914,302	2,858,086	487,479
Iowa	9,396,467	2,524,793	3,620,533	392,662,441	20,509,582	9,377,878	114,386,441	1,075,109	244,963
Kansas	1,971,003	635,419	3,050,457	90,327,040	4,053,312	2,519,452	27,630,651	158,046	129,913
Kentucky	8,103,850	9,134,658	1,421,598	311,238,916	8,572,896	10,709,382	87,477,374	1,231,385	527,329
Louisiana	2,045,640	4,003,170	977,007	68,215,421	7,159,333	11,042,789	52,006,622	142,129	176,969
Maine	2,917,793	2,224,740	695,525	102,961,951	4,809,113	2,903,292	33,470,044	874,569	266,397
Maryland	2,914,097	1,435,988	162,584	170,369,684	5,268,676	8,560,367	35,343,927	1,319,495	1,039,782
Massachusetts	1,736,221	706,714	287,348	116,432,784	5,000,879	5,821,032	32,192,378	939,854	1,980,231
Michigan	5,096,939	4,080,146	842,057	398,240,578	13,714,979	8,421,161	81,508,623	3,447,985	352,658
Minnesota	2,322,102	1,336,299	2,825,427	97,847,442	6,721,120	4,459,201	33,446,400	15,818	115,234
Mississippi	4,209,146	7,959,384	952,583	81,716,576	4,456,633	10,326,794	73,137,953	71,018	61,735
Missouri	9,180,615	8,965,229	3,611,376	392,908,047	15,596,426	8,797,487	103,035,759	2,617,463	406,655
Montana	84,674	1,198	53,665	729,193	145,438	325,213	1,676,660	....	35,130
Nebraska	647,031	213,374	1,213,376	30,242,186	1,549,716	882,478	8,604,742	9,932	30,649
Nevada	92,644	13,415	102,451	1,485,505	163,718	438,350	1,659,713	900	31,235
New Hampshire	2,334,487	1,647,090	224,417	80,589,313	3,459,943	2,319,164	22,473,547	743,552	119,997
New Jersey	1,976,474	718,335	294,702	257,523,376	7,887,991	8,314,548	42,725,198	1,295,282	2,978,250
New Mexico	143,007	106,283	584,259	2,260,139	121,114	523,888	1,905,060	13,609	64,132
New York	15,627,206	5,679,870	883,734	1,272,857,766	45,997,742	34,451,362	253,526,153	8,347,417	3,432,354
North Carolina	5,258,742	12,026,894	2,549,774	78,211,083	4,082,111	8,342,856	57,845,940	394,749	48,499
Ohio	14,469,133	6,883,575	359,712	1,054,465,226	25,692,787	16,256,967	198,256,967	5,843,679	1,289,272
Oregon	1,116,290	761,001	511,961	22,352,989	1,293,717	719,875	7,122,790	310,041	105,371
Pennsylvania	11,515,965	5,740,864	737,371	1,043,481,582	35,658,196	23,181,944	183,946,027	4,208,094	1,810,016
Rhode Island	289,030	169,399	43,879	21,574,968	786,246	1,124,118	4,761,163	43,036	316,133
South Carolina	3,010,539	6,443,851	2,650,890	44,808,763	2,282,946	7,404,297	41,909,402	47,960	127,459
Tennessee	6,843,278	10,771,396	1,966,540	218,743,747	8,199,487	7,118,003	86,472,847	571,520	301,093
Texas	2,964,836	7,662,294	7,769,393	60,149,950	3,396,793	4,777,638	49,185,170	69,172	74,924
Utah	118,755	215	29,391	2,297,922	291,390	133,695	1,973,142	43,938	8,700
Vermont	3,073,257	1,386,934	68,613	139,367,075	5,250,279	4,155,385	34,647,027	682,241	42,225
Virginia	8,165,040	8,294,734	1,686,137	213,020,845	4,924,036	9,753,041	51,774,801	891,231	505,117
Washington	192,016	291,206	165,917	3,978,341	280,551	215,522	2,111,902	71,863	74,462
West Virginia	2,580,254	4,364,405	1,583,735	101,604,381	2,112,937	1,903,788	23,379,692	848,773	69,974
Wisconsin	5,899,343	3,437,442	2,378,536	300,414,064	14,239,364	8,186,110	78,027,032	819,268	226,665
Wyoming	338	35	3,968	18,187	5,723	3,075	42,700	....	....

STATES AND TERRITORIES	Forest products.	Value of home manufactures.	Value of animals slaughtered, or sold for slaughter.	Value of all live stock.	LIVE STOCK.						
					Horses.	Mules and asses.	Milch cows.	Working oxen.	Other cattle.	Sheep.	Swine.
	Dollars. 36,808,277	Dollars. 23,423,332	Dollars. 398,956,376	Dollars. 1,525,276,457	Number. 7,145,370	Number. 1,125,415	Number. 8,935,332	Number. 1,319,271	Number. 13,566,005	Number. 28,477,951	Number. 25,134,569
Total United States	36,808,277	23,423,332	398,956,376	1,525,276,457	7,145,370	1,125,415	8,935,332	1,319,271	13,566,005	28,477,951	25,134,569
Alabama	85,933	1,124,513	4,670,146	26,690,095	80,770	76,675	170,640	59,176	257,347	241,934	719,757
Arizona	....	....	9,400	143,996	335	401	938	587	3,607	803	720
Arkansas	34,225	807,573	3,843,923	17,222,506	92,013	36,202	128,959	35,387	193,589	161,077	841,129
California	566,017	301,491	6,112,503	37,964,752	192,273	17,533	164,093	5,944	461,361	2,768,187	444,617
Colorado	....	57,658	252,394	2,871,102	6,446	1,173	25,017	5,566	40,153	120,928	5,509
Connecticut	1,224,107	53,297	4,881,858	17,545,038	34,935	190	98,889	39,639	79,485	83,884	51,983
Dakota	700	1,677	22,066	779,952	2,514	225	4,151	2,125	6,191	1,901	2,033
Delaware	111,810	33,070	997,403	4,257,323	16,770	3,584	24,082	6,888	19,020	22,714	39,818
District of Columbia	....	750	455	114,916	533	124	657	6	138	604	577
Florida	7,965	131,693	520,966	5,212,157	11,902	8,835	61,922	6,292	322,701	26,599	158,908
Georgia	1,281,623	1,113,080	6,854,382	30,156,317	81,777	87,426	231,310	54,332	412,261	419,465	988,566
Idaho	....	34,730	57,932	520,580	2,151	371	4,171	522	5,763	1,021	2,316
Illinois	1,087,144	1,408,015	56,718,944	149,756,698	853,738	85,075	640,321	19,766	1,055,499	1,568,286	2,703,343
Indiana	2,645,679	605,639	30,246,962	83,776,782	497,883	43,259	393,736	14,088	618,360	1,612,680	1,872,230
Iowa	1,200,468	521,404	25,781,223	82,987,133	433,642	25,485	369,811	22,058	614,366	855,493	1,353,908
Kansas	368,947	156,910	4,156,386	23,173,185	117,786	11,786	123,440	20,774	229,753	109,088	206,587
Kentucky	574,994	1,683,972	24,121,861	66,287,343	317,034	99,230	247,615	69,719	382,993	936,765	1,838,227
Louisiana	92,596	64,416	817,831	15,929,188	59,738	61,338	102,076	32,596	200,589	118,602	338,326
Maine	1,531,741	450,988	4,939,071	23,357,129	71,514	336	139,259	60,530	143,272	434,666	45,760

State											
Maryland	613,209	63,608	4,621,418	18,433,698	89,696	9,830	94,794	22,491	98,074	129,697	257,893
Massachusetts	1,616,818	79,378	4,324,658	17,049,228	41,039	103	114,771	24,430	79,851	78,560	49,178
Michigan	2,559,682	338,008	11,711,624	49,809,869	228,302	2,353	250,859	36,499	260,171	1,985,906	417,811
Minnesota	311,528	174,046	3,076,650	20,118,841	93,011	2,350	121,467	43,176	145,736	132,343	148,473
Mississippi	39,975	505,298	4,090,818	29,940,238	90,221	85,886	173,899	58,146	269,030	232,732	814,381
Missouri	793,343	1,737,606	23,626,784	84,285,273	493,969	111,502	398,515	65,825	689,355	1,352,001	2,306,430
Montana	918	155,357	169,092	1,818,693	5,289	475	12,432	1,761	22,545	2,024	2,599
Nebraska	36,307	36,951	854,850	6,551,185	30,511	2,632	28,940	5,931	45,057	22,725	59,449
Nevada	36,700	2,329	104,471	1,445,449	7,520	990	6,174	2,443	22,899	11,018	3,295
New Hampshire	1,743,944	234,062	3,720,243	15,246,545	39,095	37	90,583	40,513	91,705	248,760	33,127
New Jersey	352,704	144,016	6,982,162	21,443,463	79,708	8,853	133,331	3,830	60,327	120,067	142,563
New Mexico	506	19,592	224,765	2,389,157	5,033	6,141	16,417	19,774	21,343	619,438	11,267
New York	6,689,179	1,621,621	28,225,720	175,882,712	536,861	4,407	1,350,661	64,141	630,522	2,181,578	518,251
North Carolina	1,089,115	1,603,513	7,983,132	21,993,967	102,763	50,684	196,731	45,408	279,023	463,435	1,075,215
Ohio	2,719,140	1,371,409	40,498,375	120,300,528	609,722	16,065	654,390	23,606	758,221	4,928,635	1,728,968
Oregon	259,220	87,376	1,365,737	6,828,675	51,702	2,581	48,325	2,441	69,431	318,123	119,455
Pennsylvania	2,670,370	1,503,754	28,412,903	115,647,075	460,339	18,009	706,437	30,048	608,066	1,794,301	867,548
Rhode Island	254,683	37,847	755,552	3,135,132	7,770	43	18,806	5,821	9,748	23,938	14,607
South Carolina	167,253	312,191	2,507,149	12,443,510	44,105	41,327	98,693	17,685	132,925	124,594	395,999
Tennessee	335,317	2,773,820	15,856,880	55,084,075	247,254	102,983	243,197	63,970	336,529	826,783	1,828,690
Texas	66,841	293,308	4,835,284	37,425,194	424,504	61,322	428,048	132,407	2,933,588	714,351	1,202,445
Utah	800	56,891	172,382	2,149,814	11,068	2,879	17,563	3,479	18,138	59,672	3,150
Vermont	1,238,929	181,268	4,320,619	23,888,835	65,015	252	180,285	27,809	112,741	580,347	46,343
Virginia	686,862	556,307	8,375,975	28,187,669	152,899	26,903	188,471	45,987	277,285	370,145	674,670
Washington	19,705	28,890	292,280	2,103,343	11,138	943	16,938	2,181	28,135	44,063	17,491
West Virginia	363,668	615,412	4,914,792	17,175,420	90,479	2,139	104,434	18,937	178,309	552,327	268,031
Wisconsin	1,327,618	338,423	11,914,643	45,310,882	252,019	4,195	308,377	53,615	331,302	1,069,282	512,778
Wyoming	......	175	11,712	441,795	584	283	707	922	9,501	6,409	146

STATES AND TERRITORIES.	PRODUCED.									
	WHEAT.		Rye.	Indian corn.	Oats.	Barley.	Buckwheat.	Rice.	Tobacco.	Cotton.
	Spring.	Winter.								
	Bushels. 112,549,733	Bushels. 175,195,893	Bushels. 16,918,795	Bushels. 760,944,549	Bushels. 282,107,157	Bushels. 29,761,305	Bushels. 9,821,721	Pounds. 73,635,021	Pounds. 262,735,341	Bales. 3,011,996
Total United States										
Alabama	201,086	853,982	18,977	16,977,948	770,866	5,174	144	222,945	152,742	429,482
Arizona	27,052	....	....	32,041	25	55,077	....	....	100	....
Arkansas	72,347	669,389	27,645	13,382,145	528,777	1,921	226	73,021	594,886	247,968
California	16,676,702	....	26,275	1,221,222	1,757,507	8,783,490	21,928	....	63,809	34
Colorado	255,939	2,535	5,235	231,903	332,940	35,141	178	....	890	....
Connecticut	2,085	36,059	289,057	1,570,364	1,114,595	26,458	148,155	....	8,328,798	....
Dakota	170,460	202	....	133,140	114,327	4,118	179	....	....	....
Delaware	137	895,340	10,222	3,010,390	554,388	1,799	1,349	....	250	....
District of Columbia	....	3,782	3,724	28,020	8,500	....	7	....	....	....
Florida	....	....	545	2,225,056	114,204	12	....	401,687	157,405	39,789
Georgia	308,890	1,818,127	82,549	17,646,459	1,904,601	5,640	402	22,277,380	288,596	473,934
Idaho	73,725	1,925	1,756	5,750	100,119	72,316	....	....	....	....
Illinois	10,133,207	19,995,198	2,456,578	129,921,395	42,780,851	2,480,460	168,862	....	5,249,274	465
Indiana	161,991	27,585,231	457,468	51,094,538	8,590,409	356,262	80,231	....	9,325,392	3
Iowa	28,708,312	727,380	505,807	68,935,065	21,005,142	1,960,779	109,432	....	71,792	7
Kansas	1,314,522	1,076,676	85,297	17,025,525	4,097,925	98,405	27,826	....	33,241	7
Kentucky	38,532	5,690,172	1,108,933	50,091,006	6,620,103	238,486	3,443	....	105,305,869	1,080
Louisiana	1,157	8,749	984	7,596,628	17,782	1,226	260	15,854,012	15,541	350,832
Maine	274,593	4,200	34,115	1,089,888	2,351,354	658,816	466,635	....	15	....

Maryland	1,095	5,773,408	307,080	11,701,817	3,221,643	11,315	77,867		15,785,339	
Massachusetts	17,574	17,074	239,227	1,397,807	797,664	133,071	58,049		7,312,885	
Michigan	268,810	15,996,963	144,508	14,086,238	8,954,466	834,558	436,755		5,385	
Minnesota	18,789,188	76,885	78,088	4,743,117	10,678,264	1,032,024	52,438		8,247	564,938
Mississippi	66,638	207,841	14,852	15,637,316	414,586	3,973	1,619	374,627	61,012	1,246
Missouri	1,093,905	13,222,021	559,532	66,034,075	16,578,313	269,240	36,252		12,320,483	
Montana	177,535	3,649	1,141	320	149,367	85,756	988		600	
Nebraska	2,109,321	15,765	13,532	4,736,710	1,477,562	216,481	3,471		5,988	166
Nevada	147,987	80,819	310	9,660	55,916	295,452	985		25	
New Hampshire	189,222	4,399	47,420	1,277,768	1,146,451	105,822	100,034		155,334	
New Jersey	2,099	2,299,334	566,775	8,745,384	4,009,830	8,283	353,983		40,871	
New Mexico	338,930	13,892	42	640,823	67,660	3,876	10		8,587	
New York	1,834,330	10,344,132	2,478,125	16,462,825	35,293,625	7,434,621	3,904,030		2,349,798	144,935
North Carolina	405,238	2,454,641	352,006	18,454,215	3,220,105	3,186	20,109	2,059,281	11,150,087	
Ohio	256,400	27,625,759	846,890	67,501,144	25,347,549	1,715,221	180,341		18,741,973	
Oregon	1,794,494	546,252	3,890	72,138	2,029,909	210,736	1,645		3,847	
Pennsylvania	322,328	19,350,639	3,577,641	34,702,006	36,478,585	529,562	2,532,173		3,467,539	
Rhode Island	588	196	20,214	311,957	157,010	33,559	1,444		796	
South Carolina	317,700	465,910	36,165	7,614,207	613,593	4,752	312	32,304,825	34,805	224,500
Tennessee	375,400	5,813,516	223,335	41,343,614	4,513,315	75,068	77,437	3,399	21,465,452	181,842
Texas	66,173	348,939	28,521	20,554,538	762,663	44,351	44	63,844	59,706	350,628
Utah	543,487	14,986	1,312	95,557	65,650	49,117	178		72,671	22
Vermont	438,155	16,548	73,346	1,699,882	3,602,430	117,333	415,096		37,086,364	
Virginia	7,389	7,391,398	582,264	17,649,304	6,857,555	7,259	45,075		1,682	183
Washington	186,180	30,863	4,453	21,781	255,169	55,787	316		2,046,452	
West Virginia	3,395	2,480,148	277,746	8,197,865	2,413,749	50,363	82,916		960,813	2
Wisconsin	24,375,435	1,230,909	1,325,294	15,033,998	20,180,016	1,645,019	408,897			
Wyoming					100					

PRODUCED

STATES AND TERRITORIES	Wool.	Peas and beans.	POTATOES.		Wine.	DAIRY PRODUCTS.			Hay.	SEED.	
			Irish.	Sweet.		Butter.	Cheese.	Milk solid.		Clover.	Grass.
	Pounds.	*Bushels.*	*Bushels.*	*Bushels.*	*Gallons.*	*Pounds.*	*Pounds.*	*Gallons.*	*Tons.*	*Bushels.*	*Bushels.*
Total United States ...	100,102,387	5,746,027	143,337,473	21,709,824	3,092,330	514,092,683	53,492,153	235,500,599	27,316,048	639,657	583,188
Alabama	381,253	156,574	162,512	1,871,360	5,156	3,213,753	2,732	104,657	10,613	17	139
Arizona	679	3,417	575	16	......	800	14,500	4,800	109	......	......
Arkansas	214,784	47,376	422,196	890,631	3,734	2,753,931	2,119	31,350	6,839	42	143
California	11,391,743	380,010	2,049,227	202,035	1,814,656	7,969,744	3,395,074	3,693,021	551,773	1,353	976
Colorado	204,925	7,500	121,442	60	67	392,920	33,626	19,520	19,787	......	......
Connecticut	254,129	13,038	2,789,894	867	27,414	6,716,007	2,031,194	6,253,259	563,328	1,725	4,471
Dakota	8,810	456	50,177	......	......	209,735	1,850	......	13,347	......	......
Delaware	58,316	3,123	362,724	85,309	1,552	1,171,963	315	758,603	41,890	2,228	60
District of Columbia	......	40	27,367	5,790	900	4,495	......	126,077	2,019	......	......
Florida	37,562	64,846	10,218	789,456	681	100,989	25	3,002	17	......	......
Georgia	846,947	410,020	197,101	2,621,562	21,927	4,499,572	4,292	109,139	10,518	143	540
Idaho	3,415	610	64,534	......	......	111,480	4,464	11,250	6,985	......	14
Illinois	5,739,249	115,854	10,944,790	322,641	111,882	36,083,405	1,661,703	9,258,545	2,747,339	10,486	153,464
Indiana	5,029,023	35,526	5,399,044	150,705	19,479	22,915,385	283,807	936,983	1,076,768	61,168	17,377
Iowa	2,967,043	42,313	5,914,620	34,292	37,518	27,512,179	1,087,741	688,800	1,777,339	2,475	53,432
Kansas	335,005	13,109	2,342,988	49,533	14,889	5,022,758	226,607	196,662	490,289	334	8,023
Kentucky	2,234,450	119,926	2,391,062	802,114	62,360	11,874,978	115,219	1,345,779	204,399	2,551	35,896
Louisiana	140,428	26,888	67,695	1,023,706	578	322,405	11,747	833,928	8,776	1	......
Maine	1,774,168	264,502	7,771,009	354	7,047	11,636,482	1,152,590	1,374,091	1,053,415	5,255	3,859

Maryland	435,213	57,556	1,632,205	218,706	11,583	5,014,729	6,732	1,520,101	223,119	35,040	2,609
Massachusetts	306,659	24,690	3,025,446	917	10,956	6,559,161	2,245,873	15,284,057	597,455	252	464
Michigan	8,726,145	349,365	10,318,799	3,651	21,832	24,400,185	670,804	2,277,122	1,290,923	49,918	2,590
Minnesota	401,185	46,601	1,943,063	1,594	1,750	9,522,010	233,977	208,130	695,053	126	3,045
Mississippi	288,285	176,417	214,189	1,743,432	3,055	2,613,521	3,099	17,052	8,324	6	82
Missouri	3,649,390	43,986	4,238,361	241,253	326,173	14,455,825	204,090	857,704	615,611	2,494	12,246
Montana	100	2,414	91,477	......	470	408,080	25,603	105,186	18,727	......	31
Nebraska	74,655	3,332	739,984	762	711	1,539,535	46,142	95,059	169,354	......	133
Nevada	27,029	414	129,249	......	......	110,880	......	63,850	33,855	7	64
New Hampshire	1,129,442	58,375	4,515,419	160	2,446	5,965,080	849,118	2,352,884	612,648	697	1,775
New Jersey	336,609	56,221	4,705,439	1,550,784	24,970	8,266,023	38,229	5,373,323	521,975	26,366	72,401
New Mexico	684,930	28,856	3,102	......	19,686	12,912	27,239	813	4,209	......	......
New York	10,599,225	1,152,541	28,547,593	10,656	82,607	107,147,526	22,769,964	135,775,919	5,614,205	98,837	57,225
North Carolina	799,667	532,749	738,803	3,071,840	62,348	4,297,834	75,185	75,145	83,540	651	1,002
Ohio	20,539,643	45,443	11,192,814	230,295	212,912	50,266,372	8,169,486	22,275,344	2,289,565	102,355	48,811
Oregon	1,080,638	12,575	481,710	1,970	1,751	1,418,373	79,333	107,367	75,357	10	1,210
Pennsylvania	6,561,722	39,574	12,889,367	131,572	97,165	60,834,644	1,145,209	14,411,729	2,848,219	200,679	50,642
Rhode Island	77,328	9,920	669,408	142	765	941,199	81,976	1,944,044	89,045	954	1,938
South Carolina	156,314	460,378	83,252	1,342,165	13,179	1,461,980	169	241,815	10,665	5,830	1,878
Tennessee	1,389,762	194,535	1,124,337	1,205,683	15,778	9,571,069	142,240	415,786	116,582	8,564	11,153
Texas	1,251,328	42,654	208,383	2,188,041	6,216	3,712,747	34,342	62,771	18,982	7	497
Utah	109,018	9,291	323,645	163	3,131	310,335	69,603	11,240	27,305	......	5
Vermont	3,102,137	95,242	5,157,428	96	1,038	17,844,396	4,830,700	3,835,840	1,020,669	785	4,613
Virginia	877,110	162,102	1,293,853	865,882	26,283	6,979,269	71,743	266,812	199,883	11,367	12,709
Washington	162,713	15,790	280,719	425	235	407,306	17,465	21,060	30,233	179	1,387
West Virginia	1,593,541	31,449	1,053,507	46,984	6,093	5,044,475	32,429	144,895	224,164	3,939	3,868
Wisconsin	4,090,670	388,425	6,646,129	2,220	9,357	22,473,036	1,591,798	2,059,105	1,287,651	2,906	13,016
Wyoming	30,000	4	617	......	......	1,200	......	4,980	3,180	......	......

STATES AND TERRITORIES	Hops	Hemp	Flax	Flaxseed	Silk cocoons	SUGAR			MOLASSES			BEES	
						Cane.	Sorghum.	Maple.	Cane.	Sorghum.	Maple.	Wax.	Honey.
	Pounds.	Tons.	Pounds.	Bushels.	Pounds.	Hhds.	Hhds.	Pounds.	Gallons.	Gallons.	Gallons.	Pounds.	Pounds.
Total United States	25,456,669	12,746	27,133,034	1,730,444	3,937	87,043	24	28,443,645	6,593,323	16,050,089	921,057	631,129	14,702,815
Alabama	32		37	2		31			166,009	267,269	3	22,767	320,674
Arizona	25												
Arkansas		200	420	104		92		1,185	72,008	147,203	75	12,789	276,824
California	625,064		31,740	13,294	3,587					333		4,903	294,326
Colorado	1,004												
Connecticut			300	4				14,266		6,832	168	1,326	32,158
Dakota										1,230		6	110
Delaware	800		878	356						65,908		800	33,158
District of Columbia													
Florida						952			344,339			6,052	50,884
Georgia	2					644			553,192	374,027		31,233	610,877
Idaho	21		983	48	14								
Illinois	104,032	174	2,204,606	280,043				136,873		1,960,473	10,378	46,262	1,547,178
Indiana	63,884	22	37,771	401,931				1,332,332		2,026,212	227,880	12,049	395,278
Iowa	171,113	4	695,518	88,621			15	146,490		1,218,636	9,315	2,225	853,213
Kansas	396	35	1,040	1,553				938		449,409	212	2,208	110,827
Kentucky	947	7,777	237,268	14,657	45			269,416		1,740,453	49,073	32,557	1,171,500
Louisiana					1	80,706			4,585,150	180		2,363	37,646
Maine	296,850		5,435	227				160,805			28,470	5,253	155,640

State	1	2	3	4	5	6	7	8	9	10	11	12	13
Maryland	2,800		30,760	1,541				70,464		28,563	374	3,439	118,938
Massachusetts	61,910	2	930	52				399,800			2,326	1,195	25,299
Michigan	828,269		240,110	5,528				1,781,855		94,686	23,637	14,571	280,325
Minnesota	222,065		122,571	18,635				210,467		38,735	12,722	3,963	92,606
Mississippi		3	100	2	31	49		125	152,164	67,509		9,390	199,581
Missouri	19,297	2,816	16,613	10,391	3	49		116,980		1,730,171	16,317	35,248	1,156,444
Montana													
Nebraska	100		54	404				10		77,598		707	28,114
Nevada										3,651			363
New Hampshire	99,469		177	6				1,800,704			16,884	2,668	56,941
New Jersey	19,033	5	234,061	6,095				419		17,424	5	2,021	60,636
New Mexico										1,765			
New York	17,558,681	6	3,670,818	92,519				6,692,040		7,832	46,048	86,333	896,286
North Carolina	101,236		59,552	6,756	95	35		21,257	33,888	621,855	418	109,054	1,404,640
Ohio		25	17,880,624	631,894				3,469,128		2,023,427	352,612	22,488	763,124
Oregon	9,745		40,474	10,988				11			30	1,207	66,858
Pennsylvania	90,688	571	815,906	15,624	1		9	1,545,917		213,373	39,385	27,033	796,989
Rhode Island	249									20		498	6,290
South Carolina	1,507		80,930	4,612	153	1,055		2	436,882	183,585		11,404	194,253
Tennessee	565	1,933	25	2		1,410		134,968	3,629	1,254,701	4,843	51,685	1,039,550
Texas	51	5				2,020			246,062	174,509	5,032	13,255	275,169
Utah	322		10							67,446		13	575
Vermont	527,927		12,899	444				8,894,302		329,155	12,023	5,235	142,932
Virginia	10,999	31	130,750	9,699	7			245,093		245,093	11,400	26,438	505,239
Washington	6,162							612		612		629	25,636
West Virginia	1,031	37	82,276	2,393				490,606		780,829	20,209	9,917	376,997
Wisconsin	4,630,155		497,398	112,019				507,192		74,478	31,218	9,945	299,341
Wyoming													

The Growth of

Commercial Agriculture,

1870-1914

Introduction

The first American agricultural revolution, triggered by the Civil War, led to the rapid commercialization of northern and western agriculture. This had occurred earlier in the South. The period from the Civil War to World War I saw a major expansion in acres farmed, number of farms, and total production. The nation's farm population reached its peak about World War I and declined thereafter. Between 1870 and 1880, farmers became less than one-half of the nation's workers even though the number of persons in farming continued to increase until World War I.

Many farm leaders believed that the nation had achieved its ultimate goal in land policy with the passage of the Homestead Act of 1862. Farmers henceforth would own the land that they worked. The goal came true for some, but for others it did not. The act was not suited to the region to which it applied. In the arid West, 160 acres was too much land for irrigated farming and too little for dry farming or grazing. For many years, Congress passed first one law and then another in an attempt to handle these problems.

Opportunities to establish easy and inexpensive methods of irrigating land were very limited. Congress responded in an attempt to ease the increasing per-acre cost of irrigation with the Desert Land Act of March 3, 1877. Under this law, a farmer could hold up to a section of land under promise to attempt to irrigate it. It proved of little benefit.

The Cary Act of 1894 granted each arid state up to a million acres of land to be sold at fifty cents an acre. The receipts were to be used to construct irrigation facilities. By 1902, only about 250,000 acres had been claimed under the act. Congress turned to the National Reclamation or Newlands Act of 1902. Basically, the act provided that the United States should plan and construct irrigation projects, with the water users paying back the cost over a period of time.

Timber was scarce in much of the West, but a valuable rescource in some areas. Congress, in the Timber Culture Act of 1873, offered homesteaders in relatively treeless areas an additional 160 acres of land if the claimant would plant trees on one-fourth of the area. The requirement was changed from time to time, but by 1904, less than 10 million acres had been granted under this law. On the other hand, the Timber and Stone Act of 1878 provided for the sale of 160-acre tracts of non-farm land for $2.50 an acre. Immense tracts of the nation's most valuable timber lands were virtually given away under these provisions.

In 1890, Congress limited the total amount of land any person could enter under the Homestead, Desert, Timber Culture, and other acts to 320 acres.

Congress granted larger homesteads in western Nebraska in 1904 in an effort to provide the grazing in areas not suited to farming. The provisions were later extended to other areas. The goal was desirable; the actions, late. By World War I, land policy was still being debated.

The other agricultural reform laws passed in 1862 — the Morrill Land Grant College Act and the law setting up the Department of Agriculture, as well as the Transcontinental Railroad Act — provided the bases needed for developing a more scientific approach to farming. Both the agricultural colleges and the Department were criticized in their early years. Their proponents had offered more than could be accomplished at once. However, over the years these institutions made possible an increasingly productive agriculture. This was particularly true after the passage of the Hatch Experiment Station Act in 1887. It provided for the establishment of at least one agricultural experiment station in each state.

The reports of the experiment stations indicate the broad scope of their investigations. They studied soil fertility and the effects of erosion, the usefulness of new machines and new seeds, the cure of animal diseases and the conquest of plant pests. But the stations won public support when their researchers reached farmers with useful, comparatively simple results that added to the productivity and profitability of farming. Soil analysis and recommendations of fertilizers to be used, means of controlling plant and animal diseases and pests, and the development of such simple and profitable marketing aids as the Babcock test for butterfat won farm support for the experiment stations and the colleges.

Both the stations and new Department of Agriculture sometimes urged the cultivation of crops that never became established. The Department's suggestions that farmers raise opium poppies and silk and its experiments with sorghum sugar had no effect on farming, although its work with sugar beets helped establish that industry.

The Department of Agriculture soon went far beyond simple experimentation and the collection of statistics. Its fight against animal diseases led to the establishment of a Bureau of Animal Industry. The Bureau found remedies for several diseases and controlled others by quarantine. European refusals to admit American meat on sanitary grounds led to the passage of the Meat Inspection Law of 1890 and the assignment of inspecting meat for export to the Bureau. Over the next several years, sentiment grew for meat inspection for U.S.-consumed meat. Novelist Upton Sinclair, in The Jungle, portrayed packing houses as unsanitary and worse. The Meat Inspection Act of 1906 instituted nationwide inspection by the Bureau of Animal Industry.

In 1881, pure-food laws were passed by Illinois, Michigan, New Jersey, and New York. A chemist in the Department of Agriculture, Harvey W. Wiley, began calling attention to food adulteration in the 1880's. In 1906, over strong opposition, Congress passed a Food and Drugs Act. Its enforcement was assigned to the Department of Agriculture until 1940.

The early 1900's was a period of many changes in government agricultural policy. In the field of conservation the Forest Service was established in 1905, with Gifford Pinchot as its chief. Both the state colleges and the Department became concerned with getting the results of research to farmers. Farm journals and fairs continued to encourage the adoption of better practices, but the public agencies realized that they had to make greater efforts. Boy's and girls' agricultural clubs were started in a number of states — the forerunners of the 4-H movement. State colleges and experiment stations carried their work to local farmers by means of institutes, using lectures and exhibits to get their messages across.

The need to control the cotton boll weevil led Seaman A. Knapp of the Department of Agriculture to carry the latest research results directly to farmers by local demonstrations, with the help of county agricultural agents. This led in 1914 to the passage of the Smith-Lever Act, establishing cooperative extension work carried out by county argricultural agents.

New lands were opened and improved farming practices were developed between the Civil War and World War I, but both economic problems and inadequacies in farm life plagued many farm families. The Bacon family, for example, in its efforts to establish a wine industry near Pasadena, California, had problems both in developing a good quality product and in marketing it.

The westward movement, now a part of American folklore, saw new lands become productive. At the same time, such families as that of John A. Sanborn, which left Illinois for Nebraska in 1885, faced a land that often seemed hostile. The family, because of economic pressure and isolation, sometimes did without not only amenities but what to many would have been necessities.

From the 1870's to the terrible winters of 1886 and 1887, the open-range cattle industry dominated the Great Plains. Thereafter, the open range gave way to ranching, where controlled grazing permitted better use of the grass and upbreeding of the herds. Many cowboys turned to farming; others spent much of the time between roundups and caring for the cattle in cutting hay and building fences of the newly-invented barbed wire. Around the turn of the century, the organization of national cattle growers' organizations was further evidence of the commercialization of the industry. Attempts continued to encourage Indians to turn to agriculture, but with little success.

Southern agriculture had a commercial orientation even in colonial days. After a period of some confusion after the Civil War, cotton, grown by tenants working under fixed contracts, dominated the economy. Southern farm journalists and scientists at the experiment stations urged diversification but with only limited success.

Over the years, beginning in 1867 with the establishment of the National Grange or Patrons of Husbandry, farmers attempted to alleviate economic and social problems through national organizations. The Grange emphasized improved farming methods, more opportunities for a wholesome social life, and cooperative marketing and purchasing. As the Grange declined in numbers and influence after 1875, the new Farmers' Alliances undertook many cooperative activities. After 1902 the Farmers' Union and the American Society of Equity aided the movement.

In the 1890's, the feeling on the part of many farmers and farm leaders that agriculture was not sharing in the national prosperity came to a head in the Populist political movement, growing out of the Alliances. In 1896, the Populist Party reached its high point. Failing to elect its candidate for President, the new political movement declined rapidly, although some of its goals were later achieved. For example, the free delivery of rural mails, Federally-sponsored rural credit facilities, and Federal regulation of futures trading developed within the next two decades. At the same time farming, so far as income and prices were concerned, about 1900 moved into a period of comparative equilibrium with the rest of the economy. This lasted through World War I.

Farm life, as portrayed in the Sanborn diaries and those of the Loomis family of Ionia, Michigan, had both its pleasures and its handicaps. In 1908, President Theodore Roosevelt appointed a Country Life Commission to report "upon the present condition of country life." Although the Commission's report, submitted to the President on January 23, 1903, had no immediate effect on policy, the government eventually took many of the actions recommended. Over the years, the report has remained one of our best comprehensive discussions of farm life in the years just before World War I, and one relevant to many problems of the 1970's.

Land Policies

Timber Act of 1873

From 17 U.S. Statutes at Large 605.

AN ACT TO ENCOURAGE THE GROWTH OF TIMBER ON WESTERN PRAIRIES

Be it enacted by the Senate and House of Representatives of the United States of America in Congress assembled, That any person who shall plant, protect, and keep in a healthy, growing condition for ten years forty acres of timber, the trees thereon not being more than twelve feet apart each way on any quarter-section of any of the public lands of the United States shall be entitled to a patent for the whole of said quarter-section at the expiration of said ten years, on making proof of such fact by not less than two credible witnesses; *Provided*, That only one quarter in any section shall be thus granted.

SECTION 2. That the person applying for the benefit of this act shall, upon application to the register of the land-office in which he or she is about to make such entry, make affidavit before said register or receiver that said entry is made for the cultivation of timber, and upon filing said affidavit with said register and receiver, and on payment of ten dollars, he or she shall thereupon be permitted to enter the quantity of land specified: *Provided however*, That no certificate shall be given or patent issue therefor until the expiration of at least ten years from the date of such entry; and if at the expiration of such time, or at any time within three years thereafter, the person making such entry, or if he or she be dead, his or her heirs or legal representatives, shall prove by two credible witnesses that he, she, or they have planted, and for not less than ten years have cultivated and protected such quantity and character of timber as aforesaid, they shall receive the patent for such quarter-section of land.

SECTION 3. That if at any time after the filing of said affidavit, and prior to the issuing of the patent for said land it shall be proven after due notice to the party making such entry and claiming to cultivate such timber, to the satisfaction of the register of the land-office that such person has abandoned or failed to cultivate, protect and keep in good condition such timber, then, and in that event, said land shall revert to the United States.

SECTION 4. That each and every person who, under the provisions of an act entitled ''An act to secure homesteads to actual settlers on the public domain'' approved May twentieth, eighteen hundred and sixty-two, or any amendment thereto, having a homestead on said public domain, who, at the end of the third year of his or her residence thereon, shall have had under cultivation, for two years, one acre of timber, the trees thereon not being more than twelve feet apart each way, and in a good, thrifty condition, for each and every sixteen acres of said homestead, shall upon due proof of said fact by two credible witnesses receive his or her patent for said homestead.

SECTION 5. That no land acquired under provisions of this act shall, in any event, become liable to the satisfaction of any debt or debts contracted prior to the issuing of patent therefor

SECTION 6. That the commissioner of the general land-office is hereby required to prepare and issue such rules and regulations, consistent with this act, as shall be necessary and proper to carry its provisions into effect; and that the registers and the receivers of the several land-offices shall be entitled to receive the same compensation for any lands entered under the provisions of this that they are now entitled to receive when the same quantity of land is entered with money.

SECTION 7. That the fifth section of the act entitled ''An act in addition to an act to punish crimes against the United States, and for other purposes'' approved March third, eighteen hundred and fifty-seven, shall extend to all oaths, affirmations, and affidavits required or authorized by this act.

Approved, March 3, 1873

Desert Land Act, 1877

From 19 U.S. Statutes at Large 377.

AN ACT TO PROVIDE FOR THE SALE OF DESERT LANDS IN CERTAIN STATES AND TERRITORIES—

Be it enacted by the Senate and House of Representatives of the United States of America in Congress assembled, That it shall be lawful for any citizen of the United States, or any person of requisite age ''who may be entitled to become a citizen, and who has filed his declaration to become such'' and upon payment of twentyfive cents per acre—to file a declaration under oath with the register and the receiver of the land district in which any desert land is situated, that he intends to reclaim a tract of desert land not exceeding one section, by conducting water upon the same, within the period of three years thereafter, *Provided however* that the right to the use of water by the person so conducting the same, on or to any tract of desert land of six hundred and forty acres shall depend upon bona fide prior appropriation: and such right shall not exceed the amount of water actually appropriated, and necessarily used for the purpose of irrigation and reclamation: and all surplus water over and above such actual appropriation and use, together with the water of all, lakes, rivers and other sources of water supply upon the public lands and not navigable, shall remain and be held free for the appropriation and use of the public for irrigation, mining and manufacturing purposes subject to existing rights. Said declaration shall describe particularly said section of land if surveyed, and, if unsurveyed, shall describe the same as nearly as possible without a survey. At any time within the period of three years after filing said declaration, upon making satisfactory proof to the register and receiver of the reclamation of said tract of land in the manner aforesaid, and upon the payment to the receiver of the additional sum of one dollar per acre for a tract of land not exceeding six hundred and forty acres to any one person, a patent for the same shall be issued to him. *Provided*, that no person shall be permitted to enter more than one tract of land and not to exceed six hundred and forty acres which shall be in compact form.

SECTION 2. That all lands exclusive of timber lands and mineral lands which will not, without irrigation, produce some agricultural crop, shall be deemed desert lands, within the meaning of this act, which fact shall be ascertained by proof of two or more credible witnesses under oath, whose affidavits shall be filed in the land office in which said tract of land may be situated—

SECTION 3. That this act shall only apply to and take effect in the States of California, Oregon and Nevada, and the Territories of Washington, Idaho, Montana, Utah, Wyoming Arizona, New Mexico and Dakota, and the determination of what may be considered desert land shall be subject to the decision and regulation of the Commissioner of the General Land Office.

Approved, March 3, 1877.

Act for Sale of Western Timber Lands, 1878

From 20 U.S. Statutes at Large 89.

AN ACT FOR THE SALE OF TIMBER LANDS IN THE STATES OF CALIFORNIA, OREGON, NEVADA AND IN WASHINGTON TERRITORY

Be it enacted by the Senate and House of Representatives of the United States of America in Congress assembled, That surveyed public lands of the United States within the States of California, Oregon and Nevada and in Washington Territory, not included within military, Indian, or other reservations of the United States, valuable chiefly for timber, but unfit for cultivation, and which have not been offered at public sale according to law, may be sold to citizens of the United States, or persons who have declared their intention to become such, in quantities not exceeding one hundred and sixty acres to any one person or association of persons, at the minimum price of two dollars and fifty cents per acre; and lands valuable chiefly for stone may be sold on the same terms as timber lands: *Provided,* That nothing herein contained shall defeat or impair any bona-fide claim under any law of the United States, or authorize the sale of any mining claim, or the improvements of any bona-fide settler, or lands containing gold, silver, cinnabar, copper, or coal; or lands selected by the said States under any law of the United States donating lands for internal improvements, education, or other purposes: *And provided further,* That none of the rights conferred by the act approved July twenty-sixth, eighteen hundred and sixty-six, entitled "An act granting the right of way to ditch and canal owners over the public lands, and for other purposes", shall be abrogated by this act; and all patents granted shall be subject to any vested and accrued water rights, or rights to ditches and reservoirs used in connection with such water rights, as may have been acquired under and by the provisions of said act; and such rights shall be expressly reserved in any patent issued under this act.

SEC. 2. That any person desiring to avail himself of the provisions of this act shall file with the register of the proper district a written statement in duplicate, one of which is to be transmitted to the General Land Office, designating by legal subdivisions the particular tract of land he desires to purchase, setting forth that the same is unfit for cultivation, and valuable chiefly for its timber or stone; that it is uninhabited; contains no mining or other improvements, except for ditch or canal purposes, where any such do exist, save such as were made by or belong to the applicant, nor, as deponent verily believes, any valuable deposit of gold, silver, cinnabar, copper, or coal; that deponent has made no other application under this act; that he does not apply to purchase the same on speculation, but in good faith to appropriate it to his own exclusive use and benefit; and that he has not, directly or indirectly, made any agreement or contract, in any way or manner, with any person or persons whatsoever, by which the title which he might acquire from the government of the United States should inure, in whole or in part, to the benefit of any person except himself; which statement must be verified by the oath of the applicant before the register or the receiver of the land-office within the district where the land is situated; and if any person taking such oath shall swear falsely in the premises, he shall be subject to all the pains and penalties of perjury, and shall forfeit the money which he may have paid for said lands, and all right and title to the same; and any grant or conveyance which he may have made, except in the hands of bona-fide purchasers, shall be null and void.

SEC. 3. That upon the filing of said statement, as provided in the second section of this act, the register of the land office, shall post a notice of such application, embracing a description of the land by legal subdivisions, in his office, for a period of sixty days, and shall furnish the applicant a copy of the same for publication, at the expense of such applicant, in a newspaper published nearest the location of the premises, for a like period of time; and after the expiration of said sixty days, if no adverse claim shall have been filed, the person desiring to purchase shall furnish to the register of the land-office satisfactory evidence, first, that said notice of the application prepared by the register as aforesaid was duly published in a newspaper as herein required; secondly, that the land is of the character contemplated in this act, unoccupied and without improvements, other than those excepted, either mining or agricultural, and that it apparently contains no valuable deposits of gold, silver, cinnabar, copper, or coal; and upon payment to the proper officer of the purchase-money of said land, together with the fees of the register and the receiver, as provided for in case of mining claims in the twelfth section of the act approved May tenth, eighteen hundred and seventy-two, the applicant may be permitted to enter said tract, and, on the transmission to the General Land Office of the papers and testimony in the case, a patent shall issue thereon: *Provided,* That any person having a valid claim to any portion of the land may object, in writing, to the issuance of a patent to lands so held by him, stating the nature of his claim thereto; and evidence shall be taken, and the merits of said objection shall be determined by the officers of the land-office, subject to appeal, as in other land cases. Effect shall be given to the foregoing provisions of this act by regulations to be prescribed by the Commissioner of the General Land Office.

SEC. 4. That after the passage of this act it shall be unlawful to cut, or cause or procure to be cut, or wantonly destroy, any timber growing on any lands of the United States, in said States and Territory or remove, or cause to be removed, any timber from said public lands, with intent to export or dispose of the same; and no owner, master, or consignee of any vessel, or owner, director, or agent of any railroad, shall knowingly transport the same, or any lumber manufactured therefrom; and any person violating the provisions of this section shall be guilty of a misdemeanor, and, on conviction, shall be fined for every such offense a sum not less than one hundred nor more than one thousand dollars: *Provided,* That nothing herein contained shall prevent any miner or agriculturist from clearing his land in the ordinary working of his mining claim, or preparing his farm for tillage, or from taking the timber necessary to support his improvements, or the taking of timber for the use of the United States; and the penalties herein provided shall not take effect until ninety days after the passage of this act.

SEC. 5. That any person prosecuted in said States and Territory for violating section two thousand four hundred and sixty-one of the Revised Statutes of the United States who is not prosecuted for cutting timber for export from the United States, may be relieved from further prosecution and liability therefor upon payment, into the court wherein said action is pending, of the sum of two dollars and fifty cents per acre for all lands on which he shall have cut or caused to be cut timber, or removed or caused to be removed the same: *Provided,* That nothing contained in this section shall be construed as granting to the person hereby relieved the title to said lands for said payment; but he shall have the right to purchase the same upon the same terms and conditions as other persons, as provided hereinbefore in this act: *And further provided,* That all moneys collected under this act shall be covered into the Treasury of the United States. And section four thousand seven hundred and fifty-one of the Revised Statutes is hereby repealed, so far as it relates to the States and Territory herein named.

SEC. 6. That all acts and parts of acts inconsistent with the provisions of this act are hereby repealed.

Approved, June 3, 1878.

Act Limiting Entry of Public Lands, 1889

From 25 U.S. Statutes at Large 854.

AN ACT TO WITHDRAW CERTAIN PUBLIC LANDS FROM PRIVATE ENTRY, AND FOR OTHER PURPOSES

Be it enacted by the Senate and House of Representatives of the United States of America in Congress assembled, That from and after the passage of this act no public lands of the United States, except those in the State of Missouri shall be subject to private entry.

SEC. 2. That any person who has not heretofore perfected title to a tract of land of which he has made entry under the homestead law, may make a homestead entry of not exceeding one-quarter section of public land subject to such entry, such previous filing or entry to the contrary notwithstanding; but this right shall not apply to persons who perfect title to lands under the pre-emption or homestead laws already initiated: *Provided,* That all pre-emption settlers upon the public lands whose claims have been initiated prior to the passage of this act may change such entries to homestead entries and proceed to perfect their titles to their respective claims under the homestead law notwithstanding they may have heretofore had the benefit of such law, but such settlers who perfect title to such claims under the homestead law shall not thereafter be entitled to enter other lands under the pre-emption or homestead laws of the United States.

SEC. 3. That whenever it shall be made to appear to the register and receiver of any public land office, under such regulations as the Secretary of the Interior may prescribe, that any settler upon the public domain under existing law is unable by reason of a total or partial destruction or failure of crops, sickness, or other unavoidable casualty, to secure a support for himself, herself, or those dependent upon him or her upon the lands settled upon, then such register and receiver may grant to such settler a leave of absence from the claim upon which he or she has filed for a period not exceeding one year at any one time, and such settler so granted leave of absence shall forfeit no rights by reason of such absence: *Provided,* That the time of such actual absence shall not be deducted from the actual residence required by law.

SEC. 4. That the price of all sections and parts of sections of the public lands within the limits of the portions of the several grants of lands to aid in the construction of rail roads which have been heretofore and which may hereafter be forfeited, which were by the act making such grants or have since been increased to the double minimum price, and, also, of all lands within the limits of any such railroad grant, but not embraced in such grant lying adjacent to and coterminous with the portions of the line of any such railroad which shall not be completed at the date of this act, is hereby fixed at one dollar and twenty-five cents per acre.

SEC. 5. That any homestead settler who has heretofore entered less than one-quarter section of land may enter other and additional land lying contiguous to the original entry, which shall not, with the land first entered and occupied, exceed in the aggregate one hundred and sixty acres without proof of residence upon and cultivation of the additional entry; and if final proof of settlement and cultivation has been made for the original entry, when the additional entry is made, then the patent shall issue without further proof: *Provided,* That this section shall not apply to or for the benefit of any person who at the date of making application for entry hereunder does not own and occupy the lands covered by his original entry: *And provided,* That if the original entry should fail for any reason, prior to patent or should appear to be illegal or fraudulent, the additional entry shall not be permitted, or if having been initiated shall be canceled.

SEC. 6. That every person entitled, under the provisions of the homestead laws, to enter a homestead, who has heretofore complied with or who shall hereafter comply with the conditions of said laws, and who shall have made his final proof thereunder for a quantity of land less than one hundred and sixty acres and received the receiver's final receipt therefor, shall be entitled under said laws to enter as a personal right, and not assignable, by legal subdivisions of the public lands of the United States subject to homestead entry, so much additional land as added to the quantity previously so entered by him shall not exceed one hundred and sixty acres: *Provided,* That in no case shall patent issue for the land covered by such additional entry until the person making such additional entry shall have actually and in conformity with the homestead laws resided upon and cultivated the lands so additionally entered and otherwise fully complied with such laws: *Provided, also,* That this section shall not be construed as affecting any rights as to location of soldiers certificates heretofore issued under section two thousand three hundred and six of the Revised Statutes.

SEC. 7. That the "act to provide additional regulations for homestead and pre-emption entries of public lands," approved March third, eighteen hundred and seventy-nine, shall not be construed to forbid the taking of testimony for final proof within ten days following the day advertised as upon which such final proof shall be made, in cases where accident or unavoidable delays have prevented the applicant or witnesses from making such proof on the date specified.

SEC. 8. That nothing in this act shall be construed as suspending, repealing or in any way rendering inoperative the provisions of the act entitled, "An act to provide for the disposal of abandoned and useless military reservations," approved July fifth, eighteen hundred and eighty-four.

Approved, March 2, 1889.

Law Limiting Public Land Entries to 320 Acres, 1890

From *Limitations*, **August 30, 1890; 26 U.S. Statutes at Large 391.**

No person who shall after the passage of this act, enter upon any of the public lands with a view to occupation, entry or settlement under any of the land laws shall be permitted to acquire title to more than three hundred and twenty acres in the aggregate, under all of said laws, but this limitation shall not operate to curtail the right of any person who has heretofore made entry or settlement on the public lands, or whose occupation, entry or settlement, is validated by this act: *Provided,* That in all patents for lands hereafter taken up under any of the land laws of the United States or on entries or claims validated by this act west of the one hundredth meridian, it shall be expressed that there is reserved from the lands in said patent described, a right of way thereon for ditches or canals constructed by the authority of the United States.

Law Limiting Entries on Public Lands

From *Commutation Clause,* March 3, 1891; 26 U.S. Statutes at Large 1098.

. . . the Revised Statutes, be, and the same are hereby, amended, so that they shall read as follows:

SEC. 2289. Every person who is the head of a family, or who has arrived at the age of twenty-one years, and is a citizen of the United States, or who has filed his declaration of intention to become such, as required by the naturalization laws, shall be entitled to enter one-quarter section, or a less quantity, of unappropriated public lands, to be located in a body in conformity to the legal subdivisions of the public lands; but no person who is the proprietor of more than one hundred and sixty acres of land in any State or Territory, shall acquire any right under the homestead law. And every person owning and residing on land may, under the provisions of this section, enter other land lying contiguous to his land, which shall not, with the land so already owned and occupied, exceed in the aggregate one hundred and sixty acres.

SEC. 2290. That any person applying to enter land under the preceding section shall first make and subscribe before the proper officer and file in the proper land office an affidavit that he or she is the head of a family, or is over twenty-one years of age, and that such application is honestly and in good faith made for the purpose of actual settlement and cultivation, and not for the benefit of any other person, persons or corporation, and that he or she will faithfully and honestly endeavor to comply with all the requirements of law as to settlement, residence, and cultivation necessary to acquire title to the land applied for; that he or she is not acting as agent of any person, corporation, or syndicate in making such entry, nor in collusion with any person, corporation, or syndicate to give them the benefit of the land entered, or any part thereof, or the timber thereon; that he or she does not apply to enter the same for the purpose of speculation, but in good faith to obtain a home for himself, or herself, and that he or she has not directly or indirectly made, and will not make, any agreement or contract in any way or manner, with any person or persons, corporation or syndicate whatsoever, by which the title which he or she might acquire from the Government of the United States should inure, in whole or in part, to the benefit of any person, except himself, or herself, and upon filing such affidavit with the register or receiver on payment of five dollars when the entry is of not more than eighty acres, and on payment of ten dollars when the entry is for more than eighty acres, he or she shall thereupon be permitted to enter the amount of land specified.''

SEC. 6. That section twenty-three hundred and one of the Revised Statutes be amended so as to read as follows:

"SEC. 2301. Nothing in this chapter shall be so construed as to prevent any person who shall hereafter avail himself of the benefits of section twenty-two hundred and eighty nine from paying the minimum price for the quantity of land so entered at any time after the expiration of fourteen calendar months from the date of such entry, and obtaining a patent therefor, upon making proof of settlement and of residence and cultivation for such period of fourteen months,'' and the provision of this section shall apply to lands on the ceded portion of the Sioux Reservation by act approved March second, eighteen hundred and eighty-nine, in South Dakota, but shall not relieve said settlers from any payments now required by law.

Carey Irrigation Act, 1894

From 28 U.S. Statutes at Large 422.

SEC. 4. That to aid the public land States in the reclamation of the desert lands therein, and the settlement, cultivation and sale thereof in small tracts to actual settlers, the Secretary of the Interior with the approval of the President, be, and hereby is, authorized and empowered, upon proper application of the State to contract and agree, from time to time, with each of the States in which there may be situated desert lands as defined by the Act entitled ''An Act to provide for the sale of desert land in certain States and Territories,'' approved March third, eighteen hundred and seventy-seven, and the Act amendatory thereof, approved March third, eighteen hundred and ninety-one, binding the United States to donate, grant and patent to the State free of cost for survey or price such desert lands, not exceeding one million acres in each State, as the State may cause to be irrigated, reclaimed occupied, and not less than twenty acres of each one hundred and sixty-acre tract cultivated by actual settlers, within ten years next after the passage of this Act, as thoroughly as is required of citizens who may enter under the said desert land law.

Before the application of any State is allowed or any contract or agreement is executed or any segregation of any of the land from the public domain is ordered by the Secretary of the Interior, the State shall file a map of the said land proposed to be irrigated which shall exhibit a plan showing the mode of the contemplated irrigation and which plan shall be sufficient to thoroughly irrigate and reclaim said land and prepare it to raise ordinary agricultural crops and shall also show the source of the water to be used for irrigation and reclamation, and the Secretary of the Interior may make necessary regulations for the reservation of the lands applied for by the States to date from the date of the filing of the map and plan of irrigation, but such reservation shall be of no force whatever if such map and plan of irrigation shall not be approved. That any State contracting under this section is hereby authorized to make all necessary contracts to cause the said lands to be reclaimed, and to induce their settlement and cultivation in accordance with and subject to the provisions of this section; but the State shall not be authorized to lease any of said lands or to use or dispose of the same in any way whatever, except to secure their reclamation, cultivation and settlement.

As fast as any State may furnish satisfactory proof according to such rules and regulations as may be prescribed by the Secretary of the Interior, that any of said lands are irrigated, reclaimed and occupied by actual settlers, patents shall be issued to the State or its assigns for said lands so reclaimed and settled: *Provided,* That said States shall not sell or dispose of more than one hundred and sixty acres of said lands to any one person, and any surplus of money derived by any State from the sale of said lands in excess of the cost of their reclamation, shall be held as a trust fund for and be applied to the reclamation of other desert lands in such State. That to enable the Secretary of the Interior to examine any of the lands that may be selected under the provisions of this section, there is hereby appropriated out of any moneys in the Treasury, not otherwise appropriated, one thousand dollars.

Approved, August 18, 1894.

House Debate on Newlands Act, 1902

From *Congressional Record,* 57th Cong., 1st Sess., XXXV, pp. 6673, 6745, 6749.

FRANCIS NEWLANDS (Dem., Nev.): Mr. Speaker, I had hoped that the House would immediately adopt this rule and that we would proceed to debate the pending irrigation bill pursuant to its terms; but the gentleman from Indiana [Mr. ROBINSON], on the consideration of this rule, has seen fit to arraign his party associates upon this side of the House, his party associates on the Committee on Rules, his party associates on the Committee on Irrigation, his party associates on the Democratic Congressional campaign committee, and has seen fit to assure this side of the House that all these gentlemen have been deceived into the support of a purely Republican policy and a purely Republican measure which has the advocacy and support of President Roosevelt.

Now, I contend, Mr. Speaker, that this is a nonpartisan measure; that it is in harmony with the platforms of all parties in the last campaign; that it is in harmony with the enlightened sentiment of the country, which has gradually been formulating itself upon this subject and which found its expression in the party platforms.

It is also in harmony with the opinion of the Senators and Representatives from the arid and semiarid States and Territories regardless of politics. Every Senator and every Representative from that great region has supported this measure.

Now, the gentleman insists that we have been driven by the President into this report of a Republican measure. Let me give the gentleman the history of this measure. For years the arid States have been insisting upon some action by the Federal Government in reference to the arid public lands, composing as they do in some States 95 per cent of their entire area, and they have been insisting that it is the duty of the Government to prepare these lands for settlement, so that the States in which they are located may become populated.

They urged for a long time the cession of these lands to the States. But Congress, regarding this great public domain as a public trust, not to be lightly turned over to sparsely settled States to be managed according to the judgment or lack of judgment, the discretion or indiscretion, the honesty or dishonesty, the providence or improvidence, of State legislatures, regarding it as a heritage for the entire Union, to be preserved for our unborn millions, has refused in its wisdom a cession to the States. So, at last, after the subject had been debated in and out of Congress for twenty years or more, the two parties in 1896 met in their respective conventions and formulated their expression on this subject, almost identical in terms—certainly identical in spirit.

Both parties declared in favor of the reclamation of these arid lands by the National Government and the holding of such lands for actual settlers, and in so declaring they but followed the general sentiment of the country, which was against any abandonment of its trust by the National Government and its surrender to the States.

As soon as that campaign was over I sought to shape a measure which would be in harmony with the two platforms and in harmony with the general sentiment of the country. At the last session of Congress, and before Mr. Roosevelt came into power, I introduced a bill which was the result of careful study of legislation prior to that time, and of consultation with the Secretary of the Interior, the Secretary of Agriculture, the Director of Geological Survey, the chief hydrographer of the Survey, the chairman of the National Irrigation Association, and other well-informed and experienced men on this subject.

Its purpose was to present a settlement of the entire question, to relieve the Treasury of the United States of any burden and simply to devote the proceeds of the sales of lands in the arid regions to the conservation of flood waters, so as to make the waters available for settlers, who would do the actual work of reclamation. The purpose was to present a comprehensive plan, which would impose no burden on the taxpayers of the country, which would enable the West to reclaim itself, and which would preserve this vast domain for home builders, and save it from concentrated and monopolistic holdings.

And if the gentleman will examine that bill—introduced in Congress before Mr. Roosevelt became President—he will find that it is identical in its provisions, though differing somewhat in phraseology, with the bill which is now before us for consideration. That bill, after its introduction, was presented to a meeting

JOHN SNOOK (Dem., Ohio): Mr. Chairman and gentlemen of the committee, the part of section 4 which I seek to amend now reads as follows: that upon the determination of the Secretary of the Interior that any irrigation project is practicable, he may cause to be let contracts for the construction of the same, in whole or in part, providing the necessary funds therefor are available in the reclamation fund, and thereupon he shall give public notice of the lands irrigated under such project. If amended will read as follows: "That upon the determination of the Secretary of the Interior that any irrigation project is practicable, he may cause to be let contracts for the construction of same, providing the necessary funds for the entire completion thereof are available in the reclamation fund, and thereupon he shall give public notice of the lands irrigated under such project."

It has been claimed by the friends of this bill in every part of the debate so far as I have heard that they do not intend, or at least they have intimated that they do not intend, to fasten upon the Government as a permanent policy the making of appropriations from year to year for the purpose of reclaiming these lands.

It was urged against this bill by the able gentleman who made the minority report that this section, as reported by the committee, would permit the commencement of these works, and that after they were commenced these people would come to Congress and say, "You have now invested a large sum of money in commencing these works; we do not want to see that money lost by the decay or falling down of the work; and we would like to have Congress make a permanent appropriation."

I have offered this amendment so that the Secretary of the Interior can not commence the work of reclamation or of building these reservoirs or dams until there is in this fund named in the bill sufficient money to wholly complete each project upon which he is about to enter.

It seems to me that if the gentlemen who favor this bill are in earnest in their declarations or intimations they should be in favor of putting into the measure this amendment to provide that the Secretary of the Interior can not enter upon this work until he has in hand the money on which to draw to fully complete the work.

To my mind the most dangerous part of this measure is that, as I believe, it commits this Government to the permanent policy of making an appropriation of from five to ten million dollars a year in the future for the reclamation of arid lands.

I heard the gentleman from Illinois [Mr. CANNON] challenge the gentlemen who were urging this measure to rise in their places and say to this Congress that they did not intend to come to future Congresses and ask for these direct appropriations. But the silence which has followed that challenge has been death like. No man who is in favor of this bill has yet said in this debate that he does not intend to ask in the future that this country shall be bound to a general policy of permanent appropriations to carry on this work, although without committing themselves they would like us to so understand until the vote is taken on the adoption of the bill. I think, Mr. Chairman, that is the worst feature of the bill, and for that reason this amendment of mine ought to be adopted.

But there are many other reasons why I oppose the adoption of this measure as a whole. The district which I have the honor to represent in this body is made up largely of low, level lands. They were originally covered with vast forests. When the farmer came to that country in search of a home he was confronted at the outset with the almost insurmountable task of felling and clearing away these forests.

This was accomplished only by the most incessant and severe toil. When he had cleared away the forest he found that his land was so level that at many seasons of the year it was wholly covered with water, so that it was impossible to raise a crop. At first he had no money with which he could pay for the drainage of his lands. He was compelled to rely on his own resources. So he hitched his horses to the plow and scraper and constructed the outlet ditches necessary to commence the work of drainage. Soon he was enabled to raise small crops, and he began at once to burden himself with taxation in order to raise further means to carry on the work. He then found that if he would be at all successful he would be compelled to arrange a complete system of drainage by placing tile drains in the land at intervals of eight rods apart.

He has accomplished all this by his own efforts. And every acre so improved has cost him in labor and money from twenty to forty dollars. As a result of this sacrifice he has had the satisfaction of knowing that he has developed and built up one of the richest and most productive agricultural districts in the world. I believe that the difficulties with which he was confronted were fully as great as those which confront the home seeker in the arid regions. He overcame all these difficulties unaided and alone. He never received, yea, more than that, he never asked, for a cent of Government aid.

And now you propose to tax him and the fruits of his unaided toil to build up a great farming section where products will be raised to compete with those that he raises on the farm that he has made tillable without any assistance on the part of the Government whatever.

* * *

THOMAS GLENN (Pop., Ida.): Irrigation, instead of being an injury to the Eastern and Southern farmer, will prove of incalculable benefit to them, in that we are informed by the most recent census statistics that the agriculturists of the country furnish the manufacturers with products equal in value to nine-tenths of the cost of all factory products. Conceding this to be true, any increase in consumers would of necessity create additional demands for manufactured products, which in turn would require an additional number of men to increase the output commensurate with such demands, and the Eastern and Southern farmers would have to supply products equal to nine-tenths of the cost of the additional factory products. Thus it is seen that the farmer and manufacturer are mutually dependent on each other, and that any improvement in the one works an advantage to the other. In other words, the farmer is largely dependent on the factory for the market for the products of the farm, whereas the manufacturer is dependent on the farmer to the extent of all necessary farm products with which to conduct his business and largely dependent on the farm for a market for the products of the factory. In this the Eastern, Central, and Southern farmers will have the advantage of being the greatest beneficiaries, in that they will furnish an amount equal to the cost of nine-tenths of all factory products, a demand for which will be created by the reclamation of the arid region, it being a well-established fact that when the farmer is prosperous it means prosperity for all other industries. . . .

In the United States irrigation was introduced by the Mormons under Brigham Young in 1847, and the wisdom and great business ability of this man as a leader are demonstrated by the great State of Utah in all her resources of every character. Under his guidance and direction the sagebrush plain and the rugged mountain side have been transformed into beautiful farms, gardens, orchards, homes, and magnificent cities, and this has been brought about alone through the application of the methods of irrigation. Yet this great inland empire has hardly been touched. From Utah this system radiated to the States of Idaho, Montana, Nevada, California, and the Territories, to which system is due the wealth of said States and Territories, but this has taxed the ordinary flowage susceptible to appropriation by the individual to its utmost extent, and further development and improvement is impossible without a conservation of forest and stream, so as to furnish additional waters for extending to unreclaimed lands the blessings of irrigation.

Mr. Chairman, the next query that may be made by gentlemen of this House is this: Is it possible to compensate the reclamation fund by distributing the cost of constructing reservoirs, canals, conduits, and dams among the purchasers or homesteaders? And for reply to this query, will say I sincerely believe that but few, if any, of the many investments will fail to reimburse the fund, and that, taken as a whole, the proceeds of the sale of lands under all the reservoirs will more than reimburse the reclamation fund; and this fund, when reimbursed, will be enabled to construct additional reservoirs, the cost of which will again be replaced by the sale of lands under these new and additional reservoirs. Thus will the fund revolve until all available waters shall have been exhausted, and the original amount will at the close of this great work remain in the Treasury Department, subject to the disposition and will of some future Congress. . . .

Newlands Act, 1902

From 32 U.S. Statutes at Large 388.

AN ACT APPROPRIATING THE RECEIPTS FROM THE SALE AND DISPOSAL OF PUBLIC LANDS IN CERTAIN STATES AND TERRITORIES TO THE CONSTRUCTION OF IRRIGATION WORKS FOR THE RECLAMATION OF ARID LANDS

Be it enacted by the Senate and House of Representatives of the United States of America in Congress Assembled, That all moneys received from the sale and disposal of public lands in Arizona, California, Colorado, Idaho, Kansas, Montana, Nebraska, Nevada, New Mexico, North Dakota, Oklahoma, Oregon, South Dakota, Utah, Washington, and Wyoming, beginning with the fiscal year ending June thirtieth, nineteen hundred and one, including the surplus of fees and commissions in excess of allowances to registers and receivers, and excepting the five per centum of the proceeds of the sales of public lands in the above States set aside by law for educational and other purposes, shall be, and the same are hereby, reserved, set aside, and appropriated as a special fund in the Treasury to be known as the ''reclamation fund,'' to be used in the examination and survey for and the construction and maintenance of irrigation works for the storage, diversion, and development of waters for the reclamation of arid and semiarid lands in the said States and Territories, and for the payment of all other expenditures provided for in this Act: *Provided,* That in case the receipts from the sale and disposal of public lands other than those realized from the sale and disposal of lands referred to in this section are insufficient to meet the requirements for the support of agricultural colleges in the several States and Territories, under the Act of August thirtieth, eighteen hundred and ninety, entitled "An Act to apply a portion of the proceeds of the public lands to the more complete endowment and support of the colleges for the benefit of agriculture and the mechanic arts, established under the provisions of an Act of Congress approved July second, eighteen hundred and sixty-two," the deficiency, if any, in the sum necessary for the support of the said colleges shall be provided for from any moneys in the Treasury not otherwise appropriated.

SEC. 2. That the Secretary of the Interior is hereby authorized and directed to make examinations and surveys for, and to locate and construct, as herein provided, irrigation works for the storage, diversion, and development of waters, including artesian wells, and to report to Congress at the beginning of each regular session as to the results of such examinations and surveys, giving estimates of cost of all contemplated works, the quantity and location of the lands which can be irrigated therefrom, and all facts relative to the practicability of each irrigation project; also the cost of works in process of construction as well as of those which have been completed.

SEC. 3. That the Secretary of the Interior shall, before giving the public notice provided for in section four of this Act, withdraw from public entry the lands required for any irrigation works contemplated under the provisions of this Act, and shall restore to public entry any of the lands so withdrawn when, in his judgment, such lands are not required for the purposes of this Act; and the Secretary of the Interior is hereby authorized, at or immediately prior to the time of beginning the surveys for any contemplated irrigation works, to withdraw from entry, except under the homestead laws, any public lands believed to be susceptible of irrigation from said works: *Provided,* That all lands entered and entries made under the homestead laws within areas so withdrawn during such withdrawal shall be subject to all the provisions, limitations, charges, terms, and conditions of this Act; that said surveys shall be prosecuted diligently to completion, and upon the completion thereof, and of the necessary maps, plans, and estimates of cost, the Secretary of the Interior shall determine whether or not said project is practicable and advisable, and if determined to be impracticable or unadvisable he shall thereupon restore said lands to entry; that public lands which it is proposed to irrigate by means of any contemplated works shall be subject to entry only under the provisions of the homestead laws in tracts of not less than forty nor more than one hundred and sixty acres, and shall be subject to the limitations, charges, terms, and conditions herein provided: *Provided,* That the commutation provisions of the homestead laws shall not apply to entries made under this Act.

SEC. 4. That upon the determination by the Secretary of the Interior that any irrigation project is practicable, he may cause to be let contracts for the construction of the same, in such portions or sections as it may be practicable to construct and complete as parts of the whole project, providing the necessary funds for such portions or sections are available in the reclamation fund, and thereupon he shall give public notice of the lands irrigable under such project, and limit of area per entry, which limit shall represent the acreage which, in the opinion of the Secretary, may be reasonably required for the support of a family upon the lands in question; also of the charges which shall be made per acre upon the said entries, and upon lands in private ownership which may be irrigated by the waters of the said irrigation project, and the number of annual installments, not exceeding ten, in which such charges shall be paid and the time when such payments shall commence. The said charges shall be determined with a view of returning to the reclamation fund the estimated cost of construction of the project, and shall be apportioned equitably: *Provided,* That in all construction work eight hours shall constitute a day's work, and no Mongolian labor shall be employed thereon.

SEC. 5. That the entryman upon lands to be irrigated by such works shall, in addition to compliance with the homestead laws, reclaim at least one-half of the total irrigable area of his entry for agricultural purposes, and before receiving patent for the lands covered by his entry shall pay to the Government the charges apportioned against such tract, as provided in section four. No right to the use of water for land in private ownership shall be sold for a tract exceeding one hundred and sixty acres to any one landowner, and no such sale shall be made to any landowner unless he be an actual bona fide resident on such land, or occupant thereof residing in the neighborhood of said land, and no such right shall permanently attach until all payments therefor are made. The annual installments shall be paid to the receiver of the local land office of the district in which the land is situated, and a failure to make any two payments when due shall render the entry subject to cancellation, with the forfeiture of all rights under this Act, as well as of any moneys already paid thereon. All moneys received from the above sources shall be paid into the reclamation fund. Registers and receivers shall be allowed the usual commissions on all moneys paid for lands entered under this Act.

SEC. 6. That the Secretary of the Interior is hereby authorized and directed to use the reclamation fund for the operation and maintenance of all reservoirs and irrigation works constructed under the provisions of this Act: *Provided,* That when the payments required by this Act are made for the major portion of the lands irrigated from the waters of any of the works herein provided for, then the management and operation of such irrigation works shall pass to the owners of the lands irrigated thereby, to be maintained at their expense under such form of organization and under such rules and regulations as may be acceptable to the Secretary of the Interior: *Provided,* That the title to and the management and operation of the reservoirs and the works necessary for their protection and operation shall remain in the Government until otherwise provided by Congress.

SEC. 7. That where in carrying out the provisions of this Act it becomes necessary to acquire any rights or property, the Secretary of the Interior is hereby authorized to acquire the same for the United States by purchase or by condemnation under judicial process, and to pay from the reclamation fund the sums which may be needed for that purpose, and it shall be the duty of the Attorney-General of the United States upon every application of the Secretary of the Interior, under this Act, to cause proceedings to be commenced for condemnation within thirty days from the receipt of the application at the Department of Justice.

SEC. 8. That nothing in this Act shall be construed as affecting or intended to affect or to in any way interfere with the laws of any State or Territory relating to the control, appropriation, use, or distribution of water used in irrigation, or any vested right acquired thereunder, and the Secretary of the Interior, in carrying out the provisions of this Act, shall proceed in conformity with such laws, and nothing herein shall in any way affect any right of any State or of the Federal Government or of any landowner, appropriator, or user of water in, to, or from any interstate stream or the waters thereof: *Provided,* That the right to the use of water acquired under the provisions of this Act shall be appurtenant to the land irrigated, and beneficial use shall be the basis, the measure, and the limit of the right.

SEC. 9. That it is hereby declared to be the duty of the Secretary of the Interior in carrying out the provisions of this Act, so far as the same may be practicable and subject to the existence of feasible irrigation projects, to expend the major portion of the funds arising from the sale of public lands within each State and Territory hereinbefore named for the benefit of arid and semiarid lands within the limits of such State or Territory: *Provided,* That the Secretary may temporarily use such portion of said funds for the benefit of arid or semiarid lands in any particular State or Territory hereinbefore named as he may deem advisable, but when so used the excess shall be restored to the fund as soon as practicable, to the end that ultimately, and in any event, within each ten-year period after the passage of this Act, the expenditures for the benefit of the said States and Territories shall be equalized according to the proportions and subject to the conditions as to practicability and feasibility aforesaid.

SEC. 10. That the Secretary of the Interior is hereby authorized to perform any and all acts and to make such rules and regulations as may be necessary and proper for the purpose of carrying the provisions of this Act into full force and effect.

Approved, June 17, 1902.

Act for 640-Acre Homesteads in Nebraska, 1904

From 33 U.S. Statutes at Large 547.

AN ACT TO AMEND THE HOMESTEAD LAWS AS TO CERTAIN UNAPPROPRIATED AND UNRESERVED LANDS IN NEBRASKA

Be it enacted by the Senate and House of Representatives of the United States of America in Congress assembled, That from and after sixty days after the approval of this Act entries made under the homestead laws in the State of Nebraska west and north of the following line, to wit: Beginning at a point on the boundary line between the States of South Dakota and Nebraska where the first guide meridian west of the sixth principal meridian strikes said boundary;

thence running south along said guide meridian to its intersection with the fourth standard parallel north of the base line between the States of Nebraska and Kansas; thence west along said fourth standard parallel to its intersection with the second guide meridian west of the sixth principal meridian; thence south along said second guide meridian to its intersection with the third standard parallel north of the said base line; thence west along said third standard parallel to its intersection with the range line between ranges twenty-five and twenty-six west of the sixth principal meridian; thence south along said line to its intersection with the second standard parallel north of the said base line; thence west on said standard parallel to its intersection with the range line between ranges thirty and thirty-one west; thence south along said line to its intersection with the boundary line between the States of Nebraska and Kansas, shall not exceed in area six hundred and forty acres, and shall be as nearly compact in form as possible, and in no event over two miles in extreme length: *Provided,* That there shall be excluded from the provisions of this Act such lands within the territory herein described as in the opinion of the Secretary of the Interior it may be reasonably practicable to irrigate under the national irrigation law, or by private enterprise; and that said Secretary shall, prior to the date above mentioned, designate and exclude from entry under this Act the lands, particularly along the North Platte River, which in his opinion it may be possible to irrigate as aforesaid; and shall thereafter, from time to time, open to entry under this Act any of the lands so excluded, which, upon further investigation, he may conclude can not be practically irrigated in the manner aforesaid.

SEC. 2. That entrymen under the homestead laws of the United States within the territory above described who own and occupy the lands heretofore entered by them, may, under the provisions of this Act and subject to its conditions, enter other lands contiguous to their said homestead entry, which shall not, with the land so already entered, owned, and occupied, exceed in the aggregate six hundred and forty acres; and residence upon the original homestead shall be accepted as equivalent to residence upon the additional land so entered, but final entry shall not be allowed of such additional land until five years after first entering the same.

SEC. 3. That the fees and commissions on all entries under this Act shall be uniformly the same as those charged under the present law for a maximum entry at the minimum price. That the commutation provisions of the homestead law shall not apply to entries under this Act, and at the time of making final proof the entryman must prove affirmatively that he has placed upon the lands entered permanent improvements of the value of not less than one dollar and twenty-five cents per acre for each acre included in his entry: *Provided,* That a former homestead entry shall not be a bar to the entry under the provisions of this Act of a tract which, together with the former entry, shall not exceed six hundred and forty acres: *Provided,* That any former homestead entryman who shall be entitled to an additional entry under section two of this Act shall have for ninety days after the passage of this Act the preferential right to make additional entry as provided in said section.

Approved, April 28, 1904.

Act for Transferring Forest Reserves to the Agriculture Department, 1905

From 33 U.S. Statutes at Large 628.

AN ACT PROVIDING FOR THE TRANSFER OF FOREST RESERVES FROM THE DEPARTMENT OF THE INTERIOR TO THE DEPARTMENT OF AGRICULTURE

Be it enacted by the Senate and House of Representatives of the United States of America in Congress assembled, That the Secretary of the Department of Agriculture shall, from and after the passage of this Act, execute or cause to be executed all laws affecting public lands heretofore or hereafter reserved under the provisions of section twenty-four of the Act entitled "An Act to repeal the timber-culture laws, and for other purposes," approved March third, eighteen hundred and ninety-one, and Acts supplemental to and amendatory thereof, after such lands have been so reserved, excepting such laws as affect the surveying, prospecting, locating, appropriating, entering, relinquishing, reconveying, certifying, or patenting of any of such lands.

SEC. 2. That pulp wood or wood pulp manufactured from timber in the district of Alaska may be exported therefrom.

SEC. 3. That forest supervisors and rangers shall be selected, when practicable, from qualified citizens of the States or Territories in which the said reserves, respectively, are situated.

SEC. 4. That rights of way for the construction and maintenance of dams, reservoirs, water plants, ditches, flumes, pipes, tunnels, and canals, within and across the forest reserves of the United States, are hereby granted to citizens and corporations of the United States for municipal or mining purposes, and for the purposes of the milling and reduction of ores, during the period of their beneficial use, under such rules and regulations as may be prescribed by the Secretary of the Interior, and subject to the laws of the State or Territory in which said reserves are respectively situated.

SEC. 5. That all money received from the sale of any products or the use of any land or resources of said forest reserves shall be covered into the Treasury of the United States and for a period of five years from the passage of this Act shall constitute a special fund available, until expended, as the Secretary of Agriculture may direct, for the protection, administration, improvement, and extension of Federal forest reserves.

Approved, February 1, 1905.

Problems of Public Land Disposition, 1905

From United States Public Lands Commission, *Report*, pp. iv–v, xiv–xv, xvii–xviii, xx–xxiv.

Magnitude of Problem

In approaching the question of attaining the largest practicable disposition of the public lands to actual settlers, and the equally important question of securing the most effective use of these lands, we appreciate that extremely difficult and far-reaching problems are involved. The public lands embrace in area very nearly one-third of the entire extent of the United States and are widely scattered, extending from the Gulf of Mexico to the Pacific and from Canada to Mexico, including every variety of topography and climate. Excluding Alaska there are 23 States and 3 Territories containing public land. This includes approximately from 5 to 95 per cent of the area of these States.

Often in any one State the conditions are so diverse that the man who argues for certain points is usually found to base his argument upon conditions which exist in his locality. If not limited by geographical environment the view point is almost always that of a special industry such as sheep or cattle raising, irrigation, etc., and the arguments are based upon a knowledge of conditions which affect that industry. It is this condition which has led to the presentation before the Commission of irreconcilable statements of existing conditions, and the divergence of opinion as to the remedies to be adopted. Certain able men insist that the public land laws are sufficient, and that however the lands are disposed of they will ultimately be put to the best use.

Others go to the other extreme and assert that nearly all of the public land laws should be repealed or modified, that they are incompatible with good administration, and that the lands now being disposed of are held in such a way that they will never furnish homes to people who might otherwise enjoy their use.

Between these two extremes there is a broad middle ground, occupied by the majority of persons who have carefully considered the subject and who agree that changes should be made and that the land laws should be simplified and codified.

Antiquated Land Laws

The information obtained by the Commission through the conferences in the West and the hearings in Washington discloses a prevailing opinion that the present land laws do not fit the conditions of the remaining public lands. Most of these laws and the departmental practices which have grown up under them were framed to suit the lands of the humid region. The public lands which now remain are chiefly arid in character. Hence these laws and practices are no longer well suited for the most economical and effective disposal of lands to actual settlers.

The States and Territories where lies the greater part of the public domain are progressing rapidly in population and wealth, but not in proportion to the disposal of land. In spite of this fact and of the recognition that the land laws might be improved, there is a general fear of change and a wide demand that the present laws be allowed to stand. This is due to dread of the introduction of unfamiliar requirements and to the fear that new enactments may recognize physical conditions even less than the present ones, and may be even less suited to the needs of the country. By the use of practices sanctioned by custom, the people have heretofore been able to get along fairly well; any change in their minds is associated with more difficult requirements, and they dread innovations which may hinder rather than help home making.

The changes suggested at this time have principal bearing upon the control, use, and disposal of the forest lands, as these are among the most valuable of the lands remaining in public ownership. The repeal of the timber and stone act will unquestionably cure the most obvious defect in the administration of the public lands. Next in importance to this is the desert-land law. The Commission is not at present prepared to suggest radical changes in this law, but we believe that the change recommended hereafter in this report, together with a more careful enforcement of the law itself, and especially of those provisions which relate to the adequacy of the permanent water supply, will suffice to insure good results.

Timber and Stone Act

Under the act of June 3, 1878, generally known as the timber and stone act, there has lately been an unusual increase in the number of entries, which can not be accounted for by an increase in the demands of commerce or by any unusual settlement of the localities in which the greater part of the entries were made. In 1902 there were 4,022 entries under this act, aggregating 545,253 acres, while in 1903 there were 12,249 such entries, aggregating 1,765,222 acres. A very large proportion of these entries were upon timbered land. The law was enacted to meet the demands of settlers, miners, and others for timber and stone for building, mining, and other purposes. There is much evidence, however, going to show that many entries have been made for purposes not contemplated by the Congress.

Land Classifications

The agricultural possibilities of the remaining public lands are as yet almost unknown. Lands which a generation or even a decade ago were supposed to be valueless are now producing large crops, either with or without irrigation. This has been brought about in part by the introduction of new grains and other plants and new methods of farming and in part by denser population and improved systems of transportation. It is obvious that the first essential for putting the remaining public lands to their best use is to ascertain what that best use is by a preliminary study and classification of them, and to determine their probable future development by agriculture.

Until it can be definitely ascertained that any given area of the public lands is and in all probability forever will remain unsuited to agricultural development, the title to that land should remain in the General Government in trust for the future settler.

For example: The passage of the reclamation act (June 17, 1902) made certain the disposition to actual settlers of large areas of land which up to that time had been considered as valueless. Other areas, which are too high and barren to have notable value even for grazing, are now known to have importance in the future development of the country through their capacity to produce forest growth. The making of wells will give an added value to vast tracts of range lands for which the water supply is now scanty. In short, because of possible development, through irrigation, through the introduction of new plants and new methods of farming, through forest preservation, and grazing control, the remaining public lands have an importance hitherto but dimly foreseen.

In view of these facts it is of the first importance to save the remaining public domain for actual home builders to the utmost limit of future possibilities and not to mortgage the future by any disposition of the public lands under which home making will not keep step with disposal. To that end your Commission recommends a method of range control under which present resources may be used to the full without endangering future settlement.

After the agricultural possibilities of the public lands have been ascertained with reasonable certainty, provision should be made for dividing them into areas sufficiently large to support a family, and no larger, and to permit settlement on such areas. It is obvious that any attempt to accomplish this end without a careful classification of the public lands must necessarily fail. Attempts of this kind are being made from time to time, and legislation of this character is now pending, modeled on the Nebraska 640-acre homestead law, which was passed as an experiment to meet a certain restricted local condition. This act (33 Stat., 547) permits the entry of 640-acre homesteads in the sand-hill region of that State. Whether in practice the operation of this law will result in putting any considerable number of settlers on the land is not yet determined.

Your Commission is of opinion, after careful consideration, that general provisions of this kind should not be extended until after thorough study of the public lands has been made in each particular case, because to do so controverts the fundamental principle of saving the public lands for the home maker. Each locality should be dealt with on its own merits. Even if it should ultimately appear that this law has worked beneficially in Nebraska it would by no means follow that such a law might be safely applied to other regions different in topography, soil, and climate. No arbitrary rule should be followed, but in each case the area of the homestead should be determined by the acreage which may be necessary to support a family upon the land, either by agriculture, or by grazing if agriculture is impracticable. Until such acreage is determined for each locality, any new general law providing a method of obtaining title to the public lands would, in the opinion of your Commission, be decidedly unsafe.

* * *

Sale of Timber on the Public Lands

Necessity for the enactment of a law authorizing the sale of timber on nonreserve public land is becoming more evident, and the recommendations made in the preceding report of this Commission are reiterated. For the best use of the public lands it is absolutely essential to hold public timber for sale when needed and in quantities necessitated by the continuous growth of prevailing industries. Provision should also be made for a limited free-use right by miners and actual settlers.

Commutation Clause of the Homestead Act

In the preceding report a statement was made that our investigations respecting the operations of the commutation clause of the homestead law were still in progress. We were not at that time prepared to recommend its repeal. Investigations carried on during the past year have convinced us that prompt action should be taken in this direction and that, in the interest of settlement, the commutation clause should be greatly modified.

A careful examination of the districts where the commutation clause is put to the most use shows that there has been a rapid increase of the use of this expedient for passing public lands into the hands of corporations or large landowners. The object of the homestead law was primarily to give to each citizen, the head of a family, an amount of land up to 160 acres, agricultural in character, so that homes would be created in the wilderness. The commutation clause, added at a later date, was undoubtedly intended to assist the honest settler, but like many other well-intended acts its original intent has been gradually perverted until now it is apparent that a great part of all commuted homesteads remain uninhabited. In other words, under the commutation clause the number of patents furnishes no index to the number of new homes.

To prove this statement it is only necessary to drive through a country where the commutation clause has been largely applied. Field after field is passed without a sign of permanent habitation or improvement other than fences. The homestead shanties of the commuters may be seen in various degrees of dilapidation, but they show no evidence of genuine occupation. They have never been in any sense homes.

Investigations have been carried on where the commuted homesteads are notable in number. The records of some of the counties examined show that 90 per cent of the commuted homesteads were transferred within three months after acquisition of title, and evidence was obtained to show that two-thirds of the commuters immediately left the State. In many instances foreigners, particularly citizens of Canada, came into this country, declared their intention of becoming citizens, took up homesteads, commuted, sold them, and returned to their native land.

The reasons given for adhering to the commutation clause are diverse and many of them are cogent when applied to individual cases. It is said, for example, that the commuter desires to raise money for use in improving his place. This is often true, but in the majority of cases the records show that the commuter immediately leaves the vicinity. The frequency of loans is traceable in many places directly to the activity of agents of loan companies, who are often United States commissioners also, eager first to induce settlement and then to make these loans on account of the double commission received. Later they secure the business which accrues to them through the foreclosure and transfer of the property. The true working of the commutation clause does not appear until after foreclosure upon the maturity of the loans.

One significant fact brought out by the investigation is that a large portion of the commuters are women, who never establish a permanent residence and who are employed temporarily in the towns as school-teachers or in domestic service, or who are living with their parents. The great majority of these commuters sell immediately upon receiving title, the business being transacted through some agent who represents his client in all dealings and prepares all papers.

The commutation clause, if it is to be retained to cover special cases, should be effective only after not less than three years' actual — not constructive — living at home on the land. Under present practice, the commutation period being fourteen months, six months of this time is generally taken to establish residence, so that only eight months remain. This time is usually arranged to include the summer, so that the shack built need not be habitable in severe winter weather, and the residence on the land may consist merely in a summer outing. Obviously it is essential that residence should be far more strictly defined. It is probable that lax interpretation and enforcement of the provisions of the law regarding residence is responsible for more fraud under the homestead act than all other causes combined.

It may be urged that the frauds which have taken place under the operations of the commutation clause are due largely to lax administration. The fact is that the precedents established by decisions rendered on special cases have so far weakened the powers of administration that additional legislation is necessary.

* * *

Grazing Lands.

The great bulk of the vacant public lands throughout the West are unsuitable for cultivation under the present known conditions of agriculture, and so located that they can not be reclaimed by irrigation. They are, and probably always must be, of chief value for grazing. There are, it is estimated, more than 300,000,000 acres of public grazing land, an area approximately equal to one-fifth the extent of the United States proper. The exact limits can not be set, for with seasonal changes large areas of land which afford good grazing one year are almost desert in another. There are also vast tracts of wooded or timbered land in which grazing has much importance, and until a further classification of the public lands is made it will be impossible to give with exactness the total acreage. The extent is so vast and the commercial interests involved so great as to demand in the highest degree the wise and conservative handling of these vast resources.

It is a matter of the first importance to know whether these grazing lands are being used in the best way possible for the continued development of the country or whether they are being abused under a system which is detrimental to such development and by which the only present value of the land is being rapidly destroyed.

At present the vacant public lands are theoretically open commons, free to all citizens; but as a matter of fact a large proportion have been parceled out by more or less definite compacts or agreements among the various interests. These tacit agreements are continually being violated. The sheepmen and cattlemen are in frequent collision because of incursions upon each other's domain. Land which for years has been regarded as exclusively cattle range may be infringed upon by large bands of sheep, forced by drought to migrate. Violence and homicide frequently follow, after which new adjustments are made and matters quiet down for a time. There are localities where the people are utilizing to their own satisfaction the open range, and their demand is to be let alone, so that they may parcel out among themselves the use of the lands; but an agreement made to-day may be broken to-morrow by changing conditions of shifting interests.

The general lack of control in the use of public grazing lands has resulted, naturally and inevitably, in overgrazing and the ruin of millions of acres of otherwise valuable grazing territory. Lands useful for grazing are losing their only capacity for productiveness, as, of course, they must when no legal control is exercised.

It is not yet too late to restore the value of many of the open ranges. Lands apparently denuded of vegetation have improved in condition and productiveness upon coming under any system of control which affords a means of preventing overstocking and of applying intelligent management to the land. On some large tracts the valuable forage plants have been utterly extirpated, and it is impracticable even to reseed them. On other tracts it will be possible by careful management for the remaining native plants to recover their vigor and to distribute seeds, which will eventually restore much of the former herbage. Prompt and effective action must be taken, however, if the value of very much of the remaining public domain is not to be totally lost.

The conclusions as to grazing reached by your Commission were based:

First. Upon the results of long acquaintance with grazing problems in the public-land States on the part of each member of your Commission.

Second. Upon the results of careful examinations made for the Commission of the grazing systems of the State of Texas, the State of Wyoming, the Union and Northern Pacific railroads, and of the Indian Office in the case of permits to stockmen for the use of Indian lands suitable for grazing, and of the grazing conditions throughout the West. A map has been prepared showing the general location and area of the summer, winter, and year-long ranges, and the sections which are largely dependent upon a temporary water supply for their utilization in grazing, and those where there has been extensive development by wells and windmills. We believe that this map will be found exceedingly valuable and interesting in the consideration of all grazing problems, and it is therefore submitted in the appendix.

Third. Upon the results of a meeting called to confer with the Commission by the National Live Stock Association in Denver early in August, 1904, which was attended by the Secretary of Agriculture and by representative stockmen from all the grazing-land States and Territories. The opinion of the stockmen present was almost unanimous in favor of some action on the part of the Government which would give the range user some right of control by which the range can be kept from destruction by overcrowding and the controversies over range rights can be satisfactorily eliminated, the only question being as to the most satisfactory method by which such right may be obtained.

Fourth. Upon 1,400 answers received to a circular letter addressed to stockmen throughout the West. These answers show that under the present system the pasturing value of the ranges has deteriorated and the carrying capacity of the lands has greatly diminished; that the present condition of affairs is unsatisfactory; that the adoption of a new system of management would insure a better and more permanent use of the grazing lands; that a certain improvement in range conditions has already been brought about by range control on the forest reserves, and that the great bulk of the western stockmen are definitely in favor of Government control of the open range.

Fifth. Upon facts presented at many public meetings held throughout the West and upon innumerable suggestions which have been received and considered.

Your Commission concurs in the opinion of the stockmen that some form of Government control is necessary at once, but is opposed to the immediate application of any definite plan to all of the grazing lands alike, regardless of local conditions or actual grazing value. The following plan is intended to bring about the gradual application to each locality of a form of control specifically suited to that locality, whether it may be applicable to any other locality or not. Your Commission recommends that suitable authority be given to the President to set aside, by proclamation, certain grazing districts or reserves. To the Secretary of Agriculture, in whose Department is found the special acquaintance with range conditions and live-stock questions which is absolutely necessary for the wise solution of these problems, authority should be given to classify and appraise the grazing value of these lands, to appoint such officers as the care of each grazing district may require, to charge and collect a moderate fee for grazing permits, and to make and apply definite and appropriate regulations to each grazing district. These regulations should be framed and applied with special reference to bringing about the largest permanent occupation of the country by actual settlers and home seekers. All land covered by any permit so given should continue to be subject to entry under reasonable regulations notwithstanding such permit.

* * *

Large and Small Holdings

Detailed study of the practical operation of the present land laws, particularly of the desert-land act and the commutation clause of the homestead act, shows that their tendency far too often is to bring about land monopoly rather than to multiply small holdings by actual settlers. The land laws, decisions, and practices have become so complicated that the settler is at a marked disadvantage in comparison with the shrewd business man who aims to acquire large properties. Not infrequently their effect is to put a premium on perjury and dishonest methods in the acquisition of land. It is apparent, in consequence, that in very many localities, and perhaps in general, a larger proportion of the public land is passing into the hands of speculators and corporations than into those of actual settlers who are making homes.

This is not due to the character of the land. In all parts of the United States known to your Commission where such large holdings are being acquired the genuine homesteader is prospering alongside of them under precisely the same conditions. Wherever the laws have been so enforced as to give the settler a reasonable chance he has settled, prospered, built up the country, and brought about more complete development and larger prosperity than where land monopoly flourishes. Nearly everywhere the large landowner has succeeded in monopolizing the best tracts, whether of timber or agricultural land. There has been some outcry against this condition. Yet the lack of greater protest is significant. It is to be explained by the energy, shrewdness, and influence of the men to whom the continuation of the present condition is desirable.

Your Commission has had inquiries made as to how a number of estates, selected haphazard, have been acquired. Almost without exception collusion or evasion of the letter and spirit of the land laws was involved. It is not necessarily to be inferred that the present owners of these estates were dishonest, but the fact remains that their holdings were acquired or consolidated by practices which can not be defended.

The disastrous effect of this system upon the well-being of the nation as a whole requires little comment. Under the present conditions, speaking broadly, the large estate usually remains in a low condition of cultivation, whereas under actual settlement by individual home makers the same land would have supported many families in comfort and would have yielded far greater returns. Agriculture is a pursuit of which it may be asserted absolutely that it rarely reaches its best development under any concentrated form of ownership.

There exists and is spreading in the West a tenant or hired-labor system which not only represents a relatively low industrial development, but whose further extension carries with it a most serious threat. Politically, socially, and economically this system is indefensible. Had the land laws been effective and effectually enforced its growth would have been impossible.

It is often asserted in defense of large holdings that, through the operation of enlightened selfishness, the land so held will eventually be put to its best use. Whatever theoretical considerations may support this statement, in practice it is almost universally untrue. Hired labor on the farm can not compete with the man who owns and works his land, and if it could the owners of large tracts rarely have the captal to develop them effectively.

Although there is a tendency to subdivide large holdings in the long run, yet the desire for such holdings is so strong and the belief in their rapid increase in value so controlling and so widespread that the speculative motive governs, and men go to extremes before they will subdivide lands which they themselves are not able to utilize.

The fundamental fact that characterizes the present situation is this: That the number of patents issued is increasing out of all proportion to the number of new homes.

Respectfully submitted.

W. A. RICHARDS
F. H. NEWELL
GIFFORD PINCHOT

Act for Entry of Agricultural Lands within Forest Reserves, 1906

From 34 U.S. Statutes at Large 233.

AN ACT TO PROVIDE FOR THE ENTRY OF AGRICULTURAL LANDS WITHIN FOREST RESERVES

Be it enacted by the Senate and House of Representatives of the United States of America in Congress assembled, That the Secretary of Agriculture may, in his discretion, and he is hereby authorized, upon application or otherwise, to examine and ascertain as to the location and extent of lands within permanent or temporary forest reserves, except the following counties in the State of California, Inyo, Tulare, Kern, San Luis Obispo, Santa Barbara, Ventura, Los Angeles, San Bernardino, Orange, Riverside, and San Diego; which are chiefly valuable for agriculture, and which, in his opinion, may be occupied for agricultural purposes without injury to the forest reserves, and which are not needed for public purposes, and may list and describe the same by metes and bounds, or otherwise, and file the lists and descriptions with the Secretary of the Interior, with the request that the said lands be opened to entry in accordance with the provisions of the homestead laws and this Act.

Upon the filing of any such list or description the Secretary of the Interior shall declare the said lands open to homestead settlement and entry in tracts not exceeding one hundred and sixty acres in area and not exceeding one mile in length, at the expiration of sixty days from the filing of the list in the land office of the district within which the lands are located, during which period the said list or description shall be prominently posted in the land office and advertised for a period of not less than four weeks in one newspaper of general circulation published in the county in which the lands are situated: *Provided*, That any settler actually occupying and in good faith claiming such lands for agricultural purposes prior to January first, nineteen hundred and six, and who shall not have abandoned the same, and the person, if qualified to make a homestead entry, upon whose application the land proposed to be entered was examined and listed, shall, each in the order named, have a preference right of settlement and entry: *Provided further,* That any entryman desiring to obtain patent to any lands described by metes and bounds entered by him under the provisions of this Act shall, within five years of the date of making settlement, file, with the required proof of residence and cultivation, a plat and field notes of the lands entered, made by or under the direction of the United States surveyor-general, showing accurately the boundaries of such lands, which shall be distinctly marked by monuments on the ground, and by posting a copy of such plat, together with a notice of the time and place of offering proof, in a conspicuous place on the land embraced in such plat during the period prescribed by law for the publication of his notice of intention to offer proof, and that a copy of such plat and field notes shall also be kept posted in the office of the register of the land office for the land district in which such lands are situated for a like period; and further, that any agricultural lands within forest reserves may, at the discretion of the Secretary, be surveyed by metes and bounds, and that no lands entered under the provisions of this Act shall be patented under the commutation provisions of the homestead laws, but settlers, upon final proof, shall have credit for the period of their actual residence upon the lands covered by their entries.

SEC. 2. That settlers upon lands chiefly valuable for agriculture within forest reserves on January first, nineteen hundred and six, who have already exercised or lost their homestead privilege, but are otherwise competent to enter lands under the homestead laws, are hereby granted an additional homestead right of entry for the purposes of this Act only, and such settlers must otherwise comply with the provisions of the homestead law, and in addition thereto must pay two dollars and fifty cents per acre for lands entered under the provisions of this section, such payment to be made at the time of making final proof on such lands.

SEC. 3. That all entries under this Act in the Black Hills Forest Reserve shall be subject to the quartz or lode mining laws of the United States, and the laws and regulations permitting the location, appropriation, and use of the waters within the said forest reserves for mining, irrigation, and other purposes; and no titles acquired to agricultural lands in said Black Hills Forest Reserve under this Act shall vest in the patentee any riparian rights to any stream or streams of flowing water within said reserve; and that such limitation of title shall be expressed in the patents for the lands covered by such entries.

SEC. 4. That no homestead settlements or entries shall be allowed in that portion of the Black Hills Forest Reserve in Lawrence and Pennington counties in South Dakota except to persons occupying lands therein prior to January first, nineteen hundred and six, and the provisions of this Act shall apply to the said counties in said reserve only so far as is necessary to give and perfect title of such settlers or occupants to lands chiefly valuable for agriculture therein occupied or claimed by them prior to the said date, and all homestead entries under this Act in said counties in said reserve shall be described by metes and bounds survey.

SEC. 5. That nothing herein contained shall be held to authorize any future settlement on any lands within forest reserves until such lands have been opened to settlement as provided in this Act, or to in any way impair the legal rights of any bona fide homestead settler who has or shall establish residence upon public lands prior to their inclusion within a forest reserve.

Approved, June 11, 1906

Act for Enlarged Homesteads, 1904

From 35 U.S. Statutes at Large 639.

AN ACT TO PROVIDE FOR AN ENLARGED HOMESTEAD

Be it enacted by the Senate and House of Representatives of the United States of America in Congress assembled, That any person who is a qualified entryman under the homestead laws of the United States may enter, by legal subdivisions, under the provisions of this Act, in the States of Colorado, Montana, Nevada, Oregon, Utah, Washington, and Wyoming, and the Territories of Arizona and New Mexico, three hundred and twenty acres, or less, of nonmineral, nonirrigable, unreserved and unappropriated surveyed public lands which do not contain merchantable timber, located in a reasonably compact body, and not over one and one-half miles in extreme length: *Provided,* That no lands shall be subject to entry under the provisions of this Act until such lands shall have been designated by the Secretary of the Interior as not being, in his opinion, susceptible of successful irrigation at a reasonable cost from any known source of water supply.

SEC. 2. That any person applying to enter land under the provisions of this Act shall make and subscribe before the proper officer an affidavit as required by section twenty-two hundred and ninety of the Revised Statutes, and in addition thereto shall make affidavit that the land sought to be entered is of the character described in section one of this Act, and shall pay the fees now required to be paid under the homestead laws.

SEC. 3. That any homestead entryman of lands of the character herein described, upon which final proof has not been made, shall have the right to enter public lands, subject to the provisions of this Act, contiguous to his former entry which shall not, together with the original entry, exceed three hundred and twenty acres, and residence upon and cultivation of the original entry shall be deemed as residence upon and cultivation of the additional entry.

SEC. 4. That at the time of making final proofs as provided in section twenty-two hundred and ninety-one of the Revised Statutes the entryman under this Act shall, in addition to the proofs and affidavits required under the said section, prove by two credible witnesses that at least one-eighth of the area embraced in his entry was continuously cultivated to agricultural crops other than native grasses beginning with the second year of the entry, and that at least one-fourth of the area embraced in the entry was so continuously cultivated beginning with the third year of the entry.

SEC. 5. That nothing herein contained shall be held to affect the right of a qualified entryman to make homestead entry in the States named in section one of this Act under the provisions of section twenty-two hundred and eighty-nine of the Revised Statutes, but no person who has made entry under this Act shall be entitled to make homestead entry under the provisions of said section, and no entry made under this Act shall be commuted.

SEC. 6. That whenever the Secretary of the Interior shall find that any tracts of land, in the State of Utah, subject to entry under this Act, do not have upon them such a sufficient supply of water suitable for domestic purposes as would make continuous residence upon the lands possible, he may, in his discretion, designate such tracts of land, not to exceed in the aggregate two million acres, and thereafter they shall be subject to entry under this Act without the necessity of residence: *Provided,* That in such event the entryman on any such entry shall in good faith cultivate not less than one-eighth of the entire area of the entry during the second year, one-fourth during the third year, and one-half during the fourth and fifth years after the date of such entry, and that after entry and until final proof the entryman shall reside within such distance of said land as will enable him successfully to farm the same as required by this section.

Approved, February 19, 1909.

Senate Debate on Land Policy, 1912

From *Congressional Record*, 62nd Cong., 2nd Sess., Vol. 48, pp. 1013–15. Jan. 17, 1912.

WILLIAM BORAH (Rep. Ida.): Let us look at our land laws and their administration. The original public domain in this country, all told, amounted to 1,849,072,587 acres. Of that vast domain only about 731,000,000 acres, in round numbers, are left. Some 368,000,000 acres of it are in Alaska.

There have been different methods of disposition of our public lands. The old Continental Congress provided in the first instance for bounties out of the public lands to be paid to the officers and privates in the army of King George in case they should see fit to resign from that army and join the American forces. Shortly after a bounty was also provided for our soldiers and for the general officers in the Army.

The second method of disposition was that of sale. It will be remembered, of course, that a number of States deeded large tracts of land to the Government after the Government was organized, and it was deeded primarily for the purpose of enabling the National Government to secure revenue to take care of the indebtedness then existing. A number of large sales were made, but it came to be the observation of those of that day that settlement and development were of vastly more importance than the amount of revenue which was obtained from the public lands. And so gradually they drifted into the policy of settlement and development rather than of sale.

The first recognition of this principle was in 1813, when we find the first indication of a preemption law, and finally, in 1841, a preemption law, somewhat complete in its terms, was passed by Congress.

In 1846 began the agitation for the homestead law. The movement had its real origin with a tailor, who resided in Philadelphia — a Scotchman, who had come to this country and had observed intelligently and comprehensively the condition of affairs which prevailed in the old country by reason of the land holdings. After agitation for some years on the part of this gentleman, isolated in his effort, it was taken up by the public, and what is known as the Free Soil Democracy — in 1852, I think it was — for the first time placed a declaration in its platform in favor of free homesteads. The matter was discussed from time to time from 1846 to 1862. Very great opposition was found to it in Congress, but the law was finally enacted, and the first homestead law very appropriately bears the signature of Abraham Lincoln. From that time until this the controlling policy with respect to our public lands has been that of settlement and development.

I am bound to say, however, that within the last 10 years there has been a very studied and persistent effort — and, in my judgment, independent of the law — without changing the law, to change the policy. There was a disposition to go back to the idea of revenue, and jealousy seemed to exist on the part of the Government apparently against all men who should enter upon the public domain. A desire seemed to exist to make a charge in every conceivable way against those who were seeking either to acquire land or to develop our natural resources. I do not believe, however, that the idea of going back to a revenue basis will find lodgment generally in the mind of our people.

I notice that the Secretary of the Interior in his last report, filed a few days ago, said:

> The general theory under which the Government has proceeded and is now proceeding is that the public domain should be utilized for actual settlement and development rather than as a source of revenue for the General Government. In my judgment this theory is entirely correct. The essential thing is to see that the theory is, in fact, carried into effect and that under the guise of settlement we do not permit mere exploitation, which, in the last analysis, retards and prevents both settlement and development.

This is a very clear and succinct statement of the policy of the Government for a number of years and what I hope will continue to be the policy of the Government for some years to come.

The conditions which prevailed at the time of the enactment of the old homestead law were entirely different to the conditions of to-day. At that time the great, rich prairies of Illinois and Wisconsin and all those Middle Western States were open to settlement. The lands were rich and accessible. They were easily obtainable by those who desired a portion of the public domain. It cost little to reclaim them. But that condition has entirely changed. No one can at this time secure title to public domain under the homestead law who does not more than pay for it in his effort and his energy to get it. Though the law at the time it was passed was humane and in every way commendable, wise in its provisions, and beneficent in its execution, the time has come when we ought to consider the proposition of ameliorating the terms of the law.

Our homestead law provides for a residence period of five years. During that time the settler is chained, like Prometheus to his rock, and regardless of what misfortune and unwonted condition may overtake him, he forfeits his title if he is not found there acting in full compliance with the law for the long period of five years.

We require a man to stay upon a farm on the public domain in order to show his good faith longer than the term for which we elect a man President. If he goes upon the public domain, in the first place, without money, we do not allow him any opportunity or chance to secure sufficient funds to continue to develop and reclaim the land.

The result is, Mr. President, that these land laws have come to be in their operation extremely harsh, forbidding to go upon the public domain those who have not the means to remain there for a long period of time and continue to develop and reclaim their land at a comparatively heavy expense.

What the Government wants, and all the Government wants or should want, is a bona fide settler, a man who is upon the land in good faith for the purpose of reclaiming it and making it a home, and I maintain that 2 or 3 years will test a settler's good faith just as efficiently and completely as 5 years or 10 years.

The very fact that he is there, the fact that he has removed his family from more pleasant surroundings and environment out into the places where public lands are to be found, the fact that he goes there for the purpose of remaining through years, meeting the adversity and the harshness of the situation, the very fact, I say, that he is there under these conditions is the most conclusive evidence of his good faith, and only upon the strongest evidence and the most conclusive proof ought a man's title be challenged for good faith after he has given this evidence of his intention to reclaim a part of the desert.

I want to read in this connection a statement from the Public Lands Commission, which was appointed by President Roosevelt, I think, and report of which was made several years ago. I read only a general statement to show the view which they took of the land laws at that time:

> The information obtained by the commission through the conferences in the West and the hearings in Washington discloses a prevailing opinion that the present land laws do not fit the conditions of the remaining public lands. Most of these laws and the departmental practices which have grown up under them were framed to suit the lands of the humid region. The public lands which now remain are chiefly arid in character. Hence these laws and practices are no longer well suited for the most economical and effective disposal of lands to actual settlers.

This report is signed by Mr. Pinchot and by Mr. Newell and, I believe, by Mr. Richards.

Mr. Fisher, the Secretary of the Interior, while on a visit to the West last summer, stated, in a clear and convincing way, the condition of the settler under our present land laws, and I desire to read a portion of his address delivered at Boise City, Idaho. The Secretary said:

> Let us forget the quarrels of the past; get down to concrete facts, and face actual present and future problems, and solve them. There has been too much bickering over what has been done and too little constructive work for what is being done and for what should be done.
>
> First of all let it be known that the man on the land is the man who interests me. If you understand what that means, you will understand my position, as briefly as I can state it. It is the man on the land who is essential.

The man on the land, says the Secretary, is the man who interests him, and that ought to be the true policy. The Government should have no desire to hold the public lands if there is a bona fide settler or a citizen who desires to reduce them to cultivation and to make them taxable and to bear their proportion of the burdens of the county and State and National Government. Therefore the Government should be interested in the individual who puts forth his efforts and endeavors to reclaim any part of the public domain; and instead of being anxious to know whether technically every phase of the law has been complied with, we ought to be anxious to know whether or not the citizen is there in good faith, and if he is we ought not to search for technical and harsh reasons to drive him away, but rather should we aid and encourage and protect him.

> It is the man on the land who is essential. It is he that builds up the country and develops the resources and produces wealth and makes everything else possible for a community. I believe that you should make it easier for him to get the land; and I believe just as hard, on the other side that you should make it harder for the man who holds the land and will not develop, but just waits so that he can get a higher price from the man who is the actual settler and is the actual man on the land.
>
> And, furthermore, I want to say that I and my department, while I am in it, will do everything in our power to accomplish the realization of those two principles — help the man on the land; make it harder for the speculator.

I think that we should give the settler title under the reclamation act as soon as we give the man on the land title on homesteads. I think that the settler should get title to his homestead just as soon as he has shown good faith and has convinced the Government that he sincerely means to develop the land and help build up the community. I do not believe in making him wait and wait for years.

> WILLIAM SMITH (Rep., Mich.): From whom are you reading?
> MR. BORAH. From the speech of the Secretary of the Interior.
> Again, says the Secretary:

Here we find that a man comes on the land, puts his money into necessary buildings, a house and outbuildings and sheds, and buys implements, then starts to clear his land. He comes in good faith, meaning to do everything the Government asks of him, and he works ahead and pretty soon his money is all gone and he is up against it hard. There is no mercy for him. He faces ruin and the loss of everything. His hard years of toil and effort and sacrifices and isolation and struggle have netted him what? Nothing! Tell me that is right? Tell me that is just? I say, no! It is wrong — dead wrong — and the fact that the United States Government does it and allows this sort of thing to go on, knowing the terrible injustice of it, makes no difference to me. I have come that far to the western view.

In other words, that far toward a sound view. That is a true, moderately but graphically drawn picture of the situation. For, remember, when the homesteader loses he not only loses his land, but he loses his improvements and his years of hard toil. I think it cruel and brutal, contrary to every principle which should control a government in dealing with its citizens to take a homestead from the settler, except upon clear proof of willful disregard or violation of the law. So long as he is acting in good faith the Government should help and not hurt the settler.

I say that the payments are too high. The fact is, the settler has too great a burden to bear in the first place, during the early years. The Government should only want a guaranty of continuous and progressive cultivation. The law should only require what can reasonably be expected from an ordinary man. But I do think that before he gets title the Government has the right to make him show that he intends to stay.

I have no sympathy for the hardy pioneer who sits in his mahogany chair in his office in Chicago or New York or Cleveland, and talks about the "awful hardships of the early pioneer on a homestead." That kind of talk does not sound good to me.

But the man who goes on the land deserves all consideration, and he will get it from me.

Now, that was like the announcement of a new gospel to the western people. No single speech of late years has been delivered in the West that sounded better to the ears of those who were seeking to make homes upon the public domain than this deliverance of this Secretary of the Interior. I hope that the policy which he suggests will be enacted into law and administered accordingly.

> WELDON HEYBURN (Rep., Ida.): What is the date?
> MR. BORAH. My colleague asks the date of the speech. It is September 18, 1911. I am not sure that that is the exact date of the deliverance, but it is the date of publication.

I read also some views of the Secretary of the Interior, as found in his late report:

It is now clear, however, that it contains certain serious disadvantages for which there is no longer any adequate excuse. What we desire is actual settlement. We should have no desire to impose any unnecessary hardships upon the actual settler. What has happened is that the law has failed to take into account the conditions under which the actual settler is required to work.

Irrigated lands, as a rule, are in their natural state but parts of the desert. They are usually covered with the growths which the desert produces. These must be cleared and the land graded and otherwise prepared for the application of water before any crops whatever can be raised. In many instances each tract must also be fenced, and where it is adapted for actual residence on the ground itself the home must be constructed, together with the necessary outbuildings and shelters for the agricultural implements and machinery essential to cultivation. All of this requires a considerable expenditure, which is usually a heavy drain upon the resources of the settler. The land itself can seldom be made to produce any immediate revenue. If it is fruit land, the trees must be planted and reach a certain growth before they will bear fruit. Subsidiary crops can often be raised, but frequently not with profit until after one or two years' preliminary cultivation. It is often essential to plant the land in alfalfa or other leguminous crops before it is suitable for the raising of grain, sugar beets, or other crops for which it is ultimately intended. All of this means that where the settler has not accumulated a considerable capital and is without other means of livelihood, the requirement of actual residence upon the land during the first two years after entry is a serious hardship and a real obstacle to settlement. Many men who would make admirable settlers and citizens of the Western States are prevented from acquiring the homes and the substantial livelihood which would otherwise be opened to them. I see no reason whatever for insisting upon the requirement of actual residence at the outset in such cases.

It has been suggested, Mr. President, that instead of shortening the homestead period from five years to three years we permit the homesteader to leave his homestead for the first two years; that is, relieve him of residence during that period. This suggestion is made by the Secretary of the Interior, I believe, in his report. I have no doubt of the good faith of the Secretary in making the suggestion, and that it was intended to benefit the homesteader. But in my opinion, Mr. President, it will not have the desired effect. The homesteader must still continue to improve and develop his land. He must, unless he has means to employ it done, give his time to it anyway. While he is not required to actually reside upon the land, he is nevertheless required to continue to make the expenditure, to incur the indebtedness or the obligations necessary to its development, and he must wait for the long period of five years in order to have a basis of credit for what he is doing. For the most needy, the poorer class of home builders, for those who really want a home and have no other place to go, it would help them little if at all.

It does not help, Mr. President, the man in whom I am particularly interested, and that is the man who desires to go directly upon a piece of land and remain there until he can secure a title to his home. It might aid those who were engaged as clerks or mechanics or in some other kind of an occupation. They could remain with their business and continue to improve their ranch or their homestead; but, Mr. President, it would not aid the one in whom we ought most primarily to be concerned, and that is the man for whom the homestead law was originally enacted; the man who has no other home, no other occupation, no other means, but who desires to go and avail himself of a part of our public domain, and to do it under such circumstances as to enable him to have a home without debts and distress, which will not permit him to hold or enjoy it.

I want to read a letter from a homesteader upon this particular subject, because it states the situation perhaps more tersely than I could state it, as he has had actual experience. It is a letter from Mr. M. C. Turner, who resides at Caldwell, Idaho, a former resident of Iowa, who went west for the purpose of availing himself of the homestead law under a reclamation project. Speaking of this proposition of not reducing the time but to relieve the homesteader from actual occupancy, he says:

I believe that our Secretary is much interested in the "struggle for existence," of we homesteaders, but I am sorry to say that I do not think his desired changes will give us homesteaders the desired relief, neither will it offer any inducement to the home seeker who has heretofore objected to our present five-year homestead law. We bona fide settlers do not ask for a "relaxation of the rule requiring residence during the first two years," for that rule has always been the common practice of the insincere homesteader. We want relief for the present homesteader, and at the same time offer an inducement to the prospective home seeker, and that is exactly what your three-year bill provides. I wish that Secretary Fisher could understand that no homesteader of moderate financial means can give Uncle Sam his time, accumulated money, and future earnings for the long period of five years without a basis of credit. Why have — I think it safe to say — three-fourths of the original homesteaders been forced to give up their homes and let the next man receive the benefits of their money, time, and labor? It was not because he did not have more time, nor was not able to perform more labor, but because his money, time, and labor were assets of Uncle Sam rather than assets of his own. I think that your three-year bill offers the only real remedy to this long-existing evil. Our Secretary says that (in some cases) three years is long enough time to till the land, and the tilling of the land is the one thing that establishes good faith on the part of the homesteader. So, why not give him his patent at the expiration of the good-faith period?

What I have said, Mr. President, relates more particularly to the general homestead law. I desire, briefly, now to mention some additional facts with reference to the homestead law as it applies to our reclamation projects.

Under these reclamation projects a man must first reside upon his land for five years, just the same as under the old homestead law. In addition to that, he is not permitted to take title until the Government is paid in full for the expenditure made in reclaiming the land, putting water upon the land, and this may result in his having to remain out of title from 10 to 12 or 14 years, as the payments may be made in annual installments.

What is the result? The result is that the Government requires a man to go upon the land and build his home. He must necessarily build his barn, outbuildings, and stable. He must necessarily make those improvements which are essential to show good faith for the purpose of reclaiming his land. He must reclaim one-half of the land. He must pay not only the maintenance expense, but he must pay the annual charge of the Government, without any basis of credit, without anything upon which to base a business transaction. His assets, his labor, his land, may remain in the Government, under its control, and subject to forfeiture for 10 or 12 years. We require him to do a vast amount of work, to incur a great deal of expense, yet we provide no means in the world by which he can get the benefit of his labor for almost a quarter of a lifetime.

Now, what is the result? The result is, Mr. President, that this law which was passed by Congress and intended to be a poor man's law, and was advertised from one end of the country to the other as a poor man's law is distinctly a rich man's law.

CLARENCE CLARK (Rep., Wy.): Mr. President ——

The PRESIDING OFFICER (Mr. GALLINGER in the chair). Does the Senator from Idaho yield to the Senator from Wyoming?

MR. BORAH. I do.

MR. CLARK of Wyoming. I want to supply what, perhaps, the Senator inadvertently omitted when he spoke of refunding or repaying to the Government the money necessary to reclaim the land. I should like him to indicate somewhere the specific amount it ordinarily requires for reclamation.

MR. BORAH. You mean per acre?

MR. CLARK. Yes; per acre.

MR. BORAH. I have not the figures, and of course they vary with different projects. On one project that I have in mind it amounts to $26 an acre, on another to $30 an acre. If I remember correctly, the figure may be reasonably estimated at from $26 to $40 an acre.

MR. CLARK. I have known none less than the first sum mentioned by the Senator.

MR. BORAH. I think $26 is the lowest figure, because it was one of the first projects. This large amount of money, together with the money which he must necessarily have to develop his place, must come from some one. He must have it before he goes there or he must get it in some way.

I venture to say that there is not a business man in the Senate or within the sound of my voice who would engage in any kind of business in the world, even with the guaranty of the Government behind him, where he was not permitted to have the benefits of his efforts and his labor for 10 years or even for 5 years. The men who have fortunes would not undertake such a proposition. Yet we require of those who are supposed to be without means, those whom we especially desire to benefit, who are supposed to be limited in their holdings, to go upon these lands and develop them and pay out this enormous expense, and we withhold from them all basis of credit. The homesteader goes to the groceryman, or to the general merchant, and asks that which the most prosperous farmer asks time and again; that is, for credit during the season of crop raising. He is told that he has nothing upon which to extend the credit. The Government of the United States has extended him no credit, and the individual has no basis upon which to figure, because that which you have may to-morrow become the property of the Government of the United States. By no possible means can he go into the business world and represent his efforts as a basis for his credit. The result is, just as Mr. Turner so well says in his letter, that the first homesteaders, those who went upon the projects and upon the public domain under these circumstances, are in large numbers driven away, and the second and third homesteader comes along, who has a little more money and avails himself of the other man's work; it becomes distinctly and in every sense a law for the benefit of those who would have money enough to buy a home without taking it from the public domain.

I know of homesteaders who have gone upon these homesteads and spent $5,000 and $10,000 and $15,000 in trying to reclaim them, leveling down the ground, putting the soil in such a condition as to raise a crop, and still were unable to secure title after that large investment.

Mr. President, it is far better for the Government, looking at it as a business proposition, that the homesteader be given his title within a reasonable time and that the Government simply take a lien, if necessary. As was said by Mr. Fisher in his western trip last summer, the sooner the bank becomes the creditor of the homesteader the sooner the Government can gets its money. Give him an opportunity in accordance with his energy and his efforts, according to the ordinary business rules, and he will the more quickly pay the Government than if you tie him down to an impossible transaction. The Government can not hope to get the money until the homesteader gets it, and the homesteader can not hope to get it so long as the title is in some one else. A man can not make a success of a thing made impossible by unreasonable laws and regulations.

I say, Mr. President, give the man upon the public domain, who is trying to secure a home, a home as soon as he evidences his good faith, and do not hold him there until he is impoverished and unfitted to continue to manage his farm. I would give no man his title until he shows his good faith, and then I would give it to him before I pauperized him.

Now, just a word or two, Mr. President, with reference to the administration of our land laws. Congress can not avoid its portion of the responsibility for the condition of these laws. They are in the condition that they are in because we have failed to give them the consideration they are entitled to have.

But the trouble rests not alone with the Congress of the United States. I said a while ago that there has been a disposition for the last 10 years to return to the revenue basis, to get money out of the public lands, to sell or to lease them, to replenish the revenue and to supply the large and growing expenses of the department. This has resulted, Mr. President, in a most harsh administration of the public-land laws.

PORTER McCUMBER (Rep., N.D.): Mr. President ——

The PRESIDING OFFICER. Does the Senator from Idaho yield to the Senator from North Dakota?

MR. BORAH. I yield.

MR. McCUMBER. The Senator has indicated in his discussion so far that he would close with the subject that he has now under consideration. I want to suggest to him that he has so far omitted a most important feature in the matter of the administration of our laws.

Congress is to blame in one respect. Congress is employing to-day a corps of people known as special agents, but whose general duties seem to be those of detectives, for the purpose of arresting every possible farmer in the country who is upon public land. These men are employed with the idea that has been very prevalent of late that every man who is upon a homestead is necessarily there because he wants to steal it from the Government without paying a proper price. Assuming that to be the case, we have assisted the departments in furnishing them with a great army of detectives who feel that they can not earn their salaries unless they do it at the expense of the man who is on the farm and upon Government land in attempting to show that he is trying to steal his land.

Further than that, if the Senator will pardon me one moment, we have gone so far in the administration that instead of allowing the claimant upon public land to make his proof before the register and receiver of the land office, as in the old way, we have a fixed date on which he can have his hearing, and that date must be fixed to agree with the convenience of the detective who is there and must investigate whether or not he has any right. Then the detective goes there, and he has the right, and the administration accorded him that right, to hold it up for further consideration. So his proof has been held up from year to year at the suggestion of a detective employed for the purpose of disturbing him, until he has become so discouraged about getting his title that in many cases he has been compelled to leave it. In that respect the Congress of the United States is very much at fault.

MR. BORAH. I agree with the views of the Senator, so well stated. I remember upon one occasion, where there was a contest over a homestead title, to have seen seven special agents in one town waiting upon the trial, to watch a homesteader who did not have money enough to pay an attorney $5 to take the evidence before the land office.

But I think there is a little daylight upon the subject. I am looking forward to an entirely different administration. I stated there had been a disposition to return to the revenue basis, and this, in my judgment, which has been suggested by the Senator, is one of the evidences of it. I am of the opinion the regulation has been abandoned now — at least, I have not seen the effects of it so much of late — but there was a time when the homesteader would go into the public-land office and make his proof. The next day, after the homesteader had gone his way, assuming that the representatives of the Government had all that they desired to have and he had made the complete proof, the special agent would come along, without any facts or knowledge in his possession whatever of any defect upon the part of the title, and he would simply file a contest or a protest in the hope that there might be something he could find in after years.

Education and Experimentation

General Education for Farmers, 1872

From *Southern Cultivator* (Athens, Ga., January, 1872), XXX, pp. 17–18.

Columbus, Miss., Dec. 1871

EDITORS SOUTHERN CULTIVATOR:

To guard against misapprehension, I feel called on to make a few remarks on your comments on my article. When an agricultural department is attached to another institute of learning, it should only be to an ordinary college, and *never* to a University. An ordinary college offers sufficient facilities for learning, for such young men as desire to make agriculture their calling. The vocation of an agricultural college is, as stated in your comments, instruction in scientific matters relating to agriculture, but allow me to assert, JUST AS MUCH to give instructions in practice. Your reference for instruction to the young men's father's farms, or if their father's are no farmers, to their father's neighbors, would hardly prove to be very beneficial. What kind of instruction would they be likely to receive? How many farmers, for instance, understand the simple matter of cleaning a horse thoroughly and properly? or know how to use a harrow and a roller? or have a correct idea of spading? or of economizing time? or of having their work done systematically? or of having their tools and implements placed and cared for properly, and repaired well and in time? How many do you suppose, understand the proper care of stock? Let me assure you that the majority of farmers need instruction in all these and hundreds of other practical things. Of course every one will say, and actually thinks, that he knows all about it. Yes, he knows all he has been taught by his father and the customs of the country, but let me assure you that they have a great deal more to learn than they know at present, if they desire to be counted among the progressive and successful tillers of the soil? We all know and must acknowledge that agriculture is in its infancy at the South, and such being the case, agricultural colleges are required, where the growing up generation of farmers can learn PRACTICE as well as science. There is more in practice than most people think or imagine.

L. A. HANSEN

We are glad to find that our correspondent recognizes the importance of a *general education* to an agricultural student. He does not give his reasons for preferring the "ordinary College to the University," for giving that general education, and we cannot divine what they are; for our part, inasmuch as a University offers greater opportunities for learning than the ordinary College, we should always give *it* the preference in preparing a young man for any department of life. We do not yield to our correspondent in his estimate of the importance of *practice*. We served a seven years *apprenticeship* on a farm and know full well how often the general indications of theory must be modified by the stubborn lessons of experience. But that is not the point at issue between us — it is where and how practical knowledge is to be obtained. We unhesitatingly say that the *farm*, not the school, is the proper place. And we are very far from agreeing with our friend that "agriculture is in its infancy at the South," if by this he means that it is so in comparison with agriculture in other parts of the world. There are ignorant farmers here as elsewhere, but we venture the assertion that more real cultivated intellect has directed farming operations at the South than in any population of equal numbers anywhere else in the world. Because the methods pursued in connection with particular products and under peculiar local conditions, were not the same as those practiced in densely peopled countries like Germany, it by no means follows that ignorance guided in the one case and wisdom in the other. The complete disorganization of our political, social and industrial systems produced by the late war, necessitated a change in our modes of farming, and our people, with wonderful sagacity and rapidity, are adjusting themselves to the new regime. Compare the success of the Southern farmer since the war, with that of Yankee adventurers who came South, thinking they knew a thousand times more than the poor benighted Southerner, who was without churches and school-houses, and did not know the value of implements, or of time, or of anything else particularly.

We are sorry also to be compelled to differ from our friend in holding that an agricultural college is necessary to teach our young men how to "clean a horse," or "take care of stock," or "how to spade," or to "save time," or to "care for tools and implements," &c., &c. Somehow or other every livery stable keeper learns how to dress a horse thoroughly, and the best spaders we ever saw, (Irishmen not excepted) were the ignorant half savage negroes of the plantations along our coasts. Place upon a farm, a man of trained intellect — well acquainted with mechanical principles and with the laws of physiology and hygiene — and he will very soon learn the proper use of machinery and implements — the care of stock and the breeding of stock — and with the assistance of his father or his neighbor, the best management of crops also. — EDS. SO. CULT.

Criticism of Department of Agriculture, 1872

From *American Agriculturist* (New York, February, 1872), XXXI, p. 49.

The Department of Agriculture — Report for 1871.

Mr. Capron resigned his position as Commissioner of Agriculture, to take office under the government of Japan, and Mr. Frederick Watts, of Pennsylvania, was appointed successor, and assumed the duties of Commissioner in August last. All that we know about Mr. Watts is, that he is highly esteemed in his own locality, as an excellent citizen and a good farmer; that he is over seventy years of age, and that he was President of the Board of Trustees of that much mismanaged institution, the Agricultural College of Pennsylvania. The appointment having been made and confirmed, nothing is to be said upon its fitness. The public acts of the officer and the official documents emanating from him are proper subjects of notice and criticism by the agricultural press.

In his first report Mr. Commissioner Watts labors under two difficulties: he has nothing to say, and he takes 14 pages to say it in. We do not often meet with so much commonplace, even in government reports.

Upon page 4 of the Report we find the following:

"It will be remembered, that by the act of the 2d of July, 1862, Congress donated to the States public lands to 'provide colleges for the benefit of agriculture and the mechanic arts.' This was a new and important era, and may be said to mark the beginning of scientific knowledge as it pertains to agriculture."

If this language means anything, it means that previous to the year 1862 there was no "scientific knowledge as it pertains to agriculture," but that this knowledge had its beginning in that year. Later in the report, the Commissioner, in speaking of the works in the Department library, says, "Many of them are not accessible in any other library in the country." It must have been from some of these remarkable books that the Commissioner obtained this remarkable information in regard to "scientific knowledge as it pertains to agriculture."

Those who read only accessible books, suppose that Davy, Berzelius, Liebig, Boussingault, Way, Johnstone, Voelcker, Lawes, Gilbert, Pugh, and a host of others, long before 1862 contributed something to "scientific knowledge as it pertains to agriculture." But the head of our Department of Agriculture says differently, and he *ought* to know. We are informed that the various literary colleges spoil farmers' sons, while the agricultural colleges turn them out good boys, willing to stay upon their fathers' farms. Neither of these propositions is sufficiently established to make it safe to assert it in an official report. Detraction of "universities, colleges, and schools" seems to be a hobby with Mr. Watts. He was "down on them" in 1864, and is after them again in 1871. . . .

Warmed-over dinners are often necessary and tolerable, but are not we entitled to something better than warmed-over reports?

We have not time to notice the Commissioner's peculiar views concerning Agricultural Colleges; but we think it will be long before they send the results of their experiments to Washington to be worked up, as he suggests they do.

The Commissioner thinks that the Annual Volume should not be published, in which we can only in part agree with him. In the main, the Annual Reports for the past few years have been creditable and useful, and if the Commissioner's suggestion that they be placed on sale at cost be adopted, the objection of free book distribution at Government expense would be removed. But the Commissioner proposes to run opposition to the agricultural journals by means of his monthly reports. In referring to the foreign journals received at the Department he says: "They furnish the results of the very latest investigations in entomology, botany, agricultural geology, and microscopy, as well as experiments in agriculture, which could be abridged and published in the monthly reports of the Department before they could be reproduced by the agricultural journals of the country." How do our brethren of the press like this?

The seed business is to be continued in its objectionable features, and, instead of pints and quarts, bushels and half-bushels of grains are recommended. We are in favor of a properly managed distribution of seeds. New varieties, not yet in commerce, may be obtained by the Department and distributed, but we do object — and so does every right-thinking man — to furnishing to Members of Congress, at public expense, innumerable packages of seeds with which to court favor with their constituents. These seed packages are a thorough fraud; they contain the seeds sold everywhere, of the commonest sorts. It is a flagrant injustice to the seedsman, and no one can tell why Government should interfere with their business any more than with that of the druggist or grocer. If we are to have a general free seed distribution, let us have one also of family pills and spices. Let us also have the hoes, and rakes, and all other implements necessary to cultivate the plants sent by mail with the seeds. The "Tabular Statement" of seeds sent out includes under *"Cereals,"* 113 varieties of vegetables and 54 varieties of flowers. In the same table, under *"Textiles,"* we have peanuts. We once knew a pompous man who spoke of a potato as an excellent *condiment*, but it takes an official report to call a peanut a *textile*. We might show up more of the weaknesses of this weak report, but we leave it with a feeling of melancholy that the official representative of American agriculture should make so poor a showing. We have no high hopes for the Department of Agriculture under its present administration. We await in patience further developments. It may be that one who makes a weak report with his pen may prove a good executive officer. One of these days the farmers will make themselves felt; then the Department of Agriculture will be quite different from what it ever has been.

Georgia Agricultural College

From *Southern Cultivator* (Athens, Ga. November, 1874), XXXII, pp. 428–30

Our readers will pardon a brief allusion to the above Institution. Agricultural education has acquired considerable prominence within a few years past, in consequence of the endowment of Agricultural Schools by the U.S. Congress. From that source Georgia has received two hundred and forty-three thousand dollars, which, invested in 7 per cent bonds, yields an annual income of about *seventeen thousand* dollars. — This fund, under legislative sanction, was given to the University of Georgia, and accepted by its Trustees, with the following proviso:

"The interest of which shall be inviolably appropriated to the endowment, support and maintenance of the College organized by the Board of Trustees of the University of Georgia, as hereinbefore set forth. That the leading object in said College shall be, without excluding other scientific and classical studies, and including military tactics, to teach such branches of learning as are related to Agriculture and the Mechanic Arts, in such manner as the Legislature of this State may prescribe."

A part of the organization alluded to in the above, and which is included in the Governor's order turning over the fund, is as follows:

"The officers of this College shall be as follows:

1st. A President, who shall be charged with the special oversight of the College, under the direction of the Chancellor.

2d. A Professor of Agriculture and Horticulture, who, besides performing the usual duties of his chair, shall deliver each year, in different parts of the State, such popular lectures on Agriculture and Horticulture as may be found practicable.

3d. A Professor of Analytic and Agricultural Chemistry.

4th. A Professor of Mineralogy and Economic Geology.

5th. A Professor of Natural History and Physiology.

6th. A Professor of Industrial Mechanics and Drawing.

7th. A Professor of Physical Geography and Meteorology, with the assigned duty, in addition to his work of instruction, of making, as far as possible, a physical survey of the State, with reference to the development of its natural resources.

8th. A Professor of English Language, who shall give special attention to the training of the students in those branches that constitute an English scholar.

9th. A Professor of Military Tactics.

We have cited the above facts that the reader may appreciate what follows. When the proper appropriation of this fund was under discussion in the Georgia State Agricultural Society and elsewhere, its donation to the State University was opposed by many, on the ground that there ought to be an Agricultural College apart and distinct from any literary institution; that if attached to one of these, it would be merged into it and lose its distinctive character. In common with other friends of the State University, we took ground against this, and contended that its association with the University would give it many advantages and increased usefulness. Among these advantages were: a good library, physical and chemical laboratories with their appliances, and all the requisites for teaching the preparatory studies tributary to the mastering and applying of the higher branches of science to the useful arts.

We are pained to confess, however, that the expectations which the agriculturists of Georgia had a right to entertain, under these promises and the contract between the State and the Trustees of the University, have not up to this time been realized, and that there is danger of the agricultural fund being diverted from the objects intended by Congress, as embodied in the extract above from the Governor's order. It is a part of the contract — first between Congress and the State, and secondly between the State and the Trustees of the University — that the income arising from the donation should be inviolably appropriated to teaching *"such branches of learning as are related to Agriculiure and the Mechanic Arts."* The object is specific. It will not answer to say that *all* knowledge is tributary to agriculture. This is true in a certain sense, but every candid person will admit is not a legitimate version of the language of the contract.

The agriculturists of Georgia have a right to demand that the fund in question should be *strictly* used in their interest and that of those who cultivate the Mechanic Arts. Has this been done? We propose briefly to lay the facts before the reader. In the first published Report of the Georgia State College, now before us, the Treasurer reports having received from collected interest on land scrip fund, from May 1st, 1872, to Jan. 6th, 1874. . . . . $16,034 15

And paid out:

For salaries	13,802 33
For Chemical Apparatus	1,800 00
For books, stationery, printing, advertising, experiments and labor on farm, fuel and incidentals	2,653 95

The salary expenditure is not itemized. We will, as well as we can, supply this omission. — In August, 1872, Prof. Broun was elected President of the College, at a salary of $3,000 00 a year, still retaining his former Professorship in the literary department, the salary of which is $2,250 00. There is chargeable, therefore, to land scrip fund 1½ year's *increase* of salary at

$750 00 a-year, ...	$1,125 00
The Professor of Engineering being transferred to State College, his salary, $2,250 00, for same time, is chargeable to same	3,375 00
Three assistants at $500 each, from August, 1872 to August, 1873	1,500 00
Three assistants from August 1873, to Jan. 1874, at $616 each, a year	925 00
Prof. Pendleton's salary, from Jan. 1873, to Jan. 1874	2,250 00
	$9,175 00

This, taken from $13,802 33, leaves $4,627 33, which has been paid, we suppose, as part salary of other officers of the University. Prof. White's salary we do not charge against the fund, because he is *Terrell* Professor, and is therefore paid in part by the Terrell endowment, and besides, filling an *old* chair in the literary department, his pay is no more chargeable to the land scrip fund, than that of any other Professor in the literary department.

Is it right to appropriate the income from the land scrip fund to the payment of salaries of officers in other departments of the University, who taught the *same* things *before* the Agricultural College was established that they do *now?* Clearly not. In all discussions antedating the bestowal of the fund upon the State University, its friends promised that whatever aid the then existing organization could give the new College, should be given it gratuitously. — Indeed, the strength of their argument was, that so much expense could be saved in this manner — that all *preparatory* studies could be taught without a dollar's additional expense, and the income of the fund could thus in its entirety be devoted to agricultural education proper. That such was the understanding, is shown also by the language of the contract. We quote again from the Governor's order:

"Free Tuition in this College is hereby guaranteed to as many students, residents of the State, as there are members of the General Assembly of Georgia; and in addition to this free tuition in the College, all such students are likewise entitled to the advantages of the different Departments of the University of Georgia, without charge."

It will thus be seen that whatever the different departments could do for the agricultural student, was to be done *without charge*. The work thus done was not to be paid for in money — the remuneration was to consist in the incidental advantages arising from having the Agricultural College connected with the University.

In the contract with the Governor quoted above, an itemized organization is included, and the special officers of the Agricultural College designated. As the whole of the interest from the land scrip fund did not become available until some time last year, we attributed the fact of the election of but *one* additional Professor in the new College, (Prof. Pendleton,) to the lack of means. But how shall we interpret the action of the Board of Trustees at their recent meeting, (August, 1874.)? With an income of $17,000 00, and with salaries to be paid, amounting, according to the above schedule per year, to $7,100 00, and incidentals less than $2,000 00, and with a balance of about $8,000 00 income, strictly belonging to the Agricultural College, they failed to elect, or take steps looking to the election of, either of those Professors designated in the contract, and whose business it should be to teach subjects *specially related to Agriculture and the Mechanic Arts*. What is to be done with this $8,000 00 surplus? Is it, as the interest from the Terrell Endowment has been, to be merged into the *general* funds of the University? We hope our agriculturists through the State will look well into this matter, and through their representatives in the Legislature, see that the terms of the contract are strictly carried out.

Beginning of Connecticut Agricultural Experiment Station, 1876

From Connecticut Agricultural Experiment Station, *Preliminary Report*, in Connecticut Board of Agriculture, *Annual Report* (Hartford, 1876), pp. 359–65.

The Committee of the Trustees of Wesleyan University, to whom has been entrusted the organization of a "work appropriate to an Agricultural Experiment Station," contemplated in the legislative appropriation for that purpose, take pleasure in presenting the following report of the Director.

That the portion thus far expended of the installments which have accrued has been economically and profitably employed will, they trust, appear from the fact that, while considerable other and no less useful labor has been performed, analyses of fertilizers have been made during the first half year which, at the prices charged by leading chemists, would alone have cost more than the appropriation from the State for an entire year.

The Committee are happy to bear testimony to the skill, faithfulness and zeal with which the chemists of the Station have performed its work. . . .

To attempt any report of the work of the Experiment Station, when but little more than half a year has elapsed since its first organization, would be some like giving an account of the operations of a farm before a single summer had passed since the clearing of the land. The plan of operations and the incipient stages of the work might be explained sufficiently for comment and criticism, but the prospect of success or failure would be more certain when a season's crops had been harvested.

In the following brief preliminary report are described some of the main features of the organization and first labors of the Station.

The bill making an appropriation of $2,800 per annum to Wesleyan University "to be used in employing competent scientific men to carry on the appropriate work of an Agricultural Experiment Station," was approved July 20, 1875, during the summer vacation at the College.

Prompt efforts were made by the trustees of the University to secure the services of proper men for the work. Early in October, very shortly after the opening of the fall term, a chemist was on the ground, and as soon as practicable two assistants were secured. Arrangements were also made by which the professor of chemistry in the College was relieved of a part of his regular labor of instruction and enabled to assume charge of the work as Director.

Feeling that this enterprise should be entirely for the benefit of the farmers of the State, and that their counsel, sympathy, and coöperation were indispensable to its success, the Committee of the Trustees of the University to whom the organization of the Station had been referred, invited the State Board of Agriculture and the Farmers' Experiment Station Committee to meet at the college, October 12, 1875, and advise concerning plans for carrying out the purpose of the appropriation. . . .

It has been felt from the first that more abstract scientific investigations would afford not only the proper, but also the most widely and permanently useful field of labor. But the need of a fertilizer control system was so pressing and so vital to the interests of a considerable portion of the farmers of the State that it seemed absolutely necessary to turn the first efforts in this direction. Accordingly analyses of fertilizers sold in the State were undertaken, and circulars giving directions for the selection and forwarding of samples were widely distributed. Some of the further efforts made to introduce into this State a system of trade in commercial fertilizers by which the same shall be "bought and sold upon the basis of their commercial value as shown by their composition," are given herewith.

The following is a copy of a circular which was sent to a large number of persons interested, and published in the press of the State:

Dear Sir: WETHERSFIELD, CONN., Dec. 28, 1875.
    "It is plainly for the interest of both dealer and consumer that fertilizers should be bought and sold upon the basis of their actual value as determined by their composition. To further such a regulation of the trade in commercial fertilizers, arrangements will be

made with those dealers who wish to place their stock under the supervision of the Agricultural Experiment Station, whereby their wares will be inspected, samples taken for analysis, and results of same reported under authority of the director.''

As harmony of action is necessary to insure confidence, you are requested to be present at a meeting of Farmers and Dealers, to be held at Orange Judd Hal Middletown, Conn., at 11 o'clock, A. M., Thursday, Jan. 13th, 1876, to devise and accept means by which these desirable results may be attained.

S. M. WELLS, CHAIRMAN,

Of Advisory Committee, Connecticut Agricultural Experiment Station.

The success of this meeting was greater than any but the most sanguine had hoped. Not only were over seventy farmers, representative men from all parts of the State, present, but a large number of leading manufacturers and merchants connected with the fertilizer trade in this and other states, showed their interest in the matter by attending themselves, or sending special representatives to the meeting. Among the latter, were parties from Boston, New York, Baltimore and intervening places. A report says:

Many of the merchants here represent other large concerns, so that it may be affirmed that the fertilizers trade generally gives this Experiment Station its entire and cordial support. And I may add that farmers are more than satisfied with the action of this meeting. The good feeling manifested here between all parties in the warmest terms is worth coming to Middletown to see.

"The following resolutions, drafted by a joint committee of dealers and farmers, were adopted after full deliberation and with entire harmony. They were emphasized by the gentlemen present, without a dissenting voice, and in a manner that promises their fulfillment'':

WHEREAS, An Agricultural Experiment Station has been established at Middletown for the promotion of the interest of the agriculture of the State; in order to avail ourselves of the benefits of said institution, be it
Resolved, That all fertilizers sold in the State should be sold under a guarantee of their composition, to be determined by analysis at the Station.
Resolved, That we recommend to all manufacturers and dealers to place their stocks under the supervision of the Station, subject to their examination at all times.
Resolved, That as consumers of fertilizers we will give the preference in our purchases to those dealers who offer their goods under this guarantee.

At the close of the meeting, in a conference of the manufacturers and dealers present with the Director of the Station, the outlines and general tenor of an agreement between the Station and the sellers of fertilizers were decided upon. It was then proposed that, as soon as the details could be arranged by needed and proper consultation, a form of agreement should be drawn up and presented to the sellers of fertilizers in this State for approval and signature. . . .

The analysis of fertilizers is by no means the most important work of an Agricultural Experiment Station. Such an institution will be worthy of the name in proportion as it carries on accurate and thorough investigations and experiments in agricultural science. The knowledge thus gained of the principles that underlie the right practice of agriculture, has a very much wider and more permanent value than exposure of frauds or regulation of the trade in fertilizers. This is simply in accordance with the fact that the knowledge of any principle is of more consequence than any one special application of it. It is important for the farmers of Connecticut to know whether they get the worth of their money in the manures they buy, but is of equal consequence that they should know how to use them. And it is of still more importance to them to learn how they shall manage their fertilizers, their crops, their fodder materials, and their stock, so as most economically and profitably utilize the products and the productive power of their farms. That these facts are appreciated by our best farmers is very gratifying. That such knowledge is becoming increasingly valued for its own sake is still more so.

During the last summer some experiments were undertaken with the hope of making new contributions to our knowledge of the development of sundry of our common farm plants, and throwing some light on the question of rotation of crops and the feeding values of the products. Specimens of grass, clover and cereal crops, grown on different soils, and with different methods of manuring and culture, were cut at different periods of growth, from plots of known size, weighed and portions reserved for analysis. Samples of the roots and of the soils in which they grew were also gathered. Over forty specimens of roots and tops, and several of soils were thus collected. It was hoped that opportunity would be found during the winter for proper investigations in the laboratory of these products of the fields, but the various details of labor incident to getting the work of the Station systematized and, more especially, the analyses of fertilizers, have demanded so much attention that little time has yet been found to prosecute these investigations.

But few persons have any adequate conception of the amount of labor needed for accurate scientific researches. In the experiments above mentioned, the separation of a single lot of roots from the soil, required, in each of a number of cases, the painstaking labor of a whole week.

A number of specimens of muck and of natural manures of various sorts have been received, and investigations upon them begun. So soon as the stress of work upon artificial fertilizers is over, these and studies other will be continued.

Large numbers of letters of inquiry have come to the Station. These have been replied to, as fully as the time and opportunity of the laborers would permit. We ask those who may feel that their communications have not received as ready and full answers as their importance would demand, to remember that many of their inquiries can not be answered without previous study and experiment, and that even were the knowledge at hand, the putting of it in satisfactory form in individual letters consumes a great deal of time that is needed for other work. Still these inquiries are always welcome, and will be answered as well as is in our power.

The cordial sympathy which has been manifested on all sides in behalf of this enterprise has been very encouraging. Thanks are especially due to a number of persons for valuable assistance in various ways. . . .

W. O. ATWATER, *Director*.
Orange Judd Hall, Wesleyan University.

Agricultural Societies

From William H. Brewer, "Agricultural Societies, What They Are and What They Have Done," in Connecticut Board of Agriculture, *Annual Report*, 1880–1881, pp. 98–116.

The two great means of diffusing knowledge among men are *societies* and the *periodical* press. These are the two great engines of modern progress; but as the Agricultural Press will be discussed by others at this convention, I will drop it entirely with merely the remark that in praising the functions and results of the one, I do not wish to be misunderstood as to the merits or usefulness of the other. . . .

The changes in farming in these latter times have been so marvelously great that it is probable that there are men now living who have seen in their lifetime greater changes in the methods and appliances of farming than took place in all the centuries before, down from the time when Abel tilled the soil. This change in farming has been one of the developments of the age in which we live, and has gone along with the progress of science and invention, but it has been mostly through societies that the knowledge acquired in modern times has been carried to the men actually on the farms, and moreover, these same societies have stimulated farmers in a great variety of other ways.

We now see so many separate societies at work, with such a variety of aims, that it is hard for us to appreciate how very modern they mostly are, at least in their present form. So, a few words on the development of societies in general, and of Agricultural Societies in particular, will be a fit introduction to what I wish to say of their past work and present uses. . . .

Late in the last century, a "Board of Agriculture" was formed in Great Britain, and it was the earnest wish of Washington, while president, to have such established in this. In his message to Congress in Dec., 1796, he recommended the establishment of a national "Board of Agriculture" for the United States. More than two years earlier, writing to Sir John Sinclair, the president of the British Board of Agriculture, he used language which might well form the motto of any modern society: "I know of no pursuit in which more real and important service can be rendered to any country, than by improving its agriculture, its breed of useful animals, and other branches of a husbandman's care." Had Congress listened to his recommendation, and then, when three months later that prince of farmers retired from the presidential office, had he been placed at the head of such a board, we cannot help but picture to ourselves "what might have been," in such an event, and contrast it with what has been in our later developed national "Agricultural Department."

I know of no agricultural societies proper, being organized in the American colonies, before the Revolutionary War. But long before that date there were societies formed in the mother country, to promote special objects pertaining to the agricultural resources of the colonies. For instance, a society was instituted in London in 1753, *for the Encouragement of Arts, Manufactures and Commerce.* which published in 1761 a list of "Premiums offered for the advantage of the

British Colonies," the object of which was to make the colonies more profitable to England herself, by stimulating the production of certain raw materials she wanted. Such premiums or prizes as these were offered: £100 sterling, first prize, for the production of *cochineal*, not less than 25 lbs., in South Carolina, within three years of 1759. For *silk* in Georgia, (3d. per lb.), for planting and securing *olive* trees southward of the Delaware river, for the production of hemp, barilla, wine, raisins, opium, scammony, etc., etc. Under the stimulus of prizes, and with the facilities offered in part by such societies and in part by the great commercial companies, spices and many commercial and agricultural plants were tried in all the colonies, from Georgia to Massachusetts. Cotton, hemp, millet, rape, kohl, lucerne, sainfoin, poppies, woad, are among the plants tried over and over again in this State, and allspice, pepper, cinnamon, indigo, nutmegs, etc., etc., in the southern colonies long before the Revolutionary War. Some of these failed because of the natural defect of climate, some because not suited to the wants of the colonists, and some, indeed many, would-be industries or productions were smothered by government interference or forbidden outright. . . .

There was a society for the promotion of silk culture in this State, formed about the middle of the last century. I do not know the precise date, or whether it related to the whole State, or only New Haven County. Eliot speaks of it in 1759, when he was one of the officers to distribute the premiums it gave. The attempts to grow silk were prolonged for many years, particularly about New Haven, and statements occur which lead us to think that at one time mulberry trees were planted along the north side of the public green in that city, and the Connecticut Journal, of August 25, 1790, says that "about sixty families within the city of New Haven, during the present season of 1790, wherein about 420,000 silk worms were raised by the following persons," etc., and then follows a list of the persons, and the number of worms raised by each.

It was not until after we had achieved our national independence, and the country began to rapidly grow under the stimulus of its newly acquired liberty, that any of the agricultural societies began to be formed, which were the parents of those we have now. Even after the political state of the country was favorable, it took a long time for the people to learn how to form such societies, how to run them successfully, and how to profitably use them.

It is uncertain where the first American Agricultural Society was formed, or when. Some say that the first was formed in Charleston, S.C., in 1784, while others date the founding of this society in 1795, thus making it the fifth in point of time.

As to others begun in the last century, we have fuller data.

"The Philadelphia Society for the Promotion of Agriculture" was instituted in 1785, and is still in existence. So far as I know, this is the oldest agricultural society in America.

Of more interest is the experience of the next society, as it illustrates so well both the changes as adapted to suit the times, and also the results.

The next movement was "At a Meeting of a respectable Number of Citizens, at the Senate Chamber, in the City of New York, for the Purpose of instituting a Society for the Promotion of Agriculture and Manufactures; Mr. Chancellor Livingston, Mr. Simeon De Witt, and Mr. Samuel L. Mitchell," were appointed a committee to prepare rules and regulations. At a subsequent meeting, held February 26, 1791, the celebrated *"Society for the Promotion of Agriculture, Arts, and Manufactures"* of New York was formally organized, adopted rules, and chose officers. The eighth "Rule, provided for a Committee of Publication," to select such of the papers and works of the society as merited printing, and in 1792, the first volume of *"Transactions"* appeared, followed from time to time by others. These were small quartos, and, so far as I know, were the beginning of that great mass of literature, officially put out since by our various agricultural societies and kindred organizations, and in quality of material and soundness of doctrine might well stand as a pattern for some of its modern descendants. These "Transactions" were so sought after, that a second edition was published in 1801, in the more convenient octavo form which all the official "agricultural reports" I am acquainted with, have since followed.

The seventh "Rule" provided that "the society shall parcel the State into districts" with a special secretary in each, and this led in due time to the formation of county societies, of which more anon.

The society was incorporated by act of legislature, March 12, 1793, but the society expired in 1804 by the limitation of its charter, and April 2d of that year an act was passed incorporating a new "Society for the Promotion of Useful Arts, in the State of New York," with essentially the same officers that the old one had, the Hon. Robert R. Livingston being president from the beginning in 1791, until his death in 1813, after which he was succeeded by Simeon De Witt, formerly vice-president. Three octavo volumes of "Transactions" were published between 1807 and 1818, at which date it closed its existence. It was less distinctly agricultural than its predecessor, but "although the title of the society points at the useful arts generally, it is intended to consider agriculture the chief."* But, as a matter of fact, the society interested itself more in manufactures, and in 1808 an act was passed giving prizes or premiums for the manufacture of woolen goods, to stimulate both agriculture and manufactures. The first awards, in 1809, went into twenty-two counties, in 1810 thirty-two counties competed, and in 1811, thirty-nine counties. Meantime, merino sheep began to be grown, and the next year, 1812, a new law was passed giving premiums for broadcloth, to encourage the raising of merino sheep as well. This society expired by limitation, and Governor Clinton, in his annual message, January, 1818, recommended the establishment of a "State Board of Agriculture," a measure long before advocated by leading farmers. The politicians opposed it, and combining with such suspicious farmers as feared that such a board might lead to a landed aristocracy or some other evil, they in March of that year killed the bill by this amendment: "Be it further enacted that the farmers of this state be permitted to manage their own farms in their own way." You notice that the fathers of the modern politicians were already in the field, and a writer of the time says that the amendment "was carried by a thundering majority." But the matter would not rest and the next year, April 19, 1819, a "State Board of Agriculture" was created and an appropriation of $10,000 was made from the State treasury to aid the county societies in offering premiums. This was, I think, the beginning of State aid to county societies. This board published three volumes of "Memoirs," the first in 1821, the last in 1826. This board ceased to live in 1825, and a legislative committee reported that in the six years of its existence the total amount appropriated by the State and expended by the societies amounted to upwards of $52,000,* of which over $46,000 was paid to county societies. These various agricultural societies, more than any one other cause, secured to New York the leading rank in agriculture, population, and wealth. I find, in the publications of that time, very frequent allusions to the importance of preventing the "depopulation," by farmers emigrating further westward, as was then going on to such an extent from New England. And the argument then used was that, the way to do this was to improve the agriculture at home. It was then claimed that this action of the agricultural societies was not only improving the agriculture but was preventing this depopulation (as it was called) and that it called emigrants from other states. As a matter of fact, New York, which was the fourth state in population in 1790, and the third in 1800, had come to the front by 1810, and has since remained the "Empire State." The act creating the State Board was amended March 24, 1820, and the charter expired in 1825. There was no society organized to take its place until 1832. Feb. 14th of that year a convention met at Albany, at which thirty-one counties were represented, and means taken to organize a society, and as a result, the "New York State Agricultural Society" was incorporated by act passed April 26, 1832. This act was amended Feb. 10, 1841, giving the society essentially the shape it now has. Now it began to hold annual exhibitions, since so noted, and to publish those volumes of "Transactions" so familiar in all agricultural libraries.

To return to the earlier societies. The next society in the United States was "The Massachusetts Society for Promoting Agriculture," which was incorporated in 1792, and "diffused much practical information by means of a series of papers known as the *Agricultural Repository*," and afterwards by a publication styled the *Massachusetts Journal of Agriculture*. This, too, after changes suggested by experience, is, I think, still in existence.

The next society was organized in this State in 1794, of which I will speak more fully by and by.

So far as I have learned, these five societies were all that were formed in the first twenty-five years of our national existence. Some of them extended their operations beyond their own State, the Philadelphia society awarded a gold medal in 1790 to a Rhode Island farmer and the Massachusetts society did the same to Col. Humphries in this State, for his importation of merino sheep.

In the centennial year, the U.S. Commissioner of Agriculture published a "List of Agricultural Societies and Farmers' Clubs * * * on the books of the Department of Agriculture, July 4, 1876, being the Centennial year of American Independence." I have enumerated the only societies, five in number, formed during the first quarter-century. According to the list referred to, of organizations in existence in 1876, and on the books of the Department, sixteen were formed in the next quarter-century, 1802 to 1826 inclusive; 376 in the next quarter, 1827 to 1851; and over 1,500 were formed in the last quarter, 1852 to 1876. In this list, forty-seven societies are enumerated in Connecticut, of which only six were organized before 1850, and seventeen before 1860.

Inasmuch as one of the original five societies on this grand list started in this State, something more of its history may interest you. Its "Transactions" published in 1802 tells us that "A number of citizens, from different towns in the State of Connecticut, convened at Wallingford, on the 12th day of August, A.D. 1794, for the purpose of forming a society for promoting agriculture; and having shown their approbation of the plan proposed, appointed a committee to draft a constitution for the society and report to the next meeting. On the 11th day of November, 1794, the committee, before appointed, reported," etc. In short, the society was organized. They published one volume of "Transactions of the Society for Promoting Agriculture in the State of Connecticut," in 1802, a quarto pamphlet of but nineteen pages of printed matter. I infer that its first president was James Wadsworth, as I find his name under the advertisements calling meetings in 1796 and for some years later. It met at various places, at Wallingford, Cheshire, New Haven, etc., and extended its influence and operations over various parts of the State, although most of its meetings (if not all) were held in New Haven county. A new constitution was made in 1803, and its business records exist in manuscript from that date. A library was started in 1807, but I cannot find what became of it or that the papers read at the meetings have been preserved. Advertisements for calls of meetings as early as 1799 speak of it as "The Agricultural Society of the State of Connecticut," and the manuscript records state that Sept. 10, 1817, a committee was appointed to apply to the Legislature for an act of incorporation, which committee reported at a meeting on March 10, 1818, that the Legislature had "declined incorporating us by the name of The Connecticut Agricultural Society, but were willing to grant an act of incorporation under the name of The Agricultural Society of New Haven." The society voted "to accept such act and name," and it still exists as the flourishing *County Society* of New Haven. But two societies in the United States are older, but this has had a continuous, living existence from the time of its first organization to the present without other break than came from the act of incorporation which changed its name and in effect restricted its operations to one county.

But its influence has been much wider. What it has been on the state and on the world we can never know; but my belief is that it has been especially great and far-reaching. Col. Humphreys was long an active member, and for a time its president, but the society had been in existence, and was moving our farming interests for eight years before the importation of his merinos, and nearly twenty years before those other importations of merinos into New Haven, which several importations practically laid the foundations of the so-called American Merino Sheep, which breed has done more during the last forty or fifty years to improve the wool of the world than all the other breeds combined.

And we can trace its influence in other directions also, not only in the prosperity of this State, for it was active just at the time when Connecticut was powerfully influencing the West through emigration from our farmers, and perhaps the South also, through the cotton-gin.

It will be noticed that during the first twenty-five years, the few societies were general, and belonged to states. If any county societies were formed before 1800, I have no account of them, but very soon after that we hear of them, and their formation characterizes this second period. I think it probable that the first county societies were started on the Hudson river. The famous Berkshire (Mass.) society started in 1807. The beginning may be said to have been the exhibition of two merino sheep, "under the big elm tree," in the fall of that year, by Elkanah Watson. Its first formal cattle-show, however, was held in September, 1810. This was not the first cattle-show in the country (as many believe), for the *Ulster County Plebeian,* (Kingston, N.Y.), in a notice of that show, says, that "the laudable example exhibited by our sister county of Dutchess, in instituting a society for agricultural fairs, has been adopted in various parts of the country, with a zeal that insures the most extensive benefits," etc. The work went on actively, and Elkanah Watson says, "on the 22d of October 1819, the first boat sailed on the Erie Canal from Rome to Utica. It was drag'd by a single horse, trotting on the embankment, in the tow-path. It was an elegant boat, constructed to carry passengers. . . . The scene was truly sublime. . . . This was a proud month for the State of New York. While *new agricultural societies were exhibiting in every direction,"* etc., etc.

The fact that at the organization of the State Board of Agriculture of New York, January 10, 1820, twenty-six county societies were represented by their officers, gives us another view of the activity of that period, and an article "on the utility of cattle-shows," by the President of the Massachusetts Agricultural Society in the *Massachusetts Agricultural Repository and Journal* for January, 1825, says, "it is no longer necessary to justify these exhibitions, since fifty millions of men in Europe and America have sanctioned them by their adoption," that in France there are about ninety (one in each department), in England not so many, but they are numerous and very efficient, "and the United States have at this moment nearly fifty public exhibitions of this description."

Plowing matches also began about this time, along with the fairs. The first plowing match I know of in this State is described in the *Connecticut Journal* (New Haven) of July 12, 1810. It took place on the Fourth of July, started by "the farmers, shepherds, mechanics, and manufacturers, in Col. Humphreys' employ." The account says, that "at dawn of day, in a field of eighteen acres marked out into lands of one acre each, fourteen plows started, each in its own land," etc. The first prize was won by a farmer who used oxen and had come three miles, and who finished his acre before nine o'clock. Horse, mule, and ox teams were used. The dinner for one hundred and fifty-two persons was "prepared hot on the ground by means of a portable Rumford kitchen." The account cited goes into full details of the affair, which, although not under the auspices of a *society*, yet shows the drift of the times.

Agricultural balls too came into fashion during this period, in connection with local societies, and Mr. Watson gives some amusing anecdotes of the haps and mishaps arising from them, particularly of his sending a package of such ball-tickets to the president of a county society in New York State, who chanced to be a Quaker, and the package was unfortunately opened by his good wife, who was a Quakeress preacher of some repute, to the great dismay of the family and confusion of the zealous sender.

During the next quarter century, 1827 to 1851, societies multiplied by hundreds, and town societies and farmers' clubs began to be noticed. It is possible that farmers' clubs began much earlier, for I have found in the *Connecticut Journal* of March 30, 1791, reprinted from the *Gazette of the United States,* a letter about a *Farmers' Club*, but whether this describes a genuine club in operation, or merely what might be, I do not know, nor have I any data as to when these useful organizations actually began.

I have spent so much time on this historical sketch, because I felt that it was important for an intelligent grasp of the real uses and functions of agricultural societies, and under this head, I include all organizations which have for their immediate object the promotion of the interests of the tiller of the soil or grower of live-stock. They are so numerous, so varied in their character, so wide-reaching in their operations and influences that it would take more than one lecture to describe their mere characters and special aims.

We have national societies and associations of various kinds. State agricultural societies, boards of agriculture, regional societies (like the New England Society, or that of the Ohio Valley), county and town societies, farmers' clubs, horticultural societies and fruit-growers' associations. Cotton-planters and cane-growers have each their associations. There are dairymen's associations and various kinds of organizations devoted to live-stock. Nearly every improved breed of live-stock has its particular and separate society to promote its interests, Ayrshires, Merinoes, Short-horns, Berkshires, trotters, etc., etc., has each its society or association. There are poultry societies and pigeon associations. There are granges and congresses, and so on — indeed, it seems as if each and every department and sub-department of this great industry had its special organization, to promote its particular interests in such ways as the associated wisdom of the society can suggest, and the combined powers of its members effect. And these differ as widely in their scope as in their aims. Some are as broad as the nation, others as narrow as a neighborhood. Some are so general as to relate to everything that is grown on the farm or that can be used there by the farmer and his family. Others are as special as a single breed of pigs. In numbers, probably more than 2,500 of one kind and another exist to-day in the United States.

Now, how have they operated to promote agriculture and educate the farmer?

I will not claim to tell *all* the ways, nor give in detail all their beneficent workings. I hope to call attention to enough of them to make you all think of other ways which I have left out, and which possibly may have not occurred to me.

First, and most important, they get farmers together to learn from each other, each to see what others are doing and how they do it, and to have their wits sharpened by the rubbing of mind against mind.

The farmer's work is most of it solitary, or nearly so; at least, it is not performed by large numbers of men together. From the very nature of the vocation, farmers see little of each other directly in their business. The merchant, the manufacturer, the professional man, each is thrown in contact with many other men of various vocations, and with men of their own calling. They are also thrown into very sharp face to face competition, amounting to almost conflict. The battles in the professions and in the arenas of trade are mostly battles between *men*. It is individual intellect opposed to individual intellect. But from the necessities of his calling, the farmer's battles are mostly with the forces of nature, and where he carries on his fight comparatively alone and in silence. He thus learns to rely so much on his own private judgment, or it may be on his individual whims, that he is particularly liable to overrate his own judgment as compared with his neighbor's, and as a consequence to think that his own ways and methods are the best, and that his own experience is better than that of others. It is this that makes the calling so very conservative.

This tendency is perhaps increased by their actual intelligence in this country, where the farmers as a class are more intelligent, in the best sense of that word, than any other class which has so much of hand labor (or, as we call it, "hard work"), to perform. Combining the offices of overseer and manager of the business with that of the skilled workman, he is at once the employer and the laborer. He must be personally familiar with a greater variety of manual operations than any other laboring man or mechanic is required to know, he must exercise his judgement in a greater variety of ways, and, as before said, with less contact with other men than other business men have, — all this makes him peculiarly liable to underrate the experiences of others and to become prejudiced in favor of his own ways.

Now, there is one, and only one way to remedy this, and that is, to meet his equals, his peers in his own calling, see what they do, how they do it, and with what success. For this purpose no other plan has yet been found so efficient as agricultural societies and exhibitions, of one kind and another.

Theoretically, it would seem as if all this could be got from the printed book or agricultural newspaper. These should be in every farmer's house, and have their effect; but they do not and cannot do the work I am speaking of. We need to meet men face to face, talk with them, wrestle with them in argument. It is so in all other vocations; it must be so in ours. It is just as in teaching and spreading religious truths: the printed tract can never take the place of the preached word, nor the religious newspaper ever take the place of the living preacher. Actual progress is most rapid when both go together.

Next in importance, men are educated by seeing things. It may be tools or machines to do work, it may be animals, it may be fruit, and along with this is the stimulus of prizes to establish standards of excellence. The stimulus of premiums is not to be measured by the money value of the prizes won. Here, as everywhere else, a *prize* won, means a victory won, and it is this which gives it its chief value. I question if all the money won at agricultural fairs more than half pays the actual expenses of the winners in entering the object exhibited, caring for it there, and getting it home again. It is not the *cup*, won at a boat-race, that incites young men to do so much labor, spend so much time and money, and exercise so much self-denial while training, but its possession is the sign of *victory* — and so of the prizes won at our fairs.

In previous ages the stimulus of rivalry did not work so strongly among farmers as among men in most other vocations, partly because of oppressive laws, and partly because of the state of society, but now agricultural societies and exhibitions are stimulating this, because of the call for excellence in such a variety of products; indeed, a successful fair must offer many premiums, for many things, and be attended by many people. The very *crowd* educates itself, and what a remarkable kind of crowd it calls together! Where else and when else do we see such vast crowds with so little disorder, and so little need of police repression, as at our modern fairs or exhibitions?

Again, with modern means of production, competition is sharper than ever before. Steam transportation has put the farmers of widely separated regions into direct competition with each other, and now they need societies and exhibitions even more than before to bring them into contact with new and competing methods.

When agricultural societies began, there was but little agricultural literature, and they published but little before the second quarter-century (1802 to 1825), into which I have divided my historical sketch, and this second period is the most instructive for us to consider, as it shows so well *how* societies work in diffusing knowledge, and *what* the effect is, for that quarter closed before railroads and steam-power and other modern things had affected agriculture in this country, and before we had any distinctive agricultural press, for of all our present vast accumulation of agricultural literature, a very small proportion indeed was printed before 1826.

Three of the five original societies of the first period, ceased to exist in second period or else changed in their methods. They were either reorganized to adapt themselves to new conditions, or they simply ceased to exist, to give place to a new society better adapted to the work, for it was usually easier to form a new society than to remodel an old one. It was during this second period that the societies began to be formed of the kind we are now familiar with: meetings for papers, discussions, exhibitions and fairs, with prizes and premiums, and at the close of the period, they were well at work. A few tools and implements were exhibited at the meetings in Albany as early as 1796 or 1797, and probably at the other societies also; but regular exhibitions and cattle-shows, such as we know them, began in this second period, and at its close, it is said that fifty societies had held exhibitions.

Now, what was the actual result of all this? What was the state of agriculture in this country at the close of this period of a quarter-century in 1826, compared with its state at its beginning in 1801?

First and most wonderful was the rapid and universal introduction of better farm tools, implements, and machines. At the beginning of this period, the wicker fan, the wooden plow, wooden pitchfork, and the hand-rake, were in universal use, the cradle had as yet but partly supplanted the sickle, the grain-drill was known but not used, the flail or the tramping of animals were the almost universal means of threshing. All of these had been invented before, some long before, all were known to a few persons in this country and yet *very* few used them. To the mass of farmers at the beginning of this period they were practically unknown; at its end they were in common use, and except the grain-drill and threshing-machine, the new and improved implements had entirely supplanted the old and former kinds, and the methods of farming were practically revolutionized. Why, even four-wheeled wagons were rare in this State at the beginning of this period; many whole towns were without a single one until long after 1801. For many years I have been questioning old farmers about the tools and farm-implements of their boyhood, and the date of the introduction of improved kinds, and they all tell practically the same story, that the implements had long been known or heard of, then some would be exhibited or used at fairs, soon every one began *talking* about them, a few enterprising farmers would buy them, and then, almost suddenly, everybody else would want them. Of all these, the cast-iron plow perhaps wrought the greatest change, and met too the greatest opposition to its introduction. Yet in fifteen years from the time it began to be seen, it had found its way to perhaps nineteen-twentieths of the farms.

Remember that all these tools and machines had been invented and somewhat used before, why were they not *generally* used before, and why did they then spread so suddenly into common use? What was the moral agency which so rapidly changed this most conservative of industries? My own belief, founded on a careful study of the agriculture and agricultural features of that day, is that the great moving agent in this revolution was *agricultural societies and their exhibitions;* other elements helped, of course, but this was the great one.

The agricultural newspapers, now such a means of carrying useful information to the farmers' houses, then scarcely existed at all. It was the *seeing* of things and talking with the persons who used them that led to the rapid introduction of better tools and machines. Men would see them at the agricultural exhibitions, then would talk about them, then use them, and once used, men would never go back to the poorer methods again.

The next most important influence (perhaps the most important in the end although not so obvious at first), was that it destroyed the intense prejudice against what was stigmatized as *"book farming,"* and this paved the way for agriculture to practically apply the truths of science. When these societies began, this prejudice existed all through the masses. How very intense it was and in what contempt book farmers were held, we find hard now to appreciate.

But just before this century began, these societies began to publish papers, "memoirs," "transactions," pamphlets, and other documents. As these mostly emanated from farmers themselves, many of whom were men well known as statesmen or venerated for their patriotism, and as this printed matter was put out by societies composed of farmers, they broke down the prejudice against "book-farming," so-called — at least, against books about farming, and as that prejudice melted away it left the soil of the public mind ready to receive the truths of science; it also paved the way for the agricultural newspaper. These would have been useless before. Agricultural societies had to plow the soil first, and turn it up to the light, and it was like the breaking up of an old sod. But when well broken, science might furnish the seed and the agricultural newspapers scatter it, and find a congenial soil for it to take root. If societies had done nothing else than this, it would have been a glorious result in itself, and well paid for all the work it cost.

Moreover, the societies themselves have been a great source of agricultural literature; the immense mass of official "Reports" that have been printed doubtless contain much chaff with the grain, but in all farming operations we must clean the good wheat from the worthless chaff, we must weed our fields and weed our stock; so too, if the literature of our societies has to be winnowed, that is no sign that it lacks good grain.

Again, the getting together of the influential men of this class, tended to impress farmers themselves with the importance and dignity of their calling, and this I think was no small gain. Washington was an officer in one society, John Adams was at one time President of the Massachusetts society, Mr. Madison delivered addresses before another; it is only in modern times, and only a certain class of modern newspapers that sneers at a president of the United States for delivering "the address" at an agricultural exhibition, or even encouraging it by his presence. Many a man has been cheered in his calling when he sees what respectable company he is in.

Again, the societies did much to improve the varieties of grain; or rather, to spread the knowledge of the better kinds. In accounts of the meetings of societies at this early period, I find frequent accounts of improved varieties of grain being exhibited, and often of seed being distributed. It is mentioned that farmers took home with them new kinds of grain to try them.

Along with this was the decrease in the cultivation of certain old-world plants long tried here, but which we now hear nothing of. Indeed, in the publications of these very societies, in New York and New England, we find papers on the cultivation of lucerne, vetches, spelt, rape, spurry, poppies, madder, woad, etc., etc. Some of these plants had been under trial here for more than a hundred years; and under the old system of things we would have been trying them yet, had it not been for these influences at work which tended to eliminate the least profitable, by teaching to profit by the experiences and failures of others.

With live-stock the good effects were even more marked than with grain; for at the fairs the better kinds of animals would be seen by the farmers present, the breeds compared with each other, intelligent discussion provoked, and the public thus educated as to what good stock really was; every one could see it, and see the differences between the good and the poor. We find all over the country importations of all kinds of improved animals. Then was that great importation of merino sheep, as well as other breeds; short-horns and various breeds of stock began to come. Frank Forester says that there were more thoroughbred horses in this country before 1820 than there were thirty years later. But it was with sheep, cattle, and hogs that the effect was the most marked.

I well remember the first short-horn bull I ever saw. A new county society had just been formed, my father was one of the originators and officers; a fair was held, and a short-horn bull was exhibited. An illustrious farmer of that county, Mr. Ezra Cornell (later the founder of Cornell University), had just bought the bull "*Arab*," the first thoroughbred short-horn that was brought into that county. I was a very small lad then, for that was over forty years ago, but I well remember the crowds that stood around that animal all day, the curiosity to see a bull that cost several hundred dollars, the critical eye with which he was examined, and the comments on him. The society had offered a big prize — I mean big for such a society — for a short-horn bull to be shown at that fair, and that prize, I afterwards learned, was the incentive to that bull's introduction just then. That bull was the *lion* for that day. But the farmers were not so well satisfied with scrub stock after that; in a few years short-horns were no curiosity there, and the improvement in the quality of the stock in the next twenty years was worth several hundreds of thousands of dollars to that community. I dare say that half of the older men who now hear me could tell some similar story. Elkanah Watson bought two merino sheep in the fall of 1807, and as they were the first introduced into that county he exhibited them under the big elm in Pittsfield, and that started the celebrated Berkshire society.

I need not dwell on the influence fairs still have in spreading a knowledge of machines and appliances; the host of agents at every fair, however small, with all kinds of machines, from a patent apple-corer or pot-washer to a steam thresher or patent ditching-machine, is evidence enough that the manufacturers of to-day believe, from experience, that this is a great and sure way to get a knowledge of their wares before the people. And we all know the eagerness of breeders of fine stock to exhibit and thus advertise their animals.

Again, no other one thing has done so much to spread a knowledge of fruit and good vegetables among farmers and to stimulate their cultivation, as well as to educate the people as to the character and appearance of the different varieties. I have included the modern horticultural societies in this general sketch, for they are so intimately connected; moreover, all the principal agricultural societies have a horticultural department, and the exhibition of fruit and vegetables has so long been made a feature that the common style of cheap wit expended on agricultural exhibitions, is to allow them as mere shows of big squashes or overgrown turnips.

Not the least of the beneficent effects of annual exhibitions has been the effect on the farmers' families, particularly on the boys. After the harder work of the summer is passed, how the "fair day" is looked forward to as a grand gala day, and after it is passed, how much there has been seen and heard to talk about. It would indeed be a sad day for farmers' boys if fairs were abolished.

I shall say but little of the more special associations, important though they are, — I mean such organizations as poultry societies, horticultural societies, associations for the cultivation of special crops, or for the promotion of special breeds of live-stock. Such associations have done great work, and they must continue to increase as farming becomes more and more specialized.

This tendency to greater specialization, that is, to the growing of fewer and fewer kinds of crops, is one that is most marked, and while it is mostly brought about by modern phases of trade and commerce, fairs have tended to increase it. We do not cultivate so many kinds of crops to-day as we did fifty or seventy-five years ago. I have already explained how the societies and their exhibitions tended to eliminate or weed out our less profitable crops, until many have passed so completely out of sight that we now rarely even hear of them here, and the younger generation does not even know their looks.

Without attempting to enumerate more of the uses, — what are the duties of farmers towards societies? The answer is easy — *sustain them and attend them*. If you have anything to say, why say it. If you have anything to show, show it; above all things, don't stay at home and grumble. It is bad enough to go to the meeting or fair and grumble, but it is worse to stay at home, for at the fair the most stubborn and self conceited man may learn something in spite of himself.

There are probably 800 or 1,000 exhibitions devoted entirely or in part to the interests of agriculture, held in the United States every year, and probably five or more millions of people see something of them. It would be passing strange if in all these, voluntary gatherings as they are, and pertaining to such a variety of interests and multitude of details, it would be strange, I say, if something did not sometimes creep in that had better be left out; but how very little there is of this compared with all that is meritorious! Taken all in all, their work and their record has been a glorious one, and they will continue to be a prominent feature in our progressing civilization.

Establishment of a Bureau of Animal Industry, 1884

From 23 U.S. Statutes at Large 31.

AN ACT FOR THE ESTABLISHMENT OF A BUREAU OF ANIMAL INDUSTRY, TO PREVENT THE EXPORTATION OF DISEASED CATTLE, AND TO PROVIDE MEANS FOR THE SUPPRESSION AND EXTIRPATION OF PLEURO-PNEUMONIA AND OTHER CONTAGIOUS DISEASES AMONG DOMESTIC ANIMALS

Be it enacted by the Senate and House of Representatives of the United States of America in Congress assembled, That the Commissioner of Agriculture shall organize in his Department a Bureau of Animal Industry, and shall appoint a Chief thereof, who shall be a competent veterinary surgeon, and whose duty it shall be to investigate and report upon the condition of the domestic animals of the United States, their protection and use, and also inquire into and report the causes of contagious, infectious, and communicable diseases among them, and the means for the prevention and cure of the same, and to collect such information on these subjects as shall be valuable to the agricultural and commercial interests of the country; and the Commissioner of Agriculture is hereby authorized to employ a force sufficient for this purpose, not to exceed twenty persons at any one time. The salary of the Chief of said Bureau shall be three thousand dollars per annum; and the Commissioner shall appoint a clerk for said Bureau, with a salary of one thousand five hundred dollars per annum.

SEC. 2. That the Commissioner of Agriculture is authorized to appoint two competent agents, who shall be practical stock-raisers or experienced business men familiar with questions pertaining to commercial transactions in live stock, whose duty it shall be, under the instructions of the Commissioner of Agriculture, to examine and report upon the best methods of treating, transporting, and caring for animals, and the means to be adopted for the suppression and extirpation of contagious pleuro-pneumonia, and to provide against the spread of other dangerous contagious, infectious, and communicable diseases. The compensation of said agents shall be at the rate of ten dollars per diem, with all necessary expenses, while engaged in the actual performance of their duties under this act, when absent from their usual place of business or residence as such agent.

SEC. 3. That it shall be the duty of the Commissioner of Agriculture to prepare such rules and regulations as he may deem necessary for the speedy and effectual suppression and extirpation of said diseases, and to certify such rules and regulations to the executive authority of each State and Territory, and invite said authorities to co-operate in the execution and enforcement of this act. Whenever the plans and methods of the Commissioner of Agriculture shall be accepted by any State or Territory in which pleuro-pneumonia or other contagious, infectious, or communicable disease is declared to exist, or such State or Territory shall have adopted plans and methods for the suppression and extirpation of said diseases, and such plans and methods shall be accepted by the Commissioner of Agriculture, and whenever the governor of a State or other properly constituted authorities signify their readiness to co-operate for the extinction of any contagious, infectious, or communicable diseases in conformity with the provisions of this act, the Commissioner of Agriculture is hereby authorized to expend so much of the money appropriated by this act as may be necessary in such investigations, and in such disinfection and quarantine measures as may be necessary to prevent the spread of the disease from one State or Territory into another.

SEC. 4. That in order to promote the exportation of live stock from the United States the Commissioner of Agriculture shall make special investigation as to the existence of pleuro-pneumonia, or any contagious, infectious, or communicable disease, along the dividing-lines between the United States and foreign countries, and along the lines of transportation from all parts of the United States to ports from which live stock are exported, and make report of the results of such investigation to the Secretary of the Treasury, who shall, from time to time, establish such regulations concerning the exportation and transportation of live stock as the results of said investigations may require.

SEC. 5. That to prevent the exportation from any port of the United States to any port in a foreign country of live stock affected with any contagious, infectious, or communicable disease, and especially pleuro-pneumonia, the Secretary of the Treasury be, and he is hereby, authorized to take such steps and adopt such measures, not inconsistent with the provisions of this act, as he may deem necessary.

SEC. 6. That no railroad company within the United States, or the owners or masters of any steam or sailing or other vessel or boat, shall receive for transportation or transport, from one State or Territory to another, or from any State into the District of Columbia, or from the District into any State, any live stock affected with any contagious, infectious, or communicable disease, and especially the disease known as pleuro-pneumonia; nor shall any person, company, or corporation deliver for such transportation to any railroad company, or master or owner of any boat or vessel, any live stock, knowing them to be affected with any contagious, infectious, or communicable disease; nor shall any person, company, or corporation drive on foot or transport in private conveyance from one State or Territory to another, or from any State into the District of Columbia, or from the District into any State, any live stock, knowing them to be affected with any contagious, infectious, or communicable disease, and especially the disease known as pleuro-pneumonia: *Provided,* That the so called splenetic or Texas fever shall not be considered a contagious, infectious, or communicable disease within the meaning of sections four, five, six and seven of this act, as to cattle being transported by rail to market for slaughter, when the same are unloaded only to be fed and watered in lots on the way thereto.

SEC. 7. That it shall be the duty of the Commissioner of Agriculture to notify, in writing, the proper officials or agents of any railroad, steamboat, or other transportation company doing business in or through any infected locality, and by publication in such newspapers as he may select, of the existence of said contagion; and any person or persons operating any such railroad, or master or owner of any boat or vessel, or owner or custodian of or person having control over such cattle or other live stock within such infected district, who shall knowingly violate the provisions of section six of this act, shall be guilty of a misdemeanor, and, upon conviction, shall be punished by a fine of not less than one hundred nor more than five thousand dollars, or by imprisonment for not more than one year, or by both such fine and imprisonment.

SEC. 8. That whenever any contagious, infectious, or communicable disease affecting domestic animals, and especially the disease known as pleuro-pneumonia, shall be brought into or shall break out in the District of Columbia, it shall be the duty of the Commissioners of said District to take measures to suppress the same promptly and to prevent the same from spreading; and for this purpose the said Commissioners are hereby empowered to order and require that any premises, farm, or farms where such disease exists, or has existed, be put in quarantine; to order all or any animals coming into the District to be detained at any place or places for the purpose of inspection and examination; to prescribe regulations for and to require the destruction of animals affected with contagious, infectious, or communicable disease, and for the proper disposition of their hides and carcasses; to prescribe regulations for disinfection, and such other regulations as they may deem necessary to prevent infection or contagion being communicated, and shall report to the Commissioner of Agriculture whatever they may do in pursuance of the provisions of this section.

SEC. 9. That it shall be the duty of the several United States district attorneys to prosecute all violations of this act which shall be brought to their notice or knowledge by any person making the complaint under oath; and the same shall be heard before any district or circuit court of the United States or Territorial court holden within the district in which the violation of this act has been committed.

SEC. 10. That the sum of one hundred and fifty thousand dollars, to be immediately available, or so much thereof, as may be necessary, is hereby appropriated, out of any moneys in the Treasury not otherwise appropriated, to carry into effect the provisions of this act.

SEC. 11. That the Commissioner of Agriculture shall report annually to Congress, at the commencement of each session, a list of the names of all persons employed, an itemized statement of all expenditures under this act, and full particulars of the means adopted and carried into effect for the suppression of contagious, infectious, or communicable diseases among domestic animals.

Approved, May 29, 1884.

Work of Bureau of Animal Industry, 1884

From U.S. Department of Agriculture, *Annual Report,* 1884, pp. 5–6.

DEPARTMENT OF AGRICULTURE,
Washington, D.C., November 10, 1884.

To the President:

I respectfully submit a statement of the work done in the Department of Agriculture during the year 1884.

During the year the duties of the Department have largely increased. The extension of the work of the Bureau of Statistics has furnished the chief a large amount of matter, which he has with great diligence and skill reduced to statistical form and embodied in a monthly report, which has attracted great attention both in this country and in Europe. In addition to Mr. Moffatt, who reports from London upon the trade and industry of Europe, there are ten thousand correspondents of this Department in this country, who are constantly furnishing the materials for the statistical estimates of the Bureau. The establishment of a Bureau of Animal Industry in the Department has also added very largely to its duties, and the work required by it has been most satisfactorily performed. The Bureau of Entomology has been most efficiently represented abroad by its chief, and its investigations in this country have been conducted with great care and success. I submit extended statements of the work of these several bureaus.

Bureau of Animal Industry.

This Bureau, established by act of Congress approved May 29, 1884, has been organized during the year, and it is now in active and efficient operation. Investigations have been made in regard to the extent, nature, and means of combating outbreaks of communicable diseases among the domesticated animals of the country in the States of Maine, Connecticut, New York, New Jersey, Pennsylvania, Maryland, Virginia, Tennessee, Kentucky, Ohio, Indiana, Illinois, Missouri, Kansas, Arkansas, and Texas. While the prevalence of such diseases is probably not much in excess of what it has been in previous years, the organization of the Bureau has led to a greatly increased number of demands for information on the subject, and the existence of dangerous diseases has been more promptly and fully reported than heretofore.

Scientific investigations in regard to the nature and cause of contagious diseases among animals have been constantly in progress, and are throwing much light on the difficult problems which are encountered by those who practically attempt to reduce the ravages of these plagues. An extended microscopic investigation of American pork has been made to learn what foundation there was for the charge of trichinous infection which has been brought against it in Europe.

A great mass of information has been collected in relation to the development and needs of the various branches of the live-stock industry, with a view of enabling the owners of animals of all kinds to escape preventable losses, and to direct their efforts in the most promising direction.

The practical direction of the quarantine system, which was transferred to the Department of Agriculture by the Secretary of the Treasury in accordance with a recent act of Congress, has been made one of the duties of this Bureau. The professional knowledge of the chief, who must be a competent veterinary surgeon, taken in connection with the information which is being continually received by this Bureau as to the presence of contagious diseases in those foreign countries from which we import cattle, and the most advanced methods of controlling these diseases, makes it peculiarly appropriate that the protection of American cattle from imported diseases should be in the same hands.

In a word, the labor of this Bureau has been directed to prevent and control communicable diseases among animals in this country, to prevent the importation of such plagues from abroad, and to collect such information as is valuable to the stock-grower and necessary to the profitable development and conduct of our animal industries, and to enable us to secure free entrance for our animal products into the markets of the world.

Congress has provided for the publication of fifty thousand copies of the first annual report of the Bureau of Animal Industry. This report will be issued simultaneously with this volume, and will contain a vast amount of information of great value to breeding, rearing, and the general traffic in live stock.

The Hatch Act, 1887

From 24 U.S. Statutes at Large 440.

ACT OF 1887 ESTABLISHING AGRICULTURAL EXPERIMENT STATIONS

Be it enacted by the Senate and House of Representatives of the United States of America in Congress assembled, That in order to aid in acquiring and diffusing among the people of the United States useful and practical information on subjects connected with agriculture, and to promote scientific investigation and experiment respecting the principles and applications of agricultural science, there shall be established under principles and applications of agricultural science, there shall be established under direction of the college or colleges or agricultural department of colleges in each State or Territory extablished, or which may hereafter be established, in accordance with the provisions of an act approved July second, eighteen hundred and sixty-two, entitled "An act donating public lands to the several States and Territories which may provide colleges for the benefit of agriculture and the mechanic arts," or any of the supplements to said act, a department to be known and designed as an "agricultural experiment station": *Provided,* That in any State or Territory in which two such colleges have been or may be so established the appropriation hereinafter made to such State or Territory shall be equally divided between such colleges, unless the legislature of such State or Territory shall otherwise direct.

SEC. 2. That it shall be the object and duty of said experiment stations to conduct original researches or verify experiments on the physiology of plants and animals; the diseases to which they are severally subject, with the remedies for the same; the chemical composition of useful plants at their different stages of growth; the comparative advantages of rotative cropping as pursued under a varying series of crops; the capacity of new plants or trees for acclimation; the analysis of soils and water; the chemical composition of manures, natural or artificial, with experiments designed to test their comparative effects on crops of different kinds; the adaptation and value of grasses and forage plants; the composition and digestibility of the different kinds of food for domestic animals; the scientific and economic questions involved in the production of butter and cheese; and such other researches or experiments bearing directly on the agricultural industry of the United States as may in each case be deemed advisable, having due regard to the varying conditions and needs of the respective States or Territories.

SEC. 3. That in order to secure, as far as practicable, uniformity of methods and results in the work of said stations, it shall be the duty of the United States Commissioner [now Secretary] of Agriculture to furnish forms, as far as practicable, for the tabulation of results of investigation or experiments; to indicate from time to time such lines of inquiry as to him shall seem most important, and, in general, to furnish such advice and assistance as will best promote the purpose of this act. It shall be the duty of each of said stations annually, on or before the first day of February, to make to the governor of the State or Territory in which it is located a full and detailed report of its operations, including a statement of receipts and expenditures, a copy of which report shall be sent to each of said stations, to the said Commissioner [now Secretary] of Agriculture, and to the Secretary of the Treasury of the United States.

SEC. 4. That bulletins or reports of progress shall be published at said stations at least once in three months, one copy of which shall be sent to each newspaper in the States or Territories in which they are respectively located, and to such individuals actually engaged in farming as may request the same, and as far as the means of the station will permit. Such bulletins or reports and the annual reports of said stations shall be transmitted in the mails of the United States free of charge for postage, under such regulations as the Postmaster General may from time to time prescribe.

SEC. 5. That for the purpose of paying the necessary expenses of conducting investigations and experiments and printing and distributing the results as hereinbefore prescribed, the sum of fifteen thousand dollars per annum is hereby appropriated to each State, to be specially provided for by Congress in the appropriations from year to year, and to each Territory entitled under the provisions of section eight of this act, out of any money in the Treasury proceeding from the sales of public lands, to be paid in equal quarterly payments on the first day of January, April, July, and October in each year, to the treasurer or other officer duly appointed by the governing boards of said colleges to receive the same, the first payment to be made on the first day of October, eighteen hundred and eighty-seven: *Provided, however,* That out of the first annual appropriation so received by any station an amount not exceeding one-fifth may be expended in the erection, enlargement, or repair of a building or buildings necessary for carrying on the work of such station; and thereafter an amount not exceeding five per centum of such annual appropriation may be so expended.

SEC. 6. That whenever it shall appear to the Secretary of the Treasury from the annual statement of receipts and expenditures of any of said stations that a portion of the preceding annual appropriations remains unexpended, such amount shall be deducted from the next succeeding annual appropriation to such station, in order that the amount of money appropriated to any station shall not exceed the amount actually and necessarily required for its maintenance and support.

SEC. 7. That nothing in this act shall be construed to impair or modify the legal relation existing between any of the said colleges and the government of the States or Territories in which they are respectively located.

SEC. 8. That in States having colleges entitled under this section to the benefits of this act and having also agricultural experiment stations established by law separate from said colleges, such States shall be authorized to apply such benefits to experiments at stations so established by such States; and in case any State shall have established under the provisions of said act of July second aforesaid, an agricultural department or experiment station, in connection with any university, college, or institution not distinctively an agricultural college or school, and such State shall have established or shall hereafter establish a separate agricultural college or school, which, shall have connected therewith an experimental farm or station, the legislature of such State may apply in whole or in part the appropriation by this act made, to such separate agricultural college, or school, and no legislature shall by contract, express or implied, disable itself from so doing.

SEC. 9. That the grants of moneys authorized by this act are made subject to the legislative assent of the several States and Territories to the purposes of said grants: *Provided,* That payment of such installments of the appropriation herein made as shall become due to any State before the adjournment of the regular session of its legislature meeting next after the passage of this act shall be made upon the assent of the governor thereof duly certified to the Secretary of the Treasury.

SEC. 10. Nothing in this act shall be held or construed as binding the United States to continue any payments from the Treasury to any or all the States or institutions mentioned in this act, but Congress may at any time amend, suspend, or repeal any or all the provisions of this act.

Approved March 2, 1887 (24 Stat. 440).

Development of Agricultural Experiment Stations

From A. C. True, "Origin and Development of Agricultural Experiment Stations in the United States," in U.S. Department of Agriculture, *Annual Report,* 1888, pp. 541–47.

In the United States, as in Europe, the first organized experimental work in agricultural science was done in connection with the higher educational institutions.

It is believed that Yale College was the first American institution to officially recognize the claims of agricultural science. In 1846 John P. Norton was appointed professor of agricultural chemistry and vegetable and animal physiology. Professor Norton began his lectures in 1847, and during the five years which intervened before his death he also wrote extensively for agricultural journals, edited an American edition of "Stevens on the Farm," and published a work of his own entitled "Elements of Agriculture." After the fund which had been established by the sale of the land-scrip donated to Connecticut under the act of Congress of July 2, 1862, had been given to the Sheffield Scientific School of Yale College in 1863, a professor of agriculture was added to the working force of that institution. Samuel W. Johnson, M. A., the successor of Professor Norton as professor of theoretical and agricultural chemistry, and William H. Brewer, Ph. D., the professor of agriculture, have for many years taken an active interest in all work for the promotion of agricultural science in Connecticut and elsewhere in the United States. Under their direction experimental work for the benefit of agriculture was carried on to a limited extent at New Haven more than twenty years ago. And it is doubtless safe to say that "through the influence of the professors and pupils trained in this school, more than to any other single cause, is due the recognition of the importance of the establishment of agricultural experiment stations, first in Connecticut and subsequently throughout the whole country."

In 1870 the president and fellows of Harvard College began to organize the school of agriculture and horticulture which had been provided for in the will of Mr. Benjamin Bussey, of Roxbury, Mass. This interesting document was signed July 30, 1835, and was proved soon after the death of the testator in 1842. It bequeathed half of the income of about $300,000, and 200 acres of land in Roxbury, to the President and Fellows of Harvard College, on condition that they establish on the farm "a course of instruction in practical agriculture, in useful and ornamental gardening, in botany, and in such other branches of natural science as may tend to promote a knowledge of practical agriculture and the various arts subservient thereto." Owing to other provisions of the will, it was not deemed advisable to begin the formation of the Bussey Institution earlier than 1870. In the same year, the trustees of the Massachusetts Society for Promoting Agriculture granted to the corporation of Harvard College a considerable sum "for the support of a laboratory and for experiments in agricultural chemistry to be conducted on the Bussey estate." The laboratory of the new institution was not ready for occupation until the last week in 1871. As soon as it was completed, however, agricultural researches were begun by F. H. Storer, the professor of agricultural chemistry, and his assistants. The first report of work done was presented to a committee of the trustees of the Massachusetts Society for Promoting Agriculture, December 3, 1871. The experiments consisted of field tests of fertilizers upon the farm of the institution, and chemical analyses of commercial fertilizers. Other interesting and valuable work was done in the next few years, but the great fire in Boston, in 1872, and the commercial crisis of 1873, combined to cripple the institution financially, and it has since been able to make comparatively few original investigations. Meanwhile, agricultural colleges had been organized in a number of the States. Michigan led the way in 1857, and New York soon followed her example. After the passage of the land-grant act in 1862, Kansas and Massachusetts were the first States to avail themselves of the national gift by establishing agricultural colleges, and thereafter the formation of these institutions proceeded with as much rapidity as could have been expected when the country was recovering from the direful effects of the civil war. Experimental work in agriculture was undertaken in several of these institutions soon after their organization.

The reports of the successful and beneficial work done in the European experiment stations excited more and more attention on this side of the Atlantic, and the more advanced leaders in agricultural progress in this country began to ask for the establishment of similar institutions in the United States. In 1872, at a convention of representatives of agricultural colleges held in Washington in response to a call issued by the Commissioner of Agriculture, the question of the establishment of experiment stations was discussed, and the report of a committee in favor of such institutions was adopted by the convention.

On the 17th of December, 1873, at the winter meeting of the State Board of Agriculture, at Meriden, Conn., Professor Johnson, of the Sheffield Scientific School, and Professor Atwater, of Wesleyan University, urged the establishment of an agricultural experiment station in that State after the European pattern. A committee was appointed to consider the expediency of such a movement, and reported two days later that it was "their unanimous opinion that the State of Connecticut ought to have an experiment station as good as can be found anywhere, and that the legislature ought to furnish the means for its establishment." A permanent committee was then appointed by the board to bring this matter to the attention of the public and the legislature. This committee held meetings in different parts of the State, and the following winter secured the introduction of a bill for an experiment station, which, however, was laid over until the next session of the legislature. Another year of agitation of the matter ensued. The project had many warm and enthusiastic friends, but, as might have been expected, the great mass of the farmers took little interest in the enterprise. When it had become apparent that it could not succeed, Mr. Orange Judd, the editor of the American Agriculturist, offered on his own part $1,000 to begin the undertaking, and on the part of the trustees of Wesleyan University of Middletown the free use of the chemical laboratory in the Orange Judd Hall of Natural Science, donated by him to that institution. These offers were made on the condition that the legislature should appropriate $2,800 per annum for two years for the work of the station. It was thought that if by these means the work of agricultural experimentation could be actually begun the usefulness of the enterprise would be so clearly demonstrated that it would speedily be given more generous and permanent support. An act making the appropriation thus proposed was unanimously passed and approved July 2, 1875. Early in October of the same year a chemist was on the ground, and as soon as practicable two assistants were secured. Professor Atwater was made director, and thus the first agricultural experiment station in America was an accomplished fact.

A considerable amount of experimental work, chiefly on commercial fertilizers, was done with the limited means at the disposal of this first American agricultural experiment station. At the expiration of the two years provided for in the original bill the station was reorganized under the more direct control of the State and removed to New Haven, where it has since been in successful operation, first in rooms of Sheffield Hall, free use of which was granted by the Sheffield Scientific School, and later in buildings and grounds in the suburbs of New Haven, for the purchase and improvement of which the legislature provided $25,000 in 1882.

The success which attended this first attempt to establish an organized experiment station in the United States was sufficient to attract the attention of advanced agriculturists throughout the country, and March 12, 1877, the State of North Carolina established a similar station at Chapel Hill in connection with the State University.

The Cornell University Experiment Station was organized in February, 1879, by the faculty of agriculture of the University, as a voluntary organization.

From that time until the passage of the act of Congress of March 2, 1887, the work was carried on by the different professors in time which could be spared from other studies. For a part of that time the trustees of the University appropriated money from the University funds to pay for the services of an analyst and for the purchase of supplies. All the other work was done without compensation. The New Jersey State Station, at New Brunswick, N. J., was established March 18,1880, by an act of the State legislature, and connected with the Scientific School of Rutgers College. The movement grew in favor with the people with each succeeding year, and in 1886 the Committee on Agriculture, in reporting the Hatch bill to the House, was able to make the following statements:

Since 1881 the legislatures of several States have either recognized or reorganized the departments of agriculture in the land-grant colleges as "experiment stations," thus following substantially the course adopted by New Jersey. Such stations have been established in Maine, Massachusetts, Ohio, Tennessee, Wisconsin. In three other States (possibly more), without legislative action, the college authorities have organized their agricultural work as experiment stations. This has been done in California, Missouri, and New York; but in addition to the twelve experiment stations specifically designated by that name, a very large number of colleges established under the act of 1862 are doing important work of a precisely similar kind. Many of them began such work immediately upon their establishment, and have maintained it continuously; others have entered upon it more recently. The colleges in Colorado, Indiana, Kansas, Michigan, and Pennsylvania are carrying on what is strictly experiment-station work as a part of their ordinary duty.

The convention of delegates of agricultural colleges, which met at Washington in 1883, discussed and indorsed the project for the establishment of stations in connection with the colleges by appropriations from the national Treasury, in accordance with the terms of a bill already introduced in the House of Representatives by C. C. Carpenter, of Iowa. Congress, however, was not yet quite ready to undertake so large a scientific enterprise in this direction, and the bill was not put upon its passage. Meanwhile, the number of stations was steadily increasing, and the interest of practical farmers, as well as men of science, was more and more excited by the reports of the results of the experiments which the stations had completed. On the 8th of July, 1885, a convention of agricultural colleges and experiment stations met at the Department of Agriculture at Washington in response to a call issued by the Commissioner of Agriculture. Almost the first thing which this convention did was to pass a resolution —

That the condition and progress of American agriculture require national aid for the investigation and experimentation in the several States and Territories; and that, therefore, this convention approves the principle and general provisions of what is known as the Cullen bill of the last Congress, and urges upon the next Congress the passage of this or a similar act.

(The "Cullen bill" was in its general provisions similar to the bill afterwards passed by Congress and now known as the Hatch act.)

So earnest was the convention in this matter that it appointed a committee on legislation, which was very efficient in securing the passage of the amended bill.

In a later session the convention passed resolutions urging the creation of a branch of the Department of Agriculture which should be a special medium of intercommunication and exchange between the colleges and stations, and which should publish a periodical bulletin of agricultural progress, containing in a popular form the latest results in the progress of agricultural education, investigation, and experimentation in this and in all countries. Provision was also made for a permanent organization by the appointment of a committee to co-operate with the Commissioner of Agriculture in determining the time of meeting and the business of the next convention, and in forming a plan for a permanent organization.

At the next session of Congress the experiment-station enterprise was again called to the attention of the House of Representatives by the bill which was introduced by William H. Hatch, of Missouri, and referred to the Committee on Agriculture. This committee made a favorable report March 3, 1886, and nearly a year later the bill was passed by Congress, and approved by President Cleveland, March 2, 1887.

According to the official interpretation of the act establishing the stations they were unable to draw the appropriation contemplated in that act until after the passage of a supplementary act, which was approved February 1, 1888. This financial difficulty delayed the establishment of the stations in many of the States. At the present time, however, experiment stations are organized in all the States and in the Territory of Dakota. In several States more than one station has been organized, and in some States there are several branch stations under one management. Counting these latter as single stations the total number at present is forty-six, but counting the branch stations separately the total number is more than fifty.

The following table shows the number of separate stations and the number of the working force employed in each station, and also the sources and amount of the income which each station receives (as far as these facts have been reported to this office):

Table showing the number of officers composing the Station Staffs of the Agricultural Experiment Stations in the United States, and the revenues of those Stations for the fiscal year ending June 30, 1889, from the United States under the act of Congress of March 2, 1887, from the several States and from other sources.

State.	Name of station.	No. in staff.	Annual revenue.		
			From what source.	Am't.	Total.
Ala.....	Agricultural Experiment Station of the Agricultural and Mechanical College of Alabama..	10	Fertilizer fees......... $10,000 / United States......... 13,000		}$23,000
Ala.....	Canebrake Agricultural Experiment Station.....	2	State................ 2,500 / United States......... 2,000		} 4,500
Ark.....	Arkansas Agricultural Experiment Station......	10	....do............... 15,000		15,000
Cal......	Agricultural Experiment Station of University of California...........................	16	...do............... 15,000 / State, etc............ 13,000		} 28,000
Col......	Agricultural Experiment Station of Colorado....	12	United States......... 15,000		15,000
Conn....	Connecticut Agricultural Experiment Station ...	9	State................ 8,000 / Analysis fees, etc...... 3,100 / United States......... 7,500		} 18,600
Conn....	Storrs School Agricultural Experiment Station	5	....do............... 7,500		7,500
Dak.....	Dakota Agricultural Experiment Station........	11	....do............... 15,000		15,000
Del.....	Delaware College Agricultural Experiment Station	5	....do............... 15,000		15,000
Fla......	Agricultural Experiment Station of Florida......	....	....do............... 15,000		15,000
Ga......	Georgia Agricultural Experiment Station.......	7	....do............... 15,000		15,000
Ill.......	Agricultural Experiment Station of University of Illinois.	9	....do............... 15,000		15,000

Table showing the number of officers composing the Station Staffs of the Agricultural Experiment Stations in the United States, and the revenues, etc. — Continued.

State.	Name of station.	No. in staff.	Annual revenue.		
			From what source.	Am't.	Total.
Ind......	Agricultural Experiment Station of Indiana....	9	Proceeds of farm......	2,000	17,000
			United States.........	15,000	
Iowa....	Iowa Agricultural Experiment Station.........	11	....do...............	15,000	15,000
Kans....	Kansas Agricultural Experiment Station.......	12	....do...............	15,000	15,000
Ky......	Kentucky Agricultural Experiment Station......	8	...do...............	15,000	16,500
			Analysis fees, etc.......	1,500	
			State................	2,000	
La......	Sugar Experiment Station No. 1..............	7	Sugar planters.........	10,000	18,400
			Tax on fertilizers......	1,400	
			United States.........	5,000	
La......	State Agricultural Experiment Station No. 2.....	4	State................	2,000	8,400
			Tax on fertilizers......	1,400	
			United States.........	5,000	
La......	North Louisiana Experiment Station No. 3.....	2	State................	2,000	12,000
			Ouachita Parish.......	5,000	
			United States.........	5,000	
Me......	Maine State College Agricultural Experiment Station.	10	...do...............	15,000	15,000
Md......	Maryland Agricultural Experiment Station......	6	....do...............	15,000	15,000
Mass....	Hatch Experiment Station of Massachusetts Agricultural College.	8	....do...............	15,000	15,000
Mass....	Massachusetts State Agricultural Experiment Station.	7	State................	10,000	10,000
Mich....	Experiment Station of Michigan Agricultural College.	18	United States..........	15,000	15,000
Minn....	Agricultural Experiment Station of University of Minnesota.	12	....do...............	15,000	15,000
Miss....	Mississippi Agricultural Experiment Station.....	10	....do...............	15,000	15,000
Mo......	Missouri Agricultural College Experiment Station.	9	....do...............	15,000	15,000
Nebr....	Agricultural Experiment Station of Nebraska....	9	....do...............	15,000	15,000
Nev....	Nevada State Agricultural Station.............	5	....do...............	15,000	15,000
N.H....	New Hampshire Agricultural Experiment Station.	9	....do...............	15,000	15,000
N.J....	New Jersey State Agricultural Experiment Station.	5	State................	11,000	11,000
N.J.....	New Jersey Agricultural College Experiment Station.	5	United States..........	15,000	15,000
N.Y....	New York Agricultural Experiment Station.....	7	State................	20,000	20,000
N.Y....	Cornell University Agricultural Experiment Station.	13	United States..........	15,000	15,000
N.C.....	North Carolina Agricultural Experiment Station.	9	State................	2,200	17,200
			United States.........	15,000	
Ohio....	Ohio Agricultural Experiment Station.........	7	United States..........	15,000	15,000
Oregon..	Oregon Experiment Station..................	3	....do...............	15,000	15,000
Pa......	Pennsylvania State College Agricultural Experiment Station.	10	State................	3,000	18,000
			United States.........	15,000	
R.I.....	Rhode Island State Agricultural Experiment Station.	1	....do...............	15,000	15,000
S.C.....	South Carolina Agricultural Experiment Station.	13	...do...............	15,000	20,000
			Tax on fertilizers......	5,000	
Tenn....	Tennessee Agricultural Experiment Station......	7	...do...............	800	15,800
			United States.........	15,000	
Tex.....	Texas Agricultural Experiment Station.........	11	...do...............	15,000	15,000
Vt.......	Vermont State Agricultural Experiment Station.	8	State................	3,500	19,500
			Proceeds of farm......	1,000	
			United States........	15,000	
Va......	Virginia Agricultural Experiment Station........	5	...do...............	15,000	15,000
W. Va...	West Virginia Experiment Station.............	5	...do...............	15,000	15,000
Wis.....	Agricultural Experiment Station of University of Wisconsin.	8	...do...............	15,000	20,000
			State................	4,000	
			Proceeds of farm......	1,000	
	Total................................	369	....	....	710,400
D.C.....	Office of Experiment Stations..................	......	....	....	10,000
	Grand total............................	......	....	....	720,400

A complete report of the financial condition of the stations would undoubtedly increase this amount by several thousand dollars, so that it is safe to say that the total amount which will be expended by the stations during the current year will reach $725,000.

Most of the new stations are in actual operation. Bulletins have been published giving accounts of organization, and of experimental and other work. The investigations cover a wide range of topics, and the stations have in nearly all cases manifested their wisdom by directing their investigations towards the solution of questions of special interest to the localities in which they are situated, without neglecting subjects of more general interest and wider application.

On the 18th of October, 1887, the second convention of Agricultural Colleges and Experiment Stations convened at Washington. A permanent organization was effected, and the association was named "The Association of American Agricultural Colleges and Experiment Stations." George W. Atherton, LL. D., president of the Pennsylvania State College, was elected president of the association. This convention was deeply interested in securing the co-ordination of the work of the several stations and indorsed the action of previous conventions in urging the establishment of a central office to be a medium of intercommunication between the stations. As the result of the efforts of this association, acting in harmony with the Commissioner of Agriculture, such an office was provided for in the annual appropriation bill for the Department of Agriculture for the fiscal year ending June 30, 1889.

That in order to secure, as far as practicable, uniformity of methods and results in the work of said stations, it shall be the duty of the United States Commissioner of Agriculture to furnish forms, as far as practicable, for the tabulation of results of investigation or experiments; to indicate from time to time such lines of inquiry as to him shall seem most important; and, in general, to furnish such advice and assistance as will best promote the purposes of this act. It shall be the duty of each said station, annually, on or before the 1st day of February, to make to the governor of the State or Territory in which it is located a full and detailed report of its operations, including a statement of receipts and expenditures, a copy of which report shall be sent to each of said stations, to the said Commissioner of Agriculture, and to the Secretary of the Treasury of the United States.

The act of July 18, 1888, appropriates $10,000 —

Payable upon the order of the Commissioner of Agriculture, to enable him to carry out the provisions of section 3 of said act of March 2, 1887, and to compare, edit, and publish such of the results of the experiments made under section 2 of said act by said experiment stations as he may deem necessary; and for these purposes the Commissioner of Agriculture is authorized to employ such assistants, clerks, and other persons as he may deem necessary.

To carry out these provisions the Commissioner of Agriculture, as has already been stated, instituted, in October, 1888, an Office of Experiment Stations as a special branch of the Department of Agriculture and appointed a director at its head.

LIST OF AGRICULTURAL EXPERIMENT STATIONS IN THE UNITED STATES.

ALABAMA.

AGRICULTURAL EXPERIMENT STATION OF THE AGRICULTURAL AND MECHANICAL COLLEGE OF ALABAMA.

Department of the Agricultural and Mechanical College of Alabama.

W. L.Broun, LL. D., President.

Location of station, Auburn, Director, J. S. Newman.
Organized by State June 1, 1883; reorganized April 1, 1888.

CANEBRAKE AGRICULTURAL EXPERIMENT STATION.

Department of Agricultural and Mechanical College of Alabama.

W. L. Broun, LL. D., President.

Location of station, Uniontown. Director, J. S. Newman. Assistant director in charge, W. H. Newman, M. Sc.
Organized by State in 1885.

ARKANSAS.

ARKANSAS AGRICULTURAL EXPERIMENT STATION.

Department of Arkansas Industrial University.

E. H. Murfee, LL. D., President.

Location of station, Fayetteville. Director, A. E. Menke, D. Sc.
Organized ———, 1888.
Substations at Pine Bluff, Newport, and Texarkana.

CALIFORNIA.

AGRICULTURAL EXPERIMENT STATION OF THE UNIVERSITY OF CALIFORNIA.

Department of the University of California.

Horace Davis, A. B., President.

Location of station, Berkeley. Director, E. W. Hilgard, Ph.D., LL. D.
Organized by University of California in 1876; reorganized March, 1888.
Substations at Jackson, Amador County; Paso Robles, San Luis Obispo County; and Tulare City.
Grape culture stations at Cupertino, Fresno, and Mission San José.

Act for Inspection of Meats for Export, 1890

From 26 U.S. Statutes at Large 414.

AN ACT PROVIDING FOR AN INSPECTION OF MEATS FOR EXPORTATION, PROHIBITING THE IMPORTATION OF ADULTERATED ARTICLES OF FOOD OR DRINK, AND AUTHORIZING THE PRESIDENT TO MAKE PROCLAMATION IN CERTAIN CASES, AND FOR OTHER PURPOSES

Be it enacted by the Senate and House of Representatives of the United States of America in Congress assembled, That the Secretary of Agriculture may cause to be made a careful inspection of salted pork and bacon intended for exportation, with a view to determining whether the same is wholesome, sound, and fit for human food whenever the laws, regulations, or orders of the Government of any foreign country to which such pork or bacon is to be exported shall require inspection thereof relating to the importation thereof into such country, and also whenever any buyer, seller, or exporter of such meats intended for exportation shall request the inspection thereof.

Such inspection shall be made at the place where such meats are packed or boxed, and each package of such meats so inspected shall bear the marks, stamps, or other device for identification provided for in the last clause of this section: *Provided,* That an inspection of such meats may also be made at the place of exportation if an inspection has not been made at the place of packing, or if, in the opinion of the Secretary of Agriculture, a re-inspection becomes necessary. One copy of any certificate issued by any such inspector shall be filed in the Department of Agriculture; another copy shall be attached to the invoice of each separate shipment of such meat, and a third copy shall be delivered to the consignor or shipper of such meat as evidence that packages of salted pork and bacon have been inspected in accordance with the provisions of this Act and found to be wholesome, sound, and fit for human food; and for the identification of the same such marks, stamps, or other devices as the Secretary of Agriculture may by regulation prescribe shall be affixed to each of such packages.

Any person who shall forge, counterfeit, or knowingly and wrongfully alter, deface, or destroy any of the marks, stamps, or other devices provided for in this section on any package of any such meats, or who shall forge, counterfeit, or knowingly and wrongfully alter, deface, or destroy any certificate in reference to meats provided for in this section, shall be deemed guilty of a misdemeanor, and on conviction thereof shall be punished by a fine not exceeding one thousand dollars or imprisonment not exceeding one year, or by both said punishments, in the discretion of the court.

SEC. 2. That it shall be unlawful to import into the United States any adulterated or unwholesome food or drug or any vinous, spirituous or malt liquors, adulterated or mixed with any poisonous or noxious chemical drug or other ingredient injurious to health. Any person who shall knowingly import into the United States any such adulterated food or drug, or drink, knowing or having reasons to believe the same to be adulterated, being the owner or the agent of the owner, or the consignor or consignee of the owner, or in privity with them, assisting in such unlawful act, shall be deemed guilty of a misdemeanor, and liable to prosecution therefor in the district court of the United States for the district into which such property is imported; and, on conviction, such person shall be fined in a sum not exceeding one thousand dollars for each separate shipment, and may be imprisoned by the court for a term not exceeding one year, or both, at the discretion of the court.

SEC. 3. That any article designed for consumption as human food or drink, and any other article of the classes or description mentioned in this Act, which shall be imported into the United States contrary to its provisions, shall be forfeited to the United States, and shall be proceeded against under the provisions of chapter eighteen of title thirteen of the Revised Statutes of the United States; and such imported property so declared forfeited may be destroyed or returned to the importer for exportation from the United States after the payment of all costs and expenses, under such regulations as the Secretary of the Treasury may prescribe; and the Secretary of the Treasury may cause such imported articles to be inspected or examined in order to ascertain whether the same have been so unlawfully imported.

SEC. 4. That whenever the President is satisfied that there is good reason to believe that any importation is being made, or is about to be made, into the United States, from any foreign country, of any article used for human food or drink that is adulterated to an extent dangerous to the health or welfare of the people of the United States, or any of them, he may issue his proclamation suspending the importation of such articles from such country for such period of time. as he may think necessary to prevent such importation; and during such period it shall be unlawful to import into the United States from the countries designated in the proclamation of the President any of the articles the importation of which is so suspended.

SEC. 5. That whenever the President shall be satisfied that unjust discriminations are made by or under the authority of any foreign state against the importation to or sale in such foreign state of any product of the United States, he may direct that such products of such foreign state so discriminating against any product of the United States as he may deem proper shall be excluded from importation to the United States; and in such case he shall make proclamation of his direction in the premises, and therein name the time when such direction against importation shall take effect, and after such date the importation of the articles named in such proclamation shall be unlawful. The President may at any time revoke, modify, terminate, or renew any such direction as, in his opinion, the public interest may require.

SEC. 6. That the importation of neat cattle, sheep, and other ruminants, and swine, which are diseased or infected with any disease, or which shall have been exposed to such infection within sixty days next before their exportation, is hereby prohibited; and any person who shall knowingly violate the foregoing provision shall be deemed guilty of a misdemeanor, and shall, on conviction, be punished by a fine not exceeding five thousand dollars, or by imprisonment not exceeding three years, and any vessel or vehicle used in such unlawful importation with the knowledge of the master or owner of said vessel or vehicle that such importation is diseased or has been exposed to infection as herein described, shall be forfeited to the United States.

SEC. 7. That the Secretary of Agriculture be, and is hereby, authorized, at the expense of the owner, to place and retain in quarantine all neat cattle, sheep, and other ruminants, and all swine, imported into the United States, at such ports as he may designate for such purpose, and under such conditions as he may by regulation prescribe, respectively, for the several classes of animals above described; and for this purpose he may have and maintain possession of all lands, buildings, animals, tools, fixtures, and appurtenances now in use for the quarantine of neat cattle, and hereafter purchase, construct, or rent as may be necessary, and he may appoint veterinary surgeons, inspectors, officers, and employees by him deemed necessary to maintain such quarantine, and provide for the execution of the other provisions of this act.

SEC. 8. That the importation of all animals described in this act into any port in the United States, except such as may be designated by the Secretary of Agriculture, with the approval of the Secretary of the Treasury, as quarantine stations, is hereby prohibited; and the Secretary of Agriculture may cause to be slaughtered such of the animals named in this act as may be, under regulations prescribed by him, adjudged to be infected with any contagious disease, or to have been exposed to infection so as to be dangerous to other animals; and that the value of animals so slaughtered as being so exposed to infection but not infected may be ascertained by the agreement of the Secretary of Agriculture and owners thereof, if practicable; otherwise, by the appraisal by two persons familiar with the character and value of such property, to be appointed by the Secretary of Agriculture, whose decision, if they agree, shall be final; otherwise, the Secretary of Agriculture shall decide between them, and his decision shall be final; and the amount of the value thus ascertained shall be paid to the owner thereof out of money in the Treasury appropriated for the use of the Bureau of Animal Industry; but no payment shall be made for any animal imported in violation of the provisions of this act. If any animal subject to quarantine according to the provisions of this act are brought into any port of the United States where no quarantine station is established the collector of such port shall require the same to be conveyed by the vessel on which they are imported or are found to the nearest quarantine station, at the expense of the owner.

SEC. 9. That whenever, in the opinion of the President, it shall be necessary for the protection of animals in the United States against infectious or contagious diseases, he may, by proclamation, suspend the importation of all or any class of animals for a limited time, and may change, modify, revoke, or renew such proclamation, as the public good may require; and during the time of such suspension the importation of any such animals shall be unlawful.

SEC. 10. That the Secretary of Agriculture shall cause careful inspection to be made by a suitable officer of all imported animals described in this act, to ascertain whether such animals are infected with contagious diseases or have been exposed to infection so as to be dangerous to other animals, which shall then either be placed in quarantine or dealt with according to the regulations of the Secretary of Agriculture; and all food, litter, manure, clothing, utensils, and other appliances that have been so related to such animals on board ship as to be judged liable to convey infection shall be dealt with according to the regulations of the Secretary of Agriculture; and the Secretary of Agriculture may cause inspection to be made of all animals described in this act intended for exportation, and provide for the disinfection of all vessels engaged in the transportation thereof, and of all barges or other vessels used in the conveyance of such animals intended for export to the ocean steamer or other vessels, and of all attendants and their clothing, and of all head-ropes and other appliances used in such exportation, by such orders and regulations as he may prescribe; and if, upon such inspection, any such animals shall be adjudged, under the regulations of the Secretary of Agriculture, to be infected or to have been exposed to infection so as to be dangerous to other animals, they shall not be allowed to be placed upon any vessel for exportation; the expense of all the inspection and disinfection provided for in this section to be borne by the owners of the vessels on which such animals are exported.

Approved, August 30, 1890.

Combating Insects and Fungi, 1890

From H. Garman, "Means of Lessening Injuries due to Insects and Parasitic Plants," in Kentucky Agricultural Experiment Station, *Circular,* no. 3, pp. 3–10, 20.

MEANS OF LESSENING INJURIES DUE TO INSECTS AND PARASITIC PLANTS

The preparations and instruments for combating injurious insects and fungi have multiplied at an exceptional rate during the past five years. A good many of those now sold have stood the test of real use in the garden and orchard, and some of them are doubtless to be considered a permanent part of the farmer's equipment for the successful prosecution of his profession. It is with the purpose of calling more general attention to those which have proved good that the present account of insecticides and fungicides, and of means of applying them, is drawn up. I shall mention chiefly the spraying apparatus of three establishments, but this is not to be understood as implying that the instruments sent out by others are not also good. I should have been quite as well satisfied to commend the work of any other firm if I had chanced to have the same assurance of its excellence.

I. Insecticides

Under the head of insecticides I have included substances such as oils, soaps, poisons, and the like, which prevent insect injury by destroying the insects when applied to their bodies, when eaten by them, or which effect the same object by rendering plants obnoxious to insects.

Kerosene

Ordinary kerosene is excellent both as a repellent and as an insect destroyer. It is especially good for insects, such as bark lice and plant lice, which have piercing mouth parts, and so cannot be poisoned. An objection to its use has been that it injured foliage. It will generally do this when used pure, though some plants, it is asserted, will endure applications of the pure oil. The objection is now obviated by the use of the oil in the form of an emulsion, in which condition it may be diluted to any extent with water. . . .

Pyrethrum

Under the name "Persian insect powder" this material is sold everywhere in drug stores. It is nothing more than the pulverized flowers of a plant belonging to the same family as the solidagos, asters and sunflowers of roadsides and neglected fence rows. The powder most commonly sold is imported from Asia, but the plant (Pyrethrum roseum) is now cultivated in the United States, and a related plant, from which an insect powder known as "buhach" is made, is grown in California for commercial purposes.

The powder has the advantage over most powders recommended for the same purpose in being perfectly harmless to man, and to the foliage of plants. Indeed it is surprising to find a substance so completely harmless to man and plants having so destructive an effect on insects. The effect it has on the latter is believed to be due to a volatile oil in the powder. This is soon dissipated when the powder is exposed, consequently it is necessary to keep it in a close jar or other vessel to preserve its value as an insecticide.

Applied to the bodies of insects it has commonly a benumbing effect, followed by death, or if the powder is not good, by complete recovery. . . .

Hellebore

This is a powder sold as white hellebore by druggists, and is the powdered root-stocks of a plant (Veratrum album) which grows among the Alps and Pyrenees of Europe. We have in this country a related plant (V. viride) from which a similar but less poisonous powder is made. It is applied as a powder, or by spraying, in the latter case three or four table spoonfuls being used in an ordinary bucket of water.

Paris Green

This is a bright green powder which is valued as a pigment, and beside the above, is sold also under the names, emerald, imperial, mitis, and Schweinfurth green. Its properties as an insecticide are due to the presence in it of a compound of arsenic. It was originally tested on the Colorado potato beetle, and is now widely sold as a means of stopping the injuries of this insect, and for protecting orchards from the codling moth. It is a rank poison, a fact to be kept in mind in handling it.

London Purple

London purple also owes its virtues as an insecticide to the arsenic, in combination, which it contains. It is used in the same way as Paris green — suspended in water — in the proportion of one pound of powder to 200 gallons of water. It divides honors with the preceding in efficiency as a protection against the codling moth, and has the advantage of being cheaper.

Lime

Dusted on the leaves of plants liable to be eaten by insects, lime is often found useful in gardens. It is very commonly used to prevent the gnawing of flea beetles and the striped cucumber beetle.

Carbolic Acid

In solution this substance has little value as an insecticide when used in the small quantities necessary to avoid injury to plants. Quite recently Prof. A. J. Cook has recommended its use in combination with land plaster as a protection against the plum curculio, and says it is quite as complete a defense as Paris green or London purple. He uses one pint of crude carbolic acid mixed with 50 pounds of plaster, and throws the mixture over the trees so that it reaches all the fruit.

Gas Lime

This is a waste product in the manufacture of ordinary illuminating gas, and may be obtained at gas factories for the trouble of hauling it away. It has a powerful, and sickening odor, but possesses valuable properties for the destruction of root-infesting insects and worms. It is commonly applied to land in the fall of the year, and worked in later. By spring it has lost its caustic properties; and is changed largely to lime sulphate, a condition in which it is thought to be a valuable manure in some soils. In England it is now very extensively used by gardeners, being considered especially valuable as a preventive of the disease known as the "club-root" of cabbage.

Tobacco

This is an excellent remedy for the injuries of plant lice. In hot houses it is commonly applied as a vapor, tobacco "stems" (mid ribs of leaves) being the best part of the plant to use for burning. Hot houses or frames may be filled with the smoke for a few minutes without ill effect on the growing plants. A solution of tobacco made by placing stems in hot water and allowing them to remain there over night, is also very effective for clearing plants of aphides, and has the advantage over the other method of using, in that it can be sprayed out-of-doors. Its harmlessness to plants, its cheapness, and its efficiency, make it the best material we have for preventing plant lice injury.

Bordeaux Mixture

This preparation has for some years been employed in European countries as a preventive of fungus attacks upon grapes. More recently, at the recommendation of the Department of Agriculture at Washington, it has been tried with good effect for the same purpose in this country. From experiments made last summer at this Station I am satisfied that beside its value for this purpose it is also a valuable protection against the injuries from gnawing insects. For injury from the striped cucumber beetle, the flea beetles on turnips or potatoes, the blister beetles on potatoes, and the like, nothing better can be used. Not the least of its many valuable properties is the tenacity with which it holds to leaves, thus making unnecessary the frequent applications required of other materials. . . .

Sulphur

Flour of sulphur is a very useful substance for use against the injurious work of mites, such as the red spider. It is commonly dusted in the leaves of infested plants. It is sometimes recommended that the fumes be employed for similar purposes but in my own experience it has proved so destructive to plants when so used that I cannot recommend this manner of applying it. If it is desired to apply it by spraying or dipping plants into it, this may be accomplished after first preparing it according to a formula given by Miss Ormerod, as follows: "One pound of flour of sulphur and two pounds of fresh lime [are] boiled together in four gallons of water."

Water

It is sometimes possible to relieve plants of insects, especially if these be exposed on the leaves, by thorough and repeated drenchings with water. Mites are especially sensitive to its influence. Plants are much less sensitive to hot water than insects, and may be immersed for a few moments in water heated to 120° F. By dipping plants infested with mites or aphides in such water, the pests can be quickly removed. Peas or beans infested with weevils should be immersed for a few moments in water heated to the boiling point.

II. Fungicides

I have included here preparations which are intended to ward off or in any way put a stop to the injuries of parasitic fungi. The best of these protect both as fungicides and insecticides. It is quite important in many cases that a preparation intended to avert the injuries of a parasitic plant should be obnoxious to insects because these latter by gnawing fruit afford ready access to the fungi and may be responsible for most of the cases of invasion. So commonly are the two injuries associated on plums, for example, that it was a very common belief at one time that the curculio was the cause of the brown rot of plums.

Bordeaux Mixture

This mixture stands first in value for preventing rots and blights of fruit and leaves. It has proved especially good for the black rot and mildews of grapes. The formula for preparing the mixture which I have used is presented under the head of insecticides. Several others have been found useful, of which the following may be given:

6½ pounds, copper sulphate.
3¼ pounds, lime.
22 gallons, water. . . .

The copper sulphate sells in quantity for about eight cents per pound. Lime can be obtained anywhere for less than a cent per pound. This latter when first prepared has a caustic property by which it destroys the spores of fungi. It loses this on exposure, and in the mixture seems to act finally as a fixative and preservative for the more directly useful copper. . . .

Sulphur

Flour of sulphur is a common and useful remedy for several mildews, but when dusted on leaves is liable to be blown or washed off again, making necessary frequent applications. I would suggest that it will probably be found to retain all its qualities as a fungicide when prepared and applied as has been suggested under insecticides, — by boiling with lime, and then spraying it upon plants.

Potassium Sulphide (liver of sulphur)

One of the best of fungicides, but more costly than some others. It may be bought in quantity for thirty cents per pound. A one per cent. solution may be sprayed upon plants without danger of injuring the foliage.

Hyposulphite of Soda

This has been strongly recommended as a remedy for the scabbing of apples. It is prepared for spraying by dissolving one pound of the soda in ten gallons of water. It is injurious to foliage. It sells for about six cents per pound.

Copper Sulphate (blue vitriol, bluestone)

While very good for most of the purposes for which Bordeaux mixture is used, this compound burns foliage very badly, and is not so lasting in its effects as a fungicide. It sells, in quantities, for about eight cents per pound.

Iron Sulphate (copperas, green vitriol)

This has been recommended for certain parasitic fungi, but seems to be exceedingly damaging to the leaves of plants in any useful strength which I have experimented with. Its price, in quantity, should be about three cents per pound.

Carbolic Acid

A good fungicide in its first effects, but its usefulness is soon gone after it has been dried upon leaves, and insects are not then deterred by it from eating sprayed foliage. The crude material is catalogued by dealers at twelve cents per pound, or seventy cents per gallon. . . .

Danger to Man from Sprayed Fruit

It has been shown, both by experiment and by practice, that there is no danger to be apprehended from eating fruit sprayed either with the compounds of arsenic, or with Bordeaux mixture.

Removal of Bordeaux Mixture

A more serious objection to the use of Bordeaux mixture on such fruit as grapes, is the fact that it adheres, if applied late, so as to affect the market value of the fruit. As I have suggested above this may be obviated largely by avoiding late applications of the mixture, and, where necessary, using carbolic acid instead.

However, it has recently been shown at the Delaware Station that the mixture can be easily removed by suspending fruit in a tub of water to which has been added a couple of quarts of cider vinegar.

Fertilizer Experiments, 1890

From J. S. Newman, "Some Conclusions from Experiments with Fertilizers," in Alabama Agricultural Experiment Station, *Corn, Cotton, Rye, Chufas* (Bulletin No. 16, new series June, 1890), pp. 101–13.

Inquiries as to the needs of the soils of this station and the choice of plants as to sources of their food supplies were commenced in 1884.

A retrospective view of results during five years develops some interesting facts.

The most prominent of these is the effect of phosphoric acid, not consumed by the plants to which it is applied, upon subsequent crops, as shown by the failure of later applications to produce perceptible effects. An application of acid phosphate to corn in 1884 upon land to which none had been previously applied increased the yield seven bushels per acre upon land with clay subsoil. This land, when first taken in charge, produced only 3.7 bushels of corn per acre without manure. Four years later, after continuous cultivation in different crops, all except one of which were fertilized with phosphatic manures, the yield without manure was 13.02 bushels while the application of phosphates gave no increase. The reserve force from previous applications furnished all that the plant needed, or all that it could utilize without additional supply of other elements of plant food.

These and many other facts indicate that, on soil having clay subsoil, the phosphoric acid does not leach to an injurious extent, but remains in an available form in reach of cultivated plants.

On another class of soil having no clay within four feet of the surface different results appear. Here there seems to have been a serious loss of phosphoric acid and a decided response to new applications after seasons in which the rainfall was excessive, causing a rapid descent of the water through the porous subsoil. The last season was exempt from such leaching rains and the corn seems to have received the full benefit of the residue from the application of the previous year as well as that of the current season.

The complaint is often heard, that the phosphates do not produce the effects upon crops that were realized from their early use, and the conclusion that the phosphatic manures have degenerated in quality, is drawn from this assumption of facts. The facts are:

(a) That the phosphatic compounds are of higher grade than those sold fifteen years ago.

(b) That their effect is equally marked upon lands to which none has been previously applied.

(c) Lands, to which repeated liberal applications have been made, contain enough of the unappropriated previous applications to supply the needs of the crops.

This last is true of soils which contain enough clay to prevent injurious leaching.

We infer then that phosphates applied to clay soils, or sandy soils with good clay subsoils, are held until used by plants, or at least the larger part of them. On such soils, therefore, heavy annual applications are not wasteful.

On sandy soils, without clay foundation, however, heavy applications are not advisable, since that not appropriated by the crops to which it is applied may leach beyond the reach of the roots of cultivated plants. . . .

Some Practical Suggestions on the Use of Phosphates

Vast sums have been wasted in the cotton states by the injudicious purchase and use of commercial manures. This has resulted.

(a) From the absence of a knowledge of the needs of soils, which could be acquired only by experiment.

(b) By following the advice and practice of ignorant teachers.

Within the last twenty years the farmers and planters have learned much about the use of fertilizers, but their tuition has involved a severe tax upon their income. Commercial compounds have been purchased and applied without a knowledge either of the composition of the fertilizer or the needs of the soil or the plants. They paid twenty cents per pound for nitrogen while the cotton seed and animal manures were largely robbed of this valuable ingredient by wasteful handling before being applied to the soil.

Phosphates were applied to land already rich in phosphoric acid as are the black prairie lands of Alabama.

Mr. David Dickson made extravagant application of a low grade phosphate to his sixteen acre lot, previously enriched by animal manures, and harvested large crops; others followed his example upon impoverished fields and harvested poor crops and disappointment. This continued until experiment demonstrated that smaller application of concentrated manures gave more profitable results.

Mr. Furman caused a wasteful expenditure for kainit, to be applied to lands already abundantly supplied with potash. Except as a conservator of moisture, during severe drouth, very little benefit has been derived from the use of kainit or other sources of potash. Under a judicious rotation of crops, including those which are humus-supplying little else than phosphates need be purchased by the corn and cotton grower. The lands of this station have been rapidly improved by the following rotation:

Commencing 1st year with cotton.

    2nd year corn with peas between rows.

    3rd `` oats followed by peas same year.

    4th `` cotton again.

All of these crops except the peas are fertilized. Under this system the soil soon becomes sufficiently supplied with humus to furnish the nitrogen needed for the cotton plant in the cheapest, best possible form, so that an application of acid phosphate is sufficient to secure profitable crops.

Cotton seed and stable manure, supplemented with acid phosphate, furnishing the cheapest and best manure for corn, so that the purchase of nitrogen may be entirely dispensed with, pea vines furnishing it for cotton and cotton seed and stable manure for corn. If lands have been so denuded of vegetable matter as to require the purchase of nitrogen, cotton seed meal affords the cheapest source. This and acid phosphate mixed in equal parts, 100 lbs of each per acre, on sandy and red lands, supply the needs of plants as well as the more costly commercial compounds. They may be easily, thoroughly and cheaply mixed on the farm.

The black prairie lands should be excepted from all rules of treatment of other soils. They respond to sotton seed, stable manure and cotton seed meal but not satisfactorily to phosphates.

If cotton seed, stable manure and phosphates are composted for corn, the following formula, used for many years, has given most satisfactory results; to make one ton of the dry materials use.

    500 lbs Acid phosphate.

    750 `` Stable manure.

    750 `` Cotton seed.

    ‾‾‾‾

    2000 lbs.

The cotton seed should be protected from fermentation until used in the compost. The stable manure should remain in the stalls until needed. When the stalls are cleaned out in January, the time for making the compost, a liberal supply of litter should be spread in the stall to furnish a bed for the mules and serve as an absorbent for the first droppings. A small quantity of litter is used during the year, as found necessary, to keep the stall dry. An occasional dusting with land plaster or gypsum will also contribute to this end and prevent loss of ammonia. To those not familiar with this practice it seems at first view untidy, but on the contrary, since the manure is packed down by the tread of the mule from day to day — siloed as it were — no fermentation takes place and no disagreeable odor is emitted, while the animal has a clean, elastic bed throughout the year.

Again, the liquid manure, which contains most of the nitrogen, is absorbed by the solid excrement and no loss of nitrogen takes place. If the manure is removed daily it is almost impossible, in this climate, to prevent injurious fermentation or "fire fanging," while much of the liquid manure is lost.

Manner of Composting

Take such quantity of the cotton seed and stable manure as can be conveniently mixed with forks and shovels: stir them until thoroughly commingled, wetting them as they are stirred, using enough water to wet them thoroughly without leaching. Spread this mixture, to a depth of about six inches, and pour over it the phosphate, which should be free from lumps, and stir until the particles of phosphate adhere to the manure and seed and the three ingredients are intimately mingled. This process is repeated until all of the material is consumed, each mixed lot being shoveled into the common heap as the mingling is completed. Of course the proper relative proportions must be preserved in these several mixings.

It is important to wet the material of the compost thoroughly to retard the fermentation and prevent fire fanging.

Is Ammonia Lost During Fermentation?

It is commonly supposed that when vapor passes off rapidly from the compost heap — when it "smokes" — that a loss of ammonia takes place. Litmus paper placed immediately upon the freshly stirred compost, in the midst of the rising fumes, did not detect the presence of an Alkali, indicating that no free ammonia was present. On the contrary it discovered the presence of acid sufficient to neutralize ammonia should volatilization take place. The acid phosphate prevents loss of ammonia.

Why Is This?

Nearly half of every acid phosphate or super phosphate, as it is sometimes called, is gypsum, or sulphate of lime, which results from treating the pulverized phosphate rock with sulphuric acid. The presence of this sulphate of lime furnishes a safeguard against any loss of ammonia by being volatilized.

If stable manure or stable manure and cotton seed are fermented without the phosphate, or without gypsum added, a perceptible loss of ammonia takes place.

If the compost is to be applied to cotton, we use the following formula, mixing as before.

> 700 lbs acid phosphate.
> 650 " Stable manure.
> 650 " Cotton seed.
> ———
> 2000 lbs.

Experiments in the use of kainit in the compost heap indicated that the cotton seed and stable manure supplied enough potash.

If the compost is made for miscellaneous use, 600 lbs of phosphate per ton is used. The compost has proved during twenty years of practical experience and experiment the cheapest manure for the corn and cotton planter.

In making the first experiments with it in 1869 the materials were put up in layers, but this practice has long since been abandoned as unsatisfactory on account of the phosphate hardening into lumps.

Composting in the Furrow

Some apply the cotton seed in the furrow, over which cotton is to be planted, and sprinkle the phosphate over them early in the season and, covering them with earth, allow the seed to ferment there. If the seasons are favorable in early spring this practice gives good results, but some serious objections stand against it.

(a) In order that the seed may not vegetate they must be applied before the soil has been warmed sufficiently to supply the conditions necessary for germination. If heavy, baking rains occur, the soil where the plant is to grow becomes hard. It cannot be rebroken without disturbing the manure, and hence there is difficulty in securing a mellow seed bed.

(b) It involves extra labor in distributing the seed and phosphate as they must be distributed separately.

Cotton Seed Meal in Compost

Since cotton seed meal is cheaper at twenty dollars per ton, or even at twenty-two dollars per ton, than cotton seed at twelve, the meal has been substituted for the seed in the compost heap with perfectly satisfactory results. The following formula was used:

    500 lbs. cotton seed meal.
    500 " acid phosphate.
    1000 " stable manure.
    ————
    2000 lbs.

The stable manure is thoroughly pulverized and moistened and the meal and phosphate stirred into it until they adhere to the moist manure. The fermentation of this compost proceeds much more rapidly than that in which the seed are used and hence must be closely watched to avoid excessive heating. If this occurs, open vertical holes with a crowbar and pour in water, or turn the heap, adding water as it is turned. The plant food in the meal-compost is more promptly available than in that in which the seed are used.

Potash

So far as furnishing plant food is concerned, there seems to be little need of applying potash to these soils.

As conservators of moisture in dry seasons the potash salts are useful. During seasons in which there is sufficient rainfall, their influence is not appreciable. Plants seem indifferent as to the source from which they derive their potash. The sulphate, (in Kainit) muriate, and carbonate (in cotton seed hull ashes) have been applied under identical circumstances, using the same number of pounds of potash from each source. Cotton, corn, turnips and potatoes express indifference as to the source from which it is derived. During dry fall seasons cotton to which potash has been applied retains its leaves later than that to which none was applied. This however, is not usually accompanied by increased production, due to the potash.

Nitrogen

The following source of nitrogen have been employed alone and in various combinations, viz: Nitrate of soda, sulphate of ammonia, dried blood, cotton seed meal, cotton seed, stable manure and pea vines.

Of the four commercial sources, cotton seed meal is not only the best suited to this latitude, but is the cheapest source of supply — best, because its nitrogen is not so promptly available as in the others and hence resists the leaching influence of our heavy spring rains better than the others. Nitrate of soda and sulphate of ammonia when applied before or with the seed of spring crops are often leached beyond the reach of the roots of the young plants, on sandy soils, before the seed vegetate. If applied during the growth of the crop, either as a top-dress to small grain, or interculturally, to corn, cotton or vegetables, when the soil is occupied by root-hairs ready to appropriate the nitrates, the effect is very marked.

As remarked of phosphoric acid and potash, plants are indifferent as to the source of supply of their nitrogen, *per se,* but some of the sources carry with them conditions, inseparable from themselves, which render more certain, reliable and continuous their supply of this important factor in plant growth. We need, in our long growing season, a source which will not exhaust itself in the early growth of the plant, but give out a sufficiency for an early and vigorous growth and gradually yield up its supplies, as the season advances, and the demands of the growing plant increase. For this reason, experience and results of experiment point to the vegetable sources as the most desireable in our climate.

The cost of the commercial sources of nitrogen, and the limited supply of the domestic sources — cotton seed and animal manures — render it necessary for us to look for a cheaper and more universally available means through which to permanently improve our wasted soils. This we find in pea vines and other leguminous plants. When lands become exhausted of phosphoric acid, it must be resupplied by purchase; not so with nitrogen. This need not be purchased at all. Peas, clover, melilotus, vetches etc., may be used as factories for its production upon the very soil that needs it. On the stiff clay and calcarious prairie soils, clover, peas or melilotus may be used — on sandy soils, resort must be had to the peas. These furnish the cheapest and most permanent manure available to the cultivator of sandy soils. A crop of pea vines following oat stubble and left to protect, and rot upon the soil, until prepared for corn the following February, proved more than the equivalent of the residue of half a ton of compost and two hundred pounds of cotton seed meal and acid phosphate per acre, applied to cotton the previous year. A rotation of crops for three years, including two crops of pea vines, one cut for hay and the other left to rot upon the land, compared with clean culture in cotton for the same number of years, made a difference of *one hundred and five* per cent. in the yield of rye, following, in favor of the rotation including the peas.

How to Use the Pea Vines

In more northern latitudes the practice of summer fallowing prevails as a preparation for winter grain and hence clover is turned in, *while green,* to be followed in August by wheat or barley: Fall plowing is also practiced in climates in which the winter is sufficiently severe to freeze the surface to the depth to which the land is plowed and thus pulverize the soil and prevent decomposition. There are no deleterious effects from thus plowing sod or clover lands, in cold climates, since the low temperature, prevailing through the winter, prevents the decompostion of the vegetable matter, turned into the soil, and consequently there is very little waste possible before the planting season in early spring. The crops therefore in such climate profit both by the meliorating effects of the vegetable matter upon the physical condition of the soil and the supply of plant food resulting from its decomposition.

On the lime lands of Alabama fall plowing is admissible, and even desirable, as a preparation for spring crops, on account of the difficulty of preparing such soils in spring, and the superior physical condition resulting from the fall plowing.

Even on the prairie, lime lands, however, turning in pea vines green, has proved wasteful as demonstrated by experiment, since cutting the vines for hay has left the soil in better condition than turning them green, as shown by subsequent production, while leaving them to rot upon the land gave better results than either.

Many writers have misled farmers by recommending an imitation of northern practice on southern farms, under conditions entirely different. Under no circumstances should the soil be fallowed in this climate during summer unless it is to be covered by another crop immediately. Exposure to our summer suns is injurious even if no green matter is turned in.

If large quantities of vegetation is turned in, during our warm and long summer, injuriously rapid fermentation takes place and, on sandy soils, every vestige of organized matter soon disappears in consequence of the rapid decomposition.

The soil is benefited in three ways by growing upon it leguminous plants for its improvement.

(a). The shade afforded by the growth while it remains upon the surface and the prevention of evaporation and consequent crusting of the surface is important. Land will improve if merely covered with plank but will deteriorate if constantly exposed with a bare surface. During the severest drouth, land covered with pea vines remains porous and friable. The covering of vines also prevents surface washing which has been the most potent agent in the impoverishment of the soils of the cotton states.

(b). The presence of the decaying vegetable matter in the soil improves its physical condition and increases its power of absorbing and retaining moisture. In our warm climate, subject to long-continued drouths, this is a most important function.

(c). The decomposition of the vegetable matter upon and in the soil improves its chemical properties, directly, by addition of the chemical plant food which the decaying vegetation contains, and indirectly, by the action of the acids and alkalies, generated during and by the decomposition, upon insoluble substances already in the soil. If not turned in too long before planting, it especially supplies nitrogen in a most desirable form and doles it out gradually as the season advances and the growing plant demands it. It also darkens the soil and thus increases its capacity for absorbing heat and thereby hastens the arrival of seek time in spring.

The Time to Plow in Pea Vines

Experiments instituted for the purpose of making this inquiry have invariably indicated that the proper time is in the preparation of the land for the next crop.

Experiments instituted for the purpose of making this inquiry have invariably indicated that the proper time is in the preparation of the land for the next crop.

If a crop of small grain or grass is to be sown in the early fall, the vines may be turned in some weeks before sowing the seed. If the land is not to be planted until the next spring, then, except with stiff soils, which require fall and winter fallowing, the land should not be broken until a short time before planting. If plowed in green during the summer and the land left bare, as remarked before, injury will result from this exposure and the vegetable matter will have decomposed, and the results of such decomposition leached through the soil, before the spring crop is planted. Decomposition progresses throughout our mild winters and, unless the land is occupied by some growing crop, loss must ensue.

No one would think of applying manure in August or September for the crop to be planted the following April. The results of experiments have only served to corroborate the current testimony of practical men whose observation and experience have taught them that pea vines *pay best* when left upon the surface until the land is needed for another crop.

Conclusions From Six Years of Experiment

1. Phosphoric acid leaches but little, if any, upon clay soil or those having clay sub-soil, but does leach through sandy soils with sandy subsoils.

2. Citrate soluble phosphoric acid possesses equal agricultural value with water soluble.

3. The phosphoric acid from floats, or phosphate rock ground to an impalpable powder, gradually becomes available in the soil, but produces very little effect upon the first crop.

4. The availability of the phosphoric acid in floats is hastened by use with cotton seed meal.

5. Plants are indifferent as to the sources from which available phosphoric acid is derived.

6. Nitrogen leaches rapidly through sandy soil unless occupied by feeding roots or underlaid by clay subsoil.

7. Plants are indifferent as to the sources from which their supply of nitrogen is derived, but those sources which yield a supply gradually, as needed by the plant, are best suited to our long seasons of growth.

8. Of the commercial sources of nitrogen, cotton seed meal is cheapest and most reliable. It yields its plant food more gradually than either the mineral or animal sources.

9. Pea vines, grown upon the land, and left to protect the surface until preparation is made for the next crop, furnish the cheapest source of nitrogen in the most desirable condition.

10. Pea vines, thus grown and treated, furnish the most reliable and practicable means of improving worn lands.

11. Pea vines cut for hay, leaving the stubble and roots on and in the land, benefit the soil more than turning them in green during the summer.

12. Potash applied to the soil of this station has not been profitable except during drouth. Its principal benefit seems to result from its affinity for moisture.

13. Plants seem indifferent as to the source of supply from which they derive the potash needed.

14. Following thorough preparation of the soil, shallow cultivation produces larger crops at less cost than deep cultivation.

15. Impoverished soils may be rapidly restored to productiveness by terracing accompanied by a judicious rotation of crops involving a restoration of humus.

16. The best way to utilize the animal manures saved on the farm, and the surplus cotton seed, is in compost with acid phosphate.

17. Contrary to the general opinion, ammonia is not volatilized and lost from such compost during the fermentation.

Fruit and Stock

18. Grapes, peaches, plums, raspberries, strawberries and the oriental type of pears can be grown profitably under intelligent culture.

19. Growing wool and mutton, intelligently pursued, is more profitable than growing cotton — a profit of fifty per cent upon the value of the sheep and the cost of keeping them can be realized.

20. Pork can be grown here as cheaply as in any state in the union by cultivating our peculiar crops especially for swine.

21. Green crops for soiling cattle may be had in abundant supply, during the entire year, from the cereals, lucerne, corn, sorghum and peas. By means of these and ensilage pasturage may be dispensed with.

Second Morrill Act for Agricultural Colleges, 1890

From 26 U.S. Statutes at Large 417.

[AN ACT TO APPLY A PORTION OF THE PROCEEDS OF THE PUBLIC LANDS TO THE MORE COMPLETE ENDOWMENT AND SUPPORT OF THE COLLEGES FOR THE BENEFIT OF AGRICULTURE AND THE MECHANIC ARTS ESTABLISHED UNDER THE PROVISIONS OF AN ACT OF CONGRESS APPROVED JULY SECOND, EIGHTEEN HUNDRED AND SIXTY-TWO]

Be it enacted by the Senate and House of Representatives of the United States of America in Congress assembled, That there shall be, and hereby is, annually appropriated, out of any money in the Treasury not otherwise appropriated, arising from the sale of public lands, to be paid as hereinafter provided, to each State and Territory for the more complete endowment and maintenance of colleges for the benefit of agriculture and the mechanic arts now established, or which may be hereafter established, in accordance with an act of Congress approved July second, eighteen hundred and sixty-two, the sum of fifteen thousand dollars for the year ending June thirtieth, eighteen hundred and ninety, and an annual increase of the amount of such appropriation thereafter for ten years by an additional sum of one thousand dollars over the preceding year, and the annual amount of be paid thereafter to each State and Territory shall be twenty-five thousands dollars to be applied only to instruction in agriculture, the mechanic arts, the English language and the various branches of mathematical, physical, natural, and economic science, with special reference to their applications in the industries of life, and to the facilities for such instruction: *Provided,* That no money shall be paid out under this act to any State or Territory for the support and maintenance of a college where a distinction of race or color is made in the admission of students, but the establishment and maintenance of such colleges separately for white and colored students shall be held to be a compliance with the provisions of this act if the funds received in such State or Territory be equitably divided as hereinafter set forth: *Provided,* That in any State in which there has been one college established in pursuance of the act of July second, eighteen hundred and sixty-two, and also in which an educational institution of like character has been established, or may be hereafter established, and is now aided by such State from its own revenue, for the education of colored students in agriculture and the mechanic arts, however named or styled, or whether or not it has received money heretofore under the act to which this act is an amendment, the legislature of such a State may propose and report to the Secretary of the Interior a just and equitable division of the fund to be received under this act between one college for white students and one institution for colored students established as aforesaid, which shall be divided into two parts and paid accordingly, and thereupon such institution for colored students shall be entitled to the benefits of this act and subject to its provisions, as much as it would have been if it had been included under the act of eighteen hundred and sixty-two, and the fulfillment of the foregoing provisions shall be taken as a compliance with the provision in reference to separate colleges for white and colored students.

SEC. 2. That the sums hereby appropriated to the States and Territories for the further endowment and support of colleges shall be annually paid on or before the thirty-first day of July of each year, by the Secretary of the Treasury, upon the warrant of the Secretary of the Interior, out of the Treasury of the United States, to the State or Territorial treasurer, or to such officer as shall be designated by the laws of such State or Territory to receive the same, who shall, upon the order of the trustees of the college, or the institution for colored students, immediately pay over said sums to the treasurers of the respective colleges or other institutions entitled to receive the same, and such treasurer shall be required to report to the Secretary of Agriculture and to the Secretary of the Interior, on or before the first day of September of each year, a detailed statement of the amount so received and of its disbursement. The grants of moneys authorized by this act are made subject to the legislative assent of the several States and Territories to the purpose of said grants: *Provided,* That payments of such install-ments of the appropriation herein made as shall become due to any State before the adjournment of the regular session of legislature meeting next after the passage of this act shall be made upon the assent of the governor thereof, duly certified to the Secretary of the Treasury.

SEC. 3. That if any portion of the moneys received by the designated officer of the State or Territory for the further and more complete endowment, support, and maintenance of colleges, or of institutions for colored students, as provided in this act, shall, by any action or contingency, be diminished or lost, or be misapplied, it shall be replaced by the State or Territory to which it belongs, and until so replaced no subsequent appropriation shall be apportioned or paid to such State or Territory; and no portion of said moneys shall be applied, directly or indirectly, under any pretense whatever, to the purchase, erection, preservation, or repair of any building or buildings. An annual report by the president of each of said colleges shall be made to the Secretary of Agriculture, as well as to the Secretary of the Interior, regarding the condition and progress of each college, including statistical information in relation to its receipts and expenditures, its library, the number of its students and professors, and also as to any improvements and experiments made under the direction of any experiment stations attached to said colleges, with their costs and results, and such other industrial and economical statistics as may be regarded as useful, one copy of which shall be transmitted by mail free to all other colleges further endowed under this act.

SEC. 4. That on or before the first day of July in each year, after the passage of this act, the Secretary of the Interior shall ascertain and certify to the Secretary of the Treasury as to each State and Territory whether it is entitled to receive its share of the annual appropriation for colleges, or of institutions for colored students, under this act, and the amount which thereupon each is entitled, respectively, to receive. If the Secretary of the Interior shall withhold a certificate from any State or Territory of its appropriation, the facts and reasons therefor shall be reported to the President, and the amount involved shall be kept separate in the Treasury until the close of the next Congress, in order that the State or Territory may, if it should so desire, appeal to Congress from the determination of the Secretary of the Interior. If the next Congress shall not direct such sum to be paid, it shall be covered into the Treasury. And the Secretary of the Interior is hereby charged with the proper administration of this law.

SEC. 5. That the Secretary of the Interior shall annually report to Congress the disbursements which have been made in all the States and Territories, and also whether the appropriation of any State or Territory has been withheld, and if so, the reasons therefor.

SEC. 6. Congress may at any time amend, suspend, or repeal any or all of the provisions of this act.

Approved, August 30, 1890. (26 Stat. 417.)

Making Wine in California, 1892

From E. W. Hilgard, "General Objects and Plan of the Viticultural Work," in E. W. Hilgard and L. Paparelli, *Report of the Viticultural Work at the University of California* (Sacramento, 1892), Part I, pp. 15–23.

. . . .Among the first necessities of the present situation of California wines in the world's market, is the establishment of more definite qualities and brands, resulting from a definite knowledge of the qualities of each of the prominent grape varieties, and of their influence upon the kind and quality of the wine, in blending before, or, as the case may be, after fermentation; of the treatment required by each in the cellar during the time of ripening; and finally, of the differences caused by difference of location, climate, etc., as well as by different treatment of the wines themselves.

To this end, a definite knowledge of the character and special wine-making qualities of each kind of grape serving in the preparation of wine is indispensable. In the wine-producing countries of Europe this knowledge has been acquired by long experience; and chemical investigation has subsequently, in a great measure, ascertained the natural conditions upon which the attainment of certain results in wine-making depends. The principles thus evolved can be applied to new conditions, such as those existing in California, and thus save, to a great extent, the laborious and costly experimenting which has been gone through heretofore, by formulating into generally intelligible rules the knowledge which otherwise usually remains the trade secret of a few experts.

The first step to such knowledge is to obtain a definite idea of the material to be treated. Clearly, what is needed is that first the must, and then the corresponding wine of the more important grape varieties, should be made the subject of detailed investigation, and that the wine should have been produced from the must under definite, or definitely varied conditions, with absolute certainty of the purity of materials, as well as of the precise manner of operating in each case.

In an experimental laboratory, the qualities operated upon are of necessity relatively small; and it is highly important that allowance be made for this circumstance, as well as for other points in which the "wholesale" practice must always differ from the small-scale one. Nevertheless, we are thus enabled to obtain a very close estimate of the results obtainable from a given grape variety on the large scale, and of the part that each will play when blended either before or after fermentation.

It should be fully understood and remembered that while peculiarities and defects shown by analysis are perfectly definite indications as to the conditions that *must* be fulfilled in a successful blend, yet analysis cannot as yet take cognizance of the delicate and almost intangible flavors, or "bouquets," which must likewise be made to harmonize, in order to satisfy a cultivated palate. To that extent the determination of the proper blends must always remain with the expert wine-taster; but the work of the latter is immensely facilitated by being informed, through the analysis, of the prominent chemical peculiarities which in any case must be taken into consideration, and which ordinarily are left to laborious and more or less blind guessing or experimenting.

Even the most cursory consideration, however, shows that this cannot be the work of one or even a few years; but, like all other agricultural experiences and experiments, must be extensively repeated in order to become the basis of general practice. The same grape varieties grown in different localities, and in different years, will differ materially in their composition; and it is only by extended comparisons of these through a number of years that the accidentals can be definitely segregated from the essentials. Hasty generalization, based upon limited experience, is the bane of all experimental work, especially in agriculture."

In the earlier stages of this work a great deal of labor was bestowed on the examination of wines sent in by producers. In a large number of cases important results were thus obtained, owing to the special intelligence and care of the senders; but in a considerable proportion the results were extremely unsatisfactory, partly owing to the confused nomenclature and incorrect determination of the varieties from which the wines had been made, partly because of the very faulty methods of wine-making then prevailing, which rendered the product so different from what it would have been under correct treatment, that no valid conclusions could be drawn from its examination, whether chemical or gustatory. It was then attempted to gain better results by getting the grapes themselves from the growers and making them into wine in the laboratory, and the first thoroughly reliable results were thus obtained. But there arose great difficulty in getting the fruit picked at just the right stage of maturity during the hurry and pressure of wine-making in a large establishment; moreover, the transportation was found to involve not only heavy cost but frequent partial or total loss from injury to tender-skinned grapes in the rough handling they underwent before reaching the laboratory.

Stations under Private Auspices

It was then that under the generous initiative of Mr. John T. Doyle, of Menlo Park, followed by Messrs. E. B. Rogers, of Fresno, and John Gallegos, of Mission San José, the establishment of "experimental plots" under private auspices, planted with well-identified and important varieties, was begun and pursued with excellent results for several years. As will be seen from the record hereinafter given, the bulk of the exact information we now possess regarding the peculiarities of prominent varieties of grapes in different localities, have been the result of the work in these experimental plots established under private auspices; and among these, more particularly, the contributions from the "Cupertino Experimental Plot," under the patronage of Mr. Doyle, have been very full and important, as will be seen from the record.

The practice with respect to these experimental plots has been, that while the cultivation and general care of the vines devolved upon the patrons offering their use for experimental purposes, they were visited several times prior to the vintage by either the Director or some other competent person, in order to observe the growth and development of each variety, a full record of these observations being kept. Toward vintage time a suitable person was sent to remain on the spot and record the progress of maturity, and also to superintend the picking of the crop when at the proper stage. The mature grapes were then packed in "basket crates," such as are used for shipment of fresh fruit to the East, and then shipped mostly by express, since conveyance by ordinary freight trains would in most cases be too slow to permit the delicate-skinned and juicy wine grapes to arrive in a sound condition. It was found that in many cases even the relatively gentle handling and rapid conveyance by express would not carry certain varieties safely when in the proper condition for wine-making — that of complete maturity. The very conditions that must be fulfilled in a true wine grape, render its conveyance to any considerable distance without injury extremely difficult. As a matter of fact, almost every lot of grapes received at the laboratory has had to be picked over, in order to cull out as closely as possible all damaged, partially fermented, and moldy grapes, together with those which, as the result of coulure or other early injury, have remained only partially developed, or have become wholly or partially dried in that condition. That this tedious and laborious process was not always successful is painfully apparent from the frequency with which abnormal fermentations began to develop shortly after the first rapid fermentation was over, resulting, in the small quantities necessarily used, in frequent almost total loss of the experiment.

Limitation of Experiments as Regards Quantities Used

This limitation of quantity is one of the most serious drawbacks upon our work and its comparability with large-scale practice. The limitation is, however, unavoidable, unless there were at command an amount of financial means, which there is not the slightest prospect of being supplied. For large-scale experimentation of this character would require the establishment of several well-equipped and extensive wineries for that express purpose, in each of the several wine-making regions of the State, together with extensive vineyards, in which each of the two hundred or more varieties now under trial in the State could be grown in quantities sufficient for such large-scale work. Those who have established wineries and vineyards embracing many varieties, will readily appreciate the enormous cost and practical difficulty involved in such a scale of experimentation. It is certainly quite useless to attempt their establishment within this century; and I am satisfied that the results obtained would be so largely vitiated by the impossibility of the exact management of such complicated establishments that the heavy cost would not be repaid by them.

In fact, the main points now to be ascertained are of so elementary a character that even small-scale experiments, carefully conducted, can serve with certainty to eliminate from consideration, for practical purposes, three fourths of all the uncertainties existing as regards the adaptation of given grape varieties to the production of certain classes of wines in given districts. Except in a few localities, the wine industry of the State is still in the elementary condition in which the discriminations elsewhere made in the later stages of the development of wines are hardly thought of. The broad question to be solved is, *What classes of wines can certain regions of the State undertake to grow at all?* And this question can be solved with certainty, in the vast majority of cases, by small-scale experiments, even if the samples made should not be available for observation for more than eight months after fermentation. A practiced palate judges, without difficulty, of the possible development of a wine three or four months old. At six months most of our wines pass out of the grower's hands, in accordance with the wine-dealer's judgment and valuation, and cease to interest him.

If then, our small-scale experimentation in wine-making — the only practically possible mode of operating in so vast a State, where so many varieties are under trial — can be made to represent even approximately the character and quality of wines at the age of from six to eight months, it will have rendered the wine interest of the State a service that can, within reasonable limits of time, be rendered in no other way. *It serves to indicate with perfect plainness what trials it may be advisable to make on the large scale, and what others it is idle to think about.* If not conclusive evidence in all cases, it is assuredly in the great majority so plain that he that runs may read. It renders unnecessary the huge experimental establishments proposed by some, and relegates to private trials, on whatever scale may be thought advisable, such experiments as promise reasonable success. . . .

"Art" vs. Science

It has been alleged that "wine-making is an art, and has nothing to do with science." It would be sad for this important industry if this were in any sense true, and if at the end of the nineteenth century it had still failed to participate in the advance of all other industries — from the making of indigo and madder color from coal to that of butter and cheese, and even the feeding of hogs — to the benefit and dignity of a scientific basis. The allegation is simply untrue. It *is* true that good wines have been made for a long time in certain regions or localities, upon no other basis than long-continued experience; but it has cost centuries of time and floods of bad wine before that point was reached, and even now the vast majority of the wines made in the old wine districts of Europe is, according to the unanimous testimony of both merchants and scientific experts, *very* far from being the best that could be made from the materials given. Unless California wine-makers are willing to go through the same protracted performance that has been required to enable Europe to protect its choice vintages, they should avail themselves of the *principles* that have been deduced from the experience of centuries in the Old World, as formulated by the exact observations of experts. It is idle to pretend, at this late hour, that blind imitation is to be preferred to the intelligent application of principles that hold good under all circumstances, and that we have only to plant the same vines and follow the same modes of operating practiced in the Old World, in order to produce similar vintages, when the climatic conditions under which we operate are radically different, as are also our soils. The advocates of such a policy have much to learn from the history and development of the beer industry, which, from a mere tentative art, dependent upon personal skill and accidental conditions, and supposed to be practicable only in certain climates, has been transformed into a definite manufacturing industry that can be carried on anywhere, with proper appliances and the knowledge of the principles developed by scientific study.

So far as the application of scientific study to wine-making is concerned, one single illustration may suffice. Since it is definitely known that a sound vinous fermentation depends essentially upon the presence of a certain proportion of the natural acids of the grape to the sugar present, the most elementary common sense teaches us that when it is ascertained that this proportion is not attained by certain varieties of grapes in certain climates or localities, their culture for wine-making should either be discontinued, or other varieties that supply the deficiency should be planted alongside and blended with the other in the vat. There may be a few who might judge of such matters from the taste alone (if their tasting organs happened to be in good condition at the right time); but such cultivated taste is not at the command of every one, nor is it always infallible even with the best tasters. By the aid of investigations such as are recorded in this report, the general character of the several varieties in these respects can be ascertained, and their adaptations to blends predetermined, with at least a great degree of probability, while scores of others are at once excluded by the simplest of chemical tests. We may not, by the aid of these, be always able to tell which blends will be successful; but we *can* tell, with perfect certainty, which among two hundred varieties it would be perfectly useless to try for certain blends. The chemist cannot replace the taster or the expert cellarman, but he can save both a vast proportion of useless trouble and expense.

Viticultural Investigations Require Much Time

It need hardly be said that a definite characterization of a grape or of its wine-making qualities cannot be the work of one or two years, even for a single locality. Vintages differ notoriously with the seasons, so that until a sufficiently large number of observations can be brought into the calculation of averages it is impossible to come to valid conclusions. It is largely for this reason that the early publication of this record has not been pressed; it having been observed that the previous publications of results, covering only a year or two, have been taken as indicating established averages, and have led to injudicious investments on the part of too eager producers. In all agricultural experimentation the experience of a number of years taken together, and properly discussed, is absolutely essential to the safety of the conclusions drawn.

It is for these reasons that, notwithstanding the persistent misrepresentations that have from certain quarters been heaped upon the work and those participating in it, it has been steadily pursued, substantially on the original plan, with such modifications as experience suggested, and will so continue so long as the present Director shall have power to uphold it. Being without precedent, for the simple reason that similar questions have never been presented for investigation on so vast a scale, great difficulties have had to be overcome, and are still before us. For instance, it is not possible to tell beforehand at what precise stage of maturity the wine of a particular grape and locality should be bottled for further development; and when, by the passing of the right moment, the wine of one year is spoiled beyond recuperation, it takes at least another year to repeat the experiment. Yet, even then the particular vintage may be of a different character, and again bring to naught the effort to "catch the season" for the particular sample; and when the samples are before the cellar-master by the hundred, it is not easy to "keep the run" of each one.

Future Operations

Since the establishment of experimental culture stations in four representative agricultural regions of the State, it has not been thought advisable to expand further the policy of viticultural stations under private auspices. While extremely welcome and useful, the work thus conducted frequently involves serious inconvenience and expenditure for the patron himself; while on the other hand, at times, the impossibility of securing intelligent labor at the moment required will fatally vitiate the work and results of the Station. So soon, therefore, as it becomes possible to prosecute the same kind of work under the supervision of a competent person throughout the season, as is the case at the regular culture stations established under the Hatch Act, it is manifestly preferable that it should be done. Of course it requires time to bring the vines planted there into bearing, and, in the meantime, the material and data obtained from the private stations or from individuals will continue to be studied and utilized as heretofore. As regards the Cupertino Station, the study of the greater part of the varieties represented there has now been carried through so many years that for those varieties the local questions are probably quite definitely determined, so far as small-scale tests can do so, and their further prosecution is not called for. A few more years of work will probably place the experimental plot at Mission San José in the same category. The same, however, is not true of the Fresno plot, the distance of which, from the central station, together with other accidental conditions, have rendered the tests thus far made quite insufficient to serve as a basis for definite conclusions for more than a few varieties. As the property upon which the plot is situated has now changed hands, and is thus probably rendered unavailable, it is proposed to purchase carefully selected lots of the more important grapes now under cultivation at different points in the region, for the purpose of experiment, at least until the vines at the San Joaquin Valley Station near Tulare shall be in full bearing. This policy has been pursued for some years past, with the attainment of some important results at the Foothill Station in Amador County; but unfortunately the number of varieties as yet in bearing in that region is so limited, and on the whole so little adapted to the peculiarities of the climate, that we shall have to await the results from the culture plots at the Station to come to any definite conclusions as to the true policy to be pursued in planting wine grapes in the foothills. Nearly the same may be said of the Southern California Station and the region it represents; it is certain that thus far but very few of the high-class varieties best adapted to wine-making in that climate are in bearing there. At the Southern Coast Range Station, no grapes grown in the region will be available much sooner than those grown on the Station ground themselves.

We regret that for a number of years past, few additional data have been obtained from the great wine-making regions of Sonoma and Napa. The depression of the wine industry, which has been most seriously felt in that portion of the State, explains, in a measure, the apparent lack of active interest in the progressive improvement of the product. While, with the more general recognition of the fact that in wines it is quality and not quantity that pays in the end, there has been a very obvious and encouraging improvement in the practice of vinification and its results, there naturally has been little disposition to try experiments of uncertain issue, while little more than the cost of production could be realized by the wine-maker. Nevertheless, a number of encouraging offers of coöperation have been received; among others, from the Italian-Swiss colony of Asti, near Cloverdale, which is the more important as the grape varieties grown there are among the class to which, in our opinion, California will have to look for the production of high-class dry wines in her warmer sections, viz.: the "North Italian type."

Climatic Conditions.

The products and meteorological records of California show beyond all possible denial, that over by far the larger portion of the cultivable area, her climate corresponds most nearly to that of the countries immediately bordering upon the Mediterranean. Where the orange and olive grow alongside of the grape, the rational conclusion must be that the character of the latter will be essentially similar to that of corresponding parts of the Old World, and that the experience and practice of Spain and Portugal, Mediterranean France, Italy, Algeria, and Greece, and not that of the Rhine or the Atlantic seaboard of France, is presumably applicable to our wines. Dearly bought experience has amply verified this presumption, with all its practical consequences; and the sooner it is acted upon by our grape-growers and wine-makers the sooner will the wine industry emerge from the slough of despond into which a concurrence of unfortunate circumstances has kept it for some years past.

Keeping Qualities and Shipments.

Among the chief considerations needful to be acted upon is the fact, that in order to reach a market outside of the State, our wines have to undergo prolonged and trying transportation; if by sea, they have to undergo the most critical fourfold change of climate, and under present financial conditions they have to pass this ordeal while still far younger than is usual elsewhere in the shipment of wines to long distances. It is therefore eminently important that the keeping qualities should be among the foremost considerations, and whatever means can be legitimately employed for this purpose should be used with all diligence. It is for this reason that much space is given in this publication to the several processes for the preservation of wine that in climates like ours have become special desideratum, and to some extent the regular practice in the Old World, wherever similar difficulties are experienced. The illogical prejudice against the use of preservative processes which add nothing to the wine and take nothing from it (save, in some cases, what it is the object of all after-treatment of wines to eliminate), but which practically approves of the use of a number of antiseptics and additions foreign to the wines and injurious to its quality, is fast getting to be a thing of the past in Europe, and must soon be so everywhere; the sooner the better.

There are among the grapes now grown in California a number of varieties that are especially sturdy keepers; a similar quality is shown by a number of others not yet grown, but reported upon in our record. Special attention should be given to these, as their wines are, in numerous cases, not only of high quality, but when well made will keep perfectly without any special preservative processes being used upon them prior to shipment.

Preservative Processes.

It is freely admitted that thus far none of these processes are without some influence upon special "bouquets," and that it is undesirable to use them on the best class of wines. But as between wines of ordinary consumption, rendered safe by proper pasteurization on the one hand, and those that on the slightest provocation will start in on the way to milk-sourness — the bane of all wines of southern climates — on the other, there can be but one opinion among purchasers and consumers. In this matter, at least, we shall be perfectly safe in following the precedent and example of the countries where most of the wine of the world is produced and consumed.

But as regards sweet fortified wines, there can be no question that the ability of California to produce *all* classes, from the common to the best, is limited only by the probable demand for such wines. Now that the artificial restrictions upon their production are practically removed, and thus competition in the world's market is open, it should be our study to make them of the best quality possible, and to refrain from making this class the Botany Bay of our spoiled dry wines. The best varieties of grapes adapted to their production are mostly already in the State, and the correct process of manufacture (quite different from what has been usually practiced heretofore in California) is no secret. It is also proved that the Great Valley, the Foothills, and Southern California are particularly well adapted to their production, while the coast region, generally speaking, is decidedly less so, while much better adapted to the making of dry wines. Let each section of the State, then, produce that kind of wine for which it is best fitted by its natural condition, and cease to try to produce "everything everywhere." There can be no permanent advantage in maintaining a chronic fight against natural conditions, so long as there are other producers who are able to get along smoothly and without conflict. The latter will inevitably win in the race.

Experiments in Florida Agriculture, 1893

From Florida Agricultural Experiment Station, *Annual Report*, 1893, pp. 7–12.

My term of office as Director of the Florida Experiment Station began on September 1st, 1893, hence this report, so far as my own work is concerned, embraces only the last four months of the year 1893. When I entered upon duty there came into my hands no unpublished notes of experiments either complete or incomplete, hence it was necessary for me to initiate work.

One of the first things that came to my notice in regard to agriculture in Florida, is that the State does not produce enough forage and grain for home consumption. Large sums are now paid annually for forage and grain grown north of us. If this forage and this grain, especially the grain for feeding stock, can be grown in Florida these large sums will be saved, it will be made possible to produce the meats consumed in the State, and a large production of valuable fertilizers will result as a by-product. Hence I began immediately to experiment with the growth of winter forage. Plats have been sown with oats, rye, barley, wheat, rape, turnips, ruta-baga, kale and collards, with a view of learning the profit of growing these as forage crops during our winter season. It seems to me that with our cheap lands and our incomparable climate, we can grow better fodder and at less expense than any other State. I hope to prove this, and shall leave no means of doing so untried. . . .

The prices of cotton just now are very low, and much discouragement exists among cotton growers. It therefore becomes necessary to learn if more productive varieties of cotton of better quality can be grown at less expense. To this subject careful attention will be given.

Tobacco growing is just now in a very depressed state, owing to the uncertainty of the tariff. It has been made clear by years of successful experience that a superior article of tobacco can be grown in Florida. But much remains to be done in learning the best varieties, soil, cultivation, fertilizers and curing. To this work the Station at Lake City will give attention.

Many Florida farmers desire to grow sugar cane to make syrup and sugar for home consumption. It would not be surprising should this State again produce large quantities of sugar as a commercial article. Experiments in growing cane, including varieties, soil, fertilizers and cultivation will be made in the near future.

The production of up-land rice may become a much larger and a much more profitable industry than at present. I shall procure promising varieties from Japan, China, India and other rice growing centers. Attention will also be given to the growth of low-land rice, as there are large acres of Florida where this rice can be profitably cultivated.

The climate and soil of Florida give it unexampled facilities for the growth of truck and fruit. This industry is yet in its infancy. Much remains to be learned as to varieties, seasons, cultivation and fertilizers. We shall from year to year carry on experiments to discover what may be done in all these directions. The experiments in truck farming will be carried on mainly in Lake City.

Olive culture is so valuable an industry wherever the olive will thrive, that we should try to learn if it will thrive in this State. To this end I shall have olive trees set at our three stations, and in other parts of Florida, this spring. The fig is one of the important fruit crops of the world. We should learn if the fig can be grown and cured on a lage scale in Florida. A few trees will be set out this spring, and others as fast as I learn of promising varieties.

Investigations as to the insect pests of the various farm, orchard and garden crops, and also as to fungoid diseases, are among the most essential helps to modern agriculture. Much has been learned by investigation in all parts of the world in the last few years to aid the agriculturist to conquer these foes. But much more remains to be done. A department of our Experiment Station will devote much time to this work. This department is now led by Prof. P. H. Rolfs. It gives me much pleasure to call your attention to the fact that under him Florida is not behind other States in original valuable discoveries in this line. Prof. Rolfs is the discoverer of the cause of the disease known as tomato blight, one of the most destructive fungoid diseases to which the tomato is subject in this State. He has pointed out a remedy which promises to hold it in check. His work in this immediate direction will be carried on during the coming year with careful attention. Prof. Rolfs is not unfrequently called to different parts of the State to investigate various pests, and to advise as to remedies. He recently discovered the presence at DeFuniak Springs of a most destructive enemy to several varieties of deciduous fruits. I refer to the San Jose scale, which is found at that point diffused through several orchards. I am now in communication with the fruit growers of DeFuniak, and with the Department of Agriculture in Washington, as to the steps necessary to exterminate this scale before it has made further progress. The seriousness of the matter cannot be overestimated. If this scale is allowed to spread, the fruit industry will be ruined wherever the pest gets a strong hold. I shall give much attention to this, and hope next year to be able to report that every scale has been wiped out.

The work done and in progress in regard to tomato blight and San Jose scale, is but a sample of the immediate service the Experiment Station can do for all the agricultural industries of the State. Diseases of the pineapple, the citrus fruits, the peach, the pear, the mango, have already received attention, but all need constant study by men trained for the work.

As to the insect pests of citrus fruits, I call attention to the fact that the Department of Agriculture in Washington has a special agent in Florida for this work — Mr. H. G. Hubbard, Crescent City, who is considered the ablest man in America on the insects that infest citrus fruits. The Department of Agriculture has also a Sub-Tropical Laboratory at Eustis, for the study of the diseases of citrus fruits. This laboratory is in charge of Prof. W. T. Swingle and Prof. H. J. Webber, who are most thoroughly trained. As they have a well equipped laboratory, and are in the midst of the "Orange Belt," they have every advantage for the pursuit of these special lines. From the investigations of these three men we may expect most valuable results.

As the pests and diseases of the citrus family are thus in such competent hands, our Florida Experiment Station need not take up this line of investigation, but give its efforts in other directions.

The dependence of modern agriculture upon chemistry is most intimate. Knowledge of soils, fertilizers, the constituents of various crops, and the nutritive value to man or beast of the food crops, comes directly from chemical investigation. The chemist of the Experiment Station, Prof. A. A. Persons, is largely employed in answering the numerous questions in his department which come to my office, and in analyzing material sent in from all parts of the State. He is also at present engaged in determining the nutritive value of the orange, work which has not heretofore been done in Florida. . . .

The sub-tropical portion of Florida, including the immense area south of the 25th parallel of latitude, has a climate that enables it to grow products that cannot be produced elsewhere in the State, nor in the United States. Some of these can be profitably grown and marketed during the winter. To lead in discovering fruits, vegetables, and farm crops adapted to this section, and in learning the fertilizers and methods of cultivation, is a most important work for the development of Florida, and for the Station to enter upon. I hope that this work can go on with increasing success. . . .

Very respectfully yours,

O. Clute, *Director*

Chemistry and Agriculture in Idaho, 1893

From Charles W. McCurdy, "The Application of Chemistry to the Agricultural Development of Idaho," in University of Idaho, Agricultural Experiment Stations (March, 1893), *Bulletin*, no. 3, pp. 6–12.

THE APPLICATION OF CHEMISTRY TO THE AGRICULTURAL DEVELOPMENT OF IDAHO.

Geological Features

Idaho has an area of 84,290 square miles. The soil is volcanic, about equally divided among rolling plains, mountainous regions and lava beds.

The extent of arable land is indefinitely stated owing to the lack of proper surveys. But we are assured that the greater portion of the State will be brought entirely under cultivation for the growing of grain, grazing and horticultural purposes.

Southern Idaho is a great lava plain through which the Snake river has cut its way. Here the volcanic material is still *in situ* and comprises vast arid regions, but fertile in the extreme when irrigated. The eruptive material forms the surface soil. The Silurian formation outcrops prominently, overlaid in places by the Carboniferous and well defined areas of the Triassic, Cretaceous and Tertiary strata. The Quarternary areas are largely confined to the river bottoms constituting the arable lands, bounded by extensive grassy plains or sage brush areas. Such is the prevailing geological formation of the southern third of the State.

The Salmon river penetrates a mountainous region rich in mineral resources and timber and whose valleys offer every inducement to the husbandman; while the Clearwater flows placidly along through one of the best grazing districts in the northwest.

North of the Clearwater the soil is of alluvial formation, volcanic in origin, and requires no irrigation. It is a part of the great Palouse country, famous for its agricultural resources. The soil is deep, finely divided and extremely fertile. An extensive lake and river system adds to its desirability. Thus much is true of the greater portion of Nez Perce, Latah, Shoshone and Kootenai counties.

Indeed, the economic features of the State are most varied, from the plains of Lewiston (530 ft.), to the more elevated regions of Boise City (2490 ft.), Moscow (2569 ft.), Pocatello (4446 ft.), Idaho Falls (4712 ft.), Rathdrum, Murray and Hope, that only the hand of the trained scientific agriculturist aided by the practical irrigation engineer, is needed to make our beautiful "Gem of the Mountains" the most fruitful and wealthiest of the North-West States.

Alkali Soils

The term alkali soils is applied to those lands which contain a large amount of soluble salts in their composition, usually sulfates of soda, potash, lime and magnesia. Such soils may be known by the peculiar incrustation which appears upon the surface in dry weather, after a season of rainfall or irrigation, or, by the taste. They are finely divided soils, very dusty when dry, and will absorb large quantities of water. They are largely the product of volcanic formation; are very generally distributed over the earth, but more especially noticeable in those regions where there is insufficient rainfall.

Nearly all soils contain alkali salts, but the frequent drenchings by rain or river flow wash the soluble salts deeply into the subsoil whence they will not again soon reach the surface, except by capillary action induced by surface evaporation.

The only sure remedy, therefore, would seem to be perfect underdrainage and deep tillage; surface flooding, in any form, without such treatment affords only temporary relief, as surface exposure will cause the alkali to rise.

Vegetation requires some of the salts, named as sustenance, and they are detrimental to the plant only when present in too large quantities; in such cases the roots are corroded, the woody fibre poisoned and the plant is "set back" in consequence. When the subsoil is near the surface such is likely to be the case. Piercing the subsoil with a crow-bar will partially obviate the difficulty.

Alkali Soils of the North-West States

This question is of interest not only to the agriculturalists and scientists of Idaho, but has become an absorbing topic of discussion among farmers, stockmen and horticulturists in regions adjoining us. Dr. Hilgard of California has thoroughly investigated the subject, upwards of fifteen hundred (1500) analyses having been made by that Station of soils selected from California, Oregon, Washington and Montana; but, to my knowledge, no analytical study of Idaho soils has ever been undertaken.

Composition of Alkali

The analyses made by the California Station show a composition of the soluble parts to consist, in the main, of potassium carbonate (saleratus). sodium sulfate (Glauber's salt), sodium nitrate (Chile saltpeter) potassium nitrate (saltpeter), sodium carbonate (sal soda), sodium chloride (common salt), calcium sulfate (gypsum), magnesium sulfate (Epsom salts), sodium phosphate, potassium sulfate, ammonium carbonate and organic matter composed largely of humus or vegetable mold. The ingredients predominating are Glauber's salt, common salt and sal soda in about the order named, though subject to considerable variation in the two types of aikali.

Black and White Alkali

A very superficial study of soils sent to this department for analysis reveals the fact that there are two well marked types of alkali, the "white" and "black." Chemical analysis and practical tests made in the field prove the black soil to be the worse. It is composed largely of soda carbonate with varying proportions of humus. When a watery solution of this type was evaporated slowly over a water bath, or by exposure in mud holes, a dark ring was left about the vessel and on the soil surface. This dark ring was found upon closer examination to be largely humus that had been held in solution.

Dr. Hilgard, whose wide observation and thorough study entitles him to speak with authority, writes concerning humus: "This in itself is serious injury, for humus is one of the most important of soil ingredients. If held in solution, or washed through the soil, the producing powers of the land are seriously impaired.

"That, however, is not the end of the injury; for when accumulated by evaporation around the crown, the alkali absolutely corrodes and dissolves the bark, as it does the humus of the soil causing a dead ring around the butt, and finally girdling the stem as effectually as could be done by a knife, or even worse, because the wound is poisoned and the wood attacked after the bark is gone.

This difficulty," he continues, "does not exist in the case of "white" alkali soils; they till kindly and the only trouble lies in the accumulation of the salts at the surface in consequence of evaporation to such extent as to injure the surface roots and root crown."

How to convert the "black" alkali into the "white" type and thus eliminate the destructive properties of the former, is a serious question that confronts the agriculturist. This may be done by a liberal application of land plaster (calcium sulfate.)

Sodium carbonate (black alkali) plus calcium sulfate equals calcium carbonate plus sodium sulfate (white alkali.)

Furthermore, the gypsum renders the humus insoluble and it retains its original function as one of the soil ingredients. It is also a valuable fertilizer for leguminous and broad-leaved plants. Land plaster scattered freely upon manure heaps and in or about stables or sheds will catch and hold fast the escaping ammonium carbonate, giving it up in due time to the growing crop. Gypsum beds should, therefore, be sought for in the State that the article may be brought within the means of the consumer.

Thus far in the discussion of the alkali problem, I have endeavored to make clear to the reader the term alkali soils, their composition, their prevalence in certain sections of our State, the benefit to be derived by irrigating them, and how the effect of the alkali upon the growing crops may be modified by under-drainage and deep tillage, and the application of land plaster; also the natural deduction that the proper treatment can be decided on only after the soil has been submitted to a chemical anylysis to determine which of the injurious constituents predominates. . . .

Available Crops for Alkali Soils

based upon the ultimate purpose of said crop. Alfalfa has been found to be a most valuable and thrifty plant, the dense leaves thickly shading the ground while its deep roots absorb nearly all the water and dissolved salts, thus reducing evaporation to the minimum. Root crops, as potatoes, carrots, turnips, cabbage, beets (not intended for sugar production), sowed corn and other ensilage crops may be successfully grown. The small fruits and the grape, prune, pear, apple and peach, may be profitably raised when the alkali is not too strong. The Experimental Stations will early inaugurate such tests for the benefit of the farmer. . . .

Laboratories

The Chemical Department of the University dates from the first of the year. One small room only could be spared for class-room and laboratory instruction; supplies had to be secured from the far east; and yet, at this date, the department is very well organized and prepared to do analytical work for the State. With the completion of the university building, the department will be assigned to permanent quarters, comprising an office and weighing room, a qualitative laboratory, a quantitative laboratory, a metallurgical and assaying room and a lecture room, all of which will be available for investigation in agriculture and kindred sciences.

To meet the demand already made upon the department has necessitated a large outlay of funds for Station equipment, which will be considerably augmented during the summer.

Lines of Investigation

In the near future the management will undertake a series of systematic soil and clay analysis collected from typical sections of the State, especially from regions effected by alkali; waters intended for sanitary and irrigation purposes will receive special attention; fertilizers offered for sale within the State will be examined that the consumer may be protected against the use of the adulterated article; coal and other fuels will be analyzed to determine their value for factory and domestic purposes; the beet sugar industry will be given early consideration, so also will the examination of dairy products and various foods offered for household consumption.

The department will utilize every available means to make itself a prominent factor in the development of the resources of the State that come within its province, and requests the co-operation of all interested parties.

No investigations will be made gratutiously intended to advance the private interests of corporations or individuals only, but such experiments and research undertaken whose results will aid in increasing the material and social wealth and health of any community or of the State at large, and add to the sum total of scientific knowledge.

Chinch-Bug Experiment Station in Kansas, 1893

From University of Kansas (Lawrence) Experiment Station, *Annual Report*, 1892 (Topeka, Kan., 1893), pp. 1–4.

The act establishing the Experiment Station is as follows:

An Act to establish an Experimental Station at the State University of Kansas, to promote and conduct experiments for the destruction of chinch-bugs by contagion or infection, and making an appropriation therefor.

Be it enacted by the Legislature of the State of Kansas:

SECTION 1. That the sum of thirty-five hundred dollars be and the same is hereby appropriated for the purpose of establishing, maintaining and conducting an experimental station at the State University, at Lawrence, to propagate the contagion or infection that is supposed to be destructive to chinch-bugs, and furnish the same to the farmers free of charge, under the direction and supervision of the Chancellor, F. H. Snow, as hereinafter provided.

SEC. 2. As soon as practicable after the taking effect of this act, the said Chancellor shall procure the necessary furniture and material, with such assistance as he may require, and proceed to propagate as much contagion, on as large a scale, as may be necessary, and supply the farmers of this State with the same, when required.

SEC. 3. Of the sum hereby appropriated, two thousand five hundred dollars shall be available during the fiscal years ending June 30, 1891, and June 30, 1892, to be applied to defraying the necessary expenses for assistants, furniture, expressage, telegraphing, postage, etc. And said Chancellor is hereby authorized to issue his warrant upon the State Treasurer, upon itemized accounts, for the amounts specified by this act: *Provided*, That not more than five hundred dollars shall be drawn in any one month, except in the month of April, 1891, when the sum of eight hundred dollars may be drawn, if deemed necessary; and all accounts shall be verified. And if the experiments fail to produce the desired results, no more funds shall be drawn from the treasury, and the station shall be abandoned.

SEC. 4. If the experiments shall prove successful, or desirable to be continued, the sum of one thousand dollars shall be made available during the fiscal year ending June 30, 1893, to be drawn under the same conditions as set forth in section 3 of this act.

SEC. 5. The Chancellor shall also report the results of his experiments to the official State paper, provided the said paper shall publish the same free of charge, beginning the first day of April next and every month thereafter, until the first day of December following. He shall also make a full report of the money expended and the results of his experiments to the Governor, on or before the first day of December of each year.

SEC. 6. This act shall take effect and be inforce from and after its publication in the official State paper.

Approved March 4, 1891.

Observations and Experiments of 1892

The first chinch-bugs for infection were received April 20. These bugs came from Texas. With these bugs the infection cases were started with the "white fungus," *Sporotrichum globuliferum*. This now makes the fourth winter through which this infection has been carried in the laboratory. Near the close of the summer of 1891, a considerable number of dead bugs, whose bodies were filled with this fungus growth, were put away in secure boxes to be used for the beginning of the following season's experiments. With the first bugs sent in a healthy growth was soon obtained in the infection jars, and as soon as the chinch-bugs began to be sent in considerable numbers from various portions of the State the large infection boxes adopted last year were again put into use.

The method of infecting and distributing during this season has been the same as that adopted in 1891. Large, shallow boxes, in which infected bugs were put from the small infection jars used in beginning the work, were kept stocked with live bugs throughout the season. From these boxes a small number of dead bugs covered with the fungus, dying bugs on the outsides of whose bodies the fungus had not yet appeared, and active, apparently healthy but presumably infected bugs, were sent in response to each request for infection.

During the season 3,500 requests for infected bugs were received, of which number more than 3,000 were from Kansas farmers. In every case where the application was accompanied by live bugs (a condition obviously necessary in order that the infection boxes might be kept stocked) infected bugs were returned. Resulting from these 3,000 applications, reports were received regarding 1,732 field experiments. Of these 1,732 experimenters, 196 report a failure to give the infected bugs a trial for various reasons; the results for 120 cases were doubtful in the minds of the experimenters; in 372 cases no successful results were obtained; and in 1,044 cases infected bugs were believed to have been used with successful results. Thus 67.9 per cent. of the experiments regarding the outcome of which reports were received were successful, 24.3 per cent. were unsuccessful, and 7.8 per cent. were doubtful. In making these percentages the "no trial" reports were of course excluded.

Of these 1,044 successful reports, 383 include specific estimates of crops saved by the experiments. The sum in cash value of these estimates is $39,481.15. If the average amount may be fairly applied to the remainder of the 1,044 Kansas experimenters, an aggregate saving of $107,615.52 may be estimated. In the two years 1891 and 1892, during which the Station has existed, an aggregate saving of crops amounting in cash value to $300,925.52 is estimated.

Infected bugs were sent to eight States other than Kansas, and also to Indian and Oklahoma Territories. Reports were received from 216 experimenters in these States and Territories, of which 153 report successful results, 16 unsuccessful, 7 doubtful, and 40 were unable to give the infected bugs a trial.

Farmers' Institutes in Kansas, 1898

From H. M. Cottrell, "Farmers' Institutes," in *The Industrialist* (Manhattan, Kans., June, 1898), XXIV, pp. 417–19.

Kansas is behind in her work in farmers' institutes. The state makes no provision for institutes whatever, and the work has been left to be carried on and to be paid for by the Agricultural College whose funds are insufficient for the needs of the regular college work and whose entire force is needed for teaching. This year the regents appropriated $500 from the college funds for institutes, a larger amount than had ever before been expended for this purpose, and thirty institutes were held — not quite one institute for each three counties in the state. Three railroads, the Santa Fe, the Rock Island and the Union Pacific granted the College half-fare rates for members of the faculty traveling on institute work when the institute was held on the line giving the reduced rate. But for this courtesy the College could not have held over twenty institutes with the money available. In addition to the thirty institutes held with the help of the College, a few were conducted in different parts of the state at private expense by local talent. Compare this record with the work of other States. The state appropriation for farmers' institutes in Wisconsin is $12,000, in Minnesota $13,500, in Pennsylvania $15,000, and in New York $15,000. In Ohio the institutes are supported by a county tax, the sum not to exceed $200 for each county. There are 105 counties in Kansas, and the Ohio plan applied to them would give an institute fund for the state of $21,000 as compared with the $500 now spent. The latest reports at hand show the following number of farmers' institutes held during the year in the states named: Kansas, 30; Indiana, 185; Ohio, 284; New York, 290.

A few facts brought out in our institutes held during the past winter will show the need and advantages of the work:

In one of our western counties the wheat yield was good in 1892 and in 1897, with almost total failures in the intervening years. In this county there is a settlement where the farmers have had fair crops every year. Inquiry was made as to whether these farmers had any advantage, in regard to soil or situation, over their neighbors whose wheat crops were failures; but it was ascertained that their success was due to the methods of preparing the ground before seeding. Think of the benefit if these farmers, who have learned to grow wheat when others fail, should be employed during the winter on an institute force, giving farmers thruout the State the benefit of their knowledge.

The "Potato King of the United States" grows the potato crops which give him his title in a section of Kansas where a few years ago, potatoes were not grown sufficient to supply home consumption, because farmers had failed to get them to grow. What would it be worth to the farmers of this state if the methods of this grower could be presented before two or three institutes in each county?

Alfalfa is essential for the cheapest production, under Kansas conditions, of beef, milk and pork. At an institute the past winter in one of our south-central counties with 500 people in attendance, it was asserted by one of their leading farmers that alfalfa could not be grown successfully in that county except on the bottom lands, and therefore that upland farmers would have to lose all the profits to be obtained from growing and feeding it. The majority of the audience agreed with the speaker, and this opinion is generally held thruout the state. A gentleman rose and pointed to the fact that he had 100 acres in alfalfa, on the highest land in the county, and raised good crops every year. If this farmer could present his methods of alfalfa raising, which are successful on uplands, before institutes in every county in the state, his address would alone be worth the entire cost of holding the institutes.

Kaffir corn grain is nearly equal to Indian corn for producing beef, milk and pork. In the severe drouth of 1897 where Indian corn yielded only one to five bushels per acre, Kaffir corn gave 25 bushels per acre; and on uplands in eastern Kansas during the past ten years Kaffir corn has averaged about one-third more grain per acre than Indian corn. Yet thousands of farmers in that part of the state, where rainfall is usually deficient, continue to plant corn; as do their neighbors on the upland farms in the eastern section of the state. How much would it save these men if the value of Kaffir corn could be thoroly presented to them thru farmers' institutes?

In one county alone the past winter $2,000,000 was invested in feeding steers — a large part of this amount by men new in the business whose methods were pronounced by experienced feeders to be sure to bring loss or at the least no profit. These new feeders could have held farmers' institutes in every township in that county for $500 and with this amount could have engaged the most successful feeders of the state to teach them the best methods of feeding. Single feeders in this county lost one to five times this amount by mistakes which others could have told them how to avoid.

Reports received last winter indicate that patrons of creameries were receiving on an average $20 per cow per year for milk. At one creamery a patron received $45 for the milk of each cow during the year, while another patron received only $12 — a difference of 275 per cent. At another creamery a patron sold his milk for $48 per cow, and his calves brought him an average of $18 each — an income of $66 per cow. What would it be worth if two or three institutes could be held in each county of the state at which these successful milk producers could teach others their methods?

The cost of holding such institutes is paltry when we consider what a slight increase in the profits obtained from each cow means. If one dollar could be added to the profits obtained from each cow it would mean over half a million dollars yearly increase for the state. One cent added to the value of each animal slaughtered or sold for slaughter in the state would add nearly forty thousand dollars: one tenth of a cent saved in the cost of producing each bushel of corn would mean a saving of one hundred and fifty thousand dollars.

Other states have the benefits that come from farmers' institutes, and Kansas farmers must have help in the same direction or they will fall behind. The college force has neither the funds nor the time to conduct the number of institutes that should be held in the state. At least three should be held in each county, making over 300 in all. A good plan would be to have a thoroly competent man appointed as director of institutes who should become a member of the college faculty with work confined to conducting institutes and preparing for them. Such a connection would give all institutes the benefit of all our experimental work. During the summer this director could familiarize himself with our experiments and prepare to put the results in the best form for presentation at institutes. Successful men in all branches of Kansas farming could be employed during the winter to give their experiences to institutes, and the college force would go whenever other duties permitted. The farmers of the town where an institute is held should furnish half the papers. Institutes conducted in this way would give the full benefits of the experience of the best farmers where the institutes are held, of the scientific knowledge of the experiment station force and of the methods of successful farmers thruout the state.

Experiments with Animal Diseases, 1899

From D. E. Salmon, "Some Examples of the Development of Knowledge concerning Animal Diseases" U. S. Department of Agriculture, *Yearbook*, 1899, pp. 93, 124–34.

Introduction

The acquirement of knowledge in the domain of animal diseases during the century now closing has been constant and amazing, and compares favorably with the advancement in other branches of science which, with the zeal and activity of investigators, has attracted the wonder and admiration of the world. While something is known even to the general reader of the progress of knowledge in this field, and of the usefulness of this knowledge in explaining and preventing the diseases of man, there are comparatively few who have an adequate conception of the vast array of facts which have been accumulated and the revolution which these facts have brought in the prevailing ideas as to the nature of the various diseases and the methods by which they should be treated. To enter into all the details of the development of this subject during the century would require the writing of a series of volumes on the respective subdivisions, which, when completed, would be of professional rather than popular interest. A review of this character is manifestly impossible, even if such detail were desirable, in a Yearbook paper. The writer, therefore, deems it wise to confine himself to the work that has been done upon a few great problems which are, or should be, of interest to the many, and the elucidation of which has done most to ameliorate the condition of mankind as well as that of the domesticated animals.

The beginning of the nineteenth century almost defines the line at which the old and fantastic doctrines on animal pathology began to crumble and to be replaced by facts and scientific principles. Previous to that time a more or less elaborate system had been compiled, based upon observations made during the past history of the world; but as the ideas in regard to the structure and activities of the animal body were in many cases crude and erroneous, it is not surprising that the conceptions of disease were often distorted and strange, as viewed from the standpoint of our present knowledge. What is it that has brought light out of the darkness and order out of the chaos of the preceding centuries? What new factor, what change of method, was introduced with this century which accounts for the overthrow of the anthrax virus into the veins is more dangerous than when inserted into the connective tissue, and is fatal with infinitesimal doses. On the contrary, blackleg virus may be inoculated into the veins in much larger doses than into the connective tissue without producing fatal effects. It was shown that one attack of either of these diseases granted immunity from that particular contagion, but that an attack of anthrax did not protect from blackleg nor did an attack of blackleg protect from anthrax.

Remedy for Blackleg

The above experimental studies consequently established the fact beyond controversy that two distinct diseases had previously been grouped together; that the germs of these two diseases were distinct and very different in their biological characters, and that different measures were required for their control.

These investigators did not stop at this point, however, but continued their researches with a view of finding a prophylactic treatment. The remarkable success of Pasteur in attenuating the virus of anthrax and fowl cholera led them to endeavor to produce an attenuated virus, or vaccine, for blackleg. This was finally accomplished by drying the virulent flesh and afterwards reducing it to a powder and subjecting it to a temperature between 85° and 100° C. for a sufficient time to properly reduce its activity. This vaccine, perfected by years of experience, is now in use in most parts of the world. It is supplied by the Bureau of Animal Industry to the stock raisers of the United States to the extent of half a million doses a year, and where used has reduced the losses on infected pastures from 10, 15, or 20 per cent, which annually occurred before using, to less than 1 per cent per annum.   .

This great practical triumph in the control of an infectious disease is due entirely to the application of the experimental method. Without experiments upon living animals and confined to clinical observation, it was impossible to determine whether anthrax and blackleg were essentially identical in nature or whether they were distinct diseases, and much less was it possible to isolate and identify the germ or so to change the activity of this organism as to transform it from one of the most deadly organisms to a harmless protective vaccine.

Texas Fever, Splenetic Fever, or Southern Cattle Fever

History of Texas Fever

In 1814 we find the first known accounts of a disease being disseminated by apparently healthy cattle from certain districts in the Southern States when these cattle were driven North to market. Attention was at that time called to this phenomenon by Dr. James Mease in a lecture before the Philadelphia Society for Promoting Agriculture, who stated that the cattle from a certain district in South Carolina so certainly diseased all others with which they mixed in their progress to the North that they were prohibited by the people of Virginia from passing through the State; that these cattle affected others while they themselves were in perfect health, and that cattle from Europe or the interior taken to the vicinity of the sea were attacked by a disease that generally proved fatal. In a paper read before the same society in 1825 he says: ''The circumstance of cattle from a certain district in South Carolina affecting others with this disease has long been known.''

The precise locality from which these cattle originated, or its extent, he was, however, unable to ascertain, notwithstanding inquiries upon the subject.

Dr. Mease gave an account of an outbreak of this disease which occurred in 1796 in Lancaster County, Pa., as a result of South Carolina cattle being brought and sold there. These cattle were penned over night in a plowed field and did not come in contact with the cattle on the farm; nevertheless, the latter commenced dying a short time afterwards. In every instance where sold they communicated the disease to the cattle with which they mixed. The symptoms were loss of appetite and weakness of the limbs, amounting to inability to stand; when they fell, they would tremble and groan violently. Some discharged bloody urine, others bled at the nose. On being opened the kidneys were found inflamed and sometimes in a state of suppuration.

Many similar outbreaks occurred in North Carolina, Virginia, and Maryland in the first half of the century, but the accounts of them are too meager to be of use. Legislation was enacted in North Carolina, however, as early as 1837 to prevent the driving of cattle into that State from either South Carolina or Georgia between the first day of April and the first day of November; also, to prevent cattle from being driven from those parts of North Carolina, where the soil is sandy and the natural production or growth of timber is the long-leafed pine, into or through any of the highland parts of the State, where the soil or growth of timber is of a different kind, between the dates already mentioned.

Very little more was heard of this disease until about 1850, when cattle bred in Texas began to be driven through Arkansas, Missouri, and Kansas for distribution to feeders in those and other Western States. A mysterious and highly fatal disease then appeared along the great roads, highways, or trails over which these cattle were driven, destroying about 50 per cent of all the native cattle. Persons living near the fording places lost as high as 90 per cent. It was two years before the origin of this disease was traced to the Southern cattle.

From 1856 to 1860 many Texas cattle were driven into the States of Kansas, Missouri, Kentucky, Iowa, and Illinois, and it was stated that the native stock in the sections to which they were taken were swept away by a "dry murrain." An epizootic under such circumstances was so unexpected and contrary to all previous experience that at first the source of the disease was not suspected, and when the Southern cattle were accused there were many who looked upon their presence as a mere coincidence. However, by 1861 the conviction that Texas cattle disseminated disease became so strong that laws were enacted by the States of Kansas, Missouri, Kentucky, and Illinois regulating the movements of Southern cattle.

The disease ceased in these States during the civil war and its ravages had apparently been forgotten, when it reappeared during 1866, 1867, and 1868 with the first droves of cattle from Texas. There was little attention given to it at first, as the number of cattle driven in 1866 and 1867 appears not to have been very large. In 1868, however, the markets and other conditions were more encouraging to those who handled this class of stock, and large herds of Texas cattle were sold for feeding in Illinois, Indiana, Ohio, Pennsylvania, New York, and other Northern States.

As the hot weather of summer came on the disease broke out wherever the Southern cattle had been taken. Of 320 head of native stock shipped from one farm to the East for slaughter, 224 died before they reached their destination, and the remainder were said to have been sent to the rendering tanks. At the little town of Tolono, Ill., from 15,000 to 18,000 Texan cattle were landed. The fever commenced its destructive work about July 20, sweeping away nearly every native animal of the bovine race in that section. Nine hundred and twenty-six head of cattle died in that township, which polled but a trifle over 200 votes, and 5,000 head succumbed in the county. Within 2 miles of the Chicago stock yards, according to the report of the medical officer of the city, but 1 cow escaped, 161 animals having perished. In the vicinity of Loda, Ill., it was estimated that not less than 1,800 cattle died. In Warren County, Ind., the losses reached about 1,500 head; in Jasper County, 400 head; in Marion County, 100 head.

These losses are simply examples of what was occurring in many parts of the Northern States. The disease was soon traced to the Southern cattle, and in the absence of specific knowledge concerning its character there was great alarm as to the extent to which it might spread and its effect upon the public health. While the direct loss from the disease was very heavy and brought disaster to many individuals, the contagion was fortunately one which did not spread from the sick native cattle, and was consequently self-limited. It was also a disease that is not communicable to the human species, and hence did not appreciably affect the public health.

Investigations of Texas Fever by the Department of Agriculture and Boards of Health

The excitement and interest aroused by the outbreak of 1868 led to extensive investigations by the Department of Agriculture and by the boards of health of Chicago and New York. These researches were sufficient to establish the symptoms, the post-mortem lesions, and some of the peculiarities in regard to the transmission of the disease. It was shown that there was intense fever, with a temperature ranging from 105° to 110° F., accompanied by great weakness and prostration. The ears and head drooped, the hind legs were advanced under the body, and the fetlocks were partially flexed, constituting, when taken together, a more or less characteristic attitude. The urine, at first tinged with red, became deeper colored, until it had the appearance of undiluted venous blood. On post-mortem examination the liver and spleen were found to be the organs most seriously affected. Both were congested and enlarged. In the liver there was bile-stasis in the ultimate biliary canaliculi, which were found distended and occluded, while the spleen was greatly engorged with blood, and its interior was transformed into a dark semifluid mass. The kidneys, also congested, presented numerous blood extravasations in the pelvic portion.

A study of these symptoms and lesions threw little light upon the nature of the disease. The condition of the spleen suggested that it might be allied to anthrax, but there was an absence of the gelatinous exudations seen in that disease, and, moreover, there was no case of the transmission of the malady to mankind. The course of the disease was also longer than in anthrax fever. A consideration of the phenomena observed relating to the transmission of the contagion only served to deepen the mystery. The cattle from the South which brought the disease were themselves apparently healthy. The sick Northern cattle did not communicate the disease. The contagion in most cases was confined by ordinary farm fences, and, indeed, it appeared to be the ground over which the Southern cattle had traveled rather than the cattle themselves which was dangerous to susceptible animals. And this infected ground retained its power to communicate disease until it was purged by the frosts of approaching winter.

Strange to say, the pastures did not always become dangerous immediately after the Texas cattle had traveled over them. In some cases it was observed that susceptible cattle had fed upon such pastures for a month or more after the Texas cattle had left them, and had then been removed to other fields without sustaining any injury, while other Northern animals of the same lot allowed to remain a few weeks longer suddenly developed the disease in a most violent form. How different from the phenomena of other contagious diseases were these manifestations! and how inexplicable in the light of the medical knowledge of that day! Of what did this contagion consist that it could be propagated by well animals and not by those affected with the disease; that it could remain upon pastures inactive and resist sun and rains for weeks and then suddenly attack in the most virulent form all Northern animals that so much as walked across them, while it respected the animals from the South? Surely they were justified who called this a "romance in pathology," since these phenomena were without precedent and to the most enlightened appeared incredible.

These investigations of 1868 and 1869 established the more apparent characteristics of the disease, though for sixteen years afterwards there were scientific men who tried to prove that no such disease existed. During all this time the cattle driven from Texas and Indian Territory to the Northwestern States and Territories for grazing left a deadly trail behind them, which was destructive to the native cattle that crossed it. The stock yards and stock cars became more and more infected, and cattle purchased in the public markets and taken back to the farms for feeding were in so many instances found to have contracted the disease that purchasers avoided such places as much as possible. Even our export cattle that were given the greatest care en route became infected, and as many as two or three hundred would sicken on a single ship. This brought American cattle into disrepute and threatened to lead to annoying restrictions or even prohibition by foreign governments.

Texas-Fever District Defined and Efforts to Separate Infectious Cattle

The almost intolerable condition described above existed when the writer took up the study of Texas fever in 1879.

The first questions were: How shall this difficult problem be attacked? and, what methods of investigation shall be adopted? One question that appeared possible of solution had reference to the extent and the exact boundaries of the district from which the cattle came that spread the contagion. This could be determined partly by collecting all the information possible as to outbreaks of Texas fever in the Northern States and ascertaining exactly where the cattle came from which caused them, and partly by ascertaining the sections of the Southern States where Northern cattle imported to improve the stock were liable to die with acclimation fever, a disease which the writer had shown to be synonymous with Texas fever.

By pursuing these lines of investigation a great section of the country was found to be already invaded by the infection. This section included half of Virginia, the greater part of North Carolina, all of South Carolina, Georgia, Florida, Alabama, Mississippi, Louisiana, Arkansas, and large portions of Tennessee, Indian Territory, and Texas. The defining of this district made it possible to separate the infectious cattle in the cars and pens, while in transit, from the Northern susceptible cattle, and thus tended to lessen the spread of the contagion. However, there were many difficulties in enforcing regulations for this purpose, as there was no way of distinguishing between these different classes of animals when they reached their destination, and the waybills and car marks could not be implicitly relied upon. It was also desirable to know of what the contagion consisted, how it was disseminated, what disinfectants could be used to destroy it and in what strength these should be present to be active, what was the true period of incubation, what measures could be adopted to reduce the losses among pure-bred cattle taken to the Southern States to improve the stock, and what safeguards could be thrown around cattle from the infected district when taken North for grazing so that they would not destroy the animals in the sections to which they were permitted access.

The people of the South said: ''What right have you to put restrictions upon our cattle when they are going to market? There is no disease among our cattle; and if the Northern cattle sicken and die, the loss should not be charged against our healthy cattle, the presence of which in certain cases was probably a mere coincidence.'' These arguments were difficult to meet, doubly so when the cases went to the courts, and it became necessary to explain the part played by the Southern cattle in originating the disease. Here, as in many other cases, observation of the. outbreaks which developed spontaneously failed to reveal the mysteries, and it was necessary to question and cross-question nature through experiments in order to obtain the information which she withheld from the ordinary observer.

Conjectures as to Manner of Dissemination of Texas Fever

There were numerous conjectures as to the manner in which the contagion was disseminated. Some thought that in driving the Southern cattle such long distances their feet became worn, sore, and ulcerated, and that the discharge from these ulcerated surfaces poisoned the grass and developed contagion. It was believed that this hypothesis was confirmed by the known fact that the Southern cattle apparently lost the power to transmit the disease after they had been upon the Northern ranges sixty to ninety days. Another conjecture was that the contagion resided in the saliva and was distributed over the grass while the infectious animals were grazing. It was also contended by some that the Texas cattle became infectious by drinking from pools of stagnant water, particularly that which contained alkali, and that the infection was distributed with the urine and excrement. Still another conjecture was that the ticks, with which most of the Southern cattle were covered, passed from these to the Northern animals, and the latter, not being accustomed to their bites, became affected with and died from the irritation and fever thus induced. A modified form of this hypothesis was also held, to the effect that the ticks dropped from the Southern cattle laid their eggs in the grass; that myriads of young ticks hatched, covered the herbage, and were taken into the stomachs of the cattle with the food, causing inflammation of the digestive organs, fever, and death.

How were we to decide which, if any, among these divergent views was the correct one? The writer was asked to make a hasty examination of the subject and prepare a preliminary report for publication. This he did, and it is at least instructive as to methods to read his views concerning the part played by the ticks in the transmission of the contagion. The following appeared to be extremely good arguments at the time the report was written (1880):

> *The tick theory.* — One of the most widely spread opinions in regard to the causation of Southern fever is the pathogenic influence of the ticks with which Southern cattle are generally covered and which migrate in large numbers to the bodies of other cattle with which they mix. But the acceptance of this view is simply an evidence of the desire of the human mind to explain the origin of mysterious phenomena. The same principle is exhibited in the popular views regarding the pathogenic nature of *hollow horn, hollow tail, wolf teeth, black teeth, hooks, etc.,* none of which have the least foundation in fact or reason. The tick theory scarcely explains a single one of the many peculiar phenomena of the disease. Ticks are found everywhere, but are simply more numerous at the South. Their attacks are not confined to the latter half of the summer, nor would they be likely to remain on a pasture from spring till August without doing harm and then suddenly cause an outbreak of the disease. Again, the post-mortem examination plainly indicates the cause of the disease to be an agent taken into the circulation and causing the most important changes in the composition of the blood.

Alas, for the limitations of human observation and reasoning when we fail to establish our premises by rigid experimentation! It has since been shown by experiments, outlined by the writer and carried out successfully by his direction, that the ticks do transmit the contagion of Texas fever, and that all of the mysteries connected with this transmission are explained by an accurate knowledge of the biology of the particular tick involved (*Boophilus bovis*), and of the other parasite (*Pyrosoma bigeminum*), which cooperates to produce the pathogenic effect.

Experiments to Determine the Cause and Dissemination of Texas Fever

The first step toward revealing the nature of the disease was evidently to determine if it could be inoculated from animal to animal. If this question were decided in the affirmative, it would be possible, by continuing the inoculation experiments, to determine how widely the virus was distributed through the body, and with what secretions or excretions it was disseminated by the affected animal. It might also be possible to identify a microorganism as the essential cause and to study its biology.

With these purposes in view, the writer, in 1879 and 1880, inoculated six head of cattle and drenched three with liquids that appeared most likely to contain the contagion. Two of these animals had an attack of fever, one being so seriously affected that it became quite weak and emaciated. In 1882 three more animals were inoculated, one of which became sick in ten days and died three days later of acute Texas fever. This was the first demonstration of the inoculability of the disease, and it proved that a mixture of blood and splenic pulp contained the contagion.

In 1886 Dr. Smith, in studying microscopic preparations from the spleen of an animal that had died of the disease, observed peculiar bodies in the red corpuscles which were suggestive of parasitic micro-organisms. In 1888 and 1889 further studies of these bodies were made, which led to the conclusion that they were protozoa. As the most prominent feature of the disease was found to be a breaking down and destruction of the red corpuscles, and as these parasites existed almost exclusively in the red corpuscles of the blood, there was some reason to think they might be the cause of the disease.

At this period, having completed the survey of the permanently infected district, the writer observed that this district corresponded almost exactly with the habitat of the tick (*Boophilus bovis*), which was almost invariably found to infest the cattle that were capable of transmitting the disease. Taking this coincidence, with the strong belief held by many cattle men of experience, that the ticks had something to do with the production of the disease, it was determined to have this aspect of the question fully investigated. Dr. F. L. Kilborne, who was at that time in charge of the Bureau experiment station, was consulted and given explicit instructions to carry through one or more series of experiments with this object in view. The first experiments were made in 1889, and the result was: (1) That Northern cattle pastured in a field with cattle from the infected district which were infested with ticks contracted Texas fever; (2) that Northern cattle pastured in a field with cattle from the infected district that were carefully freed from all ticks by hand picking did not contract Texas fever; (3) that Northern cattle pastured in a field where no cattle from the infected district had been, but over which had been scattered a large number of ticks, contracted Texas fever.

The result of these experiments was a distinct and positive advance in our knowledge of the disease. It was now known (1) that the disease was inoculable; (2) that the blood of diseased animals contained a microscopic protozoan parasite; (3) that ticks picked from Southern cattle and spread upon pastures were a means of communicating the infection.

It was next important to learn in what manner the ticks conveyed the contagion. From a medical point of view the most plausible theory was that the biting parts of the ticks became soiled with the blood of the Southern cattle, and that these contaminated ticks, migrating to susceptible cattle, carried the virus and inserted it when they began sucking blood from the latter. A study of the life history of the tick showed, however, that this theory was not consistent with the facts. The ticks do not leave one animal and go to another. When they are once upon an animal they remain there until they become mature, and then they drop off, lay their eggs on the surface of the ground, and die. There is no opportunity for this parasite to carry blood directly from the Southern to the Northern animal and inoculate it.

Another hypothesis was that with the blood sucked from Southern cattle the tick took into its body the virus of the disease, and that when the mother tick died and became disintegrated upon the pastures the contagion was liberated and the grounds infected. This supposition was entirely demolished by experiments, which proved that the disease was caused by young ticks hatched from the eggs of the mature ticks which developed upon the Southern cattle, that is, the contagion is in some manner transmitted from the adult tick through its egg to its progeny, and this progeny has the power of inserting the contagion into the circulation of the cattle upon which it happens to fasten itself.

These facts threw much light upon the propagation of the malady, but they were not sufficient to establish a scientific theory explaining the transmission. Indeed, it was yet to be proved that the Southern cattle carried the protozoa in their blood. Microscopic examination was not sufficient to decide the question. A few minute points were observed in the red corpuscles of Southern cattle, but these points were much smaller and far less numerous than the protozoa in sick Northern cattle. The Southern cattle, besides, were in good health, and it seemed improbable that they harbored so deadly a parasite.

There was but one way to decide as to whether Southern cattle carried this contagion in their blood, and that was to inoculate susceptible Northern cattle with the blood of Southern cattle. This experiment was made, and it demonstrated that a comparatively small quantity of blood from a Southern cow, injected under the skin or into the veins of Northern cattle, produced an acute attack of Texas fever. In Northern cattle infected in this manner the protozoa appeared in the blood corpuscles with the same characteristics as when the infection occurred through the medium of ticks. There could no longer be any doubt that the blood of cattle from the infected district contained the contagion of Texas fever.

It was now important to decide how long Southern cattle carried this contagion in their blood after leaving the infected district. Again, it was necessary to resort to inoculation, as the microscope was powerless to decide. The first experiments had been made with the blood of cattle immediately after they had been brought from the South. In the next experiment blood was used from an animal that had been away from the infected district seventy-four days. This also produced disease. In succeeding years experiments were made by inoculating with the blood of cattle that had been under observation, with no chance for reinfection, for one year, two years, three years, four years, five years, six years, and seven years, and in every case the disease was produced. It was concluded, therefore, that this contagion once introduced into the blood of cattle remained there in an active condition throughout the animal's life.

The Principal Features of Texas Fever

We were now in a position to understand and explain the principal features of this disease, that is, it was plain that cattle in the infected district carried in their blood the contagion of Texas fever; that this contagion was in reality a protozoan organism called the *Pyrosoma bigeminum*, analogous to the parasite of human malaria; that this parasite was transferred to susceptible cattle outside of the infected district by the Southern cattle tick *Boophilus bovis;* that Southern cattle, although carrying the contagion, were harmless unless infested by this particular tick; that the Southern cattle carried this contagion in their blood for years after leaving the infected district, and would again be dangerous to other cattle if by any chance they were reinfested with the proper species of ticks. A study of the biology of the tick showed that the time required for the eggs to hatch depends upon the atmospheric temperature, and that all the mysteries of the propagation and incubation of the disease depended upon the hatching of these eggs.

The Progress Made in the Control of Texas Fever

The above is a remarkable chapter in the progress of medical science, and has already led to extensive studies of the part played by insects in the propagation of human diseases, and particularly the malarial fevers. That it has opened up a new field of medical research is unquestionable. What has it accomplished toward the control and eradication of Texas fever? In the first place, it has given us a ready method of identifying infectious cattle found in the channels of commerce. Previous to these investigations it was often impossible to tell whether a given carload of cattle unloaded at any stock yards was from the infected or noninfected district. The point from which it was billed was no criterion, since it was common to rebill cars, often for the express purpose of deceiving the inspectors. These great centers of cattle traffic were, consequently, continually infected. To-day, if cattle are infested with the *Boophilus bovis* ticks, they are sent without question to the quarantine yards.

Another line in which progress has been made is in lessening the area of the infected district. Whole counties have been placed above the cattle quarantine line, because the ticks have been destroyed in those counties and the danger of contagion removed. In many other counties the citizens have taken up the task of tick killing and are making rapid progress in freeing their districts from this pest. The infected district, instead of advancing and enlarging in area, as before these investigations, is now diminishing. This work is of immense advantage to the people of the districts involved.

Great success has also been achieved in immunizing cattle taken to the infected district for improving the stock. In the past the greater part of the cattle taken to the infected district died of Texas fever. These losses were 80, 90, and even 95 per cent of the animals introduced. Still, it was so important to grade up the cattle in the vast herds of the South and Southwest that the people of those sections persisted and accomplished much even under such discouraging circumstances. In pursuing the inoculation experiments it was learned that young animals, particularly calves, were much less severely affected than old ones, even with the same dose of virulent blood; also, that as cold weather approached a milder form of disease was produced in the same class of animals. Putting these two facts together, it was decided to immunize some young cattle and test their resistance in the infected district. This was successfully accomplished, and proved that young stock inoculated in the late fall or early winter with virulent blood contracted a mild form of disease, from which the experimental animals recovered, and that these animals sent to the infected district the following spring were but slightly affected with the disease, although untreated animals sent with them either died or were very severely affected and barely survived.

This method of immunizing has now been adopted in practice and is proving very satisfactory. Instead of a loss of 90 per cent among breeding stock taken South, it has been shown that more than 90 per cent can be saved. This means rapid improvement of Southern herds and a vast increase in the value of the animals produced.

There is one other problem under experimentation, which, if it can be solved, will remove the last terrors of Texas fever. That problem is the rapid and inexpensive destruction of the ticks upon cattle from the infected district. Such cattle are now dangerous because of these ticks. They are not allowed to go North, except for slaughter, during ten months of the year. They are always regarded with suspicion, quarantined, and sold as quarantine cattle at a reduced price. This is a constant hardship to the people of a great section of the country; but destroy all the ticks and the cattle are harmless and can go anywhere, for any purpose, at any season of the year. The plan of destroying the ticks is to drive the cattle through a vat containing some liquid that will be fatal to the ticks without injuring the cattle. While it has proved a difficult task to find a liquid that will answer these conditions, there are some which are so nearly satisfactory as to inspire hopes that success in this line will in the near future be achieved.

Confining our argument to the facts which have already been demonstrated, Have we not abundant justification for the experimental method? With a disease so obscure and complex, depending upon two different parasites for its dissemination, one of these so small as to tax the highest powers of the microscope, it was impossible for observation, unaided by experimentation, to solve the mysteries and elucidate it. But the experimental method was invoked, and, as in many other fields of biology, has brought order out of chaos, giving an intelligent comprehension and control of phenomena, where before were only ignorance and helplessness.

Controlling Injurious Insects, 1899

From L. O. Howard, "Progress in Economic Entomology in the United States" U. S. Department of Agriculture, *Yearbook*, 1899, pp. 135, 153–55.

Introduction

At the beginning of the present century the United States, with its population of only 5,000,000, with its restricted geographical area, with its small fields and its comparatively slight diversity of crops, and with its infrequent communication and limited commercial relations with other countries, suffered comparatively little from the attacks of insects on its crops. There are old last-century records of the local destruction of the grain crops by the army worm, and as early as 1793 the cotton caterpillar did a great deal of damage to the cotton crop of Georgia and South Carolina. Similar outbreaks occurred in 1800 and 1804, while the Hessian fly, as its name suggests, made its destructive appearance soon after the close of the war of the Revolution.

With the rapid growth of the new Republic, both in geographic area and in population, and with its marvelous agricultural development, many native plant-eating insects, finding in cultivated crops an almost unlimited abundance of food greatly to their taste, multiplied rapidly and became important factors in crop production. As commercial relations with Europe and other countries increased and as the introduction of steam made international journeys more and more rapid, new injurious insects were introduced from abroad, many of them becoming readily established and assuming an importance as crop enemies surpassing that of native species. Many of them, in fact, as has frequently been pointed out, became, for reasons which need not be discussed here and which are not well understood, more prolific and injurious than in their native homes. For a long time these imported species, beginning their work on the Atlantic seaboard, traveled westward by natural spread, entering new regions after a few years, following in the track of the pioneers. . . .

It is true that in the early days of the march of the Colorado potato beetle toward the East a number of sprinklers and dusters were invented for the purpose of applying Paris green to potato plants; and two or three of these, like "Gray's improved sprinkler," invented by Frank M. Gray, of Illinois, in 1874, and "Peck's spray machine," invented by W. P. Peck, of Pennsylvania, about the same time, were prophetic of the improved knapsack sprinklers which have come into such great use, especially for diseases of the grape in France, and also to a lesser degree in this country. But it was not until the late W. S. Barnard, working under the direction of Riley, invented the admirable eddy chamber, or "cyclone system" of nozzles, following it with the construction of a number of ingenious, but since superseded, machines for the field distribution of the poison that what may be termed the "insecticide-machinery epoch" began. This work was soon after taken up in France, where it has been carried to a high degree of excellence by such firms as V. Vermorel and others, Vermorel inventing a modification of the cyclone nozzle, known there as the Vermorel modification of the Riley nozzle and in this country as the Vermorel nozzle. It was not, however, until the use of arsenical sprays in orchards, against the codling moth in particular, and also against the plum curculio and the cankerworm, became general that the full tide of perfection of insecticide machinery began. As was quite to be expected, so soon as there was a strong demand for such improved machinery intelligent manufacturers took hold of the problem and began to place machines of great excellence on the market. The demand increasing, improvement became more and more abundant, and there are at the present day many firms in the United States putting out distributing machines of a high degree of merit and of almost unending variety, from the hand bucket pump for garden use to the motor engine pumps and machinery for orchard use on a large scale. Many nozzles have been invented since Barnard produced his first rough tin model of the eddy chamber, or "cyclone," as he termed it, but the modifications of his system remain to-day the most generally used and the most efficient and economical of any that have been produced.

Work of an International Character

In 1889 was brought about by American entomologists the first example of what may be termed beneficial international work in economic entomology. The introduction of *Novius (Vedalia) cardinalis* from Australia into California, where it utterly destroyed the white or fluted scale, an insect which had damaged the citrus crops of California to the extent of hundreds of thousands of dollars, and which threatened the extinction of the citrus industry of the Pacific slope, is an event which is too well known to need description here. It was also an event which has been termed "epoch-making," and which would deserve the title could it only be often repeated. It opened up, however, in a practical way a line of work which had often been suggested by American writers on entomology (the first of them, by the way, it must be stated, being a Canadian, Rev. C. J. S. Bethune).

The first and successful importations of this beneficial ladybird were made by Albert Koebele, a salaried agent of the Division of Entomology, working under the direction of the late Dr. Riley, but whose traveling expenses were defrayed from the fund appropriated by Congress for the representation of the United States at the Melbourne Exposition. A later trip to Australian regions was undertaken by Mr. Koebele while still on the pay rolls of the Division of Entomology, but his expenses were paid from the appropriation granted by California to its State board of horticulture. The results of this second trip, although not as conclusive as those of his first trip, still demonstrated in marked degree the advantage of this class of international work, namely, the introduction of beneficial insects from one country to another. After Koebele's second trip he resigned his position, and was soon after employed by the newly established Hawaiian Republic for the purpose of continuing the same class of work for that country. From reliable accounts it seems certain that his work along the same line has resulted in great benefit to the agricultural interests of Hawaii, which, since its annexation to this country, has once more made Koebele's work a feature of the economic entomology of the United States.

The United States has been able to assist other Governments in their work against injurious insects. Sendings of the same ladybird (*Novius cardinalis*) to South Africa, to Egypt, and later to Portugal, have brought about results similar to those which proved the salvation of the citrus industry of California, while other less important exportations of beneficial insects promise good results. Through the office which the writer represents there have been several introductions of beneficial insects from foreign countries. Collections of museum specimens of injurious insects of foreign countries have also been made and brought to this country in the course of a study of the greatly increasing danger which enlarging commercial relations and rapidity of ocean traffic are constantly bringing about by the introduction of new insect pests.

A striking exemplification of the benefits to be derived from the prosecution of this international work is actually developing in California in the probable establishment in that State, through the efforts of this Department, of *Blastophaga grossorum*, an insect which in Mediterranean countries fertilizes the Smyrna fig, and which it is confidently expected will result in the building up of a fig industry in California, the output of which will rank favorably with, if it does not exceed, that of the countries which have made the Smyrna fig the standard fig of commerce. At the time of the present writing (December, 1899) four generations of the fertilizing insect have been reared under natural conditions at Fresno, Cal., and there is every probability that it will be carried through the winter successfully. The insect hibernates in so-called gall-figs upon the wild fig tree. Such figs heretofore at Fresno have fallen with the first heavy frost. The present winter, however, a certain number of trees have been protected from the action of the frost by a canvas covering, and a commercial product of American-grown Smyrna figs during the ummer of 1900 is confidently expected.

Agricultural Education, 1899

From A.C. True, "Agricultural Education in the United States," U. S. Department of Agriculture, *Yearbook*, 1899, pp. 157, 181–90.

The activity in agricultural education during the present century will seem all the more impressive if it is remembered that, after the cessation of the efforts of Greek and Roman writers to encourage agriculture by describing the processes of the art, centuries elapsed before the educated men in Europe took interest enough in agriculture to write books about it. War was the chief occupation of gentlemen, and the arts of peace were left to the ignorant and the lowly. But these centuries nevertheless marked the steady progress of civilization, and "soon after the beginning of the sixteenth century agriculture partook of the general improvement which followed the invention of the art of printing, the revival of literature, and the more settled authority of government, and, instead of the occasional notices of historians, we can now refer to regular treatises, written by agricultural instruction. The publications of the stations and of the Department in large measure supply the materials for these books, and they are written from an American standpoint. There is already a healthful competition in the production of books best adapted to special purposes of agricultural education, and thus the way is being prepared for the more general and satisfactory diffusion of such education in the twentieth century.

Development of General Agencies for the Education of Farmers

The second half of the nineteenth century has witnessed a great awakening of the farmers of this country to their educational needs and opportunities. This has led to the broadening of the work and influence of general agencies for their education. The State and local societies have been supplemented by great national organizations, such as the Farmers' Alliance and the Patrons of Husbandry (granges), which, besides doing a great deal for the promotion of their general welfare, have done much to quicken the desire of multitudes of farmers for definite education in matters relating to their art. That portion of the newspaper press which is wholly or partially agricultural has been more active and far-reaching than ever before in its efforts to disseminate useful information among the rural masses. State departments and other agencies for aiding the farmer to acquire knowledge along agricultural lines have been greatly strengthened. The limits of this article will forbid anything more than the mere mention of the origin and usefulness of these general agencies for agricultural education. In considering in any broad way the institutions for the farmers' education which now exist in this country, great credit must be given to those organizations which, though established for more general purposes, have exerted their influence to arouse the farmer to see the need of progress and enlightenment, and which have labored earnestly for the establishment and maintenance of institutions definitely organized for technical education in agriculture. Without the movement for the farmers' uplifting, begun and fostered by those general agencies, the schools and colleges of agriculture could not have reached their present promising condition.

The American System for Agricultural Education in the Year 1900

Without taking into account the general educational agencies just referred to, the American system for agricultural education as it exists at the close of the nineteenth century comprises a number of important branches whose functions may be more or less clearly differentiated.

Departments of Original Research and Graduate Study in Agriculture

At the head of this system stand the Department of Agriculture and the agricultural experiment stations now in operation in all the States and Territories chiefly as departments of the land-grant colleges. These constitute very largely the university, or graduate branch of agricultural education in this country, having for their chief functions the discovery and dissemination of new truths regarding the theory and practice of agriculture. Organized primarily with reference to research, both the Department and the stations to a considerable extent directly promote agricultural education, in the technical sense, by giving instruction to students. This is done by opening their laboratories to assistants who participate in research work while continuing their studies, or by imparting new inspiration and knowledge to students who become acquainted with the research work by indirect contact through residence at the institutions where it is being conducted. From time to time officers of the agricultural colleges and experiment stations come to work in the Department of Agriculture for a period, to carry on special investigations or to enlarge their knowledge of scientific facts and principles in special lines. In accordance with an arrangement recently made, a limited number of graduates of the land-grant colleges are admitted to the Department for advanced study and research. At the universities and colleges having courses in agriculture there are now a considerable number of persons pursuing graduate courses in agricultural subjects. This has for the most part been made possible by the establishment of the experiment stations as research departments of these institutions and the consequent employment of experts in different lines of agricultural science competent to give graduate instruction in their several specialties.

College Courses in Agriculture

Under the provisions of the acts of Congress of July 2, 1862, and August 30, 1890 (Morrill acts), sixty-four colleges are in operation in the several States and Territories. Of these, about sixty institutions maintain courses in agriculture. In fourteen States separate institutions are maintained for white and colored students. These institutions are brought together to constitute a national system of higher education in the sciences and industries through the Association of American Agricultural Colleges and Experiment Stations, the Office of Experiment Stations of the Department of Agriculture, and the Bureau of Education of the Department of the Interior. The colleges of agriculture may be divided into three classes, according to the general differences in their organization: (1) Colleges having only courses in agriculture; (2) colleges having courses in agriculture along with those in a variety of subjects, including especially mechanic arts; and, (3) colleges (or schools or departments) of agriculture forming a part of universities. The only institution in this country which is simply an agricultural college is the Massachusetts Agricultural College.

Agricultural and mechanical colleges have been organized in Alabama, Colorado, Connecticut, Delaware, Florida, Iowa, Kansas, Kentucky, Maryland, Michigan, Mississippi, Montana, New Hampshire, New Jersey, New Mexico, North Carolina, North Dakota, Oklahoma, Oregon, Pennsylvania, Rhode Island, South Carolina, South Dakota, Texas, Utah, Virginia, and Washington. Separate institutions of this class for colored students are maintained under the Morrill Act of 1890 in Alabama, Delaware, Florida, Mississippi, North Carolina, South Carolina, and Virginia. The instruction in these institutions has, however, very wisely been confined for the most part to courses below the college grade. A similar institution, maintained by private funds, is the well-known Tuskegee Industrial Institute, in Alabama.

Colleges of agriculture (or equivalent schools or departments) in universities are maintained with the aid of national funds in Arizona, Arkansas, California, Georgia, Idaho, Illinois, Indiana, Louisiana, Maine, Minnesota, Missouri, Nebraska, Nevada, New York, Ohio, Tennessee, Vermont, West Virginia, Wisconsin, and Wyoming. In Massachusetts, Harvard University has a school of agriculture known as Bussey Institution.

The college course in agriculture in most of these institutions extends through four years and leads to a bachelor's degree. The course varies considerably in different institutions as regards the requirements, both for admission and for graduation. In some cases students are admitted directly from the common schools, while in others the entrance requirements are on a level with those for admission to other college courses in high-grade colleges. The course at the Massachusetts Agricultural College may be taken as a type of a relatively high-grade college course in agriculture as given in American colleges. Candidates for admission must be at least 16 years old, and are required to pass examinations in English grammar, geography, United States history, physiology, physical geography, arithmetic, the metric system, algebra (through quadratics), geometry (two books), and civil government. The student is required to follow a definitely prescribed curriculum during three years, and in the fourth and last year of the course he is allowed wide latitude of choice among numerous specialties, English and military science being the only required studies. In freshman year the following subjects are included in the course: Agriculture, botany, chemistry, algebra, geometry, bookkeeping, English, French, military tactics, and mechanical drawing; in sophomore year, agriculture, horticulture, botany, chemistry, anatomy and physiology, trigonometry, surveying, English, and mechanical drawing; in junior year, agriculture, horticulture, chemistry, zoology, entomology, physics, English (including rhetoric and literature); in senior year, together with the required English and military science, at least three elective studies must be taken, which may be selected from the following: Agriculture, botany, chemistry, entomology, veterinary science, civil engineering, analytical geometry, calculus, English, German, Latin, political economy, history, and farm law.

In these colleges, as a rule, ample provision is made for the teaching of the sciences related to agriculture. Horticulture, vegetable pathology, economic entomology, and veterinary science are commonly taught along with agriculture, but by separate instructors. An outline course in forestry is also often given. The subject of agriculture is not infrequently divided among two or more instructors. Matters relating to soils, fertilizers, and the composition of plants, dairy products, etc., are often taught under the head of agricultural chemistry. Agricultural physics, especially as relating to soils, has been recently made a separate department of instruction in a number of colleges. The theory and practice of dairying, animal husbandry, and plant production have, in some cases, each been assigned to different instructors. Here and there some branch of animal husbandry (as sheep raising) has been deemed sufficiently important to require a special teacher. In general, differentiation of subjects hitherto grouped together under the general term ''agriculture'' is more and more followed by the employment of specialists to teach in a limited field. Much greater attention is being given than formerly to the improvement of methods of teaching agricultural subjects. This is evidenced by the employment of more thoroughly trained teachers, by individual and associated efforts to define and arrange the topics of instruction in accordance with pedagogical principles, by the general adoption of the laboratory system as applied to the field, the plant house, and the barn, as well as to the buildings constructed with special reference to the peculiar needs of instruction in agricultural subjects.

The collection and devising of apparatus and illustrative material are being pushed with much enthusiasm and success. Wherever means will permit, and in an increasing number of institutions, the housing and equipment of the agricultural department will compare favorably with that of other departments. Along with the improvement of the college courses in agriculture has come the realization of the true function of these courses. It is now well understood that they are for the training of the leaders in agricultural progress and not for the general education of the agricultural masses. For this purpose they are to be made as thorough and complete internally and externally as the manifold needs of American agriculture for well-trained and intelligent leadership may require. Their success is to be judged by the same standard that is applied to other college courses, and the number of students is not of so much importance as their quality. For the general education of the agricultural people, young and old, other agencies than the four years' college course are to be employed, which will require for their management a large share of the graduates of the agricultural colleges.

Owing to the complicated organization of many of the institutions having courses in agriculture and the fact that the students in agricultural courses in many subjects are in classes with students in other courses, and that much of the equipment is used in common by the students in all the courses, it is impracticable to show by statistics, with exactness, the means and facilities for strictly agricultural education. The general statistics of the land-grant institutions may, however, serve to show with how great an enterprise, devoted chiefly to higher education along scientific and industrial lines, agriculture has been joined in permanent alliance, and to indicate in some measure how extensive are the educational facilities at the command of the youth of the country who have sufficient intelligence, courage, and perseverance to follow out long and thorough courses of study in agriculture.

The aggregate value of the permanent funds and equipment of the land-grant colleges and universities in 1898 is estimated to be as follows: Land-grant fund of 1862, $10,170,549.99; other land-grant funds, $1,204,234.44; other permanent funds, $11,816,258.16; land grant of 1862 still unsold, $3,838,219.48; farms and grounds owned by the institutions, $6,046,500.16; buildings, $15,185,476.95; apparatus, $1,916,227.85; machinery, $1,383,137.14; libraries, $1,634,190.25; miscellaneous equipment, $1,765,243.19 — total, $53,632,852.25. The income of these institutions in 1898, exclusive of funds from the United States for agricultural experiment stations ($720,000), was as follows: Interest on land grant of 1862, $645,546.28; interest on other funds, $578,067.38; United States appropriation under act of 1890, $1,108,610.38; State appropriation (annual or regular), $1,827,924.51; State appropriation (occasional), $533,794.98; tuition fees, $480,847.32; incidental fees, $146,458.72; miscellaneous, $679,130.93 — total, $6,008,379.20. The value of the additions to the permanent endowment and equipment of these institutions in 1898 is estimated as follows: Permanent endowment, $1,424,277.64; buildings, $851,481.75; library, $105,661.11; apparatus, $132,111.90; machinery, $123,477.63; miscellaneous, $167,336.53 — total, $2,796,350.97. The number of persons in the faculties of the colleges of agriculture and mechanic arts were as follows: For preparatory classes, 254; for collegiate and special classes, 1,564 — total, 1,722. In the other departments the faculties aggregated 889, making a grand total of 2,611 persons in the faculties of the land-grant institutions. The students in 1898 were as follows: (1) By classes: Preparatory, 6,593; freshmen, 6,016; sophomores, 4,202; juniors, 3,216; seniors, 2,506; special, 4,526; post graduate, 878 — total, 31,658. (2) By courses: Agriculture, 4,181; mechanical engineering, 2,797; civil engineering, 1,504; electrical engineering, 1,698; mining engineering, 554; architecture, 411; household economy, 1,298; veterinary science, 449; military tactics, 8,952. The graduates in 1898 were 2,328, and since the organization of these institutions 34,168. The average age of graduates in 1898 was 22.1 years. The total number of volumes in the libraries was 1,221,226.

Short and Special Courses in Agriculture

In many of the colleges of agriculture provision has been made for more elementary and practical education in agriculture by establishing short courses. These may continue through two college years or be limited to a few weeks, chiefly in the winter months. Recently, successful short courses have been given at a few colleges in the summer, when the regular college courses were suspended. The short courses may either cover agriculture in general or be confined to some special line, as dairying. Now that the short courses are quite clearly differentiated from the regular college courses in agriculture the objections formerly made to them are no longer strongly urged, and in popularity and success they seemed to have entered on a prosperous career. The short courses offered by the University of Wisconsin may serve to illustrate the nature of this feature of the American system for agricultural education. "The short course in agriculture," it is stated, "is designed to meet the wants of young farmers who desire practical, helpful instruction in agriculture before taking up their chosen vocation. This course covers two terms of twelve weeks each, beginning the first of January each year." It includes lectures on feeds and feeding, breeds of live stock, agricultural chemistry, agricultural physics and meteorology, plant life, veterinary science, dairying, farm bookkeeping, horticulture, agricultural economics, and bacteriology. Laboratory practice is given in dairying, physics, plant life, stock judging, and horticulture, and practical work in carpentry and blacksmithing. The dairy course occupies one term, and includes theoretical and practical instruction in the science and practice of dairying and dairy farming. It is definitely planned to meet the needs of persons intending "to operate creameries and cheese factories," and has been very successful in training men competent for work of this kind. The students engage in milk testing, operate separators and butter extractors, and attend to the ripening of the cream, churning and packing butter, and all the operations of a creamery and cheese factory.

This dairy school has already sent out 800 trained butter and cheese makers and has also taught nearly 2,000 young men butter making on the farm, as distinct from the creamery. The short course in agriculture at this institution was reported in 1899 to have had 190 students in attendance, and its practical outcome is thus stated by the dean: "We have found places on farms this year for more than fifty young men, who will secure from $2 to $10 more per month because of their training with us."

Another interesting special school is that for training sugar experts, which has been in successful operation for a number of years at Audubon Park, New Orleans, in connection with the State university, and has received financial assistance from the Sugar Planters' Association.

University Extension in Agriculture

The term "university extension" has been used in recent years to denominate in a general way the effort of our colleges to promote the diffusion of knowledge outside of their own halls. Though not always spoken of under this head, no university extension movement in this country has actually been so widespread as that on behalf of agriculture. Broadly speaking, this would properly include the dissemination of agricultural information through the publications of the experiment stations and this Department. The stations annually issue over 400 publications, which are distributed to mailing lists aggregating half a million addresses, and this Department supplements these with some 600 others, of which about 7,000,000 copies are distributed. But confining ourselves to what would more usually be considered university extension work, we find the colleges of agriculture largely engaged in conducting farmers' institutes and home-reading courses and helping to introduce nature study into the common schools.

Importance of Farmers' Institutes as Factors in Education

The farmers' institutes are sometimes under the direct management of the agricultural colleges and sometimes are controlled by independent State officers, but in either case the colleges do much of the actual teaching in them and in various ways contribute largely to their success. These institutes are regularly held in over forty States. It is estimated that about 2,000 institutes were held in the United States last year, which were attended by half a million farmers. The importance of the institutes as factors in the general education of farmers in some of the States where they have been most successful may be indicated by the following brief statistics:

In Wisconsin there are now annually held 120 institutes, with an average attendance of over 50,000 persons. Sixty thousand copies of their annual institute bulletin, in which the best addresses are grouped together, making a book of over 300 pages, are annually distributed. A copy of this book is put into every school library in the State. For this work the State appropriates $12,000 annually.

In Massachusetts 125 institutes are held, with an attendance of about 11,000 farmers.

In West Virginia over 60 institutes are held, with a total attendance of 14,000.

In Minnesota 50 farmers' institutes are held of two or three days each, with an attendance of from 300 to 1,000, and 25,000 copies of their annual report are distributed.

In Indiana an attendance is reported of over 25,000, with an average of 272 persons in about 100 institutes.

In Kansas 135 institutes are held, with a total attendance of 20,000.

In Michigan institutes are held in nearly every county, and the total attendance is reported to reach 120,000.

In Nebraska 60 institutes are held, with a total attendance of over 26,000.

In Pennsylvania some 300 institutes are held, with a total attendance of over 50,000.

In Ohio 250 institutes in 88 counties are held, with an aggregate attendance of about 90,000.

In New York over 300 institutes are held in a single year.

In California about 80 institutes are annually held, with a total attendance of 16,000.

Home-Reading Courses in Agriculture

The agricultural colleges in a number of States, notably in Pennsylvania and New York, are carrying on courses of home readings in agricultural subjects. These at present are developing into what may very properly be called correspondence courses. Not only are lists of books furnished by the college, but series of lessons with questions are sent out, and much correspondence is had with the persons following the courses. College officers also visit classes or clubs of farmers who are pursuing these courses to give them advice and instruction along the lines in which they are reading. Thousands of farmers are already enrolled in these courses, and only lack of funds prevents their rapid extension.

Secondary Courses in Agriculture

Thus far comparatively little has been done in the United States toward the establishment of schools of agriculture of secondary or high-school grade. As previously stated, a successful school of this grade is maintained at the University of Minnesota, and a similar one has been begun at the University of Nebraska. The agricultural courses maintained in a number of the institutions for colored students in the South are of this grade. In Alabama provision has also been made for secondary schools of agriculture for white students in the nine Congressional districts. There are a few private schools in which agricultural subjects are taught.

There is some agitation in favor of the introduction of agriculture in the public high schools, but no definite movement in this direction has as yet been attempted. Meanwhile, however, books of reference and text-books on agricultural subjects suited to this grade of schools are being published in increasing number, and the way is thus being prepared for more rapid development of secondary courses of instruction in the schools in the near future.

Agriculture in the Common Schools

While there has been much agitation at different times during the present century in favor of introducing agriculture into the common schools, thus far no widespread efforts to do so have been made. Under present conditions, it appears to most persons who have made a careful study of the subject that very little can successfully be done in this direction until much preliminary work has been bestowed on the formulation of courses in nature study suited to the needs of the rural schools, on the training of teachers in this line, and on the general introduction of nature teaching in the schools. The success which is attending the movement on behalf of nature study in New York, Indiana, Pennsylvania, and elsewhere is so pronounced that there is good reason to hope that it will ere long secure the general recognition of the value of nature study for young children and its widespread introduction into the common schools. Important features of this movement are the strong indorsement which it is receiving from school officers and teachers, and the fact that nature study has already become quite generally a part of the curriculum in the graded schools of the cities. As this movement in the interest of the rural schools is being led by the agricultural colleges, agriculture seems likely to have its claim fully recognized in the formulation of nature-study courses. Already many of the lessons used in such courses are on subjects directly related to agriculture. Wisely planned and effectively taught, courses on natural objects and phenomena in the common schools will not only train the powers of observation of the children, but will interest them in the subjects included in the theory and practice of agriculture, and thus pave the way for the successful introduction of this complex subject in courses of higher grade.

Present Conditions and Prospects for the Future

In general, the century now closing has witnessed an intellectual awakening of the farmers of this country, the volume and depth of which have been increasing with greatly accelerated speed in the past few years. We now have a considerable body of well-trained investigators, teachers, and other promoters of agricultural progress who are working earnestly and with greater success each year to raise the general intelligence of farmers and give them accurate and definite information for the improvement of their art; we have the widespread dissemination of knowledge on agricultural subjects through the press and through public agencies liberally endowed by the States and the nation; we have strong local, State, and national organizations which are laboring diligently for the promotion of the general and technical education of the farmers. Strong institutions for original research and higher education in agriculture have already been built up, and hopeful beginnings have been made in the formulation and introduction of more elementary courses of instruction in agriculture in schools of various grades and among the farmers generally. We shall therefore enter the twentieth century with a reasonable expectation that the education of our farmers in agricultural lines will go on increasing in efficiency and extent, and ere long become general and satisfactory.

Controlling Plant Diseases, 1899

From B. T. Galloway, "Progress in the Treatment of Plant Diseases in the United States" U. S. Department of Agriculture, *Yearbook*, 1899, pp. 191–97.

Introduction

In looking back over the work of the past century in the treatment of plant diseases, two facts immediately enlist attention: (1) That the last fifteen years have witnessed by far the greatest advances made, and (2) that in every step taken there has been shown the characteristic American spirit of striving to get direct practical results as quickly as possible. For the first three-quarters of the century there was practically no systematic attempt to obtain light on the diseases of crops. Of course, diseases have been recognized as long as plants have been grown, but in all these earlier years it was the custom to regard them more in the nature of obstacles, against which it was practically useless to contend, than as subjects for study and thought.

Present Classification of Plant Diseases

A few words at this point in regard to present methods of classifying plant diseases will perhaps make clearer the discussion to follow. Briefly stated, diseases may be produced in three ways: (1) By living organisms acting as parasites; (2) by unfavorable environment in which the plant grows; and, (3) by combinations involving both organisms and environment. No line can be drawn between these groups, for their relations and interrelations are so intimate that sharp separation at any point is out of the question. The living organisms, such as fungi, bacteria, etc., produce diseases by attacking the higher plants and destroying them in order to build up their own structures. On the other hand, when the surroundings, such as unfavorable soil, too much or too little food, improper cultivation, excess of water, insufficient aeration of the soil, or other similar conditions occur, disease may follow without the action of such organisms as fungi or bacteria.

It might, however, be held that the plant ought not to be subject to disease produced by organisms, for if it were surrounded by conditions exactly suited to its growth and was at all times able to adapt itself to these conditions, growth would in a measure be perfect, consequently no disease could be produced by outside agencies. But the plant is always in a state of unstable equilibrium, and it is this fact that makes it subject to the attacks of organisms and likely to be injured when any marked change of environment occurs. While this appears to be an element of weakness, it nevertheless affords vast opportunities, and is really the keynote to successful plant culture, as the writer will endeavor to show farther on.

Early Theories on Plant Diseases

It is not surprising that the man who grows plants looks to the weather as the source of all that is good or bad. In his own way he learns by experience that the weather has an important relation to the success or failure of his work, and he soon begins to connect certain weather conditions with what he sees going on about him. In all the early literature, therefore, references are found to the effects of "unfavorable weather," "meteorological disturbances," etc.

Other facts gained by long experience were also brought to bear on peculiar phenomena connected with plant diseases and their treatment. Thus, it was known at the beginning of the century and earlier that the injury from wheat rust was influenced by the presence of the common barberry plant. So strong was this conviction that laws were passed prohibiting the growing of barberry for ornament or for hedges. The opinion prevailed that the barberry caused rust, but it was not until many years later that its connection with rust was shown scientifically by the investigations of De Bary in Germany. It was also believed by many of the older agriculturists that smut was the direct result of a rupture of the cells of the plant itself, and that the rust of wheat was often produced by similar causes. Not only was this the general belief among many agriculturists, but it was credited by a number of workers abroad who made special studies of the subject.

About the year 1845, largely through the efforts of one or two investigators abroad, light began to dawn upon the nature of a number of the common diseases of plants, and these efforts were destined to have a marked influence on all future knowledge bearing on this subject. Although there was as yet no systematic attempt in this country to make special investigations, the work done abroad was gradually made known here, and through the agricultural press and other sources, became more or less familiar to farmers and others interested.

The great prevalence of the potato-rot fungus about this time (1845) gave a decided impetus to work on plant diseases. The rot swept over the earth, and many attempts were made to discover its cause and to provide a remedy. The relation of the parasite to the disease was worked out in Germany, and this knowledge soon became known to the farmers of this country. The same was true of wheat rust, corn smut, etc., so that even in these early days there was some knowledge of treating diseases by the direct use of remedies or preventives. This is particularly true of the smuts, which were among the first diseases to be controlled by the use of substances designed to destroy the reproductive bodies of the fungi themselves. Aside from this, the principal efforts in the way of treatment were in the direction of giving the plants the best surroundings possible and treating wounds by the use of simple paints, wax, etc.

Experience had taught that blight of the pear and apple must be cut out, although believed to be due entirely to "atmospheric influences." This emphasizes the important fact that has already been referred to, that is, that although the growers of plants did not, as a rule, concern themselves much with the causes of diseases, their experience had taught them certain methods of treatment which in some cases are even to-day accepted as the best that can be followed.

The Beginning of Modern Research

From 1845 until 1861 there was considerable advance in knowledge concerning plant diseases, particularly as regards their causes, or in other words, the relation to them of certain parasitic organisms. This knowledge came about largely through the investigations of a few men in Europe. From 1861 to 1873 the accounts of investigators abroad were published from time to time in our horticultural and agricultural reports and in agricultural and other journals. There was an increasing interest in the subject, however, and it is not surprising that in 1873 and 1874 there was a marked tendency to advance in knowledge along these lines.

Prof. T. J. Burrill, of the University of Illinois, was one of the pioneers in this field. Early in 1874 he commenced publishing articles on the parasitism of fungi and the relation of various organisms of this kind to such diseases as leaf blights, rusts, and other maladies. The following year Dr. W. G. Farlow, of Harvard University, began a series of papers which were epoch making in their nature. These papers dealt with a number of important diseases of plants and treated them in a masterly way. Although up to this time knowledge as to combating such diseases was limited, the information obtained in regard to the life histories of the organisms and the manner in which they attack the host plants and cause their death was of great value in suggesting lines of action looking toward prevention. Farlow's papers were followed by similar ones by Halsted, Bessey, Trelease, Earle, Arthur, and others.

Early in the eighties the interest in the subject became marked, as may be seen by the increased number of papers and the fact that some of the universities and colleges were devoting time to lectures and studies relating to the work. The State agricultural experiment station at Geneva, N. Y., inaugurated some important work under the direction of Dr. J. C. Arthur, who was made botanist of the station in 1884, and whose work was almost entirely on the diseases of plants. This was really the first systematic attempt on the part of any station or organized body in the United States to undertake a thorough study of the subject. Dr. Arthur published four reports, which dealt with a great number of important diseases. He paid particular attention to pear blight, which was recognized as one of the most destructive diseases of fruit in the United States, and had already been shown by Dr. Burrill to be due to bacteria. Dr. Arthur's work tended to establish more thoroughly the parasitic nature of a number of fungi. The keynote to the practical work of treatment had not yet been struck, but was to come later as a natural result of the studies made at this time.

The Epoch-Making Period From 1885 to 1895

A careful study of events, such as are to be described here, shows that in nearly every case where a line of work stands out preeminently as having a marked influence on the welfare of a country, two things have conduced to this end: (1) Through writings, lectures, and other channels the public has been educated so as to understand its need in this direction, and (2) after the recognition of this need there has been the proper direction of the forces necessary to satisfy it.

Prior to 1885 much had been done toward educating the farmers and fruit growers to the necessity of protecting their crops. There was a well-grounded belief that many of the common and destructive diseases owed their existence to causes which could be discovered, and which if once known might be controlled. The time, therefore, was ripe for starting the work on a more extensive scale than had ever been done before. The demand at this time was largely for information as to the best methods of treatment from a practical standpoint. It was not so much a question of knowing what the diseases were as it was how to best get rid of them. Recognizing these questions and their importance, the Department of Agriculture inaugurated some work which was destined to have far-reaching effects. F. Lamson-Scribner, who was assistant botanist at the time, was active in bringing about a proper recognition of the importance of the work. He undertook the publication of papers, which appeared first in the report of the Botanist of the Department of Agriculture. Soon such an interest was awakened that the Commissioner of Agriculture, Hon. Norman J. Colman, took steps to have the work put on a sound basis. Small appropriations were obtained, and the Section of Mycology was established as a distinct branch in the Department. Fortunately, a great impetus was given to the work at this time by the efforts being made in France to find remedies for the downy mildew of the grape. When black rot, another American disease, appeared in the French vineyards, there was widespread alarm, and consequently renewed efforts to find means of checking it.

It is well to call attention to the marked difference in the conditions existing in France and in this country with respect to such matters. Our country is so great, and the possibilities of diversified culture so numerous, that many farmers and fruit growers do not feel the necessity of putting forth any marked effort in treating the diseases. In France, however, the life of the community itself depends in many cases on the success or failure of a particular crop in that community, and so it was that the greatest pressure was brought to bear on the French Government to make a determined effort to check the ravages of downy mildew.

Through a fortunate accident — the sprinkling of vines bordering a roadside with bluestone and lime in order to prevent the pilfering of the fruit — there was discovered about 1885 a fungicide which was to have a marked influence not only on the welfare of France, but also on the interests of America as well. This fungicide thus accidentally discovered is the so-called Bordeaux mixture, which is made by combining copper sulphate, or bluestone, with lime. It has long been known that copper in various forms is able to destroy fungus spores, but it was not until the discovery of the Bordeaux mixture that a great impetus was given to the study of its effects on many plants. No one could have imagined the consequences which were to come from the combined use of two such simple things. Not only was the fruit saved from the thieves, but it was protected against mildew as well.

Soon after the success in France in the treatment of grape mildew with Bordeaux mixture, its usefulness was noted in this country by the Department of Agriculture and also by others. It was difficult, however, to convince fruit growers of the importance of making thorough trials of this and other preparations. This was one of the greatest obstacles that the Department met with in the early stages of the work. However, circulars were sent out describing the preparation of the fungicide and suggesting diseases that might be effectively treated with it. The success of the work was marked. Immediately there sprang up probably one of the most remarkable series of investigations and experiments ever witnessed in this or in any other country. Fungicides of many kinds were proposed and tested on a large scale, and extensive lines of investigation were inaugurated not only by the Department of Agriculture, but also by private individuals in various parts of the country.

In 1887 Professor Lamson-Scribner severed his connection with the Department of Agriculture, accepting an appointment to the chair of botany in the University of Tennessee, and the Department's work in this line was put in charge of the writer.

The investigations were pushed forward as vigorously as possible; new lines of investigation were inaugurated, and a special effort was made to bring about practical results. Black rot of the grape was successfully treated in 1887, and the same year decisive results were obtained in controlling several potato diseases.

A great impetus was also given to the work in 1887 by the establishment of the agricultural experiment stations. By means of these stations it was made possible for many of the States to inaugurate work not only in the study of plant diseases and their treatment, but also in many other lines of investigation as well. Several of the stations immediately commenced investigations, and as a result for the next eight years the educational work done throughout the country had the most remarkable effect in putting farmers, fruit growers, and others in possession of knowledge most valuable to them. During the period under consideration a revolution was wrought in our horticultural methods, and, as a result, it is now as rare to find people who are not thoroughly convinced of the importance of spraying as it is to find those who are satisfied that the cultivation of the soil is not necessary.

This vast amount of work on the fungicides carried with it the necessity of providing suitable apparatus for the application of the various preparations, there being a great need for such apparatus when the work was started. Just prior to the beginning of the important line of work in 1885 attention had been called to the value of the cyclone nozzle, an apparatus invented by Dr. W. S. Barnard while connected with the United States Entomological Commission. Although this nozzle was designed for the application of insecticides, it was found that with some minor changes it would be equally as valuable for use in connection with fungicides. There was also an urgent need in 1887 for suitable power pumps for the application of the various preparations. Some advances had been made with such apparatus in France, particularly in the knapsack forms, but such of these as were in actual use were more or less cumbersome, and none could be obtained in this country. Early in 1887 the first American knapsack pump was put on the market, largely through the efforts of Col. A. W. Pearson, of Vineland, N. J., who was one of the pioneers in the work of treatment. The machine was somewhat complicated, however, and did not attract the attention that it really deserved. In 1888 the writer devised a new form of knapsack spray pump, which was soon put on the market, and this became the pattern from which many designs have been made. In a few years such was the demand for apparatus of this kind that numbers of machines were manufactured. The knapsack forms of sprayers have had a marked influence in the success of the work described. Through them it was made possible to apply the remedies in the most thorough manner, a feature which is of the greatest importance in such work. As a direct result of this work many other forms of sprayers were designed; in fact, in this feature of the investigation the United States can well claim to have constantly led the way.

Some Results of the Work

The ten years' work just described was unique in its way. There was a united effort to concentrate on as many practical problems as possible, with a view of solving these first and attending to the more difficult ones later. Immediate results were demanded, and by obtaining them confidence was engendered; and thus the foundation for future efforts was laid.

Eradication of Pleuro-Pneumonia, 1899

From George F. Thompson, "Administrative Work of the Federal Government in Relation to the Animal Industry," U. S. Department of Agriculture, *Yearbook*, 1899, pp. 441–46.

Preliminary Remarks

Diseases of domestic animals have been the subject of many articles and letters which have appeared in the Annual Reports for the Department of Agriculture since its organization, and even previous to that time in the agricultural part of the Patent Office Reports. The first investigations were undertaken by Department authority in 1868, at a time when Texas fever and contagious pleuro-pneumonia were creating considerable alarm among the cattle raisers of the country. In 1882 and 1883 the investigation of Texas fever was taken up with a view to ascertaining its causes and methods of prevention and establishing definitely the areas infected by it. However, no administrative work relative to the animal industry of the country was undertaken by the Federal Government previous to the establishment of the Bureau of Animal Industry in the Department of Agriculture in 1884, except the limited amount done by the Treasury Department at the quarantine stations at the ports of import. One of the purposes of the establishment of the Bureau was to inaugurate and supervise the federal administrative work relative to contagious diseases of animals, and the history of the work in the United States forms a large portion of the history of the Bureau.

The work of the State governments relative to animal diseases can not be given within the limits of this paper, but it is well to say that, even before the Federal Government took up the work, several States had enacted laws for the control of contagious diseases of animals. Such enactments, while they might not have been inefficient, were found to be inadequate, since the regulation of the movement of animals from State to State could only be accomplished by the Federal Government; hence, the necessity was apparent that the latter should take up the great work and cooperate with the States.

Authority Conferred and Scope of the Work

The authority possessed by the Department of Agriculture for enforcing measures with reference to contagious diseases of domestic animals is conferred by "An act for the establishment of a Bureau of Animal Industry, to prevent the exportation of diseased cattle, and to provide for the suppression and extirpation of pleuro-pneumonia and other contagious diseases among domestic animals," which was approved by the President on May 29, 1884. The power thus conferred is not in all cases sufficient to effect the eradication of a disease, for the reason that the Federal Government can not enforce measures within a State without the legislative consent of that State, unless the animals affected are subjects of or endanger interstate commerce. Its work, therefore, without the cooperation of the States affected, is limited to interstate traffic, and quarantine lines are thus made to follow State lines. It has always been a matter of gratification, however, that wherever the Bureau of Animal Industry has undertaken to suppress and eradicate a contagious disease the authorities of the affected States have readily lent their assistance. A State, on the other hand, can do nothing more than guard its own territory; and, while all of the States have laws for the control of live-stock traffic with a view to the prevention or suppression of disease, it could hardly be expected that they would under all circumstances cooperate with each other effectually. The work of the Federal Government is therefore necessary to the State, and the State laws are necessary to the Federal Government, if success in eradicating disease from the country is to be assured; the federal and State powers are not only supplementary, but interdependent.

Contagious Pleuro-Pneumonia Work

The success of the Bureau of Animal Industry in eradicating contagious pleuro-pneumonia from this country was a triumph that will never be forgotten by the cattle owners of the United States. This disease had become established in several States east of the Allegheny Mountains, and later broke out in Ohio, Illinois, and Kentucky, all great cattle-growing States of the Mississippi Valley. From these States it threatened to spread over the great cattle districts of the West and completely to ruin the industry. The country was thoroughly alarmed, and Congress was prevailed upon to enlarge the powers of the Bureau of Animal Industry to deal with contagious diseases of domestic animals, contagious pleuro-pneumonia being especially mentioned.

A thorough study was immediately begun of the history of the disease in this country and abroad and of the means and methods employed elsewhere for its eradication. Dr. D. E. Salmon, who became the chief of this new Bureau, speaking of this disease in 1883, had said ''that the only object kept in view should be its complete extinction by the most summary measures at our command,'' and further: ''We can recommend no temporizing measures with regard to this affection. The only ones applicable are quarantine, restriction of movement of cattle, slaughter of affected animals, and disinfection.'' The veterinary profession the world over was agreed as to the efficacy of these measures alone, and the Bureau desired to adopt them at once in entering upon the pleuro-pneumonia work. In fact, rules and regulations providing for the destruction by Bureau inspectors of affected animals and the certification of the assessed value of such animals to the Commissioner of Agriculture, who, upon approval, would order payment for the same, were issued by the Commissioner of Agriculture on April 22, 1885; but about the same time the Attorney-General of the United States rendered an opinion, based upon the organic act creating the Bureau, that there are ''no provisions for purchasing the diseased and exposed animals,'' thus rendering null and void the rules and regulations of the Commissioner. However, in the appropriation act for the fiscal year of 1887 the Commissioner was authorized to expend the appropriation ''in such manner as he may think best to prevent the spread of pleuro-pneumonia . . . and to expend any part of this sum in the purchase and destruction of diseased animals wherever in his judgment it is essential to prevent the spread of pleuro-pneumonia from one State to another.'' From that time forward the work was pushed vigorously and successfully.

In accordance with the organic act creating the Bureau and also with the appropriation act just quoted, rules and regulations, dated August 12, 1886, were formulated for prosecuting the work. Provision was made for the acceptance of these rules and regulations by the governors of the affected States, which in most instances was promptly done. In the matter of inspection, the Bureau was to furnish the necessary inspectors, who were to receive from the proper State officers the authority to make inspections of cattle under the laws of the State, to receive such protection and assistance as would be given to State officers engaged in similar work, and be permitted to examine quarantined herds wherever so directed by the Commissioner of Agriculture or the chief of the Bureau of Animal Industry. Reports upon inspections were to be made to the Bureau of Animal Industry and to the proper State authorities. When contagious pleuro-pneumonia was discovered in a herd, the owner or person in charge was at once to notify the inspector, who was to put in force the quarantine regulations of the State in which the herd was located. Every animal of an infected herd was distinctively marked with a lock and chain, which were furnished by the Bureau, but which became the property of the State when placed upon an animal, in order that anyone tampering with them would become amenable to the laws of the State. Quarantine restrictions were for a period of not less than ninety days, and were not to be removed without the consent of the Bureau. All affected and exposed animals were to be slaughtered as soon after discovery as possible, were to be appraised according to the provisions of the State law, and the representatives of the Bureau notified of the appraisement. The Department of Agriculture was to pay to the owner such portion of the appraised value as was provided by the laws of the State for cattle condemned and slaughtered by State authority. All necessary disinfection was to be conducted by the Bureau. The Bureau did not recommend inoculation for the disease, but retained supervision over the herds which were inoculated under State authority.

These regulations were modified from time to time as necessity arose. On April 15, 1887, the chief of the Bureau was authorized to inspect stock yards, cars, boats, and other vehicles of transportation lines, and to make the necessary regulations for their quarantine and disinfection. A few weeks later a notice was sent to the managers of transportation lines, calling their attention to the existence of contagious pleuro-pneumonia among cattle in Illinois, Maryland, and New York, requesting their cooperation in preventing the spread of the disease by means of disinfection and by declining to receive cattle for shipment which were not known to be free from infection. Still later this notice was modified so as to apply to all States affected.

These measures soon began to give good results, enabling the chief of the Bureau of Animal Industry to make the following statement in his report for 1888:

> The prompt eradication of pleuro-pneumonia from Chicago and vicinity is worthy of more than a simple narration of the fact. It may well be considered one of the most important results ever accomplished by the Department of Agriculture. History gives few if any cases where the dairies of a city of the size of Chicago have once been infected with pleuro-pneumonia and where the disease has been eradicated without years of constant work and the expenditure of vast sums of money. Paris was infected more than one hundred years ago, and in spite of the large number of veterinarians in that district, and of the stringent laws and regulations promulgated for its suppression, the disease still exists, and the ravages continue from year to year apparently undiminished.

At the same time the disease was eradicated from all affected districts in Maryland outside of the city of Baltimore, and in Virginia it was completely suppressed. In the other affected States the work had been most satisfactory. In 1889 the progress of the work was notable, being hampered only by lack of full authority on the part of the Bureau properly to enforce its regulations. The plague had not reappeared west of the Allegheny Mountains and no extensions occurred in the Eastern States. Cattle owners and shippers outside of the infected districts had gained such confidence in the work that the presence of the disease in this country no longer interfered with the traffic to any appreciable extent. In 1890 the chief of the Bureau reported as follows:

> The year has passed without any discovery of contagious pleuro-pneumonia outside of the districts which were recognized in the last report as infected. The regulations of the Department have been enforced without difficulty, and the progress of the work for the eradication of this plague has been continuous and rapid.

*　*　*

> The efficiency of the regulations and of the methods employed under them is demonstrated by the fact that for two years there has not been a case of the disease outside of the very restricted areas on the Atlantic seaboard which have from the first been recognized as infected. These regulations are still in force, and with the almost complete eradication of the contagion the danger of any infection extending to other sections has practically disappeared.

In 1891 the disease had disappeared from all of the States that had been infected except New Jersey, where it was restricted to a very small area, enabling the Bureau to publish the statement that "the United States is now practically free from contagious pleuro-pneumonia." On March 25, 1892, the last case of the disease disappeared from the United States, and six months later the following proclamation was issued:

PROCLAMATION — ERADICATION OF PLEURO-PNEUMONIA.

U. S. DEPARTMENT OF AGRICULTURE,
OFFICE OF THE SECRETARY.

To all whom it may concern:

Notice is hereby given that the quarantines heretofore existing in the counties of Kings and Queens, State of New York, and the counties of Essex and Hudson, State of New Jersey, for the suppression of contagious pleuro-pneumonia among cattle, are this day removed.

The removal of the aforesaid quarantines completes the dissolving of all quarantines established by this Department in the several sections of the United States for the suppression of the above-named disease.

No case of this disease has occurred in the State of Illinois since December 29, 1887, a period of more than four years and eight months.

No case has occurred in the State of Pennsylvania since September 29, 1888, a period of four years, within a few days.

No case has occurred in the State of Maryland since September 18, 1889, a period of three years.

No case has occurred in the State of New York since April 30, 1891, a period of more than one year and four months.

No case has occurred in the State of New Jersey since March 25, 1892, a period of six months, and no case has occurred in any other portion of the United States within the past five years.

I do therefore hereby officially declare that the United States is free from the disease known as contagious pleuro-pneumonia.

J. M. RUSK, *Secretary*.

It may be that those countries which are still afflicted with the plague of contagious pleuro-pneumonia are in position better to appreciate the importance of the work done in this country than we are ourselves. If the Bureau of Animal Industry, by eradicating this disease from the country, were to be given credit for the value of all losses which would have resulted from a continuance of the disease, as well as for the money which might have been expended ineffectually by the State authorities toward suppressing it, who can estimate what it would be?

In a summary of the work of the Bureau, published in 1897, the chief wrote as follows regarding the eradication of contagious pleuro-pneumonia:

It is almost impossible at this time to give an idea of the danger with which the cattle industry was menaced by the spread of that fatal and treacherous disease to a point so far in the interior as Chicago or of the difficulties under our form of Government of promptly and effectually meeting the emergency. Fortunately, although the cattle owners in the affected districts were not friendly, the State authorities cooperated in every case and supplied the power which was lacking in federal legislation, and although there were many who questioned the existence of the European lung plague in this country, who did not believe in the success of the measures that were adopted, who were positive that the disease could not be eradicated, or who were certain that untold millions of money would be squandered before the end was reached, the result was accomplished with an expenditure of less than five years of time and of $1,500,000 — a sum which is less than 5 per cent of the value of the beef exported in 1892.

When we consider that the Governments of Great Britain, France, and Germany all undertook the work of eradicating pleuro-pneumonia long before the establishment of our Bureau of Animal Industry, and that none of them have yet succeeded in freeing their territory from the plague, we can appreciate the fact that the completion of our task in a comparatively short time was a notable achievement.

In order to make this review of the pleuro-pneumonia work complete and satisfactory, the following tables, taken from the report of the Bureau for 1892, are given:

Work done in the eradication of pleuro-pneumonia, by years.

ILLINOIS.

Character of work.	September 1, 1886, to December 3, 1887	1888.	Total.
Herds inspected	7,411	140	7,551
Cattle inspected	24,059	285	24,344
Post-mortem examinations	7,267	1,712	8,979
Number diseased on post-mortem	350	4	354
Premises disinfected	677	1	678
Diseased cattle purchased	172	4	176
Exposed cattle purchased	870	129	999

Character of work.	1887.	1888.	1889.	1890.	Total.
Herds inspected............................	5,704	9,809	10,904	4,210	30,627
Cattle inspected............................	57,868	60,312	79,606	108,376	306,162
Cattle tagged	....	17,749	10,534	5,463	33,746
Post-mortem examinations	2,788	5,820	11,491	12,949	33,048
Number diseased on post-mortem	1,137	507	76	....	1,720
Premises disinfected.......................	145	145	35	1	326
Diseased cattle purchased	a1,442	459	73	....	1,974
Exposed cattle purchased................	a1,564	1,036	310	20	2,930

aIncludes all purchases of cattle from July 1, 1886, to December 31, 1886.

Agricultural Experimentation in Colorado, 1899

From "Outlines of Station Work for 1898," Colorado State Board of Agriculture and the State Agricultural College, *Annual Report*, 1898, (Denver, 1899), pp. 113–18.

Outlines of Station Work for 1898

At a meeting of the Station Council, held January 25, the schedules of station work for the year were presented, revised, and adopted. These schedules were subsequently — January 28 — adopted at a regular monthly meeting of the Executive Committee. The outlines of experimental work for the different sections of the Home Station . . . are herewith given: —

Agricultural Section

* * *

Sugar Beets

The work in this connection to be done in coooperàtion with the Chemical Section, tests of seed grown in the United States as compared with that grown in Europe, tests of the effect of alkali, early and late thinning, early and late planting, medium and late irrigation, manured and unmanured land, and alfalfa sod; all these tests to be made at Fort Collins and Rocky Ford, and part of them at fourteen other places distributed in the valleys of the Platte, Arkansas, Grand, Gunnison, and on the Divide and in the San Luis Valley.

Bromus Inermis

Tests for hay, pasture, and seed, with and without irrigation, especially with reference to fall seeding.

Alfalfa

The continuation of the tests of top dressing, with duplicate tests of plowing in stable manure; duplication of the tests of the past season on the losses of alfalfa in the stack and in the mow, and on the effect of different times of cutting alfalfa; a test of a new variety of alfalfa as compared with the common variety, to be made at Fort Collins and Rocky Ford, and if possible, at several other places.

Corn

A continuation of the second year of a three years' test on the value of seed from different climates.

Winter Wheat

A test of its use as fall pasture for sheep when sown after barley.

Gypsum

A test as a top dressing on alfalfa, as plowed in for cereals and corn, and as an addition to stable manure, in our third year of the test for the reclamation of ''poverty weed'' land.

Digestion Experiments

In connection with the Chemical Section, it is especially desired to make some digestion experiments with sheep with reference to Dr. Headden's new method for determining the feeding value of fodders by chemical analysis. The animals necessary for the experiments are already on hand. It will probably take about $75.00 to buy the necessary apparatus for performing the experiments and for fixing up the stalls to make them suitable for carrying on these lines of experimentation.

Section of Botany and Horticulture

I. The study of the Flora of the State, special attention being given to:
   1. The weeds of the farm and garden.
   2. Grasses, native and introduced.
   3. The various species and varieties of the genera, Oxytropis and Astragalus.

II. The further introduction to the garden of such wild fruits as can be obtained.

III. Nursery test of orchard fruits with a view to the study of the adaptability of varieties to this climate.

IV. Tests of varieties of small fruits.

V. Coöperative work with the Division of Forestry of the United States Department of Agriculture.

Section of Meteorology and Irrigation Engineering

I. Meteorology — To continue observations as hitherto. This includes observation and record of the data bearing on agricultural meteorology; average maximum and minimum temperatures; range; solar radiation; terrestrial radiation;

rainfall and humidity observations; barometer, wind, amount, direction, etc.; and amount and intensity of sunshine. This also includes observations by various voluntary observers and at the sub-stations. To make these of most value, the stations should be visited to examine the exposure of the meteorological instruments.

II. Evaporation determinations — The continuation of that from waters, and study of evaporation from soils and vegetation.

III. Soil moisture.

IV. Soil temperatures.

V. Continuation of examination of irrigation questions of the State — The subirrigation question of the San Luis Valley was not completed last year. The correspondence now in progress may enable its completion without taking it up as a topic for the summer. I think it is desirable to enter upon a study of the questions of the Arkansas Valley.

VI. Seepage measurements in the State — On the Arkansas and on some other streams.

Entomological Section

I. Collecting and rearing insects for the purpose of determining food-habits and life-histories.

II. Experiments for the destruction of insect eggs.

III. The beginning of work looking to an Orthopterological survey of the State.

IV. Testing insecticides.

V. Experiments to determine the value of the bandage system of combatting the Codling Moth.

VI. Experiments for the destruction of miscellaneous insect pests.

VII. Experiments in the Apiary:

1. To determine the value of sugar for winter stores.
2. Testing apiary appliances.
3. Making a collection and list of honey-producing and pollen-producing plants with notes as to their probable value.
4. Experiments to determine the nature of and remedy for the disease known as "Bee Paralysis."

Chemical Section

I. Continuation of the soil study already begun, including a study of the effect of cropping alkali soil to sugar beets, as outlined last year.

II. Coöperation with the Farm Department in the study of the sugar beet problems in Colorado, including the subjects of the influence of the seed upon the date of maturing, effect of manuring, etc.

III. Animal digestion experiments in coöperation with the Farm Department — a continuation of the study presented in Bulletin No. 39. This will entail an expenditure of about $75.00 by the Department of Chemistry.

Farmers' Institutes, 1903

From John Hamilton, "The Farmers' Institutes," U. S. Department of Agriculture, *Yearbook*, 1903, Washington, 1904) pp. 149–58.

The Development of Farmers' Institutes

Farmers' institutes are now held in all of the States except Arkansas, Montana, and South Dakota, and in all of the Territories except Alaska, Porto Rico, and Indian Territory. In no two of the States are institutes organized in the same manner or conducted by the same methods. In some the management is under the control of a central board, or institute official. Others have no central organization, but each county institute is an independent unit. Others have both a central organization and local boards, each having distinct powers and being charged with specific duties. In some States the local organizations are created by legislative acts under State laws, and consequently have continuous existence. In others they are without legal status, and are temporary in character, new associations for institute purposes being formed each year.

This diversity is due to the fact that the work is new, and its development has been by independent action by the several States, without conference, and in many instances without precedent for their guidance.

Efforts at Uniformity in Institute Work

The first attempt in the direction of securing uniformity of method in institute work was made in 1896, when Supt. George McKerrow, of Wisconsin, called a meeting of the institute workers of the country for March 13 of that year, to be held at Watertown, Wis. At this meeting a form of constitution was prepared to be submitted to a subsequent convention to be held October 14, 1896, in Chicago. At the Chicago meeting a new constitution was presented as a substitute for the one prepared at Watertown, and after extended discussion the substitute was finally adopted. The name given to the organization was "The American Association of Farmers' Institute Managers."

The condition of the institute work at that time was summed up by one of the speakers in the following statement:

As States we have been pursuing different lines with different objects in view, but in the future we should endeavor to unify our plans of work by discussing methods, criticising pet theories, and subjecting the plans followed by the various States to a sort of surgical treatment of the work and the workers. If this is done thoroughly, we can unite upon a common method which will be of great benefit to all.

In furtherance of the purpose of the organization to secure greater uniformity, the association at its meeting in Columbus, Ohio, in 1897, by formal action requested the Secretary of Agriculture of the United States to "arrange for a division in connection with that Department, to be known as the Division of Farmers' Institutes, and to appoint a suitable officer who shall be in charge."

The Secretary of Agriculture at the second session of the Fifty-seventh Congress made request for an appropriation of $5,000 for the purpose of enabling the Department to engage the services of some one to cooperate with the State directors, and to render such other assistance as the Department might be able tofurnish. Congress made the appropriation, and an official known as Farmers' Institute Specialist was accordingly appointed, who took charge of the work under the direction of the Office of Experiment Stations on the 1st of April, 1903.

The act providing for the appointment makes it the duty of this officer to "investigate and report upon the organization and progress of farmers' institutes in the several States and Territories, and upon similar organizations in foreign countries; with special suggestions of plans and methods for making such organizations more effective for the dissemination of the results of the work of the Department of Agriculture and of the experiment stations, and of improved methods of agricultural practice."

Features of Work Common to All Institutes

Notwithstanding the diversity that has existed in many respects among the directors in conducting their institutes, two leading features of the work have been common to all, and are the distinguishing characteristics. The first is an earnest purpose to carry valuable agricultural information to farming people at their homes, and the second is to effect this by means of oral instruction given by capable teachers in institute assemblies.

The faithful carrying out of these purposes will, as the work develops, and as the practice pursued in the several States becomes generally understood by the directors, naturally cause them to adopt such common methods as experience has shown to be best adapted to the accomplishment of the ends in view. These efforts, assisted by the two agencies referred to, the American Association of Farmers' Institute Workers and the Office of Experiment Stations, through its farmers' institute specialist, it is believed will secure in the near future such a degree of cooperation as will lead ultimately to substantial uniformity of methods throughout the country. The extent to which the Department of Agriculture can aid in bringing about this result is indicated in the following extract from the report of the Director of the Office of Experiment Stations for 1903, in which he outlines the general policy to be pursued respecting the institute work:

Since the work of this Department relating to the farmers' institutes is based on the principle of giving aid to the institutions maintained under the authority of the States, this Office has established the rule of working in this line through the State officers charged with the management of the institutes. It is the intention to consult freely with these officers, to welcome suggestions from them regarding the development of our work, and to recognize them as the proper authorities through whom to deal in matters relating to the institutes in the several States. It is our purpose to endeavor to strengthen the State organizations for the management of the institutes, and to create a National system of institutes by promoting the reasonable coordination of the work throughout the country, and the cooperation of the State organizations without weakening or destroying their autonomy.

Those most in need of immediate assistance are the State directors, or persons in general control of the institutes in the several States, the local managers, and the lecturers or teachers who are engaged in giving instruction in agriculture at institute meetings.

The State directors need help along the line of organizing their work that it may be most effective as an educational institution for the benefit of agriculture; the local managers need assistance in arranging for the institutes in the several localities in the matter of advertising, preparing programmes, providing proper local committees to look after minor details, such as the question box, the entertainment of visitors, the collecting of exhibits for display at institutes, the securing of suitable halls for the meetings, and other matters of like character; and the lecturers need assistance in the direction of their proper equipment as teachers of agriculture. How most effectively to assist these three great classes of workers in their efforts to elevate agriculture into a more scientific and remunerative profession is the institute problem which the Department, through its Office of Experiment Stations, has undertaken to solve.

Growth of Interest in Farmers' Institutes

The interest manifested in the farmers' institutes is seen in the action of the legislatures of the several States and of the agricultural college and experiment station officers having charge of the work in making appropriations for their support. Amounts varying from $35 in the Territory of Hawaii to $20,000 in the State of New York show the extremes, the aggregate for the 45 States and Territories which reported the past season being $187,226. The appropriations for the coming season, as shown by the reports of 40 States and Territories, amount to $210,975. If the States not reporting appropriate sums equal to those expended by them in 1903, the total for 1904 will reach $214,729, or $27,503 more than was appropriated for the year just closed.

It is noticeable that where the institutes have been longest in operation the appropriations are correspondingly large: New York, $20,000; Pennsylvania, $17,500; Ohio, $16,981; Wisconsin, $12,000; Illinois, $18,150; Indiana, $10,000; Minnesota, $16,500; Michigan, $7,500. Other States with smaller agricultural populations have been proportionately liberal: West Virginia, $5,451; Vermont, $5,000; Maryland, $4,000; Maine, $3,000; Florida, $2,500, and California, $4,000.

The attendance has also been increasing each year, that of the season just closed being 904,654, as against 819,999 for the previous year. The real advance numerically is, however, greater than these figures indicate. Upon the recommendation of the American Association of Farmers' Institute Workers, the method of computing attendance has recently been changed, with the result of reducing the number reported in attendance in 1902, in four States, by 99,481. The fact that these four States held 126 more institutes in 1903 than in 1902 shows that the falling off, as reported, was not actual, but is due to the method of computing attendance. If this correction is made, the attendance for the present year exceeds that of the year previous by 184,136. This increase was for the most part in the following States: Delaware, Illinois, Indiana, Iowa, Kansas, Kentucky, Louisiana, Maryland, Massachusetts, Michigan, Minnesota, Mississippi, Missouri, New Hampshire, and Pennsylvania.

The increase in the number of institute meetings is another evidence of progress. There were 415 more institutes held this year than last, the figures being

3,179 for the year ended June 30, 1903, and 2,764 for the year ended June 30, 1902. Of the 3,179 institutes held, 1,359 were one-day institutes, 1,637 covered two days, and 77 three days and over. A more accurate understanding of the amount of work accomplished can be had from the number of sessions held, which amounted to 9,570 during the year.

The Lecture Force

The meetings held during the season of 1902–1903 were addressed by 924 lecturers employed by the State directors, and by about three times as many more employed by the local managers, approximating 4,000 persons who gave instruction at institutes last year. One hundred and ninety-six of these were members of the staffs of agricultural colleges or experiment stations, who contributed 1,666 days of time to this work, attending in all 752 institutes.

The lecture method is used in giving instruction at the institutes, the lectures being followed by an informal discussion of the topics by the audience. These informal discussions are valuable and distinguishing features of the institutes. Any new theory or improved method suggested is thereby subjected to the scrutiny and criticism of practical men, many of whom have had a lifetime of experience along the line of the speaker's topic, and so are well qualified to discuss from a practical standpoint the subjects presented and to call attention to any impracticable features advocated by the lecturers that might prevent their adoption by the general farmer. The effect of this critical discussion is to drive the uninformed and ill-balanced lecturer from the platform, and gradually to secure for institute service a corps composed of well-qualified and conservative teachers.

That this sifting process occurs is shown by the character of the lecture force as it now exists in this country. An examination of the personal history of 623 lecturers engaged in the farmers' institutes in the United States showed that 287 had college degrees, 138 had taken partial college courses, 108 had the advantage of normal or high-school training, and 90 were practical men who had ordinary educational advantages. The men, therefore, who are now giving instruction in the farmers' institutes in this country are for the most part unusually well qualified for their work. The progress made in this respect is most striking if the qualifications of the lecture force of to-day are compared with those of the average lecturer of fifteen years ago.

Training Lecturers

It is manifest that the extension of the institutes will be limited by the ability to secure a sufficient number of capable teachers. Thus far the State directors have depended upon the agricultural colleges and the experiment stations for their supply of men for expert scientific teaching, and upon the more intelligent and successful practical farmers for giving information in regard to conducting the practical operations of agriculture.

A number of State directors appear to have given little attention to securing a supply of lecturers from among citizens of their own States, but have depended upon the services of men of reputation from other States. Some directors, on the other hand, have striven to develop capable teachers for institute work by selecting men in their own State who have succeeded in some line of agricultural practice, and giving them the opportunity of telling institute audiences the results of their own experience. In this way many excellent teachers have been secured and added to the force.

That each State director should adopt some method for discovering capable men to be developed into competent instructors is clear, for unless the teaching force can be constantly recruited and maintained at a high standard of efficiency the work must necessarily deteriorate and eventually become of little benefit to agriculture. The Office of Experiment Stations of the Department of Agriculture has taken up this question, and is now sending out to the State lecturers lists of the Department publications, from which they can select such bulletins as promise to be of assistance to them in the study of their several specialties. The agricultural experiment stations are cooperating in this work.

How far the agricultural colleges or experiment stations can go, or ought to go, in preparing men and women specially for institute work should be seriously considered by the officers of these institutions. Illinois, Michigan, New York, Tennessee, and Wisconsin have already started a movement in this direction. The plan pursued by these institutions consists in general of courses of lectures by members of the agricultural college and experiment station staffs delivered to the institute teachers of the State, continuing for from one to two weeks, with a view to acquainting them with the more important scientific truths relating to their specialties. A number of the presidents of agricultural colleges in other States have expressed their interest in this effort to educate institute teachers, and no doubt the next few years will develop, in connection with these colleges, some system that will be practicable and otherwise satisfactory in this direction.

Management of Institutes

In 27 States directors complete all arrangements for the holding of institutes, fixing the dates and places, and arranging the programmes. In 13 States one or more leading topics are prescribed by the State director to be discussed in all institutes held during the season. By this method it has been found possible to disseminate over the entire State accurate information in regard to subjects of special importance in a single year.

In 29 States the directors publish in advance of the beginning of the institute season an announcement of the dates, places, and speakers. In 10 States no such announcement is made. Twenty-four State directors attend all or nearly all of their institutes, and 21 directors permit their names to be placed regularly on the programmes of exercises.

Special institutes for women are held in 15 States. In 43 States the agricultural colleges and experiment stations furnish lecturers for institute work. In 14 States annual round-up institutes are held, and 20 States publish reports of proceedings, aggregating last year 253,700 copies.

The Cost of Institutes

Of the institutes held last year, 3,106 have reported their expenses, showing an average cost of $60.22 for each institute; 9,426 sessions cost an average of $16.85 per session, varying from $3 to $82 as the extremes. There were 4,864 days of institutes in all. The cost of 4,792 of these was at the rate of $39 per day, and the average cost per person for the year was about 2.2 cents.

In 33 out of the 44 States reporting, the institutes are supported by appropriations by the States; 10 by local subscriptions or by agricultural college or experiment station assistance; and one receives appropriations from both the State and the agricultural college.

In 10 of the States no compensation is allowed to the lecturers outside of their necessary hotel and traveling expenses. In 22 States the remuneration of the lecturers ranges from $2 per day to $50 per week and expenses.

Assisting Farmers' Boys

The work of the institute thus far has been mainly directed and planned to meet the needs of the practical farmer. The programme, the question box, the discussions by experts, have all been arranged and conducted with special reference to interesting and instructing adults, with the natural result that the institute halls are filled for the most part by gray-haired men and middle-aged women, with only here and there a farmer boy or girl.

Some managers have recognized the importance of their institutes doing something for the improvement of country children, and accordingly have arranged for holding meetings to which country boys and girls are invited, and at which they are called on to read essays or recite selections, often upon subjects having little or no direct relation to farm life. It not infrequently occurs that when such a session has been concluded none of the young people who have participated has acquired any additional knowledge of agricultural affairs or received a stimulus to a study of any problem connected with farm life.

A new movement has recently been inaugurated with the purpose of rendering the institutes specially interesting and at the same time directly useful to country children. At least three States have begun work in this direction with satisfactory results. The plans adopted are essentially the same, differing only in minor details.

A brief outline of the system at present in operation in Illinois will serve as an illustration of what is being undertaken:

Packages, each containing 500 grains of seed corn of some approved variety, are sent out by the State director of farmers' institutes to as many boys throughout the State as will agree to enter the contest. The conditions are that a boy receiving a package ''shall plant 300 grains of the seed in a square, with the balance planted in two rows on the south and west sides to fertilize and protect the inside rows; that he will cultivate and harvest it and exhibit not less than ten ears of it at his home county farmers' institute, the ten ears or more for exhibition to be taken from the inside square. It is further agreed by the boy receiving the corn that he will comply with the rules governing the exhibit of corn at his county institute, and that he will attend at least one session of the institute.'' Each boy is required to keep a record of the crop and report to the institute on the following items:

The kind of soil upon which the corn was grown; the previous crop upon the plot; the manure used, if any; the time and depth of plowing; the cultivation of the ground before planting; the time of planting; the number of times and kind of cultivation; the implements used in cultivation; the number of hills; the number of stalks in each hill; the number of ears;

the number of stalks that were without ears; the total weight at the time of gathering; the injury from cutworms and insects. All to pertain only to the hills from the 300 grains on the inside square planted.

The ten ears exhibited are expected to be uniform in appearance, true to type, to have the rows of kernels straight and parallel with the cob, and each ear to carry the same circumference from butt to tip.

The judging is performed by persons selected by the local board of county institute officers, usually some one who has taken and passed the Illinois Corn Growers' examination for skill in corn judging. The standard of excellence is fixed by the following scale of points adopted by the Illinois Corn Growers' Association:

Scale of points in judging corn.

Points.

Uniformity of exhibit 10
[Uniform type, size, shape, color, and indentation.]
Shape of ears 5
[Cylindrical, straight rows, proportional length to circumference.]
Color of ears 10
[Uniform.]
Market condition 10
[Soundness, freedom from injury, maturity.]
Tips of ears 10
[Filled out with regular-sized kernels.]
Butts of ears 5
[Kernels swelled out about shank regularly.]
Uniformity of kernels 5
[In type, shape, and color.]
Shape of kernels 5
[Wedge shape, straight edges.]
Length of ears 10
[Conformity to standard.]
Circumference of ears 5
[Conformity to standard.]
Space between rows 5
[Small.]
Space between kernels 5
[Small.]
Per cent of corn 15
[Conformity to standard.]

Rules for judging corn.

(1) The excess and deficiency in length of all ears shall be added, and for every inch thus obtained cut one point.

(2) The excess and deficiency in circumference of all ears shall be added, and for every inch thus obtained a cut of one-half point shall be made.

(3) For every per cent short of standard in proportion of shelled corn a cut of one point shall be made.

The contest is confined to boys not over 18 years of age. Premiums are offered by the county institutes for the best samples of corn exhibited, and also for the best report presented on the method of growing the crop. These premiums usually consist of some animal or article closely related to farm life, such as a well-bred calf, pig, or lamb; some farm implement; a library of selected agricultural books; an assortment of fruit trees; a collection of seeds of special worth; and choice varieties of plants, such as strawberries, small fruits, or ornamental shrubs or trees.

In one county an entire day of the institute is set apart to be known as "boys' day," and the county superintendent of public instruction recommends that the public schools be closed on the day of the boys' programme, and that teachers and children attend the institute.

It is manifest that while the State from which this example has been taken has confined the contest to the single item of Indian corn, the principle is, nevertheless, capable of being applied in many directions, embracing other crops, the growing of animals, the improvement of home surroundings, the manufacture of butter or cheese, or the care of poultry.

The experiment is full of suggestions, and no doubt other State directors will, as the success of these trials becomes assured, adopt similar means for improving their institutes so as more effectively to educate and interest the youth in their several States in agriculture.

Improvement of the Institutes

In the early stages of the institute work, and with the limited means at the disposal of the managers, the holding of a few meetings was about all that could be undertaken, but now with more funds, increased interest, and clearer views of what the institute stands for, it ought to be possible in many States to do much more. Hitherto many institute managers have seemed to feel that they had performed all of the service required when they had held successfully in their county two, three, or four institutes a year. As soon as these were over, the local institute force either entirely disbanded or settled back into a state of comparative inertia until the time was near for the next year's meetings, when a new campaign had to be organized and the public again be awakened to renewed interest in the work.

Many of the most advanced institute workers have come to the conviction that the institute work has reached a stage of progress when there should be such a degree of stability in the organization of the local institute as will keep it not only in existence during the entire year, but energetically at work as well. Delaware, Illinois, Kansas, Michigan, Ohio, and Oklahoma already have county institutes which are constituted under their laws and have continuous existence. In these States the county institute organizations are responsible to a State director or central board, and yet they have sufficient independence of action to make it impossible for any change in the personnel of the State directory to affect their integrity. Work undertaken by these local organizations for the improvement of home conditions can not be seriously interfered with by any change occurring in the State administration. This is a great improvement over the system most common, where there is either no local organization or one that is so temporary as to virtually cease to exist at the end of the institute season. The loss by death or removal of the State director in such instances is always attended with great inconvenience, and sometimes is a serious permanent injury to the work.

The establishing of a properly constituted local organization in each county has undoubtedly tended to strengthen the institutes wherever the plan has been introduced, and has made possible their expansion to meet the constantly increasing needs of the people for institute service. One direction in which such a system can be of service is shown in the Province of Ontario, Canada, where similar local permanent organizations cooperate with their experiment stations in testing the adaptability of various seeds and plants to the several districts. The report of the Experimental Union for 1903 shows that during the previous year 3,845 different persons had cooperated with their stations in conducting experiment work in agriculture.

The subjects of interest to country people which are important, and which would furnish work for the institutes during the intervals between the lecture seasons, are quite numerous. They include the preparing of the way for the introduction of the teaching of agriculture in the rural schools, the betterment of the public roads, the improvement of the live stock of the county, the securing of better county fairs, and the introduction of new and valuable varieties of seeds and plants. These and many others are subjects needing attention in every rural community, and a well-organized permanent county institute would be constantly on hand with a selected force of men and women ready to help.

The new field which the institutes thus organized could enter would expand their work far beyond its present bounds, and would compensate for some of the loss which the lack of a sufficient number of high-grade teachers has occasioned. Institute managers are now greatly embarrassed in their efforts to extend their work upward along the lines originally laid out. The broadening of the work so as to reach all of the citizens in every county during the entire year, and then reaching down and assisting country children to a better appreciation of their life and surroundings, will relieve much of this embarrassment and bring about an improvement that is urgently needed in every community in every State.

Effect of Preservatives on Foods, 1903

From H. W. Wiley, "Determination of Effect of Preservatives in Foods on Health and Digestion," U.S. Department of Agriculture, *Yearbook*, 1903 (Washington, 1904), pp. 289–95, 301–02.

Reasons for the Investigations

The Secretary of Agriculture is charged by law with the determination of the injurious effects which may be exerted upon health and digestion by preservatives, coloring matters, and other substances added to foods. It is important that decisions as to the effects of these substances shall rest upon indubitable evidence, which, in many cases, is not now at hand. To throw additional light on this subject an extensive series of experiments has been undertaken in the Bureau of Chemistry for the elucidation of some of the problems involved. In order that just decisions should be reached it was first necessary to eliminate, in so far as possible, all bias or prejudice concerning the matter. Nearly everyone has acquired, by reading the results of experiments or opinions, some definite ideas concerning the favorable or unfavorable action of these added substances, with many of which the consumer of food products is brought into daily contact. There, may be cited, for instance, the coloring matter which is added to butter and cheese, sometimes to milk and cream, and the chemicals added to green vegetables (such as peas and beans), in order to produce and maintain a deep green color. The latter are usually salts of copper or zinc, generally copper. Of late, in preserved meats, in addition to the familiar preservatives which are at the same time condimental, such as sugar, salt, and wood smoke, there are found also such chemicals as borax or boracic acid, which have high preservative properties.

In specific cases the expert testimony which is available is often contradictory, and sometimes it is open to the suspicion of bias. In these cases inquiry elicits the fact that the testimony in question was obtained as the result of a specific employment of the expert by interested parties. This does not necessarily imply any lack of care or conscientious investigation on the part of the expert, nor does it impute to him any wrong motive, but it only takes into consideration the natural tendency of man to incline toward the side of a controversy in which he is chiefly interested.

For these and other reasons, it was deemed advisable to undertake a series of independent experiments in the Department of Agriculture, in a manner as thorough as possible, to obtain new data relating to the very important questions outlined above.

Methods of Experimenting

In the specific case of preservatives added to food substances three lines of investigation may be followed.

In the first place, food products may be subjected to artificial digestion. In these experiments all the conditions of natural digestion, in so far as possible, are secured — the proper temperature, the proper subdivision of the food itself, the admixture of the digestive ferments, and the movements to imitate the peristaltic motions of the intestinal organs can all be provided for. A chemical study of artificial digestion will reveal in part the effect of the added preservatives upon human digestion. Most valuable data are secured in this way, and these studies have been thoroughly made by many different persons in widely separated localities. The only thing, however, which is determined by these experiments is the influence of the preservative upon the rate of digestion, and the question of the speed of digestion is not always the most important one. Within reasonable limits, the mere fact that one substance is digested more rapidly than another is no just cause for supposing that the former is more wholesome than the latter. It is of course, evident that if the time of digestion be so prolonged as to endanger the processes of absorption and nutrition, such delay would work injury. If, on the contrary, only a moderate delay of digestion results, it may not in any sense diminish the total amount of food eventually absorbed for the nutrition of the body nor induce any disorder in the digestive organs themselves.

The second method in which the effect of these bodies has been studied is by feeding them under controlled conditions to the lower animals. The rabbit, the guinea pig, the dog, and even the chimpanzee and the monkey have been used for these purposes. There are many advantages to be noted in working upon animals of this class. In the first place, the effect of the mind upon the process is practically eliminated, as the animals are not supposed to know that their food has been changed in any way, inasmuch as the preservatives experimented with are usually of such a nature as to impart no perceptible taste or odor to the food to which they are added. One unfavorable condition is the confinement of the animals, since experiments of this kind can not be made upon animals allowed to go at large. Long confinement has its effects even upon the lower animals, and these effects may seriously interfere with the processes of digestion; hence impaired digestion resulting from these experiments may not be solely due to the added bodies. On the other hand, the unrestricted range of experiments with the lower animals has some notable advantages, chief among them the fact that at the end of any given period of the experiment the animal may be killed and the condition of the internal organs carefully studied. It is undoubtedly true that often incipient disease of the internal organs may be induced by foods or substances added to foods without such effects being noticeable through ordinary observation; hence experiments might result in the declaration that any given substance was harmless, when, in point of fact, the foundations of serious and perhaps even fatal disease had been laid by it. It is evident, therefore, that the omission of experiments of this kind with the lower animals would be a grave mistake in experimental work.

In regard to both of these methods of experiments, it is only just to say that most careful and painstaking investigations have been carried out by competent observers, and the data which have been obtained are reasonably satisfactory. It, therefore, did not seem desirable to repeat in connection with the present investigations any of the experiments belonging to either of the classes mentioned.

Character of the Experiments Conducted by the Department

The third method of experiment is that which both the others lead up to — namely, experiments with man himself. The important point in all researches of this kind is to determine what effect these substances have upon the health of man. It might easily be that a substance which is found to be innocuous to a lower animal would prove a serious menace to man, since the digestive organisms of animals differ very widely, not only among themselves, but still more widely among different species and genera. It is well known that some of the lower animals are immune from the effects of many substances which would speedily prove fatal to man. Thus, the crucial experiment in all cases of this kind must be with man himself. The difficulties, however, of experimenting with the human animal are exceptionally great. We have here to deal with a high intelligence, a perfect knowledge of the process which is going on, and a consequent factor of mental influence; the subject under study must be placed under an observation which is annoying, and, when long continued, becomes burdensome. Nevertheless, the importance of the work was of such a nature as to warrant its undertaking.

Experiments with the human animal in regard to the effect of preservatives and other substances added to foods are not new. They have been made by many observers for many years. A study of all the experimental data reveals the fact that generally the number of persons experimented upon at any one time has been very limited, usually not exceeding two, and the time of observation has been relatively short, rarely exceeding ten or fifteen days. It seemed highly desirable, therefore, in the conduct of work of this kind, to increase the number of persons under observation, and especially to lengthen the time of the experiment. The facilities at the disposal of the Bureau of Chemistry permitted experimental work to be carried on with at least twelve persons, and that was the number finally selected.

Selection of the Experimental Class

In the selection of the subjects it was necessary, of course, to call for volunteers, and during the work of the fiscal year ended June 30, 1903, they were taken almost exclusively from among the employees in the Department of Agriculture. A full statement of the nature of the experimental work was placed before each candidate, so that no misconception of the character of the life which they were to lead could arise. Among the applicants, the number of which was far greater than could be included in the experiment, a selection was made first with regard to the use of alcoholic beverages. It was deemed advisable, at least in the first series of experiments, to secure volunteers who were not in the habit of using alcoholic beverages of any kind, and in the number selected no one was included who regularly indulged in the use of these beverages. Respecting the use of tobacco a more liberal policy was pursued. No one was selected, however, who used tobacco to excess, and among the few candidates who did use it those were taken who agreed that during the progress of the experiments they would use tobacco regularly, in constant quantities, at regular hours, and continue to use the same kind during the whole period. Thus, any possible disturbance which might be due to the tobacco would be eliminated, as such disturbance would be a constant one, pervading all periods of the experimental work.

In the conduct of this work it was also fully realized that the difficulty of controlling so large a number of individuals by any system of espionage was insurmountable. Young men, therefore, of reliable character were taken and were placed upon their honor to observe rigidly all the rules established for the conduct of the work. The candidates signed an agreement to follow explicitly the rules and regulations governing the hygienic table during their attendance thereon. While at the table of observation they agreed to use no food nor drink other than that provided, with the exception of water, and any water drunk away from the table was to be measured and reported daily as a part of the ration. They further agreed to continue as members of the hygienic table for a period of at least six months from December 1, 1902, unless prevented by illness, accident, or other unavoidable circumstance. The regulations specified that regular habits of life were to be pursued, no unusual exercise or labor indulged in, and if tobacco were used it was to be in such quantities and at such times as the subject and the chief of the Bureau of Chemistry should agree upon. It was also agreed that neither the Department of Agriculture nor any person connected therewith should be held responsible for any illness or accident that might befall the subject during his connection with the hygienic table. At the completion of each experimental period, in retiring from the observation table and passing to the recreation table, each member was required to sign a form certifying that he had fulfilled these requirements in every particular and had to the best of his ability recorded accurately the data relating to weight, temperature, pulse, and all items of food and drink received.

This feature of the work was undertaken with the full knowledge that any violation of these pledges on the part of a subject under examination would introduce very misleading data into the results. It is evident, however, that any marked variation from the schedule of life laid down for each one of the young men under observation would reveal itself in such a way in the analytical data as to attract attention, and even to arouse suspicion. Thus, the analytical data obtained from the foods eaten and from the excretions of the body constituted a reasonably reliable check upon the honesty of the individual and the fidelity with which he observed the regulations imposed.

Features of the Experiments

The food of each member of the class was weighed or measured. The liquids, such as coffee, milk, tea, and water, were measured, and their weights calculated from the density of the solutions. Samples were taken of each kind of food served with each meal, in order that a complete chemical control of the food supply might be secured. The sample of food, immediately after being taken, was placed in a bottle, stoppered, and sealed with melted paraffin, so that no moisture could escape from the sample during the necessary interval of time before the analysis could be accomplished. In the same manner the excreta from each member were carefully collected, weighed, and subjected to analytical study. In the collection of these excreta in the way described there is necessarily a small percentage of loss; it is fair, however, to presume that such losses would be uniformly distributed throughout the whole of the observation period, and that the errors would be both of a plus and minus nature, and therefore mutually compensatory throughout a long period of time.

By this system of analysis it may be said that an account was opened with each individual, who was charged with all that he received and credited with all received from him, the difference being credited to profit and loss. There are some elements of the food which are practically all secured in the excreta after having passed through the functional activity in the body for which they are particularly designed. It may occur as an objection to this form of experiment that the excreta which are secured in any one day or few days do not represent the actual foods which have been consumed in that time in their entirety. This objection is without doubt well taken. For instance, the nitrogen recovered to-day may have entered the body many days, or even weeks, previously in the food; and the same is true of the phosphoric acid. But, in point of fact, in the equilibrium which is found to exist in the healthy body, the quantity of nitrogen or phosphoric acid excreted in a given day represents very accurately the amount ingested. For instance, if one were to take a long tube filled with marbles and put another marble in at one end, one is forced out at the other end, and thus the equilibrium is restored. So in a body in a state of equilibrium, if 15 grams of nitrogen are ingested in the food an equivalent quantity is excreted.

An accurate record was kept of the temperature of the body ascertained by a standardized clinical thermometer before and after dinner. The weight of the body was determined each day by use of a delicate balance, which would easily indicate a difference of 10 grams when weighted with a man of ordinary size. A record of the pulse was also made twice a day, and any variations from the ordinary functional activities of the body carefully noted.

Periods of the Experimental Work

The experimental work in each case was divided into three periods — a fore, a middle, and an after period. During the fore period, by experimental determination there was ascertained the quantity of a well-balanced ration which would maintain the body in a state of practical equilibrium, so that there was but little, if any, gain or loss of weight. The quantity of the ration having thus been determined during a period usually of about ten days, the subject was required to live upon that exact ration during the remaining two periods.

During the middle period there was added to the food a given quantity of a preservative. During the first year the preservatives employed were borax and boracic acid. The middle period was divided into subperiods of about five days. The amount of preservative used at first was small, and was then increaseduntil practically the limit of toleration was reached — that is, until a quantity was given which manifestly produced discomfort, distressing symptoms, or positive illness. The effects of this substance upon the digestive process were carefully noted by the changes which took place in the proportions of the elements of ingested food and of the excretions.

After the middle period, which ranged from fifteen to sixty days, the members of the class entered upon the after period, during which time the same quantity of food was given, with, however, the omission of the preservative. The object of the after period was to restore the body, at least partially, if the equilibrium had been disturbed, to the state of equilibrium in which it was found at the time the middle period began. Thus, each subject at the end of all the periods, if possible, was left in practically the same state of health in which he was at its beginning. All the data obtained in this way, therefore, became valuable in determining even minute effects produced upon digestion, health, and the general metabolic processes.

Dietary of the Class

In the following table are shown the character and amount of foods eaten by the members of the experimental class during a part of one period. The table illustrates not only the variations in the amount of foods which are eaten, but also the fact that the bodily weight is not always an index of the amount of food consumed, though, in general, the larger the bodily weight the greater the amount of food required for its proper sustenance.

Amount of food consumed daily in relation to weight of subject

[January 28 to 31, 1 gram borax per diem.]

NUMBER ONE

Date	Weight of subject	Soup	Fish	Meat	Vege-tables	Cereals	Bread	Butter
1903.	Kilos.	Grams.	Grams.	Grams.	Grams.	Grams.	Grams.	Grams.
January 28........................	56.46	165	.....	140	300	125	300	75
January 29........................	56.60	170	.....	150	175	30	271	90
January 30........................	56.57	207	187	.....	300	100	238	75
January 31........................	56.12	200	.....	150	300	30	254	60
Average	56.44	186	187	147	269	71	266	75
Total......................	.....	742	187	440	1,079	285	1,063	300
Ratio......................	.....	1.31	0.331	0.780	1.90	0.505	1.88	0.532

Date	Weight of subject	Sugar	Water	Tea	Coffee	Milk	Dessert	Total weight of food
1903.	Kilos.	Grams.	Grams.	Grams.	Grams.	Grams.	Grams.	Grams.
January 28.........................	56.46	10	300	.....	450	1,135	200	.....
January 29.........................	56.60	10	500	.....	450	1,032	200	.....
January 30.........................	56.57	10	.....	.....	450	826	200	.....
January 31.........................	56.12	.....	700	.....	450	826	200	.....
Average...................	56.44	10	500	.....	450	955	200	.....
Total.......................	.....	30	1,500	.....	1,800	3,819	800	12,041
Ratio......................	.....	0.053	2.66	.....	3.19	6.77	1.42	21.33

The following table shows the same relation between the phosphoric acid ingested and that secured in the excreta:

Phosphoric acid balance, subject No. 9

PRELIMINARY PERIOD

Date	In food	In feces	In urine	In feces and urine	Balance	Total eliminated
	Grams.	Grams.	Grams.	Grams.	Grams.	Per cent.
February 10 to 27	30.35	8.066	19.44	27.50	+2.85	90.6

PRESERVATIVE PERIOD

Date	In food	In feces	In urine	In feces and urine	Balance	Total eliminated
February 28 to March 3..............	10.93	2.505	7.66	10.17	+0.76	93.0
March 4 to 7..........................	14.51	3.613	9.30	12.91	+1.60	89.0
March 8 to 11.........................	12.83	3.064	9.24	12.31	+ .52	95.9
February 28 to March 11 ...	38.27	9.182	26.20	35.39	+2.88	92.5

AFTER PERIOD

Date	In food	In feces	In urine	In feces and urine	Balance	Total eliminated
March 12 to March 19	26.02	6.665	14.29	20.91	+5.11	80.4

The above tables are given only as samples to show the character of the chemical work involved in the study of so complicated a problem. It is evident, however, that even though the problem is complicated and difficult of attack and solution, we must rely upon investigations of this kind to reach decisions of a practical character on which the policy of the official in charge of the inspection of food products may be based.

Conclusions

The detailed discussion of the data obtained in this experiment, together with the conclusions derived therefrom, will be found in a bulletin of the Bureau of Chemistry soon to be issued. Some of the more salient points, however, which are brought out by the experiment may be mentioned:

(1) The addition of small quantities of borax or boracic acid to the food of healthy subjects, even for a considerable period, extending in some cases to fifty days, produces a slight disturbance in the digestion and assimilation of the food.

(2) In larger quantities the effect produced upon different individuals varies. In some cases large quantities are tolerated with apparently little inconvenience, while in other cases, when the amount given daily reaches 2 or 3 grams, somewhat profound disturbances of normal conditions are developed. These disturbances are manifested by a feeling of depression and discomfort, attended very frequently by a dull and continued headache, with a sense of fullness in the head. In no instance, even when large doses were administered, did either borax or boracic acid produce any pronounced symptoms of diarrhea or diuresis.

(3) When pushed to the limit of toleration the quantities of the borax or boracic acid which produce nausea, vomiting, and loss of appetite vary greatly with the individual. In some cases these symptoms were produced by from 3 to 4 grams daily, while in other instances these quantities could be tolerated.

(4) The elimination of the added borax or boracic acid is accomplished mostly through the kidneys. The merest traces of the ingested substances are found in the feces, and considerable quantities in the perspiration.

(5) The effect of the added preservatives upon the metabolic processes is of such a character as to be properly discussed only in connection with the analytical data relating thereto, and this discussion will be found in the proposed bulletin.

(6) By reason of the different degrees of susceptibility to the influences of these added substances manifested by different individuals, it is evident that it is impossible to foretell in any given case what effect may be expected. For this reason the protection of those more sensitive to the influences of these preservatives seems to be a wise and just measure. Hence, without concluding from this experiment that the use of boracic acid and borax in food products should be absolutely prohibited, it is evident that if they are employed proper notice of the fact should be given to the consumer, either on the labels of the packages or otherwise.

Experiments with Silk Culture, 1903

From L. O. Howard, "The United States Department of Agriculture and Silk Culture," U.S. Department of Agriculture, *Yearbook*, 1903, (Washington, 1904), pp. 137–48.

Early Silk Culture in the United States

Silk culture was carried on to some extent by the early colonists of Virginia, South Carolina, and Georgia. Some reeling was done upon hand reels, and both reeled silk and cocoons were exported to Europe. Silk culture is said to have been introduced into New England about the year 1660 by a Mr. Aspinwall, who had nurseries of the mulberry at New Haven and on Long Island. Some trees were transplanted in Mansfield, Conn., and Mr. Aspinwall furnished the inhabitants of that town with the eggs of the silkworm. Reverend Doctor Styles, an early president of Yale College, aided Mr. Aspinwall in his efforts to introduce the culture in

Connecticut. The progress of the work was arrested by the war of the Revolution. Silk culture was also begun in Pennsylvania and New Jersey in 1771, and here also was interrupted by the Revolutionary War, but it was partly revived after the treaty of peace. A few people retained their interest in the industry during the early part of the nineteenth century, and in the late twenties a resolution was introduced into the House of Representatives directing the compilation of a manual on the culture of silk. House Document No. 226 of the Twentieth Congress, first session (1828), is a treatise on the rearing of silkworms, by Mr. De Hazzi, of Munich, translated from the German apparently by Mr. James Mease, of Washington, D.C. This seems to have been the first Congressional action favoring silk culture. In 1831 the house of representatives of the State of Massachusetts investigated the possibility of silk culture in that Commonwealth, and by resolution of February 24, 1831, the governor was requested to have compiled and printed "a concise manual to contain the best information respecting the growth of the mulberry tree, with suitable directions for the culture of silk," and directing that the manual be distributed in suitable numbers in the city of Boston and in every town of the Commonwealth, the expense not to exceed $600. Later an additional number of copies was purchased, and the Congress of the United States passed a resolution to purchase 2,000 copies for distribution by members. The result was a manual by J. H. Cobb, published in Boston in 1831 (new edition, 1833).

The Morus Multicaulis Craze

Following the publication of the book mentioned there began a determined effort to establish silk culture on a firm basis in the United States. It was estimated that 4 tons of silk cocoons were produced in 1833 in the county of Windham, Conn. Individuals in Massachusetts were said to have cultivated it with success for thirty years. This interest in silk culture soon passed beyond bounds, and there originated what is known as the *Morus multicaulis* craze. Anticipating a most profitable investment, if not speedy riches, thousands of individuals purchased mulberry plants of the Multicaulis species and planted large areas of valuable land. The investments far exceeded possible returns; heavy frosts destroyed the plantations of trees, and in the course of a few years the many failures and great disappointments caused so complete a revulsion of feeling that not only was silk culture practically abandoned all through the States, but the very name became a byword.

The Silk Industry in California

Ten years or more after the discovery of gold in California had attracted many thousands of people to that State, and at a time when its extraordinary agricultural prospects were first beginning to be exploited, the silk industry began to raise its head there. Near San Jose, in 1861, a Frenchman named L. Prevost, having begun the propagation of the mulberry, succeeded in raising excellent cocoons. In the transactions of the State Agricultural Society for 1864–65, Mr. Prevost published a short article on silk culture in California, in which he showed that his first plantings were made in 1853 or 1854, and that he had induced two ladies, named A. Packard and E. Goux, of Santa Barbara, to start a plantation of 3,000 trees, with the result that in 1864 they raised 5 pounds of silkworm eggs. Plantations had also been made in the San Joaquin Valley, and 50,000 trees had been set out near central

Utah. The profits anticipated by Mr. Prevost were largely in the sale of eggs, and he stated that he had received orders from Italy for 100 pounds and from Mexico for 500 ounces.

In 1865 the legislature of California offered a bounty for the production of mulberry trees and silk cocoons, and in the transactions of the State Agricultural Society for 1866–67 it was stated that the liberal action of the legislature and the success which attended the production of mulberry trees and silk cocoons had induced the starting of a very extensive factory at San Jose. The statement was made that the necessary machinery had been purchased and imported.

In the report of the U.S. Department of Agriculture for 1878, Prof. E. W. Hilgard showed that in spite of its favorable beginning, silk culture was almost extinct in California in 1877. He called the interest which existed in the sixties a mania, stating that it raged with unabated fury for several years, inflicting severe losses upon those who indulged in the popular delusion that the silkworm would thrive in the State without any precautions as to shelter and such intelligent care as could be given only by those versed in its treatment. "Some of the airy sheds that were supposed to be an adequate protection against the comparatively slight changes of temperature are still extant as monuments of that flush period when mulberry trees were thought to be the only nursery stock worth having."

After the subsidence of the craze silk culture was kept up on a small scale at San Francisco by Mr. J. Neumann for many years.

Efforts to Stimulate the Industry

When, in June, 1878, Prof. C. V. Riley was appointed Entomologist of the U.S. Department of Agriculture, he brought with him from Missouri a strong interest in silk culture and a conviction that this industry could be established in the United States. During his first year in office he published a manual of instructions in the culture of the silkworm. In the same year at the St. Louis meeting of the American Association for the Advancement of Science, under the title "A new source of wealth to the United States," he presented a paper, largely statistical, with tables of exports and imports of raw and manufactured silks for the previous half century, bringing out the steady growth of the manufacturing industry of the country. He showed that the failure of the attempts in California was largely due to the extravagant statements and excessive enthusiasm, verging on fanaticism, which characterized all of the writings of L. Prevost. He said: "Had he been as prone to report failure as he was to magnify success there would not have been a reactive depression which was as unnatural as over-enthusiasm." He stated that Monsieur Prevost's little work, "California silk grower's manual," was better calculated to produce another Multicaulis craze than to healthily stimulate the silk industry. Its extravagant statements and immoderate pictures earned for its author the name *blagueur*, which had been applied to him in France. Professor Riley showed that M. E. V. Boissière, a silk grower in Kansas, had established an important silk colony, whose efforts were intelligent, but that the industry lagged there for the reason that it was found less profitable than stock raising and general farming. It was further shown that several bales of cocoons had been shipped by E. Fasnach from Raleigh, N.C., to Marseilles, for $3 freight per 100 pounds. The bales, 6 by 5 feet in size, averaged about 40 pounds of stifled cocoons, and brought, in 1876, $2.50 per pound. Brokers in New York in this period offered $1.75 to $2 per pound for cocoons. This was the period of silk-culture depression in France, owing to the ravages of the silkworm disease known as pébrine. Cocoons commanded a very high price, and silk raisers in America — notably Mr. L. S. Crozier, then of Kansas and afterward of Louisiana — found it more profitable to raise eggs for export than to raise cocoons. Professor Riley also showed that the experiments of the past, and those which he had been carrying on, established the fact that the climate of the larger part of the United States is admirably adapted to silk culture, and that experience had shown that in the past the culture had failed largely because of the want of a market. The great need was the establishment of filatures or reeling factories. All attempts to stimulate the industry unduly are hurtful. He urged that each State should not only encourage the culture of silk, but offer a bounty of say 50 cents or $1 per pound for the choked cocoons, and $1 or $1.50 per pound for reeled silk. He further showed that the native osage orange makes excellent silkworm food.

Silk Culture by the Department of Agriculture

Holding the above views, it was quite natural that Professor Riley should immediately endeavor to interest the head of the Department of Agriculture in the subject of silk culture, and through him to interest Congress; but in the spring of 1879 he severed his connection with the Department and was succeeded by Prof. J. H. Comstock, who held the office for two years. In 1879 the Department made a number of experiments on the feeding of silkworms, and a few eggs were sent out to correspondents. In 1880 Commissioner Le Duc urged in his report to the President that the attention of Congress be called to the importance of affording Government aid to the industry, which should last at least long enough to educate the people to the work. He cited England's bounties for useful inventions and almost lavish expenditures to build up such industries as tea, cotton, and sugar in her colonies, as well as the aid given by France and Germany to the sugar-beet and other industries. During that year the Department ordered silkworm eggs from Japan, but the supply arrived late in the winter, and owing to the heat experienced at some period of the journey they had all hatched upon arrival, so that none were sent out to correspondents that year.

In 1881 Hon. George B. Loring, of Massachusetts, was made Commissioner of Agriculture, and Professor Riley returned to office.

In 1882 trees were sent out to correspondents of the Department, and the report was made that among the Mennonites in one of the Western States mulberry trees had been planted in thick hedges at the limits of the fields and both sides of the highways and byways. The trees were cut down one-third at a time every three years, furnishing an abundant supply of fuel and also serving as windbreaks. These people had almost 20,000 pounds of cocoons on hand for sale.

In 1883 the State of California established a State board of silk culture at San Francisco, and the board offered premiums to the amount of $150 for the best cocoons raised in the State.

During the winter of 1883–84 the interest in the subject was so strong that Congress appropriated $15,000 to the Department of Agriculture for the encouragement and development of the industry. A special agent, Mr. Philip Walker, was appointed, who, under the direction of the Entomologist, devoted his whole time to the investigation of all subjects relating to the culture of the silkworm and the raising of raw silk.

Professor Riley stated in his report for 1884 that he had studied the status of the industry in southern France during the previous summer and was surprised to find it languishing on account of inability to compete with the silk produced by the cheaper labor of other countries. Professor Riley said: "If the French silk grower can not well cope with this competition with the price of ordinary labor at 3 francs for men and 1½ francs for women how can we expect to?" Our chief hope he considered to lie in the natural advantages which America possesses and in the Serrell automatic reeling machine, which he thought might revolutionize the silk industry and greatly subordinate the question of labor.

Progress of Experiments

In the spring of 1885 some 8,000 mulberry trees were distributed, as well as a quantity of silkworm eggs. No cocoons were bought by the Department, but examinations were made of home-raised eggs. Two stations had been established after the Congressional appropriation became available — one at Philadelphia and the other at New Orleans. At Philadelphia 518 pounds of cocoons were reeled, producing 96 pounds of raw silk. The quality of the cocoons handled was thus shown to be very bad. They cost on the average 85 cents per pound, so that the raw material used in the production of a pound of raw silk cost $4.58. The raw silk produced was sold for $4.40 per pound, by which it was shown that the cost of the raw material was greater than the value of the manufactured product. This result was laid to the inexperience of the raisers.

At the New Orleans station the filature was run from the 15th of April until the 31st of August; 3,360 pounds of cocoons were purchased, at an average of $1 per pound. From 2,710 pounds were produced 641 pounds of reeled silk, an average of 4.23 pounds of cocoons to 1 pound of silk. This showed a much better grade of cocoons than at Philadelphia. The average cost of the raw silk, however, including labor, was $5.90 per pound.

The California work during this year was reorganized, and there was reeled at San Francisco 44 pounds of silk. An effort was made during the winter of 1884–85 by Mr. Joseph Neumann and some others to launch the "California Silk Culture Development Company," with a capital of $100,000, but the attempt was a failure.

It appears from the records that the appropriations given to the Department by Congress were expended during the fiscal year 1884–85 in support of the stations at Philadelphia and New Orleans and in the distribution of mulberry trees and eggs.

For the fiscal year 1885–86 Congress again appropriated $15,000. The reeling establishments in San Francisco, New Orleans, and Philadelphia were abandoned toward the close of the fiscal year. Silkworm eggs were distributed in the spring of 1886; circulars were sent out all over the country offering to purchase cocoons, and at the beginning of the fiscal year 1886–87 a Serrell automatic reel was set up under a new appropriation from Congress. Two Italian reelers were employed, and five American girls were instructed in the art of reeling. The result of this experience was to indicate a daily loss of $2.79, or approximately $1.50 per pound of silk produced, not including interest on capital invested or the cost of superintendence. The labor, however, was inexperienced, and improvements were possible in the machine, which were actually made at a later date. An effort was made during 1886 to ascertain the amount of the cocoons produced in the United States during that year. There were purchased at the Washington filature 1,313 pounds 15 ounces, valued at $1,272.04, and by the Women's Silk Culture Association at Philadelphia 3,081 pounds 9 ounces, valued at $2,720.88, making a total of 5,115 pounds 8 ounces, for which was paid $3,982.96, or nearly 78 cents per pound. These were obtained from 26 States and Territories.

In the spring of 1887, 150 ounces of eggs were distributed to 360 people, and the cocoon crop of the year was estimated at 6,174 pounds. The results of most of the raisers were very good, many persons having produced at the rate of 120 pounds of fresh cocoons for each ounce of eggs. In the meantime, however, reeling had been going on throughout the winter, beginning with October 30, 1886, and continuing at intervals until August 13, 1887. During this period 1,057 pounds of dried cocoons were consumed in the production of 263 pounds of reeled silk and 81⅔ pounds of waste. The quality of the cocoons was better than the previous year. The raw silk produced at the Washington filature during 1887 was sold for $864.81. During this same year the Kansas legislature, having established a station at Peabody, Kans., a filature of eight basins was started and information regarding the industry was disseminated throughout the State.

In the spring of 1888, again, 150 ounces of eggs were distributed, this time to 1,037 people, and the dried cocoon crop of the year was estimated at 3,913 pounds.

In 1887, 60 persons had received more than $10 each for their season's work, while 9 persons received more than $40 each. In 1888, however, only 48 persons received more than $10 each, and no one was paid as much as $40. In 1887 the average price paid for each lot of cocoons was $7.81, and in 1888 it was $4.53. The Kansas State commission continued its work at Peabody and made material purchases of cocoons, but was cramped financially. The Silk Culture Association at Philadelphia, working under an appropriation of $5,000, continued the purchase of cocoons and reeling, and distributed over 5,000 mulberry trees. The California society received an appropriation of $2,500. The sales of raw silk as the result of the work of the Washington filature during the fiscal year ending June 30, 1888, amounted to $1,889.60. In the spring of 1889, 575 ounces of eggs were distributed, and the dried cocoon crop of the year was estimated at 6,248 pounds, amounting in fresh cocoons to 18,744 pounds. Of these, 11,805 pounds were purchased at the Washington filature, 3,002 at Philadelphia, and 3,936 at Peabody, Kans.

Mr. Walker, special agent of the Department, visited certain of the Western States and established stations for the purchase of fresh cocoons at St. Louis and at Newton, Kans.

In 1890, 800 ounces of eggs were distributed to 2,250 people, and the cocoon crop of the year was estimated at 16,953 pounds of fresh cocoons. During the fiscal year ending June 30, 1889, the Washington filature had sold raw silk of the value of $708.26, and during the fiscal year ending June 30, 1890, it sold $1,627.81 worth of raw silk.

Constant improvements had been made in the Serrell silk reel, both by Mr. Serrell in France and by Mr. Walker in Washington. Toward the close of 1889 Mr. Serrell had abandoned his experiments. Mr. Walker, while not abandoning the idea that ultimately an automatic silk reel could be perfected, was beginning by this time to show some discouragement in the possibility of establishing the industry.

Discontinuance of Appropriations and Investigations

The last appropriation made by Congress was $20,000 for the fiscal year ending June 30, 1891. An estimate for a continuance of this appropriation was made by the then Secretary of Agriculture, but the appropriation was not made by Congress, and the work of the Department in silk culture ceased for the time (June 30, 1891).

From that time on very little was done in the United States in the way of raising silkworms. The Utah people formed, during the nineties, a ladies' silk association. Five persons served as commissioners, and received pay from the State. In various parts of Utah, settled by the Mormons, an abundance of white mulberry trees had been planted. The new commission bought every year a supply of eggs, which were distributed in small lots among the Mormon settlers. In the course of time a number of women were selected from among the more skilled silk growers to go from place to place and teach the reeling of silk to children. They received no salary, and their only compensation was free board from the farmers. The reeled silk was for a time sold in New York, but later the market was closed. In the meantime a small silk factory sprang up in Salt Lake City, which, in time, bought a small proportion of the silk produced in Utah. The cocoons were reeled upon hand reels built according to Japanese models, and a part of the raw silk was woven by the people themselves. Silk dyeing was not attempted, but the silk was sent to New York for that purpose.

Resumption of Silk Investigations by Department of Agriculture

In 1901 the present Secretary of Agriculture, who had been traveling extensively throughout the country, and particularly in the South, investigating agricultural conditions and possibilities, came to the conclusion that every possible effort should be made to ameliorate the condition of the extremely poor people of the Southern States, and particularly of the colored race. Among the many ideas which suggested themselves to him was that of silk culture, which he very well knew was a household industry in other countries and added materially, not only to the national wealth and prosperity of those countries in which it was carried on, but also to the family incomes of the extremely poor. He therefore, during the following session of Congress, asked for an appropriation of $10,000 for investigations in silk culture, which was allowed.

Purpose of the Present Investigations

The appropriation became available July 1, 1902, and the investigation was assigned to the Division of Entomology. The writer had been connected with the earlier work of the Department through his official position as first assistant entomologist, and was therefore thoroughly familiar with the conditions existing in the country, with the culture of silkworms, and with the difficulties in the way of establishing the industry. He realized the fact that practically no market for cocoons existed in the United States. He realized further that without such a market there is no inducement to create the supply. He realized also the practical impossibility of inducing the establishment of filatures without a guaranteed supply of cocoons. It seemed to him, therefore (and in all steps taken he has received the advice and approval of the Secretary of Agriculture), that the first step was to secure the planting of a sufficient number of mulberry trees in advantageous locations to feed the worms necessary to produce a commercial crop of cocoons; and further, to bring about the education of a sufficient number of people in the best methods of silk culture to guarantee a crop of high grade.

The first efforts of the Department were therefore directed, and are still being directed, to these ends. Large quantities of white mulberries grow here and there throughout the United States — some of them direct descendants from the Multicaulis cuttings set out in the early thirties, others planted more or less by accident, and still others resulting from the efforts made by the Department in the eighties. The seeds of fruit from these old trees, discharged here and there by birds, have given rise in many places to great numbers of young mulberry trees. Mulberry bushes or scrub will be found growing at many points, particularly through the South. The trees in existence, however, have not been pruned or cultivated according to European methods, and can not be used to the very best advantage; yet there was a sufficient quantity of the mulberry trees already growing to raise a very large quantity of cocoons. Miss Henrietta Aiken Kelly, of Charleston, S.C., who had spent several years in France, Switzerland, and Italy studying scientific silk culture, including the care of the mulberry, raising the worms, and microscopic examination of the moths, according to the most approved Pasteur methods, for the purpose of detecting disease, was employed as silk-culture expert; her first work was the preparation of a manual giving simple but sound instructions for the raising of the worms. Mr. George W. Oliver, an expert horticulturist connected with the Bureau of Plant Industry, prepared a manual for growers of silkworm food plants, indicating the methods of caring for and cultivating the different varieties of mulberry. These manuals were printed and distributed widely during the winter of 1902–1903.

* * *

Purchase of Domestic Cocoons by the Department

All of the correspondents to whom silkworm eggs were sent in the spring were notified that the Department would buy their cocoons at European market prices, and several hundred pounds were purchased in this way and were reeled during the summer. The raw silk thus produced, while excellent in quality, has not been large in quantity, and of course the expense of production has been prohibitive from a commercial point of view. It is the object of the Department in thus purchasing domestic cocoons to create what might be termed an artificial market for a time, in order to interest individuals throughout the country in learning the art of silk raising, to stimulate efforts in the production of the best possible cocoons (since the prices paid are graded), and to keep alive the interest, so far as possible, until the time comes when other and more natural markets shall be supplied.

From the experience of the Department in its early work and in the work of the past year and a half, it is plain that it is an easy matter to arouse an interest in silk culture. There are thousands of people in the United States who are eager to learn of some means of increasing their income by ever so slight an amount. It is not easy, however, to prevent the growth of extravagant ideas regarding the profits of silk culture. The majority of the people who write the Department about it have exaggerated ideas. Of those who begin the culture of the worm, many are so much disappointed by the meager sums which they receive from even the artificial market established by the Department that they abandon the work. Very many others, however, seem satisfied and interested, and at the present European market prices for cocoons it seems perfectly sure that enough people in the United States would take up silk culture and retain their interest in it to assure a very large annual crop.

The Prospects for the Silk Industry

The Department, therefore, is justified in its initiatory effort to create the conditions for a constant supply of cocoons. It can keep up its reeling work and thus keep open practically the only market existing at present for a period which must be determined by the will of Congress. The outlook for what we have termed a more natural market is problematical. People interested in the promotion of silk culture are very hopeful, but advance few definite ideas. People interested in the manufacture of silk are pessimistic to the last degree. The vice-president of one of the large Eastern silk factories is reported to have said recently in southern California that if a warehouse full of cocoons were presented to him he could not afford to reel them at the present market price of raw silk. There is no doubt in the mind of the writer that this is an extreme and exaggerated statement. The work of the Department in the eighties with the improved Serrell automatic reel, it is true, indicated a rather serious loss in the reeling operation, but the reel used was one of only six basins, and it is a well-understood fact in European reeling centers that an establishment of less than twenty-eight basins can not expect to pay running expenses. Economies enter into the administration of large establishments which vitally affect the question of profits. There are many portions of the United States well adapted to silk raising, many places which might well become silk centers, where labor can be employed practically at rates comparable to those of southern Europe. The establishment of a silk mill in such a location, with its own filature attached, with the surrounding people employed as operatives in both filature and mills, and with the otherwise unoccupied members of their households engaged in silk raising in the spring, is feasible, and can be made to pay. A beginning of this kind may possibly soon be made by foreign capital. The proprietor of a large estate in Italy is at present giving the matter serious consideration. A foreign proprietor of a silk establishment in one of our larger Northern cities states that he can count upon the employment of 5,000 of his compatriots more or less skilled in the silk industry at an average daily wage of from 20 to 25 cents. He himself would enter upon such an enterprise with an assured crop of cocoons.

That in some of these ways the natural market will come seems possible, and even more than possible. What the success of silk culture would mean to the United States is indicated by the following table, which shows the importations of raw silk into the United States during the years 1892 to 1902:

Importation of raw silk (as reeled from the cocoon), 1892–1902.[1]

QUANTITY

Countries from which imported.	1892	1893	1894	1895	1896	1897
	Pounds.	*Pounds.*	*Pounds.*	*Pounds.*	*Pounds.*	*Pounds.*
France.............................	319,673	307,872	210,813	365,986	381,749	233,005
Germany..........................	2,681	......	......	220	1,311	3,818
Italy	1,275,274	1,482,444	886,328	1,354,478	1,116,239	865,972
Switzerland......................	662	2,406	......	......	22	......
Turkey in Europe	4,997	7,101	......	935	221	5
United Kingdom	7,592	34,392	3,165	13,953	18,317	1,373
Bermuda..........................	......	90	......	......	......	......
Dominion of Canada (Quebec, Ontario, Manitoba, etc.)	1,195	687	47	......	12,477	......
Chinese Empire	1,845,555	1,880,242	1,198,304	2,419,128	2,315,873	1,907,892
East Indies–British............	921	9,509	13,830	1,463	1,352	......
Hongkong	......	......	......	30,476	201,680	26,682
Japan..............................	4,062,362	3,697,675	2,644,388	3,788,171	3,951,380	3,474,865
Turkey in Asia	430	12	......	......	......	......
Total	7,521,342	7,422,430	4,956,875	7,974,810	8,000,621	6,513,612

Countries from which imported	1898	1899	1900	1901	1902
	Pounds.	*Pounds.*	*Pounds.*	*Pounds.*	*Pounds.*
France	339,934	330,248	356,145	322,718	550,566
Germany	....	285	3,022	560	7,622
Italy	1,743,543	2,251,216	2,217,879	1,832,584	2,567,752
Switzerland	3,722	1,320	8,651	402	3,900
Turkey in Europe...............	....	....	....	....	11
United Kingdom.................	552	244	5,532	2,747	370
Bermuda...........................	....	....	....	....	....
Dominion of Canada (Quebec, Ontario, Manitoba, etc.)	16,252	4,699	36,462	18,713	256,703
Chinese Empire..................	2,916,549	2,512,299	3,854,657	2,290,680	3,027,608
East Indies–British	151	149	6,951	13,102	8,295
Hongkong.........................	30	75,569	4,920	....	....
Japan...............................	5,294,429	4,515,116	4,765,091	4,658,111	6,197,795
Turkey in Asia...................	....	....	....	....	60
Total	10,315,162	9,691,145	11,259,310	9,139,617	12,620,682

[1] Treasury Department, Bureau of Statistics, Report on Commerce and Navigation for 1902, Vol.II, pp.228, 229.

Countries from which imported	1892	1893	1894	1895	1896	1897
	Dollars.	*Dollars.*	*Dollars.*	*Dollars.*	*Dollars.*	*Dollars.*
France	1,154,087	1,383,377	840,338	1,235,815	1,465,405	751,846
Germany	10,582	....	....	350	4,928	13,991
Italy	4,912,495	7,303,239	3,628,864	4,899,330	4,587,761	3,019,515
Switzerland	2,088	12,932	....	....	68	....
Turkey in Europe	17,023	26,173	....	2,683	660	16
United Kingdom	12,434	84,716	6,083	39,527	59,109	5,550
Bermuda	....	195	....	....	....	....
Dominion of Canada (Quebec, Ontario, Manitoba, etc.)	4,510	3,741	281	....	43,141	....
Chinese Empire	5,087,858	5,427,531	3,087,749	5,511,960	6,622,692	4,642,457
East Indies–British	2,323	29,159	39,764	2,993	3,734	....
Hongkong	....	....	....	51,612	540,814	52,684
Japan	13,116,579	14,784,432	8,024,743	10,284,798	12,918,590	10,010,885
Turkey in Asia	1,515	62	....	....	....	....
Total	24,321,494	29,055,557	15,627,822	22,029,068	26,246,902	18,496,944

Countries from which imported	1898	1899	1900	1901	1902
	Dollars.	*Dollars.*	*Dollars.*	*Dollars.*	*Dollars.*
France	1,192,058	1,248,037	1,607,569	1,220,874	1,866,202
Germany	....	1,101	19,480	2,386	29,106
Italy	6,227,004	8,929,776	10,816,084	7,151,438	9,954,501
Switzerland	9,194	4,133	40,950	681	17,422
Turkey in Europe	....	....	....	....	38
United Kingdom	1,752	956	7,301	9,763	1,421
Bermuda	....	....	....	....	....
Dominion of Canada (Quebec, Ontario, Manitoba, etc.)	56,468	18,296	157,161	60,109	807,706
Chinese Empire	7,506,409	6,497,983	12,171,309	6,303,523	8,308,383
East Indies–British	389	476	24,659	33,456	27,190
Hongkong	120	205,516	17,027	....	....
Japan	15,453,406	14,920,787	19,686,132	14,571,547	20,702,101
Turkey in Asia	....	....	....	....	261
Total	31,446,800	31,827,061	44,549,672	29,353,777	41,714,331

Boys' Agricultural Clubs, 1904

From Dick J. Crosby, "Boys' Agricultural Clubs," U.S. Department of Agriculture, *Yearbook* (Washington, 1905), pp. 489-96.

The Corn Exhibit at the St. Louis Exposition.

"Grown by the farmer boys of Illinois!" "Eight thousand farmer boys in contest!"

All summer long these two legends surmounted two large pyramids of pure-bred corn at the Louisiana Purchase Exposition — pyramids made up of 1,000 little pyramids, each containing 10 beautiful ears of white or yellow corn, straight-rowed, symmetrical, uniform. The exhibit was a monument alike to the industry and intelligence of 8,000 Illinois farmer boys and to the energy and resourcefulness of Mr. Will B. Otwell, who had charge of the Illinois agricultural exhibit at St. Louis, and whose helpful work among these boys during the past four or five years made such an exhibit possible. A series of intensely interesting events leads up to this corn-growing contest, but only a brief sketch of them can be given here.

About five years ago the secretary of the Macoupin County (Ill.) Farmers' Institute, who had had some experience in advertising, undertook to get out a large attendance of farmers for the annual institute. He advertised the meeting in 13 county papers and instructed the janitor of the court-house to open the doors early to accommodate the crowd. On the day of the institute the attendance was limited strictly to the president, the secretary, and the chaplain. "And," says the secretary, "the chaplain offered a fervent prayer for the officers of the organization. I tapped him on the shoulder afterwards and told him he would oblige me by praying for the delinquent farmers who were absent; the officers were doing everything in their power."

The next year the secretary changed his tactics. After engaging the services of many noted speakers on subjects of interest to all good farmers, he had a lot of gilt-edged programmes printed. These were mailed, like wedding invitations, in nice square envelopes, to 500 farmers of the county. The day of the institute arrived, the janitor had the doors open early, and about two dozen farmers attended. The officers were disgusted, the president resigned, and the secretary was elected president. The latter, fortunately, was as resourceful as he was persistent, and his next experiment was both original and successful.

He first wrote to leading corn growers in Iowa, Indiana, and Illinois and procured 12 samples of first-class seed corn. He then called 12 farmers into the parlors of a local bank and asked them to select the variety best adapted to the soil of Macoupin County. This done, several bushels of the seed corn were secured at $2 per bushel. The president next solicited $40 in cash and divided it into $1 premiums. A plow company gave a two-horse plow to be offered as a sweepstake premium. Notices were then inserted in the county papers to the effect that every boy under 18 who would send in his name and address would receive a package of this seed corn — all that could be mailed for 1 cent postage. The president says:

Five hundred boys sent for the corn and began contesting for the premiums. All summer long these boys were talking farmers' institutes (where the corn was to be exhibited). They were comparing notes and exchanging ideas until our institute was a topic of general conversation. I decided not to advertise the institute in the papers any more than just to give the dates. The farmers were politely told they could stay away from the institute if they preferred. When I reached the courthouse on the morning of the institute there were scores of boys waiting for the doors to be opened. They had their prize corn with them, some of it in boxes, some of it in coffee sacks, tied up with binder twine, shoe strings, bedcord — any way, just so they got it to the institute. When I called that meeting to order at the appointed time I was confronted by 500 farmers. And Professor Stevenson, of Champaign, who scored the corn, said he had never seen a nicer display of yellow corn. I knew I had solved the problem, and so did the farmers. The boys were in evidence everywhere, and their presence was an inspiration to the institute.

The next year there were 1,500 farmer boys in the contest, and it took $300 to provide the prizes, which consisted of a high-grade bicycle, a three-wheel riding plow, a walking cultivator, a 10-foot windmill, a fanning mill, a double harrow, a 16-inch walking plow, a washing machine, a one-hole corn sheller, a hand plow, 2 rolling colters, a box of 100 bars of soap, and 140 one-dollar premiums.

The summer that followed was a dry one, and the president of the institute was fearful that the contest would not amount to much. But one of the objects for which he was striving had already been accomplished — the farmers of the county were interested. The fathers of the 1,500 boys donated the best spots on their farms for the growing of this corn — the hog lots, calf pastures, clover fields — and all the time the boys were studying deep and shallow cultivation and fertilizers of all kinds, and were becoming more interested in farming, "so that to-day there is a prevailing belief in this county that boys may choose farming as a profession and still be as good as anybody."

When the time for the farmers' institute came there were 1,500 farmers in constant attendance and a display of corn which, according to the judge who distributed the prizes, was finer than any he had ever seen at State fairs in Illinois, Indiana, Kansas, or Iowa. Mr. Otwell says of this meeting:

Farmers who two years before would not attend, and who boldly asserted that "they had forgotten more than those speakers would ever find out," were on the front seat and helping in every possible way. Besides the fathers and mothers and sisters and sweethearts, there were more than 300 farmer boys in attendance at this institute, and with no friction and the utmost enthusiasm and good will, we closed the largest and best farmers' institute I have ever attended. The corn was simply immense. And so were the boys. And when I mentioned the name of the poor little fellow in blue overalls, who lived on a thin, worn-out piece of white land, and who had carried water all through the long summer to water his corn, and had thereby been awarded the first prize (bicycle), no governor of the State of Illinois ever received a heartier ovation than he.

The problem of arousing an interest in farmers' institutes and in the questions discussed at them had been solved. The farmers were reached through their children, and the interest thus aroused will be handed down to their children's children.

When the president of the Macoupin County Farmers' Institute was asked to take charge of the Illinois agricultural exhibit at the Louisiana Purchase Exposition he determined that the farmer boys should take an active part in preparing the display. He got up a list of premiums costing $3,500, printed the premium list and the rules governing the contest, and mailed them to 120,000 farmer boys in Illinois. Eight thousand of these boys sent for the sample packages of corn and went to work.

The exhibit, as it was finally prepared and installed in the Palace of Agriculture, consisted of over 1,000 entries of ten ears each. The corn was of excellent quality and quite uniform in appearance and measurement. The prizes ranged from 50 cents to $500, and 1,250 exhibits received awards.

Eight thousand boys in a single State thoroughly aroused on the subject of improving corn! Think what power has been set in motion! And what possibilities for the accomplishment of good, especially when the interest thus aroused is extended to other matters, to the improvement of rural conditions generally!

Development of Boys' Clubs in Illinois

And yet, the series of corn-growing contests just described is but one of a number in Illinois, all developed more or less directly under the auspices of the State College of Agriculture, the Illinois Farmers' Institute, and the county institute secretaries and county superintendents of schools. Seed has been furnished by the college and the farmers' institute, and contests have been arranged by the local authorities. Packages containing 500 grains of pure-bred corn were sent by the State Farmers' Institute to over 5,400 boys in 1904. The need of local associations through which the county superintendents and secretaries coud work more effectually has led to the organization of clubs among the boys, usually by townships, with a county association of clubs. Probably a dozen different counties have started the club movement, and several of these have strong and very active organizations. In Winnebago County the club membership was 425 in 1904, and in Johnson County it was 535. The State superintendent of farmers' institutes estimates that the total membership for the State is not less than 2,000.

The work of the boys' clubs is not confined to growing pure-bred corn, but also includes the testing of varieties of sugar beets, institute work, the judging of corn, visits to leading farms, and excursions to the State College of Agriculture. In thirty counties of Illinois last year one session of the farmers' institute was given over to the boys. In Winnebago County the Boys' Experiment Club has a regular place on the county institute programme. Its members also meet at some of the best farms in the county to study the different crops, examine the buildings and live stock, and see the improved machinery in operation. Their experiments are something more than the growing of a small plat of corn, sugar beets, or soy beans; they include also the study of farm management, fertility, prevalence of barren stalks and smut — all of the conditions likely to affect materially the yield and quality of the crops grown. Note the points brought out by one of the boys in the corn-growing experiments in the following report to County Superintendent of Schools O. J. Kern, who has developed this work in Winnebago County:

Report of Harry M'Farland

My experimental corn was the Leaming corn. I planted my prize-growing corn on the 7th of May in a plat that contained 3 square rods. The soil was a black, sandy loam. The ground had garden truck on it last year, which left it in good condition for corn this year. The ground was plowed with a 16-inch plow at a depth of 6 inches. I planted my corn in rows 3 feet wide, the hills being 2 feet apart. The corn was up within 3 days and averaged 2 stalks to the hill. My corn had a good many suckers on, but very little smut. The corn averaged 12 feet tall, many stalks having 2 ears on. The work I put on my corn is as follows:

March 30, plowing one-half hour at 30 cents an hour	$0.15
May 6, harrowing one-half hour	.15
May 7, planting one-half hour...	.15
May 20, cultivating 15 minutes	.05
June 3, hoeing corn one-half hour	.10
June 23, cultivating..	.08
June 30, hoeing	.05
September 25, husking corn	.10
Cost of raising corn...	.83

The total yield of corn was 2½ bushels. The value of the corn was $3. The gain was $2.17.

These Winnebago boys also have their lecture courses where, among other things, they learn about corn judging, from Professor Holden, of Iowa; stock feeding, from Professor Henry, of Wisconsin; birds and their benefit to the farmer, from Professor Dearborn, of the Field Columbian Museum; and the kind of country schools for country people, from Professor Davenport, of Illinois. They have access to excellent traveling school libraries, containing a liberal sprinkling of standard agricultural books, and the bulletins and other publications of the State experiment station and of the United States Department of Agriculture, and at commencement time receive diplomas or other certificates for the reading done during the year. They have been on several long excursions, including two to the Illinois College of Agriculture at Urbana, and one to the Iowa Agricultural College at Ames. This year they go to the Wisconsin College of Agriculture at Madison. At these agricultural institutions great pains is taken to show the boys the magnificent equipment in buildings, apparatus, and live stock and to take them over the field experiments. They come home talking intelligently of high-protein corn, draft horses, and market grades of beef cattle. Gradually but surely it grows upon them that it is not all of farming to drudge; that there is abundant opportunity to plan, study, investigate; that intelligence and culture are needed on the farm, and that the proper exercise of these qualities will yield as abundant returns in the country as in the city.

Boy's Clubs in Other States

Illinois is not alone in this forward movement. Iowa, Ohio, and Texas are keeping step with her in the boys' club work, and Indiana and New York have taken up the boys' institute work — the former with 15 meetings last year and the latter with 72. Indeed, it may be said that New York, with its 20,000 or more members of "Junior Naturalist clubs," leads all other States in the children's club movement. But these are nature-study clubs, quite different from agricultural clubs, and they are for girls as well as boys. There are also girls' clubs in these other States — Illinois, Iowa, Ohio, and Texas — but the limits of this article will not permit a discussion of girls' clubs or nature-study clubs.

In Ohio the boys' agricultural club movement was started about two years ago by the organization of a club in Springfield township, Clarke County, under the direction of Superintendent of Schools A. B. Graham. The work at this place does not differ materially from that in Illinois. It includes the testing of varieties of corn, garden vegetables, and flowers, and some work with insects, wild flowers, weeds, and soils. There are now 16 boys' agricultural clubs in 10 counties of Ohio, with a total membership of nearly 700. These have been organized under the auspices of the Ohio State University, which has sent out during the past year 1,012 packages of vegetable seeds, 565 packages of corn, and 1,261 packages of flower seeds, besides a large amount of litmus paper for use in testing the acidity of soils.

The Texas club movement was organized only a little over a year ago in connection with the Texas Farmers' Congress, but the membership of the Farmer Boys and Girls' League is now over 1,200. In Iowa the first club was organized by County Superintendent of Schools Cap E. Miller, at Sigourney, Keokuk County, in March, 1904. This club now has a membership of 335 boys, and its first year has been one of remarkable activity and progress. It has held several meetings, has made several excursions, including one to Ames and another to one of the largest ranches in the State, and it has conducted a series of school fairs that are worthy of brief description.

School Fairs

Early last fall each of the 147 school districts in Keokuk County held a school fair, where the boys exhibited all sorts of fruits, vegetables, and farm crops which they had grown. The best and second best articles of each class were later entered at township fairs — one in each of the 16 townships in the county. In connection with each fair a programme was rendered consisting of talks and papers on corn, potatoes, peanuts, apples, and other fruits and crops, together with recitations and musical selections. All of the township fairs were attended by the county superintendent of schools and the president and the secretary of the boys' club of the county, the latter acting as judge of the agricultural exhibits. The first, second, and third prize articles from each township fair were then exhibited at a county school fair. This was held in the high school building at Sigourney, December 24, and was attended by over 1,000 people. The exhibit contained more than 3,000 articles and was probably the largest collection of varied agricultural products grown by boys ever brought together in this country. Professor Holden and Mr. Christie, of the Iowa Agricultural College, assisted in judging the agricultural products, and the former conducted a corn-judging school in which all of the boys took part. The programme rendered in connection with the fair included music, recitations, a debate on the subject "Resolved, That Corn is more Useful than Cotton," and a composition contest in which each graded school in the county was allowed one representative. The general theme of the compositions was "An Interesting Plant," each contestant presenting a paper on some particular plant. There were 10 compositions on corn, 3 on wheat, 3 on the tomato, and 1 or 2 on each of a dozen other common farm crops or flowers. Superintendent Cap E. Miller, who was the organizer and moving spirit in all this work, says of the fair:

It was the greatest educational meeting ever held in the county. The interest which it created has spread in its influence to all the work of our rural schools and has caused the farmers of our county to organize a farmer's institute.

* * *

The school-fair movement has been self-supporting. By means of a small admission fee all expenses of the fairs and of securing music, judges, and speakers were paid and a balance of about $50 was left in the club treasury. This is a matter of no little importance. A self-supporting enterprise, if worthy, commands greater respect than one which depends upon charity or private subscription for its support. And without doubt this is a worthy enterprise. Aside from the good which has come to its members through their activity in organizing and directing a remarkable series of educational meetings, much has been accomplished toward arousing enthusiasm for better, more wholesome country life, and toward laying the foundation for a broader educational movement along agricultural lines.

Laying the foundation is about all that can be hoped for in this direction during the next few years. It was forty years after the cornerstone of collegiate agricultural education in the United States was laid at the Michigan Agricultural College before the agricultural courses had been carried much above the basement line. But in the past four or five years the structure has gone up by leaps and bounds. The college courses have been developed and strengthened, the work of the experiment stations has been better systematized, and now greater attention is being given to extending the influence of these institutions beyond the bounds of the college campus. One of the direct results of this great forward movement in agricultural education, the aim of which is to extend agricultural education of some sort — formal or informal, advanced, intermediate, or elementary — to every grade of school attended by rural pupils, has been the organization of the boys' agricultural clubs. These clubs, though at present somewhat crude in their organization, are accomplishing much good, and are worthy of encouragement.

Summary

(1) Through their agricultural clubs the boys have been affected in many ways. Individually they have been led to observe more closely, to recognize good and bad qualities in the crops they have raised, and in the insects, fungi, and other things affecting these crops; they have met and learned to solve some of the problems in the improvement of crops; they have learned that improvement in one direction is not always, or even usually, accompanied by improvement in all directions; they have learned the value of labor, the cost of producing crops, and how to keep simple accounts with different crops; they have been encouraged to read good literature, and have learned some of the sources of agricultural literature; their views have been broadened by contact with others and by visiting institutions of learning, highly developed farms, and other points of interest, and, finally, the power of taking the initiative has in many cases been strongly developed in them. As one of the direct results of the sugar-beet experiments, a few of the Illinois boys will raise sugar beets this year as a commercial venture. One sugar factory has already contracted with boys in Winnebago County to raise 20 acres of beets.

(2) Collectively the boys have learned the value of organized effort, of cooperation, and of compromise, and the social instinct has been developed in them — a matter of great importance in rural districts, where the isolated condition of the people has always been a great drawback to progress.

(3) The influence upon the communities at large, the parents as well as the children, has been wholesome. Beginning with an awakening of interest in one thing — better seed corn — the communities have rapidly extended their interest to other features of rural improvement, with the result that in the regions affected by the boys' agricultural club movement there has come about a general upward trend to the thoughts and activities of the people.

Adams' Experiment Station Act, 1906

From 34 U. S. Statutes at Large 63.

AN ACT TO PROVIDE FOR AN INCREASED ANNUAL APPROPRIATION FOR AGRICULTURAL EXPERIMENT STATIONS AND REGULATING THE EXPENDITURE THEREOF

Be it enacted by the Senate and House of Representatives of the United States of America in Congress assembled, That there shall be, and hereby is, annually appropriated, out of any money in the Treasury not otherwise appropriated, to be paid as hereinafter provided, to each State and Territory, for the more complete endowment and maintenance of agricultural experiment stations now established or which may hereafter be established in accordance with the act of Congress approved March second, eighteen hundred and eighty-seven, the sum of five thousand dollars in addition to the sum named in said act for the year ending June thirtieth, nineteen hundred and six, and an annual increase of the amount of such appropriation thereafter for five years by an additional sum of two thousand dollars over the preceding year, and the annual amount to be paid thereafter to each State and Territory shall be thirty thousand dollars, to be applied only to paying the necessary expenses of conducting original researches or experiments bearing directly on the agricultural industry of the United States, having due regard to the varying conditions and needs of the respective States or Territories.

SEC. 2. That the sums hereby appropriated to the States and Territories for the further endowment and support of agricultural experiment stations shall be annually paid in equal quarterly payments on the first day of January, April, July, and October of each year by the Secretary of the Treasury upon the warrant of the Secretary of Agriculture, out of the Treasury of the United States, to the treasurer or other officer duly appointed by the governing boards of said experiment stations to receive the same, and such officers shall be required to report to the Secretary of Agriculture on or before the first day of September of each year a detailed statement of the amount so received and of its disbursements, on schedules prescribed by the Secretary of Agriculture. The grants of money authorized by this act are made subject to legislative assent of the several States and Territories to the purpose of said grants: *Provided,* That payment of such installments of the appropriation herein made as shall become due to any State or Territory before the adjournment of the regular session of legislature meeting next after the passage of this act shall be made upon the assent of the governor thereof, duly certified by the Secretary of the Treasury.

Sec. 3. That if any portion of the moneys received by the designated officer of any State or Territory for the further and more complete endowment, support, and maintenance of agricultural experiment stations as provided in this act shall by any action or contingency be diminished or lost or be misapplied, it shall be replaced by said State or Territory to which it belongs, and until so replaced no subsequent appropriation shall be apportioned or paid to such State or Territory; and no portion of said moneys exceeding five per centum of each annual appropriation shall be applied, directly or indirectly, under any pretense whatever, to the purchase, erection, preservation, or repair of any building or buildings, or to the purchase or rental of land. It shall be the duty of each of said stations annually, on or before the first day of February, to make to the governor of the State or Territory in which it is located a full and detailed report of its operations, including a statement of receipts and expenditures, a copy of which report shall be sent to each of said stations to the Secretary of Agriculture, and to the Secretary of the Treasury of the United States.

Sec. 4. That on or before the first day of July in each year after the passage of this act the Secretary of Agriculture shall ascertain and certify to the Secretary of the Treasury as to each State and Territory whether it is complying with the provisions of this act and is entitled to receive its share of the annual appropriation for agricultural experiment stations under this act and the amount which thereupon each is entitled, respectively, to receive. If the Secretary of Agriculture shall withhold a certificate from any State or Territory of its appropriation, the facts and reasons therefore shall be reported to the President, and the amount involved shall be kept separate in the Treasury until the close of the next Congress, in order that the State or Territory may, if it shall so desire, appeal to Congress from the determination of the Secretary of Agriculture. If the next Congress shall not direct such sum to be paid, it shall be covered into the Treasury; and the Secretary of Agriculture is thereby charged with the proper administration of this law.

Sec. 5. That the Secretary of Agriculture shall make an annual report to Congress on the receipts and expenditures and work of the agricultural experiment stations in all of the States and Territories, and also whether the appropriation of any State or Territory has been withheld; and if so, the reason therefor.

Sec. 6. That Congress may at any time amend, suspend, or repeal any or all of the provisions of this act.

Approved March 16, 1906 (34 Stat. 63).

(Section 1 of the Adams Act was clarified and construed to limit the annual appropriation under the act to $15,000 for each State and Territory in the act making appropriations for the United States Department of Agriculture for the fiscal year ended June 30, 1907 (34 Stat. 669, 696).)

Meat Packing in 1906

Upton Sinclair, *The Jungle* (New York, c. 1906), pp. 99–100, 135–37.

There was said to be two thousand dollars a week hush money from the tubercular steers alone, and as much again from the hogs which had died of cholera on the trains, and which you might see any day being loaded into box cars and hauled away to a place called Globe, in Indiana, where they made a fancy grade of lard.

Jurgis heard of these things little by little, in the gossip of those who were obliged to perpetrate them. It seemed as if every time you met a person from a new department, you heard of new swindles and new crimes. There was, for instance, a Lithuanian who was a cattle butcher for the plant where Marija had worked, which killed meat for canning only; and to hear this man describe the animals which came to his place would have been worthwhile for a Dante or a Zola. It seemed that they must have agencies all over the country, to hunt out old and crippled and diseased cattle to be canned. There were cattle which had been fed on "whiskey malt," the refuse of the breweries, and had become what the men called "steerly" — which means covered with boils. It was a nasty job killing these, for when you plunged your knife into them they would burst and splash foul-smelling stuff into your face; and when a man's sleeves were smeared with blood, and his hands steeped in it, how was he ever to wipe his face, or to clear his eyes so that he could see? It was stuff such as this that made the "embalmed beef" that had killed several times as many United States soldiers as all the bullets of the Spaniards; only the army beef, besides, was not fresh canned, it was old stuff that had been lying for years in the cellars.

Then one Sunday evening, Jurgis sat puffing his pipe by the kitchen stove, and talking with an old fellow whom Jonas had introduced, and who worked in the canning-rooms at Durham's; and so Jurgis learned a few things about the great and only Durham canned goods, which had become a national institution. They were regular alchemists at Durham's; they advertised a mushroom-catsup, and the men who made it did not know what a mushroom looked like. They advertised "potted checken" — and it was like the boarding-house soup of the comic papers, through which a chicken had walked with rubbers on. Perhaps they had a secret process for making chickens chemically — who knows? said Jurgis's friend; the things that went into the mixture were tripe, and the fat of pork, and beef suet, and hearts of beef, and finally the waste ends of veal, when they had any. They put these up in several grades, and sold them at several prices; but the contents of the cans all came out of the same hopper. And then there was "potted game" and "potted grouse," "potted ham," and "deviled ham" — de-vyled, as the men called it. "De-vyled" ham was made out of the waste ends of smoked beef that were too small to be sliced by the machines; and also tripe, dyed with chemicals so that it would not show white, and trimmings of hams and corned beef, and potatoes, skins and all, and finally the hard cartilaginous gullets of beef, after the tongues had been cut out. All this ingenious mixture was ground up and flavored with spices to make it taste like something. Anybody who could invent a new imitation had been sure of a fortune from old Durham, said Jurgis's informant, but it was hard to think of anything new in a place where so many sharp wits had been at work for so long; where men welcomed tuberculosis in the cattle they were feeding, because it made them fatten more quickly; and where they bought up all the old rancid butter left over in the grocery stores of a continent, and "oxidized" it by a forced-air process, to take away the odor, rechurned it with skim milk, and sold it in bricks in the cities! Up to a year or two ago it had been the custom to kill horses in the yards — ostensibly for fertilizer; but after long agitation the newspapers had been able to make the public realize that the horses were being canned. Now it was against the law to kill horses in Packingtown, and the law was really complied with — for the present, at any rate. Any day, however, one might see sharp-horned and shaggy-haired creatures running with the sheep — and yet what a job you would have to get the public to believe that a good part of what it buys for lamb and mutton is really goat's flesh! . . .

With one member trimming beef in a cannery, and another working in a sausage factory, the family had a first-hand knowledge of the great majority of Packingtown swindles. For it was the custom, as they found, whenever meat was so spoiled that it could not be used for anything else, either to can it or else to chop it up into sausage. With what had been told them by Jonas, who had worked in the pickle rooms, they could now study the whole of the spoiled-meat industry on the inside, and read a new and grim meaning into that old Packingtown jest — that they use everything of the pig except the squeal.

Jonas had told them how the meat that was taken out of pickle would often be found sour, and how they would rub it up with soda to take away the smell, and sell it to be eaten on free-lunch counters; also of all the miracles of chemistry which they performed, giving to any sort of meat, fresh or salted, whole or chopped, any color and any flavor and any odor they chose. In the pickling of hams thay had an ingenious apparatus, by which they saved time and increased the capacity of the plant — a machine consisting of a hollow needle attached to a pump: by plunging this needle into the meat and working with his foot a man could fill a ham with pickle in a few seconds. And yet, in spite of this, there would be hams found spoiled, some of them with an odor so bad that a man could hardly bear to be in the room with them. To pump into these the packers had a second and much stronger pickle which destroyed the odor — a process known to the workers as "giving them thirty per cent." Also, after the hams had been smoked, there would be found some that had gone to the bad. Formerly these had been sold as "Number Three Grade," but later on some ingenious person had hit upon a new device, and now they would extract the bone, about which the bad part generally lay, and insert in the hole a white-hot iron. After this invention there was no longer Number One, Two, and Three Grade — there was only Number One Grade. The packers were always originating such schemes — they had what they called "boneless hams," which were all the odds and ends of pork stuffed into casings; and "California hams," which were the shoulders, with big knuckle joints, and nearly all the meat cut out; and fancy "skinned hams," which were made of the oldest hogs, whose skins were so heavy and coarse that no one would buy them — that is, until they had been cooked and chopped fine and labelled "head cheese"!

It was only when the whole ham was spoiled that it came into the department of Elzbieta. Cut up by the two-thousand-revolutions-a-minute flyers, and mixed with half a ton of other meat, no odor that ever was in a ham could make any difference. There was never the least attention paid to what was cut up for sausage; there would come all the way back from Europe old sausage that had been rejected, and that was mouldy and white — it would be dosed with borax and glycerine, and dumped into the hoppers, and made over again for home consumption. There would be meat that had tumbled out on the floor, in the dirt and sawdust, where the workers had tramped and spit uncounted billions of consumption germs. There would be meat stored in great piles in rooms; and the water from leaky roofs would drip over it, and thousands of rats would race about on it. It was too dark in these storage places to see well, but a man could run his hand over these piles of meat and sweep off handfuls of the dried dung of rats. These rats were nuisances, and the packers would put poisoned bread out for them, they would die, and then rats, bread, and meat would go into the hoppers together. This is no fairy story and no joke; the meat would be shovelled into carts, and the man who did the shoveling would not trouble to lift out a rat even when he saw one — there were things that went into the sausage in comparison with which a poisoned rat was a tibit. There was no place for the men to wash their hands before they ate their dinner, and so they made a practice of washing them in the water that was to be ladled into the sausage. There were the butt-ends of smoked meat, and the scraps of corned beef, and all the odds and ends of the waste of the plants, that would be dumped into old barrels in the cellar and left there. Under the system of rigid economy which the packers enforced, there were some jobs that it only paid to do once in a long time, and among these was the cleaning out of the waste barrels. Every spring they did it; and in the barrels would be dirt and rust and old nails and stale water — and cart load after cart load of it would be taken up and dumped into the hoppers with fresh meat, and sent out to the public's breakfast. Some of it they would make into "smoked" sausage — but as the smoking took time, and was therefore expensive, they would call upon their chemistry department, and preserve it with borax and color it with gelatine to make it brown. All of their sausage came out of the same bowl, but when they came to wrap it they would stamp some of it "special," and for this they would charge two cents more a pound.

Food and Drugs Act, 1906

From 34 U.S. Statutes at Large 768.

AN ACT FOR PREVENTING THE MANUFACTURE, SALE, OR TRANSPORTATION OF ADULTERATED OR MISBRANDED OR POISONOUS OR DELETERIOUS FOODS, DRUGS, MEDICINES, AND LIQUORS, AND FOR REGULATING TRAFFIC THEREIN, AND FOR OTHER PURPOSES.

Be it enacted by the Senate and House of Representatives of the United States of America in Congress assembled, That it shall be unlawful for any person to manufacture within any Territory or the District of Columbia any article of food or drug which is adulterated or misbranded, within the meaning of this Act; and any person who shall violate any of the provisions of this section shall be guilty of a misdemeanor, and for each offense shall, upon conviction thereof, be fined not to exceed five hundred dollars or shall be sentenced to one year's imprisonment, or both such fine and imprisonment, in the discretion of the court, and for each subsequent offense and conviction thereof shall be fined not less than one thousand dollars or sentenced to one year's imprisonment, or both such fine and imprisonment, in the discretion of the court.

Sec. 2. That the introduction into any State or Territory or the District of Columbia from any other State or Territory or the District of Columbia, or from any foreign country, or shipment to any foreign country of any article of food or drugs which is adulterated or misbranded, within the meaning of this Act, is hereby prohibited; and any person who shall ship or deliver for shipment from any State or Territory or the District of Columbia to any other State or Territory or the District of Columbia, or to a foreign country, or who shall receive in any State or Territory or the District of Columbia from any other State or Territory or the District of Columbia, or foreign country, and having so received, shall deliver, in original unbroken packages, for pay or otherwise, or offer to deliver to any other person, any such article so adulterated or misbranded within the meaning of this Act, or any person who shall sell or offer for sale in the District of Columbia or the Territories of the United States any such adulterated or misbranded foods or drugs, or export or offer to export the same to any foreign country, shall be guilty of a misdemeanor, and for such offense be fined not exceeding two hundred dollars for the first offense, and upon conviction for each subsequent offense not exceeding three hundred dollars or be imprisoned not exceeding one year, or both, in the discretion of the court: *Provided,* That no article shall be deemed misbranded or adulterated within the provisions of this Act when intended for export to any foreign country and prepared or packed according to the specifications or directions of the foreign purchaser when no substance is used in the preparation or packing thereof in conflict with the laws of the foreign country to which said article is intended to be shipped; but if said article shall be in fact sold or offered for sale for domestic use or consumption, then this proviso shall not exempt said article from the operation of any of the other provisions of this Act.

Sec. 3. That the Secretary of the Treasury, the Secretary of Agriculture, and the Secretary of Commerce and Labor shall make uniform rules and regulations for carrying out the provisions of this Act, including the collection and examination of specimens of foods and drugs manufactured or offered for sale in the District of Columbia, or in any Territory of the United States, or which shall be offered for sale in unbroken packages in any State other than that in which they shall have been respectively manufactured or produced, or which shall be received from any foreign country, or intended for shipment to any foreign country, or which may be submitted for examination by the chief health, food, or drug officer of any State, Territory, or the District of Columbia, or at any domestic or foreign port through which such product is offered for interstate commerce, or for export or import between the United States and any foreign port or country.

Sec. 4. That the examinations of specimens of foods and drugs shall be made in the Bureau of Chemistry of the Department of Agriculture, or under the direction and supervision of such Bureau, for the purpose of determining from such examinations whether such articles are adulterated or misbranded within the meaning of this Act; and if it shall appear from any such examination that any of such specimens is adulterated or misbranded within the meaning of this Act, the Secretary of Agriculture shall cause notice thereof to be given to the party from whom such sample was obtained. Any party so notified shall be given an opportunity to be heard, under such rules and regulations as may be prescribed as aforesaid, and if it appears that any of the provisions of this Act have been violated by such party, then the Secretary of Agriculture shall at once certify the facts to the proper United States district attorney, with a copy of the results of the analysis or the examination of such article duly authenticated by the analyst or officer making such examination, under the oath of such officer. After judgment of the court, notice shall be given by publication in such manner as may be prescribed by the rules and regulations aforesaid.

SEC. 5. That it shall be the duty of each district attorney to whom the Secretary of Agriculture shall report any violation of this Act, or to whom any health or food or drug officer or agent of any State, Territory, or the District of Columbia shall present satisfactory evidence of any such violation, to cause appropriate proceedings to be commenced and prosecuted in the proper courts of the United States, without delay, for the enforcement of the penalties as in such case herein provided.

SEC. 6. That the term "drug," as used in this Act, shall include all medicines and preparations recognized in the United States Pharmacopoeia or National Formulary for internal or external use, and any substance or mixture of substances intended to be used for the cure, mitigation, or prevention of disease of either man or other animals. The term "food," as used herein, shall include all articles used for food, drink, confectionery, or condiment by man or other animals, whether simple, mixed, or compound.

SEC. 7. That for the purposes of this Act an article shall be deemed to be adulterated:

In case of drugs:

First. If, when a drug is sold under or by a name recognized in the United States Pharmacopoeia or National Formulary, it differs from the standard of strength, quality, or purity, as determined by the test laid down in the United States Pharmacopoeia or National Formulary official at the time of investigation: *Provided,* That no drug defined in the United States Pharmacopoeia or National Formulary shall be deemed to be adulterated under this provision if the standard of strength, quality, or purity be plainly stated upon the bottle, box, or other container thereof although the standard may differ from that determined by the test laid down in the United States Pharmacopoeia or National Formulary.

Second. If its strength or purity fall below the professed standard or quality under which it is sold.

In the case of confectionery:

If it contain terra alba, barytes, talc, chrome yellow, or other mineral substance or poisonous color or flavor, or other ingredient deleterious or detrimental to health, or any vinous, malt or spirituous liquor or compound or narcotic drug.

In the case of food:

First. If any substance has been mixed and packed with it so as to reduce or lower or injuriously affect its quality or strength.

Second. If any substance has been substituted wholly or in part for the article.

Third. If any valuable constituent of the article has been wholly or in part abstracted.

Fourth. If it be mixed, colored, powdered, coated, or stained in a manner whereby damage or inferiority is concealed.

Fifth. If it contain any added poisonous or other added deleterious ingredient which may render such article injurious to health: *Provided,* That when in the preparation of food products for shipment they are preserved by any external application applied in such manner that the preservative is necessarily removed mechanically, or by maceration in water, or otherwise, and directions for the removal of said preservative shall be printed on the covering or the package, the provisions of this Act shall be construed as applying only when said products are ready for consumption.

Sixth. If it consists in whole or in part of a filthy, decomposed, or putrid animal or vegetable substance, or any portion of an animal unfit for food, whether manufactured or not, or if it is the product of a diseased animal, or one that has died otherwise than by slaughter.

Sec. 8. That the term "misbranded," as used herein, shall apply to all drugs, or articles of food, or articles which enter into the composition of food, the package or label of which shall bear any statement, design, or device regarding such article, or the ingredients or substances contained therein which shall be false or misleading in any particular, and to any food or drug product which is falsely branded as to the State, Territory, or country in which it is manufactured or produced.

That for the purposes of this Act an article shall also be deemed to be misbranded:

In case of drugs:

First. If it be an imitation of or offered for sale under the name of another article.

Second. If the contents of the package as originally put up shall have been removed, in whole or in part, and other contents shall have been placed in such package, or if the package fail to bear a statement on the label of the quantity or proportion of any alcohol, morphine, opium, cocaine, heroin, alpha or beta eucaine, chloroform, cannabis indica, chloral hydrate, or acetanilide, or any derivative or preparation of any such substances contained therein.

In the case of food:

First. If it be an imitation of or offered for sale under the distinctive name of another article.

Second. If it be labeled or branded so as to deceive or mislead the purchaser, or purport to be a foreign product when not so, or if the contents of the package as originally put up shall have been removed in whole or in part and other contents shall have been placed in such package, or if it fail to bear a statement on the label of the quantity or proportion of any morphine, opium, cocaine, heroin, alpha or beta eucane, chloroform, cannabis indica, chloral hydrate, or acetanilide, or any derivative or preparation of any of such substances contained therein.

Third. If in package form, and the contents are stated in terms of weight or measure, they are not plainly and correctly stated on the outside of the package.

Fourth. If the package containing it or its label shall bear any statement, design, or device regarding the ingredients or the substances contained therein, which statement, design, or device shall be false or misleading in any particular: *Provided,*

That an article of food which does not contain any added poisonous or deleterious ingredients shall not be deemed to be adulterated or misbranded in the following cases:

First. In the case of mixtures or compounds which may be now or from time to time hereafter known as articles of food, under their own distinctive names, and not an imitation of or offered for sale under the distinctive name of another article, if the name be accompanied on the same label or brand with a statement of the place where said article has been manufactured or produced.

Second. In the case of articles labeled, branded, or tagged so as to plainly indicate that they are compounds, imitations, or blends, and the word "compound," "imitation," or "blend," as the case may be, is plainly stated on the package in which it is offered for sale: *Provided,* That the term blend as used herein shall be construed to mean a mixture of like substances, not excluding harmless coloring or flavoring ingredients used for the purpose of coloring and flavoring only: *And provided further,* That nothing in this Act shall be construed as requiring or compelling proprietors or manufacturers of proprietary foods which contain no unwholesome added ingredient to disclose their trade formulas, except in so far as the provisions of this Act may require to secure freedom from adulteration or misbranding.

SEC. 9. That no dealer shall be prosecuted under the provisions of this Act when he can establish a guaranty signed by the wholesaler, jobber, manufacturer, or other party residing in the United States, from whom he purchases such articles, to the effect that the same is not adulterated or misbranded within the meaning of this Act, designating it. Said guaranty, to afford protection, shall contain the name and address of the party or parties making the sale of such articles to such dealer, and in such case said party or parties shall be amenable to the prosecutions, fines, and other penalties which would attach, in due course, to the dealer under the provisions of this Act.

SEC. 10. That any article of food, drug, or liquor that is adulterated or misbranded within the meaning of this Act, and is being transported from one State, Territory, District, or insular possession to another for sale, or, having been transported, remains unloaded, unsold, or in original unbroken packages, or if it be sold or offered for sale in the District of Columbia or the Territories, or insular possessions of the United States, or if it be imported from a foreign country for sale, or if it is intended for export to a foreign country, shall be liable to be proceeded against in any district court of the United States within the district where the same is found, and seized for confiscation by a process of libel for condemnation. And if such article is condemned as being adulterated or misbranded, or of a poisonous or deleterious character, within the meaning of this Act, the same shall be disposed of by destruction or sale, as the said court may direct, and the proceeds thereof, if sold, less the legal costs and charges, shall be paid into the Treasury of the United States, but such goods shall not be sold in any jurisdiction contrary to the provisions of this Act or the laws of that jurisdiction: *Provided, however,* That upon the payment of the costs of such libel proceedings and the execution and delivery of a good and sufficient bond to the effect that such articles shall not be sold or otherwise disposed of contrary to the provisions of this Act, or the laws of any State, Territory, District, or insular possession, the court may by order direct that such articles be delivered to the owner thereof. The proceedings of such libel cases shall conform, as near as may be, to the proceedings in admiralty, except that either party may demand trial by jury of any issue of fact joined in any such case, and all such proceedings shall be at the suit of and in the name of the United States.

SEC. 11. The Secretary of the Treasury shall deliver to the Secretary of Agriculture, upon his request from time to time, samples of foods and drugs which are being imported into the United States or offered for import, giving notice thereof to the owner or consignee, who may appear before the Secretary of Agriculture, and have the right to introduce testimony, and if it appear from the examination of such samples that any article of food or drug offered to be imported into the United States is adulterated or misbranded within the meaning of this Act, or is otherwise dangerous to the health of the people of the United States, or is of a kind forbidden entry into, or forbidden to be sold or restricted in sale in the country in which it is made or from which it is exported, or is otherwise falsely labeled in any respect, the said article shall be refused admission, and the Secretary of the Treasury shall refuse delivery to the consignee and shall cause the destruction of any goods refused delivery which shall not be exported by the consignee within three months from the date of notice of such refusal under such regulations as the Secretary of the Treasury may prescribe: *Provided,* That the Secretary of the Treasury may deliver to the consignee such goods pending examination and decision in the matter on execution of a penal bond for the amount of the full invoice value of such goods, together with the duty thereon, and on refusal to return such goods for any cause to the custody of the Secretary of the Treasury, when demanded, for the purpose of excluding them from the country, or for any other purpose, said consignee shall forfeit the full amount of the bond: *And provided further,* That all charges for storage, cartage, and labor on goods which are refused admission or delivery shall be paid by the owner or consignee, and in default of such payment shall constitute a lien against any future importation made by such owner or consignee.

SEC. 12. That the term ''Territory'' as used in this Act shall include the insular possessions of the United States. The word ''person'' as used in this Act shall be construed to import both the plural and the singular, as the case demands, and shall include corporations, companies, societies and associations. When construing and enforcing the provisions of this Act, the act, omission, or failure of any officer, agent, or other person acting for or employed by any corporation, company, society, or association, within the scope of his employment or office, shall in every case be also deemed to be the act, omission, or failure of such corporation, company, society, or association as well as that of the person.

SEC. 13. That this Act shall be in force and effect from and after the first day of January, nineteen hundred and seven.

Approved, June 30, 1906.

Meat Inspection Act, 1906

From 34 U. S. Statutes at Large 674.

EXTRACT FROM PUBLIC — NO. 382 — 59TH CONGRESS

General expenses, Bureau of Animal Industry: For carrying out the provisions of the Act approved May twenty-ninth, eighteen hundred and eighty-four, establishing the Bureau of Animal Industry, and the provisions of the Act approved February second, nineteen hundred and three, to enable the Secretary of Agriculture to more effectually suppress and prevent the spread of contagious and infectious diseases of live stock, and for other purposes; and also the provisions of the Act approved March third, nineteen hundred and five, to enable the Secretary of Agriculture to establish and maintain quarantine districts, to permit and regulate the movement of cattle and other live stock therefrom, and for other purposes: *Provided,* That live horses be entitled to the same inspection as other animals herein named, eight hundred and thirty-seven thousand two hundred dollars; and the Secretary of Agriculture is hereby authorized to use any part of this sum he may deem necessary or expedient, in such manner as he may think best, in the collection of information and dissemination of knowledge concerning live stock, dairy, and other animal products, and to prevent the spread of pleuro-pneumonia, blackleg, tuberculosis, sheep scab, glanders or farcy, hog cholera, and other diseases of animals, and for this purpose to employ as many persons in the city of Washington or elsewhere as he deem necessary, and to expend any part of this sum in the purchase and destruction of diseased or exposed animals and the quarantine of the same whenever in his judgment it is essential to prevent the spread of pleuro-pneumonia, tuberculosis, or other diseases of animals from one State to another; for improving and maintaining the Bureau Experiment Station, at Bethesda, Maryland; to establish, improve, and maintain quarantine stations, and to provide proper shelter and equipment for the care of neat cattle, domestic and other animals imported at such ports as may be deemed necessary; for printing and publishing such reports relating to animal industry as he may direct; and the Secretary is hereby authorized to rent suitable buildings in the District of Columbia, at an annual rental of not exceeding two thousand five hundred dollars, to be used for office, laboratory, and storage purposes for said Bureau of Animal Industry for purposes other than meat inspection; and the employees of the Bureau of Animal Industry outside of the city of Washington may hereafter, in the discretion of the Secretary of Agriculture, without additional expense to the Government, be granted leaves of absence not to exceed fifteen days in any one year, which leave may, in exceptional and meritorious cases where such an employee is ill, be extended, in the discretion of the Secretary of Agriculture, not to exceed fifteen days additional in any one year: *Provided,* That the Act of March third, eighteen hundred and ninety-one, as amended March second, eighteen hundred and ninety-five, for the inspection of live cattle and products thereof, shall be deemed to include dairy products intended for exportation to any foreign country, and the Secretary of Agriculture may apply, under rules and regulations to be prescribed by him, the provisions of said Act for inspection and certification appropriate for ascertaining the purity and quality of such products, and may cause the same to be so marked, stamped, or labeled as to secure their identity and make known in the markets of foreign countries to which they may be sent from the United States their purity, quality, and grade; and all the provisions of said Act relating to live cattle and products thereof for export shall apply to dairy products so inspected and certified: *Provided,* That the Secretary of Agriculture be authorized to expend of the amount hereby appropriated, through the dairy division of the Bureau of Animal Industry of the Department of Agriculture, a sum not to exceed twenty thousand dollars in further developing the dairy industry of the Southern States by conducting experiments, holding institutes, and giving object lessons in cooperation with individual dairymen and State experiment stations: *Provided, also,*

That the Secretary of Agriculture is authorized to expend five thousand dollars of the amount hereby appropriated, to especially investigate hemorrhagic septicemia, infectious cerebro-spinal meningitis, and malignant catarrh, prevalent among domestic animals in the State of Minnesota and adjoining States, to work out, if possible, in cooperation with the Minnesota Experiment Station, the problem of prevention by developing antitoxin or preventive vaccines and to secure and diffuse information along these lines, provided that the Secretary of Agriculture is authorized to purchase in the open market samples of all tuberculin serums, antitoxins, or analogous products, of foreign or domestic manufacture, which are sold in the United States for the detection, prevention, treatment, or cure of diseases of domestic animals, to test the same, and to publish the results of said tests in such manner as he may deem best.

For experiments in animal breeding and feeding in cooperation with State agricultural stations, twenty-five thousand dollars.

That for the purpose of preventing the use in interstate or foreign commerce, as hereinafter provided, of meat and meat food products which are unsound, unhealthful, unwholesome, or otherwise unfit for human food, the Secretary of Agriculture, at his discretion, may cause to be made, by inspectors appointed for that purpose, an examination and inspection of all cattle, sheep, swine, and goats before they shall be allowed to enter into any slaughtering, packing, meat-canning, rendering, or similar establishment, in which they are to be slaughtered and the meat and meat food products thereof are to be used in interstate or foreign commerce; and all cattle, swine, sheep, and goats found on such inspection to show symptoms of disease shall be set apart and slaughtered separately from all other cattle, sheep, swine, or goats, and when so slaughtered the carcasses of said cattle, sheep, swine, or goats shall be subject to a careful examination and inspection, all as provided by the rules and regulations to be prescribed by the Secretary of Agriculture as herein provided for.

That for the purposes hereinbefore set forth the Secretary of Agriculture shall cause to be made by inspectors appointed for that purpose, as hereinafter provided, a post-mortem examination and inspection of the carcasses and parts thereof of all cattle, sheep, swine, and goats to be prepared for human consumption at any slaughtering, meat-canning, salting, packing, rendering, or similar establishment in any State, Territory, or the District of Columbia for transportation or sale as articles of interstate or foreign commerce; and the carcasses and parts thereof of all such animals found to be sound, healthful, wholesome, and fit for human food shall be marked, stamped, tagged, or labeled as "Inspected and passed;" and said inspectors shall label, mark, stamp, or tag as "Inspected and condemned," all carcasses and parts thereof of animals found to be unsound, unhealthful, unwholesome, or otherwise unfit for human food; and all carcasses and parts thereof thus inspected and condemned shall be destroyed for food purposes by the said establishment in the presence of an inspector, and the Secretary of Agriculture may remove inspectors from any such establishment which fails to so destroy any such condemned carcass or part thereof, and said inspectors, after said first inspection shall, when they deem it necessary, reinspect said carcasses or parts thereof to determine whether since the first inspection the same have become unsound, unhealthful, unwholesome, or in any way unfit for human food, and if any carcass or any part thereof shall, upon examination and inspection subsequent to the first examination and inspection, be found to be unsound, unhealthful, unwholesome, or otherwise unfit for human food, it shall be destroyed for food purposes by the said establishment in the presence of an inspector, and the Secretary of Agriculture may remove inspectors from any establishment which fails to so destroy any such condemned carcass or part thereof.

The foregoing provisions shall apply to all carcasses or parts of carcasses of cattle, sheep, swine, and goats, or the meat or meat products thereof which may be brought into any slaughtering, meat-canning, salting, packing, rendering, or similar establishment, and such examination and inspection shall be had before the said carcasses or parts thereof shall be allowed to enter into any department wherein the same are to be treated and prepared for meat food products; and the foregoing provisions shall also apply to all such products which, after having been issued from any slaughtering, meat-canning, salting, packing, rendering, or similar establishment, shall be returned to the same or to any similar establishment where such inspection is maintained.

That for the purposes hereinbefore set forth the Secretary of Agriculture shall cause to be made by inspectors appointed for that purpose an examination and inspection of all meat food products prepared for interstate or foreign commerce in any slaughtering, meat-canning, salting, packing, rendering, or similar establishment, and for the purposes of any examination and inspection said inspectors shall have access at all times by day or night, whether the establishment be operated or not, to every part of said establishment; and said inspectors shall mark, stamp, tag, or label as "Inspected and passed" all such products found to be sound, healthful, and wholesome, and which contain no dyes, chemicals, preservatives, or ingredients which render such meat or meat food products unsound, unhealthful, unwholesome, or unfit for human food; and said inspectors shall label, mark, stamp, or tag as "Inspected and condemned" all such products found unsound, unhealthful, and unwholesome, or which contain dyes, chemicals, preservatives, or ingredients which render such meat or meat food products unsound, unhealthful, unwholesome, or unfit for human food, and all such condemned meat food products shall be destroyed for food purposes, as hereinbefore provided, and the Secretary of Agriculture may remove inspectors from any establishment which fails to so destroy such condemned meat food products: *Provided,* That, subject to the rules and regulations of the Secretary of Agriculture, the provisions hereof in regard to preservatives shall not apply to meat food products for export to any foreign country and which are prepared or packed according to the specifications or directions of the foreign purchaser, when no substance is used in the preparation or packing thereof in conflict with the laws of the foreign country to which said article is to be exported; but if said article shall be in fact sold or offered for sale for domestic use or consumption then this proviso shall not exempt said article from the operation of all the other provisions of this Act.

That when any meat or meat food product prepared for interstate or foreign commerce which has been inspected as hereinbefore provided and marked "Inspected and passed" shall be placed or packed in any can, pot, tin, canvas, or other receptacle or covering in any establishment where inspection under the provisions of this Act is maintained, the person, firm, or corporation preparing said product shall cause a label to be attached to said can, pot, tin, canvas, or other receptacle or covering, under the supervision of an inspector, which label shall state that the contents thereof have been "inspected and passed" under the provisions of this Act; and no inspection and examination of meat or meat food products deposited or inclosed in cans, tins, pots, canvas, or other receptacle or covering in any establishment where inspection under the provisions of this Act is maintained shall be deemed to be complete until such meat or meat food products have been sealed or inclosed in said can, tin, pot, canvas, or other receptacle or covering under the supervision of an inspector, and no such meat or meat food products shall be sold or offered for sale by any person, firm, or corporation in interstate or foreign commerce under any false or deceptive name; but established trade name or names which are usual to such products and which are not false and deceptive and which shall be approved by the Secretary of Agriculture are permitted.

The Secretary of Agriculture shall cause to be made, by experts in sanitation or by other competent inspectors, such inspection of all slaughtering, meat canning, salting, packing, rendering, or similar establishments in which cattle, sheep, swine, and goats are slaughtered and the meat and meat food products thereof are prepared for interstate or foreign commerce as may be necessary to inform himself concerning the sanitary conditions of the same, and to prescribe the rules and regulations of sanitation under which such establishments shall be maintained; and where the sanitary conditions of any such establishment are such that the meat or meat food products are rendered unclean, unsound, unhealthful, unwholesome, or otherwise unfit for human food, he shall refuse to allow said meat or meat food products to be labeled, marked, stamped, or tagged as "inspected and passed."

That the Secretary of Agriculture shall cause an examination and inspection of all cattle, sheep, swine, and goats, and the food products thereof, slaughtered and prepared in the establishments hereinbefore described for the purposes of interstate or foreign commerce to be made during the nighttime as well as during the daytime when the slaughtering of said cattle, sheep, swine, and goats, or the preparation of said food products is conducted during the nighttime.

That on and after October first, nineteen hundred and six, no person, firm, or corporation shall transport or offer for transportation, and no carrier of interstate or foreign commerce shall transport or receive for transportation from one State or Territory or the District of Columbia to any other State or Territory or the District of Columbia, or to any place under the jurisdiction of the United States, or to any foreign country, any carcasses or parts thereof, meat, or meat food products thereof which have not been inspected, examined, and marked as "inspected and passed," in accordance with the terms of this Act and with the rules and regulations prescribed by the Secretary of Agriculture: *Provided,* That all meat and meat food products on hand on October first, nineteen hundred and six, at establishments where inspection has not been maintained, or which have been inspected under existing law, shall be examined and labeled under such rules and regulations as the Secretary of Agriculture shall prescribe, and then shall be allowed to be sold in interstate or foreign commerce.

That no person, firm, or corporation, or officer, agent, or employee thereof, shall forge, counterfeit, simulate, or falsely represent, or shall without proper authority use, fail to use, or detach, or shall knowingly or wrongfully alter, deface, or destroy, or fail to deface or destroy, any of the marks, stamps, tags, labels, or other identification devices provided for in this Act, or in and as directed by the rules and regulations prescribed hereunder by the Secretary of Agriculture, on any carcasses, parts of carcasses, or the food product, or containers thereof, subject to the provisions of this Act, or any certificate in relation thereto, authorized or required by this Act or by the said rules and regulations of the Secretary of Agriculture.

That the Secretary of Agriculture shall cause to be made a careful inspection of all cattle, sheep, swine, and goats intended and offered for export to foreign countries at such times and places, and in such manner as he may deem proper, to ascertain whether such cattle, sheep, swine, and goats are free from disease.

And for this purpose he may appoint inspectors who shall be authorized to give an official certificate clearly stating the condition in which such cattle, sheep, swine, and goats are found.

And no clearance shall be given to any vessel having on board cattle, sheep, swine, or goats for export to a foreign country until the owner or shipper of such cattle, sheep, swine, or goats has a certificate from the inspector herein authorized to be appointed, stating that the said cattle, sheep, swine, or goats are sound and healthy, or unless the Secretary of Agriculture shall have waived the requirement of such certificate for export to the particular country to which such cattle, sheep, swine, or goats are to be exported.

That the Secretary of Agriculture shall also cause to be made a careful inspection of the carcasses and parts thereof of all cattle, sheep, swine, and goats, the meat of which, fresh, salted, canned, corned, packed, cured, or otherwise prepared, is intended and offered for export to any foreign country, at such times and places and in such manner as he may deem proper.

And for this purpose he may appoint inspectors who shall be authorized to give an official certificate stating the condition in which said cattle, sheep, swine, or goats, and the meat thereof, are found.

And no clearance shall be given to any vessel having on board any fresh, salted, canned, corned, or packed beef, mutton, pork, or goat meat, being the meat of animals killed after the passage of this Act, or except as hereinbefore provided for export to and sale in a foreign country from any port in the United States, until the owner or shipper thereof shall obtain from an inspector appointed under the provisions of this Act a certificate that the said cattle, sheep, swine, and goats were sound and healthy at the time of inspection, and that their meat is sound and wholesome, unless the Secretary of Agriculture shall have waived the requirements of such certificate for the country to which said cattle, sheep, swine, and goats or meats are to be exported.

That the inspectors provided for herein shall be authorized to give official certificates of the sound and wholesome condition of the cattle, sheep, swine, and goats, their carcasses and products as herein described, and one copy of every certificate granted under the provisions of this Act shall be filed in the Department of Agriculture, another copy shall be delivered to the owner or shipper, and when the cattle, sheep, swine, and goats or their carcasses and products are sent abroad, a third copy shall be delivered to the chief officer of the vessel on which the shipment shall be made.

That no person, firm, or corporation engaged in the interstate commerce of meat or meat food products shall transport or offer for transportation, sell or offer to sell any such meat or meat food products in any State or Territory or in the District of Columbia or any place under the jurisdiction of the United States, other than in the State or Territory or in the District of Columbia or any place under the jurisdiction of the United States in which the slaughtering, packing, canning, rendering, or other similar establishment owned, leased, operated by said firm, person, or corporation is located unless and until said person, firm, or corporation shall have complied with all of the provisions of this Act.

That any person, firm, or corporation, or any officer or agent of any such person, firm, or corporation, who shall violate any of the provisions of this Act shall be deemed guilty of a misdemeanor and shall be punished on conviction thereof by a fine of not exceeding ten thousand dollars or imprisonment for a period not more than two years, or by both such fine and imprisonment; in the discretion of the court.

That the Secretary of Agriculture shall appoint from time to time inspectors to make examination and inspection of all cattle, sheep, swine, and goats, the inspection of which is hereby provided for, and of all carcasses and parts thereof, and of all meats and meat food products thereof, and of the sanitary conditions of all establishments in which such meat and meat food products hereinbefore described are prepared; and said inspectors shall refuse to stamp, mark, tag, or label any carcass or any part thereof, or meat food product therefrom, prepared in any establishment hereinbefore mentioned, until the same shall have actually been inspected and found to be sound, healthful, wholesome, and fit for human food, and to contain no dyes, chemicals, preservatives, or ingredients which render such meat food product unsound, unhealthful, unwholesome, or unfit for human food; and to have been prepared under proper sanitary conditions, hereinbefore provided for; and shall perform such other duties as are provided by this Act and by the rules and regulations to be prescribed by said Secretary of Agriculture; and said Secretary of Agriculture shall, from time to time, make such rules and regulations as are necessary for the efficient execution of the provisions of this Act, and all inspections and examinations made under this Act shall be such and made in such manner as described in the rules and regulations prescribed by said Secretary of Agriculture not inconsistent with the provisions of this Act.

That any person, firm, or corporation, or any agent or employee of any person, firm, or corporation who shall give, pay, or offer, directly or indirectly, to any inspector, deputy inspector, chief inspector, or any other officer or employee of the United States authorized to perform any of the duties prescribed by this Act or by the rules and regulations of the Secretary of Agriculture any money or other thing of value, with intent to influence said inspector, deputy inspector, chief inspector, or other officer or employee of the United States in the discharge of any duty herein provided for, shall be deemed guilty of a felony and, upon conviction thereof, shall be punished by a fine not less than five thousand dollars nor more than ten thousand dollars and by imprisonment not less than one year nor more than three years; and any inspector, deputy inspector, chief inspector, or other officer or employee of the United States authorized to perform any of the duties prescribed by this Act who shall accept any money, gift, or other thing of value from any person, firm, or corporation, or officers, agents, or employees thereof, given with intent to influence his official action, or who shall receive or accept from any person, firm, or corporation engaged in interstate or foreign commerce any gift, money, or other thing of value with any purpose or intent whatsoever, shall be deemed guilty of a felony and shall, upon conviction thereof, be summarily discharged from office and shall be punished by a fine not less than one thousand dollars nor more than ten thousand dollars and by imprisonment not less than one year nor more than three years.

That the provisions of this Act requiring inspection to be made by the Secretary of Agriculture shall not apply to animals slaughtered by any farmer on the farm and sold and transported as interstate or foreign commerce, nor to retail butchers and retail dealers in meat and meat food products, supplying their customers:

Provided, That if any person shall sell or offer for sale or transportation for interstate or foreign commerce any meat or meat food products which are diseased, unsound, unhealthful, unwholesome, or otherwise unfit for human food, knowing that such meat food products are intended for human consumption, he shall be guilty of a misdemeanor, and on conviction thereof shall be punished by a fine not exceeding one thousand dollars or by imprisonment for a period of not exceeding one year, or by both such fine and imprisonment: *Provided also,* That the Secretary of Agriculture is authorized to maintain the inspection in this Act provided for at any slaughtering, meat canning, salting, packing, rendering, or similar establishment notwithstanding this exception, and that the persons operating the same may be retail butchers and retail dealers or farmers; and where the Secretary of Agriculture shall establish such inspection then the provisions of this Act shall apply notwithstanding this exception.

That there is permanently appropriated, out of any money in the Treasury not otherwise appropriated, the sum of three million dollars, for the expenses of the inspection of cattle, sheep, swine, and goats and the meat and meat food products thereof which enter into interstate or foreign commerce and for all expenses necessary to carry into effect the provisions of this Act relating to meat inspection, including rent and the employment of labor in Washington and elsewhere, for each year. And the Secretary of Agriculture shall, in his annual estimates made to Congress, submit a statement in detail, showing the number of persons employed in such inspections and the salary or per diem paid to each, together with the contingent expenses of such inspectors and where they have been and are employed.

Total, Bureau of Animal Industry, three million nine hundred and forty-six thousand nine hundred and eighty dollars.

Approved, June 30, 1906.

Research on Hog Cholera, 1908

From M. Dorset, "Recent Work in the Bureau of Animal Industry Concerning the Cause and Prevention of Hog Cholera," U.S. Department of Agriculture, *Yearbook,* 1908 (Washington, 1909), pp. 321–32.

Previous Work on Hog Cholera

As a result of researches carried out more than twenty years ago, Salmon and Smith reached the conclusion that hog cholera was caused by a small rod-shaped bacterium, named by them *Bacillus cholerae suis.* Salmon and Smith showed that this organism is present in the blood and organs of a great majority of the animals which die of hog cholera, and they showed also that by injecting pure cultures of this organism, or by feeding such cultures, they were able to produce, in many instances, lesions which were indistinguishable from those found in hogs which died from a natural attack of hog cholera. In addition they were able to recover this organism from the organs of all hogs which died from artificial infection with *B. cholerae suis.* These findings were confirmed by bacteriologists in this country and abroad, and as a result it has been generally believed that the etiology of hog cholera was settled, the cause being *B. cholerae suis*.

The cause of hog cholera being thus regarded as definitely established, most of the scientific work concerning this disease has, during the past twenty years, been directed toward the development of a vaccine or serum to be used for purposes of prevention. It is well known, however, that although some workers claimed to attain a certain measure of success, none of the methods proposed was found to act with sufficient reliability, when applied in a practical way in the field, to warrant its general use. Practically all of the methods proposed consisted in the preparation of vaccines or serums by using cultures of *B. cholerae suis*. The vaccines were prepared by attenuating this organism, or by extracting from it various substances which were used for the production of immunity. A number of authors also claimed to have secured good results by the use of serums, these serums being prepared by injecting or feeding animals with pure cultures of *B. cholerae suis* or with various substances derived from this organism. As has been stated previously, none of these vaccines or serums gave satisfactory results in practice, and it may be said that for twenty years after the discovery of the supposed cause of hog cholera little or no progress was made in combating this disease.

The Bureau of Animal Industry has been unremitting in its efforts to secure some substance which could be used as a preventive or cure for hog cholera, but until three or four years ago little progress was made. Apparent success was attained in some instances, but at other times, and especially where the preventive was applied in the field, partial or complete failure was the result.

The Cause of Hog Cholera

It is a fact known to all who have had occasion to study the disease that hog cholera is extremely contagious. Starting with the introduction of one sick animal into a healthy herd, the disease will spread rapidly from one to another until finally the great majority of the exposed hogs will contract the disease. It is also well known to practical hog raisers that a hog which has recovered from an attack of hog cholera is subsequently immune against that disease.

During the course of an experiment being carried out by the Bureau in which cultures of *B. cholerae suis* were injected into hogs for the purpose of producing immunity, it was noticed that in certain cases the injected animals would be made sick and would die from the injection. Associating with these hogs were others which were not injected and which were susceptible to hog cholera, but which did not contract disease from this association. At that time it was considered a very remarkable fact that the uninjected hogs associating with those made sick by cultures of the supposed cause of hog cholera did not in any case contract the disease. We also had occasion to note that in certain instances where hogs recovered after being made sick through the administration of pure cultures of *B. cholerae suis* there was no evidence of an immunity having been acquired through the illness produced by the culture, for when exposed subsequently to the natural-disease hog cholera such animals, almost without exception, succumbed.

These results were considered to be of such importance that special experiments were carried out to determine beyond doubt whether or not the disease produced by *B. cholerae suis* is contagious, and also whether hogs which recover from an attack of illness produced by the administration of that organism are rendered immune against the natural-disease hog cholera. The results of these experiments completely confirmed the original observations and showed that in no case was the disease that was produced by cultures of *B. cholerae suis* transmitted to nonimmune hogs by association. It was also found that an attack of illness produced by *B. cholerae suis* did not render the hog subsequently immune to the natural-disease hog cholera.

Salmon and Smith had previously observed that hog cholera is readily transmitted from one hog to another by injecting the blood of a sick animal subcutaneously into a nonimmune animal, and more recent experiments confirmed this. These later experiments showed also that the disease produced by the injection of hog-cholera blood, in marked contrast to that produced by the cultures, possessed the contagiousness of the natural-disease hog cholera and conferred complete immunity upon hogs which recovered. The only reasonable explanation of these differences in the characteristics of the disease produced by the blood on the one hand and by cultures of *B. cholerae suis* on the other seemed to lie in the supposition that some organism other than *B. cholerae suis* is concerned in the production of hog cholera and that this unknown organism is present in the blood of hogs sick of hog cholera. In order to settle this question, the most careful examinations were made of the blood of hogs sick of hog cholera, but neither by microscopic examination nor by cultural methods were we able to find any visible organism other than *B. cholerae suis* which could be regarded as playing any part in the disease.

Disease Due to a Filterable Virus

It should be noted here that previous to this time certain highly contagious diseases, such as yellow fever, foot-and-mouth disease, and chicken pest, had been shown to be due to invisible viruses present in the blood or body fluids of diseased individuals. These viruses are invisible under the highest magnifications now available; they can not be cultivated artificially, and in addition when fluids containing these viruses are passed through porcelain or earthen filters the filtrates, though proven to be free from all known bacteria, are capable of giving rise to the disease in question in susceptible individuals. The conclusion reached by those who worked with such diseases was that they are caused by organisms of such minute size or of such structure that they may pass through the pores of porcelain or earthen filters. These organisms are spoken of as "filterable," "invisible," or "ultramicroscopic." From what has just been said it will be readily understood why, at this stage of the work of the Bureau concerning hog cholera, search was made for a filterable virus in the blood of hogs sick of hog cholera.

The results of this search, which has been described in bulletins of the Bureau of Animal Industry, showed that filtered blood serum from hogs sick of hog cholera, and proven to be free from all known bacteria, is capable of producing in hogs typical attacks of hog cholera, the disease produced in this way presenting the contagiousness, and the immunity upon subsequent exposure in the case of hogs which recover, which are characteristic of the natural disease, but which are lacking in disease artificially induced by cultures of *B. cholerae suis*. As a result of the experiments with *B. cholerae suis* and with filtered blood from hogs sick of the natural-disease hog cholera, the conclusion was reached that the filterable virus which is present in the blood serum of sick hogs is the prime cause of hog cholera. While it is recognized that *B. cholerae suis* is capable of producing many of the lesions seen in various cases of hog cholera, and that it no doubt frequently exercises considerable influence upon the outcome of an attack of the disease (that is, certain hogs sick of hog cholera might recover if not forced to combat the combined attack of *B. cholerae suis* and the filterable virus), for the reasons already given we regard *B. cholerae suis* as playing the part of a secondary invader solely.

The first announcement of the finding of this filterable virus was made in the year 1903, and an extended publication with a description of the experiments was issued in 1905. This work of the Bureau of Animal Industry and the conclusions reached have since been confirmed by investigators in various parts of the world, notably by Ostertag and associates in Berlin, by Hutyra in Austria, by the British Board of Agriculture and Fisheries in England, by Leclainche, Carré, and Vallée in France, and by Professor Uhlenhuth of the German Imperial Board of Health, after a most extended and convincing series of experiments.

The Prevention of Hog Cholera

Having found that *B. cholerae suis* is not the true cause of hog cholera, the failure of earlier attempts to produce a satisfactory vaccine or serum for that disease could be readily understood, for although we might protect hogs from the attacks of *B. cholerae suis* by means of vaccines or serums derived directly or indirectly from that organism, we could not expect to secure protection from the filterable or ultramicroscopic virus by such means.

The filterable virus which exists in the blood of hogs sick of hog cholera has never been grown artificially. For this reason it is evident that any agent which is to be a true vaccine or preventive for hog cholera must be prepared directly or indirectly from the blood or body fluids of hogs sick of hog cholera which contain this virus. Following up this idea, many attempts were made to produce a vaccine by attenuating the virus in the blood. This attenuation was attempted by means of drying, by means of heat carefully regulated, and by the use of various chemical agents. In no case were we able to procure a vaccine by such methods which could be depended upon. At times excellent results were obtained, but at others the vaccine was found to be either too weak, therefore affording no protection to susceptible animals, or too strong, thereby causing serious injury or death of the vaccinated animals.

Immunity Secured by the Use of Blood Serum

At the same time that these attempts at attenuation were being carried out efforts were made to produce a protective serum by injecting animals with the blood from hogs sick of hog cholera. For this purpose donkeys and immune hogs were employed. The serum from donkeys did not prove to be effective, but that obtained from immune hogs was found to possess remarkable immunizing properties.

It is not necessary at this time to discuss these earlier experiments, as the records of this work have been published elsewhere, and as the original methods of producing the serum have been modified in many respects. Some of the details of the process as it is now carried out may, however, prove to be of interest.

In the first place, it should be stated that the underlying principle in this process consists in increasing the protective substances in the blood of immune hogs by treating these immunes with the virus of hog cholera. Any hog that has recovered from an attack of hog cholera or that has passed through an outbreak, associating with sick hogs without contracting the disease, may be regarded as an immune. The virus of the disease is readily available in the blood of hogs sick of hog cholera. Aside from the details of the treatment to which the immune is subjected there is one point that is of vital importance: The hog-cholera blood which is given the immune for the purpose of raising the protective power of its blood serum must be of a high degree of virulence. The object sought by the injection of the immune with the virus is of course the stimulation of the defensive mechanism of the hog's body to such a degree that protective substances will be formed in excess and float free in the blood of the immune. These protective substances are then secured for use in protecting suscep-tible hogs by drawing blood from the immune. If the immune hog does not receive blood of high virulence the reaction following this injection will be comparatively slight, and the amount of protective substances produced by the immune will be correspondingly small. This would result in a serum that might be so low in potency as to be unsuitable for practical use.

To ascertain the virulence of blood from any given outbreak of hog cholera two nonimmune hogs may be injected with small amounts (2 c. c. to 5 c. c.) of the blood. If these do not sicken promptly and exhibit acute symptoms of the disease the blood is not suitable for injecting the immune. Having secured an immune hog and disease-producing blood of proper virulence, the protective serum may be produced in almost any amount after the first lot is secured, for each of the vaccinated hogs becomes an immune which is available for serum production, and the disease-producing blood can be kept available by transferring the disease regularly from the original hogs injected with it to other susceptible hogs.

The methods now in use for hyperimmunizing the immunes, for drawing blood from immunes, and for vaccinating susceptible hogs are given below in some detail, though many points which are of much practical importance in producing the serum can not be touched upon in this paper.

The Process of Hyperimmunization

The disease-producing blood may be injected into the immune in a number of different ways and in varying doses, as follows:

1. *Subcutaneous injections:*
   (*a*) Inject the immune subcutaneously with defibrinated disease-producing blood in the proportion of 10 c. c. of blood for each pound of body weight; or
   (*b*) Inject the immune subcutaneously with 1 c. c. of defibrinated disease-producing blood for each pound of body weight. After an interval of one week give a second injection of 2.5 c. c. disease-producing blood

for each pound of body weight. After another interval of a week give a third injection of 5 c. c. of disease-producing blood for each pound of body weight.

2. *Intravenous injections:*

(*a*) Inject the immune intravenously with defibrinated disease-producing blood in the proportion of 5 c. c. of blood for each pound of body weight; or

(*b*) Inject the immune intravenously with defibrinated disease-producing blood in the proportion of 5 c. c. of blood for each pound of body weight, and after an interval of a week, if the hog has recovered, repeat the injection.

3. *Intra-abdominal injections:*

Inject the immune intra-abdominally with defibrinated disease-producing blood in the proportion of 10 c. c. of blood for each pound of body weight.

It will be understood, of course, that the above directions for treating the immune hog are not inflexible, for satisfactory results could, no doubt, be secured by modifying the method of administration, the number of doses given, and to a slight extent, perhaps, the amount of disease-producing blood employed, though from our own experience there appears to be little to be gained by materially increasing or diminishing the amounts of disease-producing blood, experience having shown that larger amounts can not be conveniently injected and that smaller amounts produce a serum of lower potency than that secured by the injection of the amounts given above. Immune hogs are not greatly affected by these injections, the most noticeable symptoms being loss of appetite and listlessness for a few days after injection, and following the subcutaneous injections there may be soreness and stiffness for a few days. When properly carried out any one of the above plans for treating the immune will produce a serum that will protect hogs from hog cholera.

Drawing Blood from the Immune

As has been stated, the serum which is used for protecting nonimmune pigs is secured from the immune after this animal has been injected with the disease-producing blood and has recovered from the effects of this injection. In almost all cases the immune will have recovered and will be in condition for bleeding within a week or ten days after receiving the disease-producing blood. Immunes "hyperimmunized" by one large subcutaneous injection usually regain their health more slowly than hogs treated by other methods.

Blood may be drawn from the immune by severing the carotid artery, thus bleeding the hog to death, or by cutting off the tail. The latter method is always to be preferred for the first drawings, as the bleeding may be stopped at any time, thus permitting the immune to live and furnish more blood later on. A large number of experiments have shown that, after hyperimmunization, blood may be drawn from the tail of the immune three or four successive times, at intervals of a week between bleedings, without any perceptible effect upon the protective properties of the serum which is secured. By repeating the bleedings in this way much more serum is secured than by one bleeding from the carotid artery. As a routine procedure, very satisfactory results have been obtained by bleeding the immune three times from the tail, and then one week after the last tail-bleeding severing the carotid artery and bleeding the hog to death. The blood secured at each bleeding is defibrinated and the fluid portion, consisting of a mixture of red blood cells and serum, is preserved in sterilized glass bottles, a small percentage of carbolic acid being previously added as a preservative. Before use all of the serum obtained from one immune is mixed together. In fact, as the potency of all serum should be tested before being employed in practice, considerable saving will be effected by mixing together in a large container the serum obtained from a number of different immunes, and then testing the potency of the mixture.

Determination of the Potency of the Serum

The protective power of this serum may be roughly determined as follows:

Inject eight pigs, weighing from 30 to 60 pounds each, subcutaneously with 2 c. c. of blood from an acute case of hog cholera. At the same time give two of the pigs 10 c. c. of the serum on the opposite side of the body; give two 15 c. c. and two 20 c. c. in the same way. This will leave two untreated pigs, which serve as controls on the virulence of the blood. If the two pigs which receive only the diseased blood die, those that receive 10 c. c. of serum sicken, but recover, while those receiving the larger doses of serum remain well, the serum should be suitable for use in practice in doses of 15 cubic centimeters. As a matter of fact, it has been found that all immunes properly hyperimmunized will yield a serum which is sufficiently potent in doses of 20 c. c., and it is considered best to use this dose of serum for protecting pigs weighing between 20 and 100 pounds, even though certain lots of serum may appear to be somewhat more potent. Carrying out this idea of always using a dose of 20 c. c. for hogs weighing from 20 to 100 pounds, it is only necessary, in standardizing, to determine the action of a serum in a dose of 20 c. c.; if shoats do not sicken after a simultaneous injection of disease-producing blood and 20 c. c. of serum, the serum may be considered suitable for practical use. Of course, care is necessary to avoid misleading results. Susceptible pigs must be used for the test and the disease-producing blood must be of undoubted virulence, as shown by its effect upon pigs which receive no serum.

Methods of Vaccination

After the serum has been obtained and tested in the manner indicated above, it is ready for use in immunizing susceptible hogs against hog cholera. This immunization is carried out in the following manner:

Injection of serum alone. The hogs it is desired to protect are injected subcutaneously with the proper dose of serum as determined by the preliminary test. If these animals are now exposed immediately to virulent hog cholera along with others which have not been treated with the serum, it will be found that the serum-treated animals will survive, whereas untreated animals subjected to the same exposure will succumb. This serum injection has been found to confer an immunity which will last for three weeks, though probably not very much longer.

Farmers' Institutes in New Hampshire, 1910

From "Institutes at Hollis, Hudson, and Meredith," New Hampshire Board of Agriculture, 1909–10 (Manchester, New Hampshire, 1910), pp. 3–10.

The first of the series of farmers' institutes during Christmas week was held on Monday, December 21, under the auspices of the State Board of Agriculture at the Grange Hall in Hollis, on the invitation of the grange in that town, and the institute workers were given a cordial greeting and were accorded a large audience. H. O. Hadley, master of the State Grange and county member of the Board of Agriculture, presided. The speakers of the day were men well known throughout the state as specialists in the line of farming, and they spoke of subjects of interest to the people of the community. They included Prof. Fred Rasmussen of the New Hampshire experiment station, Prof. L. A. Clinton of the Connecticut station at Storrs, H. O. Hadley of Peterborough, and N. J. Bachelder, secretary of the Board of Agriculture. . . .

The first subject discussed was "How to Increase Profits in Dairying," and was thoroughly explained by Professor Rasmussen. The subject of his lecture will be given in a later report. He was followed by Professor Clinton on

Maintaining Soil Fertility

It is hard to establish any definite facts about the richness of the soil, and equally hard to discuss them, but there are certain truths that are common to most localities under varying conditions. There are four essential points connected with this subject and under which it is generally discussed: how the fertility gets into the soil, how it gets out, how to prevent it from getting out, and how to restore it are the subtopics into which we will divide this talk on maintaining soil fertility.

Soil is a mixture of stone that has been ground up and pulverized by the glacier period and deposited all over North America, and decayed and decaying plant and vegetable matter. The kinds of soil depend on the degree of fineness with which these rocks, the remnants of the stone age, and the organic matter have attained. There is the clay soil to which the water clings tenaciously, and the gravel loam that acts like a sieve for rain water. The fertility depends on the amount of humus, the amount of organic substance or plant food, and whether a crop can be raised on it that may be sold for more than the cost of production.

Many soils are depleted in fertility by Nature's actions, by surface erosion, by bacteria growth, leakage and surface tightness. These things rob the soil of its vitality. An average corn crop when analyzed yields but two or three percent plant food that has been taken from the soil. The main loss in New England takes place during the winter from the rains and storms, which carry off the valuable surface of the land.

This wasting of fertility can be prevented by having some crop, it makes not much difference so long as it is a living one, growing on the cultivated fields out of season, during the winter and early spring. Rye and oats are common crops that are grown. In the spring this off season should be plowed under, making its green food life available for more profitable crops. Some fields are low and contain much water, which, if allowed to stand, makes the soil logy and stagnant, and locks up the organic matter. In this case underdrains situated at the right places will carry off the superfluous moisture.

Another method along this same line is the use of lime, spread judiciously over the earth, not eight or ten tons to the acre, but two or three. The application of the lime loosens up the plant life and cures the acidulous soil. Experiments in the use of lime have shown that soil on which lime had been placed always gave the best results. The use of stable manure is questionable when it has been allowed to stand outside the barn in all kinds of weather, because it has lost most of its organic substance. If manure is to be used, it should be taken to the field, immediately spread and harrowed in. This is impossible in the winter, and then it should be stored in a square, tight pile on the field and used in the spring. A satisfactory commercial fertilizer, I have found, consists of 250 pounds of nitrate of soda, 200 pounds of acid phosphate, and 150 pounds of muriate of potash.

The next speaker was Chairman Hadley, and he discussed

Thorough Cultivation of the Soil

A large part of the success and failures in agriculture are due to the thorough or the hurried preparation of the soil, to the loosening or the tightening of the plant life in the soil. I remember when I was a small boy my father was not particular in the way he plowed his fields, and if he struck a stump or a stone the quicker he could get his plow in ahead the better. His usual recipe for harrowing used to be to take the old spike-tooth harrow and run it a couple of times each way of the field.

Under present conditions the methods of cultivation are entirely different and hardly resemble the old-fashioned ways. Today every section of the field is given a thorough plowing, not a particle of the sod is left unturned, and the soil is pulverized very fine by the use of the disk and cut-away harrows, leaving it level and dusty.

When the crop is planted, and before it comes up, harrowing is of vast importance because it stops the growth of weeds and makes the cultivation free and easy and loosens up the plant matter, giving the seed an excellent chance to germinate. The cultivation of such crops as corn and potatoes should be carried on with horse and harrow so long as it can be done without damaging the plants. This should take the place of the expensive hand hoeing. Another thing thorough cultivation does is the saving of the water originally deposited in soil. It is the natural course for the water to rise on account of capillary attraction up the stems of the plants, and then evaporate into the air. The continual harrowing leaves a thick layer of dust or a mulch subsoil, as it is called, that prevents this action, and acts as a layer of straw would when placed on a field.

I say to you farmers here today that only the thorough cultivation of the seed bed and the thorough cultivation of the growing crop will widen the cost of production and the selling price, and will make New Hampshire agriculture what it ought to be — ahead of the same industry in all the other states of the Union. . . .

Relation of the Experiment Station to the Farmer

We are all interested in this subject. The experiment station is interested and hopes that the farmer is also. The people here in Hollis are in closer touch with the New Hampshire experiment station than any other town in the state. The state does not support the station, but the maintenance falls to the federal government. Money has been appropriated yearly until we have now eleven thousand dollars for the experiment work. There are seven stations at the college prepared to give advice and assistance to the farmers of New Hampshire along the following lines: The maintenance of soil fertility, including the rotation of crops and the selection and the use of manures and fertilizers; the selection of varieties of grain, grasses, and forage crops and methods of culture; the selection of fruits and vegetables and the management of orchards; the examination of seeds, the identification of different plants; the prevention of fungous diseases; the identification of insects and control of such as are injurious; the feeding of animals, including calculations of rations and methods of feeding stuffs; the methods of milk production and the testing of milk to determine value of dairy cows; the planting and caring of trees.

There is one question that we are often asked, "Why don't you get out more among the farmers?" We reply that the money has not been devoted for that purpose, but we had rather do it and could do far better work if we did. All our results now in experiment work are circulated by bulletins. In Iowa the state has appropriated money for extension work, and short free courses and cooperative experiments in localities having the same conditions are being held all over the state. This gives the people faith in the station, and I am sure if we could get in as close touch with the farmers in New Hampshire the result would have a greater influence on agriculture than those obtained from the present methods.

There is one phase of the experiment station that the farmers are neglecting. Last summer we inspected over a hundred farms in the state and were asked many questions that have arisen during the last three years about farming that might have been answered through the mail. Sometimes even a postal will give the desired information. Even when we did get out there were some people who were suspicious of our actions. We are not trying to act as police, but are trying to find out what the people are doing, and then we will try to help them.

Besides coöperation between the farmers and the experiment station there should be local coöperation among the farmers themselves. It has been started on a small scale for the improvement of the cattle. In the northern part of the state a local dairy association has been formed by some twenty or thirty farmers, who have hired a man to test the produce of each cow once every month, measure the feed and see if the cow is up to her limit of production. The work of this man begins January 1. In other states of the Union there are these same organizations. Many problems can be solved by local coöperation that will prove beneficial to the community and to the individual.

Professor Rasmussen's discussion was followed by lectures by Professor Clinton and Mr. Hadley on "Potato Growing" and "Good Citizenship," respectively, and the important issues of their speeches will be given in a later report.

Secretary Bachelder brought the institute to a successful close with a speech on

The National Grange

When I first became connected with the State Board of Agriculture, more than twenty years ago, the conditions in this state were entirely different from what they are today. The board was at war with the grange, the grange and the board were fighting the experiment station, and the people were down on all three. I believe today that it is just as important for the board of agriculture, in this state or any other state, to support the grange, as it is to work in the interests of crop growing. Today the board is entitled to credit for the harmonious state of affairs, and the grange for the support that it has given the board in helping to unite the three different factors at work in the interests of the New Hampshire farmer.

At the present time granges are in existence in thirty states of the Union, stretched from ocean to ocean, have a membership of over a million people, have doubled their membership within the last ten years, and have added twenty thousand during the last year. The National Grange is a large institution, and in New Hampshire has members to the number of thirty thousand. New Hampshire ranks fifth among the states. The National Grange is an important organization and so are the state granges, but it is from the small subordinate ones that these two derive their power.

There is no agency in the state working in the interest of the rural people, excepting the church and the school, that has done more for the farmer than the grange. At a hearing of the "Up-Lift" commission, appointed by President Roosevelt to find out "What is the matter with the farmers," at Washington, I strongly recommended and firmly believe that the best report that the commission can make to the President is to help to establish subordinate granges in every country town and at every crossroad. The grange is playing an important part in the development of young men and is fitting them for responsible public positions, where they will be more favorable to the interests of the farmer than any other class of people.

You hear a great deal about the farmer not being able to fill public positions, but he hasn't had the chance. There are now forty thousand young men whose ages range from fourteen to twenty-one, who are presiding at grange meetings, taking part in the discussions and ritual work, that are being well trained and will be qualified to send to legislatures, to fill gubernatorial chairs, and to congress.

The grandest work, though not the important, is the legislation obtained for the farmer, through the efforts of the National Grange. During the last thirty years the department of agriculture has been established at Washington, the secretary made a member of the President's cabinet, rural free delivery, the interstate commerce, and the pure food laws have been passed. More legislation will be attempted at this session of congress. The National Grange will stand for federal appropriation for highways, parcels post and postal savings banks. If we do not get what we want this year we will try next. . . .

Beginnings of Extension Work, 1909

From S. A. Knapp, "The Farmers' Cooperative Demonstration Work," U.S. Department of Agriculture, *Yearbook*, 1909 (Washington, 1910), pp. 153–60.

Purpose of the Work

The aim of the Farmers' Cooperative Demonstration Work is to place a practical object lesson before the farm masses, illustrating the best and most profitable methods of producing the standard farm crops, and to secure such active participation in the demonstrations as to prove that the farmers can make a much larger average annual crop and secure a greater return for their toil.

This work shows also that there is no necessity for the general deterioration of farms and the too common poverty of the rural masses.

Briefly stated, the salient features of the rural lessons given by the farm demonstration work are as follows:

(1) Better drainage of the soil.

(2) A deeper and more thoroughly pulverized seed bed; deep fall breaking (plowing) with implements that will not bring the subsoil to the surface.

(3) The use of seed of the best variety, intelligently selected and carefully stored.

(4) In cultivated crops, giving the rows and the plants in the rows a space suited to the plant, the soil, and the climate.

(5) Intensive tillage during the growing period of the crops.

(6) The importance of a high content of humus in the soil; the use of legumes, barnyard manure, farm refuse, and commercial fertilizers.

(7) The value of crop rotation and a winter cover crop on southern farms.

(8) The accomplishing of more work in a day by each laborer by using more horsepower and better implements.

(9) The importance of increasing the farm stock to the extent of utilizing all the waste products and idle lands of the farm.

(10) The production of all food required for the men and animals on the farm.

(11) The keeping of an account with each farm product, in order to know from which the gain or loss arises.

Plan of Organization

The Farmers' Cooperative Demonstration Work is conducted by a special agent in charge, who reports directly to the Chief of the Bureau of Plant Industry. There are five general assistants and a full office force; also a corps of field agents is employed, classified according to territory in charge, as state, district, and county agents. These agents are selected with special reference to a thorough knowledge of improved agriculture and practical experience in farming in the sections to which appointed. The county agents are appointed mainly on the advice of local committees of prominent business men and farmers conversant with the territory to be worked. Each agent has in charge the practical work in one or more counties, strictly under such general directions as may be issued from the central office at Washington, D.C. District agents are expected to have not only a knowledge of scientific agriculture, but to be practical farmers and to have had considerable experience in the demonstration work. State agents are strong and capable men, who have shown their ability to carry out successfully the instructions of the central office over a large territory, and they are especially qualified for the work by the possession of the tact necessary to influence men.

The term "demonstration farm" is used to designate a portion of land on a farm that is worked strictly according to our instructions. This is visited by an agent as often as once a month, if possible, to see that these instructions are carried out and to give any further advice necessary.

A "cooperator" is a farmer who agrees to work a part or all of his crop according to our instructions.

The Farmers' Cooperative Demonstration Work now covers portions of 12 States, employs 375 traveling agents, has many thousand demonstration farms, and potentially influences, through boys' corn clubs, field schools, and cooperators, a much larger number than are classed as demonstrators. At present it has close cooperation with six agricultural colleges and a large number of rural schools, assisting the latter to make field demonstrations. It also cooperates with state and county superintendents of public instruction in demonstrations for boys' corn clubs.

This work is supported by Congressional appropriation, by liberal contributions from the General Education Board, by county aid, and by donations from boards of trade and private individuals.

A Real Rural School for the Man with the Plow

The demonstration work may be regarded as a system of adult education given to the farmer upon his farm by means of object lessons in the soil, prepared under his observation and generally by his own hand.

The teaching by object lessons is more effective where it is simple, direct, and limited to a few common field crops, such as cotton, corn, cowpeas, and oats in the South, so that the comparisons may be evident and accepted at a glance. If general success can be secured with these standard crops, further diversification follows as a natural result.

The instruction given for the first year mainly refers to the method of making a larger and more profitable crop at a reduced cost of production, and consists of four lessons, called "the primary lessons:" (1) The best seed bed and how to make it; (2) the best seed of its variety and how to obtain it; (3) frequent and mainly shallow cultivation of the crop — how and why; (4) the use of better teams and tools to secure more economic production.

The principal defects in the seed bed for farm crops in the South are shallow breaking (plowing), failure to fully pulverize the soil before planting, insufficient humus in the soil, and defective drainage. Such a seed bed can never produce maximum crops. It carries insufficient moisture for periods of drought and has an excess under heavy precipitation. During most of the period of growth the plants are insufficiently nourished, either from inability to obtain sufficient food through lack of moisture or a too diluted nourishment through excess of moisture. The result is a small crop.

The simple remedy is deeper breaking in the fall, thorough use of disk and harrow, plowing under of green crops at frequent periods, and an improvement of the drainage by ditches or tiles.

One cause of the general shallow breaking in the Southern States is the single mule used on many farms and the light mules where they are used double. The introduction of the disk plow, enables one man to do nine times the work in a day of the one man and do it easier. The one man with one mule is expected to break an acre a day 3 inches deep; one man with a disk plow and four large mules will average 3 acres a day 9 inches deep on rather stiff soil and do a better job.

Seed

Prior to the commencement of the demonstration work the average farmer in the South gave little attention to seed selection. Corn was culled in the spring from the crib and cotton from the gin-run pile and planted without testing. The result was a poor stand — a condition that can rarely be remedied.

The demonstration work requires seed of a known type, carefully selected, graded, and stored for the first year's planting, and for each succeeding year the planting of a small field remote from any grain crop of the same type; this seed patch to be specially prepared, fertilized, and planted with the seed selected in the field the previous fall when the grain was ripe and afterwards stored in a dry place.

Cultivation

Great use is made of the section harrow before and after planting and when the plants are quite small. Cultivation of cotton or corn in rows is at first deep, but shallow and frequent after the plants are 10 inches tall. This conserves the moisture.

In the practical application of these instructions it has been found that the best seed bed added 100 per cent to the average crop on similar lands with an average preparation; planting the best seed made a gain of 50 per cent, and shallow, frequent cultivation was equal to another 50 per cent, making a total gain of 200 per cent, or a crop three times the average. With better teams and implements this greater crop is made at less cost an acre. The profit increases faster than the yield. If the net profits on a crop of corn yielding 20 bushels an acre, valued at 75 cents a bushel, be $3, on a crop of 60 bushels the net profit would be $33 an acre; that is, the profit is tenfold where the gain in yield is threefold.

It generally requires from two to three years to thoroughly impress the farmer that this lesson of making a greater yield per acre is a practical method of farming applicable to his entire farm. The first year he rarely carries out the entire plan. He has not quite faith enough, or possibly the season is adverse, but he generally succeeds so much better than he expected that the second year's trial is more thorough, with a correspondingly increased gain.

The farmer is a natural doubter. When he has harvested the larger crop the second year, he is frequently inclined to attribute it to one thing, generally the seed, because this is most in evidence, instead of distributing the credit between the better seed bed, the better seed, and the intensive cultivation. Frequently his neighbors, full of the one-idea merit, offer $5 a bushel for the seed, thinking that the seed alone will make the crop. The third year the demonstration farmer is generally more of a convert and enlarges his trial area, frequently including his entire farm. In the meantime his neighbors have been observing and have commenced to inquire and follow his example.

It requires from three to five years to have the increased yield show a considerable average gain in the local markets. This depends, however, somewhat upon the number of demonstrations established in a county. Where one can be placed in each neighborhood the progress is rapid, because the interest soon becomes intense. If only one or two demonstration farms are established in a county, the work does not create interest enough to arouse public sentiment and produce at once a strong opinion in its favor.

As soon as the primary lessons, as above explained, have been accepted and tested by a farmer, a secondary series is commenced, which includes —

(1) Demonstrations in conserving and enriching the soil by the use of legumes and winter cover crops. These involve simple crop rotation and the turning under of green crops; also the prevention of soil waste by erosion.

(2) The value and uses of barnyard manures and commercial fertilizers, and how to apply them.

(3) Simple methods of farm drainage.

The third series of lessons relates to better pastures and meadows and how to secure them; the most economic grain crops for work animals or to produce flesh as a supplement to the pasture and meadow grasses. This line of instruction is necessary, because the economic production of farm crops depends in a great measure upon an economic support of the work teams.

The general method among the small farmers of the South was to depend mainly upon corn fodder and corn. Some had pastures, but rarely a good pasture. This method is expensive and causes a reduction in the number of animals kept for work to the smallest number possible and a corresponding substitution of hand labor. Modern methods of farming require considerable increase in the number and strength of teams. Profitable farming has become a team and implement problem. The improved pasture and cover-cured hay furnish foods of great economy and are sufficiently nutritious for the ordinary support of work stock. For heavy work a small addition of grain to the ration is required.

If it be necessary in the interests of economy to produce upon the farm the food for the work animals it is still more important to produce, as far as possible, the food required by all the laborers and their families. The family garden, the poultry, and the cow are great cash economizers and pocketbook conservers and may be classed with the better teams and tools as essential to better farm equipment.

Field Schools

A very valuable method of instruction introduced by the demonstration work is the field school. Previous to the time the local agent of the work expects to visit a demonstrator he notifies all the cooperators in the vicinity to meet him there on a certain date at a given hour. Thus, a number of good farmers discuss the methods and, by comparison, place a value upon the work done. The same method is employed in the selection of seed corn. . . . Such is the isolated situation of the average farmer that he may continue for years to believe he has the best seed of the several crops he produces unless he is brought into direct public comparison and competition with other farmers — not in a fair or exhibition where prizes are to be awarded and only the best specimens are brought, but in a mere exhibit of what the farmers expect to plant without any assorting. The farmers in the First Congressional District in North Carolina were invited to assemble in March, 1909, at central points and each bring about 50 ears of the seed corn they expected to plant. These ears were arranged on a long table in the public square, the owner's name being conspicuously attached to each pile. (See samples, Pl. III.) Expert judges were present to select and test. Some corn was brought that tested less than 45 per cent of fertile grains. At the close of the meeting over 90 per cent of the corn samples went for stock feed and was replaced by purchasing a better variety or quality.

Boys' Corn Clubs

One of the greatest problems before the American people has been how to interest in rural life and attach to the farm the young man who has acquired a liberal education and displayed a capacity for leadership. The loss of rural leaders by emigration to the city has been one of the most serious retrogressive factors in our whole civilization. The Farmers' Cooperative Demonstration Work has solved the problem. These young men left the farm because they were repelled by the hardships, excessive toil, and meager gains on the farm and were allured by a seemingly greater opportunity to acquire wealth, influence, and position in the city. The demonstration work undertakes to create in the schoolboy a love of the farm and a new hope by showing the wonderful possibilities of the soil when properly managed and the ease with which wealth and distinction are achieved in rural life when science and art join hands. This is worked out by the cooperation of the demonstration workers, the county superintendent of public instruction, and the rural teachers.

The superintendent and teachers organize the schoolboys over 10 years of age into clubs; the demonstration work furnishes the plan of organization and the instructions (which the boys agree to observe); the respective parents furnish land, teams, and implements; the merchants and bankers provide the prizes, and the local papers give the publicity. Each boy must personally work 1 acre under the same regulations governing all other contestants. The result of 300 to 400 boys entering such a contest in a county arouses intense interest. The boy learns the best way to raise corn or cotton and his appreciation of the farm is greatly enhanced.

In 1909 the boys in the corn contest of one county in Mississippi averaged a production of 74 bushels of corn per acre, while the farmers averaged less than 20. In South Carolina one boy raised 152½ bushels on a measured acre, while the state average was less than 16.

Incidental Teaching

In addition to the demonstrations made to teach the best methods of securing the largest yields of field crops with the greatest economy, incidentally there is much instruction along the lines of rural improvement, the better home, its equipment and environment, the country roads, the school at the crossroads, rural society, etc. The average farmer takes it for granted that an agent of the Department of Agriculture is an authority upon all lines of husbandry, and innumerable inquiries are made of him about the dairy, the breeding and management of farm stock, horticulture, market gardening, insect pests, etc. All this incidental teaching is done without demonstration by referring the inquirers to the several bureaus in the United States Department of Agriculture, or request is made that bulletins covering the subject of inquiry be forwarded to them by mail.

In still another way the Farmers' Cooperative Demonstration Work is helpful. The many scientific divisions of the Bureau of Plant Industry are annually making discoveries of great value, and the problem has been how to get these to the farmers in a way so effective that they will adopt them. A bulletin does not do this with the average farmer. The agents of the Farmers' Cooperative Demonstration Work can place these improvements or discoveries in the hands of men who will utilize them to advantage because these agents are in touch with all the people. Thus the demonstration work is a means of disseminating information for all the bureaus of the Department that are close to rural life.

Demonstration Work Helpful in Other Ways

In the Southern States, where there are some white and many negro farmers who can not read, there is liable to sweep over a section a wave of depression amounting to a doubt about making a crop, which may cause a perceptible reduction in the acreage planted if the depression is felt prior to planting, or if later it may reduce the tillage of the crop or may result in its total abandonment. Nor is this wave of pessimism confined to the unlettered. Where crops are made on the advance system it may take such a hold of the merchant and the banker that they refuse to make the necessary advances, which forces the laborer and the tenant farmer to remove to territory where the advances can be obtained. In Harrison County, Tex., in 1907, about 500 tenants and laborers were preparing to abandon the farms after the cotton crop was up, through fear that they could not succeed in making it. The same cause enormously reduced the cotton acreage in Louisiana and Mississippi in 1909. The agents of the Farmers' Cooperative Demonstration Work have been exceedingly influential in restoring and maintaining confidence among all classes.

Two Viewpoints

The Farmers' Cooperative Demonstration Work may be regarded as a method of increasing farm crops and as logically the first step toward a true uplift, or it may be considered a system of rural education for boys and adults by which a readjustment of country life can be effected and placed upon a higher plane of profit, comfort, culture, influence, and power.

Because the first feature of this demonstration work is to show the farmer how he may more than double his crop at a reduced cost of production, it has been regarded by some solely as a method of increasing farm crops by applying scientific principles to the problem. This would be of great value to the world and would stand as a sufficient justification for the efforts put forth and the expenditures involved, but such a conception would fail to convey the broader purpose of this work.

There is much knowledge applicable and helpful to husbandry that is annually worked out and made available by the scientists in the United States Department of Agriculture and in the state experiment stations and by individual farmers upon their farms, which is sufficient to readjust agriculture and place it upon a basis of greater profit, to reconstruct the rural home, and to give to country life an attraction, a dignity, and a potential influence it has never received. This body of knowledge can not be conveyed and delivered by a written message to the people in such a way that they will accept and adopt it. This can only be done by personal appeal and ocular demonstrations. This is the mission of the Farmers' Cooperative Demonstration Work, and it has justified its claims by the results.

It is noteworthy that the sciences adopted the demonstration method of instruction long since. The chemist and the physicist require their students to work out their problems in the laboratory, the doctor and surgeon must practice in the hospital, and the mechanical engineer must show efficiency in the shop to complete his education. The Farmers' Cooperative Demonstration Work seeks to apply the same scientific methods to farmers by requiring them to work out their problems in the soil and obtain the answer in the crib. The soil is the farmers' laboratory.

The demonstration method of reaching and influencing the men on the farms is destined ultimately to be adopted by most civilized nations as a part of a great system of rural education.

Extension Work in Utah, 1910

From Lewis A. Merrill, "The College Extension Work," *Deseret Farmer* (Lehi, Utah, August 27, 1910), VII, pp. 3, 10.

The College Extension Work

Until recently comparatively few of the people of Utah received any direct benefit from the work of the Agricultural College, notwithstanding its enrollment of more than a thousand students. It is true that the influence of the students in their respective communities and the results of the experimental work are far reaching but the man and woman on the farm, who in their earlier life were so fully occupied in clearing the sage brush and in building canals, had few educational advantages, were not influenced materially by these agencies.

For this reason the Extension Department has been organized and the responsibility of carrying the glad tidings of the new Gospel of Agriculture and Domestic Science, placed upon it. The President of the College recognizes the importance of this work and in the organization of the College made the Extension Department co-ordinate with the work of the Experiment Station or any of the schools of the College.

The work of the Department embraces:

1. Farmers' and Housekeepers' Schools

These schools are of one week's duration. Subjects of most importance to the various communities are taken up and discussed by experts from the College, separate sessions being held during the morning and afternoon for men and women. Conjoint sessions are held during the evening at which special lecturers are secured from the various educational institutions of the State.

These schools are usually held in co-operation with the Farmers' Organizations or Commercial Clubs and a small registration fee of $1.00 is charged for the course.

During the past three years these schools have been very successful and there are thousands of men and women in Utah villages today who are ready to affirm that the week spent in these schools was the most profitable week of their lives.

2. Farm and Home Lectures in the State High Schools

A course of lectures in Agriculture and Domestic Science has been outlined and professors from the College will go to the high schools, where permitted, and give a week's course of instruction in these subjects.

Most Utah villages are dependent for their commercial prosperity, yes, for their very existence, on the farms surrounding them. The high schools draw their students from the farms. The College Extension Department endeavors through these schools to promote the interests of agriculture and domestic science. The desirability and feasibility of including these subjects in the high school program is recognized throughout the State and the demands for this form of work, are already in excess of our ability to supply. There are no charges for this course, but the high school authorities are expected to arrange public meetings on Thursday and Friday evenings of the week during which the schools are held and provide a number of musical selections for the program. They are also expected to furnish a well lighted and heated hall for these meetings.

3. Farmers' Institutes

This form of extension work has been carried on in this State for some thirteen years now. Local organizations are perfected, officers are elected, and under their auspices one and two day meetings are held. At these meetings problems of most importance to the various localities are taken up and discussed for a part of the session, ample time, however, being allowed for discussion. Women's Institutes are planned co-ordinate with the men's Institutes and the evening sessions are usually held conjointly.

It is doubtful if there is a more intelligent and more intellectual body of farmers anywhere in the world that is to be found in Utah. Farmers' Institutes here are really conferences between the local farmers and some men from the Agricultural College, who happen at that time, to be carrying out experiments at the State's expense. There is a genuine respect and mutual confidence between the farmers and the professors from the College. Recently an able scientist from the U.S. Department of Agriculture, in traveling through this State, remarked to the Director of the Experiment Station that he had never been in any place where the farmers had so much confidence in the Station workers and where the Station workers were so completely in harmony with the farmers.

Owing to the other forms of Extension work, the Farmers' Institutes have not been emphasized during the recent years as much as formerly because it is felt that so much greater good can be accomplished by the Movable Schools. During this coming season it is planned to hold a large number of these Institutes, however, and members of the Extension staff are already out in the outlying counties conducting Farmers' Institutes.

4. Farmers' Demonstration Trains

A new and unique form of Extension work has recently come into existence. The Agricultural College authorities, in co-operation with the various railroad companies, now send out each year a demonstration and lecture train. Two years ago such a train was carried through this State for some fifty-six days. At the more important points the train stopped for twenty four hours. Some cars were equipped with exhibits and others were for lecture purposes.

The train carried a milking machine and at each of the points visited cows were brought and milked. Last year the Oregon Short Line Railroad, in co-operation with the College sent out a potato and orchard heating special. This train went only through the populous districts in the northern part of the State and made stops of only one hour's duration. In the evening, however, stops were made at important farming centers like Brigham City and Logan and there public meetings were held.

This train accomplished much good in educating the fruit growers regarding the proper methods of orchard heating and resulted during the past year in saving thousands of dollars to the Utah orchardists.

The Extension Department in addition to the duties outlined above, sends out field specialists to give advice to the farmers, prepares and sends out bulletins, reports and circulars, prepares articles for the public press, conducts and publishes the Deseret Farmer, provides educational exhibits for the State and County Fairs, takes part in, and assists at the various State Agricultural organizations, assists in farmers' excursions, field demonstrations, etc.

Hundreds of letters are sent out each week to the farmers of the State advising them as to the best methods of farm practices. All of these various forms of activity make the Extension Department one of the most important departments of the College.

Beef Cattle in North Carolina, 1912

From R. S. Curtis, "Beef Cattle Industry of North Carolina," in North Carolina Agricultural Experiment Station, *Thirty-fifth Annual Report*, 1911–12 (Raleigh, 1913), p. 29.

The feeding of beef cattle in North Carolina will undoubtedly become an important industry. In the western portion of the State, the mountain pastures afford excellent grazing where already very desirable types of feeding cattle are being produced. With the advent of better bred sires to use on the common cattle of that region and the improvement of the pasture lands by better management the industry is sure to develop rapidly. Prominent cattle growers state that a large percentage of the desirable grazing land is not at present utilized for pasturage purposes. Not only will the area be extended into the more remote parts, but the quality of the pastures will be improved by better methods of management.

The writer mentions North Carolina especially because the western section of the State is typical of the Appalachian region for cattle grazing purposes. The production of feeding cattle is not limited to this State alone, as Virginia and Tennessee, especially, can produce types of cattle equally as desirable, and within reach of the cattle feeders of this State. Virginia is using to a large extent her own cattle for feeding purposes and also the larger and better cattle of eastern Tennessee and western North Carolina. This is a condition which should receive the attention of the more progressive stockmen of this State. North Carolina feeders should feed all of the cattle produced in the State and, if necessary, draw on the surrounding States for surplus needs.

It need not be stated that cottonseed meal is the only commercial concentrate which at present can be used for feeding beef cattle. The cattle feeding industry furnishes a means of obtaining both the feed and fertilizer values from this commercial product and for this reason every effort should be made to use as much cottonseed meal in our live stock and general farming industries as conservative business methods will permit. It has not been definitely determined just how much cottonseed meal is most profitable for feeding beef cattle, but it is likely that the concentrated portion of the ration will consist largely of cottonseed meal for an indefinite period. Knowing the approximate quantity of cottonseed meal which will form a safe and satisfactory ration, the writer has confined his work of the last two years in determining the most profitable roughage feeds to use with the meal.

The chief roughages available in this State are corn stover, corn silage, and cottonseed hulls. Others of local importance could be named, but it is considered that these three are the most important from the standpoint of economy in beef production. As beef cattle do not return large profits in the South it is necessary to confine the roughage part of the rations to the less valuable feeds produced on the farm. . . .

Agricultural Experimentation in Wisconsin, 1913

From H. L. Russell, "Research Work of the Experiment Station," in Wisconsin Agricultural Experiment Station, *Annual Report*, 1913 (Madison, Wis, 1913), pp. 3–5, 7–11.

The Agricultural Experiment Stations, as organized here in America, were founded with the definite object of promoting agricultural science and practice. Their practical applications of many of the fundamental discoveries in the realm of the physical sciences have done much to transform the art of farming into a more scientifically controlled occupation.

In the earlier years of this movement much emphasis was laid on the study of the physical and biological problems of production. The object was to increase the returns for labor, for land resources, and for managerial ability by the improvement of breeds of live stock and varieties of crops, the development of better cultural practices, and the elimination of waste caused by diseases and pests. Great success has attended this phase of endeavor, as is evident from the results seen wherever intelligent use is made of the improved methods.

But it is the function of the experiment station to study *all* the forces which influence the farmers' activities. Besides the physical and biological factors which have properly received great attention are the economic forces which influence the farmer in determining when and how to market his produce, as well as what to produce and how to produce it most economically. These economic questions are now being given much greater attention than heretofore.

Among the present day problems which must command attention on the part of our agricultural workers are those relating to marketing and distribution. Economy in transferring products from the producer to the consumer and a fair division of the proceeds among those who produce, store, or transfer the article, constitute the problems of this field. If each farmer in this country grew twice as large a crop this year as he did last, how much better off would he be? In many portions of the country it would simply mean more rapid depletion of soil fertility without any consequent profit, for a great increase in production without a corresponding increase in demand means lower values and lower profits to the farmer.

Agriculture must of necessity be judged by the profits secured from its operation. It is, therefore, incumbent on the experiment station to undertake the studies which are necessary to understand thoroughly the economic forces concerned in the problems of distribution. This demands as keen economic insight and thorough study as do such material questions as feeding values and plant diseases. The general public too has a peculiar interest in this class of questions since the rising cost of living is determined quite as much by the costs of distribution as by the costs of production.

We, therefore, first present in the summary of the research work of the experiment station, some of the results which have been worked out here along these economic lines. . . .

Marketing of Wisconsin Cheese

Much interest is now being manifested in cooperation along various lines, but before any rational plans can be proposed that will aid in the development of the cooperative idea, an accurate picture of the entire marketing process of any product is necessary. The Agricultural Economics department is, therefore, undertaking thorough studies of the marketing of some of our leading agricultural products to serve as a basis for future development along rational economic lines.

The first of these studies was that of the marketing of Cheddar cheese, begun by Professor Taylor in the spring of 1912, the results of which were published a year later in Bulletin 231. The picture of all the middleman processes intervening between producer and consumer which is presented in this bulletin, shows that the marketing of cheese is not so simple a process as might have been assumed.

Various defects in the present system are shown, but at the same time it is pointed out that while improvements should be made in some instances, both with respect to economy of marketing and to fairness of the charge made for the middleman's service, great care should be taken in any effort to improve the present system. No institution which is efficiently performing an important function for a fair price, should be attacked, but where excessive charges are made two methods are available for establishing fair charges, (1) cooperation, for local problems, and (2) state regulation, for state-wide questions. . . .

The cheesemaker gets less for making a pound of Brick or Limburger cheese than for making Cheddar or Swiss. This difference would be offset in part by the larger amounts made from a given quantity of milk were it not for the fact that he handles less milk than does the maker of the harder cheeses. The somewhat higher cost of transportation of American cheese as compared to the other kinds is due to the fact that on an average it goes a longer distance. The wholesaler gets a narrower margin for handling American cheese than for the others because the quantity he sells is so much greater that he does not need so great a return on each pound. The dealer performs a considerable service in assembling cheese, paraffining it, handling, carting, and the like. About a cent a pound is absorbed in storage charges and shrinkage. The storage charge is one of the necessary expenses of the process and may be paid by any one of the various owners of the cheese, between maker and consumer. The shrinkage is borne in part by the farmer who usually is paid for a little less cheese than is produced from the milk he delivers.

The retailer has to stand a considerable loss due to the shrinkage, crumbling, and spoiling of cheese while in his possession, which explains in part the fact that aside from the farmer, he gets the largest share of anyone. A great many merchants handle but a small quantity of cheese and as a result are obliged to get a wide margin per pound or lose money. So long as it is necessary for cheese to pass through so many hands there is little prospect of reducing the middleman charges so that the farmer will receive a much larger proportion of the consumer's price, or the consumer be much more favorably treated than at present.

Marketing of Wisconsin Potatoes

Owing to the importance of the potato industry in Wisconsin, Professor Taylor in 1912 undertook a study of the various phases of the marketing of this crop so as to gain accurate information which would point out any opportunities for greater economy in the middleman processes. The two main services which must be rendered in marketing potatoes are (1) storing of the supply harvested in one month in order that there may be potatoes for the remainder of the year, (2) distributing the surplus potatoes of the principal potato districts to the regions where fewer potatoes are produced than consumed.

Although potato dealers maintain warehouses in which some potatoes are stored, it is the usual thing for a dealer to handle three times as many potatoes as he could store at any one time. The storing of potatoes is, therefore, a function performed largely by the producers. The work of the local dealer is primarily that of sorting, and loading into cars either in sacks or in bulk. As an active potato dealer is always shipping the product, it is only incidental that he is a storer of potatoes. If the roads are good, the price satisfactory, and the farmers have the time and the inclination to haul potatoes, the warehouse fills up more or less; then when the roads are bad or the farmer is busy in the fields the warehouse is emptied out. . . .

Potatoes are always shipped in carload lots from the local station to the distant consuming or wholesale centers. In winter, it is necessary to ship in heated cars to prevent freezing in transit. When the car reaches Chicago it may be rebilled to Cincinnati, Pittsburgh, St. Louis, or some other wholesale point, or it may be sold to a wholesaler in Chicago.

The investigations are being continued with a view of obtaining a complete description of what happens to our potatoes from the time they leave the local station until they are placed in the consumer's kitchen.

Rural Credit

The widespread interest in the subject of agricultural credit has suggested the desirability of a survey with a view to ascertaining the actual facts in selected counties in Wisconsin. It seems highly probable that the special interest developed in this subject will lead to legislative action. To take such action wisely the legislators should have before them all the necessary facts to serve as a basis for their deliberations. In securing such data, the Agricultural College should lend all possible assistance. Naturally it is impossible to cover the conditions that actually exist over the entire state in any limited period of time, but Professor Hibbard of the Agricultural Economics department has chosen the two extreme conditions to study first. Dane represents a long-settled county in which land values have reached a high figure and a high per capita of wealth obtains. Rusk, on the other hand, is a new and pioneer county in which the main development has been and probably will be agricultural.

Interest rates on farm loans in the older southern county range from 5 to 6 per cent, while in the newer northern county money brings from 6 to 10 per cent. In southern Wisconsin the highest quality of bank loans are farm mortgages on improved land. Often such loans are made to the farmer at less than his city cousin is obliged to pay for his real estate accommodation. In this section the credit wants of the farmer are usually easily met at reasonable rates, for farm loans are eagerly sought by those who have money to lend.

In southern Wisconsin undoubtedly much additional capital could, however, return profitable income on the investment if it was utilized in further development of lands already occupied. For drainage, both surface and tile, and for clearing and breaking woodland large amounts of money are yet needed even in southern Wisconsin.

In the undeveloped North there is not sufficient accumulated money to meet the needs of these communities, although it must be kept in mind that the fortunes amassed in the harvesting of the first crop, the wonderful stand of pine and hardwood forests, in many cases have contributed much to the agricultural development of these cut-over sections. These regions need large amounts of money for further development, and the probabilities are that the settler frequently exhausts his credit and yet is unable to finance at cheap rates his real monetary needs. To aid in meeting this demand a law authorizing the creation of cooperative land mortgage banks was passed by the last legislature and three of these were organized this past year.

These studies bring out the interesting fact that although the indebtedness of farmers is constantly growing, this increase is not so great as the increase in wealth. . . .

Smith Lever Act, 1914

From 38 U. S. Statutes at Large 372.

AN ACT TO PROVIDE FOR COOPERATIVE AGRICULTURAL EXTENSION WORK BETWEEN THE AGRICULTURAL COLLEGES IN THE SEVERAL STATES RECEIVING THE BENEFITS OF AN ACT OF CONGRESS APPROVED JULY SECOND, EIGHTEEN HUNDRED AND SIXTY-TWO, AND OF ACTS SUPPLEMENTARY THERETO, AND THE UNITED STATES DEPARTMENT OF AGRICULTURE

Be it enacted by the Senate and House of Representatives of the United States of America in Congress assembled, That in order to aid in diffusing among the people of the United States useful and practical information on subjects relating to agriculture and home economics, and to encourage the application of the same, there may be inaugurated in connection with the college or colleges in each State now receiving, or which may hereafter receive, the benefits of the Act of Congress approved July second, eighteen hundred and sixty-two, entitled "An Act donating public lands to the several States and Territories which may provide colleges for the benefit of agriculture and the mechanic arts" (Twelfth Statutes at Large, page five hundred and three), and of the Act of Congress approved August thirtieth, eighteen hundred and ninety (Twenty-sixth Statutes at Large, page four hundred and seventeen and chapter eight hundred and forty-one), agricultural extension work which shall be carried on in cooperation with the United States Department of Agriculture: *Provided*, That in any State in which two or more such colleges have been or hereafter may be established the appropriations hereinafter made to such State shall be administered by such college or colleges as the legislature of such State may direct: *Provided further,* That, pending the inauguration and development of the cooperative extension work herein authorized, nothing in this Act shall be construed to discontinue either the farm management work or the farmers' cooperative demonstration work as now conducted by the Bureau of Plant Industry of the Department of Agriculture.

SEC. 2. That cooperative agricultural extension work shall consist of the giving of instruction and practical demonstrations in agriculture and home economics to persons not attending or resident in said colleges in the several communities, and imparting to such persons information on said subjects through field demonstrations, publications, and otherwise; and this work shall be carried on in such manner as may be mutually agreed upon by the Secretary of Agriculture and the State agricultural college or colleges receiving the benefits of this Act.

SEC. 3. That for the purpose of paying the expenses of said cooperative agricultural extension work and the necessary printing and distributing of information in connection with the same, there is permanently appropriated, out of any money in the Treasury not otherwise appropriated, the sum of $480,000 for each year, $10,000 of which shall be paid annually, in the manner hereinafter provided, to each State which shall by action of its legislature assent to the provisions of this Act: *Provided*, That payment of such installments of the appropriation hereinbefore made as shall become due to any State before the adjournment of the regular session of the legislature meeting next after the passage of this Act may, in the absence of prior legislative assent, be made upon the assent of the governor thereof duly certified to the Secretary of the Treasury: *Provided further,* That there is also appropriated an additional sum of $600,000 for the fiscal year following that in which the foregoing appropriation first becomes available, and for each year thereafter for seven years a sum exceeding by $500,000 the sum appropriated for each preceding year, and for each year thereafter there is permanently appropriated for each year the sum of $4,100,000 in addition to the sum of $480,000 hereinbefore provided: *Provided further,* That before the funds herein appropriated shall become available to any college for any fiscal year plans for the work to be carried on under this Act shall be submitted by the proper officials of each college and approved by the Secretary of Agriculture. Such additional sums shall be used only for the purposes hereinbefore stated, and shall be allotted annually to each State by the Secretary of Agriculture and paid in the manner hereinbefore provided, in the proportion which the rural population of each State bears to the total rural population of all the States as determined by the next preceding Federal census: *Provided further,* That no payment out of the additional appropriations herein provided shall be made in any year to any State until an equal sum has been appropriated for that year by the legislature of such State, or provided by State, county, college, local authority, or individual contributions from within the State, for the maintenance of the cooperative agricultural extension work provided for in this Act.

SEC. 4. That the sums hereby appropriated for extension work shall be paid in equal semiannual payments on the first day of January and July of each year by the Secretary of the Treasury upon the warrant of the Secretary of Agriculture, out of the Treasury of the United States, to the treasurer or other officer of the State duly authorized by the laws of the State to receive the same; and such officer shall be required to report to the Secretary of Agriculture, on or before the first day of September of each year, a detailed statement of the amount so received during the previous fiscal year, and of its disbursement, on forms prescribed by the Secretary of Agriculture.

SEC. 5. That if any portion of the moneys received by the designated officer of any State for the support and maintenance of cooperative agricultural extension work, as provided in this Act, shall by any action or contingency be diminished or lost, or be misapplied, it shall be replaced by said State to which it belongs, and until so replaced no subsequent appropriation shall be apportioned or paid to said State, and no portion of said moneys shall be applied, directly or indirectly, to the purchase, erection, preservation, or repair of any building or buildings, or the purchase or rental of land, or in college-course teaching, lectures in colleges, promoting agricultural trains, or any other purpose not specified in this Act, and not more than five per centum of each annual appropriation shall be applied to the printing and distribution of publications. It shall be the duty of each of said colleges annually, on or before the first day of January, to make to the governor of the State in which it is located a full and detailed report of its operations in the direction of extension work as defined in this Act, including a detailed statement of receipts and expenditures from all sources for this purpose, a copy of which report shall be sent to the Secretary of Agriculture and to the Secretary of the Treasury of the United States.

SEC. 6. That on or before the first day of July in each year after the passage of this Act the Secretary of Agriculture shall ascertain and certify to the Secretary of the

Treasury as to each State whether it is entitled to receive its share of the annual appropriation for cooperative agricultural extension work under this Act, and the amount which it is entitled to receive. If the Secretary of Agriculture shall withhold a certificate from any State of its appropriation, the facts and reasons therefor shall be reported to the President, and the amount involved shall be kept separate in the Treasury until the expiration of the Congress next succeeding a session of the legislature of any State from which a certificate has been withheld, in order that the State may, if it should so desire, appeal to Congress from the determination of the Secretary of Agriculture. If the next Congress shall not direct such sum to be paid, it shall be covered into the Treasury.

SEC. 7. That the Secretary of Agriculture shall make an annual report to Congress of the receipts, expenditures, and results of the cooperative agricultural extension work in all of the States receiving the benefits of this Act, and also whether the appropriation of any State has been withheld; and if so, the reasons therefor.

SEC. 8. That Congress may at any time alter, amend, or repeal any or all of the provisions of this Act.

Approved, May 8, 1914.

Changes in Farming and Farm Life

On Fencing, 1871

From U.S. Department of Agriculture, *Annual Report*, 1871, pp. 497–512.

STATISTICS OF FENCES IN THE UNITED STATES

It has been a mooted point, in the past, whether fences were intended to avert the destruction of corn by the cattle of neighbors, or to restrain one's own stock from similar depredations. For a long time the popular idea, logically interpreted, appeared to be that corn should be restrained to prevent depredations upon cattle. Another question, of which a solution has been desired, is whether the money invested in farm-stock or that in farm-fences is the greater sum. It is certain that the fence investment is a large one, and strongly suspected that much of it is avoidable and unprofitable. While rapidly paying the national debt, it is possible that the American people may discover a means of reducing another of almost equal proportions. In the one case the annual tax is a fixed sum, which is less than legal interest upon the entire principal; in the other, it is legal interest on the whole amount, and a still larger tax for depreciation of the principal, thus more than doubling the tax, and rendering the fence debt a heavier burden than the war debt.

It is beginning to be seen that our fence laws are inequitable in a greater degree than is required by the principle of yielding something of personal right, when necessary, for the general good. When a score of young farmers "go West," with strong hands and little cash in them, but a munificent promise to each of a homestead worth $200 now, and $2,000 in the future, for less than $20 in land-office fees, they often find that $1,000 will be required to fence scantily each farm, with little benefit to themselves, but mainly for mutual protection against a single stock-grower, rich in cattle, and becoming richer by feeding them without cost upon the unpurchased prairie. This little community of twenty families cannot see the justice of the requirement which compels the expenditure of $20,000 to protect their crops from injury by the nomadic cattle of their unsettled neighbor, which may not be worth

$10,000 altogether. There is also inequality in the tax which fencing levies upon the farmers, the rate of which increases with the decrease of the area; for example, a farmer inclosing a section of land, 640 acres, with a cheap fence costing but $1 per rod, pays $1,280 for as many rods of fence, or $2 per acre; another, with a quarter section, 160 acres, pays $640, or $4 per acre; while a third, who is only able to hold 40 acres, must pay $320, or $8 per acre. Thus the fencing system is one of differential mortgages, the poor man in this case being burdened with an extra mortgage of $6 per acre which his richer neighbor is not compelled to bear. All these acres are of equal intrinsic and productive value, but those of the larger farm have each but a fourth of the annual burden thrown upon the smaller homestead, and the whole expense may be for protection against trespassing cattle owned by others.

But it is not proposed to discuss the fence question. It is necessary, first, to obtain possession of its facts, ascertain what kinds of fence are used, the number of rods of each, and the cost of each. The census furnishes no light upon it, and local collections of these essential facts are few and imperfect. The best that can be done at present is to seek county estimates of kind, amount, and cost, from careful analysis of ascertained facts. As a preliminary effort in this direction, in the absence of a thorough census, the following series of questions was addressed to the regular statistical correspondents of this Department:

1. What descriptions of farm-fences are made in your county; if of more than one kind, the proportions of each, expressed as percentages of the total quantity?
2. What is the average height and prevailing mode of construction of each kind?
3. What is your estimate, for the farms of your county, of the average number of rods of fence to each one hundred acres of farm-lands, including together improved and unimproved lands?
4. What is your estimate, for the whole county, of the average size (number of acres) of inclosures or fields?
5. Average price of boards used for fences, per thousand?
6. Average price of rails per thousand?
7. What proportion of openings have bars and what proportion gates; style and cost of gates?
8. Average cost per rod of worm-fence; of post and rails; of board-fence; of stone wall; of other kinds?
9. Average cost per hundred rods of annual repairs of all farm-fences?
10. What kinds of wood are used as fence material, and what the relative cost of each?
11. What is the comparative durability of each kind?

Returns were made from 846 counties, nearly all answering every question, some very fully. As a sample of the most exhaustive, the following, from Hon. John M. Millikin, of Butler County, Ohio, is given in full:

1. Our farm-fences consist of common worm rail fence, and (what can hardly be called a fence) of osage-orange hedge. There are no data by which to determine accurately the proportion of each. My estimate is 80 per cent. rail-fence, 15 per cent. board-fence, and 5 per cent. hedge-fence.

2. Our worm rail fence varies in height. They are from seven to nine rails high, including riders. Our board-fence is usually made of 16-foot boards, 1 inch thick and 6 inches wide. Posts 8 feet apart. Black locust posts always preferred. Red cedar, white cedar, and oak posts all used, and esteemed for durability, in the order named. Most people make their board-fence five boards high, and then cap it. Recently many are only using four boards, and capping with the fifth.

3. In 1857 I made a very careful estimate of the number of rods of fence in this county, and the cost of the same. I also estimated the annual interest on the same, and the annual expense of keeping the same in repair. These estimates were made for the purpose of showing the necessity of having a law enacted to prevent cattle from running at large. I presented my statement to the State Agricultural Convention, and the ultimate result was the passage of a very valuable law restraining cattle from running at large. As yet, it is not generally enforced, but is accomplishing good results. My data, then used, I cannot find, and must, therefore, hastily make another estimate. So much preliminary. Our farms, of 100 acres each, will average from 875 to 950 rods of fence — say fully 900 rods.

4. We have in this county about 4,000 farms, varying in size from 30 acres to 400 acres. Of the latter we have some thirty or forty. Each farm, on an average, will have about eight fields, and we have, therefore, "of inclosures or fields," at least 32,000. This estimate does not include numerous small lots which every farmer has in immediate connection with the barn-yard.

5. The average price for fencing-boards is about $22 per thousand.

6. Good oak rails are worth $70 per thousand.

7. Nearly all inclosures are now provided with gates. There are scarcely more than one pair bars to fifteen gates. In some neighborhoods bars have been entirely superseded by gates. Gates are usually made with common fencing-boards, one inch thick and six inches wide; a post 3 by 4 at one end and 2 by 3 at the other end. Braces of boards of like size, extending from bottom of the larger post to the top of the smaller. Cost about $3.

8. New worm-fence will cost about $1.75 per rod. Post and rail fence has almost gone out of use. I have seen none made within the last twenty years, with the exception of one string. It would cost per panel of ten feet, about $1.80. Board-fence per rod, good lumber, and locust or red cedar post, will cost about $2 four boards high, and $2.15 to $2.20 five boards high. Stone walls are not constructed and used as fences in this county.

9. I know of no way of answering this question satisfactorily, as the annual repairs will so much depend upon the age, material, &c., of the fence. From the investigations I have made, I am satisfied that it will take 15 per cent. per annum of the original cost of the fence to pay interest and keep up repairs.

10. Farmers prefer oak and walnut rails. The latter would probably cost $120 per thousand, and are not now used. Where rails are used now, farmers are willing to make them out of almost any kind of timber. Where board-fence is made, pine boards are preferred. Locust and red cedar posts are preferred, costing about 35 cents each. Oak posts are somewhat cheaper but less durable.

11. Locust posts are believed not only to e stronger than cedar, but they hold nails better and are more durable.

Permit me to add further. We have in this county 293,000 acres of land, all inclosed. We have at least 1,600,000 rods of fencing, some costing largely more, yes, four-fold the price at which I have estimated our fences per rod. But for the purpose of estimating the annual cost of maintaining our fences, including interest, let me put the average at $2 per rod; 2,600,000 rods of fence, at $2, will cost $5,200,000. Annual cost of maintaining same, (including interest,) at 15 per cent. on original cost, $780,000. These figures are astounding, and yet I believe that they are not too high. Material for rail-fences will soon be out of the question, and lumber of every kind is annually becoming scarcer, and necessarily will increase in price. Is it not, therefore, highly important that laws restraining stock from running at large should meet with more favor; that fields should be enlarged; that soiling should be more practiced, and that farmers should thereby be relieved from the great burden of paying such immense sums for fencing?

Kind of Fences and Mode of Construction

The replies are necessarily monotonous from their repetition of details; they show that the common forms of fencing are substantially alike in all parts of the country, yet varied everywhere to accommodate the differences in kind, quality, comparative scarcity, and cost of timber; and present the Virginia rail-fence as the pioneer in all timbered districts, from the simplicity of its construction, not even requiring nails, but rails only. The tendency to supersede this form with a fence requiring less timber and occupying less space, while presenting to the eye more artistic features, is manifestly growing. The following extract from the returns of our correspondent in Rutherford County, Tennessee, shows that this tendency is already pervading a State which has yet half its farm-lands in forest:

> There can be no objection to the red cedar rail-fence on the score of first cost or durability; but there is a most serious objection to all worm-fences. The writer has, upon a farm of 475 acres, about five and a half miles of worm-fence and one mile of plank-fence; also one-fourth mile of good stone fence. The stone and plank fences occupy only the ground they stand on. The five and a half miles of worm-fence occupy five acres of land, and keep out of cultivation nearly if not quite eleven acres of land. The cost of keeping down weeds, briars, &c., along these five and a half miles of fence — eleven miles of fence-corners — is a tax greater than my State and county tax for this year, and was poorly done at that.

A description in detail of the minute differences in construction, even as reported from the counties of any single large State, would require a score of printed pages; and the additional information in drawings and descriptions necessary to a thorough understanding of the peculiarities and variations of each kind of fence would fill a volume. Only a brief classification of the more essential facts embraced in these returns will therefore be given at present, with the hope of approximating the total amount and cost of the fences of the United States.

The fences of Maine are of many kinds and of various construction. Stone-wall is more generally distributed than any other substantial fence, about one-fifth of the inclosures being walled in, York County reporting 30 per cent., Hancock 29, Waldo 25, and other counties a smaller proportion. The post and rail style is next in prominence, especially in Somerset and Hancock, surrounding nearly three-fourths of the inclosures of those counties. Board-fence is used for four-tenths of the fields of Cumberland; for one-fifth of those of York and Oxford; and one-fourth of the farms of Waldo. Brush-fence predominates in Oxford, being used for three-fourths of all inclosures. The height of Maine fences ranges from 4 to 4½ feet. There are structures which pass as fences that are still lower. The board-fences are of various patterns. In Oxford a desirable style is made of 8-inch boards, nailed to posts 8 feet apart, and battened with a perpendicular strip upon each post. In York, except near buildings, the boards are confined with withes. In Sagadahoc, where timber is getting scarce, three or four boards to each length are used, and posts are set on stone, iron dowels entering the wood 8 inches. A "cap and bunk" fence of cedar is the style in Aroostook; the rails cut 18 feet long, and lapped to make each length a rod; a "bunk," or block, about 4 feet long, laid under the end of each length, and a cap at the top, holds the stakes together. "Hedge-fence" is made of fallen trees. In Waldo half the inclosures have worm-fences. As material for fencing, cedar is used wherever it can be obtained, and hemlock, spruce, oak, pine, poplar, and other woods.

A similar variety is found in New Hampshire. The worm-fence (Virginia) surrounds one-fourth of the fields of Coos. Board-fences predominate in Coos and Strafford, half of all being of that sort. The post and rail is largely used in all parts of the State; and brush, stump, pole, log, &c., are common. Stone-wall is largely used in all rocky districts, both single and double, of all widths, from 2 feet to 6 or more, according to the quantity of stone for which no other disposition is so convenient. In Hillsborough it constitutes three-fourths of the fence; in Strafford, one-half; and a large proportion in all other counties.

Worm-fence is common in several counties in Vermont, the proportion being 90 per cent. in Grand Isle, 65 in Addison, 25 in Washington. In the latter county the rails generally rest on stone 8 inches high, and six rails to the panel are used. Boards are used for half the fences of Washington and Essex, and are largely employed in Orleans and Windsor. One-fifth of Addison fences are made of stumps, standing about 5 feet high, roots upward. About one-fourth of the fencing of the State is made with stone, the proportion in Essex and Windsor being fully 50 per cent., and 25 in Washington, 20 in Orleans, and in Addison and Grand Isle scarcely more than 5 per cent. Stone at bottom, with stakes and rails above, is used to some extent. Cedar rails are common in Orleans.

Stone-wall is the main fence in Massachusetts, its proportion reaching to 75 per cent. in Essex, 67 in Norfolk, 40 in Dukes and Bristol, in Plymouth 60 per cent. stone and wood combined, and 10 per cent. of stone alone. Nearly half the fences are of stone, or stone and wood combined; fully one-third post and rail fence, 3½ to 4½ feet high, of which Dukes has 60 per cent., Hampden and Bristol 40, Norfolk 33, Plymouth 30, and Essex 20. In Hampden stone-walls are very substantial, many being 4 feet wide at bottom, and 3 at top.

Rhode Island is mainly fenced with stone, scarcely any other material being known in Newport, Bristol having 75 per cent., and Washington 60; height, about 4½ feet. A foundation two feet deep is sometimes laid with small stone. The rail-fence is 4½ feet high, of 5 rails; and the posts of board-fence are set 2½ to 3 feet in the ground, 8 feet apart. All fences and gates are comparatively substantial and thorough in construction.

Stone is the material for one-third of the fences of Connecticut, New London having 70 per cent. of wall, Fairfield 50, and other counties a smaller proportion. Post and rail fence incloses three-tenths of the fields; worm-fence nearly one-fourth; board-fence one-eighth; height, 3½ to 4½ feet. In Middlesex, where a poor quality of stone is available, walls 3 feet high are common, with stakes and rails above. In New Haven similar fences are made, the wall 2½ feet high. These walls are preferred to the regular stone-wall for sheep-pastures. Six rails are said to make a legal worm-fence; heavy rocks are often placed under the corners; and a fence built with 1½ to 2 feet of stone, with 3 rails above, is deemed a good fence.

An averaging of thirty-three reports from New York indicate a predominance of worm-fence, of which there appears to be 45 per cent.; 18 per cent. of post and rail, and 19 of board; 18 per cent. being stone-wall and other kinds, including a small amount of wire, picket, hedge, &c. Orange has 80 per cent. of wall; Putnam 75, and Greene, Dutchess, Columbia, and Delaware, 50 per cent. each. Of post and rail, Kings has 95 per cent., Warren, 80, Cattaraugus, 70, Saint Lawrence, 67, Steuben, 65, Saratoga, 50. Worm-fence is found in large proportion in the following counties:

Orleans, 90 per cent.; Yates, 85; Niagara, Jefferson, Monroe, 80; Wayne, Genesee, Schuyler, Otsego, Livingston, Ontario, Lewis, 75; Wyoming, 70; Chenango, 60; Seneca, 55; Onondaga, Cortland, Queens, Greene, 50 per cent. Madison reports 80 per cent. of board-fence; Schenectady, 50; Tioga, 45; Fulton, 33; Cattaraugus, 30; Saratoga, Washington, and Onondaga, 25 each. A part of the worm-fence is staked and ridered, and some is wired, and varies from 4 to 5½ feet high, the latter only in Livingston. Post and rail is usually 4 to 5 feet high, averaging about 4½ feet; breadth of worm, usually 4 feet. Where poor stone prevails rived sticks are used in stone-wall, to bind it. Stone-wall is built entirely of stone, or is combined with rails or boards for the upper portion of the fence. In Seneca, wire and picket fence meets with general commendation for cheapness and durability. Board-fences differ considerably in length of panel and number and quality of boards. Hemlock is much used, in the scarcity of other material. In Erie, "a beginning has been made to dispense with fences." A large proportion, not less than 60 per cent., of New Jersey fences, are of the post and rail style; the posts of white oak, chestnut, white and red cedar, and "fat" pine, 6 or 7 feet long, round or sawed, set 2½ feet in the ground, 11 feet apart, some having three or four mortises for the rails, (which are cut 12 feet long, and sharpened,) and others are nailed to the posts. About 30 per cent. of inclosures are surrounded by the worm-fence, of chestnut or cedar rails chiefly, which are laid in angles of 25 degrees, with stakes set in the ground, and double ridered.

The post and board fence is found in Hunterdon, Ocean, Morris, and other counties, being used in the former for one-fifth of the inclosures. The osage-orange hedge is employed to some extent. A few stone-walls may be seen, and brush, turf, and other modes of fencing. In Bergen and Union all the fence is reported to be of posts and rails, and 90 per cent. in Essex and Hudson, and 60 in Morris.

Two-thirds of the fences reported in thirty counties in Pennsylvania are of the zigzag "Virginia" style, one-sixth are of post and rail variety, one-eighth constructed of boards, and the remainder stone-wall, osage-hedge, stump, pole, or other kinds: Most of them are 4½ feet high, some 4 feet, some 5. In Luzerne worm fence is 5½ feet, and in Westmoreland it is 6 feet. In Beaver there is no other fence reported; little else in Butler, in Warren, or in Somerset; 90 per cent. in Crawford, Armstrong, and Elk; 85 in Westmoreland and Lehigh; 80 in Cambria and Clearfield; 75 in Berks, Snyder, and Washington; 65 in Lawrence and York; 60 in Clinton and Susquehanna. Montgomery claims 70 per cent. of post and rail; Sullivan, 67; Dauphin, 50; Union, 42; Clinton, Huntingdon, and York, 30. Bradford reports 90 per cent. of board-fence, Lycoming 50, Clearfield and Luzerne 20, and others declining to 2 per cent. Wayne has 50 per cent. of stone-wall, Susquehanna 35, Sullivan 16, Tioga 15. There is a small amount of osage-hedge in Chester, Bucks, Northumberland, Montgomery, Washington, York, and other counties. There is a style of fence known as "rough and ready," used in some counties, made by setting rough posts dressed with an ax on both sides, upon which rails about 9 feet long are nailed alternately on either side; in Fayette 18 per cent. is of this kind. The stone-fence is usually quite substantial, rarely less than 2½ or 3 feet wide at bottom, and 4½ to 5 feet high, though some is lower. The material is various as the kinds of wood in the Pennsylvania forests. Locust and cedar are preferred for posts, and for rails much use is made of chestnut, white-oak, cherry, cucumber, pine, ash, and basswood. The growing scarcity of timber tends to decrease the amount of worm-fence, which is often replaced with post and rail, and with board-fence in districts of greater scarcity of timber; and still more substantial forms, as the stone-fence, or osage or other hedge, are growing in favor.

The farms of Delaware are inclosed with worm and post and rail fence, with a small proportion of osage-hedges and other modes of fencing. Kent County reports 60 per cent. of post and rail fence. White oak or chestnut posts, with cedar rails, are much used; and osage-hedges are popular and of thrifty growth.

The zigzag rail-fence surrounds nearly two-thirds of the inclosures of Maryland; post and rail one-sixth; board-fence, stone wall, pole-fence, and other styles making up the remainder. Chestnut rails and locust posts are largely used. In Kent the osage-hedge is plashed and wattled upon stakes until well grown.

As indicated by returns from forty-one counties, four-fifths of the fence of Virginia is that to which her name is commonly given. Few counties report more than a small proportion of other kinds. Albemarle, Fauquier, and Culpeper have 20 per cent. of post and rail, which is the largest percentage reported. Chesterfield has 60 per cent. of post and board, and Botetourt and Culpeper 20. Rappahannock, Scott, Albemarle, and Fauquier, among other counties, return a fair proportion of stone-wall. In King George the wattling or brush-weaving style is extensively employed, being used for one-fifth of the inclosures. In Scott County black-walnut rails are still used, costing $15 per thousand. Among the material used are found locust, cedar, several kinds of oak, chestnut, poplar, walnut, cucumber, pine, ash, and nearly all other woods of the forest. The legislature of the State has enacted a no-fence law, subject to acceptance by each county, and many have ratified it, and find no inconvenience in the exemption from fences, but the change is received with great satisfaction by the people. The correspondent in Buckingham says of those counties which have no fences that "more crops are raised, and nearly as much stock as before." One correspondent in King George County thus describes the lawful fence of that State:

A lawful fence must be 4 feet high if made with stone, and 5 feet high if made with any other material, and so close that the beast breaking into the same could not creep through; or with an hedge 2 feet high upon a ditch 3 feet deep and 3 feet broad; or, instead of such hedge, a rail-fence of 2½ feet high, the hedge or fence being so close that none of the creatures aforesaid can creep through.

Throughout the Southern States, a section in every State of which more than one-half of the farm area is woodland, the worm-fence is almost the exclusive mode, except in the vicinity of the better class of buildings. Garden fences are usually of palings. In returns from thirty-seven counties in North Carolina, there is only one record of post and rail fence, 10 per cent. in Sampson County; and in Chowan one-half is board-fence. In Caldwell the "Van Buren" fence is coming into use; the worm 3 feet in width, panels 5 to 10 feet long. A very little of stone-wall and of other kinds appears in a few of the reports. The proportion of worm-fence is 96 per cent. In South Carolina the proportion of crooked-rail fence rises to 98; it is 95 in Georgia and 94 in Florida. In the latter State, stone is placed at 10 per cent. in Gwinnett, and hedge of Cherokee rose is reported in Wilkes and Monroe. The reported height varies from 4 to 6 feet in South Carolina; in most of the counties 4½ and 5, and more reports place the height of North Carolina fences at 5 to 5½ feet than from 4 to 5. Georgia, which represents fairly all this section, makes the average height 5 feet in nineteen counties,

5½ feet in six counties, 6 feet in six counties 4½ feet in four counties, and 4 feet in two counties. Five feet is the legal height fixed for fences in most if not all of the cotton States. The proportion of worm-fence in Alabama is 90 per cent., 10 per cent. representing many kinds, no one of which has much prominence in any locality, except board-fence in Colbert, 20 per cent., and post and rail in Montgomery, 15 per cent. Osage-hedge is marked 10 per cent. in Montgomery. The height of fences is placed quite uniformly at 4½ and 5 feet in this State. For posts, chestnut, oak, and heart-pine are much used.

In Mississippi 95 per cent. are worm-fences, the remainder osage and rose hedges, wire, board, and post and rail; Claiborne County having 28 per cent. of the latter. Half of the counties report all worm-fences. In Claiborne, post and rail fence is made by setting two posts, dropping the rails between, and fastening with caps; wire-fence, by stretching wire upon posts eight feet apart, with a rail or slab-cap from post to post.

Only about two-thirds of the inclosures of Louisiana are surrounded with the Virginia fence. In the parish of La Fayette all fences are post and rail. There are many hedges of Cherokee and McCartney rose, and of osage-orange. In the Creole section, a fence made of cypress, and known as *Pieux* fence, is the prevailing style, as in Iberia, where no other is known, and in Saint Landry it amounts to 60 per cent. of the aggregate fencing. It is 5 to 5½ feet high. Slabs of cypress, 9 feet in length, are split from the circumference of the log, in size about 10 by 2 inches, one of which is mortised as a post, for every four tenoned, to be used as boards, making a rough but strong and durable board-fence. In West Feliciana, nearly all inclosures were surrounded by Cherokee-rose hedges; and they were so effectual and popular that most planters cut down all wood except what they reserved for fires and plantation repairs. They died out during the war, probably from frost, and now poles and other make-shifts are common, and every year the destruction of a portion of the crops results. Sugar-planters on the river often fence only on the levee.

Worm-fence constitutes three-fourths of all fencing in Texas. Rail, board, brush, and picket are styles frequently employed, and osage-orange, or *Bois d'Arc*, (from its employment in making bows,) is used in many portions of the State as live fence. Cedar, live-oak, and mesquite are used for posts. The latter, *Prosopis (Algarobia) glandulosa*, is used extensively in brush-fence. Ditches, 5 feet deep, 6 feet wide at top, and 3 feet at bottom, the earth thrown up on the side of the field inclosed, are made where timber for fencing cannot be obtained readily. In some counties there is only a small area inclosed; ''not one rod to one hundred acres'' in Hardin. There are sections where stone is obtainable for walls; one-fifth of the fences of Lampasas being made of that material. In De Witt a Mexican fence is built, constructed of logs and brush, piled together 18 inches in thickness, between parallel rows of posts, 7 feet long, set 18 inches in the ground, and 3 feet apart. A citizen of Williamson County proposes the present season to fence five thousand acres with wire, for pasturage.

The worm is almost the exclusive fence of Arkansas, not more than 2 per cent. of other kinds being used, generally 5 feet high; in some cases less, very rarely more. Tennessee has 95 per cent. of the prevailing style; Giles has 15 per cent. of post and rail, and 10 per cent. of stone-wall; Haywood 20 per cent. of lath and orange-hedge, and a small proportion of other kinds is found scattered through the State.

In West Virginia the worm-fence amounts to 85 per cent., the remainder being of almost all kinds in use; some having but seven to nine rails to the panel; in Kentucky about the same proportion, from 4 to 5½ feet high, with post and rail, board, and stone, 4 or 5 per cent. of each. Worm-fences, of eight to ten rails to the panel, are common.

In forty-seven counties in Ohio, the percentage of worm-fence is also about 85, board-fence about 10 per cent., post and rail, stone, picket hedge, and patent fences making the remainder. The height in most localities is from 4½ to 5 feet. The proportion of worm-fence in Michigan is about four-fifths, board being also used quite generally, with a small amount of stone, brush, log, and other structures, and some hedging. The height is in most counties 4½ feet. Indiana, which is well wooded, uses the Virginia style for four-fifths of all fencing. In Lake County there is little else than board-fence; 50 per cent. in Newton, 40 in Warren, and 20 in Switzerland, Fountain, Jefferson, and Vanderburgh. Small quantities of osage-hedge are found in all sections of the State. Worm-fences vary in height from seven to eleven rails to the panel, being highest in the cattle-farms of the southwestern part of the State.

In the prairie States the worm-fence has less prominence. The scarcity of timber limits the use of rails, except for a fence of three or four rails to the panel, with posts, where native wood is to be obtained at all, from margins of streams or artificial plantations of forest-trees. The open prairies, having railroad communication, are fenced with boards from the northern pineries, with cedar and locust posts, if obtainable without great cost, otherwise with oak and sometimes chestnut. In Southern Illinois timber is abundant, and the old-fashioned rail-fence is largely used. From fifty-six counties of Illinois, which may be assumed to represent the State quite fairly, returns make a percentage of 43 for worm-fence and 32 for board, osage-hedge standing next in prominence. Some counties already have a very large proportion of this hedge, viz: Kankakee, 75 per cent.; Henderson and Stark, 50; Marshall, 40; Macoupin,33; Knox, 30; Rock Island, Warren, Lee, Adams, Madison, Whiteside, 25; and Bureau, Fulton, Peoria, Crawford, 20. It is coming into general use with great rapidity. In Richland osage-hedge is not popular, the expense of trimming being deemed greater than repairs of other fences. In thirty-four counties in which osage-hedges are particularly mentioned, the average percentage is about 20.

Worm-fence constitutes 54 per cent. of the reported fencing of Wisconsin, and board fence 32 per cent. Post and pole, log, brush, stone, ditch, "Shanghai," and various fancy styles, are made. Ingenuity is exercised in prairieregions for the invention and building of fences requiring the smallest possible amount of material. A hurdle-fence is popular in Rock, supported by short stakes which reach to the third rail, which is longer than the others, thus lapping over and connecting one panel with another.

In Minnesota the proportions of the principal kinds are as follows: worm, 33 per cent.; post and rail, 27; board, 26; and 14 per cent. of other kinds, including (tamarack,) pole, wire, "leaning," and other fences. Average height, about 4½ feet. Oak and pine are used in construction of board fence, while walnut, ash, cottonwood, tamarack, elm, linn, and other woods are used for rails.

No greater variety of fencing exists in any State, than is found in Iowa. An average of 48 county returns indicates 24 per cent. of worm, 23 of board, 14 of post and rail, and 39 of a miscellaneous list of styles, among which osage-hedge is most prominent, reaching 60 per cent. in Cedar, 33 per cent. in Clinton, 25 in Scott, and smaller proportions in many other counties. In Muscatine the proportion of board is 90 per cent., 80 in Harrison, 75 in Scott, and 50 in Henry and Jasper. In Mitchell 63 per cent. is post and rail, and 50 in Carroll and Floyd. The "Shanghai" fence is made of rails, three to five to the panel, laid on the crotches of forked stakes driven into the ground, staked and surmounted with riders. In Mahaska, as in other counties, some inclosures include a dozen farms in a tract of 2,000 acres or more. A "leaning" fence is used in some places, the posts set at an angle of 40°. The "Bloomer" is made with three rails and stakes to the panel. Several counties have no fences, animals being prohibited by law from running at large. Five wires, 8 inches apart, stretched upon posts 8 feet apart, with one stay midway, makes a popular fence in some places.

The worm-fence again predominates in Missouri, amounting to 74 per cent., while there is 26 per cent. of board-fence, and "corduroy" (poles nailed to posts) hedge, post and slat, stone, palings, o "rough and ready," and fancy styles. There is 30 per cent. of osage-hedge in Henry, 20 in Greene, and a large amount of growing hedges in different part of the State. From seven to twelve rails to the panel are used in worm-fences. Post and rail fence is often made with three rails for cattle and six for hogs, and board-fence with three or five boards.

It is difficult to calculate the comparative prominence of styles in Kansas. Averaging the returns, the worm-fence appears to constitute but 18 per cent., board 12, and post and rail 9: leaving 61 per cent. for a great variety of fences reported somewhat indefinitely. The osage-hedge is very prominent, apparently bidding fair to be the principal fence of the State. It is reported at 100 per cent. in Cloud; 50 in Bourbon, Franklin, Linn, and Osage; 40 in Leavenworth; 33 in Douglas; 30 in Anderson. Dickinson reports 400 rods of stone-wall, built at $2 per rod. The Shanghai fence is also found in Kansas. Cherokee county reports fences with names hitherto unheard of, "the eccentricity of whose construction language very feebly conveys."

In many counties of Nebraska few fences are to be found. About 30 per cent. of existing fences are post and rail, 25 per cent. board, and the remainder hedge, wire, Shanghai, and earth-walls 3½ feet high; Hall County having 25 per cent. of the latter.

Board-fence appears to predominate in California; two-fifths being of that style in the counties reported, nearly one-fourth post and rail, and the remainder brush, picket, worm, &c., including a small amount of live willow. Napa and Humboldt have a considerable proportion of worm-fence.

A large proportion, fully 90 per cent. in the returns received, of the fencing of Oregon, is of Virginia style. The remainder is mainly constructed with boards. A few picket-fences are reported.

In Washington Territory wood is abundant; worm-fence is the prevailing style. Utah has poor material for fencing; is inclosed with poles, brush, post and rail, and inferior forms of fences. Red pine is much used for rails, and aspen poles are abundant. Fence material is scarce in Colorado, except among the mountains. In the dry atmosphere of the mountains, pines, firs, aspen, and other soft woods last well. A Utah correspondent says the aspen will last twenty years if not resting on the ground. There are few fences in New Mexico. There is a law against trespass, and each county is allowed to regulate the time when cattle may be turned loose, which is generally from November 1 to March 1. From corn-planting till harvest is finished cattle must be herded, and the owner is made responsible for any damages they may commit. The Doña Aña correspondent says there is not a rail in New Mexico. Walls are built for small inclosures of adobe, or unburned brick. A fence is sometimes built of cedar poles, set upright and close together, with a horizontal pole bound to each upright, near the top, by strips of raw-hide an inch wide. In Arizona and Nevada small poles are much used for fencing, though a small area only is inclosed.

In recapitulation it will be seen that worm-fence predominates in Vermont, New York, and in all the States west and northwest of New Jersey, except Kansas, Nebraska, California, and Nevada, and the Rocky Mountain region, though but slightly in Vermont, Minnesota, and Iowa. Its proportion in the former States exceeds that of all other kinds combined, except in Vermont, New York, Illinois, and Iowa, in the latter constituting scarcely one-fourth of the total fencing. It may fairly be ranked as the national fence, though it is temporary, giving way gradually to kinds requiring less lumber, and covering less land, as well as making a less awkward appearance not at all indicative of the straight-forwardness of the American character. Board-fence is the prevalent style in California, and next to worm in Vermont, New York, in all the Southern States south and west of Maryland, (though the percentage is still small,) and in all the Western States in which worm-fence predominates, except Minnesota and Nebraska. The post and rail style is the main fence in New Jersey, and stands second to other kinds in Maine, Massachusetts, Pennsylvania, Delaware, Maryland, Minnesota, and Nebraska. Stone-wall is the principal fence in Maine, New Hampshire, Massachusetts, Rhode Island, and Connecticut; and the next in prominence in New Hampshire, Rhode Island, and Connecticut, is board-fence. For hedges, the osage orange stands first, being already in efficient condition in Illinois, and largely planted west of the Mississippi; while it is coming gradually into use in all of the Middle and Western States south of the fortieth parallel of latitude, and, to some extent, for ornamental purposes in the Southern States. The Cherokee and McCartney rose (botanically, *Rosa laevigata* and *R. Macartnea,*) are preferred by many as hedge-plants in the States of the Gulf coast. The white willow, *Salix alba,* and other plants are employed for hedging purposes to a very limited extent. The table on the following page shows the proportion of the principal kinds of fence in the several States, as averaged from the reports.

Gates. — Many descriptions are received of different styles of gates used, with plain drawings in many cases; but the variations are so numerous and wide, even in the same State, and the description in many instances so indefinite and incomplete, that it would be impossible to attain perfect accuracy in an exhaustive exposition. The gates of wooded regions are of a heavier pattern, and those of the settled States which have not given place to recent improvements are very clumsy in construction and movement. The common slat-gate is in very general use. The balance-pole is largely employed in nearly all sections of the country, especially in the older settlements. Gates turning upon hinges, fastened with "hook and eye," moving in a socket, those with wooden latches and every imaginable style of fastening, are found of such variety and form of material and mode of construction as almost to defy description. Lattice-gates and fancy styles are common near dwellings and in the vicinity of towns. The tendency in the new farming regions is to lightness of material, facility of

Proportion of each kind of fence

States.	Worm.	Post and rail.	Board.	Other kinds.	States.	Worm.	Post and rail.	Board.	Other kinds.
Maine.................	5	17	11	67	Texas	74	—	7	19
New Hampshire	8	6	35	51	Arkansas	98	—	1	1
Vermont	30	11	27	32	Tennessee.............	95	1	2	2
Massachusetts........	6	31	3	60	West Virginia........	85	5	6	4
Rhode Island	—	10	11	79	Kentucky.............	87	4	5	4
Connecticut..........	24	30	13	33	Ohio	86	1	9	4
New York	45	18	19	18	Michigan.............	79	—	8	13
New Jersey	29	62	4	5	Indiana	81	1	10	8
Pennsylvania	67	17	12	4	Illinois................	43	2	32	23
Delaware.............	50	45	—	5	Wisconsin............	54	2	32	12
Maryland.............	65	14	3	18	Minnesota............	33	27	26	14
Virginia	79	2	4	15	Iowa	24	14	23	39
North Carolina.......	96	—	3	1	Missouri..............	74	2	10	14
South Carolina.......	98	—	1	1	Kansas................	18	9	12	61
Georgia..............	95	—	—	5	Nebraska.............	3	29	25	43
Florida...............	94	—	3	3	California	5	22	41	32
Alabama	90	1	1	8	Oregon	92	—	8	—
Mississippi...........	95	1	1	3	Nevada and				
Louisiana	61	8	—	31	Territories..........	5	14	5	76

movement, and cheapness, with the requisite degree of strength. Many of them are patented. Large numbers of new patterns are built in the Western States at $1 to $2 each. Perhaps the most popular is a slide-and-swing gate, which moves back on rollers part way, balances on a pivot in the post, and turns round at right angles. In many counties in the South, few, if any gates, are reported, while in others nearly all the openings are gates; in a few there are neither gates nor bars, but "slip-gaps." The correspondent in Henry County, Virginia, says that the fields there are entered by pulling down a corner of the fence; that it becomes less substantial every time it is taken down, until it will no longer restrain stock, when "the exasperated farmer rights it up, props it, and perhaps cuts thorn rushes to lay upon it, and finally pulls down another portion of the fence where the same experiment is repeated."

The following table gives the estimated percentage of openings guarded respectively by gates and bars, and the average cost of gates. A small proportion of the inclosures of certain States have neither gates nor bars. It is, of course, understood that these statistics include only farm-gates.

The average proportion of bars, in the whole country, is about 53 per cent.; of gates, 43; leaving about 7 per cent. of openings for slip gaps or other mode of entrance.

Cost of Farm-Fencers

Cost of material. — A great variety of material is used for board-fences. Of course, inferior qualities of lumber are taken — that which is rough and knotty, or those kinds of wood less in request for house-finishing or furniture-making. Where oak is abundant, it is often employed; hemlock and spruce are used largely in New England, New York, and elsewhere, as other timber increases in value; and the

States.	Percentage of gates.	Percentage of bars.	Cost of gates.	States.	Percentage of gates.	Percentage of bars	Cost of gates.
Maine	34	65	$2 33	Texas	35	47	$4 81
New Hampshire	33	66	2 66	Arkansas	29	45	5 22
Vermont	19	80	3 50	Tennessee.............	37	36	4 50
Massachusetts........	10	90	6 25	West Virginia........	33	67	2 71
Rhode Island	31	68	7 66	Kentucky..............	36	55	5 17
Connecticut..........	22	78	4 12	Ohio	49	47	3 89
New York	27	72	3 85	Michigan..............	33	65	3 47
New Jersey...........	24	76	6 25	Indiana	52	45	3 60
Pennsylvania	24	76	4 55	Illinois................	67	29	3 54
Delaware.............	25	75	4 50	Wisconsin.............	43	53	3 15
Maryland	48	51	4 96	Minnesota	29	71	2 66
Virginia	52	43	4 71	Iowa..................	36	62	2 96
North Carolina.......	40	57	3 33	Missouri	49	40	3 75
South Carolina......	49	45	4 14	Kansas................	43	51	3 60
Georgia	37	46	3 10	Nebraska..............	31	68	2 04
Florida	47	53	3 25	California	74	26	7 00
Alabama	33	61	3 21	Oregon	40	60	8 00
Mississippi	64	35	4 53	Nevada and			
Louisiana	44	45	6 00	Territories	38	62	4 53

cheaper grades of pine are extensively used in the Northwest, and culls from oak, poplar, ash, and other woods.

The average cost, as reported, is given in the accompanying table, from which it appears that boards used for fences are dearest in Texas, costing $29.53; $28.95 in Kansas; $27.88 in Nebraska; $27 in Delaware, and $25.66 in Rhode Island. The cost is least in Georgia, $12; $12.37 in Oregon; and $12.85 in Florida. The cost of rails are highest in New Jersey; next in order, Nevada, Rhode Island, Massachusetts, and Connecticut. The lowest figure is $8.12 per M, in Florida; then Georgia, Alabama, South Carolina, and Mississippi.

Price of material

States.	Boards, per M.	Rails, per M.	States.	Boards, per M.	Rails, per M.
Maine	$9 80	$74 66	Texas	$29 53	$39 32
New Hampshire.....................	11 25	60 00	Arkansas	17 78	15 06
Vermont..............................	12 33	47 50	Tennessee	15 29	19 50
Massachusetts	21 64	106 42	West Virginia	15 86	22 27
Rhode Island	25 66	120 00	Kentucky	18 75	27 56
Connecticut	24 61	102 85	Ohio................................	17 58	35 20
New York	16 01	68 12	Michigan	12 72	23 60
New Jersey	23 00	130 00	Indiana	16 50	30 69
Pennsylvania........................	15 99	56 26	Illinois..............................	21 00	45 51
Delaware	27 00	65 00	Wisconsin	14 81	28 56
Maryland	22 88	59 51	Minnesota	18 88	37 00
Virginia	15 74	16 51	Iowa................................	24 51	59 56
North Carolina	11 45	10 44	Missouri	23 25	37 20
South Carolina	13 50	11 83	Kansas..............................	28 95	67 91
Georgia	12 00	10 95	Nebraska............................	27 88	64 44
Florida...............................	12 85	8 12	California	19 54	99 28
Alabama..............................	13 88	11 64	Oregon..............................	12 37	48 00
Mississippi	19 07	12 50	Nevada and		
Louisiana.............................	24 00	23 00	Territories	53 50	120 00

Cost of fences per rod. — There is a great difficulty in estimating the cost of fences, from the variety and differing value of material used, and the many kinds of fences built, as well as the differences in their height, massiveness, and thoroughness of construction. The best built fences in the United States are in Rhode Island, if the returns are correctly made, and their average cost is the highest. The best fences are of stone, and they are also cheapest, repairs costing little, though their first cost exceeds that of any other kind.

The cost of fences, as stated below, is lowest in the Southern States. It is deemed best to give the averages of the figures returned for those States, though they do not adequately express the real cost. It is stated in many of these returns that the price per rod returned is simple the cost of "mauling the rails" and laying them, without counting expense of teams for hauling, and in some cases of board while doing the work. Nothing is reckoned usually for the value of timber, and the estimate is often based on the bare wages of hands employed by the month. The work is done by tenants as odd jobs, or in the winter interval between cotton-picking and cotton-planting, as one of the requirements of their contract, and so the expense is scarcely considered. While giving these averages as they are made in this table, an enlarged estimate, intended to include all the actual elements of cost, is used in calculating the total cost of farm-fences, which may be found in a subsequent table. The returns are very complete as to the cost per rod of worm, post and rail, board, and stone fences, but not so full as to the various other kinds. The estimate of average cost per rod in each State is based upon prices and proportions of each kind of fence.

Cost per rod

States.	Worm	Post and rail.	Board.	Stone-wall.	States.	Worm.	Post and rail.	Board.	Stone-wall.
Maine..................	$0 66	$0 83	$0 72	$1 64	Texas	$0 87	$0 80	$1 44	$2 47
New Hampshire	65	82	86	1 37	Arkansas	43	1 25	1 21	1 50
Vermont	95	91	1 00	1 52	Tennessee.............	50	77	1 09	3 27
Massachusetts........	1 38	97	1 31	2 75	West Virginia........	67	1 27	1 48	2 96
Rhode Island	2 00	2 06	2 58	2 33	Kentucky..............	71	1 71	1 64	4 22
Connecticut...........	1 37	1 64	1 67	2 42	Ohio	79	1 06	1 38	3 20
New York	1 10	1 25	1 47	2 45	Michigan..............	71	1 06	1 26	2 16
New Jersey	1 61	1 61	1 61	2 50	Indiana	75	1 07	1 39	2 95
Pennsylvania	95	1 35	1 26	2 34	Illinois.................	99	1 27	1 31	3 56
Delaware..............	1 00	1 33	1 70	—	Wisconsin.............	63	77	99	2 75
Maryland..............	1 08	1 94	1 96	2 66	Minnesota.............	65	72	99	—
Virginia	43	1 17	1 16	2 13	Iowa	91	94	1 31	—
North Carolina	33	44	93	—	Missouri...............	88	1 02	1 43	2 81
South Carolina	35	43	76	—	Kansas.................	1 08	96	1 27	2 96
Georgia................	31	49	99	—	Nebraska..............	1 00	97	1 42	—
Florida.................	30	37	78	—	California	1 22	1 59	1 30	3 50
Alabama	34	1 04	1 05	—	Oregon	96	—	1 02	—
Mississippi...........	43	87	1 57	—	Nevada and				
Louisiana	60	1 25	3 00	—	Territories..........	1 38	1 75	2 20	—

Amount and cost of fencing. — The inquiry was made for "the number of rods of fence to each one hundred acres of farm-lands, including together improved and unimproved lands." As a few in the older States, and many in the South and West, answered with reference only to the "improved" acres, it was deemed proper, in calculating the acres fenced, to avoid an exhibit erroneously large, to exclude one-fourth of the unimproved area in the New England States, (with the exception of Maine,) the Middle States, and Maryland; one-half in the unimproved portion of farms in the States of the Ohio Valley and lake region, between Kentucky and Wisconsin, and in Maine; three-fourths of unimproved lands in the States between Virginia and the Mississippi, where only the "improved" area is usually reckoned as the farm; all of the unimproved land in Virginia, (where a no-fence law has been enacted,) Florida, and Louisiana, where water boundaries save much fencing; and in Minnesota, Iowa, Kansas, Nebraska, and California, where some improved land is unfenced, only three-fourths of the improved area was taken.

In calculating the number of rods of fencing, the estimate of the number of rods to each one hundred acres was carefully made from the returns, as follows:

States.	Rods to 100 acres.	Cost per rod.	States	Rods to 100 acres.	Cost per rod.	States.	Rods to 100 acres.	Cost per rod.
Maine	713	$1 00	South Carolina	500	$0 80	Indiana..............	680	$1 05
New Hampshire...	875	1 20	Georgia.............	546	75	Illinois	475	1 20
Vermont...........	775	1 33	Florida.............	464	72	Wisconsin	525	85
Massachusetts	850	1 75	Alabama............	610	80	Minnesota..........	400	88
Rhode Island	1,000	2 20	Mississippi.........	420	96	Iowa.................	420	1 10
Connecticut	910	1 70	Louisiana..........	400	1 00	Missouri	525	1 00
New York..........	825	1 35	Texas	440	1 10	Kansas..............	425	1 10
New Jersey	925	1 60	Arkansas	590	95	Nebraska	400	1 05
Pennsylvania.......	955	1 15	Tennessee	655	95	California	425	1 40
Delaware	625	1 20	West Virginia	900	90	Oregon..............	450	1 05
Maryland..........	630	1 25	Kentucky..........	600	95	Nevada	400	1 50
Virginia	500	90	Ohio................	860	1 00			
North Carolina	560	75	Michigan	800	95			

From all this data, the calculation of amount and cost of fences in the United States leads to the result shown in the table on following page.

Cost of repairs. — The annual cost of repairs of fences varies with the cost of material of which they are constructed, and the durability of that material. It is comparatively low in the New England States, on account of the large proportion of stone-wall in that section; and low in the South because of the abundance and cheapness of material. It is undoubtedly too low in that section, few of the reports recognizing any value whatever in the wood used for rail-splitting. The cost is relatively high in the older States, where timber is becoming scarce, and in the prairie States, which are nearly destitute of home supplies. In the Rocky Mountain section the cost is increased in consequence of the perishable nature of the material employed, much of it being brush or poles of soft woods. The true average, as nearly as possible, of the figures received from the several counties reporting in each State, have been taken as a basis of the calculation, and the resulting total cost of repairs for all the States, (not including Territories,) is $93,963,187 — a total which may be

States.	Acres fenced.	Rods of fencing.	Total cost of fencing.
Maine	4,377,925	31,214,605	$31,214,605
New Hampshire	3,288,117	28,771,023	34,525,227
Vermont	4,164,917	32,278,106	42,929,880
Massachusetts	2,481,767	21,095,019	36,916,283
Rhode Island	448,988	4,489,880	9,877,736
Connecticut	2,185,000	19,883,500	33,801,930
New York	20,549,909	169,536,749	228,874,611
New Jersey	2,736,251	25,310,321	40,496,513
Pennsylvania	16,374,641	156,377,821	179,834,494
Delaware	963,770	6,023,562	7,228,274
Maryland	4,112,936	25,911,496	32,389,370
Virginia	8,165,040	40,825,200	36,742,680
North Carolina	8,902,909	49,856,290	27,392,217
South Carolina	5,284,224	26,421,120	21,136,896
Georgia	11,035,877	60,255,888	45,191,916
Florida	736,172	3,415,838	2,459,403
Alabama	7,536,947	45,975,376	36,780,300
Mississippi	6,437,137	27,035,975	25,954,536
Louisiana	2,045,640	8,182,560	8,182,560
Texas	6,822,757	30,020,130	33,022,148
Arkansas	3,294,189	19,435,715	18,463,929
Tennessee	10,027,762	65,681,841	62,397,748
West Virginia	4,067,289	36,605,601	32,945,049
Kentucky	13,381,978	80,291,868	76,277,274
Ohio	18,090,776	155,580,673	155,560,678
Michigan	7,558,040	60,464,320	57,441,104
Indiana	14,111,963	95,961,348	100,759,415
Illinois	22,606,406	107,380,428	128,856,513
Wisconsin	8,807,332	46,238,493	39,302,719
Minnesota	1,857,681	7,430,724	6,539,037
Iowa	7,517,173	31,572,126	34,729,338
Missouri	12,274,766	64,442,521	64,442,521
Kansas	1,576,802	6,701,408	7,371,548
Nebraska	517,624	2,070,496	2,174,020
California	4,974,504	21,141,642	29,598,298
Oregon	1,116,290	5,023,305	5,274,476
Nevada	74,115	296,460	444,690
Total	250,505,614	1,619,199,428	1,747,549,931

Average rods per acre, 6.46. Average cost per acre, $1.08.

accepted at a low estimate. A proper allowance for low estimates in the Southern and some of the Western States, would make it fully equal to the annual interest on the cost.

This exhibit makes the cost of fences nearly equal to the total amount of the national debt on which interest is paid, and about the same as the estimated value of all the farm animals in the United States. For every dollar invested in live stock, another dollar is required for the construction of defenses to resist their attacks on farm production. Experiment has proved that at least half this expense is unnecessary. Wherever it has been tried, wherever farm-animals are restrained, and their owners are placed under (fence) bonds for the good behavior of their restless dependents, the system is regarded with general and growing satisfaction, capital is released from unprofitable investment and made available for farm improvement, soiling is encour-

States.	Cost per 100 rods.	Total cost.		States.	Cost per 100 rods.	Total cost.
Maine	$3 06	$955,166		Kentucky	$5 15	$4,035,031
New Hampshire	3 80	1,093,298		Ohio	5 25	8,167,985
Vermont	4 00	1,291,124		Michigan	4 00	2,418,572
Massachusetts	4 50	949,275		Indiana	5 40	5,181,912
Rhode Island	5 75	258,168		Illinois	9 50	10,201,140
Connecticut	7 50	1,491,262		Wisconsin	4 55	2,103,851
New York	7 06	11,969,294		Minnesota	5 10	378,966
New Jersey	9 80	2,480,411		Iowa	9 80	3,094,068
Pennsylvania	6 32	9,883,078		Missouri	4 90	3,157,683
Delaware	7 50	451,767		Kansas	6 75	452,345
Maryland	7 80	2,021,096		Nebraska	8 50	175,992
Virginia	3 51	1,432,964		California	8 50	1,797,039
North Carolina	3 40	1,695,113		Oregon	7 50	376,747
South Carolina	4 00	1,056,844		Nevada	9 00	26,681
Georgia	4 00	2,410,235				
Florida	3 80	129,801		Total cost of annual repairs	—	93,963,187
Alabama	4 65	2,137,853				
Mississippi	5 26	1,422,092		Interest on the original cost at 6 per cent	—	104,852,995
Louisiana	6 51	532,684				
Texas	8 50	2,551,712				
Arkansas	5 92	1,150,594		Grand total, exclusive of rebuilding of fences	—	198,806,182
Tennessee	5 00	3,284,092				
West Virginia	4 50	1,647,252				

aged, the manurial resources of stock husbanded, and the way prepared for larger production and higher profit. Even where a herd law of some sort has not been enacted, the tendency is strong, as many correspondents assert, toward the reduction of the amount of fencing; as repairs are needed, division fences are taken down and the material used to keep outside fences in repair; fields are almost everywhere becoming larger; in the younger States, a single field often answers all requirements, and sometimes a single inclosure embraces within its bounds many farms. The entire town of Greeley, in Colorado, with its suburbs for gardens and small market farms, is surrounded with a single fence, the cattle being excluded and kept outside upon the illimitable plains. It is possible to dispense with fencing to the value of one thousand million dollars, and the advantages of the change would greatly overbalance the inconvenience of it. Let the farmers discuss the subject in the light of actual experiment, rather than under the influence of ancient prejudice, and their views will soon coincide with their true interests.

Irrigation in Colorado, 1871

From U.S. Department of Agriculture, *Annual Report*, 1871, pp. 254–75.

There has been a great lack of experienced irrigators in the United States, and consequently irrigation is carried on in a very primitive manner. The Eastern States generally have not realized its importance, while in the Western the usual slovenly mode of farming has deferred what was erroneously supposed to be a very costly improvement. In the drier climates of the far West farmers have been compelled to adopt a *quasi* style of irrigation, based upon a slight knowledge of European modes. Even here they have supposed that the modes practiced in England, France, Italy, and Germany were equally adapted to this climate. This was a great mistake, and many have been obliged to unlearn all they had read and heard of European irrigation, and begin from the "bed-rock" to acquire, by experience, a better mode. Sometimes they would put in too much water, sometimes too little; tender plants, requiring little water, would be deluged, on the supposition that they required as much as the hardier kinds.

There is scarcely a farm in the United States but is susceptible of irrigation in some way or other. It is a very easy matter to plow a ditch from some stream to the highest point of your farm, or as high as you can get the water to run. If the distance to the stream is too great for your own work, and you are afraid of the expense, let the neighbors club together on a mutual co-operative or joint-stock plan. Any intelligent farmer can supply the details. If it is one, two, three, six, or a dozen miles, it matters not. By the co-operation of the whole township, pecuniarily and by sympathy, success will attend it. In Colorado, California, and the Pacific slope ditches are sometimes built fifty miles in length. The only water supplied to Denver for irrigation during eleven years has been by a ditch twenty-four miles long; and such a ditch can be built by the combined work of farmers, with a very small cash outlay. Let not the distance of the farm from an available fall of water deter any one in the outset from investigating the matter. If there is an elevated point on a farm upon which it is impossible to bring the water by an open ditch from a distance, a well may be sunk on the crowning point, an ordinary suction-pump put in, and with a small windmill, which one can make himself if he cannot afford to buy an improved patent, a constant stream can be obtained for use whenever needed. A reservoir or pond near by will economize a body of water as a reserve in case of drought. If the strata of water is too low for a suction-pump, a belt of cups may be used. Leather or rubber belting, with cast-iron cups, is made for the purpose; but rawhide belting and tin oyster-cans have answered temporarily; and the success of this expedient was astonishing. If one is not disposed to use a windmill, a common gin, or whim, as it is called in the mountains, or a thrashing treadle-machine, with power supplied by a donkey, oxen, mule, or horses, will answer the purpose. With very slight appliances of such a character many a magnificent field of golden grain may be saved from absolute loss on the occurrence of a drought. The more wealthy farmer can easily improvise more extensive machinery to meet a larger demand, or almost any exigency. The old Archimedean screw has been utilized for raising water, and an immense body, 10,000 gallons per hour or more, can be raised from almost any depth by the application of a corresponding ratio of motor power. There is no necessity of losing a crop by drought. If it is lost, it is by improvident or ignorant farming. There is scarcely a spot on the great plains where water cannot be obtained in sufficient quantity to irrigate 80 acres of land at a maximum cost of $500.

The occasional high winds in Colorado are very disastrous to ordinary windmills, unless protected from the prevalent wind blasts. Mr. Butters, a farmer on Cherry Creek, nine miles from Denver, has used one of the ordinary windmills for pumping water with a two-inch pipe and a cistern-pump. It worked admirably for five days with a common breeze, but on the sixth day a high-pressure blast carried away the vane, fans, and all the wind apparatus, leaving the machinery for pump, &c., standing naked and alone. A windmill with adjustment for opening and closing the fans, as the wind is increased or decreased, is the only kind adapted to Colorado.

The Levels

The farmer must ascertain the altitude of his farm at different points. The best way would be to engage a surveyor, and let him take the levels at various points; ascertain the highest, and run a line in the direction of the nearest stream, if possible avoiding plowed fields, and, when practicable, keeping on fence-rows or on the sides of roads. The surveyor should be judicious in his selection of the ground for his ditch; if he can choose, he should select a good, solid, clayey soil, as nearly impervious to water as possible. Judgment in this matter should be cautiously exercised. A fall of about 2½ feet to the mile should be obtained, if possible; 1 foot to the mile may barely suffice. Water will run at a fall of 8 inches to the mile, corresponding with the curvature of the earth; but in a small volume of water it is not enough. The smaller the stream the greater the fall allowable, up to about 3 feet. Above that, it is not desirable, as it will fill up with *detritus*, sand, or gravel. A ratio corresponding with a medium fall of about 2½ feet to the mile is preferable, neither permitting vegetable growth in the channel nor carrying down sand or gravel to choke it up and cause the breaking of the banks of the ditch.

It may be very probable that one survey will not be sufficient to locate a good and permanent line of ditch. A dozen lines have sometimes been run before a determination is arrived at; and it is good economy to examine each line critically, because, by the expenditure of a few hours' work at this initial point, a great deal of expense may be saved in the future. An hour or two of due consideration on the part of the surveyor may save a thousand yards of excavation, and he should therefore be allowed his own time and plenty of help. The width of the stream from which the water is taken should be as narrow as possible, to save money in the construction of the dam. The solidity of the bank should also be regarded in the choice of locality for dam and sluice-gate, as the washing of the water round the timbers of the sluice or head-gate must be guarded against, or at the first high water the whole structure may be deposited piecemeal in a potato-patch or wheat-field. It is possible for a farmer to get along without a surveyor in his survey of a ditch; especially if he provides himself with one of those elegant little drainage and irrigating levels which are in the market at a low price. An ordinary carpenter's or mason's spirit-level might suffice, as it very often does, where the farmer is compelled to exercise the most rigid economy.

The Dam or Weir

The selection of a place for a dam should be guided by the character of the bed of the stream, the narrowness of the channel, the rapidity of the current, &c. It can be made of any size or character, from the magnificent structure of historic fame down to the little sandy dam we used to construct in our boyhood to float our tiny crafts upon the gutter. If an expensive dam is desired, a mill engineer should be engaged for the purpose. A log-dam can be constructed cheaply when occasion requires it, but for a small irrigating ditch nothing of so costly a character is ordinarily used. A row of piles may be driven close together across the stream, varying in size according to circumstances, from 12 to about 3 inches in diameter. In Cherry Creek a farmer has been known, in the dry season, to throw up a little dam of horse-manure, sand, and willow branches, and with it turn the water into a ditch carrying about 150 square inches of water, by which he saved an excellent crop of farm and garden produce and several hundred fruit trees. The farmer is his own best judge of the kind of dam he needs, especially when he is aided by the advice of a careful and judicious engineer.

Mr. Magnus has twice changed the whole volume of the Platte River by a simple brush-dam, and it can still be seen near Denver as a monument of the fact, with the brush sprouting out and a bunch of nice cottonwood springing from it. The river bottom was of loose gravel and sand. He says he has more success with brush than with anything else. Large stones and logs increase the current too much, and cause washing. Brush and hay are particularly effective in constructing dams on shifting sand. A low dam should be as wide at the top as the height; the front or breast slope should be three feet to one, and the back slope two feet to one. These dams are called perfect dams when the top is above the water, and imperfect, or submerged dams, when the surplus water runs over the top or sill.

Wing-dams extend partly across the stream, and these are most generally used for temporary farm irrigation. The difference of their span across the stream is the only peculiarity. They, of course, do not raise all the water in the bed; but if they point diagonally up the stream from the head-gate, they can raise all the water necessary for the purpose of the farmer. This statement must be taken with caution, as wing-dams will not pay on a moving bottom of sand. With a substantial bed-rock or clay strata, a permanent wing-dam may be good; but on the sand of the torrential streams of Colorado they will ruin any farmer who expends a large amount of money on their construction. One of the most enterprising millers of Colorado has been ruined by the outlay expended on wing-dams in such a connection. A simple bar may be all that is needed to pen up the water and divert it into the sluice. This must be left to be improvised according to existing circumstances, as it would be but a very temporary structure, and liable to be carried off every night. Calculations should also be made for floods and freshets.

The Sluice, Hatch, or Head-Gate

This is a very important part of the economy of irrigation, and should be located in a bank with a firm, solid ground of the most compact material, so as to obviate the necessity of repairs from the degrading influence of the water. It is usually made of a square frame, well bolted, primed, and dovetailed together, like the window-frame of a house, only of sufficient strength to withstand a heavy pressure of water; and in place of sash, some 2-inch plank, about six inches deep, one above the other, fitted in, and capable of working up and down by means of a lever or chain-pulley in a groove on the sides of the frame. This will let out the water from the dam and main stream in quantities to suit demand or exigency. If the bottom of the sluice-gate is placed down level with, or even a little below, the bed of the stream, it is better, as then a choice of either bottom or surface water can be obtained, and can be employed at any time to keep the collection of silt or accumulations as low as desirable. Sometimes, and it is certainly better, a double sluice-gate is arranged with one at each end; a strong plank box, flume, or aqueduct between. This makes the whole structure stronger, and is a better protection against floods and freshets. These hatches or sluices can be raised from the top or bottom, and the amount of water graduated to accommodate circumstances. Another kind of movable frame is made of planks, working upright or on end. The water by these can only be admitted at the floor of the sluice. These gates are so commonly used in connection with mills that a further description is unnecessary, as any person can see one but a short distance from his own door.

In building a sluice it is better to excavate a little deeper than run the risk of the embankment being below high-water mark, or of poor material. The initial cut at the head-main should not be at a right or acute angle, as it tends to create resistance to the current, and occasion rebounds from one side to the other, which probably may cause undermining. The line of the ditch should be, as near as circumstances will allow, with a due regard to permanency, continued with the line of the mother stream, so that the current will be uninterrupted in its easy flow. If the water is taken out at a tangent with the supply stream, mischief and disaster by impingement is inevitable. The angle should be rounded as near as Hogarth's line of beauty as is possible.

Artificial embankments, of which there are several forms, such as earthen, sod, or rock-wall, either dry or cemented, earthen mounds with reversed slopes, faced with stones, piles, brush, sod, or wicker-work, all can be used for the purpose. Where the escarpment of the bank is of a sandy or gravelly character, the willow, osier, and a thousand other plants and trees which will bind the bank in a solid mass, and compact the drift-sand with a surface of alluvial soil, can be used with success. In Colusa County, California, the Agricultural Report of October, 1871, says:

> Our farmers are making flood-gates out of wrought iron instead of wood. Where there is no rain for six months, wooden gates shrink, and are apt to break the next season. We are now making round tubes, one to six feet in diameter, with the gate in the upper end.

The Head Main Ditch

This ditch is first marked out by the surveyor's stakes, usually 100 feet apart, and followed by a good plow to mark the line; it is not essential to follow the surveyor in every minute turn in the line, as the difference of level in 100 feet, at a fall of 2½ feet to the mile, is only about half an inch; so if a close approximation is arrived at, it will be sufficient. The eye of an intelligent farmer or teamster can save quite a distance in a mile, by watching these corners, without any loss of fall. When the line of the ditch is well marked, then return and run a parallel line to mark the width of the ditch; then the heavy ditching plow and scraper should be used. Some very excellent ditchers are made, both in Europe and in the United States, which make ditching a very easy job.

In regard to the size of the ditch, calculation must be made as to the number of acres to irrigate; 50 inches for 80 acres would usually suffice for ordinary farm crops; garden crops want more; the rice crop still more. Then, again, other matters must be taken into consideration, such as the quality of the soil and the amount of evaporation and seepage. If it is very sandy, more water must be used, as it will lose by percolation more than an impervious clay soil.

The amount of evaporation is a large item in a long ditch. Mr. J. W. Smith, of Denver, one of the stockholders in the Platte Water Canal Company, informs me that out of about 1,700 inches of water at one point in their ditch, not above 1,000 are sold and utilized when it reaches a point eight miles below; the remainder, about 700 inches, is lost by evaporation and seepage. This is a wide and shallow ditch. In some places it is eight feet, in others six, and down to eighteen inches of fall to the mile. It is a well established principle that the deeper the amount of water carried by a ditch, in proportion to its width, the less fall is necessary, and the loss is much smaller from evaporation and seepage. According to the best authorities, a velocity of seven or eight inches per second is necessary to prevent the deposit of slime and vegetable growth, and about fifteen inches per second the deposit of sand. Thus the mean velocity need not exceed, over a slimy bed, 8 inches per second; over a common clay bed, 6 inches per second; over a river sand-bed, 15 inches per second; over a gravelly bed, 18 inches per second.

A superficial observer might suppose that seepage is influenced very much by atmospheric or even the water's own vertical pressure; but it is not so, except in a very minute degree. Let us remember that an oak flume or channel, water-tight, holds water without seepage; flumes and channels of other material can be made impervious to seepage. There are many kinds of material used in the construction of ditches that will prevent seepage, and different materials can be found, on a graduating scale, calculated upon acknowledged scientific formulas, of every kind of porosity, including white sand, fine gravel, coarse gravel, shingle, small bowlders, up to large ones, through which the water will percolate as through a sieve. In fact, all soils are really sieves of different degrees of fineness.

Materials properly prepared can be found other than wood, stone, iron, &c., which will prevent the seepage of water, at least to any great extent. A ditch can be constructed over a sand-hill, where 50 inches will be lost in running 100 feet. The same ditch can be prepared by artificial bottoming which will carry the 50 inches of water for a length of ten miles with scarce any perceptible loss.

A deeper ditch can be run at a less fall, thus economizing surface exposed to the heat of the sun's rays, and thereby decreasing the evaporation. In constructing ditches of a small fall, the deposit of slime, sand, and vegetation diminishes the sectional area, and impedes the current. They should be always kept well cleaned. The course of a ditch should be as straight as possible, if velocity is desirable; the more frequent the curves the greater the loss of velocity; the actual loss by curvature has been calculated and tabulated. The ditch should not be made too large, too wide, or too deep; it can always be enlarged either by widening or deepening, when necessity requires. When practicable it is better to construct a ditch by plowing two or three furrows, which can be done by unaided labor with a span of horses, than to pay out ready cash for assistance when it really cannot be afforded. A very useful size of ditch in a hard, compact soil is six feet wide at the surface, three feet at the bottom, and three feet deep. If the soil is loose, the slope to the banks must be more extended.

If a lumber channel is desired as a flume, a square-sided box will do, as the object in the slope of a ditch is to prevent its washing or degradation. Such a ditch will irrigate, at 50 inches to 80 acres, 3,200 acres. This will cost about $400 per mile in Colorado, calculating the excavation at 15 cents per cubic yard. If several neighbors join together to construct such a ditch, it may decrease in size as each in succession draws from it. For instance, if twelve neighbors join together, they can each drop off six inches in width, or its equivalent of width and depth, and have plenty of water for all their purposes. The price of the whole ditch can be equalized between them, making the aggregate expense very light.

Fall of the Main Ditch

A fall of 1 in 9,288 gives a mean velocity of 6 inches per second in an artificial canal; 1 in 27,000 gives a mean velocity of 7 inches per second in a drain near Conde. Ancient aqueducts show a fall of 1 in 432 to 1 in 643. The fall of the new river or canal which conveys water to London is on a scale of 0.21 foot per mile, or 1 in 21,120. Its motion is a half mile per hour. This is too slow, since, during the summer, the temperature of the water is raised in consequence. The fall of the grand Ganges Canal is 1 in 3,520; that of the culvert of the Croton waterworks equals 1.125 feet per mile. The artificial canals in the Dutch and Austrian Netherlands are 30 to 40 feet per minute mean velocity, and from 2 to 9 inches to the mile. The Illinois River, in a distance of two hundred and twenty miles, has a fall of only 28 feet. The Platte River below Denver has a fall of 11 feet per mile; but it gradually decreases as it approaches the Missouri River. Cherry Creek, from its source to its mouth, at Denver, has a fall of 35 feet to the mile; but it is filled with sand all the year round, except at the time of the spring floods, after a heavy fall of snow in the mountains, or a peculiarly rainy season.

Colorado, on account of the great fall to her streams, is singularly fortunate in regard to irrigation. In all mountainous countries, the plains gradually slope toward the larger water-courses or great arteries of the different hydrographic systems of the globe. Like the plains of Lombardy and Abyssinia, the Great Plains of Colorado, gradually sloping gradually decrease in fall. The Adda and the Ticino, in Italy, in some of their characteristics, are much like, the torrential streams of Colorado. As the mountains of Egypt are to the plains of Abyssinia, so is the Sierra Madre of the American continent to the Great Plains of Colorado and Kansas.

Some of the hydraulic ditches in the mountainous districts of Colorado employed for ground-sluicing, &c., have an immense fall, and tax the great rubber and canvas hose to the very utmost. The ditch of the Platte Water Canal Company, with its heavy fall in some places, is of course choked with sand, and its banks are continually breaking. If a main ditch is very rapid, and the fall heavy, the slope of the banks must be considerable, or the washing will work serious trouble and break through, cutting crevasses by its action, and disfiguring the farm. It is best, therefore, to sow grass on the slopes and banks; it holds the whole together, and is a great help to the beauty and permanence of your ditch. A main ditch should never have over 2½ feet fall per mile. This pinches old prejudices of a few farmers, but long experience and all scientific authorities prove the accuracy of the statement.

Flume, Chute, or Aqueduct

In ditching, there may be gullies, cañons, streams or depressions in the surface of the farm, over which you want to carry the water, where it will be cheapest to construct a flume or aqueduct either of lumber, logs, earthwork, rock, or pipes. In such case, the cost of each should be carefully computed. A lumber flume will not last above five or six years, and if the water does not run all the year round, the sun, when it is dry, will so warp and twist the planking as to make it leaky, and act like a colander, or sieve, thereby losing a great many inches of water. There is a tendency among Americans to construct everything with an eye only to the present. Europeans generally build with reference to permanency. The old buildings now standing in England, monuments of durability, constructed eleven hundred years ago, bear witness to this fact. The tendency to put up works of a temporary character should be checked as much as possible. Foundations should be more substantial, and every flume, aqueduct, dam, bridge, or work of public improvement should be built of rock. Lumber flumes are only like shells or toys; earthwork flumes are like sugar and salt arrangements, at the mercy of the gophers, winds, and storms; sheet iron is better, but not so good as rock, which will scarcely require repairs. The water-way should be lined with cement or puddle, to prevent the walls from being saturated.

Puddling, or Artificial Bottoming

In Europe this is known as puddling, and requires an intimate knowledge of the composition of soils, their compactness, their durability, the exact amount of their porosity, and their solubility. There are two kinds, constructive puddling and puddling by deposition.

Constructive puddling. — It is useless for a novice to attempt this description of work on ditches. A mere puddle of water or clay is not sufficient. It requires working with as much care as the clay for a well molded brick. Surface alluvial soil, found on the banks of our streams, will not do. It wants a light loam, very different from clay, with a slight admixture of course sand or fine gravel, well worked with a spade to a proper consistency with water, so as to form a kind of concrete, though it does not partake of the character of concrete. In California and Utah, horses, oxen, and even men are used to work the puddle to a proper consistency with their feet. Putting it when properly compounded into a brick-machine will do better than anything to prepare it for plastering or daubing (to use a common expression) the bottom and sides of a ditch. If a ditch does not run water all the year, puddling may as well be omitted; for the cracking from exposure to the sun will be so great as to make it almost useless. A brick-maker, who would naturally be supposed by the novice to be the best person to select puddling stuff, is the worst, as he would select the same material which he would use for making brick. In fact, it is only by experience that one can learn to choose good puddling stuff. It is true that farmers in Colorado are using the common alkali bottom clay to puddle their ditches, and have approximated to a *quasi* success; but in every instance where it has been used the ditch cannot be relied upon for economical work. Probably, however, this alkali clay, if the farmer is short of water, and does not understand the better process, will suffice in a rough way, for ordinary purposes, but certainly not for a permanent and substantial structure.

This artificial bottoming, or puddling, is of vital importance where the scarcity and the great evaporation makes water valuable. The farmer of the western side of our continent should experiment and acquire a practical knowledge by observation in regard to it, as the greater the density of population, the more urgent will be the necessity for its use. He cannot afford to look hastily over this part of the economy of irrigation.

Puddling by deposition. — Every current of water carries with it certain sedimentary deposits of *debris,* which are the accumulations from localities disintegrated by certain influences, oftentimes by the stream itself. These deposits are of a great variety of composition and material, from small rocks down to the gravel, sand, clay of various densities, mineral earths, alluvial soil, and vegetable matter. The kind or description of the sedimentary deposit depends on the velocity of the current or the fall. These deposits can be used as a lining or cement for ditches, if proper care is used in the depth of fall and the choice of ground for your ditch courses. After the deposit of one kind of earth, an experienced engineer will, by a change of fall, bring down a different kind of sediment, which, deposited along, will make a cement, capable of resisting the action of water from either seepage or leakage. A popular scientist of the present day says: "By this gradual cementing process, already alluded to, or by an interruption of the aqueous action, the alluvial layers may become so hardened as to form a new bed-rock."

The immense evaporation of water from ditches is a serious loss, which should be obviated as far as possible by the protection of the water in the ditches from the action of the powerful rays of a vertical sun. Covering the ditches by planking or arches, of course, would not be economical, therefore not feasible. This loss may be decreased by reducing the evaporating surface — making the ditch as narrow as practicable. Trees are a very important material to use for this purpose — the cottonwood, box elder, locust, and the willow. The last is probably the best for this purpose, as it grows very rapidly, especially the basket or osier willow.

Measuring Water

What is an inch of water? Some of our engineers will tell you an inch of water should be measured with a six-inch, some a five-inch, some a four-inch head, and so on, according to the whim of the party, or the object sought to be obtained. Why is there so much confusion? It is simply because every one measures an inch of water to suit his own particular views.

The pressure doctrine no doubt originated in countries or localities where hydraulic force was required, and not where used for simple irrigating purposes. In mountainous sections, where hydraulic mining is carried on, of course they stipulate for a certain pressure at the head; so also with water for power in our mills; but, if an inch of water without stipulation as to head is contracted for, the contractor would not be compelled to furnish more water than the efflux of a stream through a square inch orifice, with a head only of a line above the surface of the opening. The most proper way to measure water, to buy or to sell it, is by the gallon per second, per minute, per hour, or per day. This can be calculated to a nicety, as every kind of velocity has been reduced by the ablest mathematicians to minute formulas. Take a bottle partially filled with water, let it float down the stream to be measured, between two points designated by poles or ropes thrown across, say for 100 feet, then take a good stop-watch, and note the length of time the bottle is floating between the given points; get the mean width and depth of the stream forming the sectional area; then multiply the velocity per second by the sectional area, and you obtain the volume in inches or feet as you think best; then divide by the cubic inch contents of a gallon, and the result is ascertained for any time you wish, per second, per minute, &c., &c. An "inch of water" is not the same as a cubic inch of water. Many irrigators who are not versed in mathematics or engineering, are apt to call it "a cubic inch of water;" this is a mistake; a square inch of water would be correct as irrigation is measured in the far

West. The old German mode of measuring an inch of water was by a round orifice one inch in diameter. The Platte River Canal Company obviates the trouble of disagreement on the measurement of water by stipulating how it shall be measured at the hatchway, where the water is taken out. They do not agree to give an "inch of water," or inch of water under certain pressure; but merely a volume of water running from their ditch filling a hole of certain dimensions.

Reservoirs

In connection with the head main ditch, it is oftentimes desirable, if you have favorable depressions in the land, to form reservoirs into which you can have a continuous stream of water running during the time not devoted to irrigation, and for the purpose of getting rid of your waste or surplus water. These reservoirs, lakes, or ponds, are useful for a multitude of things; for instance, as a reserve in case your stream of water may fall short at your head main, or by reason of accident or other emergency. A reservoir may be made at the head of a ravine, by throwing a temporary dike or embankment across from side to side, with a sluice level with the bottom, for draining or irrigating lands below it. Fish can be kept within it, aquatic fowls can be bred there, and a fine stock watering-place can be assured all the year round, besides furnishing all the ice for the neighborhood during the summer months. The main ditch may be tapped to fill it at any point in its line by a hatch or sluice-way, to open or close at pleasure.

Dr. Bell, in his "New Tracks in North America," says:

About six miles south of Fort Union is situated what, even in a civilized country, might be called a model farm. Mr. Kronig, the owner of this farm, came to the conclusion, from his own observation, that the rainfall along the base of the mountains was quite sufficient to supply artificial reservoirs from which tracts of land could be successfully irrigated. Notwithstanding the chance of such an experiment turning out a costly failure, he set to work, and has formed on the open plain two or three lakes or reservoirs, from which he now irrigates 2,500 acres of land. I bathed in one of these lakes in passing, went over a fine house he was building near it, and saw with pleasure the groves and avenues of young trees which he had planted, all thriving beautifully. The yield last year was an average of 35 bushels of maize, 40 of wheat, and 50 of oats to the acre. He is now a rich man, and hopes soon to have another lake and several hundred acres more land in good working order. He also states that he feels convinced that the rainfall has increased since he commenced to irrigate and form the lakes.

Different Modes of Irrigation

There are several different modes of irrigation, and each of them has its peculiar crops and lands to which it is best adapted: 1. Bedwork; 2. Catchwater; 3. Warping; 4. Flooding; 5. Subterraneous.

Bedwork irrigation. — This is done by a series of hatches or sluices in the main ditch, on either side, opening into lateral branches, generally at right angles, and much smaller in size than the main, and generally, though not necessarily, at regular distances from each other; the land between each forming planes of sometimes 30, 40, or 50 feet each, with a water-branch running down their slopes, upon the old ridge and furrow principle, though the draining-branch of the feeder-ditch is slightly more marked than the old shallow furrow. These planes or ridges must vary in width and extent, according to the necessities of the case. If it is a soil hard to irrigate and hard to absorb, they must be smaller in measure across them. If the soil absorbs moisture readily, a longer distance across them will be sufficient. The crown of the ridge should not be over 15 inches higher than the furrow. These lateral branches must all be carefully regulated as to the quantity of water necessary to effect the object, and, if possible, not have any waste or surplusage when the object is accomplished and the lowest point properly watered. A careful farmer, who has executive ability and understands the principle, can so regulate the water as to have scarce any surplusage, which is a very great consideration in dry localities. Care must also be taken that the surplusage, if any, should be carried off immediately, by proper drains, as standing water on crops is quite as disastrous as no water at all. Bedwork irrigation, however, will not pay in Colorado, because the land requires beveling and so much expense to be laid out upon it to prepare it for the water. The best irrigators there have entirely given it up, and prefer a medium plan of embodying the catchwater and flooding modes.

Catchwater irrigation. — This is carried on upon quite a different principle. Lateral branches are used from the main ditch, as in the bedwork plan, but not in such numbers. Only one hatch and lateral is ordinarily used for one class of altitude slope or declivity. The water is taken from the main and passes down the slope a short distance, then takes a turn horizontally along the side or face of the slope, and sometimes parallel with the main ditch, continuing to the farthest point of the slope; it is then let down to a lower point, and returns on a lower parallel, say 20 or 30 feet, to just below the starting-point; thence it again doubles at a lower point, and repeats the process until the whole of the water is exhausted or the land irrigated. This process is carried on at different places in the field, according to the topography, contour, or profile. If there is one locality or one description of crop which needs more water than this plan gives, the water in the channel can be stopped or dammed up by sods or little board sluice-gates, and the water made to run over the edges and flood the neighboring area, the next parallel below catching the surplus. It is not sound policy or economy to dam up the main ditch in this manner, which should be used as a head-main and source of supply alone.

Another plan can be adopted, and is usual in Colorado, to construct laterals down the slope from the main ditch, with diagonal furrows, about every four or six feet, more or less, as circumstances may require, to carry the water on either side of the laterals. In this case, a mere plow furrow is sufficient, and is temporary, being plowed every year, and locations changed as the experience of the farmer may determine. Another plan is to throw laterals from the main ditch down the face of the slope, and draw a harrow in various directions from the laterals, continuing the teeth-marks with the grade of the slope. This is a very good arrangement, and perhaps is better than flooding for ordinary crops, as the little rivulets caused by the harrow-teeth can be better controlled than by flooding, though for permanent, sound, compact, close old grass sod, the flooding is preferable.

Flooding. — This system is very commonly used in connection with the catchwater plan, and is really the very cheapest and easiest understood of either. It is done by closing the laterals with temporary dams or boards, and flooding the water over the edge. This is as cheap as any of the systems, and finds much favor, though great caution is necessary, as, if the slope of the ground is too heavy, washing of the soil and the seed with it may result. This mode by some is called terrace-work, and

Governor Hunt at Denver has practiced it to some extent on clover, with admirable success. Another kind of flooding is by letting a body of water from one side of a river run all over a low piece of land, and letting it off into the parent stream at a lower point.

Warping. — This is applied to lands submerged with water, and is scarcely ever used, except on the seaside, where the tides can be employed. It is done by embankment of the land, and letting in the water; allowing it to stand until the sediment or warp is deposited.

Subterraneous irrigation. — This is done entirely by letting the water into deep drains, or ditches, to reach down into the sub-soil, and is admirably adapted to a very dry climate, and for crops which extend very deep, as it does not appear on the surface, except by absorption or upward percolation. This kind can be used any time in the day, when the sun is ever so hot, and it does not scald the plants like the other systems. The ditches are usually made the same as underdrainage, by brush or large stones to fill the ditch, allowing the water to soak or seep through the soil. The only difference between subterranean irrigation and underdraining is in the location of the ditches; in the first you place them on the highest, and in the latter on the lowest point of the land.

Irrigation as a Vehicle for Fertilizers

Water can be used as a vehicle for various fertilizing mixtures or substances; a stream of water through the stable, hennery, piggery, back-house, or cow-pen, may be used in conveying food to farm-plants. Spring or well-water should never be directly turned upon seeds or plants, unless moderately warm, or of the temperature assimilating to river-water or rain. Cold well or spring water should be exposed in a reservoir to the action of the sun, so that it may acquire a temperature equal to the atmosphere and the earth.

A good liquid fertilizer for plants may be made by mixing twelve gallons of water with four pounds of Peruvian guano, and allowing it to stand for twenty-four hours. This may be applied to flowers in pots. The guano administered in a dry state might kill the plants. The same guano will serve three times, each time being covered with twelve gallons of water.

The Germans have a popular proverb, that "he who has water has grass." The irrigators in the vicinity of Northern Spain need no manure where they use water by irrigation. In that section the water is loaded with the abraded deposit of the granite rocks, held in solution until, by warping and flooding, it is deposited on their farms. Near Antwerp, the meadows are never manured, but highly improved by the application of water alone. In the manipulation of his soils the farmer can take advantage of knowledge gained by study of their peculiarities and experience in their treatment. If he has a too stiff and heavy clayey soil, he may apply a thin layer of calcareous or silicious sediment, or warp. If it is too light, sandy, and lacks compactness, a solution which will give a deposit of clay will prove advantageous. Water in such cases must be used as an infiltrater and not for superficial deposition alone; where water is used as a fertilizer as well as a refreshing medium, reservoirs must be dispensed with, unless the intention is to replenish the bottom of the reservoir for the ultimate object of reclaiming it for farm or garden purposes. Water is prized for irrigation purposes just in the ratio of its amount of extraneous matter contained in solution. River and swamp waters are always preferable to spring waters for other reasons besides fertilizing. Spring waters are always colder than river water, and, therefore, not so well adapted to cereals and small plants particularly. To test the necessity of a proper temperature for irrigating water, let the gardener and farmer try the experiment of watering plants of the same kind, part of them by warm and part by cold water, and they will easily see what a difference there will be in favor of the warm water.

On the Ganges or Nile, it is usual to make dikes or embankments to keep the waters confined within certain limits, in order that they may have sufficient time to deposit their alluvial sediment. This is known as "warping" all over the world. In Egypt these deposits are alluvial in their character; in England and Germany they are chiefly salt and marine deposits.

The amount of matter which comes down from the Rocky Mountains is immense, and cannot be estimated; and the same process has been going on from time immemorial. How, then, can the great plains ever be exhausted, if the farmer will use the waters that come heavily laden with the nutrition which furnishes the every-day food for plants?

Irrigation cannot be complete without proper judicious underdraining. It requires good subsoiling, if the depth of soil will admit it, and thorough underdraining. Simple water-furrows are not sufficient in every instance. The water must be carried off as effectually and with as much care as was devoted to bringing it on to the land. Water, standing in pools on the land, should be immediately got rid of. In the winter such pools are apt to accumulate; then the plow and the spade should be brought into requisition, even if it is in midwinter, upon winter crops.

Meadow grass has, as yet, received but little attention in Colorado, simply because the farmers there have tried the European plan of very heavy watering. It must be borne in mind that a tenth part of the water used in England is not required in Colorado, for the reason that the compact turf, the growth of many years in England, will bear a continued flooding. If the same amount was used on the thin grass of our plains it would kill it out, the soil being more porous and the plants not growing so closely together. The English turf-sod is almost impervious, and it requires a long time ere the roots of the grass receive the nourishment necessary. In time, when the farmers of Colorado have made a rule to plant timothy and the grasses peculiarly adapted to irrigation, they may then with impunity use the quantity of water recommended by English and Italian irrigators.

How Much and When to Irrigate

The best time to irrigate is early in the morning, before the sun acquires very great power, or in the evening, when it is about to go below the horizon. A good time to water land is when a cloud comes up and you expect a shower. In nine cases out of ten the shower does not give all the water needed, so the work will not be uselessly expended. In the spring the work of irrigation commences in earnest. It is not necessary to use water in May as a fertilizer, but simply to moisten the earth as a germinator. Probably it may not need any water if a large quantity has fallen during the winter. The water which comes down from the mountains then is the melted snow and surface water; but in June and July the sedimentary deposits are running, and the streams are laden with fertilizers, which decrease as the winter approaches and the streams are lower. When the waters are laden in this way and the crops want the fertilizer, the farmer should irrigate by flooding; and in the fall, when the streams are limpid, it should be done by catch-work. The soil should not be kept continually moist; dryness on the surface does not always indicate dryness below. It will not hurt crops to let them get occasionally partially dry. Some crops require more water than others, and some will bear very little at a time; twenty-four hours' watering will not hurt wheat and other small grains, nor beans, peas, turnips, and rutabagas; beets and cabbages will not bear more than twelve hours of continuous moisture, as their root-fibers are so delicate that they soon get choked up and rotten. In such cases they will sometimes shoot out more fibers, but often they will die, and a retardation of growth is certain. It should be continued in August, as in that month the rainfall is usually less; in September also, and, in fact, until early winter, or the ordinary rains and snow appear. If an ordinary or sufficient quantity does not fall, it should be continued all the winter at intervals, as it prevents the frost from extending too deep into the soil.

The Economy of Irrigation

The history of irrigation warrants the statement, beyond all contradiction, that without it, in certain dry climates, no successful crops of any kind can be raised; and, also, that in ordinarily humid climates, all over the American continent, there occur periods when droughts are experienced and the crops are almost a complete failure, while with irrigation properly and industriously conducted, double the yield attained without it can be assured. It is, therefore, logically true that irrigation, properly conducted, either in a dry or humid climate, may be decidedly profitable. The testimony of California, Colorado, New Mexico, Missouri, Pennsylvania, Massachusetts, and almost any State and Territory of the American Union, places the matter beyond dispute. The Pacific Rural Press, of California, in speaking of the Woodland Ditch Company, which is but the mirror of hundreds of similar institutions, says: ''All the grain irrigated by this company will produce a fair average crop. The same grain, without irrigation, would have been an almost total failure. The cost to the farms for water is about $4 per acre, and the grain will probably be worth $25 to $30.''

In Colusa County, California, the alfalfa or Chili clover, probably lucerne, produces ordinarily, without irrigation, three tons per acre at each cutting, twice a year; but, with irrigation, it reaches to three tons three times a year. Mr. Safford, of Hope, Maine, says he has 40 acres of meadow which he irrigates from a small stream. He does not allow water to go on it in the winter, as it kills the roots of the grass. Of two fields, side by side, one without irrigation yielded 400 pounds to the acre; the other, irrigated, from two to three tons. He uses no manure.

In some localities, but not usually in Colorado, the charge for water is $1.50 per inch, which astonishes parties who come from the East, and wonder how a farmer can possibly afford to pay such a price for the irrigating season. It is easily explained. The employment of irrigation doubles the product. Where, in the United States, except in Colorado or California, (as is popularly claimed,) is the average yield so high as 26 or 28 bushels of wheat to the acre? If they did not irrigate, the crops would yield probably only 12 or 20 bushels, as in Iowa, Illinois, and other portions of the favored West. If they have to put more labor upon their farm, it yields immensely more in proportion. A farmer in Colorado, who for seven years has steadily stuck to business and worked only half as hard as the slaving husbandman of the older States, will be found to be wealthy, and not actually compelled to work another day. In the East it takes thirty years to acquire a competency, which the Colorado farmer secures in seven or ten years. There is no necessity for a farmer to remain poor in Colorado, even if he starts without a penny.

In Boulder County, Colorado, the cost of irrigation is not more than 5 or 10 cents per acre, outside of a share in the works, costing, probably, from $50 to $100 each. The cost of repairs in the main ditch is paid by a tax on the shareholders, which usually amounts to $5 per annum; this, added to the interest for money, is the actual cost of the water. The lateral branches are owned by each individual, and built at his own expense, which amounts to but very little, and that only in labor when the men and teams have nothing else to do. The representation that irrigation is expensive is a mistake calculated or intended to depreciate the country and institute unfavorable comparisons with eastern agriculture. In any country which is subject to occasional drought, a crop cannot be assured without irrigation; with it the yield may be doubled. The expense of irrigation is probably less by 50 per cent. than average loss by drought in any State in the Union. The rain-fall is not enough in any section of our country at all seasons of the year to meet the want of the crops. With irrigation, the quality of Colorado wheat is far superior to the wheat of any Eastern State. With irrigation, the quality of every specimen of wheat sent to Colorado has been wonderfully improved — a fact substantiated by the reports of this Department.

Mr. G. H. Church has a ditch whose terminus is eleven miles from Denver, on the Boulder road. It was taken out from Coal Creek, at the foot of the mountains, and runs 10 miles east to his farm. The average fall is 13 feet to the mile — too much. The size is 5 feet wide and 1 foot deep; cost about $1,000, reckoning team and man at $4 per day. This ditch is a proof of the efficacy of the reservoir system. It does not run enough water from the head for the entire season, but is kept running all the time while water can be obtained from the head, and stored in a lake or reservoir, to be used as a reserve in dry seasons. He has one lake from which he draws his irrigation water, but he has another which he keeps for fish-breeding, and has stocked it with sun-fish and cat-fish from the Pancross Lake at Valmont, and they are multiplying enormously. Mr. C. is going to the States in the spring to bring out some black bass to stock another lake. He thinks that all through the season, such a dry season as 1871 for garden and farm produce, it cost him for spreading and manipulating the water on 40 acres about $1 per acre; in ordinary seasons it will not cost half that amount. The lake is one and a half miles from his house. The irrigation lake is about 1,000 to 1,200 feet square. This water supplied last year 40 acres of land, leaving plenty for fish and for watering stock.

Mr. Magnus says of the Upper Platte and Bear Creek Ditching Company, in which he is a shareholder, that it costs him about $30 to $35 per annum for repairs, and his share of water is about 144 square inches, which irrigates 140 acres of land, comprising about equal quantities of bottom land, second bottom, and upland. It costs the person near the head of the ditch only about $5 or $6 per annum, and the last person on the line of the ditch it costs about $50 per annum. This ditch is five or six miles long in Arapahoe County, though it commences in Jefferson County, 16 feet wide at the head and 20 inches deep, tapering gradually as it passes down the line. Mr. Everett, on the divide between Clear Creek and Platte, says that it costs a great deal less in proportion for water to irrigate 160 acres than it does for 40 acres. To illustrate this in his own case, he says he irrigated 180 acres of land with 90 inches of water, and it is generally conceded by the whole community, in his neighborhood, that 30 or 40 inches is required to irrigate about 40 or 50 acres. He says he has always averaged over 25 bushels of wheat to the acre before this year. Last year (1870) he had 50 acres, and averaged over 25 bushels per acre. This year his average on 120 acres was 16 bushels to the acre; but some of his crop, not being irrigated, was so poor it was never harvested, and about 12 or 15 acres not cut at all. He says, if the farmer is well situated for irrigating, and can employ his water to advantage, 25 bushels per acre of wheat is a very low average.

It may be said, after reading the statements as to the cost of irrigation, that there is a discrepancy per acre. This can be accounted for thus: Where the amount extends to $1 per acre, or in that neighborhood, the farmer hires the water of a ditch company, who realize a large profit on the investment. The mere manipulation of the water, when the main ditch is built, will probably not cost above 50 cents per acre for 160 acres, but rather more in proportion for 40 acres. Platte Water Canal Company charge about $3 per inch; Table Mountain, $1.50; Farmers' Ditch, Jefferson County, $1.50; Ralston Creek Ditch Company, $3.

Mr. Meeker, of Greeley, gives, in the Greeley Tribune, an estimate of the cost of canal No. 1, as follows: Length of surveyed line, thirty and a half miles; completed length, twenty-six miles; cost of excavating 107,949 cubic yards, at 21 cents per yard, $22,669.29; head in Larimer County, section 11, township 6 north, range 68 west; terminus in Weld County, section 15, township 6 north, range 65 west; distance from head to terminus, (air-line,) seventeen miles; lost by sinuosity, 53 per cent.; total fall in twenty-six miles, 75 feet 9 inches; fall per mile, about 3 feet; cost per mile, $872. Irrigation is found on a grander scale of expense in the older countries of Europe; one may scarcely find a system there more economical, or more subservient to the wants of the masses, than is found in the little community of Greeley. The lack of an equal humidity in the atmosphere with other sections, is the cause also of a lack of a great mass of those pestiferous insects well known in the United States, and the disadvantage in one case becomes an advantage in another. The lack of moisture on the plains cures the grass into hay, while the excess of moisture on the eastern seaboard, and even in the garden of the Mississippi Valley, saturates and rots the grass, which is lost to utility for everything but manure, when left on the ground during the winter.

Ditches in Colorado

According to the most authentic information, without an exact and complete examination, it is estimated that there are about four hundred miles of main irrigating ditches in Colorado. General Lessig, surveyor general of Colorado, estimates 10,000,000 acres of land as susceptible of cultivation in the Territory, and says, "The amount is only limited by the facilities of irrigation." There are many hydraulic mining ditches which do not properly come in the province of irrigation, and are therefore omitted in this calculation.

The Platte Water-Canal. — This canal or ditch was commenced in 1859, and is twenty-four miles long. Its cost was said to be, at the time it was built, $100,000; but this is exaggerated, as it can be duplicated in 1871 at $25,000. It is estimated that 50,000 acres are covered by this ditch, though probably not more than 15,000 are under cultivation. It commences near the mouth of the Platte Cañon, on the line of Douglas and Jefferson Counties, and extends northerly partly across Arapahoe County, to a point about two miles east of the city of Denver. Its original width at the head was about 10 feet, and depth 2 feet, gradually decreasing in size as it nears the city. The fall is various; in some places 6 feet, and in others as low as 18 inches. This ditch was constructed in a very unscientific manner, from lack of facilities, and, in consequence, a large amount of water is lost. The company are enlarging the volume of the ditch to meet the requirements of the city of Denver for irrigation purposes, and the width at the head is now 30 feet, with a depth of 3 feet.

[The compiler deems the great capacity of the new works unnecessary, as well as calculated to give the impression that the entire volume of water in the river will be monopolized, and tending to discourage the work of irrigation in the new West.]

Table Mountain Ditch Company. — This ditch is taken out of Clear Creek on the south side, about one and a half miles from Golden City. Originally it was 6 feet wide at the bottom, 2 feet deep, and from 12 to 15 feet wide at the surface. Head-gate 12 feet wide, with partitions between waste-gates, 10 feet wide. The fall is about 19 feet to the mile in the first two miles, which is very much too great a fall in any ditch whatever; and, in consequence, it is gradually washing and degrading its banks every year. It is nearly twenty miles in length. The south branch is about two and a half miles long, and is taken out eight and a half miles from the head. The charge is $1.50 per inch per annum, with a pressure of about 3 inches, making the cost of irrigation about $1 per acre. It was built in 1864 and 1865, and cost about $15,000; but everything then was very much higher in price than now; probably it could be built for $8,000 now.

The Farmers' Ditch. — This ditch leads out of Clear Creek, and is intended to irrigate 30,000 or 40,000 acres. Its head is one and a half miles above Golden City; in size it is 6 feet wide at the bottom, 8 to 12 feet on the surface, and 18 inches deep. In length it is eleven miles, and runs down on the ridge and uplands between Clear and Bear Creeks and the Platte River, toward Denver. The probable cost is $10,000; it is not yet completed the whole length. The charge will probably be the same as the Table Mountain Water Company, $1.50 per inch.

Canal No. 2, of Saint Louis Western Colony, Evans, Colorado. — Mr. W. H. McDonald, the surveyor of the canal, furnishes the following items respecting this improvement: The main trunk will be nine miles long, from a point on Warren Batchelor's farm on Platte River, to a point four miles below Stover's Ranch, on Denver Pacific Railway, with a falling grade of 7 feet per mile. The canal is 10 feet wide on the bottom, with slopes of 1½ to 1, giving an area of water-section of 53.37 square feet. At the end of the first nine miles the main trunk will be divided into two branches; each branch will be 7 feet wide on the bottom, slopes 1 to 1, fall 6 feet per mile. The east branch will cross under the Denver Pacific Railway to its east side, thence northeast twenty miles parallel with the railway, and along the western base of the divide between Box Elder and Platte; the west branch will run parallel to the Denver Pacific Railway on its west side, and generally along the old stage-road from

Denver to Atchison and Saint Joseph, Missouri, at a point near to and east of Mr. Holon Godfrey's ranch; this branch will cross to the east side of the railway, thence northeast to a point south of Evans, its terminus for the present. It will be eleven miles in length; making a total length of forty miles, at an estimated cost of $23,750, covering an area of five townships of land, or 115,200 acres. The colony also constructed the past season six and a half miles of canal to supply the town and irrigate residence and garden lots; also two and a half miles of street ditches, costing about $7,000. This canal was constructed also with a view to milling purposes. The colony proposes to construct another canal, No. 3, to be taken from Big Thompson, 7 feet on bottom, slope 1 to 1, and nine miles in length, to cost $8,000, in time for spring crops.

Alkali Lands

In many parts of Colorado there are patches scattered here and there of what is known as "alkali lands." They are common all over the Great Plains on both sides of the Cordilleras, and are a great bugbear to the farmers, who generally suppose that nothing can be raised upon them; but this is wrong, as in Colorado places where alkali abounds raise magnificent crops. The whole of the Great Plains is, in a great measure, saturated with it. The Commissioner of the General Land Office, in his report to the Secretary of the Interior for 1868 and 1869, says:

The table-lands afford excellent winter pasture in the white sage which they produce, but are of doubtful capacity for the raising of cereals by irrigation. The alkali lands are beyond the power of reclamation by any means now known to man.

If the Commissioner had resided in Colorado, or had examined the matter critically in person, he would not have hazarded that statement. Practical experience has demonstrated that the sage-brush land is capable of raising large crops of timothy, clover, alfalfa hay, and the general cereals. In Colorado the produce of alkali land has been as high as 70 and 80 bushels of wheat to the acre, and it can easily be made to yield 40 or 50 tons of beets per acre.

A gentleman, through one of the agricultural papers, speaks as follows in this connection:

In traveling across the continent last summer, we began to hear of alkali, when we were a few hundred miles west of Missouri, and the evidences of its presence in the soil and in the water grew stronger as we advanced, till, in the Humboldt Valley, we ran for hours through the alkali flats, a region made hopelessly desolate by the excess of noxious elements. The action of air and rains has been to dissolve the salt and remove a part of it, carrying away the chlorine, but not the soda nor the magnesia. In Utah they have had a long contest with what they call saleratus land. Time, cropping, and water are the remedies for the soil. Mr. Meeker, in his prosperous colony, spoke of finding some, but not enough to be mischievous; besides, he draws his water from the snow-clad peaks of the high mountains one hundred miles west of the plain, where Greeley is situated, and needs no wells. Irrigation is the sovereign remedy where water can be obtained. The bitter stuff can be washed out. Probably the best way in Kansas would be to plow these spots in a ridge furrow late in the fall, and let the winter rain leach through the earth.

An ox, bloated with alkali on the plains, can be cured by the administration of fat bacon or vinegar. Governor Gilpin tells us that when he went across the plains with the Doniphan expedition, he served double rations of vinegar to the soldiers, and they experienced none of the effects usually known from drinking the alkali water. Onions, also, are a specific, and the pioneer feels an absolute longing and desire for onions and vinegar in preference to any other food, on crossing the plains. To thoroughly cure alkali lands, in the first place irrigate them, then well drain them with good underdraining of brush, round stones, or tiles and deep subsoiling; this will wash the alkali quite out of the soil and make it clean, mellow, and free from a deleterious quantity of these salts.

In irrigating, of course the farmer will take care that he does not add more alkali to his land in large quantities. It is deposited by precipitation and evaporation, but a current of water will remedy the trouble very shortly.

Questions on Irrigation

The following questions on practical irrigation, propounded through the columns of the Greeley Tribune, are thus answered by our correspondent, Mr. Stanton:

1. Does a dam across an irrigation canal have any effect on the water above the first ripple?

The reaction of the water consequent upon the obstruction offered by a dam is called "regurgitation," and is effected in extent up the stream in the ratio of the height of obstruction. The surface of the water is, however, raised a little above the level by the action of the volume above coming in sudden contact with the still water. This swell backwater, or regurgitation, sometimes should be allowed for so as not to overflow a neighbor's land. It has been contended that the stagnation of the water extends to a sensible height above the horizontal line of the regurgitation from the dam or sluice, or any other fixed obstacle. This is accounted for by the compression or closer adhesion of the particles of the water. This has been for many years a subject of philosophical discussion among hydraulic savans, and is not even yet fully established as a dogma.

2. Will more water pass into an *acequia* by placing a board diagonally and upward across the lateral than by making a dam straight across?

No. You cannot get more water through a channel, from a lateral, than the volume contained in it. If you confine the water, and divert it from its natural course, you may compress it into a smaller space, but the same quantity will be found below the compression as is found above it. A funnel-shaped ajutage, or channel, will discharge the same amount of water after the narrow portion of the funnel is passed. In illustration: Let an orifice of one inch square be made in a board, with a head of water six inches above the orifice; more water will be discharged than if the water was only level with the upper edge of the orifice; therefore it is always considered that more than an inch of water is passed under those circumstances.

3. Is it not cheaper to sow wheat and all small grain in drills, with furrows for water-courses between; that is, granting the crop equal, will not the greater facility afforded by irrigating in furrows compensate for the extra labor of drilling?

In the first place, I cannot believe that flooding grain is so good as allowing the water to run in channels between the drills. It is not best to allow the water to touch plants above the ground if it can be avoided. It is unnecessary, certainly, as the nourishment to the plant is derived from the roots alone. By drilling grain, with irrigation, you can have a better control of it. I think that "granting the crops equal" is not a fair supposition, as I cannot imagine they could be so. Flooding over a standing crop must injure it more than by letting the water down on either side of the plants. A crop *might* be irrigated by flooding without sensible injury, but it would require much greater care to prevent the plants from being washed out. You can certainly with the same labor irrigate more land by drilling grain than otherwise, as the quantity of the water above must be excessive, almost dangerously so, for it to reach the lower part or bottom of a long slope.

4. Is one time in the day better for irrigating than another?

This all depends upon the system of irrigation that is used. If you use subterraneous irrigation, like underdraining, you can irrigate at any time in the day or night; but it is always more expensive, and where the land is so cheap as in Colorado there is no necessity for it. By the other systems, crops should never be irrigated in the heat of the sun. When a storm is coming, and clouds obscure the sun, then would be a good time to irrigate. Nine times out of ten the showers are not adequate to give all the water needed. Such an opportunity should never be neglected. Early in the morning, though the sun may be shining, is a good time, as it is not strong enough to scald the plants. In the evening, also, and all through the night, would be a proper time to irrigate; the extra value of the result will justify, even if it does cost more. It might be possible, in crops planted in rows or drills, to irrigate in the heat of the sun; but it would require great care to prevent the water from touching the plants. I am inclined to believe that if the water can be kept from moistening the plants the increase of temperature over the heated surface would do good.

5. How often should a garden be watered, and do some kinds of vegetables require more water than others?

The quantity of water depends upon the kind of soil, the amount of rain-fall, the description of the subsoil, and the kinds of plants to be watered. Some vegetables are more tender than others; some have such minute tendrils in their roots that complete saturation for twenty-four hours would rot them entirely. This question can be met only by the good judgment of the irrigator, without going through the whole catalogue of plants, grain, and vegetables. Again, crops may be watered twice a week; sometimes, according to the circumstances named above, they may want it only once a week; sometimes possibly once a fortnight; it is impossible to prescribe for every patient or every case; all depends, as the doctors say, on the diagnosis.

6. Over how many rods broadcast can water be made to flow with advantage, and what is the limit of distance where the grain on the upper side of the field will receive positive injury?

This question can be answered only by the farmer himself, as the limit is governed entirely by the slope or declivity. If the land is nearly level and the water is not in danger of degrading the soil when it leaves the lateral, the water can be carried over it for a very long distance. But if the slope is a heavy one, common sense would deem it the height of folly to throw a heavy sheet of water over it, or even sufficient, perhaps, to carry the water over five or six rods, or even less. The kind of seed must also be taken into consideration; light grass seeds must be very carefully flooded, if ever, on any kind of slope whatever. A strong, heavy sod of turf, like the English meadows, will bear a rush of water which would utterly ruin a newly planted grass-patch.

7. How much less water is required for land cultivated the year previous, and what, if any, is the increase of production in grain, potatoes, and vegetables?

This is a very important question, and involves more of careful thought than has yet been given to it. On sod-lands it is usual to calculate your crop about two-thirds less than can be ordinarily raised the second year; and in some cases very much less, though I have known, in Colorado, larger crops raised than ever afterward. This is due to the extra amount of good farming and good work expended upon it. The opinion is borne out by isolated cases of practice and experience, that if sod-land is plowed well in the fall and again in the spring, and plenty of water used, the crop will be equal in every case. The crop will be found to be graduated in the ratio of mellowness and thorough pulverization of the soil, and in the same ratio will be the amount of water required. Plants require aeration as well as moisture, and a baked soil will never allow a proper germination of any but the hardiest seeds. The expenditure of force required to break the crust of a harsh soil will result in dwarfed and truncated plants. Farmers generally settle down into the belief that sod-land will only raise a meagre crop, so they do not devote the care necessary; and, of course, the result only equals their expectation, and scarcely ever exceeds it.

8. What is the value of the gramma grass for hay, when irrigated, and is it likely that clover, timothy, and other tame grasses can be grown to advantage instead?

Very little is known about the irrigation of our native grasses in Colorado, and I have heard of no experience in the matter. But I am inclined to believe that, if a crop of clover and timothy were sown and harrowed in upon our wild grass-lands, that it would be the means of insuring a fine crop; when, if our wild grasses were irrigated as they now stand, the yield for a year or two would not be nearly as great.

9. Does the fertility supposed to be given by the water of an irrigating canal come from the soil through which it flows or from the mountain rock, or from both, or is it due in part to chemical changes, induced through the action of the air and sun, corresponding to fermentation.

I am satisfied that the chief, if not entire fertility of our irrigating water, coming as it does from The Rocky Mountains, and, as soon as it debouches on the plains, rushing over a bed of clean sand, is caused by the disintegration and washing down of the properties contained in the rocks. The fertilizing agents which are contained in the water can come from no other source, as the water of our canals does not run over alluvial soils until the main ditches are opened; and then the distance is so short that no large accumulation of its properties could result from it. The beds of our alkali lakes, as I view them, are but the accumulated deposits of many, many years of filtering and precipitation, as it were, like the accumulations of sediment on the filtering-paper in the funnels of our laboratories.

10. If we could choose, would we or would we not prefer rain, as it comes in the States, to irrigation?

In answering this question, it requires to be prefaced by a half apology to the farmers and residents of older countries, in offering an opinion which is so much at variance with all their old pet prejudices and preconceived notions of the relative value of the two sections. The answer is, unhesitatingly, that our people, with scarce an exception, would not prefer the rain, as it comes in the States, to irrigation in Colorado. There is no uncertainty in raising a crop with irrigation, properly conducted, with even a very ordinary amount of hard, common sense, and without any scientific or engineering ability whatever. There is such a difference between the two systems, in view of their products, that there can be no dispute about it in the minds of any who have tested both.

A Great Western American Canal

Some of the most important works of both ancient and modern times have been accomplished in all the great divisions of the globe, from east to west, north to south, in every one of the old monarchies, in connection with irrigation and water-supply; and these works were conducted under the auspices of the Government.

Mr. Stanton favors, in the suggestions following, a grand enterprise for the reclamation of the "Great American Desert," and says that, with very few exceptions, every foot of land lying in Colorado and Kansas, known on our old maps and the maps of Europe as the Great American Desert, between the base of the Rocky Mountains and Kansas City, on the Missouri River, is susceptible of irrigation.

From the head-waters of the Platte River down to Kansas City there is plainly a continuous water gradient, as is evident by the Platte River itself, which empties into the Missouri. The altitude of the head-waters of the Platte is 9,600 feet, while the altitude of Kansas City is only 648 feet above tide, thus making a difference of 8,952 feet fall. There is certainly, then, no point upon the great grassy plains of Colorado and Kansas which is above the waters of the Platte River. Take a lower point of the Platte River, in the interior of the mountain chain, from the calculations of Professor Engelmann and Dr. Parry: They give 9,153 feet of altitude; eleven miles lower down, 8,657 feet; three miles lower, 8,435 feet; six miles lower, 8,028 feet; Plum Creek, which is an affluent, and joins the Platte about fifteen miles south of Denver, these gentlemen say, is 6,409 feet. The mouth of Plum Creek is at least six miles from the Platte Cañon, where the river debouches upon the plains, and where the Platte becomes quite a large and important stream. At the cañon it is at least 6,000 feet above sea level. We will take this as an objective point or base of calculation, because we know, and it has been abundantly demonstrated, that the river can be tapped there, as a ditch is now running twenty-four miles from thence round to Denver. There is no point on the plains anywhere in the area of Colorado and Kansas so high as this initial point at the mouth of the cañon.

A preliminary survey and approximate levels have actually been run from this place in an easterly direction across Plum Creek, Cherry Creek, Cole Creek, Box Elder, Kiowa, Bijou, Beaver, to the head-waters of the Republican; and the fact of its practicability along this route, keeping along the Kansas Pacific Railway, and covering their lands, is beyond a doubt. From this place, which is near the line of Colorado and Kansas, there is no point higher in the whole area of Kansas, proving that Kansas lands are as susceptible of irrigation and of a water gradient as are those of Colorado. If the supply of water from the Platte River should at any time not prove sufficient, all the streams which the canal may cross by aqueduct, sluice, tunnel, or otherwise, can be made subservient as lateral branches, supply affluents, or feeders. All the streams are torrential in their fall, and in every case a mile of feeder will be all-sufficient to take from those streams as much water as is required to keep up the supply in the head main.

Again, a doubt may arise as to whether there is enough, or indeed any water, in these every one apparently dry streams. If any person will take the trouble to dig down in the bed of these streams, they will find abundance of water at a very little depth. If the water is there, and above the level of the head-main, it can be used as a supply-feeder. If a canal, then, is constructed, covering the whole of the lands of the Kansas Pacific Railroad, it will enhance the value of those lands at least 50 per cent., and in most cases, especially in Colorado, 100 per cent., as it is a well-known fact that every acre of land covered by a ditch of however limited a size is worth at least $10 per acre.

A grand work has been accomplished by British engineers: at an enormous expense, borne entirely by the government of India, (and amounting, if we remember correctly, to ten millions of dollars,) a dam was thrown across the great river Godavery, which enters the Bay of Bengal on the Coromandel coast; and thus not only was the river itself made navigable, but thousands of square miles of fertile land were supplied with water for irrigation. The mere increase of revenue from the districts benefited by that great work is reported to have more than compensated the government for its outlay. Should the necessity for similar works ever arise in this country, American engineering skill will be found equal to the task of constructing them. When the population of the North American continent shall have increased to hundreds of millions, even our deserts must be utilized. The system which, on a small scale, has made a garden at Salt Lake City, where once scarcely a shrub grew, can be indefinitely extended. The engineer, to whom nothing is impossible, will demand merely the size of the reservoir desired, and the millions to be spent in its construction, and he will undertake to irrigate all Frémont's Basin from the melting snows of the Sierra Nevada. Such tasks as those of irrigating the arid plains of Western Texas or the valley of the Rio Grande would be more ordinary performances, and the day may not be very far distant when, under laws adapted to the object, American energy and capital will undertake such works as profitable private enterprises.

This great work of the reclamation of the Great American Desert will not cost a hundredth part so much as the works of European engineers, and will put the gigantic Suez Canal and its compeers in past ages into the deepening shade. It remains to be seen whether the Congress of the United States will place alongside her magnificent work of uniting the Atlantic and Pacific with an iron band the equally magnificent work of wiping out from the map of the world the bar-sinister upon her escutcheon — the "Great American Desert."

Agricultural Statistics

From U.S. Bureau of the Census, *Ninth Census, III, The Statistics of the Wealth and Industry of United States* (Washington, 1872), pp.588–89.

Tables on following pages.

	ESTABLISHMENTS			STEAM ENGINES 1870		WATER-WHEELS 1870		HANDS EMPLOYED									
STATES AND TERRITORIES	1870 Number	1860 Number	1850 Number	Horse-power	Number	Horse-power	Number	1870 All	Males above 16	Females above 15	Youth	1860 All	Males	Females	1850 All	Males	Females
	2,076	1,982	1,333	15,873	676	10,209	426	25,249	24,634	12	603	14,814	14,810	4	7,220	7,211	9
The United States	2,076	1,982	1,333	15,873	676	10,209	426	25,249	24,634	12	603	14,814	14,810	4	7,220	7,211	9
1 Alabama	3	18	2					9	9			84	84		23	23	
2 Arkansas	1	7	4					16	16			10	10		14	13	1
3 California	10	5		15	1			68	68			12	12				
4 Connecticut	38	47	35	48	3	1,278	50	593	591	2		498	497	1	297	296	1
5 Delaware	10	17	4	126	4	23	2	56	52		4	116	116		20	20	
6 District of Columbia			2	58	5							12	12		3	3	
7 Florida	10	3						59	54	1	4	15	15				
8 Georgia	294	17	26	70	3	130	5	3,935	3,911	1	23	37	37		205	201	4
9 Illinois	124	201	84	2,575	91	620	14	1,268	1,257		11	1,790	1,790		646	646	
10 Indiana	55	103	58	860	33	165	6	552	546		6	709	709		210	210	
11 Iowa	3	44	5	457	27	20	1	29	29			208	208		15	15	
12 Kansas	44	1															
13 Kentucky	32	65	45	270	10	505	24	624	567	1	57	3	3		217	217	
14 Louisiana	34	13	11			10		15	15			462	462		29	29	
15 Maine	37	46	49	31	2	964	31	219	217	1	1	28	28		325	325	
16 Maryland	164	35	76	189	14	317	20	295	295			189	189		333	332	1
17 Massachusetts	27	56	56	221	8	50	2	477	471	1	4	368	368		786	786	
18 Michigan	11	108	13	948	52			969	960	2	9	630	630		35	35	
19 Minnesota	38	12		126	6			167	166		1	666	666				
20 Mississippi		34		24	3			34	34			42	42				
21 Missouri		43	37	325	14			537	497		40	127	127		113	112	1
22 Montana								1	1								
23 Nebraska	2							9	9								
24 New Hampshire	24	29	28	26	2	458	24	184	181	1	3	96	96		147	147	
25 New Jersey	30	33	24	139	8	208	6	366	366			260	260	1	80	80	
26 New York	337	333	135	2,529	106	2,722	116	4,953	4,678		274	2,905	2,904	1	923	923	
27 North Carolina	20	22	15	31	16	16	15	78	78			100	100		52	52	
28 Ohio	219	182	161	3,581	110	283		5,124	5,026		98	2,239	2,239		765	765	
29 Oregon	4	5		8	1	21		10	9		1	7	7				
30 Pennsylvania	286	260	222	2,041	104	581	43	2,286	2,248		38	1,465	1,465		947	947	
31 Rhode Island	5	3	3	15	1	154	4	81	81			10	10		70	70	
32 South Carolina		13	13									30	30		53	53	
33 Tennessee	25	15	53	102	10	6	2	110	109	2	1	110	109		143	143	
34 Texas	12	46						44	44			138	138				
35 Vermont	45	32	35	162	4	1,251	45	372	367	2	3	155	155		178	178	
36 Virginia	37	53	98	157	9	323		267	267			418	417		374	374	
37 West Virginia	11			53	5	15	1	55	55								
38 Wisconsin	82	81	31	669	31	89	6	1,387	1,360	3	24	666	666	1	178	177	1

| CAPITAL | | | WAGES | | | MATERIALS. | | | |
1870 Dollars.	1860 Dollars.	1850 Dollars.	1870 Dollars.	1860 Dollars.	1850 Dollars.	1870 Dollars.	1860 Dollars.	1850 Dollars.	
34,934,600	11,477,239	3,564,202	12,151,504	5,070,674	2,167,868	21,473,925	5,625,169	2,445,765	
3,800	68,620	8,000	1,975	28,692	5,544	1,849	31,057	12,000	1
12,500	1,975	10,200	1,340	3,096	4,380	5,050	1,973	3,460	2
79,450	6,100		43,725	10,620		43,370	9,250		3
1,061,100	346,500	233,460	328,718	190,380	86,340	455,849	185,955	100,140	4
57,800	70,000	9,000	18,850	41,112	6,504	13,864	34,560	5,662	5
		4,500			960			1,800	6
39,550	13,500		12,436	6,240		23,904	5,700		7
19,715	19,715	112,835	1,813,835	11,124	57,984	3,598,897	5,584	65,523	8
5,350,978	1,968,995	254,515	484,526	673,388	216,060	951,714	649,637	200,530	9
1,622,769	462,049	66,950	182,138	268,200	52,776	401,372	241,312	38,826	10
543,040	126,202	4,810	8,951	74,364	4,044	10,163	71,118	6,338	11
30,750	2,000			1,440			1,000		12
633,025	331,095	88,200	287,590	173,464	61,200	673,176	148,752	49,352	13
5,000	31,500	14,685	5,000	10,620	9,240	5,000	7,650	3,918	14
241,250	132,350	227,300	72,742	62,472	98,436	86,480	90,604	110,356	15
281,300	329,900	100,150	117,311	99,673	89,232	276,257	120,761	103,572	16
499,400	365,250	542,100	243,112	188,599	289,284	487,460	374,549	390,200	17
1,254,759	689,272	13,450	362,844	199,164	11,940	714,933	263,121	8,698	18
190,712	19,650		72,520	14,364		92,656	11,870		19
21,150	105,500	67,770	8,950	45,252	25,608	22,586	32,923	22,328	20
791,435	170,550	15,550	403,847	88,476	10,032	699,376	127,471	8,932	21
500			100			440			22
									23
3,800	46,100	77,500	3,210	29,868	45,900	10,570	30,877	43,379	24
174,550	202,850	33,730	78,505	74,508	22,944	77,714	114,300	27,312	25
517,250	2,364,846	448,500	181,687	920,201	311,424	202,361	1,237,051	500,448	26
7,824,656	76,250	14,019	2,513,317	26,016	11,256	4,594,316	26,002	10,285	27
34,520	1,633,825	287,595	16,914	800,260	216,048	34,348	793,845	166,318	28
7,570,320	5,600		2,841,518	4,680		5,240,550	3,009		29
15,700	1,004,520	457,294	3,800	499,002	270,876	7,075	519,561	334,152	30
3,387,949	13,200	95,000	1,025,618	3,374	24,180	1,278,805	6,338	30,902	31
252,500	15,800	9,815	37,450	6,420	10,808	42,806	4,957	5,717	32
62,900		46,632	36,717		37,884	49,782		25,240	33
12,559	64,650		13,370	43,740		18,165	42,935		34
518,150	61,055	99,550	138,327	42,756	43,752	212,964	35,119	51,813	35
187,128	118,400	130,077	102,886	60,144	79,836	153,694	61,207	66,586	36
57,650	205,700		24,283	132,276		19,640	116,669		37
1,494,700	403,720	91,075	663,392	236,689	63,396	966,739	218,452	51,978	38

1870

STATES AND TERRITORIES.	Cane-mills. No.	Clover-hullers. No.	Corn-planters. No.	Corn-shellers. No.	Cotton-planters. No.	Cultivators. No.	Fanning-mills. No.	Grain-cradles. No.	Grain-drills. No.	Hand-rakes. Dozens.	Harrows. No.	Harvesters. No.	Hay and straw cutters. No.	Hay-forks. No.	Hoes. Dozens.	Horse-powers. No.	Horse-rakes. No.	Lawn-mowers. No.
The United States	108	5,206	21,709	12,941	2,000	88,740	19,772	103,646	32,033	207,310	9,150	3,566	30,879	1,298,260	135,139	4,541	80,619	2,536
Alabama																		
Arkansas											145							
California						95												
Connecticut						230		300		7,167			5,380	500	30,350		4,780	
Delaware						18			50		251			86,000			9	36
District of Columbia											50		475					
Florida							33											
Georgia			15,244	1,262	2,000	42,945	1,626			3,888	50							
Illinois				196		1,030	1,076	39,324	4,750		1,890	2,860	3,634	66,000	9,400	654	6,475	
Indiana						2,700	3,027		5,931		1,088		1,808	147,600		97	25	
Iowa											300		300	200				
Kansas											95							
Kentucky	100			50		50	50				92	700			12	100		
Louisiana								57										
Maine											8							
Maryland		40	100	1,290		1,437	200	2,040	505	4,200	475		8,050	8,400	2,000	61	1,520	
Massachusetts			1,000	1,700		625		2,400		371	800		162	30	50	73	400	
Michigan				1,150		2,200	2,410	16,536	240	13,530	650			102,600	40,000	706	3,013	
Minnesota						13,636	1,940		580	140,100	30			96,000	7,000		10,932	
Mississippi						156											38	
Missouri			3,500			100	680		100		30							
Montana							8											
Nebraska																		
New Hampshire				100				110			140		1,750			6	752	
New Jersey				63		492					75		1,766			192		
New York		208	100	664		1,412	4,481	34,539	2,068	6,710	994	6		300	27,000	1,505	15,541	2,500
North Carolina	8			158		11,492	10			54				308,823				
Ohio			1,100	1,026		5,683	1,425	2,428	11,793	19,447	6		4,190	144,000	2,085	380	30,004	
Oregon						821					25							
Pennsylvania		4,958	665	4,547		300	1,660	4,972	1,881	3,450	100		271	203,807	11,000	573	5,276	
Rhode Island										1,801							60	
South Carolina										200	200							
Tennessee							266											
Texas				85		25												
Vermont				250		415	105	100		6,292	1,595			134,000	6,200	173	1,385	
Virginia				400		300	50	840	885		1		3,000		42		225	
West Virginia						2,007											12	
Wisconsin						571	725		3,250	100	60						172	

PRODUCTS.

No.	Mowers. No. 39,486	Plows. No. 864,947	Reapers. No. 60,388	Reapers and mowers combined. No. 59,645	Rollers and scrapers. No. 4,803	Seed-sowers. No. 6,900	Scythes. No. 881,244	Scythe-snaths. No. 17,680	Separators. No. 1,131	Shovels.* Dozens. 25,756	Sickles. Dozens. 300	Stump-pullers. No. 124	Thrashers. No. 22,931	Other products. Dollars, 5,206,789	1870 All products. Dollars, 52,066,875	1860 All products. Dollars, 17,487,960	1850 All products. Dollars, 6,842,611
1		200												7,500	10,059	75,636	34,500
2	50	867												12,000	12,000	8,350	11,900
3	4,025	18,091	175										14	49,450	118,540	23,375	
4		1,278	54				342,000		175					138,239	1,183,947	611,934	258,047
5									240					13,430	41,325	104,181	15,175
6																	6,550
7	170	1,190											6	6,500	77,450	19,700	
8	4	236,783					72,000							449,641	8,880,390	27,300	228,837
9		62,700											647	158,245	2,128,794	2,379,362	761,970
10		25,314											206	215,750	829,965	865,436	146,025
11		1,235												8,714	31,252	233,248	17,900
12	350	147,189	1,381	11,500	1,405				55				154	78,630	1,384,917	3,670	
13		1,000	25	1,460	762										14,000	619,355	184,615
14	23	32,229	8				44,400	780					135	68,115	231,991	27,300	25,610
15	164	16,608								11,000			81	181,829	549,085	210,404	239,787
16	2,050	14,600			80		49,200							103,601	1,033,590	340,430	257,656
17	20	20,794				750							806	407,658	1,569,596	842,980	840,141
18		5,980			694					6			1	42,223	267,841	684,913	30,600
19		10,450												4,575	51,800	45,150	
20		52,490	34,200	5									8,021	96,970	1,588,108	111,813	109,260
21																320,236	37,550
22														1,000	1,640		
23														17,000	17,000		
24	1,025	425				5,300	86,400						299	12,545	254,470	86,414	119,096
25	1,473	1,760				850	186,300		101				4,101	122,578	633,875	310,460	72,636
26	19,005	12,700	802	21,027	997								50	879,604	11,847,037	3,454,082	1,266,276
27		28,809	12,885											17,125	82,110	86,155	32,930
28	4,691	12,650	7,485	24,518				3,900	25	14,500	300		5,610	1,036,315	11,907,366	2,820,626	557,932
29		61,941					95,544							8,300	19,950	12,330	
30	6,094	125	1,833	1,135					15			124	2,067	777,339	3,652,295	1,582,071	853,513
31		52,696											24	12,040	92,464	15,845	72,000
32		600															
33		16,064											183	28,605	132,772	117,260	29,939
34		2,030					5,400		20					6,295	42,420	100,200	97,570
35	292	21,545						13,000					384	120,858	523,669	167,347	133,355
36		2,290											41	56,485	403,457	429,824	213,906
37															58,281		
38	50	6,734	1,540		865				500	250			99	76,530	2,393,428	735,198	187,335

*See table for shovels and spades on next page.

The Granger Movement, 1872

From Timothy H. Ball, *Lake County, Indiana, From 1834 to 1872* (Chicago, 1873), pp. 221–22.

This order was organized in Washington City, in August, 1867. It now comprises a National Grange, State Granges, and Subordinate Granges. It is a secret organization, designed for the pecuniary, social, intellectual, and moral improvement of the agricultural community. It seems to be rapidly gaining favor in this country. In February, 1872, the State Grange of Indiana, and seventy-nine Subordinate Granges were organized. In this county are now three of these organizations:

Eagle Grange, No. 4, organized June 28, 1871; number of members, 80. Lowell Grange, No. 6, October 12, 1871: number of members, 80. Leroy Grange, No. —, ——, 1872; number of members, 26.

The organization in this county owes its existence to the enterprising spirit of Oscar Dinwiddie, First Special Deputy, who is still active in carrying it on, aided very much by the earnest zeal of C. L. Templeton, and other energetic farmers. O. Dinwiddie, and C. L. Templeton are both officers in the State Grange, and members of its Executive Committee.

I am at liberty to say that the Grange has a beautiful ritual, and that its practical teachings are fitted to improve and ennoble the families of the owners and cultivators of the soil; and the Grange influence in the south part of the county, where some of our wealthiest, most intelligent, and most energetic farmers reside, is certainly a felt and living power.

State Grange Officers

O. Dinwiddie, Overseer; C. L. Templeton, Treasurer; E. M. Robertson, Gate-Keeper.

There are other *ex-officio* State Grange officers in the county.

There have been Grange burials of the following members of the order: Charles A. Kenney, burial November 1, 1871; religious services conducted by Rev. J. Harrison. Norman Stone, burial September 24, 1872; religious services by Rev. T. H. Ball. The Grange Burial Service is touching, instructive, and impressive; but Christianity only can give a certain answer to that great question, "If a man die shall he live again?"

The Grange interest is on the increase in the county. It is probable other Granges will soon be organized. It is time that the farmers were more energetic and united in promoting their interests, cultivating their social natures, and gaining useful knowledge. To the Granges of Lake I take the liberty of dedicating the following little poem:

"THE INDEPENDENT FARMER.

"Let sailors sing of the windy deep,
Let soldiers praise their armor,
But in my heart this toast I'll keep
'The Independent Farmer.'

When first the rose in robe of green,
   Unfolds its crimson lining,
And round his cottage porch is seen
   The honeysuckle twining;
When banks of bloom their sweetness yield,
   To bees that gather honey,
He drives his team across the field,
   Where skies are soft and sunny.

"The blackbird clucks behind the plow,
   The quail pipes loud and clearly,
Yon orchard hides behind its bough
   The home he loves so dearly;
The gray old barn, whose doors enfold
   His ample store in measure,
More rich than heaps of hoarded gold,
   A precious, blessed treasure;
But yonder in the porch there stands,
   His wife, the lovely charmer,
The sweetest rose on all his lands —
   'The Independent Farmer.'

"To him the spring comes dancingly,
   To him the summer blushes.
The autumn smiles with mellow ray;
   He sleeps, old winter hushes.
He cares not how the world may move
   No doubts nor fears confound him;
His little flocks are linked in love,
   And household angels round him:
He trusts in God and loves his wife,
   Nor griefs, nor ills may harm her;
He's nature nobleman in life —
   'The Independent Farmer.' "

Farming in California, 1872

From Letters, F. P. Bacon, Marengo Ranch near Pasadena, Calif., to H. D. Bacon, 1871–1872. These items are reproduced by permission of the Huntington Library, San Marino, Calif.

Marengo Ranch, Sunday, October 22, '71

MY DEAR FATHER

   I have been so busy, and harassed with work and the loss of house help this week, that I have had no time before to-day to answer yours. The wine has turned out thus far, better than I could expect, though I must not be too sanguine yet, as it is in the most critical time now. Since the first of last week have been racking off the wine. And a wine maker who came to see me, complimented it highly, said he had not seen wine in California, clarify itself so well after the first fermentation. I think the cause of this is my having used a fine sieve, which had to be disused after the third day, as it did not let the wine run from the vat as fast as the trampers tramped. The wine made from the coarser sieve is not near as clear. The vineyard yielded about 98,600 lbs. of grapes, from which were filled — to within ten inches of the top — seventy-two pipes of White and ten of strong Red wine. Up to this time have not drawn off, but one barrel of the lighter red. Having no one to assist me, but unreliable mexicans, have been unable to visit Mr. Rose, to ascertain in regard to the orange seed, or even to see how he manipulates his grapes. One day not very long ago, our loquacious friend Shorb, came over to see me, and how I was getting along. Upon tasting the wine, he wanted to secure all of it, for a friend in the East. He feels very sore towards the Lake Vineyard Co., ever since they bought him out.

We have thirteen good size Olive trees, six of them are bearing their first fruit. The plan of planting cuttings along the banks of the ditches, I have tried with orange and lemon, and find to work very well.

When I was having the place cleaned up, five thrifty but forgotten Almon trees were discovered in amongst some scrubby peach trees, the way I know they are the Almon is: one of them had three nuts on it. The leaf is very similar to the peach, and it is only at second sight that you see the laf of the nut tree is shorter and of a lighter green.

I have had to hire a four horse team to haul sheep manure for the trees, if an other pair of horses could have been procured, I could have saved the expense of four, two could not haul and place it where it was needed without handling twice. The cost will be about sixty dollars.

Have had a great deal of corn destroyed by my neighbor's trespassing cows; the fence around the inclosure being in the point of security to myself a failure, and only securing stray cattle from starvation, I have, after repeatedly telling the owners, tried what they call down here "a dose of blue pills", which has made the thieving owner a little more watchful, but has not abated the depredations of the brutes, but little.

About the end of November will have to pay one hundred dollars for having the vinyard [sic] pruned, that is cheap as it can be done. Shall have the same man that pruned it last year.

The sky for the last few days has been overcast, and large bodies of black clouds have swiftly traversed the heavens, foreboding the approach of rain; hope that we may have our full share of this blessing once more this year.

WITH MUCH LOVE, I REMAIN AS EVER
YOUR LOVING SON
F. P. BACON

Marengo Ranch, Nov. 14, '71

MY DEAR FATHER,

Yours of the 24th, 28th, and 29th are at hand, also the one brought me by William Graham. He and his wife have concluded, they cannot stay longer than the month. He must have misrepresented his capabilities, for outside of gardening &

pruning he knows nothing of farming. Acknowledge him self when he told me he was going — "that he was not accustomed to ranch routine". The motive of their unexpected departure, is the discontentment of the wife. I did not think she would stop long with me when she, on entering the house, observed, "they were not used to living in this manner" but "thought (very dubious) they *could* get along". I for my part will not be sorry to lose them, for it was very disagreeable to hear what they had up in Napa, of the carriage and horses they had at their service, of the large amounts of money with which they were trusted etc, etc. I have a man and wife — English — in view, who I think will do me.

Except, seeng [sic] that the pipes are full, have finished with the wine making. Have 47 casks of white, but think that if the hot weather don't subside before long, the evaporation will leave but 45 for me to rack off from next spring. There are besides, the eight of strong, and seven of light Red wine, six barrels of vinegar. Have been told the Red wine should be shipped to market as soon as possible, on account of its bad keeping qualities. If I have to send it to San Francisco, what disposition do you want made of it? It is as good as any made from the Mission grape, which is not saying much for it, the wine (Red) from the grape being not very good. The taxes on the place Real & Personal are as follows: 30 acres vineyard land at $600, 130 acres farming land valued at $1300, 211 acres grazing land val. at $1105, 400 acres timber land val. at $300. House, fence & other improvements val. at $500. 30,000 vines val. at $600 Fruit trees val. at $40. Yd & St. furniture val. at $100. 4 improved horses val. at $160. American Cow val. at $15. 5 hogs val at $10. 9 hives of bees val. at $20. 1 wagon val. at $100. 1 spring wagon val. at $100. harness val. at $45. farming utensils val. at $45. male dogs $2.

Summary: Value of Real Estate	$ 7075
Value of improvements on R.E.	$ 1170
Value of personal property	$ 665
Total value of property	$ 8910

Total tax $245.03. The tax is payable any time from now until the 18th of Dec, which is the last day of payment.

In my next will write in full, giving map of grounds and estimates of the cost of each, for setting out the trees & vines you spoke of.

Mr. Rose said it was more sure when you planted the pulp with the orange seed.

Think you must have forgotten to send the Wheat seed as I have not heard from it. Please direct hereafter, P.O. Box No. 344.

Hoping that you are well & had a pleasant trip,

REMAIN WITH MUCH LOVE,
YOUR SON
F. P. BACON

Marengo Ranch, April 13th, '72

MY DEAR FATHER,

After the usual disagreeable sea-trip, arrived here last Tuesday. Found everything about the ranch looking fine, except (would that word and its attendants were no where to be found) the last "sown wheat, which unless we soon have rain, will not make hay. Our barley crop is heading out splendidly & the orange trees are doing well.

Gen. Stoneman has been making himself very neighborly during my absence, by appropriating the material on the old division fence. Have not seen Gen. "B" about it yet, but have sent him word to desist from any further aggressions.

Mr. Schliefer, who has control of the Lake Vineyard wine this year, came over and examined my wine. Soke [sic] in high terms of it, and also said that in a year or two it would be splendid.

Mr. Swanson the surveyor said he would sue us for his money. If he should I suppose you would prefer Mr. Howard to act as our lawyer.

I inclose the account-current for month ending April 12th.

WITH MUCH LOVE
I REMAIN YOUR'S IN HASTE
F. P. BACON

Marengo Ranch

In a/c current with
The Land and Loan Company

1872

Jan	29	On hand this day	256 98	
"	"	50 lbs Salt 1.25 Matches .25		1 50
"	"	Blacking		25
Feb.	3	Seeds .75 Chlorid of lime .25		1
"	"	Sold 4 doz eggs @ 30¢	1 20	
"	"	Sold 5½ lbs butter @ 40¢	2 20	
"	"	Axle grease .50 Balance scale 1.00		1 50
"	"	100 lbs Flour		4
"	5	50 lbs Potatoes .88 Oysters .50		1 38
"	"	Sugar .50 Crackers .25		75
"	9	Shot .25 Corn starch .25		50
"	"	Sharpening plow point		3
"	"	Grinding corn		25
"	"	Rec'd of H.D. Bacon	500	
"	12	10 lbs Coffee		2 20
"	14	7672 lbs. of hay @ 23.00 per ton		88 25
"	"	Castile soap		50
"	"	Thermometer		75
		Amt. Forward	760 38	

			Amt. Forward	760	38	105	83
Feb	15	Nails .25 2 plow points No. 2B 2.00				2	25
"	"	1 plow 5½ 13.00 1 pick handle .50				13	50
"	"	1 wheel 2.50 1 plow 12.50				15	
"	24	97 lbs potatoes @ 2¢				1	94
"	"	1 Bx candles 4.00 Oysters .75				4	75
"	"	Corn Starch .25 Apples .50					75
"	"	Sugar 1.00 5 Gals. Vinegar 4/2.50				3	50
"	"	1 Keg 2.00 67 lbs beans 4½¢ 3.02				5	02
"	"	Labor				17	50
"	29	Juan Calefan — wages —				38	
"	"	Fixing tape-line				1	50
"	"	Grinding corn					40
"	"	3052 lbs of corn @ 1.25¢				38	15
"	"	Laborer				6	25
Mar	5	100 lbs Flour 4.00 9 lbs coffee 2.00				6	
"	15	Wm. P. Reynolds — survey —				76	
"	"	E. J. Weston — map of survey —				10	
"	"	Laborer				6	
		Amt. Forward	760	38	352	34

			Amt. Forward	760	38	352	34
Mar	18						
"	"	1 sk. salt .75 4 yds table damask 2.00				2	75
"	"	Fixing plow point					50
"	"	Stone-jar 1.50 Sulphur-matches .50				2	
"	"	Edward — cook — 2 months				60	
"	"	Laborer				4	
"	19	Personal expense				14	
"	23	100 lbs flour 4.00 Matches .25				4	25
"	25	12 lbs rope 3.00 Broom .50				3	50
"	"	1 scythe stone					15
"	26	Rec'd of H.D. Bacon	200				
Apr	3	100 lbs flour 4.00 Dryd Apples .50				4	50
"	"	Rec'd of H.D. Bacon	1420				
"	"	O.W. Childs — as per bill —			1420	
"	"	Personal expense — trip to city			214	49
"	9	Post Office box rent				1	
"	"	25 lbs meat 2.50 Dish pan 1.00				3	50
"	10	seed corn 3.50 Freight on seed-corn 1.50				5	
"	"	Juan Calefan wages				30	
		Amt. Forward	2380	38	2121	98

Marengo Ranch a/c
continued

			Amt. Forward	2380 38	2121 98
Apr	10	Casuse Calefan wages			10
"	12	Jose "			5 75
"	"	Personal expense			8
"	"	Wood-choppers			10
"	"	S.L. Page on a/c work			20
"	"	Chinamen			123 05
"	"	On hand this day			81 60
				2380 38	2380 38

Disbursements

For the month ending April 12th 1872

Cash	878 78
Order on H. D. Bacon	1420
	2298 78

Marengo Ranch, Sunday
(probably May 28, 1872)

MY DEAR FATHER,

Yours of the 14th ultimo is at hand, enclosing Mr. Keller's list; also your estimate of trees, etc. The orange trees had what they call the black scale on them, which was gradually [sic] extending all over the young grove. I was informed that it was caused by lack of nutriment and cultivation. As they had been cultivated and worked every two weeks through-out the summer, the only inference I could draw, was starvation. Knowing the cause, I applied the remedy in the shape of sheep manure. The effect of which was not only to rid the trees of the disease, but to give them a new start. The manure was hauled some two miles. All the ranch work is progressing nicely. The wheat and barley is planted and already coming up. You were right; I did not use diligence enough in trying to find the wheat. For in fact no inquires were made for it until the receipe of yours stating that it was shipped. The vineyard pruning and cleaning is finished. The wine is in good condition. Herewith is the business card of Ellis & Curtis, to whom the cellar-man of Lake Vineyard — Mr. Meletta — directed me, as likely buyers. If you go to them, it would be well to give his name as speaking well of the wine. Am happy to say I found on my return that my new man Mr. Christensen, had been very faithful and attentive to his duties. Edward — the man-of-all-work in the house — likewise, had been very busy cleaning and whitewashing the house. Nothing comes amiss and nothing is wasted by him. Even some white skirts, which Mother left, he made up into window curtains. Have rented to a sheep man, for the sum of two hundred dollars, all the outside land except sixty acres, for the sum term of eleven months. Half of the amount is paid, the remaining one hundred will be paid in May. That together with fifteen dollars he paid for pasturage during the last month, will go a good way toward paying taxes.

The feed being very high this year, the plow work is consequently higher than what I estimated. Will have to pay three dollars an acre, they to furnish themselves in everything. I think it would be well to prepare sixty acres at a cost of one hundred and eighty dollars. Thirty of which could be planted to orange and lemon and the rest after a second plowing at an expense of ninty [sic] dollars, could be used for, the vineyard. There would however be about a weeks work for six men, before plowing could be done on thirty of the sixty acres. The lemons being thirty-five dollars and the oranges forty dollars a hundred, instead of fifty dollars respectively as you estimated. It leaves a difference of one hundred and sixty eight dollars and twenty-five cents less, even when we pay three dollars an acre for plowing. Then my idea would be, unless you wish to put them on the other half, to plant thirty (estimated) acres on the now enclosed portion with almond. This land is or will be in two days, all plowed and in splendid condition for the trees. Or we may let it lay summer-fallowed for next year's crop, in waiting for the almond nut to mature. By the by, will you please to see that man Meek at San Leandro, as while I was up it rained so I could not get down there. I would suggest that together with the trees a barn to be put up, useing [sic] the materials in old — formerly a school-house — barn. It would with a corn-crib cost in the neighborhood of three hundred dollars. This years hay crop will need a cover. If you should conclude to have one, please return the plan with your ideas pro or con as to it. Mr. Rose very cleverly loaned me one of his Cow's an excellent milker, to buy or not just as it pleased me. Have had her now over two months. The cow that Mr. Page advised me to purchase, got so that do her best, only half a tea cup of milk would she give. I thought it would be best to keep her till after she calfed and then if her milking qualities did not improve to sell her. She is in excellent condition, being very fat. Mr. R's price for cow is seventy-five dollars. Am unable to give you an estimate for the fence as of yet, and as matters stand it may be long before I can. Will explain what I mean, you see immediately after yours came, I went to the ex county surveyor — said to be the best down here — Handson, to get him to locate the boundaries, as the points given to me by Mr. Page were very unsatisfactory. He agreed to do the work for thirty-five dollars supposing there would be only one days work. After spending a day, the job was not half done and the lines on the map did not agree with the land marks in the field. So they said they would come again next day, but they wanted fifty dollars instead of thirty-five, as there was an extra day. I agreed to it, not however without a protest, for what was I to do? This was Monday, the next day came and so did the following, until Saturday came round without the surveyor. You can imagine that I was in a high state of anger at them, as it kept me at home, when there was other outside business to attend to. Well I went to them prepared to tell them I did not want their services, if they could not come when they agreed to. But they met with an excuse that made me forget my ire in the greater danger of trouble about lines. They gave as reason, for not putting in an appearance, that on comparing the deed, township survey and my map, that all three differed. That if they followed the deed sixty acres on the west and they thought the Western spring would be left out. But the whole drift and issue of it, to use their words is that ''there has evidently been *a fraud* somewhere.'' Now they propose to survey the land and make a correct map of it for One hundred & fifty dollars. One point more the line on the East, cuts through and off about 8000 vines, on what will be Gen. Stoneman's place, when the division is made between him and Wilson in the month of March. As the location of boundaries demands immediate attention, you will please to telegraph me if shall have the survey done at the above figures or not, so there will be no delay.

As all the stack was gone, have had to buy four tons of hay, paying twenty-three dollars per ton. Hope that will be the first and last hay I have to buy for the ranch.

Will during the week send you one quarter of the first crop Sicily lemons on the ranch, together with them some malago lemons. I hope you will find them good.

Hoping That You Are Well, I Remain As Ever

H. D. Bacon
Oakland, Cal.

Your Loving Son
F. P. Bacon

Patrons of Husbandry, 1872

From *Southern Cultivator* (Athens, Ga., February, 1872), XXX, p. 76.

Patrons of Husbandry.

The above is the title of a *secret* organization which originated *North* some time ago, and which is trying to extend its organization through the Southern States. We have been surprised to observe that even a *few* Southern farmers are disposed to join it. It would seem as if we had had "entangling alliances" enough already with the North, to warn us against going blindfold into an organization with a great *central head* at Washington City, exacting tribute from local organizations all over the country. The true policy of the South is to resist *centralizing* tendencies of all kinds — attend to her own business and let other people attend to theirs.

Supplying Milk to Cities, 1872

From "City Milk Supply," U.S. Department of Agriculture, *Annual Report*, 1872 (Washington, 1874), pp. 332–47.

The milk supply of our cities is a subject of rapidly increasing importance not only to the consumer, but also to the agricultural regions which are being called on to furnish this staple of food. It is but about thirty years since our largest city commenced to receive milk regularly by rail, and twelve years ago its longest line of milk supply did not extend one hundred and fifty miles. Now New York receives daily from

Rutland, Vermont, distant two hundred and forty-one miles, and from Pittsfield, Massachusetts, distant one hundred and sixty-seven miles on another route. Three years ago, Saint Louis, with a population of 310,000, obtained all its supply from its suburbs; now an estimated proportion of one-eighth of its supply is received by rail from distances up to ninety-five miles.

Adulterated Milk

In view of the fact that the trade in fresh country milk for the single market of New York represented, in 1871, a yearly gross income to producers of $4,170,000, while the entire expenditure for city consumption exceeded $15,000,000, it will be perceived that fraudulent and deleterious enlargements of the volume of supply seriously affect the interests of agriculturists while bearing more directly on the consumers. As concerning the latter class, the adulteration of milk is attracting increasing solicitude in the larger cities of our own country as well as those of Europe. Milk inspectors and chemists, acting under direction of boards of health, have repeatedly called attention to the current depreciation of this important article of human food, and the injuries resulting to the public health, especially in increase of infant mortality. The ills of adulteration fall most heavily on the poorer classes who constitute the mass of city population; but medical testimony has shown that they affect the young life of the higher ranks of society to a much greater extent than is commonly understood. The apathy consequent on an imperfect appreciation of these evils has much impeded the execution of State and city laws concerning watered and impure milk. Experience has also shown that a common tendency has been to embarrass the statute by unwise qualifications. Boston, a pioneer in the matter of milk inspection, tried the proviso of "guilty knowledge" on the part of sellers at intervals of several years, and the results induced the State legislature to return in 1869 to the unqualified liability of the person selling or intending to sell, with heavy penalties for infringements of the law. . . .

Action of the Press

* * *

A marked instance of the power which a leading journal can exert in exposing to general notice abuses affecting the public welfare was exhibited in the issue of the New York Tribune for May 21, 1872, containing material which had been collected during several days by a corps of employés of that paper, assisted by a few city officials. These employés visited the depots of milk-receipt at railroad termini in New York and Jersey City, stores of milk dealers, and a portion of the "swill-milk" stables of Brooklyn and vicinity. At the depot of the Erie road, in Jersey City, the depot of largest supply, the milk was delivered between midnight and 4 a.m. Specials sent to this point reported that watering was freely carried on while the milkmen were crossing in the ferry-boat to New York, and additions of salt, saleratus, chalk, &c., were observed. Samples purchased of thirty-four named venders were afterward subjected to chemical tests. In all these cases the milk had been skimmed before receiving liberal additions of water, and in seven or eight of the samples was found "a large amount of salts, showing adulteration by foreign substances.'' The reporter who visited the depot in Forty-eighth street, New York, the point of next largest receipt, having disguised himself as a milk-dealer's assistant, witnessed the pouring of milk into large receivers containing water, and obtained samples from sixty-eight named venders. The milk in all these cases had been much skimmed before watering, some of the samples showing scarce a trace of the buttery substance of the original milk. In Brooklyn and vicinity, twelve swill-milk stables were visited, containing at the time over one hundred and fifty cows, the number per stable ranging from three to thirty-six, excepting in two, which had been emptied by distemper. Bad ventilation and the grossest filth were the general rule. Milk odorous with the smell of distillery-slops, and drawn into dirty vessels from unclean animals, was being made ready for conveyance in wagons which stood by, bearing in large letters the labels of ''Pure Country Milk,'' ''Pure Long Island Milk,'' &c.

In New York itself, where the feeding of distillery-swill for milk was formerly carried on to a most alarming extent, this nuisance is now mostly abated. The report of the board of health for 1870 says that, so far as is known to the board, there are no milch cows in that city fed on distillery-swill or other deleterious substance.

Substitution of Condensed Milk

In view of the prevalence of depreciated milk in our large cities, recourse has been recommended to the use of condensed milk, particularly the ''plain condensed,'' or milk condensed without addition of sugar. A late report of Dr. C. F. Chandler, chemist to the New York board of health, showed that large amounts of an excellent article of this description were used by various hospitals and charitable institutions of that city. But the necessity of exercising care in selecting an approved brand is illustrated by his statement in the report of the board for 1870, giving the following analyses of good milk of average quality, the same article condensed ''plain,'' and plain condensed milk sold by a certain New York company:

	Pure milk.	Pure milk condensed.	Condensed milk sold by a New York company.
	Per cent.	Per cent.	Per cent.
Butter	4.00	16.00	1.75
Caseine	4.00	16.00	15.80
Sugar	5.00	20.00	18.90
Salts	0.65	2.60	2.21
Water	86.35	45.40	61.34
	100.00	100.00	100.00

In the latter case there remained not more than one-eighth of the butter contained in the original milk, seven-eighths having been skimmed off and sold for cream. He adds: ' It is a notorious fact that most of the condensed-milk companies regularly send cream to the New York market.''

Analyses of samples of the plain condensed milk of several companies, presented by Dr. Chandler in May, 1872, are as follows:

	American.	Borden.	Rockland.	Eagle.	Accepted standard of condensed milk.
	Per cent.	*Per cent.*	*Per cent.*	*Per cent.*	*Per cent.*
Butter......................	13.74	11.39	11.67	11.77	13.12
Caseine....................	14.12	12.96	12.63	13.03	14.44
Sugar	17.24	14.12	13.89	14.38	16.30
Salts........................	2.64	2.30	2.24	2.36	2.60
Water......................	52.26	59.23	59.57	58.46	53.54
	100.00	100.00	100.00	100.00	100.00

Average Adulteration, and Its Effect on Prices

It is calculated by Dr. Chandler, from long-continued investigation, that the milk supply of New York and Brooklyn receives, on an average, one quart of water to every three quarts of pure milk before reaching consumers. It cannot be otherwise than that this artificial extension of supply should depreciate prices obtained by producers. Recent tabular statements, published by milk associations concerned in the New York market, go to show that the average net price obtained by farmers shipping to that city had fallen fully one cent per quart during the three years from 1869 to 1871, inclusive. Reports for 1871, received by the Department, indicate the total receipts by rail during that year, for the city of New York and vicinity, to have exceeded 27,800,000 gallons. With the addition of water in the proportion of one to three before delivery to consumers, we find milk-growers deprived of a business which would return to them $1,390,000 yearly, at an average first price of 15 cents per gallon, city consumers, on the other hand, paying more than $3,700,000 annually for water; and these losses are increasing. This calculation does not touch the supply of swill-milk from the city suburbs, stated at about 1,800 gallons daily in 1872. Putting aside extension by water, this deleterious stuff causes an additional forestalling of country production to the amount of 657,000 gallons of milk yearly, an item of comparatively small consequence to the great milk-growing region, but quite significant in city health reports. It has been stated that, in 1841, swill-fed milk constituted nearly the whole supply of New York.

Supply by Rail

The statistics of milk supply by rail include the most important relations between the producer and the consumer. This medium of conveyance, in opening a market to regions hitherto comparatively isolated, has compelled dairy-farmers to study more carefully questions of feeding and the home management of milk, and has made charges of transportation and handling by middle-men and city milkmen points of constantly growing consequence. . . .

Shipments to New York

In the New York trade the milk is shipped by the producers at the country stations on milk-cars fitted up and cared for by the railroad company. The farmer furnishes his own cans, each of ten gallons' capacity, and costing him $6 or more. The shipments are to dealers who have contracted to pay a certain price for a designated season, or they are on commission. Freight charges are paid by dealers at the city terminus. On the Erie road, the line of largest shipment, and on the New York and Oswego Midland, the charge is 55 cents per can, for all distances; on other roads, 60 cents per can, excepting shipments from points on the Harlem Extension, one hundred and thirty miles to two hundred and forty-one miles from New York, which are charged 80 cents per can. The following summary of average prices received by farmers at stations of shipment is derived from replies to circulars addressed to station-agents and others on the various lines of supply: At points distant about thirty miles from New York, 3½ cents per quart in summer, 5½ cents in winter; at fifty miles, 3 cents in summer, 5 cents in winter; at one hundred and fifty miles to one hundred and seventy miles, on the Housatonic route, 3 cents in summer, 4 cents in winter; at one hundred and fifty miles to two hundred and forty miles on the Harlem Extension, 2½ cents in summer, 4 cents in winter. The averages of the regions of largest shipment are very nearly 3 cents in summer and 5 cents in winter. Taking the whole supply, the cost per quart laid down at the depots in New York City ranges from 4½ cents in summer and 6 cents in winter, for receipts from points distant one hundred and fifty miles or more, to 5 cents in summer and 7 cents in winter for receipts from distances of about thirty miles.

The following will give an idea of variations in average prices at different points:

| Points of shipment. | Distance from New York. | Price per quart. | | Freight per quart. | Points of shipment. | Distance from New York. | Price per quart. | | Freight per quart. |
		Summer.	Winter.				Summer.	Winter.	
	Miles.	Cents.	Cents.	Cents.		Miles.	Cents.	Cents.	Cents.
Chappaqua, N.Y....	33	3½	5½	1½	Attlebury, N.Y......	97	3	5	1½
Croton Falls, N.Y.	48	3½	5	1½	Stissing, N.Y........	96	3	5	1½
Monroe, N.Y........	50	3	5	1⅜	Pine Plains, N.Y. ..	100	3	5	1½
Chester, N.Y.	55	3¼	4¾	1⅜	Husted, N.Y.........	108	3½	4¾	1½
Cornwall, N.Y......	56	3	5	1⅜	Stephentown, N.Y.	170	2¼	4½	2
Goshen, N.Y.	60	3	5	1¾	Canaan, Conn.......	130	3	4	1½
Lagrange, N.Y.....	74	3½	5	1½	Sheffield, Mass.	136	3	5	1½
Billings, N.Y........	76	3	4½	1½	Pittsfield, Mass.	167	3	4	1½
Moore's Mills, N.Y.	78	3¼	4⅜	1½	East Dorset, Vt.	216	2½	4	2
Verbank, N.Y.......	81	3	4½	1½	Clarendon, Vt.......	235	2½	4	2
Millbrook, N.Y....	86	3	4½	1½	Rutland, Vt.........	241	2¼	4½	2

*   *   *

Reports received from freight agents and superintendents give the following as the shipments over the several named roads above for the year ending December 31, 1871: Erie, 11,733,500 gallons, including 306,092 gallons of cream and 14,217 gallons of condensed milk; New York and New Haven, 3,144,330 gallons; New York Central and Hudson River, 1,925,557 gallons; Central New Jersey, 543,770 gallons; South Side Long Island, 359,944 gallons; United Railroads of New Jersey, 365 cans per month. No report has been received from the New York and Harlem. Recent estimates have placed the shipments on that road at six-sevenths of the amount shipped on the Erie, which, on the above basis, would show about 10,057,280 gallons for 1871, making the total receipts in New York and vicinity, in 1871, by the named roads, over 27,800,000 gallons. Receipts by the New York and New Haven road were (excepting three stations) from Connecticut and Massachusetts, and included 1,858,497½ gallons by the Housatonic road and 581,487½ gallons by the Naugatuck.

History of shipments by the Erie road. — In 1843, soon after the opening of the Erie road, it carried 795,376 gallons; in 1851, 3,152,639 gallons; in 1861, (year ending June 30,) 6,103,652 gallons; in 1871, 11,733,500 gallons; in 1872, 11,720,580 gallons, including 332,340 gallons of cream. . . .

Shipments to Philadelphia

Mr. Benjamin T. Lovett, secretary of the Dairymen's Association of Philadelphia and Camden, writes that the receipts of milk in Philadelphia are chiefly by rail and from within forty miles of distance, the limit of shipment being about fifty miles; a small percentage of the total receipt is by wagons. He gives the following statement of receipts by the several named roads: By the North Pennsylvania road, for the year ending October 31, 1871, 2,498,438 gallons; the Philadelphia and Reading road, for the nine months ending September 30, 1872, 2,105,080 gallons; the Philadelphia, Wilmington and Baltimore road, for the year ending October 31, 1872, 765,580 gallons; the Philadelphia and Baltimore Central road, for the nine months ending October 31, 1872, 462,500 gallons; the West Chester and Philadelphia road, for the year ending at the same date, 488,500 gallons; the Pennsylvania Central road, for five months ending August 31, 1872, 283,835 gallons. The city retail prices per quart are, in summer, 8 cents; in winter, 10 cents.

Mr. Lovett reports the prices paid by dairymen to farmers in 1872 as follows: From January 1 to March 31, 5½ cents per quart; for April, 5 cents; from May 1 to October 31, 4 cents; from November 1 to December 31, 5½ to 6 cents. An analysis of this statement shows 4 cents for the six months ending October 31, and an average of 5½ cents for the other months. Replies to inquiries made by the Department bring out the fact that the rating of the cans is very generally by dry measure. Taking this into consideration and deducting freight-charges of ⅜ cent per quart, paid by the farmer, net prices to producers at stations of shipment are exhibited at about 3-1/10 cents for the six summer months, and an average of 4-2/5 cents for the remainder of the year. . . .

Shipments to Boston

The business of supply for the Boston market is chiefly managed by contractors, who, conferring with the producers just before the commencement of each season of six months, fix the price per can at the farmer's door, and assume provision of cans, collection of the milk, and transportation by rail. The contractor leases a car of the railroad at a fixed yearly rent; the actual cost of transportation is therefore to be deduced from the average amount of milk carried. The capacity of the milk-car is stated at 1,000 cans, the capacity of the cans being, on some routes, the Fitchburgh road for example, 8½ quarts; on other roads, as the Boston and Albany, 9½ to 9⅝ quarts. Average amounts carried on established routes, 750 cans and upward. The yearly rental per car has ranged from $5,000 for a running distance of twenty miles to $9,000 for about fifty miles.

A careful summary of reports received from points along the chief lines of supply presents the following exhibit of prices received by the farmer at his door, clear of charges for collection of milk and rail transportation, as well as cost of cans: At distances of about twenty miles from the city, summer price, April 1 to October 1, 3¾ cents per quart; winter price, not over 4-2/5 cents. Concord, twenty miles from Boston, reports 4-5/17 cents in winter. At distances of twenty-five to forty miles, summer prices, 3½ cents to 3-1/5 cents; winter, 4⅓ to 4⅛ cents generally diminishing as the distance increases. For larger distances, up to fifty-eight miles, the extreme of shipment, summer prices generally fall within 3-1/5 cents and winter prices within four cents; as exceptions, Mason, South Lyndeborough, and New Ipswich, in New Hampshire, report winter prices of 4⅓ to 4½ cents, as in the season of 1870–'71.

At distances of ten to twelve miles from Boston the milk is commonly taken up by milkmen who carry to the city in wagons. Prices at the farmer's door 4⅛ cents in summer and about 5 cents in winter. The correspondent at Woburn, ten miles from Boston, writes that retailers pay at the car in the city 40 cents per can of 8½ quarts in summer, and 50 cents in winter, and that he is acquainted with farmers raising 40 cans per day and delivering to retailers in the city at these prices. In that vicinity 5 cents per can have represented the cost of collection and transportation either by wagon or rail.

The conditions of first prices and charges of transportation affecting the bulk of supply are presented in the following table, the two last columns giving the cost of the milk laid down at the depot in Boston:

Distance of points of shipment from Boston.	Price per quart at farmer's door.		Cost of collecting per quart.	Cost of rail transportation per qt, (car rent.)	Cost laid down in Boston, per quart.	
	Summer.	Winter.			Summer.	Winter.
	Cents.	*Cents.*	*Cents.*	*Cents.*	*Cents.*	*Cents.*
20 miles	3.75	4.4	0.4	.25	4.4	5.05
25 to 40 miles	3.5 to 3.2	4.33 to 4.12	.4	.33 to .5	4.23 to 3.95	5.06 to 4.97
40 to 58 miles	3.2	4	.4	.5	4.1	4.9

* * *

The legislature of Massachusetts, a little more than twelve years ago, passed an act requiring the use of sealed cans, showing capacity in wine quarts, under penalty of fine in case of neglect. This law is generally observed in that State, but an exception appears in the report from the Harvard correspondent, who says: "Not a single sealed can has been left with me lately; I do not think I have seen one for five years, certainly not for two years. The law is a dead letter in this vicinity." He complains that this illegal usage operates, through irregularity in size of cans, to reduce the price received by the farmer to a rate below the nominal one. On New Hampshire portions of the routes, South Lyndeborough and Amherst report that few of the cans are sealed, other points reporting sealed cans.

In May, 1872, the Massachusetts law respecting adulteration of milk was made still more stringent, and a clause was inserted making the seller of milk which has been skimmed or partly skimmed liable to a fine of not less than $20 for the first offense, and not less than $50 for each subsequent offense.

Shipments to Chicago

Comparatively little milk is received in Chicago from points distant more than fifty miles from that city. On the Chicago and Northwestern Railway fifty-three miles is reported as the extreme distance of regular milk shipment, and on the Chicago, Burlington and Quincy road seventy-seven miles. Producers ship to city dealers, the former paying freight and generally furnishing cans.

Dr. J. H. Rauch, of the Chicago board of health, writes that during the six winter months of 1871–'72 city dealers paid farmers 4⅛ cents per quart and retailed at 7 cents; during the summer of 1872 farmers received 3⅛ cents, city retailers obtaining 6 cents. Farmers had received in the preceding year 5 cents per quart, gross, in winter, and 3¼ cents in summer; city retail prices, 8 cents and 7 cents. To show net receipts by farmers at points of shipment freight-charges must be deducted from gross prices. Reports received by the Department from the Chicago and Northwestern Railway give transportation charges per can of 8 gallons, for distances reaching twenty miles, 16 cents; for twenty to forty miles, 20 cents; for more than forty miles, 24 cents. The Chicago, Burlington and Quincy road reports 15 cents per eight gallons up to about forty miles, 20 cents for fifty miles, and 25 cents for seventy-five miles. A summary of information on net prices received in 1872 by farmers at country stations shows 2½ cents in summer and 3½ cents in winter, at points of largest shipment, correspondents at other points reporting variations reaching ¼ cent, in some cases more. . . .

Shipments to St. Louis

The first regular shipments of milk to St. Louis were from the neighboring counties of Saint Charles and Warren, on the line of the North Missouri road, in the latter part of 1870. Colonel N. J. Colman, of Colman's Rural World, writes that the city receipts by rail now reach an estimated proportion of one-eighth of its total supply. "The business by rail is still in its infancy, owing to the large number of swill-milk dairies in the immediate vicinity, the owners of which are able to purchase brewers' grains at 2 cents per bushel, and distillery-slops at a proportionate price. Perhaps no city in the United States is so favorably situated for receiving its milk-supply directly from the country. Numerous railroads, radiating from Saint Louis in every direction, penetrate sections of country admirably adapted to milk-production." City retail prices are 5 cents to 8 cents per quart throughout the year. [In 1870 the price was 10 cents per quart.]

Railroad returns indicate ninety-five miles as the extreme distance of shipment. Price per quart generally received by farmers at stations of shipment, clear of freight, 3⅛ cents throughout the year. Freight-charges on the different roads range from ⅜ cent to ½ cent, without regard to distance. The correspondent at Sandoval, Illinois, sixty miles from Saint Louis, reports prices averaging fully ⅜ cent lower, and adds that the cans contain more than their nominal measure. Only about six months had elapsed since the commencement of shipments, which would not exceed on an average 30 gallons per day.

Shipments by the Ohio and Mississippi Railway for 1871 amounted to 157,356 gallons, all from stations in Illinois. Freight ½ cent per quart. . . .

Management of Milk on the Farm

One of the greatest obstacles to success in new enterprises of shipment is the difficulty of impressing producers with the absolute necessity of perfect cleanliness in milking, and care of milk vessels, and of establishing themselves in accurate methods of cooling. The looser management which may suffice for milk not subjected to transportation will not suffice for milk which is to be carried long distances and made liable to considerable delay before consumption. Shippers who are not careful to inform themselves fully on points of management are often surprised, if not indignant, at having milk returned on their hands as sour which left their hands apparently in good condition, while their neighbors meet with no such misadventure. Return of milk sometimes occurs through efforts of dealers to relieve themselves of a surplus; on the other hand it is frequently the result of improper management on the farm. And when a producer has once established a reputation as a prompt, skillful dairyman, his account with the dealer generally suffers little deduction for sour milk. Participants in new enterprises should exert themselves to diffuse among all concerned a knowledge of the requisites of the business, since the difficulties arising from ignorance in this respect tend to depreciate prices and imperil the success of the whole undertaking. . . .

Sealed Cans

There can be no just reason for the use of one description of measure between the producer and the dealer, and another between the dealer and the consumer. Such usage is in effect a deception. It is plainly desirable that cans should be sealed, showing their capacity in standard or (in common phrase) wine measure.

Organized Association

The circumstances of the milk trade point plainly to the desirability of some general organized communication between producers. Accurate and widely diffused information concerning home management and cost of production, conduct of transportation and charges of middle-men, evidently tends, by steps however slow, to an equalization of the several contending interests involved in the business of milk shipment. Such complete information can be attained only through judicious organization.

At the annual meeting of the New York Dairymen's Association in January, 1873, Mr. X. A. Willard, the president, said that the dairy conventions of the country are chiefly attended by cheese manufacturers and others (dealers, &c.) not actually engaged in farming. The consequence is that while cheese manufacturers have become highly educated in their employment, dairy-farmers have not advanced in a proportionate degree. If farmers would come together and interchange ideas freely, many of the now-existing evils would soon disappear. Mr. T. D. Curtis, in speaking of the efforts toward better systems of marketing, urged the importance of strengthening the bonds of union among producers by the establishment of farmers' clubs in every school-district, these to be represented in town clubs, and the latter in county clubs sending delegates to State organizations.

In comparing the systems of milk-shipment pursued in different regions, there will be perceived a decided advantage in the New England system of transportation by car-contract in lessening the difference between prices to first hands and prices to consumers. This system has also brought heavy profits to contractors on the lines supplying the Boston market. Under the stimulus of the high cost of winter production, energetic efforts have been made to divert a portion of these profits to producers. For a time the project was entertained of the assumption by associated producers of the entire business of shipment up to delivery to city retailers.

Limited enterprises of associated shipment have been carried out successfully in different parts of the country. Failures have occurred, as they do in all other descriptions of business. They enforce the caution that in all such undertakings the field of operation with its local conditions should be adequately studied, and that the one person to whom must be committed the superintendence should possess the business qualification which will enable him to cope with those details which lie between the barn-yard and the city peddler's payments. Absence of such competent superintendence being the natural precursor of failure, its presence should be secured by that liberal compensation which will be in effect the truest economy. The disposal of a car-load of milk daily from a tolerably compact region of production would not appear to involve serious difficulties, granted a united sentiment among shippers and a trusty and capable manager; otherwise, the case is quite different. The variations in prices found within the same region of production of themselves evince the minuteness with which individual operators watch the sails of their enterprise, and the agent of associated shipment must have a similar appreciation of the value of "margins" and the various other particulars which constitute the interval between success and its opposite, in new regions including especially the securement of reliable railroad service.

As to enterprises involving heavy capital and extending over large areas of country, risks would obviously be increased by the more complex service and the greater distance between managers and individual stockholders. For the present a preference is indicated for undertakings of moderate dimensions, which, in succeeding, would make more feasible the success of larger operations in the future.

The Patrons of Husbandry, 1874

From *American Agriculturist* (New York, January, 1874), XXXII, pp. 9–10.

How the "Grangers" Appear to One Who Lives Among Them

[The following article is by a resident of that portion of Illinois where Granges are numerous, and may be regarded as an impartial view of one not identified with the order. — Ed.]

It is assumed by some that the Patrons of Husbandry are necessarily violent partisans. Can any one imagine the abruptly courteous and hospitable farmer of the West as a violent partisan, determined on a narrow-minded course toward any particular class? The man who believes so thoroughly in his Western soil, and who is always glorying over his big corn and the rapid development of the country, can not be, in the nature of things, such a man as he is often painted by writers who associate so many unheard of things with the name "Granger."

The farmers of the West are, as they have been, open-hearted, generous; in the main contented. They nursed a special interest beyond its natural growth, and were surprised to see this interest turn against them. Indignation followed naturally, and discussion caused them to look about for a remedy. They found interests combined against them, and they found it necessary to combine in their own interest. But before this combination that made them a power had taken place, the order known as Patrons of Husbandry was at work in its own special field. It now became the basis of combination, and afforded no very great opportunities for display of ill-nature. It appealed to the farmer with a touch of idealism in his nature rather than to the prosy, discontented croaker. It became strong with the intelligent and progressive rather than with the stubborn, old fogyish, and non-reading classes. In short, the organization made a direct appeal to all the better classes of farmers not conscientiously opposed to secret societies, and formed into an active body the good elements in rural society.

The sentiment of the order is generous, and there is nothing to suggest the harboring of a policy that could grow into a violent one. Although it has been dragged into the discussion of puzzling questions, its general attitude has been consistent, and it has encouraged the growth of a healthy sentiment among farmers. Under the cover of the organization, new combinations of extraordinary strength have been formed. These are not the consequences of the working of a resentful spirit, but are the first organized attempts to remedy a great evil; the first general evidence of a common business shrewdness on the part of Western farmers.

A desire to meet a wrong face to face and make it right, and the ability to protect self, do not make violent partisans. The truth is, the Western farmers are just as generous as Grangers as they are as neighbors or entertainers of new-comers, and they are no readier to become the blind instruments of designing men than before.

It has pleased some people to make something of a bugbear of the Grange movement, and persons really in sympathy with it as a matter of principle, have turned away and hesitated to investigate. That the present status is promising, all must admit. That there must be a strong inward growth in the future to make the order satisfying, its warmest friends do not deny. In many cases there is a shallowness in the forms that annoys the thoughtful. In other cases there is too much of what we denominate a "gushing element," to satisfy the earnest business man. There is possibly too much machinery of the simply ornamental kind to wear well. But none of these are serious objections. If the order is to have a future it will have a better future in this respect, and will depart from whatever experience has demonstrated of questionable utility. The growth of the order was not as rapid from the first as many people imagine. The rapid growth did not commence until the organization had been on trial some years. The necessity for thorough organization brought its machinery into use, and the order at once became popular as no other order had ever been among farmers.

Seen from a distance the ground occupied by the Grangers suggests contention, aggressive lines, and general confusion. Seen from the place of operations there is nothing of this. We see simply farmers striving after a better social life, like other men; seeking a higher standard of education and seeking to make their business as profitable as possible. All these objects are commendable, and when we consider their attitude on the railroad question, we must take the order as an order, not select certain irate and thoughtless men as representatives. Farmers stand committed to war against monopolies, and they have conducted an aggressive campaign on their own plan. The great majority of farmers realize the advantage of railroads, and have familiarized themselves with expenses and with difficulties in the way of successful management. They made demands that were treated with contempt. Railroad companies resented the making of any demand as an impertinence, and this policy precipitated a struggle which can not end to their advantage. It is often declared that the farmers have been hasty, resentful, and short-sighted. But in this respect their conduct will stand comparison with that of corporations directed by wise heads and financiers who have indulged in no small amount of railroad policy. In the present conflict with the farmers will the present policy of the railroads win? We answer no. Because their interest is, in this case, identical with that of the farmers. Many of the roads want farmers on their lands, want producers along their lines, want the country developed by a policy that encourages rather than discourages farming. Any one act discouraging or persecuting farmers, reacts to their disadvantage, and it will be simply to the interest of great Western lines to do in common what many individual roads must do — make reasonable concessions to men who have a lasting interest in the success of our railroad system. The sooner this is done the better, and then will it be discovered that the Grangers are not wanton assaulters of any interest, but that they are quiet, good-natured people, seeking to make life pleasant by ordinary and legitimate means.   X. Y. Z.

The Attractions of Agriculture, 1874

From Southern Cultivator (Athens, Ga., March, 1874), XXXII, pp. 95–96.

This curious and indescribable charm which surrounds agriculture, even in the minds of those who know but little of its processes, and still less of its scientific laws, is remarkable and interesting. This may undoubtedly be attributed to the fact that man's love of nature is one of his foremost sentiments — next to his love of kindred and home; and also to the peculiar radiance of all the bright days which dawn upon a farmer's life, and all the cheerful events which surround his occupation. Man's pathway thro' the world is not always pleasant and easy. — Perhaps, as in nature, the darkness of night and the shadow of the cloud occupy by far the larger portion of passing time, leaving for the sunshine a smaller share, so in human life the weary and heavy hours abound. But while even the sorrows prevail, the memory of the bright and joyous days will remain, and they will cast their cheering rays through all the darkness. There is no such thing in all God's creation as unmitigated gloom. And so around every condition and calling in life, the bright days will gather, the remembrance of which makes life dear to all men. Where then does the sun shine brightest? — where do the most delightful associations cluster? — where do the sweetest memories throng? Not where man with his artificial ways is supreme; but where he divides his power with nature, and submits to her influence over one half of his life. The morning may dawn brightly on him who pursues his way to his mill or his office; but with what surpassing radiance it breaks for him who in the early sunlight walks a field, and who even in the midst of his toil, feels the sudden and perhaps momentary sense of awe and inspiration, and freedom, and joy, with which nature fills all the souls of her sons, and from which the dullest and most material cannot always escape. A resplendent sun-rise over one's native hill — once seen and realized, do you think it is ever forgotten? — Never! But all down the long and tiresome journey, even to the close, will that ray of morning beauty stream, and irradiate many an hour, which, but for that God-given picture might be unsupportable in its gloom. The associations too of the field and the fireside — how they endear! And as the festal and anniversary days come round, where on all the earth do they mean so much as they do to him, who, gathering his generations about him, points to the fruits of his copartnership with nature, and traverses those lands which were his father's and which he intends shall be his son's. It is because the bright days of the farm are the brightest given to man, in all his occupations, that the charms of nature are always recognized, and its fascinations are felt even by the weary farmer, who, when worn with toil for his land and animals, loves them still, and also by the poet, who knows and feels what beauty and truth God has written on the face of earth and sky. — *Extract from Address of Dr. Geo. B. Loring, to Hampden Ag'l Society.*

Georgia Patrons of Husbandry, 1874

From *Southern Cultivator* (Athens, Ga., October, 1874), XXXII, pp. 391–92.

DEAR PATRONS:

It becomes my duty, being so prominently identified with the great farmers' movement in Georgia, to invite your serious attention to the demands of the time upon our noble order. Our efforts as producers of the soil, under a protecting Providence, to render our farms self-sustaining, have, to a great measure, proven successful.

Our good Lord and Master has sent us early and late rains, and fruitful seasons, and our so long empty granaries will soon groan with more cheering abundance than they have since the unfortunate war. The excessive hot and dry weather, curtailing our cotton crop, it is to be hoped will prove a blessing in disguise. The shrewd and sharp-sighted speculator, who has been so vigilant in heralding through the press the crop of four and a half millions of bales, will be hushed, and the cotton ring, who true to their instincts, were forging chains to fetter us — let us prepare to rend asunder, and, true to ourselves, families, and country, rally under our bright and floating colors, the only promise to the tillers of the soil. We should take time by the forelock, using our utmost influence with our friends who have so kindly come forward and contributed to our necessities, furnishing food, etc., to hold our cotton until developments are made that are satisfactory as to the extent of the growing crop.

Heartily congratulating you upon the spirit of self reliance and fortitude which you have so nobly manifested under privations and disappointments, grievous to be endured, and for which we were totally unprepared, let me earnestly and affectionately entreat you not to abandon the policy of making an abundance of supplies for home, and heed earnestly the resolution as passed by the Cotton States Convention of November last year, and impressively reiterated in its session of July last, of planting one-third of our arable land in small grain, one-third in corn and one-third in cotton:

Hearken to the warning voice of the past whose syren song of planting all cotton, hurled us into bankruptcy of property and well nigh of credit and character. Soon the season of sowing of fall and winter crops — turnips, wheat, oats, rye, etc., will be upon us, and remember earnestly that the judicious and prudent farmers, the good and faithful Patrons will gather into their granaries, that themselves, families and animals may have feed in winter. Our brother Patrons of all the cotton growing States, pledge their hearty concurrence in the one-third system, and, therefore, while our cotton production will be diminished, you may yet hope to realize a greater amount of profit by the advance price of the same. Efforts are being made through established agencies to secure supplies of grain for seed at reduced cost; and can't I ask, with some confidence, where are the good and true Patrons who have a surplus and will refuse to open their hearts and granaries in furnishing seed to promote the laudable end we have in view?

Though the hardships, privations and disappointments of the farm are galling, let us bear it with Christian fortitude, promising ourselves by such sacrifices a better day will soon dawn, and to hasten that better time we will do all in our power to promote the interest of our noble undertaking. We propose soon to divide our State into districts, over these put wise and discreet deputies of our order, whose duty will be to canvass, lecturing and organizing Granges. — In this I invoke the free and hearty co-operation of every Patron in Georgia. Believing the weal or woe of the South, yes, of the whole country, is depending upon the success or failure of the Grange movement, I propose, in addition to the deputy movement, to devote my entire time to the work of our order, and will visit, as I have been doing, all parts of Georgia where duty and my good brothers have called me. Brothers, we have a great work to do. Let us set about it in earnest, and kindle a flame of brotherly love throughout our proud old State, and not be content until we enlist under our bright and flying colors every tiller of the soil in our midst.

The political parties of the country will soon be arrayed, and the sagacious politicians will attempt to allure us into the entangling alliances of party. Let us prove to them we are true to our profession and faith in adhering strictly to our fundamental law, doing nothing that will savor in the least of committing our Order to politics.

Let me, in conclusion, exhort you to cherish and practice the cardinal precepts of our Order in every detail of life, and we, under the guidance of the ever-merciful Husbandman above, may confidently anticipate for our distressed and dispirited class a bright era of propserity, plenty and contentment.

YOURS, FRATERNALLY, ETC.,
T. J. SMITH, MASTER OF G.S.G.

Farming in New England, 1874

From "Does Farming in New England Pay?" U.S. Department of Agriculture, *Annual Report*, 1874 (Washington, 1875), pp. 187–193, 197–201, 203–04, 210–11, 214.

This question has been much discussed in the Eastern States, and answered variously in accordance with the views of those canvassing it. It has been put to our correspondents, who have answered it almost unanimously in the affirmative, as to systematic and enterprising operations — otherwise the average success being moderate, yet sufficiently liberal for the half-hearted and feeble effort put forth. Before presenting the views of several progressive farmers, fortified by facts illustrating well the difficulties and the possiblities of New England agriculture, a few suggestive statistics will be presented.

The farm-lands of New England include 19,569,863 acres, of which 61 per cent. are improved, 31 in woodland, and 8 in unimproved or waste areas. The details are:

States	Improved.		Unimproved.			
	Acres.	Percentage of total acreage.	Woodland acres.	Percentage of total acreage.	Other un-improved acres.	Percentage of total acreage.
Maine	2,917,793	49.9	2,224,740	38.1	695,525	11.9
New Hampshire	2,334,487	64.7	1,047,090	29.	224,417	6.2
Vermont	3,073,257	67.8	1,386,934	30.6	68,613	1.5
Massachusetts	1,736,221	63.5	706,714	25.8	287,348	10.5
Rhode Island	289,030	57.5	169,399	33.7	43,879	8.7
Connecticut	1,646,752	69.6	577,333	24.4	140,331	5.9
Total	11,997,540	61.3	6,112,210	31.2	1,460,113	7.4

Only seven States have a larger proportion of improved land — Illinois, 74.6 per cent.; New York, 70.4; Ohio, 66.6; Delaware, 66.3; New Jersey, 66.1; Maryland, 64.5; Pennsylvania, 63.9.

Lands are low in price, averaging $29.90 per acre; lower than in settled Western States, viz: Ohio $48.56; Michigan, $39.74; Illinois, $35.56; Indiana, $35.03; much lower than in five other States, viz: New Jersey, $86.14; Pennsylvania, $57.98; New York, $57.35; Delaware, $44.39; Maryland, $37.75. With unexampled market facilities, this small capital in land would be cheap for a bed of sand as a matrix for the development of plants, by means of added fertilization. A total capital of $100 per acre, or $6 per acre rental per annum, would not indicate very high farming, and yet it would admit of adding $1,371,000,000 for stocking and improving New England farms to the $585,000,000, the present value of the farm-lands.

Though the tilled area is comparatively small, and the breadth in cereals still less, the rate of production in New England will bear comparison with that of any other section. The average annual yield of corn for the past ten years is greater than in the Western States; Vermont surpasses Ohio, and only two of the six States fall behind Illinois. In wheat a larger yield is obtained than in any of the other divisons of our country; and the same is true of potatoes and tobacco. Look on this picture of average yield for ten years:

	Corn.	Wheat.	Rye.	Oats.	Potatoes.
Maine, bushels.................................	29.6	13.1	16.4	25.9	122
New Hampshire, bushels.................	34.9	15.	16.7	31.6	112
Vermont, bushels............................	36.7	17.	16.2	34.9	141
Massachusetts, bushels	34.2	16.8	16.3	29.4	111
Rhode Island, bushels	27.3	16.3	16.8	31.6	93
Connecticut, bushels.......................	31.1	17.3	14.2	32.9	100

And on this:

New York, bushels..........................	30.6	14.8	14.7	32.4	100
Pennsylvania bushels	35.1	13.1	13.6	31.	91
Tennessee, bushels.........................	22.5	7.6	9.5	17.5	71
Illinois, bushels..............................	30.	11.9	16.	30.6	74
Iowa, bushels	35.	13.1	18.4	35.8	97
Kansas, bushels..............................	33.8	15.4	20.	33.1	96

Now compare the prices of these products in December, 1874, in the same States, and note the advantage of New England in that regard:

	Corn.	Wheat.	Rye.	Oats.	Potatoes.
Maine..	$1 13	$1 54	$1 19	$0 67	$0 54
New Hampshire...........................	1 12	1 55	1 20	65	59
Vermont.....................................	1 10	1 43	1 06	57	43
Massachusetts	1 10	1 45	1 11	67	69
Rhode Island	1 18	—	1 16	73	82
Connecticut................................	1 17	1 45	1 21	72	72
New York...................................	93	1 26	92	57	57
Pennsylvania	76	1 21	90	59	79
Tennessee..................................	68	1 06	1 05	57	97
Illinois......................................	56	86	71	45	83
Iowa	43	65	63	38	50
Missouri....................................	74	83	69	47	85

These figures show a fair return for agricultural labor. Taking the whole number of persons in the United States engaged in agriculture in 1870, as reported by the census, and the aggregate return of value of the annual products of agricultural labor, it is found that the average is $413 to each man. Now very many of the agriculturists of New England work in winter at shoemaking and other mechanical labor, having only a very short summer for farming, and yet the average return per man is $490, $77 more than the general average, without counting the proceeds of other labor. Making such a calculation for all these States, the result would be as follows:

	Value of products.	No. of agriculturists.	Earnings per capital.
Maine	$33,470,044	82,011	$408
New Hampshire	22,473,547	46,573	482
Vermont	34,647,027	57,983	597
Massachusetts	32,192,378	72,810	442
Rhode Island	4,761,163	11,780	404
Connecticut	26,482,150	43,653	606
	154,026,309	314,810	490

The Middle States having good markets also, and a longer term of labor, exclusively agricultural, during the year, average $686; the States of the Ohio Basin, with a fertile soil, yielding only $498; and the Southern States average but $267. Need the eastern farmer despond?

After giving an interior view of the agricultural economy of this section, with the aid of original facts from reliable sources, a summary of practical conclusions will be presented.

Farming in Northern New England

Maine. — Mr. H. G. O. Smith, a farmer in York County, states that he knows of cases of successful farming in that region, but acknowledges the existence of a listless and despondent spirit in agricultural circles. He thus illustrates the situation, and distinguishes between real and pseudo farmers:

Webster says a farmer is "one who cultivates a farm;" but usage includes others than cultivators. For example, we have grocery-farmers, who spend their time discussing better methods. Road-farmers sow their seed by the wayside, and the fowls devour it. Mixed farmers do a little skimming and much bragging in addition to their egular business. Fast-horse farmers run our agricultural societies, seed in October, landlords gathering the harvest. All these classes fail to make farming pay, and should be counted out.

Least known, but not least in numbers or importance, are working farmers. They furnish bread and meat, pay the taxes, and live comfortably, unless, like Issachar of old, they voluntarily crouch down between the social and political burdens of the day. Farming does not yield as much income as mechanical or mercantile pursuits, yet farmers, being more economical, lay up the most, seldom compromising with creditors. I suppose three-fourths of the regular farmers in York County to be substantially free from debt, while one-fourth, at least, have money at interest. I estimate the average income at 3 per cent. on the capital invested, and $20 per month for the man's labor, after deducting farm expenses. The remuneration is sufficient to support a family comfortably, provided they live from the farm instead of the store; but not sufficient to permit leisure or luxuries. Lack of these, the concentration of educational and religious privileges in the villages, fancied loss of social equality, heavy taxes, and, most of all, abandonment of the homestead by children, combine to weaken the courage of New England farmers.

Mr. Robie Whitney, of Sebago Lake, Cumberland County, gives as the opinion of a majority of the farmers of his county, that "farming is not a paying occupation at the present time.'' He says that it was undoubtedly remunerative during the war, when currency was inflated, produce in demand, and prices high, but now that prices have fallen, Government bonds exempted from taxation, and capital in railway and other securities secreted so extensively to evade taxation, the burden falls with crushing force upon the farmers; and the men of capital, energy, and skill, who should lead the van of enterprising cultivators, leave the ranks, hide their money, or invest it in other enterprises less heavily taxed or more remunerative. With faith in the capabilities of agriculture in Maine, and a recognition of certain advantages over the West, he still thinks the preent time unfavorable for buying farms on credit and paying for them out of the profits of their culture. He supposes the purchase of a stocked farm by a young man at $3,000, with interest at 8 per cent., or $240, cost of clothing and other outside necessities, $365; annual depreciation of property $100; unjust taxes, $50; a total of $755 to pay annually before a dollar of the principal can be discharged. He thinks the prospect of clearing the farm a poor one, and desires the exemption of mortgaged farms from taxation. He gives the following example of the more prosperous class of farmers, Mr. Charles Johnson, of Gorham, whose work is done by himself and a son sixteen years of age:

My farm consists of about 115 acres of improved land, divided into about 55 acres of grass and tillage, and 60 of pasture. I cut about 55 tons of hay; keep 8 cows, using 2½ tons of hay each to winter them, 20 tons; one pair of oxen, 5 tons; two horses, kept the whole year, 6 tons; four young cattle, 4 tons; 12 sheep, 3 tons. Total 38 tons.

This leaves a surplus of 17 tons, worth, in the barn, $14 per ton	$238 00
3 acres sweet corn, 8,300 cans, at 4½ cents	373 50
Milk from eight cows	600 00
Profit on oxen	50 00
Growth of young cattle, estimated at	30 00
Profit of 12 sheep	84 00
100 bushels of potatoes	50 00
Total	1,425 50

The land on which I raised my corn was clay loam; one acre was ground newly-broken, on which I put about eight cords of barn-yard manure, and spread and worked it well with plow and harrow, also 400 pounds of phosphate to the acre. The other two acres were planted to potatoes the year before, manure applied in the fall, and plowed in very shoal; applied 400 pounds of phosphate to the acre. The expenses of meal for the stock, phosphate, carriages, harnesses, fencing material, repairs on buildings and all other incidental expenses, are to come out of the above amount. I did my work with my son, sixteen years old. This statement is for the year 1873.

Mr. W. H. Johnson, of East Corinth, Penobscot, says farming has always paid, if properly conducted, and will pay even if done in a shiftless and half-hearted way, for such a farmer could not get a living in any other business. Half of the cultivators of his county do not farm well, for want of energy, skill, and a proper knowledge of tillage. He thinks the remuneration as certain as in any part of the country east of the Rocky Mountains. He cannot give an example in complete detail, as he does not know of a farmer who has kept an account of yearly expenditure and income. . . .

New Hampshire. — The secretary of the New Hampshire Board of Agriculture, Mr. J. O. Adams, sent to towns, in obedience to legislative requirement, a statistical circular, involving the question of the profits of farming, that of the comparative tendency to emigration, and other practical inquiries, answers to which are published in his last annual report. Not all of the towns made returns, and some of the returns were silent or indefinite as to the profit of farming enterprise; but a classification of one hundred and forty-one such answers presents a list of fifty-five towns in which none of the farmers are "making money," and one of fifty-three in which a few only are making headway in accumulation. Four counties are represented by one prosperous farmer in each; others by "one or two," "occasionally one," or "one in a hundred;" seven give percentages of money-makers ranging from 1 to 25; one reports one-third, another one-half, a third "more than half," and still another "a bare majority;" while in others " a majority are saving a little," "farming pays," "some stock-farmers" are prospering. This gives a fair idea of the report, and probably an estimate lower than the real proportion of farmers that save money in the several counties, because the reports are evidently, in some instances, tinted with the bright hopefulness or tinged with the despondency of the reporters. New Durham illustrates well the prevalent combination of agriculture with other industries, having seventy-five who are both farmers and shoemakers, and only thirty who are farmers solely; and in Atkinson, these classes are respectively thirty and fifty-five. In Dandia few farmers are prospering, because, among other reasons, they "neglect their farms, and do not devote the time and money to them that they would to other business." At the same time the reporter acknowledges that farm-buildings are better than in former days, that such conveniences as sewing-machines in the house, and mowing-machines out of doors are common, and that there is more money at interest and less economy than formerly. In Hampton Falls, where farmers are said to be merely "supporting their families," it is said that they "do not work all the time," and that farming, "for the time and labor bestowed upon it, probably pays better than any other business conducted in a similar manner." The high price of labor is very generally deemed an obstacle to profitable farming, but in Kensington it is acknowledged that "those farmers in town who have had plenty of help in the house and out of doors, are about the only ones who have made any money by farming in the last few years." No farmers are making money in Sandown, for the reason that "their lands are worn out, or grown over with wood and bushes." In Rollinsford none are growing poor by farming, and nearly all are increasing their means, their cash products being garden-vegetables, milk, fruit, and hay. The money makers in Centre Harbor are stock-growers. The town clerk of Freedom is free to say, and sorry to say it, that no one in town is living solely from the farm, and that "there seems to be a lack of energy and enterprise." One farm in Tamworth is earning a profit without deterioration in growing white beans for market. In Dunbarton the best farmers agree that none are "making money solely by farming and at the same time keeping up the value of their farms and supporting their families." They may not know an equally indisputable fact, that scarcely one in a hundred of the laboring men of the world can do more than support their families; and certainly not half of them can give their families as good a support as that enjoyed by Dunbarton farmers.

Near the cities a spirit of enterprise is caught from the prevailing activity. Market facilities are improved more wisely. In Manchester "Many of the small farms pay better than the business of mechanics." In Claremont, farmers "are saving more money than the average of mechanics and men engaged in mercantile pursuits who have an equal amount invested in their business and houses.'' The estimate of interest on farm-capital in Rochester and Rollingsford is 6 per cent. Unfortunately there is no return from Concord, Nashua, Portsmouth, or Dover, where similar facts might be supposed to exist. In Bedford, near Manchester, 6 per cent. is realized, largely from milk, of which $85,000 worth annually is sold, and ''young people stay at home generally, because they can make farming pay.''

In nearly all these reports the continued exodus of farmers' sons is affirmed. In more than half specific estimates are made of the proportion emigrating. It amounts to nearly six-tenths, and it would probably be safe to say that more than half of the boys of the farms of New Hampshire leave their paternal acres. As might be expected, where the profit is largest the migration is least. It is said that ''farming pays in Hollis.'' Sequence: ''Boys stand by the old homestead better than in neighboring towns.'' This town is near Nashua, a manufacturing city; and Hudson on the other side, yields ''5 or 6 per cent., and fewer boys leave the farm than in many other towns.'' In Farmington ''no farmers are making money and supporting their families;'' consequently ''all leave town who know enough.''

The return of estimated percentage of profit or real rental value of farms is an exceedingly gloomy exhibit, in most cases making the profit nothing, and in a score or more of towns where profits were definitely estimated the average is about 3 per cent. In the whole State, on the basis of these returns, the average could not be 2 per cent. — indeed it could scarcely be more than 1. Very little reliance should be placed upon them, the universal idea being that one hundred days' labor in the fields, and two hundred or more in warming and feeding inmates of the house and barn, should support and clothe and school a family, with advanced views of necessary comforts and admissible luxuries, and the surplus, if any, after deducting an additional sum to represent the profits of *labor*, should be credited as profits of *capital*. It is asking too much for the real productive labor done, the half a dozen or half a score of acres actually tilled, especially if a systematic starving of these acres is practiced.

Examine, for example, the labor-account and the list of products of that labor in the Dunbarton report:

Average income. — One hundred bushels corn, one hundred and fifty bushels potatoes, $190; 25 bushels of wheat, 75 bushels of oats, $95; growth of stock, $150; income of five cows, $200; pork sold, $30. The growth of wood on this farm is small, say $50; improvements, $50; fruit, $100; income of kitchen-garden, $15. To this might be added 20 cords of wood, for fire, worth on the stump $20; making a sum total of $900. To this amount may be added house-rent, which I think should be reckoned in favor of the farm.

Expenditures. — Labor of man and wife, $500, (a low estimate;) first-class hired man, $25 per month; board in addition, $12, amounting to $37 per month, or $444 per year; taxes, which are lower in this town than in most towns, $100; blacksmith's bills, $25; wear and tear of tools, carts, carriages, harnesses, &c., $50; fertilizers, seeds, and grain, $50; annual repair of buildings, $50; to this should be added the help of two boys belonging to the family, with some extra help by the day, &c., also the help of two girls in the house, who take the place of a girl hired, the whole being reckoned low at $200; thus making the whole amount of the really necessary expenses of the farm $1,419, leaving a balance against the farm of $519. The question then comes, how does this farmer live? Well, how does he? Five hundred and nineteen dollars against him in the management of the farm, to which may be added the interest of a $6,000 establishment, including farm, tools, carriages, stock, &c., $360 more, amounting to $879. Then there are the necessary expenses of the family, such as clothing, books and papers, schooling, groceries, and many other things, swelling the amount, perhaps, to the round sum of

$1,500. To live, in the first place, the man and wife must cross out their salaries of $500; that of the children must also be erased, making $700, save a few dollars paid for extra help by the day and otherwise. Then the interest on the estate must not be reckoned — $360 more, and we have $1,060. The board of the hired man is also reckoned out, $144 more, giving a sum total of $1,204. There is still a deficiency which must be made up in various ways, of nearly $300: sometimes, by taking a few boarders in the summer, or by cutting and selling a little extra wood and timber, or more often, at the neglect of the educational interests of the family, or in the necessary rest or clothing of the housewife, or it may be sometimes by a little outside speculation.

Here are three acres in corn, three in oats, one and a half in potatoes, about the same in wheat, or nine acres in cultivation, with the care of five cows; and two men and two boys, with the wife and two girls, assigned to do the work, and $1,144 placed to their credit in payment for this work. One black man in the South would be required to care for twice as many acres, and a white one in the West three times as many. This looks too much like playing at farming, and, perhaps, supposes the training of a Black Hawk trotter in summer, and a carnival of sleigh-riding in the long winter. It is diluting labor too much for profitable results. . . .

Another farmer, Mr. B. Frank Brown, of Tilton, tells us how in seven years he brought up a farm that could feed but one cow to the point of carrying twelve to twenty:

There is only now and then a farmer in New England who makes his business pay, for the reason that he does not go at it with that energy, forethought, and perseverance which characterizes the actions of our merchants and business men generally. The average farmer works well a few months and takes his ease the rest of the year. Most of them tread the beaten paths of their forefathers; they do not think for themselves and act on the result of thought, like merchants. The farmer should understand his soil and know what it is adapted to raise to the best advantage; then concentrate his force in the right direction. Seven years ago I purchased some worn-out soil, (light,) about thirty acres. I raised only enough to keep one cow the first winter. I began to turn everything about the premises adapted to fertilizing to the best account. I turned the sink-water into the barn-cellar upon plenty of loam, and put a few hogs to work upon the loam. At first I bought corn to feed my hogs, and was careful to have loam enough for the absorption of all liquids which came in contact with it. The hogs brought enough to pay for the corn, and what they did for me was profit, as I was able to raise my fodder. I bought more cows and put loam for bedding and to absorb the liquid manure which went into the cellar, where the hogs could work it over. I have not kept many hogs, but generally from five to ten. I have bought very little of the commercial fertilizers, and what I have bought has cost at least double what it would have cost me to produce its value with loam and hogs. I have bought some ashes, and would much rather have money laid out in ashes at 25 to 30 cents per bushel than any commercial fertilizer at any market-price. I keep the dressing as near the top as possible and harrow it in. I believe in top-dressing grass just before the fall-rains, or in the spring after the grass is up far enough to shield it from the sun. I have treated my land as above stated, and now I am raising enough to keep from twelve to twenty cows from the same land that only produced enough for one seven years ago. If I raised corn I should buy a little superphosphate of lime to give it a start in the spring, unless my ground was very rich. As a rule it costs so much that the farmer cannot afford to buy it. Grass is usually the best crop in New England. Farmers should have a few tons of hay to sell, and buy western corn with the proceeds, and if they can hire money at 5 per cent. (its real cash-value) they may find it profitable to hire it to buy corn at 75 cents to $1 per bushel to feed hogs. But they must keep the dirt-cart busy, and they must keep the manure-heap under cover where it will not go to waste. A farmer may as well put his bank-notes in the fire as leave his manure-heap under the eaves-droppings of the buildings. . . .

Vermont. — The enterprising and systematic farmers of the Green Mountains are prosperous, although the State is almost exclusively agricultural. General or mixed farming is in vogue, usually with some prominent crop for a cash surplus, and such specialties as gilt-edged butter, pedigree merinos, and Morgan horses.

Mr. Z. E. Jameson, of Irasburg, Orleans, reports the management of a worn-out farm near his own, purchased nineteen years ago by Mr. G. B. Brewster, who, after a series of discouragements and failures, increased the productive capacity of his sterile acres to 25 bushels per acre of wheat, 70 of oats, 70 of corn, 300 of potatoes, and 900 of turnips, and the value of his estate from a few hundred dollars to $15,000.

Mr. Safford, whilom a member of the Vermont Board of Agriculture, bought contiguous tracts of land for $6,500, which are now worth $20,000, with a manifold increase of stock-carrying capacity, and large additions of barn accommodations and improvements.

Mr. J. A. Child, of Weybridge, Addison, says, after extensive observation east and west, that he has never seen anywhere better evidences of prosperity and wealth, as shown by fertile and well-kept farms and substantial buildings, than in the counties bordering on Lake Champlain, where farms sell at $40 to $50 per acre, and not unfrequently at $100.

Mr. Jonathan Lawrence, of Passumpsic, Caledonia, says that hundreds of farmers in his region made money during the war, while many bought additional farms, and find it less easy to pay for them than they had hoped. He gives a statement from Mr. E. A. Parks, showing an income of $2,265 from 325 acres, and expenses, amounting to $1,400, including $600 as interest on investment, leaving $865 above legal interest on cost of farm. One item is $1,490 from fifteen cows.

Mr. Samuel S. Kelton, of East Montpelier, Washington, thus gives his views and facts in illustration:

> I will say that farming pays as well as any other business would in the same hands. As a class the farmers are as well off as any other; and in proportion to numbers there are less very rich and less very poor, a much larger proportion well-to-do. Their position, financially and socially, is very much better than fifty years ago. Enterprising young men, who do not receive parental or other assistance, work for hire until they save a thousand or two, buy a farm worth $4,000 to $8,000, put on ten to twenty cows, and by middle age are out of debt and have reared a family bred to industry. A large proportion do not do so well; neither would they in any other business. It is the *man*, not the business, that tells. You ask for an example of success. In 1857 the writer's near neighbor died. His estate, appraised at $8,000 real, $2,000 personal, was bought by his oldest son, (aged twenty-three years,) who gave his notes for $8,000, took an incumbrance of $1,500, (the estimated support of a relative,) and paid $500 = $10,000. He kept a dairy stock, a few sheep, raised some colts, paid all his debts, bought an adjoining farm at $6,000. This man is now forty years of age. His farm of over three hundred acres would sell for $16,000. He has forty head of cattle, five horses, and some sheep, and does not owe as much as his personal property is worth. This I call success. You may think it small business, but remember we live in a small State, and do business in a small way.

Southern New England

Massachusetts. — Returns from all parts of Massachusetts are full of illustrations of successful effort in agriculture, were further proof necessary. In one instance a farmer says he purchased 350 acres seven years previously for $12,000, with stock and tools $15,000, and could pay but $2,000 down. He had a dairy of 40 cows, and made some maple-sugar. His expenses at the start were $100 per month, and his receipts $200. He had no difficulty in paying his notes as they became due, and eventually resold the place to the former owner, who had returned disgusted from the West.

Mr. Allen Look, of West Tisbury, Dukes, acknowledges many instances of agricultural industry in his county, and believes it would be general if farming were properly conducted. He finds sheep-husbandry a profitable branch, and reports a flock of 100 ewes that had the previous year 100 lambs that were sold for $300, and 300 pounds of wool for $150 more; the cost of keeping being but a small portion of the gross proceeds. He mentions a field of three acres of bush-land, dressed with a compost of fish and peat, and sown with clover and timothy, yielding twelve tons of hay, sold for $240. With a similar top-dressing the next year, twelve tons and $360 were obtained. The land unbroken was considered nearly worthless for any other purpose. From a strawberry-patch of 25 rods, 15 bushels and 20 quarts of fruit brought $100.20, at the rate of $641 per acre. He declares it to be easier to get $100 in cash now than $50 twenty-five years ago. He hits the nail which confines this whole secret of farm-profits in saying, ''I think extravagance has very much to do with the success of farmers, for it does not matter how much one gets from his farm if he is bound to spend it all.''

Mr. William Sutton, of Ipswich, Essex, adds the following testimony to the success resulting from intelligent effort:

It is undoubtedly true that negligent farming is everywhere unprofitable, but I think it is equally certain that in New England, as elsewhere, the industrious, economical, and intelligent farmer is amply repaid for his toil. We may not here be able to boast of the remarkable crops which are sometimes exhibited in sections where a more generous soil awaits the labor of the husbandman, but steady, unremitted cultivation of our better class of farms has in repeated instances resulted in prosperity and wealth. I have now in mind the cases of two families, in my own immediate vicinity, (the Wares and Kings,) who have acquired ample fortunes in legitimate farming. The several brothers of these families, (and they number six in the latter instance,) are among the most prosperous of our people, and they have gained their fortunes entirely by the cultivation of the soil. They have been, in both families, engaged in the specialty of market-gardening, which they have followed from their youth up. And their success answers affirmatively and decidedly the question, ''Does farming pay in New England?'' I may mention also that in this town of Ipswich are instances of very successful farming in the hay-crop.

Mr. N. S. Hubbard, of Brimfield, Hampden, makes the following statement:

In reply to the first question I answer in the affirmative and also in the negative. And the same can be said of any other branch of industry. If the farmer puts forth the same energy that is exerted in other branches of industry, and uses his brain as well as his muscles, he will be sure of fair success although he cannot become suddenly rich. But there are advantages not to be found by the professional or business man. He partakes of the fruits of his own garden, field, and orchard, fresh, and which his own hands have cultivated, and is also comparatively free from the cares and perplexities of the business and professional man. In this immediate vicinity the dairy, perhaps, pays the best of anything in farming. Milk is sold for the city market or manufactured into butter and cheese, and is worth for that purpose 2½ cents per quart in summer, and in some cases a trifle more; in winter from 3½ to 4 cents for the city markets. This gives a product of from $45 to $75 per cow, and in some cases as high as $100. These prices, although low, give the farmer a fair income, and were it not for the fact that taxes fall proportionately heavy on the farmer, he would feel greater courage in his business. The most valuable of all crops in this vicinity, or even in Massachusetts, is the grass and hay crop. . . .

Connecticut. — Rev. William Clift, the well-known "Tim Bunker," of the Agriculturist, furnishes the following positive views and significant facts upon this question:

Answering for the State of Connecticut, the immediate field of my observation, I have no doubt that the men engaged in agriculture receive as fair a compensation for their labor in this occupation as they would in any other. The term "pay" does not mean simply the pecuniary rewards of labor, but all of comfort and thrift that labor brings in any shape — shelter, food, raiment, and the social and religious privileges without which money is of little use to the possessor. This comprehensive meaning of the term "pay" is generally overlooked in the discussion of this question. I will use it in this sense in what I have to say. Five hundred dollars a year in the city or village will not procure for the professional man or mechanic what most Connecticut farmers have directly as the result of their labor and of their location without any exchange of money.

Farming in Connecticut is in a transition state from the old style to the new; and probably not more than half of the agricultural population are out of the ruts and availing themselves of the improved methods and improvements of husbandry. I had occasion in the summer of 1873 to inquire for a horse-reaper to cut a large field of rye, and after diligent search and much riding I could hear of but a single implement of that kind, and that was a Buckeye of the old pattern, that had been laid upon the shelf several years. It is probably now the only horse-reaper owned in the county of New London, one of the richest counties in the state, that has had an agricultural society and yearly fairs for twenty years and more. Most of the rye raised in the county is still cut with the cradle, and farmers are exceedingly slow in adopting the new implements that transfer the labor of tillage and harvest from their own muscles to the horse. But even for the lower grades of intelligence and labor applied to the farm, there is a fair reward and more of comfort gained than the same individuals could secure in any other calling. The old style farmer is intensely conservative, and wary of all new ideas and new implements. If he has abandoned the old wooden mold-board in the plow, it is rather because mechanics have forgotten how to make them, than his want of faith in them. He finds it difficult to get anything else than the iron plow, and adopts it under protest. He is shy of agricultural societies, of county and State fairs; of blooded stock, and of agricultural papers. He does not believe in new crops or new machines. His farm is cultivated just as his father worked it fifty years ago. He raises corn, potatoes, and oats, and his "woman," as he still calls his wife, makes butter and cheese, and raises poultry and eggs, and exchanges them at the village store for all the coffee, sugar, and tea used in the family. They are both saving and honest, and keep their side of the ledger-account at the store good year after year. No man ever lost a cent by them, and there is not the least chance for such a calamity in the future. A short account of one dozen in the eggs would keep them awake at night and spoil their thanksgiving. He raises nearly all his breadstuff except one barrel of flour a year, and the main staff of life is the Indian brown loaf, and johnny-cake; meat from the butcher's cart is the rare exception. He corns beef and pork, more than enough for his own use, and pays a part of his labor bills from the meat-casks in the cellar, which are always well filled and packed with Turk's Island salt. If he wants variety in spring, he kills a calf; if in the fall, he kills a sheep or fowls. He is always ready to exchange fresh meat with a neighbor, and only deals with the butcher on the credit side. He is easily seduced by that plausible caterer for village tables into selling his best calves, lambs, and turkeys. He is not yet fully persuaded in his own mind about barn-cellars, and continues to adorn the sides of his barn under the stable-windows with pyramidal paintings of manure-heaps. He carts dirt into the open yard every summer and carts it out again in the spring, with such additions as the stock may have made to it. He sells pork at the market-price and cannot tell whether it has cost him 6 or 10 cents a pound. He gets his best manure from the pig-stye, and guesses it pays to raise pork, because he thinks he gets the manure as clear profit.

Now I claim that this pretty large class of farmers, who do not know whether farming pays or not, are better rewarded for their labor upon the farm than they would be in any other calling. They get for their toil their house-rent, their fuel, their meats, fruits, and vegetables; live in great comfort, and usually save money after all their expenses are paid. This class of farmers not infrequently have considerable sums in the savings-bank. They are, with few exceptions, near to the school, the mill, the church, the library, and all the privileges which the village or city confers. The State has a mile of railroad to every five square miles of land, and six or eight miles' ride will bring almost every farmer to the depot, which is exactly in the center of the world. The mechanic, who generally resides in the village or city, and is paid in money for his labor, has to pay out nearly all that he receives for the means of living, which the farmer produces upon his own premises. He handles more money in the course of the year, but he has procured no more enjoyments for body or mind than the farmer.

But the husbandry of the state is by no means confined to the slow, conservative class I have described. There are many thoughtful, stirring men among the tillers of the soil, who take the papers and digest what they read. They are not afraid of new ideas, new crops, and new methods in husbandry. They comprehend the changes which have come over society in the last twenty-five years, and have adapted themselves fairly to their new circumstances. They study their location and the markets, and raise those crops which they can most economically turn into money. They comprehend the vast changes which railroads, canals, and steamers upon the great lakes and rivers have wrought in our communications with the fertile plains of the West, and do not attempt to compete with the crops which the new States must necessarily raise, and can raise much cheaper than we. They do not raise much grain or pork for the general markets, but cultivate those crops that are consumed near home.

The tendency of our farming is every year more and more toward specialties. Some one or more staple articles are selected that always command a remunerative price, and the whole force of the farm is concentrated upon the production of these special crops. The supplies for the family are not overlooked. It is taken for granted that a cultivator of the soil can raise the fruits, vegetables, eggs, poultry, butter, and most of the meats consumed on the place cheaper than he can purchase them. The number of these special crops is already quite large, and is constantly increasing. . . .

Mr. T. S. Gold, secretary of the Board of Agriculture of Connecticut, gives the following explicit and satisfactory statement concerning the substantial farmers of his neighborhood and their prosperity:

Does farming pay in New England? — You ask a question which is often discussed in this age of inquiry, and your remark which follows explains the whole matter. It pays, "if managed with energy and skill and the use of necessary capital." Where brush is allowed to overrun the pastures and meadows, and weeds to choke the crops, we hear the cry that farming does not pay; that it is cheaper to buy corn and other products than to raise them.

It is true, I admit, that little judgment was used in first settling the country, and that many farms, or even larger districts, were cleared from the forests that should have been allowed to remain, to furnish timber for manufacturing and building, and shelter for fruits and crops. The introduction of agricultural machinery is rendering the culture of these rough portions and the gathering of the hay relatively more expensive than upon smoother land, and there is no doubt that some entire farms thus circumstanced fail to return to their owners a fair equivalent for the labor and capital employed, and that many other farms have some portions which are a drag upon their better parts, a sinking-fund to swallow up the profits derived from successful culture elsewhere. I do not refer to those expensive labors in clearing rocky land, or draining wet land, or reclaiming sandy land by ashes and lime or green crops, but to the continued culture of rough and impoverished lands, the gathering of hay from rough meadows, still mowed because they were once productive, and other like practices followed because under other circumstances they were profitable. Lands so situated that they cannot profitably be manured or even cultivated, because they are so difficult of access, must be classed here as not paying for the labor required. Wherever we find farmers laying aside these old-time ways, concentrating their energies upon their better lands, adapting their farming to the changing conditions of the times in stock, crops, and improved implements and machinery, we find them thrifty, enjoying the comforts and luxuries of life, with means to support society, to educate their children, laying up a comfortable competency for old age, and to give their children a better start in life than they themselves enjoyed.

Again, if farming does not pay, how is it that all the cultivators of the soil live? They always get their living by their occupation, not by dependence upon other callings. The agricultural laborer always has his sustenance and always secures his wages. The failure of a farmer to meet his obligations, unless he becomes involved by some outside venture, is a rarity so great that it may be said never to occur, while every community can show examples of ruined fortunes, involving many other parties, in the more enticing walks of trade and manufactures. Agriculture absorbs and employs all men who fail in other avocations either from physical disability or other causes. The disjointed parts of lives spent in other callings, which absorb their mental powers and their physical training in periods of rest, are mostly spent in the culture of the earth. Agriculture has to feed all these and their families. Adventurers of every kind take rest and find renewed strength on the farm for new enterprises, and come back again often with blasted hopes and shattered health and fortunes.

The amount of physical labor expended in agriculture is large, the amount of mental is often small. The return for the quality and amount of labor and the risk incurred will compare favorably with, yes, even surpass, that in other departments of human industry. Agriculture, manufactures, commerce, and mining are the four great divisions. If some give greater average returns for the risks, labor, mental and physical, capital and skill, than others, I claim that this is in the order named. The returns of agriculture are slow but sure. Manufactures, giving employment to varied ability, furnish some examples of splendid success. Commerce and trade have their merchant-princes, but these are rare. The miner finds a vein of ore, a rich nugget, or a gem, but of all mining the baser metals afford the surest and best profits; so we are driven back to the conclusion that agriculture, the basis of national strength and wealth, is also the most sure and liberal in its support of those who practice it. As the other callings make greater demands for mental daring and capacity, so they give the corresponding examples of success.

Mr. T. G. Kingsley, of New London, correspondent of the Department, reports concerning his county:

Gardening pays the best of any kind of crops in this county. Selling milk in the cities also pays well. The soil in this county requires fertilizing to a considerable amount, or our crops are small, but by using phosphate, guano, fish guano, or plaster, the crop is increased from one-third to one-half per acre. Many of our farmers purchase western cattle in the spring of the year and sell them in the fall or winter for beef, and in that way are making money; selling the cattle for from 50 to 75 per cent. more than cost by keeping them from six to nine months. In one instance a man planted six acres of the Early-Rose potatoes and used 2,400 pounds of phosphate besides 100 loads of stable-manure, and he raised 300 bushels of marketable potatoes per acre, making 1,800 bushels. Some were sold for $1.50 per bushel; the balance, at $1. I know of a young man who purchased a farm for $7,500, and by attending to his business, using good judgment, energy, economy and prudence, in fourteen years sold sufficient from the farm to pay its cost.

Conclusions

1. Farming in New England pays well if conducted with skill and enterprise, combined with the use of sufficient capital.

2. It is unremunerative to those who starve the soil, decline the use of improved implements and labor-saving processes, and fail to adapt their crops to soil, situation, and circumstances.

3. Those who employ the least possible labor, because of its high price, receive smaller net returns than those who use enough of it for good culture and large yields.

4. The popular estimate of the receipts of the farm is erroneous in failing to reckon house-rent, carriage-hire, and fruits and grains and vegetables used at home, and in assuming that a large portion of the gross receipts should be net savings, however small the annual expenditure of labor.

5. Proximity to numerous markets compensates for lower natural fertility; contiguity to the sea-coast renders available large supplies of cheap marine fertilizers, and the manufacturing villages furnish equivalent advantages to interior farms; and while the average yields of crops are thus made equal to those of the most fertile portion of the country, the prices obtained are greater.

6. The statistics of production show that for the labor employed no section of the country, excepting only three of the Middle States, enjoys a larger net return.

7. Lands are cheaper than in any equally populous and improved section of the country, with a probability of future increase in price, greater productiveness, the employment of a larger capital and more labor in their cultivation.

8. The necessity is indicated, before high prosperity can become general, for increased fertility, better drainage, more machine-labor and brain-work and less drudgery, and more feeding of farm-animals for flesh and milk and less for the bare support of animal existence.

Agriculture in the South, 1874

From C. W. Howard, "Condition of Agriculture in the Cotton States," in U.S. Department of Agriculture, *Annual Report*, 1874 (Washington, 1875), pp. 215–24, 227, 229–31, 237–38.

The condition of the agriculture of a country is to be determined by the salable value of its lands, the prices of its products, whether remunerative or the reverse, and the system of farming, whether ameliorating or exhaustive to the soil. The first two of these tests are sometimes variable and, therefore, not always accurate. War, with its immediate results, and panics in the money-market may affect injuriously both the value of lands and the prices of agricultural products. Allowances must be made for the effects of these causes; but the last test never varies or is inaccurate.

The agricultural condition of a country is never solidly prosperous in which a system of farming is practiced which exhausts the soil. This is destroying capital, for which destruction no temporary annual returns, however large, are an equivalent. The seeming prosperity based upon large results from a soil in course of impoverishment is always fallacious and, therefore, hurtful in the end.

We may arrive at the condition of agriculture in the cotton States by these tests. In ascertaining this condition, it is proper to say that the writer is most familiar with the State of Georgia. A large proportion of his remarks and estimates will be based upon his knowledge of this State. Georgia is generally considered to be the most prosperous of the cotton States. Any coloring which may unintentionally be given from this cause to southern agriculture will certainly not be to the disadvantage of the other States.

From North Carolina to Louisiana there is a strong uniformity in the physical structure of the soil, and in the character of the staple crops. There is also a decided uniformity in the system of agriculture which is pursued wherever cotton is raised. One State may, therefore, very well represent the rest of these cotton-States. The writer is a native of Georgia; his sympathies are with his brethren of the South, and, therefore, when he condemns existing practices it is with the temper with which an attached relative should point out the errors of a kinsman.

Salable Value of Land in the Cotton States

It is proper to say that Texas is not included in this estimate among these States, because it is yet in progress of settlement. This examination will be confined to those of the cotton States which have been long and fully settled, and where land has attained a determinate value.

The value of land in the settled portion of the older cotton States is less than in any other country in Christendom. This was the case before the war. Take the State of Georgia, for instance, as a representative State.

In 1860, the average value of land was $4.85. The highest value of the richest county was $10.66 per acre. The lowest value was 68 cents per acre. If we contrast these values with those of the Northern, Middle, or the new Northwestern States, as Illinois, the difference is striking.

Since the war we might have supposed that the depression, in average value, would have been greatly increased; but this has not been the case to any great extent. In Georgia in 1866, immediately upon the close of the war, the average value of land was $3.42, showing a diminution from the value of 1860 of $1.43 per acre. There has been a slow advance in value from 1866 to the present time, the average value nearly, if not quite, reaching that of 1860. The lands of some sections have actually increased in value, in many instances to $50 per acre, while others have decreased from $20 to $30 per acre to from $3 to $5 per acre. The causes of this difference will be hereafter pointed out. The average value has, however, not materially changed. That which is true of Georgia, as to the value of her land, is true also of the other cotton States.

Why were these lands so low in price before the war? It was not the climate of these States, because while portions of the territory were sickly the larger portions were perfectly healthy. The sickly sections extended along the line of the coast, including the rice-lands and the level pine-lands, which were very difficult of drainage; but all the rolling lands of the interior, (including the greater bulk of the territory,) the mountainous portions, were extremely healthy.

It was not the poverty of the soil, because while a portion of this territory was poor the larger portion was originally very fertile land. With the same manure and the same culture, there is not an agricultural product of use to man, raised at the North, which cannot be raised in equal perfection at the South, independent of the products which are peculiar to the South, as cotton, rice, sugar, and the semi-tropical fruits. In fact the largest recorded yield, within the knowledge of the writer, of the cereals has occurred at the South, as 212 bushels of corn, 58 of wheat, and 100 of oats to the acre.

It was not the amount of taxation. The State tax in Georgia was about one-tenth of one per cent. This, perhaps, was a fair average of the other cotton-States.

It was not the amount of cheap land at the West, because those cheap lands were equally within reach of northern land-holders, and those lands did not sink in value on that account, by reason of emigration from them.

It was not slavery, because those lands were highest in value where most slave-labor was used. The rice-lands, for instance, requiring a hand to every 4½ acres, sold at from $150 to $300 per acre, while in the upper portions, where slave-labor was almost unknown, the lands would not command $5 per acre.

It was not because the farmers did not make money. They did accumulate under a most ruinous system of agriculture, because at the end of the year there were no wages to be paid, and if the crop covered expenses, their profit was large in the mere increase of their slaves.

What, then, was the cause of the low price of land? Clearly the bad system of farming. The value of the land was scarcely considered. It was cultivated in cotton and corn until it was unable to produce either, and was then thrown out to grow up in briers, sassafras, and scrub pines. A purchaser looking for land, if he found a field without a stump in it, considered that fact *prima facie* evidence that it was worn out.

Of course land, considered as something which was to become less valuable every year until it became worthless, was of little market value. There were some exceptions, as the rice-fields, where the annual flooding or "warping" was an annual heavy manuring. These lands maintained their high valuation.

Since the war the same system of agriculture has been generally, but not universally, pursued. It is pleasant to observe an increasing departure from the old practice. Wherever this departure occurs, the lands are rising rapidly in value.

Market Value of Crops

Cotton is considered almost exclusively the money-crop. It is almost the only crop which is sold. Planters, since the war, have, for the most part, bought their provisions with the proceeds of their cotton. The exceptions are the truck farmers, who supply the towns, &c., with a certain class of provisions. Besides these there are occasional instances of large farmers who not only make their own provisions, but have a surplus to sell. These men are almost always prosperous.

The question naturally arises, does cotton, with the present labor, pay the producer at present prices? The cost of raising a pound of cotton has been a mooted point. In order to settle it, the writer addressed letters to several of the most successful farmers in Georgia. But a small proportion of the parties addressed have returned replies. The letters of those who have replied are very valuable. These gentlemen are from different sections of the State, and are all gentlemen of experience, practical good sense, and successful farmers. One, Mr. Hardaway, resides in Thomas County, on the Florida line, while Colonel Winn's residence is near the northern border of cotton culture. Mr. Hardaway cultivates a very small farm, but does it perfectly. This gentleman took the premium on corn at the State fair, making 119 bushels of corn on an acre, while the average product of the State is 5½ bushels per acre.

Dr. Lavender is, perhaps, our best representative of successful mixed farming, raising clover, the grasses, live stock, and, among other things, 15 to 20 acres of turnips annually. At the same State fair he received the premium on turnips, having grown 1,550 bushels on an acre.

Mr. Dickson's name is a household word among southern cotton-planters. Upon anything relating to cotton, he is our highest authority. Before the war, this gentleman cultivated 1,000 acres in cotton, 800 in corn, and small grain in proportion, expending annually $10,000 for commercial fertilizers. His large experience, remarkable success, and his exact business habits give great weight to his opinions. The whole South will read his letter with surprise. His estimate of producing a pound of cotton being correct, (and it would require a hardy man to doubt it,) it follows that since the war, for the most of the time, the South has grown cotton at a positive and serious loss. The different estimates of cost, ranging from 11 cents to 17 cents per pound, may be easily accounted for. The lower estimates are based upon the practice of comparatively small farms with high manuring and under exceptionally skillful culture. They rather represent what may be done than what is generally done. Mr. Dickson bases his estimate upon the general practice of cotton-planters. . . .

Griswold, Ga., November 7, 1874.

DEAR SIR: Yours of the 1st instant only came to hand yesterday, and, in compliance with your request, I give you my estimate of the cost of raising cotton with negro labor.

I have kept an account of the production on my small place, with the actual outlay, for several years, and have made estimates each year. The cheapest cotton I ever made cost about 9½ cents and the highest about 12 cents. I think the average about $11^3/_{10}$.

My land is light, sandy loam, and with 180 to 200 pounds phosphate will average 200 pounds lint cotton. The only profit I get is from my corn, oats, fruit, potatoes, and grapes. I must make some cotton in order to get the seeds for my compost heap.

In the estimate above given, I have charged nothing for personal services; the remuneration comes from grain and seed for manure.

As ever, yours, truly,

E. C. GRIER.

Thomasville, Ga., November 7, 1874.

DEAR SIR: It gives me pleasure to promptly answer your question as to the cost per pound to raise cotton. I give you the cost for seven years, to wit: 1866, 14.50; 1867, 12.50; 1868, 12.25; 1869, 10.90; 1870, 8.60; 1871, 13.61; 1872, 10.77. The average is 11.88. This includes interest on value of land, repairs, interest on team, taxes, fertilizers, labor of cultivating, picking and packing, but nothing added for personal supervision. The latter would be hard to estimate. This year's crop has not been marketed, but will not exceed 10 cents. I keep a record of my crops annually, and it simply required the copying, as the calculation was already made and entered on my memorandum-book.

Respectfully,

R. H. HARDAWAY.

Barnesville, Ga., November 5, 1874.

DEAR SIR: In answer to your inquiries I will state that I have carefully counted the cost of making cotton from 1866 to 1874 each year. 1866, the cost per pound, 8¾ cents; 1867, 7¼; 1868, 9⅞; 1869, 12⅛; 1870, 13½; 1871, 13⅞; 1872, 14⅝; 1873, 17½; 1874, 14, or about that, as the cotton of 1874 is not yet all gathered; but I will not miss the figure by ½ cent. The other accounts are from a diary kept of expenses and profits. I mean that includes all the costs; and all over the figures was clear profit, and all under clear loss to the producer. So you see that in 1873, when we got 13½ cents per pound, my actual loss was 4 cents per pound, and in 1866, my actual profit was 20 cents per pound, as I sold for 28½ cents. The great difference of cost from 1867 to 1873, 10¼ cents per pound, was caused by my inability to govern and control labor and make it effectual, the high price of labor, and the great demand for it, with the use of high-priced guano. This has no reference to any one else but my own farm.

I am, very truly, your obedient servant,

J. S. LAVENDER.

Sparta, Ga., November 15, 1874.

DEAR SIR: You ask me what it costs me to make cotton. At one time I could have told you its cost per pound; but what it costs to make it now depends on so many contingencies it cannot be estimated beforehand. I have sixty or seventy tenants, and it costs no two the same to make cotton. It depends on the price of labor and its efficacy, direction of the sun and rain, time and quantity; worms, caterpillars, storms, frost, and land, as well as many other things. Crops vary from one bale to eight bales per hand.

There is one thing certain: When cotton is below 16 cents, the tenant and landlord, in four cases out of five, lose money. For example: Two hands, on an average, in Georgia, without manure, will make about 3 bales each, making 6 bales, planting 12 acres each in cotton, making 24 acres; 6 acres each in corn, making 12 acres; that is, per each mule, 36 acres. You may say this is low average, but it is high enough as Georgia now is.

6 bales cotton, 2,400 pounds lint, 16 cents	$384	00
6 bushels corn per acre on 12 acres, at $1 per bushel	72	00
Fodder	7	20
	463	20
Less rent of land	115	80
	347	40

1 mule and feed	$175	00		
Tools, machinery, and horses	20	00		
Hire of two hands	240	00		
Use of house, board, and wood	120	00		
	555	00		
Loss			207	60

You may say my estimate is too low. Then add to the product 33⅓ per cent., making $463,20: still a loss of $91.80. Add on 50 per cent., making 4½ bales per hand and 9 bushels corn, and amounting to $521.10; still a loss of $33.90.

Who will say a hand will make 4½ bales of cotton without manure and 54 bushels of corn, which is in the last estimate? I can see very plainly what causes so much loss and hard times. The planter furnishes every thing — houses, gardens, patches, and the best wood on his place, free of charge. The true plan is to pay for all you get, and get pay for all you let go. The planter furnishes house, wood, fruit, garden, and patches, for three persons, to get poor labor out of one — out of proper time, poor in quality, &c.

Very respectfully,

DAVID DICKSON.

In view of the statements contained in these letters, it cannot be said that for the last ten years the price of the great staple of the South has been remunerative. On the contrary, taking the average of cotton-planters throughout the South, has not the cotton-crop been produced and sold at a positive loss? The mere fact that this question is even debatable proves that, if there has been a general profit, it has been very small. It is worthy of notice that in none of these letters is there an allowance made for the personal supervision of the planter. A large portion of cotton-planters are educated men, who could command salaries in other pursuits. Their time is money, and its value should be included in the estimate of the cost of cotton-culture.

Improvement or Deterioration of the Soil

This point has been partially met in the foregoing remarks. A very large proportion of the cotton-lands of the South contains a material admixture of sand. In fact, a certain proportion of sand is indispensable to successful cotton-culture. Wherever such a soil is undulating, and is submitted year after year to shallow plowing, it must not only become poor by the surface being washed away, but hideous and deep gullies are formed. The writer, who has passed his three-score years, well remembers lands that were originally covered with wild-pea vines, luxuriant grasses, and magnificent forests which now, in their excoriated and gullied surface, are sad mementos of the wasteful improvidence of their owners.

Since the war there has indeed been a vast expenditure of money for the purchase of commercial fertilizers. Three or four years since the farmers of Georgia expended, according to the testimony of the state inspector of fertilizers, $10,000,000 in one year for these fertilizers. These were not designed or expected to improve the land. They were homeopathic doses to increase a single crop. Under this system of exclusive cotton-culture, accompanied by shallow plowing and the use of commercial fertilizers merely to increase a single crop, the lands of the cotton States are growing annually poorer instead of richer. There are of course honorable and marked exceptions to this hurtful practice. The general usage, with the general result, has, however, been correctly stated. The traveler who passes through the cotton-belt of the southern states will be struck with the constant recurrence of worn and impoverished plantations, with here and there a pleasant exception.

Judging by the test given, it must be conceded that the agricultural condition of the cotton States is generally far from being prosperous. The value of the lands is low, the price of the staple crop is unremunerative, and the lands are in a course of impoverishment.

Methods of Improvement

The remedy for this low condition of southern agriculture is to be found in the abandonment of exclusive cotton-culture and the devotion of a much larger area to the growth of the cereals, the grasses, and the raising of live stock.

It is not designed to advocate the abandonment of cotton. This would be a supreme folly. In many respects this plant is the most beneficent boon of a kind Providence to man. No other plant is capable of so great a variety of uses. Its seed affords an excellent oil for the table, and for lubrication, or for conversion into soap. The meal left after the oil is expressed possesses greater flesh-forming properties for the domestic animals than any other food which can be given them, Indian corn not excepted. The seed in its natural state, or when converted into meal, has greater manurial value than any other single substance. . . .

A country in which cotton is judiciously grown, and in which the various manufactures for which it affords the raw material are in successful operation, and which supplies the food for its own laborers, can support a more dense population than any other portion of the globe. Yet this invaluable blessing, like other misused blessings, may be converted into a scourge. Although capable of this vast utility, it may be questioned whether the cotton-plant has been of greater benefit or injury to the Cotton States. Few persons not living in these States can form an idea of the extent to which it has monopolized the attention of southern land-holders. For instance, the comptroller-general of the state of Georgia informs us that in 1873 there were produced in the state 504,253 bales of cotton, worth, at 15 cents per pound, $75 per bale, amounting to $37,818,975. Yet it cannot be doubted that its agricultural population, taken as a whole, were poorer at the end than at the beginning of the year. Little of the proceeds of the crop remained in the State, except that which was paid in money for labor; almost the whole was expended in fertilizers, bacon, corn, flour, mules, &c.

The population of Georgia, in round numbers, is 1,200,000. The crop of corn, in 1873, was 10,025,013 bushels; of wheat, 847,455 bushels; of oats, 1,553,003 bushels. The number of horses and mules was 171,223. Allowing 50 bushels of corn a year to the horse or mule, they would require at that rate 8,561,150 bushels. Deducting this amount from the whole corn-crop, it would leave for the support of the 1,200,000 people 1,463,863 bushels of corn for a year. This would be at the rate of less than 1.4 bushels of corn and about .7 of a bushel of wheat for the sustenance of each person, leaving nothing for the 794,527 hogs and 608,379 oxen and other cattle. There must have been at least 12,000,000 bushels of corn brought into the state during that year. This is about the condition of things throughout the cotton states. Can it be a matter of wonder that they are in a depressed condition? Every one who handles a cotton-bale prospers except the man who produces it. Three years ago the writer by careful estimate ascertained that $26,000,000 worth of the necessaries of a farmer passed over the Western and Atlantic Railroad from the West *via* Chattanooga to Atlanta, all of which could have been produced in Georgia. They consisted of horses, mules, hogs, cattle, sheep, corn, wheat, bacon, flour, &c. Can we wonder that the cotton-planter is poor and in debt? We see what becomes of the proceeds of the cotton-crop. The exclusive culture of cotton demoralizes the negroes.

In this connection it will not be improper that the writer, as a southern man, while he condemns the faults of the blacks, and they are very numerous and vexatious, should do justice to that which is praiseworthy in their character and conduct. During the war, while the men were in the army, our wives and children were at the mercy of our servants. Their conduct generally was beautiful. Never were they more orderly, subordinate, industrious, and respectful. The southern people owe them a debt of gratitude, which they will repay, if they are left free to act. This, without question, is the general, not universal, feeling among former slaveholders. No sensible man would venture an assertion like this, in a way so public, without being assured of its correctness.

It was apprehended if the war terminated unfavorably to the south, that the scenes of Saint Domingo would be re-enacted among us. This apprehension was based upon the well-known fact that among ignorant persons, new-found liberty is often followed by a temporary intoxication leading to great excesses — to violence and bloodshed. These apprehensions were unfounded. There has been rarely violence, bloodshed, or excess, save in those instances in which they have been incited by crafty and bad white men of southern as well as northern origin. If there had been no wicked interference on the part of these men, the "enteinte cordiale" between the blacks and the whites by this time would have been nearly or wholly restored.

Exclusive cotton-culture demoralizes the blacks in this way: The labor on a cotton-plantation where a full crop is planted is without intermission, and it is excessive in the quantity required, often exceeding in cost in a single year the whole salable value of the plantation. For instance a plantation of 1,000 acres which could not be sold for more than $5,000, if 500 acres are planted in cotton would require thirty hands. These at $12 per month and rations, say, including both, would be $15 per month, or $180 per annum. The wages of thirty hands would amount to $5,400 per annum. Fifteen horses or mules would be required to plow these 500 acres. Allowing $100 as the annual cost of each horse or mule, including wear and tear, loss and food, the aggregate amount would be $1,500. Adding this to the cost of human labor, it gives the amount of $6,900 for labor on a plantation worth $5,000. This condition of things is anomalous and ruinous. To this should be added the fact that the average yield of cotton in Georgia, according to the sworn returns to the tax-receiver, is one bale to three and one-half acres.

Such is the demand for labor in those sections in which exclusive cotton-culture is practiced, that the planter is compelled to take any labor that offers, whether it be good, bad, or indifferent. The exclusive cotton-planter belongs practically to the negro, as the negro once belonged to him. He is at the mercy of the negro and the latter knows it. It is human nature, whether white or black, to presume upon such knowledge. The planter cannot demand a certificate of character, for he is only too glad to obtain the labor on any terms. If the laborer behaves badly and is discharged, he is indifferent to it, because he can get employment on the next plantation. This condition of things is eminently hurtful, both to the laborer and the employer.

If but half the usual quantity of cotton were planted, the value of the crop would be about the same, and but half the labor would be required. From this surplus the planter could make selections, employing the industrious and rejecting the idle and worthless. He could demand certificates of character as is usual in other countries in the employment of servants. This would make character valuable among the blacks, as without it they could not obtain work. So long as the laborer thinks he is conferring a favor on the person who employs him, so long his position is not dependent on his good conduct, so long will he be insubordinate, unreliable, and his employer will suffer. The interest of the planter and a due regard to the improvement of the laborer, require the reduction of the cotton area one-half.

While pointing out this great defect in our labor system, it is not designed to advocate any change except the improvement of the labor we now employ. The attempt to introduce hired white men from any quarter to carry out the exclusive cotton system is, from various causes, preposterous.

In the southern climate, with the habits of the people and the wages they can afford to pay, no laborer can be a substitute for the negro. He, as such, may and must be improved. A prominent method of this improvement has been pointed out, viz, by creating competition and thus giving value to character.

The cotton states do greatly need skilled white labor in the dairy, the orchard, the vineyard, the mine, the manufactory, and the trades. If a judicious system of farming were adopted, such as is practiced at the North and in Europe, in which the amount of plowed crops bears but a small proportion to the land in the cereals, meadow, and pasture, the present farm-labor of the South in number is abundant.

If they would improve their farm-labor, planters must live on their own estates. Absenteeism must be abandoned. Formerly, it was the practice of many planters to live in the towns and cities, while their plantations, managed by overseers, were perhaps hundreds of miles distant. . . .

The writer has devoted anxious and prolonged thought to the solution of the labor-question at the South. In the cotton states, we can use in farm and household work no other servant than the negro. He was placed here, not by us, but by persons in other states and from other countries, who derived the profit of his importation. We cannot remove him if we would, and we would not remove him if we could. Though, as a general rule, with some, and it might be said, with numerous exceptions, he is thievish, indolent, unreliable, improvident, and without regard to contracts, still he is very capable. As he cannot be removed, he must be improved. The attempts at this improvement thus far have been mere surface-efforts. No attempts at intimidation, no forms of contract, no combinations among planters, no penalties of the law, can effect this improvement. It must include the whole present system of southern agriculture. It will require such changes in our mode of farming as will enable us to accomplish our ends with less than one-half of the labor which we at present employ. The negro must be made to feel that in order to eat he must work, and that in order to obtain work he must be honest and industrious. The landholders have it in their power to accomplish this result by requiring on their farms less labor, and in their selection employing laborers only of good character. Self-interest and humanity both require this change. . . .

There are, however, alleged difficulties in the proposed change in southern agriculture. It is said that we cannot grow the artificial grasses common in England and at the North, and that therefore we cannot raise hay and live stock to advantage. . . .

But it is not true that artificial forage, plants, and grasses will not flourish at the South. They will not thrive on very sandy land or poor land of any kind; but where the soil has a substratum of good clay, and where it is naturally or artificially rich, and proper seasons for sowing are adopted, and proper precautions taken afterward, and the soil in proper tilth, the uncertainty of success is not greater than with a crop of cotton, corn, wheat, or oats. It is true that the hot summers are against them, but not more than the intense cold of the northern winter. Proper care will ordinarily obviate the bad effect of the summer's sun; that care is not to allow these grasses to be grazed during the summer, allowing the grass to fall and cover the roots from the sun's rays. Even with this loss of June, July, and August, the period of grazing is longer at the South than at the North, because it includes the whole of the spring, autumn, and winter. Lucern, red and white clover, orchard, timothy, herds, or red-top, tall meadow-oats, Italian rye-grass, and blue-grass will all grow on soils suitable for them. This is not mere theory; the practical proof is found in every one of the cotton states.

But the cotton-planter objects that he has attempted and seen others attempt the cultivation of these grasses, and that both he and they have failed; so they have failed, perhaps, for successive years with cotton, and yet they continue to plant it. One or several failures do not discourage them. The fact is, that the whole subject of grass-culture is so new to them, it is so foreign to their practice, which has been to kill grass, that it is no wonder that they make mistakes; by reading and inquiry they should learn how to correct these mistakes, and persevere until success has crowned their efforts; others, who once thought as they do, have persevered, and now they are the pleased owners of meadows and pastures.

One plant, in this connection, deserves the especial attention of the southern planter; that plant is lucern, the alfalfa of Chili and California. Lucern is a child of the sun, suffering less from heat and drought than, perhaps, any other forage-plant. Its tap-root, which becomes in three or four years as large as a medium-sized carrot, penetrates a number of feet in the ground and pumps up moisture and nutriment from below. Its requirements are very rich, clean, and dry land. These requirements being filled, it will, after the first year, yield from three to six, and even eight tons of hay, preferred by horses, cattle, and sheep to any other hay whatever. It will thrive from Texas to Virginia. It is the great reliance of the Swiss and French farmers. It will not succeed in England, as there is not sufficient sun; neither does it succeed at the North, because it is too cold in winter. It should be the main reliance of the southern farmer for soiling and hay. . . .

Our ordinary method of raising hogs, letting them run in the woods until they are two years old, and then putting them up to fatten, is very expensive. After they are put in the pen, they require usually ten bushels of corn to fatten them, besides the other food which they have previously destroyed. An additional and serious item of previous cost arises from the sagacity with which woods hogs ascertain all holes and rotten rails in the planter's fences, and by which they are enabled to maraud upon the growing crops. The same ten bushels of corn, if fed to a pig confined in a pen or lot near the dwelling, would make the same amount of pork in one year as is made in the ordinary way in two years. If the pen or lot is well littered, although the cost of the pork might be even a little greater than the market-price, the manure will give a moderate profit. It is a good deal cheaper to obtain manure from our own farm-pens than from the Chincha Islands. If hogs are raised in this way, which on the whole is the cheapest way, he must be a very sleepy-headed planter who cannot protect them when they are within gunshot of his house. . . .

If there be one class of men rather than another throughout this great country, whose duty and inclination it is to forget the painful past and to cultivate and maintain peaceful relations with their fellow-beings, it is the tillers of the earth, which brings forth its fruits alike to the industrious wherever found, and which is the handiwork of Him whose great glory it is to dispense ''peace on earth and good will to men.'' In the exhibition of this kindly temper, no portion of the great brotherhood of farmers will be more decided than the planters of the South.

The Montgomery Ward Catalog, 1875

From Montgomery Ward & Co., *Catalogue*, 1875.

In offering you this (our 13th) Catalogue, we feel called upon to thank our friends for their kind support.

We have now, in consequence of liberal patronage, reduced our prices on every article where there was any chance to do so (as you will find by comparing), and have added largely to our list.

You will find full instructions regarding the manner of making out your orders, etc., on the succeeding pages, which *we desire you will follow*, and thus avoid, as nearly as possible, all delays, errors and misunderstandings.

The original plan of conducting our business, suggested by the growing combination of farmers to deal directly with a house near the base of supplies, was to ship goods by Express, collect on delivery (*i.e.* C.O.D.) only; but as time passed and strangers became friends, the necessity of reducing the expenses of transportation became apparent, and we allowed goods to go by Freight to Granges, when the Grange seal was affixed to the order.

COTTON GOODS.

Numbers.		Price per yard.
1	Standard Prints, good style	7½
2	Best Prints, new work	8½
3	Best Prints, in Pink, Purple, Blue and Green figures	9½
4	Ginghams	9
5	Ginghams, best	11
6	Chambrays in all colors, (give color)	25
7	Fine Brown Sheeting	8
8	Fine Brown Sheeting	10
9	Fine Brown Sheeting, 1 yard wide, extra	12
10	Fine Brown Sheeting, 40 inches wide	12

HOOP SKIRTS AND CORSETS.

		Each.
965	Lotta Hoop Skirts, white, 20 springs, 5 tape	50
966	Lotta Hoop Skirts, white, 25 springs, 5 tape	75
967	New Style Hoop Skirt, no hoop at the top	75
968	Belle Bustles, good style	25
969	Good Satin Jean Corset	45
970	Champion Corset, imported expressly for Montgomery Ward & Co.	60
971	Fine French Corsets, 48 bone & nicely trim'd	1 25

BUTTONS.

980	72 dozen White Agate Shirt Buttons for	35
981	72 dozen large White Agate Buttons for	55
982	72 dozen extra large White Agate Buttons for	80
983	12 dozen Pearl Shirt Buttons	75
984	12 dozen clear Pearl Shirt Buttons	1 00
985	12 dozen fine Pearl Shirt Buttons for	1 25
986	12 dozen black Horn Vest Buttons for	37½
987	12 dozen black Horn Coat Buttons, medium size, for	75

Of the many other advantages which MURRAY'S CELEBRATED WAGONS claim to have over all others manufactured in this country, the following are the principal ones, viz:

1st. The Wagons are better Ironed than all others now manufactured in the country; the Bolsters are all plated on top.

2d. The Axles are plated in the centre, where the Reach and the King-Bolt are working, which prevents the Axle from being worn out.

3d. The front bounds are braced solid to the axles, which will hold the hounds solid until the Wagon is worn out.

4th. All Axles are turned out by the Axletree Lathe Machine, and are therefore, exactly alike in every regard, which gives the great advantage over those made by hand, that every axle has the same set and gether, which enables us to furnish a new axle in the place of such as may be broken by some accident; and, as it is exactly a duplicate, any farmer can put it in in a few minutes, and the wagon will run as easy and light as ever before, saving time and expenses in going to a mechanic.

DESCRIPTION OF WAGONS AND PRICE.

Delivered on board Cars, at Niles, Michigan.

No. 1. One-horse, Thimble Skein, 2¼ in. Spindle, with Spring Seats and Thills, 1¼ × ⅜ Tire..............................$50 00

No. 2. One-horse, Iron Axle, 1¼ in. Spindle, with Spring Seats and Thills, 1¼ × ⅜ Tire...................................... 55 00

No. 3. One-horse, Thimble Skein, 2¼ in. Spindle, with Spring under Box and Spring Seats and Thills, 1¼ × ⅜ Tire 60 00

No. 4. One-horse, Iron Axle, 1¼ in. Spindle, with Spring
   under Box, and Spring Seats and Thills,
   1¼ × ⅜ Tire 65 00

No. 6. Two-Horse, Thimble Skein, 3 in. Spindle, 1⅜ × ½
   Tire, with common Double Box...................................... 63 00

No. 7. Two-Horse, Thimble Skein, 3¼ inch Spindle,
   1½ × 9-16th Tire, with common Double Box 70 00

No. 8. Heavy Two-Horse, Thimble Skein, 3½ in. Spindle
   1½ × 9-16th and 1⅝ × ⅝ Tire, with common
   Double Box or Cotton Bed 72 00

No. 9. Two-Horse, Iron Axle, 1½ in. Spindle, 1⅜ × ½
   Tire, with Double Box 70 00

No. 10. Two-Horse, Iron Axle, 1¾ in. Spindle, 1⅝ × ⅝
   Tire, with common Double Box...................................... 75 00

Accompanying each Wagon, to make it complete, are 1 Doubletree, 2 Singletrees, 1 Neck-Yoke, 1 pair of Stay-Chains, 1 Wrench and 1 Spring Seat.

All Thimble Skein Wagons have Hickory Axles, and the Wheels and the Gearing are made of the Best Quality of Oak and Hickory, all *Thoroughly Seasoned and Warranted*

Brake...............$4.50 Extra.

––––––––––

DESCRIPTION OF BUGGIES, AND PRICE,

Delivered on board of Cars, at Niles, Michigan.

No. 1. Piano Box, Open ....$125 00   With Top...............$230 00
No. 2. Coal Box, Open .... 125 00   With Top.............. 230 00
No. 3. Yacht Box, Open............ 125 00   Wiyh Top 230 00
No. 4. Square Box, Open.. 110 00
No. 4. Square Box, Open, with Top 180 00
No. 5. Two-seated Open Carriage 150 00

All Fine Buggies with SARVENT'S PATENT WHEELS. and the best Axles and Springs that are made.

All Light Bodies are made of Hard Wood, and the Gearings are all of Second-growth Hickory.

We can put from 22 to 25 Wagons on a Car. No Wagons shipped, unless the order is accompanied by the money, or has the "Grange Seal" attached. We shall require our money within 10 days from date of shipment.

MONTGOMERY WARD & CO.

Agricultural Products in Nevada, 1874

From John J. Powell, *Nevada: The Land of Silver* (San Francisco, 1876), pp. 187–89.

Table Showing the Agricultural Products for 1874.

GRAIN, ETC.	ACRES SOWN.	GROSS YIELD, BUSHELS.	AVERAGE PER ACRE.
Wheat	4,346	73,600	17
Barley	26,651	506,790	19½
Oats	5,372	74,695	14
Rye	100	1,000	10
Corn	493	3,450	28
Buckwheat	12	200	17
Peas	326	3,450	10½
Beans	53	590	11
Potatoes	4,136	290,458	70
Sweet potatoes	¼	24	96
Onions	76	4,216	55½
Hops	1	125 lbs	125

Beets, number of tons raised 314
Turnips, number of tons raised 320
Pumpkins and squashes, number of tons raised 5,352
Butter, number of pounds 22,200
Wool, number of pounds 668,738
Honey, number of pounds 7,400
Acres of hay cut, 72,101 .... yield, 77,626 tons.

Fruit Trees

Apple, 25,782; peach, 5,069; pear, 2,874; plum, 3,364; cherry, 1,506; nectarine, 276; quince, 316; apricot, 158; fig, 97; lemon, 2; gooseberry, 13,024; raspberry, 5,500; strawberry, 74,100; grape vines, 32,526.

Domestic Animals

Horses, 22,131; mules, 4,530; asses, 202; cows, 49,895; calves, 28,005; beef cattle, 75,082; oxen, 5,793. Total number of cattle, 185,638.

Live Stock

Sheep, 185,486; Cashmere and Angora goats, 2,439; hogs, 5,290; chickens, 49,202; turkeys, 2,050; geese, 355; ducks, 4,444; hives of bees, 662.

Improvements

Grist mills, 14; lumber mills, 27; lumber sawed, 3,480,000 feet; quartz mills, 143; tons of quartz crushed in '73 and '74, 1,263,392; mining ditches, 7; miles in length, 35.

California Agriculture, 1878

From E. W. Hilgard, "The Agriculture and Soils of California," U.S. Department of Agriculture, *Annual Report*, 1878, pp. 476–507

Agriculture in California possesses many peculiarities, arising partly from climatic causes, and partly from the somewhat exceptional history of the industrial development of the State. From the condition of total neglect in which it was left during the prevalence of the mining fever, it has, in the course of a few years, risen to be the commanding industry of the State. But unlike the great agricultural States of the Mississippi Valley, California has not undergone the slow and regular process of settlement by pioneer farmers, who, fleeing from the too close approach of towns and neighbors, as well as from soil exhaustion, keep selling out and moving west as part of their normal existence. The great tide-wave of the rush for gold cast a far different material on the shores of the Pacific; and when the placer mines ceased to yield fortunes to the men of small means, and agriculture began to attract their attention as a surer mode of acquiring the coveted metal, very many of the hands that grasped the plow had never felt its touch before, while their owners would have been at a loss to distinguish a grain-field from a meadow; but among these, as well as among those who at that time returned to the plow after a few years' digression, there was an unusual proportion of progressive, thinking, and reading men, whose ambition and energy had carried them forward when others fainted by the wayside. Both classes of men soon discovered that in a great many respects the rule-of-thumb experience and practice of the older countries would not avail them here; and casting loose from precedent, they tried a "new deal" in constructing for themselves a practice adapted to the new conditions. One of the controlling features being the scarcity and high price of labor, the introduction of labor-saving machinery was among the very first needs, instead of being a late fruit of long discussion and costly experience. Inasmuch as all such implements had to be brought from the East at great expense, it was the obvious policy to bring only the best. But many even of these were soon found to be behind the requirements of California progressiveness, and home invention and manufacture soon set to work, hand in hand, for still farther improvements. The great Moline plow and the sulky cultivator of the Western States were combined into the gang-plow, and the self-binding reaper was rendered superfluous by the gigantic header, which dispenses with both binding and stacking. Finally, to save time and handling still farther, we are threatened with a combination of the header and thrasher, whereby the grain is almost automatically sacked, ready for shipment to Liverpool, within a minute or two of its removal from the stalk on which it grew. The steam-plow and steam-wagon, whenever their time comes, will nowhere find as warm a welcome as in California. In curious contrast to this refinement of perfected appliances stands the crude system of culture in which they are employed. In direct proportion to their efficiency they aid in robbing the soil more rapidly of the accumulated treasures of a thousand years; and soil-exhaustion progresses with long strides, leaving far behind the puny efforts of the growers of wheat and corn in the Western States, and successfully emulating the ruinous system of cotton-planting in the South. Outside of truck-gardens, vineyards, and to some extent orchards, the only means of soil improvement thus far practiced on a large scale is the summer-fallow, not even the rotation of crops being as yet recognized in any great degree as a necessary means of husbanding the resources of the soil. Nothing can in this respect be more eloquent than the fact that the two establishments in San Francisco now manufacturing bone and meat manures from the slaughter-house offal have to seek and do find a ready market for their products in New Zealand and Australia. But it is not an easy task to persuade the Californian farmer that his methods are not what they should be. Having been obliged to discard a good many of the old-country practices, his conviction that things in California are altogether different, exceptional, and without precedent, is strong and deep-seated; and certain experiences had with "experts" at the mines in olden times have left him a strong impression that not only a new practice but a new science will have to be set up to meet the case of California.

It is undoubtedly true, that suggestions for advantageous changes in time-honored practice have to be made with unusual caution by any one not thoroughly familiar with the peculiarities of a California climate and its possible unexpected developments. It is proverbial that "no two seasons are alike," and that "the oldest citizen" is apt to be more cautious in his predictions of the weather than the novice, who allows himself to be misled by his eastern experience, while neither usually comes very near the mark. It is impossible to discuss intelligently the peculiarities of agriculture in California without adverting somewhat in detail to the climatic features upon which the former depend. It is self-evident that within a coast State, stretching through ten and a half degrees of latitude (as far as from Boston to Southern Georgia), and diversified with mountain chains, local climate must vary greatly; and he who cannot find within these limits some spot to suit his tastes must be fastidious indeed. In matter of fact, the seasons in the most northerly counties of the State resemble much more nearly those of Oregon than those of Middle and Southern California in the amount and distribution of the rainfall, the governing influence which chiefly determines agricultural peculiarities everywhere. It is, therefore, mainly the southern three-fourths of the State of California I propose to consider here. Within these limits, which embrace the most populous and most generally known portions of California, there is also, of course, a wide diversity of local climates. The salient climatic feature of the whole, however, is that practically all the water relied on for the production of crops fall between the middle of November and the first of April. The rains come from the south, often accompanied by strong but steady winds; some times in storms lasting but a day, more frequently three days, and sometimes, with little interruption, for two or more weeks; they are unaccompanied by lightning, and thunder is rarely heard more than once a year in Middle and Southern California. It is during this rainy period that crops are made or undone; the impetus then given to vegetation must carry it to maturity, and the kind intensity of that "start" will, in the majority of cases, determine the ultimate yield. Rains of brief duration may fall before or after the epoch mentioned, or exceptionally in any month in the year; but if so, they are looked upon with indifference at best, and mostly with well-founded apprehension of harm, since they interfere with the plan of agricultural operations established on the average supposition that fully six months in the year will be practically rainless. When, moreover, it is understood that in a large portion of the region under consideration the average annual rainfall barely comes up to the minimum of 10 inches estimated to be necessary for the growth of a crop, while over most of the remaining portion the average does not exceed (except locally) twice and a half that minimum, it will be readily conceived that the California farmer watches the rain-gauge with the same feelings with which the Egyptian regards the nilometer; and as the latter counts his seasons by Nile-inundations, so the California farmer reckons his time by "seasons" instead of calendar years. It is of comparatively little interest to him how much rain has fallen from January to January, as exhibited in the usual form of meteorological tables; for the 40 inches of rainfall so shown as the aggregate of two consecutive years may have been so distributed as to leave him "high and dry" during one growing season, with an excess for the other.

In order to exhibit the "fat" and "lean" years of California, it is necessary to tabulate or plot the rainfall by "seasons"; and after some unsuccessful attempts to connect their recurrence with the eleven-year period of the sun-spots, a discussion of the observations of twenty-eight years now on record, Prof. G. F. Becker, of the University of California, seems to show the existence of a thirteen-year period between consecutive minima, the second minimum within the time of the American occupation having occurred in the season of 1876–'77, with a rainfall of only 10 inches at San Francisco, where the average is 23½ inches; while in some portions of the upper San Joaquin Valley, as at Bakersfield, as well as in the region of the Mojave Desert, there was not rainfall enough to start vegetation at all, and no ground not irrigated was broken that season. In autumn, 1877, much of that region resembled a well-swept barn floor. There is an Indian tradition that at one time toward the end of summer water was only found in pools in the Sacramento River, so little snow having fallen the previous winter that all streams ceased to flow. From information kindly furnished me by H. H. Bancroft, esq., of San Francisco, it appears that in the records of the early explorers of California, the year 1805 is known as the "hungry year," the drought having been extraordinarily severe; and nearly the same account is given of the year 1817. It will be observed that these dates indicate a period of twelve years between themselves, and that the interval from the latter date to 1877 — for those drought-years as yet no data have been found — is also divisible by the same number. It is quite intelligible that as the result of several concurrent causes the period may vary between such limits as twelve and thirteen.

It has been suggested that a study of the growth-rings of the ancient Redwoods and Sequoias might lead to the recognition of the laws governing the seasons through past ages; it being probable that the dry years would be represented by a smaller growth than the wet ones. Unfortunately, it appears that in California, as well as in other countries where there is no well-defined season of rest for vegetation, the formation of several growth-rings within the year is of frequent occurrence, so that even the estimate of the age of the great trees is thereby materially vitiated. I have seen on the face of a redwood plank, 8 feet wide, groups of three, seven, twelve, and even thirty closely contiguous rings, occupying spaces but little larger than the intervals between two rings elsewhere, making it appear clearly that the unraveling of their record requires more than mere counting and measuring. But whatever may be the precise period in general, the fact that the average rainfall in so many regions nearly approaches the minimum required for any crop, gives exceptional importance to the minor, or annual, as well as local variations of its amount and distribution. It thus happens that in each region experience has shown a certain average expectation of successes and failures of unirrigated crops, which is taken into account by the farmer in his calculations. It is not, of course, easy to obtain perfectly impartial figures in this regard, the more as each valley may differ from its neighbor, and differences of crops, cultivation, and soil come in for a large share of influence. Besides, the shortness of the rainfall during one "season" may be materially supplemented, and fair crops made, when the preceding season has been one of abundant rain, it being popularly said that there is a chance for a crop whenever the moisture rising from below and that coming from above have met. This naturally happens much sooner in land kept tilled than in such as has been left to crack open — given free access to the hot, dry air of summer. In such soil, in the San Joaquin Plains, no perceptible moisture is to be found at depths of three, and even four, feet at the end of the dry season, while in deeply tilled land it may be reached at 12 or 15 inches. Again, a slow and gentle falling of a small amount of water will do as much good as a larger amount falling violently and largely draining into the streams; while, on the other hand, a few days' prevalence of a dry "norther" may completely wipe out the effect of spring showers that otherwise would have turned the scale in favor of the producer.

For the middle San Joaquin Valley, with from 9 to 10 inches of average rainfall, the usual estimate for cereals is that about two full crops out of five will be made without irrigation, the proportion increasing toward the north and decreasing toward the south, until in the Mojave Desert, with only about 3 inches of rain, the chances of making a crop without irrigation are too remote to be considered. Since, however, the rainfall increases pretty regularly with the elevation, the slopes and valleys of the foot-hills of the Sierra will frequently bear crops when there is failure in the valley. On the seaward slope of the coast range, where the rainfall is considerably greater than at a corresponding height and latitude in the interior, the average proportion of successes to failures varies greatly with locality and soil. The summer fogs brought in regularly by the trade-winds, as well as the coolness of that season, serve to eke out largely a scanty rainfall wherever the coast winds have access. Thus Santa Barbara, with about 12 inches of rain, only claims at least two crops out of three. The country bordering on the Bay of San Francisco, six out of seven or eight, each of the tributary valleys differing in this respect; and one, that of Napa, with 30 to 34 inches on an average, claims that crops never fail for want of sufficient moisture.

Irrigation

It will thus be readily understood that it is difficult to overestimate the importance of artificial irrigation in the middle and southern parts of California. In the entire valley of the San Joaquin it is the condition-precedent of assured success in farming; which otherwise is nearly as full of risks as speculation in mining stocks, and to many has proved equally seductive and fatal; for in favorable seasons, the cereal crops of that region are prodigious, and successes therein have made many fortunes, which too often have again vanished into thin air on a repetition of the venture. The bordering mountains supply water enough for the irrigation of the whole region, at least so long as the forests on the Sierras shall be preserved; and where this supply has been made available, as in a number of the "irrigated colonies" of Fresno, Los Angeles, and other counties, the results have been most satisfactory in every point of view. Not only does the irrigated land produce certain and large crops, but also several such in a single season, if so desired. The land is thus rendered very valuable, is naturally divided into small parcels, and thus invites and favors a system of conservative and intense culture, which is the exact reverse of the general practice of American farmers, and cannot fail to exert a beneficial influence in improving the latter by the example of success thus set.

At the head of the Great Valley, in the tributary valleys on its east side, and in the comparatively narrow strip of land lying between the rivers and the Sierra, irrigating ditches are rapidly multiplying, though unfortunately, so far, not generally upon any comprehensive plan. In the vast and, when watered, profusely fertile plains on the west side but little has been done as yet toward irrigation, the cost of bringing water being too great for either a private purse or even for that of a corporation; for the small streams of the coast range can only be locally utilized. The projected great "West-side Irrigation Canal," which is to be fed by the headwaters of the San Joaquin, is now the subject of extensive surveys ordered by the State, and when constructed will, it is expected, redeem the whole of the valley from its scourge of drought and render it the garden of California. At many points, both in the valley and on the coastward slope, artesian wells have been successfully resorted to as sources of water for irrigation, even on a large scale.

The Climates

Taking as a convenient point of view the central portion of the State, the climates of California may, for agricultural purposes, be roughly classified as follows:

1. *The bay and coast climate.* — Its prominent characteristics are, first, the small range of the thermometer, caused by the tempering influence of the sea, the prevailing winds being from the west. The average winter and summer temperature at San Francisco thus differs by only about 5° Fahrenheit (50° and 51° respectively). Snow rarely reaches the level of the sea, and is sometimes not seen for several seasons even on the summits of the Coast Range. A few light frosts, with the thermometer at between 28° and 32° Fahrenheit for a few hours during the night, is the ordinary expectation for winter, while in summer the number of "hot" days on which the thermometer reaches 80° or more rarely exceeds eight or ten. These occur chiefly in September, and under the influence of the "norther," which causes the hot, dry air of the interior valleys to overflow the barrier of the Coast Range. Under a brilliantly clear sky, it sweeps over the mountains, accompanied by clouds of dust, and, like the hot breath of a furnace, it licks up all moisture before it, wilting and withering the leaves of all but the most hardy plants, cracking and baking the soil, loosening the joints of all wooden structures, whether wagons, furniture, or houses, and causing the latter to resound at night with the splitting of panels and similar unearthly noises, to the discomfort of the nervous sleepers, that at such times comprise the vast majority of the population. This universal infliction fortunately lasts but rarely more than three days, when the welcome sea-fog, which has been kept standing like a wall forty or fifty miles in the offing, gradually advances, and with its grateful coolness and moisture infuses fresh life into the parched vegetation and the irritable, panting population.

During the winter months the north wind is equally dry, but at the same time cold; and while it then sometimes lasts a week or more, it causes but little discomfort or damage, save occasionally to the young grass and grain. The second distinctive feature of the coast climate is the fogs brought in from the sea by the prevailing west winds or summer trades, as the result of their crossing the cold Alaskan current inshore. The sea-fogs, coming in regularly almost every afternoon from the latter part of June to that of August, and more or less throughout the year, often with a gorgeous display of cloud pictures, temper materially not only the heat, but also the summer drought; so that under their influence plants requiring but a moderate degree of moisture can, in a loose soil, grow throughout that season. In the latitude of San Francisco it thus happens that in the coast climate sub-tropical and northern plants may thrive side by side; the latter (such as currants and cranberries) ripening with ease and in great perfection, while the fig, grape, orange, &c., though growing luxuriantly, can ripen their fruit only in valleys protected by mountain ridges from the direct influence of the summer trade-winds. Thus while a broad river of fog may be pouring in at the Golden Gate, covering the two cities and spreading out on the opposite shore to a width of eight or ten miles, the hamlet of San Rafael, only fourteen miles to the north, but under the lee of Mount Tamalpais, and the old town of San José, under the protection of its seaward mountains, forty miles to the south, are mostly basking in full sunshine, and ripen to great perfection not only the grape, but also the more tender fruits of their groves of fig and orange.

2. *Climate of the great interior valley.* — The *average* winter temperature is lower than that of corresponding portions of the coast, although the *minimum* is little, if at all, below that of the latter. Sub-tropical plants, therefore, winter there almost as readily as on the coast. In summer, however, the average temperature is high, often remaining above 100° Fahrenheit for many days, the nights also being very warm. At the same time, however, the air is so dry as to render the heat much less oppressive than is the case east of the mountains, sunstroke being almost unknown. Standing on the summits of the Coast Range in summer, and looking down upon the thick shroud of fog covering all to seaward, the white masses can be seen drifting against the mountain side, and, rising upward, dissolving into thin air as soon as, on passing the divide, they meet the warmth of the Great Valley. From points in the latter the cloud-banks may be seen filling the mountain passes and sometimes pouring like a cataract over the summit ridges, but powerless to disturb even for a moment the serenity of the summer sky, or to yield a drop of moisture to the parched soil of the San Joaquin Plains. The unwary traveler, starting from Sacramento or Stockton on a hot summer's day without the thought of shawl or overcoat, may find himself chilled to the bone on crossing the Coast Range, and runs imminent risk of rheumatism or pneumonia. On the other hand, the San Franciscan, feeling the need of having his pores opened by a good perspiration, can have his wish gratified in an hour or two by taking the reverse direction. The ''norther'' is, of course, more frequent in the great valley than on the coast; but its dryness and high temperature are not so much of a change from the ordinary condition of things, and it therefore does not cause such general remark, disturbance, or damage unless unusually severe.

3. *Climate of the slope of the Sierra Nevada.* — The essential features of the climate of the Great Valley may be roughly said to extend to the height of about 2,000 feet up its flanks into the ''foot-hills,'' with, however, an increasing rainfall as we ascend, and therefore greater safety for crops and less absolute dependence upon irrigation. Higher up, the influence of elevation makes itself felt; snow falls and lies in

winter, while the summers are cool; and we thus return to the familiar *régime* of seasons as understood in the Middle and Northern States, including, especially in the more northern portion, the phenomenon of summer thunder-storms, which are almost unknown on the coast and in the San Joaquin Valley. The same general features come into play more and more as we advance northward in the hilly and mountainous regions lying north of San Francisco Bay, toward the Oregon line, marked also in general by a gradual increase of timber growth. The features of the three principal climates described intermingle, or are interspersed, according as the valleys are open to seaward, run parallel to the coast, or are in communication with the great interior valley. We thus find numberless local climates, ''thermal belts,'' and privileged nooks adapted to special cultures which may be impracticable in an adjoining valley, and almost insular as regards the region where similar conditions are predominant. To the southward, the chief climates above defined are modified by three factors, viz: the increase of temperature, the decrease of rainfall, and the decrease, from about San Francisco southward, of the feature of summer fogs. As regards temperature, the extreme range is still very nearly the same at Los Angeles as at San Francisco; but the averages are very considerably higher at the former point, that of the winter being 60°, that of summer about 75° Fahrenheit. At intermediate points along the coast, local variations excepted, the averages vary as sensibly as the latitude. As to rainfall along the coast, its decrease is slow, descending from 24 inches at San Francisco to 15 at Santa Barbara, 12 at Los Angeles, and 9 to 10 at San Diego. But in the interior valley the decrease is much more rapid, as previously stated, modified locally, according as the divide of the Coast Range is so high as to preclude the access of moisture from the sea, or low enough to admit its influence. The same factor influences also the cooling and moistening effect of the summer winds and fogs, which temper the summer climate of the Los Angeles Plain, but fail to reach the Mojave Desert or the fervid plains of the upper San Joaquin Valley.

Soils of California

In a region of such vast extent, traversed by mountain ranges formed of rocks of all kinds and ages, there is of course an endless variety of soils, to describe all of which would be beyond the limits of the present article, even if the data were available. Unfortunately this is far from being the case, the geological survey having paid but little attention to the examination of soils, which, it is true, is a subject requiring special qualifications and care on the part of the observer to insure useful results. There are, however, some general features developed on a large scale in the more thickly settled parts of the State, a brief summary of which may find a place here.

It is well known that the main axis of the Sierra Nevada is formed by granitic rocks, which in the northern portion of the range, as well as on the slopes, are usually overlaid by clay slates and shales, forming the proverbial ''bed-rock'' of the gold-placers and gravel-beds. The soil derived either directly from the granites or from the older portion of the slates — in other words, the gold-bearing soil of the Sierra slope — is an orange-colored (commonly called ''red'') loam, more or less clayey or sandy according to location, and greatly resembles, on the whole, the older portion of the ''yellow loam'' subsoil of the Gulf States. Of course it contains much more of coarse materials in the shape of undecomposed rock, and its sand-grains are sharp instead of rounded. It is the predominant soil of "the foot-hills," and where ridges extend from these out into the Great Valley they are usually characterized by the red tint, which gradually fades out as the ridges flatten into swales in their approach to the San Joaquin and Sacramento Rivers, being lost in the gray or black of the "adobe," or the buff of the river-sediment soils. Its admixture is everywhere, I believe, found to be advantageous to the other soils; and in the foot-hills themselves it proves to be highly productive, as well as durable, easy of tillage, and what is termed a "warm" soil. The rocks of the lower slope of the Sierra, but more especially those of the Coast Range opposite, are predominantly of a very clayey character, soft gray clay shales and laminated clays alternating with ledges of soft clay sandstone and brittle horn-stone. Their mechanical and chemical decomposition results, therefore, in the forma-tion of gray, buff, or sometimes almost white clay soils, which occupy the hillsides and higher portions of the valleys, while in the lower portions the admixture of vegetable matter, especially in the presence of a comparatively large amount of lime, causes them to appear dark, and often coal-black. These soils constitute the "adobe," so often mentioned in connection with California agriculture. They are substantially the same, both as to tilling qualities and chemical composition, as the prairie soils of the Western and Southern States. Like these, they are rich in plant food, durable, and strong, yielding the highest returns of field crops in favorable seasons and under good culture, but sensitive to extremes of wet or dry seasons, and of course more in cultivation, as well as more liable to crop failures, than lighter soils. During the dry season the adobe soil, unless it has been very deeply and thoroughly tilled, becomes conspicuous by the wide and deep gaping cracks which traverse it in all directions, sometimes to a depth of several feet, precisely as in the "hog-wallow prairies" of the Southwestern States. Of course the effect of rains is here also similar in causing a bulging up of the masses between the cracks when the material which has fallen into the latter expands forcibly on wetting. Hence the "hog-wallow" surface is as familiar in California as in Texas; and the fact that a traveler outside of the Sierras in the dry season is rarely out of sight of some such land is eloquent as to the wide prevalence of the "adobe." On the steep hillsides of the Coast Range the sun-cracks aid in giving foothold to stock; and during the rainy season the water running into them to the bed-rock causes numberless land-slides, such as gave rise to the memorable case of Hyde *vs.* Morgan. As it is well ascertained that at a former geological period the entire interior valley, as well as the bay of San Francisco, was fresh-water lake basins, the bulk of the adobe soil would seem to represent ancient lake, or rather, perhaps, swamp deposits, which are therefore found in corresponding positions in most of the connecting valleys. On the bay we find usually only a narrow strip of sandy soil running along the beach; inland of this a level belt of black adobe (or at times salt marsh), from which there is a gradual ascent toward the foot of the Coast Range, the soil becoming lighter colored and mingled with bowlders and rock fragments. The nature of the materials, as well as the form of portions of this slope, characterizes them almost inevitably as the result of glacial action.

The peninsula on which San Francisco is situated is overrun with the dune sand drifted from the ocean beach for a distance of several miles south from the Golden Gate, so that the fixing of the sand and its conversion into soil is one of the chief problems of the gardens and parks of that city. The city of Oakland, also, is situated on a somewhat sandy, but nevertheless quite productive, soil; and land of a similar character, but stronger by admixture of the adobe, yet easily tilled, forms the soil of the fertile valleys in the plain lying between the eastern shore of the bay and the coast range, which are largely devoted to market-gardens and fruit-culture, and, farther from the cities, to that of barley. The comparative difficulty and more or less of uncertainty attendant upon the cultivation of the adobe soils, unless very thoroughly tilled, has caused a preference to be very commonly given to the lighter soils found nearer to the streams, which are formed of a mixture of the adobe with the river sediment, or, nearest the water-courses, of that sediment alone. It is suggestive of the character of the majority of California streams that the word ''bottom,'' used east of the mountains to designate the well-defined flood-plain, is scarcely heard in the State, the more indefinite and general term ''valley'' being in general use. The obvious reason is that there is in most cases no very definite terrace, but a rather gradual slope from the bank to the bordering hills. The Sacramento and San Joaquin have not, as a rule, raised their immediate banks perceptibly above the rest of the flood-plain, because the sediment they carry is not such as will subside at the slightest diminution of velocity, but is apt to be carried some distance inland. At the points of its upper course the San Joaquin, and in the lower portions both it and the Sacramento, subdivide into numerous sloughs traversing wide belts of more or less marshy flats, subject to overflow, and covered with a rank growth of ''tule.'' This name applies, strictly speaking, to the round rush *(Scirpus Lacustris)*, which occupies predominantly the tide-water marshes, here as well as on the Gulf of Mexico. The farther from salt water, however, the more it is intermingled with (or locally almost replaced by) other aquatic grasses, sedges, and cat-tail flag *(Typha)*, affording, together with the young ''tule,'' excellent pasture nearly throughout the the year. Here, as elsewhere in such districts, the cattle soon acquire the art of keeping themselves from getting bogged, by maintaining a sort of paddling motion when on peaty ground, while draught-horses require to be provided with broad ''tule-shoes.'' These tule lands, embracing a large number of rich and partly reclaimed islands, such as Union, Brannan. Sherman. and others, forming part of the counties of Sacramento, San Joaquin, and Solano, continue with varying width along the east shores of Suisun and San Pablo Bays, and up the tributary valleys of Napa, Sonoma, and Petaluma, nearly to the limit of tide-water. It is noteworthy that, as regards salubrity, the tules, at least so far as they are within reach of brakish tide-water, are less liable to malarious fevers than the upper portions of the great valleys.

The soil of the tule lands is of two principal kinds: sediment land, found chiefly along the Sacramento and other streams, carrying much ''slum'' from the hydraulic mines; and peaty land, more prevalent along the San Joaquin and its branches. The latter kind consists almost entirely of tule roots, in various stages of freshness and decay, to a depth of from two to twenty and more feet; in the latter case we have the ''float land,'' which rests on the water-table and rises and falls more or less with it. Like the ''Prairie Tremblante,'' near New Orleans, it often trembles under the tread of a man, but will nevertheless sustain herds of cattle without the least danger, its bulges forming places of refuge for them in time of high water. An excellent fuel has been made by pulping this mass and forming it into bricks like true peat. The tule lands were long thought to be worthless except for pasture purposes; but it has now come to be well understood that they are in large part of extraordinary fertility, and, if protected from overflow by levees, are almost sure to yield abundant crops every year, even in seasons when those of the uplands fail for want of moisture. In their reclamation the construction of levees is of course the first thing needful. The sediment land can then be taken into cultivation at once by the use of large sod-plows, resembling the prairie plows of the Western States. It is usual to burn off the rushes and native grasses previous to plowing, especially in the peaty lands where the blow would otherwise find no soil. But here the fire penetrates several feet down, either to the underlying soil or to moisture, leaving behind a layer of ashes so light that the plow is useless. At the proper season grain is then sown upon the ashes, and either brushed in or trodden in by sheep, and extraordinary grain crops are thus produced during the first years, the duration of fertility depending, of course, upon the soil underlying after the ashes have been exhausted. The tule lands bordering upon Tulare Lake are of a different character from those of the lower rivers. The soil is heavy, consisting of fine sediments mixed with gray clay and shell *débris,* contains a large supply of plant food, and with proper cultivation will doubtless prove as highly productive as are the soils of the Great Tulare Plains themselves.

The soils of the Mojave Desert seem on the whole to be rather light, whitish silts, of whose possible productiveness little can as yet be said, except that without irrigation culture is hopeless. In striking contrast with these close soils of the San Joaquin Valley are those which prevail south of the Sierras, San Fernando, and San Gabriel, in the Los Angeles Plain and its tributary valleys, the home of the orange, lemon, and olive in their perfection. The fine rolling uplands ("mesas") of that region are generally covered with a brownish, gravelly loam, from 8 to 20 feet in thickness, which, with tillage, assumes the most perfect tilth with ease. It is a generous, "strong" soil, varying locally so as to adapt itself to every variety of crop, yet readily identifiable by its general character from Los Angeles to San Diego. In most respects it may be considered a variety of the red soils of the Sierra slope already described, like which it appears to be pre-eminently adapted to fruit culture.

The soils of the plain to seaward of Los Angeles, and of the coast plains south of Santa Barbara generally, so far as not modified by the sediments of the streams, seem to be uniformly characterized by a very large amount of glistening mica scales, distributed in a rather sandy, dark-colored mass, destitute of coarse materials. They are easily cultivated and highly productive when irrigated, although not unfrequently afflicted with a certain taint of "alkali." This, however, when not too strong or salt, is here readily neutralized by the use of gypsum.

"Alkali" soil is the name used in California to designate any soil containing such unusual quantities of soluble salts as to allow them to become visible on the surface during the dry season, as a white crust of efflorescence. They are of course found chiefly in low, level regions, such as the Great Valley, and the plains to seaward of the Coast Range; sometimes in continuous tracts of many thousands of acres, sometimes in spots so interspersed with non-alkaline land as to render it impossible to till one kind without the other. The nature and amount of salts in these soils is of course very variable. Near the coast the "alkali" is often little more than common salt, and can be relieved only by drainage or appropriate culture. At times we find chiefly magnesian salts, when liming will relieve the trouble. But in the Great Valley the name "alkali" is in most cases justified by the nature of the salt, which almost always contains more or less carbonate of soda, and sometimes potassa. The presence of these substances, even to the extent of a fourth of one per cent., while it may do but little harm during the wet season, results in their accumulation at the surface whenever the rains cease, and the corrosion of the root-crown, stunting, and final death of the plants. But when stronger, as is too often the case, the seed is killed during germination. Moreover, land so afflicted cannot be brought to good tilth by even the most thorough tillage. Fortunately, a very effectual and cheap neutralizer of this, the *true* "alkali," is available in the form of gypsum, which transforms the caustic carbonates into innocent sulphates. Wherever the amount of alkali present is not excessive, the use of gypsum relieves all difficulties arising from the presence of the former. Moreover, analysis shows that in many cases large amounts of important mineral plant-food, such as potash, phosphates, and nitrates, accompany the injurious substances; so that when the latter are neutralized, the previously useless soil may be expected to possess extraordinary and lasting fertility. Abundant deposits of gypsum have been shown to exist in many portions of the State since attention has been directed to its importance in this connection.

On the eastern affluents of the Sacramento River, the American, Bear, Yuba, Feather, and other streams heading in the region where hydraulic mining is practiced, a new kind of soil is now being formed out of the materials carried down from the gold-bearing gravels. The enormous masses of detritus washed into the streams, filling their upper valleys to the height of 60 feet and more with bowlders and gravel, while a muddy flood of the finer materials overruns the valley lands in their lower course, have given rise to a great deal of complaint on the part of farmers; and the "mining *débris* question" has been the subject of numerous lawsuits, and of much angry debate in the legislative halls. In some cases the lands so overrun are definitively ruined; in others the new soil formed is of fair quality in itself, but as yet unthrifty; in many, the best quality of black adobe is covered many feet deep with an unproductive "slum." By the same agency, the beds of the Sacramento and its tributaries have become filled to such an extent as to greatly obstruct navigation and to cause much more frequent overflows, whose deposit, however, appears to improve, in general, the heavy lands of the plain, as well as the tules. It is difficult to foresee a solution of this question that would be satisfactory to all parties concerned; the more as the navigation of the bay itself is beginning to suffer from the accumulation of deposit, the reddish sediment-bearing waters of the Sacramento being always distinguishable in front of the city from the blue water brought in by the tides.

Natural Pastures

The most obvious agricultural consequence of the climatic features previously outlined is that meadows and permanent grass pastures, and even clover, are practically eliminated from the agricultural system of the State. They are possible only where artificial or natural irrigation supplies moisture throughout the season; and lands possessing this advantage are, thus far, as a rule, too valuable to be devoted to grass crops or pasturage. This sounds paradoxical in view of the fact that California is noted as a stock-raising country, and that her mountainsides and valleys may be seen dotted with herds and flocks throughout the season. The newcomer instinctively pities the poor beasts who seem to be turned out on these brown slopes to starve from June to December. And yet when he examines them more closely he finds to his surprise that they are sleek and fat, and are contentedly occupied in picking up from the parched and fissured soil something that satisfies hunger; varying their diet occasionally by browsing on the foliage of shrubs and the lower branches of trees. Several circumstances contribute toward rendering these "dry pastures" available. First, and perhaps chief among them, is the rapid transition from the growing season to the dry in May and June; whereby the grass and other eatable herbage is cured into hay *in situ,* instead of withering slowly and losing its nutriment by withdrawal into the roots, or washing into the soil by rains. Hence the occurrence of any heavy rain subsequent to the setting-in of the dry season is regarded as a calamity by stock-men; for it leaches the dry pasturage of its nourishment, renders it unpalatable to stock, and sometimes causes it to become moldy in part. From the same cause, the real lean and hungry season for stock is from the time when the rains have begun (October or November) to that when the new grass becomes strong enough to afford adequate pasture. The latter epoch, so anxiously looked for, varies greatly from year to year. A universal welcome greets the first rain (usually about the middle or end of October), washing the dust of months from the evergreen oaks and laurels, and allaying that of the roads, which has long shrouded every team in an earthy cloud. But it will not please the farmer if it exceeds the moderate amount needed to wash the face of nature, or possibly to enable him to start his plow; for if it should be sufficient to start "the grass" into rapid growth at that early period, the chances are that no more may fall until Christmas, or even later, and that instead a succession of dry northers may sear the tender blades, or even dry up their roots. When the rains set in later, in November, they are more likely to continue at short intervals; and then the grass will be in good condition for stock by Christmas. But at times (as in 1878–'79) they may be delayed until near Christmas; or having commenced early, they may be interrupted by a dry season (as in 1876–'77), when the grass may not be available until February, and stock, as well as meat-eaters, will have a hard time indeed. During the growing season numerous native and introduced grasses contribute to pasturage. On roadsides and in waste grounds one of the commonest and earliest is the wild barley (*Hordeum jubatum*), commonly called by an unfortunate misnomer "Foxtail Grass", which is relished by cattle in its early stages, but later becomes not only useless but a serious nuisance, in consequence of the tendency of its barbed and pointed spikelets to adhere to any moderately rough object, and, if penetrable, to penetrate it by a crawling process, which in the case of clothes soon brings it into unpleasant contact with the skin of the wearer; while as a component of hay, or in dry pastures, it is really dangerous. Among the best ingredients of the spring pastures are six or seven species of native clovers, mostly annuals, and perishing at the setting-in of the dry season.

Apart from sun-cured herbage, properly so called, an important ingredient of the "dry pastures" is the dry pods of the "bur clover" (*Medicago denticulata*). This hardy plant flourishes under difficulties that would discourage most other forage plants from even attempting to make a living. When in its season it disputes even the hardest trodden paths, roadsides, and pastures with such hardy weeds as the bird grass (*Polygonum aviculare*) and the yellow centaury (*Centaurea solstitialis, Tocalote* of the Mexicans). It lies close to the ground, with small leaves and flowers; but in time becomes noticeable from being crowded with its prickly pods, spirally rolled into pellets, whose hooked bristles cling tenaciously to the wool of sheep and impart to it the commercially unprofitable epithet of "burry."

But however objectionable from the woolgrower's point of view, these burs are among the most substantial ingredients of the "dry pastures," and are eagerly picked up by all animals, from the hog to the horse. This bur-clover is among the many plants of European derivation which have become so naturalized over the largest part of the State that few think of them otherwise than as native weeds. The Argonauts of 1849 already found the hills waving with the wild oat (*Avena fatua*) yielding a wild hay which at that time was sold at fabulous prices, and even now continues to be held in high esteem. Two species of crane's-bill (*Erodium cicutarium* and *moschatum*) are even more common here than in Southern Europe, and the first-named is esteemed as one of the most important natural pasture plants, being about the only green thing available to stock throughout the dry season, and eagerly cropped by them at all times. Its Spanish name of Alfilerilla (signifying a pin, and now frequently translated into "pin-weed") shows that it is an old citizen, even if possibly a naturalized one.

Weeds

To the process of naturalization of Old-World plants familiar to mankind, the California climate seems to be peculiarly adapted; for the commonest and most troublesome weeds of fields and roadsides are originally at home on the Mediterranean and Black Sea shores, and not usually found growing wild elsewhere. Thus the colza or rape-seed, under the common names of white mustard and wild turnip, everywhere takes possession of fields and waste places. The same is true, to a less extent, of one or two species of mustard proper (*Sinapis nigra* and *adpressa?*) and of the hedge-mustard (*Erysimum officinale*). Even the garden radish (*Raphanus sativus*) has escaped from cultivation to become a troublesome weed, often forming large patches, of a delicate rose-tint, in a landscape otherwise yellow with mustard and native poppies (*Eschscholtzia*). The larger mustard, often growing so high as to hide from view a man on horseback, is a formidable weed in portions of the San Joaquin and Sacramento Valleys, covering whole sections of land as a thicket, through which man or beast penetrates with difficulty. While the plants above mentioned embrace those immigrants whose coming and displacement of the native vegetation has exerted an important influence upon the face of the landscape and the operations of agriculture, there are numerous other weeds which, locally, give considerable trouble to the husbandman and gardener. The pimpernel (*Anagallis arvensis*), the spurrey (*Spergula arvensis*), several Old-World chickweeds, the omnipresent dog-fennel, hog-weed, or wild chamomile (*Anthemis Cotula*), and among the grasses the soft chess or brome grass (*Bromus mollis,* not unfrequently miscalled "buffalo grass"), the annual spear grass (*Poa annua*), the darnel (*Lolium temulentum*), a numerous contingent of the Goose-foot family (*Chenopodium album, Bonus Henricus, anthelminthicum,* several Amaranths (*A. retroflexus, spinosus,* and others), the two cockle-burs (*Xanthium spinosum* and *strumarium*), and other homely weeds, both of Europe and the Atlantic States, greet the immigrant with their familiar, if not altogether welcome, faces. The number of these is continually increasing, some being as yet confined to a few localities, as, *e.g.,* the mouse-tail (*Myosurus*) to the peninsula north of the Golden Gate; the Canada thistle to the neighborhood of Chico; while the common purslane (*Portulaca oleracea*) appears dotted, here and there, all over the State. The advent of some of these is still historically traceable to the importation of some particular lot of seed, or to the unpacking of a box or crate of goods packed in straw; and in view of the direct communication of California by sea with all parts of the world, there is, of course, no limit to the possibilities of the importation of both foreign weeds and insects, save such as is imposed by climate. The latter, however, is so peculiarly cosmopolitan and tolerant, permitting both the currant and the orange to flourish in the same orchard, that we may fairly expect the weeds and insect pests of India and Siberia to unite in worrying the Californian farmer hereafter, unless some preventive measures are taken. Even now, the weed question has assumed exceptional importance in the agricultural practice of California, in interfering with the otherwise so desirable practice of dry sowing in summer-fallowed ground; and it is notable that, among the weeds so interfering, there is scarcely one of material importance that is a native. The legislative action so far taken refers only to the Canada and Scotch thistles; and, curiously enough, the law misses its mark so far as the latter is concerned, the plant intended to be reached by it being in reality not the true Scotch thistle (*Onopordon*), but the milk thistle (*Silybum*). Among the many resinous, clammy plants popularly designated as "Tar-weed," formidable from their effects on the pants or skirts that brush by them, there are several native composites, and (on the Sierra slope) one of the Mimosa family, but none is more troublesome than the imported Madia (*M. Sativa*), which is everywhere found in fields and waste grounds, though nowhere, so far as I know, in cultivation for its oily seeds.

Forage Crops

As already stated, the rainless summers in the part of California under consideration exclude from its agricultural system, at least on unirrigated land, both permanent meadows and clover. The search for forage plants suitable for such climatic conditions was early begun and is far from being as yet concluded. The most obvious expedient, adopted at the outset and still supplying the bulk of dry forage, is the cutting of the ordinary cereal crops for hay before the grain ripens. "Wheat hay" and "barley hay," which with oats similarly cured constitute the main mass of the hay crop, are among the Californian oddities that first strike the agricultural immigrant. Most of the late-sown grain, as well as so much of the early sown as from any cause does not promise a good grain crop, and the "volunteer crop" that commonly springs up from the seed shed in harvesting the previous season's grain on land left untilled, is devoted to this purpose, for which it generally becomes fit some time in May, according to location. Oddly enough, embarrassment not uncommonly arises on fresh and strong land from the fact that the straw is so strong and tall as to render it unsuitable for curing into hay. A great deal, also, is cut at too late a period, when the grain is almost full grown — it being well known that it is then that the greatest total weight is harvested; the quality, however, is in that case of course injured.

During hay-making time (end of April to that of May) the weather is usually so dry that there is little difficulty about curing. There are no sudden thunder-storms to call for a hasty garnering of the hay. Sometimes, indeed, a late shower will give a superficial wetting to the shocks, necessitating their being scattered for drying; but with ordinary care in this respect there is rarely any excuse for damaged or musty hay. So little danger is there that injury from rains will occur after May, that the shocks are often left exposed for many weeks to the bleaching action of dew and sunshine. The regular practice, however, is to gather them into large rectangular ricks, built without much reference to protection from rain, but mainly with regard to the convenience for pressing into bales. This is mostly done by contract with gangs or "pressers," usually consisting of four men with a wagon and press, who perambulate the country from June to October. These men generally take up their lodgings under a hut of bales, which is all the protection needed at that season; and do their own cooking at some point outside of the ring of plowed ground with which, as a safeguard against fire, the ricks are circumscribed. Such hay-baling campaigns are sometimes chosen by persons needing a change from sedentary life as an opportunity for recruiting their health without expense, if not with much pecuniary advantage.

Even in this country, but little hay is handled in California without baling; and thus "bale-rope," from cut bales, is the universally recognized material for "tying up things," from a bundle to a broken wagon. Of late years soft iron wire has, to a considerable extent, come into use for baling hay; so that to stumble over a bundle of discarded "bale-wires" in the back yard is not at all out of the ordinary range of events.

Alfalfa. — Undoubtedly the most valuable result of the search after forage crops adapted to the California climate is the introduction of the culture of alfalfa; this being the name universally applied to the variety of Lucerne that was introduced into California from Chili early in her history, differing from the European plant merely in that it has a tendency to taller growth and deeper roots. The latter habit, doubtless acquired in the dry climate of Chili, is of course especially valuable in California, as it enables the plant to withstand a drought so protracted as to kill out even more resistant plants than red clover; as a substitute for the latter, it is difficult to overestimate the importance of alfalfa to California agriculture; which will be more and more recognized as a regular system of rotation becomes a part of the general practice. At first alfalfa was used almost exclusively for pasture and green-soiling purposes; but during the last three or four years alfalfa hay has become a regular article in the general market, occasional objections to its use being the result of want of practice in curing. On the irrigated lands of Kern, Fresno, and Tulare Counties, three and even four cuts of forage, aggregating to something like twelve to fourteen tons of hay per acre, have frequently been made. As the most available green forage during summer, alfalfa has become an invaluable adjunct to all dairy and stock farming, wherever the soil can, during the dry season, supply any moisture within two or three feet of the surface.

Grasses. — Of the ordinary pasture and meadow grasses of Europe and the East, but a few have to any extent gone into cultivation. One of the most unsuited to the climate, viz., Kentucky blue grass, is carefully nurtured by daily sprinklings as the chief ingredient of lawns, for which the Eastern immigrant generally maintains a preference, often satisfied at an inordinate cost of money and labor, and sometimes of health. As water for household purposes is almost universally kept under pressure from elevated tanks or water-works, the hose and lawn sprinkler are probably in more general use here than in any other country; and innumerable attacks of rheumatism and malarious fever are traceable to their intemperate use, even to the injury of the coveted grass itself. But few attempts have as yet been made to find an acceptable substitute for the costly blue-grass lawn. Among those which promise best are the Italian rye grass, which remains green all summer without irrigation in the bay climate; and, with proper treatment, doubtless the Bermuda grass could also be used. In either case, fully six out of seven weekly sprinklings might be dispensed with. This rye grass (*Lolium Italicum, multiflorum*) has in some districts become so naturalized as to be cut for "volunteer hay," while at other points it is regularly cultivated with irrigation, if needed. In the tule lands and other naturally or artificially irrigated regions, the soft meadow grass (*Holcus lanatus*), under the singularly inappropriate name of "mezquite," as well as the orchard grass (*Dactylis glomerata*) have come into use for pasture as well as hay; but the latter is not found in market. So of the millets (*Panicum Italicum, Germanicum*), which are locally in use. Of late various species and varieties of sorghum are coming into favor; among these especially the Dhoura, or Egyptian corn, and the pearl millet (*Pennicillara spicata*). Other forage plants are under trial in various portions of the state; but thus far none can compare in importance with the cereal grasses and alfalfa. It is probable that hereafter some of the native grasses and clovers, now considered as weeds only, will be found profitable for culture.

Stock-Breeding and Dairying

Prior to the American occupation, the breeding of sheep, horses, and, to a less extent, of neat cattle, roaming in flocks over the extensive ranches, was the chief occupation of the inhabitants; and to a great extent the remnant of the original Spanish-Mexican population still clings to the old pursuit, which affords an easy livelihood, and permits of indulgence in that *dolce far niente* which seems to be impossible to the "Americanos," however varied may be the nationalities that compose the population of the United States. It thus happens that even where the "ranch" and stock are owned by Americans, the herders are to a great extent still the native "vaqueros," who, mounted on their hardy mustangs, and with the old-time lasso (more properly "lazo"), coiled around the horn of their high Mexican saddles, and rarely more than a rope to guide their steed, may be seen careering around the steep hillsides with a disregard of all the ordinary precautions against the breaking of necks that is quite straining to the nerves of novice lookers-on. As a matter of fact, accidents very rarely happen to these wild riders; and their efficiency in keeping in bounds and "corralling" the cattle intrusted to their care, on the most rugged ground, is remarkable. It is but fair to say, however, that their practice has been quite successfully imitated by other nationalities, and that many a swarthy herdsman nowadays responds more promptly to the Saxon or Norse salutation than to that of the Mexican-Spanish dialect.

The purely pastoral method of stock-raising is, of course, gradually receding before the advance of agriculture proper to the more thinly settled regions; maintaining itself, however, in some of the large ranches owned by parties declining to sell to small farmers. The obvious disadvantage of being entirely at the mercy of the seasons, thus sometimes losing in a single dry year all the increase of a previous succession of favorable ones, has gone far toward the introduction of a safer system, in which the hardy and nutritious alfalfa serves to carry reduced numbers of stock of correspondingly higher quality safely through the dry months. In few States, probably, is the value of improved breeds more highly appreciated than in California; and nowhere, probably, can the best strains of the more important breeds be seen in greater perfection. The one domestic animal of common note, not as well represented in California as elsewhere, is the hog; the obvious cause of the comparative neglect being the absence of a sufficiently long and regular period of freezing weather, whereby the safe packing and curing of pork, hams, &c., is rendered too precarious. While, therefore, fresh pork of excellent quality is commonly found in the markets, the supplies of bacon, ham, and lard are, as a rule, furnished by the Western States, and partly by Oregon. Foremost in numbers among the rest is undoubtedly the *sheep,* in its double capacity of wool-bearer and producer of some of the best mutton in the world; a combination which has doubtless contributed much to the preference given it on the part of the somewhat inert native population. Easily satisfied with scanty pasturage, and in the southern part of the State scarcely needing shelter, the sheep is the very animal for the swarthy inhabitant of the adobe house, who loves to take his ease lounging on the airy veranda, asking of fate no luxury beyond a due allowance of cigaritos, and not at all envious of the greater comforts and riches of his unquiet, hard-working, and ever-scheming Saxon neighbor.

The common sheep of the country, while far from being a high-bred animal, is yet superior in many points to the stock commonly found in other countries, and its adaptation to the climate has rendered it profitable in cases where improved stock failed to pay. The Spanish Merino, whose blood doubtless runs in the veins of the native stock, seems to be best adapted to its improvement, and the best of this breed has been imported into the State. The wool-clip is among the most important products of South California; but it would seem that the attainment of the highest quality requires some change from the natural conditions of pasturage, which present too great a contrast between the wet and dry seasons to insure perfect uniformity of the fiber. This, however, can undoubtedly be accomplished by the introduction of the proper forage plants. In dry seasons, such as that of 1876–'77, the mortality among the larger flocks has sometimes amounted almost to annihilation. The sheep-owners of the plains, in order to save something, have driven their flocks to the foot-hills and valleys of the high sierras, leaving their route marked with the festering carcasses of the weaker animals, and sweeping every green thing before them, to the dismay of the dwellers in the invaded regions, who were thus sometimes themselves reduced to extremities. In ordinary seasons, this migration has its regular methods and routes, the herds ascending the mountains in the wake of the summer's drought, and returning to the foot-hills or plains to winter.

Of other fleece-bearing animals the Angora or Shawl goat has attracted considerable attention, and seems to succeed well; but the industry has not as yet assumed large proportions, chiefly, it seems, on account of the want of a regular market sustained by competition among the purchasers.

Of horses. — The Mexican mustang, a rather undersized yet hardy and serviceable, but proverbially tricky, race, descended from the Spanish breed, and therefore far from being inferior blood, still forms the greater portion of the horses in common use in California. The larger American horse brought from the Eastern States, although preferred for heavy work, is not so well adapted to the mountains and requires higher feeding. The two varieties are of course rapidly mixing, and better blood than that of many California studs it would be hard to find anywhere. Fast horses and fast men have here, perhaps, more than elsewhere been the bane of the agricultural fairs, whose real and important objects have, until lately, been most frequently swallowed up in that of an opportunity for betting and horse-racing, to the disgust of the agriculturists. The introduction of the more useful breeds has not, however, been neglected, as is evidenced by the fine Norman and Percheron dray-horses seen on the streets of San Francisco. A tolerable riding-horse can probably be bought for less money in California than anywhere else in the United States, the mustangs (which are generally of light build) being bred in large herds on pastures, with little care and therefore little expense. But when the excursionist pays twenty or thirty dollars for his steed he must not expect to find it trained to gentleness and affection, for the "breaking-in" process which these animals undergo on the ranches has but few of the features that Mr. Rarey would recommend. The unwary horseman will pay for his experience by many an unexpected nip or kick, or by being left on foot at inconvenient distances from his destination, in consequence of a dexterous slip of the rein from his arm, a sudden rush under a tree with low branches, or a "bucking" process of exceptional suddenness and violence. The mustang will, ordinarily, abandon these practices in proportion as it feels that the rider is "up to" its tricks; but the latter should never be found altogether off his guard against them, as he might safely do with a well-educated horse.

The *neat cattle* of California, previous to the American occupation, were chiefly of a type whose ancestry may still be seen on the pastures of Andalusia — a middle-sized race, lightly built, bearing medium, long, but aggressively-pointed horns, which, combined with an irritable temperament and a fair capacity for speed, render the proximity of a herd of these cattle not altogether pleasant to the novice. Like its cousin, the Texas Long-horn, now familiar to the West, it is a hardy, prolific race, yielding a fair quality of beef, and a thick and tough hide, well adapted either to the production of sole leather or to that of the strong rawhide thongs, which serve the Mexicans in place of rope, twine, nails, and other domestic appliances deemed indispensable by more pampered nations. As milkers, however, its cows are a failure; nor are its oxen remarkable for either docility or disposition to engage in agricultural pursuits, being the natural result of a nomadic life on wild pastures, from which they were driven in and "corraled," for branding or slaughtering, only a few times in the course of the year. All this, of course, has materially changed since the advent of the American. The immigrants brought their cattle with them over the plains, and found no reason to exchange the progeny of these for the pugnacious natives. The latter have, therefore, greatly diminished in numbers, and are little seen in the more populous regions, retiring before the advance of culture like their original masters. The gentler race that accompanied the Americans across the Rocky Mountains now dots the plains and foot-hills of the Great Valley of California; and since their weaker brethren mostly perished on that trying and weary voyage, a process of selection has taken place, as a result of which the worst breeds of "scrubs" are rarely seen in the State. Moreover, the tendency to improvement that is so apparent in the use of perfected appliances of every kind has manifested itself at least equally in the importation of the best breeds of neat cattle, among which the Short-horn, Jersey, Alderney, and Ayrshire, and to some extent the Devon, have found especial accept-ance, and are represented by some of their best strains. Much discussion prevails as yet in regard to the relative merits of the various breeds under the peculiar climatic conditions of California; but already they are beginning to become localized in accordance with their several adaptations to local climates, which can be found to suit all; and perhaps in time the tawny race of the Swiss Alps will find a congenial range on the Sierra Nevada.

The production of beef is as yet limited by the requirements of home consumption; but the dairy interest is rapidly assuming a wider range, and with an increasing knowledge of the modifications of the processes demanded by climatic conditions, the quality of dairy products is improving so much that as a market for all but the choicest kinds, California will soon be closed to the Eastern producer, and will, perhaps, compete with him in foreign markets. The average quality of the milk supplied to San Francisco and Oakland, from the numerous "dairy ranches" on the coast and bay and in the Coast Range, is greatly superior to that generally found in Eastern cities; one obvious reason being that in the absence of distilleries there is no opportunity or temptation to feed the cows on unhealthy offal; nor do the sleek and healthy cows that range the breezy hills of the coast ever need to be propped or slung up in order to enable them to stand the milking process. It is believed that an undue increase of bulk from a too free use of the pump is all that the milk consumers of these cities ever have to complain of.

Butter is now very generally of fair quality, some brands being quite up to the "gilt-edge" standard. It is usually sold in rolls supposed to weigh two pounds, but in reality always several ounces below that weight — a circumstance so well understood, however, that the practice hardly amounts to deception. The price per roll rarely falls below 50 cents to the consumer, and ranges more generally from 60 cents to $1.10 about Christmas time, when even that which has been packed in casks with salt during the spring and summer brings 70 cents.

The intimate connection (to the housekeeper at least) of butter with *eggs* suggests a few words on that subject in this place. The demand for eggs is unusually large in California cities, in consequence of the commonly prevailing practice of not only single men and women, but also small families in moderate circumstances, living in lodgings, and taking an easily made breakfast of eggs, bread, and coffee, thereafter going to the restaurant for dinner, and thus avoiding the pains and pleasures of housekeeping. Whatever may be said of the desirability of this practice in a social point of view, it manifests its effects in the price of eggs, which rarely falls below 30 cents per dozen to the consumer, and is more frequently among the fifties and upward; even so, *fowls* cannot often be bought at less than 80 cents apiece, and $1 is a common price. Poultry-keeping is therefore a very remunerative pursuit when judiciously managed, since feed is as cheap as elsewhere; and it is one of the industries which have not, as yet, been overdone. There are no special difficulties to be overcome in poultry-raising in California; yet a great deal of money has been lost in attempts made by persons unfamiliar with its proper management. There is no lack of the improved breeds, but among them the Leghorns seem to enjoy the widest acceptance at this time.

Apiculture is common throughout the State, and nowhere is the product of the bee of finer flavor, or marketed in a more attractive form. The best of improved hives are in common use, and the market is always supplied with the frames filled with the delicate, almost white, comb. Of course the improved varieties of bees have been introduced, and in the southern part of the State especially this industry is practiced on a scale not often to be met with elsewhere, as can readily be seen from the figures showing the export, amounting in 1878 to no less than three and a half millions of pounds. How kindly the honey-bee takes to even the desert region of that country is well illustrated in what has been supposed by many to be a "snake" story, but what is an unquestionable fact; namely, that some miners prospecting in Arizona struck a regular "fissure vein" of honey in a rocky ridge, where the bees had been making deposits for years, and, although the vein-contents were not what they had been searching for, they took to it kindly and worked it, extracting therefrom a fabulous amount of honey. Another adventurous colony took possession of the court-house cupola at San Bernardino, and had accumulated several hundred pounds of honey when discovered. The bee is very fond of the flower of the mountain sage (*Artemisia*), as well as of a number of other desert plants, and is thus afforded unlimited pasture through three-fourths of the year. It seems that certain kinds of flowers, not yet identified, impart to the honey a tendency to become turbid after straining, from the separation of minute white crystals, whose nature has not as yet been ascertained. Such honey, whose other qualities are generally of the highest, has been unjustly suspected of adulteration in Eastern and English markets. The prejudice arising from this merely conventional defect will soon be overcome, and South California will doubtless become one of, if not the largest, honey-producing country of the world.

Silk-culture is at present almost extinct in California in consequence of the reaction against the mania for this industry that began in the State some eighteen years ago and raged with unabated fury for several years, inflicting severe losses upon those who indulged in the popular delusion that the silkworm would thrive in the State without any special precautions in the way of shelter and such intelligent care as can be given only by those versed in its treatment. Some of the airy sheds that were supposed to be an adequate protection against the comparatively slight changes of temperature are still extant, as monuments of that flush period when mulberry trees were thought to be the only nursery stock worth having. It can hardly be doubted that the advantages offered by a climate in which the food of the worm is available during all but two or three months in the year, yet free from the excessive heat that elsewhere militates against the insect's well-being, will ultimately assert themselves in the resumption of silk-culture in a calmer mood. It has been very successfully kept up, on a small scale, by Mr. Gustavus Neumann, of San Francisco, showing pretty conclusively that it is not the nature of the climate, but adverse commercial and industrial circumstances that at present keep the rise of silk-culture in check.

Alongside of the useful animals of California, some mention of the injurious ones should also be made. The grizzly bear and puma, or California lion, have ceased to possess more than an occasional local interest to farmers; but the sneaking coyote, freed from the competition of the stronger animals, finds the conditions of his existence rather improved than otherwise by the multiplication of flocks on the mountain sides, where the thick "chaparrel" affords him a refuge from which it is not easy to dislodge him. Both he and the wildcat still range in sight of "the city," and make their presence felt in occasional inroads upon valuable flocks. But the damage thus done is insignificant in comparison with the ravages of a much more peaceful animal, to which civilization has afforded additional safety and means of subsistence. This is the ground-squirrel (*Sciurus Fossor*), which the immigrant at first is inclined to greet as an old acquaintance, it being very like the gray squirrel of the Western woods. It lives, however, exclusively in underground burrows, each occupied by from two to thirty individuals; and from this safe retreat it levies its assessments upon the grain-fields with all the certainty and pertinacity of the tax-gatherer, not unfrequently harvesting as its share over one-half of the growing crop, and pursuing the grain into the stacks and sacks, and even to the barn itself. Passing through the grain-fields after harvest, one may see the wary little animals scattering hastily to their holes by hundreds, like young spiders from a nest; then, turning on their heels in the burrow, they will sit erect at the entrance, uttering a peculiar whistle, the signal of danger to their neighbors. The pot-hunter, imagining that he has a fine chance, will find them drop into their holes at the very instant that he pulls the trigger; and should he succeed in putting a few shot through its tough hide, the chances are that the wounded animal will wriggle into its hole, out of reach, before the marksman has time to reach the spot. While not first-class eating, yet both their carcasses and skins find a ready sale; but even skilled hunters appear to make but little impression upon their numbers in favorable ground. Wheat poisoned with strychnine is the remedy that has been thus far most used for their destruction, but the want of coöperation by neighbors renders all efforts for their extermination futile, and other domestic animals, as well as the farmers' friends, the birds, too often fall sole victims to the poison. Legislative enactments also have failed to prove efficient in compelling united action. Of late the use of carbon bisulphide has been introduced with a fair degree of success; and whenever the home manufacture shall so reduce the price of this substance as to bring it within the farmers' reach, there may be reasonable hope that the "squirrel nuisance" will be abated.

Another animal equally destructive on a smaller scale is the gopher (*Thomomys Umbrinus*), an animal of the aspect of a small rat, with a short, stumpy tail. Its shallow, winding burrows are marked by small piles of earth-crumbs at their outlets, and by the unaccountable dying-out of trees, shrubbery, and flowers when at their best, the animal feeding on their roots unperceived. The gopher can do little damage where the ground is kept in perfect tilth, and leaves in disgust when it finds its burrows falling in behind it. But in plantations of young trees, in lawns, and the like, its ravages are most grievous, and difficult to check.

Of insects, the *Phylloxera,* and the "scale-bugs" attacking the pear and orange, are those most complained of. The Colorado potato-bug does not seem to have made its way across the mountains. The Rocky Mountain locust-grasshopper is reported to have made its appearance occasionally in the mountain counties; but it is possible that other species have been mistaken for it when, as sometimes happens, they have appeared in unusual numbers. This year an invasion by one of these (*Oedipoda Atrox*) is reported as doing serious damage in Sierra and Tulare Counties. The caterpillar, which occasionally appears in countless numbers, completely denuding the live-oaks, and is then scarcely seen for several years, seems to be gradually enlarging the scope of its appetite, and attacks the orchards. The cut-worm and codling-moth also are increasingly complained of; yet, on the whole, insect pests do not as yet excite much alarm in California, despite the fact that they are undeniably on the increase, both in numbers of the same species and in new ones being constantly introduced by sea and land.

Cereal Crops

Of all the field crops grown in the State, wheat is the most important at this time. It was the first culture on a large scale introduced on the subsidence of the gold fever, and the returns received proved to be so much greater and more certain than those from the placer mines that it extended rapidly, and has ever since remained the largest and most generally appreciated product of California agriculture. The amount produced in 1878, an average year, was 22,000,000 of centals, of which 8,069,825 were exported as grain, and about 500,000 barrels of flour. In the markets of the world the wheats of the Pacific coast are noted for their high quality — the plumpness and light color of the ''berry,'' and the high percentage of first-class flour it furnishes in milling. At home the extraordinarily high product per acre of forty to sixty bushels, and even more, under very imperfect tillage, for a number of consecutive years, forms a strong incentive to this culture. Nor is the California wheat-grower obliged to be very careful in the choice of his seed. Probably every known variety of wheat has in the course of time been brought and tried here; but all, in a short time, seems to assume very nearly the same peculiar California type, upon which, in fact, it would seem hard to improve materially. It is almost ludicrous, at times, to compare the eastern seed with its California offspring, which has undergone the ''swelling process'' of one season's growth in her generous soil and climate. It is but fair to say that substantially the same peculiarities are observable in the wheats of Oregon, grown in the valley of the Willamette and on the plains of the Upper Columbia. Since the growing season in the greater part of California extends, with little interruption from cold, from the beginning of November to June, the distinction between winter and spring grain is also in a great measure lost. The farmer plows and sows as early as practicable, watching his chances between rains, in November and December if he can, in March if he must, or at any convenient time between; increasing the amount of seed sown per acre in proportion as there remains less time for the grain to tiller. Should the ears fail to fill, he can still make hay.

Much discussion has been had concerning the merits of early as compared with late sowing. The objections against the former practice are that copious early rains may start the growth too rapidly, the chances being that in that case but little more water will fall until Christmas. It is true that the weather-wise may sometimes gain materially by delay in sowing; but the general result of experience seems to be that it is better in the long run to take the risk of having to sow twice, rather than that of being kept from sowing at all, until too late, by persistent rains. It has therefore become a very common practice to ''dry-sow'' grain in summer-fallowed land in September and October. The seed lies quiescent in the parched and dusty ground until called forth by the rains, and in clean fields and ordinary seasons such grain generally yields the highest returns. The preparation of the ground for the crop on the large wheat farms is usually made by means of gang-plows with from two to six shares, drawn by from three to five horses or mules, three animals very commonly walking abreast. At the critical season it is not uncommon to see half a dozen such implements and teams at work in a single field, closely followed by a wagon carrying seed-grain and the centrifugal sower, which showers the grain upon the fresh-turned furrows, in strips thirty or more feet wide. Before the day ends the great (usually flexible) harrows have also performed their work, and 30 or 40 acres of what was a stubble field in the morning have been converted into a well-seeded grain field. Of late, appliances for seeding and covering have been attached to the gang-plows themselves, so that the whole task is performed in one operation — certainly the perfection of labor-saving machinery. Seed drills are as yet in but limited use; although nowhere, probably, would drilling be more desirable, in order to admit of subsequent culture, for want of which crops often totally fail on the heavier soils. During the rainy season the covering is often done by rolling alone, and on harrowed ground the roller is frequently used later in the season, in order to compact the surface so as to mitigate the drying effects of "northers."

In the grain harvest (which begins in the second week of June) the "wholesale" mode of procedure is equally prevalent. The scythe is used only to cut the way, and that on small farms; then follows the reaper, hired if not owned by the farmer himself. But the binding and shocking process that is to succeed is far too slow for the large grain-grower, who has his hundreds, and sometimes thousands, of acres to reap within the short time allowed by the exceedingly rapid maturing, which threatens him with serious loss by shedding, the air being at that season very dry even at night. His implement is the giant header, pushed into the golden fields by from four to eight horses. Its vibrating cutters clip off the heads with only a few inches of straw attached, on a swath 16 and even 28 feet wide, while a revolving apron carries the laden ears to a wagon driven alongside, and having a curious, wide, slanting bed for their reception. Several of these wagons drive back and forth between the swaths and the steam thresher, where, within half an hour, the grain that was waving in the morning breeze may be sacked ready for shipment to Liverpool. Even this energetic mode of procedure, however, has appeared too slow to some of the progressive men in business, and we have seen a wondrous and fearful combination of header, thresher, and sacking-wagon moving in procession side by side through the doomed grain. If this stupendous combination and last refinement shall prove practically successful, we shall doubtless next see the flouring-mill itself form a part of this agricultural pageant. Where farming is not done on quite so energetic a plan, the reaped and bound grain being at that season perfectly safe from rain, is left either in shocks or stacks until the threshing party comes around, mostly with a portable engine often fed with straw alone, to drive the huge "separator," whose combined din and puffing will sometimes startle late sleepers, as it suddenly starts up in the morning from the most unexpected places. Two wagons usually aided by some "bucks" (a kind of sledge-rake, which also serves to remove the straw from the mouth of the thresher) feed the devouring monster. In an incredibly short time the shocks or stacks are cleared away and in their stead appear square piles of turgid grain-sacks and broad, low hillocks of straw. Both products often remain thus for six or eight weeks, the grain getting so thoroughly dry in the interval that there is frequently an over-weight of five or more per cent. when, after its long passage in the damp sea air, the cargo reaches Liverpool. The moral question thus arising as to who is entitled to the benefit of this increase I will not pretend to determine; but the producers say that they rarely hear of any differences in their favor.

The manner of disposing of the straw is one of the weakest points of California agriculture. Near to cities or cheap transportation, much of it is baled like hay, and finds a ready market, but in remote districts it is got rid of by applying the torch; and these "straw fires" habitually redden the autumn skies as do the prairie fires in the western States, covering the whole country with a smoke haze, as a faint reminis-cence of the Indian summer, which is not otherwise well-defined on the Pacific coast. This holocaust of valuable materials, which might be made the means of some slight return of plant-food to the soil, is a standing reproach to those who practice it; yet they have some excuse in the fact that the peculiarities of the climate do not make it as easy to convert it into manure as is the case in countries having summer rains. For in winter the temperature is, after all, too low to favor rapid decay, while during the summer months, the intense drought soon puts an end to fermentation. It therefore takes two seasons to render the straw fit for plowing in; and in the mean time, as left by the thresher, it occupies considerable ground. As yet, the conviction that straw-burning is penny-wisdom and pound-foolishness has not gained sufficient foothold to induce the majority of wheat-growers to take the pains of putting the straw into stacks with concave tops, to collect and retain the water. But those who have done so report that the resulting improvement of the soil pays well for the trouble. The practice of burning will, of course, disappear so soon as the system of large-scale planting gives way, as it soon must, to that of mixed farming on a smaller scale.

Of the other cereals, *Barley* and *Oats,* are the only ones that can as yet lay claim to general importance; and the methods of culture are much the same. Like the wheats, so the barleys of California are of exceptionally fine quality, that of the "Chevalier" variety being so eagerly sought for by eastern brewers that but little of it finds its way into California-brewed beer. The common (six and four rowed) barleys are, however, themselves of such high quality that the absence of the highest grade grain is certainly not perceptible in the quality of the beers, into which, unlike most of its eastern brethren of Saint Louis and Chicago, nothing but barley and hops find their way. The various kinds of *Oats* are produced for home consumption only, the difficulty being very commonly that the straw becomes so strong as to interfere seriously with its use for forage. Rye is grown to some extent in the mountain counties, and yields a splendid grain, called for chiefly by the taste of the German population for rye bread. Some Polish wheat (*Triticum polonicom*) is grown under the name of "white rye." *Maize* is thus far grown, but to a small extent compared with wheat, barley, and oats; not, however, because of any difficulty in producing corn, which, both as to quality, size, and yield per acre, can compete with any in the Mississippi Valley. The large foreign element in the population limits the demand for corn-meal, and, as before remarked, on account of the mild winters, hog-raising on a large scale is not likely to become important in the State. A good deal, however, is planted for green-soiling purposes in connection with dairies. The planting is generally done very late in April, and in May after everything else has been attended to, since in the coast climate a crop of corn is often made without a drop of rain from the time of planting, when the season has been one of abundant moisture. Of late, several millets, and among them especially the *Dhoura* or Egyptian corn, are coming into favor. The Dhoura, though not as much relished by cattle as maize fodder, will admit of three cuttings each season, when irrigated, and the meal made from its grain is by many preferred to corn meal, while as a chicken-feed it is, apparently, superior to anything else.

Miscellaneous Field Crops

Of other field crops, the *"beans"* that formed the chief solace of the Argonauts of early days are still prominent, especially where the Mexican element is somewhat strong. To them "frijoles" are still the staff of life, supplemented by the "tamales," the native preparation of the "roasting ears" of green corn.

The *Irish potatoes* grown in California are not, as a rule, of first quality, but incline to be watery. The tuber is largely imported from Utah under the name and style of "Salt Lake potatoes," albeit much that is sold under that brand is of California growth. The *sweet-potato* flourishes especially in the lighter soils of the coast south of San Francisco; its quality would not be likely to be criticised by any but those who have been accustomed to the product of the Gulf States or of the Antilles.

The big *pumpkins* of California have acquired a world-wide reputation not unlike that enjoyed by the sea serpent. The unprejudiced observer, however, readily appreciates the fact that when a well organized pumpkin has ten months' time to grow instead of three or four, it has every reason to give a corresponding account of its stewardship. But while a laudable ambition to excel may result in the production of three-hundred-pound pumpkins, it is but fair to say they are not the rule; being inconvenient to handle, and, like other organisms exceeding a certain age, inclined to be hard and tough. The same is true of mammoth beets (mangel-wurzel), carrots and turnips, which, when left out in the field during a mild winter, continue incontinently to grow and develop until the time comes to put in another crop. The dairy-men and stock-breeders raise these crops largely and are chiefly responsible for the production of the monsters.

The *sugar-beet* succeeds admirably in a large portion of the State, and in appropriate locations yields a juice of extraordinary richness; as much as 19 per cent. is clarified in some cases (but I can vouch for 15 only from personal experience), and a fair degree of purity. Several prosperous beet-sugar factories already exist, the failures reported having apparently been due to mismanagement. It is difficult to see why, with such material and the possibility of keeping up the supply for nine months by the planting of successive crops, this industry should not become one of the most important and lucrative in the State, and fully able to compete with any sugar-cane planting that may hereafter be introduced in the southern portion of the coast.

Hop growing is an important industry in the middle portion of the State, especially in the Sacramento Valley and in the Russian River region, north of San Francisco Bay. The product is of excellent quality, and is much sought after by Eastern brewers.

Of other crops of minor or only local importance may be mentioned the culture of *pea-nuts,* chiefly in the coast region south of San Francisco; of the chiccory root, in the neighborhood of Stockton, supplying a large amount of the parched and ground "old government Java coffee" sold by grocers. In the same neighborhood the culture of the *"Persian insect-powder plant"* (*Pyrethrum carneum*) is being success-fully carried out, the product being in very general requisition on account of the prevailing abundance of fleas. This neighborhood supplies a quality of *mustard* that is somewhat overwhelming to the novice, and even for plasters should be diluted with flour. Were *rape-seed* oil in demand, the fact that the whole State is overrun with the plant that produces it, as a most troublesome weed, proves what could be done with it if fostered.

Horticultural Products

Nothing, probably, strikes the new-comer to California more forcibly, and nothing certainly more agreeably, than the advantages offered by a climate where plants can ordinarily be kept growing from ten to twelve months in the year, provided water is supplied. The immigrant desiring to make a home for himself is delighted to find that the rapid growth of shrubbery and flowers — and among them many that he has so far seen only nurtured in greenhouses — will enable him to create around him in the course of three seasons, on a bare lot, a home atmosphere that elsewhere it would have required ten or more years to establish. The housewife, however industriously disposed, is not ill-pleased to find herself relieved from the annual pressure of the "preserving season" by the circumstance that fresh fruits are in the market at reasonable rates during all but a few weeks in the year; so that a few gallons of jellies is all that is really called for in the way of "putting up." It is not less pleasing to her, as well as to the rest of the family, that a good supply of fresh vegetables is at her command at all seasons, and that the Christmas dinner, if the turkey *does* cost 30 cents a pound, may be graced with crisp lettuce, radishes, and green peas just as readily as it may be celebrated by an open-air picnic on the green grass under blooming bushes of the scarlet gooseberry. Of course there are seasons of preference for each vegetable, but among the great variety naturally introduced by the various nationalities there are few that cannot be found in the San Francisco market at almost any time in the year — if not from local culture, then from some point between Los Angeles and the mouth of the Columbia. The truck-gardens are largely in the hands of the Italians and Portuguese, who have brought with them from their home habits of thrift; and their manure piles, windmills for irrigation, and laborious care of their unceasing round of crops on a small area, render their establishments easy of recognition. Their products are distributed partly by themselves, partly by the ubiquitous Chinese huckster, trotting with his two huge baskets under a weight that few Caucasians would carry for any length of time. Not a few Chinese also are engaged in the truck-farming business. The vegetables are in general of excellent quality, and it may be truly said that in no city in the United States is the general quality of fare so good, so well adapted to every variety of taste, and, last but not least, so cheap, as in the city of the Golden Gate; and nowhere is the decoration of even the humblest homes with flowers and shrubbery more universal and at the same time so generously aided by nature.

In no department of industry, probably, is the reputation of California better established than in regard to *fruit culture*. Its pears seem to have been the pioneers in gaining the award of special excellence; grapes and cherries have rapidly taken a place alongside, and, last, oranges and lemons have come to dispute the palm with Sicily and the Antilles. The most striking peculiarity of California fruit culture is its astonishing versatility, not to say cosmopolitanism; for the variety of fruits capable of successful culture within the limits under consideration in this article probably exceeds, even at this time, that found elsewhere in any country of similar extent, and is constantly on the increase by the introduction of new kinds from all quarters of the globe. Doubtless, in time, each district will settle down to the more or less exclusive production of certain kinds found to be most profitable under its particular circumstances, so far as the large-scale cultures are concerned; but whosoever raises fruit mainly for home consumption will hardly resist the temptation offered by the possibility of growing side by side the fruits of the tropics and those of the north temperate zone — the currant and the orange, the cherry and the fig, the strawberry and the pineapple, the banana and plantain, as well as the apple and the medlar. It would be supposed that the quality of these products must of necessity suffer grievously under the stress of their mutual concessions of habit; and this, of course, is true as regards the highest qualities of the extremes, under the judgment of the expert, but unperceived to a surprising degree by the taste of the public in the general market.

The oranges grown in some of the sheltered valleys of the Coast Range, and on the red soils of the Foot Hills, as far north as Butte County, often successfully dispute the precedence of the product of Los Angeles and San Bernardino.

In view of the short time within which this industry has developed, and of the multitude of nationalities which have taken part therein, it is not surprising that many important questions relating to it should still remain unsettled, and that the best regular routine for the several districts, or even for general practice, should as yet not have been established. Too many different varieties, whose adaptation to the local and general climate is undetermined, fill the orchards, and give rise to immense quantities of unmarketable fruit, that ultimately fall to the share of cattle and hogs. The high price of labor and of transportation from remote districts condemns another large part to a similar fate, especially in favorable seasons, when the local market soon becomes glutted with fruit unable to bear shipment to the East. Curiously enough, even at such times, the prices of fruit to the consumer are generally higher than is the case at corresponding times in the Western States, showing irrefragably that the cost of production is higher, and consequently that only fruit of high quality can bear exportation. Inattention to this point has rendered unprofitable, or worse, many of the refrigerator-car shipments heretofore made, and the same want of proper care in assorting the various qualities is one of the chief causes of frequent business failures of those supplying the markets of San Francisco. This practice, however, is fast being improved upon, and the disposal of the surplus fruit by drying is beginning to relieve, to a very great extent, the glut that has often depressed prices below the paying point. The exportation of dried fruits of all kinds is doubtless destined to become one of the most important branches of agricultural industry in the State, both on account of quality and of the natural facilities for the drying process offered by the dry summer air. It is found to be absolutely necessary to exclude in the drying operations all access of insects, which otherwise lay their eggs on the fruit and spoil it within a year. This is now very generally and effectually accomplished by the use of the best drying apparatus, not uncommonly in co-operative factories erected by companies or granges. The quality of the prunes, plums, apricots, pears, &c., cured by some of these establishments is not behind the best of the kind imported from France and Italy, but as yet the neatness and convenience of the packages is not so generally what would be necessary to render them equally attractive to the purchaser.

While the orange, lemon, lime, and other sub-tropical fruits are more or less in cultivation up to the northern third of the State, they form the specialty of Los Angeles, San Bernardino, and adjoining counties, where also the pineapple, banana, guava, and other more strictly tropical fruits are mainly under trial. In a measure, what has been said above of the more northern fruits applies here also. While much fruit of the highest quality is produced, much also is still in the experimental stage, and some very poor lots are occasionally thrown upon the market. The subject has lately, however, been earnestly taken in hand by the young but proportionally energetic Horticultural Society of South California, in which a number of the most intelligent men have combined to determine in the shortest possible time, by systematic experiments, discussion, and scientific investigation, in connection with the agricultural department of the university, the practically important questions relating to this culture. While the orange and lemon product is marketed without difficulty and at good prices, the millions of excellent limes borne by the hedges customary in the southern part of the State are still mostly allowed to decay where they fall. The manufacture of citric acid can hardly fail before long to put an end to this waste of precious material. The pomegranate, which is to some extent similarly used, generally finds a ready sale for its fruit. The olive, so generally found around the old missions as a relic of the past, has not so far found its place in general culture; and on the shelves of the grocers in the cities we still find the same mixtures of cotton-seed, peanut, and other oils, with a modicum of the genuine product of the olive, that form the standing complaint of salad-eaters throughout the United States. The subject of olive culture has of late attracted considerable attention, and small quantities of excellent oil have been made in various parts of the State, proving beyond cavil that its production can be made an important industry. The culture of the fig in California is coextensive with that of the vine, and both fresh and dried fruit of the highest quality is found in the market.

As to *nuts,* the European *walnut,* Italian *chestnut,* and *almond* are those whose culture on a large scale has been successfully carried out. The filbert may also be mentioned. Of these, the almond has been made the subject of the largest experiments, and, as might be expected, there have been numerous disappointments in consequence of the selection of unsuitable localities, subject to light frosts at the time of bloom. The best results have been obtained in situations moderately elevated above the valleys, ''thermal belts,'' where the cold air cannot accumulate. The quality of the product leaves nothing to be desired, where proper care is had in selection of varieties.

The *Japanese persimmon* promises here, as in the Southern United States, to prove an important acquisition. The *jujube,* the *carob,* the *pistachio nut,* and many others are under trial.

Of small fruits, the *strawberry* is in the market during the twelve months of the year. *Raspberries* and *blackberries* are largely grown, both for market and canning. The *currant* is of especial excellence and size, and is extensively grown between the rows in orchards. *Gooseberries* have not been altogether successful in general culture.

A good deal has been said and written about *coffee* culture. It was currently reported that a kind of coffee grew wild in the foot-hills, and of course the real coffee must succeed. The ''wild coffee,'' however, is simply the California buckthorn (*Frangula Californica*), and of course no more suitable for a beverage than turnip-seed. True, coffee trees are now growing at numerous points in the State, but it is not probable that the culture will prove a success outside of South California.

Grape Culture and Wine-Making

The grape-vine was among the culture plants introduced earliest by the Catholic missionaries. The similarity of the California climate to that of the vine-growing regions of the Mediterranean would naturally suggest the probable success of vine culture, corroborated by the fact that a native vine, albeit with a somewhat acid and unpalatable fruit, grows abundantly along the banks of all the larger streams. The grape variety introduced by the missionaries, and still universally known as the ''Mission'' grape, was probably the outcome of seed brought from Spain; it most resembles that of the vineyards which furnish the ''Benicarlo'' wine. It is a rather pale-blue, small, round berry, forming at times very large and somewhat straggling bunches. It is very sweet, especially in South California, has very little acid, very little astringency, no definite flavor, and, on the whole, commends itself as a wine-grape only by the abundance of its juice and its great fruitfulness. The American immigrants found this vine growing neglected around the old missions, along with the olive, fig, and pomegranate. It soon attracted the attention of the European emigrants from wine-growing countries, was resuscitated and propagated, and still forms the bulk of the vineyards of California. We have good testimony to the effect that the wines made by the missionaries were of very indifferent quality, owing partly, of course, to the inferiority of the grape used, but chiefly to the primitive mode of manufacture; the entire caskage consisting of a few large, half-glazed earthenware jars (*tinajas*), from which the fermented wine was rarely racked off, being mostly consumed the same season. Still, the luscious grapes and refreshing wines of the missions are dwelt upon with all the delight that contrast can impart by travelers just from the fiery ordeal of the Arizona deserts or the thirsty plains of the Upper San Joaquin. The European wine-makers soon improved vastly upon the processes and product of the padres, but, in accordance with the fast ideas of the early times of California, they imprudently threw their immature product upon the general market, and thereby damaged the reputation of California wines to such a degree that it is only of late years that the prejudice thus created has been overcome, not only in consequence of better methods of treatment, and greater maturity of the wines when marketed, but also, and most essentially, by the introduction of the best grape varieties from all parts of the world. The result is that, at this time, a large part of the wines exported are either partially or wholly made of foreign grape varieties, and, as a whole, will compare favorably with the product of any European country, while among the choicer kinds now ripening there are some that will take rank with the high-priced fancy brands of France. It is true that so far all California-grown wines are recognizable to experts, a peculiar flavor difficult to define, which has been called "earthy," recalling to mind that of the wines of the Vaud and of some of Burgundy. But this peculiarity remains unperceived by most persons, and is not comparable in intensity to the "foxy" aroma of wines made from the American grape varieties.

Another prominent peculiarity of the California wines is that they are generally of considerable alcoholic strength, as the result of the intense and unremitting sunshine under which they invariably ripen. This is especially the case in the Los Angeles region, whose natural wines are by many, at first blush, thought to be "fortified," since they not only reach the maximum alcoholic strength attainable by fermentation, but even then retain a very perceptible amount of unchanged sugar. This circumstance interferes, of course, with the safe daily and sanitary use of the native wines at home, and explains the fact that as yet a not inconsiderable amount, of French clarets especially, is imported into California for table use by the foreign-born population. This folly (for such it must be considered in this point of view) has already been in a measure remedied by the use of such varieties as the Hungarian "Yinfandel" and others of a more acid and tart character; and it is quite probable that it will be found desirable to limit the time of exposure of the ripe grapes to the sugar-making autumn sun in order to restrict still further the alcoholic strength of some of the wines. Of course, the German and French vintners are difficult to convince that there may be in California too much of the blessed sunshine, every hour of which, in their native climes, adds to the market value of their product. This is but one of the many points in which the vinicultural practice of California seems susceptible of improvement. We find elsewhere that long experience teaches the vintners of each country how to obtain the best possible results under their particular conditions; and it is not surprising that during the short period of experience had in California, and with the tendency of Spaniards, Portuguese, Italians, French, and Germans to introduce each the practice of his own country under circumstances so different, the best methods and uniformity in quality should not yet have become fixed. What is true of wine-making proper is equally so of the modes of culture. The padres naturally adopted the system of short pruning prevailing in their own country, and the later comers as naturally continued it, and, oddly enough, applied it almost indiscriminately to the other grape varieties brought from Northern France, Germany, and Hungary, in some cases even to the varieties of the native American stock, altogether unused to such summary treatment. The experimental stage in California wine-making is also strikingly evidenced by the great variety of grapes still found in the vineyards of progressive growers, as the result of which we find in the markets and in fairs a most tempting and beautiful display of the grape varieties of all countries; and nothing can be more convincing as regards the peculiar adaptability of the State to this industry than the excellence of most of these often surpassing in this respect the best of their kind in their original homes. Yet we can hardly wonder at this in a climate which allows the currant and the orange to ripen side by side.

Another drawback to the quality of the wines thus far is the tendency of each vine-grower to make his own wines, involving not only an unnecessary multiplication of costly buildings, caskage, &c., but also the unfounded assumption that wine-making is an easy thing and can be managed by any one having a moderate amount of common sense; whereas, on the contrary, the production of the best possible result from a given material requires in this case, as in other manufacturing industries, a very considerable amount of knowledge and good judgment, which can be in some degree replaced by mere practice only in countries where long experience has settled all into a regular routine. The introduction of large wineries, managed by professional experts, (like the magnificent establishment of Buena Vista, near Sonoma Town), has gone far toward redeeming the wines of California from the reproach cast upon them by the hasty marketing of first crude efforts, which has, until lately, caused much of the native product to be sold under foreign labels. They have always possessed at least the merit of being made of the grape pure and simple, ungallized and unpainted, not so much, perhaps, as the result of superior virtue of wine-makers on the Pacific coast as because the superabundance and low price of grapes reduces the temptation to adulterate or ''correct'' the natural product to a minimum. Even within the last few years some vineyards in the interior have been in part harvested by turning in hogs; and other uses for the surplus product have been sought and found in the making of an excellent sirup by evaporation of the must. The growing appreciation and consequent better price of California wines will probably hereafter prevent recourse to such expedients.

A detailed consideration of the methods of wine-making is beyond the limits of the present article, but it should be said that after the picking of the grapes (usually by Chinese) the means and appliances used in the succeeding processes are generally (as in other branches of agriculture in California) of the most approved and efficient kind, and the operations conducted in the most cleanly manner. The reported treading of the grapes by the feet of "Greasers" in the southern part of the State applies only to the pommace destined for distillation into brandy; albeit for certain kinds of wine (*e.g.*, Port) the treading process is deemed indispensable in Europe, and, after all, feet can be washed as clean as hands.

Again, there are in California, as elsewhere, regions whose soil and climate favor the development of the highest qualities in wines, while there are others whose product, however abundant, good-looking, and pleasant to the palate when fresh from the vine, will fail, even with the best management, to yield a beverage fit for exportation.

The volcanic soils of the beautiful valleys of Napa and Sonoma have thus far achieved the highest general reputation for wines of fine bouquet; yet even there the products of adjacent vineyards sometimes differ widely, and these differences are not yet, as a rule, sufficiently considered by the producers, or by those who blend the several products for market. The red soils of the foot-hills of the Sierra also give high promise of fine wines, and in the Coast Range those of the valley of San José are noteworthy. The wines made from the sugary berries of Los Angeles are, of course, very similar to those of South France, Spain, and Portugal — fiery, and with a heavy body, but less "bouquet" than those grown farther north. Its least deserving wine (if it may be so classed at all) is perhaps the far-famed Angelica; and the mission grape almost alone is in bearing there as yet.

The vineyards planted on the heavier soils of the Sacramento Plain yield a large part of the table grapes for the home and Eastern markets, and seem destined to become one of the chief regions for the raisin-making industry, to which the climate of the great interior basin is, of course, especially adapted in consequence of its rainless summers and intense, dry heat, sweetening the grape to the utmost and rendering the curing process easy. Owing probably to a combination of favorable soils and good management some of the Muscatel raisins from near Woodland, in Yolo County, have proved fully equal to the highest quality of those imported from Malaga. Unfortunately the commercial standing of California raisins, like that of its wines, has been injured by putting into market such as, from the mode of curing, did not possess the requisite keeping qualities. The efficient drying apparatus now introduced obviates this objection, and it is highly probable that raisin-making will hereafter take its place, alongside of wine-making, among the most important industries of the State.

Brandy-making, also, has not been neglected, but in consequence of unfavorable Federal legislation has until lately labored under great disadvantages. Most of the native "Aguardiente" has been distilled from pommace, and is, of course, rather hot and rank-flavored. In the Los Angeles region it is, to a great extent, the "first run" of the grapes only that is made into wine, no presses being used; hence, the brandy made from the residue is of higher quality. The distillation of brandy from wine itself (now so rare in France) from the best of foreign grapes has been made a specialty by General H. Naglee, of San José, and the quality of the product is far above that of any imported now in the market. That the extensive importation of grape varieties should result in the introduction of their formidable enemy the *Phylloxera* is not surprising; but we may well wonder at the indifference with which that now well-known fact is regarded by the majority of wine-growers, even in districts in which the insect has already made its appearance and has shown its power for harm. This is due largely to the fortunate, as well as unexpected and hitherto unexplained, circumstance that the progress of the pest has been remarkably slow as compared with its sweeping advance in Europe, though evidently not less sure. It is as though the winged form were either not produced at all or very much restricted in its powers of locomotion. It, therefore, seems quite possible to check, and perhaps stamp it out by timely precautions. But nothing of the kind has been done, and the penalty of this neglect has already been dearly paid in the Sonoma Valley, the region chiefly afflicted. Sonoma Mountain seems to have proved an effectual barrier against its transmission to the Napa Valley. The ravages of the insect are also reported from some other localities, but no noteworthy damage has thus far been heard of. Of other vine pests, the *Oidium* and a kind of black-knot are the chief; but, on the whole, the damage done has been merely local and easily checked, and it may truthfully be said that to the grape-vine, as to the human race, the climate of California is exceptionally kind.

Indiana Farming and Manufacturing, 1878

From W. B. Seward, "Manufacturing and Agricultural Interests Inseparable," in Indiana State Board of Agriculture, *Annual Report,* 1878, pp. 161–68.

The relations that should exist between the two great industries of the world, namely, agriculture and manufacturing, do not seem to be properly understood by those who would seek to array one against the other. They are, to a limited extent only, independent industries, as neither could be carried on with profit without the other. How can there be any real conflict between them? And yet I regret to say that there are persons who claim that there is a conflict of interest between the two, and that the profit that one may make must come off the other. While this is true, to a certain extent, yet it does not prove true the point these chronic grumblers would make; but it does prove true that those who use the argument do not understand or comprehend the true relations that must exist between them in order that both may be the most successful. It is true that agriculture is the foundation, the very bed-rock upon which all other industries are erected; and yet with all this, what would it be without its twin brother, manufacturing? If all men were engaged in agricultural pursuits, as some persons seem to think they should, there could be no market for any surplus products that we might have. One farmer could not sell wheat and corn to another farmer, who himself had a surplus of these things, any more than one plow-maker can sell plows to another. In order to furnish a market for our products, be they what they may, there must be a division of labor, so that one will produce what another wants. The farmer can exchange his products with the manufacturer, because each has something that the other does not produce, and that each wants. This makes the market so necessary to each, and in proportion as these two great industries are carried on largely in close proximity to each other, are both benefited.

This brings me to the main point intended to be made, namely, that as the interests of agriculture and manufacturing are identified, there can be no conflict of interests between the two, and that each should encourage the other in every possible way, for the mutual benefit of both.

Let it be understood that a home market is the best market that can be had. If we find a market at our own doors for any surplus that we may have to sell, then we have solved the problem as to how to secure cheap transportation, and need not longer spend our time pondering over this question.

The best results that have ever been secured to labor is where there is the greatest diversity of it. If an entire community were engaged in making pins, we might have a good supply of these useful articles; but all other things required would have to be purchased and brought to the community. We could not go to a neighbor and exchange pins for a barrel of flour, or potatoes, because our neighbor, like us, has plenty of pins, but no flour or potatoes. It is only by the statement of an extreme case like this that we are able to see the results and consequences of concentrating all our labor to the production of one article, as is now being done in many places in the world, but I will have more to say on this part of the subject further on in this paper.

The first great industry that would naturally be developed in a state like ours is agriculture; in some of the extreme Western states mining was first developed, then agriculture, and lastly manufacturing. Notably was this the case in California, but the development of agriculture was so necessary to the success of the other, that it soon followed, and now California is in some respects the greatest agricultural state in the Union, and notwithstanding the immense amount of gold taken from her hills and valleys, the yield of golden wheat and fruits of various kinds, now exceeds in value each year that of the gold taken any year since its discovery there. The gold supply in California is being rapidly exhausted, but the annual supply from her cultivated fields is being increased all the time. Nature is not now manufacturing gold in her great laboratories, as all that work was completed millions of years ago, but she has an inexhaustible supply of material on hand of one kind and another from which is being manufactured in her cultivated fields that which is of more value to us and greater necessity than gold. At one time in California we had a fair illustration of an entire population devoted to one particular industry. There was a large and growing population to supply with food, clothing and implements, without there being any development of the industries that produce these things. All these necessary articles must be transported a great distance at an immense expense, and sold at such prices that none but those who were fortunate and industrious could buy what was absolutely needed to sustain life. Had the gold supply become suddenly exhausted, great distress must have prevailed, as there was no other means of procuring the necessaries of life only to buy them with the gold as it was produced. But what a change has taken place here; diversified labor has made these people, once so helpless, notwithstanding the wealth of gold some of them had, to one of true independence. We must have diversified labor to the greatest extent possible, otherwise we can not have that exchange one with another so necessary in order to prevent the disastrous results that always follow, when from any cause whatever the particular industry of one section is paralyzed. . . .

If there is all the diversity of labor that is possible in a state like ours, there can hardly come a time when agriculture, manufacturing and mining will be depressed to such an extent that willing hands can not find something to do to earn and secure a living. We have had several times in this state partial, and in some sections almost total, failures of crops that have caused hardships and distress; but they were always felt less severely in sections of the state where the manufacturing interests have been most developed, because money circulates more freely in such places, being drawn there by the manufacturing interest; but, unfortunately for us, these manufacturing places are too few and far between. We are at this time paying not less than half a million dollars each year to other states for agricultural implements alone, and what the aggregate amount is that we pay for other manufactured goods I have no means of telling, owing to our lack of statistical information; but I have no doubt that a large part of our last immense crop will be required to foot the bills. If money is constantly drawn from our state at this rate, to pay for goods that we might as well make ourselves, we are losing that amount all the time, and can not expect to increase in material wealth and independence as we should.

We have a number of very large manufacturing establishments in this state that would be a credit to any state, and we have a great number of smaller ones. But as yet their numbers are so small, as compared to what they might be, that it becomes a matter of serious consideration to do something to encourage this great industry.

Some years ago, an organization in this and other states was gotten up, composed exclusively of agriculturalists, for the purpose of mutual protection and the curing of some real and some fancied wrongs. I have no doubt that all who went into this organization did so with the very best intentions. It is believed by many persons that serious injury has been done to the manufacturing as well as the agricultural interests by this organization, without any such result being intended or expected. I am not prepared to say that it has had an injurious effect on either of these great industries, but it can not be claimed that it has accomplished for its members the good results that were expected. Organizations of this kind must necessarily partake, to some extent, of the nature of trades unions; they must be in favor of some particular interest and against some other interest, and, like trades unions, almost always injure most those they were intended to benefit. This organization, although not so intended, has been used by those who are so foolish as to try to keep alive the old jealousy that still crops out from time to time between agriculturists and manufacturers, when, in fact, there is no conflict of interest between them. You can not benefit or injure one or the other, without both being benefited or injured, as the case may be. As well might we expect to fatten and improve one end of a mule without the other end being improved, as to improve the conditions of a farmer or a manufacturer, without both being improved.

Indiana has long since taken prominent rank as an agricultural state. May we not hope that before long she will also rank high as a manufacturing state. We have within our borders all the elements of a great manufacturing state, except enough of capital and skilled labor. When our resources in iron, coal, timber, clay, stone, etc., become better known, and with proper encouragement from us, capital and skilled labor will be attracted here, and find one of the best fields for investment in enterprises of this kind to be found in the Union. Here we can combine manufacturing and agriculture in that close proximity to each other so necessary to make both the most profitable. The value of our manufactured, as well as agricultural products, are regulated in part by the distance they have to be transported to find a market. If wheat is worth one dollar per bushel in New York city, it can not be sold in central Indiana for more than eighty cents. This large difference is the cost of transportation, commission, etc., and is unavoidable so long as we have to go so far for a market. We can not have New York city here, but we can have that which will give us as good a market if we will do something to increase the demand for wheat at home, as the price of it, like all other products, is regulated by supply and demand. It is a well known fact, that land is worth more when situated near a large city or manufacturing district than when situated remote from such places. Why is this? It is not because the land is better, or that it will produce any more corn or wheat, but because that which it does produce is worth more, because of a home market. When lands are situated a great distance from market, only such crops can be raised as will bear transportation a long distance with safety, and at least expense. An acre of corn or wheat in Indiana is not worth, on an average, more than fifteen dollars per acre, while it is possible to raise crops on a single acre worth three hundred dollars, and even twice that amount has been received for the product of a single acre. But such crops as these can only be raised to a limited extent, as yet, in Indiana, because we have not a market that can be reached. These crops that pay so largely, for the most part, must find sale at the exact time they are ready, otherwise they are worth nothing. Situated as we are, the farmer can not vary the monotony of almost one continual routine in the crops he raises. He has no chance to renew the fields worn out with repeated crops of corn or wheat, except to rest them, and wear out other fields while they are recuperating. He has not at hand, and can not get without great expense, fertilizers that will keep up the drain in the large fields he must cultivate. This necessitates large farms with quite a large part of it lying idle more than half of the time, or at least if not quite idle, so nearly so that little can be expected from it. If we had a large demand for market-garden products, small farms, under a high state of cultivation, would be the rule. A few acres could always be kept up, with the fertilizers that could be readily procured, and from these few acres an increase could be had, larger than many persons make from a quarter section of land. There is no doubt but there are many farms in some of the Eastern states containing not more than fifteen or twenty acres, from which the owners not only make a good living, but actually get rich. The tendency to have large farms and poor tillage has been too much the rule in this State, but the cause of it, in part, is the one before mentioned, that owing to the nature of the crops that must be raised in order to find a market, we are compelled to take such as pay the least and exhaust the soil the most.

If we had a large population of non-producers to feed, as they have in many places, then we would have a change, in part at least, in the crops we would raise, and this change would not only lighten the labor of making it, by giving a pleasing change and variety to it, but it would result in more money in our pockets and smaller mortgages on our farms.

It is not enough for us to merely say that it is all right to try and bring about a better understanding between the two great industrial interests of the world; but we must act. If there is anything in the way that can be removed, that prevents a more rapid development of either of these two great interests, we must remove it. If legislation is needed, let us not only ask for it, but see that we get it. There are so many ways in which we can do something to help ourselves and neighbors that it would seem useless to name them here; but above all things, let us encourage home productions. If a poor, struggling mechanic is trying to establish a business near you, give him your right hand and patronage, and even if his productions cost you more than those of same kind made at a distance, do not stop for this. He may not be an angel in disguise; but he is a public benefactor if he only makes wooden nutmegs from wood that would otherwise go to waste, if there is still a market for such things. Many of our largest and most important manufacturing establishments had very small beginnings; and there is no doubt that there are many places deprived of the advantages derived from what is now a large establishment, because the poor, insignificant beginner did not meet with the encouragement that he deserved when he tried to build up a business at these places. After a prolonged struggle he was compelled to abandon the enterprise, and go to some other place where his efforts are better appreciated. This is but the history, in short, of many cases that could be mentioned. The disposition on the part of many persons to always send to some other place for such things as they want is an evil that can and should be cured. It is an evil that strikes at the very foundation of a new beginner, as it not only deprives him of the profit he could make from the sales he should make, but he loses reputation and courage by it.

If we would prosper as a state, and have that degree of independence that we should have, we must pay more attention to the development of our resources. We can not afford to have this constant drain on us for manufactured goods that we might as well make ourselves. We are grumbling all the time at high taxes, and yet do almost nothing in the right direction to reduce them.

Each county must have money to meet certain expenses, and this amount we must raise, whether we are rich or poor. If we have a large amount of property, in proportion to our population, the assessment is small, and, if a small amount of property, the assessment is large. Then if we can do anything to increase the value of our property, or bring more of it into the state, we are doing that which will result in a reduction of taxes.

The peculiar geographical position Indiana bears to the balance of the states in the Union, makes us the half-way house between the east and the great west. We were at one time a border state; now our position is changed, as though some great convulsion of nature had lifted us up, and placed us down again, much further east than we were before. All the great through lines of railroads from east to west pass through our state, and if we could examine the contents of each car, and see the amount of manufactured goods, of one kind and another, with which they are filled, that have come so far and have still further to go, we might learn a lesson, or at least take a hint, that if we could only make these goods, what an immense advantage it would be to us. Much of the raw materials from which they are made have to be transported as far to reach their present manufacturers as they would if we made them here. The great advantage we have over eastern manufacturers, in the way of cheap grounds, building material, food and fuel, and our nearness, as compared to them, to this great western market, would be greatly to our benefit. We have a large amount of raw material of our own, and our network of railroads, that reach almost every county in our state, gives us great facility for gathering raw material and distributing finished goods, and bringing them to shipping centers for transportation. We are met sometimes with the argument that we can never compete with the east in manufacturing, because we have not got reliable water-power. This is too large a question to be discussed by me fully at this time; but I will say, that the time will come when we will no longer hear the assertion made that we can not compete with the east on this account. It is true that we do not have reliable water-power; but we do have that which is more reliable. The immense beds of mineral coal, under our fertile soils, will furnish power for manufacturing purposes equal to that of the best water-power in the east, and quite as cheap, all things considered. When water-power is used, we have to contend against floods, droughts and ice; besides, we have no choice in the selection of a site for our manufactories. The distance the raw material has to be transported, or the finished goods taken to a market, can not be considered in establishing manufactories when water-power must be used. We must go with them to where the power is to be had, regardless of all other conditions or circumstances. . . .

Indian Agriculture, 1878

From "Report of Kiowa and Comanche Agency, Indian Territory," U.S. Commissioner of Indian Affairs, *Annual Report*, 1878, pp. 58–61.

KIOWA AND COMANCHE AGENCY, INDIAN TERRITORY,
August 15, 1878.

SIR: In compliance with instructions contained in circular letter of July 1, 1878, the following is respectfully submitted as my first annual report of the condition and affairs of the agency under my charge for the year just past.

Having relieved my predecessor, Mr. J. M. Haworth, so late as the 1st day of April last, I will not be able to present to you a statement that may prove to be as full and as accurate as is desirable. But I shall endeavor to detail all the more important events of the year; and while imparting information as to the character and extent of progress made, I will present as clear a view as I can of the condition, habits, and disposition of the Indians over whom I have been placed.

It is shown by the census recently taken that the Indians of this reservation number: *Comanches*, 1,475; *Kiowas*, 1,120; *Apaches*, 344; in all 2,939, of which 802 are men, 1,166 women, and 971 children, divided into 345 families.

Since the trouble of 1874 these Indians have been at peace with the whites, and have shown no disposition to move from their reservation. While many of them complain that the western boundary-line of the reservation has been drawn in too close, contending that it should be even far beyond the 100th meridian of west longitude, and that the settlers upon the Pan Handle of Texas are encroaching upon this territory, they manifest no disposition to violate orders by crossing the line. . . .

Agriculture

When I reached the agency in April, the Indians were actively engaged in breaking and preparing the ground for planting. This I found quite an undertaking, as their ponies, besides being small, were very poor, and the ground very hard from want of rain and from being trodden during the winter by their stock; the fodder stalks having been left standing, and the fencing down, they were permitted to feed upon their fields. This I shall endeavor to prevent next winter, and have them plow their fields late in the fall or early in the winter, before their ponies lose their flesh.

Heretofore corn has been planted for the most of them, with the planter, and I found it was expected this year. They protested strenuously against undertaking it themselves, pleading their inability to accomplish it, and the fact that they had been promised it should be planted for them, and for a while it seemed as if they would hold out in their refusal. A few, however, attempted it, and others seeing how well they did, all were soon planting, being instructed by two farmers and two regular employés engaged for the purpose. Many of them were entirely ignorant of the process, and the most difficult part was in running a straight furrow, as both themselves and ponies were very awkward. Sometimes would be seen three Indians with one team, one at the head of each pony and another hold of the plow. Various improvements upon the white man's plan were suggested. One fellow, having made several ineffectual efforts at a straight furrow across his field, stopped at the end of a row and casting his eyes back at his work exclaimed ''no good,'' and unhitching hurriedly one of his team and mounting he galloped off, apparently in disgust at his efforts at following the white man's way. He appeared, however, before a great while with a coil of rope, which he had purchased at the store, and this he soon had stretched across his field as a guide to his plow in marking the ground. Considering the fact that the ground was exceedingly cloddy, with all other circumstances, they succeeded, I think, remarkably well, the majority of the rows being so they could be cultivated with the plow.

The prospect the first of the season was very bad, as no rain fell on most of the fields until the 23d of May, and a large portion of the seed failed to sprout. Later rains brought up all the replant, and now I am pleased at being able to state that they are promised an excellent crop. The yield would have been better could they have been prevailed upon to thin the corn; but they cannot be made to see the wisdom of this, and were indignant when advised to do it.

Very few have before used the plow in the cultivation, while this season all we had have been constantly in use, and all the time there was a demand for more. The Indians are much encouraged at the prospect, and pleased at what they themselves have accomplished in the planting and the cultivation, and allude to their work seemingly with much pride. It is certainly gratifying to me to know that, besides harvesting a good crop, they will have learned sufficiently to make them in a measure independent of any instructions from the farmers in another year.

The supply of garden seeds I found at the agency was the donation of Mr. Benjamin Coates, a benevolent gentleman of Philadelphia. These were carefully distributed and at the time seemed to be appreciated, but the dry weather the first of the season caused a failure with most of their gardens; some, however, who had seed to replant with, have good gardens.

I had placed in bed several bushels of sweet potatoes, intending to introduce among the Indians the cultivation and use of this potato, but unfortunately some stray bug destroyed the bed. I am satisfied this crop might be made to go far toward subsisting these Indians, as in this country they yield abundantly, will keep well, and are easily cultivated. I shall endeavor to grow next season an abundance of these and other plants.

The patches cultivated by the Kiowas have been all in one inclosure, and this situated about 14 miles from their camp, which is a favorite one with them. This is a source of inconvenience to them as well as trouble to the agent, and I hope soon to have it remedied by assisting them in opening farms elsewhere. While doing this, I shall hope to remedy another evil. I take it that no very great improvement can be looked for among any Indians until their custom as to bands is broken up, and certainly not as long as large bodies of them are in one camp. The different bands of Comanches and Apaches have their camps and fields, in most cases, located at suitable distances apart but the Kiowas are encamped together, and its bad effect is to be seen nearly every day. Less inroads can be made upon their savage rites and customs while so living; they are often in a state of excitement for days at a time by the circulation of some idle story or maybe they all appear at the agency requesting a council upon a trivial matter, the result of a "talk" at their dance the night before. I was enabled to locate some men for the contract for breaking 250 acres of sod this spring, but I regret it did not allow me to settle more of them, or all who wish to be. I annex herewith the report of the farmer.

Having previously received authority from you, I gave, during the month of June permission to a portion of the Comanche and Apache Indians, a few from each band, to go out to the western part of their reservation to hunt buffalo. The Kiowas desired while out to engage in their annual medicine dance waited until the close of the school the last Thursday in June, when they moved out to a point they had selected for the erection of their medicine lodge. General Davidson sent out with them one company of cavalry, under the command of Captain Nolan. The buffalo, after being hunted awhile, moved off beyond their reach, but yet they succeeded in obtaining a very good supply of meat and robes. The robes at this season can only be used for covering their tepees. The Comanches and Apaches returned several weeks since, remaining there but a short while, and the Kiowas are now on their way in.

Progress

While I am not able to report any very great advancement toward civilization of the Indians during the few months they have been in my charge, I believe I am justified in hoping that another year will show a marked improvement. The desire to enter into the cultivation of the soil is very general, and many more are inclined to settle off by themselves, and away from the main camps, than was the case several months back. Some of the chiefs have expressed a willingness to give up their chieftainship and settle down with their families on their farms. Moh-a-way, for a long time a prominent Comanche chief, has recently formally abdicated, saying he desires to spend the rest of his life with his family on his farm. I hope and believe that many others will soon follow his example. Another favorable indication is that they show a more correct appreciation of the rights of individual property and a desire to accumulate. They seem lately to be impressed more with the fact that their subsistence must depend upon their own labor, and that the government will not always supply them. I am satisfied that until recently many of them believed they were always to be fed, and with such rations as they could consume, and have not understood that there was any ration prescribed by the authorities at Washington. The disappearance of buffalo has doubtless had its effect in directing their attention to agriculture and the preservation and increase of their herds of cattle.

Those who have houses and lands to cultivate are taking considerable interest in the improvement of their places. Until recently, few have lived in their houses, preferring their tepees, but now, since they have received some beds, chairs, &c., they have moved into them, and seem desirous of adding to their comforts.

They are very anxious to increase their herd of cattle, and some have sold some of their ponies and brought the money to me to be invested in cattle for them. They have many more ponies than they need, and I shall endeavor to have them exchange their surplus for cattle. As the crops in the country are very uncertain on account of the drought and therefore not always to be depended upon as a means of subsistence, it becomes the more important that care should be taken with their cattle. The country is well adapted to raising stock, and could their herds be added to in some way, for instance by devoting a portion of their annuity to the purchase of cattle for two or three years; this, with the natural increase, would in a comparatively short while make them independent of any support of the government.

Farming in Michigan, 1880–97

From Excerpts, *Loomis Family Farm Diaries*, Ionia, Michigan, 1880–1897. Diary kept by Arthur Perkins Loomis, 1880–1892, and by his father, James W. Loomis, 1893–1897. Reprinted by permission of Frances Loomis.

Thursday, March 4, 1880. Warm and Cloudy. I trimmed appletrees in the afternoon. Mortimer received Dunham's catalogue. Mr. Munn sent after his derrick and ropes. Pa went to town after the boys. . . .

Saturday, May 8. Ditto. I plowed all day. Pa and Bertie Ebb's stayed all day. Clarence Tucker came after some bantam eggs this afternoon. Pa went to town in the P.M. . . .

Monday, May 10. Rained hard last night and some today. I plowed some this forenoon. Pa and I went to Eri Le Valley and got some trees set them out this afternoon. Ma and Trad went to the city this evening got Lon and I a suit of clothes. Jack Corey called here today to see about getting seed corn.

Tuesday, May 11. Pleasant. I plowed all day. Pa made garden until 4 o'clock and then went to town. Lillie and Ada were here a short time tonight.

Wednesday, May 12, Pleasant. I plowed all day. Mrs. White was here this morning. Uncle Dick and Fred were here this A.M. Pa hoed in garden some this forenoon and went to town with A.F.K. in P.M. Schoolma'am was here this morning. J. W. brought me some shoes. A.H. Tibbitts' children were in the afternoon.

Thursday, May 13. Colder but pleasant. I plowed the remainder of the corn field got done at 10.30. dragged until night. . . .

Friday, May 14. Very pleasant. I dragged until 5 o'clock. Mrs. White's hired man used Dick 3/4 of today to mark corn ground. Ma got dipper of the peddler. Book agent was here today. Pa commenced marking corn ground tonight. Thomas went to hear Frank Beard in the evening. Pa cleaned out the old house today.

Saturday, May 15. Same as yesterday. Pa marked corn ground all day. I sowed plaster in the orchard and fixed fence in same place in the forenoon. The little boys and I planted corn in the afternoon. Old Harmon was here after Ida this P.M.

Sunday, May 16. Same as yesterday. Mortimer and Bertie went to church this morning. Mort went around by E.P.'s who all came over after dinner. Uncle Dick was here a little while tonight. F.G. Cornell was here to day. I went to F. Keen's and after Ida in P.M. Ed the Irishman was here this P.M. Steve came with Uncle Eb's folks.

Monday, May 17. Same as yesterday. Pa marked corn ground til 3 o'clock. Bertie and I with some help from Pa and Mort finished planting corn tonight. J.M. Babcock got "Bill" this afternoon. I received Biblical Biology from Estil. Pa received his appointment as enumerator. Lon left for Colorado today.

Tuesday, May 18. Very pleasant. Bertie and I planted two rows of potatoes around the cornfield. Pa and Ma went to Mr. Benedict's after seed potatoes I plowed in the old garden this afternoon. Pa went to town this afternoon. S.V.R. came home with Pa and Mort tonight. Rag peddler here this P.M.

Wednesday, May 19. Very pleasant. Rained some this afternoon. Pa and I set out tomato and cabbage plants this afternoon. I commenced plowing the corn stubble at 2 o'clock. . . .

Friday, May 28. Pleasant. Ed and I dug ditch and postholes today. Wurster and Chauncey worked on windmill. W.S. Bates was here today. Pa went to town in the A.M. after feed. A.F.K. was here tonight. A man was here to get job of painting windmill. . . .

Sunday, July 4. Conrad here today to put up reaper.

Monday, July 5. Warm. Charley made road in barnyard in A.M. cultivated corn in P.M. I picked some cherries and loafed around some. Pa went to town in forenoon bought some beef. Cut around first wheat field.

Tuesday, July 6. Commenced harvesting. Albert Errisige, Elonzo Sherrard and myself bound, Charlie and the lads set it up. A fruit tree agent was here today.

Wednesday, July 7. Warm. Cut wheat. Albert, Robinson and Charles bound. Aunt Theresa and Lily called tonight.

Thursday, July 8. Rained some in afternoon. I didn't work today. Finished cutting "back twenty." Myron Graves called after milk and eggs tonight. Lon picked cherries for "Lind."

Friday, July 9. Hottest day of the season. Completed harvesting about 4. . . . Mort stayed down to attend ice cream festival at Public square.

Saturday, July 10. Very hot. Charlie drew manure. I fixed rack. . . .

Tuesday, July 13. Same. hard thunder shower in evening. Drew wheat all day. Lon helped. Mr. Cornell was here to dinner.

Wednesday, July 14. Hot. Rained hard in afternoon. I went to town after feed this morning. Lon picked some cherries this forenoon. I repaired road fence today. Charles spread manure and hoed in garden. Pa went to T.E. Smith's with Lon and bought a span of horses of him. Mr. and Mrs. Canfield were here this morning.

Thursday, July 15. Warm, rained some at night. Drew in Lon's wheat tonight. Charles plowed in forenoon. Hoed in garden in afternoon.

Friday, July 16. Cooler. Rained a little tonight. Completed drawing wheat about 2.30 and then Charles and I went to help A.H. Tibbitts draw wheat. . . .

Saturday, July 17. School started today.

Tuesday, July 20. Cooler. Charles plowed. I cultivated garden in the afternoon and painted some on windmill. . . .

Wednesday, July 21. Cool. Rained some in afternoon. I fired log heap in 40 stirred hay and raked up windrows in A.M. Charles plowed in forenoon. . . .

Thursday, August 26. Rained this forenoon. I got a load of bran at Lyons this forenoon. Pa and I went to Grange picnic in afternoon.

Friday, August 27. Very hot. I threshed at A.H. Tibbitts in the forenoon and at Joe Babcock's in the afternoon. Bertie left for Milwaukee this afternoon. . . .

Tuesday, September 7. Cooler. I cultivated in the little lot with the "Arnold cultivator." Bert cultivated in the 40. Mortimer did not work in bank. Mortimer went to the cantata in the evening. . . .

Sunday, September 12. Bright and pleasant. My birthday. 21 years old today.

Monday, September 13. Rained a little. Cold. I dragged. Pa went after drill teeth. Had em sharpened at Arnold's. . . .

Tuesday, September 14. Cool. I drilled all day. Pa went to town about 4.30. Jack Corey and Jim Kinney fixed cistern. . . .

Wednesday, September 15. Pleasant. I drilled until 4.30 and then went to Joel Benedict's to tea. Pa and Ma went to Mr. Bates to visit with Mr. and Mrs. Lathrop.

Thursday, September 16. Drilled. Pleasant.

Friday, September 17. Pleasant. I drilled. School closed today. . . .

Wednesday, September 22. Pleasant. I dug potatoes in forenoon. Bertie and I drew in corn in afternoon. Pa went to town this forenoon.

Thursday, September 23. Ma had two teeth pulled today. Ada and Lily were here this forenoon.

Friday, September 24. I finished digging potatoes today. Pa and Ma went to Uncle Ebb's in afternoon.

Saturday, September 25. Pa went to town today. I took 30 barrels of apples to John Durkee this afternoon.

Sunday, September 26. Rained all day. S.V.R. came here last night stayed all day.

Monday, September 27. I husked corn all day.

Tuesday, September 28. Pa and Ma visited at Uncle Ebb's in afternoon, Jess and I went to hear Captain Allen.

Wednesday, September 29. Show day. Jess and Bertie and I husked corn in forenoon drew in afternoon. Have got 200 bushels drawn now.

Thursday, September 30. Picked apples. . . .

Tuesday, October 5. First day of the Fair.

Wednesday, October 6. Pleasant. I went to the Fair today.

Monday, Jan. 3, 1881. A pleasant day. I went to Abe Benedict's and bought forty cords of wood this morning. Ma and I went to town in the afternoon. Annual meeting of the Agriculture Society at 2 P.M. today. Snowed a very little last night, as much more would make good sleighing. Bertie commenced school again today. Jess did not go, stayed at home and done most all the chores. Mort stayed down tonight to go to dancing school.

Tuesday, Jan. 4. A pleasant day. Looked like snowing this morning but did not. Jess and I went over to Uncle Ebb's in the forenoon and from there we went to town. Jess started at 2 o'clock for Lansing. I took 6.85 worth of butter to town. . . .

Thursday, Jan. 6. Snowed enough last night to make good sleighing. Returned Uncle Dick's sausage cutter this morning. Ma made head cheese all day.

Friday, Jan. 7. Colder. I took some corn down to Bush's this morning. I got a load of wood in the forenoon, churned, made brine, went to town in afternoon. . . .

Wednesday, March 23. I split some wood in the forenoon. Went after Pa tonight, took a bushel of apples down to the office and sold 21 pounds of butter at 20 cents a pound. Rag peddler here this noon. Mort did not come home, went to a social or somewhere else. Bert cleared out the hall closet today carried in some wood but did not get any rats. Roads are very muddy.

Thursday, March 24. Thawed considerable this afternoon. I went after Pa and Mort tonight. Bert and I made a figure 4 trap this P.M. Sewing machine agent was here this afternoon. . . .

Thursday, April 14. I churned. Took 22 bags of corn down to the mill this afternoon. . . .

Friday, April 15. I split some wood today. Bert and I took some parsnips to Mrs. Balcom. Mr. Corell and Mr. Monroe, the patent fence men were here this afternoon, made about 50 feet of fence, stayed to supper.

Saturday, April 16. Warm and pleasant. I went down to the mill this morning after the meal but it was not ground. Expected Jake Perkins today but he did not come. I went to town three times today. Took 8 dozen eggs down today. Got 5 pounds of sugar for 'em.

Monday, May 2. I had the ague today, high fever until 5 o'clock. School began Monday. Mr. Davis is the schoolma'am. Ada and Myrtie are coming to school here.

Tuesday, May 3. I loafed around all day. Lillie was here this morning after some grafts. Bert cut 'em.

Wednesday, May 4. I am a good deal better but haven't commenced work yet will go for it in a day or two. I went to town this afternoon, took down some butter and eggs, got a new hatchet today. The state agent of the Myers windmill was here tonight.

Thursday, May 5. I went to town this afternoon. Bertie went fishing. Uncle Eb raised his straw barn today. I got the 14 foot stuff to make fence with.

Friday, May 6. Very warm. Bertie churned this forenoon. I made fence standards this A.M. Bert and I laid over the fence between us and Mr. Balcom in the afternoon.

Saturday, May 7. Warmer. Bert and I made fence standards all day. Sheep shearing festival on the Fair Ground today.

Sunday, May 8. Looked like rain all day but didn't. Bert went to church this morning. Pa and Ma went over to Uncle Ebb's a little while this forenoon. Uncle Dick was here. Josie has the diptheria. Mortimer went to town a little while this afternoon.

Monday, May 9. Very warm, rained several times in the afternoon. Commenced plowing for corn this morning. Barringer sent a sulky plow up here this morning. W.E. Williams came to operate it. Uncle Dick, Will Taylor, Hub Babcock, Mr. Hubbell and Mr. Barringer were here this forenoon to see the plow run. Mr. Munn fixed the pump this morning. Mr. Patrick got two bushels of corn here tonight.

Thursday, May 26. Very hot. Sheep shearers were here all day. Dragged the garden and planted some potatoes, Bert and I did. El. Tew's man borrowed our corn planter.

Friday, May 27. Very, very hot. McQuillen and Co. finished shearing sheep at two o'clock. Lon Sherrard was here this afternoon after some seed corn.

Saturday, May 28. Bert and I planted corn all day 2d time. . . .

Monday, May 30. Rained some this afternoon. Bert churned this morning. We planted corn. Mrs. Rogers was here this afternoon, got a bushel of corn.

Tuesday, May 31. Cool. I worked on the road today. Bert finished planting corn about 3 o'clock. Lon returned the wool packer.

Wednesday, June 1. Rained some last night. Bert and I cleared out the cellar and made garden today. I laid up the fence in the 8 acre lot. Mort and I went to town tonight. I got a pair of shoes. Went around by Uncle Eb's. Expected to work on road today but as the pathmaster didn't come we come home.

Tuesday, June 7. The long wished for rain came last night, was raining this morning when I got up, stopped about 9 o'clock. I took Trad down, Pa did not go until after dinner. I plowed from nine A.M. until night. Myron Smith and Philo Bates were (here) tonight to buy wool. Paid 31 cents a pound "docking" 8 fleeces. Rag peddler here also wind mill agent. Bertie took the hired girl home tonight.

Wednesday, June 8. Rained some today, cloudy since yesterday morning. I took the wool down this morning, 518 pounds. Plowed ¾ of a day. Two seed corn customers. Got a barrel of salt.

Thursday, June 9. Plowed. Lon called to borrow a grub hoe. Aunt Theresa and Lillie to borrow the corn planters. Bert finished spreading manure this afternoon. . . .

Wednesday, June 17. Bright and pleasant. I went to Grange in the evening. was elected Secretary.

Thursday, June 18. Warm. Bert dragged on the cornfield until noon. I went over to M. Overhiser's sorted out seed corn this A.M. I plowed in the corn stubble after dinner. Ada came after Lillie tonight. George Townsend marked corn ground for us this afternoon. Mr. Overhiser returned our corn planters this evening.

Friday, June 19. A bright pleasant day. Bertie and I planted corn, tried the planters but did not like 'em, used the hoes. Lillie and Ada came tonight. Trad spent the evening in town. Albert and I went over to Mrs. Sellick's after some butter. George Townsend finished marking the corn ground at noon. . . .

Tuesday, June 20. Cool and pleasant. I plowed until three and then went to town after a new corn cultivator. Bert cultivated corn while I went to town.

Wednesday, June 21. I plowed this forenoon. Bert and I cultivated corn until night.

Thursday, June 22. Hottest day of the season. I plowed this A.M. Bert and I finished cultivating corn north and south. Mrs. Cutler was here after flowers.

Friday, June 23. I cultivated potatoes until ten o'clock then went to plowing. Plowed until five P.M.

Saturday, June 24. Rained hard about 11 A.M. and again about 2 P.M. I plowed about half a day, took the wool down this afternoon, had 542 pounds from 66 sheep. . . .

Monday, July 3. Finished plowing the back twenty at noon, commenced on the other, quit about 3 on account of the rain.

Tuesday, July 4. Pleasant, rained this afternoon. We were all at Uncle Ebb's to dinner, went to the races this afternoon. . . .

Saturday, July 8. I plowed about half a day. Barringer and Wentworth's men set up our McCormick binder.

Monday, July 10. Pa came home at noon to help Bertie and I draw hay, got in four loads. I commenced mowing about five o'clock, got run away with and broke the machine.

Tuesday, July 11. I took the mower down to Arnold's to have it fixed, went down after it after dinner, cut some. Bought a potato cultivator of Mr. Arnold.

Thursday, July 13. Pleasant. Bert and I drew hay this afternoon, cultivated corn until noon.

Friday, July 14. Finished drawing in hay this P.M.

Saturday, July 15. Pleasant. Started the self binder this afternoon. I picked cherries, went over to Uncle Ebb's after some potatoes, then went around by town after Pa. Uncle Ebb came over to see the binder. . . .

Sunday, January 14, 1882. I took Mrs. Whipple and Lizzie over to Mr. Balcom's. Pa, Trad and I went over to Uncle Ebb's a little while.

Monday, January 15. Two degrees below zero this morning. I went down town this morning, had Dick and Bill shod. Drew one load of wood this afternoon. Went after Pa and the boys. Trad did not come home. Mr. Arnold sent his bull here this morning, came home at night. Trad went to the concert this evening.

Wednesday, January 18. I drew one load of wood this forenoon. Lillie stayed all night, took Lizzie down this morning, I went after them.

Friday, January 19. I drew one load of wood. Went around by Uncle Ebb's to town. Trad stayed down.

Saturday, January 20. Snowed this afternoon. I took them down this morning, went after them at night. Bertie went over to Uncle Ebb's this morning, spent the day.

Sunday, January 21. Very cold and windy, worst day yet, 5 below all day. We all stayed home all day.

Monday, January 22. Another awful day. 12 below this morning and about 6 all day. I did not do much, went to town after Pa and Jess. Trad did not come home. Jess froze his ears.

Tuesday, January 23. 15 below this morning. 20 below in time. I took them down this morning. I broke the stove cover this afternoon. Went over to Uncle Ebb's this afternoon. Bert went down after them.

Wednesday, January 24. I went to Grange this evening, got home from Uncle Ebb's this forenoon.

Thursday, January 25, 1883. I went to the Farmer's Institute this afternoon.

Friday, January 26. I went to the Institute all day. Went to the Bailey House to dinner. Rained some this evening.

Saturday, January 27. Went to the Institute, went up to Uncle Ebb's to dinner, went down town again, rode up (with) Uncle Tip and Aggie, took supper there, went up to Uncle Ebb's, stayed all night. . . .

Wednesday, February 7. Very cold. Trad, Jess and Bertie went to Dan Sturtevant's to a dance tonight. Grange meeting and New Orleans minstrels tonight.

Monday, June 18. Rained all last night. I set a leach this forenoon. Went down town this morning, brought home a new Tiger rake. I plowed this afternoon. Very windy all day.

Tuesday, June 19. A pleasant day. Rained some this P.M. I got a spring tooth corn cultivator at Willett's. Bert and I cultivated corn. Pa came home at noon, went down to see the sheep shearers at John Sessions.

Wednesday, June 20. Sheep shearers came this afternoon. Bert and I cultivated corn until they came.

Thursday, June 21. Sheep shearers here all day. Bertie cultivated corn.

Friday, June 22. Very pleasant. George Grinnell and Charlie Oliver finished shearing sheep about two o'clock. I went around by town, got a new hat, a gold pen for Ada, then went up to Uncle Ebb's.

Saturday, June 23. Hard rain this afternoon about three. Bert cultivated corn this forenoon. I hoed the early Vermont potatoes. . . .

Saturday, January 5, 1884. Last night about 10.30, Canfield's house burnt. Jessie Benedict drove over here after us. We got there in time to help get out the most of the things. This morning, Bert took the folks down and I went over to Canfield's, helped pick up things, drew two loads of studd over to Mr. Benedict's. Went to town tonight, got lumber for another sheep rack. Two sheep got in the tank.

Monday, January 7. Yesterday, Pa, Jess and I went over to Uncle Ebb's. Today has been pleasant though cold. I went to town this afternoon, attended the annual meeting of the agri. society, got 50 pounds of patent flour. School commenced again today.

Tuesday, January 8. Pleasant, splendid sleighing. I went up to Uncle Dick's a while this afternoon, went to town from there. Pa and I, Mrs. Whipple and Lizzie went to hear the Fisk Jubilee Singers this evening, a splendid show.

Wednesday, January 9. Done chores and that is about all. Bert and Lizzie went to the installation of the Grange officers, Jess and I over to Uncle Ebb's to a rehearsal of "Off the stage."

Tuesday, March 5, 1889. Warm and pleasant. Pa went down town after the corn meal. Lizzie went down to take a painting lesson. Uncle Elliot and his wife spent the evening here. Am reading Dombey and Son, the late Mrs. Null and Ben Hur. . . .

Tuesday, May 7. I finished rolling the corn ground about ten o'clock. Uncle Dick's man came after the roller. I started to plant corn after dinner but the planter would not work. I went after Barringer's man, took him back after supper.

Wednesday, May 8. Commenced to plant corn this morning but the machine wouldn't work. Went after man at Barringer's, he couldn't fix it. After dinner I commenced plowing potato patch. Pa brought Hub Babcock down to fix planter, got it to working about four o'clock.

Thursday, May 9. Very warm, need rain. I planted corn, quit early, went to the Presbyterian church to see Mr. Lindsay installed, took Mrs. Whipple and Lizzie. Rev. Herrick Johnson preached.

Friday, May 10. Warm. I finished planting corn at noon, plowed and dragged for potatoes this afternoon. Pa and Mrs. Whipple went to town this P.M. to do some trading. Hub got four bushels seed corn here yesterday.

Saturday, May 11. Pa and I got up the sheep this morning, cut off lambs tails, then went back to the forty and marked out potato patch, planted after dinner and got done at four o'clock, then I went to town, got the buggy, had cart tires set. . . .

Monday, May 13. I drew manure on garden, planted it, dragged it. Pa and I plowed out grape vines. Burt Babcock got some seed corn here this afternoon. I went to town this evening.

Wednesday, June 12. George Grinnell and Ed Felton sheared sheep all day. I cultivated corn. Ed cultivated the potatoes. Pa done up wool. Uncle Dick and Hug

Babcock here this forenoon. Mrs. Root and son here to see the pony this afternoon. Sheep sheared drove Zara home. Lizzie sick. Pleasant day.

Thursday, June 13. Pleasant, warm. Sheep shearers got done at noon. Ed went to town this forenoon after the doctor for Lizzie. Dr. Allen came this afternoon. I cultivated corn. Ed drew manure. Pa went to town this afternoon, took tea at Uncle Chauncey's. Two fires in town last night.

Friday, June 14. Warm. I cultivated corn and the potatoes in the forty, got done at noon. Uncle Dick borrowed our cultivator this afternoon. Pa went to town after Dr. Allen for Lizzie. Ed drew manure this forenoon, spread this afternoon. I plowed this afternoon.

Saturday, June 15. I plowed. Ed drew manure. Ed and I went to town this evening.

Monday, June 17. Warm. I plowed. Ed drew manure. Pa went to town this afternoon. Dr. Allen here this forenoon. Flora Balcom here this evening.

Tuesday, June 13. I plowed. Ed drew manure. Mr. and Mrs. Balcom here to dinner, had strawberry shortcake. "Las" Smith here to look at the wool tonight. Pa went to town this afternoon. A very hard rain about five thirty P.M. Pa sold the wool for thirty two cents a pound.

Tuesday, January 14, 1890. I split some wood today. Went to town this afternoon. This evening I went to see Nelse Cole to get him to help us butcher. Stopped at Mr. Balcom's.

Wednesday, January 15. Pa and I drew a load of hay this forenoon. Miller here this afternoon, wants to chop some wood. Mrs. Whipple and Lizzie went to town this afternoon. Nursery agent here this forenoon. I split a little wood.

Thursday, January 16. Nelse Cole helped Pa and I butcher our two hogs. I went down town after the mail about five.

Friday, January 17. I helped about the butchery work this afternoon. Lizzie and I went to town. In the evening, we called at Mr. Bates.

Saturday, January 18. I took a load of wheat to Hoag's, got sixty cents a bushel, brought home a ton of middlings. In the evening, Pa and Mrs. Whipple went down to Uncle Elliot's. Clate Root here this morning.

Sunday, January 19. Mrs. Whipple and Lizzie went to church this morning. Pa went over to Uncle Ebb's this forenoon. Uncle Ebb brought him home at night. I spent the evening at Uncle Dick's.

Monday, January 20. I went down town this morning after the sausage, drew two loads of wood and then went down after a load of bran.

Sunday, March 1, 1896. Cold and windy. No one went to church from here. Mr. and Mrs. Balcom here to dinner. And Alva Bessie came to do chores for eight dollars per month until April when he commences work at sixteen and a half dollars.

Friday, October 30. It rained last night so we couldn't draw stalks. The men took Frank's apples to train in the forenoon and made cider in the afternoon. Art went to town in the forenoon and came home by way of Eb's. I took him down town in the afternoon on his way to Lansing. Warm and rainy in the morning and colder at night.

Saturday, October 31. The men went to Chamberlain's after a load of straw, then put away the tools and littler in the yard. I went to town for art in the forenoon, in the afternoon he and Lizzie went to town and in the evening we all went to the Republican blow out. Weather disagreeable in the morning, pleasant in the evening. . . .

Monday, November 2. We dehorned the cattle in the forenoon. The men drew cornstalks in the afternoon, finished the back lot (24 loads). Art went hunting and I went to town in the afternoon. Weather pleasant.

Farming in Connecticut, 1880

From William Clift, "Tenant Farming," in *Connecticut Board of Agriculture, Annual Report,* 1880–1881 (Hartford, 1881), pp. 232–37.

Tenant Farming

Connecticut has the reputation of being the richest state in the Union, according to its population. However this may be, a large part of its wealth is invested outside of the State, in railroads, in mines, and in mortgages upon real estate in the cities and farming districts of the West. A capitalist, recently deceased, had nearly a half million in loans upon real estate in that region. In the past it has been thought better to make these loans, because the rate of interest has been high, running from eight to twelve per cent. Now, that government bonds pay only four per cent., and interest on good security is much lower, a new factor comes into the calculation of the capitalist, and he has to consider whether he may not find paying investments in home enterprises. There can be no doubt that Connecticut agriculture has suffered very much in the past from lack of capital. So great has been the demand for Eastern money to develop the enterprises, and especially the farms of the new states and territories, and so high have been the rates of interest, that the Connecticut farmers have not had the requisite capital to carry on their own business to advantage. While land and rents have been cheap enough, and markets reasonably good, they have lacked money to invest in labor, fertilizers, stock, tools, drainage, and other improvements. So great has been the disadvantage under which they have labored, that farms, as a rule, have diminished in value, and have been the most unsalable of property. Excepting the farms that lie in the immediate vicinity of cities and villages, and whose value is affected by this nearness to markets, it is doubted if the capital invested in farming has paid three per cent. during the last ten years. The exceptions are in cases where capital has been judiciously used and new methods have been adopted. The problem now to be solved is to bring capital and labor together, on such terms as shall give to each a better and surer reward.

There prevails to some extent, in the eastern part of New London county, a system of tenant farming, which we think helps to solve this problem. If the capitalist can get legal interest for his investment in farm lands and stock, he need not send his capital abroad. If a skillful farmer can get fair pay for his labor and skill, support his family, and save a few hundred dollars every year, he need not go out of the State to find employment.

We recently visited the farm of William B. Hull of North Stonington, and went over it with the proprietor, to study the workings of the system, where it had been in operation for a term of twenty-two years, a period long enough to fully test its value. We were favorably impressed with the system, as a fair thing both for the capitalist and for the farmer. . . .

The Character of the Soil

The farm consists of 160 acres, old measure, which means 178 by actual survey. The heart of the farm is a large swale with several copious, never failing springs, which indicates grazing and dairying as the leading branches of its industry. This swale-land is wet and stony, and runs rapidly to brush and wood. It requires constant attention to keep the grass in sight. It is the he ad-waters of the south branch of Assekonk brook, one of the feeders of Shunnock river. The eastern part of the farm, a hundred acres or more, slopes gently to this swale, and the western part, some forty-five acres, slopes to the east. The most of the swale is so thickly strewn with boulders that drainage would not be a paying investment at present prices of land. But a large part of the eastern slope is comparatively free from large boulders, and could be drained to good advantage. During the spring months it is so saturated with water as to make late plowing and planting a necessity. There are moist and wet patches of land on other parts of the farm, where tiles are greatly needed. The soil is a gravelly loam, with a retentive yellow loam beneath, and beneath that, in many places probably, a hard-pan that prevents good natural drainage. Some of the meadows, however, are sufficiently drained naturally, and always yield fair crops. There is an inviting field for the investment of capital in tile drainage on at least a quarter of the whole area of the farm. But no improvements of this kind have ever been attempted, and the methods of cultivation, crops, fertilizers, are mainly in the old style of husbandry. About sixty acres are kept in mowing and grain crops, seven acres in woodland, and the balance pasture.

Leasing on Shares

The system adopted on this farm, and which prevails in this region, is the following: The owner of the farm furnishes the stock of manure in the yard at the beginning of the lease, which is measured by the cart-loads, as it is drawn out to the fields for use. He furnishes one-half of the stock, cattle, sheep, swine, poultry, which is undivided property, so that there may be no temptation to feed one part of the stock better than another. The tenant, on his part, binds himself to leave as much manure in the yard as he found there, to furnish one half the stock, and to keep it in as good condition as when he took it, to keep a strict account of all sales from the farm, and of all products consumed in his family, and to pay one-half of the receipts to the owner of the farm. He has the use of a garden, his fuel, and some other small perquisites, as may be agreed upon. The time of settlement is usually Christmas or New Year's. He is to keep the fences in good repair, and to conduct the business according to the rules of good husbandry. The lease runs for one year or indefinitely, as long as both parties are satisfied. It is considered best for all parties to have the lease a long one. If the tenant is expecting to leave at the close of the year, he does not look much at the future condition of the soil. He is tempted to skin the farm for his present advantage. If he expects to occupy for several years, his interest is more identified with the owner in keeping the farm in good condition.

The Stock

The stock kept upon the farm the present year, which is about the average, is 25 sheep, which have produced 23 lambs, 19 cows, 5 two year olds, 4 yearlings, 1 yoke of cattle, two horses, 2 old swine, sows, which have produced two litters of pigs, and will make from 2,500 to 3,000 lbs. of pork, a dozen hen-turkeys, and about 40 hens.

Crops and Products

There are seven or eight acres of corn, an acre of potatoes, three acres of oats, and the sixty acres of meadow, producing probably seventy tons of hay, though it is never weighed. Sales of hay are rarely made, and there are this year nine stacks left over, estimated to contain twenty-five tons of hay. This large surplus of hay is kept as a safeguard against years of drought, which affects a well-cultivated farm much less than one in poor condition. When sales are deemed expedient, it is in years of scarcity, when it brings twenty dollars a ton.

The Money Crops

are almost exclusively animal products, which is a cardinal doctrine of good husbandry. These are butter, calves, beef, pork, pigs, lambs, wool, poultry, oats. The oats are sold for the purpose, mainly, of buying corn. All the corn raised upon the farm is fed out to the animals, and considerable quantities in addition. While the price of oats is about the same as corn, the feeding value to fattening animals is much less. The wood is principally white oak, hickory, white wood and chestnut, which furnishes timber and fencing, but is not sold for fuel. The vegetable crops are nearly all consumed upon the farm, which keeps up its fertility, notwithstanding the defective arrangements for making manure.

Fertilizers

The main reliance for fertilizers is the manure of the stock. The principal barn is in the old style, and the common receptacle of the manure is the open yard, where the contents of the stable in the winter, and the droppings of the cattle, are mingled with dirt and refuse matter carted in. A new barn, and barn cellar with modern improvements are very much needed. They would not only save much labor in the making of the manure, but a third at least would be added to its value. Room also would be furnished for the numerous stacks of hay, which are inevitably damaged, by exposure to the weather. The wasteful process of foddering at the stack-yard would be prevented, and pine boards would be made to do the work of hay, in keeping up the animal heat of the stock during the winter. Two-thirds of the fodder fed under cover, would bring the cattle out in the spring in better condition than the whole now does. This lack of shelter for manure, crops and stock is noticed, because the success attained here is in spite of a radical deficiency in good husbandry. If anything is settled in New England farm practice in the last thirty years, it is that shelter pays abundantly. The enlargement of barn room and the very general introduction of farm cellars in our own most thrifty farming districts, attest the general belief that shelter pays. But little attention is paid to

The Orchard

although parts of the farm are well adapted to the raising of fruit, and success with apples is attained in the neighborhood. Some four or five acres have been devoted to an orchard, which is kept in grass, and bears fair crops in alternate years, and adds something to the income. The varieties are the Rhode Island Greening, and the Prentice Russet, which is the local name for Roxbury Russett. These two winter apples have been in this region from the early settlement of the country, and notwithstanding the introduction of new sorts, they maintain their popularity, and are more generally planted than any other varieties. . . .

The Result of Twenty-two Years Tenant-Farming

As nothing but figures are satisfactory to men who have money to invest, we give the receipts of the farm which were kindly furnished us by Mr. Hall, taken from his account-book.

Receipts for one-half the products in 1872:

For calves, $93.47; pigs (18 in number) $72.62; lambs (12 in number), $51.75; apples, $20.00; oats, $37.20; potatoes, $12.00; cheese, $15.21; eggs ($70^3/_{12}$ dozen), $17.56; butter, (from 19 cows 845 lbs.) $308.20; turkeys, (445 lbs.) $114.20; chickens, $17.00; wool (61¼ lbs.), $39.29; beef, $39.81; pork (1010 lbs.), $75.75. Total, $909.06.

For the twenty-two years for which the farm has been rented, he has received $15,824.20, making an average of $719.28, as the annual rent of the farm.

The farm, with the stock, came into Mr. Hull's possession at the valuation of $9,000. The annual rent is very nearly eight per cent. upon the principal. Allowing one per cent. for taxes, it would give eight per cent. interest upon the original valuation. The farm has been kept up in good heart, and will bear as good crops as when it came into his possession, and probably better. There has been some depreciation in the farm buildings, but these are still in fair condition, and will probably survive the owner.

What Show for the Tenant

The first tenant made money steadily for thirteen years, and retired because he had money enough to buy a $6,000 farm for himself, and the larger part of it paid down. The present tenant has been on the farm nine years and seems contented, which is pretty good evidence that he is satisfied with his investment. This system of working the land upon shares offers many advantages to a young farmer, who has small capital and does not want to run in debt for a farm. It gives him at once a home with pleasant surroundings and a living business, without the burden of a heavy interest account.

Sharecrop Contract, 1882

From "Grimes Sharecrop Contract, 1882," in *Grimes Family Papers* (#3357), Southern Historical Collection, University of North Carolina Library, Chapel Hill, North Carolina.

To every one applying to rent land upon shares, the following conditions must be read, and *agreed to.*

To every 30 or 35 acres, I agree to furnish the team, plow, and farming implements, except cotton planters, and I *do not* agree to furnish a cart to every cropper. The croppers are to have half of the cotton, corn and fodder (and peas and pumpkins and potatoes if any are planted) if the following conditions are complied with, but — if not — they are to have only two-fifths ($^2/5$). Croppers are to have no part or interest in the cotton seed raised from the crop planted and worked by them. No vine crops of any description, that is, no watermelons, muskmelons, c . . . . or squashes or anything of that kind, except peas and pumpkins, and potatoes, are to be planted in the cotton or corn. All must work under my direction. All plantation work to be done by the croppers. My part of the crop to be *housed* by them, and the fodder and oats to be hauled and put in the house. All the cotton must be topped about 1st August. If any cropper fails from any cause to save all the fodder from his crop, I am to have enough fodder to make it equal to one half of the whole if the whole amount of fodder had been saved.

For every mule or horse furnished by me there must be 1000 *good sized* rails m . . . . . , hauled, and the fence repaired as far as they will go, the fence to be torn down and put up from the bottom if I so direct. All croppers to haul rails and work on fence wherever I may order. Rails to be split when I may say. Each cropper to clean out every ditch in his crop, and where a ditch runs between two croppers, the cleaning out of that ditch is to be divided equally between them.

Every ditch bank in the crop must be shrubbed down and cleaned off before the crop is planted and must be cut down every time the land is worked with his hoe and when the crop is "laid by", the ditch banks must be left clean of bushes, weeds, and seeds. The cleaning out of all ditches must be done by the first of October. The rails must be split and the fence repaired before corn is planted.

Each cropper must keep in good repair all bridges in his crop or over ditches that he has to clean out and when a bridge needs repairing that is outside of all their crops, then any one that I call on must repair it.

Fence jams to be done as ditch banks. If any cotton is planted on the land outside of the plantation fence, I am to have *three fourths* of all the cotton made in those patches, that is to say, no cotton must be planted by croppers in their home patches.

All croppers must clean out stables and fill them with straw, and haul straw in front of stables whenever I direct. All the cotton must be manured, and enough fertilizer must be bought to manure each crop highly, the croppers to pay for one half of all manure bought, the quantity to be purchased for each crop must be left to me.

No cropper to work off the plantation when there is any work to be done on the land he has rented, or when his work is needed by me or other croppers. Trees to be cut down on Orchard, House field & Evanson fences, leaving such as I may designate.

Road field to be planted from the *very edge of the ditch to the fence*, and all the land to be planted close up to the ditches and fences. *No stock of any kind* belonging to croppers to run in the plantation after crops are gathered.

If the fence should be blown down, or if trees should fall on the fence outside of the land planted by any of the croppers, any one or all that I may call upon must put it up and repair it. Every cropper must feed, or have fed, the team he works, Saturday nights, Sundays, and every morning before going to work, beginning to feed his team (morning, noon, and night *every day* in the week) on the day he rents and feeding it to and including the 31st day of December. If any cropper shall from any cause fail to repair his fence as far as 1000 rails will go, or shall fail to clean out any part of his ditches, or shall fail to leave his ditch banks, any part of them, well shrubbed and clean when his crop is laid by, or shall fail to clean out stables, fill them up and haul straw in front of them whenever he is told, he shall have only two-fifths (2/5) of the cotton, corn, fodder, peas and pumpkins made on the land he cultivates.

If any cropper shall fail to feed his team Saturday nights, all day Sunday and all the rest of the week, morning/noon, and night, for every time he so fails he must pay me five cents.

No corn nor cotton stalks must be burned, but must be cut down, cut up and plowed in. Nothing must be burned off the land except when it is *impossible* to plow it in.

Every cropper must be responsible for all gear and farming implements placed in his hands, and if not returned must be paid for unless it is worn out by use.

Croppers must sow & plow in oats and haul them to the crib, but *must have no part of them*. Nothing to be sold from their crops, nor fodder nor corn to be carried out of the fields until my rent is all paid, and all amounts they owe me and for which I am responsible are paid in full.

I am to gin & pack all the cotton and charge every cropper an eighteenth of his part, the cropper to furnish his part of the bagging, ties, & twine.

The sale of every cropper's part of the cotton to be made by me when and where I choose to sell, and after deducting all they may owe me and all sums that I may be responsible for on their accounts, to pay them their half of the net proceeds. Work of every description, particularly the work on fences and ditches, to be done to my satisfaction, and must be done over until I am satisfied that it is done as it should be.

No wood to burn, nor light wood, nor poles, nor timber for boards, nor wood for any purpose whatever must be gotten above the house occupied by Henry Beasley — nor must any trees be cut down nor any wood used for any purpose, except for firewood, without my permission.

Pioneer Ranching in Montana, 1882–83

From Lucia B. Mirrielees, ed., "Pioneer Ranching in Central Montana: From the Letters of Otto Merdian," *The Frontier* (Missoula, Mont.), pp. 243–57.

St. Paul, May 28, 1882.

DEAR SISTER

We just arrived about ten minutes ago, 9.15 P. M. We had a splendid day. The weather was fine and as warm as could be. Everything is O. K. Don looks kind a dirty just now. Will take him to the river tomorrow and clean him.

By the Letter head you will see we are stopping at the Merchants Hotel. We have a Room together. It is very nicely furnished. I guess if we would be in one that is furnished one quarters as nice out there, we might call it a Palace. We met a fellow on board that is going out to the same place we are.

Tell all the girls to write two or three sheets of fools cap so I will have something to read when I get there. I know I will be kind-a lonesome.

Hope you have forwarded the tent because we want to cut down all expense possible. Have got a Cook Book.

Will write when I get to Miles City and tell you how we passed the time and how near we came to being Recked.

Hoping this will reach you and the rest all well. I will close by sending my love to all.

From your true brother and strayed Sheep —

OTTO

Miles City June 1/82

DEAR SISTER

We arrived yesterday evening about nine o'clock; had a long and tiresome ride. The train went rather slow and we lay on a side track all night. Tuesday we passed over some very nice country and the scenery was grand. Can see prairie for five hundred miles. You can look over fifty miles of prairie in some places and not a tree to be seen. Every thing looks green and every here and there it is dotted with an old buffalo scull that some body has killed, and the wolves have made a feast of what was left on it. I saw lots of prairie dogs; some places there are regular villages of them. They dig up the ground and it looks as though it had been plowed. Saw thousands of ducks going through Minnesota a few snipe and chickens. Saw about twenty antelope and one white tailed deer, one Jack rabbit and some plover.

In the western part of Dakota we passed through what is called the bad lands; it is the roughest country ever I saw, and the hills are straight up and down. No body could ever get up there, they are high, and all this gray colored ground looks like tile but makes the scenery grand. The hills are covered with grass on top and the sides are bare. We passed some places where for miles we could see nothing but sage plants. I don't like the land right around Miles City. We are going farther west in a day or two.

Every thing costs about two prices. I went in a dry goods store this morning. They sell calico that we used to sell for 8 cts at 12. Lonsdale muslin is .17. Washington oil calico 3/4 wide we sold for 12c is 25c. We wanted to go to Ft. Keogh and they wanted five dollars for a horse & buggy. It is three miles; guess we will walk it. Have not seen any Indians since we left St. Paul; saw two Indian Squaws. I have enclosed samples of flowers I got on the prairie while walking around this morning.

Guess I will have to quit writing or it will cost me six cents if I get too much paper in it. Direct all mail same as before until farther notice and write soon. Ed got two letters this morning from home. Give my regards to all.

YOUR BROTHER,
OTTO

Excuse bad writing done in haste. It is as hot as it can be, 75 in shade. How is that for high?

Miles City June 9/82

DEAR SISTER

We have moved our headquarters from the hotel to a tent. We bought a mans outfit team wagon harness and cooking utensils. We moved yesterday afternoon slept in the tent last night and have done our own cooking.

It is awful hot here. I have been putting our tools together and put handles on all of them. We are waiting for my tent and Ed is waiting for a draft from home. We bought our team with out money from a man in Wisconsin. He left yesterday and is trusting us with them they are two fine horses big and strong. One is Black and the other sorrel. Give my regards to all the Boys & Girls and write soon. Excuse scribbling, for it was written on wagon seat in camp.

FROM YOUR BROTHER
OTTO

I was going to have a tintype taken of myself but the price was too high, $1.00 a piece.

Hot Springs June 25/82

DEAR SISTER

We are now about fifty miles from Bozeman. We would have been there last night but we were off of the road one whole day, and last Thursday we camped on White Beaver creek all day to look at the land in the valley. Ed went out in the morning and I in the afternoon. We took our rifles along. He saw some antelope and shot eighteen times at them but did not get any. I went in the afternoon saw three, but they saw me first so I did not get a shot this time. Then I watched their course and made the horse go pretty fast until they stopped running; then I drove pretty close to them and stopped the horse, slid off and ran around the hill. They watched the horse and I had a good chance to sneak on them. I got within 25 yds of them and they saw me. I let drive with my gun but shot over them and they saw the dust of the bullet and turned towards me. I shot four times and the fifth time I fetched one of them. We have eaten him up. He was boss, young about 3 months old. I am going to send the hide home when I get to Bozeman. Ed says he will take antelope every time in place of veal so will I; it was fine.

Yesterday was my birthday; did not celebrate, am celebrating it today. It being Sunday, we concluded not to travel. One of our horses is sick. I am afraid we will lose her. I cut the cake this morning the one that had been cut but I gave Ed a big piece about twice as large as I used to cut at home. After he eat it he said, ''Golly, that is good; lets have some more,'' and he cut another piece. We see how it is. We have been living high here lately. Everything costs pretty much. I have eat bread that cost twenty-five cts a loaf, and it is not one half as good as the worst bread ever you baked. It looks dark and tough as old beef. The loaves are small like those long loaves you get at the store. Although the bread is poor, I am getting fat, I believe. I tried on my stiff hat this morning, the first time I had it on since we left Miles City. It looked natural only I am sunburnt like the dickens. Look like a nigger.

We expect to get to Bozeman tomorrow eve or Tuesday. Will not say there any longer than we can help. We saw lots of land that suits us, but the ranch men tell us that it is all taken up; so I guess it will be hard for us to get land worth much. The land up here is very good but you can't raise anything on it unless you irrigate it, which will take quite a lot of work. We are going to try and get a place in Sweet Grass valley if we can.

This is the best way to travel ever I saw, you can see everything and look as long as you want to at it. We don't travel at night so we see lots of sights. We are use to it now and enjoy it. The bigest scare we had was the first night after we left Miles City. We camped on the Yellowstone in the wood, and on the opposite side there was an Indian camp. We did not know it when we stopped or nothing would have made us. There, two men that were freighting came about eleven o'clock that night and told us that the camp was on the other side of the river about two hundred yds from shore. The river is not much wider than our yard is long, about forty yards wide. The first day went over two rivers and through two canyons and across the table land for 25 miles. Second day we made good time until noon when it rained and the roads were sticky and bad. We have rain every day for about half an hour; this is the rainy season.

Next day we were off the road; drove pretty hard; and at night we had only made two miles.

This is the greatest place for saloons and restaurants ever seen. We passed one place called Youngs Point. There were 4 houses in the place and 3 of them were saloons and the other a restaurant.

I think I will go down to the hot springs this afternoon and get a drink of the hot water. The folks around here say it is just like that in Arkansas.

Sending my love to all I will close from

YOUR BROTHER,
OTTO.

Bozeman July 1/82

DEAR SISTER

I was very glad I heard from you for we are going to leave Bozeman tomorrow morning. Are going back to Sweet Grass. We are going up the valley in search of ground for our ranch. They say it is all taken up, but if we can't find land there we are going up on the Musselshell river, about 50 or 75 miles north of the Yellowstone river, where we think we can get a place. We met a man at Hot Springs that was going up there. He seems to be a very nice man. He gave us lots of information, told us several men from whom we could learn more about sheep and the land. He wanted us to go with him, but we had to come here for our mail and provisions so we could not go. He said he would show us around the country and help us lay out our ranch and give us all the information he could. He told us to buy all we needed at Bozeman, for flour was $12.00 a hundred lbs, and here it is $3.50; so you see we will save $8.50 if we buy it here. He seemed to take a lot of interest in us and told us all we asked of him.

I think we will like the Musselshell valley all but one thing. The Indians are not as much civilized as they are around here. If we find a place up there we will be Booked in this country for five years; then if we want to we can stay or leave. We will have what land we are on and do with it what ever we want to.

We have been having plenty of fresh meat. On the way I killed an antelope, and this man gave us a big piece of Elk meat it was fine. He was a lawyer and lived in Colorado for 2 years; then came here and opened a ranch on the Musselshell.

We arrived here Thursday eve at six o'clock. It is a very nice place, the nicest place I have seen since I left St. Paul. It looks like a civilized town a long side of the rest. There are 2 Churches, Court house, fine large brick school and the nicest lot of small dwelling houses all painted white with green lawns and level as a floor. There are lots of brick store buildings here. That is something you don't see the whole length of the Yellowstone river. We only saw one brick house on our trip from Miles City, and that was at Stillwater.

We stopped at the Hot Springs for three days, Sun. Mon. & Tuesday. One of our horses was sick and we could not move; so we had to take care of it. The springs are on the side of a hill. They are a ditch about 10 feet long and three feet wide. The water comes up out of the rocks and boils like it does on a stove. The steam rises off it and is terrible hot. I shoved my hand in it and was glad to pull it out again. I drank some of the water. It don't taste very nice; it is too hot to drink. You have to let it cool off first. It has iron and sulphur in it, they say, and will cure rheumatism and a great many more diseases. The man that owns them, Mr. Hunter, is building a hotel. There is going to be a dance there on the fourth; so we will be there I guess to take it in. There is going to be a big time here on the 4th I see by the paper. Base Ball & Horse racing. We can't spare the time or we would stay here.

I will send the Bozeman Paper home. When we leave Bozeman, which will be in the morning, we will not be back for a month or over. We have rented a Box at the Post Office and are coming back here for our mail and provisions. We can buy cheaper here than any other town & it is not any farther; so we will stop all our mail here. There is no post office where we are going, so this is the best we can do at present. We see snow every day and have just as hot a weather as you have at home. On last Monday I rode one of the horses. I was going up in the mountains to get a bit of snow to see what it looked like in summer, but I saw some antelope and they took too much of my time so I did not do it. I shot at one antelope but missed him. I have got the boss horse to hunt with. I shoot off of his back and he don't move. When I see an antelope I take him ontop of the hill and slide off on the opposite side, so the antelope don't see me, and then sneak around the hill. The horse won't go off. He grazes until I come back. Antelopes are very easy to hunt in this way. They will stand and look at an object for hours and you can sneak on them, if the hill they are on is not too wide on top.

Give my regards to all and write soon and often for there is nothing like news from home. Tell Rude if he wants to come out here he will have to quit smoking. Cigars cost 25c each. I have not drunk a drop since I left St. Paul. It costs too much. Beer is 15c a glass and I can't stand that when there is good water with in ten minutes walk.

I AM YOUR LOVING BROTHER, OTTO.

The strawberries will be ripe in about 2 weeks. I saw a bed of them last night; they look fine.

DEAR SISTER

We are now on the Musselshell river and don't like the country as well as we thought we would. It is a very nice Valley, but there is no timber nearer than fifteen miles; so we are going back on Sweet Grass creek. I think we can find some good land there, but it will be a job to irrigate it. It is a very nice valley. The water in the creek is clear as crystal. You can see the bottom of it any place. There are lots of trout in it. I caught one last Saturday evening that was sixteen and one half inches long, and I tell you it was fine eating. That same day I killed a Grouse; so we lived high that day. Today we baked, or rather fried, our first batch of bread. You ought to have seen it. My dog would not eat it. We had fried potatoes, tea and bread for supper. The bread we laid on the cloth and every time we looked at it we would laugh so tears would come in our eyes. Some fellow showed us how to bake this fine bread. It took the cake. We satisfied our appetite by laughing. Ed broke the loaf open and smelled it. He said the smell reminded him of how he used to steal hot biscuits at home when his mother baked them. He blamed the poor bread on the flour like all women do. When they don't have good bread they always say the yeast did not rise or the flour was poor. We have been living on pan cakes in place of bread. We like them and have them twice a day. We have not eaten any bacon for two weeks, are tired of it.

I will go to Bozeman some time the latter part of this month as soon as we get our cabin built. We are going to Sweet Grass, have given up the notion of buying sheep this fall unless we can buy them cheaper than $3.00. We are thinking of waiting until spring, and I will go to California or Oregon to buy them. We can buy them for $1.50 & $1.75 per head there and drive them over. The only expense is I will have to get a pony to go on. We can drive them over in one year and a half, and while I am gone Ed will do the farm work so we can make things work in that way. Ed will have to get sheds built, hay put up, and every thing ready for them.

We think it best to go there, for we can get twice as many and there will be no more expense. The wool pays all expenses, and they can graze on the way just as well as if they were in this part of the country.

The first time I get a chance to send you a Spanish bayonet plant I am going to do it. They have the prettiest flower I have seen in this part of the country. They have a long stem and it is covered with white flowers. They are about the size of a tulip; some of the stems are a yard long and look real pretty. If they will grow down there, it will take the eye of a good many. The hill and mountains around the Hot Springs are covered with them and they look as though they were made of wax. The stem is covered with them. Everything is all right. We keep healthy and are about to settle down in a few days.

Say, will you go to the store and buy me about six yds of cottonade or mole skin for two pair of pants, make them and send them by mail? I would like the mole skin if you can get it. They had a piece of slate color with a narrow white stripe very dark and a brown stripe they were both striped alike and were about 30c or 40c a yard. Don't send anything good, for I will not have any use for it. Have worn out one pair of those light pants. Line the mole skin pants with some of papa's old pants so they will be warm. Send me a pair of buckskin gloves with them; have it registered so it will come safe. Send by mail, and if I ever get rich enough to pay you I will send the money.

I AM YOUR LOVING BROTHER

T. O. M.

Puetts Ranch   July 28, 1882

DEAR SISTER

I am now on the land where I intend to settle. We have found a place that suits us and are waiting for Mr. Puett to get back from Ft. Benton to survey it for us. We had his compass the other day and tried to survey it, but some of the cornerstones were gone so we could not do it. I am awful tired. I was up in the mountains yesterday cutting timber for our house. I tell you it was a hard job, but I stuck to it and brought a load with me. It is nine miles from here, and it is a very lonesome place; there is no sound to be heard but your ax and the wind blowing in the pine trees. There is one place about five hundred yds from where I chop where you go down in a hollow about one hundred and fifty feet and there you find a creek of the finest and coldest water ever I drank. I make ice tea every time I go up to chop. It is boss. I put Ed on to it. He thinks it is quite a treat to have ice tea. The creek goes down into the rocks and you ought to see how fast it runs; don't know whether it ever comes out any place or not, but it is in a very lonely place. There are lots of tracks of wild animals. I guess that is about all there is that ever goes around it. I don't feel safe when I go there, and yesterday I forgot my revolver and I felt "kinder weak in the knee."

I have to go and see how the bread is now. Wait a minute and I will finish.

By the way did you send those pants? If you have not, send them by mail. I think I forgot to tell you how to send them. When you send my things, always send it by mail. If it is too heavy to send in one package make two of it. It will cost twice as much either by express or freight. There are no railroads or boats here so it cost a great deal to have any thing sent here.

I think I will go to Bozeman next week to get the mail; hope there will be a sack full for me. It seems as though I haven't heard from any body for six months.

Mena says in her letter that Chat Russel is back again and he thinks there is no place like Illinois. He is right. That is where I am going if I ever make money enough to live there. I want money, though, before I go back. If we have good luck in raising sheep and I make enough money in the next five or six years to go back and start a little Biz of my own I am going to do so.

I am going to try and get four hundred and eighty acres of land. I can do it out here: 160 acres under the homestead law, 160 under the timber, and 160 under the Desert act. After that if I want to take 160 under the preemption act, I can do so; then I will have a whole square mile of land or one section. All the difference would be they would be in different places.

After I go to Lower California* and drive over what sheep I buy, I am going to try and come home on a visit. I expect to go on horse back. Will leave here about the first of January. It will be kind of cold but I will have two or three Buffalo robes to roll up in. We had ice night before last, and yesterday it was hot as the dickens.

---

*This trip was never taken. It was not, however, an unusual one.

That is one thing I like about this country; you can always sleep at night no matter how hot it is during the day, and the mosquitoes do all their work in the day time. There are plenty of them in the low lands. What do you think I have struck? An old lady. She is a widow, and she said she wanted to be my mother while I am out here. She came from St. Louis out here seventeen years ago. She is about forty in years. It is Mrs. Peuet. She is a fine lady, and she gave us several pies and told us to come and see her often. The pie struck me natural right where I live. We ran out of lard so she gave us as much as we got at Miles City for $1.00. She has no daughter or I would think there was something at the back of it. Her nephew is with her; he is an Illinois boy. He is about twenty five. He is quite a nice young fellow. He watches her sheep. They have nine hundred and some over, I have forgotten just how many. They sheered five hundred and thirteen sheep and got over four thousand lbs of wool. How is that for high? Sheep sheared 13 lbs of wool, and they had an old ram that sheared 17 lbs. If we can only get a flock that will do that well, we will be all O. K. The general average of wool to a sheep is six lbs and their average eight. Oh I am bound to be a stock raiser for the next five or six years!

Say, send me a box of this kind of writing paper. I am very nearly out and we are over 150 miles from a place to buy it so I wish you would. You can buy it cheeper there and send by mail. I wish you would keep an account of what you buy for me and if I ever get the money, I will pay it back.

I have done all kinds of work already: have sewed my clothes, shoed one of our horses, mended the wagon, tended Peuets sheep, doctored our horse, cut wood, and am going to help build our house — and lots of things I have done.

Fishing is fine. I went out every day last week and caught a fish for dinner. Caught one trout that measured nineteen and three-quarter inches. He was a monster; broke my pole at the joint, but I fixed it again and I caught eight or ten that measured over 15 inches. They are the prettiest fish to catch ever I saw. You see them swimming along the bottom of the creek, drop in your fly, and it hardly touches the water when he has it. In your next letter send me some light green zephlyr split, some medium red, some blue, and a spool of button hole silk, orange color. Take it off of the spool so you can put it in an envelope.

Tell Rude to shoot a red bird and send me the feathers. Tell him not to muss them any more than he can help. I want to make some flies to fish with. Send three or four yards of the Zephyr or German town wool. I think I can make the flies. They are fifty cts a piece, and if you get them snaged it comes off. You don't use any bait, nothing but the feather. The fish think they are bugs and bite like good fellows. The La-da-das ought to come up here. If they wouldn't open their mouths when they caught one of those salmon colored trout about fifteen inches long I don't want a cent! They are pretty fish, salmon color with dark blue back and spotted all over on the sides and top. They have teeth three row of teeth on the lower jaw and three on the upper; the teeth are very small and sharp as a needle. The first one I caught I put my finger in his mouth and he closed on it. It felt kind a queer a long side of the fish at home; so I took it out in a hurry.

We are going to change our Post Office Box to Big Timber after I go to Bozeman. It is but 18 miles and Bozeman over 150. That will be our Sunday ride.

It takes all the spare time I get to write to you at present. After we get our house built I think I will have more time.

Hoping this will find you all well and wish to receive an abundant supply of mail when I get to Bozeman, I will close.

Sending my love and regards to the girls and boys. I am your loving

BROTHER,

OTTO.

All seems to be going on well. The work is awful hard but I am going to nuckle down to it and put it through. Hope the Lord will reward me in the end.

Extra Suppliment

We have been living like Chinese for the last week on boiled rice. It went fine. Today we will have antelope. A man by the name of Andrew brought us a half of one last night so we will have saratoga potatoes and antelope stake for dinner. Sometimes I go out along the creek and pick wild goose berries. They are splendid; just like tame ones only not so large. Beans are pretty good when you can't get anything else. Mrs. Peuet says she will make butter in a few weeks and then we can have all the butter-milk we want.

Will write the balance some other time. I have to go about a mile and a half to mail this and see a man about his mower to cut our hay. Write often and tell the girls to write. I will have more time after I get the house built.

YOUR BROTHER.

Puetts, Aug. 11/82.

DEAR SISTER:

I received your letters dated June 27th and July 9th. Was very glad to find you all well and am very thankful for the money you sent me. I was really in need of it when I got it. I left here for Bozeman Friday A. M. with seven dollars in my pocket, and with that I had to get the horse shoed and buy some nails, an ax handle, and my lunch besides. I did not know how in the world I would get any lunch out of that amount after having paid for them; so I thought I would have to live on hopes of getting some thing when I got to camp. Thought I would have to take Dr. Tanner's method of living on water, but when I opened the letter & found the P. O. Order I was all O. K. and began to feel fat. Every thing is so high out here you have to have a pocket full of money to get any thing.

I have sent to H. Filley to send me some sole leather. My boots are played out, and there are quite a lot of snake in this country; so I don't trust shoes much. Ed killed a big rattle snake about fifty yds from our camp while I was gone. It had seven rattles and a button. I have the dinamite yet and if any should get over my shoe tops I will use it to blow it down. As yet I have not pulled the cork. You seem to worry a good deal about me going too near the Indians. Why I have not seen any since I left Miles City & I saw but six or eight there. There are two families of half breeds about a half mile from us, but they are civilized and are better neighbors than most white people. Folks call people "neighbors" if they live within ten miles from them. We have ten families with in five miles of us. Two old Batchelors are about as far as from our house to Levises from where we are; so we aint out of calling distance. One of them, Mr. Andrews, was here this A. M. All the people around here are real nice folk; you ask them any thing and they give you all the information they can, and if you want any thing they lend it to you in a minute. We are going to help Puetts make hay to day and to morrow, and they are going to let us have there mower; so it won't cost us any thing to cut our hay.

The Indians don't come through only in the fall and spring, and the settlers watch them so close that they don't get a chance to do any thing. Last year some went through that did not do just as the settlers wanted them, and they were driving off there horses; so the settlers made for them and took the scalp of one. He is in the sod near the mountains. The setlers make them walk chalk when they come around here.

Ed did not do any thing on the house while I was gone so it is not done yet. When I got back I found him fast asleep.

I think we have a pretty honest lot of people out here. We have left the tent several times and have been gone all day and not a thing has been touched.

I almost forgot there is going to be a young lady and her brother out here in the spring. They have taken up some land near us. She is rather nice looking, too. I had an introduction to her mother; she seems to be a nice lady. I have been clubbing myself because it was not her daughter instead of her, but I will get around that. I will go and see her brother and perhaps I may get a chance to know her. I made a big mash on Di Hunter's daughter. I took dinner there on my way to Bozeman and she set down near by and waited on me. After dinner we had quite a long talk and she told me to come & see her some time. She just came out here last fall and is a fine looking girl. Her father has the Hot Springs & is putting up a hotel there.

By the way, we are going to have a cook next year. Ed is going to have his girl come out. He is going to build a big house in spring while I am gone to California. Wont that be a fine trip to Lower California? I am awful glad Ed has to stay and build so I can go. Rude thinks I am joking but I am not. I saw two bands of sheep that came from there while on my way to Bozeman. The fellow wanted 4.00 a head. You can buy them there after shearing for from 1.25 to 1.75 a head; so it will pay us to go there for them. I will leave about the first of January; then I will see some fine country.

I got eleven letters when I got to Bozeman, seven from home and four elsewhere. Was glad it panned out so well, and you don't know how much good it does to hear from home.

I am not particular when Pa sends the money now but I would like about $35 to enter my land with. I think we have got a good lot of hay ground. I am going to try and get some of this rail road land; it is fine. The rail road will pass Sweet Grass this fall about 18 miles south of us.*

We are on the Sweet Grass Creek on what is called Cayouse flat. There is a spring runs through our land of nice clear water full of fish but too small to catch.

Tell Bob to save the brass wire that comes around white shirt linen and send it to me. It is very fine and braided, or to send me some of this gold colored trimming they use for masquerade suits. I want it for flies; also send a small piece of guta percha. Get it at the drug store. I want to make me some flies to fish with. Guta percha about the size of a walnut, hammer fine, and put in an envelope.

BROTHER,
OTTO.

Write often.

*The Northern Pacific.

DEAR SISTER:

Ed has gone to Big Timber today to get the mail. Hope I don't get left. We have not got our house done yet. It seems as though we never will. We have been helping Mr. Puett make hay for the last seven days; so I have got some hay seed in my hair already.

We wrote to a man that has 5000 sheep. He wants to let them on shares. If we can get them on halves we intend to take from 1000 to 1500 head. Then what money we have we will buy cattle and horses with so we will have quite a stock farm if we get the sheep. If we do in the spring, we will get about $750. worth of wool and about 700 lambs for our share; that is if we have any luck at all.

I think we have got in a nice part of the territory. We have nice folk all around us, and they try to do all they can to help you along. We were down to Puetts the other day and Ed happened to mention that we had run out of bacon. When we started for home, she brought us a piece rolled in paper that weighed 12 lbs and told us if there was any thing else we were out of we should tell her and she would let us have it. We did not ask for it; she gave it on her own accord. Bacon is the thing that costs us more than any thing else; it is 25c a pound — just 4 times as much as at home. They don't raise pigs here, no corn to fatten them on. We are going to buy a quarter beef at six cents. That is the cheapest thing I have seen in this country.

I don't believe I have told you where we have settled yet. It is about 20 miles from the Yellowstone river (north) on Couyout's flat about 1.4 miles* east of Sweet Grass creek. It is about nine miles from the Crazy Mountains (east) and one mile east of Porcupine bute. We are in townshp 4, range 14, section 2, south half.

There is a nice spring running through our land of good water. I think we have got a good piece of land for sheep. There are a row of hills north that will break the north winds and will be a good place to let the sheep run on in the winter. The wind blows all the snow off of the hills so the sheep can eat the dry grass.

I am sorry I brought my gun and dog with me, for there is no small game out here. There are lots of Antelope, but I have not had time to go out after them. One day when we were building our house an old Antelope came within fifty yds of us. Ed shot at him with his revolver but missed him and off he went. One day when I was up in the mountains I went down in a hollow about 150 feet deep to get some water, and while I was down there I walked up the creek for 300 yds and I saw lots of rocks turned over. Some I could not begin to lift one side of. I looked around and happened to think there might have been a bear did this looking for insects; and when I thought of bears, you ought to have seen me get out of there. I got out in a hurry, for I had no gun or any thing to defend my self with. I asked a half breed the other day if bears ever turned over any stones and told him what I had seen, and he said he thinks it was a bear, for that is the way they do. I guess I will take my rifle along after this. I also saw an old Indian wigwam made of bark down in the hollow.

We have found a good substitute for eggs. When we make corn cake we use yellowcorn meal and it look as though it was filled with eggs. Eggs are 8 1-3c apiece, pretty cheap.

I AM YOUR LOVING BROTHER,
OTTO.

*It was two and a half miles from the present city of Melville.

DEAR SISTER:

I was down to Big Timber Sunday and got a letter from you dated July 30th. I cant imagine what kept it so long on the road. I also got the pantaloons. I like them very much; think I will be in style when I wear them. They are the first Old Gold pantaloons I ever saw. I am sure that is not the style now out east is it?

I suppose you learned through Pa that we lost one of our horses. Well, we have bought two, not near as big as our other one was, and we are going to use our first one for a third one should we have a big load. We have not paid for them yet. Wish you would tell Pa to send my money so we can pay for them, and we will have to get some blankets for cold weather. We have not got a cent left; all the money we have is five dollars & eighty five cents, and that is the balance I have left from the spending money you sent me.

I had quite a hard time of it the other day when I went to Big Timber. I left here Sunday noon. It rained all the way and next morning I went to Sweet Grass town to have our horse shoed, but when I got there the horse shoer was not there; so I had to go without. I thought I would go a nearer road. Some men told me that the road up Sweet Grass creek was nearer than the one I came on. So it is, about 20 miles shorter, but I got on the wrong road and kept it all after noon in the rain and at night I found myself in the wilderness miles away from home. I walked about for 3 hours trying to find where I was, but without success. I found nothing. I was afraid to lie down in those hollows where there was nothing but trees & hills around me. I was afraid of bears & wolves or other wild beasts, so I walked for fully 3 hours when I came on a big hill and, looking down in the valley below, I saw a lot of cattle. Thinks I, there are no bear around here or I would not see cattle here if there was. So I went down in the valley to find a place to lie down, for I was awful tired. When I got where the cattle could see me, they all snorted and ran away. I felt awful lonesome in a hollow, no body around & I had a strange horse. I did not know whether he would stay where I was or not, was afraid he would break loose and leave me. So I tied him to a big log where he could get plenty to eat & sat down along side of a big tree. I was not there more than five minutes when I was fast asleep slept until ten minutes to 12. I got up and looked to see if the horse was all right, and he was; so I went back and sat down again, but sleep I could not until 3 o'clock. I sat there thinking and wondering where I was and what in the world I was treated in that way for. I could not think what in the world I should have been led off in this way, for I knew not what direction to go in; had no compass; the sun was not out; and there I was — nothing to eat since breakfast Monday morning. So I sat there until I fell asleep again. When I woke, it was six o'clock by my watch. I got up, saddled my horse, and went on top of the butte. The sun had not got out from the clouds; so I could not tell which was east or west. I saw the mountains, but the rain the day before had covered them with so much snow I could not tell whether they were the mountains west of us or south of us on the other side of the Yellowstone; so I was in a fix. I at last made up my mind to go strait for them. If they were those west of us I would be going in the right direction, and if they were south on the other side of the Yellowstone I would strike the Bozeman road & then I would know where I was. I walked a while until the sun came out & then I knew what direction I was to go; so I got on the horse & went over one hill after the other on a straight line west until I came to Sweet Grass creek at 10 o'clock. I followed it up for about 4 miles when I came to Cooks. Mr. Cook was just coming home to fix dinner, and he invited me in. I was awful glad he did. I told him that hit me just in the right place; so I went in sat down and had some dinner. Told him my adventure & ate a square & talked awhile & then made the rest of the way home, a distance of 4 or 5 miles. When I got there I made some more dinner & slept the rest of the day from 3 o'clock. While I was on the wrong road, I saw 4 white tail deer & two elk. I shot two loads at the deer with my revolver & four at the elk. I hit one of the elk twice, but the bullet was so small it had no effect on them. I got right close to the elk. I led my horse right up to them with in thirty yards. If I had had my rifle I could have killed both of them, for they did not run until I shot the fourth load. They are awful big game. They are as tall as a horse & have horns on them. If they were set on the ground they would be very near as tall as I am. Just wish I had my rifle with me. I would have felt a little safer and would have killed one of those elk & I would not need to fear Indians or bear. Indians go through this country in the fall & spring. My revolver is too small for this country. I ought to have one that shoots a 45 cartridge & 10 in barrel like all the men out here carry. I will have to take my rifle here after, but it is so much trouble & it is awful unhandy on horse back.

The horse I was riding is a dappled Grey, a fine fellow, price $150, the best rider in the country, and he makes the dust fly. All I don't like is he shyes at every thing he sees. I thought I would see if he would let me shoot off of his back. I shot twice and he jumped like he had been shot, but he has got so he does not take much notice of it.

We have about got our house done. We put poles on top today & tomorrow we will plaster the roof with mud & then we will shovel dirt on it. That is the way they put roofs on houses out here where shingles are scarce. We will finish it this week if we can keep at it.

YOUR LOVING BROTHER
OTTO.

Sept. 28, 1882.

DEAR SISTER:

I received your letter and would have answered it before but thought I would wait until Ed went to Big Timber so he could take it down.

I have written a pretty stiff letter to the Post Master at Bozeman about the other Hdkfs and that letter of yours and Lulu's. I think a little talk will bring him to time. Your letter was there over a month and a half.

About the money, we are rather hard up at present. Have bought two horses but have not paid for them. The man ticked us for them. They are two brothers and are nice men. We owe them 175 dollars yet. This is a hard country on a poor man. They all are independent and wont sell any thing unless they can get a price for it, and us poor chaps have to stand it. If we ever get fixed, we will do just the same. The horse we got goes all right in harness. I tried him the other day and he did not make much fuss.

I have not worn the pants yet. I have made one mash on Mrs. Puett's niece. She is an Illinois girl from Lexington. She came on a visit and bought a round trip ticket, but she liked it so well that she sent her ticket home and her father left Sunday for home so she is going to stay. The old lady says she is going to buy a piano for her. Wont we have a jolly time when the 'pianner' gets here?

She called on us instead of us calling on her, and invited us down to see her. She sent for us to come down last Friday and spend the evening with her pa before he left. Ed went but I stayed at home and watched the children. You want to know how far it is to Puetts? Only two miles. I used to think it was far, but when I got to getting milk for nothing it seemed only half so far. They are not the nearest neighbors. There are two others but they are bachelors. There is another family about 1½ miles west, Mrs. Roberts. She is a fine lady about 25 years old and a very nice girl, but Puetts is on the road and we leave our mail there so it is the handiest.

I wish we had half even one eighth of the fruit you put up, for I have not tasted a bite so far.

Our house has three rooms. One we live in the other we cook in and one the length of the house but narrow at the back of the house we use for a work shop. You ask what we do for windows. Puetts gave us one window sash and we bought six lights and put it in the door. We have 4 more lights; so we will make a sash for them. Will send a plan some day of our palace.

You must think people out here live awful queer, asking if they have stoves. You can get stoves by paying for them. We intend to send east for ours; we save from 10 to 20 dollars on it, but houses are not furnished very nice. The country is too new yet; can't get them. We cook in our fire place so far. It is a poor way. We are not in our house yet. I am kind afraid of it. We have a dirt roof & it is pretty heavy; am afraid it will cave in on us.

FROM YOUR LOVING BROTHER,
OTTO.

Tell Rude to send me a pound of walnuts in a cigar box by mail. I want to plant them to see if they will grow.

Puetts, Dec. 13, 82.

DEAR SISTER:

I received your letter quite a while back and would have answered them, but we have been camping in the mountains the past 3 week getting out timber for sheep sheds before the snow got too deep. We got about 400 trees out & about 300 pulled out & hauled where the snow wont bother them. The rest we will have to leave. The snow is so deep that we could not do any thing; so we moved down Monday and I started to haul the timber home today.

You ask where I put up for the nights when I go to Bozeman. Why I sleep in the wagon & take chuck enough to last me on the way. It is quite a tiresome job, I should remark. It is riding for 10 days* If it was not for the scenery I think I should die on the road. You want to know what kind of a place Big Timber it. It is a fine town 3 buildings built of logs one is a store & saloon, one a dwelling & the other a feed stable the Marble fronts are so numerous I wont stop to mention them. That horse you think we ought not to have bought goes fine & I am going to try & ride

---

*Bozeman was "over 150 miles" from the ranch, as stated elsewhere in the letters.

him some day. We just saved about $50 dollar buying him unbroke. I got the cake you sent by mail. It was kind of dry. It would have tasted better if we had had some wine with it. We did not make it look sick at all. All there was left of it was the box & string; came very near eating them.

I have not cut my other fruit cake yet, will sample it Christmas. Ed could not wait so cut his some months ago. I will have a picnic on it.

You say our old cat died. I wish there was a way to send a cat by mail, for the mice are awful bad out here. They spoilt one of Ed's woolen shirts & a pair of socks for me & carried off about a bushel of oats for us. They are thick as flees on a dogs Back. You say that paper smelt of bacon. Smell this and see if it dont smell of elk. Our neighbor killed one the other day not far from our house. I am going to try & take a hunt during the holidays from Christmas to New Years. I went out deer hunting one day while we were up in the Mountains but did not see any.

I sent for some strychnine for wolves; hope you have send it. I saw four yesterday morning. I can buy it out here, but they ask $8.00 an ounce & you can get it for $1.60, want the crystalized. I would like to have it before I go on that hunt if I can get it. Their fur makes nice robes & I want an overcoat out of them. They are pretty thick around here you can hear them every morning & evening. Most of the rabbits out here are white. There are few other kind. I have not killed much game, have no time to hunt. I have killed quite a number of chicken; I would kill them on my way to Puetts.

The rail road has been at Big Timber for some time & is about 40 miles beyond toward Bozeman.*

Ed was going up on the Musselshell this morning to see what we could do in the way of buying sheep, but the weather was so bad he gave it up. I hope Pa has sent the balance of my money. If not, tell him a St. Louis draft will be best. Money orders can not be sent in larger than fifty dollar sums & I would have to go to Bozeman to get them cashed.

Send me one of my Cabinet photos if there are any of them at home. I want one of them. Also have Rude & Pa get some taken I would like one of theirs & yours send them together so they will not be so likely to get damaged. Dont wait six months to send them.

Don seems to enjoy Montana life only he look as though his appetite had left him, poor fellow, I wish I had left him at home where he could hunt. The game out here can't be hunted with a dog.

Wishing you all a Merry Christmas & a Happy New Year with love & regards to all I remain your loving Bro,

OTTO.

P.S. — Send me a pair of common slippers, some Almanacs, & ink blotters. I did not get to mail this today. Ed left for the Musselshell river this afternoon, will be gone 4 or 5 days; so I am all alone in my glory. Send a pair of heel plates for my skates.

Puetts, Jan. 7, 83.

DEAR SISTER:

Your letter was received all O. K. but not when you expected in the New Year. I got it a few days after Christmas. I also got the cake; got it New Years eve. It was fine, beats the one I had all hollow.

*The Northern Pacific was completed Sept. 8, 1883, when the line built from the East met the line from the West near Garrison, Montana.

I spent my Christmas going to the Party. Had an immense time. There were about seventy ladies there and you ought to see how they dress. I was perfectly surprised when I entered the hall to see women in this country dress so fine. Nearly every one had on a silk or satin Dress & they were made real neat. They come from all parts of the Country and cold as it was, every body seemed satisfied for going. We left home at daylight and got there at about Eight o'clock. We stopped about 2 hours at Big Timber to feed the team and get some thing ourselves.

New Years I put in at Big Timber. We bought a stove so we had to stay there all day. I helped the P. Master get out his quarterly report. I did all the writing for him. He called off the numbers & I filled the blanks. After we were done he said I would make a good Post Master. It is the queerest Job I ever saw. They have to keep an account of all the stamps they sell — cancel — & buy and every 3 months send it to Washington. They came out $42.00 behind last quarter; so it aint very profitable.

I got on to our colt today, the one we broke to harness. He did not want me there so he thought he would dump me off, which he did. I had no saddle so I put on a blanket and it came off, I with it. I dont think I would have slid off if it had not come loose. I held on to the bridle & got Ed to help me up on to him again, & he went all right then. I am going to Big Timber tomorrow; so I got a saddle today & I will try him again tomorrow.

I tapped the Dynamite Christmas eve. It is pretty slick. There is more in a table spoon full of it than there is in a whole bottle of what you get out here.

We are having quite a little winter, plenty of snow. Ed is making a sleigh & we have some sheep bells; so we will have some music & a ride day after tomorrow. I made a pair of heel plates yesterday. The creek in front of our house has overflowed & is frozen & slick as glass; so I am going to try my skates someday when the wind don't blow. It has been blowing awful hard the last few days, and the snow has drifted in some places about 5 ft deep in other places the ground is as clear of snow as can be.

Wishing to hear from you soon, I am your loving brother,

OTTO.

Melville, Jan. 22, 83.

DEAR SISTER:

I have nothing to read so I thought I would put in a little time writing. We got some good ink now & I feel a little more like writing.

Ed got a letter from his father the other day & he says there is a young officer at the same fort where he is who wants to invest ($5000) Five thousand dollars in stock & wants some one to keep it on shares; so a few days ago Ed got a letter from the officer himself asking all about our ranch & on what terms sheep are raised & if we would take some should he want to go into sheep. We sent him a letter next night. We figured up the profits & told him a lot more so all we want now is an answer saying that he will furnish us with sheep, & then we will be fixed. We also got a letter from Kirsch & Schiess wanting to know some thing about the country & our ranch. We gave them a blast; so we expect to hear from them in the near future & I hope it will be favorable.

Please don't say any thing about this to any body. Don't tell Pa about it. Keep it to your self & when we are in the business (that is if they do any thing) then I will let you tell him, but don't let any one know it before hand, for we might not get any; so keep it mum.

We were not able to get any sheep this fall. We tried several places but no one wants to sell until after shearing; so we will wait and buy then if we don't hear from the above parties.

I want to build me a house next month if I can on my homestead claim, but I am afraid the snow won't let me do any thing in the mountains. It is pretty deep up there now, about 3 feet deep. The snow dont lie long down in the valley. Where we are the wind blows it all away. One day you wade through six inches & next day the ground is as bare as in summer & dry as can be. It blows it into large drifts & into gutters. I have walked over gutters that I knew if I had gone through I would have gone down all of 15 feet. It blows in so hard & tight you can drive over with a team & wagon & there wont be any signs or track in it; it is hard as ice. I was out Sunday morning & I saw a big drift. I had on those buffalo over shoes & I had put on a half sole so they are slick. I would go up on one side & slide down on the other. It went boss. I would go a sailing down. I tried my skates to day. I made a pair of heel plates and went on our creek. The wind was blowing & I went down to see our neighbor in a hurry. The wind took me a kiteing. One old batch did not know what my skates were. I called on him; I had them in my hand & he said, "What kind of a trap is that?" He thought they were steel traps to catch wild animals with. I told him they were skates & he said, "That is a new wrinkle in skates, ain't it?" He said they were different to what they had when he left the states & wanted to know if that was all there was to them. I told him it was. He looked at them & wanted to know how I kept them on & I showed him. He thought they were fine.

I took dinner with an old Batch who is pretty well off. We got our horses from him. He & his brother own about 175 horses & a lot of cattle & neither one of them are married. The other one was, but his wife died. They live in separate houses about 2 miles apart & own about 160 acres apiece. The one I took dinner with let me have a horse & saddle to ride home on so it saved quite a long skate, about six miles. I did not want to take it but he insisted on me doing so.

I have not got any wolf hides yet; they are too smart for me. I put some strychnine in to a piece of liver, cut a hole in it, & made it so they could not smell the S nine, but they wont eat it. They go up to it & smell it & then walk a way.

I wish you would subscribe for the American Agriculturalist for me; it don't cost more than 1.50 a year. It is a good book & show lots of ways to build all kinds of gates, fences, & how to make hay racks, sleighs for heavy work & lots of useful things. If you send it begin with January; we have one for December.

Ed is going to start for Bozeman Friday. His box is there & he is going there after it. It has been on the road since last October. It went by way of Utah* & who knows where. If it had come by way of St. Paul it would have got here in about 3 weeks & not cost one tenth as much. Every thing is all O. K. Don has been living a little better since we got the Antelope & Elk.

Dont mention any thing about those sheep to any body.

Hoping to hear from you soon I will close remaining your loving brother,

OTTO.

*The Utah and Northern was the first railway built in Montana. By 1880 the road reached Silver Bow, approximately 125 miles north of the Idaho line.

DEAR SISTER:

We have been having some very fine weather the past week. It has been pretty warm and no snow on the ground. I left Friday for Fish creek to see if I could not cut some timber for fence posts; went with one of our neighbors. We took my tent along and I stayed until this morning. The timber is not what I want so I gave it up. I hunted Friday afternoon. We saw one deer. I did not get a shot at it, but the fellow that went with me shot at it but did not kill it. I also found a Deer's horn. It is the prettiest ever I saw & I wish I could have found the mate to it. I looked high and low for it; it has four prongs on it and long and slender.

Our place or neighborhood is to be called Melville. We have a post office & will have a service next spring. Send my mail to Big Timber as usual, and when we have a service I will change it.

So hoping to hear from you soon I will close remaining your loving brother,

OTTO.

April 11/83.

DEAR SISTER:

All is well & we are having splendid weather. We had to plow the other day and you ought to have seen the bold break we made at it. We just made the dirt fly. I have plowed a ring around my five acres that I am going to put in timber. I just marked it off so I can plow it up some other time. I am going to raise Oats on it this year & next I will put in the trees.

I bought a dozen chickens and they only cost six ($6.00) a dozen. Folks out here think I bought them cheap, bought them of Mrs. Marshal. She gave me a doz eggs and a bucket of milk in the bargain.

I don't think I told you that I went to Livingston & had a lady go with me. It was a picnic, had a high old time. It was Cora Marshal, one of our neighbors and a little daisy too. We stopped two days at Hunters Hot Springs and, while there, there were two young ladies visiting Hunters. Mrs. Hunter took me up in the parlor and knocked me down to them. It was a grand treat. Old Dr. he was there and he gave us some history of Montana, and she set em up to hot water and after that we played a few games and adjourned next day. We left about 4 P. M. for this young lady's sister's about six miles from the Springs. Got there just before dark and in time for supper. I did not eat. Just imagine me eating. I have forgotten how to eat. We had a time after supper. I have never had so much fun since I left home as I did that night. They have a parlor organ and singing and dancing till noon. It was a picnic for this country. The young lady stayed up there and is not coming home until May 1st. I felt sorry when I left there for home and had to go alone. She has been out here but a short time, came last fall from Iowa.

Hoping this will find you all well and wishing to hear from you soon I am your loving bro

OTTO.

DEAR SISTER:

I suppose you think something is wrong with me, for I have not written to you for a long time; but I hear from you so seldom that I don't feel as though I ought to write often. I think it will hurry you up a bit.

The Indians stole about 150 head of horses from one of our neighbors Cook Bro. They have about 200 head on the range and can't find but about 50 head. They don't know what Indians they were but think it was the Flatheads. They stole a lot of the Crow Indians' ponies and Cook think they run theirs with them. There has been several lodges of Flatheads passed through this section here lately; there were seven (7) lodges of Crows went through here on their way looking for the Flatheads who stole their ponies. There was also a company of soldiers from Ft. Ellis* went through here today. They were after the ponies. Also there is another company stationed at Big Timber waiting for orders.

Say I believe I would like to have you send my light suit out for I have nothing to wear this summer only my black suit & Montana broadcloth [overalls]. Also send my watch. Make me a few chamois skin bags to carry it in. I need a watch bad, for when I go any place half the time I can't find what time it is, and while out at work I can't tell when noon comes and we lose more time than a little by it. When you send it, send it by Express and have the agt give you a receipt for it. Put the clothes in a box and put the watch inside of the clothes where it won't slip to the side or corners of the box. Have pa bind the box around the edge with hoop iron and to take a good strong box. Please pay Express charges on it.

Have it send Via Chicago to St. Paul care N. P. railroad Exp. Have this put on one corner of the box; then I will get it in a short time. Otherwise it may go by way of Utah and N. and nobody will know when it will get here.

YOUR LOVING BROTHER,
OTTO.

DEAR SISTER:

We have a regular mail service through here now three times a week so you can direct my mail to Melville, M. T. (Via Big Timber). We are getting quite civilized here lately. After a while we won't know ourselves.

Tell Mrs. Johnson I think if her Nephew was out here, he could get work but he would find it a very rough place and in regards to Christianity, it makes no dif. He would have to do as the rest of the fellows out here. It is all day and Sunday too. He would find the cowboys a hard set to work with. Stock raising out here is so different from what he is used to that experience in that country would do no good out here. All the experience he wants, to know how to throw a rope and ride. They turn there cattle out and in spring and fall they round them up and brand them and turn them out again. Sheep is different. He might find his experience in raising them to help him, but winter herding would be hard on him; it is so cold. I advise her not to let him come to this country unless he goes into business for himself, for they don't have any mercy on any body. The cow boys are all right if you get acquainted with them and treat them all

*Fort Ellis, near Bozeman, was built in 1867 to protect the settlers from the Indians.

right, but otherwise they are not; and if you bother them it is better if you look a 'letle oud.'

You ask about Mrs. Puett. I tell you about her and leave the girl out. This time she is quite well and goes out horseback every day. She is riding the range now seeing to her horses. She has two bands of horses and they keep her busy.

All is well. Have been plowing for over a week. I was down to the creek today and got a lot of gooseberry bushes and some tree cuttings to plant. When raspberry bushes come up I am going to get a lot of them.

If you get this before you send the box with my suit, have Pa send me a sack of shot 25 lbs of No. 8. I can't get it out here. If not too late, how is cake? Put in my Christmas cake and candy. It will come all O. K. but pack it so it won't get on the clothes, and fix the shot so it won't fall from one end of the box to the other when they move or roll it.

Give my regards to Kate and all the girls and love to Pa and Rude and write soon.

YOUR LOVING BROTHER,
OTTO.

Indian Boarding School, 1883

From Letter, George W. Hunt, Superintendent, Kiowa, Comanche and Wichita Agency, to P. B. Hunt, Indian Agent, Aug. 17, 1883, Kiowa Agency Letterbook, Indian Archives Division (Oklahoma Historical Society, Oklahoma City, Okla.), XV, pp. 288–90.

SIR:

The following is respectfully submitted as my *annual report of the Kiowa and Comanche Manual labor and boarding School for the year ending June 30, 1883*.

The school has been in succeful operation throught out the year nothing having occurred to interfere with the school.

The health of the pupils has been good.

The average attendance during the ten months was 89½ and the largest attendance any one month was 112.

During the fall and winter months the children attended school very regularly but when the weather grew warm in the spring they were much disposed to visit the camps and escape from the confinement of the school rooms. We found it very difficult then to keep the children at their work and especially so, as many of the Indian Camps were very near the School house.

The advancement of the pupils in a literary way has been very satisfactory. Many of them had not attended school before this year but some of these before the close of the term had learned to read, in the first reader. Most of these who had attended school last year read and write understandingly and some have martered the first four rules of Arithmetic.

The industrial part of our work has also been satisfactory — the pupils have worked willingly and well. The house has been swept every morning, and upon certain days of each week has been scrubled by the detail of boys. The grounds worked and the house was cleaned and the wood and water carried by the smaller boys. The wood was cut and hauled by the larger boys and the required considerable labor as the timber was about three miles from the school house and during cold weather 19 fire places had to be supplied with fuel. Two boys were detailed with each wagon and one of these gathered the commissary supplies for the School going every day two miles after the beef.

We found much work for the boys in the school field which was very convenient to, only a few yards from the house.

Last years crop of corn was gathered and housed in September and October.

A second crop of Millet grown on the same ground the first grew on was cut and stacked.

During October also the crops of Irish and sweet potatoes, and the squash and common field pumpkins were gathered and housed these crops were all large, and was carefully lifted and laid away in the root house, which had been built by the boys under my direction. It was 12 × 24 feet dug four feet in the ground and built three feet above making seven feet in the inside and covered entirely with earth.

The ground for this years crop after having been throughtly cleaned by the smaller boys, was deeply ploughed and got in readiness for planting by the larger boys. About 18 acres was planted in corn 2 sowed in Millet and 4 devoted to the growing of vegetables. The corn was planted by hand, the smaller boys dropping the seed, and the larger boys covering with the hoe. A remarkably good stand was secured, and it was well cultivated, the boys having gone over the crop twice with the hoe, besides giving it three ploughings. The result is a crop such as has rarely been seen in this Country. The crop of Millet was very heavy, and was put into the rick in good order. The yield in vegetables was very large. A failure was made ine crop only. The boys destroyed about 300 hills planted in winter squash.

Eight bushels of Irish potatoes were planted and about 7500 Sweet potato plants set out, one and one half acres has been sowed in Ruta Baga and common turnips. Beans are growing in about seven acres of the corn crop. Besides these crops there are Cabbages, beets, tomatoes, cucumbers and etc., about 400 hills were planted in melons, and the yield was very large.

The girls were taught all kinds of household work. Under the direction of the Matron, they every morning made up the beds and cleaned the rooms.

The worked by details in dining room and kitchen and also under the instruction of the Seamstress.

We have endeavored to the children the use of the English language but this we find difficult to do, because of the nearness of the Camps to the school and the fact that the children spent so much of their time when out of the school room, with their own people. Many of the children however speak the language very well.

Very Respectfully

(Signed)   Geo. W. Hunt

Superintendent

Utah in 1884

From J. H. Ward, "Utah, Past and Present," *Latter-Day Saints' Millennial Star* (Salt Lake City), XLVI, pp. 520–21.

When, a little more than thirty-eight years ago, a band of persecuted exiles were seen fleeing from their beautiful homes (which were left in the hand of a bloodthirsty mob), carrying with them their sick and wounded, halt and blind, and slowly disappearing behind the western horizon, how few realized that this little band, so few in numbers and so feeble in strength, would soon become the nucleus of a mighty people! Yet so it was.

Leaving behind them the buds and boughs and bloom of an advanced civilization, the shelter of homes, the sympathy of friends, and the fierce scorn of their enemies — across deserts so prostrate under the throbbing light, that the very silence seemed to cry out at the approach of a human footstep — over barren mountains and through rugged canyons, this little band came at length to the shores of the American Dead Sea. And here, in the solitude of the desert, with only the bleak mountains, the gilded morning, the painted sunset, and the glimmer of that tideless sea about them, they gave obedience to the commands of God, the fulfillment of which has compelled even the reluctant admiration of their enemies. The desert has been made to blossom as the rose, and they who were considered too vile to dwell among so-called Christian people have, in the providence of God, built up a civilization so far superior to all that has preceded it, that travelers from distant lands are struck with admiration on beholding it.

When the pioneers entered the Valley of the Great Salt Lake in 1847, there was little attractive in it. The soil produced little else than sage brush and wild sunflowers. The rainfall was so light and infrequent that no crops could be raised without irrigation. No foliage could be seen except in the narrow rock-ribbed gorges of the Wasatch Mountains. Fuel could only be obtained at great distances from where habitation was possible. Nearly or quite a thousand miles intervened between the pioneers and the nearest civilization, and even from this they were frequently cut off by savage and inhospitable Indians.

Thirty-seven years have passed since then, and what a wonderful change has taken place! Instead of dreary and monotonous wastes, we see fruitful fields, smiling gardens, and happy homes. Utah now contains more than two hundred prosperous communities, some of them amounting to the dignity of cities, where the various arts, sciences and industries flourish, and where are found places of worship, schools, libraries, and all the requisites for mental culture.

Utah Territory lies in the same latitude as Spain and Portugal, and about three-fourths of the way from New York to San Francisco. The Wasatch Mountains intersect it from north to south, dividing it into two substantially equal parts. Of the parts lying east of this range, and drained by the Green and Colorado rivers and their tributaries, little use has yet been made. The settlements are few and small. The Denver and Rio Grande Western Railroad, lately constructed, runs across this section, which makes it accessible and its resources available. Of the twenty-four counties comprised in the Territory, only eighteen may be considered as settled, and even these could sustain many times their present population.

The range of climate in Utah is favorable to the growth of crops of all kinds. There are valleys where frosts are almost of nightly occurrence, but which are well adapted to grazing; there are others where for many months frost is not felt, and still others where it is rarely if ever experienced. In Southern Utah the climate is congenial to the growth of cotton and semi-tropical plants and fruits.

In some localities good crops are raised without irrigation, but generally it cannot be dispensed with. It involves preliminary outlay and the labor of applying the water; but, on the other hand, the husbandman is safe from storms that might damage or ruin his crop.

The blessing of God has rested upon the efforts of the pioneers in reclaiming the desert. Many streams have been greatly increased in volume, and in some places new springs have burst forth in the desert. In some places where, twenty years ago, there was scarcely water sufficient for the needs of a few families, now there are large streams capable of irrigating thousands of acres. The rainfall has greatly increased in some localities. A few years ago it was considered impossible to raise crops without irrigation; now quite a proportion of the land under cultivation is tilled without artificial irrigation, which system is commonly known as dry farming.

Thirty-seven years ago the land on which Salt Lake City now stands, and that in its vicinity, was considered barren beyond redemption. Indeed, Col. Bridger, an old mountaineer, offered $1,000 for the first bushel of corn that could be raised in the valley, so confident was he that agriculture would be a failure in such a region. In 1882, Bishop S. A. Woolley, on ten and eight-tenths acres of this same soil, raised an average of seventy-three and one-half bushels of grain to the acre! He also sowed six and seven-tenths acres with wheat, and obtained four hundred and twenty-six bushels; five and five-tenths acres with barley, and realized five hundred and seventeen bushels; three and one-half acres with oats, and received three hundred and ten bushels; making a total of one thousand two hundred and fifty-three bushels of clean grain from fifteen and seven-tenths acres of land, or seventy-eight and four-fifths bushels per acre.

Stock-raising has always been a profitable pursuit in the Territory, and in the matter of stock Utah is improving. At present the most prominent breeds of horses that are being introduced are the Hambletonians, the Normans, the Clydesdales, and many crosses of these animals. Of cattle, the prominent breeds are Shorthorn, Devon, Jersey and Ayrshire. Of sheep, there are more than six hundred thousand, from which were sheared, last year, two million seven hundred thousand pounds of wool.

Ranch Cattle Business in 1885

From Joseph Nimmo, Jr., *Report in Regard to the Range and Ranch Cattle Business*, (Washington, 1885), pp. 19–22, 53–54.

Capacity of the Ranges for Grazing Purposes

The capacity of the range and ranch lands of the United States for grazing cattle, differs widely in the several States, Territories, and sections as the result of differences in the quantity and quality of nutritious grasses produced, the water supply, and the extent to which natural shelter is available for cattle during storms. In Texas from five to thirty acres of land per head are required, and on the northern ranges almost the same differences are observable in different localities.

The ultimate limit of the capacity of the entire range and ranch cattle area of the United States for grazing, and the magnitude of its possible annual product can of course only be ascertained from the results of experience. It is evident, from the best available information, that the number of cattle on ranches and ranges in Texas might be greatly increased. Mr. George B. Loving, of Fort Worth, Tex., in reply to inquiries addressed to him by this office, expresses the opinion that by providing reservoirs, sinking artesian wells, and destroying the prairie dogs, which, in certain parts of the State, consume a larger quantity of the nutritious grasses than is consumed by cattle, the number of range and ranch cattle pastured in that State might perhaps be doubled.

It is impossible at the present time even approximately to estimate the proportion of the available range lands in the northern part of the great dry area which are as yet unoccupied, or the extent to which the supply of grasses within the nominally occupied portions exceeds the supply necessary for the sustenance and fattening of cattle now grazing thereupon.

There appears to be a tendency on the part of those who have already occupied the ground to promulgate the idea that the ranges are well stocked, and that there is, therefore, no room for additional herds. Most intelligent observers who have prospected the different parts of the great cattle area north of Texas assert that two, three, or even four times the number of cattle now upon the ranges can be fed upon them.

Experience proves that cattle cannot advantageously graze more than 6 or 8 miles from water. The result is that vast areas now well grassed are of little value on account of their remoteness from water. The rendering of such lands available for the cattle business of course depends largely upon the practicability of procuring thereupon adequate supplies of water by means of artesian wells or by reservoirs for collecting rain-water.

Profitableness of the Range Cattle Business

The range cattle business of the western and northwestern portions of the great cattle area of course differs widely in the various localities and sections as to its profitableness. This is due to differences of conditions as to water supply, the quantity and quality of grasses, shelters, the number of calves produced, extent of winter losses, and the management of herds. As a rule the business has yielded large profits.

It is clearly indicated by the large amounts of capital which have been invested in it during the last fifteen years. Many large fortunes have been made at the business within a comparatively brief period. Hundreds of men who embarked in the business a few years ago, with exceedingly limited means, are now ranked as ''cattle kings.'' In certain instances women also have successfully engaged in the enterprise and two or three of their number have already won the soubriquet of ''cattle queen.''

But like all enterprises yielding extraordinary results in the beginning, competition has in many sections already reduced the average profits approximately to the limits usually attained in commercial enterprises.

Mr. E. V. Smalley states that the usual profits on long-established ranges in Wyoming and Montana vary from 20 to 30 per cent. per annum on the capital invested. The following is from his statement in Appendix No. 1:

''The average cost of raising a steer on the ranges, not including interest on the capital invested, is usually estimated by the large stock owners at from 75 cents to $1.25 a year. Thus a steer four years old ready for market has cost the owner $4 or $5 to raise. When driven to the railroad he is worth from $25 to $45. A recent estimate, approved by a number of Wyoming ranchmen, places the profit at the end of the third year on a herd consisting of 2,000 cows with 1,000 yearlings, and 35 short-horn bulls, representing in all, with ranch improvements and horses, an investment of about $70,000, at $40,000.''

The completion of the Northern Pacific Railroad, and the construction of other railroads in the Territories during the past two or three years, caused the price of range cattle to advance. Thus large profits were realized from the sale of herds.

Generally it is found that the average cost per head of the management of large herds is much less than that of small herds. The tendency in the range cattle business of late years has therefore been toward a reduction in the number of herds, and generally toward the consolidation of the business in the hands of individuals, corporations, and associations. It is stated that a single cattle company in Wyoming advertises the ownership of ninety different brands, each one of which formerly represented a herd constituting a separate property.

In opposition to the tendency toward consolidation, there is also the tendency toward separate ownerships on the part of homestead, preemption, and ''desert land'' settlers, through the privileges afforded them under the public land laws of the United States.

The Breeding of Cattle on the Northern Ranges

As already stated, the northern ranges were originally stocked with young cattle, chiefly steers, driven from Texas. For several years it was supposed that Texas must continue to be almost exclusively the breeding ground, and that the northern ranges would for all time be the maturing and fattening ground for Texas cattle. But an important change has taken place in this regard. The raising of cattle on the northern ranges has met with an encouraging degree of success. At the present time many of the large cattle-owners and herdsmen of Montana, Dakota, Wyoming, Nebraska, and it is believed also of Colorado, are of the opinion that it is more profitable for them to raise their young cattle than to import them from Texas.

It is a well-established fact that cows in Texas produce more calves than cows on the northern ranges. The general opinion appears to be to the effect that about 90 per cent. of the cows of Texas drop calves every year. Wide differences of opinion are, however, expressed as to the increase on the northern ranges. The estimates vary from 50 to 70 per cent. of the number of cows. Hon. Martin E. Post, late Delegate in Congress, from Wyoming, estimates the average increase at from 50 to 60 per cent. of the total number of cows, and the increase from two-year-old heifers at 40 per cent. He adds, however, that every two-cattle raised in Wyoming are worth three raised in Texas.

While Texas cattle are largely purchased for stocking ranges at the north, the policy upon the well-established ranges appears to be quite generally favorable to maintaining and increasing the stocks upon the ranges by keeping a sufficient number of cows and bulls for breeding purposes. This change of policy has led to a disposition on the part of the northern-range cattlemen to oppose the driving of young cattle from Texas to the north, which spirit of opposition has manifested its own hostility to the proposition for the establishment of a national cattle trail. In so far as such opposition is based upon considerations of commercial nature, namely, the shutting off of the competition of Texas cattle-breeders from the northern ranges, it could not, of course, need any co-operation whatever from the National Government, as that would be to favor the restriction of free competition in a legitimate trade. Nor does it appear to be becoming in the northern owners of herds to seek such protection so long as they enjoy the privilege by suffering or of allowing their cattle to graze upon the public domain.

The practical effect of breeding cattle on the northern ranges and the efforts made to raise the grade of such cattle by the importation of high-grade bulls is seen in the improved quality of the beef already shipped to market from the northern ranges.

The Improvement of the Breed of Range and Ranch Cattle

During the last ten or twelve years the thought of the leading ranchers and ranch cattle herdsmen, as well as of settlers, within the great cattle belt has been turned toward the subject of improving the quality of their stock. This has been accomplished, first, by the shipment of young "native" cattle of the States east of the Missouri River to the western and northwestern ranges, there to be matured and fattened for market. Efforts in the direction of improving the breed of range cattle have also been made by crossing the "native" and the Texas cattle with bulls of the higher breeds of beef cattle, and chiefly with those of the Short-horn, Hereford, Polled Angus, and Galloway breeds. To what extent it is practicable to improve the grade of cattle on the range that are compelled to seek their own food and water, and such shelter against storms as they can find in valleys and mountain gorges and in the "coulees" of the broken ranges from the time they are dropped until they are driven to the railroad depot for shipment to market, are permanently to maintain such improvement under the conditions mentioned, is yet to be ascertained. . . .

General Remarks in Regard to the Range and Ranch Cattle Business of the United States

The occupancy of the public lands throughout the central and northern portions of the great dry area for range cattle purposes is a legitimate and laudable branch of the national industry. It has subdued and utilized such lands for the production of a cheap and nutritious article of food now brought within the means of purchase by the laboring people of this country, and it has contributed greatly to the foreign commerce of the United States by swelling the volume of our exports. It has also served as an indirect but effectual instrumentality in keeping the Indians upon their reservations, by expelling their game — chiefly the buffalo — from the ranges, and thus removing the main inducement for the Indians to go on hunting expeditions outside of their reservations. Besides, it has supplied in the cow-boys an effective police force, which is ever alert to prevent ostensible hunting excursions by Indians, such excursions in times past having oftentimes been but the pretext to cover schemes for going ''on the war path.''

It is not a strange thing that a great branch of industry like the range cattle business, which within the space of a few years has assumed gigantic proportion, should in the course of its development have been subject to frictional resistances and embarrassments. But difficulties beset all human enterprises, especially those which are new and have not become fully adjusted to the conditions which complete their environment.

As hereinbefore stated there are several important features of the range and ranch cattle business which deserve a full and careful investigation by Congress with the view of devising some definite and carefully considered line of policy regarding the disposition of the public land, now so extensively used for the pasturage of cattle ''on the range.'' Such an investigation would, of course, tend to determine the respective rights of cattlemen and of settlers, and it would also embrace incidentally the consideration of the question as to the practicability of increasing the rain fall of the great dry area, and of securing additional supplies of water for cattle and for the purposes of irrigation by means of artesian wells.

These subjects in their summation constitute one of the largest and most important lines of inquiry which have ever yet commanded the attention of the Government of the United States.

Farming in the Midwest, 1885–98

From Excerpts from Diaries of John A. Sanborn, 1885–1898, near Polo, Illinois (1885) and near Franklin, Nebraska (1885–1898). Reprinted by permission of the Nebraska State Historical Society.

Thursday, January 1, 1885. New Year opens clear & cold. Did not get above zero all day. I went to Brookville after 32 bu. of grist, barley, and oats. The roads are very rough and hard.

Friday, January 2. Cold and clear still. Went over and helped Father's folk kill a beef. Brought home a quarter. The beef was very fat and nice.

Saturday, January 3. Hazy and cold but moderating. Got my grinder to work and ground 10 bu. corn. I went to Polo to see Dr. Scott. The baby is not improving fast enough to suit me.

Sunday, January 4. Clear and pleasant. The baby is much better in morning and beginning to feel like herself.

Monday, January 5. Clear at sunrise. Clouded up warm and commenced to rain at 2 o'clock and by night it rained hard. I went to the grove and got a load of wood cream money $7.00.

Tuesday, January 6, 1885. Rained hard all night but at daylight: it commenced to snow and kept it up sometimes hard and sometimes light till afternoon. Then broke up and now is clear and cold. Went to Horace Magne's sale. Took Old Tom up but couldn't sell him.

Wednesday, January 7, 1885. I traded 5 barrows with Father for 5 sows. I now have 16 sows. I hope I will have better luck than last year. Went to Polo in evening.

Got crackers	.25
window glass	.09
traded caps, book	.25
thread	.10

Thursday, January 8, 1885. Went to Polo in morning. Took two loads of corn to Joe Bingaman 40 cts. per cwt. amt. — to 14.38. Got $1.80 worth of beef. Thawing all day.

Friday, January 9, 1885. Butchering. Killed 5 hogs. Jasper, All Miller, and Joe helped. I am writing this at one o'clock at night. N. W. wind and quite cold.

Monday, January 12, 1885. Clear and cold and getting colder. Helped Emma shake carpet and c. Cut some wood &c. Went to Polo in evening. Emma and I bought a stove for our dining-room, a small one price, $9.00. Ran up a bill at Beards of $4.55. Forgot to take money with me so no pay.

Tuesday, January 13, 1885. Did not get above ten all day and is 10 below at sundown. Cut some wood and did chores.

Wednesday, January 14, 1885. Wind N. E. Commenced to snow about 3 o'clock & is still hard at it. I ground chop for calves nearly all day. Fixed the grinder and now have it in pretty good shape. I put about 6 bu. of barley & corn & oats in with the corn in Ear & it ground pretty good if we do not put it in too fast, but it makes slow work.

Thursday, January 15, 1885. Cloudy and cold. Went to Polo and paid G. B. Treat's bill of $12.00 for fixing Will's & Minerva's teeth. Paid Treat $8.00 on stove & c. Paid H. A. Fiem's $1.00 for Delineator next year (till/Oct.). Got

coffee	1.00
tea	.40 Beards
axe helve	.25 chgd
kerosene	.40

Tuesday, January 20, 1885. Not quite so cold. Cut some wood at wood pile. I have to cut down some of my old apple trees and it is going to spoil the looks of the yard.

Wednesday, January 18, 1885. I am 35 years old, but I do not feel very old yet. 18° below at sunrise. 12° below at noon. 20° below at 7 p.m. and getting colder. Wind Northwest. Sat by fire most of the day.

Friday, February 6, 1885. Not very cold. Sleety forenoon. Took my hams over to Father's smokehouse. Looked over our accounts and find myself $25.00

behind. We had a long talk and I may go to the West if I can close up here without too great a sacrifice.

Saturday, February 7, 1885. Snowed quite hard all day. Emma and I cleaned cellar and I sorted our apples. Found them pretty badly softed. Went to Polo. Took a bushel of apples to Mrs. Foulk who has made some button holes in a nice dress for Emma. Sold 5½ dozen eggs. 7 cts. 93 cts. Got $1.00 worth of sugar. 25 cents for tabaco.

Thursday, March 19. Raw cold day. High west wind. Grinding corn. Splitting wood. Father and Mother came over on a visit and we talked over the subject of going west they favor Dakota and I am in favor of Nebraska. Will decide tomorrow.

Friday, March 20, 1885. Cold weather. Snowed about 1 inch. Hauled 1 load of hay from Rutlands will have 2 more. Hired John Rukendall for $4.00 per week untill Spring then he gets $18.00 per month. He commences work next Monday.

Sunday, March 22, 1885. Fine clear cold day. The water started to run a little. Went over home. Pick the day for starting West — it will be either Tuesday or Wednesday.

Monday, March 23, 1885. The boys hauled home 2 loads of hay from Rutlands. I went to Polo with Father and got 100 sale bills struck off and engaged Sol Beard to cry my sale on the 8th of April.

Paid Clinton for printing sale bills	$5.00
Paid bill at Shoop	.35
Paid bill at Stricklers	.70
Got me a coats and paid for it	$7.00
and paid bill at Allens of	3.75
Postal Cards 10 cts. and etc.	.25
Paid Rutlands boy for hay etc.	7.15

Tuesday, March 24, 1885. Chilly raw day. Freezing hard tonight. Father gave me $25.00. Emma and I went to Polo. Got her carpet paid the bill. 31⅔ yd. 15 cts. $4.75. Mr. R. gave her $10.00 pension money to pay it with. Stamp .02 cts. Father paid me $25.00 yesterday for 100 bu. Barley and gave me 25 more on account.

Wednesday, March 25, 1885. Started from home to go to Nebraska. Crossed the river in evening got to Lincoln at noon the next day. To Lincoln is $22.25. Left the snows at middle of Iowa. Father is with me.

Thursday, March 26, 1885. Left Lincoln at noon got to Riverton at ½ past 8. We have passed through some beautiful country but everything looks new, *very new* and raw but I expected that. People are plowing, seeding, and rushing into the beginning of storing work. We can hardly realize the change in climate.

Friday, March 27, 1885. Took a drive 10 miles NW of town to see the country, particularly a 180 acre tract of land. Found it all that could be asked for in a lay of land, soil and c. but its 6 miles from market. No improvements whatever. No school house within 2 miles at least and price $12.00 per acre. Also viewed one 1¾ miles from town 120 acres. Good house, farm barn sheds and c. but a good deal of rought land on it. Quite a snow storm this evening. 1 in fell but it has stopped and is warmer.

Tuesday, March 31, 1885. Alex took us to Franklin. When we arrived about noon after dinner Mr. James F. Zediker took us a drive of about 20 miles and showed us a lot of desirable land. We saw a spring running out of the side of a bluff and run through a trough of fence boards which could not carry 1/5 of it the finest we've seen in the state. Came to Riverton tonight.

Wednesday, April 1, 1885. Made a purchase this morning. Took the N.E. Q Sec. 5 town, 7 R. 14. Franklin Co. Neb. Price $1895.00. It lies 5 miles north and 1½ miles East of Franklin about 2½ miles S.E. of Macon P.Q. As smooth as a piece of land can be and be good. Father sent checks home for the money. The bank will send them to me and pay the money. Mr. Grove took Father out riding and he and Father called on Mr. Eaton, a relative of Alex's wife.

Thursday, April 2, 1885. Started for Lincoln last night at ½ past 9. Got here at 7:35 this morning. Were promised a thunder storm, coming up form Red Cloud but it fizzled out and only laid the dust. Went out to Mr. Pecks. Having a first rate time visiting Mr. Peck. He took us in his buggy and hauled us around the city all afternoon. I caught a cold.

Sunday, April 5, 1885. A beautiful, warm, sunny day the finest day we have had this spring. Uncle Henry Neff and wife came over. My trip to Nebraska has cost including Father's expenses viz:

Fare to Lincoln	$44.50
Fare Lincoln to Riverton	15.00
Hotel bill Franklin	1.50
Hotel bill Riverton	7.00
Lunch at Lincoln	.50
	68.50
Cigars and lunch on road	.50
Price paid for land	$1895.00
	68.50
	$1963.50

Tuesday, August 18, 1885. Wrote to Freeport Machines countermanding my order for a windmill. Went to Polo and ordered my sale bills. Paid Treats bill for oile stove by check. $21.80. Cigar 0.5 Salt 15. Tobaco for John .50. Clark says he will furnish me a car for 85.00 to Franklin. John Lawson come home. Bought land near Riverton. Wrote for Alex Landon to engage welldiggers.

Wednesday, August 19, 1885. Went to Polo and got my sale bills and put up a dozen or so about town. Emma came home on the 5 o'clock train. Stopped off in Freeport and had a visit with Mother. She has had a good time. She says. Brought home $4.50 and some trinkets and keepsakes.

I paid for sale bills	$1.00
Royal Arch dues	1.00
Bot Mason pin of Treat	2.50
Gave John	1.00

John threshed for Gavin by noon and is now at Jasper Scotts. He is working by the day.

Thursday, August 20, 1885. John helping Jasper thresh. I put sale bills East and North and Will went to Brookville. Stopped at Maryland Station and sent for rates on a car to Nebraska. Received letter from Freeport Machine Co. saying they could not let me of on windmill write back that I can't help myself.

Friday, August 21, 1885. Emma and I did a big washing and c. Took all day. John helped Milton thresh. So did Will.

Saturday, August 22, 1885. Sent Will up toward Foreston and c. to put up bills. John went to Polo and tonight is going to Leona to Camp meeting. I went to Polo in afternoon. Gave John $10.00. Got kerosene, 2 gals. .50. Sugar, 1.00. Got a card from Maryland Station giving me a car for Nebraska for $25.00.

Sunday, August 23, 1885. Rained so the folks could not go to Camp meeting at Chambers Grove untill evening when it cleared. I wrote letters and c. one to Freeport Machine Co. about windmills.

Monday, August 24, 1885. Heavy rain during the night and rained nearly all day. Sent Will after Mrs. Kockendarfer Mother's aunt who was left at the Camp ground. I packed up some of my tools and c. and c. Went to Polo in evening and got some sugar and rice. 2.25.

Tuesday, August 25, 1885. Went around and fixed up some of my bills. Was told the sale would be $25.00. But think there is some mistake. Mother went home afternoon.

Wednesday, August 26, 1885. Helped Emma wash and c. Setting out things for sale. Went to Polo and got two boxes to pack in $1.25. Got some paper with a ledger. .50 ct. and nails .30 cts.

Thursday, August 27, 1885. Old settlers picnice at Polo. A beautiful day and about 3000 people in attendance. Gave John a piece of my mind and $1.00. He is getting lazy and saucy but it won't last long. Lester Brand called and told us they had a baby at their house born at 11 o'clock last night all right. Leavitt and Eddie staid at home and did the chores and I gave each a nickel. Bought a cigar, .5 ct.

Friday, August 28, 1885. Lent the boys and got 3 sacks of flour and some hay at fathers. I took the red Roan and Lill to Foreston with All. Miller and others sold them Monday to Will Pringle for $80.00 Nellie Van Santford and Tom Ormston form Neff called this evening with Joe and Laura.

Saturday, August 29, 1885. Rained like split all day forenoon I put on a rubber coat and worked at setting things in shape for sale. Went over and got the young cattle after it cleared up. Then went to Polo and got 31 lb. beef for Monday. 9 ct. per lb. $2.80. Emma gave Minnie 1.00. Cigars, .25 ct. Ordered 26 loaves bread of L. Beard to be sent out. Paid Will $1.00 I owed him.

Friday, September 4, 1885. Busy packing. Mother came over to help. I went to John Lawsons sale in afternoon and expected to see some parties to finish settlements but they were not there. His sale ran very much like mine. I think I did some the best. John is planning to move to Nebraska at the same time I do.

Tuesday, September 15, 1885. On the road at Galesburg 8 p.m. Horses etc. all right. Laid 4 hours at Galesburg.

Wednesday, September 16, 1885. Left Burlington 8 o'clock evening. Lawson lost his dog. Got off the train with him and forgot to look after him when train started. Carelessness on both our accounts.

Thursday, September 17, 1885. Left Platsmouth 8 a.m. Showery. Warm. All right. Lincoln noon. Exeter sundown. Clear warm.

Friday, September 18, 1885. Arrived safely at my journeys end. Found Uncle Ruben at the Grand Central Hotel and he helped me unload the horses etc. Paid $150.00 to the Agt. for my cars. 10 cts for cigars. Arrived 9 o'clock a.m. Left Lawson at Riverton.

Saturday, September 19, 1885. Left Platsmouth. Got unloaded at night. Alex Landon came along by noon and rendered effecient service. Bought a shirt .75. Cigars .10.

Sunday, September 20, 1885. Went out and viewed the farm. Saw Mr. Smith and he will commence boring a well next week at 50 cts per foot complete.

Monday, September 21, 1885. Set up the wagon brought up the last of my truck from the station. Drumming up bids on mason work. Let the job to Mr. Ogden at 3.00 per hr. for laying brick wall. 15 cts yd. for plastering. 25 cts per foot for chimney. Put my plow and mower together. Got bill shod in from 50 cts tobaco 10 cts.

Tuesday, September 22, 1885. took out some truck tank plow mower and c. to the place. Staked off the house. Emma got here at ½ past seven. All right. Stay tonight at Mr. Fagers. Emma had $13.00 left.

Wednesday, September 23, 1885. Took Emma out to the farm. Thank the Lord she likes the country so far. We stay tonight at Mr. Fagers. Sent a load of brick out by Sam Smith. Clear warm and dusty.

Thursday, September 24, 1885. Took out two loads of brick. 1280 I now have 2460 out and think it enough. Found Smith busy at the cellar but not very deep yet. Paid mini host of the Grand Central 27.50 for lodging and .05 for a loaf of bread. My wagon [illeg] was loose and bothered me a good deal. Emma went home with Alex Landon. I stay at the Hotel. Sent the boys to Fagers. Bought 2 bu. oats 80 cts

Friday, September 25, 1885. My lumber came and half unloaded. Had to get my tires set in morning and was only able to get a few lath out by noon but I made Uncle Ruben hump himself afternoon he handed it out of the car and I piled. We loaded doors, windows, and some lath and shingles on the wagons.

Monday, October 5, 1885. Moved out to our new home. Sleep here tonight. Paid Hovey for keeping horses 2 weeks and 3 days.

Breakfast	$00.25
Groceries	$00.25
Bread	$03.25
Horses	$14.70
	$18.45

Got lumber for stable of White Lake L. Co. Smith made 2 trips and took the masons in tonight. The foundation is done.

Tuesday, October 6, 1885. Sam and Rube brought out a load and I went in afternoon. They brought out 2 6 × 6 × 12 ft. stick for posts in cellar. I got some battens to stop the cracks in shanty made a stable on south end. 240 ft 24 $5.76. White Lake. Got some bread. .50 Gloves and matches $1.25. Glycerin .10.

Wednesday, October 7, 1885. Sent Leavitt in to town after some 2×14×14 30 of them working at frame got part of it up. Cool and clear. Wind north. Sent for 2 gallons gasoline.

Thursday, October 8, 1885. Working on the house. Got it partly sided up with Shiplap (?) The boys helped Mr. Clapp pick potatoes and I bought about 10 bu. at 25 cts. He had near 50 bu. off less than ½ acre. Smith came along and I paid him $30.00 on the well. I still owe him $20.00. Heavy post.

Friday, October 9, 1885. Warm and windy. Plowed fireguard in forenoon with sulky the Casaday is not a complete success as a breaker.

Friday, October 16, 1885. Putting on roof sheeting and c. Quite warm. Sent Eddie to town with Mr. Clapp for 2 gallons gasoline from Fagers .50 cts.

Saturday, October 17, 1885. Working at the house. Sam and I put on Cornice and Rube made windows, blinds and c. Sent Lall and Ed to town after coal and barrels and c. They got 650 lb of coal cost $2.65.

Sunday, October 18, 1885. raining all day. A cold North Easter. Rube and Sam drove to town towards evening. I don't see as this is a very drouthy country so far.

Monday, October 19, 1885. Bought 3½ bu. potatoes of Mr. Clapp. I now have 20½ bu. of him. Also some cabbage I did not ask how much they were. The potatoes are 26 cts per bu. Commenced shingling at noon. Rube and Sam got back from town at 11 o'clock. Quite a hard frost last night. The boys brought out my pump with them. Mr. Ogden the plasterer came along to see how we were coming on and he and I went to hunt for some good sand. Found it about 2½ miles east of here in Thompson Creek. Mr. Warner showed us the place.

Tuesday, October 20, 1885. Mr. Fager came out and put in a pump for me. It is a good pump but 150 feet is a long distance to lift water and I told him to send for a Woodmanse wind mill at once.

Tuesday, October 27, 1885. The weather suddenly changed about 10 o'clock from warm to cold. Clouded up and spitted rain all day and part of the night. Had hard work to keep warm. Wind blew from north like fury. Emma and Lall went to town and nearly froze. Got 1400 lath. Bbl. gasoline and tank. 50 cts worth salt. Ethel a pair shoes. Emma had a dollar and Lall had 50 cts.

Wednesday, October 28, 1885. Lathing ceiling, stairs fitting door frames and c and c down stairs fixed for wainscoating kitchen. Put in pieces in between stradding(?) their scaffolding brands and their helpers will come back in Mon. The boys hauled two loads of sand. Pete is not very well yet but is better. Got scratches.

Thursday, October 29, 1885. Heavy white. frost. Otherwise fine and cool. Plasterers are hard at work. I got the chambers nearly done. Put porch frames in place. Stairs also. Paid Wm. Clapp 6.00 this morning for 20 bu. potatoes at 25 cts. Hauling a load of lumber 1.00. Cabbage .50. He met Mr. Chitwood and paid him for a load of corn. for me. $5.20 very kindly. Emma bought a chicken of Clapp for our dinner 25 ct.

Friday, October 30, 1885. Plastering. Putting up porches and c. and c. Beautiful day. Clear and cool. Started to use gasoline out of our barrel. Want to see how long it lasts.

Saturday, October 31, 1885. Got the plastering done. Chimneys built by 2 o'clock. Took in the plasterers.

Paid Ogden	$40.00
Paid Rube	10.00
to Wm. Clapp	5.20
Linseed oil and ochre brush	6.50
P.O. Box rent	.15
vinegar oatmeal and mittens	1.90
coal	7.80

brought home coal. Stove pipe. Barrel of soap and c. and c. Got ammunition gun fixed. tuns (?) for door and roof and cof. Fager ch'g'd.

Sunday, November 1, 1885. Yesterday brougth Landons trees out and huled (?) them in for him. Also brought Clapps trees out from town for him. Paid for Landons. $6.40.

Monday, November 2, 1885. I went to [illeg] got big cupboard and a lot of jars and c. 8½ gallons of paint.

Paid Smith the balance on well digging	$20.00
for paint	11.00
writing paper	.25
stamps	.25

Got 10 lb spikes at Fagers. Overalls for Ed and Lall 2.00. Fine weather.

Tuesday, November 3, 1885. Worked all day at the house.

Wednesday, November 4, 1885. Worked on house. Put roof and cornice on porches. Got the north one done. Ed and Leavitt hauled 3 small loads of hay from Mr. Dakes stack. Got all of the stack we started one.

Thursday, November 5, 1885. Got the roof on the south porch by noon. Just in time for it came up misty and settled into a regular North Easter not cold but very wet without heavy rain. Wind in N.E.

Friday, November 6, 1885. Heavy rain during the night. But stopped before morning. Cloudy all day. Sun peeked through very little. Towards night it turned colder with snow squalls and high winds from North. Ripping out caseing stuff and c. Put on corner boards and sided up the south cable above chamber windows. Emma says we must hurry and get inside. Got some corn of Clapp 5 bu.

Saturday, November 7, 1885. I painted shutters all day. Rube worked till noon on Caseings then he and Leavitt went to town. I sent for Door locks, Hinges from Fager. Wainscoating, Plank from White. Lake Lumber Co.

Monday, November 9, 1885. Warm and clear. A beautiful day. Leavitt plowed. Rube and I put on siding. My horses have caught cold. Bought 20 bu. corn of Clapp at 16 cts. Did not pay as I had no change. Insured my house in Farmers and Merchants Ins. Co. to the amount of $1500 giving my note for premium on one year 54.40.

Tuesday, November 10, 1885. Fine day. Putting on siding. Leavitt plowed.

Wednesday, November 11, 1885. Warm in morning and foggy. Got some colder and windier tonight the wind is howling. Wind blows from north. Not so cold but I sided up in the wind all day. Leavitt plowed. Rube is putting on caseing.

Thursday, November 12, 1885. A little snow fell during the night. Enought to whiten the ground gone by noon. Quite cold all day. 26° in morning. Freezing tonight. Clear and bright. I put on siding on east end of kitchen. Rube wainscoated kitchen. Melted the grate out of our little stove.

Friday, November 13, 1885. Busy at the house. I got the kitchen sided up and paper on north end. Chilly all day.

Saturday, November 14, 1885. Fine and warm. I got the north end done.

Tuesday, December 1, 1885. Cleaning house a awful job the lime is clear through the floor and takes lots of muscle. Fager and Co. came along at noon and commenced to put the windmill and tower together.

Friday, December 4, 1885. Jerusalem! How it blows. A howling windstorm set in during the night and I realized what is meant by "wind swept prairies" My tower rocked and swung about and I felt very anxious about it. Finally went up on it and tied rope to the top and anchored it. The weighted at the N.W. corner. And it stood the storm. The wind died away after sundown and I hope it won't come again very soon. It came from the North West.

Thursday, December 24, 1885. A fine warm day so much unlike the usual weather [illeg] that we hardly can believe it to be winter. Finished foundation and vault for a privy etc. Set up a Christmas tree in schoolhouse. I played Santa claus. We had a nice time. Some fifty of us present.

Friday, December 25, 1885. Christmas. We went up to Alex Landons' to spend the day. A ten mile drive. A fine day. A good dinner. A pleasant visit. Staid all night.

Saturday, December 26, 1885. Got home at 1 o'clock. Cloudy and damp but not cold. Cut windows and a door in the stable.

Friday, January 1, 1886. Had a New Year dinner of our own. Mr. Clapp and wife, niece and nephew present. Pleasant time. Joe Fager and Miss Morrish drove up too late for dinner but we fed and warmed them any how.

Saturday, January 2, 1885. Heavy snow storm from northwest. A genuine blizzard. Made cupboard door and dressed lumber for closet door and library.

Sunday, January 3, 1886. Still hard at work, snowing, blowing, drifting. We can hardly see anything out of doors.

Monday, January 4, 1886. Blowing hard but no snow falling. Afternoon the wind slackened a little so we could see some. No drifts except around buildings. I'm done working at Library doors.

Tuesday, January 5, 1886. Pleasant again. The snow is 4 feet between house and barn. Hauled one load of hay from east stack. Good sleighing if I had my sleigh.

Wednesday, January 6, 1886. Hauled 5 loads of hay cleaning up the stack making 6 loads from one stack. Bought for 4 tons. Heavy bank of clouds in west N.W. all afternoon. Wind rose at sunset and by 8 o'clock we had a genuine blizzard.

Thursday, January 7, 1886. A genuine unadulterated blizzard and no mistake. Wind north west 40 miles per hour. Sun shines some but the air is full of snow. Terrible day. I made closet door for upstairs closet and quit.

Friday, January 8, 1886. Strong wind all day. Getting cold in the cellar, 35 above put a lamp in at night.

Saturday, January 9, 1886. Clapp and I went to Franklin in buggy, wished for sleigh. Sent $3.80 to Prairie Farmer for Prairie Farmer, Inter Ocean Godey Ladies Book, sugar $1.00, Calico dress $1.05, Tea $.25, Flour and meal $1.50, Hanger screws. Ear medicine.

Sunday, January 10, 1886. Clear and still.

Monday, January 11, 1886. Rose to 4° above, clear cold and still. I painted the kitchen and oiled the doors of sitting room.

Saturday, January 16, 1886. Went to town for mail. Got a two weeks supply. Big blockade on all railroads all over the land. Salt 25 cts. Washing powder 10.

Saturday, January 23, 1886. Took Rube in to town. Got glass for library doors and 1 window $1.95, mouse traps $.30. Took in $2 lb. butter. $.15 per pound. My first income in Nebraska.

Tuesday, February 9, 1886. Still thawing and clear, no wind. Finished putting on siding.

Monday, February 15, 1886. Cut out steps for out side cellar stairs and finished my outhouse. Got cellar steps done, put corn in crib.

Thursday, February 18, 1886. Went and bought 3 sows of James Grout. Am to pay 4 cents per lb. He has as good stock as I have seen.

Wednesday, February 24, 1886. Went for lumber for pig pens and paid $8.50 for it. Exchanged shoes and yarn. $1.30 for sugar and thread. tobacco 25 cents.

Thursday, February 25, 1886. Made hog pen and got my hogs in it. Paid Jim Grout $20.60 for 3 sows and $11.25 for 25 bushels wheat.

Thursday, March 4, 1886. Snowing like fun. South East wind, not much of it.

Friday, March 5, 1886. Went to town, Good sleighing, six inches deep. Clear and bright. Bought coffee $1.00, slat $.25, Candy $.10, Pins $.05, stockings and tacks $.40, Collars $.75. Emma and Mrs. Clapp visited at Jimmy Grouts. I rented 50 acres of land of him.

Saturday, March 6, 1886. Snowing hard all day, no wind to speak of. The boys and Ethel went to Macon with Mr. Clapp leaving Emma and I alone. The first time we ate dinner alone since we were married I believe.

Sunday, March 7, 1886. Took a sleigh ride over to Mr. Laraways.

Monday, March 8, 1886. Went to Franklin with Clapps — Emma and I. Got a sack of flour and one of Graham $1.85. Got very cold coming home. Bought 50 bu. wheat of Elder Grout. 50 cts. per bu. and paid him $15.00 on it.

Sunday, March 21, 1886. Warm and pleasant, walked over to Briggs and Warriners.

Monday, March 22, 1886. Started spring work, fixed seeder on wagon, started to plow.

Tuesday, March 23, 1886. Went to Jim Grouts and got 40 bushels sea island wheat and sowed about 15 acres with the Strowbridge seeder, it works well.

Wednesday, March 24, 1886. Sowing wheat and working it in the sod. My seeder works well so far.

Thursday, March 25, 1886. Seeding, my sod is well rotted but I have to plow it as it was not all backset.

Friday, March 26, 1886. Seeding, slow work, day cool, heavy frost in morning, ground froze almost too hard to drag.

Friday, April 30, 1886. The boys plowing for corn. I do chores, fix windows, tool closet. Clapp brought out a box of plants from home.

Saturday, May 1, 1886. Warm and clear. Planted about 400 soft maple trees.

Monday, May 3, 1886. Finished plowing for corn, burned off prairie, raining tonight.

Tuesday, May 4, 1886. Started to break sod on southeast corner a 12 acre lot that has been cropped some time.

Tuesday, August 10, 1886. Thrashing wheat 27 acres produced 275 bushels, 2 loads of oats 70 bushels, Jim Grout 2 hands and team, Briggs 2 hands and team, Shively 1 hand and team, Warrinen 1½ day and team.

Wednesday, August 11, 1886. Stacking my wheat, 2 teams Shively and Elmer Grout helping.

Thursday, August 12, 1886. Finished stacking at 5 o'clock and put up a stack for Shively.

Friday, August 13, 1886. Stacking for Shively, Leavitt and I got done at sundown, all in good shape.

Monday, August 23, 1886. Stacking Hay and millet, fine hay weather, Clapp got my mower at noon.

Tuesday, August 24, 1886. Got my millet stacked have about 5 tons.

Friday, September 10, 1886. Went to the Fair, tickets $1.00. A fair display for a young country. Brought home a cook stove bought at Fagers, cost $27.75.

Tuesday, October 5, 1886. Finished backsetting, took a load of wheat to town 22.40 bushel $.41 = $9.35, sent plow box to Hastings to be exchanged $.25, socks for 3 for $.25, mustard $.10, pepper $.10.

Thursday, October 7, 1886. Dug potatoes. We have about 25 bushels a very light crop. Hauled some dirt in stable.

Saturday, October 9, 1886. The boys husked two loads of corn, 8 rows, 90 rods long. I butchered a pig last night. Dressed over 100 lbs. and 4 months old.

Thursday, October 28, 1886. Sold 50 bu. 50 lbs. wheat 45 ct. $22.90.

Monday, November 1, 1886. Plowing orchard and garden ground. Planted some walnuts and butternuts.

Thursday, November 18, 1886. Went to Franklin with buggy, got felt boots for Leavitt and myself also leather ones for him, molasses, sugar. Snow is drifted badly and a good deal of suffering among stock and some loss is reported.

Saturday, November 27, 1886. Took a load of hay to Fager. Upset and had an all days job. Settled up for it. 2¾ tons $4.50 = 12.25. Bought 2 gals. vinegar 60 cts tea 1 lb. 60 ct. Copy book for Ed, 15 ct.

Monday, December 13, 1886. Ethel suffered with tootheache last night and I took her to the dentist and had 6 cavities filled $2.00, broom $.25, candy and elastic $.10, got 850 lbs, coal for school and lumber for box.

Tuesday, December 14, 1886. Helped Emma wash clothes and partly made a coal box for the school house. High northwest wind.

Wednesday, December 15, 1886. Cold and windy. Fixed water barrel and well. Fine in morning but got cloudy. Went to schoolhouse in evening to arrange for Christmas tree.

Thursday, December 16, 1886. Helped Emma iron clothes and took coal to schoolhouse and put it in the new box.

Friday, December 17, 1886. Mending shoes — I am getting to be quite a shoe maker. Rev. Mr. Durham called on us.

Friday, December 24, 1886. Getting ready for the night. A Christmas tree in the schoolhouse about 60 of us had a pleasant time.

Saturday, December 25, 1886. A fine clear day for Christmas, spent it at home.

Sunday, December 26, 1886. Cold as Greenland all day, 8° below at night and 10° below at night, some snow flew in, just enough to whiten the ground.

The year closes leaving us in a fairly satisfactory condition. Very little money on hand but enough to eat and wear. During the season we have put in 57 acres of wheat and 10 acres of oats. Also 30 acres of corn. Have broke up 70 acres of prairie . . . also put up 30 tons of fine hay. 30 acres of wheat raised at home yielded 15 bu. per acre or 450 bu. 27 acres on rented land only made 10 bu. per acre. My oats yielded 30 bu. per acre or 300 bu. My corn averaged about 20 bu. all told. My sod corn, 12 acres, makes me 27 bu. per acre . . . I raised 13 pigs form 4 sows and will have 7 sows and 3 barrows left after killing my meat. Bought 2 cows and raised 2 calves. One cow hung herself in rope and I now have one cow and two steer calves.

Saturday, January 8, 1887. It is cold, the mercury rose no higher than 12° below all day, wind from north, some snow flying all day. We all sat by fire and then we feel cold.

Tuesday, February 1, 1887. Stayed 12° below all day — 2° at noon, snow flying part of time. Took 4 bushels corn to school house for fuel, shall ask $.18 per bushel for it. Reading Othmar by "Ouida".

Thursday, February 3, 1887. 2° at noon, still cold, wind north, churned and read stories. Reading 2nd volume of Grants Memoirs.

Friday, February 4, 1887. Clapp and I went to town after the mail. Took down 4½ pounds butter and sold it to Ezra Fager for $.75, got thread $.25, comb $.05, candy $.05.

Wednesday, March 16, 1887. The boys plowing, I help clean house. A big prairie fire started at Jones and swept over the prairie north and east of us and we had to fight fire several hours. It is burning tonight and is a grand sight since danger is past. Prairie fires are burning all the time in some direction. We can count 25 different ones at night sometimes.

Saturday, April 9, 1887. Very high wind. Air so full of dust can't see the sun. Cloudy part of time and just before sunset we had a shower. Wet the ground a little. Then cleared off. Went to town with Peterson. Bought 6 pr. hose got us boys and 3 pr. for Emma cost $1.00 pr. plow shoes $2.00. Candy .05. Copy book for Ed. .15. Got box of crayons for school .25 and 15 lb. nails .90. Sold 7 lb. Butter 15 ct. $1.05.

Monday, April 11, 1887. Wind still in south, clouding up some. Marked out my orchard in forenoon. The wind was so high and dry I did not set out any. Leavitt plowed afternoon.

Friday, May 13, 1887. Light rain during night again. The grass grows so you can see it move.

Tuesday, June 7, 1887. 6 years ago today was our wedding, now we have two children one 5 and over, the other 5 days. Plowing corn, got 15 acre field done.

Wednesday, June 8, 1887. Leavitt plowed corn. I sowed about 30 acres of millet on sod, going to make my fortune raising the seed.

Thursday, June 16, 1887. Took 5 hogs to market. Weighed 1130 lb. Price $4.15 per cwt. Amt. $46.90.

Wednesday, October 26, 1887. Husking or Jerking corn. Leavitt and I picked about 5 acre today. Fred and Alex Lawson stopped here for dinner. Very pleasant.

Sunday, November 6, 1887. Went up to see Alex Landon, fine day. Alex gave us a lot of squash and pumpkins.

Thursday, November 10, 1887. Clear and beautiful, helped clean pantry. Emma says she has her house cleaned now.

Saturday, November 26, 1887. Wind shifted to the old place, northwest, during the night, and a blizzard of the first water is upon us. Mercury fell all day and the wind rose. Reading Scott and tending fire and baby.

Sunday, November 27, 1887. Clear and bright, no wind but cold, 24° below.

Monday, November 28, 1887. Cold and clear, sent boys to town for mail, mended horse blankets.

Wednesday, December 21, 1887. Colder and clear, high wind. Hard work to keep stove warm.

Another year is closed and leaves us in good health and an increase of one in family. My crops have been very poor on account of drought and chinch bugs. My wheat yielded 2½ bu. per acre. Oats 20 bu. per acre. Corn from 0 to 15 . . . Have broke out 20 acres and now have nearly 120 under cultivation. My sales for the year are: Wheat, 19.75. Butter and eggs, 29.78. Oats, 9.90. Corn, 6.95. Hogs, 113.70. Hay, 12.85. Calves, 20.00. Labor (cash) 12.50. Boarders, 90.00. Total, $325.43. Our espenses for household purposes up to about 225.00. I bought a drag, corn plow, and Shively's interest. in the binder, in all about 180.00.

Tuesday, January 3, 1888. Moderating some during the day, quite warm, wind west and south, washed. Took eggs to town 6 dozen, 18 cents, $1.10, 2½ yards Denim for Eddie's pants $.18 $.45, candy and cards $.15.

Monday, December 3, 1888. 1st day of school. The boys and Ethel started off in good style. I put in my time shelling corn, watching cattle. Clear and cool, froze quite hard during night. We have clear bright days right along with cold enough at night to freeze ice ½ inch thick, not much wind.

Memoranda: Another year has closed and leaves us in good health as before and a good deal better off otherwise. Crops have been fair and although prices are low I will have enough to pay my debts in Nebraska and some if not entirely enough to settle up with father. I have sold as follows: corn 171.13, wheat 119.10, oats 198.25, stock 89.31, butter and eggs 21.27, other sources 103.81, total $693.87.

Wednesday, January 2, 1889. Took 51 bushels white corn to town 51×1.17 $8.65. Paid Fager $25.10. This makes me out of debt to anyone in Nebraska.

Tuesday, March 5, 1889. Hauling manure, I went to town after noon and bought of Gittle and Chitwood a corn plow. John Deere, maker, am to pay $20.00. A mad dog got on a tare on the street and finally was killed, he had a tussle with my dog "Tip" and I had him killed. Several dogs and a little girl was bit.

Monday, April 1, 1889. Sowed 12 acres oats, this finishes the sowing, 40 acres of wheat, 20 acres of oats, 12 acres of rye. Annual school metting, reelected director.

Thursday, January 30, 1890. Took a load of hogs to town 5 of them. Weighed 1370 lbs, was docked 40 lbs on one as being piggy. 1330 × $3.25 = $43.20. Paid box rent at post office $.15, 5 lbs. sulphur $.50, writing paper $.30, traded for soap and soda a bill Emma left at Chitwoods of $.75, gave Eddie $4.50.

Friday, January 31, 1890. Took 39.10 bushels wheat to market, price $.30 — $11.75. got 96 feet lumber for making a bin $2.20. A basket $5.00, cloudy, cold and raw.

Tuesday, March 18, 1890. Commenced seeding, sowed the White Bonanza Oats that father sent to me on about two acres, then sowed nearly 25 acres of wheat, cultivating with one team, raking stalks with another. Warm and pleasant until just night when a cold wind sprang up from the northeast.

Friday, September 26, 1890. The boys cutting cane. I went to the Fair, small attendance, the show shows the effect of the drougth. Stock especially hogs was pretty good. I spent for Fair $.50, salt $.10, glycerin $.10, envelopes $.55, paper $.25. Sold to Fager 8 lbs. butter at $.10 $.80. Got for it coffee 2 lbs. $.55, prunes $.25, total $.80. Mr. Daggett paid me for 8 lbs. butter which he got a month ago, $.80.

Saturday, November 29, 1890. Went to Franklin, the box from Father had come. It had nuts, two flour sacks full of dried apples, some old clothes. Such things make us think of the old home. Charlie Gorham and I divided our hay. I got ½ lb. powder $.20, pen, pencil for Ethel $.05, Tobacco $.10, Harness menders $.25. Sold beef hides 62 lbs. $1.25

Memoranda: This year has been a tough one for us. The long severe drougth killed our crops and it will be as much as I can do to have feed enough to see me through. Grain raised: Corn 80 acres 250 bushels, wheat 35 acres 67 bushels, rye 12 acres 83 bushels, oats 22½ acres 8 bushels. Cut 20 acres oats for hay too short or light to harvest. Raised 2 colts, 7 calves, 40 pigs.

Wednesday, May 18, 1891. Cleared off by morning, a high wind from the northwest has dried up the mud so that we can get in the fields tomorrow. Took 18 head of hogs to Franklin weighed 3700, price $3.90 per cwt, total $144.30. Bought Kerosene $.30, Nails $.30, Thermometer $.20, Rule $.35. Paid Gilber Grays on horse bill $20.00, mending springseat $.10.

Sunday, July 16, 1893. A still warm day until about 4 o'clock when a thunderstorm came from the north west with hail in it and in half an hour 40 acres of winter wheat, 40 acres of oats, and 120 acres of corn was harvested. Wheat and oats are ruined, corn badly hurt.

Monday, July 17, 1893. A cool cloudy day took a look over the place in morning and fell pretty blue. $1000.00 damage is not far out of the way. Went to town. Found the storm had been worse west of us 12 miles by 4 is about the size of it. Bought some window screen of Gettle on "tick" $1.20.

Wednesday, August 30, 1893. Plowing. Emma went to Franklin to get tooth filled and do trading, spent $5.00. I went to the Populist convention at Macon.

Thursday, August 31, 1893. Plowing on millet ground for rye. Went to see a road grading work on trial afternoon. The town will probably buy it.

Saturday, September 30, 1893. Heavy mist till 10 o'clock, plowed. L.E. Furry took dinner with us and sold me a carload of steers to feed this winter. Deliver them next week.

Saturday, October 7, 1893. Finished sowing my wheat. I have now 75 acres in. Have to drag over 2 acres yet. I went after my cattle — 20 head of 2 year olds. Weighed 16450 lbs., pay $2.75 per cwt. Gave note for $452.37 to J. M. Barber for them. Ezra Fager helped me drive them home. Bought 1 sack flour $1.00, thread and Bologna $.10.

Saturday, March 3, 1894. Drove my steers to Riverton delivering them to P. Carnahan. 23 head steers 23745 lbs, 1 bull 1910. I got $3.00 per cwt for steers, $2.40 cwt for bull. Amounting to $758.20. The steers averaged 1032 a gain of only 200 lbs. for 150 days feeding. One, the largest of the lot only made 100 lbs. or I was cheated on his weight when bought him.

Friday, March 9, 1894. Seeding has commenced. Sowed 10 acres of oats and partly cultivated them. I took 7 pigs to market, weight 460, price $4.25 per cwt, amounting to $72.05. Bought lumber $10.43, tobacco $.10, hat $1.00, sent 52 lbs. butter to E. C. Budlong, Denman.

Saturday, March 10, 1894. Went to see Lizzie Grube married. Stayed during evening to dance awhile. Beer galore.

Saturday, March 17, 1894. The boys finished the oats. I went to Franklin to get my new plow but it was not there yet. Bought 3¼ bushels potatoes at 85¢ — $12.85. tobacco $.10, dried fruit $.80, soap $.25, coffee $.50, tea $.25, Codfish $.20, sugar $.50. Sold 10 dozen eggs $.70, garden seeds, $.85. A furious dust storm blew afternoon from south — worst in long time.

Friday, August 17, 1894. Cutting corn. Took 7 hogs to town weighed 1140, price $.04 = $45.60. Mr. Furry paid me $80.00 on hogs and I sent $238.50 to the B & M R.R. Co. to pay the last payment on land.

Tuesday, September 25, 1894. A windy day, drilling in wheat. Tried the press drill in cornfield, find it works nicely if we go angling through the field. Will finish with it. Hugh wind from south all day — had to quit at noon.

Saturday, October 27, 1894. Wind — Oh, no, about 50 miles an hour from the south. Dust till you could not see the horses heads. Took 30 bushels wheat to mill, brought home 10. Bought 20 bushels of potatoes. Shively paid my $10.00 for 12 bushels rye he got for seed at $.75, the extra money to go on account.

Sunday, October 28, 1894. A big change, cold and windy and a misty rain. Just enough to wet the side of a house, sat by fire.

Thursday, November 29, 1894. A beautiful day. We do not make any display today. We can hardly eat a feast with the same relish which we could in ordinary years. The boys went to Macon to a social in evening.

Monday, December 3, 1894. I went to town got some glycerin and a slat $.25. Tried to sell my hogs but failed. Brought home the last grist from Gettles mill.

Friday, December 7, 1894. A nice day till afternoon. Wind turned to northwest. Blows strong but not cold as yet. Gets very smokey. We have hard work to find enough to do to keep us in good nature. A party of young folks spend the evening with us.

Wednesday, December 26, 1894. A bright clear day but with a high north west wind, 12 to 16 above. Sat by fire. Help wife make patterns with dress pattern machine, thinks I will make a dress maker in time.

Thursday, December 27, 1894. Clear and cold, strong northwest wind. 8° below in morning. 8° above at night but going down with the sun. Sat by fire.

Saturday, December 29, 1894. The boys went to town. I worked a wash bench for Emma. A cold day but fine and clear — no snow.

Sunday, December 30, 1894. Went to church — a cold job. No preacher, bright and clear. Visited with Dr. McElwee and paid him $2.00 for his visit July 26th.

Monday, December 31, 1894. A beautiful day choring about yard. The close of this year leaves us in good health but otherwise in anything but a prosperous condition. Almost total loss of crops, lack of feed and consequent lack of means has diminished our resources sadly.

Tuesday, January 1, 1895. A beautiful day. Eddie and I went to town for the mail and I ordered a milk tank made by Thos. Gettle. Received letter from father with check for $100.00 and a note for me to sign, also one from Mrs. Kreidler with $11.00 on Butter account. Also $4.60 from Mrs. Dunn for butter. Paid box rent $.15, tracing wheel $.15. Got shoes for Edith but did not pay until tried or returned. Coffee $.15, cloth $.75, same bill.

Friday, January 11, 1895. The wind got on its ear during the night. Blowed big gusts and snowed a little in morning but soon cleared off leaving the air full of frost and wind. Cut up meat, made sausage.

Thursday, February 21, 1895. Wife and I went to call on Mrs. John Larraway who has a little boy. Warm day, thawing. A revival in progress at Macon, went up in evening.

Friday, February 22, 1895. A beautiful warm clear day. Sent 22½ lbs of butter to Mrs. T. R. Acres in Denver. The finest 22nd I've seen in the state.

Tuesday, February 26, 1895. Cloudy and warm mist, rain some of time. A lot of rain fell during the night, nearly 2 inches. The first good rain since June 23rd. A warm gentle rain.

Thursday, April 4, 1895. Hot and windy from south very dry. Was out looking at my winter wheat. It is gone up. Oats sprouting, ground like road dust. Boys are plowing to make a garden.

Friday, April 5, 1895. How it blows, a furious wind from the north has filled the air (and house) full of dust. Still hard at it. Mercury fell from 68 this morning to 50 at 4 o'clock. The boys plowed. I trimmed the trees in orchard, my apricot tree is full of bloom.

Monday, April 15, 1895. Plowed till noon and washed. Commenced to rain about 2 o'clock and is still raining at 10 o'clock. Part of the time it has poured down. Everything is flooded. It rains in Nebraska once more.

Tuesday, April 16, 1895. Cleared off by noon. Stopped raining towards morning over 2 inches of rain. Borrowed two breaking plows and broke sod in south east corner of farm. A five acre patch — the last.

Wednesday, April 17, 1895. Warm and clear, breaking sod done, churning, etc. I went to Franklin with Mr. Clapp. Bought garden seeds $1.00, vanilla and tobacco $.25. Except the pasture of 30 acres, my farm is all broke out — about 270 acres is all under plow.

Tuesday, October 1, 1895. Have charged the boys each $100.00 for a team. They start out for themselves today.

Wednesday, October 2, 1895. Dug my potatoes. 75 bushels from ⅔ acre, nice ones, large and smooth. Warm and clear — south wind.

Tuesday, November 19, 1895. High north, cold in morning but afternoon it calmed down and turned to the south. 8 loads corn in pile, cribs are full — 3000 bushels.

Thursday, November 28, 1895. Thanksgiving Day. We roasted a turkey and made mince and pumpkin pies and had a nice dinner.

Memoranda. Taken as a whole the year has been a fairly good one. Have 300 bu. corn on hand, 30 good shoats, 10 head cattle, and 10 horses and colts. We have plenty to eat, drink, and to wear, but very little to pay debts with. Hard times of last year has left its mark on us. We are in our usual good health.

Monday, January 20, 1896. Took 12 hogs to market, weighed 2480 lbs., price $3.35 amount $83.10. Sent draft to Harry Shryock to pay threshing bill $24.00, pain on "Youths Companion" for last year and this $3.50, "State Journal" and "Inter Ocean" $1.35, Flour (2 sacks) $2.00, Shoe tacks $.15, Crackers $.25, A.O.U.W. $1.00, Exchange on Draft $.10, Shively paid for corn shelling (680 bushels) $5.40, my share $3.40, took 7 bushels along to send to Eugene but Railroad difficulties were too great so I sold them to Austin on account $2.40.

Tuesday, January 21, 1896. 46 years old today and still feel young. Cloudy and foggy. The boys shelled corn for Reimer Grube.

Monday, March 30, 1896. I tramped about the fields looking at my rye, if it rains and quits blowing it will live otherwise not. Wash day forenoon, warm and clear but windy strong. Paid Chris Detefsen $.70 for helping me shell corn Friday.

Thursday, July 23, 1896. Took grist of 12 bushels corn and rye to mill for chop for pigs. Bought cupboard $6.00, nails $.30, lumber $1.90, sugar $1.00. Cashed check of H. L. Rodenburg $4.25. Got a little oil of mullien from Dr. Lenox to use in my ears $.25, had no change.

Wednesday, August 19, 1896. Cool and cloudy. Wash day. Rented 145 acres of land to Charlie Maska ⅓ rent delivered in bin and crib. Charlie Gorham rents 32 acres ⅓ in bin. Leavitt Rubendall rents 100 acres ⅓ delivered in bin and crib. Leavitt got martins corn shelled 550 bushels. Paid me $2.75.

Tuesday, September 22, 1896. Making hay, I took a trip in morning to Macon to see a land agent who was there to get him to look at my farm. Cool and clear.

Monday, December 28, 1896. Took 46.4 bushels corn to town times 8½ cents = $3.90. The lowest price I ever sold corn. Paid for 6 gallons of kerosene and a lamp, shade and chimney at Gettles $1.65, Coffee, 2 lbs. $.50. A fine warm day.

The year closes leaving us in good health except Ethel who is somewhat indisposed. I have on hand about 2500 bushels corn, 400 bushels oats, 25 bushels rye, 50 head hogs weight 150 lbs., 7 head cows, 6 spring calves, 2 yearling heifers, 1 bull, 6 horses, 30 tons hay. Have rented the farm during the year except 25 acres which I planted to corn. Corn yielded about 40 bushels, oats 15 bushels, rye 4 bushels.

Thursday, March 4, 1897. Today McKinley is president. No more of Grover. A cool cloudy day. Threatening rain. Doing chores. Leavitt shelled 300 bushels corn for Charles Gorham.

Friday, March 26, 1897. Warm. The weather is all one could ask. The last day of our school. Had quite an entertainment in evening. Miss Austin's mother and aunt, Mrs. Hyatt were here. Edith and Ethel feel very bad because Miss Austin is leaving us, and cried themselves to sleep.

Thursday, May 13, 1897. Working at the hog lot fence. Did not get the fence quite done. Leavitt finished planting corn. He has 18 acres to list yet. Quite cool tonight. Fear we'll have frost.

Monday, May 31, 1897. Decoration Day. We went to Franklin, hot windy and dusty. A big procession for the place — nearly 100 teams. Bought some trifles $.50. Shipped 25 lbs. butter to H. L. Hodenburg.

Thursday, July 8, 1897. Picked cherries and helped pit them. We have about 40 quarts canned. Very hot and dry. No wind.

Saturday, February 12, 1898. Wife, Leavitt and I went to Franklin to see the new Creamery Station start up, took along 15 lbs. of milk. Attended a meeting of the stockholders. Wife traded out the butter I took in yesterday. I paid my February assessment in A.O.U.W. $1.00. Sent to mother a draft for $400.00 and a note for $350.00.

Tuesday, February 15, 1898. Hauling fodder and digging post holes. Only got 14 dug — find from 2 to 6 inches of frost. Clear and warm. Beatrice Creamery Co. collector called.

Wednesday, February 16, 1898. Dug post holes till noon. Left Leavitt dig the last 20 and I went to town for the posts. Got 70 at 12 × 14½, 28 × 14½ — $9.45. Bought 3 rolls, 343 ft. of barb wire at Guttles at 2½ cents, unpaid $8.40. Tobacco and candy $.35.

Friday, March 11, 1898. Cloudy and chilly, snow going off slowly. Fixed fence, choring about house and yard. Fred Custer the milkman brought me my 1st check from the creamery $11.00, paid him $1.79 for hauling milk.

Wednesday, March 30, 1898. Leavitt and I took two loads of hogs to town. 14 head weighed 2710 × $3.20 = $86.70. A cold south wind blowing not very hard. We all went to a A.O.U.W. banquet in evening at Franklin — fine affair. Enjoyed ourselves highly.

Friday, April 15, 1898. Hot and clear but windy. Set out a lot of peach trees, going to have a peach orchard.

Friday, May 20, 1898. Cloudy till noon. Clear and warm afternoon, heavy thunderstorm off East tonight. Plowed my potatoes forenoon. Put in the afternoon mending the corn sheller. The 1st cheese came out of press all right — put in another.

Saturday, June 4, 1898. Heavy rain 1 inch during the night and early morning. I sorted potatoes. I find a cave to be an ideal place for potatoes — mine are sound and hard yet not sprouted very badly.

Monday, June 6, 1898. Ground too wet to do good work in corn field. Sowed 5 acres of millet and dragged it during forenoon. Edith drove one team on drag — her first attempt. Got done just as it commenced to rain. ¼ inch fell in a drizzle, churned.

Tuesday, August 2, 1898. An inch of rain fell during the night saving the corn, four weeks drouth is broken. Painting wagon and window shutters. Leavitt brought me $1.35 from John Eichoff for the use of my planter last spring. A skunk got into the henhouse and killed 24 fine chickens.

Tuesday, August 16, 1898. Drove into see Mr. Conklin about my land. He has a buyer coming in tonight and wanted to arrange terms with me. Tobacco $.20. The dry winds are killing the corn badly. Cashed check from Ed. Phelan $8.50.

Saturday, August 20, 1898. Took 48.20 bushels wheat to Franklin. Sold for $47 per bushel, amount $22.72. Got tire set at John Ivins. Paid A.O.U.W. fee $1.50, sugar $1.00, Spices $.35, sold eggs $.60, Glour $1.10, mending harness $1.50, Freight on organ $2.29. Got my new Harwood organ from Kansas City.

Wednesday, August 24, 1898. Warm again. I have sold my farm to a Mr. Porter if he don't back out by morning. I am to get cash $6100.00 down $1300.00 1st January. He takes the cattle for $400.00. Fred Devous helped Leavitt haul hay afternoon.

Thursday, August 25, 1898. We all went to the A.O.U.W. picnic at Bloomington — splendid. Cost about $1.00.

Wednesday, September 7, 1898. Picked a small load of corn forenoon. Pretty good for this year. Raked my millet and put a small load in feed rack. Millet poor.

Went to a camp meeting at Macon. Mennonite. Hard lot. Sermons consist mostly of abuse of everybody else.

Saturday, September 10, 1898. Steady rain 2½ inches has fallen since yesterday morning and still it comes — every drop going where it is needed. Wind northeast. Doing chores.

Wednesday, September 21, 1898. Came to Omaha. Took all day, Fare $9.50. Found W. H. Brodey place and stayed with them. Left Edith at Austins and Ethel at Mr. Clapps.

Thursday, September 22, 1898. We went to the exposition. It is grand is all I can say. Had to carry Willie most of the time and am used up. Tickets $1.00.

Tuesday, September 27, 1898. Left Omaha 4:30 p.m. for Mound City. Arrived 8 p.m. The run over the Missouri bottom shows some fine farms. Some new fine houses are going up.

Friday, September 30, 1898. Took team and George and wife and Emma and I took a long drive — looked over a 100 acre farm that suits me to a T. 10 acres timber, 85 plowland, balance orchard and house lot. $50.00 per acre, 5 miles from town. Dinner with Fred Lawson. Cigars and candy $.35.

Saturday, October 15, 1898. Sold out. The deed is done. Met Porter in town and made transfer. He then came out and bought my pigs and 3 year old colt, paying me $140.00 for them. $100.00 for 5 pigs, $40.00 for colt. He assumes the $1500.00 mortgage, paying balance in cash less interest to January 1st. Land $7000.00, Pigs and colt $140.00, Cattle $400.00 = $7540.00. Less Mortgage $1500.00, Interest $37.50, 60 bushels wheat $30.00 = $1567.50. Balance Cash $5972.50.

Tuesday, December 6, 1898. Worked hard at packing in evening 40 of the neighbors came in on us with baskets filled to bid us goodbye. Gave Emma $25.00.

Wednesday, December 7, 1898. Loaded car. Had eight good loads and two horses. Charlie Gorham, Mr. Wicklund, Dunkin, Clapp, Mr. Perry, Leavitt, Fred Devries and I got car loaded and ready for horses by dark. Stayed with D.A. Fager, bought padlock $.25, Paid A.O.U.W. $2.75, Lumber $2.10.

Memoranda: The year closes showing great change for us. Sold out in Nebraska bought in Missouri. Time will show the wisdom of it. But we feel as if we would be satisfied so far. 100 acres of rich land, 10 of it in fine timber. Am about to purchase 36 acres as good to add to it. I have no debts except the one owing to my mother of $350.00. I have $1550.00 in cash and we all have good health.

Wages of Farm Labor, 1866–88

From U.S. Department of Agriculture, *Annual Report*, 1887, pp. 579–88.

The result of the May investigation of wages of farm labor is almost identical with that of three years ago. The changes are very slight, though local differences occur, the averages of the geographical sections or groups of States being changed very little. The average rate per month, where the laborer boards himself, is a few cents lower in the Middle and Western States and in California, and a very little higher in the South and in New England.

The highest rates obtained in 1866 in the Northern and Western States. In California and in the South there was a positive advance between that date and 1869. The investigation of 1875, a year or two after the monetary crisis appeared, showed decline in each section, which continued for several years, culminating in 1879, the date of lowest prices of all American farm products. The decline from 1866 to 1879 amounted to 39 per cent. in the Eastern States, 35 in the Middle, 30 in the Western States, and 17 in the Southern States. In California the rate of averages was well sustained, rising at first but standing in 1879 higher than in 1866.

The following statement presents the sectional averages for each period:

Sections.	1888	1885	1882	1879	1875	1869	1866
Eastern States	$26.03	$25.30	$26.61	$20.21	$28.96	$32.08	$33.30
Middle States	23.11	23.19	22.24	19.69	26.02	28.02	30.07
Southern States	14.54	14.27	15.30	13.31	16.22	17.21	16.00
Western States	22.22	22.26	23.63	20.38	23.60	27.01	28.91
California	38.08	38.75	38.25	41.00	44.50	45.38	35.75
Average United States	18.24	17.97	18.94	16.42	19.87	20.98	21.71

The accompanying diagram (K) illustrates the course of prices for more than twenty years, and forcibly shows into what a gulf wages fell during the five or six years of panic, from which a slow recovery commenced in 1879. The sharp decline from 1886, except in California — where the highest point after the war is noted in 1869 — is a fall from an era of inflation, in which speculative values were all the higher from being stated in a depreciated currency. The present values appear to be on a more natural and stable basis.

It will be seen that the rise was coincident with the return to specie payments, reaching the natural level by a leap as soon as the pressure which depressed was removed. It is curious to note, further, that at the lowest ebb of wages rates were higher in the West than in the Middle States, and slightly above the lowest point reached in the Eastern States, because the soil was still cultivated and crops were grown in their usual quantity, while much of the manufacturing industry was suspended. This Western line of wages would not have dipped so low but for the immigration to the West of Eastern operatives and artisans out of work seeking employment and future homes.

Wages Per Month by the Year

This statement gives the result of the present investigation, in connection with those of five prior inquiries at intervals from 1869 to 1888:

States and Territories.	1888. Without board.	1888. With board.	1885. Without board.	1885. With board.	1882. Without board.	1882. With board.	1879. Without board.	1879. With board.	1875. Without board.	1875. With board.	1860. Without board.	1860. With board.
Maine	$24.64	$17.20	$23.09	$16.00	$24.75	$16.15	$18.25	$11.08	$25.40	$15.94	$26.25	$16.50
New Hampshire	24.38	17.00	22.80	15.75	25.25	16.72	19.75	12.30	28.57	18.25	32.66	22.16
Vermont	23.25	16.40	23.00	16.20	23.37	16.00	19.00	11.50	29.67	19.37	32.40	21.40
Massachusetts	29.50	18.00	28.75	17.85	30.66	18.25	25.00	15.33	31.87	20.25	35.95	22.16
Rhode Island	27.75	17.50	28.50	17.70	27.75	17.00	23.00	13.25	30.00	19.00	32.25	20.00
Connecticut	27.40	17.17	27.67	17.20	27.90	17.37	23.29	14.23	28.25	18.50	33.00	20.75
New York	24.13	16.30	24.00	16.52	23.63	15.30	20.61	13.19	27.14	17.80	29.28	18.64
New Jersey	23.33	15.73	23.60	14.10	24.25	14.20	20.22	11.53	30.71	16.78	32.11	19.02
Pennsylvania	22.24	14.50	22.52	14.12	22.88	14.21	19.92	11.46	25.89	16.10	28.68	18.05
Delaware	18.00	12.25	18.33	12.63	18.20	12.50	17.00	9.50	20.33	11.67	22.00	13.00
Maryland	18.48	11.84	18.20	11.50	16.34	9.89	14.00	8.95	20.02	11.42	21.55	12.00
Virginia	13.82	9.25	13.95	9.34	13.96	9.17	11.00	7.66	14.84	9.21	15.28	9.65
North Carolina	13.41	9.00	12.85	8.91	12.86	8.80	11.19	7.66	13.46	8.82	12.76	7.91
South Carolina	12.25	8.00	12.00	8.25	12.10	8.10	10.25	6.66	12.84	8.19	11.54	7.34
Georgia	12.60	8.81	12.47	8.73	12.86	8.70	10.73	7.38	14.40	8.79	14.70	9.70
Florida	18.00	11.33	17.80	11.37	16.64	10.20	13.80	8.73	15.50	10.75	16.10	10.91
Alabama	13.59	9.49	13.00	9.10	13.15	9.09	13.20	8.30	13.60	9.40	15.19	10.52
Mississippi	15.03	10.09	14.60	10.00	15.10	10.09	13.31	9.28	16.40	11.25	17.11	11.21
Louisiana	15.37	11.12	16.05	11.26	18.20	12.69	16.40	11.27	18.40	12.20	21.37	12.62
Texas	19.20	12.60	18.87	13.72	20.20	14.03	18.27	11.49	19.50	13.37	18.83	13.21
Arkansas	18.34	12.50	17.33	12.25	18.50	12.25	17.12	11.31	20.50	13.00	25.25	16.60
Tennessee	14.00	10.00	13.88	9.74	13.75	9.49	12.73	8.69	15.20	10.00	16.81	11.00
West Virginia	18.74	12.25	19.00	12.40	19.16	12.46	16.98	10.94	20.75	13.10	21.39	13.87
Kentucky	16.51	11.33	16.80	11.90	18.20	11.75	15.17	10.00	18.12	12.00	26.35	12.57
Ohio	22.21	15.00	23.00	15.50	24.55	16.30	20.72	13.34	24.05	16.33	26.35	16.74
Michigan	25.20	17.00	24.00	16.14	25.76	17.27	22.88	14.64	28.22	18.46	31.01	20.03
Indiana	22.50	15.30	22.20	15.30	23.14	15.65	20.20	12.76	24.20	16.14	25.42	17.93
Illinois	23.20	16.00	23.50	16.60	23.91	17.14	20.61	13.01	25.20	16.87	27.32	17.69
Wisconsin	24.65	16.80	23.54	16.78	26.21	17.90	21.07	13.81	25.50	16.45	30.08	18.47
Minnesota	25.75	17.68	25.50	16.75	26.36	17.75	24.55	15.62	26.16	16.36	28.61	17.94
Iowa	25.60	17.34	25.33	17.00	26.21	17.95	22.09	13.90	24.35	16.11	28.39	17.87
Missouri	21.00	14.20	21.35	14.50	22.39	13.95	17.59	11.84	19.40	13.15	24.47	16.38
Kansas	24.25	16.05	24.70	16.00	23.85	15.87	20.67	13.28	23.20	14.65	28.96	18.38
Nebraska	25.59	17.18	25.00	16.50	24.45	16.20	23.04	14.86	24.00	14.75	33.25	19.18
California	38.08	25.67	38.75	25.00	38.25	23.45	41.00	26.27	44.50	28.60	46.38	28.69
Oregon	32.56	23.00	34.00	21.25	33.50	24.75	35.45	23.86	38.25	25.67	.....	.....
Nevada	38.00	27.00	.....	.....	.....	.....	.....	.....	.....	.....	.....	.....
Colorado	36.00	23.00	33.00	21.25	36.50	27.08	35.00	20.00	38.50	21.14	.....	.....
Arizona	25.00	16.00	.....	.....	.....	.....	.....	.....	.....	.....	.....	.....
Dakota	25.85	18.21	25.55	17.00	.....	.....	28.56	16.57	32.50	20.50	.....	.....
Idaho	39.00	26.25	.....	.....	.....	.....	.....	.....	.....	.....	.....	.....
Montana	40.00	27.50	.....	.....	.....	.....	.....	.....	.....	.....	.....	.....
New Mexico	28.75	18.25	28.75	17.50	.....	.....	22.10	13.80	22.75	14.25	.....	.....
Utah	33.50	22.30	30.00	21.00	.....	.....	28.87	20.50	35.50	25.33	.....	.....
Washington	35.20	25.00	38.33	26.25	.....	.....	.....	.....	.....	.....	.....	.....
Wyoming	37.00	25.00	.....	.....	.....	.....	.....	.....	.....	.....	.....	.....
Average	18.24	12.36	17.97	.....	18.94	.....	16.42	.....	19.87	.....	20.98	.....

Day Wages in Harvest

The following exhibit of average day wages in harvest time, with and without board, corresponds in its periodical changes with those in the statement of monthly wages of labor employed by the year.

States and Territories.	1888. Without board.	1888. With board.	1885. Without board.	1885. With board.	1882. Without board.	1882. With board.	1879. Without board.	1879. With board.	1875. Without board.	1875. With board.	1869. Without board.	1869. With board.
Maine	$1.65	$1.30	$1.58	$1.19	$1.52	$1.22	$1.42	$1.89	$1.99	$1.49	$2.17	$1.65
New Hampshire	1.67	1.37	1.65	1.32	1.71	1.35	1.25	.95	2.06	1.64	2.37	1.95
Vermont	1.65	1.35	1.68	1.30	1.75	1.35	1.29	.97	2.28	1.85	2.46	2.00
Massachusetts	1.80	1.38	1.70	1.31	1.75	1.35	1.50	1.00	1.90	1.50	2.37	1.95
Rhode Island	1.75	1.35	1.60	1.25	1.60	1.30	1.30	.95	2.00	1.50	2.37	1.75
Connecticut	1.70	1.40	1.65	1.33	1.65	1.33	1.60	1.25	2.06	1.53	2.40	1.90
New York	1.80	1.37	2.00	1.54	1.89	1.47	1.53	1.18	2.25	1.75	2.53	1.99
New Jersey	1.88	1.50	2.04	1.65	2.09	1.74	1.55	1.30	2.56	2.03	2.63	2.09
Pennsylvania	1.51	1.13	1.65	1.20	1.73	1.30	1.33	.99	2.01	1.51	2.23	1.73
Delaware	1.40	1.10	1.88	1.52	1.60	1.25	1.37	1.00	1.83	1.41	1.87	1.50
Maryland	1.46	1.15	1.74	1.38	1.52	1.15	1.48	1.12	1.81	1.34	2.16	1.67
Virginia	1.30	1.10	1.33	1.06	1.27	.99	1.16	.96	1.48	1.21	1.48	1.13
North Carolina	.96	.75	1.15	.82	1.20	.85	.99	.76	1.17	1.00	1.37	1.04
South Carolina	.95	.72	.87	.64	1.08	.78	.89	.68	1.17	1.01	1.15	.90
Georgia	.99	.77	1.04	.80	1.10	.80	.98	.61	1.29	.99	1.24	.90
Florida	1.04	.78	.96	.70	1.12	.80	1.02	.73	1.00	.72	1.25	.87
Alabama	.97	.72	.99	.76	1.05	.80	.96	.77	1.40	1.15	1.24	.95
Mississippi	.97	.73	1.00	.79	1.23	.95	1.00	.85	1.40	1.00	1.56	1.27
Louisiana	.92	.72	.95	.75	1.10	.85	1.03	.77	1.30	1.05	1.54	1.13
Texas	1.23	.96	1.32	1.04	1.39	1.08	1.30	.94	1.52	1.20	1.58	1.26
Arkansas	1.30	.97	1.30	1.03	1.34	1.02	1.38	1.08	1.50	1.25	1.67	1.40
Tennessee	1.20	.93	1.28	1.04	1.30	1.00	1.28	.98	1.62	1.20	2.10	1.59
West Virginia	1.20	.92	1.31	1.03	1.30	1.00	1.26	.95	1.55	1.20	1.78	1.29
Kentucky	1.35	1.07	1.51	1.17	1.54	1.18	1.49	1.15	1.79	1.46	1.83	1.38
Ohio	1.56	1.23	1.75	1.40	1.79	1.41	1.51	1.17	2.05	1.60	2.15	1.72
Michigan	1.80	1.40	1.90	1.57	2.13	1.76	2.02	1.55	2.50	2.00	2.76	2.25
Indiana	1.64	1.32	1.85	1.55	1.89	1.58	1.68	1.28	2.20	1.75	2.16	1.77
Illinois	1.60	1.25	1.80	1.40	1.91	1.54	1.52	1.18	2.20	1.83	2.34	1.94
Wisconsin	1.80	1.44	1.89	1.57	2.50	2.10	2.11	1.70	2.40	1.92	2.45	1.96
Minnesota	2.20	1.75	2.29	1.89	2.61	2.16	2.63	2.25	2.82	2.30	2.90	2.36
Iowa	1.81	1.46	2.00	1.61	2.25	1.81	1.66	1.57	2.57	2.10	2.85	2.24
Missouri	1.43	1.13	1.62	1.30	1.59	1.23	1.47	1.17	1.75	1.43	2.30	1.84
Kansas	1.60	1.25	1.87	1.48	1.70	1.35	1.70	1.32	1.86	1.46	2.08	1.63
Nebraska	1.80	1.42	1.98	1.55	1.95	1.57	2.17	1.66	2.40	1.98	2.41	2.00
California	2.25	1.85	2.20	1.80	2.30	1.86	2.27	1.76	2.50	2.00	2.82	2.04
Oregon	1.94	1.45	1.95	1.50	1.92	1.50	2.02	1.54	2.11	1.72	.....	.....
Nevada	1.80	1.37	.....	.....	.....	.....	.....	.....	.....	.....	.....	.....
Colorado	1.87	1.35	2.05	1.50	2.21	1.80	2.08	1.55	2.33	1.50	.....	.....
Arizona	1.70	1.20	.....	.....	.....	.....	.....	.....	.....	.....	.....	.....
Dakota	2.12	1.64	1.38	1.00	2.65	2.19	.....	.....	2.37	1.90	.....	.....
Idaho	2.00	1.52	.....	.....	.....	.....	.....	.....	.....	.....	.....	.....
Montana	2.20	1.50	.....	.....	.....	.....	.....	.....	.....	.....	.....	.....
New Mexico	1.31	1.00	1.31	.88	1.65	1.40	1.00	.67	1.35	.90	.....	.....
Utah	1.72	1.30	1.75	1.36	2.00	1.56	1.82	1.43	2.20	1.75	.....	....
Washington	2.10	1.60	2.05	1.50	.....	.....	2.15	1.61	2.40	2.00	.....	.....
Wyoming	2.00	1.80	.....	.....	.....	.....	.....	.....	.....	.....	.....	.....
Average	131	1.02	.....	.....	.....	.....	.....	.....	.....	.....	.....	.....

Day Wages of Ordinary Farm Labor

Table showing the average rate of wages per day in transient service other than harvesting.

States and Territories.	1888. Without board.	1888. With board.	1885. Without board.	1885. With board.	1882. Without board.	1882. With board.	1879. Without board.	1879. With board.	1875. Without board.	1875. With board.	1869. Without board.	1869. With board.
Maine	$1.25	$0.92	$1.19	$0.88	$1.18	$0.91	$0.97	$0.72	$1.46	$1.05	$1.48	$1.05
New Hampshire	1.27	.95	1.30	.95	1.30	.97	.98	.74	1.50	1.12	1.79	1.41
Vermont	1.16	.90	1.15	.88	1.20	.90	.91	.64	1.51	1.11	1.76	1.28
Massachusetts	1.42	1.00	1.50	1.00	1.45	1.08	1.05	.75	1.41	1.12	1.92	1.37
Rhode Island	1.42	1.02	1.25	.94	1.28	1.00	1.00	.50	1.62	1.18	1.73	1.18
Connecticut	1.33	1.00	1.32	1.00	1.30	.98	1.50	.88	1.50	1.16	1.87	1.37
New York	1.21	.90	1.26	.93	1.29	.93	.92	.68	1.48	1.00	1.64	1.19
New Jersey	1.20	.87	1.47	.83	1.21	.86	.99	.68	1.45	1.00	1.63	1.15
Pennsylvania	1.10	.82	1.10	.80	1.20	.85	.96	.63	1.37	.95	1.43	1.04
Delaware	.95	.70	1.00	.78	1.10	.80	.75	.50	1.04	.70	1.30	.95
Maryland	.90	.64	.93	.62	.83	.55	.75	.48	1.06	.71	1.20	.77
Virginia	.73	.51	.71	.49	.70	.48	.63	.44	.78	.51	.80	.55
North Carolina	.61	.45	.67	.47	.68	.46	.58	.41	.72	.51	.74	.49
South Carolina	.65	.43	.60	.45	.65	.45	.53	.41	.71	.55	.70	.50
Georgia	.75	.50	.66	.47	.70	.49	.58	.41	.83	.60	.83	.60
Florida	.95	.70	.85	.60	.75	.55	.76	.53	.93	.70	.96	.72
Alabama	.72	.53	.73	.52	.72	.51	.69	.50	.75	.53	.86	.61
Mississippi	.75	.55	.80	.60	.75	.55	.78	.55	1.07	.80	1.10	.90
Louisiana	.85	.65	.82	.64	.80	.60	.85	.62	1.00	.74	1.44	.83
Texas	.95	.71	.98	.76	.93	.70	.92	.66	1.14	.84	1.16	.84
Arkansas	.93	.65	.80	.64	.88	.62	.86	.60	1.10	.80	1.36	1.02
Tennessee	.74	.53	.71	.52	.72	.50	.69	.50	.95	.60	1.05	.88
West Virginia	.85	.62	.83	.60	.82	.59	.80	.55	1.05	.75	1.14	.79
Kentucky	.82	.60	.84	.59	.87	.60	.77	.53	1.03	.72	1.10	.77
Ohio	1.07	.82	1.11	.85	1.19	.89	1.00	.83	1.35	1.00	1.44	1.05
Michigan	1.20	.90	1.28	.92	1.30	.96	1.16	.82	1.55	1.10	1.66	1.17
Indiana	1.10	.82	1.08	.80	1.08	.78	.90	.69	1.30	.95	1.36	1.01
Illinois	1.12	84	1.14	.87	1.19	.90	1.01	.73	1.37	1.01	1.50	1.13
Wisconsin	1.22	.97	1.20	.95	1.33	.99	1.12	.79	1.42	1.00	1.56	1.15
Minnesota	1.30	1.00	1.25	.90	1.37	1.02	1.27	.94	1.50	1.07	1.64	1.18
Iowa	1.27	.97	1.31	.97	1.34	.99	1.12	.80	1.38	1.01	1.52	1.13
Missouri	.94	.80	.95	.68	1.00	.70	.67	.59	1.07	.73	1.44	1.02
Kansas	1.17	.85	1.20	.87	1.12	.80	1.05	.72	1.30	.90	1.56	1.12
Nebraska	1.37	1.00	1.35	.97	1.21	.91	1.29	.90	1.43	1.00	1.62	1.26
California	1.60	1.18	1.57	1.15	1.71	1.29	1.65	1.23	1.84	1.30	2.13	1.50
Oregon	1.35	.98	1.30	.95	1.33	1.00	1.44	1.08	1.47	1.15	.....	.....
Nevada	1.65	1.20	.....	.....	.....	.....	.....	1.23	.....	.....	.....	.....
Colorado	1.60	1.12	1.55	1.10	1.63	1.14	1.83	1.19	1.75	1.16	.....	.....
Arizona	1.25	.90	.....	.....	.....	.....	.....	.....	.. .	.....	.....	.....
Dakota	1.35	1.10	1.31	1.08	1.50	1.11	1.34	.92	1.62	1.08	.....	.....
Idaho	1.50	1.15	.....	.....	.....	.....	.....	.....	.....	.....	.....	.....
Montana	1.70	1.25	.....	.....	.....	.....	.....	.....	.....	.....	.....	.....
New Mexico	1.35	1.00	1.25	.81	1.28	1.00	.81	.56	.85	.50	.....	.....
Utah	1.42	1.10	1.52	1.14	1.57	1.10	1.46	1.12	1.80	1.40	.....	.....
Washington	1.45	1.15	1.70	1.17	.....	.....	.....	.....	.....	.....	.....	.....
Wyoming	1.50	1.10	.....	.....	.....	.....	.....	.....	.....	.....	.....	.....
Average	.92	.67	.....	.....	.....	.....	.....	.....	.....	.....	.....	.....

Comparative Labor Supply

There is a sufficiency of farm labor in this country as a whole, with a comparatively even balance between the geographical divisions. There are localities in perhaps every State where scarcity exists, and others having a superabundance. There is in some places a scarcity of agricultural labor caused by demand at higher wages for labor in some specific local industry. There is reported now, as always heretofore, a tendency to exercise distinctive preferences and encourage peculiar aptitudes for professions and avocations outside of agriculture, generally leading away from the country to the town or city.

On portions of the coast the fishing industry, or other seafaring pursuits, are mentioned among those which compete with agriculture for labor. In many of the counties bordering on Chesapeake Bay the supply of labor for farming purposes is somewhat scanty during the oyster season. In Maine, in portions of New York and Pennsylvania, in the yellow-pine regions of the South, and in the forest regions of the Northwest, lumbering creates a demand for labor which is sensibly felt in adjacent agricultural districts. Other forest industries whose competition is felt within certain limits are chopping cord-wood, the gathering of tan-bark, and in the Southern yellow-pine region the turpentine business. The extension of mining and the establishment of additional furnaces and iron-works have had a like effect upon agricultural labor within the sphere of their influence. The construction of railroads and various public works has created a considerable demand for labor, drawing to an inconvenient extent in some cases on the agricultural labor in their vicinity. Temporary disturbance of the relation between supply and demand has been caused by changes in rural industries from arable to pastoral, from farming to fruit-growing or market gardening. The preference of negroes to renting or owning land has caused local scarcity, and a movement to richer lands or newer settlements has had a similar effect.

Depression in manufacturing industries, total or partial suspension of work in some establishments — such as factories, iron-works, or mines — and strikes of miners, iron-workers, railroad men, or others, as causes of increased supply, are mentioned by a number of correspondents in the States bordering the Ohio and Mississippi Rivers, including West Virginia, Kentucky, Ohio, Indiana, Illinois, Wisconsin, and Missouri. It must not be inferred, however, that such conditions are extensively prevalent in those States, as the reports in question apply to only a few counties or parts of counties.

Low prices of farm produce have caused a reduced demand for hired labor, farmers and members of their families doing more of their own work than they formerly did, while there are some cases in which farmers of the poorer class have abandoned the cultivation of their own land and accepted employment from others. Increased use of machinery or improvement in its character is another cause of reduced demand referred to in many cases.

It is worthy of notice that in some of the reports from the States and Territories of the farther West the labor of the Indians is referred to as a prominent factor in the supply for farming purposes.

Rent of Farms

The marked peculiarity of American agriculture has been the fact that owners of farms are the cultivators of the land. A large proportion of the farm proprietors do not employ farm laborers or pay farm wages. There are fewer laborers working for wages than owners cultivating their own acres. The whole number of farms reported in the last census was 4,008,907, the number of farmers 4,225,945, and the number of laborers 3,323,876. Since then our population has increased 20 per cent., and the number of persons, exclusive of the wives and children of farmers, who are actively employed in agriculture must be about 9,000,000. Including non-laboring children and others in the families of farmers, the agricultural population is not less than 26,000,000. The class of farm laborers must now number about 4,000,000.

In 1880 the number of farms rented was 1,024,601, of which 322,357 were taken at a cash rental and 702,244 on shares. Those that were cultivated by owners 74.4 per cent., say three-fourths to one-fourth rented. Even this proportion of rentals is more apparent than real, as 47 per cent. of all are found in the cotton States, arising from the counting by census enumerators of individual laborers or "freedmen," to whom sections of plantations were distributed for cultivation on shares, simply because they refused to work for wages and insisted on a semblance of independent management; and thus a single farm, not to be alienated from its single owner or even divided by any permanent lines of division, was reckoned as half a dozen farms or more. Very few of these individual laborers on shares, working under various terms of contract, can be considered independent renters of farms. They are rather temporary tenant-workers of fractional parts of farms, and can not be fairly cited in proof of the gradual decadence of cultivation of lands by farm proprietors. It is an available form of cultivation, by paying wages in produce instead of cash, with a certain degree of independence of the freedmen, and a measure of protection to the farmer against the unreliability of the laborer.

The following is the census subdivision of farms by tenure:

Sections.	Total farms.	Farms cultivated by owner.		Tenant.	
		Number.	Per ct.	Cash rental.	Shares.
New England	207,232	189,572	91.5	10,230	7,430
Northern Middle	488,907	395,275	80.8	38,781	54,851
Southern Middle	167,783	116,550	69.5	17,781	33,452
South Atlantic	413,537	244,181	59.0	52,723	116,633
Southern	720,195	443,130	61.5	88,268	188,797
Western	1,214,400	956,881	78.8	73,886	183,633
Trans-Mississippi	699,766	553,608	79.1	36,066	110,092
Pacific	53,555	41,016	82.2	4,013	5,526
The Territories	43,532	41,093	94.4	609	1,830
Total	4,008,907	2,984,306	74.4	322,357	702,244

Aside from the peculiar and temporary tenures of the Southern States, about four-fifths of the farms are cultivated by their owners. There is comparatively little difference in the several geographical divisions, except that there is less tenant-holding in New England than elsewhere, there being but 17,660 farms held by any system of tenantry in the six States, and a very small proportion in the Rocky Mountain region.

The number of farms in each class, with the percentage of all cultivated by owners, for each State, is given in detail:

States and Territories.	Farms.	Farms cultivated by owner.		Farms cultivated by tenant.	
		Number.	Per ct.	Cash rental.	Shares.
Maine	64,309	61,528	96	1,628	1,153
New Hampshire	32,181	29,566	92	1,237	1,378
Vermont	35,522	30,760	87	2,164	2,598
Massachusetts	38,406	35,266	92	2,292	848
Rhode Island	6,216	4,980	80	989	247
Connecticut	30,598	27,472	90	1,920	1,206
New York	241,058	201,186	83	18,124	21,748
New Jersey	34,307	25,869	75	3,608	4,830
Pennsylvania	218,542	168,220	79	17,049	28,273
Delaware	8,749	5,041	58	511	3,197
Maryland	40,517	27,978	69	3,878	8,661
Virginia	118,517	83,531	70	13,392	21,594
North Carolina	157,609	104,887	67	8,644	44,078
South Carolina	93,864	46,645	50	21,974	25,245
Georgia	138,626	76,451	55	18,557	43,618
Florida	23,438	16,198	69	3,548	3,692
Alabama	135,864	72,215	53	22,888	40,761
Mississippi	101,772	57,214	56	17,440	27,118
Louisiana	48,292	31,286	65	6,669	10,337
Texas	174,184	108,716	62	12,089	53,379
Arkansas	94,433	65,245	69	9,916	19,272
Tennessee	165,650	108,454	65	19,266	37,930
West Virginia	62,674	50,673	81	4,292	7,709
Kentucky	166,453	122,426	74	16,824	27,203
Ohio	217,189	199,562	81	14,834	32,793
Michigan	154,008	138,597	90	5,015	10,396
Indiana	194,013	147,963	76	8,582	37,468
Illinois	255,741	175,497	69	20,620	59,624
Wisconsin	134,322	122,163	91	3,719	8,440
Minnesota	92,386	83,933	91	1,251	7,202
Iowa	185,351	141,177	76	8,421	35,753
Missouri	215,575	156,703	73	19,843	39,029
Kansas	138,561	115,910	84	4,438	18,213
Nebraska	63,387	51,963	82	1,948	9,476
California	35,934	28,810	80	3,209	3,915
Oregon	16,217	13,938	86	741	1,538
Nevada	1,404	1,268	90	63	73
Colorado	4,506	3,922	87	165	419
Arizona	767	666	87	42	59
Dakota	17,435	16,757	96	72	606
Idaho	1,885	1,796	95	32	57
Montana	1,519	1,439	95	17	63
New Mexico	5,053	4,645	92	22	386
Utah	9,452	9,019	95	60	373
Washington	6,529	6,058	93	209	262
Wyoming	457	444	97	5	8
District of Columbia	435	269	62	150	16
Total	4,008,907	2,984,306	74.5	322,357	702,244

Share Contracts

There is great variety in the terms of rental for a share of the products. It is a system more popular than renting for cash in every part of the country except in the Eastern States. The three main forms of the share contract may be stated, in general terms, as (1) land only is furnished; (2) land, horses or mules, and implements; (3) all these, and feed for horses, the laborer doing the work and usually boarding himself.

In the Eastern States the preferable mode is to take the farm "at the halves," the tenant having house rent, fire-wood from the woodland, keeping the fences in condition, and dividing equally such products of the farm as are not used upon it. It is usually required that hay and coarse fodder shall be fed upon the farm, as the barnyard manure is the only ordinary resource for maintaining fertility. In some cases the owner pays for half the seed, and the tenant pays half the taxes, though required to work out the road tax. In some cases in Maine the owner receives in lieu of shares 8 to 10 per cent. of the value of the farm in cash, he paying the taxes.

The usual share of the tenant in New Hampshire is one-half: on less valuable lands, or those remote from market, he receives five-eighths. Conditions vary in minor details.

Similar terms of the shade contract prevail in Vermont. One of the diversions from the regulation form of the contract is a money rent per cow on dairy farms of from $15 to $20. The tenant "at the halves" is sometimes required to furnish half the stock and tools, or to pay interest on the investment if furnished by the proprietor.

There is very little share farming in Massachusetts, most occupiers owning the lands they cultivate; yet in a few instances in every town the share system is employed, practically the same as in the neighboring States. There are probably less than three hundred share tenants in Rhode Island, working generally for half, with considerable variation in the details of the contract.

In Connecticut the tenant getting half sometimes pays a share of the taxes and of the fertilizers, if any are used beyond the resources of the farm. Where only labor is furnished, the farm being fully equipped by the owner and work animals fed, the laborer gets one-third, or if the land is in a high state of cultivation, a fourth will sometimes suffice.

One-half is usually obtained by tenants in New York, or one-third with a minimum of provision or responsibility beyond mere labor. In some instances the taxes or the thrashing bill may be divided between the farmer and the tenant, or interest may be charged for use of stock and tools.

In New Jersey one-half is the rule in share contracts, with somewhat variable conditions, and labor alone receives one-fourth to one-third. The item of fertilizers is always important here, always considered in leases, and the quantity required affects the terms of the contract. The tenant is usually required to furnish implements, teams, and seed. In some cases the tenant is allowed two-thirds of the grain and one-half of the hay.

Pennsylvania has a great variety of forms of share contracts, allowing the tenant one-half, two-thirds, and even three-fourths of the produce, according to the value and productiveness of the land and its equipments. One-third is the usual proportion for labor only. In some cases the tenant is required to pay half of the taxes.

In Delaware the tenant gets half of the produce, and from that proportion down to one-third and one-fourth, according to his limitation of responsibility and personal expense beyond labor.

The tenant's share in Maryland, on poor or medium soils, is ordinarily two-thirds, and on more productive lands and those near to good markets one-third where only the land is furnished; but with teams and implements supplied by the owner, he gets two-fifths to one-third. Fertilizers are extensively used here, and when procured beyond the farm the tenant is usually required to pay for at least his share.

The usage varies in Virginia from one-half to two-thirds to the tenant, in some cases three-fourths. But the owner often deems it desirable to provide for the work animals when they go with the farm, especially with colored tenants, or risk the starvation of his stock. The share of labor alone is from one-fourth to one-half, according to the value of the average product of the land.

The cotton States have had a serious labor problem to solve during the past twenty years. It may not be fully solved yet, but the tendency is toward cash wages rather than a share of the crop. At first it was the only available method, as the freedman would not work for wages, preferring to become a planter himself, grow his own crops, control his own movements, and sell his own produce. The result was not altogether satisfactory to himself and not at all to the owner of the land he cultivated. Not accustomed to self-restraint, he took too much time for amusement or idleness, entertained too much company, and ran in debt for subsistence. There were more industrious and wiser men among them who managed to accumulate something, and these, to secure greater independence and larger savings, have bought land. It is the statement of many of our correspondents that the once universal system is far less popular, is rapidly waning, and slowly becoming superseded by a return to the wage system, or to a cash rent, or its equivalent in cotton, at a certain number of pounds per acre, or a given amount, a bale, a bale and a half, and in best lands 2 bales, or 1,000 pounds of lint cotton, for a one-horse farm, say 30 or 35 acres of cotton land, in some cases including other lands for pasturage.

The share of the tenant who receives land only, and furnishes implements and supplies as well as labor, in the cotton States, is quite generally three-fourths of the cotton and two-thirds of grain or other products. Where the owner furnishes stock and implements, entirely or partially, his share of the crop increases to one-half, and in some cases two-thirds. The range of allowance for land alone may be stated at one-third to one-fifth for cotton, which is very exacting in its labor requirements, from seed to gin.

In some parts of South Carolina the laborer works four days for the use of a mule two days in cultivating his own crop. The charge for rent of horse or mule ranges from $25. to $40, as reported. Where land is rented, from $1 to $3 per acre is the usual range, according to quantity and productiveness; and the returns of lint cotton as rent of land is equally variable, from 500 to 1,000 pounds for a one-mule farm (say 35 acres), and in one instance 100 pounds per acre is reported, which appears to be an extreme rent. The tenant is usually allowed land for a garden, the privilege of taking fire-wood, and often pasturage for a cow or two or several hogs.

The share of the tenant in West Virginia is one-half to two-thirds, according to value and capabilities of the farm, he providing the stock and implements. Various forms of contract are made, in which the owner furnishes more than the land and obtains a larger share of the products.

One-half to two-thirds is the ordinary rule in Kentucky; in some cases one-half of the tobacco and two-thirds of the corn. Some correspondents say one-half of the corn and two-fifths of the tobacco. In some counties half of the corn is taken by the tenant and two-thirds of the oats.

In Ohio one-half to two-thirds is usually taken by the tenant. In same cases one-half of the hay and two-thirds of the other crops is the rule. There are various modifications of the contract. A tenant who has house, garden, and pasture may receive only half, when he might obtain two-thirds if he had the land alone. The Ottowa reporter says the most satisfactory plan is for the tenant to furnish half the stock, half seed, and pay half the tax on personal property and half the repairs, and divide equally the products.

In Indiana the farm is usually taken ''at the halves.'' Sometimes two-fifths or two-thirds is the custom. Where uplands are farmed for two-thirds or three-fifths, bottom-lands are sometimes taken at one-half. For labor alone the tenant gets one-third; in best lands one-fourth. Similar practice prevails in Illinois, the tenant receiving one-half, two-fifths, and sometimes two-thirds, according to land and requirements aside from labor. In Douglas County one-third of small grain goes to the tenant and two-fifths of the Indian corn and broom-corn. On well-drained bottom-lands one-half is the tenant's share, while he gets two-thirds on less productive soils.

The renter gets from one-half to two-thirds in Wisconsin. There is considerable variation in Minnesota, from one-half, to three-fourths to tenant being reported. In Mower County ''the usual contract is for owners to furnish land, seed, grain, and sometimes part of machinery, and give one-half of crop.'' In Rice ''one-half is given when the laborer furnishes his team, seed, etc.'' This plan is reported for several counties. If the bare land or land with house is furnished, the tenant gets the larger proportion, two-thirds at least. In Dodge the prevailing usage is to furnish land, seed, and pay half the thrashing bill, owner and tenant dividing equally. The main cause of variation is the relative productiveness of the farm; otherwise conditions depend upon what is furnished besides the land.

The contract in Iowa is generally for one-third to the owner and two-thirds for the tenant, if the renter furnishes everything; otherwise the tenant gets half. In some cases it is half the hay and two-thirds of the grain, both harvested and garnered. In some cases the owner furnishes seed and pays half the thrashing bill, getting half of the crop.

In Missouri two-thirds to the tenant is usual, when only land is furnished, one-half to two-fifths when horses and implements go with the land, and one-third when the horses are fed in addition, and sometimes only one-fourth.

The prevailing custom in Kansas is to give two-thirds to the tenant who furnishes everything but land, though the rule varies, and the range is from one-half to three-fourths. The compensation for labor alone is one-fourth to one-third. One-third to the owner for land alone, and one-third for labor done, the other third going for outfit and feed of animals, to owner or tenant, whoever furnishes it. In some counties it is said that there is more land broken than is cultivated, and land can sometimes be had free, especially tree claims before the trees are set out. Two-thirds to the tenant furnishing all is the usual custom in Dakota. When the owner furnishes land, house, barn, all seed, and pays for half the thrashing, the crop is equally divided.

Similar terms are given in other Territories. In Idaho a tenant can get land the first year free if he does the breaking. For labor alone one-third is usually given. Land and teams command one-half the product. When only land is rented three-fourths of the crops are sometimes taken by the tenant.

The contract most in vogue in California gives two-thirds to the tenant who furnishes the farm equipments, using only land. In extreme cases he gets three-fourths. In San Benito the tenant pays 50 cents per acre and one-fourth of the produce. In Alameda and other counties he receives three-fourths of the grain and two-thirds of the hay. Similar terms prevail in Oregon, in most cases the tenant receiving two-thirds of the crops. Very few farms are occupied by tenants in Washington Territory. Where the practice prevails the terms are like those of Oregon and California.

Surplus Products of American Agriculture.

From U.S. Department of Agriculture, *Annual Report*, 1887, pp. 574–78.

There is no country in the world which furnishes an agricultural surplus at all comparable with that of the United States, and none with a surplus in such proportion to its production. In fact, it is rarely the case that a country has any excess above consumption, except in occasional crops or in years of exceptional abundance. That this country should regularly have a surplus of not less than 10 per cent. of the value of all its immense production, after supplying with profuse liberality the wants of 60,000,000 people, is a matter of surprise and wonder elsewhere. It is more noticeable from the large proportion of certain crops that can be exported, notably cotton and tobacco, amounting to two-thirds of the former and half of the latter. Of provisions, pork products have always been abundant for export, and cheese has been largely exported since the rise of associated cheese-making. The beef exportation was not known a dozen years ago, except in the salted forms. These articles constitute nearly all of our agricultural surplus; other items are numerous, but small in detail and in the aggregate.

The agricultural production of the country includes all that is grown in the temperate climates of the world, and a great variety of subtropical products. The variety is increasing as the Department of Agriculture and enterprising individuals introduce new plants and animals as foundations of new rural industries.

The census has never attempted to enumerate and value all these forms of production. This Department has attempted to indicate approximately the quantities or values of such products, but has not exhausted the investigation. The following table is given as a tentative estimate of farm values of the products and exports of agriculture:

Products	Production (farm value).	Exportation (farm value).	Per cent.
Breadstuffs:			
Corn................................	$610,311,000	$11,790,046	1.9
Wheat.............................	314,226,020	87,668,833	27.9
Oats	186,137,930	343,659	.2
Barley.............................	31,840,510	691,809	2.2
Rye.................................	13,181,330	197,687	1.5
Buckwheat	6,465,120	....	....
Rice	5,000,000	26,284	.5
Total	1,167,161,910	100,718,318	8.6
Meats	748,000,000	62,522,185	8.4
Poultry products	186,000,000	71,176	....
Hides, hair, etc.	93,000,000	825,902	.9
Dairy products:			
Butter.............................	192,000,000	1,487,773	.8
Cheese............................	32,000,000	6,455,438	20.2
Milk................................	156,000,000	181,279	.1
Total	380,000,000	8,124,490	2.1
Textile fibers:			
Cotton	257,295,327	177,895,501	69.1
Wool...............................	77,000,000	70,202	.1
Hemp, flax, etc.	9,000,000	....	....
Total	343,395,327	177,965,703	51.8
Vegetables:			
Irish potatoes	78,441,940	238,694	.3
Sweet potatoes	20,000,000	....	....
Peas and beans.....................	13,800,000	450,291	3.3
Market gardens.....................	68,000,000	256,518	.4
Fruits...............................	175,000,000	1,601,979	.9
Hay.................................	353,437,699	130,804	....
Tobacco	39,082,118	2,510,386	52.5
Hops	3,500,000	46,725	1.3
Sugar and sirup, including honey.......	33,500,000	....	....
Clover and grass seed..................	15,000,000	638,329	4.3
Wines................................	10,000,000	129,103	1.3
Grand totals...................	3,727,218,994	374,230,603	10.1

In the statement of value of agricultural products is included meats, hides, milk, and fruit consumed, in addition to those enumerated in the census. There are minor products, such as medicinal herbs, peppermint, teasels, and many others of small value, which are not included. The corn fodder and straw of cereals, and various kinds of green forage, ensilage, etc., are not included, because a large part of it goes into the production of meat, dairy products, wool, etc., while a considerable part of it goes to the sustenance of work-animals and the betterment of stock, and is fairly entitled on that account to be considered as a part of the unduplicated products of agriculture.

On the other hand, about half of the corn is duplicated in other enumerated products. The other cereals do not enter into meat and milk products. Making all necessary allowance for unenumerated products on one side and duplications on the other, I assume that the net agricultural production of the country amounted in 1886 to $3,600,000,000 in round numbers, and possibly to the full aggregate of the table above. These values are the values on the farm or of primary markets. They represent what the production is worth to the farmers. The value of exports, which are those made from the crops of 1886, are not those of the sea-ports, but of the farm. It is manifestly unfair to compare the exported products with the whole production on a different basis of value for each. In reducing to farm value the export values of wheat and corn, which come mainly from beyond the Mississippi, the average farm values of the district of production are taken.

It appears that the proportion of all agricultural products exported is about 10 per cent., or exclusive of cotton and tobacco, 5 per cent.

The tables below show an aggregate value of agricultural exports of $520,820,758, as reckoned in sea-port values, including all the cost of transportation and other commercial expenses. The farm value of those products would fall below a total of $400,000,000. On the other hand, the imports of agricultural products, mostly food products, amount to $287,542,266, plus the cost of ocean transportation and commercial charges and profits, and whatever of undervaluation may exist in the import prices. The real value is therefore not less than $350,000,000 at least, leaving possibly an actual balance of $50,000,000 in favor of net agricultural exports after the payment for imports of agricultural productions. This is a handsome annual balance, but not the munificent sum with which our net surplus of agricultural production is credited by the exaggerations of the patriotic orator or editor.

Exports of the products of domestic agriculture, 1886 and 1887.

Articles.	1886.		1887.	
	Quantities.	Value.	Quantities.	Value.
Animals living:				
Cattle..number	119,065	$10,958,954	106,459	$9,172,136
Hogs...do	74,187	674,207	75,383	564,753
Horses...do	1,616	348,323	1,611	351,607
Mules..do	1,191	148,711	1,754	214,738
Sheep..do	177,594	329,844	121,701	254,725
All other, and foals	....	58,531	....	40,403
Animal matter:				
Bones, hoofs, horns and horn-tips, strips, and				
waste	....	127,735	....	162,958
Casings for sausages.................................	....	700,382	....	538,236
Eggs...dozen	252,202	46,105	372,772	60,686
Glue...pounds	297,653	42,137	275,362	39,773
Grease, grease scraps, and all soap stock........	....	921,337	....	849,908
Hair, and manufactures of..........................	....	407,672	....	835,548
Hides and skins, other than furs...................	....	873,925	....	765,655
Honey	....	44,735	....	67,154
Oils:				
Lard...gallons	973,229	500,011	975,163	519,274
Other animal ....do	360,223	218,643	570,376	291,396

Exports of the products of domestic agriculture, 1886 and 1887. (Continued)

Articles.	1886. Quantities.	1886. Values.	1887. Quantities.	1887. Values.
Provisions, comprising meat and dairy products:				
Meat products—				
Beef products—				
Beef, canned	....	3,436,453	43,050,588	3,462,982
Beef, fresh ....pounds	99,423,362	9,291,011	83,560,874	7,228,412
Beef, salted or pickled ....do	58,903,370	3,544,379	30,287,188	1,972,246
Beef, other cured.......................do	824,955	89,593	192,191	17,942
Tallow.....................................do	40,919,951	2,144,499	63,278,403	2,836,300
Mutton ....do	1,059,435	93,082	371,572	18,397
Oleomargarine—				
Imitation butter ....do	928,053	93,363	834,574	88,848
The oil ....do	27,729,885	2,954,954	45,712,985	4,676,131
Pork products—				
Bacon.....................................do	369,423,351	26,899,111	364,417,744	27,338,948
Hams ....do	50,365,445	4,741,100	55,505,211	5,975,727
Pork, fresh................................do	70,749	3,985	23,930	1,233
Pork, salted or cured ....do	87,196,966	5,119,426	85,869,367	5,640,094
Lard.......................................do	293,728,019	20,361,786	321,533,746	23,703,921
Poultry and game.............................	....	28,484	....	28,284
All other meat products	....	947,524	....	956,534
Dairy products—				
Butter.....................................do	18,953,990	2,958,457	12,531,171	1,983,693
Cheese....................................do	91,877,235	7,662,145	81,255,994	7,594,633
Milk	....	255,864	....	258,971
Wax bees' ....do	136,179	36,626	90,350	24,997
Wool, raw ....do	2,138,080	476,274	257,940	78,002
Total value of animals and matter..............	....	107,539,458	....	107,115,245
Bread and breadstuffs:				
Barley ....bushels	252,183	166,330	1,305,300	853,405
Bread and biscuit ....pounds	16,778,850	725,476	15,060,061	659,924
Indian corn ....bushels	63,655,433	31,730,922	40,307,252	19,347,361
Indian-corn meal ....barrels	293,546	858,370	265,333	705,343
Oats..bushels	5,672,694	1,944,772	440,283	179,634
Oatmeal ....pounds	29,495,008	755,973	16,818,330	456,023
Rye ....bushels	195,725	133,105	357,256	216,190
Rye flour.....................................barrels	3,329	12,733	3,341	11,781
Wheat ....bushels	57,759,209	50,262,715	101,971,949	90,716,481
Wheat flour..................................barrels	8,179,241	38,442,955	11,518,449	51,950,023
All other bread stuffs and preparations of, used as food.......................................	....	813,207	....	672,384
Total value of bread and breadstuffs..........	....	125,846,558	....	165,768,662
Cotton and cotton-seed oil:				
Cotton—				
Sea island ....pounds	4,613,675	1,176,025	8,021,497	1,798,272
Other unmanufactured.......................do	2,053,423,769	203,909,617	2,161,435,833	204,423,785
Cotton-seed oil..............................gallons	6,240,139	2,115,974	4,067,138	1,578,935
Total value of cotton and cotton-seed oil	....	207,201,616	....	207,800,992
Miscellaneous:				
Broom corn...................................	....	134,185	....	170,534
Fruits:				
Apples, dried.............................pounds	10,473,183	548,434	8,130,396	413,363
Apples, green or ripe....................barrels	744,539	1,810,606	591,868	1,382,872

Exports of the products of domestic agriculture, 1886 and 1887. (Continued)

Articles.	1886. Quantities.	1886. Values.	1887. Quantities.	1887. Values.
Fruits, preserved:				
Canned	....	580,422	....	506,794
Other	....	28,339	....	29,489
All other green, ripe, or dried	....	340,507	....	337,447
Hay ....tons	13,390	237,902	13,873	218,006
Hops ....pounds	13,665,661	1,714,488	260,721	54,970
Oil cake and oil-cake meal ....do	585,947,181	7,053,714	622,295,233	7,309,691
Oils:				
Linseed ....gallons	78,885	41,963	119,840	57,136
Other vegetable	....	43,519	....	65,689
Rice ....pounds	256,311	14,241	644,384	20,204
Seeds:				
Clover...do	2,652,438	264,882	7,932,390	630,850
Cotton ....do	11,793,411	112,782	11,232,141	121,441
Timothy...do	4,023,937	175,754	6,500,004	281,048
All other	....	1,396,572	....	874,070
Tobacco:				
Leaf ....pounds	281,737,120	26,926,544	293,666,995	25,637,983
Stems and trimmings ....do	11,036,770	231,913	11,253,128	310,204
Vegetables:				
Onions....................................bushels	68,811	75,838	71,689	73,515
Peas and beans................................do	408,318	570,153	387,222	562,864
Potatoes ....bushels	494,948	346,864	434,864	318,259
Vegetables, canned	....	190,339	....	228,567
All other, including pickles	....	134,293	....	125,448
Wine:				
In bottles....................................dozen	6,051	24,813	4,426	23,490
Not in bottles..............................gallons	119,085	93,297	282,607	191,672
All other agricultural products	....	154,132	....	181,154
Total value of miscellaneous products.........	....	*43,246,496	....	*40,135,859
RECAPITULATION.				
Total value of animals and animal matter	....	107,539,458	....	107,115,245
Total value of bread and breadstuffs.................	....	125,846,558	....	165,768,662
Total value of cotton and cotton-seed oil	....	207,201,616	....	207,800,992
Total value of miscellaneous products...............	....	43,246,496	....	40,135,859
Total agricultural exports	....	483,834,128	....	†520,820,758
Total exports	....	665,964,529	....	703,022,923
Per cent. of agricultural matter	....	73	....	74

*In this compilation of agricultural exports sugar and molasses are not included, because they are mainly re-exports of foreign sugar.

†This total of agricultural exports differs for 1887 from that given by the Bureau of Statistics of the Treasury Department ($523,073,798), they having included "ginsing and roots, herbs, and barks not otherwise specified," ($834,848), more properly forest products, and "glucose or grape sugar," ($118,620), properly and always before classed as a manufactured product.

Imports of agricultural products, 1886 and 1887.

Articles.	1887.	1887.
Sugar and molasses:		
Sugar.............	$80,773,744	$78,411,224
Molasses	5,595,670	5,355,475
Total sugar and molasses.............	86,369,414	83,766,698
Tea, coffee, and cocoa:		
Tea.............	16,020,382	16,771,802
Coffee	42,672,937	56,347,000
Cocoa.............	1,793,398	1,670,012
Total tea, coffee, and cocoa.............	60,486,718	74,789,414
Animals and their products:		
Cattle	1,281,765	1,392,032
Horses	4,312,636	4,872,982
Sheep	1,006,785	1,245,782
All other and fowls.............	338,840	305,402
Bristles	1,087,137	1,174,333
Butter	28,421	38,125
Cheese.............	855,570	874,261
Eggs.............	2,173,454	1,960,396
Hair.............	2,469,237	2,617,156
Hides.............	26,699,313	24,219,101
Meats—		
Preserved.............	271,512	272,651
All other.............	220,532	162,202
Milk.............	72,410	459,060
Oil, animal.............	3,488	3,387
Wools.............	16,746,08	16,424,479
Total animals and their products.............	58,207,181	56,021,289
Miscellaneous:		
Breadstuffs:		
Barley.............	7,177,887	6,173,208
Indian corn.............	8,785	16,636
Oats	30,792	29,579
Oatmeal	49,347	37,857
Rye.............	128,180	10,720
Wheat.............	331,393	218,867
Wheat flour	6,274	3,302
All other breadstuffs and preparations of, used as food, not elsewhere specified.............	202,818	150,059
Cotton	672,508	533,928
Farinaceous substances, etc., not elsewhere specified ...	93,210	721,404
Flax, hemp, jute, etc., unmanufactured:		
Flax	1,576,518	1,922,182
Hemp and all substitutes	3,817,376	4,041,522
Jute.............	2,267,023	2,616,128
Sisal-grass and other vegetable substances.............	2,299,450	3,733,001
Fruits and nuts	17,318,259	20,608,486
Hay.............	1,035,533	790,394
Hops	444,989	3,404,669

Imports of agricultural products, 1886 and 1887. (Continued)

Articles.	1887.	1887.
Malt, barley	237,843	143,363
Oils, vegetable:		
Fixed or expressed—		
Olive..	651,590	662,107
Other..	1,272,026	1,023,059
Volatile or essential.......................................	941,645	1,012,819
Rice...	2,047,916	2,060,379
Seed..	3,266,208	1,448,307
Spices:		
Ground	179,423	168,760
Unground—		
Nutmegs..	458,379	539,291
Pepper	1,644,383	1,819,609
All other..	678,936	953,752
Tobacco:		
Leaf—		
Suitable for wrappers	37,175	. . . .
All other..	7,792,832	8,704,950
Vegetables:		
Beans and peas...	585,461	607,853
Potatoes	649,009	543,091
Pickles and sauces.......................................	323,362	387,177
All other—		
In their natural state or in salt or brine	528,830	516,319
Prepared or preserved...................................	465,517	295,911
Wines:		
Champagne and other sparkling..........................	3,110,292	3,382,907
Still wines—		
In casks..	2,519,624	2,345,565
In bottles	1,310,125	1,327,613
Total miscellaneous	66,757,918	72,964,564
RECAPITULATION.		
Sugar and molasses	86,369,414	83,766,699
Tea, coffee, and cocoa	60,486,718	74,789,414
Animals and their products	58,207,181	56,021,289
Miscellaneous	66,757,918	72,964,804
Total imports of agricultural products	271,821,231	287,542,266

Cattle Raising in Montana, 1887

From *Yellowstone Journal* (Miles City, Mont.), Jan. 15, 1887 and Mar. 26, 1887.

Condition of Range Cattle

The protracted cold and stormy weather causes no little uneasiness among our cattlemen. A wide-spread opinion exists that there is a steady increase in the number of range cattle. Notwithstanding the unusual severity of the past winter, which was the cause of heavy losses, there are still too many cattle on the present limited range, considering the extended drouth during the past season. The limit of the capacity is fast being approached. Taking the whole range country into view, it seems plain that there is little prospect for the further expansion of range cattle interests under the present methods, and until some change and improvement in management is found possible there is not likely to be any perceptible increase in the supplies of range cattle offered on the markets above those which have already been afforded. Whatever increase there may be, therefore, in cattle supplies, must mainly come from the farms and not from the range. The losses for '86 will figure close to 25 percent for Colorado, Wyoming and Montana. The estimate may be thought large by some but the condition of the cattle at the beginning of winter had a great deal to do with the heavy losses during the season. There was a large area of country wherein drouth prevailed for a period of five months previous to the winter season. This was the cause of the unprecedented losses. This winter promises an improvement on the preceding one, but should the present weather continue the mortality will be great. The decrease in supply, so far, has failed to advance the value of the beef steer to the producer, but when next season arrives, the output will doubtless be eagerly taken at higher prices. With such burdens to bear, it is not surprising that ranch men have felt depressed in spirit, but rather a marvel that they have held up so well as they have. Of course, this heavy mortality was the result of a combination of circumstances. A severe winter and poor grass is generally alleged as the prime cause, but we are inclined to think that too much crowding of the ranges had more to do with it that the severity of the climate.

The Range Outlook: A Bad Winter and a Promising Spring

As reports from the different range localities come in, the situation is found to be very much better than was anticipated at any time since the first of February, and owners who a month ago were prepared to believe that the major portion of their herds had succumbed to the unparalled severity of the winter, are now in a much happier frame of mind and inclined to regard their losses as inconsiderable, considering the length and rigors of the winter season, and the condition of the range last fall. Had there been no snow or cold weather, there would still be a more than ordinary loss in range cattle, owing to the scarcity of feed and the overcrowding of the ranges. The long continued drouth of last summer reduced the feed on many ranges to a minimum, especially where a feverish haste to get rich had induced owners to turn loose more cattle than the locality could support at its best, and while there was some compensation in the fact that owing to the drouth, cattle were forced to remain near water courses and kept from ranging on the winter feeding grounds, the depth of snow that prevailed during the last two months of winter, made winter feed so inaccessible as to be practically useless for the time being, but with their natural food locked up under crusted snow, the "rustlers" quickly turned their attention to sage brush, which by a wise provision of nature was unusually well laden with seed last year, and presumably more nutritious than it ordinarily is. At all events, it was a heap better than nothing, and no doubt prolonged life in many an animal that would otherwise have yielded up his claim on the future. The avidity with which sage brush was eaten is evident by the fact that all over the range are stumps as thick as one's wrist, from which all above has been devoured. To the timely relief afforded by the despised sage brush may be attributed the fact that a very satisfactory percentage of range cattle have succeeded in pulling through the worse winter ever experienced on the Montana ranges. But there is no cloud so dark but has sunshine behind it, and the long and hateful winter has been succeeded by a spring that could not thus far, have been more favorable to range interests, if gotten up to order. The unusually heavy fall of snow has gone off so gradually, that much of the moisture resulting from it has penetrated the ground, which being but superficially frozen, was in excellent condition to receive it. Following the disappearance of the snow came winds which rapidly dried up the surplus moisture, giving the worn and feeble cattle dry spots to lie down on, easy travel while feeding, and materially reducing the chances of miring while weak. These conditions with the added advantage of being able to fill up on old grass before new grass comes, is daily adding to the strength and vitality of range cattle, and if continued for a short time longer (and the indications are favorable) will soon place them beyond danger of set backs by storms and unseasonable weather that may come later.

The prospect for grass was never better since the country was opened to range cattle. The ground which was thoroughly saturated by late fall rains, froze but lighty before it was covered by a November snow, which was added to in the succeeding three months, keeping it protected from the low temperature that was experienced later in the winter, and left it porous and capable of absorbing an unusual amount of moisture from melting snow this spring; the swelling roots are already putting forth their tender shoots of green, and a re-stocking of the entire range with an abundant growth of grass seems to be assured. Even a dry spring cannot interfere with the present favorable outlook, and should we have our rains at the proper time, the whole face of the country will respond with an excess of fertility not experienced in many years. But in contemplating this favorable prospect for the future, the experience of the past should not be forgotten by cattle men. This experience has demonstrated, at severe cost, that there is a limit to the feeding capacity of the range, and that when two head are turned out on a tract that can support only one, they cannot be profitably run. Many owners in the past two years have over-taxed the capacity of their own ranges and their neighbors' as well, and having paid the penalty in excessive losses, it is presumed that they have learned the leason and will not again attempt to crowd nature, but there may be those who see in the excellent grass prospect a reason for running in an excess of cattle to feed it off. It would seem that this is a question for the association to take up and settle on the broad principle of the "most good to the largest number," and in so doing, protect those who first established themselves in the country and acquired all the rights that it is possible to acquire under present conditions.

The Cattle Range in Montana, 1885–1887

From Granville Stuart, *Forty Years on the Frontier* (edited by Paul C. Phillips) (Cleveland, 1925), II, pp. 227–39.

During the summer of 1885 more than one hundred thousand head of cattle were brought into Montana, most of them trailed up from the South. There were also many bands of sheep driven in and these together with the natural rapid increase (under the most favorable conditions) trebled the number of sheep in the territory and by the fall of 1885 the Montana ranges were crowded. A hard winter or a dry summer would certainly bring disaster. There was no way of preventing the over-stocking of the ranges as they were free to all and men felt disposed to take big chances for the hope of large returns. The range business was no longer a reasonably safe business; it was from this time on a "gamble" with the trump cards in the hands of the elements.

During the summer we kept our beef cattle in the grassy cañons and along the rolling foothills at the base of the mountains. In these favored places the grass was good and water plentiful and the cattle did not lose flesh traveling long distances to water as they did when left down in the plains.

These cañons were very beautiful and there were many lovely wild flowers growing here that I had not found anywhere else in Montana. There were tiger lillies, Maraposa lillies, white purple clematis, laurel, several varieties of the orchid family, wild primroses, the Scotch bluebells, several varieties of larkspurs and lobelia, and the most fragrant and beautiful wild roses that I had ever seen. There were also choke-cherries, huckleberries, wild raspberries, and gooseberries.

The autumn foliage was beautiful; groves of golden quaking aspen, orange cottonwood, scarlet thornbushes, crimson rose briers, and the trailing clematis with its white cotton balls intermingling with the evergreen of the pines, fir, and spruce.

In the fall we had two thousand head of beef cattle ready for shipment when a great rush of half fat range stuff from Texas, Indian Territory, and New Mexico flooded the markets and the price of beef cattle fell to a low water-mark. We cut out all of our three year old steers and turned them back on the range and only shipped nine hundred and eighty-two head. This left us eighteen thousand eight hundred and eighty head of stock on the range after the fall shipment.

This year the National Cattle Growers' Association met in Chicago on November 17–18. The Montana delegation devoted their time and energies to two subjects, namely:

To have the government perfect and take charge of a system of quarantine against diseases of animals in all the states and territories; and to have the Indians allotted their lands in severalty and the rest of their immense reservations thrown open to actual settlers. We succeeded in having our resolutions adopted and a delegation appointed to take them to Washington and have them presented before Congress.

There was a big fight led by the delegations from Texas and Indian territory, to set aside a wide strip of country from Texas to the British line for a cattle trail and to allow the leasing from the government of the public domain. These measures did not pass.

I returned from Chicago to the range late in December accompanied by the Marquis De Mores and we stopped off at Glendive and hunted for a week. The country was dry and dusty with only an occasional snow drift in the coulees and in deep ravines. The Marquis was anxious to visit Butte, our then flourishing mining town, and as I was going there on business he continued on with me to Helena and then to Butte.

In 1885, Butte was a hustling, bustling, mining town and everything ran wide open. We arrived at seven o'clock in the evening on a little local stub from Garrison. Volumes of yellowish sulphuric smoke rolled up from the heaps of copper ore that was roasting on the flat east of Meaderville and spread over the town like a pall enveloping everything in midnight darkness and almost suffocating one. The depot was little better than a box car and the light from the windows did not penetrate the darkness. We could not see and we could scarcely breathe.

The Marquis grabbed my arm and between sneezes gasped — "What is this to which you have brought me?"

As the cab slowly crawled along the street, music from the saloons and dance halls floated out to us but we could not even see the lights in the windows. Next day it was no better and I began to feel that our visit to Butte was destined to be a disappointment in so far as seeing the town was concerned. About ten o'clock a stiff breeze blew up from the south and scattered the smoke and we were able to visit our friends, transact business, and then view the novel sights of a big mining camp.

At the meeting of the Stock Growers' Association at Miles City, Dr. Azel Ames, F. C. Robertson, Marquis De Mores and myself were appointed a committee to confer with the people of St. Paul for the purpose of inducing them to establish stockyards and a cattle market at that city so as to relieve us from the monopoly held over us by Chicago. We succeeded in our mission and the following autumn the St. Paul yards were ready to receive shipments of cattle.

This spring we lost quite a number of cattle from their eating poisonous plants. It was the first trouble of the kind that we had encountered. These poisonous plants made their appearance after the drouths and when the grass was eaten out. Being drouth resisting they come up early, grow luxuriantly and are the first green things to appear in the spring and the cattle will eat them.

The spring roundup did not start until May 25, because with the continued drouth the green grass would not start. The cattle were in fine condition and the "calf crop" unusually large. Our outfit branded thirty-eight hundred and eighty-one calves on this roundup.

At this time a group of eastern capitalists offered to purchase our entire herd. Negotiations reached the point where we were to turn the outfit over to them, when Mr. Elkins, the man who represented the eastern company, died suddenly and the sale was not consummated.

The drouth continued and in July the short grass was dry and parched, streams and water holes drying up; but in spite of the drouth and short grass, cattle were being brought in from Washington and Oregon and the herds from the south were coming in undiminishing numbers and they were all thrown on the already over-stocked ranges of Montana.

Added to the drouth was unprecedented heat. The thermometer stood at one hundred to one hundred and ten degrees in the shade for days at a time and then would come hot winds that licked up every drop of moisture and shriveled the grass. There was nothing to be done but move at least a part of the herd.

In July I started out to look for better range and after going through the lower Judith basin, Shonkin, Highwoods, Belt creek, Sun river, and Teton ranges, finally decided to drive some of the cattle north of the Missouri river, along the foot of the Little Rockies. There was more water over there and some good grass.

In spite of every precaution range fires would start and as it was so hot and dry it was very hard to put them out when they did start. Big fires along the foot of the Judith range and on the Musselshell filled the air with smoke and cinders. Crews of fire fighters were kept busy all summer.

On arriving home, I found a telegram from Conrad Kohrs stating that he had leased range in Canada and to prepare to move. He failed to state where the leased range was located. I was not in favor of taking the herd north of the British line because of the severe blizzards that swept the open treeless plains that afforded no shelter for stock and was too far north to get the warm chinook winds. It was too late in the season to move the cattle a great distance. It always injures range cattle more or less to move them and it would never do to throw them on a strange range too late in the season.

A meeting of the stockholders of the Pioneer Cattle Company decided that we would reduce the herd as much as possible by shipping to market all the cattle fit for beef, gather the bulls and feed them at the home ranches and move five thousand head across the Missouri river to the foot of the Little Rockies. To G. P. Burnett was given the difficult task of gathering and moving the herd.

The beef could not be shipped until fall so the fat steers must not be disturbed and it was very hard to drive out the others and not disturb them, for all were as wild as antelope. Extreme care had to be used so that the herd would reach the new range in as good condition as possible.

August 10 we began gathering the cattle that were to be moved. Ordinarily one could see for miles across the range in our clear atmosphere, but not so at this time. Dense smoke obscured everything and this together with the cinders and the clouds of hot dry alkali dust almost choked and blinded us, causing much suffering to men and horses.

Moving a mixed herd is always hard. The young cattle travel fast and the old cows and young calves go slowly, so the whole herd has to be driven to suit the pace of the slowest animal in it. The drive to the new range was not a long one but under the existing circumstances it was a hard one and taxed to the fullest the ingenuity of the plucky young Texan in charge of the herd.

The weather continued extremely hot, and creeks, water-holes, and small lakes, never before dry, were completely so now. The water in all the flowing streams was very low and strongly alkaline, so much so, that in places the tired and thirsty horses refused to drink. It was so bitter that one could not drink the coffee made with it. Nearly every man with the drive was ill from drinking it. For days the herd moved forward through the smoke and stifling dust across the dry parched country.

At last we were nearing the Missouri river, intending to cross at Rocky Point. The wind was from the north and the cattle smelled the water and broke for it. No power on earth could stop the poor thirsty beasts; bellowing and lowing they ran pell-mell for the water, with the cowboys in hot pursuit. There was a point of quicksand in the river just above the ford and before the men could prevent it the cattle had plunged into it and were miring down. A small steamboat tied at the landing used their donkey engine to help drag out some of them, but we lost seventy head in spite of our best efforts.

After this mishap we crossed the herd without further trouble and from here on there was more water and better grass. The herd reached its destination in splendid condition. This fall we branded two thousand and seventy-four calves.

Seven thousand head of cattle belonging to the Powder River Cattle Company crossed the Missouri river at Great Falls and were driven through the Judith basin destined for our range, but when they saw the condition of the range and found that we were moving cattle out, they continued on north across the British line and threw their herds on the range near Fort McLeod.

John H. Conrad also had two thousand seven hundred head that he intended to bring in, but later drove them north of the line to the Cypress hills.

These changes, together with the very heavy shipments of beef to the markets relieved the over-stocked condition of the range and could we have had copious rains early in the fall to start the grass and a reasonably easy winter, all would have gone well.

We did not get the fall rains. There was quite a severe storm in November. On the sixteenth the thermometer fell to two degrees below zero, with a cutting northeast wind and on the seventeenth and eighteenth six inches of snow fell, but blew into drifts. The cattle north of the Missouri being unaccustomed to the range drifted badly and kept working back to the river.

This year we noticed that the wild animals moved south. The wild geese and ducks and song birds started south early and many that were accustomed to stay with us all winter disappeared: even the range cattle seemed to take on a heavier, shaggier coat of hair. For the first time since I had come to the range, the white Arctic owls came on the range and into the Judith basin. The old Indians pointed to them and drawing their blankets more closely about them, gave a shrug and ''Ugh! Heap Cold!'' expressive of some terrible experience in the long past that still lingered in their memory. One old Gros Ventre warrior assured me that not since he was a small boy had he seen the owls on their reservation. Everything pointed to a severe winter and we made what preparations we could to meet it with as little suffering to the stock and loss to ourselves as possible.

December 5, there was another storm, with the thermometer twelve degrees below and four inches of snow. I returned home from Chicago December 14 and rode from Custer station to the ranch, distant one hundred and twenty miles, in a blizzard, the thermometer down to zero and high east wind that pierced to the marrow of my bones.

Between the Musselshell and Flat Willow the snow blew in our faces so that the driver could not keep the road. There were two other passengers on the stage besides myself and we took turns walking ahead of the horses with a lantern to guide them. This storm lasted three days and then cleared up warm and bright and remained so until January 9, 1887. On that day a cold wind blew from the north. It began to snow and snowed steadily for sixteen hours, in which sixteen inches of snow fell on a level. The thermometer dropped to twenty-two degrees below zero, then twenty-seven degrees, then thirty degrees, and on the night of January 15 stood at forty-six degrees below zero, and there were sixteen inches of snow on the level. It was as though the Arctic regions had pushed down and enveloped us. Everything was white. Not a point of bare ground was visible in any direction. This storm lasted ten days without abating. The cattle drifted before the storm and fat young steers froze to death along their trails.

Conditions were so changed from what they were in 1880–81. The thick brush and tall rye-grass along the streams that afforded them excellent shelter at that time was now all fenced in and the poor animals drifted against those fences and perished.

Our herd was one of the first large herds brought into northeastern Montana, consequently had been on the range longer than others. They were all northern grown range stock and occupied the best range in the northwest. We kept plenty of men on the range to look after them as best they could, keeping them back from the rivers, and out of air holes and open channels in the ice, helping them out of drifts and keeping them in what shelter the cut banks and ravines offered. The herd could be said to be a favored one, yet we lost fifty per cent of them in this storm.

There was a series of storms in February and while not so severe yet they came at a time when the cattle were least able to withstand them and there were heavy losses then. The cows were all thin and the losses in spring calves was about thirty per cent.

The herds that were driven up from the south and placed on the range late in the summer, perished outright. Others lost from seventy-five to eighty per cent of their cattle.

It was impossible to tell just what the losses were for a long time as the cattle drifted so badly in the big January storm. We did not get some of ours back for a year. Our entire losses for the year were sixty-six per cent of the herd. In the fall of 1886 there were more than one million head of cattle on the Montana ranges and the losses in the "big storm" amounted to twenty million dollars. This was the death knell to the range cattle business on anything like the scale it had been run on before.

Charles Russell, "The Cow Boy Artist" told the story of the "snuffing out of the big ranges" most graphically in his charcoal sketch, "The Last of 5000." Charlie was in charge of a herd in the Judith basin, when the owner, who lived in Helena, wrote and asked how his cattle was getting along? For answer Charlie sent him the sketch.

The large outfits were the heaviest losers as they could not feed or shelter their immense herds. Most of the big outfits had borrowed large sums of money at a high rate of interest and the cattle that they had left would hardly pay their indebtedness. They had to stay in the business and begin all over again. Eastern men who had large sums of money invested, closed out the remnant of their herds and quit.

The rancher with a good body of hay land and from one hundred to two hundred head of cattle was the man that profited. He had hay enough to feed through storms and could gather his cattle around the ranch and partially shelter them, and in the spring he was enabled to buy cattle cheap. Here again I wish to say a word in defense of the "cattle barons" whom our leading newspapers abused so unmercifully at the time, accusing them of driving settlers from their homes and of "hogging" all the land. There were a good many settlers who had milch cows and a few "dogies" and did not have hay enough to feed them. The big ranches all had more or less hay and could have saved a few cattle by feeding, but instead they let the man with a family and a few cows have the hay to save their domestic animals; and they did not sell it to them at ruinous prices either but let them have it at cost of production.

In the spring of 1887 the ranges presented a tragic aspect. Along the streams and in the coulees everywhere were strewn the carcasses of dead cattle. Those that were left alive were poor and ragged in appearance, weak and easily mired in the mud holes.

A business that had been fascinating to me before, suddenly became distasteful. I wanted no more of it. I never wanted to own again an animal that I could not feed and shelter.

The spring was very wet, one heavy rain followed another in succession and the grass came on luxuriantly. We moved the remainder of the herd over on the Milk river range. I did not like the country and did not move over there. Conrad Kohrs took the management of the herd.

Much has been said and written about the extravagant mismanagement of the big cow outfits, of the selfish arrogance of the cattlemen, of the wild and reckless irresponsible cow boy.

I began at the beginning and was with it to the end and I want to say that there was never a great business that was systematized and worked more economically than the range cattle business. Some of the big outfits were owned by eastern capitalists who invested for their sons, boys who were fascinated with the free untrammeled life of the west, others were owned by men who, like myself, had been more or less in cattle in Montana for years and these small herds became the nucleus for the big outfits. Then there were men like Conrad Kohrs who had never done anything but raise cattle, and there were cattle breeders (range men) from the southwest.

It was apparent from the first that to be successful the entire range business must be run as one outfit, hence the two strong organizations, The Montana Stock Growers' Association and the Board of Stock Commissioners. These two organizations acted as Boards of Directors and they ran the cattle business absolutely. Their administration was just, honest, and economical, so much so that they have been in operation for thirty-five years and are still in operation.

The young men, scions of wealthy and influential families, loved the business and were anxious to learn, and under the leadership of older and more experienced heads, developed into splendid business men, many of them still in the state and numbered among our best citizens.

The handling of the herds on the range was entrusted to the cow boys from the southwest. These men were bred and born on the range and knew how to handle range cattle. It is impossible for me to describe one of them and do him justice. Their understanding of cattle was almost supernatural, their patience, ingenuity, faithfulness, and loyalty to their outfit cannot be described. They were to their outfit what a good mother is to her family and their way of handling herds has never been improved upon.

The idea of lavish expenditure was an erroneous one. I have described the headquarters ranch of a big outfit; few rude log cabins, comprising a bunk house, a cook house, a blacksmith shop, stable and corral, with hay land enough fenced to cut a hundred tons of hay. The food provided was beans, bacon, coffee, syrup, bread and beef. A can of tomatoes or oysters was a luxury.

The big outfits never imposed on the smaller ones or on the ranchers or squatters, but helped them in every way. In fact it was the big outfits that protected the little ones and made it possible for them to settle in the uninhabited country.

The big outfits brought millions of capital into a sparsely settled country and their herds converted the millions of tons of grass that had for thousands of years gone to waste into millions of dollars worth of beef. Their heavy taxes built roads and schools and did much for the advancement of civilization.

Silos and Ensilage, 1888

From "Silos and Ensilage," in University of Minnesota Experiment Station, Bulletin No. 2, April, 1888, pp. 3–7, 17–19.

Silos

The silos of the Station, two in number, were erected in 1884. . . . These silos are located on the right and left side of the main threshing floor of the barn and are 16 feet by 16 feet square, and extend from the level of the feeding floors of the basement stables, to the third floor of the barn, a height of 21 feet. Doors open into them from the threshing floor for filling, and out of them on a level with the basement for facility of feeding. The walls to the level of the second floor of the barn, 11 feet, are of stone, 18 inches in thickness, — above that are double studded with 2 × 6 inch scantling, well "bridged." The floor of the silo was made with a bed of concrete, composed of one part of Louisville cement, and two parts of sand, with water enough to make the mixture the consistency of thick cream; then adding coarse gravel and small pebbles thoroughly incorporated until the mass was like stiff mortar, when it was spread evenly over the bottom of the pit, three inches thick and well rammed down, and finished off smoothly with a wooden float. A slope of one inch to the foot was given to the floor, towards the centre, where a well two feet in diameter and four feet deep, was sunk into the underlying gravel formation, for the purpose of giving thorough drainage to the silo. The sides of this well were cemented, but the bottom was left open and then filled up to the level of the floor with pebbles the size of a hen's egg. The walls of the silo were listed up and down with 2 × 4 scantling, 16 inches from centre to centre, and boarded up with matched flooring — thus leaving an air space of two inches around all the sides. Over this lining I placed two thicknesses of tarred building paper, and over this a covering of matched flooring nailed on vertically. This construction gives an air-tight, water-tight, and frost-proof silo, and most conveniently placed for filling, feeding, and the preservation of its contents.

I wish to call especial attention to one point in the construction of these silos. The sides do not extend to the bottom, but stop short one and one half inches all around. Before filling the silo, a strip of tarred paper is folded lengthwise and doubled, so that one half of it will lie against the wall and the other portion on the floor, and is held in place by a strip of board. This makes an air tight joint, when the pit is filled. When the ensilage is fed out, this strip of board and the lining of paper removed, and there is a free circulation of air around all the sides of the silo between the wall and lining, which keeps the wood work dry and adds greatly to its durability. The air chamber provided by this method of construction has preserved the ensilage from freezing during the two past winters, although located on the north side of the barn, and exposed to a temperature of forty degrees below zero.

The Ensilage Crop

The plat of ground devoted to the growth of the crop designed for ensilage in 1887 contained three and two-thirds acres. The land was prairie land, with a light clay subsoil, mingled with gravel, giving thorough drainage. The ground has been under tillage continuously for twenty-five years, with only an occasional light dressing of manure until 1884, when the lot was in wheat, and seeded down to clover. In 1885, a heavy crop of clover was plowed under in June, and in 1886, was again used for the experimental plats of wheat. In the fall of that year, one-half of the field was covered with well-rotted barnyard manure at the rate of twenty tons to the acre, and plowed down. The remaining half was manured at the same rate during the winter, and the ground plowed in the spring of 1887. The whole field was put in fine tilth by repeated harrowing and rolling and the use of the "disc harrow" and was planted May 30th. The seed used was the "Burrell & Whitman Ensilage Corn," and was planted with a "Buckeye" grain drill, by "stopping off" all but two tubes, making the rows forty-five inches apart, and so regulated as to drop about four grains to the foot. The depth was regulated by a "drill roller" attachment so as to plant two inches deep. The field was well rolled after planting and the corn came up evenly by June 8th. The smoothing harrow was passed over the field from time to time until the corn was from five to six inches high, when a fine tooth cultivator was used for the after tillage. The crop was hand-hoed once to remove the weeds from between the stalks. A marked difference was observed in the condition of the two portions of the field. The one manured and plowed in the fall, was almost free from weeds and grass; the corn came up one day earlier than on the plat manured and plowed in the spring, and maintained its more vigorous growth for the entire season, — and at harvest yielded two tons more to the acre.

In the latter part of July, the "chinch bugs" swept over the farm, destroying many of our experimental plats of grain and grasses, and covering the ensilage field so that the stalks were almost black with them for two or three feet from the ground, but the growth was so vigorous that but little injury seemed to be done.

There was a marked difference in the yield and quality of the crop this year from that of 1886. The corn was planted last year in drills twenty-five inches apart, and the stalks stood four to a foot, and the yield on the same quality of ground and with the same fertilizers and method of cultivation, was twenty-two tons per acre. This year the drills were forty-five inches apart, and three stalks to a foot, and the yield was thirty-five tons pr. acre, and a much larger proportion of the stalks bore well matured ears of corn, which were in the "milk". when harvested.

Harvesting

We commenced filling the silos, Sept. 13, and the work was continued from day to day until Sept. 26. The corn was too heavy to cut with any machinery available, as it stood on an average thirteen feet high, and had been blown down by a severe storm in August. It was cut by hand, placed in open gavels, on the ground, and laid from twenty-four to thirty-six hours, to wilt and dry out a portion of the moisture. It was hauled in and weighed on the road to the silo. It was found on careful trial that the loss of weight by drying was about one sixth in thirty-six hours. The yield of green corn was One hundred and twenty-seven and one half tons or nearly thirty five tons pr. acre.

Filling the Silo

The corn was cut with a "Ross Ensilage Cutter," into half inch lengths, and delivered by an "Angle Carrier" to the silo, where it was leveled and firmly packed. The filling was done in the afternoon of each day from September 13th to 26th, not only to permit the fermentation to become well established but to prolong the work so as to allow its inspection by the numerous visitors who were interested in the operation.

The East silo, or No.1, was filled to the depth of 16 feet, with 142,600 lbs. of cut fodder which gave 35 pounds to the cubic foot. It was carefully leveled and covered with plank, placed side by side, and but one inch shorter than the width of the silo, so as to allow easy settling; this was covered with two thicknesses of tarred building paper, and over this a covering of inch boards, and the whole weighted with one hundred and thirty pounds to the square foot. On December 1st the mass had settled four feet or one fourth. There was no further settling, and on March 30th a cubic foot of the ensilage taken six feet from the surface weighed forty-three pounds — showing a loss of 10,504 pounds or seven per cent. in curing. Silo No. 2 was filled in the same manner as No. 1, with thirty-eight tons of the same kind of fodder corn, and the balance with ensilage corn from other experimental plats. This was packed and covered the same as No. 1, except it was *not weighted*. The amount of settling was only six inches less.

Both silos were opened early in December and their contents examined. The silage in No. 1 was perfectly preserved, not a cubic inch injured, and as bright under the covers and around the sides of the wall and in the corners as when put in. It was light brown in color, slightly acid — and with an agreeably vinous odor.

In silo No. 2 the contents were decayed about twelve inches from the top and nearly as much around the sides, and the silage had a strongly acid taste and smell. The sound fodder from the silo was readily eaten by all the stock, but not with the relish or results as that from No. 1.

Experiments are still in progress, showing the value of this food, in the production of milk, butter and flesh, which will be reported in a future Bulletin.

Cost of Growing Ensilage

As every hour of labor performed at this station has to be paid for at full market rates, and an account is kept of all weights and measurements, we are prepared to show the exact cost of growing this crop the past season. The average haul of manure and produce was one thousand feet.

COST OF GROWING ONE ACRE

Hauling and spreading 20 loads of manure	$5.50
Plowing the ground	1.00
Harrowing and rolling	1.00
Planting with wheat drill	1.00
Seed ½ bushel	1.25
Cultivating four times	2.00
Hand hoeing and weeding	4.00
	$15.75
Equal per ton	.45

COST OF HARVESTING AND FILLING SILO

Capacity of machine 50 tons per day of 10 hours.

Six men in field cutting and loading	@$1.33	$7.98
Two teams hauling	@ 2.00	4.00
One driver	@ 1.33	1.33
Two men feeding machine	@ 1.33	2.66
Two men packing in silo	@ 1.33	2.66
One man at the engine	@ 1.33	1.33
Coal used, one-fifth ton	@ 8.00	1.60
Cost of harvesting 50 tons	$21.56	
Cost of harvesting one ton		.43
Total cost per ton		.88

* * *

Silos

(1) A silo is only a preserving can on a large scale, and the same conditions necessary for success prevail in both.

(2) A good silo may be built with very rough lumber and with ordinary labor, by a liberal use of tarred building paper, the "pioneer's friend."

(3) The location, form and construction of the silo, the arrangements for filling, covering, weighting and feeding must be governed by local circumstances, but it is always better to fill above the feeding floor, than below, as it is easier to elevate the ensilage, at the time of harvesting, when it can be done by automatic machinery, than to do so day by day by hand through a long winter, with the mercury below zero.

(4) Of whatever material the silo is built, the walls must be perpendicular, and the inner faces smooth, so that the ensilage may settle easily.

(5) The walls of the silo must be strong enough to withstand the lateral pressure of the enclosed mass.

(6) Water tight and air tight bottoms, and air proof walls are prime essentials in building a silo.

(7) It is advisable to divide the space intended for a silo into three compartments of equal size, so that they may be filled to the depth of four or five feet, alternately, and thus allow time for fermentation to set in, and the heat to raise to

125 to 140 degrees, before again filling. This temperature aids in the digestion of the food, kills the germs which promote fermentation, partially expels the air, and secures comparatively sweet ensilage.

Ensilage

(8) While any plant or vegetable fit for cattle food when green or undried may be preserved in the silo for an indefinite period, Indian corn is the cheapest and best for ensilage in this country.

(9) Plant such varieties of corn for ensilage as will reach maturity in an ordinary season in your section. Plant in rows wide enough to admit of easy cultivation, and just thick enough in the row to allow each stalk to form a well developed ear.

(10) The best time to cut corn for ensilage is when the grains are fully formed, and in the doughy or glazing state; the fodder then contains the largest amount of digestible matter.

(11) Corn partially dried before packing in the silo gives equally good fodder, and at a reduced cost.

(12) The best results are obtained by cutting the ensilage into half-inch lengths, especially for well-grown and nearly matured cornstalks.

(13) In filling the silo, care should be taken to spread it evenly as put in, to pack the corners and sides firmly, to cover the top with a layer of boards or plank, spread over this a double layer of tarred paper, and then a layer of rough boards, and on the whole a moderate weight of from 50 to 100 pounds to the square foot. The weighting material may be anything convenient, sand, gravel or dirt in barrels, stone, fire wood, farm implements, for storage and the like.

(14) Pits should not be opened until fermentation has ceased and the mass has cooled, which will be in from six to eight weeks from the time of filling.

(15) In feeding from the silo, it is better to feed day by day from the top in uniform layers, rather than from top to bottom, as by this method the surface is not exposed long enough to the air to sour.

Value of Ensilage

(16) Ensilage can be grown and preserved much cheaper than root crops, by the ordinary farmer, and will successfully take their place in feeding value.

(17) Corn ensilage is not a complete feeding ration, as it is deficient in protein, and this must be supplied by some bye-fodder, as bran, shorts or oil cake.

(18) The tests of the laboratory and the feeding stables do not agree as to the value of ensilage. The practical results of its use are so satisfactory as to surprise the chemist, and thus far he has failed to give them a satisfactory explanation.

(19) The best results of feeding ensilage are obtained by using it in combination with dry fodder, the best of which is clover hay.

(20) We *do* get more out of the silo than we put in it, for the reason that the chemical changes which take place in the process of curing are identical with those that take place in the first stages of digestion, and consequently there is a saving of vital energy to the animal, and an economy of food consumption.

(21) Ensilage furnishes a succulent and easily digested food, greatly relished by all animals, during the long winters of our Northwest, when they would otherwise be confined to an almost uniform ration of dry provender.

Conclusion

(22) The ease with which silos may be constructed, the certainty with which they will preserve feed from injury, the low cost of raising and storing the crop, and its value as a cattle food, render this the cheapest provender a stockman can raise.

Opening of the Alliance Exchange, 1890

From "The Alliance Exchange Open for Business," *Rural Californian*, January, 1891, XIV, p. 35.

LOS ANGELES, *Calif., December, 21, 1890.*

TO ALLIANCE MEMBERS:

The urgent need of a farmers' organization in Southern California was (1) to find new and remunerative markets for Southern California farm productions, and (2) to buy all farm supplies, including implements and machinery, in wholesale lots and supply the same to the individual members at nearly cost, only a sufficient advance being charged to pay the business representative's salary and office expenses. Chief among its missions the Farmers Alliance in Southern California seeks to ameliorate the producers' condition in these two important items, and the Los Angeles County Farmers Alliance has shown a commendable bit of enterprise in establishing an agent in Los Angeles at 224 South Main street to look after the interests of the Alliance members. The plan is a very simple one and may be briefly explained as follows:

The business representative will make arrangements with several business houses of whom the most liberal concessions are to be had in the various lines of trade. Credentials will be furnished from the business office of the Alliance to each member desiring to purchase any particular line of goods. On all small purchases the charge will be 25 cents to pay the expenses of the office, while the larger purchases, and especially on machinery, wagons, etc., from 2 to 5 per cent will be demanded. The reduced rates from the various business houses so far consulted vary from 15 to 30 and even 40 per cent from list prices. This of course only goes to show what an immense field for good there is before the Alliance from a pecuniary point of view. In each and every case the consideration is *spot cash*. The Alliance or its representative will not consider any proposition but that of coin on the counter when the goods are delivered.

When it comes to handling farm produce, it will be the aim of this office to dispose of the same at the highest ruling market price with as little expense to the producer as possible. As in case of buying supplies, this office will make a like charge of from 2 to 5 per cent for selling the produce of Alliance farmers. As in the former case, spot cash upon the delivery of goods is the only basis upon which farm productions will be disposed of.

Let it be borne in mind that in order to make this venture a success all members of the Alliance must patronize their own established institution. If this office can be the means of bringing trade to the business houses that have made us liberal concessions, it will be the result of securing still larger discounts. It will also be wise if buyers will bunch their purchases, for it is obvious that the larger and more varied the amount of goods bought at each transaction, the more satisfactory it will be to all concerned. The main consideration is to convince the merchants and manufacturers that the Alliance movement is no ephermal affair, but has come to stay, and by a spirit of fairness and liberality not only help the farming classes in their commercial transactions, but also stimulate trade by enlarging and developing our horticultural and agricultural resources.

It is urgently requested that all members make their purchases through the Alliance and dispose of their produce through the same channel.

Very truly yours,

L. A. FARMERS ALLIANCE,

R. SHERER, Manager

No. 224 South Main St.

Mail Delivery in the Country

From "Mail Delivery in the Country," *Rural Californian*, December, 1891, XIV, p. 721.

The movement to have daily delivery of mail throughout the more thickly populated sections of the farming communities is one that has merit and should be heartily encouraged by every patriotic citizen. There is no just reason why the city people should enjoy the privilege of daily mail delivery at the expense of the growers, since all are taxed alike to maintain the system. The benefits to be derived are incalculable. Daily mail delivery will enable the farmer to take a daily paper, and greatly lessen the isolation from the rest of the world which now forms so conspicuous an objection to farm life to many people. Besides it will greatly stimulate a larger intercourse with the outside world, and greatly facilitate an increased circulation of farm literature.

Some $10,000 was voted at the last session of Congress to give the plan a trial. For a period of five months daily delivery of mail has been practiced in many sections embracing most every state and territory in the Union. That it has been successful and appreciated be the farmers is best attested by the fact that the increase of mail business in places where it is being tried, has, in many cases more than covered the additional expense. Detailed results have not yet been obtainable through the postoffice department as the five months have not yet expired; nevertheless, enough has been learned to demonstrate that the scheme is feasible and can be successfully inauguarated.

To bring about a permanent free delivery of mail in the farming districts of the country means agitation and a persistent demand for it on the part of the farmers from their representatives at the national government. This can best be done by peronal effort and by means of numerous petitions praying for the same.

Wages Paid Farm Hands in Illinois, 1894

From Illinois State Board of Agriculture, *Statistical Report for May 1, 1894*, Springfield: Illinois State Journal Co. 1894., pp. 8–10.

Owing to the closing of factories and reduction of force in industries of all kinds, there is an unusually large number of idle men this spring, so that farmers have no difficulty in obtaining all the help they need, but the trouble is to find capable, willing hands. Many of those out of employment do not want work, and are glad of an excuse to remain idle. Farming, as well as every other business interest, feels the effect of the hard times, and many farmers are hiring just as little help as possible this spring.

The excess of farm hands is 7 per cent., and is very equally distributed throughout the State.

Wages paid to farm hands this season are a very little less than for a few years past. More difference is noticed in southern Illinois than in the other divisions of the State.

The average wages paid farm hands during the past fifteen years in the three grand divisions of the State, are given in the following table:

The wages paid farm help in the three divisions of the State, during the past fifteen years, is given in the following tables:

DIVISION	PER DAY.		PER MONTH.	
	With board.	Without board.	With board.	Without board.
Northern....................	$1 00	$1 30	$19 75	$27 65
Central.....................	85	1 10	17 95	24 75
Southern....................	65	90	14 60	20 70
Average	$0 85	$1 10	$17 45	$24 35

The wages paid farm help in the three divisions of the State, during the past fifteen years, is given in the following tables:

NORTHERN DIVISION

	Per Day.		Per Month.	
Year.	With board.	Without board.	With board.	Without board.
1880.........................	$0 95	$1 15	$17 55	$25 25
1881.........................	95	1 25	19 55	27 25
1882.........................	1 05	1 40	21 40	29 75
1883.........................	1 05	1 35	21 15	29 75
1884.........................	1 00	1 25	20 50	29 00
1885.........................	1 00	1 25	19 50	27 75
1886.........................	1 00	1 30	19 20	27 80
1887.........................	95	1 30	19 10	27 50
1888.........................	95	1 25	18 50	26 10
1889.........................	1 00	1 30	19 35	26 90
1890.........................	95	1 25	19 10	26 30
1891.........................	1 00	1 30	19 80	27 25
1892.........................	1 05	1 35	20 70	28 15
1893.........................	1 05	1 35	21 60	30 05
1894.........................	95	1 25	19 30	26 60
Average	$1 00	$1 30	$19 75	$27 65

CENTRAL DIVISION

	Per Day.		Per Month.	
Year.	With board.	Without board.	With board.	Without board.
1880.........................	$0 75	$1 00	$16 15	$22 65
1881.........................	85	1 10	17 85	24 75
1882.........................	90	1 20	18 65	25 80
1883.........................	90	1 20	18 90	26 25
1884.........................	1 00	1 25	18 75	25 75
1885.........................	75	1 00	17 75	25 00
1886.........................	85	1 10	17 45	24 45
1887.........................	85	1 10	17 55	24 50
1888.........................	85	1 10	17 60	24 25
1889.........................	85	1 10	17 65	24 15
1890.........................	85	1 10	17 25	24 05
1891.........................	85	1 15	17 95	24 50
1892.........................	85	1 15	18 70	25 45
1893.........................	90	1 15	19 10	25 65
1894.........................	85	1 10	17 90	24 00
Average	$0 85	$1 10	$17 95	$24 75

SOUTHERN DIVISION

YEAR.	PER DAY.		PER MONTH.	
	With board.	Without board.	With board.	Without board.
1880.........................	$0 65	$0 95	$14 00	$20 45
1881.........................	65	90	14 75	21 05
1882.........................	65	90	14 55	21 00
1883.........................	70	95	15 30	22 10
1884.........................	75	1 00	15 25	22 25
1885.........................	75	1 00	15 00	21 25
1886.........................	65	90	14 25	20 90
1887.........................	65	90	14 30	20 50
1888.........................	65	90	13 95	20 55
1889.........................	65	90	14 20	19 95
1890.........................	55	90	14 05	19 80
1891.........................	65	90	14 65	20 90
1892.........................	65	90	15 00	21 45
1893.........................	70	95	15 50	18 50
1894.........................	60	85	14 35	20 20
Average	$0 65	$0 90	$14 60	$20 70

Labor Contract of 1896

From: Contract between Antony Butler and John W. Moody, from the John W. Moody Papers, 1896 (#1424), in the Southern Historical Collection, University of North Carolina Library, Chapel Hill, North Carolina.

COURT CONTRACT WITH LABORER.—Printed and for sale at The Echo Office, Lexington, Ga.

GEORGIA, OGLETHORPE COUNTY.

THIS CONTRACT, Made and entered into this *30* day of *December* 189*6*, between _John W. Moody_ and _Antony Butler,_ both of said State and County,

Witnesseth. That for and in consideration of _____ _Seventy Two_ Dollars, to be due and payable on the *25* day of *December*, 1898 and in consideration further of a sufficient and wholesome supply of provisions such as are customarily furnished to laborers for the sustenance of the said _Antony Butler._ during his term of service, to be supplied as his necessities require, the said _Antony Butler,_ hereby contracts and agrees to work for and in the service of the said _John W. Moody,_ in the capacity of _Farm Laborer_ for and during the space of _12_, months, to begin _Jany first_, 1898, and to terminate on the *25* day of *December*, 1898, the said _John W. Moody,_ to have the exclusive control and benefit of the labor of the said _Antony Butler_ in the capacity aforesaid, and any and all loss of time, negligent, willful or providential, shall be accounted for by the said _Antony Butler,_ in a deduction of his per diem wages under this contract.

It is understood and intended by the parties hereto that this contract shall take and have all the force of a Court Contract when filed in proper office for filing Court Contracts, and it is further hereby expressly acknowledged by me that the above and foregoing contract has been fully and fairly explained to me in my hearing, the said _Antony Butler,_ upon signing the same, and that it is a fair and faithful expression of my agreements with the said _John W. Moody_ Witness my hand and seal.

Witnessed by _____

John W. Moody

Antony his Butler
    mark

Fruit Farming, 1896

From L. H. Bailey, "The Improvement of our Native Fruits," U.S. Department of Agriculture, *Yearbook*, 1896, pp. 297–304.

Introduction

It is a popular subject, this evolution and amelioration of our native fruits. Everyone is convinced that there is promise in these fruits, and writers are always demanding that some person other than themselves shall take up the improvement of them. Now, the chief reason for supposing that these fruits should be domesticated seems to be the most obvious fact that they have merit in themselves; and yet, paradoxical as it may be, this is not sufficient reason to recommend their amelioration. It is not the thing which is intrinsically the best that necessarily deserves the most attention, but the thing which is most needed. We shall find our most helpful suggestions from a reflection upon what has been accomplished and how it has been done, rather than from a mere objective study of the kinds of our wild fruits. It is proposed, therefore, to divide this article into two parts: (1) What has been done, and (2) what probably should be done.

What Has Been Done

The most obvious truth that strikes one when he attempts to make a reflective or historical study of the improvement of our native fruits is the fact that in nearly every case the amelioration has come from the force of circumstances and not from the choice or design of men. The colonists, in common with other good people, knew and loved wine. The beverage has been a hand to hand (or more truthfully a hand to mouth) companion of the human family from the first. The attempt was therefore early and heroically made to grow the European or wine grape in eastern America; but the attempt failed. In sheer distress of failure, the grape grower was driven to the use of the native grape. How literally true this was the reader may learn by reading the history of the grape colony of the Dufours in Kentucky, and then in Indiana late in the last century and early in this, and noticing the fact that the existence of the colony as such depended upon the success of the wine. The salvation of the colony was the Alexander, or Cape, grape, which, in a most surreptitious way, had transferred itself from the wild into the plantations which were at first designed to grow the European varieties; and later on, John Adlum's famous Catawba, a product of the Carolina highlands, added the crowning glory and success to the experiment, and thence spread itself along the Ohio and over the Union. At the very time that the Alexander and the Catawba were driving out the Old World types, the grape growers were making a most determined opposition to the native grapes. The fact is that the native grapes, the types which we now cultivate, came into domestication in spite of us.

The native plums, of which several hundred horticultural varieties are now described, came into domestication because the Old World plums, with which we are chiefly familiar in the Northeastern States, will not thrive in the prairie States or the South. The cultivated native plums had been widely disseminated before horticultural annalists discovered the fact; and there is no evidence that the early introducers of them had any suspicion that they were making history when they planted them. These plums were, no doubt, looked upon as a makeshift in a new country, as a fruit which was better than none when the good could not be had.

The reason why the native raspberries came into cultivation was because the European species is tender in our climate and demands too much care and petting to make it succeed. The native types of gooseberries drove out the foreign ones because the latter were injuriously infested with the mildew. The native crab apples are now demanding attention where the climate is so severe that the cultivated apple can not thrive. The wild red mulberry has been improved because the Old World black mulberry is tender, and we have been so ignorant of the fact that we have all along supposed that these natives are forms of the Old World species. The Chilean strawberry — the foundation stock of our commercial varieties — brought itself into domestication while men were bent upon impressing the Virginian berry into service, and many of our writers still insist on calling the common garden strawberries descendants of the latter species, so ignorant are they of the true course of the evolution.

The obverse of this picture is likewise instructive in showing how difficult it is to introduce and to improve fruits which are not forced upon us. For a century or more the native nuts have attracted the attention of economic writers. Their merits for food have been praised without stint for years and years. Within the last twelve months two nut-culture books have been written. Yet, they have made very little progress toward amelioration. The simple reason is that we have not been pressed by any necessity to grow them. None of the nuts are staple articles of food among the peoples who have chiefly settled the United States. They are essentially subsidiary and incidental features in our lives. So, while we all like hickory nuts and walnuts, we are nevertheless not impelled by any overmastering necessity to gather the trees into the garden or the orchard. We associate them more with the woods and the landscape and the outings than we do with the kitchen and the larder. They have no conspicuous places in our heritage of custom and association, as the apples and grapes and berries have.

Much the same observation could be made respecting the native huckleberries, fruits which have been recommended time and again as proper subjects for amelioration, and yet practically nothing has been done toward their improvement. The chief reason of this neglect seems to be that the imperative needs which the huckleberries may be supposed to satisfy are already supplied in large measure by other berry-like fruits.

There are apparent exceptions to all this in the cranberry and blackberry, for neither of these fruits has ever before been an important food for the human race. Yet, the very abundance of these fruits and their adaptability to the common needs of life forced them on the attention of the settler and colonist. It was but natural that, as the wild areas became constricted, attempts should be made to grow the plants.

The minor small fruits which have recently come into notice from the West have been chiefly impressed into domestication because of the comparative scarcity of domestic fruits in the regions whence they come. Some of these are the buffalo berry, the dwarf juneberry, the Crandall currant type, and the dwarf cherries and plums.

While the fact has been that the reigning types of improved native fruits have come into cultivation largely as a result of the force of conditions rather than as a direct or designed choice on the part of man, it nevertheless does not follow that an intelligent choice of species has not played an important part in the evolution, and that it may not count for still more in the years to come. Yet, the student should bear in mind the fact that all the most needful types of native fruits have now been impressed into cultivation, and that those which yet remain in an almost wholly unimproved condition, as many of the nuts, the elderberries, the Asimina, and others, will come into cultivation, if at all, only through the expenditure of great effort to make their merits and possibilities known. From now on the attempt to introduce new types of native fruits must be, broadly speaking, a forced effort. But if this is true, it does not follow that our efforts at amelioration should cease, but rather that the most promising and most useful expenditure of energy is to be found in still further improving the species which are already thoroughly established in cultivation. None of these types are yet, and in fact never will be, brought to that condition when they may be said to be good enough; and this conclusion, while apparently the only logical one, is one which does not seem to have been reached by writers upon the improvement of our native fruits. The tendency of our writers has always been, unfortunately, to urge the importance of undeveloped species, forgetting that the really important things are the ones which we already have, and all of which are far from perfect. The whole question, then, is simply that of the best methods of improving fruits in general without respect to their nativity.

Having now seen that new types of plants are impressed into cultivation largely because they are needed, and in an undesigned or almost fortuitous way, let us ask how these particular domestic fruits which are native to North America have been ameliorated. The process has been a most simple one: Attractive varieties, or forms, have been found, and men have transferred them to the garden. This, in essence, has been the method of the amelioration of most domestic plants. It is first the discovery of a good form, and then the perpetuation of it. What has been called plant breeding is mostly discovery, or, in other words, so far as the cultivator is concerned, it is accident. In one place, an attractive wild blackberry is found. The bush is taken to the garden, and it is called, after the name of the town, the Dorchester. In another place, another form is discovered, and this, when transplanted, becomes known as the Lawton or New Rochelle. Another form is found upon the prairie and is called Western Triumph. Now and then one comes up about an old plantation and is similarly cared for; occasionally a man sows seeds and picks out a good variety from the seedlings; still more rarely a man keeps a record of the parentage of the seed he sows; and very, very rarely one makes crosses and sows the seeds therefrom.

But, while the new varieties are mostly discoveries, it does not follow that there is no skill represented in novelties. The skill is expressed in giving the plants the very best of care when once they have been transferred to the garden, and the force of this domestication is likely to express itself in better or more tractable offspring in each generation. While the tendency toward betterment is constantly augmented by the habitual selection of the best new forms, that tendency could be much more rapidly hastened if, in addition to selecting the best seedlings which chance to appear, the operator should also select the seeds from the best plants with which to raise the seedlings.

It is interesting to recall how a few prominent varieties of native fruits have originated. The old Alexander, or Cape, grape, which first introduced a successful viticulture into eastern America, was found wild in the woods of Pennsylvania in the last century. The Catawba, which is still a popular commercial variety, was found in the woods in South Carolina in 1802. There are, no doubt, as good forms of the native fox grape in the woods now as there were then, but we have now obtained a start in grape growing and we are no longer looking to the wild for our varieties. The fox grape is known to be widely variable in its wild state, and the author has this year obtained no less than a half dozen types of large and handsome wild fruits of it, varying from deep purple to amber red. The Concord was a chance seedling in a Massachusetts garden, and it is supposed to have sprung from a seed of the wild fox grape of the neighborhood. The Worden was raised from a seed of the Concord. The Delaware was found in the garden of a Frenchman in New Jersey, about fifty years ago, but its genesis is wholly unknown. It is probably a product of an accidental cross between the European grape which the Frenchman cultivated and some variety of native grape. The Brighton is the product of a hand cross made between the Concord and the Diana-Hamburg (the latter itself a hybrid) by Jacob Moore, then of Brighton, N.Y. The Diana, which was a prominent variety for many years, was grown from a Catawba seed in Milton, Mass. Moore Early was grown from a seed of the Concord. The Clinton came up where a handful of grape seed had been sown at Hamilton College, Clinton, N.Y., and the old vine, now about 75 years old, is still growing on College Hill. The Norton Virginia was found wild in 1835, near Richmond, Va. The Isabella was brought into the North early in the century. Its origin is wholly unknown and has been the subject of much speculation. The botanical evidence shows that it is probably a native form of the Southern fox grape.

All these specific illustrations of the origin of varieties are fairly typical for all native fruits. Most of the forms are random or chance discoveries, and they show that the natural tendency toward progressive variation in the indigenous fruit species must be great, else the domesticated forms could not have reached their present state. If so much has been done by mere chance, so far as the horticulturist is concerned, there is certainly reason for believing that the rewards of plant breeding must some day be great.

What Probably Should Be Done

What has been done need not be done over again. That is, the best results in the amelioration of any species are to be expected by working with the highly improved forms rather than with the original wild stock. The quickest response to the plant breeder is to be expected in those species which are already most amelio-rated, and it is in these species, also, that the greatest efforts are needed, because they are the species which have the most useful qualities for man. One can not specify how the native fruits may be improved without going into the whole subject of the amelioration of plants,[1] but it may be useful to designate some of the things which seem necessary to be done.

In the first place, we need more varieties of every native fruit now cultivated — of grapes, raspberries, plums, cranberries, and the rest. This is be-

[1] This subject is fully discussed in Plant Breeding, by L. H. Bailey.

cause new needs are always arising and the fruits are being grown in new regions, and new varieties are needed to adapt the species to these new wants. Those persons who are looking for the coming of the perfect all-around variety are behind the time and are constantly getting further behind, for it is becoming more and more apparent that it is impossible to combine all the varied and contradictory specific desires of men into one plant form. There must be a best variety for every particular use and locality and soil. The cosmopolitan variety must become more and more restricted in range and usefulness as time goes on and as more refined and specific needs arise. People are always saying that we already have too many varieties, and an effort is being made to reduce the number. Even the experimenters in the stations usually conceive it to be a part of their duty to endeavor to reduce the number of varieties; but what they are really doing, or might be doing, is determining the merits of varieties for specific uses. If a given variety does not satisfy the ideal of the experimenter, that fact is no proof that it may not satisfy the ideal of someone else, or that it may not be a positive acquisition in some other place or for some other purpose. We shall always need to test varieties, to be sure, and the testing must be the more exact and personal the more critical we become in our demands. It is out of the many new varieties that we shall find the particular ones which we ourselves desire.

In the second place, we need a greater range of variation — more divergent and widely unlike varieties. These can be had by selecting out of the annually recurring batches of new varieties those which are most unlike the existing types, provided, of course, they are worthy to be perpetuated. But they can be most surely obtained by raising seedlings from the most unlike types and by the crossing of various types.

In the third place, we need to secure more incidental or minor strains of the most popular and cosmopolitan varieties. The Concord grape, for example, is a most virile and useful type, and minor varieties of it, even if they were still called Concord, might adapt the variety more completely to some particular purpose or locality. In many districts, for example, a Concord a week earlier or a week later than the standard variety might be more useful than a variety wholly new in kind. This class of facts is introduced to show that, while we need more varied types in our native fruits, we also need to increase the usefulness of regnant types by inducing secondary variations in them. There are two means of securing these variations. The surest means is to take cuttings or buds from those particular plants in our plantation which most nearly fit our purposes. In almost every large Concord vineyard, for example, there are some vines which are earlier or later, more or less productive, or otherwise different from the type. In many cases the cuttings will perpetuate these differences. The second means of securing these incidental forms is by crossing between plants of the same variety. The writer is convinced that this type of plant breeding is, in general, quite as useful as that of crossing unlike varieties; and after a wide range of variation has been secured and when men's ideals have become critical through education and business competition it will be the more promising field.

In the fourth place, it should be said that the greatest effort should be made to preserve or intensify those desirable attributes which are characteristic of the wild species. Such attributes are likely to be more virile and permanent than similar ones which originate under domestication, because they have been impressed upon the species for a longer period of time. The intending plant breeder can save himself much time and strength by throwing his own efforts into line with the direction of evolution of the species rather than against it. He can not afford even to be indifferent to the natural capacities of the type. For example, other things being equal, the domesticator will generally find better results in breeding plants for a dry region by selecting those types which naturally grow in such regions. The adapting of the grape to limestone soils can no doubt be more quickly accomplished by endeavoring to breed up acceptable varieties from *Vitis berlandieri*, which thrives in these lands, than by attempting to overcome the pronounced antipathies of the *Vitis labrusca* types to such soils. The first attempt in impressing new fruit species into cultivation should be to secure a type which will thrive in the given region; the production of ameliorated varieties is a secondary and usually a much simpler matter. The first consideration in breeding plums for the dry plains regions, for example, is to secure a type which will endure the climate — the long droughts, the severe winters, and the hot summers. This fundamental desideratum should be looked for in the indigenous plums rather than in the domestic types. One of the most promising lines of effort in the improving of the native fruits is to work with the species which are indigenous to the locality, if they possess coveted features and if they are naturally variable.

All this means, as has been said, that there should be a general improvement all along the line in our native fruits, the same as there should be in any other fruits; and the greatest improvement is needed in those very types which are already most improved. In other words, we need more to augment the amelioration of types already domesticated than to introduce wholly new types, although this latter enterprise is also of the greatest importance. The new types may be expected to come into use as the demand for them arises, and they will come in gradually, and obscurely at first, as the other types have.

The grape, in the estimation of the writer, needs the first and the greatest attention. The types which we grow are still much inferior to the Old World types. Our commercial varieties, like the Concord, Worden, Catawba, Niagara, Norton Virginia, are generalized types, and the market is now overrun with general-purpose grapes. We shall soon be driven into specializations in grapes, as people have in older countries, and special varieties will then be needed. Aside from the further improvement of the domesticated native species, we are now being driven, by the settlement of the South and West, to the improvement of other species, as *Vitis lincecumii, Vitis champini,* and the like.

The second greatest need is in the development of our native plum flora; the third is in the further evolution of the brambles, like the raspberries, blackberries, and dewberries; the fourth in the amalgamation of the Western crab apples with the domestic apples, for the plains and the Northwest. Beyond these four emphatic needs, it is believed there are none which stand out clearly and unmistakably above all others, although there are a score of native fruit types which are crying out for attention. Among them may be mentioned the chestnuts, pecans, gooseberries, currants, cranberries, huckleberries, juneberries, cherries, mulberries, elderberries, and all the tribes of hickory nuts and walnuts.

The stimulus of the improvement will be found in the increasing demands made by a high civilization, and the actual work of improvement will be done by a few patient souls whose love of the work far outruns all desire for applause or pecuniary reward.

Irrigation on the Great Plains, 1896

From Frederick H. Newell, "Irrigation on the Great Plains," U.S. Department of Agriculture, *Yearbook*, 1896, pp. 167–96.

Introduction

The success of agriculture in a distinctly arid region, like the valleys of Utah, where perennial streams flow from snow-capped peaks, is a self-evident proposition. There the climate renders irrigation absolutely essential, and widely distributed, even though small, water supplies make it practicable. No settler thinks for a moment of trying to cultivate the soil until he has provided a means of applying water.

In contrast to these conditions are those surrounding the farmer on the Great Plains, especially upon the western half. Here the climate is far from arid. In certain seasons it may be called humid. The settlers coming from the Mississippi Valley have brought with them the methods of agriculture adapted to a wet country. In some years success is attained by these methods, and wonderful crops encourage the breaking up of increased areas next year. Total loss of crops and bitter disappointment inevitably follow, however, and the unfortunate settlers, if not driven from the country, alternate between short periods of prosperity and long intervals of depression.

The soil of the Great Plains region as a whole is wonderfully rich. The irregular and scanty rainfall has not leached out the natural salts, so valuable to plant life, and yet has been sufficient to bring about a disintegration of the soils to great depths. The sparse herbage, luxuriant at times, is not sufficiently rank to make perceptible drafts upon this supply of plant food, and when at long intervals the rainfall occurs in proper seasons and quantities the yield from the cultivated fields is surprisingly large.

The area of this fertile land is far greater than that of any one of the States of the Union, and while the outlines can not be drawn with exactness, yet, in a general way, it may be said that the extent is from one-eighth to one-sixth of that of the whole United States. Within this vast tract, which embraces portions of Montana, North Dakota, South Dakota, Nebraska, Kansas, Colorado, New Mexico, Oklahoma, and Texas, thousands of families are resident, and there is "room for millions more." The one condition requisite for success is that of obtaining and utilizing a sufficient amount of water to supplement the deficient rainfall.

The Great Plains can be characterized as a region of periodical famine. Paradoxical as it may be, the countries where great famines occur are not those of sterility, but rather those of excessive fertility and of salubrious climate, inviting a dense population. Like other parts of the globe where dearth is apt to occur, the soil of the plains is extremely rich, the climate agreeable, everything physical invites a large population and an increase of animal and vegetable life, save in one essential, and that water. Year after year the water supply may be ample, the forage plants cover the ground with a rank growth, the herds multiply, the settlers extend their fields, when, almost imperceptibly, the climate becomes less humid, the rain clouds forming day after day disappear upon the horizon, and weeks lengthen into months without a drop of moisture. The grasses wither, the herds wander wearily over the plains in search of water holes, the crops wilt and languish, yielding not even the seed for another year. Fall and winter come and go with occasional showers which scarcely seem to wet the earth, and the following spring opens with the soil so dry that it is blown about over the windy plains. Another and perhaps another season of drought occurs, the settlers depart with such of their household furniture as can be drawn away by the enfeebled draft animals, the herds disappear, and this beautiful land, once so fruitful, is now dry and brown, given over to the prairie wolf. Then comes a season of ample rains. The prairie grasses, dormant through several seasons, spring into life, and with these the hopes of new pioneers. Then recurs the flood of immigration, to be continued until the next long drought. This alternation of feast and famine is in Europe and the East as old as history and bids fair to be repeated upon our Great Plains unless American ingenuity, patience, and skill shall devise means of successful irrigation.

The first question that the farmer on the Great Plains asks when confronted with the problem of irrigation is, "Where can I get the water?" Sometimes the reply is obvious. There is a perennial stream which can be reached. But in a great majority of cases this is the first and greatest difficulty to be overcome. For each locality there are various solutions to the problem. In some cases water can be found underground at moderate depths. For example, in many of the valleys, especially in those of the larger streams, wells reach an abundant supply at depths of from 10 to 20 feet. But the area of the valleys is relatively small as compared to the whole extent of the Great Plains, and on the "uplands," as the broad divides between the rivers are commonly known, water can be had, if at all, only at depths of from 100 to 300 feet, or even more. Here, where the supply is small and must be lifted through considerable heights, the storage of storm waters must be considered. In rare instances it is possible to obtain a supply from deep artesian wells, which flow continuously a stream of fresh water. Unfortunately, the conditions governing the distribution of artesian wells are comparatively restricted, and these can be had only here and there throughout this region. The methods of water supply may, as far as the Great Plains region is concerned, be classified as those by gravity from perennial springs and streams, by pumping from rivers or underground sources, by storage of storm waters, or from artesian wells. Sometimes it is possible for the farmer to choose between two or even more of these ways of obtaining water, but as a rule he is limited to one.

Comparing the Great Plains and the arid region, there are to be noted many contrasted points which modify the practice of irrigation. These arise from the strikingly different forms of each country, its physical character or topography. In the arid regions the arable lands are mainly in the valleys or partly surrounded by mountains from which perennial streams issue with rapid fall. This facilitates the construction of canals built above the level of the fields, furnishing by gravity a relatively large amount of water. On the other hand, on the Great Plains are boundless tracts of fertile soil with no water within sight except at rare intervals after heavy storms. The underground supplies, usually small in amount, are widely distributed and can not be concentrated at any one spot.

The temptation to the settler is to make his farm as wide reaching as the horizon, and to spread his efforts over hundreds of acres. The ever-recurring droughts stimulate him to try and till more land, in the hopes that he may recoup his losses in a fortunate year. He is in a certain sense a gambler, staking everything upon luck, and with the chances against him. With his desperate eagerness to regain in one season what he has lost through many years, it is almost impossible for him to see that his only hope of permanent success lies in limiting his operations to a comparatively few acres, and in cultivating these carefully and safely by using the small amount of water which, with great care and some expense, he may be able to secure. With his large conception he can not content himself with petty details. The stern logic of facts, however, is slowly convincing him that, in spite of the wealth of land, success lies only in attention to little matters. He must go back to the trivial economies of older lands, saving and using with judgment every drop of water which falls upon his field, or which can be brought to the surface from underground. This is the hardest lesson, and one which many men can not learn, preferring to emigrate rather than adopt what seems to them an un-American intensive farming.

Western Kansas

The conditions, upon the Great Plains are epitomized in western Kansas, and therefore a brief discussion of this area may not be out of place. It may be asked, why should further efforts and encouragements be given toward the development of agriculture in such regions? Has the world not heard enough of droughts and crop losses, of famines and suffering, of abandoned farms and worthless Kansas mortgages? Why interpose to prevent the country from going back to its former conditions? It was, and can be, a magnificent grazing land. As a stock range it will contribute to individual and general wealth without great risk of hardships and losses.

In answer to such questions and assertions, it is not enough to point to the hopes of persons desirous of selling out or to the too sanguine expectations of those who, encouraged by occasional success, have persisted in their efforts to make homes. It must be shown that there are substantial foundations for such hopes and expectations; that there actually exist resources worthy of better directed and more prolonged endeavors.

The conditions prevailing in western Kansas are not unique. The rich soil and capricious rains are found over vast areas, embracing, as before stated, portions of at least ten States. Ultimate success or failure in this locality encourages or retards home making in others. The struggles in western Kansas are, therefore, not without interest to the nation as a whole, for if once victory is assured, hundreds of communities will be benefited. Public interest is drawn here because attempts at settlement have been made in greater numbers than elsewhere, experiments have been conducted on a larger scale and in a character more varied, and the difficulties now appear to be more nearly overcome. Thus, it seems proper, as an introduction to general investigations in the subhumid Great Plains region, to give first attention to western Kansas, to mention the results of trials and failures, and to outline what seems to be the road to success.

At least two things have been clearly proved. One of these is that the soil is very rich; the other is that the ordinary methods of farming are not adapted to the climatic conditions, and the farmer must laboriously unlearn much that he has acquired elsewhere. By repeated failures it has been shown that he must adjust his methods to fit more nearly the requirements of nature.

Hilgard has emphasized the fact that the soils of the arid and subhumid regions are, as a rule, as good as, if not better than, the best of those of humid lands. It is incredible that, with these great natural advantages of soil and sunshine, American ingenuity and persistence can not find a way to overcome in some degree the evil results of deficient or capricious rainfall. This is the great problem which the inhabitants of the subhumid plains have before them, and one to which the General Government can properly give attention. Not only is the prosperity of several States concerned, but, even more than this, the United States is the great land owner, still possessing many millions of acres of rich soil which should be put to better use than that of furnishing scanty forage. Such lands "deserve the most earnest attention both of agriculturists and of students of natural economy, for in them lie possibilities for the abundant sustenance and prosperity of the human race that have thus far been almost left out of account. While it is true that irrigation water may not be practically available for the whole of the arid (and subhumid) regions of the globe, so much remains to be done in the study of the most economical use of the water, of appropriate crops, and of methods of culture that even an approximate estimate of actual possibilities in this direction can not yet be made. At all events it is of the highest interest to study the problem of the reclamation of this intrinsically rich land in all its phases."

Irrigation Essential

The settlements upon the Great Plains have proceeded gradually westward from the well-watered Mississippi and lower Missouri, advancing step by step up the gradual slope which extends toward the base of the Rocky Mountains, and pushing by slow degrees into the well-defined subhumid regions. The farmers have been tempted on and on by the fertility of the soil, which, instead of decreasing in richness, has been found to be equal, if not superior, to the lands washed by frequent rains. During the years or series of years in which the rainfall was more abundant or better distributed through the growing season the agricultural areas have leaped forward from county to county toward the west, and the farmers have deluded themselves with the belief that with the breaking of the prairie sod, the building of railroads, and the advent of civilization the climate was becoming more favorable to their operations.

Succeeding years, with a rainfall at or below the average, have beaten back or driven out many of the financially weaker or more easily discouraged of the settlers, and thus the tide of emigration has ebbed and flowed, each succeeding wave in general less vigorous than the first. Such vicissitudes, however, can not lead to prosperity and contentment. It is evident that they can not continue indefinitely, and that there must be a better adjustment of man to his environment, or he will be the loser in the end. Temporary or trivial expedients will not suffice. The heavens have been bombarded in vain, both with supplication and with dynamite. Somewhat slowly and unwillingly public attention has at last settled itself upon irrigation, and in this seems to be the salvation of the country. The water supply at best is small and its source and availability have by no means been self-evident. There are a few perennial streams within this vast area, but these attain notable size mainly at points where the conditions are such that the water can not be diverted and used economically or efficiently.

The widely distributed and yet relatively small supplies of water to which reference has been made are in the pervious, unconsolidated rocks or sands underlying portions of the Great Plains, especially along and in the vicinity of the broader river valleys. The problem of how best to bring these waters to the surface and utilize them is that which peculiarly distinguishes the Great Plains. The solution is best seen in western Kansas, for here hundreds of individual efforts have been made and success has been attained to a larger degree than elsewhere.

Almost anyone can irrigate with plenty of water. In other words, where a considerable volume is to be had at any one point within the arid or subhumid region a very moderate exercise of skill and judgment will enable the farmer to produce a crop of some kind. He can hardly fail to raise something, even though he drowns out a part of his field and leaves another part too dry. There must generally be some portion upon which the crops are remunerative. On the other hand, where, as in western Kansas, the water must be pumped from underground or stored in reservoirs, every gallon means a certain outlay. The quantity is usually limited, and a high degree of skill and judgment is required in order to utilize this water to the largest possible degree and produce a crop whose value shall repay not only the labor of cultivating, but also the cost of the water applied. In the case of the little ditches constructed from the mountain torrents in the arid region, a comparatively small outlay of labor was required in order to bring a considerable stream to the agricultural land. Where the water is to be pumped, however, not only labor, but some capital, must be invested and continued to be employed until the crop is ready for the harvest. Since this first investment is usually large, and severely taxes the ability of the individual farmer, it is of vast importance to him that every step be taken in the right direction and that he make no mistakes.

In the subhumid region, especially where crop failures year after year have discouraged the farmers and have brought them almost to penury, the few hundred dollars required to start a small irrigating plant is a very great sum, and if not rightly expended may mean absolute ruin and loss of homestead. It is therefore especially important that in such undertakings no mistake be made. In the valleys of the arid region, if a farmer has not properly located his ditch, it may be possible for him to alter and improve it by his own labor or by assistance from his neighbors, but in the case of machinery or appliances used for raising water changes or alterations are far more difficult, if not impossible.

The attitude of the people of the subhumid region toward irrigation has been peculiar. They at first deemed it absurd, injurious, or impossible, and the man who held that irrigation was the proper and best thing was denounced as a public enemy and as casting discredit upon the region by advertising its disadvantages to the world. If he persisted in his unpatriotic course, it was considered enough to ask the question, "Where is the water to be had; even if irrigation is of value, where are the rivers from which to derive the supply?" If for answer attention was drawn to the ground waters and to the possible storage, the idea was regarded as laughable, and the advocate of irrigation was again asked, "How can you irrigate a section or even a quarter section by such trivial means?" If in reply the scoffers were told that it was not proposed to irrigate large areas, but to confine the attention of the farmer to 40 acres or even to 10 acres, contempt for such methods could scarcely find expression in words.

The idea that any man on the boundless plains would concentrate his energies on 10 acres has seemed ridiculous. Yet this is what stern necessity is compelling the farmer to do, and is making him unlearn his old habits and methods, relentlessly forcing him to abandon the cultivation of great areas, turning them over perhaps to grazing, and giving his main attention to the few acres almost within a stone's throw of his door. As a rule, the most successful men are those who have learned this lesson well, who have tried to do a little less than they considered could be done well, and who have practiced an untiring perseverance in adopting better methods in applying water and in cultivating the soil.

Within the past few years, or even months, public sentiment has undergone so great a change, from ridicule and skepticism to confidence in irrigation, that there is danger of rushing to the other extreme. It is now generally recognized that irrigation is practicable at many localities, and with the enthusiasm that characterizes new movements, its sanguine advocates make excessive claims. They attempt to show that a great part, if not all, of the country can be irrigated, that water can be had almost anywhere, and that with a suitable irrigation plant the farmer is insured against all future loss and discouragement. The actual conditions are far otherwise. It is hardly probable that more than a small percentage of all the fertile land can be profitably irrigated, and experience has shown that, while irrigation is feasible and profitable, it is so only when something besides a supply of water is obtained. Successful irrigation means high-grade farming. It means the employment of intelligence and persistent labor. Unlike wheat farming, for instance, the work of the year is not concentrated into a few weeks or months, but for good results must be continued in one form or another almost every day. It is not sufficient to raise a single crop or a single kind, but if practicable two crops at least every year should be raised, one immediately following the other, and the diversity should be such that the water can be used to good advantage at short intervals. In other words, successful irrigation means diversified farming and the highest type of agriculture.

In order to start right, to employ the best device for getting the water, to use the water most efficiently and economically, to cover the largest area of ground thoroughly, to raise the best crops of fruits, and to carry on all the higher specialized methods which make irrigation farming profitable, it is necessary to have a larger knowledge than is possessed by the ordinary farmer and to keep abreast of the changes or improvements constantly being made. For this reason there is a wider field of study required and more opportunity for investigation both by the individual, the agricultural experiment station, and the experts of the General Government. In many respects our knowledge of irrigation has as yet advanced little beyond that of the early Egyptians. The process has been one of imitation or of individual tests through repeated failures.

Sources of Water

The first and greatest problem is where and how to obtain sufficient water. Considering irrigated regions as a whole, the source of water, outweighing in importance all the rest, is that of the surface streams — the creeks and rivers. Secondary to this are the waters of intermittent streams or of occasional storms held by systems of reservoirs or huge tanks; and, third, the waters pumped or lifted from beneath the surface. A fourth class might be added, that of flowing wells, but these are so unusual in character and occurrence that they can hardly be considered as important factors in this method of agriculture. In western Kansas, and in the Great Plains region in general, stream waters, as has been pointed out, are exceptional in occurrence, and can play but a relatively small part, while on the other hand the widespread distribution of water-bearing rocks renders wells of importance.

Streams

The typical river of the Great Plains, and one of the first as regards the quantity of flood waters, is the Arkansas. This rises in the mountains of Colorado, flows in a course a little south of east into Kansas, continuing this direction for about 140 miles, then turns toward the northeast, and, describing a huge loop or bend, finally passes out of Kansas toward the south into Indian Territory. It drains, in round numbers, 24,600 square miles of Colorado before reaching Kansas. Of this area, that above Pueblo, 4,600 square miles, may be considered as mountainous, yielding a large perennial supply of water. The remaining 20,000 square miles are mainly plateaus and undulating plains from which an insignificant amount of water flows, except in time of flood, when vast volumes are poured into the stream, swelling it in a few hours to a raging torrent. The average discharge of the river at Canyon City, 70 miles above Pueblo, is a little over 800 second-feet, and at Pueblo 1,200 second-feet. The greater part of this water is used for irrigation, and during the spring and summer little, if any, passes into Kansas except that from a local storm or a cloud-burst. At one such time a quantity of water amounting to 30,000 second-feet or more was discharged for several hours, washing out bridges and causing general destruction. This amount was doubtless increased to 40,000 or 50,000 second-feet by the time it reached the Kansas line.

Along the Arkansas River in Colorado almost innumerable ditches and canals are taking out water, and in particular below Pueblo are the large irrigating systems under which is a considerable part of the agricultural population of the State. Many of the larger canal companies have constructed tight dams across the river capable of diverting the entire low-water flow of the stream. These are placed at intervals of from 10 to 20 miles or more. In the case of those possessing priority of rights, the entire discharge of the stream is taken and the bed of the river is left dry below the dam. In the case of others a certain portion of the water is allowed to pass by the dam under the direction of the water commissioners. Even though all the water is taken at one point, there is usually a sufficient amount of seepage to supply a small stream in the river bed, and this, increasing in the course of a few miles, furnishes, even in times of extreme drought, a small amount to the canal heading next below.

The aggregate capacity of the canals constructed or partially complete is far in excess of the ordinary flow of the river, and even by the employment of all the seepage water there must apparently be less than the amount needed for the cultivation of all the arable lands under the extensive systems. Reservoirs are already being built to hold a part of the flood waters of the river, and it is highly probable that larger undertakings must be shortly inaugurated if a permanent supply is to be assured for canals now under construction.

Owing to the large and increasing utilization of the water of the Arkansas River in Colorado, the bed of the river is dry, through the greater part of the year, at points above the Kansas line, and there are comparatively few weeks during which a notable stream is flowing. As a whole, the time during which water is flowing in the river must decrease as irrigation above increases, and there will ultimately be a condition of things in which only the excess water of floods will pass down. Thus little dependence can be placed on the surface waters of the Arkansas River, and if irrigation in Kansas were dependent upon these it would be doomed.

The same general statement applies to the Platte River and to other lesser streams coming from high mountains and crossing the plains. The head waters of the Platte interlace with those of the Arkansas, and the minor tributaries flowing eastward and northward are to a large extent diverted into canals within the foothill region. The South Platte is thus deprived, for the greater part of the year, of all water long before reaching the Nebraska line. The North Platte, on the other hand, flows through a less populous region, and its waters have not been taken out in Wyoming to an extent to appreciably affect the annual flow. With the completion of many projects now on foot it appears probable that the large irrigation canals in the lower part of the river may at times be deprived of the full flow of the stream.

Besides the mountain rivers there are a considerable number of streams whose sources are well within the Great Plains. These derive their supply from springs fed by the rain water caught in thick deposits of sands and gravels. The waters thus obtained percolate slowly toward the lowest points, and are discharged in springs often perennial in character. These streams, however, have usually a gentle grade and can not readily be diverted into canals. Their waters, as a rule, are available only through some method of pumping.

Storm Waters

The localities which can be supplied by ditches from perennial streams are, as may be inferred from what has been said, relatively small when compared with the total extent of fertile land. Even along water courses which on a map appear to be of considerable size a careful survey shows that there are not many points where a reliable supply can be had. On the other hand, it is evident that from the size of the catchment basin and the known rainfall there must be a considerable volume of flood waters. The question at once arises whether a portion at least of this excess can be held for a few weeks or months until the time of need. It is well known that in other countries irrigation is successfully practiced by means of water storage, and a large agricultural population prospers in a dry country where no living streams are to be found. Fortunately there are a number of examples of the utilization of this source of supply. Instances can be cited showing its feasibility and also indicating the disadvantages attending it and the obstacles to be overcome.

The reports showing the quantity of water flowing in the streams from time to time give the gross amount, both in flood and in time of drought. These figures, however, may be somewhat deceptive, especially those which give the maximum discharge of the stream; and estimates of reclamation of arid lands should not be based wholly upon the maximum quantities, for the reason that it is obviously impracticable in many instances to store this great quantity of water. Storage projects at best are expensive, and to repay their cost and be of benefit to the farmers each reservoir should receive yearly a sufficient quantity of water to nearly fill it.

There are few localities where it will be possible to hold water from one year to another on account of the expense involved, and by far the greater number of projects must depend upon a constant supply of water. To do this it will be impracticable to construct reservoirs of such size as to hold the greatest flood, and as a general rule it may be said that engineers will favor a reservoir whose content is somewhat less than the average storm discharge of the stream. To illustrate: If the stream from which the water is to be taken discharges in one year three times as much as in the year preceding or the year succeeding, it will rarely be profitable to construct a reservoir of size sufficient to hold more than the smaller flood mentioned; for if built to hold the highest flood it may be only partially filled for several years in succession. Theoretically, it would be better to hold the highest flood and keep the water over from year to year; but practically there are so few localities where this can be done that these places may be regarded as exceptional.

The construction of reservoir dams of any considerable size should not be undertaken without consulting an experienced engineer. In fact, there should be a provision in the law of every State requiring supervision of such construction by competent State engineers. A dam is in one respect a defiance of nature, and all its forces conspire to pull the structure away sooner or later. It must therefore be carefully watched and afforded every protection, for a slight leak or the overtopping of the dam by an excessive flood may mean destruction of property, and even of human life.

The possible dangers from dams should not, however, act as a deterrent, any more than the occasional accidents upon railroads should be considered as sufficient argument for their restriction. With proper care storage reservoirs can be made, as shown by the history of India, to last for many centuries, benefiting great communities. By using proper precautions a farmer may build upon his own land earth, rock, or timber dams which, if properly kept in repair, will be of incalculable benefit.

Wells

The most important source of supply for the Great Plains region is, and probably always will be, wells. There is reason to believe that considerable areas will be irrigated by gravity systems from the rivers and from storage reservoirs, large and small, built to catch the intermittent streams and flood waters; but taking all things into consideration, it will be conceded that ordinarily wells can be had over a larger area and possess such advantages that they must come first in the development of agriculture by irrigation on the plains.

Irrigation by water from a well, if the latter yields a good supply at moderate depth from the surface, possesses certain advantages over that from a gravity supply, in spite of the usually greater annual cost of procuring the water. The wells and the source of water are, as a rule, under the individual control of the irrigator. It is not necessary for him to combine with other men and to invest large capital in a complicated undertaking before he can receive any benefit. It is often possible for the farmer to dig or drill the well himself, and he can purchase, sometimes on credit if necessary, the machinery, windmill, or pump for bringing the water to the surface. Being under his own supervision, he can apply the water whenever in his judgment the plants need it, not being compelled to wait his turn or to take water at inconvenient times, whether day or night, according as it may be allotted under a large irrigating system.

Considering any one locality or farm, the question whether the water supply can be obtained is one for determination on the spot. It is often possible for the farmer to judge from the experience of his neighbors whether he can sink a well successfully at one point or another. If, however, his place differs widely in general location or in other conditions, so that he can not safely use the experience of others, then he must either trust to chance and dig his well at a point where it will be most convenient or, if practicable, consult some geologist or other person who has made a careful scientific study of such matters. In determining upon the location for a well it is generally useless to consult the professional well driller, unless he has put down other wells within a few miles and has considerable local knowledge. It seems hardly worth stating in this connection that money expended in the employment of the so-called "water witches," or men who use the divining rod, is worse than futile, as it merely encourages fraud.

It is often assumed that because the plains have such a uniform outward appearance their underground structure must necessarily be as featureless. But, on the contrary, there is a considerable diversity in the order of arrangement beneath the surface. In some places there are thick beds of sand and gravel filled with water, from which such quantities can be obtained as to lead to the popular statement that the wells are inexhaustible. On the other hand, large tracts have, at a short distance beneath the surface, impervious beds of shale of a thickness of a thousand feet or more, containing little water, and this usually brackish or strongly saline, so that wells sunk into it are valueless. All these conditions of underground structure are the results of different conditions prevailing in past geologic ages and are capable of exact definition and mapping by the skilled geologist, so that when once the area has been thoroughly studied there should be no uncertainty to perplex the individual farmer as to whether it will pay him to invest money in wells, or whether by going deeper he could improve his supply.

It has sometimes been asserted that water from wells is not as valuable for purposes of irrigation as that from rivers, because the latter, especially during spring floods, bring a considerable amount of silt, which, during irrigation, is carried out on the land and being deposited serves as a fertilizer. The importance of this effect is in the popular mind often greatly exaggerated. The greater part of the silt brought

into a canal is deposited in the main ditches and laterals, filling these, and necessitating a considerable annual outlay to keep them clean. The amount of material
which actually is deposited upon the cultivated land is in general insignificant, not
being equal to a few loads of ordinary fertilizer. This has been pointed out by Prof.
E. W. Hilgard.[1] He shows that even in the case of the Nile the mud deposited
amounts to only about 5 tons per acre, and that similar lands irrigated by clear water
are just as productive. It is not so much the fertilizing character of the sediment as it
is the scarcity of rainfall and the consequent freedom of the soil from leaching, as
well as the beneficial effects of the warm, dry climate, which produce the great
crops.

Well waters possess a more decided advantage in their freedom from noxious seeds. In the waters of the ordinary ditches, deriving their supply from a stream
flowing through several valleys, there is usually to be found a great variety of seeds
blown in by the wind or picked up during floods. These are carried along into the
laterals and out over the fields, causing plants to start, some of which are exceedingly difficult to eradicate. This is especially true if a new crop of weeds is allowed
to gain headway after each irrigation.

Methods of Obtaining Water

After the farmer has settled upon the source from which water for irrigation
can be obtained, the next problem which he encounters is that of bringing the water
to the point where it is to be used. If the source of supply is at a higher level than the
land to be irrigated, this is usually a simple matter. This may be considered the rule
throughout the greater part of the irrigated area of the arid region, as the water is
brought by gravity through canals and ditches from streams diverted at some point
higher than the lands to be irrigated and carried often by circuitous routes to secure a
gentle grade. If water is stored in a small reservoir or tank on the farm, it can of
course be conducted either through earthen ditches or by pipes or flumes, according
to the undulations of the ground. In the Great Plains region, however, the greater
part of the water for irrigation is to be found either underground or in ponds or
streams whose banks are of such character that, as before stated, gravity ditches are
out of the question, or where the lands to be irrigated lie above the usual water level.
The great problem, then, of obtaining water is that of pumping it at a cost so low
that this operation can be performed with profit.

The question of pumping water merely is not a difficult one. Devices for
lifting water are older than written history, and various forms of pumps are used on
almost every farm in the country, every citizen being familiar with a number of
ways of lifting water. But the question is not simply to lift the water. It must be
lifted in large quantities, and, more than this, the cost of so doing must be extremely
low — so low that it shall bear but a small proportion to the value of the crops
produced. This last requirement is really the obstacle to the widespread development of agriculture by irrigation upon the Great Plains. There the distances are great
from farm to town and from the producer to the consumer, and the value of the
crops are correspondingly low; so low, in fact, that undoubtedly many products are
not worth what they have cost if the farmer's labor were considered as being paid

[1] Popular Science Monthly, March, 1896, p. 605.

for at moderate wages. To pump water, therefore, to increase the yield of wheat or corn which must compete with that raised in humid regions is obviously out of the question.

The cost of pumping the great quantities of water used in irrigation prohibits the raising of water to heights of much over 50 feet. There are, of course, exceptions to any such rule, especially in the case of windmills and of hydraulic engines or water wheels. Claims are made that irrigation water has been pumped or lifted to heights of 200 feet, but such instances are rare and not well authenticated.

Pumps

In considering what kind of a pump to use, the farmer must of necessity determine at the same time upon the motive power, for, while some pumps are independent and may be driven by almost any kind of an engine or even by animal power, others are inseparably connected with the actuating mechanism or are designed for some particular purpose, as, for example, a windmill.

The simplest device for raising water is the open bucket. This when suspended from a well-sweep or hung in various ways has been used from long before the dawn of civilization down to the present day. In India and Egypt, where human labor is exceedingly cheap, considerable areas are irrigated by water lifted by men using buckets or woven baskets. Such methods are of course inapplicable to this country, but by having the buckets driven by machinery there results one of the simplest and most efficient devices. This idea occurred to primitive man, and there are to be found throughout the Old World water wheels carrying buckets on their rims lifting water into elevated troughs, or buckets tied together in an endless chain by ropes and lifted by animal power. This latter is known as the Persian wheel, perhaps one of the most widely employed mechanisms for irrigation, of great antiquity, and yet reinvented in almost every rural community. These wheels, or bucket pumps, as now used for irrigation, consist of an endless chain of small buckets extending down into the well and up vertically to the height to which water must be delivered to flow out to the land. This height is in practice limited to about 20 feet. The buckets descending empty and ascending filled are discharged at the highest point. The machinery for raising them may be driven either by horse power, as in the case of a thrashing machine, or by a steam engine. Windmills have been used but little for this purpose, owing to their varying speed. In this kind of pump the water is lifted with the minimum amount of friction and useless expenditure of energy.

A modification of the common Persian wheel used to a small extent for irrigation is the form in which the buckets, instead of moving freely upward, pass through a pipe or a long rectangular box in which they fit quite closely. Instead of being of bucket form, they may be flat, and are then known as "flights." These, ascending with considerable rapidity, carry ahead of them a body of water of which only a small proportion has time to run backward in the course of its progress from the bottom to the top.

By far the greater number and variety of ordinary pumps may be classed under the head of piston or plunger. These are almost infinite in number and are the kind ordinarily employed with a windmill. They depend for their action upon two or more valves and upon the lifting or displacing of the water by the alternate forward and back, or in and out, movement of the piston rod. In general principles these pumps are too well known to require description. In size they range from the ordinary pitcher pump, to be found at almost every country house, up to the massive water cylinders of the compound condensing engine built for great cities or for draining extensive mines. Their cost is as varied as their size and intricacy, and can best be ascertained by each individual consulting for himself the nearest dealer or the catalogues of well-known manufacturers. For irrigation such pumps are driven by windmills, by steam engines, or by gasoline or hot-air motors, and in some instances, notably in the vicinity of Grand Junction, Colo., and on the Yakima River in Washington, by water wheels. Although widely known and generally used for pumping, yet for purposes of irrigation they are apparently being supplanted to a considerable extent by valveless pumps, such as the Persian-wheel type or the centrifugal form.

The centrifugal pumps possess an advantage not only in being valveless, and therefore less liable to injury by sand and floating obstacles, but also in the fact that they run continuously in one direction and do not have the reciprocating motion of the various forms of plunger. The principle of their action is that of a rapidly whirling body throwing objects from its surface. Blades of suitably proportioned fans are caused to revolve rapidly in the water, and the masses thrown away are confined in a box or pipe in such manner as to be forced upward or outward, their place being supplied by succeeding quantities. These pumps are designed not only for purposes of lifting water, but even for transporting mud, sand, and gravel, and therefore can not be seriously injured by the muddy water often used for irrigation. As a rule, they are driven by steam power, as their efficiency depends upon the rapidity of motion. Some forms of centrifugal pump, however, have been designed for use with horse power and even for windmills.

Closely related to the centrifugal pumps are various forms of rotary water engines, in which the moving parts, instead of traversing forward and backward the length of the cylinder, revolve around in it or in several portions of cylinders lying side by side. These also depend for efficiency upon rapid motion, and are so constructed that ordinary muddy water does not injure them.

Besides the types above described there are a number of hydraulic engines, such as rams or modified siphons, which depend for their efficiency upon the momentum of a column of water suddenly brought to rest. The ramming force of this large column sends forward a small part of the total amount to a higher elevation than that of the source of the main supply. These devices are useful wherever they can be installed, but they only deliver from one-seventh to one-tenth or less of the water which falls from a higher to a lower elevation, and they have therefore a limited use.

There are also offered to the irrigators a few pumps of low lifting power whose action is due to the condensing of steam and the consequent inrush of water to fill the vacuum created. These pumps, though extremely simple in principle, are often complicated in construction, and have in many instances failed to operate properly when not under the direct charge of a skilled mechanic.

In placing any form of pump in a well, care must be taken that the water flows freely toward it. For this reason it is desirable that wells from which considerable quantities of water are pumped shall be of sufficient size and shape to enable observation to be made of the behavior of the pump and of the level of the water surface. In many cases irrigators, misled by the common use of the term "underflow," have assumed that the water underground must flow rapidly to their wells and have sunk pipes into the water-bearing strata, connecting pumps to these as though they led directly to an open body of water. Powerful windmills have been provided and strong pumps attached in utter ignorance of the fact that the water can percolate but slowly through the ordinary sands and gravels. As a result, disappointment and loss of investment have ensued, and the farmer, instead of digging out a suitable well, has condemned the pumping machinery as defective. If an open pit had been provided in the first instance, he would at least have seen where the source of trouble lay and probably have been able to secure a larger supply of water by sinking numerous connecting wells.

Windmills

Of the devices for operating pumps for irrigation upon the Great Plains, windmills are undoubtedly the most important, and they will always remain so from the fact that the winds blow almost incessantly over this vast country. The power of the wind in the aggregate is something that can not be comprehended, and the windmills at best utilize only a small fraction of the force available in an infinitely small part of the moving air. As far as the total power is concerned, it is impossible to build machines too big, but mechanical skill soon reaches a limit. Practical application stops far short of the theoretical possibilities. A high degree of efficiency is not as essential as in the case of steam and other motors, because of the fact that there is power in excess and costing nothing. In the ordinary steam engines, however, fuel is the great item of expense, and the amount used must be cut down even at considerable outlay in first cost of machinery.

The forms of windmill are so diverse that a volume would be required to describe them, but for the purpose of raising water for irrigation the available types are comparatively restricted. There are, however, a considerable number of windmills on the market, many of which are being used successfully for raising water for agricultural purposes. It is, of course, impossible to recommend specifically any of these, but the farmer intending to introduce irrigation should ascertain what kind of windmills, if any, are used in his locality or county, and endeavor to make use of the experience of others. If this can not be done, negotiations should be entered into with reputable firms who have been handling windmills for a number of years and whose business standing is such that they can not afford to sell or erect an inefficient machine. By taking these precautions the farmer will be reasonably sure of obtaining a good mill.

All things considered, the simpler the mechanism of a windmill the better. For use upon the Great Plains a complete metal construction is preferable to wood. One warning should be given, however, that extreme lightness and cheapness of construction should be looked upon with suspicion. There are a considerable number of mills on the market whose first cost is low, but whose expense for maintenance and repairs is extremely great.

The cost of a good windmill erected in place and attached to an efficient pump will of course be dependent not only upon the kind of machinery, but also upon the location of the pumping plant, the cost of freightage and handling being a relatively important item. In round numbers it may be said, however, that upon the Great Plains, at moderate distances from a railroad, a windmill with wheel 8 feet in diameter and suitable pump placed at a depth, say, of from 20 to 40 feet from the surface can be had complete for from $70 to $125, a 12-foot mill will cost from $100 to $200, and a 16-foot mill from $175 to $300. The cost of the individual items can best be ascertained from dealers' catalogues, as these fluctuate with the changes and improvements introduced. It is, as a rule, wiser in procuring an irrigating plant of this character to purchase a moderate-sized or small wheel at first, this being properly proportioned to the size of the pump and the amount of water to be had. If the farmer is successful with this smaller machinery, he can readily supplement it by other windmills at a later time, and by giving careful attention to the details of a small mill and limited acreage he will have greater chances of success.

Attention to details is, in fact, the keynote to good fortune, not only with the windmills and other machinery, but in the practice of irrigation itself. The windmill is a piece of machinery which, with moderate care and the exercise of common sense in keeping it oiled and properly adjusted, will last for many years. But no matter how simple or how strong, it can not be expected to run month after month without care. It has sometimes been assumed that irrigation is the lazy man's way of farming, and that all there is to be done is to procure a supply of water and let it flow upon the ground. It is through this mistaken idea that so many failures have been made upon the Great Plains. It does not follow that where the rainfall is slightly deficient all that has to be done is merely to supply this shortage. Far more than this is essential. Not only must all the devices for getting the water to the ground be kept in constant order, but the soil itself must be given unremitting attention in cultivation after each watering.

As a general rule, it may be said that the fast-running windmills with backgearing are most successful. In these the pump rod is not connected directly with the shaft of the mill, making a stroke for every turn of the wheel, but a gearing is interposed, with the result that usually two or more revolutions of the wheel are required in each stroke of the pump. This reduces the resistance to the turning of the wheel, allows it to run in a lower wind, and thus results in the pump being operated on an average for a greater number of hours per day. If a plunger pump is used, it is desirable to have one with a relatively long stroke, so geared that in moderately high winds the motion will not be so rapid as to cause the machinery to pound at the beginning and end of each stroke. As ordinarily constructed, a considerable portion of the force of the windmill is employed destructively in a rapid succession of sudden jerks on the pump rod in its alternate up and down motion. For this reason a continuous-running pump, such as a centrifugal, would be more efficient if the driving power were uniform.

Steam and Other Engines

The most obvious means of driving a pump, after the windmill, is the steam engine. Many farmers have already an engine for thrashing purposes or for other work on a farm. It is comparatively a simple matter to use this in driving a suitable pump, and the expense is in many localities so low that it is done with success. Where, however, fuel is expensive, as it is liable to be upon the Great Plains, or where it is necessary to employ a man of some considerable skill to run the engine, the cost may be prohibitory. Theoretically, it would be practicable for a number of farmers having moderate capital to join together in the erection of a pumping plant similar to that constructed for city purposes. Many estimates have been made showing that under certain conditions of cost of fuel and efficiency of engines the first and annual expense for water is less than that from the average of the larger canals throughout the country. Practically, however, this condition has not yet been realized, and so far as can be ascertained there are no steam pumping plants in successful operation upon the Great Plains. A few have been erected, but from one cause or another these have not proved financially successful.

Next to steam come the gas or gasoline and hot-air engines. The makers of these claim that they can be used with great efficiency, and in a number of instances they are reported to be in active operation. Either the first cost or the cost of the gasoline and of repairs must be greater than admitted by the owners or else there are practical difficulties in their operation. The fact seems to be that up to the present time few of these pumping plants have been installed. These engines usually require very little care and attention while in good order.

Storing and Conducting Water

Having determined upon a well or similar source of supply and a method of raising the water to a height sufficient to cause it to flow to the land to be irrigated, the next point to be considered is that of reservoir and ditches. Where storm waters are employed, the location of the reservoir is governed by the slope of the land, and the construction of this, if of considerable size, should be under the supervision of a competent engineer. With the ordinary windmill irrigation it is usually the case that the reservoir can be placed where most convenient. It is therefore desirable to so locate the point of storage that the ditches leading from it will carry the water to all points of the fields to be irrigated rapidly, and yet without such great fall as to wash the earth.

Ponds and Tanks

The necessity of a place for storing water where it is pumped or obtained in small quantities at a time arises from the fact that irrigation is only possible when a sufficient "head" of water is at hand to produce a stream of as great size and velocity as can be readily controlled by one man with a hoe or spade. It is impracticable to irrigate directly from the ordinary windmill, because of the fact that the stream of water turned into a ditch may continue for hours or even days without wetting the ditch for a distance of more than 50 to 100 feet from the well. The water soaks into the ground as fast as it is pumped upon it. But if this same amount of water is held in a tank or earthen reservoir of sufficient size, and is allowed to accumulate during several days and nights of continuous pumping, there is then at hand a sufficient volume to make it possible to irrigate even the most porous of soils. The gate of the reservoir, when opened, allows a stream of such size to issue that only a relatively small proportion can soak into the ground on its way to the cultivated lands.

Upon the Great Plains the method in most general use for holding water is that of utilizing small artificial ponds with earthen walls. In a few instances wooden tanks are used, constructed of staves held in place by iron bands, and similar to the water tanks constructed by railroad companies. The size of these latter, however, is limited and their cost relatively great, their disadvantage in this direction more than outweighing the economy effected by reducing the loss from leakage and evaporation.

In locating and constructing a small earthen pond it is necessary to consider not only the convenience of getting water into and out of it, but also the conditions which determine the losses. The greatest of these is through leaks in the sides or seepage through the bottom, and next to this is evaporation. This takes place only from the surface of water, and therefore the waste in this direction can be reduced by making the surface as small as possible relatively to the volume of water held. If two reservoirs are constructed, one 100 feet square and holding water to the depth of 1 foot, the other 50 feet on each side and holding 4 feet of water, the loss by evaporation from the first will be four times as great as from the second, because it exposes four times the surface area. That this loss from evaporation is a matter worthy of consideration may be seen from the fact that in the Great Plains region, with its dry winds and bright sunlight, the loss of water each day during the summer may be from one-quarter to one-half inch in depth, and during windy days may be upward of an inch. If, however, the depth of the reservoir is increased in order to diminish losses by evaporation, there is danger of increasing the pressure to such an extent as to force water out in leaks through the banks or bottom. Greater care must therefore be taken in construction.

In order to prevent loss of water by leaking, it is desirable to select, if practicable, a place where the soil or subsoil is composed of a rather compact clay or of clayey loam. If, however, it is impracticable to find the right kind of soil at the desired elevation, then the reservoir can be built, but greater caution must be exercised. The size must depend upon the amount of water to be had. As a rule, the reservoirs on the Great Plains are from 50 to 100 feet across. In shape they are circular, oblong, square, or rectangular. The circular form offers the advantage of presenting the least amount of surface for a content of a given quantity. The same is true of the square form as compared with the rectangular. Some irrigators, however, consider that either the oblong or rectangular shape is preferable to the circular or square form, because, if constructed with the long diameter or width across the path of the prevailing winds, the waves created are smaller and less destructive to the banks. This is a matter of considerable importance where these are built of extremely fine, friable material.

Having determined upon the location, shape, and size of the reservoir, the first operation is to plow up and strip off the sod and surface soil where the banks are to be placed. All the sods, roots, and litter should be cleared away and the ground plowed, in order to make it possible to bind the new earth thoroughly with the undisturbed subsoil. Earth is then hauled in by scraper or wagon and dumped upon the foundation thus prepared. It should always be brought in small quantities and thoroughly trampled by the horses or pressed down by the wagon wheels before another layer is put in place. If practicable, it is desirable, in building the reservoir walls, to raise the outside edges slightly above the center of the wall and let in, from time to time, sufficient water to thoroughly wet the earth, causing it to settle more compactly.

The width of the foundation will depend upon the height of the wall to be built. It is usually at least three times the latter, so as to allow gentle slopes both on the inside and outside of the reservoir. It is preferable to have slopes of at least 1½ to 1, that is, for a distance measured horizontally on the ground of 1½ feet the rise should only be 1 foot. The top of the reservoir banks should be at least 2 feet wide. If, therefore, the bank is 5 feet high, the slopes on each side will extend 7½ feet. Adding to this the width of the center will make 17 feet in all for the foundation. Earth for building a wall should not as a rule be taken from inside the reservoir, as this serves to lower the bottom and may cause it to leak, or by being below the general level the pond can not be completely drained.

In building the walls one of the first things to consider is the outlet. This should be placed in such a position that the water will be delivered conveniently to the ditches, and its position should be so low that it will completely empty the reservoir. This outlet should be provided with a valve or gate on the inner side, so arranged that it is accessible at all times. It is usual to construct this outlet of boards or plank in the form of a long box of from 8 to 18 inches in width and height. For permanence it might be better to use a metal pipe, but it is probable that the wooden outlet will serve for a sufficient number of years.

Having placed the outlet box or pipe in proper position, great care must be taken in building the wall at this particular place to secure a tight joint. Clay should be carefully tamped around and under the box, and as an additional precaution it is well to provide the box with wings or ribs projecting outward into the earth bank and preventing the percolation of water along the contact plane between earth and the wood or metal. The gate on the inside end of the outlet may be of any one of a great variety of forms, from a simple board placed securely against the end to the expensive metal valve used for city purposes. One of the simplest and most efficient gates in use consists of a broad plank covering the end of the box, which is cut off in such a position as to slope diagonally upward and toward the bank. The place of contact between the end of the box and plank covering it is lined with leather or some similar substance, insuring a tight joint. The plank covering is hinged on the upper side and is extended diagonally upward by a stout bar. When this is grasped and pulled toward the bank, the valve is opened against the pressure of the water, and when the bar is released it is automatically closed.

After the reservoir walls are built they should be protected against the washing of the waves. This can be done by placing heavy sod upon them, or, better, by covering them at the water line with broken rock if this can be had. An efficient form of protection is made by roughly weaving willow twigs into a mat and holding this in place by stone or large sod. In course of time the willow takes root and holds the soil in place. In a small reservoir old pieces of plank thrown upon the water will often suffice, as these drift over to the side exposed to the waves and break their force.

The next step is to render the bottom thoroughly tight by what is known as puddling. If the soil is clayey, it may not be necessary to resort to this, but if composed of a light, sandy material there may be necessity for considerable care and for the exercise of much patience before the reservoir will be made reasonably tight. Puddling is accomplished by letting in an amount of water sufficient to make mud and then driving animals round and round until with their feet they have completely worked up all portions of the bottom, destroying the porosity by trampling fine material into every minute orifice. If there is not a sufficient amount of clayey material to form a muddy mass, then it will be necessary to haul in a few loads of clay. Short straw, litter, and manure can also be used to advantage in a sandy soil. By continuing this process of puddling and adding such materials a reservoir, even on extremely loose soil, can be made reasonably tight.

Ditches and Flumes

From the reservoir, whether constructed on a large scale to hold storm water or of small size to receive the discharge from a pump, there must be provided suitable means of conducting the water to the land. The simplest, cheapest, and most widely used is the open earth ditch built in such a way as to have a gentle, uniform grade sufficiently great for the water to flow with rapidity and yet not to wash the banks. As no natural surface is absolutely uniform, it is necessary, in order to secure this grade, that the ditch wind about, following the contour of the surface. It is desirable, however, on account of economy of expense and of water, that all ditches should be as nearly straight as possible, and to save distance it is sometimes necessary to build up the ditch upon a mound or, if the depression to be crossed is too great, to construct a flume. It would of course be better to use a pipe laid directly from the reservoir to the point where water is to be distributed, but the expense, even of the cheapest forms, is too great to justify their use to any considerable extent for such crops as are raised upon the Great Plains. In California where the citrus and other semitropic fruits are produced, with a value of from $100 to $200 or more per acre, and where water is exceedingly expensive, pipes of wood, earthenware, and wrought and cast iron are largely used.

To lay out a ditch, if a considerable distance is to be traversed, it is desirable to use a surveyor's level and run upon a determinate grade. If this is not practicable and the farmer has not had sufficient experience to judge grades by the eye, a simpler device can be used. This consists of a straightedge or stiff board 16 to 20 feet long, so arranged that a carpenter's level can be attached. If the fall is to be one-fourth or one-half of an inch per rod (about the usual grade), a little pin is fastened to one end of the board projecting downward this distance. At the starting point a small stake is driven into the ground and the end of the straightedge placed upon it. The other end carrying the projecting pin is swung on a level until it strikes the ground, then a small stake is driven down until with the projecting pin of the straightedge upon it the leveling bubble is in the center. The straightedge is then carried forward, the upper end placed upon the second post, and the end with the grade pin on it swung about to determine the new position. After this series of posts or pins has been driven into the ground, the farmer can go over the line, straighten it out, or determine upon the necessity of constructing elevated ditches and flumes.

The ordinary flumes consist simply of open troughs or endless boxes forming a portion of the ditch. They are built of boards or plank held in position and supported by timbers. Joints are usually made tight by pitch and oakum or by similar means. While in many cases flumes are indispensable and save the construction of long lines of earth ditches, they are usually a continual source of annoyance from leaking and require considerable attention to keep them in repair. The points where the flumes join the earth ditches are particularly difficult to maintain. It is necessary that the earth be very carefully tamped and that the flume be provided with wings in such a way as to make the union perfect. The section of the flume is usually rectangular, but it may be of a V shape, and occasionally, as in California, it is semicircular, this latter form requiring least lumber, but necessitating the use of iron bands or brackets.

Applying Water

The methods of applying water differ widely, being dependent upon the character of the climate, crops, and soil, and upon the experience of the irrigator. The principles underlying the practice have never been clearly stated, and with the present knowledge of plant physiology and of soil structure it appears impossible for them to be. The greatest advance of irrigation will probably be along the line of exact information as to the behavior of water in the soils and of the influence of moisture upon plant growth and disease. This knowledge is needed, and although there is a large mass of statements of methods in vogue there has never been a comprehensive discussion of the matter such as leads to the presentation of simple and direct rules. It has been found, for example, that by applying water at one time and withholding it at others certain beneficial or injurious results have been obtained, but why these are so it is not possible to state clearly.

Rules for applying water applicable within the arid region may not be suitable for the Great Plains region or for localities farther east. There is considerable difference in the amount of sunlight received and in the dryness of the air. For this reason it has been found that so-called practical irrigators from Colorado and Utah have not made as great a success on the plains as men who have learned the art from experience on the spot. These farmers must in many instances unlearn the maxims they have acquired and note more carefully certain conditions which before they have neglected.

One of the first questions the farmer asks, after he has determined to try irrigation and has settled upon a source of water supply, is how much water will be needed or how much land can be irrigated with a given amount. This question appears simple, but like many others of its kind it is capable of a great variety of answers. It is a good deal like asking what is the average size of a boy. So much depends upon the surrounding circumstances of soil, climate, character of crop and means of applying water that most, if not all, of these must be known in advance. It is of course possible to take the statements of a great many farmers and, averaging them up, draw general conclusions, but these can not be applied to any special case without the exercise of considerable judgment, and before doing so certain technical terms or definitions of quantities must be clearly in mind.

Duty of Water

The phrase "duty of water" is a term which has been devised to convey the idea as to the relation between the quantity of water and the area which can be irrigated by it. The duty of water may be expressed in three ways: First, by the rate of flow of a stream for a certain number of days necessary for the irrigation of 1 acre; second, by the actual volume of water in gallons, cubic feet, or acre-feet which, if properly applied, will suffice for an acre; or, third, by the total depth of water put at various times upon the surface. This third expression is similar to the second, but takes no account of the extent of the field, as, for example, we may say that a certain piece of ground requires 21 inches, that is, during the irrigating season a depth of water of 21 inches has in the aggregate been applied to the surface, usually in a number of waterings at intervals of several weeks. One of these expressions may be converted into the other conveniently by simple computations based upon the relation of one unit to another. In speaking of inches in depth, these must not be confused with the miner's inch, which is simply a rate of flow independent of the quantity.

The duty of water varies widely and can only be given in the most general terms. As before stated, it depends upon the climate, the amount of rainfall, the variations of temperature, the character of the soil and subsoil, the methods of cultivation, the kind of crops, and perhaps more than all upon the skill of the irrigator. Theoretically, it might be possible to ascertain just how much water a given plant requires under the ordinary range of temperature, and from this deduce the least quantity that can be used, but so many other matters must be considered that estimates of this kind have little more than a theoretical value. A certain quantity of water must be lost on the way from the stream or source of supply to the field, and again in the field before reaching the roots of the plant.

Although the duty of water varies widely in actual practice and is such an uncertain quantity, yet it is convenient to make certain assumptions in order to estimate the possible extension of irrigation from the given source of supply. There is a theoretical limit as to the amount of water required by plants, and it is impossible to successfully produce crops with any smaller quantity, but this limit is so far removed from present practice that it does not seem probable it will ever be reached. Moreover, as different varieties of plants require different amounts of water, it may be possible to introduce kinds which will require a minimum supply and thus enable a larger acreage to be cultivated by employing the given quantity of water.

In the arid region, upon land irrigated for the first time and where water is to be had in abundance, a duty as low as 30 acres to the second-foot has been reported. This quantity of water flowing for, say, sixty days would cover an acre to the depth of about 4 feet. This may be regarded as one extreme. This amount, however, could not be used unless the surface drainage were perfect or the subsoil were largely composed of open gravels or sands, allowing water to escape freely, as it would quickly result in converting the country into a marsh. The excessive water would tend to carry away the rich qualities of the soil and wash it out until little of value remained. In some localities, where the earthy alkaline salts abound, this excessive irrigation or washing is resorted to in order to take away the injurious superabundance of soluble material.

The ordinary duty of water, as measured in the ditches leading to the fields in Utah, Idaho, and parts of Colorado, ranges from 60 to 70 acres to the second-foot. This quantity of water flowing for sixty days is equivalent to a depth of about 1⅔ to 2 feet, and for ninety days to a depth of from 2½ to 3 feet. This is very nearly the minimum duty as fixed by the State law of Wyoming, which requires that no allotment of water shall exceed 1 cubic foot per second for each 70 acres.

The highest duty of water is reached in California, where the quantities are usually given in miner's inches. The ordinary practice is 2 acres to the miner's inch, or 100 acres to the second-foot. From this as a minimum the quantity runs up to 4 or 5 acres to the miner's inch, and in some cases, as in the cultivation of orchards where water is very scarce and expensive, it is reported to be as high as from 8 to 15 acres to the miner's inch, or from 400 to 750 acres per second-foot. This quantity flowing for sixty days would cover the ground to a depth of from 3½ to 2 inches, or for ninety days to from 5⅓ to 3 inches. Where the soil is naturally retentive of moisture and has been once thoroughly saturated, it has been found possible by careful and continuous cultivation to attain success with orchards, vines, and some of the field crops with but one slight watering, or even without any, for a number of years in succession. In such cases the water duty may be given as extremely high. But it is hardly proper to consider such cases in connection with ordinary irrigation.

In the Great Plains region as a whole, where water is derived from underground sources or is held in storage reservoirs, it is necessary to reach a duty of water higher than that commonly found in case of water from large perennial streams, from the fact that the first cost is usually larger, the quantities to be handled are smaller, and the land irrigated is generally in the immediate vicinity of the source of supply. For irrigation during the first year the duty can hardly be estimated, because the thirsty soil is almost insatiable in its demand for water, but after the ground has once been fairly well saturated an application of 20 inches of water in depth for the second year should suffice, and after that less and less, depending upon the amount of rain and the humidity of the air. The question of quantity of water is so closely connected with that of cultivation that no estimate can have any great value beyond giving broad impressions.

One of the most important points for the farmer to have in mind when planning his methods of irrigation is, in any event, to provide a sufficient supply of water. On the Great Plains, especially, and to a less extent throughout the arid region, there is a tendency to underestimate the duty of water and where expenditures are concerned to try to make a small supply go too far. This is not the case with the older irrigation ditches built by farmers from streams of considerable size, for there water is lavishly used and often to the detriment of the crops; but where pumping or storing water is concerned, or where the farmers purchase water rights, the tendency is to go to the other extreme and, relying upon theoretical considerations, try to cultivate land with an entirely inadequate supply. Between these two extremes lies the intermediate ground of success. Too much water will reduce the amount and quality of the crop, while too little will result in waste of energy and in disappointment through utter failure. Great injury has already been wrought to the development of irrigation through the excessive sale of water rights in storage enterprises or canals, where farmers have purchased acreage rights to which an inadequate supply was allotted. The proper development of pumping has also been retarded by overestimates of the capacity of the pumps and underestimates of the amount of water required, so that in actual performance, where ordinary difficulties and accidents were encountered, the pumping plants have been serious disappointments if not actual losses.

The methods of applying water can best be learned by the individual farmer through experience. They are not at all difficult, although in each locality certain details are to be observed, dependent upon the character of the climate, soil, and crops. The methods in common use throughout the West have been so often described and are so well given in an article by L. R. Taft in the Yearbook for 1895 that further discussion is hardly necessary. Emphasis should be given, however, to the fact that the first essential for an economic application of water is that of having the ground properly leveled or graded before cultivation and irrigation are begun. When this has been thoroughly done, the irrigation can be carried on rapidly and efficiently with a small quantity of water and the supply can be evenly distributed, each portion of the field receiving its share.

Cultivation

The whole object of irrigation is to supply a sufficient amount of water at the right time, so that the plants will reach their highest development or produce the finest fruit. This object will, however, be defeated unless irrigation is accompanied by proper cultivation. In fact, if one can be said to have more importance than the other, it is cultivation. This must be carried on usually to a far higher degree of perfection than in the case of nonirrigated crops, from the fact that in the practice of irrigation a considerable expenditure is involved, even at the best, and the largest returns should be realized in order to recompense this outlay. With ample water at hand, many of the conditions affecting crops are under control, and it should be possible by proper care to realize an ideal condition of yield and fruitage.

The farmer who imagines that by procuring suitable irrigating machinery or devices and by pouring water upon the fields he is thereby doing all that is necessary to insure a profitable yield is almost certain to be disappointed. This is only the beginning of his labors, for, except in the case of the forage crops or small grains, the application of water must be followed by thorough tilling, and this should be kept up until the soil is in a perfect condition of mulch. There are to be found all over the plains region farmers who have gone so far as to procure a windmill or other pumping machinery, and who have for a season let the water flow over their fields without care or judgment, drowning out parts of the crops, washing the soil in places, and allowing it to bake in others. These men, as may be expected, denounce irrigation as impossible or useless, not being willing to acknowledge that the fault lies in their own lack of attention to the soil after water has been applied.

In trying irrigation for the first time the farmer should attempt it upon only a small area, from 3 to 5 acres, and put as much labor upon these as he has been accustomed to spend upon many times that number in dry farming. If this is done intelligently, the larger yield will more than compensate for the added exertion. By giving careful attention to the needs of crop over a small area the farmer will soon learn to judge for himself as to when, with his conditions of soil and climate, plants actually require water. It is almost impossible in the present stage of our knowledge to give these definite directions, but it is practicable for the observant man to learn for himself while carrying on the cultivation so essential to success.

It should not be assumed from what has been stated that the benefits of irrigation are felt only in the more arid portions of the Great Plains. Such localities undoubtedly possess a certain advantage in that the sunlight is more intense, but this is a difference of a relatively small degree. On the eastern side of the Great Plains, and in fact over the adjacent prairie regions, irrigation can be and is being introduced with success. Viewed merely as a method of insurance against crop loss, the expense of procuring suitable methods of applying water at the right time can not be regarded otherwise than as a businesslike investment.

Introduction of Domestic Reindeer into Alaska, 1895

From Sheldon Jackson, *Introduction of Domestic Reindeer into Alaska. (Washington, 1896)*, pp. 9–11, 13–18.

DEPARTMENT OF THE INTERIOR,
BUREAU OF EDUCATION, ALASKA DIVISION,

Washington, D.C., December 31, 1895.

SIR:

When in the year 1890 I visited arctic Alaska for the purpose of establishing schools, I found the Eskimo population slowly dying off with starvation. For ages they and their fathers had secured a comfortable living from the products of the sea, principally the whale, the walrus, and the seal. The supplies of the sea had been supplemented by the fish and aquatic birds of their rivers and the caribou or wild reindeer that roamed in large herds over the inland tundra.

The supply of these in years past was abundant and furnished ample food for all the people. But fifty years ago American whalers, having largely exhausted the supply in other waters, found their way into the North Pacific Ocean. Then commenced for that section the slaughter and destruction of whales that went steadily forward at the rate of hundreds and thousands annually, until they were killed off or driven out of the Pacific Ocean. They were then followed into Bering Sea, and the slaughter went on. The whales took refuge among the ice fields of the Arctic Ocean, and thither the whalers followed. In this relentless hunt the remnant have been driven still farther into the inaccessible regions around the North Pole, and are no longer within reach of the natives.

As the great herds of buffalo that once roamed the Western prairies have been exterminated for their pelts, so the whales have been sacrificed for the fat that incased their bodies and the bone that hung in their mouths. With the destruction of the whale one large source of food supply for the natives has been cut off.

Another large supply was derived from the walrus, which once swarmed in great numbers in those northern seas. But commerce wanted more ivory, and the whalers turned their attention to the walrus, destroying thousands annually for the sake of their tusks. Where a few years ago they were so numerous that their bellowings were heard above the roar of the waves and grinding and crashing of the ice fields, last year I cruised for weeks seeing but few. The walrus, as a source of food supply, is already very scarce.

The sea lions, once so common in Bering Sea, are now becoming so few in number that it is with difficulty that the natives procure a sufficient number of skins to cover their boats, and the flesh of the walrus, on account of its rarity, has become a luxury.

In the past the natives, with tireless industry, caught and cured, for use in their long winters, great quantities of fish, but American canneries have already come to some of their streams, and will soon be found on all of them, both carrying the food out of the country and, by their wasteful methods, destroying the future supply. Five million cans of salmon annually shipped away from Alaska — and the business still in its infancy — means starvation to the native races in the near future.

With the advent of improved breech-loading firearms the wild reindeer are both being killed off and frightened away to the remote and more inaccessible regions of the interior, and another source of food supply is diminishing. Thus the support of the people is largely gone, and the process of slow starvation and extermination has commenced along the whole arctic coast of Alaska.

To establish schools among a starving people would be of little service; hence education, civilization, and humanity alike called for relief. The sea could not be restocked with whale as a stream can be restocked with fish. To feed the population at Government expense would pauperize and in the end as certainly destroy them. Some other method had to be devised. This was suggested by the wild nomad tribes on the Siberian side of Bering Straits. They had an unfailing food supply in their large herds of domestic reindeer. Why not introduce the domestic reindeer on the American side and thus provide a new and adequate food supply?

To do this will give the Eskimo as permanent a food supply as the cattle of the Western plains and sheep of New Mexico and Arizona do the inhabitants of those sections. It will do more than preserve life — it will preserve the self-respect of the people and advance them in the scale of civilization. It will change them from hunters to herders. It will also utilize the hundreds of thousands of square miles of moss-covered tundra of arctic and subarctic Alaska and make those now useless and barren wastes conducive to the wealth and prosperity of the United States. . . .

Upon the failure of the Fifty-first Congress to take action, and deprecating the delay of twelve months before another attempt could be made, I issued, with the approval of the Commissioner of Education, an appeal in the Mail and Express of New York City, the Boston Transcript, the Philadelphia Ledger, the Chicago Inter-Ocean, and the Washington Star, as well as in a number of the religious newspapers of the country, for contributions to this object. The response was prompt and generous; $2,146 were received.

As the season had arrived for the usual visit of inspection and supervision of the schools in Alaska, in addition to my regular work for the schools I was authorized to commence the work of introducing domestic reindeer into Alaska. The natives of Siberia who own the reindeer, knowing nothing of the use of money, an assortment of goods for the purpose of barter for the reindeer was procured from the funds so generously contributed by benevolent people.

The honorable Secretary of the Treasury issued instructions to Captain Healy to furnish me every possible facility for the purchase and transportation of reindeer from Siberia to Alaska. The honorable Secretary of State secured from the Russian Government instructions to their officers on the Siberian coast also to render what assistance they could, and on May 25, 1891, I again took passage on the revenue cutter *Bear*, Captain Healy in command, for the coast of Siberia. . . .

However, notwithstanding all difficulties and delays, Captain Healy, with the *Bear*, coasted from 1,200 to 1,500 miles, calling at the various villages and holding conferences with the leading reindeer owners on the Siberian coast. Arrangements were made for the purchase of animals the following season. Then, to answer the question whether reindeer could be purchased and transported alive, I bought 16 head, kept them on shipboard for some three weeks, passing through a gale so severe that the ship had to "lie to," and finally landed them in good condition at Amaknak Island, in the harbor of Unalaska. . . .

On the 2d of May, 1892, I started for my third summer's work on the coast of Siberia and Arctic Alaska in the United States revenue cutter *Bear*, Capt. M. A. Healy, commanding, and, upon the 29th of June following, selected in the northeast corner of Port Clarence (the nearest good harbor to Bering Straits on the American side) a suitable location for the establishment of an industrial school, the principal industry of which is the management and propagation of domestic reindeer. The institution is named the Teller Reindeer Station.

During the summer of 1892 I made five visits to Siberia, purchasing and transporting to Port Clarence 171 head of reindeer. I also superintended the erection of a large building for the officers and residence of the superintendent of the station, Mr. Miner W. Bruce, of Nebraska.

Returning to Washington in the early winter, agitation was at once commenced before Congress, resulting in an appropriation by the Fifty-second Congress, second session (March 3, 1893), of "$6,000, to be expended under the direction of the Secretary of the Interior, for the purpose of introducing and maintaining in the Territory of Alaska reindeer for domestic purposes." The management of this fund was wisely laid upon the Commissioner of Education and was made a part of the school system of Alaska.

During the spring of 1893, 79 fawns were born to the herd at the Teller Reindeer Station, and during the summer 127 deer were purchased in Siberia and added to the Alaska herd. . . .

During April, May, and June, 1894, 186 fawns were born to the herd, of which 41 were lost by being frozen or deserted by their mothers. During the summer I purchased in Siberia 120 head, which were added to the herd.

Siberian herders were employed at the beginning of the enterprise, not because they were considered the best, but because they were near by and were the only ones that could be had at the time. It was realized from the first that if the Alaskan Eskimo were to be taught the breeding and care of the reindeer, it was important that they should have the benefit of the most intelligent instructors and of the best methods that were in use. By universal consent it is admitted that the Lapps of northern Europe, because of their superior intelligence (nearly all of them being able to read and write and some of them being acquainted with several languages), are much superior to the Samoyedes deer men of northern Europe and Asia and the barbarous deer men of northeastern Siberia. Intelligence applied to the raising of reindeer, just as to any other industry, produces the best results.

Therefore, when in 1893 it was ascertained that the herd at Port Clarence had safely passed its first winter (thus assuring its permanence), I at once set about securing herders from Lapland. There being no public funds available to meet the expense of sending an agent to Norway in order to secure skilled Lapp herders, I had recourse again to the private benefactions of friends of the enterprise, and $1,000 was contributed.

Mr. William A. Kjellmann, of Madison, Wis., was selected as superintendent of the Teller Reindeer Station and sent to Lapland for herders. He sailed from New York City February 21, and landed upon his return May 12, 1894, having with him seven men, their wives and children, making sixteen souls in all. This was the first colony of Lapps ever brought to the United States. They reached the Teller Reindeer Station safely on July 29, having traveled over 12,500 miles. Upon reaching the station Mr. Kjellmann took charge, relieving Mr. W. T. Lopp, who desired to return to the mission work at Cape Prince of Wales.

In 1894 the Fifty-third Congress, second session, increased the reindeer appropriation to $7,500, and the same amount was appropriated in the spring of 1895, at the third session of the same Congress. . . .

The experience of the past year has demonstrated the wisdom of procuring Lapps for herders. Their greater intelligence, skill, and gentleness in handling the deer, and the introduction of their improved methods of treatment, have greatly promoted the welfare of the herd. In 1894, 41 fawns out of the 186 born were lost under the supervision of the Siberian herders. This spring under the care of the Lapps but 22 fawns were lost of 298 born at the three stations, and 7 of these were from the 75 born at Cape Prince of Wales, where no Lapp was present, thus reducing the percentage of loss among the calves the past spring from 22 per cent in the previous year to about 6 per cent for the present year. This great saving is due to the greater skill of the Lapps, and would alone pay the extra expense of procuring them as herders. It has also been found that there is a hearty agreement in the work between the Lapps and the Eskimo.

Last fall a commencement was made in the distribution from the central herd at the Teller Station. In August, 1894, 119 head of deer were given to Mr. W. T. Lopp, in charge of the mission of the American Missionary Association at Cape Prince of Wales. This spring the herd was increased by the birth of 75 fawns.

Instructions were left in fall of 1895 to furnish similar herds to the Swedish Evangelical mission at the head of Norton Sound and to the Episcopalians and Roman Catholics on the Yukon River.

The Eskimo have been so little accustomed to assistance from the whites that they have been somewhat skeptical concerning their being permitted to ultimately own the reindeer. As evidence of good faith, in February last a herd of 115 head was entrusted to three or four of the most experienced native apprentices, with an agreement that they were to own the natural increase. This spring during fawning season a Lapp was sent to their assistance, and they lost only 2 fawns out of the 79 born.

The experience of the past four years has demonstrated the fact that the present system of procuring reindeer is too slow, and will take many years to accomplish the purpose of the Government. To expedite matters I would respectfully suggest the propriety of placing, with the consent of the Russian Government, a purchasing station somewhere on the Siberian coast, to remain through the year. If successful such a station ought to gather together 2,000 or 3,000 head and have them ready for transportation during the summer. Another plan, and a more feasible one, will be to contract with responsible parties for the purchasing and delivering of so many head of reindeer annually at certain designated points in Alaska. This latter plan will relieve the office of much anxiety. . . .

Effect Upon Alaska

The stocking of Alaska with reindeer means —

First. The opening up of the vast and almost inaccessible region of northern and central Alaska to white settlers and civilization.

The original purpose in 1890 to introduce reindeer into Alaska was inspired by a desire to provide a new and more permanent food supply for the half-famishing Eskimo.

Since then the discovery of large and valuable gold deposits upon the streams of arctic and subarctic Alaska has made the introduction of reindeer a necessity for the white man as well as the Eskimo. Previous to the discovery of gold there was nothing to attract the white settler to that desolate region, but with the knowledge of valuable gold deposits thousands will there make their homes, and towns and villages are already springing into existence.

But that vast region, with its perpetual frozen subsoil, is without agricultural resources. Groceries, breadstuffs, etc., must be procured from the outside. Steamers upon the Yukon can bring food to the mouths of the gold-bearing streams, but the mines are often many miles up these unnavigable streams. Already great difficulty is experienced in securing sufficient food by dog-train transportation and the packing of the natives. The miners need reindeer transportation.

Again, the development of the mines and the growth of settlements upon streams hundreds of miles apart necessitates some method of speedy travel. A dog team on a long journey will make on an average from 15 to 25 miles a day, and in some sections can not make the trip at all, because they can not carry with them a sufficient supply of food for the dogs, and can procure none in the country through which they travel. To facilitate and render possible frequent and speedy communication between these isolated settlements and growing centers of American civilization, where the ordinary roads of the States have no existence and can not be maintained except at an enormous expense, reindeer teams that require no beaten roads, and that at the close of a day's work can be turned loose to forage for themselves, are essential. The introduction of reindeer into Alaska makes possible the development of the mines and the support of a million miners.

Second. The opening up of a vast commercial industry. Lapland, with 400,000 reindeer, supplies the grocery stores of northern Europe with smoked reindeer hams, 10 cents per pound; smoked tongues, at 10 cents each; dried hides, at $1.25 to $1.75 each; tanned hides, $2 to $3 each, and 23,000 carcasses to the butcher shops, in addition to what is consumed by the Lapps themselves.

Fresh reindeer meat is considered a great delicacy. Russia exports it frozen, in carloads, to Germany. The Norwegian Preserving Company use large quantities of it for canning.

The tanned skins (soft and with a beautiful yellow color) have a ready sale for military pantaloons, gloves, bookbinding, covering of chairs and sofas, bed pillows, etc.

The hair is in great demand for the filling of life-saving apparatus (buoys, etc.), as it possesses a wonderful degree of buoyancy. The best existing glue is made of reindeer horns.

On the same basis Alaska, with its capacity for 9,200,000 head of reindeer, can supply the markets of America with 500,000 carcasses of venison annually, together with tons of delicious hams and tongues, and the finest of leather.

Surely the creation of an industry worth from $83,000,000 to $100,000,000, where none now exists, is worth the attention of the American people.

Third. The perpetuation, multiplication, and civilization of the Eskimos of that region. The Eskimos are a hardy and docile race. Their children learn readily in the schools, and there is no reason why they should not be made an important factor in the development of that land. The density of population in any section being largely dependent upon the quantity of the food supply, the increase of food supply will naturally increase the number of hardy Eskimo. . . .

REINDEER FUND, 1894–95.

Received from Congress		$7,500.00
Disbursements:		
Supplies and general expenses of station, Port Clarence	$3,811.83	
Trade goods used in purchasing deer	1,767.26	
Extra coal used by the *Bear* in transporting deer	1,081.50	
Maps used in report	150.00	
Salaries of employees at station	683.80	
Total		7,494.39
Balance		5.61

I desire to acknowledge my indebtedness to Mr. John P. Haines, president of the American Society for the Prevention of Cruelty to Animals, for illustrations of driving and loading reindeer, and to Messrs. William Hamilton, Tappan Adney, John M. Justice, Francis Barnum, Winter & Pond, and to the Woman's American Baptist Home Missionary Society for photographs.

Thanking you for your deep interest and hearty cooperation in the work, I remain, with great respect,

Your Obedient Servant,
Sheldon Jackson,
United States General Agent of Education in Alaska.

Hon. W. T. Harris, LL. D.,
Commissioner of Education, Washington, D.C.

People's Party Platform, 1896.

From Arthur M. Schlesinger, Jr., Fred L. Israel, and William P. Hansen, eds., *History of American Presidential Elections* (New York, 1971), II., pp. 840–44.

The People's Party, assembled in National Convention, reaffirms its allegiance to the principles declared by the founders of the Republic, and also to the fundamental principles of just government as enunciated in the platform of the party in 1892.

We recognize that through the connivance of the present and preceding Administrations the country has reached a crisis in its National life, as predicted in our declaration four years ago, and that prompt and patriotic action is the supreme duty of the hour.

We realize that, while we have political independence, our financial and industrial independence is yet to be attained by restoring to our country the Constitutional control and exercise of the functions necessary to a people's government, which functions have been basely surrendered by our public servants to corporate monopolies. The influence of European moneychangers has been more potent in shaping legislation than the voice of the American people. Executive power and patronage have been used to corrupt our legislatures and defeat the will of the people, and plutocracy has thereby been enthroned upon the ruins of democracy. To restore the Government intended by the fathers, and for the welfare and prosperity of this and future generations, we demand the establishment of an economic and financial system which shall make us masters of our own affairs and independent of European control, by the adoption of the following declaration of principles:

The Finances

1. We demand a National money, safe and sound, issued by the General Government only, without the intervention of banks of issue, to be a full legal tender for all debts, public and private, a just, equitable, and efficient means of distribution, direct to the people, and through the lawful disbursements of the Government.

2. We demand the free and unrestricted coinage of silver and gold at the present legal ratio of 16 to 1, without waiting for the consent of foreign nations.

3. We demand that the volume of circulating medium be speedily increased to an amount sufficient to meet the demand of the business and population, and to restore the just level of prices of labor and production.

4. We denounce the sale of bonds and the increase of the public interest-bearing debt made by the present Administration as unnecessary and without authority of law, and demand that no more bonds be issued, except by specific act of Congress.

5. We demand such legislation as will prevent the demonetization of the lawful money of the United States by private contract.

6. We demand that the Government, in payment of its obligation, shall use its option as to the kind of lawful money in which they are to be paid, and we

denounce the present and preceding Administrations for surrendering this option to the holders of Government obligations.

7. We demand a graduated income tax, to the end that aggregated wealth shall bear its just proportion of taxation, and we regard the recent decision of the Supreme Court relative to the income-tax law as a misinterpretation of the Constitution and an invasion of the rightful powers of Congress over the subject of taxation.

8. We demand that postal savings-banks be established by the Government for the safe deposit of the savings of the people and to facilitate exchange.

Railroads and Telegraphs

1. Transportation being a means of exchange and a public necessity, the Government should own and operate the railroads in the interest of the people and on a non-partisan basis, to the end that all may be accorded the same treatment in transportation, and that the tyranny and political power now exercised by the great railroad corporations, which result in the impairment, if not the destruction of the political rights and personal liberties of the citizens, may be destroyed. Such ownership is to be accomplished gradually, in a manner consistent with sound public policy.

2. The interest of the United States in the public highways built with public moneys, and the proceeds of grants of land to the Pacific railroads, should never be alienated, mortgaged, or sold, but guarded and protected for the general welfare, as provided by the laws organizing such railroads. The foreclosure of existing liens of the United States on these roads should at once follow default in the payment thereof by the debtor companies; and at the foreclosure sales of said roads the Government shall purchase the same, if it becomes necessary to protect its interests therein, or if they can be purchased at a reasonable price; and the Government shall operate said railroads as public highways for the benefit of the whole people, and not in the interest of the few, under suitable provisions for protection of life and property, giving to all transportation interests equal privileges and equal rates for fares and freight.

3. We denounce the present infamous schemes for refunding these debts, and demand that the laws now applicable thereto be executed and administered according to their intent and spirit.

4. The telegraph, like the Post Office system, being a necessity for the transmission of news, should be owned and operated by the Government in the interest of the people.

The Public Lands

1. True policy demands that the National and State legislation shall be such as will ultimately enable every prudent and industrious citizen to secure a home, and therefore the land should not be monopolized for speculative purposes. All lands now held by railroads and other corporations in excess of their actual needs should by lawful means be reclaimed by the Government and held for actual settlers only, and private land monopoly, as well as alien ownership, should be prohibited.

2. We condemn the land grant frauds by which the Pacific railroad companies have, through the connivance of the Interior Department, robbed multitudes

of *bona-fide* settlers of their homes and miners of their claims, and we demand legislation by Congress which will enforce the exemption of mineral land from such grants after as well as before the patent.

3. We demand that *bona-fide* settlers on all public lands be granted free homes, as provided in the National Homestead Law, and that no exception be made in the case of Indian reservations when opened for settlement, and that all lands not now patented come under this demand.

The Referendum

We favor a system of direct legislation through the initiative and referendum, under proper Constitutional safeguards.

Direct Election of President and Senators by the People

We demand the election of President, Vice-President, and United States Senators by a direct vote of the people.

Sympathy for Cuba

We tender to the patriotic people of Cuba our deepest sympathy for their heroic struggle for political freedom and independence, and we believe the time has come when the United States, the great Republic of the world, should recognize that Cuba is, and of right ought to be, a free and independent state.

The Territories

We favor home rule in the Territories and the District of Columbia, and the early admission of the Territories as States.

Public Salaries

All public salaries should be made to correspond to the price of labor and its products.

Employment to Be Furnished by Government

In times of great industrial depression, idle labor should be employed on public works as far as practicable.

Arbitrary Judicial Action

The arbitrary course of the courts in assuming to imprison citizens for indirect contempt and ruling by injunction should be prevented by proper legislation.

Pensions

We favor just pensions for our disabled Union soldiers.

A Fair Ballot

Believing that the elective franchise and an untrammeled ballot are essential to a government of, for, and by the people, the People's party condemns the wholesale system of disfranchisement adopted in some States as unrepublican and undemocratic, and we declare it to be the duty of the several State legislatures to take such action as will secure a full, free and fair ballot and an honest count.

The Financial Question "The Pressing Issue."

While the foregoing propositions constitute the platform upon which our party stands, and for the vindication of which its organization will be maintained, we recognize that the great and pressing issue of the pending campaign, upon which the present election will turn, is the financial question, and upon this great and specific issue between the parties we cordially invite the aid and co-operation of all organizations and citizens agreeing with us upon this vital question.

On Watermelons, 1897

From "*Watermelons*", Georgia Experiment Station, Bulletin No. 38, December, 1897, pp. 67–70, 72–78, 84.

Culture

Over the entire area covered by the yellow pine forests of Georgia, known locally as the "Wire-grass" region, and, in the main, corresponding geologically with the Tertiary formation, the watermelon (*Citrullus vulgaris*) appears to be always and impressively "at home to its friends," — and who has the hardihood to admit that he is not ranked among them?

Other regions may produce certain calabashes which through courtesy are styled "watermelons"; but to see and know the genuine watermelon, arrayed like Solomon in all his glory, one must come to Georgia. Here the melon is indeed king and its empire is the Wire-grass! In no other section of the State, in no other State of the South, in no other division of the Union does this luscious cucurbit flourish as it does on the gray Tertiary sands between the Savannah and the Chattahoochee.

Yet in spite of this — or possibly because of it — very little has ever been written on the watermelon. Its bibliography is strangely barren. A small handbook by W. Atlee Burpee & Co., containing some valuable suggestions, casual mention in a few text-books and a page or so in each of half a dozen Station Bulletins cover, so far as the writer can ascertain, all that has ever been penned on the subject. It cannot be, however, that no one needs information thereon. The commercial growers of the great melon centers of this and other States are doubtless so well posted in every detail of melon culture that they are practically independent of outside information and this Bulletin would consequently prove to them of little value. But where one man grows melons for market, a hundred plant for home consumption and this

Station is constantly in receipt of letters asking for definite information concerning varieties, fertilization, distance, cultivation and other ordinary details. Hence it is for the better instruction of the grower on a small scale — for him who plants his half-acre or his square rod in the rear of the kitchen garden, and not for the melon prince who ships by the train-load, that this Bulletin is prepared.

But it must be distinctly understood before going further, that when in Georgia a "melon" is referred to, it means a *Watermelon* — not a Cantaloupe or Muskmelon. Whatever may be the proper conception of the term, to the average citizen here there is but one production worthy of either the dignity or glory of the name Melon — to wit, the Watermelon — and that is the sense in which the word will be used in this Bulletin. We would not wittingly do violence to the feelings of anyone.

1. Soil and Location

As previously stated, a warm, sandy soil is the melon's delight, but it must be light and dry, not damp and "soggy." Like the grape the watermelon is a veritable cat in its abhorrence of "wet feet." Yet, at the same time, the soil should not be too dry. Sufficient capillarity must exist to keep the roots of the plant well supplied with their proper modicum of moisture during a drouthy period — yet not enough to evaporate the entire reservoir of water in the subsoil into the atmosphere. Any land wanting in this nice adjustment of consistency is almost, if not quite as badly adapted to melon culture as a soil that is sodden.

For all that the watermelon is extremely cosmopolitan and will readily accommodate itself to a variety of soils, and (particularly in its own native region) will stand a great deal of rough and unscientific (I had almost said unsympathetic) treatment without rebelling.

But a warm, light-gray, well-drained topsoil, with a strong clay subsoil that will daily give up its moisture, little by little, when called on, affords an ideal location for a melon plat. The latter requisite, however, it has to forego over a considerable portion of the melon belt; yet somehow it appears to dispense with it quite philosophically, and will, notwithstanding, produce profitable crops.

A soil too rich in humus is not desirable. Sufficient nitrogen for its use can be readily supplied artificially when it does not exist naturally. A surplus may (and generally does) produce larger melons but at the expense of quality. They will prove soft, watery, and insipid, poor shippers and with a small per cent. of saccharine matter.

Rotation is all important, too. In no case should melons follow melons the next season, and at least four years should intervene before the land is again planted in this crop. By that time insect depredators, attracted by the first melon crop, will have probably become exterminated and the drain from the soil of specific plant-food (especially potash) will also have been, to a certain extent, at least, made good.

2. Preparation

This should be thorough, though not necessarily deep. The roots of the watermelon, while sometimes extending quite a distance laterally, are always close to the surface. The deeper the land is broken, the deeper the roots will penetrate, and this perversion of habit will cause the plant to grow off slower, and, while in case of a drouth it might possibly withstand the season better, it would certainly entail a series of complications that could easily be avoided. Deeper breaking would be permissible with red land in Upper Georgia than on the gray, sandy soil of the Wire-grass, though the general consensus of opinion appears to be that shallow preparation is preferable for any locality.

But, while the plowing need not be deep, for that very reason the pulverization must be thorough and effective. What is saved on the subsoiler should be expended on the harrow. After breaking, two, or even three pulverizations with a cutaway harrow will leave the plat in excellent condition — especially if a crop of cowpeas has been grown on the land the previous year, as is always advisable. In such case the soil is well stocked with nitrogen and filled with vegetable matter; is loose and friable and pulverizes like an ash bank.

3. Distance

The richer the soil or the higher the fertilization the more luxuriant will be the growth of vines and hence the distance apart at which the hills should be located must correspond. On very rich land twelve feet apart each way is none too much; in fact many growers prefer this distance even on poor land. Each planter must determine for himself in the matter, according to circumstances. Probably ten by ten is the distance most frequently employed, and in no case should it be less than eight by eight — and this very rarely. Whatever the distance, the land should be checked in squares so that the hills will be equidistant in both directions. . . .

5. Fertilization

The best fertilizer for melons is a crop of cowpeas on the land the year previous to planting. After cutting for hay or ensilage the stubble should be left to die and turned under in the fall. This leaves the soil light and open, stored with a good supply of nitrogen and ready for the harrowing in the spring.

Next to this preparatory "cowpea treatment" — and, indeed, supplementary to it — nothing, perhaps, is better than stable manure, applied in the furrow in the fall and listed on as described under a previous head. But stable manure is always variable in its composition and content of plant-food, and the probability is, that used by itself in considerable quantity, especially when following a cowpea crop, there will be a disproportion of phosphoric acid and potash, which must consequently be artificially supplied. Therefore an addition per acre of some 400 pounds Acid Phosphate and 400 pounds Kainit (or 100 pounds of either Muriate or Sulphate of Potash) would in great measure balance the fertilizer and make a vast deal of difference in the result.

In Upper Georgia, or anywhere that a retentive clay subsoil is found, these "mixed minerals" — as we may term them — may be drilled in along with the stable manure in the fall. In this way not only will the stable manure have rotted by spring, rendering its content of plant food immediately available, but the phosphoric acid and potash of the commercial fertilizer will also have become completely soluble and ready for use.

But where the soil is light and porous and no subsoil exists within a reasonable distance from the surface, as is the case over a large portion of the Wire-grass, the land, in consequence, leaching badly, it has been found best not to manure in the fall, with either stable manure or commercial fertilizers, but to wait until late winter or early spring. This, of course, minimizes the loss from leaching, but the crop also fails to receive the full benefit of the fertilizer. . . .

6. Planting

On putting in the seed they should not be spared. Field mice, crows, pigeons, poultry and other depredators frequently prevent a perfect stand when but few seed are used, and the time lost, when replanting is found necessary, can never be regained. Twenty seed to the hill is not too many; thirty would be preferable to less than twenty. They should be planted by hand, and the method ordinarily pursued is to push each seed, separately, down into the mellow soil with the forefinger. The seed is scattered loosely over an area on the center of the bed as large as the crown of a hat and then each seed "punched in" where it lies, to the depth of about an inch. While this appears to be, from the description, a rather slow process, it is astonishing how rapidly a skilled darkey can operate as he shuffles down the row. This forces the depredating agent to discover and destroy each seed in succession, which gives some a chance to escape; whereas, if planted together, as soon as the pocket was found the seed would all be scattered or devoured at once.

Some growers, instead of making one planting of a large number of seed prefer to put in half a dozen seed, only, at a time, say on the south side of the hill, and, in a week or so, without waiting for the first seed to come up, making another planting on the west side, followed by a third and fourth planting, at intervals, on the other two sides, until a stand is secured. Thus no time is lost.

Be sure to plant shallow! Pushing the seed in to too great a depth is a very common fault, even with experienced manipulators. It must be remembered that the ground is comparatively cold at planting time, and, as the surface of the soil of course warms up sooner than the lower strata, the seed should receive the benefit of the daily increasing temperature as soon as possible. Therefore an inch is abundantly deep; this will ensure sufficient moisture and yet leave the seed close enough to the surface to respond readily to the sun's warmth as the season advances.

Frequently, after planting, a few weeks of drouth follow, accompanied by heavy winds, which parch and bake the surface. This is more apt to be the case in Upper Georgia than in the Wire-grass region, and in such case, to secure rapid germination, it is sometimes necessary to go over the plat and with a hoe to throw a "dab" or two of dirt on each hill. This presents a new surface for evaporation and drying out, and secures the retention of sufficient moisture in contact with the seed to induce germination. It of course prevents the hill from warming up as soon as it otherwise would; but, between two evils, it is advisable to choose the lesser. The "dab" of soil should of course be removed after sprouting has taken place and before the young plants begin to push up through the mounds.

7. Forcing for Earliness and Size

If very early melons are wanted, it is necessary to start the plants under glass. Of course this process is only permissible on a small scale or where the assurance of a market for a fancy production of this sort will justify the expense. The simplest method of procedure consists in employing a cold frame, in which small pots are sunk, after the seed are planted, in late winter or early spring — say from January 15th to March 1st, according to locality. Protected by glass, watering may be frequent and the plants, thinned gradually down to one vigorous vine in each pot, will be ready to transplant as soon as all danger of frost is over. The root system of each vine will be strongly developed by this time and a rapid growth will commence as soon as it is set out. Clay pots can of course be used, but they are not nearly so inexpensive or serviceable as a manufacture known as the "Neponset" pot made of stiff paper or pasteboard with an adjustable side flap or catch — as in accompanying figure — which may be slipped out readily and the transfer to the hill effected without the slightest danger of rupturing a rootlet. This is their main advantage, but they are also cheap, light and sufficiently durable to be used for several seasons. . . .

8. Cultivation

As soon as the seed are well up they should be thinned down to three or four plants to the hill, and a little later to one vigorous plant. Some growers are in the habit of leaving two vines to the hill, but, while by this practice they certainly get more vines, and sometimes, too, more melons, the latter are always smaller and less salable than when one lusty vine has the hill and the fertilizer all to itself.

After the first heavy rain following planting, with its compacting effect, it will be well to break out the "middles." This should be done with a "twister," throwing the furrow to the bed on either side and finishing with a "water row," which will serve, on low, level land, to thoroughly drain the beds. After this the crop should be worked entirely with the cultivator or scrape, and very lightly. The first working may be across or at a right angle to the rows; the next parallel with them. These two workings will, if the vines grow rapidly, probably be all that can be given, for as soon as the vines have run sufficiently to get in the way cultivation should cease.

Old melon growers never plow their plats while the dew is on the vines, but wait until midday before putting in the plow. To what extent the crop would be injured (if at all) by early morning cultivation yet remains to be proved — and to search for the cause before the fact is established, would be useless. Yet general customs can usually be traced to some logical cause and it is just as easy to observe this practice of our forefathers as to violate it — until it is proved to be unnecessary or inadvisable.

Never, under any circumstances, turn a vine! More will be lost by so doing than will be gained by giving the plat an extra cultivation. This is another ancestral practice and doubtless arises from the fact that vines when turned are apt to be carelessly handled. If returned gently and deftly to their original position it is difficult to realize how they would be injured. Any weeding that is found necessary after this time should be effected with a scythe blade, lopping off the tops of the weeds above the vines. They should not even be pulled out by hand on account of the danger of mutilating the vines, which generally hold them in a tight embrace with their tendrils. Indeed, rather than risk disturbing a vine it would be preferable to leave the weeds and the melons to "have it out" between them; for a few well-anchored weeds, here and there, prove rather a benefit than a detriment, since they prevent the winds from rolling up and matting the vines. . . .

9. How to Tell a Ripe Melon

With all other fruits (if, indeed, the melon may be termed a fruit and not a vegetable — and it would be treason in this section to doubt it) a change of color indicates the approach of the ripening period. With many species the ripening process continues after gathering without detriment to quality. With the melon it is different. Appearance, to the uninitiated, indicates little, and it cannot be shipped half green, like a Le Conte pear, for it resembles the grape in not improving much after pulling. It must be taken from the vine "sight unseen" — so to speak — yet it must be sent to market with absolute confidence as to its proper state of maturity — for it would never do to risk the ruin of a shipment and the reputation of the shipper by bungling green or over-ripe melons into it.

Fortunately the knowledge of a ripe melon to a native Georgian appears to come as a sort of intuition or inspiration which is almost infallible. He may not be able to tell you just *how* he knows a melon to be ripe, but he will go into a field and pick them out as fast as he comes to them and not miss one in a thousand. It seems to be largely an inherited instinct — this in sober seriousness. For it is difficult for even the adept to put in words a reliable method for distinguishing a properly ripe melon. The knowledge is mainly gained, of course, by experience and observation, and doubtless through many lamentable errors of judgment and humiliating mistakes, coupled with the loss of divers promising melons at the outset. Boys, and sometimes an adult darkey, often resort to the nefarious practice of "plugging" — feeling their inability to wrestle successfully with the problem. Many persons claim that they can decide by an inspection of the "curl" (tendril) on the stem: if this is dead the melon is ripe; if green, so is the melon. It is needless to say that this is altogether unreliable.

Aside from intuition, possibly the simplest advice that could be given, after all, would be that of the old negro "mauma" in the ballad, rating her grandson for stealing a *green* melon: "Be shore When you thumps 'em dey allus soun' 'plunk'!"

Unquestionably the flat, dead sound emitted by a melon when "thumped" is the readiest indication of ripeness, and the one most universally depended on. If the resonance is hollow, ringing or musical, it is a certain proof of immaturity. . . .

10. Gathering and Marketing

As with the grape, so with the melon the length of the wagon haul to the point of shipment is one of the main factors affecting profits. The industry would be a lucrative one, despite high freights, glutted markets and unreliable middlemen, if this item could be always eliminated. Hence the importance of locating the field within easy distance of a station or siding, in order that the haul may be reduced to a minimum. Skillful handling in the field, the use of bolster springs, careful selection and judicious loading in the car often reverse the narrow margin between loss and profit.

Undersized melons never pay for shipment. No crop responds more emphatically to severe culling. Uniformity in size or weight is an essential and should be in all cases strictly enforced.

In the second place, in loading, the smaller melons should be laid down first on the floor of the car — the larger (when there is any noticeable difference) racked on top — not for the purpose of deception or the sake of appearance, but because the smaller sizes better withstand jolting and pressure, and there is also less loss if undue bruising should ensue.

But the chief point in shipping is to select an advantageous market. Shipments cannot be made blindly. A glutted market means always that a belated shipment will not pay freight. The melon is by far the most sensitive of all perishable horticultural products. A cold northeaster over lake Michigan has dumped many a fine carload into the Chicago river. On a chilly day in summer the public will not invest largely in watermelons — and hence on such occasions an insignificant shipment of a few carloads will glut beyond hope a market that on a hot, dry day would swallow them by the trainload and eagerly call for more. In order to secure a sale at all it is absolutely necessary to select the market from day to day, and to divert shipments *en route* without hesitation. The telegraph is therefore indispensable and many a melon shipper's account with the Western Union runs up to over ten dollars a day during the season — and this is the sort of man, too, who generally comes out ahead.

But much better than attempting to singly wrestle with the problem of selecting a market judiciously would be a reliance, for this purpose, on some one of the co-operative shippers' unions, of which the American Fruit Growers' Union is decidedly the most prominent, and to Georgia growers the most convenient. This association, which is national in its scope and operation, has recently absorbed the Georgia Fruit Growers' Association, which has been in the past of such inestimable value to our fruit men and shippers. The new American Union is doing some excellent work for our people and section. Full information in regard to its methods and operations may be obtained by addressing its President — Hon. John D. Cunningham, Marietta, Georgia.

* * *

15. Varieties

For shipping many different varieties have, from time to time, contested for first place. Perhaps the melon best known to the markets of the North and West is the *Georgia Rattlesnake*, and at the head of this strain stands the sub-variety known the country over as the *Augusta Rattlesnake*. This distinction it has enjoyed for many years, and deservedly, but of late its popularity has begun to subside and other famous shippers are coming to the front. For a long time the *Kolb Gem* seemed destined to supersede it as a popular shipper. But in its turn it has had to share the market with *Jones' Jumbo* and *Duke Jones* followed by *Lord Bacon*, which is unquestionably the most notable recent introduction and appears to have "come to stay." It is a solid, thick-rined, excellent shipper and keeper and of good quality.

If forced to list the three best melons for shipping purposes it would be safe to rank *Lord Bacon* at the head, closely followed by *Kolb Gem* and *Augusta Rattlesnake,* with *Jones' Jumbo* a good fourth. None of these are of first quality, but they will all "get there"—if it's anywhere within a thousand miles—and sell, too, after they have arrived.

It is not so easy a task to decide on what variety is best in quality and superior for the local market or the home table. Taste varies greatly and so do the characteristics of the different varieties from season to season, while soil, local climatology and other conditions present another set of disturbing factors. The following are recommended as from "very good" to "excellent" in quality, of good size and sufficiently reliable in productiveness and other features to warrant a careful test: *Sibley's Triumph, Seminole, Dixie, Jordan's Gray Monarch, Phinney's Early.* Part III of this Bulletin contains a descriptive list of melons which may be consulted for details. The Station has this year no seed for either sale or distribution.

Farming in the Southwest, 1898

From Edith M. Nicholl, *Observations of a Ranchwoman in New Mexico* (New York, 1898), pp. 51–54, 57–63.

It is no easy task for an enthusiastic farming person to tell of the agricultural methods, the fruits, the vegetables, the crops, of this productive Valley without waxing tedious to those for whom farming matters are simply a bore. Yet there is one process, that of preparing for, sowing, and harvesting alfalfa, which may not be wholly uninteresting in the telling, even to him who loves not the land.

In the first place, Alfalfa is the stand-by of the Arid Belt. Without going into botanical distinctions, it is sufficient to say that it is a variety of clover, but in those sections where it flourishes the superior of both clover and timothy. Ton for ton it yields more than either; not only that, but here in New Mexico four cuttings in one season are not uncommon, and a yield of three tons per acre is considered by good judges a conservative estimate. In nutritive and muscle-forming qualities as hay it has no equal. . . . Personal experience goes to prove that cows fed on alfalfa hay, supplemented only by a nightly ration of bran, produce butter excellent as regards both quality and quantity. Needless to dilate on the trouble and expense spared the dairyman in this detail alone. Hogs and chicken graze it, and with little additional food in summer time are remunerative to their owners. Whatever may be affirmed to the contrary, however, alfalfa will not bear very close grazing, and although, if properly irrigated and not grazed too long at one time, it will last an indefinite number of years, enriching instead of impoverishing the soil, it is doubtful if it will endure flagrant neglect. Compared with other crops, however, it needs but little attention. Its one and only serious disadvantage lies in its dangerous properties where cows are concerned; that is to say, there are but few weeks in the year when cows can be turned loose with safety in an alfalfa meadow. It is no exaggeration to say that there is not a farmer in this vicinity who has not lost one or more cows from the deadly 'alfalfa bloat.' When growing it is very succulent, and the cows eat it greedily — the result: bloat and speedy death. Scrub cows suffer comparatively little — horses and mules not at all — and careful investigation goes to show that the pure-bred or graded Jersey, of small stomach and voracious habits, is the common victim.

A prettier spectacle than a meadow of well-established alfalfa ripe for the harvest, running like a purple sea under a fine May breeze, it would be difficult to picture, even for the man who cares nothing about farming. The first cutting takes place in May, and, provided there is a good supply of water, at intervals of from six to seven weeks during the season. The harvesting of fourteen acres occupies at the most four days, there being, as a rule, more danger of the hay drying too much than too little. If stacked too dry, the leaves, its valuable element, are apt to fall and be wasted in the hauling. There is occasional loss in the 'rainy season.' . . .

As regards improved orchards, the Valley is yet in its infancy. The first shipments of 'improved' fruit were not made until 1891, and yet 'Mesilla Valley peaches' are already considered 'gilt-edged,' and are sold on the trains as far East as Chicago. Last season, shipped for the first time to Los Angeles, they drove the Californian product out of the market, for the peach and apple of California, though fine to look at, are, except when mountain-grown, without flavour — a defect, some say, due to over-irrigation; others, to a lack of stimulating quality in the atmosphere — whereas the fruit of New Mexico, since being taken hold of and improved by Americans, possesses both looks and inward merit. It is also said that the superior altitude of the Territory gives its fruit the flavour so much relished, and that when the dam is built, which will enable the high mesa lands, at present barren, to be irrigated and set out in orchards, not only will the fruit be still finer, but the danger resulting from occasional late frosts will be greatly lessened. In California it is already proved that the orange groves set out on the mesas enjoy almost entire immunity from frost. Orange and lemon groves are, of course, out of the question in this climate, but in their stead we have not only peaches and apples in perfection, but apricots, plums, quinces, prunes, pears (the latter fruit so far only of medium quality), nuts of different varieties, and grapes by the ton. If this were a farming treatise or an advertising pamphlet, exact statistics of the bearing capacity of trees and vines might be of interest, and even in this place they are not altogether superfluous. The chief objection to such details lies, of course, in that question of accuracy. One successful American grape-grower estimates that each vine yields him on an average twenty-five pounds of grapes. This is the Mission grape, taken all in all the most satisfactory grape to grow here. It was brought to the territory several hundred years ago by Spanish priests, and is certainly a delicious grape, purple in colour and very juicy, devoid of the solid flesh which makes some high-priced varieties such uncomfortable eating. It ripens some time in August, is not subject to disease, and when more widely known, owing to improvement in transportation facilities — our present bugbear — should command an immense market. Here comes in, again, the need of co-operation — co-operation as it is practised in California and elsewhere. It is easy enough to make fruit grow in New Mexico; to sell it to profit and advantage, especially in the case of small or moderate growers, is another matter. The small grower, under present conditions, finds himself at a disadvantage. He is not able — railroad charges on the one and only railroad being so high — to ship with profit, and the local market is soon glutted. He either sells his grapes at a cent a pound, makes the crop into wine, or tears up his vineyard in wrath and sows the land to alfalfa, vowing that grapes cost more to irrigate, prune, cultivate, and bank up for the winter than they bring in the market. Co-operation alone will bring relief, and with the influx of intelligent farmers, who understand that in union is strength, prosperity is bound to come. Even in peach-growing the small farmer cannot be sure of his market. The large grower is, of course, safe enough.

Last June I was in a peach orchard containing about sixty trees in full bearing. A lovely display it was indeed, the great round fruit glowing in the evening sunlight, and bending the branches almost to the ground. But the owner did not share my enthusiasm. There was no market, and the peaches were spoiling, for the peach is the most perishable of crops. There were not enough for a carload, too many for village peddling. Even the markets of the neighbouring city were so crowded that prices were down, and shipping would not pay.

'Well, we must combine,' I cried, 'and ship to distant points like the big growers do individually.'

'There's no combine in this place,' was the retort; 'it's every man for himself, and — the Old Gentleman take the hindmost!'

I regret to have to say that this was but a rather vigorous summary of a reply I received from the President of our Agricultural College, whom I consulted as to the feasibility of forming a Farmers' Association, not merely for the marketing of fruit, but of all farm products, and I added that I thought that the College, placed here with the idea of guiding and instructing the farmer, ought to take the initiative. The President expressed himself warmly in favour of my view, but also as to the utter hopelessness of any such happy consummation. 'Someone would have to be at the head of such an association,' he wound up by saying, 'and no one trusts anyone in this community.' A nice state of affairs in a community which claims to be of the great progressive West! It is no marvel that some intending settlers prefer the effete East, and return whence they came. The President might have added that as an institution planned for the benefit of the people is run to a large extent — some persons maintain entirely — in the interest and for the benefit of the politicians, any such independent move on his part in the direction indicated would be considered distinctly officious. However, when 'the old order changeth, yielding place to new,' and the dam is built and the farmer comes to the front, then we may yet live to see the politician drowned out.

Farming Development by 1899

From George K. Holmes, "Progress of Agriculture in the United States," U.S. Department of Agriculture, *Yearbook*, 1899, pp. 307, 314–34.

Crude Beginnings by Indians

Indians carried on agriculture in a primitive and very limited way in the region now embraced in the United States before the country was inhabited by the white race, and to their crude agriculture they joined the harvesting of the wild products of nature.

Some Crops and Methods of Cultivating and Gathering

Indian corn. — The farming practiced on the eastern side of North America by the Indians was to burn off the forest, scrape up the top soil into little hills, and, if corn was to be raised, to plant the seed therein. Indian corn, or maize, was indigenous, and the Indians raised it from time immemorial. Women did the work, and the only implements employed were their fingers, a pointed stick for planting, and a clam shell or the scapula of an animal for a hoe. At the time of harvest the ears of corn were stored in a cache, or were hung up to dry, held together by the braided husks.

Tobacco. — Tobacco was another plant indigenous to America, and the Indians, who had learned its narcotic property, were in the habit of smoking the leaves after they had been dried.

Food and textile plants. — The Indians of northern California gathered the seeds of wild plants and roasted them on hot stones, to be ground afterwards into coarse flour by a stone operated in a hollow in a rock. Mojave Indian women planted gourd seeds in the crevices of rocks, and when the gourds were ripe gathered enormous quantities of them. Especially along the whole western coast of North America, Indian women gathered wild hemp, agave, and other textile plants; they dried the leaves or stalks, macerated them in water, extracted the fiber, and spun it on their naked bodies without the use of any implement whatever, and then made fabrics for domestic use.

Wild rice. — Throughout the Great Lake country the Indian women beat the heads of the wild rice plants while holding them over their canoes; having fanned the chaff away by using a large tray, they ground the rice in a mortar and cooked it in much the same way as corn.

Causes of Increased Production

While the country has been developing as above indicated, the great nonagricultural populations of European countries have been relatively increasing, and have exhausted in their consumption the farm production of their own countries, especially with respect to the items of wheat, corn, and other cereals, animal and dairy products, and, to the very small extent of cultivation, tobacco and cotton, thus opening up a foreign market, which has in a large degree warranted the expansion of the agriculture of the United States, along with the other causes or opportunities mentioned.

The decided decline in the cost of transportation has also contributed largely to the transformation under consideration.

Implements and Machines

The most prominent feature in the development of American agriculture is the immense improvement that has taken place in agricultural methods and machines — indeed, the word improvement is not adequate to express the change that has taken place in the methods of agriculture in this country, because the implements and machines are creations rather than improvements, and their mission has been radical and far-reaching. They have reduced the amount of human labor required to produce a given quantity of crops and to cultivate given areas of land,

and they have been largely, if not chiefly, instrumental in converting local markets into world markets for the principal cereals, cotton, tobacco, and animal and dairy products.

A technical description of these implements and machines can not be attempted here, and it will be sufficient merely to indicate generally changes in their character and in the results of their work. Dependence must be placed upon the reader's knowledge of these machines and upon his mechanical mind to understand how and why they have contributed so much to the realization of the present agricultural era.

Vehicles. — At the beginning of this century carts were used on the farms and chaises on the roads. Stagecoaches were used on the main roads of travel, and a few wagons were found here and there. Carts were more convenient for use with oxen on the farms. For many years discussion was active as to the comparative economy of oxen and horses for farm use, and wagons came in with the increased use of horses and the improvement of the country roads. Buggies and trotting horses grew up together. Light one-horse wagons first appeared in Connecticut about 1830, but it was not until 1840 or later that they became common enough not to attract notice when seen on the roads.

Plows. — In 1637 there were but 37 plows in the colony of Massachusetts Bay. Twelve years after the landing of the Pilgrims the farmers around Boston had no plows, and were compelled to break up the ground and prepare for cultivation with their hands and with rude and clumsy hoes and mattocks. It was the custom in that part of the country, even to a much later period, for anyone owning a plow to do the plowing for the inhabitants over a considerable extent of territory. A town often paid a bounty to anyone who would buy and keep in repair a plow for the purpose of going about in this way.

Mr. C. C. Coffin thus mentions the plow that his father used: "I think it was about 12 feet long. I know that it required eight to ten oxen to draw it, one man to ride upon the beam to keep it in the ground, and a man to follow behind with a heavy iron hoe to dig up the baulks."

A writer in the Rhode Island American in 1820 describes the plow generally in use in the Eastern States at that time, known as the Old Colony plow, as follows: "It had a 10-foot beam and 4-foot land side; your furrows stand up like the ribs of a lean horse in the month of March. A lazy plowman may sit on the beam and count every bout of his day's work. Six of these plows cost me on an average, last year, $5 each to keep the shares and coulters fit for work, and the wear of the other parts could not be less than $1 more — $6 per year for each plow."

The first patent for a plow in this country was taken out by Charles Newbold, of New Jersey, in 1797. His was the first cast-iron plow ever made, but the farmers in those times entertained great prejudices against it. There was a general idea throughout the country that a cast-iron plow would "poison" the land. Mr. Coffin remembers the first cast-iron plow used in his neighborhood in New Hampshire in 1837 and the assemblage of farmers who objected to it for the reason mentioned. He says that it required from 1797 to 1842 for the inventive genius of this country, together with the observations of farmers and mechanics, to arrive at any just conclusion as to what would be the best form for the plow.

Without mentioning intermediate plows, it will be sufficient to pass on to the Oliver chilled plow, which first appeared in 1870. This was a light, durable plow with a mold board of proper shape to economize draft and suitably turn the furrow, and this plow in a marked degree promoted the economy of plowing. It was stated by Mr. Coffin in 1878 that this invention, if used throughout the United States in the preceding year, would have effected a saving of $45,000,000 to the farmers of the country in the expense of plowing.

And then invention followed invention and improvement followed improvement, until we have sulky plows, gang plows, plows combined with harrow cultivators and with seed drills, side-hill plows, vine-yard plows, beet plows, sub-soil plows, double land-side plows, and lastly, what has been the aim, and seems to be the end, of plow invention, we have the steam gang plow combined with a seeder and a harrow, which has reduced the time required for human labor (in plowing, sowing, and harrowing) to produce a bushel of wheat, on an average, from 32.8 minutes in 1830 to 2.2 minutes at the present time, and which has reduced the time of animal labor per bushel from 57 to 1½ minutes; at the same time it has reduced the cost of human and animal labor in plowing, seeding, and harrowing per bushel of wheat, from 4 cents to 1 cent.

Corn planters. — Hundreds of patents have been issued for corn planters. The earlier ones were adjustments to the hoe, which permitted the release of grains of corn when the hoe was struck into the ground; then came the hand planter, and the next step was the horse drill. Next came the idea of marking rows in both directions with a drag. A long beam with pins in it was dragged both ways across the field by horses, and then the farmer would go along with the hand planter and plant the corn at the intersection of the rows. Still, again, followed an improvement, and this was the corn planter which planted two rows at one time with the rows running in both directions. A man sat on the machine, and, at every point where the drag had crossed at right angles, he moved a lever that dropped the corn, which was covered by wheels that turned and pressed down the soil upon the seed. The check rower followed; it was a simple implement, consisting of a wire chain or knotted rope stretching across the field and anchored at both ends. This passed through the machine as it was driven across the field and dropped some grains of corn every time the knot passed through a slot in the machine. It was only necessary to drive backward and forward all day long until the acres were planted, and then the corn could be cultivated in both directions. Subsequently, numerous check-row planters for corn have been invented with and without fertilizer adjustments, so that several rows of corn may be planted at the same time in places at regular distances apart, permitting cultivation in both directions.

Cultivators. — Cultivators have been the subject of several thousands of patents. The original cultivation of corn and other crops planted in rows was by means of the hoe, but in the course of time a plow was used to loosen the earth and to suppress weeds and grass, being drawn twice between the rows and turning the soil against one or the other. Next a tooth harrow was employed, and this was drawn one way between the rows, and afterwards a cultivator with small double plow-shares was used. Then followed the double-shovel cultivator, cutting deep or shallow, as desired, and turning the earth toward two opposite rows at the same time. The implement is now variously made, but it has reduced the economy of cultivation apparently to a minimum; the farmer may now ride while the cultivator is doing its work. He cultivates the rows of his crop in both directions, and the use of the hoe has been nearly, if not entirely, discontinued throughout large agricultural areas.

Harrows. — Much attention also has been devoted to the invention of implements for harrowing and pulverizing the soil. The farmer no longer drives a brush harrow over his field as of yore, nor does he need to use a tooth harrow, but he has at his command disk harrows, screw pulverizers, smoothing harrows, spring-tooth harrows, and harrows combined with plows and seeders.

Corn husker. — The mechanical corn husker is a machine of recent invention. Previously the husking of corn was done only by hand, and a peg strapped to the hand was often used for opening the husks; but there is now a machine that husks the corn and at the same time cuts the husks, stalks, and blades into feed, the motive power being steam.

Corn harvester. — Again, we have the recent corn-harvesting machine drawn by horses that cuts the cornstalks and binds them into bundles at the same time.

Cornshellers. — The steam cornsheller caused a remarkable change in the time and expense of the shelling of corn. In the olden time corn was shelled by hand, a frying-pan handle or shovel being used, the ears of corn being scraped against it, or perhaps the cob of one ear was used to shell the corn from another. Then came the first machine for shelling corn, a cylinder turned by a crank, by which a man might shell about 40 bushels in a day. Thousands of patents have been issued for cornshellers, and the culmination of them is the steam-power or horse-power cornsheller, which will shell a bushel a minute, carry off the cobs to a pile or into a wagon, and deliver the corn into sacks or wagons.

Seeders. — From the time when wheat was first sown, up to a comparatively recent period, the only method of sowing it was to throw it into the air by the hand. In this way it is impossible to sow evenly, especially if the wind blows with considerable force; and if clover seed is to be sown, the ground must be gone over a second time, while a third time is required if fertilizer is to be distributed. Then, when the harrow comes some of the grains are buried too deeply and some are not covered with earth enough. But not so many years ago inventors set to work to construct mechanical seeders, and the result is an almost complete abandonment of broadcast sowing by hand and the substitution of such seeders. They sow all kinds of grain and seeds at once, with fertilizer if required, and they harrow at the same time. They make the crop more certain. It is the general opinion that the wheat crop is increased one-eighth or more by the use of the mechanical seeders, especially in the case of winter wheat.

Mowers and reapers. — In 1794 a Scotchman invented what was described as a most marvelous and wonderful machine for cutting grain, doing as much in one day as seven men could do with the sickle. This marvelous machine was only the cradle. The reaper followed, and the first patent for one issued in this country was given to Hussey in 1833. McCormick took out his first patent in 1834, although he had constructed and tested a machine in Virginia in 1831 with some success; but the world heard little of reaping machines until 1845, when 150 of them were built at Cincinnati; by 1846 fully 300 had been built. There was a general trial of mowers and reapers at Geneva, N.Y., in 1852. Nine machines contested, for other inventors had taken out patents. Nineteen years had passed since the first patent had been issued. Out of the nine machines exhibited, not one could start in the grain without backing to get up speed. There was a heavy side draft, the machines were clumsy, and they could not turn easily.

By 1855 about 10,000 mowers and reapers had been built by different makers, nearly all being one-wheeled machines. There was an exhibition of reapers at the French exposition in 1855, in which there was one English, one French, and one American. The French machine did its allotted work in 72 minutes, the English in 66, and the American in 22.

Two years later, in 1857, there was a trial at Syracuse, N.Y., at which nineteen machines contested. Of these, all except three started in the grain without backing to get up speed. There was a trial at Auburn, N.Y., in 1866, at which forty-four different machines were entered, and of these, forty-two did their work in a satisfactory manner.

The mower and reaper combined cut the grain and left it on the ground bunched up in proper size for a sheaf, subsequently to be bound by hand. The harvester was supposed to be an improvement upon this, because it had a place for one or two men to ride to bind the grain as fast as it was cut; but the self-binder went beyond that and by means of a mechanical attachment did the binding without the aid of human labor. It was not until 1870 that the self-binder was a mechanical success; but that was not the end of invention for constructing machines to harvest wheat.

It remained for the ingenuity of man to construct a combined reaper and thrasher, with which it is necessary only to drive across the wheat field in order to obtain the grain ready for transportation to the elevator or elsewhere.

Cotton gin. — Without the cotton gin it would be practically impossible to raise and market the cotton crop of this country, which now commonly amounts to 10,000,000 bales and more annually. Before Whitney's invention it is said that the labor of one person was required for about ten hours to pick the seeds from 1½ pounds of cotton lint. At the present time one machine will gin from 1,500 to 7,500 pounds of lint in the same time, the quantity varying according to the size and power of the gin.

Influence of Patent Laws on Development of Agricultural Machines

The development and creation of agricultural implements and machines by the inventive genius of this country is one of the most remarkable features of progress of the century. Its history is one of evolution and revolution — a revolution of incalculable consequences to human labor and the production and distribution of wealth, with an immense bearing upon the trend and character of industry, social life, and civilization.

This development has been encouraged by the patent laws of the country, and perhaps nothing could be more tersely expressive of the influence of these laws in promoting mechanical agriculture than a mention of the number of patents that have been granted. Under date of November 17, 1899, the Patent Office reports that patents for agricultural machines had been granted to the number indicated in each of the following classes: Vegetable cutters and crushers, 701; fertilizers, 822; bee culture, 1,038; trees, plants, and flowers, 1,102; care of live stock, 3,749; dairy, 4,632; thrashers, 5,319; harrows and diggers, 5,801; fences, 8,404; seeders and planters, 9,156; harvesters, 12,519; plows, 12,652.

It is no longer necessary for the farmer to cut his wheat with sickle or cradle, nor to rake it and bind it by hand; to cut his cornstalks with a knife and shock the stalks by hand; to thrash his grain with a flail, nor to drive horses over it to tread it out, nor to scrape the ears of corn against a shovel or the handle of a frying pan. It is no longer necessary for him to dig potatoes, nor to cut his grass with a scythe and to spread it with a pitchfork that it may dry, nor to pitch the hay from the wagon to the haymow in the barn, nor to pick the lint from cotton seed by hand, and so on with numerous operations throughout the whole range of agricultural work.

Mechanical contrivances have largely supplanted human labor in many respects, or have improved the application of labor and increased the product of agriculture, reduced the cost of production, augmented the farmer's gross income, and made his life an easier one than it was before the machine period.

This country has come to be without a peer in the manufacture of agricultural implements and machines, both in quality and number. The manufacturing establishments for producing them in 1890 numbered 910, with a capital of $145,313,997 and 42,544 employees, receiving wages to the amount of $21,811,761, turning out a product valued at $81,271,651. One of these establishments (the largest in the world), making various kinds of mowers and reapers, corn harvesters, corn huskers and shredders, and hayrakes, turned out 187,760 machines in 1898, or, on an average, one in less than a minute for every working day.

Agencies for Agricultural Experiment and Information

Along with the application of invention, have grown up numerous agencies for educating and training the farmer in agriculture, for disseminating information with regard to improvements, and for stimulating among farmers the associative spirit and increasing the benefits to be derived from cooperation.

The first of these agencies, chronologically, consisted of voluntary organizations for the promotion of agricultural interests. These, under various titles, existed in the colonies even before the beginning of this century. We have records of five established during the decade of 1785–1794, in the following States and in the order named: Pennsylvania, South Carolina, New York, Massachusetts, and Connecticut. This method of aid to agriculture has constantly increased during the nineteenth century, and agricultural societies, the name generally applied to them, have multiplied so that at the present day there are probably few counties in the United States where some form of agricultural society does not exist, while all the leading agricultural industries are represented by State, and, in many cases, by national organization.

Many of these voluntary associations receive State aid, and especially is this true of those organized mainly for the purpose of holding annual fairs. About 1,500 such associations are now in existence, extensively distributed throughout the country, but more especially throughout the North Central and North Atlantic States. Of farmers' clubs, it is sufficient to say their name is legion. Another of these agencies consists of the commissioners of agriculture or boards of agriculture of the different States, and almost every State has some official organization in the interests of agriculture. To these must be added the agricultural colleges and the experiment stations, in which the Federal and State governments cooperate.

Finally, the most important of the agencies referred to is the Department of Agriculture itself, which began as an insignificant division in the Patent Office,

Department of the Interior, in 1839, became a Department under a Commissioner in 1862, and in February, 1889, was erected into an Executive Department under a Secretary, who is a member of the Cabinet.

Statistics

Agricultural Censuses

Important and extensive collections of statistical information with regard to farms and their products have been made by national and State censuses.

The first statistics of agriculture collected by a United States census were obtained in 1840, within limits much narrower than those adopted in the censuses of 1890 and 1900.

At the present time it is the policy of the Census Office to procure an inventory of farm property and products, with detailed statements for acreage, values, quantities, and numbers of live stock, as far as applicable. It is expected that the national census of this year will procure many facts with regard to the farms of this country, which are now supposed to number about 5,000,000. No other country takes such a thorough, extensive, and detailed census of agriculture as does the United States.

The use of the censuses of agriculture might be the subject of extended discussion, but comparatively little can be said here. Not a day passes that the Department of Agriculture does not need to use census statistics of agriculture in many ways and for many purposes, not only in its own routine work of crop estimates and in the preparation and conduct of statistical investigations, but also in response to numerous letters received from residents of the United States and foreign countries.

Some of the States are required by their constitutions, or by legislative enactments, to take censuses, but not all of them comply with the requirement. The most elaborate State census of agriculture is taken by Massachusetts. Among the other States required to take censuses are Indiana, Iowa, Kansas, Michigan, Oregon, Oklahoma, and Wisconsin.

Useful agricultural statistics are collected and published also by the boards of agriculture of the several States, notably by the States of Texas and Kansas.

Boards of Trade and Cotton Exchanges

At least twenty-five boards of trade publish statistics of the movement, distribution, prices, etc., of agricultural products, and the following is substantially a complete list of the cities in which these boards of trade are situated, the variants of the name being sometimes merchants' exchange, chamber of commerce, produce exchange, or commercial exchange: Baltimore, Md.; Boston, Mass.; Buffalo, N.Y.; Chicago, Ill.; Cincinnati, Ohio; Denver, Colo.; Detroit, Mich.; Duluth, Minn.; Indianapolis, Ind.; Louisville, Ky.; Memphis, Tenn.; Milwaukee, Wis.; New York, N.Y.; Omaha, Nebr.; Peoria, Ill.; Philadelphia, Pa. (commercial exchange and also produce exchange); Portland, Oreg.; Richmond, Va.; St. Louis, Mo.; San Francisco, Cal. (chamber of commerce and also produce exchange); Seattle, Wash.; Toledo, Ohio, and Washington, D.C.

Besides the foregoing boards of trade, there are many in the United States whose object is to stimulate concerted action by manufacturers, merchants, financiers, and persons especially concerned in carrying on the distributive processes. About 800 of these boards of trade have a national association, which speaks powerfully for interests representing many hundreds of millions of dollars of capital, and which substantially represents the class of persons known as middlemen, who distribute the products of the farm. But this national association does not include all of the boards of trade, chambers of commerce, and produce exchanges. These in the aggregate number between 1,300 and 1,400, the largest number among the States being found in New York; second to which stands Pennsylvania; third, Ohio; and, fourth, Massachusetts.

There is a class of these boards of trade especially concerned with cotton, generally known as cotton exchanges, which are associations of middlemen with the object of obtaining information in regard to the condition of the market as influenced by demand, supply, production, available cotton, and, in some cases, of dealing in futures. The cities and towns where these exchanges are situated are as follows: Eufaula, Birmingham, Mobile, Montgomery, and Selma, Ala.; Little Rock and Texarkana, Ark.; Atlanta, Columbus, Rome, Savannah, and Augusta, Ga.; Monroe, New Orleans, and Shreveport, La.; Greenville, Greenwood, Meridian, Natchez, Vicksburg, and Yazoo City, Miss.; St. Louis, Mo.; New York, N.Y.; Newbern, Wilmington, and Raleigh, N.C.; Charleston and Columbia, S.C.; Memphis and Nashville, Tenn.; Galveston, Dallas, Fort Worth, Sherman, Waco, and Houston, Tex.; Norfolk and Portsmouth, and Richmond, Va.

Statistics of Development

The progress of American agriculture up to the present time has by no means been thoroughly discussed in this paper, nor is it possible to do so within the limits of a Yearbook article; hence only a few more topics can be mentioned. First, statistics expressing development will be given.

Farms and acreage. — The number of farms increased from 1,449,073 in 1850 to 4,564,641 in 1890. During the same time the total farm acreage increased from 293,560,614 to 623,218,619 acres, of which the increase in improved acreage was greater, both absolutely and relatively, than the increase in the unimproved acreage.

Increasing importance of medium-sized farms. — The average size of farms declined from 203 acres in 1850 to 137 acres in 1890, and it has been established by a thorough statistical analysis that in the more recent years the increase in number of farms has more largely accrued to farms of medium size than to farms of the smaller and larger sizes. Why this should be so is only a matter of conjecture. It may be that the persons who acquire the proprietorship of farms, either as owners or as tenants, have become more able to acquire the possession of medium-sized farms, and so reject or consolidate the smaller farms; it may be also that the larger farms have not been found to be as profitable as medium-sized farms.

The use of machines is an important element in this country's agriculture, and possibly the medium-sized farm as it exists to-day is susceptible of being more economically cultivated and managed than either smaller or larger farms, and among the economic reasons for this the farm machine must be reckoned as highly important. But whatever the explanation may be, the fact remains that the middle-class farmer, according to the tendency disclosed by the census of 1890, is coming more and more to the front among agriculturists.

Farm real estate and machines. — The value of the real estate of farms increased from $3,271,575,426 in 1850 to $13,279,252,649 in 1890. During this period the value of farm implements and machines increased from $151,587,638 to $494,247,467; but these numbers do not adequately represent the increase in the importance of implements and machines, partly because these figures take no account of the vast increase in their efficiency, which has been infinitely greater than the figures express, and in a very large degree because of the much cheaper prices prevailing in 1890.

Farm products. — The censuses have very poorly ascertained the value of farm products, the statements undoubtedly being considerably under the facts. The published statement of the census of 1890 gives the value of farm products as $2,460,107,454, but an estimate made on the production ascertained in the census of 1890 by Mr. J. R. Dodge, former Statistician of the Department of Agriculture, places the value of farm products in the agricultural year covered by that census at about $3,500,000,000.

Farm animals have increased as follows, as shown by national censuses: Horses, from 4,336,719 in 1850 to 14,969,467 in 1890; mules and asses, from 559,331 in 1850 to 2,295,532 in 1890; milch cows, from 6,385,094 in 1850 to 16,511,950 in 1890; oxen and other cattle, from 11,393,813 in 1840 to 34,851,622 in 1890; swine, from 26,301,293 in 1840 to 57,409,583 in 1890; sheep, not including spring lambs, from 19,311,374 in 1840 to 35,935,364 in 1890. The wool clip of the census year of 1890 amounted to 165,449,239 pounds. The value of live stock increased during the period 1850–1890 from $544,180,516 to $2,208,767,573.

Farm dairy products are thus stated in the census of 1890: Entire number of gallons of milk produced on farms, 5,210,125,567; pounds of butter, 1,024,223,468; pounds of cheese, 18,726,818. It must be remembered that the production of butter and cheese on farms has been largely transferred to creameries, whose products are not included in the foregoing figures, but are included in part in the census statistics of manufactures — only in part, however, because it is known that a very large portion of the creameries and their products were omitted from the census statistics of 1890.

Poultry. — In 1890 it was reported that the chickens on farms numbered 258,871,125; other fowls, 26,738,315; and that the eggs produced and sold during the census year were 819,722,916 dozen. The poultry statistics, however, probably fall far short of the facts.

Crop production. — Coming now to the production of crops, the following extracts are made from the censuses of 1840 and 1890, to which the figures of the Department of Agriculture for 1899 are added:

Cereals. — Production of indian corn, 377,531,875 bushels in 1840; 2,122,327,547 bushels in 1890; 2,078,143,933 bushels in 1899; and the corn acreage increased from 62,368,504 acres in 1880 to 82,108,587 acres in 1899.

The wheat product was 84,823,272 bushels in 1840; 468,373,968 bushels in 1890; 547,303,846 bushels in 1899; and from 1880 to 1899 the wheat acreage increased from 35,430,333 acres to 44,592,516 acres.

The United States produces more wheat than any other country in the world.

A comparison may be made for 1898: Crop of the United States, 675,149,000 bushels; France, 371,881,000 bushels; Austria-Hungary, 170,938,000 bushels; Italy, 133,372,000 bushels; Germany, 115,000,000 bushels; United Kingdom, 77,170,000 bushels; Russia in Europe, 404,836,000 bushels; Russia in Asia, 94,000,000 bushels; total Asiatic production, 421,321,000 bushels; total African production, 44,439,000 bushels; total South American production, 72,000,000 bushels.

The oat product was, in bushels, in 1840, 123,071,341; in 1890, 809,250,666; in 1899, 796,177,713. The oat acreage was 16,144,593 in 1880, and increased to 26,341,380 acres in 1899.

The rye product was 18,645,567 bushels in 1840, 28,421,398 bushels in 1890, and 23,961,741 bushels in 1899, with a decrease of acreage from 1,842,233 acres in 1880 to 1,659,308 acres in 1899.

Cotton. — The cotton crop of 1850 amounted to 2,469,093 bales, and the crop increased decennially up to the census of 1890, and almost without a break annually since that year until the enormous crop of 1898–99, which amounted to 11,189,205 bales of considerably heavier weight than the bales of 1850. The cotton acreage increased from 14,480,019 acres in 1880 to the largest acreage yet attained, in 1898–99, which was 24,967,295. The cotton crop of the United States substantially dominates the world market for cotton, its proportion of the world's crop being from 80 to 85 per cent, and practically having little competition within the lines of its own grades and qualities. The State of Texas alone produces more cotton than any foreign cotton-producing country.

Hay. — The hay production amounted to 10,248,109 tons in 1840; to 66,831,480 tons in 1890, and to 56,655,756 tons in 1899; and the acreage increased from 30,631054 acres in 1880 to 41,328,462 acres in 1899.

Tobacco. — From 1840 to 1890 the production of tobacco increased from 219,163,319 pounds to 488,256,646 pounds, and the acreage in the latter year was 695,301 acres.

Potatoes. — White potatoes are a crop of extraordinary increase, the bushels in 1850 being 65,797,896; in 1890, 217,546,362, and in 1899, 228,783,232. From 1850 to 1890 the production of sweet potatoes increased from 38,268,148 to 43,950,261 bushels.

Agricultural Exports

The development of the agriculture of the United States has much more than kept pace with the enormous immigration, increase of population, increase of domestic consumption for food and manufactured products, and for cattle and other domestic animals. It has furnished besides an enormous surplus for export. Only the exports of the principal products can be given briefly:

Wheat. — The wheat export was 4,272 bushels in 1823; 4,155,153 bushels in 1860, and 139,432,815 bushels in 1899. During the same time wheat flour was exported to the amount of 756,702 barrels in 1823, 2,611,596 barrels in 1860, and 18,502,690 barrels in 1899.

Cotton. — The exports of raw cotton amounted to 173,723,270 pounds in 1823, to 1,767,686,338 pounds in 1860, and to 3,773,410,293 pounds in 1899. The more recent product, cotton-seed oil, had an export of 50,627,219 gallons in 1899, and the export trade in this product has chiefly grown up since 1889.

Hay and barley. — The hay export is relatively small, amounting to only 64,916 tons in 1899. The barley export also is comparatively small, amounting to 2,267,400 bushels in 1899, although it reached its maximum amount of 20,030,301 bushels in 1897.

Corn. — The corn export was 749,034 bushels in 1823; it was 3,314,155 bushels in 1860, and 174,089,094 bushels in 1899. In addition to the unmanufactured corn exports are the exports of corn meal, and these amounted to 791,488 barrels in 1899; but a large portion of the corn product is consumed by domestic animals, the exports of which are mentioned below.

Oats and rye. — In 1899 the oat export amounted to 30,309,680 bushels, and the oat-meal export was 58,042,505 pounds. In the same year the rye export was 10,140,876 bushels, and the rye-flour export 4,826 barrels.

Animals and animal products. — The following are the exports of farm animals in 1899, the figures representing numbers of animals: Cattle, 389,490; hogs, 33,031; horses, 45,778; mules, 6,755; sheep, 143,286. These numbers have grown during the last twenty-five years from almost nothing.

The exports of beef products amounted to 19,053,800 pounds in 1866, not including preserved meats, and the entire quantity of beef products exported in 1899 was 368,666,638 pounds; in the latter year the beef-tallow exports amounted to 107,361,009 pounds. In 1866 the pork products exported amounted to 97,756,169 pounds, and the number had grown to 1,700,380,357 pounds in 1899. In 1899 the mutton exports amounted to 379,110 pounds.

A large item of export has grown up within a few years under the name of oleo oil, and its export in 1899 aggregated 142,390,492 pounds.

The butter and cheese exports have in late years shown a decline, and in 1899 they amounted, respectively, to 20,247,997 and 38,198,753 pounds.

Tobacco. — For many years tobacco has been a large item of export, and its quantity has substantially remained constant for twenty-five years or so. The pounds of leaf tobacco exported in 1899 were 272,421,295 and the value of the manufactured tobacco exported in that year was $5,179,012.

Wool. — The wool export has rarely reached 1,000,000 pounds, although in 1896 it almost equaled 7,000,000 pounds.

The statistics immediately preceding, as well as the others in this paper, express forcibly and comprehensively, although tersely, the agricultural development through which this country has passed up to the present time — a development which has been unparalleled in the history of the world in its rapidity and magnitude.

Fertilizers

The decade 1840–1850 marks an epoch in the history of agriculture. The world was then making rapid strides in applied science. Railroads were rapidly extending, ocean steam navigation became established, the electric telegraph came into use, and, what was of great importance in connection with agriculture, the chemical theory of manures came to be understood. "Artificial fertilizers," made according to formulas founded on the chemical composition of the ashes of plants, began to be manufactured, and came rapidly into use. The use of nitrate of soda and superphosphate of lime was becoming common. The rapidity of this growth is perhaps best seen in the rise of the use of guano. Samples had come to Europe early in the century; next a few casks came; in 1840, Liebig, the eminent chemist, brought it into notice, and the South American merchants sold a small cargo that year. The next year some 2,000 tons were imported into Great Britain.

The use of commercial fertilizers has progressed from year to year, until, in 1896, 1,894,917 tons were used in the United States, valued at $37,688,869.

The economic advantages of the use of fertilizers are distinctly shown in an investigation conducted by the Division of Statistics of the Department of Agriculture in 1896. This was a unique investigation of comprehensive character, and was applied to the production of cotton.

Along with the increased consumption of commercial fertilizers, there has been a vastly increasing realization by farmers of the value and utility of barnyard and compost manures, especially in the parts of the country where cattle are kept in stables throughout a large portion of the year. While the average production per acre of various crops has not materially increased for many years past, yet farmers know that they not only must not, but can not, rob the soil of its fertility without restoring the elements that go to make plant growth. In some parts of the country, where the fertility of the soil is materially impaired, it is still the custom to let cultivated land lie fallow for sufficient length of time to increase its fertility, but there is also a large extent of country where this is not done, and where, on the contrary, domestic and commercial fertilizers are liberally used.

Speaking in general for the whole country, the net result of the use of fertilizers, so far, has been mainly to preserve the normal fertility and production of the soil, although farmers' experiences have numerously and extensively established the economic desirability of more intensive agriculture.

Evolution of Varieties of Foods from Products

There is one prominent feature in the agricultural development of the United States that has received little public attention (a feature which alone is worthy of an extended article), and this is the extraordinary multiplication of the varieties of foods into which farm products have been converted by the slaughterhouse, by the packing house, by the cannery, and by the manufacture of health foods. The effect of all this upon the consumption of numerous farm products has been very considerable, and has, to some extent, revolutionized the diet of the people of this country, and presumably of other parts of the civilized world, especially of people living in cities and towns.

Early Practices Regarding Food Supply

One does not need to go back more than a generation to find the meat supply derived from local farmers and butchers. Indeed, among the great mass of the people living outside of the cities and large towns the fresh-meat supply was a matter of neighborhood borrowing; a farmer slaughtered an old cow, perhaps, and distributed some of the quarters or other portions of the carcass among his neighbors, with the expectation that they would return an equivalent when it came their turn to butcher.

Until comparatively recent years the products of the farm were distributed throughout the year for food consumption in a crude and very restricted sense. Apples and green corn were dried in the sun; indian corn was preserved dry in the crib; potatoes, cabbages, and turnips were kept fresh in the cellar; some beef was dried; pork and beef were pickled in brine; squashes and pumpkins were kept for some time after the harvest without rotting, and so on with a few other products of the farm and garden.

Canning, Preserving, and Refrigerating in Recent Years

An immense change in the relation of foods to seasons has taken place within recent years. Fresh beef and mutton and pork and poultry preserved by refrigeration can now be had in all parts of the country from the farms and ranches of the Mississippi Valley, to say nothing of the improved local meat supply. Many of the principal garden products now know no season, owing to the canner and the preserver. The peach and the pear, the apricot and the plum, peas and beans, lentils and green corn and tomatoes, and many kinds of berries — and so on through almost the entire list of the fruit and vegetable products of the farm and garden — are now to be had at all times of the year, not always, perhaps, with the flavor they possessed when gathered from their vines and stalks and trees, but yet with much of their original freshness and flavor.

By means of canning and preserving the farmers' market has been enlarged both in time and space until the market for farm and garden products now extends throughout the entire year, not only to remote parts of this country, but to a large portion of the world.

If a list of the different kinds and descriptions of food were to be presented, it would, because of its magnitude, overtax the patience of the reader. An attempt was made several years ago to prepare such a list for a publisher, and the undertaking had to be abandoned on account of its unexpectedly large proportions and the time, labor, and expense required. In this paper it is proposed merely to give three illustrations of the heterogeneity that has characterized the development of farm products as foods and for other purposes.

Business of a Prominent Packing Company

One of the large Western packing companies with enormous capital and business has been selected to illustrate how the extension of the farmers' market has been promoted and elaborated in recent years. This packing company owns the cars that are used to distribute its products and to collect some of them. It has 500 tank cars for transporting blood and tankage for fertilizers and various animal oils; it has 4,000 cars for transporting dressed beef and 6,500 cars for transporting fruit. From the price lists of this company, sent to its agencies throughout the United States, the following facts are extracted:

The beef carcass is cut into many different parts in various ways, all intended to meet the demands of retailers and consumers, and the different parts so cut, including all of the parts of the animal customarily eaten, number 53. With regard to meat cuttings, the numbers are, pork 29, mutton 12, veal 5; number of boiled hams 6; varieties of sausages 43 and of delicatessen sausage 14 — total varieties of sausage 57. The dried salt meats are prepared with 16 different cuttings; the bacon meats with 16.

There are hams of many descriptions, and dried beef, mess pork, mess beef, pickled beef tongue, pork spareribs, mince-meat in packages of numerous sizes, lard, compound lard and lard oil, neat's-foot oil, and tallow oil.

The canned meats include numerous varieties, among which may be mentioned corned beef, pigs' feet, gelatin, boar's head, Oxford sausage, tongue, roast beef, boiled beef, chipped beef, deviled ham, potted ham and tongue, minced ham, chicken, turkey, chile con carne, pork and beans, ox marrow, chicken tamale, and sauerkraut and Vienna sausage, etc.

There are to be mentioned also some of the canned soups, as ox tail, mock turtle, tomato, consommé, chicken, beef, mutton, vegetable, purée of green peas, and so on.

The extracts of beef are liquid and in tablets of various descriptions. The pickled tongues, pork hocks, and pigs' feet are of nine descriptions, and there is poultry of all sorts and fresh eggs and canned eggs, ducks, quails, venison, prairie chickens, pigeons, squabs, and even frogs' legs.

Cotton Seed

Cotton seed is a very marked instance of a former by-product of the farm which has become of enormous value and of varied uses. The meats are made into oil cake and oil meal for feeding stuff and for fertilizers; into crude oil, cotton-seed stearin, salad oil, cottolene, miners' oil, and soap, and the oil is exported to Europe and brought back again as olive oil. The hulls may be used for making paper; they are made into bran for cattle food; they are used for fuel, and are an important contribution to the list of fertilizers.

Here is an enormous source of wealth which science has given to the farmers within comparatively recent years. The estimated value of the cotton seed of a 10,000,000-bale crop of cotton (to the planters) is about $30,000,000, and this value is now almost entirely appropriated by them.

Diversification of Dairy Products

Only one more instance of the elaboration of the products of the farm need be mentioned to illustrate how varied the farmers' market has become and how minutely his products have been made to create and answer the wants of mankind. The following are the varieties of the dairy products of the United States, as furnished by Maj. H. E. Alvord, chief of the dairy division, Bureau of Animal Industry:

Butter.

Dairy and Creamery: In tubs, boxes, family packages, rolls, and prints.
Imitation Creamery: Ladled, Renovated, or ''Process,'' all melted and rechurned.
Fresh or ''Sweet;'' that is, unsalted.

I. Hard: *(a)* Domestic varieties:
        Factory Standard, or Cheddar.
        English Dairy.
        Young America.
        Little Favorites. ⎫
        Picnics.   ⎬ Differing in size and form rather
        Ponies.   ⎭   than in character.
        Skim cheese.
        Pineapple.
        Sage.
   (b) Foreign forms, imitated:
        Swiss, or Gruyere.
        Edam.
        Gouda.
        Limburger.
        Munster.
        Brick.
II. Soft: Pot cheese, or smearcase.
       Neufchatel.
       Cream.
       Isigny.
       Brie.
       Camembert.
       Potted and prepared cheese, "Club-house," etc.

Milk, etc.

Condensed milk, sweetened.
Condensed milk, plain, or unsweetened.
"Evaporated cream."
Cream, sterilized and canned.
Milk and cream, Pasteurized, "Certified," "Modified," etc.
Koumys, Matzoon, Wheyn, etc.

Some Economic Results of Machines

Much remains to be said with regard to the evolution of agriculture in the United States, but only a brief reference can be made to some of the more important results of the investigation of hand and machine labor and processes as applied to agriculture, with a contrast between farming as it was practiced fifty to seventy years ago and farming as it is now carried on with the advantage of the labor-saving and perfecting implements and machines of the present time as well as with the improvements contributed by the chemist, the "book farmer," and the more enlightened experience of the last half century.

Corn Cultivation and Harvesting

Between 1855 and 1894 the following changes took place in the cultivation of corn. The time of human labor required to produce one bushel of corn on an average declined from 4 hours and 34 minutes to 41 minutes, and the cost of the human labor to produce this bushel declined from 35¾ cents to 10½ cents.

In the earlier years the plow and harrow of that period were used; the check rows were marked with the shovel plow; the seed was dropped by hand from a bucket or pouch carried by the farmer and covered with a hoe; the cultivating was done with a shovel plow; knives were used for cutting the stalks from the ground by hand; husking pegs were worn on the hand in husking; the stalks, husks, and blades were cut into fodder with an old-time machine turned by hand, and the corn was shelled by hand, either on a frying-pan handle or on a shovel or by rubbing the cob against the unshelled ears.

A radical change had taken place in 1894. The earth was loosened with a gang plow, and a disk harrow very thoroughly pulverized it. A corn planter drawn by a horse planted the corn, and the top soil was pulverized afterwards with a four-section harrow.

When it came to harvesting the corn, a self-binder drawn by horses cut the stalks and bound them, and the shocks of stalks were then hauled to a machine, which removed the husks from the ears, and in the same process cut the husks and the stalks and the blades into fodder, the power of the machine being supplied by a steam engine.

Then came the shelling of the corn, which is one of the marvels of the changes that have been wrought by machines. In this case, the machine operated by steam shelled 1 bushel of corn per minute, while in the old way the labor of one man was required for 100 minutes to do the same work.

Wheat Cultivation and Harvesting

The use of steam as a substitute for horse power in plowing, in harvesting, and in thrashing wheat has not materially contributed to economy, except from a saving due to the elimination of animal power, so the more common power supplied by horses is here selected for the comparison. The years in contrast are 1830 and 1896.

It is one of the marvels of the age that the amount of human labor now required to produce a bushel of wheat from beginning to end is on an average only 10 minutes, whereas, in 1830, the time was 3 hours and 3 minutes. During the interval between these years the cost of the human labor required to produce this bushel of wheat declined from 17¾ cents to 3⅓ cents.

In the contrast thus presented the heavy, clumsy plow of the day was used in 1830; the seed was sown by hand, and was harrowed into the ground by the drawing of bushes over it; the grain was cut with sickles, hauled to a barn, and at some time before the following spring was thrashed with flails; the winnowing was done with a sheet attached to rods, on which the grain was placed with a shovel and then tossed up and down by two men until the wind had blown out the chaff.

In the latter year, on the contrary, the ground was plowed and pulverized in the same operation by a disk plow; the seed was sown with a mechanical seeder drawn by horses; the reaping, thrashing, and sacking of the wheat was done with the combined reaper and thrasher drawn by horses, and then the wheat was ready to haul to the granary.

Haymaking

Hay is the next selection for comparison, the years being 1860 and 1894. When men mowed the grass with scythes, spread it and turned it over for drying with pitchforks, when they raked it into windrows with a hand rake, cocked it with a pitchfork, and baled it with a hand press, the time of human labor required per ton was 35½ hours; but when for this method was substituted a mower, a hay tedder, and a hayrake and hay gatherers and stackers drawn by horses, and a press operated by a horse, the time of human labor was reduced to 11 hours and 34 minutes, while the cost of human labor from the earlier to the later year was reduced from $3.06 to $1.29.

The more noticeable economy in haymaking is in the mowing and curing of the grass. In these two operations the time of human labor declined per ton from 11 hours to 1 hour and 39 minutes, while the cost of the human labor declined from 83⅓ cents to 16¼ cents.

The comparisons might be extended throughout many of the crops produced by the farmer, with a constantly recurring illustration of the saving of human labor and of the diminution of the cost of production by the dimunition of human labor. With regard to animal labor alone it often appears that an increased time is required in production, but where there is an increased cost it is principally due to the increased value of the labor of animals.

Saving in the Cost of Producing Crops

The potential saving in the cost of human labor on account of improved implements, machines, and processes, at the rate per bushel or ton, as the case may be, has been computed for seven of the principal crops of 1899; the comparison is between the old-time methods of production, in which hand labor was assisted only by the comparatively rude and inefficient implements of the day and the present time, when hand labor has not only the assistance of highly efficient and perfected implements and machines, but has been considerably displaced by them. The saving in the cost of human labor in cents, per unit of product, permits a very forcible statement of its equivalent in money by means of a computation consisting of the multiplication of the saving per unit into the crop of 1899. The result expresses the potential labor saving in the production of seven crops of that year, and is not an aggregate of the saving of human labor in the cost of producing the crops for all of the years between the earlier and the later ones, during which time this economizing and displacement of human labor has taken place. In the case of the crop of corn, the money measure of the saving of human labor required to produce it in 1899 in the most available economic manner, as compared with its production in the old-time manner, was $523,276,642; wheat, $79,194,867; oats, $52,866,200; rye, $1,408,950; barley, $7,323,480; white potatoes, $7,366,820; hay, $10,034,868.

The total potential saving in the cost of human labor for these seven crops of 1899, owing to the possible utilization of the implements, machines, and methods of the present time, in place of the old-time manner of production, reaches the stupendous amount of $681,471,827 for this one year.

Conclusion

It would be idle to claim that the progress of the agriculture of the United States and its evolution from the primitive scope and conditions in which it was found by the settlers who came from Europe have been set forth adequately, even in its important topics and details, in the foregoing pages, but perhaps enough has been presented to explain in their main features the causes and opportunities which in combination have led to an agricultural production actually too great to be grasped by the human mind.

As great as has been the growth of manufactures, mining, the fisheries, and trade and transportation, all of which tend to draw population from agriculture, yet more than one-third of the population of the country is engaged in agriculture or dependent upon agriculturists. This element in our population has proved to be a strong one. It has been conservative with regard to those things that experience has demonstrated to be good. It has been an industrial element upon which all other elements of the population have needed to depend as the cornerstone of the social and industrial structure.

The agricultural element is the one independent element in our society. Let whatever betide that may, this element has a degree of independence in subsistence and in living that no other element has, and still, as in the past, remains the chief mainstay of the nation.

The Dairy Industry, 1899

From Henry E. Alvord, "Dairy Development in the United States," U.S. Department of Agriculture, *Yearbook*, 1899, pp. 381–402

The Present Field of the Dairy Industry

No branch of agriculture in the United States has made greater progress than dairying during the nineteenth century. No other has received more direct benefit from the art of invention, the teachings of modern science, and the intelligent practice of skilled operators. Cooperative and commercial organizations have been formed to conduct the business locally and to guard its general interests. State laws and appropriations of money have been made to foster and promote this industry. Dairying has become the specialty of districts of wide area in different parts of the country. It is now regarded as among the most progressive and highly developed forms of farming in the United States.

The greater part of this country has been found so well adapted to dairying that its extension has more than kept pace with the opening and settlement of new territory. A belief was long entertained that successful diarying in America must be restricted to narrow geographical limits, constituting a "dairy belt" lying between the fortieth and forty-fifth parallels of latitude and extending from the Atlantic Ocean to the Missouri River; the true dairying districts were thought to be in separated sections, occupying not more than one-third of the area of this belt. These ideas have been exploded. It has been proved that good butter and cheese can be made, by proper management, in almost all parts of North America. Generally speaking, good butter can be made wherever good beef can be produced. Advantages unquestionably exist in the climate, soil, water, and herbage of certain sections, but these factors are largely under control, and what is lacking in natural conditions can be supplied by tact and skill. So that, while dairying is intensified, and constitutes the leading agricultural interest over large areas where the natural advantages are greatest, the industry is found well established in spots in almost all parts of the country and developing in unexpected places and under what might be considered as very unfavorable conditions.

Dairying During the Colonial Period and at the Present Time

Dairying was practiced in this country in colonial times, and butter and cheese are mentioned among the early exports from the settlements along the Atlantic coast; but this production was only a feature of general and pioneer farming. Dairying as a specialty did not appear in the United States to any extent until well along in the nineteenth century. The dairy history of the country is therefore identical with its progress in the present century. This progress has been truly remarkable. The wide territorial extension; the immense investment in lands, buildings, animals, and equipment; the great improvement in dairy cattle; the acquisition and diffusion of knowledge as to economy of production; the revolution in methods and systems of manufacture; the general advance in quality of products; the wonderful increase in quantity; the industrial and commercial importance of dairying, all constitute a prominent feature in the material progress of the nation.

Dairying During the Early Part of the Century

During the early part of the century the keeping of cows on American farms was incident to the general work. The care of milk and the making of butter and cheese were in the hands of the women of the household, and the methods and utensils were crude. The average quality of the products was inferior. The supply of domestic markets was unorganized and irregular. The milch cows in use belonged to the mixed and indescribable race of "native" cattle, with occasionally a really good dairy animal appearing singly, almost by accident, or, at the best, as one of a family developed by some uncommonly discriminating yet unscientific breeder. The cows calved almost universally in the spring, and were generally allowed to go dry in the autumn or early winter. Winter dairying was practically unknown. As a rule, excepting the pasture season, cattle were insufficiently and unprofitably fed and poorly housed, if at all. It was a common thing for cows to die of starvation and exposure, and it was considered no disgrace to owners to have their cattle "on the lift" in the spring. In the Eastern and Middle States the milk was usually set in small shallow earthen vessels or tin pans for the cream to rise. Little attention was paid to cooling the air in which it stood in summer or to moderating it in winter so long as freezing was prevented. The few who scalded fresh milk had no idea of the true reason for so doing or why beneficial effects resulted. The pans of milk oftener stood in pantries and cellars or on kitchen shelves than in rooms specially constructed or adapted to the purpose. In southern Pennsylvania and the States farther south spring houses were in vogue; milk received care, and setting it in earthen crocks or pots, standing in cool, flowing water, was a usual and excellent practice. Churning the entire milk was very common. This is still done to some extent in the Southern States, where butter is made every morning and where all the milk is buttermilk. In seasons of scarcity of milk there was no butter. In the Northern States there were some instances where families were supplied with butter weekly during most of the year, and with an occasional cheese, directly from the producers. But the general farm practice was to "pack" the butter in firkins, half firkins, tubs, and jars, and let the cheese accumulate on the farm, taking these products to market only once or twice a year. Not only were there as many different lots and kinds of butter and cheese as there were producing farms, but the product of a single farm varied in character and quality according to season and other circumstances. Every package had to be examined, graded, and sold upon its merits. It was usual for half the butter in market to be strong, if not actually rancid, and for cheese to be sharp. With the products largely low in grade, prices were also very low.

Dairying During the Middle of the Century

The above conditions continued without material change up to the middle of the century. Some improvement was noticeable in cattle and appliances, and in some sections dairy farming became a specialty, although not in a marked degree. Herkimer County, N.Y., is probably the best example of early dairy districts in this country. Of this county X. A. Willard wrote (in 1870) as follows:

Cheese making began here more than sixty years ago. For upward of twenty years its progress was slow and the business was deemed hazardous by the majority of farmers, who believed that overproduction was to be the result of making a venture upon this specialty. The fact, however, gradually became apparent that the cheese makers were rapidly bettering their condition and outstripping in wealth those who were engaged in grain raising and a mixed husbandry. About the year 1830 dairying became general in the towns of Herkimer County north of the Mohawk, and some years later spread through the southern part of the county, gradually extending into Oneida and adjoining counties. Up to this period and for several years later little or no cheese was shipped to Europe. It was not considered fit for market till fall or winter. It was packed in rough casks and peddled in the home market at 5 to 8 cents a pound.

All the operations of the dairy continued rude and undeveloped even in these "dairying districts." The cows were milked in the open yard, and the curds were worked in homemade tubs and pressed in log presses. Everything was done by guess; there was no order, no system, no science in dairy operations. The cheese-making section gradually embraced the central and western portions of New York and the adjacent parts of Pennsylvania and Ohio, and the total production became large. Toward the middle of the century the gross supply of cheese was in excess of domestic demand, and cheese exports from the United States, mainly to Great

Britain, ranged from 3,000,000 to 17,000,000 pounds a year. With the growth of cities and towns the business of milk supply increased and better methods prevailed. Yet, prior to the year 1850 no city had received any part of its milk supply by railroad transportation; near-by producers met all existing demands by hauling in their own vehicles. Butter making for home use and in a small way for local trade was common wherever cows were kept, and in some places there was a surplus sufficient to be sent to the large markets. Vermont and New York became particularly noted for butter production. "Franklin County butter." from counties of this name in those two States and in Massachusetts, was the favorite in New England markets, and the fame of "Orange County" and "Goshen" butter, from southern New York, was still more extensive.

Dairying During the Third Quarter of the Century

The twenty-five years following 1850 was a period of remarkable activity and progress in the dairy interests of the country. At first the agricultural exhibitions or "cattle shows," which were comparatively new and popular, and the enterprise of importers turned attention toward the improvement of farm animals; breeds of cattle noted particularly for dairy qualities were introduced and began to win the favor of dairy farmers. Then the early efforts at cooperation in dairying were recognized as successful, and were copied until the cheese factory became an established institution. Once fairly started in the heart of the cheese-making district of New York, the factory system spread with much rapidity. The "war period" lent additional impetus to the forward movement. The price of cheese, which was 10 cents per pound and less in 1860, rose to 15 cents in 1863 and to 20 cents and over in 1865. The foreign demand increased also, and the yearly cheese exports rose from 10,000,000 pounds in 1850 to 15,000,000 in 1860 and to almost 50,000,000 in 1865. Ten years later over 100,000,000 pounds were exported.

Establishment of Cheese and Butter Factories

Although several earlier instances of associated dairying have been authenticated, which were locally successful, it is generally conceded that the credit of establishing the first real cheese factory, which served as a model and incentive to others, belongs to Jesse Williams, of Oneida County, N.Y. Mr. Williams lived upon his farm, near Rome. He was an experienced and skillful cheese maker, and his dairy had such a good reputation and its product was so eagerly sought at prices above the average that he increased his output of cheese by adding to his own supply of milk that from the herd of a son located upon a farm near by, and then from other neighbors. This idea of bringing together daily the milk from several neighboring farms, to be made into cheese at one place by a skilled operator, was the germ from which sprang the cheese-factory system of the United States. Mr. Williams began working on this plan in 1851. He was so successful that a special building was erected the next year and fitted up with the best apparatus obtainable. The effect of this good example and the early extension of the factory system is shown by the following table, which gives the number of factories built and put into operation in New York annually during the years stated:

Number of cheese factories established in the State of New York annually,
1854–1866.

Year.	Factories.	Year.	Factories.
1854.............	4	1862.............	25
1855.............	2	1863.............	111
1856.............	3	1864.............	210
1857.............	3	1865.............	52
1858.............	4	1866.............	46
1859.............	4		
1860.............	17	Total in 1866...	499
1861.............	18		

Cheese factories were soon started in Pennsylvania and Ohio, and then in other States, East and West. In 1869 the number in the whole country exceeded 1,000, and from that time the cooperative, or factory, system practically superseded the making of cheese on farms.

Methods of Management of Cheese and Butter Factories

Independent of the matters of ownership, organization, and control, the factories and creameries differ much in methods of management and of settlement with patrons. Great progress in these particulars has been made since the introduction of the system. The first establishments received milk from patrons daily and sometimes twice a day. From near-by farms the milk was often warm from the cow at time of delivery. The milk was then kept in large vats (for cheese making) or in immense shallow pans in a cooling and creaming room until skimmed. Abundant room and expensive receptacles were necessary at the creamery. Then, for butter making, deep setting of the milk in cool water was adopted. The creameries were provided with pools or stationary vats below the floor level. Through these, cool water flowed from springs near at hand, and in them the milk was set in "shotgun" cans, immediately after arrival, for cooling and for cream to form. The pools were 18 or 20 inches deep, with racks at bottom to hold cans. The tin cans were 22 inches deep and 8 inches in diameter and filled so that when in the pool the top of the milk was just below the surface of the water. Springs with abundant flow and having a natural temperature of 48° to 56° F. were regarded as highly desirable. Afterwards came the method of mechanical cream separation (to be later described) in place of "setting," or the gravity system. Another radical change, which began about 1875, was to set and skim the milk on the farms and haul only cream to the factories. Agents from the creameries, with suitable teams and carrying cans, drove from farm to farm and gathered the cream. Hence, the name of "gathered-cream factories" for establishments of this class. This kind of factory is still the favorite in some good butter districts, and it has very decided merits. The earliest factories and creameries paid for milk by the quart or gallon and at the same price, all lots of equal bulk being regarded of equal value. The first step in advance on this line was to buy or credit milk by weight, but still all at the same price. On the gathered-cream plan, equal bulk measures of cream were long regarded as of like value, and this is still practiced to some extent. The most modern and approved plan is to pay for the milk or cream received by factory or creamery according to the pounds of fat it actually contains as experimentally determined. This will be referred to later. At first it was considered sufficient to have 200 cows tributary to a factory, and patrons were expected to be located within a mile or two, and 4 or 5 miles was the maximum haul. Larger factories were soon favored as more economical, and very large ones have been lately put in operation, each receiving the daily product of thousands of cows. Milk and cream is hauled twice as far as formerly to patronize a factory, and often by cooperation among the farmers along a "route." All patrons are now expected to cool their milk thoroughly before it leaves the farm. In the latest form of creamery management, cream is collected over many square miles of territory and transported long distances by rail to be made into butter at a central factory.

The Condensed-Milk Industry

The condensed-milk industry had its beginning coincident with the inauguration of the factory system for making butter and cheese. Some method of preserving milk had long been sought and numerous preparations of the article had been offered, but these failed to meet the requirements and win public favor. In 1846 experiments were begun in New York by Mr. Gail Borden with a view of securing a preserved milk that was pure, wholesome, and palatable, capable of being transported long distances and kept for long periods in trying climates, and then serving as a satisfactory substitute for crude, fresh milk; but it was not until 1856 that he obtained results which have since popularized the product in every quarter of the globe. The previously prevailing ideas of a dry form of milk (desiccated, solidified, or powdered) were abandoned, and it was decided that a semiliquid state was the best form for preservation. The correctness of this decision is attested by the fact that, extensive as the industry now is and numerous as are the commercial brands, all condensed milk is still prepared under substantially the system then originated. This applies to the unsweetened as well as to the sweetened article, for "plain condensed milk" was first introduced and put upon the market about the year 1861. It was then mainly in open vessels and intended for early use. At that time condensed milk in both forms had become well known, and four or five factories were in operation, each producing about 5,000 one-pound cans per day. For the year 1879 the production of condensed milk in the United States was reported as 13,000,000 pounds and for 1889 as 38,000,000 pounds.

Application of Mechanics to the Dairy

The third quarter of the century was also a period of unprecedented progress in the application of mechanics to the dairy. The factories and creameries required new equipment, adapted to manufacture upon an enlarged scale, and equal attention was paid to the improvement of appliances for farm dairies. Shallow pans were changed in shape and greatly enlarged; some were made to hold 20 or 30 gallons, and had bottom and sides double for cooling or warming by the water jacket. Then these big pans, and most others, disappeared in favor of deep setting. This system, in which deep cans were used, set in cold water, preferably iced water, was introduced from Sweden, although the same principles had been in practice for generations in the spring houses of the South. Numerous creaming appliances, or creamers, were invented, based upon this system. Butter workers of various models, most of them employing the lever, or a crank and roller, took the place of the bowl and ladle and the use of the bare hand. Churns appeared of all shapes, sizes, and kinds, the general plan being to abolish dashers and substitute the agitation of cream for violent beating. About this time the writer made a search of the United States Patent Office records, which revealed the fact that forty or fifty new or improved churns were claimed annually, and, after about one-fourth were rejected, the patents actually issued provided a new churn every ten or twelve days for more than seventy years! This illustrates the activity of invention in the dairy line. It was admitted by all that at this period the United States was far in advance of any other country in the variety and excellence of its mechanical aids to dairying.

Organization of Dairymen's Associations

The same period witnessed the organization of dairymen in voluntary associations for mutual benefit, the formation of clubs and societies of breeders of pure-bred cattle, and the appearance of the first American dairy literature of consequence in book form. The American Dairymen's Association was organized in 1863. Its field of activity was east of Indiana, and accordingly the Northwestern Dairymen's Association was formed in 1867. Both of these associations continued in existence, holding periodical conventions and publishing their proceedings for twelve or fifteen years. Then followed the formation of State dairy associations in Vermont (1870), Pennsylvania (1871), Wisconsin (1872), Illinois (1874), Iowa (1876), New York (1877), and other States, superseding the few pioneer societies, which, for the time, covered broader fields.

Introduction of Dairy Cattle and Efforts at Herd Improvement

The Shorthorn breed led in the introduction of improved cattle to the United States, and for a long time the representatives of this race, imported from England, embraced fine dairy animals. Shorthorn grades formed the foundation, and an excellent one, upon which many dairy herds were built during the second and third quarters of the century, and much of this blood is still found in prosperous dairy districts. The period named was that of greatest activity in importing improved cattle from abroad; but Shorthorns have been so generally bred for beef qualities that the demand for them is almost exclusively on that line, and very few of the breed are now classed as dairy cattle. Ayrshires from Scotland, Holstein-Friesians from North Holland, and Jerseys and Guernseys from the Channel Islands, are the breeds recognized as of dairy excellence, and upon animals graded and improved from these the industry mainly depends. The first two breeds named are noted for giving large quantities of milk of medium quality; the other two, both often miscalled "Alderney," give milk of exceeding richness, and theirs is the favorite blood with butter makers. There are also the Brown Swiss and Simmenthal cattle from Switzerland, the Normandy breed from France, and Red-Polled cattle from the south of England which have dairy merit, but belong rather to what is called the "general-purpose" class. Associations of persons interested in maintaining the purity of the respective breeds have been formed since 1850, and they all record pedigrees and publish registers or herdbooks. Pure-bred herds of some of these different breeds are owned in nearly every State, and these animals aggregate 200,000 or 300,000. Their blood is so generally diffused that half-breeds or higher grades are very numerous wherever cows are kept for dairy purposes. Therefore, although pure-bred animals form less than 2 per cent of the working dairy herds, their influence is so great that it is probable the average dairy cow of the United States at the close of the century will carry nearly 50 per cent of improved blood. The breeding and quality of this average cow, and consequently her productiveness and profit, have thus been steadily advanced.

The progress made in this respect in fifty years has been remarkable. When improvement upon the native stock began, a cow that would make a pound of butter a day for two or three months was a local celebrity. Now and then a single animal made a really noteworthy record, like that of the Oakes cow, famous in Massachusetts about 1816. This cow gave 44 pounds of milk a day and made 467 pounds of butter during one season, but she was evidently a sport and failed to reproduce her equal. The first good record of definite herd improvement was made by Zadock Pratt, of Greene County, N.Y. By careful selection and culling he increased the average butter product of his 50 cows from 130 pounds for the year 1852 to 225 pounds in 1863; for seven years the average milk yield was 4.710 pounds per cow. About 1865, when good cows sold for $40 or less, an enterprising dairyman in New England advertised widely that he would pay $100 for any cow which would yield 50 pounds of milk a day on his farm for two or three consecutive days. Not an animal was offered under these conditions. The good dairy cow has now been so long bred to a special purpose that instead of the former short milking period, almost limited to the pasture season, it yields a comparatively even flow of milk during ten or eleven months in every twelve, and if desired the herd produces as much in winter as in summer. A cow that does not average 6 or 7 quarts of milk per day for three hundred days, being 4,000 to 4,500 pounds a year, is not considered profitable. There are many herds having an average yearly product of 5,000 pounds per cow, and single animals are numerous which give ten or twelve times their own weight in milk during a year. Quality has also been so improved that the milk of many a cow will make as much butter in a week as did that of three or four average cows of the mid-century. Whole herds average 300 to 350 pounds of butter a year, occasionally more, and authenticated records of cows giving 2 pounds a day are very numerous. Rivals to the Oakes cow may now be found frequently, often several in one bovine family, the dairy merit maintained and transmitted by judicious breeding; and although animals of such excellence are none too common, they no longer excite astonishment or incredulity.

Dairying During the Closing Decades of the Century

The development of dairying in the United States during the closing decades of the nineteenth century has been uninterrupted and marked by events of the greatest consequence in its entire history. The importance of two inventions during this period can not be over-estimated.

Mechanical Separation of Cream from Milk

The first is the application of centrifugal force to the separation of cream from milk. This is based upon the fact that the specific gravity of milk serum, or skim milk, is greater than that of the fatty portion, or cream. The dairy centrifuge, or cream separator, enables the creaming or "skimming" to be done immediately after milking, preferably while the milk has its natural warmth. The cream can be churned at once, while sweet, but the better and usual practice is to cool thoroughly and then slowly cure, or "ripen," it for churning. The cream can be held at a comparatively high temperature, avoiding the necessity of much ice or cold water. The skim milk is available for use while still warm, quite sweet, and in its best condition for feeding to young animals. This mechanical method is more efficient than the old gravity system, securing more perfect separation and preventing loss of fat in the skim milk. It also largely reduces the dairy labor. The handling and care of the milk may be thus wholly removed from the duties of the household. Separators are made of sizes and patterns suited to farm use, and to be operated by hand or power — a dog or a sheep, a bull or a horse, water, electricity, or steam. The foregoing conditions apply when the separation is done on the farm where the milk is produced. In creamery practice the milk is usually aired and cooled on the patrons' farms and hauled once a day to the factory; there it is warmed to facilitate the work, passed through the separator, and the skim milk may be at once hauled back to the farms. A creamery uses one or more separators of large capacity, operated by power. This practice involves the double haul and an apparent waste of the farmer's time and labor. A movement toward economy in this respect is the establishment of "skimming stations" at convenient points, equipped with one or more power separators; to these the milk is taken for separation from the farms in the vicinity, and from these stations the cream is carried to the central factory for curing and churning.

Besides its economy and its effect upon labor, the mechanical cream separator almost eliminates the factor of climate in a large part of dairy management, and altogether has worked a revolution in the industry. The centrifuge is still a marvel to those who see it working for the first time. The whole milk, naturally warm or warmed artificially, flows into a strong steel bowl held in an iron frame; the bowl revolves at rates varying from 1,500 to 25,000 times per minute, and from two projecting tubes the cream and skim milk separately flow in continuous streams. The machines can be regulated to produce cream of any desired quality or thickness. These separators of different sizes are capable of thus skimming or separating (more properly, creaming) from 15 to 500 gallons of milk per hour. A machine of standard factory size has a speed of 6,000 to 7,000 revolutions a minute and a capacity for creaming 250 gallons of milk an hour.

The world is indebted to Europe for this invention, at least as a dairy appliance. It is the only instance in which dairy invention abroad has been notably in advance of the United States. Yet, investigations were in progress contemporaneously in this country along the same line, and many of the material improvements in the cream separator and several novel patterns have since been invented here. The machine has been vastly improved during its twenty years of existence. At first the bowl was filled with a "charge" of milk, the separation effected, the machine stopped, its compartments emptied of milk and cream, then refilled and started again. The continuously acting machine was soon invented, however, and is now universal. Most of the power machines are still operated by pulley, belting, and intermediate, but in the latest patterns steam is applied directly to a turbine wheel in the base of the standard. The first centrifugal separators were put into practical use in this country and Great Britain in the year 1879. On the continent of Europe they were used a little earlier. The century closes with more than 40,000 of these machines in operation in the United States.

Fat Test for Milk

The second great dairy invention of the period is the popular fat test for milk, being a quick and easy substitute for chemical analysis. This is one of the public benefactions of the agricultural experiment stations. In several States these stations have done much creditable work in dairy investigation, and from them have come several clever methods for testing the fat content of milk. The one which has been generally approved and adopted in this and other lands is named for its originator, Dr. S. M. Babcock, chemist and dairy investigator, first of the New York experiment station at Geneva and since of the Wisconsin experiment station. This test combines the principle of centrifugal force with simple chemical action. The machine on the Babcock plan has been made in a great variety of patterns, simple and inexpensive for home use and more elaborate and substantial for factories. By these machines from two to forty samples may be tested at once in a few moments, and by the use of bottles specially provided the percentage of fat may be determined in samples of milk, cream, skim milk, or buttermilk. Of course, the glassware appurtenances of these testers must be mathematically accurate. Besides the machine and its fittings, the only supplies needed are sulphuric acid of standard strength and warm water. Any person of intelligence can soon learn to make ordinary tests with this appliance, but care and skill are necessary to absolutely correct results.

This fat test of milk has wide application, and it may fairly be questioned whether it is second to the cream separator in advancing the economics of dairying. The percentage of fat being accepted as the measure of value for milk for nearly all purposes, the Babcock test may be the basis for municipal milk inspection, for fixing the price of milk delivered to city dealers, to cheese factories, creameries, and condenseries, and for commercial settlements between patrons in cooperative dairying of any kind. By this test also the dairy farmer may prove the quality of milk from his different cows and (with quantity of milk yield recorded) may fix their respective value as dairy animals. Cows are now frequently bought and sold upon the basis of the milk scale and the Babcock test. With perfect apparatus in competent hands the accuracy of the test is beyond question, and it is of the highest scientific value and practical use. It should be noted that although clearly patentable, thus offering to the patentee an independent income through a very small royalty, this priceless invention and boon to dairying was freely given to the public by Dr. Babcock. Recognition of this public service has taken the form of a medal voted by the legislature of Wisconsin, and a handsome testimonial has been sent by the spontaneous action of appreciative creamerymen in distant New Zealand.

Dairying at the Present Time

The advent of the twentieth century will find the dairy industry of the United States established upon a plane far above the crude and variable domestic art of three or four generations ago. The milch cow itself, upon which the whole business rests, is almost as much a machine as a natural product, and, as already shown, a very different creature from the average animal of the olden time. Instead of a few homely and inconvenient implements for use in the laborious duties of the dairy, perfected appliances, skillfully devised to accomplish their object and lighten labor, are provided all along the way. Long rows of shining tin pans no longer adorn rural dooryards. The factory system of cooperative or concentrated manufacture has so far taken the place of home dairying that in entire States the cheese vat or press is as rare as the handloom, and in many counties it is as hard to find a farm churn as a spinning wheel.

A Sample of the Changes in Dairy Practices

Here is an example of the radical change wrought in dairy practices: Northern Vermont has long been a region of large butter production. St. Albans is the business center of Franklin County. During the middle of the century the country-made butter from miles around came to this market every Tuesday. The average weekly supply was 30 to 40 tons. This butter was very varied in quality, was sampled and classified with much labor and expense, placed in three grades, and forwarded to the Boston market, 200 miles distant. During twenty-five years ending in 1875, some 65,000,000 pounds, valued at $20,000,000, passed through this little town. All of this was dairy butter made upon one or two thousand different farms, in as many churns. In 1880 the first creamery was built in this county; ten years later there were fifteen. Now, a creamery company located at St. Albans has fifty-odd skimming or separating stations distributed through this and adjoining counties. To those is carried the milk from more than 30,000 cows. Farmers having home separators may deliver cream which, being inspected and tested, is accepted and credited at its actual butter value, just as other raw material is sold to mills and factories. The separated cream is conveyed by rail and wagon — largely the former — to the central factory. There, in one room, from 10 to 12 tons of butter are made every working-day. A single churning place for a whole county! All of this butter is of standard quality, "extra creamery," and is sold on its reputation, upon orders from different points received in advance of its manufacture. The price is relatively higher than the average for the product of the same farms fifty years ago. This is mainly because of better average quality and greater uniformity — two important advantages of the creamery system.

Method of Milking Unchanged

In one respect dairy labor is the same as a hundred years ago. Cows still have to be milked by hand. Although numerous attempts have been made, and patent after patent has been issued, no mechanical contrivance has yet been a practical success as a substitute for the human hand in milking. Therefore, twice a day, every day in the year, the dairy cows must be milked by manual labor. This is one of the main items of labor in dairying, as well as a most delicate and important duty. Allowing 10 cows per hour to a milker, which means lively work, it requires the continuous service of an army of 300,000 men, working ten or twelve hours a day throughout the year, to milk the cows kept in the United States.

Organization of the Dairy Industry

The industry is becoming thoroughly organized. Besides local clubs, societies, and unions, there are dairy associations in thirty States, most of them incorporated, and receiving financial aid under State laws. The proceedings of the annual conventions are, in several instances, reported and published at public expense. In some States the butter makers and cheese makers are separately organized; in some States creamery men and dairy farmers hold separate meetings. Large competitive exhibits of dairy products are also held. . . . Eighteen States provide by law for officials known as dairy commissioners or food and dairy commissioners. These officers have a national association, and there are also two national organizations of dairymen. At several large cities and centers of activity in the commerce of the dairy there are special boards of trade. The Department of Agriculture has a Dairy Division, whose purpose is to keep informed upon and to promote the dairy interests of the country at large. Dairy schools are maintained in a number of States, offering special courses of practical and scientific instruction in all branches of the business. These schools and the agricultural experiment stations, with which most of the dairy schools are connected, are doing much original research, and constantly adding to the store of useful information as to the application of modern science to this industry. Graduates from the schools are scattered all over the country as managers of dairy farms and superintendents of creameries and cheese factories, and are contributing to the general improvement in dairy methods and results. Weekly and monthly journals in the interest of dairy production and trade are published in various parts of the country, and during the last decade or two a number of noteworthy books on different aspects of dairying have been published, so that the student of this subject may fill a good-sized case with substantial volumes, technical and practical in character.

Milk Production

The business of producing milk for town and city supply, with the accompanying agencies for transportation and distribution, has grown to immense proportions. In many places the milk trade is regulated and supervised by excellent municipal ordinances, which have done much to prevent adulteration and improve the average quality of the supply. Full as much, however, is being done by private enterprise, through large milk companies, well organized and equipped, and establishments which make a specialty of serving milk and cream of fixed quality and exceptional purity. These efforts to furnish "certified" and "guaranteed" milk and general competition for the best class of trade are doing more to raise the standard of quality and improve the service than all the legal measures. The buildings and equipment of some of these modern dairies are quite beyond precedent. This branch of dairying is advancing fast, and upon the substantial basis of care, cleanliness, and better sanitary conditions.

Cheese Making

Cheese making has been transferred bodily from the realm of domestic arts to that of manufactures. Farm-made cheeses are hard to find anywhere; they are used only locally, and make no impression upon the markets. In the middle of the century about 100,000,000 pounds of cheese was made yearly in the United States, and all of it in farm dairies. At the close of the century the annual production of the country will be about 300,000,000 pounds, and 96 or 97 per cent of this will be made in factories. Of these establishments, there are nearly 3,000, but they vary greatly in capacity, and many are very small. New York and Wisconsin each has a thousand. The former State makes nearly twice as much cheese as the latter, and the two together produce three-fourths of the entire output of the country. The other cheese-making States, in the order of quantity produced, are Ohio, Illinois, Michigan, and Pennsylvania; but these are all comparatively unimportant. A change observed as taking place in the factory system is that of bringing a number of factories previously independent into a "combination" or under the same management. This tends to improve the quality and secure greater uniformity in the product, and often reduces cost of manufacture, all being decided advantages. More than nine-tenths of all cheese made is of the familiar standard variety, copied after the English Cheddar, but new kinds and imitations of foreign varieties are increasing. The cheese made in the country, with the small importations added, gives a yearly allowance of less than 4 pounds to every person; but as 30,000,000 to 50,000,000 pounds are still annually exported, the per capita consumption of cheese in the United States does not exceed 3½ pounds per annum. This is a very low rate, much less than in most European countries.

Butter Making

Great as the growth of the associated system of butter making has been and fast as creameries have multiplied, especially in the newer and growing agricultural States, such as Minnesota, Nebraska, Kansas, South Dakota, and Washington, there is still much more butter made on farms in the United States than in creameries. Creamery butter controls all the large markets, the dairy products making comparatively little impression on the trade; but home consumption and the supply of small customers and local markets make an immense aggregate, being fully two-thirds of all. Estimating the annual butter product of the country at 1,400,000,000 pounds, not much over 400,000,000 of this is made in the 7,500 or 8,000 creameries now in operation. Iowa is the greatest butter-producing State and the one in which the greater proportion is made on the factory plan. This State has 780 creameries, only two counties being without them; about two-fifths are cooperative. In these creameries about 88,000,000 pounds of butter are yearly made from 624,000 cows. It is estimated that in the same State 50,000,000 pounds of butter in addition are made in farm dairies. The total butter product of this State is therefore one-tenth of all made in the Union. Iowa sends over 80,000,000 pounds of butter every year into other States. New York is next in importance as a butter-making State, and then come, in order, Pennsylvania, Illinois, Wisconsin, Minnesota, Ohio, and Kansas. Yet, all of these combined make but little more than one-half of the annual butter crop of the United States, and in no one of them except Iowa is half of the butter produced made in creameries. The average quality of butter in America has materially improved since the introduction of the creamery system and the use of modern appliances, and the average continues to improve. Nevertheless, a vast quantity of poor butter is made — enough to make a large and profitable business in collecting it at country stores at grease prices or a little better and rendering or renovating it by patent processes. This renovated butter has been fraudulently sold to a considerable extent as the true creamery article, of which it is a fair imitation while fresh, and several States have recently made laws to identify the product and prevent buyers from being deceived. No butter is imported into this country, and the quantity exported is as yet insignificant, although there is beginning to be a foreign demand for American butter. The home consumption must accordingly be at the yearly rate of 20 pounds to the person, or about 100 pounds annually to the family of average size. If approximately correct, this shows Americans to be the greatest butter-eating people in the world.

The people of this country also consume millions of pounds every year of butter substitutes and imitations, such as oleomargarine and butterine. Most of this is believed to be butter by those who use it, and the State dairy commissioners mentioned are largely occupied in the execution of laws intended to protect consumers from these butter frauds.

By-Products of Dairying

Within recent years there has been great development in the economical uses of the by-products of dairying. Ten years ago there were enormous quantities of skim milk and buttermilk from the creameries and of whey from cheese factories, which were absolutely wasted. At farm dairies these by-products are generally used to advantage in feeding animals, but at the factories, especially at the seasons of greatest milk supply, this most desirable method of utilization is largely impracticable. In many places new branches have lately been added to the industry, which make sugar of milk and some other commercial products from whey, and utilize skim milk in various ways. The albumen of the latter is extracted for use with food products and in the arts. The casein is desiccated and prepared as a baking supply and substitute for eggs, as the basis of an enamel paint, as a substitute for glue in paper sizing, and it is also solidified so as to make excellent buttons, combs, brush backs, handles, electrical insulators, and similar articles.

Number of Cows and Quantity and Value of Dairy Products

The cows in the United States were not counted until 1840, but have been since enumerated for every decennial census. It has required from 23 to 27 cows to every 100 of the population to keep the country supplied with milk, butter, and cheese, and provide for the export of dairy products. The export trade has fluctuated much, but has never exceeded the produce of 500,000 cows. With the closing years of the century it is estimated that there is one milch cow in the United States for every four persons. This makes the total number of cows about 17,500,000. They are unevenly distributed over the country, being largely concentrated in the great dairy States. Thus, Iowa leads with 1,500,000 cows, followed by New York with almost as many; then Illinois and Pennsylvania, with about 1,000,000 each. The

States having over 500,000 each are Wisconsin, Ohio, Kansas, Missouri, Minnesota, Nebraska, and Indiana. Texas is credited with 700,000 cows, but very few of them are dairy animals. In the Middle and Eastern States the milk product goes very largely to the supply of the numerous large towns and cities. In the Central West and Northwest butter is the principal dairy product. The following table gives approximately an exhibit of the quantity and value of the dairy products of the United States in the year 1899:

Estimated number of cows and quantity and value of dairy products.

Cows.	Product.	Rate of product per cow.	Total product.	Rate of value.	Total value.
				Cents.	
11,000,000	Butter..................	130 pounds	1,430,000,000 pounds	18	$57,400,000
1,000,000	Cheese.................	300 pounds	300,000,000 pounds	9	27,000,000
5,500,000	Milk	380 gallons	2,090,000,000 gallons	8	167,200,000

This gives the grand total of the dairy products of the country a value of $451,600,000. If to this be added the skim milk, buttermilk, and whey, at their proper feeding value, and the calves dropped yearly, the annual aggregate value of the produce of the dairy cows exceeds $500,000,000. Accepting these estimates as conservative, they show that the commercial importance of the dairying of the United States is such as to command attention and justify all reasonable provisions for guarding its interests.

Irrigation Development by 1899

From Elwood Mead, "Rise and Future of Irrigation in the United States," U.S. Department of Agriculture, *Yearbook*, 1899, pp. 591–612.

Remains of Ancient Irrigation Works

The earliest pathway of civilization on the American continent led along the banks of the streams. In various parts of the Southwest, notably in the Salt River Valley of Arizona, in northern New Mexico, and along the southern borders of Colorado and Utah are well-defined remains of irrigation works which have outlived by many centuries the civilization to which they belonged. In at least one instance the bank of an ancient canal has been utilized as a part of modern works.

Riding up the valley of the Rio Grande, in the first half of the sixteenth century, Spanish explorers found in the midst of arid surroundings beds of beautiful roses, "not unlike those in the gardens of Castile," as they noted in their diaries. They also found Pueblo Indians irrigating the thirsty soil, as their forefathers had done for centuries before them and as their descendants are still doing to-day. In this valley and along the tributary streams, and at other places in the desert wastes of the Southwest, Spanish settlements sprung up and maintained themselves by means of these life-giving waters. The ditches at Lascruces, N. Mex., have an unbroken record of three hundred years of service, the history of which is written in the banks of the canals and in the fields irrigated. This is due to the sediment with which the waters of the Rio Grande are laden. Year after year this has slowly added layer on layer to the sides and bottoms of these ditches, until from being channels cut below the surface of the soil they are now raised 2 or 3 feet above. It is here that one can yet find agriculture almost as primitive as that of the days of Pharaoh, where grain is reaped with the sickle and thrashed by the trampling of goats.

Early Irrigation in California

From these settlements and from the conquered cities of Mexico adventurous missionaries pushed their way still farther westward until they came in sight of the Pacific, teaching the Indians the crude art of irrigation, which they had learned either in Spain or of the simple inhabitants of the interior, and making oases of bloom and fruitage among the hills and deserts of the coast. So came the early churches and gardens of California and the first small impulse toward the conquest of its fertile soil, which must always be gratefully associated with the memory of the Mission fathers.

Measured by their cost or the skill required to construct them, the small, rude furrows which watered these gardens are now of little importance. Compared to the monumental engineering works which have succeeded them, they possess to-day but little interest. The best preserved of these Mission gardens is now an insignificant feature in a landscape which includes miles on miles of cement-lined aqueducts, scores of pumping stations, and acres on acres of orange and lemon orchards, cultivated with thoroughness and skill not surpassed in any section of the Old World or the New. It was far different at the end of the eighteenth century, when the thirty or more of these gardens which were scattered along the coast between the Mexican border and San Francisco were the sole resting places of weary travelers and their fruit and foliage the only relief in summer from the monotonous landscape presented by the brown and arid hills which surrounded them on every side. They were under those conditions not only successful centers of influence from which to carry on the Christianizing of the Indian tribes, but forces tending to break up the migratory impulse by the establishing of homes among the early Spanish explorers.

Beginnings of Modern Irrigation

For the beginnings of Anglo-Saxon irrigation in this country we must go to the Salt Lake Valley of Utah, where, in July, 1849, the Mormon pioneers turned the clear waters of City Creek upon the sun-baked and alkaline soil in order that they might plant the very last of their stock of potatoes in the hope of bringing forth a crop to save the little company from starvation.

Utah is interesting not merely because it is the cradle of our modern irrigation industry, but even more so as showing how important are organizations and public control in the diversion and use of rivers. Throughout the pioneer period of their history the settlers of Utah were under the direction of exceptionally able and resourceful leaders, who were aided by the fact that their followers were knit together by a dominating religious impulse. These leaders had the wisdom to adapt their methods and shape their institutions to conform to the peculiar conditions and environment of a land strange and new to men of English speech. They found that irrigation was necessary to their existence in the home that they had chosen, and that the irrigation canal must therefore be the basis of their industrial organization which was largely cooperative; hence, the size of their farms, which are less than 30 acres upon the average, the nature of their social relations, which are close and neighborly.

That the great material results which quickly followed could have been realized without the cohesion which came from an association dominated by religious discipline and controlled by the superior intelligence of the head of the Mormon Church, is doubtful; but that the character of institutions in the valleys of Utah, both industrial and social, was chiefly due to the environments in which they were placed is beyond dispute. Cooperation became the dominant principle simply because the settlers were in a land without capital, and it was beyond the power of the individual to turn the mountain current from its course and spread it upon his lands. Only the labor of many individuals, working under organization and discipline, could make the canals or distribute the waters. A small farm unit was chosen, not because men were less greedy for land than in all other new countries, but because it was quickly seen that the extent of the water supply was the measure of production, and their ability to provide this was small. Diversified farming, which is one of the leading causes of the remarkably even prosperity of Mormon agriculture, was resorted to because the Territory was so far removed from other settlements that it was compelled to become absolutely self-sustaining. The small farm unit made near neighbors, and this advantage was still more enhanced by assembling the farmers' homes in convenient village centers. One reason for adopting this plan, in the first place, was doubtless for protection against the Indians, but it has become a permanent feature, which is still adhered to in making new settlements because most satisfactory to the social instinct.

Cooperative Colonies in Colorado and California

The discovery of gold in California created the Overland Trail, which wound its tortuous course across the hitherto trackless wastes of the arid domain. Its stations were usually along the banks of the streams. In the neighborhood of these, settlers had established themselves, and by means of simple furrows turned the waters of the streams upon the bottom land. This was the extent of irrigation throughout the vast region it traversed, outside of Utah, before the Union Colony at Greeley, Colo., became the second historic instance of the beginnings of the present system, and one which furnished a different standpoint for a study of the subject.

As Utah is the result of a religious emigration, so Greeley is the creation of the town meeting. Its founding marked the beginning of a new and different industrial development in Colorado. Before this it was the wealth of the mines or the migratory and adventurous experiences of the range live-stock business which had attracted settlement. Greeley, on the contrary, represented an effort of home-making people, both to enjoy landed independence and social and intellectual privileges equal to those of the towns and cities they had left. Among its first buildings was Colony Hall, and among its first organizations the Lyceum, in which all the affairs of the community were debated with a fervor and fearlessness quite worthy of Horace Greeley's following. Cooperation was adopted in the construction and management of public utilities, of which the irrigation canal was the first and most important. The wisdom and justice of making common property of the town site, the beauty and value of which could only be created by the enterprise and public spirit of all, was recognized and put into practice with satisfactory results. The only deliberate extravagance was the erection at an early day of a school building worthy of the oldest and richest New England community. The highest methods both of irrigation and cultivation were sought out through numberless experiments, until Greeley and its potatoes grew famous together. The home and civic institutions of the colony became the pride of the State, and the hard-won success of the community inspired numerous similar undertakings and furnished an impulse which resulted in the reclamation and settlement of northern Colorado. Boulder, Longmont, Loveland, and Fort Collins were the outgrowth of success at Greeley, and each adopted many of the ideas and tendencies of the parent colony.

Twenty years subsequent to the beginning of Utah, and contemporaneously with the settlement of Colorado, similar influences began to make themselves felt in California, especially in its southern part. Anaheim is called the mother colony. This was cooperative in its inception, and its principal irrigation system has ever remained such. Riverside followed a few years later and represented a higher ideal; but the spirit of speculation in which California civilization was born soon fastened itself upon irrigation, as it had done in the case of mining, and ran a mad race through southern California. Irrigation in this State became corporate and speculative. Where Utah and Colorado had depended only upon their hands and teams for the building of irrigation works, California issued stocks and bonds, and so mortgaged its future. Men began to dream of a new race of millionaires, created by making merchandise of the melting snows, by selling "rights" to the "renting" of water, and collecting annual toll from a new class of society, to be known as "water tenants."

Corporate Canal Building

The investment of corporate capital in canals to distribute and control water used in irrigation began in California, but spread like a contagion throughout the West. For a quarter of a century it has been the leading factor in promoting agricultural growth of the western two-fifths of the United States. It has been the agency through which many millions of dollars have been raised and expended, hundreds of miles of canals constructed, and hundreds of thousands of acres of land reclaimed. It has built the largest overfall dam ever placed in a large river. It has been the chief agency in replacing temporary wooden structures by massive headworks of steel and masonry, and has, by the employment of the highest engineering talent available and the introduction of better methods of construction, promoted the economy and success with which water is now distributed and used. The question which is now to be considered is how the vast fabric created through its agency is to be directed and controlled in order that it may not crumble of its own weight.

The construction of irrigation works by corporate capital came as a natural if not inevitable evolution. There came a time in the districts first settled when the opportunities to divert water cheaply had largely been utilized, and when the expenditure required was beyond the means of either the individual or the cooperation of many individuals. The preliminary outlay was too great. In older European countries experience has shown that no agency can be so wisely intrusted with these larger expenditures as the State. Large irrigation canals have been considered as being, in their nature, as much public improvements as are works to supply water to cities and towns. Being for the service of the public, those in older European countries have largely passed under public ownership.

In this country corporations have, so far as construction is concerned, taken the place of governmental agencies in other lands. Practically all of the larger and costlier works built within the last two decades have been of this character. The High Line Canal, which waters the land surrounding Denver, Colo., with its tunnel through the mountains and its aqueduct carried along the rocky cliffs below; the canals of the Wyoming Development Company, with its tunnel alone costing more than all the Greeley Colony canals combined, and its reservoir for storing the entire year's discharge of the Laramie River; the Sunnyside Canal of Washington, which when built traversed 60 miles of sagebrush solitude, are illustrations in three States of the nature of corporate contributions to irrigation development. Even in Utah, cooperation was not sufficient to reclaim all of Salt Lake Valley. For forty years the table-land north of the lake, one of the largest and best tracts of irrigable land in the valley, remained unoccupied, while the sons of the pioneers were compelled to seek homes in the surrounding States. To reclaim this land, a canal had to be carried for 3 miles along the precipitous sides of Bear River Canyon. The flow of the river had to be controlled by an extensive dam and the Malad River twice bridged by long and high aqueducts, and the million-dollar outlay required was more than home seekers could provide.

The creation of water-right complications came with the building of corporate canals. Previous to this it had been the rule for those who built ditches to own the land they watered, and there was little difference as to whether the right to water went with the ditch or with the land, because the ownership of both was united in the same person. But when companies were organized to distribute water for others irrigate with and to derive a revenue from water rentals, there arose the question as to who was the owner of the right to the water diverted — the company transporting the water or the farmer who used it. The laws of nearly all the Western States make the ditch owner the appropriator. This has created a divided ownership of land water, and many canal companies have framed water-right contracts on the theory of absolute ownership. These have proven a source of constant irritation to farmers. Some of these contracts require the farmer to pay, at the outset, a royalty of bonus for the "right" to receive water, the charge for this right varying from $5 to $500 per acre, depending on the scarcity of the water supply or the value of land and its products. There is a very prevalent feeling among farmers that as they are the actual "beneficial users" of the streams they should be considered the appropriators, or at least that the owner of the land should share with the owner of the ditch in the right to water.

Objections to Corporate Canals

Having dealt with the benefits from corporate investment in irrigation works, it is now proper to point out their defect the most serious one is that nearly all large canals have been losing investments. The record of these losses is so stupendous that it is reluctantly referred to. A single enterprise in one of the Territories represents to its projectors a loss of over $2,000,000. The Bear River Canyon in Utah, which cost over a million dollars, was recently sold under a judgment for about one-tenth of this sum. A single canal in California represents a loss to its builders of over $800,000. These are not isolated cases. Similar instances might be multiplied indefinitely. They are not due to bad management, to dishonesty, or faulty engineering. Some of the worst failures in a financial sense have been handled by the brightest and most experienced men in the West, but they were not able to make their enterprises pay, that is, they have not paid their builders. Nearly all have been a success so far as the section interested was concerned, but the benefits have gone to the public and not to the investors. The reasons for this should be made generally understood. The following are the most important:

(1) The necessarily long delay in securing setters for the land to be irrigated and in obtaining paying customers for the water to be furnished.

(2) The large outlay and several years of unprofitable labor require, as a rule, to put wild land in condition for cultivation. Settlers of limited means can not meet this outlay and in addition pay water rentals. Nearly all of the settlers on arid public land are of mere limited means; hence, canal companies have at the outset to furnish water at small cost, or furnish to a small number of consumers.

(3) The unsuitability of the public-land laws to irrigation development.

(4) The acquirement of the lands to be reclaimed, in many instances, before canals are completed by nonresident or speculative holders, who would do nothing for their improvement.

(5) Expenses of litigation. Experience has shown that in the estimates of cost of a large canal provision should be made for a large and long-continued outlay for litigation. It begins with the adjudication of the stream and is protracted through the controversies over water rights.

Water-Right Problems of the Arid Regions

After this brief sketch of the beginnings of American irrigation, some of the lessons of which will be considered at a later point in this article, we may appropriately turn to the great arid region as a whole and the complex legal, economic, and social problems with which its agriculture will vex the future.

Mount Union rises in solemn grandeur in the Wind River Mountains of Wyoming south of Yellowstone Park. From this peak flow three streams, which, with their tributaries, control the industrial future of a region greater than any European country save Russia, and capable of supporting a larger population than now dwells east of the Mississippi River. These streams are the Missouri, the Columbia, and the Colorado. The first waters the mountain valleys on the eastern slope of the Rockies and the semiarid region of the Great Plains; the second, the Pacific northwest, including part of Montana, all of Idaho, and the major portions of

Oregon and Washington; the third, the Southwest, embracing much of Utah and western Colorado, parts of New Mexico and California, and all of Arizona.

In this vast district, when reclaimed, homes may be made for many millions of people. To effect this result is a task inferior to no other in the realm of statesmanship or social economics. It is the nation's farm. It contains practically all that is left of the public domain, and is the chief hope of a free home for those who dream of enjoying landed independence, but who have but little besides industry and self-denial with which to secure it. As it is now, this land has but little value. In many places a township would not support a settler and his family, and a section of land does not yield enough to keep a light-footed and laborious sheep from starving to death. This is not because the land lacks fertility, but because it lacks moisture. Where rivers have been turned from their course, the products which have resulted equal in excellence and amount those of the most favored district of ample rainfall.

There are only 6,000,000 acres of cultivated land along the Nile. It is all irrigated. Where there is no irrigation there is desert. This little patch of ground has made Egypt a landmark in the world's history. It supports over 5,000,000 people and pays the interest on a national debt half as large as our own. The Missouri and its tributaries can be made to irrigate three times the land now cultivated along the Nile.

The essence of the problem to be met at the outset is the control and distribution of the water supply, since not only the enduring prosperity but the very existence of the homes created will be conditioned upon the ability to use these rivers for irrigation. The diverse interest of individuals and communities, and even of different States, will all be dependent on streams flowing from a common source. To reclaim all the land possible will involve the spreading of water over a surface as large as New England with New York added. Standing now at the birth of things and looking down the vista of the future, we can see in the course of these rivers the dim outline of a mighty civilization, blest with peace and crowned with a remarkable degree of prosperity, in case wise laws and just policies shall prevail in the years of the immediate future while institutions are forming. But if it be otherwise, if greed and ignorance are allowed to govern, and we ignore the experience of older countries than ours, there will remain to us only a gloomy forecast of legal, economic, and, possibly, even civil strife.

The Appearance and Resources of the Arid Region

In discussing this phase of the subject, let us follow the Missouri, Columbia, and Colorado rivers in their lonesome courses through mountains, plain, and desert to the place where one joins the Mississippi, where another mingles its waters with the Pacific, and where a third flows into the Gulf of California. For it is not only interesting but important to see in the midst of what surroundings so large a future population must dwell, and upon what other resources than water and land it will rear its economic edifice.

The climate of the western half of the United States takes its chief characteristic from its aridity, or dryness. The heat of its Southern summers and the cold of its Northern winters are alike tempered and mitigated by lack of humidity. Neither the humid heat which prostrates nor the humid cold which penetrates to the marrow is known in the arid region. The Western mountains and valleys are a recognized natural sanitarium where thousands of invalids are sent each year by physicians to regain their health.

The dominant feature in the physical appearance of the arid regions is its mountain topography. On every hand a rugged horizon meets the view. From North to South, from Canada to Mexico, the Rocky Mountain Range makes the backbone of the continent. Along the Pacific coast the Sierra Nevada and Cascade ranges lift their barriers to intercept the moisture and condense it into snow. Between these two principal chains, with their connecting ranges and out lying spurs, are many minor systems, so that the whole country is a succession of mountains and valleys, of forests and deserts, of raging torrents and sinuous rivers winding to their sinks upon the plains or making their difficult way to the distant ocean. The far West is thus a land of the greatest scenic beauties, and widely celebrated as such.

The cultivable lands lie in the valleys, rising with gradual slope on either side of the streams to meet the foothills. Narrowing to the mountains, these valleys widen as the river loses grade and approaches the sea or its confluence with a larger stream. There are valleys which will accommodate hundreds, others, thousands or tens of thousands, and a few, like the Sacramento, in California, where millions may dwell.

In the eastern portion of the arid region, and in high altitudes farther west, the land is covered with nutritious natural grasses, which furnish ideal range for live stock. But the characteristic badge of the region is the sagebrush. This brave plant of the desert is commonly held in derision by those who behold it for the first time, and until they learn to know it as the shelter and dependence of range live stock when the terrible blizzard sweeps from the north and as the sure indication of good soil and the humble prophet of the field, orchard, and garden. Thus, it happens that to the casual traveler the appearance of the region is forbidding. It is only in localities where the work of reclamation has been in progress long enough to permit the growth of trees, with farms and homes, that the value of the soil and climate can be appreciated. There are such instances in all the seventeen States and Territories of the far West. One of the most striking is the Salt River Valley of Arizona. Here the traveler, after a long and tiresome journey through waste places, finds himself suddenly confronted with homes rivaling in taste and luxury those of Eastern States, and with orchards and gardens which resemble more the century-old gardens of France and Italy than a creation of the last twenty years.

Similar instances are the San Bernardino Valley of southern California, the Salt Lake Valley of Utah, and the Boise Valley of Idaho.

Mineral Wealth of the Arid Region

Another fact which contributes to the breadth of the economic foundation of Western agriculture is the variety and value of its mineral wealth. In this it is richly endowed, not only with the precious metals, but with the baser ones used in arts and industries, and with unusual quantities of coal, ore, and building stone, the latter of which includes many rare and valuable kinds, such as marble, onyx, and agate.

While the annual value of these products runs into the tens of millions of dollars, it is literally true that their development is yet in its infancy. With the extension of railroad facilities, the improvement and cheapening of mining processes, the extension of agriculture, and consequent increase in the volume and decrease in the cost of the home food supply, the gain in annual production will assume in the future dimensions which would now be considered beyond belief.

Sources of Future Permanent Prosperity in the Arid Region

To the mines must be added the forests which clothe the mountain sides, especially those of the northern part of this region. To a large extent this is still virgin ground, where only the foot of the hunter and explorer has trodden. It is a region unrivaled in its opportunities for the development of water power. The Shoshone Falls in Idaho are scarcely inferior to those of Niagara. The hundreds of streams which fall from the 10,000-foot level of the Rocky Mountain Range to the 4,000-foot to 5,000-foot level of the plain at their base are destined to turn more wheels of industry than have yet been harnessed west of the Mississippi River. Back of the irrigated lands are the grazing lands, of which there are probably not less than 400,000,000 acres. These lands have been the dominant factor of the pioneer life of many of the arid Commonwealths, and they are destined, under proper management, to always constitute the great nursery of cattle, sheep, and horses. The irrigated farm has back of it the mine, the furnace, and factory, and the civilization of Western America can not fail to have a prosperous and varied industrial life. Here there can be no one-sided development, no community exclusively devoted to the production of corn, wheat, or cotton, to manufactures, or to commerce. The farm, the stock ranch, the lumber camp, the mine, the factory, and the store are destined to grow up and flourish side by side, each drawing support from and furnishing sustenance to the others.

Present and Future of Irrigation

The present situation, the results secured, and the tasks ahead in securing a wise disposal of the arid lands and in preventing the rivers from becoming an instrument of monopoly and extortion, will now be considered.

We are met at the outset by an entire absence of definite information. We do not know, nor is there any ready means of determining, how many irrigation works have been built. In many States no provision is made for their record. In only two States is this record even measurably accurate or complete. There may be 75,000 completed ditches, or there may be double the number, but either as to their number or as to the number of acres of land reclaimed thereby there is only surmise and conjecture. This, however, is known, that the highest priced and most productive farm lands on this continent are in the arid region; that the largest yield of nearly every staple crop has been obtained by the aid of irrigation; that not only has the growth of agriculture furnished a market for the factories of the East and supported the railroads which unite the two extremes of the country, but it is the chief resource of nearly every one of the arid States. Colorado leads all the States of the Union in her output of precious metals, but the value of the product of her farms is nearly double that of her mines.

In California it is the grain fields and orange orchards which support the majority of her industrial population and furnish the basis for her future material growth and prosperity. The beginnings of Utah were wholly agricultural, and without the irrigated farms the cities of that interior Commonwealth would as yet be only a dream. In a less striking degree the same condition prevails in Idaho, Wyoming, Montana, New Mexico, and Arizona. This is the situation, while irrigation is as yet in its infancy. The reclaimed areas, though making a large aggregate, look very insignificant relatively to the rest of the country when delineated upon a map of the arid region. The possibilities of reclamation have but begun to be realized, yet when every available drop of water shall have been applied to the soil the irrigated lands will constitute a comparatively small proportion of the entire country. The possibilities of irrigation are, however, to be measured not alone by the possible extent of the agricultural industry, but by the development of other resources which it will make feasible. The best and largest use of the grazing lands, the utilization of the forests, the development of mines and quarries, and the maintenance of railroads and commerce in the western half of the United States, all hinge upon the control and use of streams in connection with the fundamental industry of agriculture. Since irrigation is essential to agriculture in the arid States, the extent and character of its development must surely measure the superstructure to be built upon that foundation.

Growth of Irrigation and Need of Better Laws

Some of the beginnings of irrigation have been referred to. The details of its growth can not be dealt with. It has been crude in many ways. There has been no attempt to provide for the diversion of rivers according to some prearranged plan having for its object the selection of the best land and the largest use of the water supply. Instead, each appropriator of water has consulted simply his ability and inclination in the location of his head gate. There has been an almost complete failure to realize that the time was coming when on many streams the demand would exceed the supply, and that a stable water right would be as important as a valid land title. The laws passed for recording claims are, as a rule, so loosely drawn and imperfect that they would be a source of amusement if the evil results of their operation were not so disastrous. More than half of the State laws provide for inaugurating a title to water by posting a notice on the banks of the stream. They have not aided the proposed appropriator, because the right to post other appropriations was unrestricted. They are of no use as a warning to others, because not one in ten thousand of the parties concerned ever see them. A search for these notices along the cottonwood borders of the Missouri and its tributaries would be the unending labor of a lifetime; hence, the requirement was and is ignored; it is another of the many influences tending to unsettle irrigators' just rights and bringing the attempts to frame laws for their protection into disrepute.

Looking over the field at the close of the century, we find that the United States stands practically alone among irrigation countries in having left all the work of reclamation to the unaided efforts of private capital, and in the prodigality of the surrender of public control of streams. In one respect the policy pursued has been successful. It has resulted in an enormous investment (not less than $100,000,000, and some estimates make it twice that sum) and the creation of taxable and productive wealth of many times the amount invested. We have now about reached the limit of this sort of growth. There will be few large private investments in canals hereafter until we have better and more liberal irrigation laws. Entrance on the coming century is confronted by larger problems; the storage of flood waters, the interstate division of streams, and the inauguration of an adequate system of public control, which will insure to the humblest handler of a shovel his share of the snows falling on mountains above his farm, no matter how far removed therefrom he may be.

Need of Reform in the Management of Arid Public Land

Along with better water laws should come a corresponding reform in the management of the remaining arid public land. At the outset of its settlement these problems were entirely new to English-speaking men.

Early settlers came from the humid portions of Europe and settled along the humid coast line of the Atlantic and, later, in the humid valleys of the Ohio and Mississippi rivers. The land laws which they applied to the public domain of their day produced excellent results, making homes for millions of people and effecting a wonderful development of material resources.

When settlement had proceeded under these laws to the Missouri River and beyond, it was not strange that their principles were extended to the remaining public domain, for the vast majority of the American people had no conception whatever of the conditions existing in the far West. Not only the national lawmakers, drawn mostly from regions of abundant rainfall, but the legislators in the arid States themselves were blind to the necessities of the situation. The value of gold they knew, but the value of that other element of national wealth, which will continue to sustain vast populations long after the last ounce of gold shall have been taken from the mine, they did not even dimly appreciate. So, to a large extent, they merely reenacted upon their statute books the common law of rainy and foggy England.

Homestead Law not Adapted to the Arid Region

The homestead law may have served a useful, even a beneficent, purpose throughout large sections of the Republic, but it is not adapted to the settlement of a region where practically nothing can be grown except by artificial application of water. This fact has been learned at last through many years of hardship and disappointment, at the cost of many million dollars. One of the most pitiful pages in the history of the West is that which records the story of the settlement of the semiarid belt lying between the ninety-seventh meridian and the foothills of the Rocky Mountains. This is a territory 500 miles wide, extending from Canada to Mexico, including the western portions of the two Dakotas, Nebraska, Kansas, and Texas, and also eastern Colorado. In the absence of scientific demonstration to the contrary, tens of thousands of people rushed into this territory under the delusion that it was a land of reliable rainfall, or would soon become such as the result of settlement and cultivation.

New settlements sprung up in every direction, and important towns arose almost in a night. Men hastened from all parts of the country to claim their rights under the homestead law. Remembering the prosperity which similar armies of settlers had wrung from the virgin soil of the West, unlimited capital lent willing support to this new outward surge of growing population. The capital was largely lost, but the pathetic side of the picture was seen in the bitter disappointment of the settlers themselves. Many of them wasted the most useful and pregnant years of their lives in their brave persistence in the belief that the climate would change as the land came under cultivation, and that there was some magic potency in the homestead law to overcome the processes of nature. It is recognized at last that where water sufficient for purposes of irrigation can not be had the land is useful only for grazing. It is a mistake for the Government to offer to citizens land of that character on condition that they will settle upon 160 acres of it and make a living. There can be but one of two results — either the settler must fail or he must become practically the tenant of the person or corporation furnishing water for his dry land.

Operations of the Desert-Land Law

The desert-land law was devised to promote the investment of capital rather than to encourage settlement. For this reason it did not require actual residence on the land reclaimed. Originally, whoever would irrigate 640 acres of land was given title thereto on the payment of the Government's price. Later this acreage has been reduced to one-half the original area. The operation of this law has been both useful and injurious. To give so large an area to men of small means is a mistake, because it is more than is needed to make a home and more than they can cultivate. It is not suited to corporate enterprise, or to reclaim large valleys which can be watered from a single canal, because it makes no provision for concerted or effective management of the entire area. Its field of effective usefulness has therefore been limited. While it has added somewhat to the taxable and productive wealth of Western States, it has also operated to transfer to single owners miles of water fronts which without this law would have been divided up into smaller farms with better social and agricultural conditions.

The Carey Act

What is popularly known as the Carey Act, from the name of its author, Senator Carey, gives to each State the right to segregate 1,000,000 acres of land and to control both its reclamation and disposal to settlers. The limitations of the operations of this act confine its benefits simply to the opportunity to secure better management during the time of canal building and settlement. Five States have accepted the trust, but in only one, Wyoming, have any canals been completed. These canals have been built by companies operating under a contract with the State. In Montana it is proposed to construct State canals from money obtained by selling bonds secured by the land to be irrigated. Enough progress has not as yet been made to determine whether or not this innovation on past irrigation methods is to meet with success; if it does, the third step in the evolution of canal building, which is the construction of State works, will have been inaugurated.

Influence of the Range Industries

To a certain extent there is an inevitable conflict between those who wish to use the public domain for homes and those who prefer to have it reserved for pasture, and, again, between those who wish to use the pasture for cattle and those who want it for sheep.

The range industries obtained possession of the field long before the higher utility of the lands for irrigation and settlement was generally appreciated. When irrigators did come, they worked more or less injury to the range stockmen, for each settler occupied a part of the water front and added to the number desiring to use the free grazing land. It is for the interest of the range-stock industry that access to streams be made as free as possible and that nothing be done to reduce their volume or prevent the overflow of natural meadows, while the higher interest of irrigation and settlement demands that the stream be diverted and its waters distributed over the widest possible area. The conflict is between the wasteful use of water on the one hand and its economical use on the other, and, in a sense, between a primitive and a more highly organized civilization.

This statement should not be construed as denying that the range-stock industry is of vast importance nor that it will continue to be a great source of wealth to the country. Throughout the West there are very large areas suited to nothing else. The point is that the higher interest of society lies in the most economical and profitable use of water to the end that homes may be made for the largest possible number. Neither water nor land laws have favored this result, but precisely the contrary. The object of reform should be to preserve and develop all interests, to adapt laws and institutions to the peculiar conditions and environment of the region. This can be done with far greater security to the pastoral industries than they enjoy under the present system, and at the same time land and water available for making homes and farms utilized to the best advantage.

Uncertainty as to State and Federal Jurisdiction

The pioneers of irrigation are menaced by the uncertainty which exists as to the limits of State and federal jurisdiction in the control of streams. It has heretofore been assumed that the authority of each State within its borders was unquestioned, and two of the States contain constitutional provisions asserting absolute ownership and control of all the waters within their bounds. A recent decision of the United States circuit court in Montana holds this view to be erroneous, and that the snows which fall on public land and the streams which cross it are both under the control of Congress. A similar complication has arisen in litigation over a reservoir on the Rio Grande, in which both interstate and international rights are involved. In this case the United States Supreme Court has asserted the right of the General Government to protect the interests of navigation regardless of State statutes respecting the use of water in irrigation. The assertion of the paramount importance of riparian rights and of the protection of navigation, regardless of the use of water in irrigation, will add greatly to the uncertainty regarding water rights from the tributaries of the Missouri or any other of the rivers navigable in any portion of their course. The reclamation of the arid region involves the absorption of streams, and it can not be settled too soon whether or not such absorption is to be permitted.

Complications From Lack of Uniform Water Laws

On the other hand, serious complications have arisen from the absence of any general or national regulations governing the division of water across State lines. There are many instances where one stream is a common source of supply to irrigators in two or more States. It has sometimes happened that the perennial flow of such streams has been first appropriated in a State along its lower course and utilized at a later period by other States near its source. Neither of the States concerned possesses power to remedy the evil, and each makes claim to all the water flowing upon its soil.

The conditions which govern irrigation throughout much of the arid region are practically uniform, and where this is true there is no question that a uniform irrigation law would operate with equal justice and efficiency; but, owing to the absence of such general supervision, water rights in States adjacent to each other are often as different in character as if these Commonwealths were on opposite sides of the globe. Failure to correct or regard these complications aggravates the evils to which they give rise and renders the ultimate adoption of a uniform system of laws far more difficult. There is but one thing the States have shared in common, and that is endless litigation over water rights. There is no uniformity of laws or decisions. The same issues are tried over and over again, and the precedent established in one case is overturned in another. The construction of costly works, and even the long use of water, has not always been sufficient to secure parties in their rights. Where rights have been successfully maintained, it has been done only at the price of constant lawsuits.

Usually the amount of water claimed is many times in excess of what the projected canal can utilize; frequently in excess of the entire volume of water in the stream. There is no one to protect the public interest as to the character of works to be built or to say whether they conform to good public policy. The courts confirm these loose appropriations, and the foundation for endless litigation is thus securely laid. The question soon arises as to who first appropriated the waters which do not suffice for all. There is then nothing to fall back upon except the faulty filings which were originally posted on the banks of the stream and the testimony of interested citizens. It frequently happens that old claims for very large amounts of water have not been utilized to their full extent until later comers have appropriated the unused surplus. The old claim is then enforced at the expense of the later one. The result is confusion, loss, and bitterness among neighbors.

The difficulty lies, first of all, in popular misconception regarding the nature of water rights and of property in water. This is enhanced by lack of scientific information concerning the character and extent of water supplies and of the amount required for beneficial irrigation. Still further, there is a great need for a different system of appropriating waters and of distributing a common supply among consumers. These delicate and complex issues can not be fought out among private parties without producing a condition of virtual anarchy, in which the weak must go down and the strong survive, regardless of their merits or necessities. The failure of the irrigation industry from the financial standpoint is almost wholly due to the illogical land and water laws which have been described.

Methods and Measures Needed to Develop the Arid Region

It is well to consider now by what methods and by what measures of legislation the splendid resources of the arid region may be opened to development.

The first step is to determine the proper control and just distribution of the water supply. The problem varies with different portions of the arid region. In the

South, streams are generally torrential in character, furnishing the bulk of their waters in heavy floods, which must be stored in the many natural sites available in the mountains at a distance from the places where the water is to be applied to the soil. In the North, on the other hand, the problem is not that of storage, but of the diversion of great rivers like the Yellowstone, the Snake, the Columbia, and the Missouri. Here works adequate to the reclamation of the areas of arid land which remain can only be built at great cost, rivaling those along the Ganges and the Nile.

Before such development proceeds further it is desirable that some common agreement should be reached concerning the true character of water rights. The idea of private ownership in water apart from the land can not prevail without creating institutions essentially feudal in character. A water lord is even more undesirable than a landlord as the dominant element in society. It is indisputable, as has already been said, that the man who owns the water practically owns the land. A proposition which contemplates the turning over of all the land to a private monopoly, thus making a tenantry of those who may have their homes upon it in the future, could not hope to command popular support. But the idea of a private ownership of water, amounting to a virtual monopoly of this vital element, has been permitted to grow up in the West. To a certain extent it has obtained recognition in legislation and protection in judicial decrees and decisions. In other countries the doctrine has largely disappeared, and in our country it should give place to a more enlightened conception, and to the only principle that can safely be adopted as the foundation of the agricultural industry in the West.

The right to water which should be recognized in an arid land is the right of use, and even this must be restricted to beneficial and economical use in order that the water supply may serve the needs of the largest possible number. Ownership of water should be vested, not in companies or individuals, but in the land itself. When this principle is adopted, the control of the water is divided precisely like the land, among a multitude of proprietors. Reservoirs and canals are then like the streets of the town, serving a public purpose and permitting ready access to private property on every hand. Water monopoly is impossible under this method, and no other abuse is encouraged by it. Years of painful experience have abundantly proven that peaceful and orderly development can not be realized except as water and land are forever united in one ownership and canals treated merely as public or semipublic utilities rather than as a means of fastening a monopoly upon the community. In Wyoming and Nebraska the true principle has already been adopted by the State boards of control and put into practice with the best results. If it can be maintained and speedily extended to the other States, as it surely must be in time, it would mark an economic reform of the highest significance in the life of the West.

Appropriation and Distribution of the Water Supply

Next in importance to the correct solution of the question of water ownership are the great problems of appropriation and of distribution. As soon as possible all ditches used in irrigation should be carefully measured by some public authority and the results of this measurement be given the widest publicity, in order that irrigators may know approximately how much is taken and how much remains to be taken by new canals. The need of this information is so obvious that it will perhaps be difficult for readers unfamiliar with the subject to credit the assertion that in all but four of the Western States the matter has been wholly neglected. This fact is largely responsible for the disheartening litigation which prevails so widely.

It is of almost equal importance to have a scientific determination of the practical duty of water, showing the amount required for different soils and crops. Still further, there must be some form of public control in the distribution of water. Trouble always results when this is left to rival users to determine how much they need, especially in years of partial drought, when the supply may be insufficient for all, and it is consequently necessary to recognize appropriations in the order of their priority.

Public Supervision and Control on Irrigation

The entire discussion leads up to one inevitable conclusion: This is that irrigation, over and above all other industries, is a matter demanding public supervision and control. Every drop of water entering the head gate, and every drop escaping at the end of the canal, is a matter of public concern. The public must determine, through constitutions and statutes, the nature of water ownership. The public must establish means for the measurement of streams and for ascertaining how much water may be taken for each acre of land under the principle of beneficial use. The public must see that justice is done in the distribution of water among those who have properly established their rightful claims to it. We have thoroughly tried the method of leaving all this to private initiative and management, and, along with magnificent material progress, we have reaped a large crop of deplorable financial results.

While much must be left to the action of States and communities, there is still a wide field for national effort. Only the nation can legislate as to the public lands and reform the abuses which have been referred to in connection with the present system of land laws. There is a strong popular demand in the West for legislation providing public aid in the construction of works of too great magnitude and cost for private enterprise and a growing belief that one of two things should be done: Either the arid States should be placed in a position to extend this aid, or the General Government should extend the work it is now doing in the reclamation of certain Indian reservations to the reclamation of the unoccupied public lands. One policy much discussed and widely favored is legislation which will permit of the leasing of the public grazing lands for a term of years at a small annual rental, the proceeds to be given to the several arid States and applied by them to irrigation development. If this is carried out, the settlers owning the contiguous irrigated land should be favored; the object being to unite with the lands reclaimed a certain portion of the public pasture.

The National Government alone can make the best and broadest study of the various economic questions related to the development of agriculture on arid lands. This includes not only the measurement of streams and survey of reservoir sites, but also a consideration of practical methods of applying water to the soil and of social and industrial institutions adapted to the environment of the arid region. The nation alone can deal with the conflicting rights in interstate and international streams and with the construction of great reservoirs at their head waters, with a view to benefiting the several States lying along their course. The National Government is already active along all these lines, and the field for the expansion of its efforts is wide and inviting.

Influence of Irrigation Upon People and Country

While a description of existing conditions in the far West necessarily includes references to many evils and disappointments, there is a brighter side to the picture, and the future is luminous with new hopes for humanity. A vast population will make its homes in valleys now vacant and voiceless, yet potentially the best part of our national heritage. They will create institutions which will realize higher ideals of society than the world has yet seen. Irrigation is much more than an affair of ditches and acres. It not only makes civilization possible where men could not live without it, but it shapes that civilization after its own peculiar design. Its underlying influence is that which makes for democracy and individual independence.

Irrigation Productive of Small Proprietors

Where land can only be cultivated by means of the artificial applition of water, and where that water is not under speculative control, it is owned in small holdings. This is so because irrigation intensifies the product of the land and so demands much labor. It is a kind of labor which can not profitably be left to hired hands. The result is a multitude of small proprietors working for themselves. This fact is strikingly illustrated in southern California. Here the farms are small and almost exclusively occupied by their owners. But the great wheat ranches in other parts of the State, notably in the Sacramento Valley, depend chiefly upon hired laborers, who make no homes of their own. The Sacramento Valley has less population now than it had twenty-five years ago. Of the increase of the rural population of the State between 1880 and 1890, 77 per cent went to the irrigated counties, and largely consisted of families who bought small farms and proceeded to do their own work. The influence of a great mass of small proprietors tilling their own land can not fail to have a very marked effect upon the character of the institutions.

Diversified Farming a Feature of Irrigation

Irrigation lends itself naturally to diversified farming and tends to make population self-sufficient within itself. Although in certain localities, especially those where the climate is favorable to raisins and oranges, the contrary has sometimes been true, the tendency of irrigation as a whole has been to discourage the production of single crops and make families independent by producing the variety of things they consume. This tendency is steadily gaining ground. The diversified farming which irrigation both permits and encourages will be an important element in contributing to the independence of the people who shall inhabit the arid region of the future.

Irrigation as a Training in Self-Government

Another interesting feature of irrigation is the training it gives in self-government. A farmer under irrigation can not remain ignorant and indifferent of public questions. He has to consider his interest in the river which feeds his canal and the nature of his relation to other users along its course. It is a training school in self-government and gives the first impetus to civilization in rainless regions. The capacity of the American farmer has already been demonstrated. He is the author of the best of our irrigation laws. Colorado was the first State to enact a law providing for the public control of streams and some sort of systematic procedure for the establishment of rights, but the credit of that is not due to her statesmen, but to the discussions of the Greeley Lyceum and the public spirit and independence of the irrigators under the Colony Canal. Opposed by the conservatism of the legal profession and the prejudices of those not practically familiar with the subject, they had a long and doubtful struggle to secure the adoption of a statute which for a time made the State the lawgiver of the arid region.

In Utah the practices of water users are a hundred years in advance of the State laws. This is due to the fact that irrigators recognize insensibly the community nature of their interest in the streams. The old feudal idea of privateownership in water has never made an irrigated district prosperous, and it never will.

Irrigation and Cooperation

Another feature is the tendency toward cooperation. Under the Wyoming law accepting the Carey grant this cooperation is made obligatory. Every settler under a canal becomes a shareholder therein. Not only does the right to water attach to the land, but a share in the canal sufficient to carry the water also goes with it. In fact, the need of watering many farms from a common source and of organizing a community under rules and discipline for the distribution of the supply make a nursery of cooperation. Its most conspicuous manifestation is in the widespread and successful fruit exchanges of California. There are many instances of smaller and more local organizations of a cooperative industrial character, and they are multiplying rapidly. They seem likely to deal with yet larger affairs in the future as communities gain in age, numbers, and wealth.

Effect of Irrigation on Social Life

Heretofore one of the evils of the irrigated home has been its isolation. The valleys of many streams are narrow. The broad areas which lie between these valleys are the home of cattle and sheep, but not of men. The Anglo-Saxon thirst for land, and the opportunity which the desert-land act gave to gratify it, resulted at first in a wide separation between homes, and in a loss to the pioneer of the advantages of schools, churches, and social life. Under the larger and later canals the tendency has been in the other direction. The European custom of making homes in village centers has been adopted in parts of Utah, Wyoming, Idaho, and California, and steadily gains in public favor. Where farmers live in villages, their families enjoy ready access to schools, churches, libraries, and entertainments. The agricultural society of the future in the Western valleys will realize a happy combination of town and country life — the independence which springs from the proprietorship of the soil and the satisfaction of the social instinct which comes only with community association. Such conditions are favorable to the growth of the best forms of civilization and the noblest institutions. This is the hope which lies fallow in the arid valleys of the West. Its realization is well worth the struggle which is impending for the reform of our land and water laws, and which will impose high demands upon our statesmanship and call for the exercise of the best order of patriotism.

The Commercial Importance of Irrigation

The commercial importance of the development of irrigation resources is being realized in the West at the present time as never before. Especially in California there is a new awakening, and an effort on the part of the best elements of citizenship to remove the obstacles which have formerly hampered both public and private enterprise. The East, as a whole, is beginning to realize the great part which the West is to have in the events of the twentieth century. World-wide forces are working to hasten the day of its complete development and of the utilization of all its rich resources. The Orient is awake and offering its markets to the trade of the Pacific coast. With the development of this trade there will come an impulse for the completion of the material conquest of arid America by the enlistment of public as well as private means in the storage and diversion of its streams for the irrigation of its hundred million acres of irrigable soil; the harnessing of its water powers to mill and factory wheels; the crowding of its pastures with new millions of live stock; the opening up of its mines and quarries; the conversion of its forests into human habitations; the coming of a vast population, and the growth of institutions worthy of the time and the place.

Rotation of Crops in Iowa, 1901

From Henry Wallace, "Rotation of Crops," in Iowa Department of Agriculture, *Iowa Year Book of Agriculture,* 1900 (Des Moines, Ia., 1901), pp. 56–60.

It is not at all necessary to convince Iowa farmers, at least the class which assembles at this meeting, that they should practice rotation of crops. The fact that they at least occasionally follow corn with spring wheat, oats, or barley, to rest their land, as they say, shows that in some measure even the poorest farmers believe in rotation of crops.

Nor is it necessary here to enter into any scientific discussion as to the differences between large-leafed or narrow, surface rooted or deep rooted, hoed or sown crops, viewed in their relation to crop rotations. What the farmer asks is not the scientific, but the practical; something that will work out. He has an intuition, and a very correct one, that whatever, when fairly tested, will not work out in practice is not scientific and is not worth bothering with.

All that I will now attempt to do is to show, first, why rotation of crops should be practiced, and, second, give some rotations that are practical in the different sections of the state and with different types of farms and farmers.

First, why rotation should be practiced. One of the main reasons is to maintain a supply of humus in the soil. Humus is partially decomposed vegetable matter which the Great Farmer of all farmers has been storing in the soil for ages without number and without which the best farm land is for the time being, or until it is supplied, practically a desert. Humus acts as a storehouse of available plant food, especially nitrogen, as a sponge to absorb surplus water in a wet time, to conserve it and deal it out in a dry time, to keep the insoluble particles of the soil, which are by far its greatest bulk, apart in order that the plant roots may have an opportunity to run their free course and be glorified. It also acts as an absorber of heat, adding materially to the warmth of the soil.

Every farmer, no matter how little he may observe, knows that when a soil of any of these prairies is broken up it stands dry weather and wet weather splendidly, and it is one of the commonest remarks of the new settler who has come from soils practically exhausted of their humus, that this country stands more wet weather and dry weather than any country he ever saw.

Constant plowing, harrowing, and cultivating gives free access to the air, multiplies the power of the germs whose mission it is to tear down and destroy vegetable matter and wastes humus at a fearful rate, so that in from fifteen to twenty years of continuous cultivation this partially decomposed vegetable matter is wholly decomposed, and the result is ash, which remains in the soil, and gas, which escapes into the air. The land now puddles in a wet time and bakes in a dry time, plants become enfeebled, insects live upon the sap, multiply, and the farmer who does not rotate reaches the conclusion that the climate has changed, or perhaps, if he be a partisan and his party out of power, that there is something wrong with the administration.

A crop of clover once in four years will maintain a supply of humus and nitrogen in the soil indefinitely, and if to this be added the manure usually produced on the stock farm, it will increase it gradually from year to year until the soil has more than its virgin fertility.

Rotation should be practiced to maintain the supply of nitrogen, or that element in fertility which goes to the production of those elements of the grains and grasses that build up muscle, blood, hair, wool, and which alone can be used for that purpose. Not an ounce of muscle was ever made on pure carbon.

It, therefore, becomes necessary that there should be a legume, such as clover, beans, or peas, in the rotation, and this class of plants alone, or at least almost alone, are able to use the free nitrogen of the atmosphere. This, together with the large amount of humus it furnishes by its decaying roots, is the reason why no rotation should ever be followed that does not contain a leguminous crop as its alpha and omega, its beginning and its end.

Again, rotation of crops is essential in order to prevent the multiplication of noxious insects. Whenever one crop is grown year after year on the same land, no matter what that crop may be, the insects that prey upon it multiply enormously. There is no limit to the capacity of insects to multiply and increase and infest the earth. For example, if corn is grown continuously after corn, the corn root worm and the corn root louse increase so rapidly that the crop is reduced from this cause alone from one-fourth to one-half. Soils of exceptional fertility push on the plant so rapidly that the injuries done by these insects often pass unnoticed, but they are there all the same and in time will get in their work.

The continuous growth of wheat invites the Hessian fly, the wheat stalk borer, the wheat midge, and other insect enemies. The extensive cultivation of small grain of any kind invites the chinch bug to take possession. These are given simply as samples of the command of the insects, ''Rotate your crops or we will rotate you off the farm.''

Another reason why rotation of crops should be practiced is to distribute the labor of the farm over the entire growing season. We need not even illustrate this point, but remark only that the longer the rotation, the more equitably is labor distributed, and hence the more profitably can it be employed.

Still another reason why we should rotate crops is to keep weeds in check. Land cultivated continuously to one crop or to corn and any kind of small grain, tends to become more and more weedy each year, and the more rapidly the fertility is exhausted, the more rapidly the weeds multiply, weeds being able to live where the finer grasses and grains do not. A rotation in which the grasses, particularly the clovers, form a prominent part prevents weed development in two ways. First, by increasing fertility that the finer grasses may be able to smother out the weeds; second, by preventing the seed formation, the time of cutting tame grasses being earlier than the period of most weed seeds.

Finally, a rotation of crops enables the farmer to grow live stock with profit and to establish a meat factory on his farm for which everything grown on it, with the exception of wheat, is raw material, and the shipments or sales are almost entirely finished products. This is the only way in which farming in the West can be made permanently profitable; hence, a thorough system of crop rotation is essential to success in western agriculture.

I now suggest a few crop rotations adapted some to the whole and others to different portions of the state, and to different farms and farmers in any portion. Rotations may be of two, three, four, five, six, or even seven years, the longer rotations being adapted to the larger farms and the shorter rotations to farms of smaller area. It is not easy to use a long rotation on a small farm, as it necessarily makes the field too small to be cultivated with the greatest profit. Farmers in the central and southern parts of the state who have found regular potato growing profitable, will find a rotation of corn, potatoes, winter wheat, and clover the most profitable in the long run.

It may be as well to state again that I regard red and mammoth clover as the alpha and omega, the beginning and the end of all crop rotations. If a farmer has clover to start with, he should on this clover sod apply all the manure he can gather up about the farm. The first crop in the rotation should be corn, because it is a gross feeder and can not readily be injured by any ordinary amount of manure, if it be well rotted, or by an excess of nitrogen in the soil. After a crop of corn, the land is in first-class shape for a crop of potatoes, and the thorough culture of the potatoes, without any further plowing, puts the land in an ideal condition for a crop of winter wheat, when it should be again sown to clover, thus making a four-course rotation.

In this only the red or mammoth clover should be used. Timothy might be sown with it as a precaution against an entire failure of the grass crop. If the farmer is not largely engaged in stock growing, he should use the mammoth clover and cut it for seed, which will ensure the destruction of all ordinary weed seeds, thus leaving the land clean and in elegant condition for a crop of corn.

Farmers in the central and southern sections of the state, who do not find either oats or spring wheat profitable, can use a three-course rotation to advantage; corn on clover sod, well manured, followed by winter wheat drilled in the corn-stalks with a one-horse drill, or, if the corn be used for silage or fodder, drilled after the corn is harvested, with a disk drill, and sown to clover the next spring, thus making a three-course rotation. When winter wheat is not a certain crop, oats and spring wheat are generally fairly profitable, and a shorter rotation may be used to advantage; namely, corn on a well manured clover sod, followed by oats, spring wheat, or barley, sown to clover, and this clover turned under the same fall or the next spring, and planted to corn. In order to secure a stand, however, either barley or an early variety of oats or spring wheat may be used.

In the southern and central portions of the state, corn on clover sod may be followed by oats of the later varieties and the stubble plowed under immediately after harvest, and the wheat sown on thoroughly prepared ground, clover and timothy to be sown with the wheat. This is the rotation to which I was accustomed in Pennsylvania and is the favorite four-course rotation over a large section of country.

On large farms any of these rotations may be lengthened by using two crops of corn instead of one, or by seeding heavily to clover and timothy, taking the first year, if the mammoth is used, a crop of clover hay and seed in good years, a crop of timothy hay or seed the next year, and then manuring and plowing for corn.

On rough lands, where it is not desirable to plow up frequently, corn on clover sod may be followed either by winter wheat or spring grain, using the early varieties, then sown heavily to mammoth clover and timothy, a clover seed crop being taken the first year. The second year there will be not more than a third of a stand of mammoth, but if a good catch is obtained there will be a heavy crop of timothy, which preferably should be cut for seed, and which will naturally be followed by another clover crop, the shatterings of the seed from the first year, and this rotation between mammoth clover and timothy can be kept up for several years. When either fails, the land can be plowed again and planted to corn.

In a rotation of corn, winter wheat, and clover, it will be noticed that but one plowing is necessary in the three years. The same is true in a rotation of corn, spring wheat, and clover, the spring grains doing best in this section on unplowed corn stubble. On hilly lands, it is advisable to plow as little as possible.

Any of these rotations will maintain a supply of humus in the soil, will maintain a full supply of nitrogen, and will distribute labor through the year, particularly so where live stock is part of the regular business of the farm. Any of them will keep down both noxious insects and noxious weeds. It is essential to all of them that the red or mammoth clover should have its place in the rotation.

White clover should be excluded from all rotation crops. It belongs to the permanent pasture exclusively. Alsike clover should be used only where it has not been possible to secure a stand of the larger clovers, or where land is too wet for cultivation, in which case alsike should be sown to the exclusion of the other clovers.

From the above, it will not be at all difficult for any good farmer to select a rotation that will be adapted to his location, to his taste, and to the circumstances and conditions of his farm.

Postal Service To Farm Areas, 1900

From Charles H. Greathouse, "Free Delivery of Rural Mails," U.S. Department of Agriculture, *Yearbook*, 1900, pp. 513–28.

Rapid Growth of Rural Free Delivery

The system of free delivery of mail at the farm homestead is developing in the United States by great strides. It is commonly known as "Rural free delivery." The first routes bearing this name were established on October 1, 1896, at Hall-town, Uvilla, and Charlestown, W. Va. Others followed at once, and by the close of the fiscal year the experiment showed satisfactory results. There were 44 routes in the fall of 1897; this number increased to 128 in 1898, and on November 1, 1899, had jumped to 634. These radiated from 383 distributing points and served a population of 452,735 persons. On June 30, 1900, a little more than six months later, the number of routes had grown to 1,214 for a population of 879,127, and in the next four months the system again more than doubled its proportions, showing on November 1, 1900, 2,551 routes for 1,801,524 persons; and there were also at that date 2,158 applications for the establishment of new routes. The whole of the United States is now laid out in four divisions for the inauguration and maintenance of this service, and the work is going forward with steadily increasing volume.

President McKinley in his message to Congress of December 3, 1900, states that "the number of applications now pending and awaiting action nearly equals all those granted up to the present time, and by the close of the current fiscal year about 4,000 routes will have been established, providing for the daily delivery of mails at the scattered homes of about three and a half million of rural population." The President describes this as the most striking new development of the postal service, which "ameliorates the isolation of farm life, conduces to good roads, and quickens and extends the dissemination of general information." He adds that "experience thus far has tended to allay the apprehension that it would be so expensive as to forbid its general adoption or make it a serious burden; its actual application has shown that it increases postal receipts, and can be accomplished by reductions in other branches of the service, so that the augmented revenues and the accomplished savings together materially reduce the net cost." All these results, the President says, "have come almost wholly within the last year."

The first appropriations for the service, $10,000 for the fiscal year 1894, $20,000 for 1895, and $30,000 for 1896, were not used. Subsequent appropriations have been as follows: For 1897, $40,000; for 1898, $50,000; for 1899, $150,000; for 1900, $450,000; for 1901, $1,750,000. The Post-Office appropriation bill approved March 4, 1901, carries $3,500,000 for this use in the fiscal year 1902.

History of the Development of Rural Free Delivery

Undoubtedly the evolution of the rural free-delivery service as it now exists dates back to "village delivery" which Postmaster-General Wanamaker recommended in 1890. The service he inaugurated, however, was not a "rural" delivery, but an extension of the city delivery system by carriers on foot in towns with a less population than 10,000, or less gross postal receipts than $10,000, the limit at which city delivery stops under existing law. The broad recommendations included in Mr. Wanamaker's report for an abandonment of the old colonial postal system (recently most aptly described by Postmaster-General Charles Emory Smith as a plan which "required the man to go for the mails, instead of the mails going to the man"), aroused public attention, and started an agitation in Congress and by the people for an extension of the free-delivery system into hitherto untried fields. When, on a change of Administration, the village-delivery experiment inaugurated on Postmaster-General Wanamaker's recommendation was ordered by Congress to be discontinued, after a brief experimental existence of little more than two years, the movement for free delivery on a broader basis was not suspended, but grew in intensity.

The new agitation took the form, not of a request for free delivery in villages where none of the patrons lived more than a mile or so from their village post office, but of a movement to give country delivery to farmers who lived from 2 to 12 miles from any post office, and who in consequence had to waste the best part of a day whenever they wished to mail a letter or expected to receive one, or desired to obtain a newspaper or magazine for which they had subscribed.

The State granges of Patrons of Husbandry took up the subject and brought strong pressure to bear upon Representatives in Congress from agricultural communities. Under these incentives a number of small appropriations were passed, but, as already stated, were not used. The prevailing sentiment, both in Congress and among the executive officers of the Post-Office Department, as then constituted, was that the plan of rural free delivery was impossible of general adoption, and that it would cost at least $20,000,000 a year to establish and maintain it.

Congressional Action

Postmaster-General Wilson S. Bissell declined to make any use of the small appropriation of $10,000 for experimental rural free delivery in 1894. His antagonistic views were concurred in by the Committee on the Post-Office and Post-Roads of the Fifty-third Congress, Hon. John S. Henderson, of North Carolina, being chairman. But many Representatives had become strongly interested in the project, and in spite of the committee's adverse report, the appropriation was doubled. Mr. Bissell, however, again refused to act, and it was not until after Hon. William L. Wilson became Postmaster-General that anything was done to comply with the directions of Congress. Mr. Wilson was appointed in the spring of 1895. In his first report he said that he had taken charge too late in the fiscal year to undertake the work. He agreed with his predecessor, Mr. Bissell, that the proposal was impracticable, but he added that if Congress chose to make the money available for the fiscal year 1897 he would inaugurate the experiment by the best methods he could devise. The response by Congress was a second doubling of the appropriation, putting $40,000 at his disposal.

The First Routes Established

Under this authorization, 44 routes were selected in widely differing localities in 29 States. The purpose was to make the experiment as general as possible, and to have the result represent the working of the system under as diverse conditions as possible. Fifteen routes were set going in October, 1896, 15 in November, 8 in December, 3 in January, and 1 each in February and April following. Some of these routes were in the foothills of the Alleghenies about Charlestown, W. Va., others on the prairies of Kansas and Nebraska; some among the sugar plantations of Louisiana, others among the snow and ice of Grand Isle in Lake Champlain and on the wind-swept plains of Minnesota; some were in the populous old communities of northern Massachusetts and southwestern Maine, others among the fruit orchards of Arizona and the grass lands of southern Washington. The other States represented were Indiana, Ohio, Maryland, Missouri, Arkansas, Virginia, North Carolina, Colorado, Iowa, Pennsylvania, Michigan, Alabama, Georgia, Kentucky, Illinois, Tennessee, and California.

Unfavorable Conditions

It was dead of winter before the work got fairly under way, so that the difficulties were practically at a maximum, except that of muddy roads, which would become more and more impassable as spring came on. The officials who were intrusted with the inauguration of the service were often dissatisfied and unfavorably disposed toward the work, because they had to be detailed from their regular work in such a way as to hinder their probable promotion. Accordingly some of the first reports were quite discouraging.

The inspector who laid out the route at Hartsville, Ind., wrote that the people who were reached were not asking for delivery of their mails at their homes. Their correspondence was mainly social, not demanding promptness of delivery, and only farmers living near the post office took daily papers. "The importance of the average farmer's mail," he said, "is not such as to make rural free delivery essential." The fact that the farmers near the post office took daily papers seemed to give no intimation to this inspector that free delivery would cause farmers all along the route to do the same thing.

Adoption by the Executive of Views Favorable to the System

In consequence of the discouragements just referred to, the new service was so little known when Hon. Perry S. Heath became First Assistant Postmaster-General in March, 1897, that he learned with some surprise that a trial was actually being made of rural free delivery. He took charge of the administrative division to which the experiment belonged, and determined to go into the matter exhaustively. In contradiction of the unfavorable reports from some of the agents in charge of the work came good news from other agents, and the sentiment of farmers everywhere seemed favorable to a thorough test of the system. Congress was so well satisfied with the success so far attained that the appropriation for 1898 was made $50,000.

Mr. Heath said in his second report to the Postmaster-General:

An examination of the reports on file led to the conclusion that great possibilities of social, industrial, and educational development lay behind the projected extension of postal facilities in rural communities, and that with proper care in the selection of localities, the service could be extended far and wide, with great benefit to the people and without any serious tax upon the revenues of the Government, inasmuch as the increase of postal business which had hitherto followed the granting of additional postal facilities in every well-selected rural route would go far toward the payment of the extra expense incurred, while the discontinuance of unnecessary post offices and star routes would in many cases make the improved service a source of saving instead of added outlay.

It was, of course, apparent that no accurate balance sheet of profit and loss could immediately be struck, inasmuch as no account could be kept of the saving effected by dispensing with the offices of postmasters of the fourth class, who are authorized by law to retain all their receipts up to the limit of $1,000. Their receipts do not appear in the post-office returns. They are perquisites of the postmasters, to which they cling with natural tenacity. When, under the operations of rural free delivery, their cancellations are turned into the general postal revenues, the service thus rendered becomes an item of cost charged against the rural free delivery appropriation, but the saving effected can not be credited to that account. In like manner star-route service dispensed with makes a net saving to the Government, but goes to the credit of another branch of the service, as star-route contractors are paid under an appropriation not supervised by the First Assistant Postmaster-General.

Petitions from every section of country where the service had been given a fair trial began to pour in upon the Department. Special agents were appointed to look into the claims presented and to lay out services wherever the conditions seemed favorable to an economical and successful administration. Such good results were obtained that Congress, responding to the demand of the people, appropriated $150,000 for rural free delivery for the fiscal year 1897–98 [1898–99], and gave $300,000 for the same purpose for the current fiscal year [1900]. The requests for the service multiplied like an endless chain, every new rural delivery route established bringing in three or more applications from contiguous territory for like privileges, and before four months of the present fiscal year had expired the appropriation was found to have been practically apportioned out, that is to say, the existing service, if continued to the close of the fiscal year, would require the disbursement of the whole amount appropriated by Congress. As I did not deem myself authorized to create a deficiency, even in so popular and important a work of postal development, a halt was reluctantly called in the installation of new rural free delivery service to await the further directions of the Congress.

Opposition of Postmasters and Star-Route Contractors

It must not be supposed, however, that all opposition to rural free delivery ceased with the change of attitude on the part of the Post-Office Department. It was found by the special agents in charge of the establishment of new routes that considerable sentiment against the change of method was manifested in some communities where it was about to be made. In several cases petitions were sent to Congress making protest, but upon investigation it was found in most cases that this adverse feeling had been worked up in the interest of a fourth-class postmaster or a star-route contractor who was likely to be displaced by the new routes. In some cases the fear of the postmaster was supplemented by apprehension among his village neighbors that trade would go elsewhere. In many instances signers of petitions, when called upon, repudiated the views they had been induced to indorse. They had signed out of good will to their neighbors and with little attention to the meaning of the petition. When the question of free delivery was brought before them on its merits they had little to say in opposition, and when it was presented as a direct benefit to themselves they were active in preventing the choice of some other section than their own for the location of the next new route.

The System Put To a Test

Congress without hesitation supplied the additional funds called for by the unexpectedly rapid growth of the service, and the installation of new routes went speedily forward.

Up to this point the service had been fragmentary and detached. It was Postmaster-General Smith who developed the idea of putting the service to a test of practicability by extending rural delivery over an entire county, superseding all other service, and then striking a balance sheet of profit and loss.

Four lines of investigation were laid down:

(1) To what extent can rural free delivery supersede fourth-class post offices and star routes.

(2) To what extent can it be used as a channel through which to extend to the farmer all other postal facilities, as money orders, etc.

(3) What will be the effect on the postal revenues.

(4) What the net cost to the Government as compared with that of the old system.

It seemed essential that such an experiment should be made in a strictly farming community, presenting many of the topographical and other physical conditions and obstacles likely to be encountered in a general introduction of the service elsewhere, so that its successful operation under such circumstances might be looked upon as a guaranty of its success in any other average rural locality in which it might be established.

The Carroll County Service

Carroll County, Md., was selected, with the third-class post office of Westminster as the distributing point. The results of the experiment are thus described in official reports of the Post-Office Department:

On December 20, 1899, when winter weather and snowstorms had put the roads in their worst condition, the practicability of establishing rural free delivery to extend over a wide area to the exclusion of all other service, was put to a test in Carroll County, Md. By order of the Postmaster-General, 63 minor post offices and 35 services by star-route contractors and mail messengers were discontinued, all in one day, and rural free delivery substituted in their place.

The Westminster service started with four 2-horse postal wagons, each equipped with all the appliances of a traveling post office, each accompanied by a postal clerk empowered to issue money orders, register letters, and deliver letters, and cancel stamps on letters collected. These wagons supplied mail at designated points to twenty rural carriers, for whom cross routes were laid out, so as to bring all the territory embodied in the order within easy reach of the mails. The initial service in Carroll County covered 387 square miles of the 453 square miles within the county limits. It has since been extended so as to cover the whole county and about 200 square miles of adjacent territory in Baltimore, Howard, Frederick, and Montgomery counties, Md., and York and Adams counties, Pa., this additional service being equivalent to ten ordinary rural free-delivery routes.

The total number of carriers employed is 45, and they, with the four wagon services, give a daily dispatch, as well as delivery, on every route except four, which are too far removed from railroads to be able to make connections the same day; but all letters from these points are dispatched early the following morning.

A detailed report of this service from the Superintendent of the Free Delivery System, under whose direct supervision the experiment was started, was laid before Congress on the 23d of April, 1900. It was shown by this report that during the first three months the cost of the service was $4,543; the saving by service superseded was $2,805; the increase of postal receipts directly resulting from the increased accommodation was $1,501.75, thus leaving the net cost of carrying the postal service practically to, or near to, the homes of all the people in Carroll County for one-quarter of a year only $263.

Other County Services

County services on an almost equally broad scale have since been successfully inaugurated in Washington County, Tenn., Washington County, Pa., Fairfield County, Conn., and are in process of installation in other States.

Improvements, Phases, and Incidents

The practical test of rural free delivery gave rise to many problems, and some of these are even now only in process of settlement.

Mails for Mining Camps

Among others, was the question what could be done for mining camps and similar customers of the post office. When the service was started only the farming population was considered, but it was soon evident that in several Western States settlers on mineral lands ought not to be left out of the account. What has been actually done is to establish routes for such communities the same as in agricultural sections. This service is maintained under a ruling of the Post-Office Department that the term "rural" means "communities not included in cities or incorporated villages, and does not necessarily imply that persons so situated should be engaged in farming in order to obtain the benefits of rural free delivery."

Protection of Mail Boxes

Another difficulty lay in the danger of loss of mail from boxes not directly owned by the Government and therefore completely under the protection of the statutes. It is not easy even under the most favorable conditions, to secure convictions of offenders against the Government; the lawyers for the defense in such prosecutions are prone to make use of any technicality and as a result, guilty persons often go clear. It was decided by the Department that boxes set up for farm delivery and accepted by the postal authorities as "secure and appropriate" should be regarded as within the application of the law forbidding any tampering with mails. There have been several cases of meddling with the free-delivery boxes, and one man has been held for trial in the United States courts. Further legislation has been asked of Congress so as to supply more convenient boxes to be owned by the Government and thus protected more certainly.

In comparing rural free delivery with the old system as regards safety of the mails, it must not be forgotten that abuses and carelessness are not infrequent at fourth-class post offices. At some places the mail sack is simply emptied on a table and each person hunts through it for his own mail.

Registered Mail, Money Orders, and Drop Letters

On April 12, 1900, an important advance took place. Rural carriers were authorized to receive and deliver registered mail. As the law requires such matter to be delivered personally, the carriers are obliged to go to the houses instead of dropping the letters or packages in the farm box. Rural carriers are also authorized to receipt for applications for money orders, and while they can not yet issue the orders, they can save the farmer the trip to the office by acting as his agent.

Another most satisfactory change was made on July 26, 1900, when an order was made under which postage on drop letters on rural free-delivery routes was fixed at 2 cents per ounce and carriers were required to cancel stamps on all letters collected by them. This order carried with it authority to deliver drop letters without passing them through the hands of a postmaster.

Adaptability of the Service

The effort in the incipiency of the institution of rural free delivery to put the matter to the test under as diverse conditions as possible resulted early in showing that the new way could be adapted to any section not altogether too sparsely settled. It was found possible to deliver the mails in the coldest winter of any part of this country and in the driest and hottest summer with very little interruption, scarcely more than occurs in cities by reason of snowdrifts and washouts on railways. When a heavy snow blocks the way of the rural carrier it is customary for the farmers to turn out and break the roads, and this is done several days earlier than would be the case ordinarily. In this way communication throughout neighborhoods and with the outside world is opened up promptly. In consequence the farmer is able to take advantage of good markets and the townspeople are not cut off from the supply of fresh country produce, as often has happened in severe storms. Also cases of distress in isolated farm homes are sooner reached and relieved.

The carrier's outfit is modified to suit the conditions under which his work is done, a light vehicle being used in one section while a heavier wagon is preferred in another. The Washington officials have been surprised at the rapidity of the growth of the system in remote and comparatively sparsely settled regions in the West and South.

Advantages of Rural Free Delivery

Theoretical Considerations

Rural free delivery of mails is scientific. On purely theoretical grounds the post office ought always to deliver the matter intrusted to it at the door of the addressee. The distance to be traveled from sender to receiver of mail is precisely the same whether the whole trip be made by the postal employee or he be met part way by the person for whom it is intended. Furthermore, the cost of making the trip is always paid out of the sum total of the nation's capacity to do work. It makes little difference ultimately whether the labor is paid for from Government funds collected by the sale of stamps or otherwise, or is done by each man directly without intervention of the United States Treasury at all; it all comes from the people anyhow.

The only question that need be asked is whether there will be more waste of time, a larger number of empty trips by the farmer, who never knows when there is mail for him, or by the postman, who always knows whether there is something to deliver; and to this there seems to be but one answer. The number of times the farmer would be going to the post town for other reasons and the times when several families would send for mail by the same messenger enter into the calculation, of course, but in general this would not change the answer. And whether the addressee may be a farmer or townsman really is of no consequence, if free delivery involves only a short trip for the postman in the city, it also involves only a short trip for the citizen, and the corresponding relation between length of trips exists for the farm delivery.

The Opinions of Farmers

The views of farmers as to rural free delivery are strikingly illustrated by the reception of the opening of a new route at Attica, Ind., on May 12, 1900. It was the busiest season of the year, but a large number of farmers came in, some of them 10 to 15 miles to get farm boxes at $2.60 apiece, so as to be ready for the carrier.

Further evidence of the general favor in which the system is held by farmers is found in hundreds of letters in answer to inquiries sent out by this Department. Only one in ten had any objection to offer, and frequently the objection was that the expense would be too great. In answer to this may be offered the demonstration on theoretical grounds that the real expense is much less under the new system. And more directly convincing is the demonstration by figures in the post-office reports that the cash outlay by the Government for rural free delivery is smaller than for a less desirable service through country post office and star route. The loss of work to the farming community in going to the post office for mail is shown to be absolute and total waste.

Of the letters from farmers, a few are here presented. They are selected so as to show as fully as practicable opinions of all kinds:

Jason Woodman, Paw Paw, Mich.: The daily delivery at his ''place of business'' of the farmer's letters, market reports, and daily paper are as essential to him as such things are to any business man. In my own case it saves hundreds of miles driving and days of time each year.

W. S. Jordun, North Manchester, Ind.: . . . After a trial of nearly a year we feel as though it would take away part of life to give it up.

E. D. Nauman, Thornburg, Iowa.: . . . It will greatly assist the farmer in a material and practical way by giving him the markets and United States weather forecasts daily. Of the two, I regard the weather forecasts fully as important as the markets. Under the old system the farmers, for whom to a large extent the weather bulletins are intended, do not see them with sufficient regularity to be of much value to them. And at that season of the year when the weather forecasts are of most value to the farmer (harvest time) he is too busy to visit the post office to either see the bulletin there displayed or to get his daily paper.

Jonathan B. Allen, Delavan, Ill.: . . . In November I sold 3,000 bushels of corn; there was a difference of 3 cents a bushel between the highest and lowest bid of six elevators that are located within 5 miles of me. I consider a farm on rural mail route worth 5 per cent more than a farm that is not.

W. D. H. Johnson, Holton, Ga.: . . . I would suggest that the carrier be required to carry the weather flags on his conveyance where the Weather Bureau has a signal station, as is the case at our starting point.

T. C. Badger, Smith Center, Kans.: . . . Perhaps the greatest advantage is in knowing the market prices each day. The buyers here use Kansas City markets as a basis for buying, and the farmers can be, and some of them are, just as well informed as anyone. I know of two that made the price of their daily paper on one load of hogs each. It is the forerunner of other deliveries [of grocers and the like] along the route.

W. M. Hilleary, Turner, Oreg.: . . . We have had the benefits of free rural mail delivery at Turner for more than three years. The farmers are well pleased with its benefits and pleasures. . . . Before free delivery was started there were 13 daily papers taken at Turner post office. To-day there are 113. This shows that the farmers are getting in touch with the world and are quick to avail themselves of all educational facilities. With the general extension of rural free mail delivery there will be less talk about the monotony of farm life and less desire of the boys and girls to get away from the farm. The only objectors are small retailers of merchandise and dealers in liquors and tobacco. It may injure the business of the latter, since many farmers do not drink or smoke, only when they go to the village; and their families get the benefit in more reading matter.

O. N. Cadwell, Carpinteria, Cal.: . . . It brings our daily papers promptly, so that saves us time and anxiety. The weather report is dropped in our box, and that is the first thing I look at, to see what it says about the weather to-morrow.

C. P. Waugh, Wellsburg, W. Va.: . . . We have three routes in this county that have been in operation for 18 months and are delivering mail every day to 1,275 persons. In the 18 months the increase in the amount of mail delivered and collected amounted to a little over 57 per cent. These 1,275 people live on an average about 2 miles from the office, and before the R. F. D. started only went for their mail about twice per week, and it required about one hour each week for each person to go for his mail; 1,275 hours per week, 66,300 hours per year, or 6,630 days of 10 hours each lost every year going for mail twice per week, and then not receiving half the benefits we do at the present time.

. . . By having plenty of good and cheap reading delivered at our doors every day free of charge it not only makes the farmers and their families read more, but it makes them think more.

J. S. Hollingsworth, Snacks, Ind.: . . . Here is a sample of the benefits: I get two dailies every morning. . . . On November 16, 1900, I saw a big jump in potato market. Next day I left a postal card in a United States box at the crossroads for a farmer 3 miles distant to "hold your big potato crop; a jump is on the market; don't sell too soon." In two weeks from that date he sold 1,000 bushels at 20 cents above the October market.

Matthew Williams, Verndale, Minn.: As the whole world has been drawn closer together by the inventions and uses of steam and electricity, so farmers may be drawn closer together by the universal practice of free delivery.

State Senator Thomas J. Lindley, Ind.: . . . I can say with confidence that there is no other way in which the expenditure of a like sum of money brings as great good to so large a number of the people. The farmer on a rural route is in close and constant touch with the world. He no longer feels the isolation of country life. I think the system will contribute largely to prevent the threatened congestion of population in our cities and towns. I speak after two years' experience on a rural route 7 miles from town.

Frank L. Gerrish, Boscawen, N.H.: . . . Some of the farmers got their eyes opened on the apple crop by taking papers they had not before, and made a nice thing by holding. These routes are not all they might be, but constant improvements will do much to help these back farms and keep them in touch with the near markets.

Postmaster Henry Robinson, Concord, N.H.: [At the request of Mr. Gerrish, Mr. Robinson sent letters praising the new system from 32 farmers, all living along routes radiating from that office.]

. . . If this State gets a fair allotment of the Congressional appropriation for rural free mail delivery during the fiscal year beginning July 1 next, the whole State of New Hampshire will be substantially covered, especially the principal highways, by the rural carrier service. The grangers in New Hampshire have made themselves its especial champions.

. . . The local system of rural free delivery centering at the Concord post office already comprises 26 contiguous routes. These routes, on an average, include 600 people each, which, together with the people of the city of Concord, who enjoy city and rural free delivery, include substantially 35,000 people, or more than one-half of the population of Merrimack County. These routes cover substantially 1,000 miles of highways. The rural carrier service in central New Hampshire now covers a tract of territory from the city of Franklin and the town of Salisbury, the birthplace of Daniel Webster, on the north, to the village of Litchfield, on the south, a distance of 50 miles, and from Pittsfield on the east to Henniker on the west, a distance of 34 miles.

. . . The impetus to the good-roads movement is very great, and the value of real estate generally throughout the delivery territory is increased.

G. L. Webster, Opelika, Ala.: . . . There are three routes out from this place. The first has been in operation for four years, the other two one year, and they have all proved eminently successful. . . . The amount of mail matter carried out on this route has more than doubled since their establishment, and many farmers are taking papers and getting daily crop reports that formerly only got this information once a week.

Z. Taylor Chrisman, Warwick, Pa.: . . . If rural free delivery must close our local post office and give us but one delivery a day and remove the post office so far from us that we can't go to it no matter how urgent, or should we receive a letter that required an immediate answer, it could not be answered until the next day, I can't see that it will benefit us.

Could not the Department with equal economy have a carrier from each local office distribute the mail daily, and we would still have our office, so that we could send or receive any additional mail?

John M. True, secretary State board of agriculture, Madison, Wis.: I am of the opinion that the most sanguine expectations of the friends of rural free delivery are to be more than realized. I am informed that upon lines established in my vicinity four months since the amount of mail handled has already largely increased, showing a prompt disposition on the part of farmers to avail themselves of increased facilities for general reading, which means more intelligent ideas of business, periodicals, and social questions. It measurably removes the feeling of isolation that has been one of the great drawbacks to rural life.

The whole tendency of the system is to elevate the farmer, making him a broader, more refined, happier, and more useful citizen.

S. C. McDowell, Fox Lake, Wis.: . . . Rural free delivery will encourage the people to make better roads. It has already had an influence on the price of land, which has increased $5 per acre already.

F. D. T. Hall, Lamberton, N.Y.: . . . Farmers who have all their lives been content with one or two mails a week declare they could not go back to the old way, but if the rural free delivery were to be taken away they would combine and employ a carrier at their own expense.

J. B. Cain, Aurora, Nebr.: . . . Living 9 miles from the post office, only getting our mail once or twice a week, then to have a mail route so we can take a daily, is a blessing that a few years ago was not dreamed of. Other cattle feeders as well as myself have driven hundreds of miles for reports of stock market that we now get daily.

William Schafer, Northcreek, Ohio: . . . I don't believe it will ever be a complete success. I have watched the working of it near us in Defiance County, Ohio. It works all right along the routes where there are good roads, but those goods roads are only a few, and I notice that the majority of citizens living at remote points have no accommodation; and again I see where parties go to town and right past the post office and could get their mail just the same. . . .

If the Government is inclined to do a good act for the mail service, let them extend the distance of special delivery. If a person in the country receives a letter of importance with a special-delivery stamp, if it is beyond the limit directed by law he doesn't get his letter.

Reports of Special Agents of the Post Office

The opinions of special agents engaged in introducing free rural delivery in all parts of the United States, as shown in their reports in 1899 and 1900, are invariably favorable to the success of the system. All agree that the opposition comes only from persons interested in the mail service who think they are likely to lose by the change, and from small storekeepers and saloon keepers at fourth-class post offices. Some of them mention also as difficulties to be overcome the fact that the work has been generally spoken of as experimental, and the impossibility of serving all persons precisely alike. The following expressions fairly represent the views of the special agents. The first two are reports for 1899, the others for 1900:

A. B. Smith, Eastern Division: More letters are written and received; more newspapers and magazines read; more intelligence diffused; modern methods are employed on the farm, and better crops are harvested; rural life loses its loneliness and isolation dreaded by all; lands appreciate in value; abandoned farms are again occupied; congested centers find an outlet; inducements to peculation in the postal service are diminished; the service is placed abreast of the times and in accord with the business sentiment of the age.

Thomas Howard, St. Paul, Minn.: The free delivery service offers a solution of the very serious sociological and economic problem presented by the tendency of young men and women residing in rural districts to gravitate toward the cities. I have noticed a distinct improvement in the habits and general moral tone of communities supplied with the service.

F. M. Dice, Middle Division: A great many of the localities have provided uniforms for the carriers by private donations, and have aided carriers to secure special wagons for the delivery of the mails, and are active in their efforts to obtain the best mail boxes for use on their routes.

William E. Annin, Western Division: In Iowa forty routes have been laid out in three Congressional districts during the last two months, all equipped with lock signal boxes erected on posts which are dressed, painted, and numbered. The influence of rural free delivery in stimulating the work for good roads has been powerful in not a few instances in securing appropriations for the bettering of roads, the building of bridges, the repair of culverts, and the maintenance of way.

Mr. A. W. Machen, Superintendent of the Free Delivery System, and Mr. H. Conquest Clarke, of the Southern Division, with general supervision at Washington of the rural service, concur in these views.

Method of Procedure in Starting New Routes

In order to introduce rural free delivery on a new route, a petition must be circulated and signed showing the desire of the persons along the line for the new service. This paper is then forwarded to the Representative in Congress from the district in which the route will be located, or to one of the Senators from the State, for his recommendation. If it is deemed practicable to start the service as desired, a special agent of the Post-Office Department is sent to lay out a route and make a map of it. His report and map must show that at least 100 families can be made accessible to the delivery. It also shows the character of the roads, and the agent impresses upon the persons interested that the roads must be made passable summer and winter.

A full route is considered 25 miles, but according to the country traversed may vary from 17 to 35 miles. It does not take the carrier over the same ground twice in the same day.

Carriers were paid at first only $150 a year. They now receive $500 for an ordinary route and for special short routes $100 a year for each 5 miles traveled. They are bonded, and each carrier has a bonded substitute, so that the mails may never lack a responsible carrier. The civil-service regulations have never been applied to this service, but good character and temperate habits are required. Women are acceptable, and a few are in the ranks, some of them considered very efficient. Reports to the Post-Office Department of dereliction of duty on the part of rural carriers are very few.

Summary of Advantages and Objections

Postmaster-General Charles Emory Smith in his last report summarizes the results attained as follows:

Rural delivery has now been sufficiently tried to measure its effects. The immediate and direct results are clearly apparent. It stimulates social and business correspondence, and so swells the postal receipts. Its introduction is invariably followed by a large increase in the circulation of the press and of periodical literature. The farm is thus brought into direct daily contact with the currents and movements of the business world. A more accurate knowledge of ruling markets and varying prices is diffused, and the producer, with his quicker communication and larger information, is placed on a surer footing. The value of farms, as has been shown in many cases, is enhanced. Good roads become indispensable, and their improvement is the essential condition of the service. The material and measurable benefits are signal and unmistakable.

But the movement exercises a wider and deeper influence. It becomes a factor in the social and economic tendencies of American life. The disposition to leave the farm for the town is a familiar effect of our past conditions. But this tendency is checked, and may be materially changed by an advance which conveys many of the advantages of the town to the farm. Rural free delivery brings the farm within the daily range of the intellectual and commercial activities of the world, and the isolation and monotony which have been the bane of agricultural life are sensibly mitigated. It proves to be one of the most effective and powerful of educational agencies. Wherever it is extended the schools improve and the civic spirit of the community feels a new pulsation; the standard of intelligence is raised, enlightened interest in public affairs is quickened, and better citizenship follows.

With all these results clearly indicated by the experiment as thus far tried, rural free delivery is plainly here to stay. It can not be abandoned where it has been established, and it can not be maintained without being extended.

The objections are: Fourth-class postmasters and star-route contractors are thrown out of some work, and the custom of large numbers of farmers is diverted from its former channels, a disturbance of business of indefinite proportions but of real consequence, yet soon remedied by a readjustment of relations; delay of mails of persons who have lived near enough to the country offices to send for mail early, but who are reached by the rural carrier only as he returns late in the day at the end of his route; and the impossibility of reaching very remote homesteads with rural carriers.

The balance in favor of rural free delivery is so great, the reception by farmers so enthusiastic, and the demands for its extension so widespread and urgent that the Post-Office Department now makes an estimate for it as no longer an experiment, and Congress in its liberal appropriations appears to have accepted this view, although the word "experimental" is still retained in the postal appropriation bill. The growth of the administrative work at Washington has been so great that additional room is now being provided for the force of employees.

The conditions shown justify the opinion more than once expressed by the Post-Office Department, that the United States must follow the lead of France, England, Germany, Austria, and other countries, whose closely settled lands sooner suggested it, and establish a free delivery service everywhere. It is already manifest that the service is in some respects superior to that of the older countries, and when it is fully developed and running smoothly Americans and foreigners will alike be surprised if it is not clearly superior in all its details.

Farming in the American Tropics, 1901

From O. F. Cook, "Agriculture in the Tropical Islands of the United States," U.S. Department of Agriculture, *Yearbook*, 1901, pp. 349–68.

Introduction

The tropical territory under the governmental control and within the scope of the commercial influence of the United States is an extremely small fraction of the land surface of the Tropics, but it is large enough to furnish a field for much of the American enterprise which formerly found an outlet in the Tropics under foreign flags only; it is also large enough and has sufficient natural diversity of climate and soil to produce nearly all our tropical imports, the annual value of which is about $200,000,000. As the United States is now by far the largest consumer of such products, there is no obvious reason why American interest in the agriculture, commerce, and social progress of the Tropics should remain second to that of any other nation. Americans, it is true, lack the long practical experience enjoyed by some of the European countries; on the other hand, pioneering and missionary instincts have continued from colonial times to lead Americans to the West Indies, to the "Spanish Main," and to the East, so that, as a nation, they can hardly be considered strangers in the Tropics. Valuable knowledge has been gained by individuals and firms, but it has remained local and private. We may, however, be able to compensate for lack of acquaintance with the traditional procedure in tropical agriculture by promptly recognizing and practically applying the scientific discoveries of the last decade.

Improvement of Health Conditions in the Tropics

Hope for the development of tropical resources along agricultural and other lines has recently taken on new strength through the discovery of a microscopic organism. It is now known that the air of the fairest and most fruitful regions of the earth is not charged with a "miasma" or subtle poison calculated to attack with special virulence the stranger from the North. The mysterious terror of the centuries is not even a mosquito, but the parasite of a mosquito. To compare this infinitesimal creature to the traditional millstone would be but a mild figure of speech. In all tropical countries of low elevation, except some of the Pacific islands, where the mosquito is unknown, malaria has sapped the life of man and hindered his progress, and in many regions it is a veritable scourge and pestilence, only less terrifying than cholera and other epidemics, chiefly because of its constant presence.

The knowledge that malarial infection is due to the bites of mosquitoes does not abolish the malaria, the mosquitoes, or their dangerous parasites, but it enables us to protect ourselves, and shows us that the difficulty can be overcome, in some regions very easily. In short, the discovery of the parasite of malaria is a more important factor in the progress of the Tropics than any other knowledge drawn from previous human experience in those regions. The entomologist, the drainage engineer, and those who make mosquito-proof houses and beds now hold, as it were, the keys of many paradises which civilized man has thus far been unable to inhabit or even to exploit.

Yellow fever has also yielded to investigations following the analogy of malaria, and numerous other tropical diseases are now being subjected to systematic and persistent research by modern methods. Nor will this research stop with the diseases of man and the domestic animals. The science of plant pathology, which saves millions of dollars annually to the farmer of temperate regions, may be brought to the assistance of tropical agriculture, and with every prospect of even more prompt utility, in view of the knowledge and skill already developed in investigating the diseases of temperate plants.

Importance of Plant Varieties

The study of plant diseases has also greatly increased the appreciation of the importance of varieties. It costs no more to cultivate a vigorous plant, or one which yields a product of high grade, than one which is sickly and stunted, or yields an inferior crop, and the difference between these is often merely that of the variety planted. It is highly probable that this matter of species and varieties, which are closely similar externally but widely different in their internal functions and products, is the key, or at least one of the keys, to the important and much-debated question of rubber cultivation. Trees are, in all countries, difficult subjects for botanists, and those of the Tropics are largely known only from small herbarium fragments, and are consequently especially difficult to recognize amid the tangled vegetation of the forest. If, therefore, botanists are still finding new species of oaks, hickories, and elms in the Eastern States, rubber planters should realize that it is but a reasonable precaution to reject the judgment of botanists, promoters, and natives, and insist on having seeds and cuttings from trees which have actually yielded rubber of good quality in paying quantities. To depend on the popular notion that a rubber tree is a rubber tree, to believe that some rubber trees will produce in a certain locality because others do, or that a good variety will be equally good in all localities, is to recklessly take chances of failures which no zeal in other directions can prevent.

Special Methods of Culture and Curing

That the question of quality has generally failed to receive adequate consideration in the tropical agriculture of the past is well shown by the fact that, although the coffee of some countries is two or three times as valuable as that of others, we are still in ignorance of the factors which influence quality, whether it be the variety, the rainfall, the sun or the shade, the ripeness, the fermentation, the drying, or the curing. There are some opinions on the subject, but they are widely at variance, and are generally supported only by local and superficial reasons.

With coffee, as with tobacco, cacao, and vanilla, processes of curing or fermentation influence the formation of the particular chemical compounds for which these products are valued, and though the necessary treatment may be simple, the proper application of it may require special knowledge and the skill which comes only as the result of experience and long practice. It may accordingly be believed that the development of methods and machinery for meeting these and similar requirements will exert an important influence on the development of tropical agriculture. Instead of conducing merely to the centralization of productive industry, as in the case of sugar, the existence of establishments for carrying on the manufacturing side of tropical agriculture will also make possible, as never before, the development of mixed farming in the Tropics, and will render relatively unprofitable the policy of mere exploitation, which has been characteristic of so many tropical enterprises. It will be possible for the farmer to devote himself more definitely to the work of production, and by diversifying his crops and adapting them to the climate, seasons, and other conditions, he will be able to compete successfully with enterprises which confine themselves to one specialty, and which, in many cases, import from abroad even the staple foods consumed on the plantation.

Thus, within the Tropics as well as in the temperate regions, the improvement and diversification of products and their uses will continue with increasing rapidity, made possible by the modern facilities of transportation which will certainly be a distinctive feature of all agricultural communities in which American interests are involved. A visit to the Tropics will ere long become as common a diversion for Americans as a trip to Europe, also as instructive and enjoyable, and residence in the Tropics for the whole or for a part of the year will no longer be deemed a hardship, but will become a matter of personal preference for thousands of our citizens.

Mistakes of Enterprises in Tropical Agriculture

In considering the starting of new agricultural industries it is necessary to remember that, notwithstanding the great importance and conspicuous success of many pioneer enterprises in the Tropics, the majority of them meet with more or less serious losses. Even with undertakings of excellent possibilities there are often failures, at first, for reasons that it would have been difficult or impossible to foresee. There are, however, some general requisites of success, the neglect of which often causes avoidable disasters.

The need of favorable climate, good soil, cheap transportation, and ready access to market is generally self-evident, though errors are frequently made through lack of familiarity with tropical or local conditions. Even where conditions are favorable, and where care and diligence have merited success by overcoming cultural difficulties, regrettable disappointments occur. Individual planters often try important experiments in the production of new crops, but though successful in the field they may meet with loss in the market, because the export merchants often refuse to handle an unfamiliar article, or, if they forward it to Europe or the United States at the expense of the grower, they do not take the trouble to find it a place in the market or even to bring it to the attention of those who might be able to give an authoritative opinion regarding its quality. Commercial failure may thus neutralize agricultural success; the planter has his labor and expense in vain, his experiment is discredited with his neighbors; the attempt is abandoned, and similar undertakings avoided. Such instances afford no argument against intelligent experiments, but they illustrate the point that the work of establishing new agricultural industries has a commercial side which must not be left out of account either in planning or in executing such undertakings.

Access to Markets

In being already occupied by considerable populations of civilized peoples, our tropical islands differ notably from the regions in which Americans have for so many generations done pioneer work along agricultural lines. One great advantage of this is the existence of local markets for food products for which no profits could be obtained in the uncivilized countries where many attempts have been made to establish European colonies. In Porto Rico, for example, the prices of garden vegetables average well above those of our city markets, and the quality is generally inferior. Accordingly, Americans who have been able to produce superior vegetables have not been compelled to wait for export facilities, but have disposed of their crops within a few miles of their farms. This is an important advantage for the planter of small capital, and will greatly assist in the substitution of mixed farming in our tropical possessions for the mere exploitation of a single crop, to which latter system the continued backwardness of many regions endowed with great natural resources has been very justly ascribed.

The agricultural development of such an island as Porto Rico should be sought on lines which do not, on the one hand, involve competition with already existing subtropical industries and which do not, on the other hand, throw away the enormous advantage of easy access to our Eastern markets, from which Hawaii and the Philippines are so remote. Tropical fruits are being shipped, it is true, from Bombay to London, but this is not a reason why mangoes and bananas for our markets should be grown in the Philippines rather than Porto Rico, nor why Porto Rico should be encouraged to specialize on sugar and cacao, when it can furnish tropical fruits at our door. Porto Rico should not stake too much on the possibility of being able to compete with the oranges of Florida and California in the regular season when by proper choice of varieties and cultural methods it should be possible to obtain an earlier crop than these States can grow; and neither should Porto Rico be encouraged to send to our markets indifferent oranges which will sell for 15 to 20 cents a dozen when the island could as readily produce first-class alligator pears, for which we now pay 30 to 50 cents apiece, to say nothing of the mangoes which sell at eight and ten for a cent on the south side of Porto Rico, while the far inferior fruit brought to the United States from Jamaica is held here at "three for a quarter."

Promising Crops

The Department of Agriculture receives many letters from purchasers of tropical lands who desire to be told which is the most profitable crop they can plant on them, how to cultivate the same, what the profits will be, when the profits will be realized, and other particulars of the same kind. These correspondents fail to realize that, however different in crops and cultural details, the agriculture of the Tropics resembles that of temperate regions, at least to the extent that large profits depend upon favorable natural conditions, skillful and industrious farming, adequate and cheap labor, accessible markets, good prices, and numerous other contingencies. The most important difference between agriculture in the Tropics and agriculture in temperate regions does not lie in the greater security or larger profits of tropical agriculture, but in the fact that the attendant difficulties, being less known, are less easily anticipated and less easily overcome. It is true that the profits of successful tropical agriculture are sometimes very large, but it is also plain that this would not be the case if the art by which they are obtained were as easy as often supposed.

It is not difficult to find regions in the Tropics where there are no frosts, droughts, potato bugs, or Hessian flies, but it does not follow that all seasons will be favorable or all crops sure and profitable. Other obstacles, pests, and losses should be expected, and the first months of tropical residence may well be devoted to the accumulation of experience with new plants and new agricultural conditions. Familiarity with the crops and methods of one's neighbors, however primitive, is well worth the trouble of securing, and will afford local knowledge of much value in dealing with any special cultures which may be undertaken. At the same time it is eminently desirable for the grower to widen as rapidly as possible his acquaintance with the plants which may be utilized in his locality, and to settle upon those which seem most promising from the commercial standpoint.

Alligator Pear

The alligator pear, also called butter pear, aguacate, and avocate, is a tropical fruit now relatively little known, but with every prospect of a gradually increasing popularity. It is a pear only in shape, and might better be compared to the olive, because it serves as a salad or a relish rather than a fruit in the ordinary sense, and frequently becomes a favorite, even with those who do not like it at first. The flesh has a delicate buttery consistency, and is eaten with vinegar, salt, and other condiments, or is used as an ingredient of other salad compounds. The promise of agricultural and commercial importance for this fruit lies in the fact that it already has a distinct, if limited, place in the markets of our larger cities at from 30 to 60 cents apiece, prices which might be halved or quartered and still leave good profits for both grower and dealer. Moreover, even at these large prices the supply of first-class fruit seems to be unequal to the demand.

The alligator pear is perhaps the one fruit which Porto Rico is ready to send to market in considerable quantity and of prime quality. The tree is easily propagated from seed, is a vigorous grower, and a free bearer, and there is no apparent reason why the alligator pear may not become almost as cheap and nearly as popular as the orange.

Banana

The banana may well be reckoned as the most important of all fruits, since it is one of the principal food staples of many millions of the inhabitants of the Tropics, and is also exported to temperate regions in rapidly increasing quantities, far exceeding in amount and value any similar product. The people of Porto Rico are especially dependent on bananas, which, though grown and eaten in large quantities, are not exported, so that Porto Rico receives nothing for bananas consumed in the United States, though $5,000,000 is paid annually to Jamaica and Central America. The soil and climate of Porto Rico appear to be in every way suitable for banana culture, and in early days the superiority of Porto Rican bananas was noted. Owing, however, to cultural neglect, partly due to the general use of the banana for coffee shade, the varieties now in Porto Rico are mostly inferior in quality and productiveness, and worthless for export. It is even uncertain whether the so-called Jamaica banana exists in Porto Rico, though there is a variety which is, at least, closely similar. In addition to the growing of a good variety, the opening of export trade would require production on a sufficiently large scale to secure advantageous shipping facilities, and a special effort may be needed to introduce the Porto Rican bananas to our markets unless the organized fruit trade can be induced to take an interest in the development of the island. For the future of banana culture the question of varieties is of the greatest importance, since there are even greater differences than among apples and pears. The American public is familiar with but one variety, which has been preferred in cultivation on account of its vigor and productiveness, and not because of its quality, as this is mediocre at the best.

The distress and starvation which follow a hurricane in Porto Rico on account of the destruction of the bananas could be largely avoided, as in the Fiji and other Pacific islands, by the general planting of bananas of the dwarf type, with trunk from 4 to 6 feet high, instead of from 15 to 20 feet. The dwarf banana is planted but sparingly in Porto Rico, owing to the inferior quality of the fruit of the only variety of this type now known in the island. There are, however, other dwarf sorts of a quality much superior to the large-trunked Jamaica banana, and not lacking vigor or productiveness, though possibly requiring somewhat more care in shipment. This latter feature would be an advantage rather than otherwise for Porto Rico if the new variety were to attain popularity in our markets.

Cacao

The culture of the cacao tree, from the seeds of which chocolate is made, was an important industry among the natives of Guatemala and southern Mexico before the advent of Europeans. The Spaniards found the new food beverage very acceptable, and from that time to the present there has been a gradual increase of popularity with no present indications of a limit being reached, unless through popular disgust with extensive adulteration. Unsettled political conditions have frequently interfered with the prosperity of cacao-growing regions and prevented the natural expansion of the industry, so that consumption has often been limited by high prices. Thus, although the culture of cacao is an old industry, it is still one of the most promising branches of tropical agriculture. It is also one in which there is room for much improvement in the choice of varieties, in methods of culture and preparation, and in the treatment or prevention of parasitic diseases, in all of which an intelligent and progressive community will have a distinct advantage over the backward regions which now produce most of the cacao of commerce. In the way of caution, it may be noted that while cacao was formerly, and may again be made, of some agricultural importance in Porto Rico, the growing of cacao as the only resource of the planter can not be advised, since this crop is especially liable to loss through hurricanes, owing to the fact that the large fruits are borne on very slender stems, which rise directly from the old wood, and are thus very easily broken off and destroyed.

The Philippines should be the better field for cacao, not only because of the larger extent of probably suitable land, but also because the relatively high value of cacao renders the cost of shipment proportionally much less than with sugar and other cheaper and more bulky products. Cacao has long been cultivated in the Philippines, though it is not known that care was taken to introduce superior varieties. Some of the Philippine cacao is said to be of good quality, but it seems never to have been raised in large quantities or to have become an article of export in competition with the cacao of Spanish America.

Camphor

Northern Luzon is the geographical neighbor of Formosa, the present center of camphor production. The camphor tree is relatively hardy and easy to cultivate, and has been planted in considerable numbers as a shade tree in the Gulf region of our Southern States, though it is still uncertain whether the commercial production of camphor is practicable in this region. In Algeria it has been found that although the trees appear to thrive, they contain little gum. In Luzon, and probably also in Porto Rico and Hawaii, the planting of camphor on lands unsuitable for general agricultural purposes is eminently worthy of consideration. It is, indeed, at the present time, a safer industry than rubber culture, since camphor can be grown in drier and more wholesome localities, and since the crop is less likely to be a total failure.

Cassava

The most important of the tropical root crops is the cassava, from which tapioca is made, and from which a superior quality of starch can be obtained very cheaply. Although poisonous when raw, the thick, fleshy roots furnish wholesome and palatable food when cooked. Some varieties are without noxious qualities, but are considered less productive. The yields are in some cases enormous, 12 tons and upward per acre having been claimed. Cassava should not remain unknown to any tropical agriculturist; certainly not to those who have laborers to feed.

Chayote

Porto Rico already produces in abundance a tropical vegetable for which a little persistence might create an export demand in the United States. This is a member of the squash family, called the chayote in its native country, Mexico. It is rapidly becoming popular as a winter vegetable in Paris and London, whither it is shipped in large quantities from Algeria. The chayote is worthy of a place in every tropical garden, and should be introduced into both the Hawaiian and the Philippine islands. It has a variety of domestic uses and is very easy to cultivate. It would have been widely known long since but for the fact that the fruit contains but a single seed, and must be shipped and planted whole, because the seed is soft-skinned and dries up if extracted.

Cinchona

The culture of the cinchona tree, from the bark of which quinine is extracted, has become an industry of considerable importance in India and Java, although the various species of cinchona are all natives of the mountains of South America. The mountainous regions of the southern Philippines may afford conditions favorable for the culture of cinchona, but private planters of small capital can scarcely hope to maintain competition with the enormous estates of the governments and syndicates of the English and Dutch colonies, although even at the present low prices of quinine the profits are still said to be very large. The extraction of the alkaloid from the bark is a manufacturing process of some complexity, which also favors production on a large scale.

Coca

The coca plant, from which the important medicinal alkaloid cocaine is extracted, is a native of the Andes of South America, where millions of the natives have the habit of chewing the leaves. Coca could, perhaps, be grown at high elevations in Hawaii or in Luzon, or, perhaps, in some of the frostless valleys of California, but such an industry must of necessity compete with the cheap labor and long experience of the South American Indians, who have a large home market, and who export to Europe and America only a small surplus.

Cocoanut

The cocoa palm is certainly the most characteristic object of the Tropics, and its beauty is equaled only by its utility among tropical peoples. In commerce it appears in three forms. The fresh nuts are shipped to Europe and America for eating or for use in desserts and confectionery; the dried meat is marketed under the name of copra for the extraction of the oil, and the fibers of the husk are sold as coir, and used in the manufacture of brushes and coarse fabrics. Although the cocoa palm exists in large numbers in Porto Rico, few nuts are exported and no copra or coir is made. Nearly all the nuts are picked while still green, and are bought in the cities and towns for the sake of the milk, which is the most popular beverage of Porto Rico. Copra and coir come largely from the Pacific islands and the East Indies, and both are prepared by natives in their leisure time, though machines and improved processes for extracting the fiber have been invented.

Coffee

Contrary to popular impression, the chief crop of Porto Rico is not sugar nor tobacco, but coffee, the exports of which have in some years been of more than twice the value of all other products taken together. Moreover, a majority of the people of the island are more or less directly dependent upon the coffee industry, the decay of which would mean the continuation of the distress which resulted from the conjunction of low prices, disturbed trade, and the hurricane of August, 1898. Fortunately, the natural conditions appear to be very favorable, not only for the maintenance of the present acreage of coffee, but for a still further extension of the industry, which, with the popularization of better methods of culture, would enable Porto Rico to take rank as an important coffee center. It would be entirely feasible for the island to produce one-third or even one-half of the enormous total of 800,000,000 pounds consumed yearly by the people of the United States, now imported almost entirely from foreign countries at an annual expenditure of from $60,000,000 to $100,000,000.

Although greatly subordinate to sugar, coffee culture is also established in Hawaii and in the Philippines, and with favorable conditions, so that there are no natural obstacles to the production in American territory of all the coffee required in our market.

The most conspicuous cultural problem of coffee growing is the much controverted question of shade, a preliminary report of an investigation of which has recently been published. It seems sufficiently obvious that shade is no direct nor normal requirement of the coffee plant, and that the root tubercles of the leguminous trees generally planted for shade may contribute to the fertility of the soil. Other possible advantages doubtless lie in protection against drought and in the moderation of the temperature of the superficial layers of the soil, but the relative importance of the different factors can be determined only by careful experiments.

Coffee is the most important tropical crop grown in salubrious elevated regions. The climate and natural scenery of some of the coffee districts of Porto Rico are magnificent, a fact which would doubtless have had greater weight with American investors had they not been discouraged by the distress from which the native planters have recently suffered.

Date

Date culture is a promising industry in the hot alkaline deserts of Arizona and California, but it has little prospect of commercial success in any of our tropical possessions, for although the trees do not refuse to grow, the fruit does not attain proper maturity except in hot desert climates.

Mango

The mango stands in the highest rank of tropical fruits (that is, the better varieties of mangoes), but some of the inferior sorts have been appropriately described as a mixture of tow and turpentine, because of the fibrous flesh and the resinous taste. Few Americans have seen any except the latter type, since the mangoes which reach our markets are entirely of this class. They are handled by fruit dealers merely as "novelties," and are bought by those who wish to know what a mango is like, but who generally conclude that they are worse than worthless. The difficulty of producing good mangoes lies largely in the fact that, as with the apple, the varieties do not come true to seed, but must be propagated by grafting, which, with the mango, is generally reckoned a rather difficult process, though it is now believed that the difficulties have been greatly overestimated.

The mango is a native of India and has received the largest amount of cultural attention in that country, where hundreds of choice varieties are known. Some of these are said to have reached the Philippines, but no attempt seems to have been made to bring them to Porto Rico, where chance-sown seedlings are depended upon for the perpetuation of the species. Aside from the varietal inferiority, the mangoes of the south side of Porto Rico are excellent, and there appears to be no doubt that the natural conditions are entirely favorable for the growing of this fruit to perfection.

Manila Hemp

This important fiber is extracted from the leaf bases of a species of banana, the fruit of which has large seeds, and is dry and inedible. It is a native of the Philippine Islands, to which the commercial production of the fiber is still confined, in spite of numerous attempts at introducing the industry into other tropical countries. These failures in producing the fiber elsewhere have probably been due quite as much to the lack of the skill possessed by the Philippine natives in extracting the fiber as to the refusal of the plant to thrive in other regions; and until machinery can be made to replace hand labor there is little prospect of any great change in present methods of production. There is every reason to expect that the industry will repay careful attention from agricultural, commercial, and manufacturing standpoints, but at present the steady and gradual improvement of conditions and methods of production is the only general policy which can be safely recommended. The various fiber industries have been the fields of many inventions and a great number of schemes and devices, the essential impracticability of which appears only under the test of commercial production.

Manila hemp long held the first place among the exports of the Philippine Islands, and the value of the export far exceeded the total value of all other articles except sugar. The quantity of manila hemp which came to the United States was also large and increasing, since improvements in harvesting machinery have rendered the United States the principal consumer of fibers of the class to which manila and sisal belong. The recent disturbances in the Philippines have greatly reduced the supply of manila hemp, and the sisal industry is enjoying a corresponding period of prosperity. The longer the Philippine fiber remains scarce the greater and more permanent will be the extension of the uses of sisal.

Olive

The olive is a native of the arid Mediterranean region, and seldom, if ever, fruits in the moist Tropics. Suggestions that it be planted in Porto Rico and the Philippines are therefore ill-advised.

Orange

While it is true that oranges and other citrus fruits can be grown in almost all regions where tropical agriculture is carried on, it is also true that at present but a small part of our commercial supplies of these fruits comes from the Tropics. Citrus cultures in the Tropics are accordingly still somewhat experimental, and the commercial production of high-grade fruit will remain uncertain until demonstrated by facts. Formerly there was no attempt in Porto Rico at orange growing as understood in Florida, the fruit of seedling trees supplying the local demands.

It will probably be found that some localities on the north side of Porto Rico are too wet for raising oranges, and orange culture by irrigation in some of the more arid limestone districts of the south side may possibly be worth considering, in view of the fact that the prices of the Porto Rican fruit will depend largely upon the earliness with which it can be brought to market. The season opens now in November, but a month or more may be gained by proper methods of culture and the planting of early varieties.

Pineapple

The pineapple is a native of the American Tropics, and the pineapples of Porto Rico have been noted for size and quality since the sixteenth century. One of the largest varieties, called by the Porto Ricans "cabezona," is in Florida and elsewhere called the "Porto Rico." Pineapples grow wild, or nearly so, in almost all parts of Porto Rico, so that for home consumption little in the way of regular cultivation is necessary, and under former political and commercial conditions the shipment of fruit to the United States was difficult, if not impracticable. At present, therefore, when the culture of the pineapple is being seriously taken up for the first time, there is a lack of experience and the same scarcity of good cuttings that might be expected in a country to which the plant was new.

As with many other fruits, the finest varieties do not go into trade, and the favorite pineapple of Porto Rico, the "pan de azucar," or "sugar loaf," is of too juicy a texture and decays too quickly to withstand shipment like the more acid, woody type common in our Northern markets.

In Florida, a new departure in pineapple culture has been made through the discovery that the lattice-work sheds built for protection against frost also exert a notably beneficial effect upon the size and quality of the fruits, supposedly through the medium of the partial shade. Accordingly, the building of sheds at an initial expense of from $200 to $300 per acre is now being practiced far to the south of the frost line. Whether similar measures are necessary to the best results in Porto Rico, and whether they can be attained by the substitution of shade trees like the saman (Pithecolobium) or other loose-foliaged leguminous species, commonly planted with coffee, are cultural questions which remain to be investigated.

Perfume Plants

The tropical plants from which perfumes and other essential oils are derived may be made the basis of minor agricultural industries, but production on too large a scale may render such cultures entirely unprofitable. Bay rum has long been an article of export from Porto Rico, the oil being obtained by distilling the leaves of a small tree, the "limoncillo" or "malagueta" (*Amomis caryophyllata*), native in Porto Rico, the Danish West Indies, and some of the neighboring islands. The present supplies are derived from wild trees, but cultivation would be easy and inexpensive, since the tree flourishes on rocky hillsides worthless for general agricultural purposes.

On the south side of Porto Rico the so-called "aromo" (*Acacia farnesiana*) covers many square miles of waste land. This same shrub is known as "cassie" in the south of France, where it is extensively grown for the sake of the perfume of the same name extracted from the flowers. The latter when properly dried have also a market value as an ingredient of sachet powders.

The Philippines have preeminence in the production of ylang-ylang, a perfume highly valued in the Orient as well as in Europe. The ylang-ylang oil of the Philippines is considered superior to that of the Asiatic Continent, and the higher grades command fancy prices — $50 per pound and even more. The present supply is said to be unequal to the demand, and estimates of large profits from ylang-ylang plantations have been made.

Rice

Rice is the only tropical cereal of the first rank, and is a staple article of food even in many tropical regions where it is not grown. Rice for home consumption is raised in all of our tropical islands, and large amounts are also imported. In Porto Rico only highland rice is planted, while in the Pacific islands the industry is entirely in the hands of natives and Chinese, who follow the laborious method of transplanting each individual seedling. On these lines rice culture will hardly be a subject of much interest to the American planter, but it remains to be seen whether the new methods which have recently given rice culture such an impetus in Louisiana and Texas can be applied in the Tropics. Instead of using swamps, the rice is planted on firm prairie land, where the crop can be planted and harvested with the aid of modern farm machinery, though flooding by irrigation will be necessary during the growing period.

Rubber and Gutta-Percha

Popular interest in tropical agriculture is at present largely monopolized by the possibilities of rubber culture, as set forth in glowing descriptions in various prophetic calculations and in the prospectuses of numerous companies which have been formed for establishing rubber plantations in Mexico and Central America. Some of the representations are made with every evidence of reliability and good faith, but their credibility naturally suffers from the no less obvious fact that many others are directly calculated to deceive the unwary investor. Moreover, it is known that many rubber plantations established with the most lively expectations have been abandoned because the anticipation of a profitable yield of rubber from cultivated trees proved to be fallacious.

Similar disappointments, misapprehensions, and misrepresentations have, of course, marked the early history of many finally successful and important industries. Such facts simply show that whatever may be its future, rubber production is not likely to be better able than other lines of agriculture to dispense with knowledge and discrimination.

Many of the current misconceptions regarding rubber culture result from the popular failure to realize that rubber is not like coffee, tea, or cacao, the definite product of a single species or genus of plants; rubber should be compared, instead, to starch and sugar, substances obtainable from large numbers of plants of different types, botanical and cultural. It has been estimated that 1,000 different species contain rubber, though commercial quantities have probably been obtained from only 40 or 50. The sugar cane, the sugar beet, and the sugar maple involve very distinct cultural problems, to which no general principles will apply, and the culture of the different rubber plants must be dealt with on an equally individual basis instead of through fallacious general principles. Thus far, we have little certain knowledge even regarding the identity of the plants, and the traditional rubber tree of Para has recently been described as a new species and found to be quite different from the *Hevea brasiliensis* with which it has so long been confused. A European investor who might come to New England to raise maple sugar, and who should plant his orchard from wild stock before finding out that there is more than one species of maple, or that the different species require different conditions, would not be more reckless than some of the rubber companies; nor, if he proposed to pay the expenses of the enterprise from apples and other fruit trees planted in the sugar bush and leave the sugar as a clear profit, would his agricultural ideas be more crude than those of some of these companies. In short, rubber culture is a very complex problem, which has not yet received the detailed investigation necessary to place it on a scientific and practical basis.

Notwithstanding widespread interest and the investment of millions of dollars, it can not be said that rubber culture has passed the experimental stage, if, indeed, that period has been fairly reached.

The extent to which these so-called possibilities of rubber culture have inflamed the imagination of some is well illustrated by their advocating the culture of *Eucommia ulmoides* for the sake of the gutta-percha.

Eucommia is a native of central China, and the idea of a gutta-percha tree which could be grown in the temperate regions of Europe and America promised to be especially attractive, and has been extensively advertised by the dealers in such seeds, who apparently have not undertaken to ascertain the rate of growth of the tree, and who fail to state that among the Chinese it is planted for its bark, which is valued as a medicine and brings about the same price ($1.50 to $2) per pound as gutta-percha, of which it contains about 3 per cent. On this basis, gutta-percha would need to be worth $60 a pound before the culture of Eucommia would become profitable.

Sisal Hemp

Among the current suggestions for new tropical crops is that of sisal hemp. This is a product of an agave or century plant, and is now largely imported from Mexico. It is, however, improbable that any large area of Porto Rico could be profitably devoted to growing this plant, the culture of which finds a place in soil which is too dry and rocky for ordinary crops, and consequently of so little value that it can be given up to a rather slow-growing plant like the agave. Three or four years are required before the cutting of the leaves and the extraction of the fiber may be begun. The business can be carried on to best advantage on large estates, those of Yucatan and German East Africa being from 500 to 20,000 acres or more in extent.

The dry southern slopes of Porto Rico may afford suitable conditions for sisal hemp, but most of the country is so mountainous and broken as to make difficult even the slight cultivation necessary for the agave. The roughness of the country would also render it much more expensive than in Yucatan to construct the tramways for bringing the fresh leaves to the factory. These are as necessary as in sugar plantations; but in some localities it might be possible to substitute overhead cables for surface tracks.

If the present prices could be maintained sisal would undoubtedly be a very profitable industry, since the fiber is now quoted at 7 and 8 cents per pound, while in former years from 3 to 5 cents were usual prices. The present high figures are due to the scarcity of manila hemp and to the increased use of binding twine. The demand is likely to continue, and it will require several years, at least, for manila hemp to regain its place in the market. Favorably located plantations of sisal in Porto Rico or Hawaii may remain permanently profitable; others might suffer from the natural extension of the industry in Yucatan or other communities where large tracts of nearly level desert land can be utilized at small expense.

Spices

Owing to the necessarily limited demand, the spice-growing industries are especially liable to overproduction and great fluctuation in prices. For food staples and other articles consumed in large quantities there are permanent markets, but when the normal trade requirements of special products have been filled, the surplus of even a normally high-priced article may not be worth taking, and in the Dutch East Indies it was deemed good policy to burn up spices representing thousands of dollars rather than send them to Europe to flood the market, to the permanent detriment of the industry.

The opening of new regions of production is therefore to be undertaken only when the conditions are really favorable, and when the enterprise has sufficient financial backing to survive the period of overproduction and drive the competing districts out of the business. Thus, in recent years the East African islands, Pemba and Zanzibar, have become the chief centers of clove production, while the industry is dying out in Amboina and Penang. In nutmegs, the small West Indian island of Grenada has become a formidable competitor of the even smaller Malayan islands of Banda, which long enjoyed an almost complete monopoly. Pepper is still confined commercially to the Malay Peninsula. In ginger, the traditional supremacy of Jamaica is not in serious danger, because the superior grade for which the island is famous is all scraped by hand in the leisure time of a poor but self-supporting population, with which a similar industry dependent upon hired labor could scarcely compete.

While it is thus impossible as yet to advise that the culture of spices be undertaken on a large scale in Porto Rico, Hawaii, or the Philippines, residents of promising localities should be encouraged in experimental planting, with the expectation that such crops may become useful accessories in the development of rational systems of mixed farming, so greatly needed in the Tropics.

Sugar

Sugar is the largest agricultural industry of the Tropics, and is by far the largest agricultural import of the United States, notwithstanding our extensive domestic cultures of sugar cane and sugar beets. Sugar production is an industry of the factory almost as much as of the farm, and as a manufacturing industry it can not be economically conducted on a small scale. A half million of dollars is now considered little more than a minimum investment for establishing a modern sugar plantation and mill, and the smaller enterprises of individual planters are being rapidly absorbed or combined into stock companies by large capitalists, or are compelled to leave the business of extracting the sugar, merely selling their cane to the mills. In Porto Rico many of the less accessible estates have been abandoned for several years, while in the neighborhood of the large modern factories, or centrales, there is abundant prosperity.

As might be expected with an industry requiring so much capital, sugar growing is on a much more scientific basis than other agricultural industries of the Tropics, though many improvements undoubtedly remain to be made. The most striking recent advance has been in the line of new seedling varieties bred in the British West Indies and Guiana. Some of these contain a percentage of sugar much higher than that of the sorts in general cultivation.

Tea

Tea is not, strictly speaking, a tropical plant, as shown by the success of the experiments by the Department of Agriculture in the production of a high-grade article in South Carolina. Large quantities of tea are, however, produced in elevated regions inside the Tropics, notably in Ceylon and Formosa, so that there are probably no climatic obstacles to the growing of tea in any of the tropical possessions. Moreover, the tea shrub is a hardy plant, able to make growth in rocky or sandy soils which are worthless from the standpoint of many tropical cultures.

The curing processes, which largely determine the quality of the product, are receiving scientific study which may lead to the substitution of machinery for hand manipulation, which has formed so large a part of the expense of production.

Tobacco

Tobacco has long been a staple crop of considerable importance both in the Philippines and in Porto Rico. In the latter island a considerable expansion of the industry is now taking place, and the same may also be expected in the former, though the future of tobacco growing in the Tropics has been considerably unsettled of late by the discovery of methods of culture and curing which make it possible for temperate regions to produce tobacco of qualities equal to the highest grades of Cuba and Sumatra. It is accordingly quite possible that the center of gravity of this industry may change within a few years to the temperate regions of the United States, where agricultural skill and labor-saving machinery can so easily be brought into play without having to contend with the additional difficulties attendant on all branches of tropical agriculture.

Vanilla

The so-called "vanilla beans" of commerce are the pod-like fruits of a climbing orchid, native in Mexico and Central America. The seeds are extremely small and dust-like, only the pod carrying the suggestion of beans. Moreover, the plant is never raised in culture from the seed, but from large cuttings.

Vanilla requires thoroughly tropical conditions and abundant moisture, except for two or three months of the year. Localities adapted to vanilla culture are probably to be found in Porto Rico and in the Philippines, perhaps also in Hawaii, but experiments must be intelligently undertaken, or they are sure to fail. In the first place, it is necessary outside the original home of the plant to pollinate the flowers by hand, and, in the second place, the proper curing of the fruits largely determines their market value, and, although the process is not a difficult one, it requires skill and experience. In other words, skilled labor is essential, whether obtained through special training or by importation from a vanilla-growing region. The bees which pollinate the vanilla in Mexico are known to be capable of domestication, though this knowledge seems not to have been utilized as yet.

Vegetables

The growing of vegetables in Porto Rico for the winter markets of New York and other Eastern cities has naturally suggested itself as one of the potential resources of that island. That such an industry will not reach prosperity without encountering difficulties may be expected from the fact, already noted, that the prices of vegetables in Porto Rico equal or exceed those obtainable in our Northern cities. Bermuda onions, early potatoes, eggplants, tomatoes, and other vegetables can, of course, be sold in the United States at fancy prices in the fall and winter months, but to produce these and similar crops in commercial quantity and quality in Porto Rico will be the work of specialists in market gardening and not of the general public.

Another side of the vegetable question is of more general interest to the residents of tropical countries, and especially to planters dependent upon their own estates for supplying their tables with fresh food. The Tropics are not rich in food plants corresponding to the garden vegetables of temperate regions, and these seldom thrive as well in the Tropics as in the North, even when of tropical origin, owing apparently to the fact that our long hot summer days conduce to more vigorous and fruitful growth than the more equable and continuous humid climates of the moist Tropics, where the daily exposure to the sunlight is much shorter. In the Tropics, plants which make very quick growth, like radishes and lettuce, may reach edible size before the deterioration becomes apparent, while others are weak and spindling from the first, and never attain normal growth or maturity.

It is therefore not always wise to conclude, as the newcomer in the Tropics frequently does, that the inferiority of garden products is caused merely by bad methods of cultivation. On the contrary, it will usually be found that, in spite of apparent carelessness, the native has attended to some precautions unnecessary in the North but indispensable in the Tropics. The tropical planter should rely mostly on varieties which have been tested locally, or at least in some part of the Tropics, since, in spite of their inferiority, these are often successful in comparison with the total failure of some of the best of temperate varieties. Furthermore, instead of vainly striving against the climate, he should become acquainted as rapidly as possible with the culture and uses of tropical food plants, the excellence of which is generally underestimated. Thus, cassava, yautia, and yams are the equals, and often the superiors, of the Irish potatoes and other temperate vegetables, to which Americans cling so tenaciously that they sometimes go hungry in the midst of unappreciated plenty.

The Cotton-Boll Weevil Problem, 1901

From W. D. Hunter, "The Present Status of the Mexican Cotton-Boll Weevil in the United States," U.S. Department of Agriculture, *Yearbook*, 1901, pp. 369–80.

Historical

The Insect in Mexico

The history of the Mexican cotton-boll weevil (*Anthonomus grandis* Boh.) before its advent into Texas is most obscure. Aside from the fact that the species was described by Boheman in 1843 from specimens received from Vera Cruz, and that it was recorded in 1871 by Suffrian as occurring at Cardenas and San Cristobal, in Cuba, there is but little authentic evidence concerning its early history. It is known from written documents that the cultivation of cotton was practically abandoned in the vicinity of Monclova, in the State of Coahuila, in the year 1848, on account of the ravages of an insect. But that the insect was the boll weevil appears to be by no means certain. As far as the accounts indicate, it might have been the bollworm (*Heliothis armiger* Huebn.) or the cotton worm (*Aletia argillacea* Huebn.). But there is such a mass of testimony to the effect that the boll weevil has been known in that part of Mexico for many years, that it seems not unlikely that the date mentioned really indicates about the time when the insect first became an important factor in cotton raising.

By 1885, however, we find more definite and reliable data. In that year C. V. Riley published in the Report of the Commissioner of Agriculture a brief note to the effect that *Anthonomus grandis* had been reared in the Department from dwarfed cotton bolls sent from northern Mexico by Dr. Edward Palmer. This is the earliest account associating this particular species with the damage to cotton. The bolls referred to were collected in Coahuila and probably not far from Monclova. Long before 1892 the insect had invaded all parts of Mexico where cotton is produced, and about that year it was carried across the Rio Grande, perhaps in unginned cotton, and gained a foothold at Brownsville.

Invasion of Texas by the Insect

Contrasted with the lack of data concerning the early history of the insect in Mexico, we find most complete accounts of its progress after the State of Texas was invaded. In 1894 the pest first came to the notice of the Division of Entomology as an important enemy of cotton in Texas. An agent was immediately sent to the territory affected, which then comprised only a half dozen counties, and where the total output of cotton is not large. Professor Townsend's report was published in March, 1895. It dealt with the life history and habits of the insect, then absolutely unknown, the method of its importation, its capability for damage, and closed with recommendations for fighting it and preventing its further advance into the cotton-producing regions of Texas. It is much to be regretted that the State did not adopt the suggestion, made by the Division of Entomology at this time, of establishing a belt along the Rio Grande in which the cultivation of cotton should be prohibited, and thus cut off the advance of the insect. But a failure to realize the capabilities of the pest for destruction, as well as a disinclination to deprive the few farmers of that region of the only crop the climate permits them to raise, in a region moreover that invariably produces the first bale in the United States, were factors that combined to cause the authorities to delay until the opportunity had passed.

In 1895 the insect was found to have spread as far north as San Antonio and as far east as Wharton. Such an advance induced grave fears of future injury and caused the Division of Entomology to continue its investigations during the whole season. Mr. E. A. Schwarz, Mr. C. H. T. Townsend, and Dr. L. O. Howard were in the infested region. The results of the work were incorporated in a bulletin by Dr. Howard and published early in 1896 in both Spanish and English editions.

An unprecedented drought in the summer of 1896 prevented the maturity of the fall broods of the weevil, and consequently there was no extension of the territory affected. During this year the entomologists mentioned, with the addition of Mr. C. L. Marlatt, continued their observations and experiments, which resulted in another bulletin issued in February, 1897. This bulletin was published in Spanish and German editions for the benefit of the very large foreign population in southern Texas.

During 1897 the pest seemed to have not completely recovered from the unfavorable conditions of the preceding year, increasing its range only to the region about Yoakum and Gonzales. This extension, though small, was important, because the richest cotton lands in the country were beginning to be invaded. During more than half of this year Mr. Townsend was stationed in Mexico, in the region supposed to be the original home of the insect, to discover any parasites or diseases that might be affecting it, with the object in view of introducing them to prey upon the pest in Texas. Unfortunately, nothing was found that gave any hope of materially assisting in the warfare against the weevil.

In 1898 the season was very favorable for the insect, which increased its range into Bastrop, Lee, and Burleson counties, and even across the Brazos River into Waller and Brazos counties. The investigations of the Division of Entomology were continued, and a summary of the work dealing especially with the result of experiments with poisons, conducted by C. L. Marlatt, was published in still another bulletin.

Special Investigation Authorized by Congress

At this juncture the legislature of Texas, in its 1898 session, realizing the danger that threatened the most important agricultural industry of the State, wisely made provision for the appointment of a State entomologist and a thorough investigation of the matter of combating the weevil. Upon this occurrence, and in view of the fact that at that time there was but little to indicate that the problem was any more than a local one, the Division of Entomology discontinued the work that had been carried on by having agents in the field almost constantly for four years, referring all correspondents to the State entomologist. But, unfortunately, the insect continued to spread in such a manner that other States than Texas were threatened. This caused the work to be taken up anew by the Division of Entomology in 1901, in accordance with a special provision by Congress for an investigation independent of that being carried on by the State of Texas, and with special reference to the discovery, if possible, of means of preventing the insect from spreading into adjoining States.

Present Situation and Future Prospects

Possibilities of Continued Northward Spread of the Insect

By all means the most important aspect of the invasion of the weevil into the United States has been the possibility of its continued northward spread. In 1891, as may be seen from the preceding paragraphs, the insect was unknown in Texas. In 1895, it had made its way 200 miles north of Brownsville, the point where it entered the State. At the present time it is found 500 miles north of that place, thus reaching a latitude within 100 miles of the latitude of the center of cotton production in the United States, according to the last census. The problem was serious enough when only a few counties in the most southern part of the State were concerned, because there a scanty precipitation makes cotton the only crop that can be cultivated to advantage. But as soon as the fertile and well-watered counties north of the Guadalupe were invaded the total Texas production was immediately affected, and grave fears were naturally aroused that the pest would reach all portions of the cotton-producing region of the country.

At the present time the territory affected is bounded roughly on the north by a line drawn from Palestine to Waco, on the east by the valley of the Trinity River, and on the west by the limit of cotton culture. This includes fully one-half of the total cotton-producing area of Texas. The situation is more serious on account of the fact that the most productive counties are included in the infested territory. Of the twenty-five counties that annually produce 25,000 bales or more, seventeen are now concerned. Statistics show that in these counties the devastation of the weevil has caused the amount of land required to produce a bale to be fully doubled. Where it formerly required on an average 2.3 acres to produce a bale of staple it now requires at least 4.5 acres.

No Indications of the Insect Being Killed Out by Winter

In all the area occupied at the present time the insect displays no signs of dying out, though there are instances easily accounted for where there has been a temporary diminution of its numbers. At one time it was supposed, since the weevil is of tropical origin, that it would reach a limit where the frosts of winter would annually check its advance, as is well known to be the case with the cotton worm (*Aletia argillacea* Huebn.). The winter of 1899–1900, however, bringing low temperatures that have never been equaled since records have been kept in Texas, demonstrated that such a hope is not to be relied upon. Temperatures like that of 14° F. at Austin, of 19° at Cuero, of 11° at Luling, and of 14° at San Marcos were found to have had no effect whatever upon the prevalence of the pests the succeeding season.

In this connection, it is important to notice the theory which is prevalent in some quarters, that the small number of weevils seen early in the spring indicates that the cold of winter kills the greater share of them. Many observations, however, made at Victoria and elsewhere make it evident that this phenomenon is as much due to the fact that the insects emerge gradually from their winter quarters as to any actual scarcity. As late as the 1st day of May, in southern Texas, weevils were still coming from the woods, and it required but little search to find them there. It is true that these observations were made in 1901 after an unusually mild winter; but the fact as related above, of the exceedingly cold winter preceding not lessening the insects, certainly bears out this supposition. Of course, many weevils do not survive the winter, but the dying of the debilitated individuals and the general vicissitudes of hibernation rather than cold alone seems to account for those that succumb.

Ineffectiveness of Parasites and Diseases

Though search has revealed several parasites and probably a fungoid disease of the weevil, it is not believed that these factors will ever be of much practical importance in reducing its numbers. Indeed, the habits of the insect are such as to largely preclude the possibility of effective aid from parasites. An insect occurring in such numbers as the weevil and being exposed in any stage, save the imago, to enemies, would certainly be greatly influenced by parasites; but this one, being well protected in egg, larval, and pupal stages by a dense covering of vegetable matter, remains remarkably exempt. The investigations of the Division of Entomology in Mexico indicate that even where known to exist for half a century there are few and unimportant parasites to be found. Likewise, the history of other American, as well as European, species of Anthonomus bears out the supposition that but little of value will ever result from the work of parasites.

Future Spread of the Insect

From what has just been stated it will be seen that two of the most important elements in limiting the spread of an insect, winter temperatures and parasites, in this case offer no assurance that the pest will soon be checked. It has been advancing year by year, and there are influences that seem to make it certain that the area infested will be constantly increased. The insect has extended its range eastward to within 100 miles of the Louisiana border. Though the intervening portion of Texas is not especially a cotton-producing one, several of the counties produce 5,000 bales annually, or much more than the counties toward Brownsville, in which there was enough cotton grown to make the original advance of the insect in the State quite rapid. It is certain that within the next two years Louisiana will be confronted by the same trouble that has been most seriously affecting the Texas producers. To the northward the movement will be more rapid. There is practically an uninterrupted cotton country before the insect, and its advance will be materially aided by the wind. The direction of the prevailing winds in Texas is northward, and there is an invariable equinoctial climax in their intensity in September, at the very time when the weevils are making their principal movements.

On the whole, it seems that, as the number of the pests in a certain region is practically only limited by the quantity of the food supply, so the weevil's progress will probably eventually be checked only by the limits of the distribution of cotton in the United States. This movement, however, the experience of nearly ten years indicates, will not be rapid, perhaps not much more than 60 miles per year. Moreover, it is likely that, before the pest has passed the boundaries of Texas, more will be known of controlling it, so that its damage in other regions will not compare with what was done in the parts first invaded.

Temporary Scarcity Under Certain Conditions

The fact that in certain districts where the weevil has existed for several years an unexpectedly good crop has sometimes been raised has been the cause of a supposition among some planters that there is a tendency for it to die out or migrate to other parts. The most noticeable instance of this kind occurred in the counties of Wilson, Karnes, Goliad, Bee, and Live Oak during the season of 1900. It was in that region that the weevil first reached the portion of the State where cotton is cultivated to a considerable extent, and there for several years, in the opinion of the planters, threatened to cause the entire abandonment of the industry. In 1900, however, the largest crop in the history of these counties was produced. A thorough investigation of this matter makes it clear that the explanation lies partially in the fact that several conditions reduced the number of the pests, and also as much in the fact that there were very exceptionally favorable conditions for the planting, growing, and early maturity of the crop.

For three years preceding 1900 there had been a scarcity of rains that caused not only very scant crops of cotton, but which destroyed a large percentage of the weevils which had been given opportunities for propagating. Continued dry weather is very disastrous to these insects. At Victoria it was found that during the drought in July, 1901, every larva in the square was killed in forty-eight hours, provided it was exposed in such a manner as to receive the unobstructed rays of the sun. Death resulted from the complete drying of the food supply. When the squares fell between the rows in such a way that they were shaded up to 10 o'clock in the morning and after 3 o'clock in the afternoon, under the same condition of drought, 75 per cent of the insects were killed in the same time. When it is remembered that the infested square lies upon the ground on an average ten days before the adult weevil emerges, the tremendous effect brought about by drought will be appreciated. Indeed, it appears that hot, dry, and windy weather is a far more important factor in destroying the weevils than either winter cold, excessive moisture, or any other climatic condition. There is no doubt that in 1896 an excessive drought not only prevented the weevil from spreading but actually caused the infested territory to become smaller. Accordingly, in explaining the bountiful crop raised in Bee County in 1900, the drought of the preceding seasons is most important. Moreover, in the region under consideration this drought had killed so much of the pasture grass that cotton fields into which to turn cattle to graze were at a high premium. Farmers in Bee County drove cattle 25 miles and paid high prices for the privilege of being allowed to pasture them in such fields. Consequently, practically all the larvae in squares and bolls were devoured, and what survived were reduced by literal starvation. These remarkable conditions were followed in 1900 by a season in which every factor favored the growth of cotton. In Bee County the great drawback to cotton culture is the usual very meager rainfall, but that season brought more than 20 inches of precipitation above the normal. The rains, moreover, happily descended at such times as not to interfere with planting, thinning, or cultivating the crop. But in spite of all this, it must be noted that after these most favorable conditions the few weevils that had passed through the winter multiplied at such a rate that all the bolls formed after the middle of September were destroyed by them. The following season there were apparently as many weevils as ever.

An instance of a similar scarcity, though due to quite different causes, has occurred during the present season (1901) in other counties in the valleys of the Colorado and Brazos rivers. Here the same unusual rainfall in Texas during the preceding season that made it possible to obtain a good yield west of the Guadalupe River, where a very scanty precipitation is the rule, gave the remainder of the southern portion of the State entirely too much moisture. The cotton fields, which are generally situated in the lowest portions of the valleys, were repeatedly swept by floods; for some days in the midst of the growing season these fields were under several feet of water. A more complete destruction of the crop by flooding could not have been accomplished. Moreover, in September of that year a hurricane of such intensity as to not only defoliate the plants that were left standing upon high ground but in many cases to actually uproot them, swept over this region. By these conditions not only were the weevils killed in great numbers, but the survivors found but little opportunity for propagating. The result was that the present season there were not enough weevils in the county to cause any appreciable damage.

In these two instances other influences, as, perhaps, the prevalence of parasites or diseases, may have had some effect upon the general condition, but those mentioned are certainly sufficient to account for the situation. It is needless to state that, with normal climatic conditions, the pests will in a year or two again become as numerous in Wharton County as they did in Bee County.

Methods of Combating the Insect

The investigations of the Division of Entomology for nearly ten years have all pointed toward the primary importance of cultural methods of controlling this pest. All other methods must involve some direct financial outlay, either for materials or for machinery. In the present time of low prices for the staple and consequent small margin of profit any factor that increases the cost of production in the smallest measure will be very slowly adopted, and to be adopted at all must be of perfect working. To small, renting farmers, under the present conditions, a very few dollars per acre make the difference between profit and loss. On the other hand, cultural methods involving no cash, but only a small labor outlay, are more readily adopted, and seem altogether more in accord with Southern industrial conditions.

Early Planting

Foremost among these methods is the simple expedient of early planting. All observations go to show that a small proportion of the pests pass through the winter, and that many of the individuals that do survive are late in coming from their hibernating quarters. These breed in the fruit, soon becoming numerous enough to destroy every square as it is formed. Consequently, to hasten the maturity of the plant and thus cause the development of the bolls before the pests become abundant is a manifest advantage. The chief merit of this method is that it is in accord with the whole tendency of cotton culture, that is, to obtain an early crop. Early cotton produces the best staple, brings the best price, makes the return to the planter at a time when he needs it the most, and, moreover, avoids to a great extent damage to the plant by the boll-worm, cotton worm, and sharp-shooter, as well as by a large number of fungous diseases. Northern seed produces plants that mature many days earlier than plants from local seed. Consequently, train loads of seed are annually brought from Arkansas and Indian Territory, and the competition for the first bale is as keen as ever. In fact, this bending of every factor to hasten the maturity of the crop has so taken possession of the system of cotton culture that any suggestion for fighting the weevil that runs counter to it is of very doubtful utility. The investigations of the Division of Entomology have demonstrated that it is possible to obtain a yield of the staple equal to the average production per acre in the United States — even in regions where the insects are very abundant, and where late cotton yields practically nothing — by this simple means.

Many practical illustrations of this fact are to be found in Texas. For instance, upon the plantation of Mr. F. H. Yunger, of Dewitt County, the present season (1901) there was a field, 15 acres in extent, planted early in March with seed from Arkansas of the quickly maturing King variety, that produced 5,475 pounds of lint, or about three-quarters of a bale, per acre, though the insects were so numerous by the middle of August that no top crop was made. Other cotton upon the same plantation and upon adjoining ones planted a month later, but similarly situated and otherwise treated in exactly the same manner, yielded only one bale to 8 to 10 acres. Great advantage seems to come from the use of seed of certain varieties that have been perfected to mature quickly, a matter that has received but little attention from the Texas planters.

Destruction of the Plants

The observation, noted above, of the comparative scarcity of the pests in the winter and the facility with which many may be destroyed that would otherwise go into hibernating quarters to appear the following spring, form together the basis of the recommendation insisted upon by the Division of Entomology from the beginning — that the total destruction of the plants in the field should be undertaken as soon as the gathering of a top crop should become a doubtful matter. When the plants are allowed to remain in the field they simply form a means for the insects to multiply long after there is any possibility of the cotton yielding any more fruit. In any case, the stalks have to be destroyed before planting again, and the advantage to come from fall destruction in the reduction of the number of the weevils abundantly warrants the general adoption of this measure. It appears that the maturing of a fall crop in many portions of Texas has always been more or less of a problematical matter. In Wharton County, for example, in twenty years, the planters agree, there has been a considerable top crop only in four or five seasons. Furthermore, accurate statistics for the past thirty years show an average yield per acre in Texas so low as to preclude the possibility of any important top crop. At any rate, it is now certain that where the weevil occurs there can be no dependence upon a top crop. Hence, destruction of the plants, say in October, or earlier if possible, in southern Texas should be generally enforced. This may be accomplished economically by cutting the stalks into pieces by means of a machine known as a stalk chopper, followed by burning, or the plants may be uprooted with a plow commonly used for that purpose in clearing cotton fields in the spring and then treated in the same manner.

Cattle will devour all green portions of the cotton plant, and though not, perhaps, a part of good farm practice, the turning of herds into the fields will accomplish practical destruction. This is practicable, however, only in fields that have been kept reasonably free from grasses and weeds which are preferred by live stock.

The obstacles in the way of general adoption of the destruction method are the custom of many renters to leave the land they have occupied during the crop year as soon as the cotton is picked, and the difficulty of obtaining concerted action. These obstacles, however, are not insurmountable, and it is to be hoped that a realization of the serious and permanent aspect of the situation will soon cause Texas planters to adopt the method universally.

It has repeatedly been observed that in the river valleys and in the immediate vicinity of timber the weevil causes its greatest damage, probably largely on account of more successful hibernations in such situations. In many single fields a most marked difference in yield between the outermost portion and the portion near the timber has been observed. This leads to one of the most important recommendations that can be made, namely, that the lowlands should be reserved as much as possible for other crops, like corn, cane, and rice, to which they are better adapted, and which, moreover, are far more profitable than cotton. There seems no doubt that the State of Texas will be the gainer by leaving cotton out of the region where the weevil makes it an almost certain loss and devoting that land to other crops. The greatest agricultural need of Texas is a diversification of crops, and such a system will go far toward solving the weevil problem.

Wide Planting and Hand Picking

Besides the means mentioned, there are various measures that planters may resort to upon a small scale or under certain conditions that will afford some relief. Some importance should be attached to planting the rows as far apart as the nature of the soil will permit, as thereby the sun will be able to reach the fallen squares and kill many a larva that would otherwise mature. No general rule can be given in this matter, as there will naturally be the greatest variation between the rich alluvial river lands and the sandy portions of the high lands. But it is safe to state that the great majority of planters place the rows too close together for the proper growth and consequent yield of the plants; the experiment stations in nearly every State in the cotton belt have demonstrated it. In experimental plats on upland in Victoria County the present season (1901), where no means of fighting the weevil aside from wide planting were resorted to and where the planting was purposely made very late to test the matter, it was found that one-fourth more cotton was produced with rows at a distance of 5 feet than was produced upon the same land from the same seed with rows but 3 feet apart.

Where cotton is cultivated upon only a small scale and there is an abundance of labor, much good may be accomplished by hand picking of the weevils when they first appear and later of the drooping and fallen squares when the larvae have begun their work. There is no doubt that in Victoria and other counties, where the most of the cotton is raised by small farmers, their energetic work in hand picking, induced by the offer of a bounty by the merchants, largely aided in causing a very fair crop to be made this season.

Machines

The ingenuity of many persons has been taxed to invent machines that will assist in the warfare against the weevil. Aside from poisoning machines, these devices are of two types. One is designed to jar the insects and the affected squares from the plant and to collect them, while the other is intended to pick the fallen squares from the ground. In the cases of several modifications of the first type mentioned which were examined and tested, it was found that their workings were so faulty that to collect the insects by that means was a more expensive and troublesome operation than to do it by hand. It is very doubtful if machines of this kind will ever be of much practical importance. There is some hope that a machine that may pick by suction the fallen squares from the ground may eventually be perfected, but in such an event there are very few cotton fields so free from trash as not to make it almost impossible for such a machine to work. On the whole, it must be stated that there seems but little prospect for aid from machines designed for the destruction of the weevil.

Conclusion

That the boll weevil is to be a permanent factor in cotton culture is a certainty, and that it is to spread outside of Texas is also inevitable. Local conditions may bring about temporary immunity in districts, but the general status will remain the same. Though much remains to be done in the matter of the investigation of means of fighting the pest, enough has been accomplished to show that it is not an insurmountable difficulty that confronts cotton planters. Without belittling the really serious nature of the problem, it must be stated that in many cases failure has been attributed to the weevil when it belongs to climatic conditions or to other circumstances, and attention is called to the fact that in many parts where the general loss has been very heavy, individual farmers by a few simple means have procured average crops. The seriousness of the case lies not only in the inherent difficulty of fighting an insect of the nature of the weevil, but quite as much in adapting methods of combating it to the peculiar industrial conditions of the regions concerned. A system of small, renting farmers, in most cases working only upon shares, with no cash in hand from one cotton picking to the next, with no guaranty on the part of the landowner of tenure for more than one year, or on the part of the renter of continued occupancy, presents by no means favorable conditions. But the people of Texas now realize the importance of fighting the weevil. This was shown the present season by the fact that various merchants' associations in about 25 towns expended an aggregate of nearly $5,000 in the payment of bounties for weevils and for squares in which they had deposited eggs. This beginning of cooperation between all concerned is the most hopeful assurance that these conditions will be righted, and that means for reducing the damage caused by the insect will eventually be generally adopted.

Development of Hemp, 1901

From Lyster H. Dewey, "The Hemp Industry in the United States," U.S. Department of Agriculture, *Yearbook*, 1901, pp. 541–44, 547–54

The Hemp Plant

The hemp plant (*Cannabis sativa*) is an annual, belonging to the nettle family. It grows to a height of from 5 to 15 feet, and when cultivated for fiber produces only a few small branches near the top of the slender stalk. Its leaves, of a rich dark-green color, are composed of 5 to 9 lanceolate, serrate, pointed leaflets, 2 to 5 inches in length and about one-sixth as wide. The staminate, or pollen-bearing flowers, and the pistillate, or seed-producing flowers, are on separate plants, both plants being nearly alike, but the staminate plants maturing earlier. The stems are hollow, and in the best varieties rather prominently fluted. The fiber consists of numerous series of long cells in the inner bark, firmly knitted together, which, when cleaned from the surrounding tissues, form tough strands nearly as long as the entire plant. This is a bast fiber, and is classed commercially among the soft fibers, with flax, ramie, and jute.

The hemp plant originated in central Asia, but it is now widely distributed, especially in the North Temperate Zone, growing spontaneously where it has been accidentally introduced with bird seed or cultivated for the fiber.

Other Plants Called Hemp

The name "hemp" was first applied to the plant above described, but in recent years it has unfortunately been used to designate the sisal plant, or henequen, a species of agave producing a leaf fiber, and the manila fiber plant, or abacá, a kind of banana plant producing structural fibers in the leaf petioles. Sansevieria, a tropical genus belonging to the lily family, includes three or four fiber-producing species, often called bowstring hemp, and an East Indian species, *Crotalaria juncea,* is commonly known as Sunn hemp. The name is also applied to several other species of less importance.

Principal Uses of Hemp Fiber

Hemp fiber is long, soft, very strong, and capable of almost as fine subdivision as flax. It is especially adapted for use where strength is required. It is used in the manufacture of fine twines, carpet thread, carpet yarns, sailcloth, and for homespun and similar grades of woven goods. Nearly all of the best grade of long fiber, ''dressed line,'' is used for making twines, yacht cordage, etc.; cheaper grades are made into binder twine. The tow is used for threads and for yarns to be woven into carpets, homespuns, and linen goods, and the refuse fiber combed from the tow is used as oakum for calking ships. The average annual consumption of hemp fiber in the United States is about 18,000,000 pounds, of which only about 8,500,000 pounds are raised in this country, the remainder being imported.

Regions of Cultivation

Foreign hemp. — In foreign countries hemp is cultivated most extensively in Russia, China, Japan, Italy, Austria, and France. The tallest and best hemp plants are produced in China and Japan, but the best grades of fiber are imported from Italy, where it is prepared by water-retting. It is not cultivated commercially for the production of fiber in the Tropics.

Domestic hemp. — In the United States the production of hemp is almost confined to Kentucky. Three-fourths of the American hemp fiber is produced in that State in the counties of Fayette, Woodford, Jessamine, Garrard, Clark, Bourbon, Boyle, Scott, and Shelby. These nine counties are in the famous blue-grass region, of which Lexington, the principal hemp market, is the center. The most important secondary hemp markets in this region are Nicholasville, Versailles, Lancaster, Danville, Winchester, Paris, Georgetown, Shelbyville, and Frankfort. Small scattered areas of hemp are cultivated intermittently in other parts of the State, and there are probably few counties in Kentucky in which an attempt has not been made at some time to establish the hemp-growing industry.

There are two centers of hemp cultivation in Nebraska — Fremont and Havelock. During the past two or three seasons about 100 acres have been grown at each of these places. In California, hemp is cultivated at Gridley, in Butte County. The industry has been gradually established there during the last half dozen years, and having passed the stages of experiment and loss due to new and untried conditions, there is now a tendency to develop and increase the acreage. Trials in hemp cultivation have been made on Ryers Island, near Riovista, in the Sacramento Valley, and in San Benito County. During the past two years hemp has been grown successfully on a small scale near Houston, Tex., and with improved methods of handling the crop it seems probable that it may become a profitable industry in that region. Hemp has been grown in the vicinity of Champaign and Rantoul, in eastern Illinois, and along the Missouri River, between St. Joseph and Kansas City, but its cultivation in these localities has been almost discontinued, except at Rantoul, where about 400 acres are still cultivated each year.

Soils Suitable for Hemp

In Kentucky, as stated, hemp is cultivated most successfully in the blue-grass region, where the soil is chiefly a yellow clay loam or a rich sandy loam, rather firm in texture and usually underlaid with a subsoil of yellow clay. The land is gently rolling, affording excellent drainage. Exceptionally fine crops are produced on the bottom lands along the Kentucky River and its tributaries, although it is regarded as risky to cultivate it where it is subject to overflow. A good stand of well-developed hemp plants is rarely obtained in undrained hollows in the uplands, although the soil in these hollows seems more fertile than that on the surrounding hillsides.

In Nebraska hemp is cultivated on rich, black, friable prairie loam, comparatively loose and light in texture and lying high, with good drainage. Repeated efforts to cultivate hemp on the "gumbo" and other low-lying soils there have demonstrated that while these soils may produce some large hemp plants it is practically impossible to secure on them a good, even stand of hemp stalks of the proper size for fiber. In Texas good crops of hemp have been produced on rich dark prairie soil, but on upland soils, subject to drought, the crop has proved a failure. In California hemp is grown on alluvial soils in the bottom lands along the rivers. In the testing gardens of the Department of Agriculture, where several European and Japanese varieties of hemp have been tested during the past two years, the plants have attained a good height, but they have been uneven in size, and the fiber produced is not as tough as that produced in Kentucky and Nebraska. The soil of the testing garden is alluvial, composed chiefly of sand and silt, and almost devoid of clay.

An ideal hemp soil must be rich in available fertilizing elements, especially nitrogen and potash, to insure a rapid growth; deep and sufficiently loose in texture to permit the development of the root system and also to allow good drainage; sufficiently friable to make a good, mellow seed bed, so as to insure uniform germination of seed, yet with clay enough to give it a good body and firm texture. A good supply of humus (decaying vegetable and animal matter) is necessary, not only to furnish plant food, but to retain moisture. Very few farm crops require so much water as hemp, yet it will not endure standing water about its roots. It is not grown commercially under irrigation, and the effects of inundation on crops in river bottoms indicate that it would not thrive if subjected to the ordinary methods of flooding practiced in the irrigation of broadcast crops. In soils of good capillarity, where the general level of the soil water is within 10 feet of the surface, there is little danger of injury from drought after the first thirty days, during which the root system of the hemp plant will become well established.

Preparation of Land

Rotation of crops. — In Kentucky, hemp sometimes follows hemp on the same land for two or three years, and if the stalks are retted on the same land and fertilizer applied to make up for the fertility taken off by the crops, no serious injury may result. It is the general practice, however, and doubtless the better practice, to cultivate a series of crops in rotation. A common five-year rotation is clover, hemp, corn, wheat, clover. Clover seeded in the growing wheat in spring occupies the land two years. Hemp follows clover whenever this is practicable. The stubble and roots of the clover, rich in stored-up nitrogen, furnish the desired fertilizing elements well distributed, and also the humus necessary for the development of a rapid-growing crop like hemp in soils long under cultivation.

In California and Nebraska no crop rotation is practiced for hemp, and on the deep, rich prairie soils of Nebraska, where there seems to be an almost inexhaustible supply of humus, it is claimed that the best results are obtained where hemp follows hemp through a long series of years. Hemp prevents the growth of weeds and other vegetation which would be found on such soils in most other crops or after other crops are laid by, and its cultivation also seems to make the soil more uniform in character. . . .

Harvesting

Time of harvesting. — Hemp is cut when the staminate plants are in flower. The time of harvest varies from eighty to one hundred and forty days from the date of seeding, the period of growth depending on the mean temperature and the supply of moisture, and on the variety. When sown at the proper season hemp is usually cut late in August or September (in July in California and Texas).

In some instances good fiber has been secured in Nebraska from hemp cut before flowering, but ordinarily the fiber is best when the crop is harvested just before the staminate plants are in full flower. If cut too early the fiber will be fine, but lacking in strength, deficient in yield, and wasting at every operation in its preparation. If allowed to become too mature the fiber will be coarse, harsh, and brittle.

Methods of harvesting. — In California hemp is cut with self-rake reapers or mowing machines. In Nebraska mowing machines have been superseded by self-rake reapers. Reapers have been used quite extensively in Kentucky during the past two years, and they seem to be growing in popularity there. Most of the hemp in Kentucky, however, is still cut by hand with the primitive reaping knife or hemp cutter, which is something between a corn cutter and a bush scythe, but unlike either. An experienced hand with a reaping knife will cut about one-half acre per day. With a sweep-rake reaper, under favorable conditions, from 5 to 7 acres may be cut in a day, and with a mowing machine, 7 to 10 acres. Hemp does not lodge like grain or heavy clover, but on windy days it is impossible to cut with either reaper or mower in the direction that the wind is blowing, for instead of falling back of the cutting bar the stalks drop down between the guards, where they are repeatedly cut off. The heavy, green, woody stalks, one-eighth to one-half inch in diameter and 8 to 14 feet tall, are much more difficult to handle than grass or grain, and they cause a much greater strain on the machine. Ordinary grain reapers are not entirely satisfactory for harvesting hemp; they are rarely strong enough. The experience of those who have used reapers indicates that a successful hemp-harvesting machine of the self-rake type should be made especially strong, having a cutting bar not more than 3½ feet long, arranged to cut within 2 inches of the ground, extra heavy sections with rapid motion, and driving wheel with broader rim and larger lugs than are usually made for self-rake machines. Opinions differ as to whether two or three rakes give the best results. A team of four good farm horses is generally regarded as necessary for cutting hemp with a self-rake reaper, and in Kentucky an extra hand is employed to drive. In California and Nebraska one man attends to both horses and machine. Some form of harvesting machine must soon take the place of the hemp knife, since it is ever more difficult to secure the skilled labor necessary to cut the crop by hand, and where hemp is raised on a large scale it is impossible with the slow hand methods to get it all cut at the proper season.

Drying and Stacking

After the hemp is cut it is allowed to lie on the ground from four to eight days to dry. The unbound bundles are usually turned, so as to dry both sides. To turn them a stick or fork handle is run under the tops and they are thrown endwise over the butts. When dry the hemp is usually bound in small bundles with cheap twine or the small hemp stalks and set up in shocks or stacked. If it is soon to be spread for retting on the same land it is placed in shocks without binding. When cut with a mowing machine the tangled stalks are raked into windrows like hay. In stacks properly built the hemp will remain uninjured for a period of two or three years; furthermore, the quality of the fiber is improved, and the processes of breaking and cleaning it are made easier by a kind of sweating or fermentation that the stalks undergo in the stack. In spite of the advantages to be gained in stacking, it is often omitted on account of the extra handling and the lack of skilled labor to make the stacks, which must be constructed with even greater care than stacks of wheat or oats.

Retting

Retting, or "rotting," is a process in which the vegetable gums surrounding the fiber are dissolved and the fiber is at the same time freed somewhat from the woody interior portion of the stalk and also from the thin outer cuticle. These gums are not soluble in water, but they are destroyed by a kind of putrefaction which takes place when the stalks are immersed for some time in soft water or are exposed to the weather.

Water retting. — Retting by immersing the stalks in water is largely practiced in France and Italy, and it was practiced in this country until the middle of the last century, before hemp was so completely superseded by cotton in the manufacture of fine woven goods. Water-retted fiber is lighter in color and finer in texture, and it commands a higher price than dew-retted fiber, but it requires a large amount of labor and expensive retting tanks. No process has yet been devised in America by which hemp can be water-retted so as to make it yield as great a profit as when dew-retted.

Investigations in Europe have demonstrated that certain micro-organisms are always present in flax when retting, and these agents play a most important part in the retting process. It is suggested that pure cultures of these amylo-bacteria can be made to facilitate the retting in much the same manner that fermentation is started in making wine and vinegar. In experiments conducted on a small scale flax was retted much more rapidly when the bacteria were supplied. The process of retting hemp is exactly the same as that of retting flax, and it is possible that by making use of the necessary bacteria the length of time and labor required for water-retting may be reduced to within the limits of profitable production. It seems impracticable, however, on account of the great bulk of the crop, to attempt to carry on the operation of retting under cover, as would be necessary in order to have the conditions under control. It may be possible to use the bacteria in a solution to spray on the hemp as it is spread for retting in the field.

Dew-retting. — Nearly all the hemp now produced in the United States is dew-retted. It is spread in long rows on the ground during the fall and early winter and exposed to the weather until the bark, including the fiber, readily slips from the inner woody portion. In Nebraska and California the hemp is spread in the stubble fields where it has been cut. In Kentucky it is usually spread in closely cropped blue-grass pasture land, and is sometimes hauled 2 or 3 miles from the hemp fields to the retting grounds. The plants are turned at least once to secure even retting, the tops being thrown over in the same manner as when turned in drying.

In Kentucky most of the hemp is spread for retting during the month of November, but owing to unfavorable weather and inability to secure retting lands or labor at the desired time, the retting period often extends from soon after the harvest until the following spring. The time required for dew-retting hemp depends upon the weather, and varies from two to ten weeks. Warm, rainy weather causes the hemp to ret rapidly, but it increases the danger of loss, since it is often difficult or even impossible to turn the hemp while the rains continue, and it is retted unevenly or much of it is overretted. The process which seems necessary to destroy the vegetable gums surrounding the fiber injures the fiber itself if permitted to continue too long. A period of warm rains setting in after the hemp has been spread several days and has reached an advanced stage of retting is almost sure to prove injurious to the fiber. The best fiber is obtained from hemp retted slowly during the fall, since it is then easier to secure uniformity and also to check the process before it becomes injurious. Light warm rains soon after the hemp is spread are beneficial to start the retting process. Water charged with the specific bacteria for retting and applied with spraying apparatus might perhaps be substituted for these uncertain showers. When the hemp has been retted sufficiently for the fiber to be readily separated, the stalks are raked together and set up in loose shocks to dry, or hauled to the place where they are to be broken.

Breaking

Breaking is the process by which the fiber is separated from the stalk and roughly cleaned. It prepares the fiber for market as rough hemp, and is usually the last operation performed on it by the farmer or hemp grower. The work of breaking begins as soon as the retted hemp is ready, and often continues until late in the spring. The greater parts broken during January and February.

Hand breaks. — Nearly all of the hemp is broken by hand breaks, such as have been in use many centuries. The crude heavy wooden breaks are all made by carpenters after one very simple pattern, and cost only $5 to $6 each. With one of these an experienced hand under most favorable circumstances can clean out about 250 pounds of fiber in a day. The average day's product of breaking is about 100 pounds of clean fiber. The usual wages paid for breaking is 1 cent per pound of fiber. The work is performed by alternately crushing or breaking the stalks between the long jaws of the break and beating and whipping them over the break to free the hurds from the fiber. It is a slow process, requiring not only strength, but skill. The value of the product depends largely upon the skill of the laborer. There is considerable loss of fiber in beating it against the break to shake off the hurds, and with new and unskilled laborers this loss is often an item of importance. The principal objections to hand breaking are its slowness and cost. To break an average crop of 50 acres requires the services of 10 skilled hemp breakers for two months and costs at least $500. The hand break must give way to machinery.

Hemp-breaking machines. — Several machines have been devised for breaking hemp, but they have not given complete satisfaction. Very few of them have succeeded at all in breaking hemp in commercial quantities.

A machine consisting of a series of coarsely fluted rollers followed by a rapidly revolving spiked cylinder has been in use for some years in California and Nebraska. It breaks the hemp and delivers the fiber in the form of tow. This machine seems to be particularly well adapted to the preparation of fiber from tangled hemp stalks cut with a mowing machine.

In the hemp factories at Lexington there are machines consisting essentially of long series of corrugated rollers which are occasionally used for softening the fiber. It is said that these machines may be used for breaking hemp, but they are not actually so used. These and also the break used in California are too heavy to be taken into the field, and they require more power than can be furnished by an ordinary thrashing engine.

During the past season three decorticators have been in operation near Lexington, by which the hemp stalk is crushed in passing between rollers, corrugated for unretted hemp and smooth foretted. The hurds are then loosened by a rapidly vibrating mechanism, and the fiber is partly cleaned by a kind of carrier, which gives a rapid scraping motion. These machines break the hemp well and without waste or injury to the fiber, but do not clean out the hurds as well as is desired. They are portable, weighing only 2,000 pounds, and require only 6 horsepower for operation. An ordinary thrashing engine furnishes sufficient power to run two breaks. The hurds are used as fuel for the engine. The average day's output from each of these machines is 2,000 to 3,000 pounds of rough hemp. Attention is called to these machines especially, since they are the first portable machines that have proved successful, working out in the field and producing untangled long-line fiber similar to that cleaned on the hand break.

Breaking unretted hemp. — Several hundred tons of unretted hemp stalks have been broken on the decorticators used at Lexington during the past season. The fiber thus produced is degummed and prepared for spinning by a chemical process. The finished fiber produced in this manner is of fine quality, and is used for the same purposes as the better grades of imported flax. The process is not yet in general use, however, and there is only a limited market for unretted hemp fiber. It would effect a decided improvement in the industry if the farmer could break his hemp successfully and find a ready market for the fiber without the tedious and uncertain process of retting.

Market

The rough hemp fiber is tied in bales weighing about 150 pounds each, and most of it is sold to dealers in the local markets. In some instances where it is cleaned better than usual it is shipped to the manufacturers, but most of it is hackled by the local dealers. This work is nearly all performed by hand, and consists in combing the fiber by drawing it across clusters of upright, sharp steel needles. The long fiber, nearly as long as the hemp stalks, combed out in this manner, is known in the market as "Kentucky single-dressed hemp." If the fiber is of especially good quality, it is combed still further upon a finer hackle, and it then becomes "Kentucky double-dressed hemp," which is the highest grade of American hemp quoted on the fiber market.

The price of hemp varies to a considerable degree, depending on the demand and supply of other fibers almost as much as on the production of the hemp itself. Most of the rough hemp is sold by the farmers during the winter soon after it is broken. The prices during the winter of 1901–1902 are regarded as comparatively high, being 4¼ to 5 cents per pound. The approximate average prices paid to farmers by local dealers in Lexington, Ky., during the month of February for the past seven years have been as follows:

	Per ton (2,210 pounds).		Per ton (2,210 pounds).
1896	$60.00	1901	$112.00
1897	70.00	1902	105.00
1898	75.00		
1899	90.00	Average	87.42
1900	100.00		

The minimum limit of profitable production, according to present methods, is regarded as about 3¼ cents per pound. With the present values and profits in other farm productions, a price considerably above this limit must be paid to induce farmers to grow hemp rather than devote their lands to stock raising and corn and tobacco. Even at the present time hemp is giving place to tobacco in Kentucky on many rich farms in the blue-grass region. The average production for five-year periods for the past twenty-five years, based on reports of the commissioner of agriculture of Kentucky, is as follows:

	Pounds of rough hemp.
1876 to 1880	10,793,427
1881 to 1885	6,843,367
1886 to 1890	12,541,145
1891 to 1895	7,263,713
1896 to 1900	6,354,543
Approximate average for twenty-five years	8,700,000

The generally decreasing production is not due to a diminishing yield, but to a reduced acreage. A larger acreage was planted in 1901 than during the previous two years, and allowing for loss due to drought, the 1901 crop is estimated at about 8,000,000 pounds.

Under fair average conditions an acre of hemp yields about 1,000 pounds of rough fiber, or about 6,000 pounds of dry retted stalks. At 5 cents per pound for the fiber it is a very good paying crop. It is a reasonably safe crop, aside from the uncertainties of retting. It is not often seriously injured by fungous diseases or insects. Its most serious enemy is the parasitic weed branched broom rape, mentioned under "Weeds."

Seed and Varieties

Hemp seed is produced on plants grown in checks or sometimes in drills, and cultivated like corn. These plants grow stout and coarse, with numerous branches, and they are worthless for fiber. No horticultural varieties are recognized in this country. Nearly all of the hemp grown here in recent years is of Chinese origin. The seed is obtained in small quantities from American missionaries in central China, and this is usually cultivated for two generations for seed production before it is sown broadcast for fiber. This method is pursued not only to secure a sufficient quantity of seed, but also because better fiber plants are produced after the seed has been acclimated by cultivation in this country. The hemp growers of Kentucky generally agree in the opinion that the best hemp is produced by small dark-colored seed. In Japan, on the contrary, the best varieties have comparatively large light-colored seed.

The Chinese and Japanese varieties of hemp are very similar in character. They grow to a height of 9 to 15 feet, with slender stalks, few branches, and usually with internodes 8 to 12 inches in length. The pistillate flowers on the plants grown for seed are in rather small clusters, scattered on branches of the long slender limbs. The European varieties, including the Piedmont, Neapolitan, Hungarian, and Russian, while sufficiently different in character to be readily distinguished, all conform to a general type, sometimes called the Smyrna type. This differs from the China-Japan type in a more compact growth, shorter plants, shorter internodes, and shorter and more rigid limbs, bearing the seeds in rather large, dense clusters. These European varieties reach maturity from ten to thirty days earlier than the China-Japan varieties under similar conditions.

Until comparatively recent times hemp seed of European origin was used in Kentucky, and its effects are still plainly seen in the mixed character of plants too often found in the hemp fields. These plants are so prolific in seed that the growers hesitate to throw them out when harvesting their hemp seed.

An ideal hemp plant should be 10 to 12 feet in height, one-fourth to three-eighths inch in diameter near the base, with internodes 10 inches or more in length, and stems prominently fluted, with comparatively large hollows, making them thin-shelled and more easily broken. The fiber is generally tougher on the thin-shelled stalks. The Chinese and best Japanese varieties approach most nearly this ideal. Starting with these as a foundation and practicing a rigid seed selection for a half dozen generations or longer would undoubtedly result in improved varieties of uniform plants adapted to cultivation in this country.

Organization of the Farmers' Union

From Charles S. Barrett, The Mission, History and Times (Nashville, 1909), pp. 103–05, 128–29.

The first local Union was organized at Smyrna Schoolhouse by Newt. Gresham, on the second day of September, 1902. The following officers were elected: Dr. Lee Seamster, Emory, Texas, president; J. B. Morris, Emory, Texas, vice president; O. H. Rhodes, Emory, Texas secretary; W. T. Cochran Emory, Texas, treasurer; Newt. Gresham, Point, Texas general organizer; T. J. Pound, J. S. Turner, T. W. Donaldson, Jesse Adams and W. S. Sisk, all of Emory, Texas directors. Thus it may be seen that the first local Union was made up of ten men.

The second local Union was organized on the third day of September 1902, by W. T. Cochran. Early in the work W. S. Sisk was elected secretary-treasurer. The charter of the first local Union was revoked because of the stand it took in politics. To quote Mr. Sisk: "We had quite a lot of trouble getting the Union started off right." Of the original ten, Lee Seamster was a practicing physician, O. H. Rhodes was county clerk, and Newt. Gresham a newspaper man. All owned farms, except Newt. Gresham and J. S. Turner. These were farmers living on rented farms.

A constitution and by-laws were adopted on the night of the organization. The first constitution embodied the principles which were later worked out by the various conventions that have met from time to time. The by-laws are practically the same today that they were then. Time and the needs brought about by the rapidly growing order have made these amendments necessary, and these changes have come as the organization has grown and the necessities become apparent.

Newt. Gresham was sitting on a log one day at a cross-roads country store, and observed the few woebegone and debt-depressed farmers who came and went. Doubtless Newt. Gresham recalled the time when the Grange, the Wheel and the Farmers' Alliance had made heroic but unsuccessful effort to break away from such conditions as he was then witnessing, and in his heart of hearts he desired to aid them. There came to him, as if by inspiration, a hope that he might be able to assist them and thus redress their many wrongs. He, too, was poor and, like them, had faced the credit and mortgage system then cursing the South. His influence with the rich and powerful could not be said to be of any considerable extent.

The more he thought of his and his neighbors' wretched conditions, the more determined he became to make at least one desperate effort in behalf of the farmers of his neighborhood. He did not know whether those whom he wished most to benefit would even be considerate enough to listen to his proposition. He went away from the country store with a heavy heart. He issued a call for his friends and neighbors to meet him. A few came and heard him outline his plan. Nine men besides himself thought favorably enough of the plan to agree to the formation of an organization. Some others did not think it would be of any benefit to the masses of the farmers, and Gresham was told by these that the farmers would not stick.

Sometimes I think of Gresham as being like Mahomet, who when he became imbued with the idea that there was "one God, and He was good," prepared a great feast, to which he invited his relatives, his friends and his acquaintances. When this assembly had feasted, Mahomet stood up and told them of his vision, declaring that there was but one God, and he (Mahomet) was His Prophet. This declaration was received with derision. Two only of the crowd, Kajiah, his accomplished young wife and his idiotic nephew, were all that believed in him. The others went away, laughing at Mahomet's idea.

Shortly after the first local Union was organized at Point, Newt. Gresham was invited to another community to tell about the new organization, of which he was the founder. Soon other invitations of like nature came to him, and within the next few months many local Unions were organized in Rains and other nearby communities. It soon became apparent that organizers must be sent out. The first commissions to organizers of local Unions were issued to Alex. Williams of Emory, Ed Gresham of Point, Tom Carroll of Como, R. F. Duckworth and J. J. Ross of Brinker, and with this corps of organizers in the field this new organization grew very rapidly. . . .

On August 28, 1902, Dr. Lee Seamster, O. H. Rhodes and J. S. Turner filed in the office of T. S. McGee, official notary public for Rains County, Texas, an application for charter for the Farmers' Educational and Co-operative Union of America. This application was filed in the office of John G. Todd, secretary of the state, on September 17, of the same year. The seal of the State of Texas was affixed to this charter on January 9, 1906, by O. K. Shannon, then secretary of state, at Austin, Texas.

The charter as filed and approved is here given:

Charter
THE STATE OF TEXAS,
COUNTY OF RAINS.

Be it known that we, the undersigned citizens of Rains County, Texas, hereby make application for a charter for the following purposes, towit:

1. The name of the Corporation shall be "The Farmers' Educational and Co-operative Union of America."

2. The purpose for which it is formed is to organize and charter subordinate Unions at various places in Texas and the United States, to assist them in marketing and obtaining better prices for their products, for fraternal purposes, and to co-operate with them you have not overthrown that system. You are building more rapidly than they have builded, and more solidly. They builded upon greed and graft, while you are building upon justice and equity.

Things Accomplished by the Union

Some people sometimes ask what has the Union ever done to commend it to the respect of the people and the admiration of the world? Where I to attempt to give all the incidents, and single out the repeated instances, time would fail me and the result would be a book of many thousand pages instead of a comprehensive book for the ready reference of busy people. This book is for busy ones, and must set forth in short and concise sentences what has actually been accomplished.

In May, 1907, the National President issued a manifesto requesting the membership to plow up at least ten per cent of the cotton crop. From Texas to North Carolina hundreds of members loyally obeyed the mandate and plowed up a portion of their crop. Some plowed up more than ten per cent, others a less amount. The land plowed up was planted in corn and the cotton acreage considerably decreased. A record of the names of all who plowed up their cotton has been kept, and is on file for future reference.

This sacrificial act on the part of the farmers, when many of them could not seemingly destroy a part of their living and deprive wife and children of comforts, speaks volumes for the willingness of the membership to help win the fight for better prices for cotton. This act was a severe test, but be it said to their credit that they stood it in a manner that convinces the world that the Farmers' Union stands for something.

Holding Cotton

The struggles of the membership to hold cotton for higher prices furnishes another epoch in the progress and advancement of the farming class in the South. From the days of the civil war to the present, there have been but few efforts made to maintain anything like profitable prices for cotton. These efforts have been of very little real benefit to the farmers. The Alliance did make a sporadic effort to influence the cotton market, but with few direct results. The first real beneficial movement of the kind originated with the membership of the Farmers' Union. This idea was a predominating one at the time the first State Union was organized at Mineola, Texas, and was among the principles proclaimed by every lecturer and organizer sent into the field either to arouse the membership or to plant new lodges in virgin territory.

These cotton holding movements inaugurated year by year have been the means of saving the southern farmers millions of dollars. A system of warehouses stretching like a continuous chain from the northern limit of cotton to the coast line are material aids in the movement.

Farm Management, 1902

From W. J. Spillman, "Systems of Farm Management in the United States," U.S. Department of Agriculture, *Yearbook*, 1902, pp. 343–64.

Introduction

The most successful system of farming is that which gives the largest profit, leaves the soil in condition to yield maximum crops, and brings to the farmer and those dependent on him the largest measure of happiness. In conducting a farm upon such a system, the farmer must continually answer for himself the questions: What crops shall I grow and what area of each? What care shall I give these crops and the soil upon which they grow? What disposition shall be made of the produce of the fields? If the crops are to be sold, then when and where? If they are to be fed, then to what classes of stock and to what number? What manures and fertilizers shall be applied to the soil, to what crops, in what season, in what quantities? What provision shall be made for the protection of growing crops from insect pests and fungous diseases, for storing crop products, for the protection and care of live stock? When and where shall live stock and their products be marketed? The repeated answering of these and other similar questions constitutes farm management — a business in which is found the application of many sciences, but a business so broad and complex that it must rest mainly on the accumulated experience of generations of those who have followed it. Conditions of climate, proximity to market, the character of farm labor, social conditions, and that great enigma, the soil, have all been determining factors in the development of the systems of farming that have been gradually evolved in the various sections of the country. These systems for the most part have been worked out in a purely empirical manner, and have always followed lines of least resistance. This or that crop or system of cropping has become established because it furnished the greatest immediate returns, and has remained even when it became unprofitable because of the natural conservatism of the farmer. Frequently a system established by one generation has been bequeathed to the next, to its financial undoing. One of the principal reasons for this state of affairs lies in the fact that the American farmer has until recently been drawing on soil resources accumulated by natural processes through long ages; he has not been compelled by force of circumstances to learn how to conserve the fertility of the soil. Land has been so plentiful and so cheap that when one field was exhausted he simply transferred his operations to another. No cause for alarm was felt so long as "Uncle Sam was rich enough to give us all a farm" on the fertile prairies of the unbounded West. But conditions have changed. Most of the farm lands of the West have been occupied, and the new generation finds itself under the necessity of earning a livelihood on the lands of its forefathers. In all the older sections of the Eastern and Southern States the problem of restoring the soil to its original fertility is a pressing one. Had the farmer been left to his own resources in working out this problem, agriculture would undoubtedly by this time have been in a deplorable condition. As it is, much land has been abandoned, and the profits of agriculture are very small in some regions where farming was formerly highly profitable.

Work of the Investigator for the Farmer

Fortunately the development of the agricultural press, the farmers' institute, the experiment stations, the schools of agriculture, and the Department of Agriculture during the past quarter century have contributed to the general dissemination of agricultural knowledge. These agencies have probably averted a period of agricultural depression such as afflicted England during the period which gave rise to the "corn laws." Heretofore the aid which the farmer has received from agricultural investigators has been mainly in the line of laboratory studies of chemical, physical, and physiological problems. In this way much has been learned concerning the principles involved in the production of crops, the conservation of soil fertility, and the feeding of animals. The farmer has been left largely to himself in changing his plans to fit the suggestions offered him. Too often he has been compelled to change the suggestions to fit his plans. Too little attention has been paid to the subject of farm management. A careful study of the systems of farming in vogue in all parts of the country would not only show what are the real problems that confront the farmer, but would reveal the fact that farmers themselves have already solved many very important ones. Such a study would show that in one locality there is no problem more pressing than the dissemination of the knowledge we have, and that the investigator is free to take up those fundamental problems which deal with general principles, such as the principles of nutrition, the principles of breeding, etc. Elsewhere the one great problem is the stocking of the soil with humus. The experimenter can aid the farmer in choosing the proper crops for this purpose. Again, the problem is to find a crop adapted to peculiar soil or climatic conditions, and so on. But when these problems have been solved in the laboratory or in experiment plats, there remains the problem of readjusting the system of farming. Heretofore the farmer has been left to himself in this matter, and frequently he has been slow to avail himself of the results of investigation because the problem has been too large for him. For instance, the cotton growers of the South have long recognized the necessity of introducing leguminous crops into their rotations to secure much-needed humus. But these crops can only be utilized as feed for stock. This means that the farmer must learn the characteristics of the various breeds of stock and how to care for live stock, all of which is new to him. He must have pastures, and he is not familiar with the grasses and the management of pasture lands. Again, much of the land is leased in small lots to negro tenants who are familiar with the cultivation of no other crop than cotton, or perhaps corn. It is therefore necessary, in order to secure the benefits from humus-producing crops, to revolutionize the system of farming and to change wholly the relation that has heretofore existed between landlord and tenant.

When crops adapted to the climate and soil and capable of building up the soil have been found, shall the farmer be left to readjust his system to fit them, or shall an effort be made to help him in this readjustment? To give this help the experimenter must first make himself familiar with the peculiarities of the soil and its management, climate, market conditions, character of available labor, social conditions, the character of the available live stock, and the conditions which must determine its management — all those factors that govern present practice and which must govern the new system. It is easily seen that the adoption in practice of the results of investigation may be a much larger problem than the investigation itself. These broader problems can not be taken into the laboratory; neither can they be solved by plat experiments, though these means will aid in their solution. They do not always lend themselves to laboratory methods, but require rather the methods of the statistician.

Benefits of a Study of Farm Conditions and Farm Methods

Here and there in all parts of the country farmers can be found who are highly successful. True their success is generally due to unusual executive ability; but this is simply saying that they have answered the questions propounded in the above definition of farm management and answered them correctly for their conditions. There is no more fruitful field of study than the methods and results of these men. It will usually be found that they can give satisfactory reasons for the system of farming they follow and the methods they employ. Comparison of their methods with those of other successful farmers will often give the clew to principles that underlie successful practice. There is no question that farmers everywhere would benefit by a knowledge of the methods pursued by the most successful of their fellows. Few can be originators; the majority must be imitators; hence the value of the suggestions gained by a knowledge of what others have done and are doing, The agricultural papers have realized the importance of this. Some agricultural writers have undertaken to study farm conditions and farm methods over large areas of country, with great benefit to their readers, particularly where these writers have had sufficient training and knowledge to make their deductions reliable. This study should be taken up more seriously. It should include a study of methods pursued on all classes of farms, both successful and unsuccessful, and should extend over the whole country. With the knowledge thus gained one should be in position to recognize the leading problems that confront farmers in all sections, to know what changes in farm practice are needful, and to understand how these changes may best be accomplished. With these ideas in mind, the writer during the summer of 1902 visited several widely separated agricultural sections for the purpose of studying the methods of farm management in vogue in those sections. In the present paper the methods on only a few of these farms can be given, and in order to present possible conditions and make practical recommendations only actual practices on these individual farms will be described.

Before proceeding to give the details of the management of these farms a few generalizations seem to be justified by the facts at hand. These facts tend to confirm the principles that have been advocated by leading agriculturists for many years. The agricultural sections which are most prosperous are those in which these principles are most closely followed.

Types of Farm Management

It would perhaps be premature to attempt a classification of the various types of farm management that prevail in different sections of the country. In fact the systems followed on different farms represent every gradation between the farm where a single crop is grown and the product is all sold off the farm, and that on which no crops are grown, but large quantities of feed are bought and fed, if indeed the latter may be called a farm. Nevertheless certain types may be more or less arbitrarily chosen, and each farm classed under one of these types, or considered as intermediate between them. It may be safely assumed that the development and maintenance of soil fertility is the most important problem in farming. With soil fertility assured the future of agriculture may be considered safe. Types of farm management may therefore be established on the basis of those practices which relate to soil fertility. On this basis three general types may be assumed.

(1) Live-Stock Farming

In its best development, this type of farming makes every other consideration secondary to live stock. The crops raised are practically all fed on the place, and the resulting manure is carefully utilized. Frequently more is fed than is raised on the farm, either grain or hay, or both, being purchased. When intelligently managed this system invariably results in building up the soil to the highest state of fertility. In sections of the country where it has been followed for many years there is even complaint that the land is becoming too rich for wheat and oats, since these crops, with the rank growth that occurs on exceedingly rich land, tend to be weak in the straw, and wheat particularly goes too much to leaf and too little to grain. On farms of this type commercial fertilizers are used sparingly or not at all.

These live-stock farms may be divided into subtypes, such as general live-stock farms, on which several kinds of stock are kept, no one kind having a decided preference; dairy farms; and special live-stock farms, on which one kind of stock is made a specialty. Dairy farming might be included in special live-stock farming, but it has so many distinctive characteristics that it needs to be considered separately. Every gradation between these three subtypes will of course be found. Market gardening, in which large use is made of manure obtained from cities, may be considered as intermediate between this type and the next.

(2) Grain and Hay Farming

This is a type that has grown up in certain sections where live stock has gradually disappeared, and more and more of the energy of the husbandman is devoted to the production of grain, potatoes, hay, etc., for the market. The essential feature of this second type of farming lies in its reliance on the roots and stubble of ordinary crops, including grasses and legumes grown for hay, or catch crops to be turned under as green manure, to maintain the supply of humus and nitrogen in the soil, while the mineral elements of plant food are largely supplied in commercial fertilizers. This is the system employed by many farmers in Ohio, Pennsylvania, Maryland, and New York. The farmers in this region have been driven to this system by force of circumstances. For the following facts bearing on this point the writer is indebted to Director C. E. Thorne, of the Ohio experiment station. During the eighties the price of live stock in Ohio suffered a serious decline, coincident with the opening of the Western ranges. About the same time improvement in machinery for handling grain greatly reduced the cost of producing this class of crops. The ease with which grain is marketed also contributed to the development of grain growing. Many farmers were rendered bankrupt by the decline in prices of live stock, and they naturally turned to grain growing because less capital was required in that style of farming. A few years later the development of grain growing in the Northwest reduced the price of grain, thus leaving the farmers without recourse. As a result agriculture was at a very low ebb and land values shrank nearly one-half. The turn came with the recent advance in the value of live stock, but it found many farmers without the capital required to take advantage of improved conditions. Director Thorne estimates that the amount of live stock in Wayne County, Ohio, is now about half what it was in 1870, and that $40,000 a year has been added to the bill for commercial fertilizers.

Similar conditions prevailed in all the great live-stock regions of the East. The dairy industry in this country had its birth about the time this depression began, and it proved to be the salvation of many farms. But many farmers found dairying either uncongenial or were not in a position to adopt it. As a result, a system of farming has developed which depends upon a proper rotation of crops, or upon catch crops and green manures for humus, and commercial fertilizers for mineral plant food. The ultimate effect of such a system upon the fertility of the soil has not yet been satisfactorily demonstrated. Any system which results either in rapid improvement or rapid deterioration of the soil may have its merits or demerits established in a comparatively short time. But a system which has no radical tendency in either direction must be studied through a long series of years to determine its ultimate effect. It has been quite generally assumed that unless a large proportion of the crops (the amount depending upon the strength of the soil) is fed on the farm, the fertility of the soil can not be maintained. It will perhaps be conceded that a worn out soil can not easily be brought back to its original fertility without the aid of live stock. At any rate such a process could be much more easily accomplished by feeding the crops and returning the manure to the land than in any other way, unless indeed farmers simply grow crops, especially legumes, and turn them under again. But where a soil is already in good condition, intelligent management has enabled farmers in the section referred to to maintain good yields for a generation at least by the methods outlined above. Too often, however, this system degenerates into the original system of soil robbery practiced on all new and fertile lands the world over since agriculture had its beginning.

(3) Nonhumus Farming

A third type is that in which no attention is given to the supply of humus in the soil. Commercial fertilizers may or may not be used. This type is found in a pure state in some of the newer wheat-growing regions of the Northwest and the Pacific

States, where the rich prairie soils are not yet exhausted and where no fertilizers are used, as well as in the single-crop cotton growing sections of the Gulf States. In the latter, commercial fertilizers are used extensively in the older sections and the regions of lighter soils, but only moderately or not at all in the newer or richer soils of the western portion. The vast majority of farmers in these two sections make no effort to keep up the stock of humus in the soil. The same is true of thousands of individual farmers scattered over all parts of the country.

The effects of this system are too well known. In order to maintain the fertility of the soil two things are absolutely essential: First, the soil must be kept stocked with a sufficient supply of decomposing organic material (humus) to keep it mellow and porous enough to permit of the free circulation of air and moisture; second, the soil must be supplied with sufficient mineral plant food to meet the requirements of crops. There are in general two ways of doing both these things. Humus and plant food may both be supplied by feeding more or less of the products of the soil, the proportion depending on the character of the soil itself, and returning the manure to the land; or the humus may be supplied by frequent cropping with grass and legumes or by green manures, and the mineral plant food by the use of commercial fertilizers. The first of the three systems described above uses the first and more certain of these two methods; the second system uses the last method. The third system makes no provision for a constant supply of humus, and frequently none for mineral plant food. Experience has demonstrated that no amount of plant food will compensate for a lack of humus, and lack of attention to this requirement accounts for the numerous abandoned farms in all the older sections of the country.

Distribution of the Three Systems of Farm Management

In this discussion the arid and semiarid areas devoted solely to grazing are not considered. On the irrigated lands of the Far West the second type, or grain and hay farming, prevails. No fertilizers are used ordinarily, but the supply of humus is kept up mostly by the cultivation of alfalfa and other crops. The effect of irrigation water in bringing plant food to the soil is not yet fully known, but it is probably considerable. The ultimate effect of present methods on these soils, which are all new and for the most part naturally fertile, remains to be seen. It is probable that the accumulation of salts in the soil will be more important in future on these soils than the exhaustion of fertility. The third type is found not only in those sections where single-crop systems prevail, but on individual farms all over the country. The system of live-stock farming does not cover whole sections solidly in any part of the country, but is more or less characteristic of all those parts of the country that have never been so unfortunate as to find a single crop that would make men rich in a few years. Where such crops have been discovered, they have invariably led to the general adoption of wholly unscientific systems of farming, which sooner or later lead to financial ruin.

In the main, general live-stock farming and the style of farming having beef production as its principal feature are characteristic of the great corn, oat, and clover region of the Upper Mississippi Valley. Other types of special live-stock farming are common in the same region, such as those in which horses or swine are the principal source of income. These special types are also common in all the region east of Illinois and north of Tennessee and Virginia. Isolated cases occur in the Southern States and on the Pacific coast. Dairy farming is best developed in the northern tier of States, on the whole Pacific coast, and in certain of the States of the second tier, notably Iowa. That style of farming which depends on frequent crops of grasses and legumes to keep up the supply of humus, making little use of live stock and which uses an abundance of commercial fertilizers, is found mainly north of Virginia in the East and Tennessee in the West, and east of Illinois, as already stated. It has its fullest development in Maryland, Pennsylvania, and New York.

The distribution of these various types has evidently been largely the result of the adaptability of soil and climate to certain crops. The cotton crop has determined the development of agriculture in all those regions adapted to its cultivation. It will always have an important influence in those regions, as it should. The fact, however, that it long ago excluded other excellent crops leaves us without a proper knowledge of the adaptability of the cotton-growing sections to other crops and to live-stock farming. The adaptability of the wheat plant to the prairie soils of the Northwest and the Pacific Northwest has determined until now the course of agricultural development in those regions. Corn, clover, and oats are responsible for the general prevalence of live-stock farming in the Upper Mississippi Valley, while wheat, corn, and timothy and clover, together with market conditions, are largely responsible for the systems that prevail in the East Central States. A marked instance of the adaptability of a crop to a given soil and the resulting influence on agriculture is found in the case of bluegrass in Kentucky. Taking a point 25 miles north of Lexington as a center, with a radius of approximately 55 miles, if we describe an arc of a circle in Kentucky, with both ends of the arc resting on the Ohio River, we shall include that part of the State the soil of which was formed from the dolomitic limestones of the Cambrian era. This area is the far-famed "bluegrass region" of Kentucky. Outside of it bluegrass is of no importance in that State. There is no question that the adaptability of bluegrass to this particular soil accounts for the great stock farms of the State, which are practically confined to this area.

It is not difficult to point out certain changes in prevailing systems of farming that are necessary to agricultural prosperity, both present and future. It is not so easy to indicate how these changes are to be brought about. In general, efforts in this direction must first be given to methods of supplying humus to soils deficient in this all-important constituent. This means the more general cultivation of grasses and forage crops; and since these crops must necessarily be utilized as food for live stock, and since such use of them on the farm adds greatly to the possibilities of increasing the supply of humus, it follows that a change toward live-stock farming in regions where it is now unimportant would be the most promising means of improving the soil and restoring permanent prosperity.

In this connection, certain facts revealed by the census of 1900 are not without interest. Fig. 34 shows the relative value of the live-stock products of the various States. The group of States most deeply shaded includes those in which the live-stock products exceeded 42 per cent of the total farm products. In addition to the Mountain States, this group includes Oregon, Nebraska, Kansas, the Indian Territory, Iowa, Missouri, and Wisconsin. The preponderance of live stock in the Mountain States is, of course, due to the fact that range stock constitutes their principal agricultural resource. The stock on the range lands of eastern Oregon doubtless account for the position of this State in this class also. California is excluded by her wheat fields and fruit interests, while Washington, Minnesota, and the two Dakotas are excluded from this class by their immense wheat fields. In the next group of States, extending from Illinois to Maine, live-stock products constitute from 35 to 42 per cent of the total farm products. Had it been possible to subdivide States in this discussion, much of Illinois and part of Indiana would have been classed with Iowa and Wisconsin. In the northern and eastern portion of this second group of States live-stock interests relate largely to dairying; in the western, to dairying and beef production; and in the southern, to horses and beef production.

The third group of States consists of Washington, South Dakota, Minnesota, Texas, Tennessee, Virginia, Maryland, and Delaware. In these, live-stock products constitute from 28 to 35 per cent of the total farm products. The anomalous position of Texas in this group is due to the fact that, while western Texas is devoted exclusively to stock raising, the central and much of the eastern portion is devoted mainly to cotton.

The fourth group, in which the live-stock products constitute 21 to 28 per cent of farm products, consists of California, Arkansas, Florida, and North Carolina.

The fifth group, in which the live-stock products are less than 21 per cent of the total, includes North Dakota and the cotton-producing States of Louisiana, Mississippi, Alabama, Georgia, and South Carolina.

In fig. 35 the relative amount of commercial fertilizers used is shown. In the unshaded area the fertilizer bill is less than 1 per cent of the value of the crops. It is less than one-half of 1 per cent in all these States except Michigan, where it is less than six-tenths of 1 per cent. What little fertilizer is used in these States is applied mostly to truck crops, the general farmer being ordinarily unacquainted with commercial fertilizers.

In the second group, extending from Ohio to Louisiana and including California, the expenditure for fertilizers amounts to 1 to 3 per cent of the value of the crops. In Maine, New Hampshire, New York, Pennsylvania, and Alabama the fertilizer bill is 3 to 5 per cent, and in the remaining States over 5 per cent of the value of the crops. In the two Carolinas, Maryland, Delaware, New Jersey, Connecticut, and Rhode Island over 7 per cent of the value of farm crops is used in the purchase of commercial fertilizers, and nearly 7 per cent in Georgia and Virginia.

These maps (figs. 34 and 35) furnish some interesting suggestions regarding the relation of live-stock farming to the use of commercial fertilizers. In the first place the use of commercial fertilizers has developed to large proportions in the older sections of the Atlantic seaboard and is gradually extending westward. But in its westward course it has plainly swerved toward the region in which stock farming is unimportant and away from the live-stock regions. Doubtless the course followed is partly due to differences in soil, but there can be no doubt that live-stock farming is a very important factor. Reference has already been made to the fact that during the last twenty-five years, owing to the cheaper production of beef cattle in the West in connection with the perfection of machinery for handling grain and hay crops, Wayne County, Ohio, has lost the equivalent of 12,000 head of cattle (half its live stock) and increased its annual fertilizer bill by $40,000, and that these changed conditions are typical of those in the State generally. According to Director Thorne, during the twenty years preceding this change the average yield of wheat in Wayne County increased from about 14 bushels to about 16½ bushels per acre; while during the last twenty-five years the average yield has been at a standstill, with a tendency in later years to decrease.

The very opposite of this condition prevails in parts of Wisconsin, New York, and Vermont, and other regions where the dairy industry has been greatly developed in the last quarter century. It is generally conceded that where the major part of the farm is devoted to the production of forage crops that are consumed on the farm the soil is growing richer; while in those regions where such crops are not grown and where commercial fertilizers are practically the sole reliance, the productivity of the soil has been greatly lessened. It will be noticed (see fig. 35) that in Vermont the development of the dairy industry has had considerable influence in lessening the use of commercial fertilizers.

Typical Farms

Since space will not permit the consideration here of the methods of management on farms of all types, those selected have been chosen with a view to showing how much diversity there may be in the means adopted in carrying out essentially the same idea, namely, that nothing shall be sold off the farm that would tend to rob the farm of fertility. Each of the farms selected represents a different subtype of pure live-stock farming. This class of farm is chosen purposely, because it represents the type which will most quickly build up worn-out soils. The management of the three farms of this type described is given in more or less detail, the first being a general live-stock farm, with beef production a leading feature; another purely a dairy farm, while the third is devoted to the feeding of Western range lambs and to the care of a flock of pure-bred sheep. The cropping systems followed on these farms are widely different, and one of them at least is situated on land that was at one time not as fertile as it now is. But they all agree in this one feature, that is, that all the crops produced are fed on the place, while on the last two in particular large quantities of feed in addition to that produced on the place are bought and fed.

A General Live-Stock Farm

As an example of a general live-stock farm we will take that of E. E. Chester, of Champaign County, Ill. This is situated on the rich, black prairie soil of northeastern Illinois, where corn, oats, and clover are at their best, and hence exert an important influence on methods of farming. About the same system of cropping has been pursued on this farm for the past twenty years, so that we have an opportunity to observe the effects of the system. The owner endeavors to keep enough stock to consume all the products of his farm, and to put it in his own language "takes the chances of keeping a little more and buying some feed, though some feed is sold in exceptional years." He has a 100-ton silo, the contents of which he utilizes in steer feeding, and finds it highly advantageous. Silage reduces the amount of hay required. He both raises and buys for feeding purposes horses, cattle, and hogs. He uses no commercial fertilizers of any kind. When the writer spoke of desiring to learn the methods of successful farmers in various parts of the country, Mr. Chester very quickly asked what was meant by a successful farmer, and was satisfied with the definition that a successful farmer is one who makes his farm profitable without impoverishing the soil. To quote him again: "There are two kinds of successful farmers. One is only so called, for he makes money by impoverishing his soil; the other keeps up the fertility of the soil."

The rotation on this farm is very elastic, depending on the needs of the live stock, the condition of the soil in the different fields, and the success or failure of the seeding of grass. The permanent pastures consist of bluegrass, while third-year and fourth-year (sometimes fifth-year) timothy and clover sod is used for temporary pasture. In all there are usually about 200 acres (slightly more than one-third of the arable land) in pasture. Corn is the leading cultivated crop, the usual area being about 140 acres. Part of the corn is planted on corn land of the previous year, the remainder on clover or timothy and clover sod. The amount of such sod broken up for corn each year is 30 to 50 acres. Corn is grown on the same land two or three years in succession. Each fall about 20 acres of corn land is put into wheat, the principal object of the wheat being to ''have a good place to sow timothy.'' In the spring about 35 acres more of the corn land is put into oats with clover. Clover is also sown on the wheat in the spring, care being taken to get clover seed on the vacant places where the corn shocks stood when the wheat and timothy were sown. Oats are also sown on any bare places that may appear in the clover field, and are cut with the clover for hay. Pure clover is left down two years, and mixed timothy and clover about four or five years. The following shows approximately the rotation practiced on this farm during two successive seasons:

Approximate rotation on the Chester farm.

1901.		1902	
Acres.	Crops.	Acres.	Crops.
100	Bluegrass pasture	100	Bluegrass pasture.
		90	Corn.
140	Corn..............................	30	Oats.
		20	Wheat.
		50	Corn.
100	Timothy and clover pasture......	50	Timothy and clover pasture.
50	Timothy and clover meadow	50	Timothy and clover pasture.
30	Oats	30	Clover.
20	Wheat..............................	20	Timothy and clover.

As there is no fixed order in which corn land is to be put into wheat and oats, and timothy and clover sod broken up for corn, it is not possible to represent this rotation by fixed boundaries. This is a rotation governed by mature judgment, based on the needs of the soil and the stock that are to consume the crops.

Corn. — This is the leading crop on this farm. Mr. Chester is a member of the Illinois Corn Breeders' Association, and in addition to growing corn to feed his stock he is improving his seed corn by careful selection, and in recent years has sold part of his corn crop for seed at a price that he thinks justifies him in breaking his rule not to sell his crops. He pays particular attention to the selection of corn with a view to increasing its feeding value; that is, increasing its nitrogen content. In this work he is cooperating with the Illinois experiment station.

Sod intended for corn is plowed in late fall or early winter, after the summer's heat is past. The manure is plowed under here. Most of the manure produced on the farm is drawn out directly from the barn as made and placed on sod to be broken up for corn. Some of it necessarily accumulates, owing to bad weather, pressure of work, etc.; this is drawn out in August. A manure spreader is used, one man getting out 6 to 8 loads a day on the average.

After filling a 100-ton silo, about 40 acres of corn are cut for fodder. The silo holds the corn of 10 to 12 acres. The average yield of corn for the past forty years on this farm is a little over 50 bushels per acre. This includes good and bad years alike. An ordinary good yield is considerably more than this.

Wheat and oats. — As previously stated, wheat is grown only to give a proper seed bed for timothy. The latter crop requires to be fall sown in this section. The wheat is used for feed. It is particularly valuable for pigs and poultry. The writer has fed wheat in large quantities for many years and fully agrees with this statement. The average yield of wheat for the past forty years is about 20 bushels per acre. This is evidently not typical wheat soil, and it is probable that the yield of straw is relatively larger than the yield of grain — a frequent occurrence on land too rich for wheat.

Oats are grown for feed only. The yield is from 25 to 85 bushels, averaging about 50 bushels.

Timothy and clover. — Timothy is not as much grown in this section as formerly, many farmers not sowing it at all; not that it is not appreciated, but it does not fit into the system of farming except where wheat is grown, and, as already stated, wheat is not entirely at home here. On this farm timothy is sown in the fall with wheat. In the spring clover is sown on the same land, thus giving a stand of clover in the bare places where the corn shocks stood. Clover is also sown with the oats. This clover is left down about two years and is cut for hay. The mixed timothy and clover is cut for hay two seasons, and then used for pasture two or three seasons.

The yield of hay is 1 to 3 tons per acre, averaging about 2 tons. With a liberal use of manure, an average of 3 tons is possible. About 50 acres of hay are cut each year. Corn always follows these crops, the sod being well manured before breaking.

Bluegrass. — This is used for permanent pasture. Bluegrass sod is seldom broken up, but the owner of this farm is of opinion that it accumulates so much fertility that it is best to crop it once in a while, so that occasionally a portion of the bluegrass sod is broken up and run through the usual rotation, another portion of the farm being set in bluegrass to take its place. The owner pastures bluegrass early in the season, but usually markets stock enough to give the grass comparative rest during summer, using it again in fall and winter. Last year cattle were kept on bluegrass till January.

Bluegrass seed is sown in February, in order to give it the benefit of freezing and thawing. This insures the covering of the seed.

Cattle. — Cattle are the first consideration on this farm, there seldom being less than 100 head. A herd of high-grade Shorthorns has gradually been changed into a herd of registered stock. By this means the value of the calves at weaning time has been raised from an average of $15 to an average of $100 a head. In recent years many cattle have been sold for breeding purposes. Steers are also bought and prepared for the market. Only good calves, yearlings, and two-year-olds are bought for this purpose. In buying, preference is given to young, light cattle in order that the flesh may be put on them on the farm. Mr. Chester prefers to buy a steer at 500 to 800 pounds, rather than at 1,000 pounds. When asked his method of handling calves for beef, he replied: "Never let them get hungry; but make their feed as cheap as possible till the fattening period, then stop cheapness." In the writer's opinion this sums up the principles involved in the economic production of prime beef so tersely that it deserves to be remembered. Before the fattening period begins the feed consists of pasture, cornstalks, clover hay, and silage. When the steer reaches about 1,000 pounds the fattening period begins. Several lots of one or two carloads each are fed off annually, a lot being on feed most of the time. The early winter feed of fattening steers consists of 20 to 40 pounds of silage, one-fourth to one-third bushel of corn, and all the clover hay they will eat. The corn is snapped (broken from the stalk) and is crushed — cob, husk, and grain all together. In summer, fattening steers are put on bluegrass and given about a peck of corn a day each, either crushed or in the form of fodder (stalk, leaves, and ears all together). A lot of steers were put on feed in March, 1902. When on full feed they were given 40 pounds of ensilage and a peck of corn daily, with all the clover hay they would eat. The gain during March and April averaged 3 pounds per head per day. At the end of April they were put on bluegrass, with a peck of corn a day, and fed thus till June. At the time of the writer's visit (June 30, 1902) the results had not been figured up, but Mr. Chester believed they were satisfactory. The usual length of the feeding period on this farm is from one hundred to one hundred and twenty days.

Many farmers fail to see where the profit lies in feeding steers. In the case mentioned, if we assume that silage is worth $1.50 a ton, corn 30 cents a bushel, and clover hay $8 a ton, the gain costs, approximately, 5 cents per pound. For the sake of comparison, let it be assumed that the fattened steer sells at the same price per pound he would have brought before fattening, and that this price is 4 cents per pound. The results for a 1,000-pound steer fed up to 1,300 pounds would then be as follows: Value of original carcass, $40; value of finished beef, $52. The gain here of 300 pounds adds $12 to the value of the steer. This gives a return of 4 cents a pound for the flesh added. If we assume the finished steer to be worth a cent a pound more than the stocker, we have $15 for the increased weight, plus $10 increased value on the original weight. Here the addition of 300 pounds in weight has added $25 to the value of the steer. The feeders, therefore, received 8⅓ cents a pound for the gain. If the difference in value per pound before and after fattening is 2 cents, we get $18 for the increased weight and $20 for the increased value of the original weight, or 12⅔ cents a pound for the gain. The question, therefore, is whether the value of the added flesh, plus the increased value of the original weight, is greater than the cost of gain. If it is, there is a profit. In the last case assumed, namely, where the values before and after fattening are 4 and 6 cents, respectively, a cost of 10 cents per pound of gain would still have left a profit of 2⅔ cents per pound of gain.

Hogs. — There are seldom fewer than 100 head of hogs on this farm. These are kept on pasture as much as possible, but are fed grain the year round, except when following cattle on feed. Hogs are sold at about 300 pounds. As soon as spring litters are old enough, the sows and pigs are put after cattle on pasture. As much of the growth of pigs as may be is made on pasture.

Horses. — Some 20 head of horses are kept, about twice as many as are needed for work, the idea being to make the profit on horses pay for the horse power used on the farm. As is the case with all other classes of stock, horses are both raised and bought. With the exception of a driving team, the horses are all high-grade draft animals, and are always sent to market in prime condition. No exercise is given while fitting for market except to lead them out three times a day for water.

When put on feed to be prepared for market, horses are given all the clover hay they will eat and a gradually increasing ration of corn and oats till they have all they will eat up clean. In season green corn is used instead of dry, the change being accomplished by substituting one ear of green corn for one of dry each day. Mares are sold off before they become old, unless they have exceptional breeding qualities.

Regarding the classes of horses for a farmer to handle, Mr. Chester believes the average farmer should stick to the draft breeds. If he needs road horses, it is better to buy them. Road horses must be trained before they are ready for market.

Sheep were formerly kept on this farm, but the owner dropped them because he had too many lines to look after.

A Dairy Farm

Only one strictly dairy farm, namely, that of T. E. Ellison, Allen County, Ind., was included in the list of farms visited by the writer in this investigation. This was due to lack of time to visit the more important dairy sections. The Ellison farm is located on rich alluvial soil in what was once the bed of a broad preglacial river. The soil is heavily charged with organic matter, and is drained by large, open ditches. As on the Chester farm, all the crops are fed and much additional feed is purchased. No regular rotation is practiced, the manure being placed where it seems most needed. A spreader is used, and the manure is drawn to the fields as it is produced. A little less than one-third of the arable land is in bluegrass pasture, the area of this pasture being about 105 acres. About 100 head of registered and grade Jersey cows and about 75 head of young stock are kept. No breeding stock is sold, the farm being run strictly as a dairy farm. The heifer calves are raised on skim milk, clover hay, and bluegrass pasture. About 100 fat hogs are sold annually. Six brood sows raise two litters a year each. The pigs are marketed at about 225 pounds. These pigs are fed buttermilk, rape, and corn. Sows with litters are fed all the rape they will consume, with a little grain and buttermilk. An acre of rape is sown in April near the pens, and furnishes two crops a year. It is cut and fed twice daily. These hogs were evidently in thrifty condition. This method of handling them is suggestive, as it is somewhat unusual. Thirteen head of work horses are kept on the place. The principal crop is corn, of which some 170 acres are grown annually. This crop is grown on the same land four or five years in succession, with manure applied as it seems to be needed. The average yield is about 60 bushels per acre. Five seasons the yield has been over 100 bushels. Corn land is plowed in spring, harrowed twice with a spring-toothed harrow, and rolled. After the corn is planted, a drag harrow is run over the field before the corn is up. This treatment frees the land from weeds and leaves it in good condition for the later cultivations. Forty to 50 acres of corn are cut for silage, filling a 650-ton silo. Ensiling begins about the middle of August. When the silo is full the remainder of the crop is shocked, husked, and all the stover shredded. Mr. Ellison is of opinion that this shredded fodder accounts for a larger share of the profits from his farm than any other one thing. Two varieties of corn are used, one earlier than the other, in order to prolong the cutting season.

Twenty acres of oats are grown and all cut for hay, the yield being 3 to 4 tons per acre. This crop is always grown on land previously in corn, and clover is sown with the oats. Formerly a few acres of wheat were grown, under the impression that clover could be more safely started with wheat for a nurse crop than with oats; but experience on this farm indicates that this is not the case. Wheat lodges badly on this soil, and its cultivation is to be abandoned in favor of oats.

A first cutting of 20 acres of clover and a second cutting of 15 acres produced 62 large loads of hay, probably considerably over a ton each. Clover sod is plowed up for corn at the end of the second year.

Mr. Ellison has been experimenting with alfalfa recently, having sown 10 or 12 acres on April 16, 1901, using 20 pounds of alfalfa and 1 bushel of oats per acre. This crop yielded three cuttings the same year, the first, cut June 20, being mostly oats; the second, cut August 1, mostly alfalfa; and the third, cut September 20, all alfalfa. These three cuttings combined gave over 4 tons per acre. At the time of the writer's visit (July 4, 1902), the crop had been cut once and was then 6 inches high, with a perfect stand, and very thrifty. Mr. Ellison states in a recent letter that his farmer considers alfalfa equivalent in feeding value to bran, and that he will sow 40 acres of it next spring. Soy beans have been tried on this farm but did not succeed. A few acres of potatoes are grown for market. Two acres grown last year yielded over 700 bushels per acre.

Some 50 to 60 tons of bran and gluten meal are fed annually on this farm, in addition to all crops grown, except potatoes, and the resulting manure is distributed where most needed. It is safe to say that this soil will not soon wear out with this treatment.

The owner of this farm also conducts a dairy business in a neighboring city, where he has an extensive trade in butter, ice cream, and pasteurized cream and milk. He therefore has excellent facilities for marketing the principal product of his farm — milk. The net profits from the farm last year were over $8,000.

A Sheep Farm

The farm of Joseph E. Wing, of Champaign County, Ohio, the well-known agricultural writer, is an excellent example of a special type of live-stock farming. It is noted both for its sheep and for its crops of alfalfa. Mr. Wing learned the value of alfalfa while ranching in Utah. Having returned to his native State, in 1890 he sowed one-third acre of this crop. Finding it successful, he gradually extended the area until he now has 100 acres of excellent alfalfa, from which he cuts three crops of hay a year. He regards it as the most profitable crop he grows. The soil of this farm is for the most part the ordinary upland glacial soil of that section, part of it being decidedly gravelly. It is not naturally a strong soil, but it has been demonstrated that it will produce abundant crops when intelligently managed. Mr. Wing asserts that manure is absolutely essential to profitable farming on this soil. Although located in a wheat-growing section, no wheat is grown on this farm. The owner states that he never made any money farming till he abandoned wheat and timothy. He follows no particular rotation, but suggests the following as a feasible one for his section: Alfalfa four years, corn one year, and beardless barley one year. The barley is used as a nurse crop for newly seeded alfalfa, but in case chinch bugs are troublesome he would dispense with the barley and sow the alfalfa alone. Beardless barley yields 30 to 60 bushels per acre in the region in question. Being an early crop, it can be removed in time to allow the alfalfa to make considerable growth the first season. It will be remembered that alfalfa was seeded successfully with oats on the Ellison farm, previously described.

The three crops in the rotation suggested above are the only crops grown on the Wing farm. Regarding the cost of labor, Mr. Wing states that ten years ago, with 200 acres, $200 was expended for labor in addition to the labor of the owner. The gross sales from the farm at that time were about $700 a year. At the present time, with 260 acres, the annual labor bill is $1,500, while the net profits are more than $2,500.

Alfalfa. — This is the leading crop on this farm. It is sown with barley (beardless) on land previously in corn. To insure a stand the land should be well manured for the previous corn crop, but land can be too rich for it. Mr. Wing states that it did rather poorly on old garden soil. When once established it is left down four or five years. He has occasionally plowed up alfalfa fields because they were invaded by bluegrass. In ten years he has plowed up 75 acres, always following with corn. In all cases the yield of corn is greatly increased, sometimes to double the ordinary crop. This accords fully with the experience of farmers in the Pacific States, where the yield of wheat after alfalfa is always highly satisfactory. As stated, alfalfa yields three cuttings a year. A first cutting from 80 acres this season produced about 135 tons of hay. At the time of the writer's visit (July 9, 1902) the second cutting had just begun.

Mr. Wing uses alfalfa both for hay and for pasture. Many alfalfa growers do not use this crop for pasture on account of the fact that when so used for cattle or sheep there is danger from bloat. In order to avoid this, Mr. Wing suggests that for pasture alfalfa should be sown with brome grass, and that the pasture be divided into four lots. The number of stock pastured should be small enough so that when turned from one lot to another there should still be abundant feed in the lot vacated, as stock should not go into a new lot in a half-fed condition. At the time they are turned into a new lot the alfalfa should be fairly mature. The only cattle lost from bloat were on immature alfalfa. Only two sheep were lost from bloat this year. Alfalfa grown on an old, richly manured strawberry bed gave rise to bloat oftener than that grown on other land. In this connection, it is pertinent to remark that on a large cattle farm in Nebraska a few years since, it was noticed that green corn grown on an old feed lot produced so much bloat that its feeding in the green state was abandoned.

Corn. — About 50 acres of corn a year are grown, following either corn or alfalfa. There is a liberal use of manure for this crop. In 1902 the corn on this farm was markedly superior to other corn in that section. The owner does not attempt to grow all the corn he needs, finding it more profitable to grow alfalfa and buy corn. He says he can always depend on finding others who grow corn to sell. The amount purchased varies from 1,000 to 4,000 bushels a year. This is fed mostly to Western lambs. He replants corn with pumpkins, which he uses as winter feed for breeding ewes.

Pasture. — Bluegrass is not at its best in this section, though it does fairly well; but Mr. Wing's experience indicates that an acre of alfalfa and brome grass will carry six times as much stock as an acre of bluegrass, and do it better. He is particularly favorable to brome grass in pasture mixtures, though he says it will not stand hard usage as well as bluegrass.

During the season of 1902 a field of 12 acres of alfalfa, brome grass, and bluegrass carried 30 head of steers and 140 sheep from May 1 to June 15. On July 9 this pasture was far from bare, though it still carried a considerable flock of sheep.

Sheep. — In addition to a herd of about 75 registered Dorsets, 700 to 1,000 Western range lambs are fed. When put on feed these lambs average about 40 to 55 pounds. They are fed four months, during which time their weight increases from 50 to 80 per cent. In exceptional cases 100 per cent increase has been made in this time. The lambs are fed alfalfa hay and corn, but they are never given quite as much corn as they will eat, the amount fed being about 2½ bushels a day to 100 head. A full feed of alfalfa is given, amounting to about 2 pounds per head per day. The lambs are kept in a single large barn, with no partitions, but with ample ventilation, and "there is a place for every lamb at the first table." The feed is given in racks. . . . The lambs are let out for half an hour twice a day while the feed is put in the racks, but are kept in the barn at other times to save the manure. "When lambs are on feed give them all the air they can get, and never wake them up when they are asleep." This is a maxim which it has been found advantageous to follow.

Manure. — Manure is drawn out in winter and spring, usually for corn. What is left is used as a thin top dressing for meadows and pastures.

Conclusion

The study commenced in this paper will be continued, and publications showing the methods of management pursued on different types of farms in all the principal agricultural sections of the country are under consideration.

The writer is aware that the subject is broad and complex, and that much work must be done before it can be covered in a satisfactory manner. Any suggestions that will tend to increase the value of the series of articles proposed will be thankfully received.

A Soil Culture Manual, 1902

From H. W. Campbell, *Campbell's 1902 Soil Culture Manual* (Holdrege, Nebr., 1902), pp. 5–7, 12, 22–23, 29–30, 46–47.

Introduction

Having been convinced by years of constant labor in the field, and practical results attained by soil culture experiments, that the average farm crops throughout the west are not what they might be if proper cultivation was applied; and realizing what it would signify to the great Semi-Arid Belt if every farmer in that section could grasp the fundamental principles involved in the science of soil culture, which are really plain and simple, and put them into practical use, I have been prompted to prepare the matter contained in these pages.

I desire, if it may be possible for me to do so, to in some measure supply the rapidly growing demand for a broader and more comprehensive knowledge of soil culture and the storage and conservation of the available soil waters for the increase of crops, and the greater profit thereby to the farmer; also to aid and encourage public sentiment in favor of farm life and ideal farm homes.

I believe one of the important sentiments as respects home life on the farm is the abolishment of the "Bonanza" farm idea. The small farmer has given character to agriculture everywhere and at all times. He cultivates a smaller area, produces a greater diversity of crops and practices a more intensive system of cultivation. His farm is his home, which he wishes constantly to improve by the growing of trees, fruit, flowers and shrubs. He has a better conception of economy; his wife and children are happier and better contented; in short, it is upon the comparatively small farms that many a bright young man and woman have found opportunities to develop a capacity for the higher and nobler duties and service of life.

Make the farm as comfortable and attractive as possible, and the children will love it as their home, and will feel a deeper respect for their parents, and will more fully appreciate nature in all her fruitfulness and glory.

The "Bonanza," or large scale system of farming, reverses all this; for in that case the home is not a home, but merely a place where the family stay. It is seldom beautified by trees or flowers; it is unattractive, and the very atmosphere of such a place will depress the mind of the true agriculturalist. Such a system is always barren of what is pleasing to the eye, and to the mind, and is generally a system of soil butchery.

Under the "Bonanza" system, two acres are required to do less than one should do, and, as a rule, everything is in a state of congestion; strenuous activity abounds with, generally, unsatisfactory results. Little time is given to moral, mental, or physical culture, to the school or the church, or the growth of religious sentiment in the community, and to the broader educational work, such as the "Farmers' Institute;" and the general effect of this stunted condition is to retard the development and improvement of agriculture and the people who follow it.

It is not intended to lay down in this volume a code of imperative rules to govern the farmer in every act of soil culture, but rather by explanatory illustrations to present as clearly and plainly as possible the fundamental principles which govern the movement of moisture in the soil, the development of plant life, and the quantity and quality of the crop. After these general principles have been grasped and understood, the necessary labor in detail required to make agriculture profitable becomes clear and easy to anyone who will give these pages a careful perusal.

There cannot be laid down any rule by which to be guided in the cultivation of the soil under all conditions. Soil that is too wet, naturally, must be drained, while soil that is too dry by reason of insufficient rainfall, or by reason of the fact that the rainfall in any section is not distributed seasonably, is unfavorable to the production of any crops, but in the great semi-arid area of our western country we believe a general rule may be applied, and if followed diligently the resulting storage and conservation of the natural rainfall in the soil will produce, in average years, as good crops of cereals, and of all the vegetables that are commonly grown, as can be produced in the humid central portions of the United States.

Storage and conservation of the rain waters is the basis of all this fruitful production. Has the reader not observed instances where a heavy snow drift has, by reason of some obstruction in the wind's course, lodged in a field, and where the snow was drifted the crop in the following summer was better? The usual conclusion has been that the snow drift protected the grain sown in the soil like a blanket, and the greater yield the following season was attributed to such protection; but this is an error. The reason of a greater crop on the ground so covered with the snow was that the snow melted gradually in the spring time and percolated into the soil at a much greater depth, and was stored, as in a reservoir, and, later, when the hot period and drought of summer came, supplied the roots of the plants with moisture and kept the plants growing when the plants in other parts of the field not so supplied were checked, and perhaps withered.

By that almost unexplainable movement of the moisture in the soil upwards towards the surface, under a natural law which is called capillary attraction, the roots of the growing plants on the spot where the snow had drifted were supplied from the reservoir of water below, which had come down into the lower strata of the soil as the snow in the drift had melted.

We have endeavored to show that by storage and conservation of the rain waters in this way, so as to save them for plant nourishment and growth in the summer period, like results and yields may be obtained on large fields, as have been observed on small patches of ground that happened to be covered by snow drifts. It follows, then, that the greater amount of water we can store in the soil previous to the planting of the crops, as well as during their growth, and the greater care we use in the cultivation of the surface of the ground, so as to retain and economize the moisture so conserved, the greater must be the yield at harvest time.

In connection with this fact there is another of no less importance, viz: the soil should be prepared as perfectly as possible to insure a prolific growth of roots. It is not uncommon that a single hour's extreme condition of the soil, as respects rapid evaporation, will reduce the crop one-half. If we can store and conserve in the soil a sufficient quantity of the natural rain waters and make them available during the growing season, and have coupled with the moisture a sufficient growth of roots to sustain and nourish the plants, a good crop is sure to be realized.

We are well aware it is difficult to explain what is the exactly proper physical condition of the soil for the best results in growing crops. It is important to learn how to apply the most economical mechanical work to secure such results. There are many little things and minor points to be done and observed that have a direct influence and effect in securing this condition, and many more that bear on the question as to how to maintain this good condition of the soil during the growing season, that have not been considered in the past, but which are vital and necessary to the best possible crop yields.

With these considerations fully in mind, we have tried, in the following pages, to be clear in our statements and illustrations respecting all these little points and duties we owe to the cultivation of the soil, and to make plain to the reader an explanation of our past work and the results of our years of experience and experiments in the semi-arid west, a section which at a time, not far distant, we believe will be made by our system of soil culture, to yield an abundance, and will be the abode of millions of new settlers who will found homes there that shall be blessed with peace and plenty.

Plowing

In outlining our general suggestions for securing the best possible crop results throughout this great plains country, we must of course begin with the preparation of the ground. Owing to the fact that in the settled portions the average farmer has already a sufficient area of ground under cultivation, we will start out with the preparation of ground that has been in crop the previous year. The first and all important work is the double discing of this ground in early spring, beginning as soon as the frost is out a fair depth and the surface sufficiently dry to allow of discing without having the soil adhere to the disc too much. It is not uncommon to see farmers double disc by first going over the ground one way and then cross disc it. This results in a series of ridges and trenches, leaving the surface very uneven. The trenches exposing solid soil to the surface allow of much evaporation. The proper manner of double discing is to lap half, which leaves the surface smooth and thoroughly pulverized. In the lapping of the half of the disc the last time over, the last discs revolve at right angles with the discs that precede. . . .

All these facts in connection with the movement of moisture in the soil, under different conditions of the soil, as indicated in the experiments noted and the teachings of the most eminent students of soil physics, give us the valuable lesson that the packing of the subsoil, or what may be properly termed the root-bed, aids us in these important points; increasing the water holding capacity of the soil facilitates the movement of the water from below up to this point when it is needed, is conducive to a much greater development of root growth; and still further, and quite as important, enables us to utilize the entire soil, having no waste ground caused by a loose or porous condition of the soil. . . .

This is so important that it may be stated again plainly, so that no reader may misunderstand. The process of packing the under portion of furrow or plowed ground creates three conditions to aid in carrying the growing crop over long dry periods, namely:

1. More water in the soil.
2. A stronger capillary movement of water.
3. More prolific growth of roots.

Don't pack the surface; it increases the loss of moisture by evaporation.

Less seed is needed in packed soil than in loose soil for the same crop result.

Pack the lower portion of your plowing the same day you plow, to save the moisture. . . .

Winter wheat will not winter-kill in firmed, moist soil, while in loose soil it frequently thins out or kills out entirely.

A fine, firm root bed, with a loose surface or mulch, is a condition that will withstand the extreme dry periods longest without any injury to the plant.

Study well the question of thoroughly pulverizing and packing the lower portion of the plowing; a full understanding of its importance means many dollars, because it means a larger crop result.

Sub-surface packing increases the moisture in the lower portion of the plowed ground and induces decomposition of the weeds, stubble, or manures that have been turned under, thereby adding humus, the all important soil ingredient for rapid plant growth, as well as enabling the plant to withstand drought.

If you would get your soil to a condition of fineness and firmness, do all your work to that end when the soil is just slightly moist, for it then plows better, packs better, and cultivates better. Do not go to work on plowed ground that is dried to the bottom, whether plowed in good condition or not, and expect in any way to get the lower portion of the furrow in good condition. You may improve it. The closer you keep to the plow the better you can pack the under portion.

As to Time of Cultivation

The proper time for cultivating a field is one that cannot be fixed without much thought, observation, and judgment by the farmer, especially if he would get the best results. Always cultivate immediately, or as soon after a rain as conditions will permit you on the field, and the soil is sufficiently dried so that it will not adhere to the cultivator teeth, or tools used. We do not mean by this that the soil should be absolutely dry on the surface. It is an error to wait for that time, for the moment the surface is apparently dry the crust begins to form. It is desirable to catch the ground just before this time when all the soil is simply moist and then there is a free and ready separation of all particles. In this condition the cultivator runs the easiest, the mulch made the finest and lies up light and loose. If the soil is a little too wet it settles, and not unfrequently forms absolute and perfect connection with the firm soil below, steadily carrying moisture to the surface. If too dry the cultivator produces an imperfect mulch that gives us but little protection.

Another and very important idea is that every moment's delay after the soil reaches the proper condition causes you to lose water very fast. It is at the rate of a quart or over per square foot per day providing it is clear sunny weather, and even more in case of heavy south winds. The more intense the heat the more frequent is it necessary to cultivate. A very good rule is to watch the condition of the firm soil just beneath the loose mulch or cultivated portion, and whenever the surface of this firm soil begins to show dryness it is high time to commence cultivating again. If the field is left too long during the extreme dry period the surface of the solid soil beneath the mulch will begin to form a crust, practically the same as is shown on the surface of the soil when uncultivated after a rain. . . . This is the result of the soil composing our mulch reaching a high degree of heat, causing the moisture from the surface of the solid soil to form into vapor and pass up through the mulch. The forming of a crust under these conditions, as is also true on the surface, is largely the result of the salts and alkalies that are in a soluble condition, while the soil below is wet. As the moisture from the surface begins to evaporate it leaves these chemicals deposited in the little spaces between the soil particles practically cementing them together. As the process goes on, the moisture line lowering, the surface becoming dry an eighth, quarter, or half inch, possibly an inch in depth and is filled with these chemicals which is quite detrimental in the free circulation of air.

Experience with an Orchard

We cannot impress this point more fully upon your mind than by relating our experience with the orchard at the Pomeroy Farm during the season of 1901. We began our harvest just as the extreme hot weather and high winds from the south set in. About seven days before commencing harvest we had cultivated the orchard with the Acme harrow. Our mulch was a good depth and the moisture condition perfect just beneath it. The high winds and extreme heat delayed us materially in our harvest, and sixteen days had elapsed before we were able to reach the orchard again, as help was scarce and our grain shelling badly from the fact we could not get at it. We attempted the cultivation on the 17th day after the last cultivation with the Acme harrow, but the nine days of excessive heat had so heated the mulch as to draw the moisture from the solid soil beneath until a crust of fully half an inch had formed. The crust had become very hard in this time and its resistance was so great the Acme could not break it. At about this time, or within a day or two, we noticed the color of the leaves on our trees began to change to a lighter cast. Not until noticing this did we give special attention to the soil condition, but noting this crust under the mulch we immediately ordered one-half the orchard double disced with instructions to cut a full inch and a half deeper and awaited results. About the fourth day there was a perceptible change in the color of the leaves on the portion disced, and on the seventh day the difference was perceptible to any one. The leaves again took on their bright green glossy appearance, and new leaves coming out then we ordered the balance double disced. We had nearly three weeks of extreme heat after this, and yet during all of that time the trees were pushing out new leaves, and at the close of the dry period were to all appearance in as healthy and thrifty condition as at any time during the entire growing season. The changing of the color of the leaves in this way was not due to a lack of water at the roots, but simply the lack of air. . . .

It is by the result of this wonderful movement that we are able to go well nigh the western limit of the great prairies of the semi-arid west and there store the rainfall deeply in the soil and then have it by this power return upward through the pores of the soil to feed the plant during the long dry periods, getting large yields in lieu of the oft-repeated failure of the past. When these great points are understood, together with the further fact that the loosening and drying of surface soil of a sufficient depth will practically check any further upward movement, we have a most wonderful condition. By the proper preparation of our soil, that is, the fining and firming of the portion necessary for the root bed, experience has demonstrated that we do increase the power of capillary attraction or the more rapid movement of the moisture from below up. In this soil condition we have one most favorable to the free and rapid development of root growth. Now, if we can comprehend, or be made to understand just how many stalks of corn, wheat, barley, or potatoes can be supplied by this movement to its full demand per square foot or square yard of surface soil, then with our blanket of loose soil spread over the surface to prevent any loss of this moisture so that the roots can take it all in, we have reached a condition that is most wonderful. These facts, when fully comprehended, must and will make of this great semi-arid belt the best and most desirable farming country we have in the United States.

Grape-Growing, 1902

From George C. Husmann, "Grape, Raisin, and Wine Production in the United States," U.S. Department of Agriculture, *Yearbook*, 1902, pp. 407–20.

Early History

When America was discovered the wild vine was so prominent a feature of the vegetation that the name Vineland was more than once applied to the country. Considerable wine was produced from a native grape in Florida as early as 1564. The London Company planted vineyards in Virginia prior to 1620, and many succeeding attempts at grape growing were made by William Penn and by German and Swiss settlers. Of more recent attempts to cultivate the vine on the Atlantic coast, the first were confined to European varieties, and were not successful. The

Mission Fathers in California were the first to successfully grow the European grape in the United States. They grew grapes at the missions for their own use only, the work being principally done by Indians. They had but one variety, which is still largely grown, and is known by the name of Mission. It is first heard of as introduced into Mexico in 1520. Chronologically, it was brought to the California missions, as follows: San Diego, 1769; San Gabriel, 1771; Los Angeles, 1781; and Santa Barbara, 1786. The Mission vine planted at Montecito, Cal., in 1795, was exhibited at the Centennial Exposition in Philadelphia. It was 18 inches in diameter, and in one season had produced over 5 tons of grapes. From the missions, the viticultural pioneers received their inspiration as well as their start of cuttings.

New Era in Grape Growing

Mr. John Adlum made the first really successful efforts at grape growing on the Atlantic coast. In 1820 he planted a vineyard near Georgetown, D.C., consisting mostly of native vines. His introduction of the Catawba variety into general cultivation was the beginning of a "new era in grape history." In a letter written by him to Nicholas Longworth in 1825, he says that "in bringing this grape into public notice I have rendered my country a greater service than I would have done had I paid the National debt." Since its first introduction, grape culture has gradually increased, and interest in it has become general throughout the land. Such rapid progress was made that in 1830 Mr. W. R. Prince, in his treatise on the vine, enumerates 88 varieties of American vines. To-day there are at least 1,000.

Mr. Ephraim Wales Bull is deserving of lasting gratitude for raising from seed and giving to the world the Concord grape, destined to become the most widely known, most generally planted, and, for all purposes, the best American grape yet introduced. Only a few miles from Concord, Mass., stands Bull's cottage, in the dooryard of which still grows the first Concord vine, from which stock the unnumbered millions of vines of this variety came. On one side hangs a square oak board on which these words are artistically burned:

I looked about to see what I could find among our wildings. The next thing to do was to find the best and earliest grape for seed. This I found in an accidental seedling at the foot of the hill. The crop was abundant, ripe in August, and of very good quality for a wild grape. I sowed the seed in autumn of 1843; among them the Concord was the only one worth saving. — EPHRAIM WALES BULL.

The Concord is included in nearly every collection where American vines are planted. To illustrate what a boon it has proved to be, it need only be stated that the Chautauqua grape belt, on Lake Erie, in 1900, produced 192 million pounds of grapes, at least nine-tenths of which were Concords. Mr. George Husmann, the father of the writer, in 1865, said: "One-third acre of Concord, planted five years ago, has produced me, in fruit, wine, layers, and plants, the round sum of $10,000 during that time."

In the United States there are two distinct grape-producing sections, one east of the Rocky Mountains, where the American varieties are largely and profitably grown, the other in California, where the Vinifera varieties have found a congenial home. These sections differ not only in their products, soils, and climate, but also in their methods of pruning, culture, gathering, working, and marketing of crops, so that only those familiar with both sections are able to make a just comparison.

Beginning of a Commercial Industry

The decade closing the first half of the last century witnessed the birth of commercial grape culture in the United States, leading up to the making of choice wines from American grapes. The manufacture of sparkling wine and unfermented grape juice has been developed in the Eastern States, while the Pacific coast has entered into direct competition with the choicest European wines, and has captured the raisin market of this country. The efforts of Longworth and others at Cincinnati in grape growing and wine making were followed by many in other States, especially in New York, Missouri, Virginia, Indiana, Illinois, Kentucky, Pennsylvania, the Carolinas, and Michigan. In California, where the Mission had so far been the only variety cultivated, introductions of the choicest European varieties soon followed. In 1850 the country produced almost 250,000 gallons of wine. In 1860 the product had reached over 1½ million gallons, and all the States and Territories except four were growing grapes. The census of 1860 shows California, New York, and Ohio as the three leading wine-producing States. From 1860 to 1875 rapid progress was made. In 1870 Missouri produced more than any other State, except California. With this exception, California, New York, and Ohio have taken the lead. In 1900 their combined output was 22,404,085 gallons of wine out of a total of 23,425,567 gallons for the whole country. From 1875 on, quite a decline occurred, especially in Missouri, owing to black-rot and other diseases.

To sum up, American wines and brandies have taken high honors at all important expositions, including that at Paris in 1900, and they are rapidly finding their way into all the principal markets of the world.

Grape Culture

Soil, Location, and Site

Soil, location, and site will differ greatly with the object in view. Some varieties of grapes may be grown on almost any soil. Usually those lands are selected that can be prepared and planted with the least labor, that are the easiest to cultivate, and which produce the largest crops. Quality and quantity, however, in most cases do not go hand in hand. The best soils are a gently sloping, well-drained calcareous loam, of sufficient depth, with porous subsoil; gravel or small stones in a soil are not a detriment. Some prefer a sandy soil with a gravelly substratum. The place should have a good water supply, be of easy access to market, and free from late spring frosts. The cellar or packing house should be centrally located on the place, and if possible so that the grapes can be hauled down grade, or at least on a level. For this purpose a hillside into which a cellar can be excavated, facing so that each story can be easily approached by wagon, is to be preferred.

Preparing the Soil

The soil should be well prepared. It should be cleared of large stones, stumps, and other obstructions, and not only be thoroughly and deeply plowed, but subsoiled as well. If it be virgin soil it will be of benefit to raise a crop of grain on it the season previous to planting, as this gives a better opportunity to put it in good shape. Any wet spots should be carefully drained. After being plowed and subsoiled it should be thoroughly harrowed and the clods crushed with drag or roller.

Manures and Fertilizers

On partially exhausted or poor soils such manures and fertilizers should be applied as will give them those substances in which they are deficient. Broadly speaking, if the soil lacks in fruit-producing qualities, potash is needed; if more wood growth is desired, nitrogenous fertilizers should be supplied.

Choice of Varieties to Plant

As to varieties of grapes to plant, each locality must in a measure determine this for itself, grape growing being perhaps more dependent on selection of varieties with reference to soil, climate, location, and other conditions than any other fruit industry. The writer has seen such radically different results with the same varieties, planted in vineyards only a short distance apart, that it would hardly seem possible they were the fruit from the same variety.

It must first be decided whether to grow raisin, table, or wine grapes. Usually it will be well to select such varieties as have proved valuable for such purposes in the immediate vicinity. Should a grower embark in an entirely new district, where grape growing has not been tried, he will have an opportunity for displaying good judgment, and perhaps gain the distinction of becoming a pathfinder for those who follow in his lead, or perhaps, like Mr. Bull with his Concord, will raise a new variety adapted to the locality.

The American varieties most generally grown are Concord, Catawba, Moore *Early*, Missouri *Riesling*, Elvira, Isabella, Delaware, Norton, Niagara, Herbemont, Lenoir, Ives, Clinton, and Eumelan; the Vinifera varieties are Zinfandel, Valdepenas, Petit Sirah, Beclan, Mataro, Petit Pinot, Carignan, Mission, Chablis, Semillon, Sauvignon Vert, Green Hungarian, Berger, Thompson *Seedless*, Alexandria (*Muscat of*), Sultana, Feher Zagos, Flame Tokay, Emperor, and Cornichon.

Planting, Plowing, and Cultivating

Throughout the Eastern States vineyards are usually planted in rows 8 feet apart, with the vines 8 to 10, even 12, feet apart in the rows. A plain trellis of posts, 24 by 30 feet apart, with two parallel wires, the first 18 to 20 inches from the ground and the second 36 inches, is mostly used, but in some instances a grower uses three wires. Of late years many use the Munson trellis or a modification of it. In California the usual method has been to plant 7 feet apart each way, no trellis but simply stakes being used. This enables growers to plow and cultivate lengthwise and crosswise. There is a tendency to plant farther apart, some planting 8 by 8, others 6 by 10, and others 9 by 9 and 8 by 10. The writer prefers to plant 6 by 10 in most localities. This divides the distance in such a manner as to make the plowing, cultivation, etc., better, easier, and cheaper. The vineyards are all plowed twice. In the first plowing the soil is thrown away from the vines, and in the second it is thrown up to them again. The vineyards are cultivated frequently early in the season. In the Eastern States too late cultivation, it is claimed, keeps the vines growing too late in the season, causing much unnecessary growth of wood, which does not ripen and weakens the vine. In California cultivation is abandoned after the spring rains are over.

Pruning and Grafting

So many different methods of pruning and grafting are practiced that the details of them can not be discussed in this paper. In the Eastern States the Kniffin system or some modification of it is mostly used. However, this varies greatly. In California two principal methods are practiced, commonly called cane and spur pruning. All of the systems have one underlying principle. As the grape bears its fruit mainly on shoots on the wood of the previous year's growth, the pruning should be so as to renew the wood at a given point from year to year, thereby regulating its production and keeping the plant thoroughly shaped and under constant control. With a thorough knowledge of the nature of the vine nothing is easier than to prune it correctly. Perhaps the nature of no fruit-bearing plant is so poorly understood by the average horticulturist as the vine. There are many who easily learn to prune fruit trees who fail to master the vine, and the same statement is equally true of grafting.

Insects and Diseases

In many of the Eastern States, the black-rot, anthracnose, and mildew have wrought such serious damage that many vineyards have been abandoned. In some sections the grape rootworm and the thrips have been very destructive. In California the Phylloxera and the Anaheim disease have worked very serious and extensive injury, and it will require systematic experiments and earnest work and study to cope with them.

Picking, Marketing, and Storing Grapes

In picking, the grapes are placed either in boxes or trays. Those selling in baskets accept the price of the day as satisfactory or send to commission houses to sell on commission; others who are fortunate enough to have built up a reputation sell on direct orders at fixed prices. Those disposing of the product in bulk sell the entire crop at a stipulated price per ton, delivered at the wineries or aboard cars, and receive their settlement after the last of the grapes have been delivered. Quite a few sell their crops on the vines at so much an acre, or a stipulated sum for the entire crop, the buyer in such instances doing all the work, picking, hauling, etc., and assuming all risks.

The methods of picking and packing practiced in the leading table-grape districts of the country are as follows: Grapes are picked in trays, all the stems being placed upward; the grapes are then allowed to wilt at least forty-eight hours, but are often stored away in the trays in cool, dry rooms, frequently as long as two months, and in extreme cases even longer. From these trays the grapes are carefully picked over, all decayed and inferior berries being removed; they are then packed in 4-pound baskets for shipment. In some of the less up-to-date sections, larger-sized baskets are still used. Some of the buyers have their own packing houses, but as a general rule each grower does his own packing, the baskets and labels being furnished by the buyer. In order to insure honesty and good quality, each packer receives his number, which goes on every basket furnished by him. The baskets are loaded into the cars and sent directly to the principal markets.

Late storage is practiced with good success. A leading packer at Hammondsport, N.Y., informed the writer that in 1901 he shipped his one hundred and seventy-fifth and last car the 6th of May. The different varieties are stored in separate houses. The houses are cooled by means of ventilating doors on the ground floor, around the sides and at the ends of the buildings, and also by ventilators with strong heating lamps in them overhead. The temperature is constantly watched by means of electric thermometers, and whenever there is a cool spell, either day or night, the doors and ventilators are opened, and if necessary the lamps are lighted to create a draft. In this way the temperature is often lowered as much as 10 degrees in an hour. In 1845 the first shipment of a crop of grapes (consisting of 50 pounds) was made from the Hammondsport district to New York City by way of the New York and Erie Canal. The grapes sold well, and the next year the grower shipped 300 pounds. Now, about 30,000 tons are grown in the same district, 15,000 tons of which are shipped to the different markets, and 15,000 tons converted into wine.

Cost and Returns From an Acre of Vineyard

The cost of an acre of vineyard varies considerably, owing mainly to differences in the character and price of the land. A fair average estimate would be about $200 an acre. The average annual returns are from $125 to $500 an acre, while the annual cost of maintenance, including interest on capital invested, is from $40 to $75. The yield in tons, the number of gallons of wine per ton, and the quality of the grapes and wine vary greatly with the methods pursued, the soil, climate, locality, season, and varieties. In some seasons the quality is superior, while in others the quantity is heavy. Usually the heavier the crop the poorer the quality, and vice versa.

THE RAISIN INDUSTRY

Origin and Growth

Almost all the raisins of the United States are produced in California. In fact, so few are grown outside of the State that it can be called a California industry. Few branches of horticultural industry in this country have so completely captured the home market as this one.

The introduction of raisin grapes was really only a part of the introduction of choicer varieties of Viniferas into California. In 1851 Col. Agoston Harazthy grew Muscatels from the seed of Malaga raisins. On March 25, 1852, he imported the Alexandria (*Muscat of*), and on September 27, 1861, the Gordo Blanco and Sultana from Spain and the White and Red Corinth from the Crimea. He was the first to introduce raisin varieties into the State. Another importation of Alexandria (*Muscat of*) was made by A. Delmas in 1855 and planted at San Jose, Cal. G. G. Briggs, of Davisville, imported the Muscatels from Spain, while R. G. Blowers, of Woodland, started the raisin vineyard of Gordo Blanco with cuttings received from Colonel Harazthy. These were the first two successful raisin vineyards in the State. Both of these vineyards produced raisins as early as 1867, but it was not until 1873 that their raisin crops cut any figure in the market, when they amounted to nearly 6,000 boxes. In the fall of 1873, 25 acres of Alexandria (*Muscat of*) were planted in the Eisen vineyards, near Fresno. In 1876 and 1877 T. C. White planted the Raisina vineyard with Gordo Blancos, and in 1877 and 1878 Miss M. F. Austin planted the same variety at the Hedge Row vineyards. Col. William Forsyth interested himself in raisin growing in 1882. From that time on raisin vineyards multiplied so rapidly near Fresno that in 1887 raisin production was recognized to be the leading industry of that neighborhood. In 1873 John North planted Alexandria (*Muscat of*) at Riverside, and three years later raisin-grape growing had become general there. R. G. Clark planted the first Muscats in El Cajon Valley in 1873, but most of the vineyards of that district were not planted until 1884 to 1886. In Orange County, McPherson Brothers made their first plantings in the seventies near McPherson. The industry grew so that Robert McPherson, the largest grower, became at one time not only the largest packer and dealer in the district, but the largest in the State.

Many changes have occurred since the establishment of the raisin industry in Orange County, and now Fresno has become the center, the conditions there being exceptionally well suited to the growing and the curing of raisins. The raisin-producing section comprises ten counties — Fresno, Kern, Kings, Madera, Merced, Orange, San Bernardino, San Diego, Tulare, and Yolo. The profits from an acre differ materially, varying from $50 to $500, a fair average being from $125 to $150. It takes from 3 to 4 pounds of grapes to make 1 pound of raisins. The product of about 65,000 acres is at present converted into raisins, it being desired to cure only enough to meet the demand. The demand for the last five years has been about 80 million pounds, or only 1 pound per capita for the United States.

Cultural Conditions

In the raisin-producing section of California the country is so level naturally that not much leveling is necessary. The soil varies considerably, the deep gray alluvial bottom land being considered the best for Muscatel grapes. The pruning, planting, and cultivating of a raisin vineyard is much the same as in other California vineyards.

Crops can be grown without irrigation, but it is practiced because it increases the size of the fruit, and therefore increases the yield. Two irrigations are necessary, one early in the summer and another when the berries begin to ripen. Before irrigation was so extensively practiced, water was usually found at a depth of about 18 feet; now much trouble is experienced in some localities on account of the lands becoming water-logged. In the hottest time of the summer the thermometer has stood as high as 114° F. in the shade for a day or two at a time. The highest average is about 90° F., while the average in July and August is about 85° F. in the shade. The nights are always much cooler than the days. The coldest weather in winter is 18° F. above zero. The summers are rainless and the nights are so free from dew or moisture that a piece of tissue paper after lying out all night is crisp and stiff the next morning, without a particle of moisture showing. The rainfall averages 13 inches. The principal rains occur in January and February, with some showers in October. Frequently it rains enough in November to cause considerable damage to partially dried raisins and grapes. It is then that the Japanese laborers watch the predictions of the Weather Bureau, and when rain is indicated ask as high as 50 and 75 cents an hour for turning and covering the trays of raisins that are out in the vineyards. So familiar has this practice become that the school children who are large enough get excused from school for the work. In fact, the labor question is one of the most serious problems the growers have to contend with. The Chinese and Japanese laborers (especially the Japanese) control the situation, and make from $2 to $3.50 and even as high as $4 per day picking grapes.

Harvesting and Preparing the Crop

Grapes are ripe by the middle of August, the season often lasting into November. The average time of drying and curing a tray of raisins is about three weeks, all depending on the weather. The earliest picked grapes dry in ten days, and the later ones often take four weeks and even more. The method of drying is very simple. The bunches are cut from the vines and placed on shallow trays 2 feet wide, 3 feet long, and 1 inch high, on which the grapes are allowed to sun-dry, being turned from time to time by simply placing an empty tray top side down on the full one, then turning both over, and taking off the top tray. After the raisins are dried they are stored away in the sweat boxes until they are packed and prepared for shipment. Some of the larger growers, in order not to run so much risk in drying on account of rain, and also to enable them to handle the crop fast enough, have curing houses, where the curing is finished after having been partially done outside. The seeding, grading, packing, and shipping have become separate branches. In the season of 1898 and 1899 60 plants were engaged in this part of the work, the most of them located in the Fresno district. These establishments furnished employment for 5,000 employees, and the aggregate wages paid out to them each month during the season was nearly $250,000.

Exports, Production, and Imports

The exports of California raisins first became of sufficient importance to be separately stated in the official reports of the Treasury Department in the fiscal year ending June 30, 1892. Raisins have since been sent in small, it may be said experimental, quantities to all parts of the world, and the trade has grown until in 1898 the exports amounted to 3,109,639 pounds and in 1902 to 2,323,274 pounds.

The following figures serve to show how gradually and systematically California has monopolized the raisin trade of this country:

Raisins produced and imported.

Year.	Raisins produced.	Raisins imported.
	Pounds.	*Pounds.*
1885......................	9,400,000	53,702,220
1890......................	38,000,000	36,914,330
1895......................	91,360,000	15,921,278
1898......................	80,631,000	6,593,833
1902......................	100,000,000	6,563,302

The year 1894 was the record breaker, when 103 million pounds were produced. Raisin growers claim that this was made possible by the duty of 2 cents a pound on imported raisins. Consul Ridgely says, so cheaply and abundantly are raisins grown in Malaga, that were it not for the duty Malaga exporters would undoubtedly undersell California growers. The season's opening prices for raisins the last four years have been: Per box of 20 pounds — Imperial clusters, 6 crown, $2.50 to $3; Dehesa, 5 crown, $2 to $2.50; Fancy, 4 crown, $1.50 to $3; London Layers, 3 crown, $1.20 to $1.60. Per pound in 50-pound box or bag — loose Muscatels, 4 crown, 4¾ to 7 cents; loose Muscatels, 3 crown, 4 to 6½ cents; loose Muscatels, 2 crown, 2¾ to 6 cents; seedless Muscatels, 3¼ to 6½ cents.

WINE, BRANDY, AND CHAMPAGNE MANUFACTURE

The manufacture of each of these products from grapes constitutes an important industry in itself, and can not be described in this paper. According to the United States census for 1900, of the 169,055 gallons of sparkling wines manufactured, California reported 8,880; Ohio, 15,600; Missouri, 2,940; and New York, 113,435 gallons. This shows that New York produced more than twice as much as all the other States together.

The yearly production of wine from 1887 to 1891 in California was from 15 million to 20 million gallons, and the price fell below 10 cents a gallon, notwithstanding the fact that the demand had increased a million gallons annually; notwithstanding also that half a million gallons of brandy had been made in 1886, with the same amount in 1887, and, in the three years next succeeding, a million gallons annually; that in the southern part of the State 20,000 acres had been destroyed by the Anaheim disease; that in Napa and Sonoma counties the bulk of the vineyards were wholly or partially destroyed by the Phylloxera, and that about 600 carloads of dried grapes had been shipped in 1889 and 1891. The state of affairs then existing can hardly be imagined. Many growers became bankrupt; those who had sufficient means pulled up their vines and planted other fruits or raised hay and grain; a few, who believed in the ultimate success of the industry, persevered, and replanted the vineyards which the Phylloxera had destroyed. In 1892 the heavy frost which prevailed over the leading wine districts cut the crop down to 15 million gallons, and prices went up. About this time the California Wine Association was formed for mutual protection by the largest dealers. In 1894 the California Wine Makers' Corporation was organized by the wine makers of the State for a similar purpose, and set the price in wholesale lots to the dealers at 15 cents. The corporation, which had secured enough of the State's output to control prices, entered into a contract by which an association of the principal dealers agreed to purchase from the corporation 5 million gallons annually. All went well until some of the producers became dealers and undersold the association. This resulted in a rupture of the two associations. At the next annual meeting of the members of the Wine Makers' Corporation its board of directors was instructed to enter the markets of the world. A long war of cutting prices for standard wines was the result, which was embittered by the phenomenal yield in 1897 of 27 million gallons dry and 7 million gallons sweet wine, and prices again became low. The next season witnessed a great shortage in crop, only 18½ million gallons of both dry and sweet wines being produced. This led to better feeling between the factions, and brought about higher prices. Commercial statistics show that the trade requires 22 million gallons yearly — 16 millions for export and 6 millions for coast consumption, 4 millions of this being sweet wine. The demand is increasing by 2 million gallons annually, so there is a shortage instead of overproduction, and the wines of 1900 changed hands at from 15 to 20 cents in wholesale lots from producer to dealer. The 1901 crop brought from 20 to 35 cents a gallon, and the price for the 1902 crop will be about the same.

The following prices of grapes for the last season will serve to illustrate the differences existing in the quality of grapes for wine-making purposes: In the Napa district, $30 to $35 per ton; Sonoma, $22.50 to $30; Santa Clara, $25; Livermore, black grapes $20, white $30; Contra Costa and Alameda, $25; south of the Tehachipi, from $12.50 to $15.

The investment of capital in the California wine industry may be summed up as follows:

Vineyards, at $200 an acre	$38,000,000
Nearly 500 registered distilleries	200,000
About 40,000,000 gallons cooperage	14,000,000
Cellars and machinery	10,000,000
Capital to carry on business	10,000,000
Total	72,200,000

This industry, which is not much more than fifty years old, gives employment to nearly 60,000 persons.

Some of the Large Vineyards of California

To the late Senator Leland Stanford, founder of the Leland Stanford Junior University, belongs the distinction of having had the largest vineyard in the world, comprising nearly 5,000 acres, and being over 7 miles long. The wineries on the place cover more than 6 acres of roof surface, and during the years the writer had charge of them from 2½ million to 3 million gallons of wine were made annually, from 400 to 850 tons of grapes being crushed daily.

At Asti the Italian-Swiss colony has 1,700 acres in bearing vineyards. On the place are extensive wineries, with the largest wine vat of the world, holding 500,000 gallons.

Near Cucamonga the Italian Vineyard Company has, during the last three years, planted nearly 2,000 acres in one field. The Riverside Vineyard Company during the same time planted 2,500 acres in one vineyard.

The California Wine Association, at its own wineries, in 1902, worked up 150,000 tons of grapes and at its leased wineries enough more to make 225,000 tons. In the fall of 1902 the association paid out in cash over $5,000,000 for grapes. Throughout the State there are quite a number of vineyards of 500 acres each.

Some Successes and Reverses

New York being the leading State for the growing of American grapes and California for the Vinifera varieties, a brief review of the conditions and prices that have prevailed in those States will give a fair insight into the past history of the industry.

In New York thirty years ago 5 and 6 cents a pound were received for grapes. In 1889 the price per pound for basket lots was 3 cents, in 1893 about 1⅓ cents, in 1898, 1899, and 1900 about three-fourths of a cent, and in 1901 about 1½ cents. In 1890 and 1891 bulk grapes brought an average of $20 a ton, and in 1892 an average of $18 per ton. From that time the price gradually diminished until 1896, when the average was no more than $9 a ton, and one particular lot of 100 tons was sold at $4 per ton. Since then the average price has been about $12 a ton until 1901. For some years the price of grapes failed to pay expenses of growing. The cultivation, or rather the care, of the vineyards had ceased to be a labor of love and had become one of necessity. The question was, Will the vineyards pay expenses then? In order to make them do so the vines were overcropped, expenses were curtailed, and each grower tried to do as much of the work as possible himself. Much of the work was carelessly done, much was left undone, and much was done at the wrong time, resulting in injury to the vines from which they will never entirely recover. Such were the conditions at the beginning of the 1901 vintage, when, on account of the great shortage of the grape crop in other sections and a short crop of other fruits, especially apples, with a lively demand for unfermented grape juice and cheap clarets, grapes were in great demand and much better prices were realized than for six years previous.

In California, in 1876, Mission grapes sold for from $7.50 to $10 per ton and other varieties from $14 to $18 per ton, so that many growers having poor shipping facilities turned hogs in to harvest the crop. In 1879 Mission grapes brought $10 to $12 and choice varieties $20 to $25 per ton. Prices then went up rapidly, and from 1880 to 1882 Mission grapes sold at from $15 to $20 per ton. The extreme prices had indeed been reached, and those growing grapes became rich in a few years. Everybody who could possibly plant an acre of vineyard did so, and in a few years the production far exceeded the demand, when prices dropped until in 1886 grapes brought only from $6 to $10 per ton.

After years of successes and reverses, shortages and overproductions, the industry in the East and West has gradually settled down to a more solid business basis. Grafting stocks are in good demand, the prices of grapes and wine are steadily increasing, and much new area is being planted in vines. The new plantings the last few years have been exceedingly large, and there is every indication that they will be even larger. It is to be regretted that in California, where so many thousands of acres have already been destroyed by the Phylloxera, many of those making new plantings are not using resistant stocks, and therefore many of the vineyards will not live long enough to bear a crop. In California, and the eastern section of the country as well, due regard is not being paid to the selection of the proper varieties of fruiting sorts, and returns will be diminished accordingly. This is especially to be regretted, for not only should growers, profiting by past experience, avoid errors previously made, but also improve methods wherever possible.

FUTURE OF THE INDUSTRIES

Looking back to the middle of the last century, when just a start had been made, when growers were beginning to believe something might perhaps be done in the way of a commercial grape industry, and taking a glance at what such States as Virginia, Missouri, Ohio, New York, and California have done, especially New York and California, there is good reason to believe that the industry in this country may yet reach a development proportionate to that of other agricultural interests. Achievements at expositions and on public occasions, however, are really far in advance of what has been done in the way of production. This may easily be seen when the product of this country is compared with that of other countries. In 1901 France produced of wines 1,523,233,200 gallons; Italy, 1,013,760,000; Spain, 520,080,000; Portugal, 155,760,000; Austria, 116,160,000; Roumania, 87,120,000; Chile, 85,120,000; Russia, 76,560,000; Bulgaria, 73,920,000; Germany, 60,720,000; Argentina, 55,440,000; Turkey, 50,160,000; Greece, 32,300,000; Switzerland, 31,680,000; United States, 29,500,000, and Servia, 23,760,000 gallons. However, the industry in the United States is as yet in its infancy. A beginning has just been made in a commercial and businesslike manner to improve methods and expand markets. California has produced and sold annually the last ten years an average of 20 million gallons of wine, 2 million gallons of brandy, and 80 million pounds of raisins.

So far the raisin industry of this country has only supplied the small home demand of 80 million pounds, whereas the present population, were it to consume as much per capita as some other countries, say Great Britain, would now use 400 million pounds annually, not to say anything of extending markets and exporting to other countries.

When it is considered that France in 1901 produced 1,523,233,200 gallons of wine, while this country produced 29,500,000 gallons, and that the Golden State alone has a grape and wine producing area almost equal to the whole of France, some idea can be formed of the great possibilities of the industry.

A beginning has been made; what the industry will be remains largely with those who engage in it. No reason presents itself why varieties of grapes should not be cultivated wherever the wild vines flourish, and some of these are found in nearly all parts of the Union.

Two important lines of work need thorough experimental investigation in the near future. One of these is the determination of the relative adaptability of resistant stocks to the various types of soil found in the commercial grape regions of the Pacific coast and of the congeniality of the leading commercial varieties of the Vinifera type to such stocks. The other is the development of varieties suitable for those districts east of the Rocky Mountains in which the native grapes that have developed in New England, New York, and other northern districts are not adapted to the climatic conditions. The field which is in special need of such varieties includes the South Atlantic and Gulf States. With the wealth of native grapes in this region and the improvement of the grape already accomplished through hybridizing, it appears almost certain that varieties of choice quality, resistant to the fungous diseases that prey upon the Vinifera and Labrusca types in the South, may yet be developed, and in the not distant future make grape culture as remunerative and certain in its results in this region as it already is in other portions of the country.

Development of Oil Seeds, 1903

From Charles M. Daugherty, "The Industry in Oil Seeds," U.S. Department of Agriculture, *Yearbook*, 1903, pp. 411–17.

Cotton Seed and Flaxseed in the United States

The United States has, within the past quarter century, become by far the heaviest producer of oleaginous seeds in the world. This has been wholly due to the utilization of the cotton-seed crop and the expansion of flaxseed cultivation. Previous to these developments little attention was paid in this country to this class of agriculture. None of that great variety of purely oil-yielding seeds, the oils of which are of well-known edible and industrial importance in many foreign countries, was indigenous to the United States; and, notwithstanding the diversity of tastes and customs introduced into this country by a heterogeneous immigration, little or no effort was made to transplant them for their oil-yielding properties. In fact, it is solely due to the fact that some of the oleaginous-seed plants also yield valuable fibers that their cultivation was originally undertaken in this country. Textile materials being a prime necessity of civilized peoples, the flax plant was one of the first agricultural products introduced into the American Colonies. The cotton plant is believed to be indigenous to the New as well as to the Old World. With the exception of castor beans, the culture of which is a specialized industry in a few Western States, cotton and flax are the only oleaginous-seed plants that have ever been utilized to a notable extent in the United States for oil-making purposes. Oil has been manufactured in recent years, it is true, from corn, but only as a by-product of the glucose industry. Hemp, which is raised extensively in Russia for the oil from its seed, and peanuts, large quantities of which are imported into France from Senegal and the East Indies for manufacture into oil, are also raised in the United States, but not because of their oleaginous properties; and the small esteem in which the like properties of flax and cotton were originally held is evidenced by the fact that for two and a half centuries after the settlement of this country flax was cultivated chiefly and cotton exclusively for the value of the fiber. It is only within the past half century that, by an economic revolution almost unique in an age noted for the utilization of waste, the once most valued part of the flax plant has degenerated in this country into a waste product, and the seed, formerly a secondary consideration, has become the sole object of cultivation. Within the same period, too, the rapidly increasing cotton-seed crop, previously only a troublesome waste product, has been made available as the greatest single resource for oleaginous seed in the world.

Cultivation of Oil-Yielding Seeds in Foreign Countries

The cultivation of sunflower seed, rape seed, colza, poppy seed, sesamum, ravison, mustard seed, and many other exclusively oil-yielding seeds is a factor of considerable importance in the rural economy of many foreign countries. Some of these seeds yield edible oils, and hence are ranked among the necessities of life. Sunflower seed is extensively cultivated in Russia, where sunflower oil is one of the most popular of table oils; the seeds are also roasted and eaten as peanuts are in the United States. It is stated on good authority that 700,000 acres are annually devoted to the cultivation of sunflowers in Russia, and that 150 mills turn out an annual product of upwards of 25,000,000 gallons of sunflower oil. The other seeds mentioned are objects of special cultivation in British India and other Oriental countries, and, in a smaller way, in many parts of Europe. In France, Germany, and in most of the western and northwestern sections of Europe the culture of oil seeds has greatly declined, and is now of small importance. But an import demand exists there for practically the entire surplus oleaginous-seed crop of the world. The surplus of the flaxseed crop of Argentina, of the various oil-seed and nut crops of the East Indies, of the peanut and palm-kernel crops of the European possessions on the east and west coasts of Africa, of the cotton-seed crop of Egypt, and of various other crops of oil-yielding seeds and nuts from all parts of the world is annually absorbed by the European trade and converted into oil and oil cake in European factories for the use of European consumers.

Animal Fats and Vegetable Oils

That none of the exclusively oil-yielding seeds has ever been cultivated in the United States for oil-making purposes has been due primarily to a lack of demand for their products. A distinctive characteristic of the American people, though modified in recent years, has been the use of animal fats, both in domestic and in industrial life, for many purposes for which the inhabitants of other countries largely employ vegetable oils. In domestic life there has always been in the mind of the American housewife a somewhat inexplicable prejudice against the use of vegetable oil for cooking purposes; and until recent years lard had completely usurped the functions here that from remote antiquity had been accorded in many countries to vegetable oils. That this prejudice is being gradually mollified there is no doubt, but it is a tribute to its persistency that vegetable cooking oil even now gains surreptitious access to the American kitchen only under the guise of packages and labels suggestive of lard. For most industrial purposes, likewise, animal fats have been utilized to a large extent in the United States when for the same purposes vegetable oils were chiefly used abroad. Until the discovery of petroleum, the tallow candle and animal oils furnished an illuminating power in this country that in older ones was, and to some extent still is, supplied by colza oil and divers other oils of vegetable origin. For lubricating purposes, also, animal fats have been extensively used in the earlier history of the United States when for like purposes abroad the demand has been for rape-seed oil or other vegetable oils. In the manufacture of soap, wherein large quantities and many varieties of vegetable oils have always been utilized abroad, grease has been extensively used in the United States, especially in the homemade product of the farm. In fact, though several varieties of oil-yielding seeds, such as rape seed, poppy seed, and their oils, have been annually imported into the United States in considerable quantities for special purposes, the popularity of animal fats for all uses to which they are adapted has, together with other causes, had a tendency to restrict the use of such oils, and thereby not only to place a limit upon their importation, but also to discourage the production of the exclusively oil-yielding seeds upon American soil.

Development of Flaxseed Cultivation in the United States

As late as 1860 the quantity of linseed oil manufactured from seed grown in the United States did not much, if at all, exceed 1,000,000 gallons a year; and, since the value of the oleaginous properties of the cotton-seed crop was then practically unrecognized, this quantity closely represents the total output at that date of all oil made from home-grown oleaginous seed. The use in this country of the products of oil-yielding seeds was at that time largely confined to linseed oil, valuable for its use in paint and varnish. But the domestic output of this product was entirely inadequate to the demand, and the imports of oil and seed, expressed together in terms of oil, amounted to about 6,000,000 gallons. Imports of other fixed or expressed oils, including rape seed, hemp seed, cocoanut, and palm oil, amounted to less than 2,000,000 gallons. The domestic consumption, therefore, of all oils of this class amounted in 1860 to less than 9,000,000 gallons. The marvelous advance that has been made in the production of oleaginous seeds and in the consumption of their oils in the United States since that date is illustrated by the fact that at the present time there is annually manufactured from the domestic crops of flaxseed and cotton seed a product of from 160,000,000 to 170,000,000 gallons of oil, three-fourths of which probably enters into home consumption.

The development of flaxseed cultivation on an important scale in the United States dates from the cessation of the civil war. In the activity of the westward movement of population, incident to the disbandment of the military forces, flaxseed culture, specialized and limited in territorial extent, moved with the tide of progress gradually westward and northwestward from the Ohio into the territory then known as the West and Northwest. Virgin soil seemed to be essential to its profitable cultivation. In the wake of agricultural expansion followed another economic movement, that of industrial enterprise, the course of which was marked by the building of homes and factories, the equipment of railways, and the growth of towns and cities — a movement that gave great impetus to flaxseed production in that it increased enormously the demand for paint, and hence for linseed oil, the principal object of flaxseed cultivation. The effect was immediately apparent. The flaxseed crop, which by 1869 had already increased to 1,730,000 bushels, was more than quadrupled in the next ten years. In 1879 it amounted to 7,170,000 bushels, and upward of 90 per cent of the crop was produced in the Western States, manufactured by Western mills, and consumed in territory west of the Alleghenies. There was little or no surplus, and the markets of the East were chiefly supplied by imports of flaxseed from British India. It was not until 1891, however, that the important point was reached in the history of the crop, when domestic supply overtook demand. Regular foreign imports to Eastern mills after that date ceased, and the United States took rank among exporting nations. Meanwhile the domestic demand for linseed oil had greatly increased, but the domestic production of flaxseed more than kept pace with this increased demand. The crop of 1903 amounted to 27,300,000 bushels, or 764,400 tons, and, notwithstanding the fact that the average exports of the previous five years had amounted to upward of 3,000,000 bushels annually, this crop came upon markets heavily overloaded with the surplus of the two preceding years. The industrial demand for flaxseed in the United States is practically limited to the domestic demand for oil, the export trade in the manufactured product being of small proportions. Potentially, the 1903 crop represents (after deducting 1,500,000 bushels for next year's seeding) 64,450,000 gallons of oil, or fully 15,000,000 gallons more than the country's requirements. The quantity actually manufactured each year does not exceed 50,000,000 gallons.

The United States as a Producer of Oleaginous Seeds

The position of the United States in the first rank as a producer of oleaginous seeds, however, is principally due to the utilization of the cotton-seed crop, and is the result of industrial rather than agricultural development. From the beginning of cotton cultivation in this country cotton seed had been in weight a relatively important, but in value a worthless product of the cotton belt. Constituting in weight two-thirds of the seed cotton as picked from the boll, each annual increase in valuable cotton lint resulted in a double increase of worthless cotton seed. And a few years previous to the civil war something like 2,000,000 tons of this useless and cumbersome product was a result of each year's harvest. Beyond the small quantities used for cattle feeding and for fertilizing, there was probably little thought, less prospect, of its profitable utilization. The economic field that it was afterwards to share as a cooking oil and in the manufacture of soap was completely filled in the one case by lard, and in the other by other greases. Moreover, the building up of an export trade was debarred by the liability of the seed to heat in transportation. Cotton-seed oil was then manufactured in Europe from seed imported from Egypt; and a few sporadic attempts, probably based on the hope of an export trade in cotton-seed oil, were made to establish the industry in this country. The civil war checked whatever chance there might have been of success.

Growth of the Manufacture of Cotton-Seed Oil

Within a few years after the cessation of hostilities, cotton production regained the ground lost during the war, and the utilization of the enormous waste represented by the seed became a subject of renewed interest. With the prospect of millions of tons of raw material produced without the cultivation of a single additional acre of land, without the employment of additional labor, or the investment of additional capital over and above that required for the production of the staple, cotton, the utilization of the seed presented an alluring field for exploitation. A few mills were erected late in the sixties, equipped with hydraulic presses identical with those then in common use in the North for the expression of oil from flaxseed. Probably the utilization of waste was the most active principle underlying the early experiments. Contrary to what had been the case with linseed oil, no important domestic demand preexisted for the cotton-seed product. Unadapted to general illuminating and lubricating purposes, deficient in the drying properties essential to its use in paint, its edible properties unknown, its sphere of usefulness seemed limited. Interest became centered in the export trade. The foreign demand increased with each successive year, and soon became the chief support of the new industry. In 1879–80 the quantity of cotton-seed oil manufactured in the United States had increased to about 9,000,000 gallons; and the importance of the export trade was apparent in the fact that almost 7,000,000 gallons were shipped abroad against a little over 2,000,000 gallons consumed at home.

In the following year the discovery was made that cotton-seed oil mixed with certain animal fats made an acceptable and valuable substitute for lard. This gave an immediate impetus to the industry and eventually resulted in making it one of the most important industries of the Southern States. A domestic demand sprang up that absorbed practically the entire output of the then existing mills, and foreign trade, as a result of the active domestic competition, dwindled to insignificant proportions. In 1881–82 the output of cotton-seed oil increased to about 12,000,000, and 1882–83 to about 15,000,000 gallons. Of these quantities, 11,000,000 and nearly 15,000,000 gallons, respectively, were taken by the home trade. The combined exports of the two years amounted to only 1,129,160 gallons. From the date of this discovery began a period of activity in this industry that has continued almost without abatement up to the present day. New mills were constructed year after year throughout the South until they now number upwards of 600. The quantity of cotton seed utilized, which, previous to 1881, had never amounted to one-tenth of the total crop, has increased until fully 60 per cent of the average crop is now converted into valuable products; this, too, notwithstanding the fact that the production of cotton seed has meanwhile increased in about the same proportions. New uses found from time to time for cotton-seed oil have given additional stimulus to both foreign and domestic demand. A few years after the decline in the export trade in 1882 it was restored to its old proportions. Meanwhile the domestic trade, primarily as a result of the demand from packing houses, was increasing by leaps and bounds. By 1893–94 exports had increased to 15,000,000 gallons; the domestic demand in the same year absorbed about 40,000,000 gallons.

Between 1894–95 and 1902–1903 the production of cotton-seed oil in the United States was doubled. In the former year arose a greatly increased demand for this product in Europe; in 1898–99 it culminated in exports of upwards of 50,000,000 gallons, domestic demand in the meantime averaging about 40,000,000 gallons. This remarkable increase in the foreign trade attracted to the industry new capital and enterprise and reulted in a period of the greatest activity in the erection of mills known in its history. Since 1898–99 exports have declined irregularly, and in the fiscal year 1902–1903 they amounted to only 35,642,994 gallons. But the manufacture of oil has increased steadily, and is estimated to have amounted in 1902–1903 to a total of from 110,000,000 to 115,000,000 gallons. Of this enormous output, the domestic demand absorbed from 75,000,000 to 80,000,000 gallons.

The Production of Flaxseed and Cotton Seed

The production of flaxseed and cotton seed — the two crops practically constituting the oleaginous-seed crop of the United States — now aggregates annually upwards of 5,500,000 tons. It is estimated that with every 500-pound bale of cotton picked there is gathered one-half ton of seed, and hence a cotton crop of 10,000,000 bales indicates a production of 5,000,000 tons of cotton seed. The average annual production of flaxseed for the past five years has been about 672,000 tons. A 10,000,000-bale cotton crop and an average production of flaxseed therefore result in an output of 5,672,000 tons of oleaginous seed.

Although statistics upon the production of the many varieties of oleaginous seeds in the principal producing countries are incomplete, there is no doubt that the production of the United States exceeds the combined crops of any other two countries in the world. It is true that not all of the United States crops is utilized for oil-making purposes. Probably not over 60 per cent of the cotton-seed crop finds its way to the oil mills, and of late years there has been an overproduction of flaxseed. But, assuming that 3,000,000 tons of cotton seed are now annually converted into oil, and, putting the average quantity of flaxseed crushed annually during the past five years at 500,000 tons, the total crush of these seeds may be conservatively estimated at 3,500,000 tons. Whether considered separately or collectively, these figures indicate that the United States stands first among all countries as a manufacturer of oil as well as a producer of oleaginous seeds.

Rhode Island Farming, 1905

From John G. Clarke, "Is Farming Prosperous in Rhode Island?" Rhode Island and Providence Plantations State Board of Agriculture, *Annual Report*, 1905 (Providence, 1905), pp. 95–100.

In looking over the State, one will find large areas which have the appearance of being once fertile farm lands, but now are desolate and deserted; meadows and pastures growing up to brush, houses and buildings tumbling down, all of which goes to present a very forlorn picture.

In other sections will be found thrifty looking farms with good homes and with buildings neatly painted. Some of these are dairy farms, some poultry, others market gardens, nearly every branch of agriculture being represented; the whole of which presents a most beautiful and interesting picture of industry and success. . . .

Thirty years ago, scattered all over this State were little villages, each of which had its own cotton or woolen mill. In 1870 the town of Exeter had seven of these establishments, while to-day she has none. Exeter is not alone. All of our country towns, especially those off of railroads, have witnessed the passing away of their manufacturing industries.

When all these little mills were running, the farmers in their immediate vicinity had a ready market for their milk, butter, eggs, and vegetables, without having to ship them away to distant cities; for what the village people could not use was taken to the mill store, and sold or traded for goods from the store which the farmer did not raise but had to have. Thus the village store became a sort of commission house, buying and selling farm produce, and shipping it to the city markets, taking all of that responsibility and experience from the farmers, who in the end were to be the losers by not knowing how to handle their goods.

As competition forced these little establishments out of business, the people drifted, as did the business, to the cities and large towns. With them went not only the retail markets of the farmer, but the wholesale market as well; for the country store could not live on the profits gained from handling farm produce, and were obliged to close. Thus the farmer's market was gone, and he must look elsewhere for a place to sell his produce.

Not only had the farmers lost their original market, but the railroads were opening up the great West, which began to ship its produce to our markets. All are familiar with the results which followed: Our farmers could not compete with their Western brothers who had only to plant the seed in the fertile soil and harvest the crop. Our soil had been robbed and it was necessary to supply fertility in order to grow crops, which greatly increased the cost of production. Other changes occurred.

Fifty years ago, or even thirty years ago, on nearly every farm would be seen a flock of sheep grazing over the pastures, and the farmers realized a good profit from them. My father used to say that he had kept sheep when the fleece would pay the keep of the sheep and the lambs were clear profit. Here again came Western competition, and our sheep industry has gone, perhaps due not entirely to Western competition, but largely so. In 1850 there were in this State 44,296 sheep; in 1870, 23,938; while in 1900 there were only 6,629; a decrease of 85 per cent. since 1850. There has been a great decrease in certain other farm lines; none quite equal the sheep, but swine follow closely. Statistics, however, are not all on one side.

The last United States census shows that since 1850 our farm wealth has increased $7,888,549, and that the value of our annual product has increased very rapidly during the last few years. Many of the farms that were deserted are again being improved; farms that were a few years ago regarded as totally useless are being successfully utilized for poultry farms. There is always a good demand for poultry and eggs, and the price of the home product is always in advance of that from the West. In the town of Little Compton we find a grand illustration of what can be and is being done in the poultry business. There are still many farms which can be utilized along this line to the great advantage of the State and the farmers. The production of eggs alone increased 59.2 per cent. between 1890 and 1900. This is an industry which does not demand as quick transportation as some others, and is therefore adapted to those farms that are a long distance from railroads.

The dairy industry has greatly increased during the last few years, and our farmers are producing many hundred cans of milk that are being shipped to the cities to supply our city friends with milk and cream.

Other farmers are turning their attention to raising hay for market. There is probably no more paying crop to-day than hay, and no better hay market in the world than Providence.

Near the cities and large villages, market gardens are very profitable. In 1900 there were 4,873 acres of vegetables reported. This does not include potatoes and onions, which alone were valued at nearly a million dollars. A large percentage of the former were raised on the Island of Rhode Island. This branch of our agriculture ranks second in the value of the product (hay and forage ranking first).

Fruit growing is attracting the attention of many of our farmers, and should prove a very profitable business. The consumption of fruit has increased faster than any other article of food, and will continue to increase. Good fruit put upon the market in an attractive way always brings good prices.

The greatest advancement along agricultural lines is farming under glass, which includes the growing of both flowers and vegetables. In the census of 1900 there were reported 1,397,100 square feet under glass in this State.

If the passing away of these little mills from all over the State, together with Western competition, caused many farms to be abandoned, and some branches of agriculture to diminish, what has caused others to build up and increase?

This is the most thickly settled State in the Union — 425 people to the square mile — and Providence is the richest city, per capita, in America. Thus we have the very best markets for our produce. These markets have largely been supplied from the West. Our own farmers, who had always depended upon the markets of the little villages, not being awake to the possibility of the larger and better market which existed right at their very doors.

As the great West grows in city population and manufacturing interests — and it is growing rapidly — they will consume more and more of their own produce and slowly withdraw from competition along various lines. All will admit that the West will always be a competitor in our markets, but they have for years been growing crop after crop from the soil without restoring much of the plant food removed, until now they are finding it necessary to use fertilizers, thus increasing the cost of production and reducing their profits; this will tend to cause the Western farmers to stop competing in our markets, in the more perishable products, and leave them clear for the home growers.

Not only has our large city population to be fed, but our summer resort people as well; and here we have one of our very best markets, for our summer visitors are willing to pay a good price for a good article, and our farmers must cater to this trade, supply them with water at twenty cents per quart in the form of strawberries and raspberries and other fruits, and furnish them first class vegetables put up in an attractive way.

Again, many of the farms that were once a long distance from market are being brought closer by the electric cars that are now running to all points of the State and offering quick and cheap transportation. Many country districts have been awakened again to life by the introduction of trolley lines.

Our towns and State are recognizing more and more the value of better roads. Many of our towns have taken rapid strides along this line, and now the State has taken the matter in hand and is establishing a State road system which promises to be of great value to our farming as well as to all other interests. This brief review shows clearly that, in spite of many drawbacks, agriculture has advanced slowly but surely; that while many have failed, a larger number have succeeded; and taken as a whole, farming in Rhode Island is a success; but there is still another side to the case which should be taken into consideration in order to fully measure the success of the farmers.

Under the changed conditions, newer and better methods had to be adopted; our farmers were brought in closer contact with the rest of the world, and with each other; farmers' organizations were formed which brought them together for the discussion of questions of mutual interest. And right here the Grange came to fill the long felt want, and it stands next to the church and school only, for the advancement and betterment of all mankind.

Better schools were demanded, for the farmers required a better education. Our National Government recognized this fact, and laws were passed providing for the establishment of agricultural schools in every State in the Union. A few years later, by act of Congress, the standards of these schools were raised and they were allowed to confer degrees, this making them colleges. The history of these institutions is too well known to require a long review of their work, suffice it to say that they are doing everything in their power to accomplish the results for which they were created, and their influence is being felt by all the civilized world. Not only did Congress establish schools and colleges for the study of agriculture, but experiment stations as well. These have been of unmeasurable value to the farmers, and the results already obtained from the work of our own State experiment station will fully compensate for the money already expended, and money to be expended for years to come, even though the future work they should accomplish were useless; but we have reason to believe that the work they will do in the future will far exceed in value that done in the past.

Rhode Island is to be congratulated for having the best laid out experiment plots in the United States or in the world.

Thus the whole rural community was brought up to a higher standard of life and civilization. No longer is the farmer a farmer because he does not know enough to be anything else, but a farmer because he knows enough not to be anything else. No longer is the life of the farmer looked upon as one to be despised, but as one to be desired.

The question, "Is Farming prosperous in Rhode Island," will depend somewhat upon what our ideas of prosperity are.

Development of Cream Plants, 1906

From John Michels, *Gathered Cream Plants*, South Carolina Agricultural Experiment Station Bulletin 118 (Columbia, S.C., 1906), pp. 4–11.

Introduction

In a recent bulletin published by the writer, dairy farming was suggested as a commendable means of improving the worn out cotton lands of South Carolina. This class of farming has been of untold value wherever it has been adopted as an adjunct to any form of agricultural practice. In the Northern and Middle Western States the timely attention to the cattle industry has not only made the use of commercial fertilizer unnecessary, but has resulted in such increased productiveness of farming lands in so many sections as to double the value of the land in a comparatively short period of time.

In South Carolina, dairy farming commends itself for purposes besides that of increasing the fertility of the soil. Dairy farming should be encouraged, if for no other reason than supplying our home needs of the various classes of dairy products now so largely imported from other States, notably, Tennessee, North Carolina, Kentucky, Virginia and even New York State. It seems a pity that we should permit our valuable cotton seed meal to be sent hundreds of miles away from our borders to be later returned to us in the form of milk, cream, butter and cheese. These products should be produced on our own soil. We need the valuable manure resulting from the feeding of cotton seed meal; we want the cash realized from the production and sale of dairy products. Moreover we should refuse to be made the dumping ground of inferior products which are continually being poured into our State from districts hundreds of miles removed from our borders.

Undoubtedly the prevailing high price of cotton in recent years has lead our farmers to believe that the growing of this staple crop is too remunerative to allow any other to lay any claim on their attention. The important fact should not be overlooked, however, that a dozen or more cows upon an average farm would not necessarily mean a curtailing in the cotton production on such a farm; on the other hand, the increased fertility of the land resulting from a careful saving and application of the manure produced by the cows should not only maintain or increase the yield of cotton on less acreage, but would undoubtedly also result in a curtailing of the commercial fertilizer bill and in providing ready cash from the sale of dairy products.

Value of Gathered Cream Plants

In South Carolina we have two classes of dairy farmers: those who make a specialty of dairying and those with whom dairying will largely remain a secondary matter. With the former class it is possible to make a close study of markets and provide the necessary time and skill in the production of first class products. Almost without exception, remunerative prices are realized from the sale of milk, cream and butter by this class of dairymen.

In this bulletin our entire attention will be confined to the second class of dairymen with whom dairying is only a secondary matter, and who carry on this work in conjunction with cotton growing. The great bulk of cow keepers falls within this class, and it is for them that we are now seeking more remunerative outlets for the products of their dairies. As a rule where dairying is carried on as a secondary matter, the produce is marketed in the form of butter, and the average prices realized for farm dairy butter in this State as well as in other States, do not pay for the cost of production. Taking an average price for the year, it is safe to say that not over 15 cents per pound is realized for the butter marketed by this class of dairymen. The reason for this small price is attributable to the large amount of inferior butter made and the failure to secure markets where butter is bought strictly on the basis of quality. The common market for most of this class of butter is the country grocery, which usually makes little discrimination in the quality of the butter, and hence much good butter is sold for the same prices realized for the inferior grades.

For new and undeveloped dairy districts where these small milk producers are usually found, nothing has proved so satisfactory as gathered cream plants. These plants gather the small quantities of cream from hundreds of farms and churn it into one uniform mass of butter. By employing skilled buttermakers, the butter produced is not only uniform, but of good quality, commanding on an average at least 10 cents more per pound than is realized for the average butter made upon the farm. These plants have the further advantage of relieving the house-wife of the drudgery incident to the manufacture of butter under the adverse conditions which prevail upon most small dairy farms.

Gathered cream plants are usually located at some good railroad center which enables them to gather cream from a large enough territory to supply the amount of cream needed to make the plant a success.

In proposing the construction of these plants, the writer is by no means urging an untried undertaking. Hundreds of them are scattered throughout the country and new ones are springing up almost daily. These plants are gradually doing away with the making of butter upon the farms, and serve as an impetus to dairying wherever they are located. A few of these plants located at some good railroad centers would be able to handle most of the cream produced in South Carolina. The expense of shipping cream is so small that producers a hundred miles removed from the plants could better afford the transportation charges than to undertake the task of making the butter upon the farm and selling it at the average prices paid at the country grocery.

Method of Organization

There are two distinct classes of cream plants in existence at the present time: (a) Those owned and operated by private individuals, called proprietary cream plants; (2) Those owned and operated by the patrons or milk producers, known as co-operative cream plants.

Most of the truly co-operative cream plants are found where the milk and cream are obtained within a reasonable distance from the plant. In a new dairy territory like South Carolina, it would be next to impossible to have all of the patrons shareholders in a cream plant because much of the cream must necessarily come from farmers too far removed to take an active interest in the management of the plant. It is desirable, however, to have as many as possible of the milk-producers shareholders in the plant, as well as to have them take an active interest in the management of its affairs.

If a community of farmers is interested in the establishment of a cream plant, the following method of organization is recommended:

(1) Let those most interested in the project make a thorough canvass of the milk-produces in that community to ascertain the number of cows available. There should not be less than 400 cows to start with.

(2) If the desired number of cows is available, the next step is to secure a subscription of about $3,500 by selling shares for that amount. This sum of money is necessary to build and equip a substantial fire-proof gathered cream plant containing all the modern creamery machinery.

(3) When the necessary funds have been subscribed, call a meeting of the shareholders to elect a president, secretary, treasurer, manager, and a board of directors, which should consist of the president, secretary, treasurer, and at least three other shareholders.

(4) The next step is to specify a certain time within which all subscriptions must be paid. The money is preferably turned over to a reliable banker in the form of notes bearing interest.

(5) The treasurer should be authorized to draw upon the bank for the money thus deposited whenever occasion demands, but he should be required to give security for the money that comes into his hands.

(6) When all subscriptions have been paid, a meeting of the board of directors should be called for the purpose of hiring a butter-maker, who should not only be able to make a first class article of butter, but who should also be competent to plan and superintend the construction of the plant.

(7) The cream plant is paid for out of a sinking fund created by charging the patrons, in addition to the charge necessary to cover running expenses, say one cent for every pound of butter fat delivered until the plant is paid for.

(8) After the creamery is paid for, there should be an annual dividend declared to the shareholders as interest on their investment.

(9) A sufficient sinking fund must be maintained to cover the annual dividend and the running expenses, by charging from two to four cents for every pound of butter-fat delivered.

With proprietary cream plants it is customary to pay for cream according to the ruling market prices for butter, that is, each man's dues are usually determined by multiplying the number of pounds of butter-fat he has delivered by the price quoted for butter.

Method of Construction

The best and most permanent cream plants are constructed of brick. They are the most sanitary and cheapest in the long run. The original cost may be somewhat greater than that of a frame building, but the insurance and repairs are considerably less. A brick building with galvanized iron roof, cement floors, and walls partly of cement, is practically fire-proof. . . .

All of the floor space is on the same level except the intake floor, which is elevated 3 feet to facilitate unloading and to permit the cream to flow by gravity into the receiving vat.

Care should be given to the construction of floors. Wood floors because of their porous nature and tendency to rot are entirely unsuited for creamery purposes. They are not sanitary. Well constructed cement floors are most serviceable because of their durability and the ease with which they can be kept clean. Any tendency to dampness in a cement floor can easily be overcome by constructing it upon a cobble stone and cinder foundation underlaid with drain tile.

Ventilation is another matter which should be given due consideration. Either good natural ventilation on the plan of the "King" system or some good mechanical method of the blower or fan style, should be provided. Lack of ventilation causes an accumulation of foul, moist air, which is certain to react unfavorably both upon the quality of the butter and the general health of the butter-maker.

Method of Operation

In the successful operation of a gathered cream plant, it is of prime importance to secure a first class butter-maker, a man who is not only able to make a first quality of butter, but who is capable of managing every detail connected with his business. The best skill is none too good in the manufacture of butter. A cheap inexperienced man should, therefore, never be employed if a successful business is to be established.

The cream is delivered to the plant by either wagon or rail. Obviously in a new dairy territory most of it is shipped by rail. Within a radius of ten miles of the plant, "cream routes" are established along which the cream is gathered by wagons. With good railroad facilities, cream may be successfully gathered a hundred miles or more outside of this territory.

As soon as the cream is received, it is preferably weighed in the can in which it is delivered, deducting each time the weight of the can, which is permanently marked upon it. The cans are emptied into the receiving can, from which about half an ounce of cream is withdrawn for a butter-fat test. The sample is taken either with a small dipper or a sampling tube, but only after the cream has been thoroughly mixed with a mixer kept specially for this purpose. A conical dipper with an inch opening at the bottom answers the purpose of a mixer very satisfactorily. This dipper is hung on the inside of the receiving can and will drain automatically as the cream discharges from the can.

The cream is bought on the butter-fat basis, that is, patrons receive pay according to the amount of butter-fat furnished. This is the only just way of receiving cream, since the yield of butter is in direct proportion to the percentage of fat in the cream. The amount of butter-fat is determined by multiplying the number of pounds of cream by the per cent. of fat it contains.

Butter-fat determinations are preferably made of every batch of cream delivered. However, where cream is received in good, fresh condition, the method of composite sampling may be employed with good success.

The butter-fat is usually paid for according to the ruling market quotation for butter. Some plants pay full New York quotations, others from one-half to one cent below, depending largely upon the amount of butter made. In a new dairy territory where only small amounts of cream are delivered and the daily output of butter is small, the cost of making butter is comparatively high. Cream plants making between 500 and 1,000 pounds of butter daily usually pay full New York quotations, and where the product is of exceptional quality prices even higher than this are paid.

It may be asked how cream plants can pay the farmers the same price for butter-fat which New York quotes for butter. The explanation is that one pound of butter-fat makes about one and one-sixth pounds of butter, and the one-sixth pound of butter usually pays for the cost of manufacture.

Cream should be delivered not less than four times a week. Wherever possible it should be delivered daily. Tinned steel cans of the best quality should be used for transporting cream. Cans of various sizes and patterns are always obtainable in the market.

All cans should be returned from the cream plant only after thorough washing and scalding with steam. One of the worst practices in the cream trade is to return the empty cans unwashed.

Payments for cream should be made at least once a month.

A full book account of all transactions should be kept so that the cost of manufacturing butter may be accurately determined.

So many failures in the butter-making line have resulted from swindles on the part of unscrupulous butter buyers that a few suggestions with reference to the selling of butter seem pertinent:

1. Sell butter only to well established, reputable butter firms.

2. Do not sell butter on commission, but ask for prices f. o. b. your station, based on some market quotation like New York.

3. Never send a firm a third shipment until the first has been paid for.

Farming in Tennessee

From V. S. Bright, "Opportunity for Agriculture in Tennessee," *University of Tennessee Farmer*, (October, 1906), I, pp. 15–17.

The State of Tennessee is capable of producing a greater variety of agricultural products than any state north or south. The counties bordering the Mississippi river rival Arkansas in the production of cotton while throughout the state the cereals flourish and all kinds of live stock thrive.

In 1900 the total number of farms in Tennessee were 224,628 which was more than three times as many as in 1850 and 28.8 per cent more than in 1890. In 1850 the total value of these farms was $53,030,150 and in 1900 they had reached the grand total of $265,150,750. The value of farm buildings in 1900 was $63,136,960, and of farm machinery $15,232,670. The total value of farm products for 1904 was $106,166,440 of which 33.4 per cent were animal products and 66.6 per cent were plant products which was equal to $70,750,242. In 1905 Tennessee farmers used 400,000 tons of commercial fertilizer besides the barnyard manure. This is progress, but many of our farmers have just gotten aroused to the fact that the soil can be robbed of its fertility and that in some way a portion of the plant food that has been removed in growing a crop must be replaced or else the land will steadily become exhausted.

What does a rich farming country mean? It means better corn, cotton and wheat crops. The pulse of American prosperity is not determined by the steel output or manufacturing, but by the corn and cotton crop that directly feed and clothe the people. We all know unless the farmer is prosperous all other industries must sooner or later languish, for a good corn crop means money in the farmer's pocket to purchase more luxuries; a good crop of corn means more fat beeves and hogs for market, thus greater demand for cars and engines and men to operate them.

The Tennessee farmer is the most fortunate of all farmers, for in case of a failure of one crop he has recourse to a number of others. Take for instance any region where one crop is grown to the exclusion of other crops and its fortune is imperiled every year, for a failure in the harvest means a financial crisis for the farmer.

The average young man believes that success in life can only come to him by entering some industrial field; that agriculture is a circumscribed profession, hedged about with difficulties that can not be overcome, and offering but limited opportunities for the development of his natural powers; such an idea is utterly false. No young man need hesitate in choosing agriculture for a profession under the misleading opinion that it has no future or that it is without its compensations.

Some examples bearing out the assertion just made will not be out of place. The corn crop of the United States in 1899 was grown on 94,916,911 acres. The yield was 2,266,440,217 bushels, and the total value was $828,258,326. What an enormous amount of labor must have been required to grow and harvest this crop, yet we have said that it measures the pulse of American prosperity. The question then arises, have we reached the limit of corn production? Are our American farmers growing the most desirable varieties of corn? Can't we increase the yield in some way without any further expenditure of labor and fertilizers? The successful farmer must face these questions sooner or later, and unless some action is taken the time is not far distant when we no longer can produce as much corn as we can consume. The fact has been clearly shown that the yield of corn may be increased 15 to 25 per cent per acre by the proper selection of seed and better tillage. There is no limit to opportunities for judicious breeding. In the state of Illinois there has been a company organized, for no other purpose than to breed better seed corn for the farmers of that state. Hundreds of young men that work in the shops and factories might go into the breeding of corn on a scientific basis and receive a handsome remuneration and be public benefactors as well. What has been said of corn can be said of wheat, oats, barley and potatoes.

In the last fifty years the live stock industry has been developed to a marvelous degree of perfection. In 1900 the value of live stock on the farms and ranches amounted to $3,390,000,000. The slaughtering and packing of animals and animal products has developed one of the greatest industries in the world. There are received annually in the stock yards of Chicago three million head of cattle, seven million head of hogs and four and one-half million head of sheep. When these animals are slaughtered and ready for market they are worth $390,000,000. Thus we see that fortunes are being made by men who are engaged in breeding and rearing domestic animals. But the breeding of plants has not reached such a state of perfection as the breeding of live stock. In fact the breeding of plants has just begun, and it can be safely said that there are as great opportunities offered to the plant breeder today as were offered the breeder of live stock fifty years ago. Take for example Tennessee's leading crop, which is corn. In 1899 3,374,574 acres were devoted to the culture of corn and the yield was 67,307,574 bushels. The value of the crop was $28,059,508, which was more than one-third the value of all farm crops. Assuming that the acreage for 1905 was 3,374,574 acres, an increase of one bushel per acre would mean 3,374,574 bushels, which at a value of 65 cents per bushel, would be worth $2,195,573. Those who have studied the culture of corn know that it is not impossible to increase the yield five bushels per acre, and in view of the large money value it would represent there is no reason why the farmer should not put forth every effort to increase the yield of his corn crop, especially if he can do so with a small expenditure of money.

Range Management, 1906

From J. S. Cotton, "Range Management," U.S. Department of Agriculture, *Yearbook*, 1906, pp. 225–38.

The Present Situation

At the present time the greater part of western grazing lands is badly overstocked. Some of the ranges are so crowded that the stockmen are experiencing difficulty in getting sufficient grazing for their herds. Many herds have been cut down in order to meet these conditions, while in some instances, rather than run the risk of an unusually hard winter or a period of drought, stockmen are going out of business entirely.

When the first stockmen drove their herds on the western range lands there was a great abundance of feed, and it was generally believed that this feed would never be fully utilized. As a consequence these men increased their herds as much as possible, so as to use all of the feed they could. Others, seeing the prosperous condition of these men, began to bring in large herds, that they also might get their share of the free grass. Thus it was only a few years until the range was carrying more stock than it could properly support.

During the past few years there has been a heavy immigration of settlers to several parts of these grazing lands. These settlers have taken up large bodies of the very best grazing lands for farming purposes. The men ranging their stock in these areas were for the most part crowded back to the ranges of other stockmen, thus greatly aggravating the already crowded condition of the range. As a necessary result of all this overcrowding the range began to deteriorate.

The rate of this deterioration has been governed somewhat by accessibility, a range that is easily accessible being much more likely to be overstocked than one that is difficult to reach. It has, however, been governed much more largely by climatic conditions. In the northern range States, where the severe winters and the liability of a heavy fall of snow acted as a check, and where the rainfall is sufficient for the growth of a good crop of grass, the deterioration of the range has been rather slow until the past few years. In the South, where the stock can be grazed the year round with perfect safety, the range has been stocked to the highest number it would carry during favorable seasons. When a period of drought has occurred, with a consequent shortage of grasses and other forage plants, the same number of animals has been still on hand to be supported. This has resulted in severe grazing of the native grasses and other forage plants, preventing the vegetation from yielding seed with which to reproduce itself, thus greatly lowering the carrying capacity of the range. This carrying capacity is, of necessity, governed largely by the amount of rainfall. In years when there are ample rains there is an abundance of vegetation for grazing, but in the periods when the rainfall is light the growth of vegetation is much less. Much damage has been done to the ranges through the inability of the stockmen to reduce their herds during periods of drought.

With the exception of the western portions of Oklahoma, Kansas, and Nebraska, the carrying capacity of the range is much lower at the present time than it was in the early days, or even a decade ago. Reports from various stockmen indicate that the majority of the ranges are not carrying one-half as many animals as formerly. Ranges which formerly required from 8 to 12 acres to support a single steer throughout the entire year now usually require from 20 to 35 acres. Instances are cited in Arizona where from 50 to 100 acres are needed to support a single beef animal. In western Nebraska the carrying capacity of the range is considerably higher than formerly. This is because the stockmen of that region have protected their ranges from the ravages of prairie fires.

Overcrowding the public ranges has caused considerable friction. In many sections there have been bitter fights between the sheepmen and the cattlemen. The majority of these fights were eventually settled by a division of the range and the establishing of dead lines. There have also been serious difficulties between the stockmen and the homesteaders. In some instances the stockmen tried to keep the settlers out; in other places the settlers have taken up the watering places or settled on land adjoining them, and have kept the stock from watering in their accustomed places either by building fences or by driving them away.

The stockmen have tried in many ways to adjust themselves to these conditions. Some have obtained virtual control of their ranges by buying up or leasing all the watering places. Others have been able to buy railroad land and deserted homesteads or to lease school lands, and thus bring their ranges under direct control.

In other regions, where the land could not be brought under control by these methods, stockmen have divided the ranges by mutual consent. Later they began to build drift fences on these lines in order to prevent their cattle from straying from their ranges. These drift fences were gradually extended until large tracts of Government land were inclosed. The fencing in of large pastures proved to be so convenient to the stockmen in the handling of their stock that it became quite general in several of the range States.

Attitude of Stockmen Toward Legislation

Recently an Executive order was issued requiring that these fences be removed. The results of this order have greatly emphasized the necessity for some legislation which will effect a distribution of range land among those having stock on the ranges, so as to secure to them by lease, purchase, or other legal means the possibility of managing their ranges with a view to maintaining their productiveness. The stockmen, who in the absence of legislation had gradually developed a system of range division among themselves, all recognize that this division was a primitive arrangement, devoid of legal status, but made necessary by the exigencies of the business. For the most part they are heartily in favor of legislation which will give stockmen a legal right to protect whatever range may be assigned to each.

A few years ago the stockmen were bitterly opposed to any form of legislation for the division of the public domain through leasing or any other system. They felt that if they were deprived of free feed they would be unable to make a living from the range, for they could not afford to lease or purchase the feed. All they wanted was that the range should be "let alone."

Now, with the greatly changed conditions caused by overstocking and the taking up of large areas of the best range lands for farming purposes, the more progressive stockmen realize fully that unless some such step is taken the open range will soon be destroyed.

Although the majority of the stockmen now favor some form of legislation for the future disposal of that part of the public domain which is suitable for range purposes only, there is still a great diversity of opinion concerning the character of the laws needed. The greater number seem to be in favor of some system of leasing the land in individual pastures for terms of five to ten years. Nearly all believe that the area of land leased to a given person should be some multiple of the area to which he holds title in the vicinity, but that there should be a maximum limit in order to prevent any one man or company from securing control of too much land.

Range Improvement

So long as it remains public domain, and is consequently free to all without restriction, nothing can be done to improve the range land of the country, for whatever improvement might be effected would almost immediately be destroyed by the stockmen in their eagerness to be the first to profit by it. But when the land is brought under control by lease, purchase, or other means the problem of handling the range is radically changed and the stockman is on an entirely different footing. Instead of living in uncertainty as to when his range will be a thing of the past, he will know just how much land he can use and depend upon. Then he will not feel that he must graze this land as hard as he can while he has the opportunity. Instead, he will be in position to protect it and get the greatest amount of good from it from year to year. He will then be able to fence the land and keep off all outside stock, and to regulate the number of his own grazing thereon.

Many stockmen are firmly convinced that stock can not be run at a profit in pastures that are owned or leased. Numerous citations of large cattle companies that have lost heavily in leasing grazing lands on Indian reservations are made. It is true that many of the cattle companies have lost large sums of money in leasing these lands. Careful investigation, however, will usually show some special reasons for such losses. First, the majority of these companies were handling a very poor grade of cattle. These yielded so small a margin between the cost of putting them into the pasture and the returns from putting them on the market that they could not stand the extra expense incurred in leasing. Then the cattle seemed to be unadapted to such pasturage conditions. Instead of grazing contentedly in the pastures they spent the greater part of their time wandering along the fences. Another reason for this failure, and a very important one, is that the number of acres allotted to an animal was usually placed too low, and overgrazing resulted.

In other words, these stock companies did not adapt themselves to the changed conditions. While a few men or companies have not made a success of running stock in inclosed areas, a very large number have succeeded. At the present time the most successful stockmen of such States as Texas, California, and Washington, where the free range is almost a thing of the past, run their stock in pastures.

Avoidance of Overgrazing

In making the change from the open range to the inclosed pastures stockmen must not lose sight of the fact that when they have thus shut out all stray stock they have not changed the carrying capacity of the land in the least. They must therefore be careful not to overgraze the inclosed areas, which is often done from a mistaken idea that the mere fencing of a range increases its carrying capacity. The majority of stockmen using the public domain place a very conservative estimate on its carrying capacity. Yet when they come to inclose an area and pasture it, they are quite inclined to put in more stock than their estimate calls for; consequently their pastures are badly overstocked, and in some instances are actually grazed closer than the outside range. This means not only that the pasture has been seriously damaged, but that the stock are in poorer condition at the end of the season than if they had run outside. It is safe to say that nine out of ten men changing from the outside range to pastures will overgraze their land the first season. Many of these will change their methods immediately and soon get their pastures on a supporting basis; others will take two or three years to really learn the true carrying capacity of their pastures; and still others, who can not get out of the rut, will continue to overgraze, with the result that their pastures will continually run down, while their stock grows poorer in quality from year to year.

Resting the Land

Where an area of land has been very severely overgrazed in the past it will be absolutely necessary that it be very carefully pastured for the first two or three years. The native grasses and forage plants must have a chance to regain their former vigor and to go to seed. A very large number of stockmen advocate resting the land — that is, keeping all stock off for a period of three or four years. That this remedy will bring about the desired results has been definitely proved in numerous instances. In Arizona the Department of Agriculture has a large area of land in the Santa Rita Forest Reserve that is entirely protected from stock. This area contains about 50 square miles, and includes range country that varies from very poor mesa to fairly good mountain range. Before it was fenced this area was in a very badly denuded condition. In less than two years, under protection, it has improved wonderfully. A large percentage of the new vegetation is of little value, however, as many of the seeds present were of plants not relished by stock. But the better kinds of grasses scattered among this vegetation are increasing.

In the State of Washington experiments and observation of inclosed areas covering a period of five years have shown conclusively that a given range can be very greatly improved and in some cases brought back to its original carrying capacity in from two to five years if it is properly protected. The length of time required for the range to be fully restored depends partly on how complete the overgrazing has been and largely on the amount of rainfall.

While resting will bring about the desired results, there are very few men who can afford to allow their land to remain idle for so long a period, as the taxes, interest on the investment, and cost of maintenance go on just the same whether the land is in use or not. Resting would in the end be cheaper than to continue overgrazing the land, but it is really not necessary. There is no reason why, by judicious management, the feed on such an area should not be utilized. If such a pasture be grazed very lightly during the early part of the season until the grasses can get their growth and go to seed, it will then have a chance to improve, although this improvement may be slight. It would be much better if the pasture could be protected until the grasses have gone to seed and the seed has fallen to the ground. Then the dry feed can be utilized without damage to the range.

Alternation of Pastures

This improvement can best be accomplished by dividing the pasture into a number of smaller ones and alternating the stock from one to another. The number of pastures will depend somewhat on the size of the range and how it is watered. In order to secure the best results there should be not less than three pastures, while four, or even more, would be much better. In all parts of the country the more successful stockmen have a fenced area that they reserve for winter pasture, while those who run their stock entirely on their own land nearly always subdivide to the extent of a summer and a winter pasture. It is noticeable that in nearly every instance the winter pasture shows an excellent stand and produces much more feed than the summer pasture. This is solely because the grasses, being grazed only in the winter, have a chance to remain in healthy condition and also to produce a crop of seed with which to supply new plants as the old ones give way. Again, there being a good covering of vegetation, the ground is protected so that the wind and hot sun do not take all the moisture out of the ground. Instead, the moisture is utilized in growing vegetation for feed.

In Texas many of the stockmen have found that it pays them to alternate their pastures. Some even assert that with their pastures in the best of condition they carry more stock on a given area where alternation of pasture is practiced than where one big field is used. Even in the East, where there is plenty of moisture, alternation of pastures is being more strongly advocated each year, as the farmers are gradually learning that their pastures can be made to carry more stock by this method.

Reseeding the Worn-Out Range

The problem of reseeding the range has received much attention from the Department of Agriculture. So far, experiments have shown that in the extremely arid portions of the range country reseeding is impracticable. The only method of restoring such areas is to rest the overgrazed portions. In case such ranges are grazed the year round, alternation of pastures is the only solution that can be offered at the present time. Fortunately, on account of the scarcity of water, the great majority of these areas are used only for winter pastures. In this way these areas have a chance to make a good growth and to go to seed during the summer season. Thus they have ample opportunity to restore themselves in case they are not over-grazed.

In the semiarid regions, such as the bunch-grass hills of Washington, Oregon, and Idaho, and the grama-grass regions of Montana, the Dakotas, and Wyoming, alternation of pastures will be equally useful.

Ordinarily, unless the overgrazing has been very severe, the restoration process will not take many years, in some instances only four or five. If, however, the overgrazing has been complete enough to practically destroy all the native plants and has been so long in duration that no seed is left in the ground, the process will be very slow indeed, for there is nothing left on which to base improvement. Under such conditions weeds of almost no forage value are very likely to take the place of the valuable forage plants that have been destroyed. In order to prevent this, it might be feasible in some localities to gather seed of these native grasses and scatter it on the overgrazed portions. In the State of Washington, farmers have taken seed of the tall lime-grass (*Elymus condensatus*), called rye-grass by stockmen, and sown it on areas where it formerly grew. Instances are known where these men are now cutting lime-grass hay from these same areas. Experiments carried on by the Washington Agricultural College in cooperation with the Bureau of Plant Industry have shown that this could probably be done in favorable seasons with bunch-grass. In the Dakotas and eastern Montana it is quite noticeable that wherever a part of the prairie land is plowed up and then allowed to revert it will in time be covered with wheat-grass (*Agropyron occidentale*). If it is plowed and nothing else is done the wheat-grass will take possession of the area very quickly. This and the rapidity with which this grass works into overgrazed places that are rested a little show very plainly that the overgrazed areas where it grows naturally can be easily restored by reseeding with this grass. Whether the grama grasses of these regions could be restored by this process is not known. Many of the leading stockmen are inclined to believe that they could, but think it would be a difficult matter to procure the seed.

Reseeding in the Mountain Areas

In the mountain areas, where the rainfall is much greater, the problem of restoring the range is not nearly so difficult. Where the devastation has not been too complete the range will soon restore itself if protected. On those areas where overgrazing has left the range in a denuded condition the restoration will take a number of years. It can, however, usually be greatly hastened by reseeding with some of the cultivated grasses. Experiments carried on during the past four years in the mountain areas of Washington have thoroughly demonstrated that timothy can be used to excellent advantage in the mountain meadows and in the parks of that

State where the original vegetation has been destroyed by sheep. This grass proved to be the best of a number used in reseeding the devastated mountain meadows (1) because it made the best growth and stood pasturage well, and (2) because it was the cheapest and easiest to start.

According to these experiments, the cost of reseeding land is from 60 cents to $1 an acre, depending on the amount of seed used and on the cost of getting it into the mountains. Eight pounds of seed per acre ought to give a stand that if cut for hay would yield approximately three-fourths of a ton of hay per acre. That would mean that it would yield nearly enough forage the second season after it was sown to pay for the reseeding. If the seed were sown in the autumn before snow falls it would need no further treatment, but if sown in the spring it should be harrowed in, which would greatly increase the cost.

These experiments have also proved that orchard grass and tall fescue would do well on those areas that are a little too dry for the successful growth of timothy, and that *Bromus inermis* will be of very great value in range improvement along the drier edges of the meadows and parks, provided the seed can be secured at a price that does not make it prohibitive. Redtop has given good results, but it has been very slow in establishing itself. It made almost no showing until the third year, but by the fourth season it had attained an excellent stand and was beginning to crowd out the native vegetation growing in the meadow with it. It will furnish a large amount of excellent feed in the mountain meadows.

In the Sierra Nevadas of California redtop and timothy have shown themselves to be of great value in reseeding along the edges of the worn-out and badly overgrazed meadows, provided they are not sown on those areas where there is standing water throughout the greater part of the year. Redtop seems to do especially well in the mountain areas. Judging from the results of experiments, when once introduced it will spread over a great part of the meadow and will form a dense sod that will in time crowd out other vegetation.

Orchard grass also grows very well in meadows, and also will apparently do well on some of the drier hillsides where there is not enough moisture for timothy or redtop. In fact, one of the rangers of the Sierra Forest Reserve has succeeded in growing a fair crop of orchard-grass hay for his saddle horses just on the lower edge of the timber belt, where the land has been cleared of chaparral and the conditions are quite arid.

Conservation of Water

The water problem is of extreme importance in range improvement, for without plenty of good water stock can not be expected to make good gains. When the land is once brought under control the stockmen can afford to go to considerable expense to secure plenty of water. In many instances, as in parts of Montana, Wyoming, and the Dakotas, large reservoirs, or "water holes," can be made, which, with the local showers during summer, will insure plenty of water throughout the year. In other sections, as in the sandhills of Nebraska or in southern California, the water can be easily obtained by means of wells and storage tanks, the water being pumped by windmills or gasoline engines. In many sections of the country, as in Washington, Oregon, and Nevada, there are numerous springs which formerly watered a large number of cattle, but which have gone dry through the incessant tramping of stock about them. If these springs were dug out and fenced and the water conducted to troughs they could again be made to furnish an abundance of water for a considerable number of stock. The water thus stored in troughs will be kept clean for the stock and none of it need be wasted through seepage. In Nevada the digging out and protection of the springs is considered to be of the greatest importance.

Every opportunity should be taken to increase the number of watering places, so that the stock using them would need to travel only comparatively short distances. In this way the range can be improved greatly, as the stock will not need to tramp over so much ground in traveling from the grass to the water and back. It will also be beneficial to the stock themselves, as the time spent now in traveling for water can be spent in resting or in feeding, and thus in making larger gains.

Premature Grazing to be Avoided

One of the great dangers in handling range stock is the tendency of many of the stockmen to put their stock out on the range just as soon as the grass begins to start in the spring and before the ground is thoroughly settled. The vegetation, being nipped off before it gets a fair start, or, as the stockmen say, "gets strong," is greatly retarded in its growth and does not produce as much feed that season as it would if it had a better chance. Where the soil is clayey the damage caused by the premature grazing is greatly increased by the tramping of the stock, which tends to pack it into a hard layer that is impenetrable to plant roots. This packing of the soil has been one of the greatest factors in the destruction of the feed in many mountain meadows.

Raising Winter Feed

In order to obtain the greatest returns from his land, the stockman of the future will need to grow enough feed to carry his stock through the winter without danger of loss and to keep them in good growing condition. With the extra cost of running his stock in pastures he must keep them constantly gaining, or they will prove a loss. If he can not get water for irrigation either from some stream or through storage reservoirs, such as are common in the Dakotas, that will catch enough surface water to insure sufficient pasture, he will need to grow grain hay.

Of the different cereals that can be used for hay, rye will probably prove to be the surest to yield a good crop over the greatest area of country. It will stand the hard winters of the North as well as any of the other cereals and requires the least moisture of any of them to mature a crop of hay. It can also be made to yield a fair crop with as little effort as any of the other cereals, and can thus be grown at the least cost. Many of the stockmen are greatly prejudiced against this plant as forage. This is probably very largely due to the fact that they have allowed it to get too ripe before cutting. If cut when just in the milk it makes excellent hay with which to winter stock. Beardless barley is another excellent crop to grow for grain hay. It produces a better quality of feed than rye and in some localities is preferred to any of the cultivated grasses for feed. It probably could not be depended on to produce as large a yield as rye, nor is it so certain a crop. In some sections of the country, as in the Dakotas, durum wheat will produce a considerable amount of forage in the more favorable years. In other sections many of the farmers seem to be well pleased with spelt. These last two plants are not so desirable for stock as some others on account of their heavy beards. These beards will often cause sore mouths, especially when fed to horses, and will also cause losses among sheep. In the more favorable localities wheat, barley, and oats can be grown.

In the Dakotas and eastern Montana a number of stockmen raise corn for forage and find this to be exceedingly profitable. These men are thoroughly convinced that by feeding corn fodder to their calves and yearlings they get enough better gains to pay them well for their extra work. It is noticeable that the men who are doing this are topping the markets with grass-fed cattle from their sections. This they ascribe largely to the fact that they get better gains on their young stock. In most instances these men are really raising a better grade of cattle than their neighbors, which must also be taken into consideration.

Where a little water can be stored for irrigation, brome-grass (*Bromus inermis*) produces a fair crop of hay and is becoming quite popular. This is especially true of the western half of the Dakotas. It is quite probable that with the same amount of water alfalfa would give a larger yield. Alfalfa will grow on much drier land than is often supposed. In many parts of the West the stockmen have been trying to start this plant. Some succeed, while others fail. A large number get very poor results, as their alfalfa seems to "winter-kill" badly. Experiments that are being carried on at the substation at Dickinson, N. Dak., appear to indicate that much of the winter-killing is due to a lack of nitrogen-gathering bateria, which are essential for the successful growth of alfalfa. Alfalfa is really worth a considerable effort in order to get it started. In case of failure it should be tried again on a small scale until it has been determined whether it can be made to succeed.

Area of Land Needed

The area of land required to justify engaging in the stock business, without other source of revenue, varies greatly in different sections. In the northern range States, where stock must be fed for a period of three or four months during the winter season, and where the rainfall is fairly abundant, 2,500 to 4,000 acres of land would ordinarily be needed to make a fair living for a family. If the settler were fortunate in selecting a range that had not been very much overgrazed and on which there was very little waste land, he might be able to get along with only 2,000 acres. Such areas will, however, be difficult to find. In the more southern range States, where the rainfall is much less and not so well distributed throughout the season, the number of acres required for an animal will be much greater. Here the area required to support a family will vary from 16,000 acres in the better sections to 25,000, and in some cases as much as 40,000 acres are required.

Improving the Grade of Stock

Improvement of the class of stock using the grazing lands is becoming constantly more important. In the old days, when there was plenty of free range, almost any kind of animal could be sold at a profit. Under the present crowded conditions the cost of maintenance is much higher, and the poor-grade animal, or "scrub," will no longer yield satisfactory returns.

The man who is running his stock in inclosed areas or contemplates so doing in the future will find it necessary, if he is to be successful, to carry that class of stock that will net him the greatest returns. This statement holds equally true for the outside range. In fact, there are only two methods whereby the man who expects to continue running his stock on the public domain can meet the existing conditions successfully. One is the raising of sufficient feed to carry his stock through the winter safely; the other, to run a grade of stock that shall make the largest possible returns in the shortest time.

A cattleman can no longer afford to run steers until they are 4, 5, or 6 years old, but he will need to raise quick-maturing animals that will be ready for market by the time they are 2 or 3 years old — 4 at the very latest. Not only must these cattle mature early, but they must be of a quality that will dress a good percentage of beef.

This means that the cattleman will need to raise high-grade cows and supply the very best bulls he can secure — if pure bred, so much the better. In many instances the cattlemen are so crowded for range that they find it difficult to produce beef because the grass is insufficient for the steers to make rapid gains. Men in other sections find the grass of too poor a quality to fatten steers. These men will need to grow cattle for the eastern feed yards, to be sold to the feeder in the autumn as calves, yearlings, 2-year-olds, or 3-year-olds. In producing such cattle many of these men will find it necessary to improve their herds greatly, for quality and not quantity is what the eastern feeder wants. Many of these feeders complain bitterly because they can not obtain the class of cattle they need. It is noticeable that in the sales of "feeders and stockers" at Omaha, Chicago, and other stock yards those of poor quality are hard sellers and ordinarily go at very low figures.

In the South the cattlemen realize that they must cut down their herds and instead of large ones of low-grade cattle they must raise smaller and better herds. Many of the cattlemen are making this change by culling out their poor-grade cows and heifers as fast as they can.

As an example of what may be done on the open range under present overcrowded conditions, the methods of a stockman living near Reva, S. Dak., may be mentioned. A few years ago this man, becoming dissatisfied with the kind of cattle that he was running, bought a registered bull and began to grade his cattle up. By using good registered Shorthorn bulls, which he changes every three years, and by selecting good-grade cows, he has been grading up his herd until now his cattle outweigh and outsell those in his immediate neighborhood. At first his neighbors made considerable sport of him for importing registered stock and prophesied that he would make a failure of it. Instead of a failure his cattle are so much better in quality that they may be distinguished a long distance away merely by their body outline and their increased size. In order to get the most good out of his animals this man was, of course, obliged to do a good deal more work in taking care of them. He found it necessary to "line ride" his range every day in order to keep his stock from straying and to see that his bulls served his own cows and not those of his neighbors. This extra work has paid him well, as he rarely loses cattle through straying and does not need to belong to any of the round-up associations. The prime value of this work is shown in his calf crop, which averages about 95 per cent, while that of his neighbors averages only about 60 per cent.

Now that the range is becoming so crowded that it is difficult to get sufficient grass to fatten steers, he is preparing to increase his breeding stock and cut down the number of his beef steers, so that when he can no longer grow beef he will be in a position to dispose of a high class of feeding cattle, which he will aim to sell as yearlings or 2-year-olds to eastern feeders. This he can do without any sacrifice whatever, as he has a type of cattle that is exactly such as the feeders want but find it difficult to obtain.

What has been said of cattle holds equally true of horses. To-day there is almost no place for the small horse or "cayuse," while good animals are in demand. That one can afford to raise good horses on the range has been demonstrated by a stockman living in western North Dakota. During a period of low prices for range horses this man bought a high-priced stallion. With this animal and nine range mares of average size and quality as a nucleus he built up a fine herd. When the stallion died he was replaced with two registered Percherons, which continued to build up the herd until it was one of the finest herds of range horses in the United States. When this man got his first horse his neighbors believed that he had made a serious mistake in buying so expensive an animal. For several years, while he was building up his herd, at which time horses were of almost no value, he was considerably in debt. As his stock began to improve and the price of horses increased he began to realize well from this herd, and during the last two years he has sold geldings in carload lots at $125 a head, unbroken. In the summer of 1906 he sold his entire herd, 227 head, at $85 a head straight for all branded stock — an unusually high price for range horses. There were two mares of his own raising in this herd for which the buyers refused $550 unbroken. This man estimates that his first stallion made for him many times what he paid for it.

Movement Toward Farming Range Lands

With the first extension of the railroads through the Western States large areas of land that had been previously inaccessible except for stock were taken up for farming purposes. At first only the choice areas that would grow good grain crops or those places that could be easily irrigated were selected. Within the last ten or twelve years people have learned that, by careful tillage and the use of machinery, land that had hitherto been considered of no value except for grazing can be made to produce paying crops of grain. This, together with the vast extension of irrigable lands through private enterprise and the different Government projects, has caused a heavy immigration to these regions. If the present demand for western lands continues it will be only a short time before all of the public domain except the mountainous portions and the extremely arid sections will be taken up for farming purposes.

While the rapid strides that have been made in arid-land cultivation make it impossible to tell exactly what lands will produce successful crops for a period of several years, it would seem that many of the people who have settled in the arid regions will eventually be compelled either to give up their places or combine stock raising with their dry-land farming.

Probable Future of Range Stock Industry

Present tendencies indicate that the range-stock industry of the future will be confined to those regions that are too rough for cultivation or too arid for the successful growth of crops. Except in the high mountain regions, where the grazing season is very short, or in the desert areas, where, on account of the scarcity of water, grazing can be carried on only during the winter months, the grazing will eventually be carried on in inclosed fields or on definitely assigned tracts. The stockmen will endeavor to get bodies of land large enough to support their stock, either by purchase, leasing, or, in case the homestead act should be amended to fit range conditions, by homesteading. Many living in close proximity to forest reserves will secure grazing permits, allowing them to run stock in these areas during the summer season. Wherever possible these men will raise enough feed to carry their stock safely through the winter season.

American Dietary Habits

From C. F. Longworthy, "Food and Diet in the United States," U.S. Department of Agriculture, *Yearbook*, 1907, pp. 361–64, 373–78.

Introduction

The food of any individual or family is to a very large extent determined by circumstances. Anthropologists claim, and with good reason, that in the earliest days of the human race man lived without much choice on the food which he could obtain, being fitted by his inheritance from earlier forms of life to use a large variety of foodstuffs. If he happened to be an inhabitant of sea coast regions, shellfish and other sea food, which could be readily procured, were eaten in quantity. If he lived in inland regions where nuts, wild roots, and seed-bearing grasses were abundant, such foods were used, and no one can doubt that game birds and their eggs and such other animal foods as were available were eaten.

In general, the food habits of the human race to-day are an expression of the thousands of years of experience in which man has sought to bring himself into harmony with his environment, and food habits have been determined, as regards materials selected, by available supply, man being by nature omnivorous.

Popular Ideas Regarding Diet

The majority of persons get their ideas of the food habits of a race or region from popular writings, and often the source of information is inaccurate or incomplete. If a writer states that the diet in New England is pork and beans and brown bread, or that in the South it is corn meal and pork, we all know that the statement is very inadequate. But when such statements are made about the diet in less familiar regions the error is not so obvious.

It is often said and is generally believed that we have a generous diet in the United States and that the range in variety of food products is unusually large. Our dietary results from many customs and food habits of the races which have helped to make up our population, but in its general character it is British, as is natural, for the bulk of the earliest settlers were from Great Britain and brought the customs and manners of the old home with them, adapted them to the new country, and passed them on to the succeeding generations. As time has passed there have been marked changes in the character of the diet, owing to improved methods of cultivation of food crops, to better methods of transportation and storage, to improvement in house construction and kitchen appliances, and to similar factors. Whether the value of the daily diet has changed when considered from the standpoint of nutritive material supplied is another matter, and one which it is more difficult to decide.

It is not without interest to consider in more detail some of the factors which have modified dietary habits. In northern regions of the United States, in earlier times, the vegetable supply in the summer was fairly abundant, but in the winter was limited to a few varieties, chiefly root crops, which were of good keeping quality. Eggs, salt meats, and less commonly poultry were staple summer foods, but fresh beef, mutton, and pork were much more abundant in winter, when they could be kept frozen in good condition, than in summer. The lack of variety of vegetable foods in winter and of fresh meat in summer was without doubt the reason for the great variety of preserves and pickles which every housewife deemed necessary, and for the great number of kinds of pastry, cake, and similar dishes. In other words, there was a craving for variety, and it was satisfied by using in many different ways the comparatively small number of food materials which were most commonly obtainable.

As regards different regions, we find that the available food supply very largely determines the food habits for the family or group, as it was stated earlier that it does for the race. Thus we find that in rural regions in the Southern States beef and mutton, which must be kept with ice after slaughtering, are less common food than poultry, which may be easily raised and kept alive until needed. In the same way, corn meal and other corn products, which are readily available, have always been popular foods, as have cowpeas, gumbo and collards, sweet potatoes, and the large variety of other southern vegetables which are so palatable.

In the case of Germany, England, and other European countries the information which is available regarding foods and food habits is large in amount, and the popular statements which are made concerning them are accurate in the main. It is by no means unusual, however, to find misstatements which only too often pass without question. For instance, the writers who describe the potato diet in parts of rural Ireland not infrequently omit to mention the skim milk or the bacon which goes with it. The peasants in many regions of the Continent "taste meat hardly once a year," we are often told. A study of their diet usually shows that cheese, milk, and other foods are used to replace the meat they find too expensive, and the diet is not actually so limited as at first sight it would seem to be. Mention is much less commonly made in popular writings of the great number of the wage-earners of these countries who have a generous and varied diet, as is evident from a study of the available data on the subject.

Erroneous statements regarding food and diet in different eastern countries are very frequently met with, though in many cases the question has been so often studied that reliable information is readily accessible. For instance, it is commonly said that Chinese, Japanese, and other oriental races live upon rice, and that large amounts of severe physical work are performed on a few handfuls of this cereal per day. Careful study of oriental dietetics shows that although rice is undoubtedly one of the most important foodstuffs, it fills much the same place in the diet that wheat and other common starchy foods do in the diet of western races. In other words, it is the most common and abundant starchy food. Food customs vary in the different oriental countries, but on the whole it may be said that eggs, fish, poultry, meat, and legumes are well-known nitrogenous foods and that the diet as a whole is usually adequate, particularly when considered in relation to body weight.

It is generally true that the more we learn about diet in remote regions, and the more accurate our knowledge regarding kinds and amounts of food eaten, the fewer the anomalies and the closer the resemblance in nutritive value to more familiar conditions.

Dietary Studies and Their Object

If really reliable information regarding the food of a family or a race is wanted, it must be secured by means of carefully conducted studies of the kind and amount of food eaten, the results being so expressed that they may be readily compared with other similar data.

With the growth of the scientific spirit and method and its application to all branches of learning, it is not surprising to find that the attempt should be made to carefully record and express in chemical terms the food habits of man in different countries, the underlying idea being that such a summary of data should show the practice of those who are in health, comfort, and vigor, whose lives are long and whose offspring are healthy, and that this would be valuable as a guide for others. Such an inference seems natural and reasonable, for it is difficult for those who believe that the human race has developed and improved as it has lived to conclude otherwise than that the customs of a race represent the accumulated wisdom of the ages of experiment and experience which have gone before.

European investigators began about 1850 to collect such information regarding dietetics and to reduce it to chemical terms, and the average values which they found, often interpreted in the light of laboratory work, were commonly called dietary standards. Such compilations were new in form rather than in practice, for earlier students and thinkers had collected similar data and made deductions therefrom, though the results were expressed in different terms.

American investigators followed the lead of European scientists, Prof. W. O. Atwater, who was so long in charge of the nutrition investigations of this Department, being a pioneer in the work, and a great deal of information was accumulated regarding the foods eaten by individuals and groups living under different circumstances. . . .

Adequacy of the Average American Diet

It is interesting to note that the results of dietary studies made throughout the United States do not indicate any probability of general undernutrition. In many cases families were living on a very limited diet that might be much improved as regards the kinds and amounts of food eaten, but such cases were almost exclusively found in studies made with people of such limited incomes that they were living below what has been termed the "poverty line." In the great majority of families and groups which have been studied the food was abundant, though it can be said with equal fairness that there were many opportunities for improvement as regards the rational selection of foods, economical preparation and use, and similar lines.

That persistent overfeeding is harmful no one would deny. That grave errors may also attend the long-continued use of a diet which is markedly deficient especially in nitrogenous material seems clear from the conditions noted in families or larger groups forced by circumstances to live for long periods of years on such a diet. It seems almost invariably the case that such persons are in less satisfactory physical condition and have a lower productive capacity for useful work than similar families and groups living under more generous conditions. As an instance may be cited poor families studied in New York, whose diet was limited and whose physical condition was much inferior to that of families similarly situated except for a more generous diet.

The numerous inquiries made under State or Government auspices into the question of physical deterioration and the almost unanimous conclusion that it is connected with undernourishment give additional point to the view that a reasonably generous diet is desirable.

The question of physical deterioration, which has attracted attention in Europe and has been much discussed in relation to undernutrition, can not be raised with reference to our people as a whole. A large capacity for useful labor and a high average as to the grade of work performed are conceded to Americans by careful students of this subject in this country and elsewhere. The comparatively high standard as regards family and community hygiene and sanitation, and other similar factors, undoubtedly have a bearing on these questions, but no one can doubt that diet exercises an influence, certainly not inferior to any other single factor, and the American diet as a whole is liberal.

Kinds of Food Eaten in American Homes

Owing to wide range in climate and agricultural conditions, the United States yields food products in great variety as well as in great abundance. Methods of transporting, storing, and distributing food products have kept pace with improved methods of cultivation, and perhaps at no time and in no country has there been a greater variety of products of the farm, field, ranch, and garden from which to select than in the United States to-day.

In connection with the dietary studies which have been made under the auspices of this Department, data have been summarized which show the proportionate amounts of different foods which make up the diet of the average American home and the relative proportion of the total nutrients and energy which the principal foods and food groups supply. A summary of such data based on the results of about 400 studies is presented in the table on page 375. As will be seen, the number of foods which may be called staples and which make up the bulk of the diet is small, including, among others, such articles as wheat flour, meat, milk, butter, and vegetables.

It will be seen further that animal and vegetable foods are about equal in rank as sources of protein, some 48 per cent of the total being supplied by animal foods and 52 per cent by vegetable foods, of which 43 per cent is contributed by the cereals. Little fat is furnished by vegetable foods, the group as a whole supplying only 11 per cent of the total amount in the diet. Animal foods and dairy products are the most important sources of fat, milk and cream furnishing 26 per cent of the total fat of the diet and meat, as a whole, furnishing a little over twice as much as all other animal foods. Of the different meats, pork is the most important source of fat. Meats and poultry together furnish about twice as much protein as the other animal foods, and beef and veal together furnish about half of the total amount supplied by the entire group.

Proportion of nutrients furnished by different food materials in the average American dietary.

Food material.	Total food material	Protein	Fat	Carbo-hydrates.
ANIMAL FOODS.	P. ct.	P. ct.	P. ct.	P. ct.
Beef and veal...............................	7.2	16.7	13.2	....
Lamb and mutton............................	.9	2.1	2.6	....
Pork, including lard........................	7.2	9.3	42.1	....
Poultry......................................	.7	1.6	.9	....
Total meats	16.0	29.7	58.8	....
Fish	1.8	3.5	1.0	....
Eggs...	2.1	4.1	2.9	....
40,				
Butter.......................................	1.6	.3	16.6	....
Cheese.......................................	.3	1.0	1.1	....
Milk and cream	16.5	8.7	8.0	3.6
Total dairy products........................	18.4	10.0	25.7	3.6
Unclassified animal foods...................	.2	.2	.2	.3
Total animal foods	38.5	47.5	88.6	3.9
VEGETABLE FOODS.				
Wheat flour, patent.........................	12.2	19.4	1.5	2.6
Wheat flour, entire	.1	.1	....	.2
Wheat flour, graham	.1	.2	....	.2
Wheat preparations..........................	.3	.5	.1	1.0
Wheat bread, patent.........................	5.8	8.1	1.6	12.4
Wheat bread, entire	....	....	....	.1
Wheat bread, graham	.1	.1	....	.2
Crackers.....................................	.3	.5	.5	1.0
Sweet cakes, etc	.6	.8	.9	1.4
Corn meal and flour.........................	8.7	10.1	3.8	13.7
Corn preparations...........................	.2	.2	.1	.4
Oatmeal and preparations	.5	1.0	.5	1.1
Rice...	.3	.3	....	.9
Rye..	1.3	1.6	.1	3.1
Barley and buckwheat	.1	.1	....	.5
Total cereals...............................	30.6	43.0	9.1	61.8
Sugar, molasses, etc.	5.4	....	....	17.5
Starch (prepared)	....	....	....	.1
Dried legumes...............................	1.0	2.9	.2	1.7
Fresh legumes...............................	.6	.4	.....	.3
Tubers and yams.............................	12.5	3.8	.3	8.3
Other vegetables	6.2	1.6	.5	1.7
Total vegetables............................	20.3	8.7	1.0	12.0
Fresh fruits................................	3.8	.3	.3	2.5
Dried fruits	.6	.2	.1	1.2
Total fruits................................	4.4	.5	.4	3.7

Nuts	. . . .	. . . .	.1	. . . .
Unclassified foods	.5	.1	.2	.6
Total vegetable foods	61.	52.3	10.8	95.7
Miscellaneous food materials	.3	.2	.6	.4
Total food materials	100.0	100.0	100.0	100.0

The table on page 375 does not show the relative amounts of the different foods which are expensive and which may be classed as luxuries rather than staples, but it is obvious that such foods do not supply a very large proportion of the total nutrients and energy, since the groups (e. g., "other vegetables," "fresh fruits," etc.) in which many are included are not large factors in the totals.

Variety in Diet in Relation to Cost

In general it may be said that, other things being equal, the cost of the daily food is determined by the proportion of the total expended for such staple articles as bread, meat, butter, eggs, and common vegetables, and the expenditure for accessory foods, such as expensive fruit, out-of-season vegetables, fancy sweets, etc., which, as ordinarily used, contribute more to the attractiveness of the diet than they do to its nutritive value. As an instance, may be cited the results obtained with a workingman's family in New Jersey in comfortable circumstances. The total expenditure for food during the period covered by the dietary study was $34.95. Of this, $5.16, or 14.8 per cent, was paid for oranges and celery, which together furnished only 150 grams protein and 6,445 calories of energy or about 1 per cent of both total protein and total fuel value. During the same period the expenditure for cheaper vegetables and fruits, such as potatoes, cabbage, sweet potatoes, apples, canned tomatoes, canned peaches, etc., was $5.75, and this supplied 1,909 grams protein and 58,000 calories of energy. The expenditure of $5.16 for cereal foods and sugar furnished 3,375 grams protein and 184,185 calories of energy, or about 25 times the amount supplied by the celery and oranges. The oranges and celery undoubtedly added to the attractiveness of the diet, and nothing can be said against their use provided the cost of the diet is reasonable in proportion to the family income. It is true, however, that such foods could have been omitted from the diet without materially changing its nutritive value, while the cost of the daily food would have been considerably lowered; or other articles perhaps equally attractive but of lower cost might have been used in place of the oranges and celery.

It is in the combination, with due reference to economy, of staple articles, many of which are lacking in distinctive flavor, with foods and dishes which possess marked flavor that one of the greatest opportunities for skillful management in the household occurs.

Another problem of importance is the ease and economy of preparation of food in relation to its cost. A cheap cut of meat, like shoulder clod, can not be so readily served in attractive form as a choice steak. The cheaper cut requires much longer cooking and consequently more fuel and labor, and to be at its best should be cooked with seasoning vegetables or prepared in some similar way which secures flavor. Other cases like this are too well known to need mention. True economy consists in so adjusting such matters to the family income that palate and purse may each have its due.

The housewife who can appreciate and apply the available knowledge regarding the relative cost of different methods of cookery, fitting combinations of food, the relation between composition and cost, and similar factors can supply wholesome diet suited to her family needs at a much more reasonable cost than is the case when such knowledge is disregarded.

Importance of Scientific Data in Home Management

Many housekeepers are very wise in questions of home management and understand the art of housekeeping so well that they secure the desired results with the empirical knowledge gained by experience and handed down from mother to daughter. The problems pertaining to food and diet have received a very large amount of study during the last fifty years, and the explanation of many facts on which empirical knowledge was based has been learned, and there is now a large body of valuable information, much of which has been so systematized that it can be readily taught. That this is the case is shown by the large number of high schools and other educational institutions which give courses in home economics and the success which has attended this kind of teaching. It is certainly true that system and coordination can be taught with respect to the purchase of food and the management of dietetic problems in the same way that they can be taught with reference to manufacturing problems or other business enterprises. In both cases, some of the facts systematized and arranged have been newly acquired by experimental study, while others are the result of experience and are as old as the race.

The problems of economy in living differ in town and country. The farmer's wife has her vegetables, fruits, poultry, dairy products, etc., without a cash outlay, while the housewife in the city must purchase everything. Considering market facilities, however, and the prices which must be paid for many staple and fancy foods, the advantage with respect to such foods seems to lie with the careful buyer in the large town or city. The small town with its garden and other opportunities for home production of food products is, of course, midway between the city and country. Each region has its attractions and its special advantages, but the underlying principles with respect to economical home management are the same in every locality. It is with a view to helping the producer to provide the food supplies which are most needed and the housewife to solve her problems that studies of the kind and amount of food eaten, the relative nutritive value of different foods, the comparative economy of different methods of cooking, and related questions have been undertaken by this Department.

Conclusion

An extended survey of the literature of food supply and the food habits of many races makes it plain that in no country is there a greater variety of readily accessible foods of good quality than in the United States and in none is there a more general use of a wide range of articles. Thanks to our varied climate, our ready means of transportation, and our facilities for marketing and handling food products, the contributions of any given locality are readily accessible in other regions.

Skill in selecting from this great variety of food products and in the preparation of foods after they are purchased is essential if out of our abundance a diet is to be secured which is best suited to the needs of the American people. The dietary studies herein summarized and other similar reliable data seem to show that the people of the United States as a whole are adequately nourished as compared with other races. The acknowledged energy and achievement of the American people, together with their general good health and physical well being, certainly indicate that we have in the main used our food resources advantageously.

Development of Truck Farming, 1907

From L. C. Corbett, "Truck Farming in the Atlantic Coast States," U.S. Department of Agriculture, *Yearbook*, 1907, pp. 425–34.

Introduction

The development and extension of truck farming in the Atlantic coast States has been coincident with the development of transportation facilities throughout that section. In the beginning the points affording water connection with the great consuming centers of the North were those at which truck farming first became established. Later the railways became feeders to the steamship lines, and following this came the development of express shipment, which has been almost entirely supplanted by fast freight and refrigeration in the handling of extensive truck shipments from distant fields of production.

The phenomenal growth of the great consuming centers of the country has stimulated a corresponding growth and extension of the food-producing territory, especially that capable of producing perishable truck crops. The demands for vegetables out of season, followed later by the continuous demand for fresh vegetables throughout the year by the great cities, led first to the market gardeners located near the cities supplementing their field operations by extensive forcing-house enterprises. Naturally, the products from the greenhouses were expensive and available only to the few who were able to pay fancy prices for green products out of season. The improvement and extension of the transportation facilities which came with the great railway-building era of the United States made it possible to take advantage of the wide diversity of climate offered along the Atlantic coast of the United States to furnish these perishable products to the great cities of the North and East.

Transportation facilities, together with cheap labor and cheap lands at the South, have made it possible to produce in extreme southern locations products out of season at the North in competition with greenhouse products. The greater land area and the smaller amount of capital involved in the production of crops at the South, even though transportation charges were high, have enabled southern growers to produce much larger quantities of the desired crops than could be grown profitably under glass. It was therefore not many years before lettuce, celery, tomatoes, radishes, beets, and bunch beans came to be regular winter and early spring products of gardens located at great distances from the centers of consumption.

The first development of truck farming, as we now recognize it, as distinguished from market gardening, took place about Norfolk, Va., and Charleston, S.C. Both of these places were provided with steamship connections to northern ports before rapid railway transportation became a feature in the moving of perishable products, and as a result of these advantages for reaching the markets these two ports became important truck-producing centers for supplying the northern trade.

Besides these advantages, the peculiar geographic formation of the territory immediately surrounding Norfolk gives it a winter climate characteristic of sections many miles southward. The fact that the coast line of the United States at this particular point is very broken, together with the proximity of the Gulf Stream, gives this area a winter climate which enables it to produce some of the standard garden crops without protection and many of the more tender crops with only slight protection during the winter months. The islands off the coast of South Carolina, in the vicinity of Charleston, are so protected by the warm currents and by the atmosphere of the sea that orange trees are grown successfully in the open, and in some favorable seasons are known to produce fruit. It is therefore possible to grow the hardier truck crops in the open and the more tender ones with very slight protection during the winter.

The advantages of the Norfolk region for truck work appealed to a Jerseyman by the name of Hugh Bates, who went to this section about 1840. Naturally he followed the practices of his home people of New Jersey in the new territory, and, while he found some of his precautions unnecessary, his work on the whole was successful. He was followed later by other growers from the same territory, and in 1854 the steamer *Roanoke* carried the first 200-barrel shipment of garden truck from Norfolk to New York.

Thirty-six hours were required to make the voyage, and difficulty was experienced in keeping these perishable products from heating during this period. Four hundred packages was the capacity limit of the boats in use at that date, while at the present time the increased tonnage of vessels in this service enables them to carry as high as 25,000 packages on a single trip, which can be made in eighteen to twenty hours.

It was not until thirty years later that the first all-rail shipments of truck were made from this territory. Railways began carrying the products from Norfolk to northern markets in 1885, and from Charleston in 1888. About the same time Florida sent her first carload of oranges to the New York market, and in 1889 was shipped her first carload of strawberries under refrigeration. With the adaptation of refrigeration to car and steamship service and the lessened time required to transport perishable commodities, the territory tributary to the great markets of the North has been wonderfully increased, and the doors of the market, as it were, now open direct into the gardens of the South. From the small beginnings just indicated, the industry has grown until the products are measured in thousands of carloads instead of hundreds of barrels.

Variety of Crops Grown

Besides the staple market-garden crops of the North which are now extensively grown as truck crops throughout the South Atlantic coast region, there are crops which are more or less peculiar to certain localities. As illustrations, the watermelons of Georgia, the kale of Norfolk, and the sweet potatoes of eastern Maryland and of New Jersey stand out preeminently. The northern areas of the trucking region also are characterized by particular crops adapted to comparatively restricted areas. Eastern Long Island is the seat of the cauliflower and Brussels sprouts industry of the eastern United States, as well as the center for the production of practically all the American-grown cabbage seed.

In general, however, the great commercial trucking industry is based on staple crops which are in continuous demand in the markets, and which, owing to differences in latitude and climatic conditions, may be grown in successive crop zones from southern Florida to Maine. Such crops as lettuce, radishes, peas, beans, potatoes, cabbage, summer squash, and beets are characteristic products of nearly every developed trucking zone along the whole coast. These crops may, indeed, be considered the staple truck crops, as they furnish the basis for profitable truck farming throughout the country. Those few areas which are peculiarly fitted for the production of some special crop, such, for instance, as kale, cauliflower, or Brussels sprouts, have an advantage over other areas which must depend solely on growing the staples.

Methods of Handling Some Staple Truck Crops

The methods of growing the staple truck crops differ somewhat in the various crop zones. While no attempt will be made here to present a detailed statement regarding the important truck crops for each of the several crop zones covered by the Atlantic coast States, some of the differences existing between the methods of handling certain standard crops in the various portions of the area will be pointed out.

Lettuce

Lettuce is grown as a field crop in Florida. . . . In the vicinity of Charleston, S.C., and Wilmington, N.C., it is handled almost exclusively as a frame crop, while near New York and Boston it is chiefly grown in forcing houses. While the products of Florida and Charleston come in competition to some extent with the New York and Boston crops, as a rule these products are quite easily distinguished and naturally gravitate to different districts in the great consuming centers.

Cucumbers

In Florida cucumbers are grown as a field crop. In the vicinity of Charleston and Wilmington they are extensively grown as field crops; at Charleston the plant first appears as a forcing crop, and in the neighborhood of Norfolk it is distinctively a frame crop early in the season, followed by a large field production later on. In the northern portion of the territory cucumbers are grown not only in forcing houses but asa frame product, and also as a field crop for the use of salting stations and pickle factories.

Cabbage

Cabbage is even more cosmopolitan than either of the foregoing crops. The methods employed to adapt it to the requirements of the market and to the different areas in the trucking region are very distinct and each forms a chapter in the cultural history of this important truck crop. For instance, at the South cabbage is a winter crop, seeds being sown during September and October, the plants transplanted to the field at the beginning of winter, and kept in a slowly growing condition throughout the colder portion of the year, to be forced rapidly by the addition of stimulating fertilizers early in the spring to supply the demands of the market as the warm weather comes on. This product is naturally very soft and must be consumed with little delay; and, since it is grown on a very extensive scale it must be so distributed as to meet only the immediate demands of the market to which it is sent. The importance of this industry can be judged from the fact that it is found in the crop zones from Florida to Norfolk and in areas commensurate with the needs of the market during the periods when the product is supplied by particular zones. As the supply of northern stored cabbage disappears from the market, the product from the extreme South follows closely. This in turn is followed by an intermediate crop grown around Charleston, S.C., where is found the largest acreage of purely truck-crop cabbage in the United States. The area surrounding a single shipping point in this region in 1905 produced a head of cabbage for every inhabitant of the United States.

Farther up the coast, cabbage partially gives way to kale; and, while cabbage is a very important crop, it does not hold supreme sway, as it does in the Charleston region. At the North the crop is of a very different character, both in variety and in the method of its cultivation. The great bulk of the northern-grown cabbage may be considered as a truck-crop feature of the general farming in sections where the industry has gained a foothold. The cabbage crop takes a regular place in the farm rotation in those communities where the industry has become a permanent feature. In some sections it forms the chief money crop of the fall season, occupying a position similar to that held by potatoes in other sections.

As a truck crop at the North cabbage follows immediately on the passing of the southern supply, which is marked by the clearing of the fields in the neighborhood of Norfolk. This in turn is followed by domestic cabbage for home consumption or for the manufacture of sauerkraut. In this northern territory only a very small percentage of the crop is produced from fall-sown seed and plants carried through the winter in cold frames. A large part of the early product is produced from plants grown in hotbeds or greenhouses and transferred to the open as soon as weather conditions will permit. The great bulk of the crop which forms the supply of the storage houses and sauerkraut factories, however, is grown as a farm crop from seed sown in seed beds in the open, the plants being transplanted to the field about the 1st of July.

This great crop is measured by thousands of acres and millions of tons. At harvest time, in October and November, it is shipped to the great consuming centers in bulk in carload lots. It is stored by thousands of tons in specially constructed warehouses, to be sent out as the demands of the market will justify during the winter season. It is also manufactured into sauerkraut, which finds its way to the great cities as rapidly as there is a demand for it. . . .

Potatoes

The potato must be looked upon as one of the standard commercial crops of the country. While its acreage is not as vast as that of wheat or corn, it holds high rank as a money-producing crop throughout a very large part of the territory of the United States. . . . In this section sloops are loaded by the farmers and the barrels of potatoes are transferred to railway trains or to steamships at some convenient port.

With this crop the rule that at certain seasons of the year certain localities or sections are relied upon to supply the demands of the market holds good. What is true of the cabbage in regard to methods of handling and marketing is to a less extent true of the potato. The acreage of potatoes is undoubtedly much greater than that of cabbage, but the methods of treatment are not so varied, because, owing to the tender nature of the plant, even in the extreme southern portion of our continental area, the potato can not be cultivated as a winter crop, as can cabbage and onions. The planting of potatoes must be delayed until the time of hard spring frosts has passed. This places it on the basis of a spring crop, even in Florida, where it is extensively grown to meet the demand of northern cities. In this territory, however, advantage is taken of the use of quick-maturing varieties in order that the demand at the North for early potatoes may be met as the season warms up. Besides the use of early varieties the growers of this territory depend largely upon seed grown in extreme northern localities, it being a well-known fact that seed potatoes from such sources germinate more readily and mature a marketable crop of tubers in less time than home-grown seed. For a number of years, however, there has been considerable interest in and use made of a so-called "second-crop" potato which has been produced in the South, notably in Virginia, Tennessee, and the Carolinas. These second-crop potatoes are normally immature and produce a somewhat earlier crop when used for seed than do the first-crop potatoes of the same region, when it is possible to hold them over for the next spring's planting. One great difficulty which confronts the producers of potatoes in southern territory is the fact that the early-crop potatoes do not keep through the hot weather, and can not, therefore, be retained for seed the next season, the seed supply for this industry being drawn largely from the northern potato-producing sections or from home districts where a second crop is produced. During the last two years, however, the second-crop seed has not been as satisfactory as has the northern-grown seed, particularly where several generations of second-crop seed have been employed. This, therefore, makes the great early-crop territory from Baltimore southward along the Atlantic coast almost wholly dependent for its seed supply upon the northern potato-producing territory.

Strange as it may seem, these large acreages of potatoes which are grown for the early northern market are handled — probably because of the abundant supply of comparatively cheap labor which has always been available — upon a very simple system, the work being done with the crudest tools and chiefly by hand. Potato planters and potato harvesters are practically unknown throughout the South Atlantic coast region. North of Baltimore, however, the character of the potato industry takes on a very different aspect. In this territory improved machinery is the rule on soils adapted to its use. Potato planters, potato-spraying devices, and potato-harvesting implements are extensively employed. The work is done in the most systematic way for the purpose of economizing labor, which in these areas is such an expensive factor in farm management at the present time.

New Jersey and Long Island constitute an intermediate crop zone in which potatoes are produced that can be harvested to meet the market demands immediately following the close of the season at Norfolk and the Eastern-Shore of Virginia. This crop is of such a character, however, that it not only meets the immediate demands but can be stored; thus the growers in this territory share a portion of the high profits of the potato as an early crop which are characteristic of the southern fields, and to some extent also the storage advantages which are characteristic of the northern portion of the Atlantic coast country. The varieties which are selected for this zone are those which mature at the proper season to meet the demands of the market after the southern crop has disappeared and which will bear storage for a portion of the winter at least. If the market at the time the crop comes to maturity is not such as to justify the growers' placing the product in the hands of dealers at once, it is stored, usually on the farm where it is produced, to be gradually disposed of throughout the late fall and early winter months.

Farther north and to the west of this intermediate section, the potato is recognized as a staple money crop with an established place in the farm rotation, taking the place of cabbage in some localities and of celery in others. It is here produced solely to be harvested at the close of the season and either shipped immediately to the centers of consumption or stored upon the farms or at shipping points to be sent to the markets as the demands will warrant. Improved machinery which is adapted to potato growing has been one of the main factors in placing this crop in the regular farm rotation of this territory. Potatoes in this section are grown chiefly for table consumption, for starch manufacture, and for seed to be used throughout the southern truck-farming areas. Immense quantities of this crop find their way to the markets at harvest time, the potatoes being dug, gathered from the field, and transported directly to the cars on which they are shipped in bulk to various cities with population sufficient to handle potatoes in carload lots. In other sections the crop is handled somewhat more conservatively and is stored on the farm or is purchased by dealers and stored in large warehouses, where it is held to meet the demands of the home or export markets. It is only the northern crop which can be looked upon as a staple crop to be held for a suitable market or to be handled as are grains.

The product of southern truck fields is always marketed before it is fully matured. It is, therefore, very perishable and must be handled strictly as a truck crop.

In many southern localities the large acreage of potatoes is handled in a very interesting way through the organization of truck-growing associations, the officers of the associations being in a position to dictate the destination of the product of any grower, to determine whether or not the product is suitable for placing under the trademark of the association, and to control fully the output from day to day. Because of the different character of the crop at the North such organization and methods are not generally adopted. The northern growers are to a certain extent independent of the market and, since the crop is not perishable to a high degree, can await the time when the market will warrant the sale of the crop.

Celery

It is interesting to trace the cultivation of celery in various portions of the trucking region under discussion. In Florida, celery is grown extensively as a winter crop, being placed in the field in October, November, or early December, to be harvested during the spring months. This crop is strictly a truck crop and is highly perishable in its nature, as are many other standard truck crops when grown at the extreme southern limit of their cultivation. The approach of warm weather and the consequent rapid development of many truck crops at the South just as they reach marketable maturity render them highly perishable. At the North, however, many of these same crops begin their period of existence in warm weather and mature as the days grow shorter and the weather cooler. This inversion of the seasons in the two localities produces the result of a perishable crop at the South and one possessing more or less decided keeping qualities at the North. This is true, as has been noted, of potatoes and cabbage, and it is also true of celery.

The main celery crop of the North is usually started in moderately warm weather. It makes a portion of its growth during this season, but makes its most satisfactory development as the cool nights of autumn come on. This makes it possible to produce a celery which can be held either in the ground or in a storage house for a considerable period. While it is possible to store celery, the great bulk of the celery grown at the North finds its way to the market immediately from the field, a small percentage only being placed in storage houses and a small percentage also being trenched in the field. While celery is restricted to comparatively small areas, both at the South and at the North, it is a highly remunerative crop, and in those localities where the soil and climatic conditions favor its development it forms the basis of a very important and profitable trucking industry.

Onions

The onion-growing industry of the United States, as represented in the territory now under discussion, is almost strictly confined to the North. Onions are produced from sets to a small extent for bunch purposes through portions of the southern half of the Atlantic coast trucking region, but it is in the northern half that the onion crop forms an important factor in the trucking industry. Here on soils adapted to its cultivation the onion is handled as a field crop. It may be grown either from seed sown directly in the field where the crop is to mature or by transplanting to the field, after the ground has received careful cultivation and become thoroughly warmed, young plants which have been brought forward in hotbeds or cold frames. The great bulk of the onion crop, however, is produced from seed sown where the crop is to stand.

This crop is handled in much the same way as the potato. While the work connected with its production is almost entirely hand labor, the product is of a nature which admits of placing it in storage and holding it for the demands of the market, thus avoiding the necessity of putting the entire product on the market during the comparatively restricted season of harvest.

Beans

Beans figure as a market-garden and truck crop throughout the trucking area under discussion. In the frost-free portion of Florida beans are planted as a fall vegetable to reach the northern markets for the Christmas holidays. These are followed in succession by beans from more northern localities as soon as danger from frost is past, so that the successive crop zones of the Atlantic coast region are capable of maintaining a continuous supply of snap beans in the market throughout the year. At the North the bean figures not only as a market-garden crop to be used as a fresh vegetable but also as a farm crop for canners' use. In that portion of the truck-growing area where the soil is of glacial-drift origin the bean plays an important part as a farm crop. The dry beans, being a staple product, produce a high revenue in many localities.

Asparagus

Asparagus is practically the only truck crop of a perennial nature. Most plants of this character have well-defined climatic limitations, but asparagus, fortunately, lends itself to a wide diversity of climatic conditions, and while exacting as regards soil is less so than most other perennials. The methods of culture at the South do not differ in any essential particular from those followed at the North. Seasonal differences constitute the foundation for the cultivation of this crop in different zones.

Tomatoes

The tomato is one of those truck crops which play a double role in the hands of the truck grower and the market gardener. At the North the tomato is an important field crop both for market and cannery purposes and is also extensively forced for winter use. At the South the tomato is grown in the frost-free areas in competition with the forced crop and in anticipation of the field crop of the North. As soon as the field crop from near-by localities becomes available distant shippers are as a rule at a disadvantage.

Peas

Peas are an important truck crop both at the South and at the North. The pea presents its chief points of interest not in its methods of culture, but in the matter of harvesting and transportation. When grown for immediate consumption as a green vegetable the pea can be most successfully and profitably handled from localities near the market. There is greater risk connected with the transportation of this crop than any other truck crop save strawberries. Peas when packed in barrel-high Delaware baskets, which are an almost universal package for such use, are very likely to heat in transit if the period exceeds twenty-four hours. The crop is therefore best adapted to quick handling. At the North, where the crop is extensively grown for canning purposes, these objections do not hold, for as a rule the crop is sown broadcast, harvested as is hay, and carried, pods, vines, and all, to the factory, where the peas are thrashed, cleaned, and graded by machinery. The bulk of the product will not stand shipment, and there are usually only a few hours between the time of harvesting and canning the peas. The improved methods of handling the pea crop grown for the canneries are in great measure responsible for the improvement in the quality of the processed product.

Conclusion

From what has been said an idea of the varied adaptations of the different truck crops can be formed. Most of these products occupy the land for a short period only and move with the season through the successive crop zones from southern Florida to Maine. The industry is new and the markets are growing and multiplying, but the crops and the cropping areas must always be kept within the capacity for consumption of the markets. Truck crops are quickly grown and must as a rule be consumed immediately.

With such hazardous crops profits must be high in order to justify the risk. It is an intensive industry, involving a maximum risk and maximum profits. Truck farming offers none of the security of other lines of farming in which staple products are produced.

Irrigation Problems in the West

From George Rothwell Brown, ed., *Reminiscences of Senator William M. Stewart of Nevada* (New York, 1908), pp. 348–52.

In traveling over the arid regions of the West during the twelve years from 1875 to 1887, during which time I was not in the Senate, I was strongly impressed with the vast extent of country west of the one hundredth meridian that required irrigation to produce crops.

Immediately upon reentering the Senate in 1887 I agitated the subject, and by speeches and articles in the magazines brought to the attention of the Senate the fact that two-thirds, if not three-fourths, of all the agriculture which had supported civilized and semi-civilized people had been pursued by means of artificial irrigation. The conflict between man and the desert has been unceasing since the dawn of history. When Egypt was the granary of the world, much of the Sahara Desert was irrigated from the Nile, and the dams and aqueducts which once turned that mighty river consisted of masonry so perfect in material and construction as to defy modern imitation. The ruins of irrigation works, such as dams, reservoirs, and aqueducts, are everywhere visible in the ancient land of Palestine. The waters of the Euphrates were spread over hundreds of acres that fructified what is now a vast desert, while the ruins of Babylon and other ancient cities challenge the curiosity and admiration of the scientists of our own time.

It was evident to me that the arid region of our country could only be made habitable by irrigation, and that the snow-capped region of the Rocky and Sierra Nevada Mountains furnished a more abundant supply of water for irrigation of the valleys than was found in the ancient empires once so densely populated.

I offered a resolution in the Senate creating a Committee on Irrigation, and, following a full discussion, the resolution passed, and soon after a like committee was organized in the House of Representatives. I then offered a resolution in the Senate authorizing the Committee on Irrigation to travel over the arid region, investigate conditions, and report to the next session of Congress. I was made chairman of the Senate committee.

The two men on that committee who manifested the greatest interest and took the most active part were Senators John H. Reagan of Texas and James K. Jones of Arkansas. I invited Major Powell, Director of the Geological Survey, to accompany the committee. We visited every State and Territory of the arid regions.

In many places we found people residing on the banks of streams which flowed through valleys of fertile soil, actually suffering for the products of the farm which they could easily have acquired if they had known the elementary principles of irrigation. To these we imparted such information as we had, and passed on to Colorado and Utah, where deserts were being converted into fertile regions by diverting the streams.

Utah furnished a marvelous lesson. Whatever might have been said, or may now be said, of the Mormons, when they entered Utah from the agricultural lands of the North and the East where rain-fall supplied moisture, they had no knowledge of irrigation. But they experimented by diverting the water upon the land, while they had very little food except roots, wild game, and fish.

The hardships they endured while they were working out for themselves the problem of irrigation have done much to cement and build up the Mormon church. When polygamy is eliminated and forgotten, as it must be as time passes, the history of the Mormons who created a great State in a desert, more than a thousand miles from supplies, will be read with sympathy and admiration.

Our committee found that irrigation had been practiced under the supervision of the Catholic priests who established missions in California, Arizona, and New Mexico, and that the American people who were occupying those countries at the time of our visit were improving upon the ancient systems, and gradually appropriating the water available in developing agricultural resources.

The committee found that in Idaho, Montana, Wyoming, and Nevada some progress had been made in agriculture by irrigation. The larger portion of Texas is in the arid and semi-arid region, and Senators Reagan and Jones took a lively interest in the development of irrigation in Texas, New Mexico, and Arizona, their immediate Western neighbors. These Senators were very influential throughout the South, and made irrigation popular in nearly every State south of Mason and Dixon's line.

Before the organization of the Committee on Irrigation, Senator Teller and myself appreciated the necessity of withdrawing from sale reservoir sites required for the storage of water for irrigation. The extent of the reservations for that purpose was not sufficiently guarded, for we did not anticipate that more land than was necessary would be withdrawn from the market by the Interior Department.

The ambition of Major Powell to manage the whole subject of irrigation, without regard to the views of others, led him to induce the Interior Department to withdraw vast regions of the public lands preparatory to the selection of the necessary sites. This withdrawal of public land from settlement practically closed many of the land offices in the West, and created much complaint. It became necessary to secure legislation to restore the public domain to settlement.

The result was that Major Powell was removed from his powerful position as Director of the Geological Survey. Great dissatisfaction existed on the part of the Major and his friends on account of the action of Congress, and as if by some general and secret understanding articles appeared throughout the Northern States unfriendly to irrigation. The farmers were told by writers who gained access to the agricultural press that the irrigation of the arid region would ruin the agriculture of the North by bringing in competition a vast region of country, the products of which were of the same character as those of New England, New York, Pennsylvania, and all the Northwestern States. At nearly every session of Congress, however, the Senators of the Mountain States of the West continued to agitate the question, and with the aid of the Senators from the South would put upon various appropriation bills amendments providing for National aid to irrigation. But our amendments were never considered in the House of Representatives; in fact, the rules of the House were such that the Republicans of the North prevented any discussion of the question of irrigation in that body.

When President Roosevelt became the Chief Executive of the Nation by the deplorable death of President McKinley, irrigation had a powerful friend in the White House. He had lived in the mountain regions of the West, and was more familiar with Montana, Wyoming, Colorado, and New Mexico than any Representative from any of those States or Territories. In his first message he urged Government aid in irrigation in the West, and in private conversation with all who approached him on that subject he was earnest in his advocacy of the measure he recommended.

Senator Hansbrough of North Dakota introduced a bill providing for National irrigation, and referred it to the Committee on Public Lands, of which he was chairman, because it was considered by the friends of irrigation that that committee was more familiar with the subject, and more enthusiastic in support of a measure of that kind, than the Committee on Irrigation.

After the bill was introduced the President suggested various amendments to perfect it. Senator Hansbrough in time reported the bill to the Senate, and after full explanation and debate it passed the Senate unanimously, went to the House of Representatives, and was referred to the Committee on Irrigation. That committee, as well as the Committee of the Senate, kept in close touch with the President, and took his advice at every stage of the proceedings. It required no argument to secure the support of Representatives of the Southern States, as they had been in favor of irrigation for many years. It was not necessary to educate the President, as he was as well informed as anybody in the United States. He sent for the leading Republican members of the North, and appealed to them to cease their opposition and permit the bill to pass as an Administration measure. The bill was passed.

Many men both in and out of Congress deserve credit for assisting in this great enterprise, but to Theodore Roosevelt the country owes the final success of the measure.

American Farming in 1908

From W. J. Spillman, "Types of Farming in the United States," U.S. Department of Agriculture, *Yearbook*, 1908, pp. 351–66.

At no previous period in the history of America have city people evinced so much interest in farming as at the present time. Large numbers of city toilers are looking longingly to the country as an avenue of escape from the uncertainties of city employment. At the present time there is practically no literature that will give these people, unacquainted with even the rudiments of farming, a general view of the possibilities of farm life. To meet the needs of persons of this class the various types of farming to be found in this country are outlined in this paper. In addition some discussion is given of the factors which determine the type of farming under given conditions.

Students of farm management in the colleges and high schools will also find this outline advantageous in giving them some idea of types of farming with which they are not acquainted, the conditions determining these types, and the distribution of the types in the United States.

Bases of Classification

Types of farming may be classified on several different bases.

Relation to Maintenance of Fertility

Those types of farming which make no provision for maintaining or building up the fertility of the soil are called exploitive types. They exploit the soil. Exploitive farming is characteristic of regions in which farming is new. Nature has spent ages in excavating the soil by means of plant roots and filling the soil with decaying organic matter. Insects have made their burrows deep into the soil and thus opened it up for the circulation of air and water. When first put into cultivation most soils are rich and can be farmed for many years without attention to fertility. Such farming is usually quite profitable as long as the fertility of the soil lasts. History shows that exploitive farming may continue without serious consequences on rich soils for twenty to fifty years, depending on the character of the soil and the climate; the farther south one goes the quicker the humus (decaying organic matter) rots out of the soil.

Generally speaking, after exploitive farming has reduced the fertility of the soil to the point where paying crops are no longer produced, types of farming are introduced which build up the soil and make it fertile again. Usually these conservative types of farming produce forage for live stock and put the manure back on the land. There is some evidence that the soil may be brought back by growing green crops, especially certain leguminous crops — cowpeas, crimson clover, vetch, bur clover, and the like — and turning them under. Where it is possible to grow forage crops only and to buy grain or other concentrated feed at a reasonable price, good strong land may be built up and made highly fertile without the use of chemical fertilizers; but generally, in those sections of the country where farming has been followed for more than half a century, commercial fertilizers are used to a greater or less extent.

There are some instances where exploitive types of farming have remained after the soil has been very greatly exhausted, resulting in more or less abject poverty on the part of those who till the soil. The most striking instance of this kind is on the small cotton farms of the South, on most of which no effort is made to keep a supply of humus in the soil, cotton being grown year after year, chemical fertilizers being relied upon to keep up the land. The production of corn and wheat in southern Missouri, of wheat in southern Illinois, and of hay in New England are other examples of exploitive types of farming that have continued beyond their legitimate life.

Intensity of Operation

Farming is said to be extensive or intensive according to the amount of capital and labor used upon a given area. On the grain fields of the West one man farms a large area. The amount of work done per acre is small and the income per acre is usually comparatively small. Extensive farming is usually exploitive, though not always so. It is more or less characteristic of newly settled regions. Almost any system of farming may be carried on in an intensive way. The farmer who grows 100 bushels of corn, 40 bushels of wheat, or 3 tons of hay per acre is doing intensive farming. Ordinarily, however, the term "intensive farming" applies to such types as truck and fruit growing, poultry raising, etc., where a large amount of capital and a large amount of labor are used per acre. As a general rule, the more intensive the type the larger the income from a given area of land.

Diversity of Crops or Industries on the Farm

We frequently hear such terms as "single-crop" farming and "diversified" or "mixed" farming. The most striking instances of single-crop farming in this country are to be found in the cotton plantations of the South, the grain farms of the Plains region and parts of the Pacific coast, the rice-growing areas along the Atlantic and Gulf coasts, the tobacco-growing sections in the Atlantic States, and the cornfields on many farms in the Middle West. The term does not mean to imply that only one crop is grown, but one crop brings in practically the whole income of the farm family. Such types of farming are nearly always exploitive and usually extensive. In diversified or mixed farming there are several sources of income, usually several crops are grown, and frequently live stock is kept in addition to the animals needed to work the farm. As a rule, farms are more or less diversified in their industries, and it is usual to find two or more types of farming carried on together on the same farm.

In the outline which follows, it is not to be understood that these numerous types of farming exist distinct from each other on different farms except in cases where it is so stated. Most successful farms combine two or more types.

Sources of Income

The source of income is the usual basis for classifying the types of farming. For instance, when we speak of a hog and seed-corn farm, we mean one on which the principal sources of income are hogs and seed corn. According to sources of income we may divide types of farming into crop farms, mixed stock and crop farms, live stock farms, and miscellaneous farms, with various subdivisions of each of these classes.

Classification Based on Source of Income

Crop Growing

Those types of farming in which the principal income is from crops sold may be divided into (1) truck farming, (2) fruit growing, (3) single-crop systems, (4) dominant-crop systems, and (5) a miscellaneous group for which there is no appropriate name and described here as "other crop systems."

Truck Farming

The production of garden vegetables, commonly called truck farming, is one of the most intensive types of farming, and requires a comparatively high capitalization as well as a large amount of labor. At the same time, where markets are good, the income is so large that a family can make a living on a very small area of land. In fact, 10 acres would be a large truck farm, and 2 or 3 acres properly managed, with good markets, will bring a fair living to an ordinary family. There is abundant literature about the cultivation of the various truck crops, and this type of farming is a desirable one for beginners, although a great deal of study and some experience are necessary before success can be attained. Truck farming assumes three phases: First, every farm should have a garden which produces such vegetables and small fruits as are needed for home use. Second, in the vicinity of every city, town, and village there is room for a small number of truck farmers who can supply local markets. This is a much safer form of trucking than the one mentioned later, and is, generally speaking, to be recommended. The crops to be grown must be determined by climate, soil, and market demand. The third system of trucking, which is widely developed along the Atlantic seaboard and is found to some extent in other sections, is that of growing vegetables for shipment to distant markets. This type of trucking requires not only a large capital and great expense, but it also requires a large amount of reserve capital on account of the great fluctuations in receipts for products shipped. Some years enormous incomes are obtained per acre; other years there is a dead loss. The business is very uncertain and is not recommended to beginners.

Fruit Growing

There are so many types of fruit growing that they can not be appropriately discussed within the space available for this article. What has been stated concerning truck farming may be said in a general way concerning the production of berries and of small fruits. Where there is a local market, these fruits may be quite profitable; but, when one must depend upon shipping to the large cities, the results are very uncertain. The production of winter apples for shipment to the large markets has proved in the main a profitable industry. Generally speaking, the production of any kind of fruit for market, especially tree fruits, necessitates waiting several years before any income is obtained, and it is usual to combine truck farming with orchard growing, gradually abandoning truck crops as the fruit comes into bearing. There is much good literature to be had about practically all phases of fruit growing. The beginner is especially warned against embarking his capital and time in new ventures in the line of fruit growing. It is better to stick to those things which have demonstrated themselves to be successful.

Single-Crop Systems

The principal crops found on single-crop farms in the United States are cotton, wheat, corn, hay, tobacco, rice, sugar cane, and hops. Other crops are grown as practically the only crop in small areas in various parts of the country. Generally speaking, the equipment required for conducting a single-crop farm is less than for any other type of farming. On the ordinary one-horse cotton farm of the

South the cost of buildings, work stock, and farm implements will average about $8 per acre; on the exclusive grain farm with a moderate equipment the cost is about $20 per acre; with corn as a principal crop the cost is about the same; on an exclusive well-equipped hay farm, the cost of equipment, including buildings and fences, is approximately $40 per acre; on farms where tobacco, rice, sugar cane, or hops are grown the cost is considerably more.

Cotton farming is confined to our Southern States, extending into southeastern Virginia, all of North Carolina except the western portion, south-central and western Tennessee, southeastern Missouri, central Oklahoma, and west into western Texas. A small quantity of cotton is grown in New Mexico and Arizona. An average family, with one horse, can cultivate about 20 acres of cotton and 10 acres of corn. The average yield of cotton is two-fifths of a bale, or 200 pounds of lint cotton, worth, say, $20. Twenty acres of this crop would therefore produce an income of $400. On tenant farms, where the tenant furnishes the labor, the custom is for the tenant to take half the crop and to pay half the fertilizer bill, making the income of the family about $175 per annum. This is for average conditions. By growing winter cover crops and by this means supplying the soil with humus, this income may easily be doubled.

Exclusive wheat farming was formerly practiced over wide areas, but this system of farming has exhausted the soil in regions where it has prevailed for half a century to such an extent that, with one or two exceptions, the system has been replaced by better ones. As it will undoubtedly be replaced in the near future in all regions where it now prevails, except possibly the semiarid Plains regions, it is not necessary to dwell further upon this type of farming. It is found in the upper Columbia basin of Oregon, Washington, and Idaho, in the Sacramento Valley of California, in the Dakotas, and in the semiarid Plains regions. Wheat growing is not the exclusive type of farming in these sections, but it is the prevailing type.

Exclusive corn growing is confined to individual farms scattered throughout the Middle West. It is also found in the hill country of the South to some extent. Farmers who follow this type of farming are usually poor and are getting poorer.

Exclusive hay growing is also found on individual farms in many parts of the country — east, west, north, and south — but is hardly the prevailing type of farming in any large section. It occurs on a good many farms in New England, on some alfalfa farms in the West, occasionally on a farm in the Middle West in the midst of the corn belt, and on an occasional farm in the South. When proper attention is given to fertilizing the land, hay farming is a legitimate industry. The ordinary crops grown for hay provide a fair amount of humus and their roots penetrate the soil in such a way as to keep it fairly open. By the use of commercial fertilizers it is possible to maintain the yield on a hay farm for a long period of time. For the past few years the price of hay has been fairly remunerative and hay farming has been profitable.

At the present time one of the best opportunities for those entering upon farming is hay growing in the South. In that section comparatively little hay is produced for the market and a good deal is shipped in from the North. There are many crops which may be grown very successfully for hay in the South, and there should be a large development of this type of farming in the next few years. The reader is especially referred to Farmers' Bulletin No. 312, entitled "A Successful

Southern Hay Farm," as an indication of the possibilities of this type of farming in the South. The results secured could hardly be duplicated under average conditions, but even half the profit obtained by this farmer would justify one in undertaking the business.

Exclusive tobacco growing is found in Connecticut, parts of Maryland and Virginia, and in one locality in northern Florida and southern Georgia. When proper attention is given to keeping up a supply of humus in the soil, fair yields of tobacco are obtained. One man can cultivate about 5 acres of this crop. It is estimated that it costs about 8 cents a pound to grow tobacco when the average yield is 700 pounds per acre. By proper management 1,000 pounds per acre may easily be produced, and in some sections much more than this is grown. Generally, however, tobacco growing does not offer an inviting opportunity to those entering upon farming for the first time.

Along the Atlantic coast there are certain lands which at high tide are covered by fresh water from the adjacent rivers, but which at low tide are above water. Large areas of these lands have been reclaimed by diking and are devoted to rice growing, no other crop being grown upon them as a rule. In this section it is estimated that it costs about 70 cents a bushel to grow rice, a large part of the expense being for keeping up the dikes. These dikes are frequently broken by storms while growing crops are on the land and involve great expense in their repair. The price of rice for the last few years has made the rice industry on the Atlantic coast a precarious one. The largest rice-growing region in this country is found in southern Louisiana and the Gulf coast of Texas. In this region irrigation of the rice fields is accomplished in a different manner from that on the Atlantic coast, namely, by canals taking water from rivers or from artesian wells. Rice is produced more cheaply, but the price of rice in recent years has checked the development of the industry. At the present time it is developing slowly and more conservatively than was the case a few years ago, and while the business is a fairly good one it should not be entered upon without due consideration.

Sugar cane, for the production of cane sugar and cane sirup, is grown more or less in all the Gulf Coast States. By far the largest production of this crop is in southern Louisiana, but a good deal is grown in adjacent parts of Texas. In other sections the crop is grown only for sirup making. On plantations where sugar cane is grown for sugar, enormous capital is required for successful operation, as the crop must be produced on a large scale.

Hops are grown principally in one or two counties in New York, in central and western Washington, western Oregon, and California. The areas grown are usually small. The income from the hop crop is perhaps the most variable of all crop incomes in America because of wide fluctuations in the price of dried hops. Exclusive hop growing is an exceedingly risky enterprise. It is far safer to grow a few acres on a farm devoted mainly to other crops, so that if there is a loss there may be other resources to tide over the period of low prices.

Dominant Crop Systems

In several sections of the United States there is a rotation of crops containing one crop which is the principal source of the farmer's income. Tobacco is grown in this manner in parts of Kentucky, Ohio, and Tennessee, and to a slight extent in other tobacco-growing sections. The rotations in which tobacco is grown are so variable that it is thought unnecessary to enter upon a discussion of them here.

In Aroostook County, Me., the prevailing type of farming is one in which the rotation covers a period of three years, the crops being (1) potatoes, (2) oats, and (3) clover. The land is usually divided into three approximately equal areas, so that each of these crops is grown every year. In some parts of Pennsylvania and Ohio a similar rotation is found in which wheat is substituted for oats. This is known as the Terry rotation, for the reason that it has been widely advocated by Mr. T. B. Terry, a well-known writer and farmers' institute worker.

In certain sections of the West, sugar beets are grown as the dominant crop in the rotation. In the alfalfa regions of the West the rotation generally consists of two or more years of alfalfa, followed by one year of potatoes or grain in order that the alfalfa roots may become decomposed, and then one or two years of sugar beets, followed by grain with which alfalfa is sown. The rotations used on sugar-beet farms in Nebraska, Michigan, and eastward are highly variable.

These types of farming in which one crop in the rotation is the principal source of income are very satisfactory, especially where the remaining crops are fed to live stock and the manure is put back on the land. Most of them require considerable capital for equipment, and require considerable labor compared with the single-crop systems previously outlined, but they are fairly remunerative, and in some instances exceedingly so.

Cotton occupies the position of a dominant crop on a few farms in the South in one of the best crop rotations to be found in this country. The rotation consists of cotton, followed by corn in which cowpeas are sown at the last cultivation, the next crop being winter oats, followed by cowpeas the succeeding summer. This rotation gives two opportunities for winter cover crops to be turned under to supply humus, namely, between cotton and corn and between cowpeas and cotton. Crops available for use as winter cover crops in this rotation are rye, oats, bur clover, crimson clover, common red clover, hairy vetch, and common vetch. This rotation builds up the land very rapidly, the yield of cotton going up more rapidly than that of the other crops. Many farmers, following this rotation and using a moderate quantity of commercial fertilizer, secure a bale to a bale and a half of cotton per acre. Such farming is quite profitable and is to be recommended generally for the Southern States. Even where the winter cover crops are omitted the system is a fairly good one.

Other Crop Systems

Scattered here and there over the country are farms devoted to the raising of seeds for sale. These farms are of two classes, namely, those which raise vegetable seeds, usually on contract for some large dealer, and those which make a specialty of growing improved seeds of ordinary field crops. The latter class of farming, that is, the growing of improved seeds of corn, cotton, potatoes, wheat, oats, etc., offers at the present time one of the best opportunities to be found in farming in this country. The ordinary farmer will not take the trouble to breed up the seed of his field crops, yet he will buy improved seeds, and is justified in so doing. The crops which are most easily improved by selection of excellent individuals for seeding are corn, cotton, and potatoes, and there is room for much development in the growing of improved seeds of these crops practically wherever they are grown. Improving the seed of wheat, oats, barley, and other crops in which the individual plant is small is a very difficult task, and requires technical training for its successful conduct. Such work must be left to the trained specialist. The breeding of improved strains of corn, cotton, and potatoes does not require large equipment, and there is much valuable literature to aid the beginner in this line of endeavor. The growing of seeds of garden vegetables is a specialty which requires a good deal of training and a comparatively large amount of capital and labor. It is not an inviting field for the beginner, yet it is a profitable type of farming when properly conducted.

In many parts of the country rotations of ordinary crops are grown in which no particular crop stands out as preeminent, only such portions of the crops being used on the farm as are necessary to feed the work stock, the remainder being sold. The most common form of rotation on such farms is corn, followed by wheat; this by timothy and clover, which is cut for hay one or two years and then used for pasture for one or more years. Where a large quantity of commercial fertilizers is used, a rotation of this character usually keeps the land in a fairly fertile condition, and a moderate profit is to be obtained. Generally speaking, however, on farms where such a system prevails the land, especially on rented farms, has been exploited with scant attention to its fertility, until there is little profit to be had. It is seldom a desirable type of farming, for even where yields are kept up by the use of commercial fertilizers the expense of the fertilizers eats up a large part of the profits. This system of farming, however, is one which does not require as much technical knowledge as most types of live-stock farming, and for this reason it may be justifiable for a beginner to grow such a rotation for a few years until he has had the experience necessary to succeed with some form of live-stock farming to which the rotation mentioned is fairly well adapted.

Mixed Stock and Crop Farming

The general type known as mixed stock and crop farming is perhaps the most common type found in the Northern States. It is hoped that it will also ultimately prevail very generally in the Cotton Belt, where the rotation already mentioned in discussing cotton as a dominant crop in a rotation is well suited to this type of farming. In the Northern States the common rotation found on farms of this character is one which has already been described, namely, corn, followed by small grain, and this by timothy and clover for hay and pasture. Many variations of the rotation are found. For instance, corn may be grown two years before seeding the land to wheat or oats. In the northern tier of States oats are usually grown in this rotation in preference to wheat, while in central latitudes wheat usually replaces oats. In some sections oats follow corn and wheat follows oats. In some localities wheat is grown for two years after corn before seeding down to timothy and clover. In some sections timothy is omitted, clover being sown alone after wheat, or rather sown in the spring on the wheat crop. In a few localities clover is omitted and timothy is grown alone, though in sections where this practice prevails there is usually considerable trouble in keeping up the fertility of the soil. Clover, like all of the legumes, helps to supply the land with nitrogen, the most expensive form of plant food. The legumes secure an abundance of nitrogen from the atmosphere, while other crops must secure their nitrogen from decaying organic matter in the soil.

The live stock found on the largest number of farms of this character in the southern half of the Corn Belt are beef cattle, usually with hogs, while in the northern portion of the section dairy cows are kept. On the better class of mixed stock and crop farms the only crop sold is the small grain. This is especially true in those sections where wheat is grown in the rotation. Where oats are grown it is not unusual for all the crops to be fed on the place. In either case, if the corn and hay are fed to live stock and good use is made of the manure, the fertility of the land is fairly well maintained, though after two or three generations of such farming the use of commercial fertilizers becomes necessary. The equipment on farms of this class, including cost of buildings, fences, implements, live stock, etc., will ordinarily run from $50 to $75 per acre. About one work horse is required for every 25 acres in cultivation, and one laborer for 25 to 40 acres. A family living on a quarter section of land devoted to mixed stock and crop farming, with a fair amount of industry and intelligent management, may be expected to make a good living, and perhaps to lay by a little profit. With the highest type of management a satisfactory profit may be obtained.

In the Southern States where cotton is grown in a rotation consisting of cotton, followed by corn and cowpeas, then oats, followed the next summer by cowpeas for hay or seed, or both, stock farming combines excellently with crop farming. If all the crops except cotton are fed to stock and the manure is intelligently used, large yields of cotton are obtained at comparatively small expense, and the work of the farm is better distributed through the year than on exclusive cotton farms. This is an excellent type of farming in sections where the cattle tick has been eliminated so that cattle can be kept without danger from tick fever. This tick is now gradually being eradicated by the joint efforts of the United States Department of Agriculture and the State authorities, so that an important development of this type of farming is looked for in the future. It is to be highly recommended.

Before passing from this phase of the subject it might be well to mention the use of live stock as adjuncts to sugar factories, canneries, distilleries, etc., which produce large quantities of by-products suitable for feeding to stock. Beef cattle and sheep are usually the stock kept. By feeding these factory products along with a certain amount of grain or other concentrated feed considerable profit has been made. Sometimes dairy cows are fed in this manner with very satisfactory results.

Live-Stock Farming

The various types of live-stock farming here outlined are usually found on farms which are not devoted exclusively to them, though occasionally a farm is found which sells only live-stock products, especially the better class of dairy farms and many farms where beef cattle are fed.

Beef Cattle

The growing and fattening of beef cattle is an industry found perhaps on a larger number of stock farms than any other. Generally, the profit from this type of farming is small, and a great deal of special knowledge is required to make it profitable at all. It is not a type of farming for a beginner. The most profitable form of beef-cattle raising is the production of pure-bred stock for sale as breeders, but it is only the experienced breeder who has a reputation as a breeder of good stock who can sell young stock at satisfactory prices. Many men embark in the raising of pure-bred beef stock, paying high prices for their foundation stock, and then fail because the lack of a reputation makes it impossible for them to sell their young stock at a satisfactory price.

A great many men raise beef cattle for sale as feeders. A large proportion of these cattle are raised on the ranges of the West. Ranging cattle was formerly a very profitable business, but the best ranges have now been turned into farms, and on the poorest ranges sheep are gradually replacing beef cattle, so that the range-cattle industry of the West is not so satisfactory as some years ago. A good many farmers who follow a mixed system of stock and crop farming keep a few cows of the beef breeds and raise the young for sale as feeders. This type of beef-cattle farming is perhaps the least profitable of all.

Fattening steers for market is one of the leading industries of the Middle West. On some farms steers are bought in the spring and grazed during the summer, the best of them being sold for meat before winter comes on, the others being sold as winter feeders. Some farmers who make a business of fattening steers buy their steers in the fall and fatten them during the winter. Others combine summer grazing and winter feeding. Usually the farmer who makes a business of feeding steers does not expect to make much profit directly from his feeding operations. He justifies his course, however, by the fact that through this disposition of his crops he secures a fair price for his grain and hay and retains the manure on his farm, thus keeping up the fertility of his land. It is customary to keep a few hogs on farms where the winter feeding of steers is practiced, in order that the hogs may consume the waste grain in the droppings from the cattle. When hogs and cattle are thus combined there is usually some profit in the feeding operations.

A few farmers keep cows of the beef breeds and force the young stock by heavy feeding, selling it early as "baby beef." Beef of this character sells at the highest price, but is expensive to produce. The profit from it is not great, yet this type of farming serves to maintain the fertility of the land and returns a fair price for the crops consumed.

Sheep

There are four types of sheep farming: (1) The raising of stock for sale as breeders, which is perhaps the most profitable form of sheep raising on the ordinary farm. (2) The raising of sheep for wool and mutton — a type found both on farms and on the ranges of the West. Usually the range man clips the wool and sells his young stock to farmers of the Middle West to be fattened during the winter. (3) Early winter lambs. Some sheep raisers have the lambs produced very early in the season and send them to market late in winter, at which time they sell for very high prices. Frequently these lambs when in proper condition will sell for much more than they would bring three or four months or even a year later. (4) Fattening sheep for market. This industry prevails extensively in the Middle West, where range lambs from the western country are bought and fed during the winter. Extensive feeding operations of this character are conducted in the alfalfa-growing regions of the West, and this type of handling sheep returns a very satisfactory profit to those who understand the business. As is the case with all kinds of live-stock farming, considerable expert knowledge is necessary for a high degree of success.

Hogs

There are two general types of hog raising, namely, (1) the raising of pure-bred stock for sale as breeders and (2) the production of meat. Most hogs that are raised for meat are sold on foot and sent to the large packing houses. A few farmers cure their own meat, and when they have a good market make a very satisfactory profit from the operation. A still smaller number of farmers butcher their own hogs and sell them as fresh meat, sausage, etc. Hog raising is perhaps the least difficult of all the types of live-stock farming, and the most profitable considering the amount of labor and capital involved. The equipment for hog raising costs considerable. Including buildings, fences, and live stock, a hog farm requires an expense of about $70 an acre before it is perfectly equipped for the business.

The one great danger in this type of farming is the introduction of cholera in the herd. Cholera is a contagious disease. Frequently it may be kept out by strict quarantine. A few years ago the writer was able to keep his hogs healthy while hogs died from cholera on every adjacent farm. When hogs are sick from this disease their excreta contain the germs of the disease. In walking through an inclosure containing sick hogs, these germs adhere to the shoes and may be carried from one farm to another in this manner. While strict quarantine, when hogs are known to be sick in a community, may not always prevent contagion, it greatly lessens the liability to it.

There is much valuable literature to be had concerning hog management and the various breeds of hogs.

Dairy Cattle

There are three more or less distinct types of dairy farming, namely, (1) the selling of milk and cream, (2) the production of milk for butter and cheese making, and (3) the raising of pure-bred dairy stock for sale as breeders. Generally speaking, when dairy farming is intelligently conducted it is quite profitable, though it requires more labor than other forms of live-stock farming and a larger investment of capital. By beginning in a small way the capital necessary can be earned, and this is usually done by men who embark in dairy farming. In fact, it is much safer to begin any intensive form of farming on a small scale in order to learn the details of the business with as little risk as possible. Dairy farming maintains the fertility of the soil perhaps better than most other types of farming. This is especially true where only the coarser feeds are grown and the concentrates are bought. In recent years the prices of farm labor and concentrated feeds have risen to such an extent as to reduce materially the profit from dairying, but it is still one of the best forms of live-stock farming for the beginner.

By having a good garden and plenty of small fruits, the small dairy farmer has most of his living at home, thus being assured against want. It is best to start in with a good quality of grade cows rather than to begin by purchasing high-priced, registered stock. But it is highly important to use pure-bred sires in building up and maintaining the efficiency of the herd. Generally it is not safe to depend upon maintaining a herd by buying regularly. It is much more satisfactory to raise the cows on the farm.

As between the various types of dairy farming, local conditions must determine which is most desirable. If one is located near a large city or near a railway station which gives direct connection with a city, the selling of milk or cream is the usual form of dairying followed. In sections where a market for milk is not to be had, butter making is the more usual type of dairying. Even near the large cities a few farmers find it desirable to make butter for supplying private customers, and this form of the industry is a very satisfactory one where the butter can be sold at a reasonable price. Cheese making is not often conducted on the farm, but is usually confined to factories. Most of the butter is also made in factories, and even where milk can not be sent to a city in most regions where dairy farming prevails it can be sold at a local creamery or cheese factory. Concerning the raising of pure-bred dairy stock for sale as breeders the same principles apply as in the raising of other classes of stock. It is only the breeder who has a reputation who can sell his young stock for high prices. Most of these breeders began in a small way, purchasing a few registered cows and gradually allowing their produce to replace the grade cows in their herds.

Horses and Mules

The raising of horses and mules is not generally an exclusive industry on a particular farm. For the most part these animals are raised incidentally in connection with other kinds of farming. A great many farmers keep brood mares with which they do their farm work. It is hardly advisable for the small farmer to engage in this industry, but, where one has an abundance of land and must keep a considerable number of work stock, it is entirely proper to keep a number of brood mares. In some sections of the country, especially in the Middle West, farmers either buy horses in a thin condition and fatten them for sale in the cities as draft horses, or they take horses of this kind to feed at a given price per month. The different types of horse and mule farming are the raising of draft animals, roadsters, saddle horses, ponies, the fattening of thin horses, running horses on the range, and the boarding of city horses. Most of these types of farming should not be undertaken by the beginner, as they require considerable capital and a great deal of knowledge of the industry. Boarding horses is a fairly profitable industry near the large cities.

Poultry Farming

The raising of poultry is an industry found perhaps on more farms in the United States than any other. Most farmers keep a few chickens which find their living from the waste products of the farm. They are thus practically no expense and all of the product is profit. From 30 to 75 hens can thus be kept on an ordinary farm. The magnitude of this form of the industry is so great that it interferes materially with the special poultry farm. It is probable that more failures are made in poultry farming than in any other type of farming undertaken by beginners, yet it is decidedly one of the best and most profitable types of farming when properly conducted. It is highly essential to begin in a small way in order to learn the details of the business before much capital is invested in it. There is an enormous amount of good literature relating to poultry raising easily available to anyone who wishes to learn the industry.

There are five common types of chicken farming, namely, (1) the production of eggs for the general market, (2) the production of eggs for hatching, (3) the production of broilers, (4) the breeding of fancy poultry, and (5) the hatching of chicks for sale as soon as they are hatched. Nearly all successful poultrymen began in a small way by producing eggs for the general market. By carefully breeding up the flock and developing its egg-laying capacity they have finally been able to embark in the production of eggs for hatching purposes, for which there is a ready sale for men who have earned a reputation for producing good stock. The breeding of fancy poultry is, as a rule, not a very profitable industry. It requires a large amount of special knowledge, and, while a few men have made an eminent success in this branch of the business, a very large proportion of those who have tried it have failed.

The poultry business is a legitimate one in all parts of the country. The market for strictly fresh eggs is practically always good. If the hens are so managed that a large supply of eggs is obtained during the winter, the business may be made highly profitable.

Only a few farms are devoted to ducks, geese, turkeys, or squabs as a more or less specialized industry, but there is an abundance of literature relating to these forms of poultry farming by means of which the beginner may learn the details of the business with a comparatively short experience.

Miscellaneous

There are a few types of farming found occasionally which can not very well be classified in the foregoing outline, and which the beginner should usually avoid. He can, however, make himself familiar with them by means of available literature which can always be obtained by addressing the United States Department of Agriculture and the various State agricultural experiment stations.

The raising of bees is one of these industries. It is usually combined with fruit raising. The raising of flowers for the city trade is perhaps the most intensive type of farming we have, requiring considerable money for equipment but producing a large income from a given area of land when intelligently conducted. The production of mushrooms is an industry which is conducted in a small way by a considerable number of people. There are a few ostrich farms in Arizona, southern California, and Florida. Fox farming has developed to some extent in the extreme Northern States in the past few years. Not much is known as yet about the management of these animals, but there is a possibility that foxes may become an important source of revenue to a few people in the States bordering on Canada. Farmers' Bulletin No. 328, entitled "Silver Fox Farming," gives an excellent account of the methods used by the most successful growers of foxes and points out the principal difficulties in this type of farming.

Conclusion

It is hoped that the foregoing outline of the types of farming prevailing in this country may be of some assistance to those who are embarking in farming, by way of aiding them in choosing a suitable type. Nearly every type of farming mentioned has its literature in the bulletins of the State agricultural experiment stations and the United States Department of Agriculture and in the many agricultural books and periodicals published in this country. Before undertaking to farm, one should become familiar with the literature of the type of farming chosen. In comparing farming with other industries, the fact should not be overlooked that the intelligent farmer produces a large part of his living on the farm, thus rendering the expense of living in the country much less than in the city. It should be further remembered that the independence of farm life goes far toward balancing its disadvantages when compared with city life; nor should it be forgotten that the farmer requires both experience and at least a rudimentary knowledge of several sciences in order to attain the best success. It is only recently that farming has profited by the discoveries of the scientist, and even yet there is much to learn, especially about the soil. There is growing up, however, a science of farming, and in so far as this science has been reduced to rule, it takes the place of experience to a certain extent. A diligent study of agricultural literature, therefore, may enable the beginner to be successful with comparatively little experience.

Transporting Meat Animals, 1908

From Frank Andrews, "Cost and Methods of Transporting Meat Animals," U.S. Department of Agriculture, *Yearbook*, 1908, pp. 227–44.

Historic Periods

The advent of railroads marked a turning point in the growth of the live-stock industry. Scarcely more than a half century ago the carrying trade of the United States was practically limited to passenger traffic and to what is now known as "dead freight." Relatively few live animals were then carried, and even on boats, which were the chief carriers of bulky merchandise, suitable facilities were not provided for live stock. It was generally preferable to drive animals on foot, and this was the prevailing way of taking them to market.

The history of live-stock transportation in the United States since the establishment of railroad traffic may be divided into two periods. A marked characteristic of the first period was the injury caused to stock by lack of proper accommodations and by faulty methods of managing the traffic. The suffering and death of animals on the way and the unhealthy condition of many delivered at their destinations called forth much comment and many efforts for relief during the first few decades of live-stock traffic on railroads. The second period, the present, is characterized by the extension of railroads throughout the range country of the West, and by changes in roadbed, cars, and traffic methods which are continually making the transportation of live stock more humane and economical.

Elements of Cost

Of the influences which during the last half century or more have affected the cost of marketing live stock, some of the most important were those relating to their transportation. The cost of transportation, as discussed in this article, includes not only charges for freight, feed, attendance, yardage, and other expenses of the road, but also losses in transit and other items involving more or less directly the expenditure of money, labor, and time in moving meat animals from their native farms or ranges to places of slaughter.

Driving and Hauling

Conditions in Early Days

Prior to 1850 it was generally the practice to drive live stock to market on foot. At that time, over routes in many portions of the country, pasturage was free and cattle could be grazed along the way as they were slowly driven to market. One route from the blue-grass region of Kentucky to New York City covered about 800 miles, and, according to a man who drove over it about the year 1847, the time consumed was a few days more than ten weeks. The particular route followed on one occasion by this man led from the neighborhood of Lexington, Ky., to the Ohio River just above Maysville, Ky.; thence northeasterly through Chillicothe; thence across the Ohio River below Wheeling, W. Va. The course then passed through Connellsville and Bedford, Pa., to Carlisle; thence to Harrisburg. Here the road turned southeasterly, passing within sight of Lancaster, through West Chester, to Philadelphia. From this point the cattle were driven northeasterly through Trenton, Princeton, and Newark to the Hudson River and were ferried across to New York City. The drove referred to contained 119 cattle, and three men were required to care for them. Another route from the neighborhood of Lexington, Ky., extended to Charleston, S.C., a distance of 550 to 600 miles. The way led southeasterly through Cumberland Gap to the French Broad River. Then the river was followed as far as Asheville, N.C. The route then turned again southeasterly, crossing the South Carolina line at Saluda Mountain, and thence passed on to Charleston.

In those days driving to eastern seaboard cities from points as far west as Iowa was by no means uncommon, and cattle from Texas were also among those on the road. A news item of 1855 mentions a drove of several hundred cattle from Texas passing through Indiana County, Pa., on the way to New York City. They had left Texas four months previously.

From about 1845 to 1855, and possibly at other times, large numbers of sheep were driven from Vermont into Virginia. A resident of Prince George County, Md., writing in 1854, said that in 1847 he commenced driving Spanish Merinos, mostly from Vermont, to Virginia, and that during the following five years he sold upward of 13,000 head.

Large numbers of hogs also were driven to market before the railroads were built. In 1827 the keeper of a turnpike gate near the Cumberland River certified that 105,517 hogs had during that year been driven through the gate on the way to South Atlantic States.

Trails West of the Mississippi River

Among the most important live-stock trails west of the Mississippi River were those which led from Texas. One trail extended to pasture lands in the Kansas River valley on the line of one of the Pacific railroads. Near Abilene, Kans., a station on this railroad, thousands of cattle were wintered annually in the late sixties and early seventies. Another destination of the cattle trails from Texas was grazing lands along a railroad extending through the Dakotas and Montana. One of the routes from the Southwest to northern pastures over which cattle were driven from 1865 to 1884 led from the Gulf coast of Texas northward, passing west of San Antonio; thence to the Red River at Doan's Store, in Wilbarger County, Tex. Here the trail branched, one part going northward to a point now included in Beaver

County, Okla., and thence west to the Colorado ranges. The other fork of the trail led northeasterly through Fort Sill Reservation, now in Oklahoma; thence across the Washita River at Anadarko, Okla.; thence northeasterly to the Canadian River, which was crossed, and the route extended through Fort Reno and Kingfisher, and thence northward, following here the same general route as the present railroad, through Caldwell and Wichita, to the Kansas River just above Abilene.

The increase in farming and the accompanying restriction of the open range, together with the westward extension of the railroads, tended to move the northern terminus of a trail westward. This movement was going on when railroads from the North and East reached southwestern Texas and New Mexico.

The largest number of cattle driven in any one season from the Southwest to northern ranges has been estimated at 416,000 head. This was in 1884, about the time of the opening of a through railroad line over that route, and from that year the number moving over the long trails rapidly diminished.

The valley of a river was often found a convenient course, although not always a direct one, over which to drive sheep from their native ranges to pastures along the railroads which reached eastern markets. One route from Oregon led up the valleys of the Columbia and the Snake rivers, across the mountains of Idaho, and down the valley of the Platte to shipping points in Nebraska.

Cost of Trailing or Driving

Cattle driven to Abilene, Kans., from Texas ranges, an average distance of some 700 miles spent about two months on the trail. It has been estimated that the average cost of bringing cattle over the trail was $2 per head, in addition to a loss of 20 per cent, due to stampeding, stealing, and other misfortunes of the road, making a total of $2.40 per head, or somewhat less than the freight rate over about the same route in 1908.

According to one estimate, the wages and cost of subsistence of eight men engaged in trailing 350 cattle from range to shipping point in 1908 would average $72, or about 20 cents per head. Another estimate of cost of trailing from range to shipping point for the same year was from 5 to 25 cents per head, including the cost of the roundup but not allowing for losses on the trail.

The trailing of sheep involves relatively less expense. It has been stated that less than half the number of men will be required for a given number of carloads of sheep than for the same number of carloads of cattle. The cost of trailing sheep in 1908, not including losses on the way, has been estimated as about $130 per month for a flock of 2,000 to 3,000 sheep, or from one-half to four-fifths of 1 cent per head for a trail of average length.

Over long distances the commercial advantage of the railroad over the trail is well illustrated by the readiness with which the latter is abandoned whenever railroad service is available. One important advantage in favor of the railroad is the saving of time. From southwest Texas to the most remote ranges of the North but a few days' haul now intervenes, while under the old conditions two or three months of trailing were necessary. The decline in the supply of free pasturage and inaccessibility to water along the way over a number of the old routes, due to the settlement of the country, have added much to the difficulty of trailing.

Hauling Hogs in Wagons

Throughout the States where hogs are raised in largest numbers they are usually hauled to shipping points in wagons. In 1906 an estimate of the cost of hauling live hogs to market was made by this Department, based upon data furnished by county correspondents of the Bureau of Statistics. Three hundred and sixteen counties, 291 of which were in the North Central and 25 in the South Central States, reported that the average distance hogs were hauled from farm to shipping point was 7.9 miles and the average time seven-tenths of a day. The average weight of a load was 1,941 pounds, and the average cost was $2 per load, or 10 cents per 100 pounds.

Primitive Transport Service

An Early Shipment

One of the first shipments of cattle by rail from Kentucky to eastern markets, made in 1852, is described by the shipper as follows: One week was consumed in driving the cattle, 100 in number, from the neighborhood of Lexington, Ky., to Cincinnati. Here they were loaded in box cars and shipped by rail to Cleveland, whence they were taken by steamboat to Buffalo. After a stay of several days at Buffalo, the animals were driven to Canandaigua, N.Y. Thence they were hauled in immigrant cars to Albany, where they were unloaded in the freight house. After spending two days in a feed yard near Albany the stock was taken by boat to New York. The freight on these cattle from Cincinnati to Buffalo was at the rate of $120 per car, and the total expense from Kentucky to New York was $14 per head.

Old Routes From Texas

Among the routes over which cattle were moved from Texas to eastern markets about 1870, three will serve as illustrations. One way led by coastwise steamer to New Orleans, whence the animals were taken northward on river boats. At Cairo, Ill., the railroad journey was begun, northward to Chicago, thence to the East. A second route from Texas was over a trail to shipping points on Red River, whence the cattle were forwarded on steamboats to Cairo, thence to be shipped by rail northward. A third route followed the trails from Texas to feeding grounds along the railroads in Kansas and in regions farther north. From stations along these railroads the animals were forwarded to eastern markets.

River Trade

Statistics of the receipts and shipments of meat animals at St. Louis will illustrate the relatively small importance of steamboats as carriers. At St. Louis the total number of cattle received by rail during the three years ending 1867 was 207,000 and the number received by river 65,000. During the three years ending with 1907 the number of cattle received by rail was 3,783,000 and the number by river 46,000. So it appears that in the earlier period, when railroads were just beginning to handle this traffic, they carried more than three times as many cattle into St. Louis as the established river service, and forty years later the cattle traffic by rail was more than eighty times that on the river.

Of the sheep received at this market, the railroads brought twice as many as steamboats in 1865–1867, and forty-five times as many in 1905–1907. River boats carried 18 per cent of the hogs received at St. Louis in 1865–1867 and less than 4 per cent in 1905–1907.

Sources of Supply of Live Stock

Number of Meat Animals, 1840–1900

The number of cattle, not including calves, in the United States east of the Mississippi River increased from 14,000,000 in 1840 to 19,000,000 in 1900, but the average per 1,000 population in 1840 was 861 and in 1900 only 349 head. On farms and ranges west of the Mississippi there were 33,000,000 cattle in 1900, an average of 1,584 head per 1,000 population. This average was 2,153 in 1890 and 1,713 in 1880.

The average number of swine per 1,000 inhabitants east of the Mississippi River decreased from 1,496 in 1840 to 556 in 1900. The average west of this river was 1,540 in 1900 and 1,881 in 1880. The corresponding averages for sheep, excluding lambs, per 1,000 population east of the Mississippi River were 1,162 in 1840 and only 230 in 1900; in the West there were 1,298 sheep per 1,000 population in 1900 and 1,938 in 1880, a decrease of one-third in twenty years.

Location of Range Country

Of the relatively large supply of meat animals west of the Mississippi River, a considerable fraction of the cattle and sheep is on ranges. With the development of the country, grazing lands have been more and more restricted by the extension of agriculture.

Of the grazing regions in which cattle predominate, the largest extends northward from the mouth of the Rio Grande, with but one interruption, to the Canadian border, and westward for varying distances from a line corresponding roughly with the one-hundredth meridian. A second group of ranges on which cattle are greatly in excess of sheep extends along the Pacific coast from the Mexican border to the Columbia River; while a third group reaches from southern Utah through western and southern Arizona into southern New Mexico. Of the other ranges used chiefly for cattle, one group is located in the southwestern corner of Texas, another is in Wyoming south of Yellowstone National Park, a third touches the eastern shore of Great Salt Lake, and a fourth includes parts of northern Nevada and southern Oregon.

The principal region in which the grazing lands are used chiefly for sheep is shaped roughly like the letter "T," with the top extending westward from central Wyoming to central Washington, and the stem reaching south from Montana to southern Nevada. Two other groups of sheep ranges are in central Montana and central New Mexico, respectively. . . .

Routes and Markets

Important Routes

It has been noted above that the per capita meat supply east of the Mississippi River has been rapidly decreasing and that part of the meat consumed in this region is drawn from the farms and ranges of the West. For this reason the general tendency is for long-distance shipments of live stock from the West toward the East, even as it was in the earliest days of the western live-stock industry. The old routes from the ranges of the Southwest to northern grazing lands are still followed, the railroad taking the place of the trail. From the big markets along the Missouri River, and also from Chicago and St. Louis, live-stock routes lead to the Atlantic coast, a large number of shipments passing through Cincinnati, Pittsburg, or Buffalo.

In addition to the through routes of live-stock shipments, many lines of local traffic center at each market. The number of animals received at a market from various local shipping points within the radius of a day's hauling is sometimes larger than the number coming over long-distance routes.

Illustration of Train Service

An example of the complex nature of live-stock movements is furnished by a service consisting of one or more through trains made up at Jackson, Mich., and run to Buffalo via Detroit and Niagara Falls. These are composed of cars from four local trains which come to Jackson from as many different directions. One train leaves Bay City at 10.30 a.m. and is due in Jackson at 6 p.m. the same day; another from Ceresco, about 8 miles east of Battle Creek, is due to arrive half an hour later, having spent five and one-half hours on the way. A third train from Grand Rapids is due at 7 p.m., and the fourth leaves Battle Creek at 10.30 a.m., proceeds southwest as far as Fairfax, then turns northeastward and runs to Jackson, the entire running time being scheduled as eight and one-half hours. The through trains for Buffalo are expected to leave Jackson about 9 p.m., or two hours after the last local is due. The distances traversed by these local trains range from 37 to 115 miles and their average rates of speed, including stops, from 6.8 to15.8 miles per hour.

Shipments of Cattle and Sheep in Texas

The importance of the local shipments of cattle within the State of Texas is illustrated by figures covering practically all of the railroads of the State for the six months ending May 31, 1908. According to these returns the total number of cattle shipped during those months was about 350,000 head, more than two-fifths of which were consigned to points within the State and less than three-fifths to points beyond. Of the 130,000 to 140,000 sheep received by railroads in Texas during this period, four-fifths were carried beyond the State line.

Live-Stock Movement at Kansas City

An illustration of live-stock movement through a large center is afforded by conditions at one of the chief markets. Of the total number of steers received at the Kansas City Stock Yards in 1907, 59 per cent came from the State of Kansas, 15 from Oklahoma, 11 from Missouri, 6 from Texas, and nearly all the rest from Colorado, New Mexico, and Nebraska. The small part credited to Texas may be explained by the fact that Texas cattle are often sent to pastures and feed lots in Kansas, there to be fattened before shipment to the packing houses.

Of the sheep received at Kansas City, 29 per cent came from Colorado, 22 from Kansas, 10 from Missouri, 9 from Texas, and the rest from a number of other regions. This market was furnished by Kansas with 67 per cent of the hogs received in 1907, by Missouri with 27 per cent, Oklahoma 10, and Nebraska 5.

The destinations of cattle shipped from Kansas City in 1907 were distributed over many States. Missouri received 12 per cent, or more than any other State; Kansas 10, Illinois 5, Iowa 4; a large number of other States received smaller amounts, and 15 per cent was consigned to the various large markets. The number credited to each State does not include shipments to large centers, such as Chicago or St. Louis.

Receipts at Large Markets

At the four largest cattle markets in the United States the average number of cattle received yearly during 1905–1907 was 8,000,000 head, of which the receipts at Chicago were 3,300,000; Kansas City, 2,300,000; St. Louis, 1,300,000; and Omaha, 1,100,000 head. Chicago is the largest market for hogs also, an average of about 8,000,000 head per year having been received there during the three years ending 1907. Markets whose receipts of hogs averaged in these years from 2,000,000 to 4,000,000 head per year included Kansas City, St. Louis, Omaha, and in 1905 Buffalo.

The number of sheep received at Chicago during the three years ending 1907 averaged 4,600,000 per year. Omaha's receipts were next in size, averaging 2,000,000 head; then came Kansas City, with 1,500,000; then, for the two years ending 1906, Buffalo averaged 1,300,000; and New York, 1,100,000.

Receipts of calves were smaller than those of any other class of live stock, the average annual number at Chicago during 1905–1907 being 400,000; at Kansas City, 260,000; at Fort Worth, 230,000; and for 1905–6 at New York, 390,000.

Disposition of Cattle and Sheep

A live-stock center serves at least two important purposes: It is a meeting place for dealers, and it is also a place of slaughter on a large scale. The degree to which each of these two functions is developed at a given market is generally shown by the relative number of animals shipped as compared with the number received. A group of markets whose chief business is forwarding cattle includes Denver, St. Paul, Buffalo, and New York, each of which shipped at least 70 per cent of the number received during 1905–6.

Centers whose shipments during this period were less than 70 per cent but more than 50 per cent of the number received included Sioux City, Pittsburg, Philadelphia, Boston, and Baltimore. The largest cattle markets are in the class which slaughter more than one-half of the number received. Besides Chicago, Kansas City, St. Louis, and Omaha, this third group included, in 1905–1907. Indianapolis, Fort Worth, Louisville, Cincinnati, and St. Joseph.

The important centers which shipped out 50 per cent or more of the sheep received included, in 1905–1907, Louisville, Denver, St. Paul, Cincinnati, Omaha, and, in 1905–6, Pittsburg, Buffalo, Baltimore, and New York. Of the sheep received in 1905–1907 at Kansas City, 71 per cent were retained; at Chicago, 72; at St. Joseph, 74; and at St. Louis, 85 per cent.

Reshipments of Hogs Relatively Small

The combined yearly receipts of hogs at thirteen principal markets in the United States averaged 25,000,000 head in 1905–1907, and of this number

20,000,000, or 80 per cent, were retained for slaughter. At St. Louis 73 per cent of the hogs received during this period were slaughtered, at Chicago 77, at Omaha 93, and at Kansas City 96 per cent.

Cattle Exports

Most of the meat animals exported from the United States are cattle which are shipped principally through North Atlantic ports. The average number exported yearly from the United States increased from 139,000 during the fiscal years 1878–1882 to 514,000 in 1903–1907, and the exports from the Atlantic coast grew from 90,000 to 354,000 in the same time. During the year ending June 30, 1908, Boston exported 107,000 cattle, New York 76,000, Philadelphia 46,000, Baltimore 30,000, Portland, Me., 22,000, and Detroit 18,000. Exports of sheep and swine from the United States are relatively unimportant, their average value in 1903–1907 being only 4 per cent of the cattle exports.

Stock Yards and Feeding Stations

Facilities

The facilities for handling live stock at large markets may be illustrated by the capacity of the Union Stock Yards at Chicago. These yards in 1907 covered an area of 500 acres and contained 13,000 inclosures. Separate accommodations, except at unloading and loading platforms, were provided for each kind of stock; sheep and hogs were kept in sheds of two or more stories each, while cattle occupied open pens, each holding from one to several carloads. The inclosures at the loading and unloading platforms each held slightly more than one carload of stock. These yards could hold at one time 75,000 cattle, 125,000 sheep, 300,000 hogs, and 6,000 horses and mules. The movement from one part of the yards to another was facilitated by overhead viaducts and by miles of alleyways among the pens. The water system which supplied the pens had a reservoir holding 10,000,000 gallons and pumps whose daily capacity was 8,000,000 gallons.

In addition to the large stock yards, there are minor feeding stations along the routes from local shipping points to large markets. The area devoted to feeding purposes at these stations varies from small feed yards, where only hay and grain are furnished, to large pastures of 1,000 to 3,000 acres, such as are found at some points west of the Missouri River. Facilities at feeding stations vary greatly. At some places scarcely more than a chute is available, while at others there are platforms and chutes for unloading and loading, pens for feeding and watering, scales, and other appliances for handling the stock.

Handling Traffic

The time and labor required to unload live stock from a train at a stock yard and to place the animals in a convenient location for selling is an element in the cost of transportation. Live-stock trains are so run as to arrive at Chicago or other centers in time for the animals to be fed, watered, and weighed before the morning market opens. On reaching the yards a train is stopped alongside a platform across which are a number of chutes. The distance between the gateways of pens is approximately equal to an average car length, so that each car door on one side of a train may be opposite a gateway, and the stock may be readily moved from the train across the platform and into the pens. As each car is unloaded a record is made of the number of animals as they enter the chutes, and another record is made when they are driven from the unloading pens. These records include also the names of the consignor and consignee, the numbers of cars and chutes, and other data necessary to identify the stock. Each consignment is kept separate as it is driven from the place of unloading along alleyways and over viaducts to the cattle pens, hog houses, or sheep barns, where the animals are fed and watered and where sales take place.

The owner of stock is usually represented in the market by a commission man. Buyers may be divided into at least four classes. One consists of men employed by the local packing houses; another is purchasing for farmers and feeders; a third represents the exporters, and still another class consists of speculators or traders who buy cattle, classify, and sell them to packers, exporters, or feeders. By the middle of the afternoon the market is usually over, and the animals that have been sold for shipment are generally driven to the loading chutes and placed on trains which leave the same afternoon or night. Those purchased by local packing houses are promptly slaughtered.

At Chicago the movement from cars through the chutes and pens to the alleyways beyond is estimated to average for all stock one minute per carload. This includes counting the animals, making the required records, and waiting in the unloading pen for a place in a procession of consignments moving through the adjoining alleyway. The actual movement from car to chute requires little time, a train of 40 to 50 cars being unloaded easily within fifteen minutes.

Charges for Yardage and Feed

Charges at stock yards include two general items: One is the use of the yards, together with the scales, and the other is the feed. In the Middle West a common rate for the first item, or "yardage," is for cattle 25 cents per head, calves 10, hogs 8, and sheep 5 cents. At Buffalo in 1908 "yardage and scale" was for cattle 15 cents, calves 8, hogs 6, and sheep 4 cents. The stock yards in San Francisco grant free use of the yards for twenty-four hours after unloading. After the expiration of this time the charge for each twelve days or fraction thereof for cattle is 25 cents per head, hogs 6, and sheep 5 cents.

The charge for feeding stock in a number of the larger stock yards in 1908 ranged from $1 to $2 per 100 pounds of hay, $1 to $1.50 per bushel of corn, and 60 cents to $1 per bushel of oats.

Minor feeding stations fix rates for hay and grain not greatly differing from those in force at large stock yards. For pasturing sheep en route to the East from Wyoming, Idaho, and Oregon the rates per head at feeding stations ranged in 1908 from 0.5 to 1.5 cents per day.

Shippers or Attendants

In the absence of complete service at some unloading points over a given route it is necessary for attendants or "shippers in charge" to accompany stock trains to assist in unloading, feeding, watering, and reloading the animals; but on through shipments between large centers, such as Chicago and Buffalo, it is not usual for shippers to accompany the stock. In the early days attendants were much more necessary than at present. When cars were overcrowded and the animals thrown down, one of the principal duties of the shipper was to aid them to their feet.

Number of Unloading Points on a Given Route

Legal requirements are such that thirty-six hours may be taken as the maximum running time between feeding stations. From southern Idaho to Omaha three or four unloading points are usually necessary, one from Omaha to Chicago, and one from that point to Boston or New York. From Chicago to Pittsburg the schedule time of important live-stock trains on two routes, in July, 1908, was twenty-five to twenty-nine hours, and the average rates of speed from 17 to 19 miles per hour, including stops. From Kansas City to Buffalo via St. Louis and Detroit the time was fifty-six and one-half hours and the average rate about 18 miles per hour. For traffic moving as fast as this, unloading points could be nearly 650 miles apart.

Carrying Capacity of Railroads

Number of Live-Stock Cars

The total number of live-stock cars owned by railroads in the United States in the year ending June 30, 1907, was 69,997. Besides these a considerable number were owned by private car companies. The average capacity of a stock car in 1907 was 29 short tons, and the total for all the stock cars owned by railroads was 2,013,170 tons. This capacity is the weight of dead freight that the car is permitted to carry and not the weight of the live stock that can be comfortably loaded therein.

Double-Deck Cars

Double-deck live-stock cars were first used upon railroads in the United States before 1860. The advantage of a double-deck car depends largely upon the size of the individual shipment. When a single consignment of small animals is large enough to load two ordinary single decks, the use of one double-deck car will be a saving to the carrier. Freight rates are frequently lower in double than in single-deck cars.

Of a total of 44,000 live-stock cars owned in June, 1908, by 17 principal live-stock carrying railroads, 7,800, or 18 per cent of the total, were fitted with double decks. If this percentage applied to the total number of stock cars owned by railroads in this country in 1907, there were then about 13,000 double and 57,000 single-deck cars.

Average Carloads

From reports of stock yards and railroads it is estimated that an average number of meat animals to the carload at Kansas City and Omaha is for cattle about 25, hogs in single-deck cars about 75, and sheep about 120 per deck. Allowing as an average 25 cattle per car, the 57,000 single-deck cars owned by railroads in 1907 would carry at one time 1,425,000 head, and the total weight of these cattle, at 955 pounds per head, would be 680,000 tons, or 41 per cent of the total dead-weight carrying capacity of the cars. If 680,000 tons of dead freight were substituted for the same weight of live stock, only 23,000 instead of 57,000 cars would be required.

Taking as an average number of sheep 120 per deck, the 57,000 single and 13,000 double-deck cars would carry at one time 9,960,000 head of sheep, which at an average of 100 pounds per head would weigh 498,000 short tons. The full capacity of these cars being 2,013,000 tons, the equivalent in dead freight to 70,000 carloads of sheep could be carried on 17,000 cars, thus saving 53,000, or 76 per cent, for other service. The 70,000 cars, if loaded with hogs of an average weight of 220 pounds and numbering 75 head per deck, would contain the equivalent of only 24,000 full carloads of dead freight.

Railroad Freight Charges

The first railroad freight rates on live stock were quoted in dollars per car, regardless of the weight or number of the animals carried. This method of charge has been blamed for much of the trouble due to crowded cars, but with the establishment of charges depending upon weight, dealers have no longer much inducement to load too many animals in one car. From Chicago to New York, as early as 1879, rates on live stock were quoted in cents per 100 pounds, and nine years later rates from the Missouri River to Chicago and St. Louis were changed in the same way. In 1908 the rates over most of the leading routes east of the Rocky Mountains were quoted in cents per 100 pounds. West of the Rocky Mountains and over routes from the southwestern ranges through Denver northward in 1908 rates were still expressed in dollars per car.

Cattle in 1908

For a large number of shipping points and destinations the principal items of transport cost for cattle from Texas ranges to Chicago via Montana are shown in the statement below.

Principal items in the average cost per head of moving steers from Texas to ranges in Montana, North Dakota, and South Dakota, and thence to Chicago, June, 1908.

Item of cost.	Low.	High.
Stock Cattle.		
Trailing (driving) from ranges to local shipping points, Texas	$0.05	$0.25
Freight, Texas to Montana, North Dakota, and South Dakota, at $100 to $137 per car	2.86	3.91
Feed en route at $2 per car at each of three or four unloading points	.17	.23
Shippers in charge, estimated at $2 per car	.06	.06
Trailing from railroad station to ranges, Montana, North Dakota, and South Dakota	.05	.25
Total of items given, Texas to Montana, North Dakota, and South Dakota	3.19	4.70
Beef Cattle.		
Trailing, ranges to shipping points, Montana, North Dakota, and South Dakota	.05	.25
Freight, Montana, etc., to Chicago, at 35 cents to 66 cents per 100 pounds	3.85	7.26
Feed en route with an assumed average of $2 per car at two to four unloading points	.16	.32
Shippers in charge, estimated at $2 per car	.08	.08
Switching charges, Chicago, at $2 per car	.08	.08
Feed, stock yards, Chicago	.25	.25
Yardage at Chicago	.25	.25
Total, Montana, etc., to Chicago	4.72	8.49
Total, Texas to Chicago via Montana, etc.	7.91	13.19

The average cost per head of shipping steers over a particular route is given by one of the prominent cattlemen of northwestern Texas as follows:

Per head.

Freight from Texas to Fallon, Mont., $125 per car,

40 head per car	$3.125
Hay, $8 per car	.20
Shipper in charge, $2 per car	.05
Average losses in transit, $5 per car	.125
Total, Texas to Fallon	3.50
Cost Montana to Chicago, including freight, hay,	
shipper's expense, and yardage	5.90
Total, Texas to Chicago, via Fallon, Mont	9.40

For transporting steers from northwestern Texas to feed lots west of the Missouri River and, after fattening, to London, England, via Chicago, the following estimates are made:

Principal items in the average cost per head of moving steers from Texas to feed lots in Kansas, Colorado, and Oklahoma, and thence to London, England, June, 1908.

Item of cost.	Low.	High.
Stock Cattle.		
Trailing, ranges to shipping points in Texas..	$0.05	$0.25
Freight, Texas to feed lots in Kansas, etc., at $26 to $78 per 36-foot car...........................	.87	2.00
Feed en route at one to three unloading points, at an assumed		
average of $2 per car.	.07	.20
Yardage at station near feed lot..	.00	.25
Unloading at destination and driving to feed lot	.05	.05
Shippers in charge	.05	.07
Total, Texas range to feed lots in Kansas, etc.	1.09	3.42
Beef Cattle.		
Driving from feed lot and loading on car	.05	.05
Freight, feed lots in Knasas, etc., to Chicago, at 27 to 55		
cents per 100 pounds..	3.38	6.88
Feed en route at two or three unloading points; assumed average,		
$2 per car	.20	.30
Shippers in charge; assumed average, $2 per car..	.20	.20
Switching charge, Chicago, at $2 per car	.10	.10
Yardage and feed at Chicago...	.50	.50
Total, feed lots in Kansas, etc., to Chicago	4.43	8.03
Freight, New York to Chicago, at 28 cents per 100 pounds..............................	3.50	3.50
Feed en route at one unloading point	.25	.40
Feed at New York..	.25	.50
Total, Chicago to New York	4.00	4.40
Ocean freight, New York to London..	6.60	7.20
Hay, 14 days, including 3 or 4 days at London	2.50	4.50
Shippers in charge	.50	.60
Total, New York to London...	9.60	12.30
Total of items specified, Texas range to London	19.12	28.15

Sheep in 1908

From Texas and New Mexico to feeding grounds in Colorado and Kansas, thence to Chicago, the total cost of moving sheep, including trailing, freight, feeding, and shippers' wages, averages 50 cents to $1.50 per head; and the additional cost to New York, from 35 to 45 cents per head.

Hogs in 1908

The cost of moving live hogs, weighing about 200 pounds each, from farms in Illinois, Indiana, Wisconsin, Missouri, Iowa, Minnesota, and South Dakota to Chicago includes the following items: Hauling in wagons from farm to shipping point, 20 cents per head; freight, from 20 to 70 cents; shippers' wages, feed, yardage, and similar items, 30 to 60 cents; making a total of 70 cents to $1.50 per head.

Ocean Transportation

Losses on Shipboard

Since 1891 cattle shipping across the Atlantic from the United States and Canada has been attended with comparatively small loss. In 1892, out of 98,731 cattle shipped to Europe from Montreal, 646, or about seven-tenths of 1 per cent, were lost at sea, and in the following three years the percentages of loss grew less. The number lost in any one voyage was rarely more than three or four.

The rate of insurance in 1908 on cattle shipped from New York to England was quoted at one-fourth of 1 per cent, of which one-tenth of 1 per cent was on account of the risk due to the ship's chance of being lost, and three-twentieths of 1 per cent for the risk of the cattle dying in transit. On this basis it may be assumed that the average loss of cattle on the trans-Atlantic routes is less than 5 in every 2,000 shipped. Prior to the establishment of satisfactory steamship facilities and to the present Government inspection, insurance rates on cattle, according to a prominent New York exporter, varied from 2 to 10 per cent, thus indicating that the losses in those days were from eight to forty times as great as at present.

Freight Costs From the United States

Ocean freight rates in 1908 from the United States to England were quoted at $6 to $7.20 per head for cattle, and 72 cents (3 shillings) per head for sheep. Twenty years ago, according to an exporter, rates on cattle reached $9.60. The actual rates paid are subject to private contracts, the terms of which are not usually made public. Other items of cost of ocean transportation are attendants' wages and feed for the stock. En route from New York to England the foreman of attendants is paid about $50 or $60 per trip, experienced hands from $25 to $30, and inexperienced men often no money wages, their passage being earned by work on shipboard. Sometimes, however, the exporter pays at the rate of $3 per man to secure these men through shipping agents. The total cost of labor from New York to London or Liverpool is estimated at 50 or 60 cents per head for cattle and about 10 cents per head for sheep. Enough hay is provided to feed the stock throughout the ten or eleven days on the ocean and for several days at the landing place in England.

Rates From Argentina

Before the United Kingdom prohibited the importation of cattle from the River Plate freight rates from Argentina to England sometimes reached as high as $28.50 per head and as low as $16.80. During the few months in 1903 when the quarantine was suspended in England rates ranged from $18.32 to $22.58 per head.

Unfavorable conditions, sometimes involving serious loss, are reported to have existed on the long voyages from Argentina to England before this traffic was stopped. With improved accommodations, however, many of these difficulties might be overcome, but long voyages necessarily require more food and greater cost for attendance than the short ones from United States ports to London or Liverpool.

Economy in Transporting Meat Rather Than Live Animals

Rail

It costs the carrier less to transport a given amount of meat than the live animals necessary to produce that meat. Seven carloads of live cattle yield on an average 5 minimum carloads, 20,000 pounds each, of fresh beef, or 2 carloads of 49,000 pounds each. Packing-house products other than fresh meat are carried in still larger loads and the saving to the carrier as compared with live-stock transportation is correspondingly greater.

From Chicago to New York in 1908 the freight and other expenses of the road on an export steer of average weight (1,250 pounds) were $4 to $4.40, while the freight on the average amount of fresh beef yielded by the animal, 700 pounds, would amount to only $3.15, not including the expense of icing. From Kansas City to New York the corresponding difference between live and dead freight is still greater, amounting possibly to $2.25 or $2.50 per head.

Ocean

The total cost of shipping a live steer from Chicago to Liverpool, including freight, feed, and attendance, is estimated at $13.60 to $16.70, or considerably more than double the cost of shipping the average weight of fresh beef yielded by the animal.

Over the long voyage from Argentina to England the difference in cost between live cattle and dressed meat would be great. Compared with the freight rates on live cattle, quoted in 1903 when the last exports over this route were made, the cost of shipping fresh meat is small. A rate quoted by a leading steamship company carrying dressed beef from Argentina to England in 1908 was equivalent to $7 for the average quantity yielded by an export steer, or about one-third of the freight and a still smaller fraction of the total transport cost for the live animal, which total included, besides freight, the risks of passing through the Torrid Zone and the expense of feed and attendance for a voyage of more than three weeks.

Conclusion

The growth of economy in the transportation of meat animals has taken place along at least three general lines. One is the saving to the railroads and steamships handling the traffic, which phase of improvement is reflected in lower freight rates. The size and efficiency of cars and vessels have been increased and cheaper methods have been devised for handling traffic in stock yards. A second phase is the reduction of loss in transit, a saving which may be credited to mechanical improvements, to legal regulations, and to the change over a large number of routes whereby the freight charge depends upon the weight of the live stock shipped and not upon the number of cars used. The third direction of this growth of saving is found in the tendency to transport meat instead of live animals. This movement is illustrated by the establishment of new slaughtering centers nearer the sources of supply than are the older meat-packing cities east of the Missouri River.

Report of the Country Life Commission

From U.S. Country Life Commission, *Report*, 1909, pp. 3–65.

SPECIAL MESSAGE FROM THE PRESIDENT OF THE UNITED STATES TRANSMITTING THE REPORT OF THE COUNTRY LIFE COMMISSION

To the Senate and House of Representatives:

I transmit herewith the report of the Commission on Country Life. At the outset I desire to point out that not a dollar of the public money has been paid to any commissioner for his work on the commission.

The report shows the general condition of farming life in the open country, and points out its larger problems; it indicates ways in which the Government, National and State, may show the people how to solve some of these problems; and it suggests a continuance of the work which the commission began.

Judging by thirty public hearings, to which farmers and farmers' wives from forty States and Territories came, and from 120,000 answers to printed questions sent out by the Department of Agriculture, the commission finds that the general level of country life is high compared with any preceding time or with any other land. If it has in recent years slipped down in some places, it has risen in more places. Its progress has been general, if not uniform.

Yet farming does not yield either the profit or the satisfaction that it ought to yield and may be made to yield. There is discontent in the country, and in places discouragement. Farmers as a class do not magnify their calling, and the movement to the towns, though, I am happy to say, less than formerly, is still strong.

Under our system, it is helpful to promote discussion of ways in which the people can help themselves. There are three main directions in which the farmers can help themselves; namely, better farming, better business, and better living on the farm. The National Department of Agriculture, which has rendered services equaled by no other similar department in any other time or place; the state departments of agriculture; the state colleges of agriculture and the mechanic arts, especially through their extension work; the state agricultural experiment stations; the Farmers' Union; the Grange; the agricultural press; and other similar agencies; have all combined to place within the reach of the American farmer an amount and quality of agricultural information which, if applied, would enable him, over large areas, to double the production of the farm.

The object of the Commission on Country Life therefore is not to help the farmer raise better crops, but to call his attention to the opportunities for better business and better living on the farm. If country life is to become what it should be, and what I believe it ultimately will be — one of the most dignified, desirable, and sought-after ways of earning a living — the farmer must take advantage not only of the agricultural knowledge which is at his disposal, but of the methods which have raised and continue to raise the standards of living and of intelligence in other callings.

Those engaged in all other industrial and commercial callings have found it necessary, under modern economic conditions, to organize themselves for mutual advantage and for the protection of their own particular interests in relation to other interests. The farmers of every progressive European country have realized this essential fact and have found in the cooperative system exactly the form of business combination they need.

Now whatever the State may do toward improving the practice of agriculture, it is not within the sphere of any government to reorganize the farmers' business or reconstruct the social life of farming communities. It is, however, quite within its power to use its influence and the machinery of publicity which it can control for calling public attention to the needs and the facts. For example, it is the obvious duty of the Government to call the attention of farmers to the growing monopolization of water power. The farmers above all should have that power, on reasonable terms, for cheap transportation, for lighting their homes, and for innumerable uses in the daily tasks on the farm.

It would be idle to assert that life on the farm occupies as good a position in dignity, desirability, and business results as the farmers might easily give it if they chose. One of the chief difficulties is the failure of country life, as it exists at present, to satisfy the higher social and intellectual aspirations of country people. Whether the constant draining away of so much of the best elements in the rural population into the towns is due chiefly to this cause or to the superior business opportunities of city life may be open to question. But no one at all familiar with farm life throughout the United States can fail to recognize the necessity for building up the life of the farm upon its social as well as upon its productive side.

It is true that country life has improved greatly in attractiveness, health, and comfort, and that the farmer's earnings are higher than they were. But city life is advancing even more rapidly, because of the greater attention which is being given by the citizens of the towns to their own betterment. For just this reason the introduction of effective agricultural cooperation throughout the United States is of the first importance. Where farmers are organized cooperatively they not only avail themselves much more readily of business opportunities and improved methods, but it is found that the organizations which bring them together in the work of their lives are used also for social and intellectual advancement.

The cooperative plan is the best plan of organization wherever men have the right spirit to carry it out. Under this plan any business undertaking is managed by a committee; every man has one vote and only one vote; and everyone gets profits according to what he sells or buys or supplies. It develops individual responsibility and has a moral as well as a financial value over any other plan.

I desire only to take counsel with the farmers as fellow-citizens. It is not the problem of the farmers alone that I am discussing with them, but a problem which affects every city as well as every farm in the country. It is a problem which the working farmers will have to solve for themselves; but it is a problem which also affects in only less degree all the rest of us, and therefore if we can render any help toward its solution, it is not only our duty but our interest to do so.

The foregoing will, I hope, make it clear why I appointed a commission to consider problems of farm life which have hitherto had far too little attention, and the neglect of which has not only held back life in the country, but also lowered the efficiency of the whole nation. The welfare of the farmer is of vital consequence to the welfare of the whole community. The strengthening of country life, therefore, is the strengthening of the whole nation.

The commission has tried to help the farmers to see clearly their own problem and to see it as a whole; to distinguish clearly between what the Government can do and what the farmers must do for themselves; and it wishes to bring not only the farmers but the Nation as a whole to realize that the growing of crops, though an essential part, is only a part of country life. Crop growing is the essential foundation; but it is no less essential that the farmer shall get an adequate return for what he grows; and it is no less essential — indeed it is literally vital — that he and his wife and his children shall lead the right kind of life.

For this reason, it is of the first importance that the United States Department of Agriculture, through which as prime agent the ideas the commission stands for must reach the people, should become without delay in fact a Department of Country Life, fitted to deal not only with crops, but also with all the larger aspects of life in the open country.

From all that has been done and learned three great general and immediate needs of country life stand out:

First, effective cooperation among farmers, to put them on a level with the organized interests with which they do business.

Second, a new kind of schools in the country, which shall teach the children as much outdoors as indoors and perhaps more, so that they will prepare for country life, and not as at present, mainly for life in town.

Third, better means of communication, including good roads and a parcels post, which the country people are everywhere, and rightly, unanimous in demanding.

To these may well be added better sanitation; for easily preventable diseases hold several million country people in the slavery of continuous ill health.

The commission points out, and I concur in the conclusion, that the most important help that the Government, whether National or State, can give is to show the people how to go about these tasks of organization, education, and communication with the best and quickest results. This can be done by the collection and spread of information. One community can thus be informed of what other communities have done, and one country of what other countries have done. Such help by the people's government would lead to a comprehensive plan of organization, education, and communication, and make the farming country better to live in, for intellectual and social reasons as well as for purely agricultural reasons.

The Government through the Department of Agriculture does not cultivate any man's farm for him. But it does put at his service useful knowledge that he would not otherwise get. In the same way the National and State Governments might put into the people's hands the new and right knowledge of school work. The task of maintaining and developing the schools would remain, as now, with the people themselves.

The only recommendation I submit is that an appropriation of $25,000 be provided, to enable the commission to digest the material it has collected, and to collect and to digest much more that is within its reach, and thus complete its work. This would enable the commission to gather in the harvest of suggestion which is resulting from the discussion it has stirred up. The commissioners have served without compensation, and I do not recommend any appropriation for their services, but only for the expenses that will be required to finish the task that they have begun.

To improve our system of agriculture seems to me the most urgent of the tasks which lie before us. But it can not, in my judgment, be effected by measures which touch only the material and technical side of the subject; the whole business and life of the farmer must also be taken into account. Such considerations led me to appoint the Commission on Country Life. Our object should be to help develop in the country community the great ideals of community life as well as of personal character. One of the most important adjuncts to this end must be the country church, and I invite your attention to what the commission says of the country church and of the need of an extension of such work as that of the Young Men's Christian Association in country communities. Let me lay special emphasis upon what the Commission says at the very end of its report on personal ideals and local leadership. Everything resolves itself in the end into the question of personality. Neither society nor government can do much for country life unless there is voluntary response in the personal ideals of the men and women who live in the country. In the development of character, the home should be more important than the school, or than society at large. When once the basic material needs have been met, high ideals may be quite independent of income; but they can not be realized without sufficient income to provide adequate foundation; and where the community at large is not financially prosperous it is impossible to develop a high average personal and community ideal. In short, the fundamental facts of human nature apply to men and women who live in the country just as they apply to men and women who live in the towns. Given a sufficient foundation of material well being, the influence of the farmers and farmers' wives on their children becomes the factor of first importance in determining the attitude of the next generation toward farm life. The farmer should realize that the person who most needs consideration on the farm is his wife. I do not in the least mean that she should purchase ease at the expense of duty. Neither man nor woman is really happy or really useful save on condition of doing his or her duty. If the woman shirks her duty as housewife, as home keeper, as the mother whose prime function it is to bear and rear a sufficient number of healthy children, then she is not entitled to our regard. But if she does her duty she is more entitled to our regard even than the man who does his duty; and the man should show special consideration for her needs.

I warn my countrymen that the great recent progress made in city life is not a full measure of our civilization; for our civilization rests at bottom on the wholesomeness, the attractiveness, and the completeness, as well as the prosperity, of life in the country. The men and women on the farms stand for what is fundamentally best and most needed in our American life. Upon the development of country life rests ultimately our ability, by methods of farming requiring the highest intelligence, to continue to feed and clothe the hungry nations; to supply the city with fresh blood, clean bodies, and clear brains that can endure the terrific strain of modern life; we need the development of men in the open country, who will be in the future, as in the past, the stay and strength of the nation in time of war, and its guiding and controlling spirit in time of peace.

THEODORE ROOSEVELT.

THE WHITE HOUSE, February 9, 1909.

Appendix A

One of the most illuminating — and incidentally one of the most interesting and amusing — series of answers sent to the commission was from a farmer in Missouri. He stated that he had a wife and 11 living children, he and his wife being each 52 years old; and that they owned 520 acres of land without any mortgage hanging over their heads. He had himself done well, and his views as to why many of his neighbors had done less well are entitled to consideration. These views are expressed in terse and vigorous English; they can not always be quoted in full. He states that the farm homes in his neighborhood are not as good as they should be because too many of them are encumbered by mortgages; that the schools do not train boys and girls satisfactorily for life on the farm, because they allow them to get an idea in their heads that city life is better, and that to remedy this practical farming should be taught. To the question whether the farmers and their wives in his neighborhood are satisfactorily organized, he answers: "Oh, there is a little one-horse grange gang in our locality, and every darned one thinks they aught to be a king." To the question, "Are the renters of farms in your neighborhood making a satisfactory living?" he answers: "No; because they move about so much hunting a better job." To the question, "Is the supply of farm labor in your neighborhood satisfactory?" the answer is: "No; because the people have gone out of the baby business;" and when asked as to the remedy he answers, "Give a pention to every mother who gives birth to seven living boys on American soil." To the question "Are the conditions surrounding hired labor on the farm in your neighborhood satisfactory to the hired men?" he answers: "Yes, unless he is a drunken cuss," adding that he would like to blow up the stillhouses and root out whisky and beer. To the question "Are the sanitary conditions on the farms in your neighborhood satisfactory?" he answers: "No; to careless about chicken yards (and the like) and poorly covered Wells, in one Well on neighbor's farm I counted 7 snakes in the Wall of the Well, and they used the watter daily, his wife dead now and he is looking for another." He ends by stating that the most important single thing to be done for the betterment of country life is "good roads;" but in his answers he shows very clearly that most important of all is the individual equation of the man or woman.

The humor of this set of responses must not blind us to the shrewd common sense and good judgment they display. The man is a good citizen; his wife is a good citizen; and their views are fundamentally sound. Very much information of the most valuable kind can be gathered if the Commission is given the money necessary to enable it to arrange and classify the information obtained from the great mass of similar answers which they have received. But there is one point where the testimony is as a whole in flat contradiction to that contained above. The general feeling is that the organizations of farmers, the grangers and the like, have been of the very highest service not only to the farmers, but to the farmers' wives, and that they have conferred great social as well as great industrial advantages. An excellent little book has recently been published by Miss Jennie Buell, called "One Woman's Work for Farm Women." It is dedicated "To farm women everywhere," and is the story of Mary A. Mayo's part in rural social movements. It is worth while to read this little volume to see how much the hard-working woman who lives on the farm can do for herself when once she is given sympathy, encouragement, and occasional leadership.

REPORT OF COMMISSION ON COUNTRY LIFE.

WASHINGTON, *January 23, 1909.*

To the President:

The Commission on Country Life herewith presents its report, covering the following topics:

Introductory review or summary:
    I. General statement—
    The purpose of the Commission.
    Methods pursued by the Commission.
    (Circulars, hearings, school-house meetings).
    II. The main special deficiencies in country life—
      1. Disregard of the inherent rights of land workers.
        (a) Speculative holding of lands.
        (b) Monopolistic control of streams.
        (c) Wastage and control of forests.
        (d) Restraint of trade.
        (e) Remedies for the disregard of the inherent rights of the farmer.
      2. Highways.
      3. Soil depletion and its effects.
      4. Agricultural labor.
        (a) Statement of the general problem.
        (b) The question of intemperance.
        (c) Development of local attachments of the farm laborer.
      5. Health in the open country.
      6. Woman's work on the farm.
    III. The general corrective forces that should be set in motion—
      7. Need of agricultural or country life surveys.
      8. Need of a redirected education.
      9. Necessity of working together.
     10. The country church.
     11. Personal ideals and local leadership.

Introductory Review or Summary

The Commission finds that agriculture in the United States, taken altogether, is prosperous commercially, when measured by the conditions that have obtained in previous years, although there are some regions in which this is only partially true. The country people are producing vast quantities of supplies for food, shelter, clothing, and for use in the arts. The country homes are improving in comfort, attractiveness, and healthfulness. Not only in the material wealth that they produce, but in the supply of independent and strong citizenship, the agricultural people constitute the very foundation of our national efficiency. As agriculture is the immediate basis of country life, so it follows that the general affairs of the open country, speaking broadly, are in a condition of improvement.

Many institutions, organizations, and movements are actively contributing to the increasing welfare of the open country. The most important of these are the United States Department of Agriculture, the colleges of agriculture and the experiment stations in the States, and the national farmers' organizations. These institutions and organizations are now properly assuming leadership in country-life affairs, and consequently in many of the public questions of national bearing. With these agencies must be mentioned state departments of agriculture, agricultural societies, and organizations of very many kinds, teachers in schools, workers in church and other religious associations, traveling libraries, and many other groups, all working with commendable zeal to further the welfare of the people of the open country.

The Most Prominent Deficiencies

Yet it is true, notwithstanding all this progress as measured by historical standards, that agriculture is not commercially as profitable as it is entitled to be for the labor and energy that the farmer expends and the risks that he assumes, and that the social conditions in the open country are far short of their possibilities. We must measure our agricultural efficiency by its possibilities rather than by comparison with previous conditions. The farmer is almost necessarily handicapped in the development of his business, because his capital is small and the volume of his transactions limited; and he usually stands practically alone against organized interests. In the general readjustment of modern life due to the great changes in manufactures and commerce inequalities and discriminations have arisen, and naturally the separate man suffers most. The unattached man has problems that government should understand.

The reasons for the lack of a highly organized rural society are very many, as the full report explains. The leading specific causes are:

A lack of knowledge on the part of farmers of the exact agricultural conditions and possibilities of their regions;

Lack of good training for country life in the schools;

The disadvantage or handicap of the farmer as against the established business systems and interests, preventing him from securing adequate returns for his products, depriving him of the benefits that would result from unmonopolized rivers and the conservation of forests, and depriving the community, in many cases, of the good that would come from the use of great tracts of agricultural land that are now held for speculative purposes;

Lack of good highway facilities;

The widespread continuing depletion of soils, with the injurious effect on rural life;

A general need of new and active leadership.

Other causes contributing to the general result are: Lack of any adequate system of agricultural credit, whereby the farmer may readily secure loans on fair terms; the shortage of labor, a condition that is often complicated by intemperance among workmen; lack of institutions and incentives that tie the laboring man to the soil; the burdens and the narrow life of farm women; lack of adequate supervision of public health.

The Nature of the Remedies

Some of the remedies lie with the National Government, some of them with the States and communities in their corporate capacities, some with voluntary organizations, and some with individuals acting alone. From the great number of suggestions that have been made, covering every phase of country life, the commission now enumerates those that seem to be most fundamental or most needed at the present time.

Congress can remove some of the handicaps of the farmer, and it can also set some kinds of work in motion, such as:

The encouragement of a system of thoroughgoing surveys of all agricultural regions in order to take stock and to collect local fact, with the idea of providing a basis on which to develop a scientifically and economically sound country life;

The encouragement of a system of extension work of rural communities through all the land-grant colleges with the people at their homes and on their farms;

A thoroughgoing investigation by experts of the middleman system of handling farm products, coupled with a general inquiry into the farmer's disadvantages in respect to taxation, transportation rates, cooperative organizations and credit, and the general business system;

An inquiry into the control and use of the streams of the United States with the object of protecting the people in their ownership and of saving to agricultural uses such benefits as should be reserved for these purposes;

The establishing of a highway engineering service, or equivalent organization, to be at the call of the States in working out effective and economical highway systems;

The establishing of a system of parcels posts and postal savings banks;

And providing some means or agency for the guidance of public opinion toward the development of a real rural society that shall rest directly on the land.

Other remedies recommended for consideration by Congress are:

The enlargement of the United States Bureau of Education, to enable it to stimulate and coordinate the educational work to the nation;

Careful attention to the farmers' interests in legislation on the tariff, on regulation of railroads, control or regulation of corporations and of speculation, legislation in respect to rivers, forests, and the utilization of swamp lands;

Increasing the powers of the Federal Government in respect to the supervision and control of the public health;

Providing such regulations as will enable the States that do not permit the sale of liquors to protect themselves from traffic from adjoining States.

In setting all these forces in motion, the cooperation of the States will be necessary; and in many cases definite state laws may greatly aid the work.

Remedies of a more general nature are: A broad campaign of publicity, that must be undertaken until all the people are informed on the whole subject of rural life, and until there is an awakened appreciation of the necessity of giving this phase of our national development as much attention as has been given to other phases or interests; a quickened sense of responsibility in all country people, to the community and to the State, in the conserving of soil fertility, and in the necessity for diversifying farming in order to conserve this fertility and to develop a better rural society, and also in the better safe guarding of the strength and happiness of the farm women; a more widespread conviction of the necessity for organization, not only for economic but for social purposes, this organization to be more or less cooperative, so that all the people may share equally in the benefits and have voice in the essential affairs of the community; a realization on the part of the farmer that he has a distinct natural responsibility toward the laborer in providing him with good living facilities and in helping him in every way to be a man among men; and a realization on the part of all the people of the obligation to protect and develop the natural scenery and attractiveness of the open country.

Certain remedies lie with voluntary organizations and institutions. All organized forces, both in town and country, should understand that there are country phases as well as city phases of our civilization, and that one phase needs help as much as the other. All these agencies should recognize their responsibility to society. Many existing organizations and institutions might become practically cooperative or mutual in spirit, as, for example, all agricultural societies, libraries, Young Men's Christian Associations, and churches. All the organizations standing for rural progress should be federated, in States and nation.

The Underlying Problem of Country Life

The mere enumeration of the foregoing deficiencies and remedies indicates that the problem of country life is one of reconstruction, and that temporary measures and defense work alone will not solve it. The underlying problem is to develop and maintain on our farms a civilization in full harmony with the best American ideals. To build up and retain this civilization means, first of all, that the business of agriculture must be made to yield a reasonable return to those who follow it intelligently; and life on the farm must be made permanently satisfying to intelligent, progressive people. The work before us, therefore, is nothing more or less than the gradual rebuilding of a new agriculture and new rural life. We regard it as absolutely essential that this great general work should be understood by all the people. Separate difficulties, important as they are, must be studied and worked out in the light of the greater fundamental problem.

The commission has pointed out a number of remedies that are extremely important; but running through all of these remedies are several great forces, or principles, which must be utilized in the endeavor to solve the problems of country life. All the people should recognize what those fundamental forces and agencies are.

Knowledge. — To improve any situation, the underlying facts must be understood. The farmer must have exact knowledge of his business and of the particular conditions under which he works. The United States Department of Agriculture and the experiment stations and colleges are rapidly acquiring and distributing this knowledge; but the farmer may not be able to apply it to the best advantage because of lack of knowledge of his own soils, climate, animal and plant diseases, markets, and other local facts. The farmer is entitled to know what are the advantages and disadvantages of his conditions and environment. A thoroughgoing system of surveys in detail of the exact conditions underlying farming in every locality is now an indispensable need to complete and apply the work of the great agricultural institutions. As an occupation, agriculture is a means of developing our internal resources; we can not develop these resources until we know exactly what they are.

Education. — There must be not only a fuller scheme of public education, but a new kind of education adapted to the real needs of the farming people. The country schools are to be so redirected that they shall educate their pupils in terms of the daily life. Opportunities for training toward agricultural callings are to be multiplied and made broadly effective. Every person on the land, old or young, in school or out of school, educated or illiterate, must have a chance to receive the information necessary for a successful business, and for a healthful, comfortable, resourceful life, both in home and neighborhood. This means redoubled efforts for better country schools, and a vastly increased interest in the welfare of country boys and girls on the part of those who pay the school taxes. Education by means of agriculture is to be a part of our regular public school work. Special agricultural schools are to be organized. There is to be a well-developed plan of extension teaching conducted by the agricultural colleges, by means of the printed page, face-to-face talks, and demonstration or object lessons, designed to reach every farmer and his family, at or near their homes, with knowledge and stimulus in every department of country life.

Organization. — There must be a vast enlargement of voluntary organized effort among farmers themselves. It is indispensable that farmers shall work together for their common interests and for the national welfare. If they do not do this, no governmental activity, no legislation, not even better schools, will greatly avail. Much has been done. There is a multitude of clubs and associations for social, educational, and business purposes; and great national organizations are effective. But the farmers are nevertheless relatively unorganized. We have only begun to develop business cooperation in America. Farmers do not influence legislation as they should. They need a more fully organized social and recreative life.

Spiritual forces. — The forces and institutions that make for morality and spiritual ideals among rural people must be energized. We miss the heart of the problem if we neglect to foster personal character and neighborhood righteousness. The best way to preserve ideals for private conduct and public life is to build up the institutions of religion. The church has great power of leadership. The whole people should understand that it is vitally important to stand behind the rural church and to help it to become a great power in developing concrete country life ideals. It is especially important that the country church recognize that it has a social responsibility to the entire community as well as a religious responsibility to its own group of people.

Recommendations of the Commission

The commission recommends all the correctives that have been mentioned under the head of "The nature of the remedies." It does not wish to discriminate between important measures of relief for existing conditions. It has purposely avoided indorsing any particular bill now before Congress, no matter what its value or object.

There are, however, in the opinion of the commission, two or three great movements of the utmost consequence that should be set under way at the earliest possible time, because they are fundamental to the whole problem of ultimate permanent reconstruction; these call for special explanation.

1. Taking stock of country life. — There should be organized, as explained in the main report, under government leadership, a comprehensive plan for an exhaustive study or survey of all the conditions that surround the business of farming and the people who live in the country, in order to take stock of our resources and to supply the farmer with local knowledge. Federal and state governments, agricultural colleges and other educational agencies, organizations of various types, and individual students of the problem should be brought into cooperation for this great work of investigating with minute care all agricultural and country life conditions.

2. Nationalized extension work. — Each state college of agriculture should be empowered to organize as soon as practicable a complete department of college extension, so managed as to reach every person on the land in its State, with both information and inspiration. The work should include such forms of extension teaching as lectures, bulletins, reading courses, correspondence courses, demonstration, and other means of reaching the people at home and on their farms. It should be designed to forward not only the business of agriculture, but sanitation, education, home making, and all interests of country life.

3. A campaign for rural progress. — We urge the holding of local, state, and even national conferences on rural progress, designed to unite the interests of education, organization, and religion into one forward movement for the rebuilding of country life. Rural teachers, librarians, clergymen, editors, physicians, and others may well unite with farmers in studying and discussing the rural question in all its aspects. We must in some way unite all institutions, all organizations, all individuals having any interest in country life into one great campaign for rural progress.

The Call for Leadership

We must picture to ourselves a new rural social structure, developed from the strong resident forces of the open country; and then we must set at work all the agencies that will tend to bring this about. The entire people need to be roused to this avenue of usefulness. Most of the new leaders must be farmers who can find not only a satisfying business career on the farm, but who will throw themselves into the service of upbuilding the community. A new race of teachers is also to appear in the country. A new rural clergy is to be trained. These leaders will see the great underlying problem of country life, and together they will work, each in his own field, for the one goal of a new and permanent rural civilization. Upon the development of this distinctively rural civilization rests ultimately our ability, by methods of farming requiring the highest intelligence, to continue to feed and clothe the hungry nations; to supply the city and metropolis with fresh blood, clean bodies, and clear brains that can endure the strain of modern urban life; and to preserve a race of men in the open country that, in the future as in the past, will be the stay and strength of the nation in time of war and its guiding and controlling spirit in time of peace.

It is to be hoped that many young men and women, fresh from our schools and institutions of learning, and quick with ambition and trained intelligence, will feel a new and strong call to service.

I. General Statement

Broadly speaking, agriculture in the United States is prosperous and the conditions in many of the great farming regions are improving. The success of the owners and cultivators of good land, in the prosperous regions, has been due partly to improved methods, largely to good prices for products, and also to the general advance in the price of farm lands in these regions. Notwithstanding the general advance in rentals and the higher prices of labor, tenants also have enjoyed a good degree of prosperity, due to fair crops, and an advance in the price of farm products approximately corresponding to the advance in the price of land. Farm labor has been fully employed and at increased wages, and many farm hands have become tenants and many tenants have become landowners.

There is marked improvement, in many of the agricultural regions, in the character of the farm home and its surroundings. There is increasing appreciation on the part of great numbers of country people of the advantage of sanitary water supplies and plumbing, of better construction in barns and all farm buildings, of good reading matter, of tasteful gardens and lawns, and the necessity of good education.

Many institutions are also serving the agricultural needs of the open country with great effectiveness, as the United States Department of Agriculture, the land-grant colleges and experiment stations, and the many kinds of extension work that directly or indirectly emanate from them. The help that these institutions render to the country-life interests is everywhere recognized. State departments of agricultural, national, state, and local organizations, many schools of secondary grade, churches, libraries, and many other agencies are also contributing actively to the betterment of agricultural conditions.

There has never been a time when the American farmer was as well off as he is to-day, when we consider not only his earning power, but the comforts and advantages he may secure. Yet the real efficiency in farm life, and in country life as a whole, is not to be measured by historical standards, but in terms of its possibilities. Considered from this point of view, there are very marked deficiencies. There has been a complete and fundamental change in our whole economic system within the past century. This has resulted in profound social changes and the redirection of our point of view on life. In some occupations the readjustment to the new conditions has been rapid and complete; in others it has come with difficulty. In all the great series of farm occupations the readjustment has been the most tardy, because the whole structure of a traditional and fundamental system has been involved. It is not strange, therefore, that development is still arrested in certain respects; that marked inequalities have arisen; or that positive injustice may prevail even to a very marked and widespread extent. All these difficulties are the results of the unequal development of our contemporary civilization. All this may come about without any intention on the part of anyone that it should be so. The problems are nevertheless just as real, and they must be studied and remedies must be found.

These deficiencies are recognized by the people. We have found, not only the testimony of the farmers themselves but of all persons in touch with farm life, more less serious agricultural unrest in every part of the United States, even in the most prosperous regions. There is a widespread tendency for farmers to move to town. It is not advisable, of course, that all country persons remain in the country; but this general desire to move is evidence that the open country is not satisfying as a permanent abode. This tendency is not peculiar to any region. In difficult farming regions, and where the competition with other farming sections is most severe, the young people may go to town to better their condition. In the best regions the older people retire to town, because it is socially more attractive and they see a prospect of living in comparative ease and comfort on the rental of their lands. Nearly everywhere there is a townward movement for the purpose of securing school advantages for the children. All this tends to sterilize the open country and to lower its social status. Often the farm is let to tenants. The farmer is likely to lose active interest in life when he retires to town, and he becomes a stationary citizen, adding a social problem to the town. He is likely to find his expenses increasing and is obliged to raise rents to his tenant, thereby making it more difficult for the man who works on the land. On his death his property enriches the town rather than the country. The withdrawal of the children from the farms detracts from the interest and efficiency of the country school and adds to the interest of the town school. Thus the country is drained of the energy of youth on the one hand and the experience and accumulation of age on the other, and three problems more or less grave are created — a problem for the town, a problem for the public school, and also a problem of tenancy in the open country.

The farming interest is not, as a whole, receiving the full rewards to which it is entitled, nor has country life attained to anywhere near its possibilities of attractiveness and comfort. The farmer is necessarily handicapped in the development of social life and in the conduct of his business because of his separateness, the small volume of his output, and the lack of capital. He often begins with practically no capital, and expects to develop his capital and relationships out of the annual business itself; and even when he has capital with which to set up a business and operate it the amount is small when compared with that required in other enterprises. He is not only handicapped in his farming but is disadvantaged when he deals with other business interests and with other social groups. It is peculiarly necessary, therefore, that Government should give him adequate consideration and protection. There are difficulties of the separate man, living quietly on his land, that government should understand.

The Purpose of the Commission

The commission is requested to report on the means that are "now available for supplying the deficiencies which exist" in the country life of the United States and "upon the best methods of organized permanent effort in investigation and actual work" along the lines of betterment of rural conditions.

The President's letter appointing the commission is as follows:

OYSTER BAY, N.Y., *August 10, 1908.*

MY DEAR PROFESSOR BAILEY: No nation has ever achieved permanent greatness unless this greatness was based on the wellbeing of the great farmer class, the men who live on the soil; for it is upon their welfare, material and moral, that the welfare of the rest of the nation untimately rests. In the United States, disregarding certain sections and taking the nation as a whole, I believe it to be true that the farmers in general are better off to-day than they ever were before. We Americans are making great progress in the development of our agricultural resources. But it is equally true that the social and economic institutions of the open country are not keeping pace with the development of the nation as a whole. The farmer is, as a rule, better off than his forbears; but his increase in well-being has not kept pace with that of the country as a whole. While the condition of the farmers in some of our best farming regions leaves little to be desired, we are far from having reached so high a level in all parts of the country. In portions of the South, for example, where the Department of Agriculture, through the farmers' cooperative demonstration work of Doctor Knapp, is directly instructing more than 30,000 farmers in better methods of farming, there is nevertheless much unnecessary suffering and needless loss of efficiency on the farm. A physician, who is also a careful student of farm life in the South, writing to me recently about the enormous percentage of preventable deaths of children, due to insanitary condition of southern farms, said:

"Personally, from the health point of view, I would prefer to see my own daughter, 9 years old, at work in a cotton mill than have her live as tenant on the average southern tenant one-horse farm. This apparently extreme statement is based upon actual life among both classes of people."

I doubt if any other nation can bear comparison with our own in the amount of attention given by the Government, both Federal and State, to agricultural matters. But practically the whole of this effort has hitherto been directed toward increasing the production of crops. Our attention has been concentrated almost exclusively on getting better farming. In the beginning this was unquestionably the right thing to do. The farmer must first of all grow good crops in order to support himself and his family. But when this has been secured the effort for better farming should cease to stand alone, and should be accompanied by the effort for better business and better living on the farm. It is at least as important that the farmer should get the largest possible return in money, comfort, and social advantages from the crops he grows as that he should get the largest possible return in crops from the land he farms. Agriculture is not the whole of country life. The great rural interests are human interests, and good crops are of little value to the farmer unless they open the door to a good kind of life on the farm.

This problem of country life is in the truest sense a national problem. In an address delivered at the semicentennial of the founding of agricultural colleges in the United States a year ago last May, I said:

"There is but one person whose welfare is as vital to the welfare of the whole country as is that of the wage-worker who does manual labor, and that is the tiller of the soil — the farmer. If there is one lesson taught by history, it is that the permanent greatness of any State must ultimately depend more upon the character of its country population than upon anything else. No growth of cities, no growth of wealth can make up for loss in either the number or the character of the farming population."

*   *   *

"The farm grows the raw material for the food and clothing of all our citizens; it supports directly almost half of them; and nearly half the children of the United States are born and brought up on the farms. How can the life of the farm family be made less solitary, fuller of opportunity, freer from drudgery, more comfortable, happier, and more attractive? Such a result is most earnestly to be desired. How can life on the farm be kept on the highest level, and, where it is not already on that level, be so improved, dignified, and brightened as to awaken and keep alive the pride and loyalty of the farmer's boys and girls, of the farmer's wife, and of the farmer himself? How can a compelling desire to live on the farm be aroused in the children that are born on the farm? All these questions are of vital importance not only to the farmer but to the whole nation.

*   *   *

"We hope ultimately to double the average yield of wheat and corn per acre; it will be a great achievement; but it is even more important to double the desirability, comfort, and standing of the farmer's life."

It is especially important that whatever will serve to prepare country children for life on the farm and whatever will brighten home life in the country and make it richer and more attractive for the mothers, wives, and daughters of farmers should be done promptly, thoroughly, and gladly. There is no more important person, measured in influence upon the life of the nation, than the farmer's wife, no more important home than the country home, and it is of national importance to do the best we can for both.

The farmers have hitherto had less than their full share of public attention along the lines of business and social life. There is too much belief among all our people that the prizes of life lie away from the farm. I am therefore anxious to bring before the people of the United States the question of securing better business and better living on the farm, whether by cooperation between farmers for buying, selling, and borrowing; by promoting social advantages and opportunities in the country; or by any other legitimate means that will help to make country life more gainful, more attractive, and fuller of opportunities, pleasures, and rewards for the men, women, and children of the farms.

I shall be very glad indeed if you will consent to serve upon a commission on country life, upon which I am asking the following gentlemen to act: Prof. L. H. Bailey, New York State College of Agriculture, Ithaca, N.Y., chairman; Mr. Henry Wallace, Wallace's Farmer, Des Moines, Iowa; President Kenyon L. Butterfield, Massachusetts Agricultural College, Amherst, Mass.; Mr. Gifford Pinchot, United States Forest Service; Mr. Walter H. Page, editor of The World's Work, New York.

My immediate purpose in appointing this commission is to secure from it such information and advice as will enable me to make recommendations to Congress upon this extremely important matter. I shall be glad if the commission will report to me upon the present condition of country life, upon what means are now available for supplying the deficiencies which exist, and upon the best methods of organized permanent effort in investigation and actual work along the lines I have indicated. You will doubtless also find it necessary to suggest means for bringing about the redirection or better adaptation of rural schools to the training of children for life on the farm. The national and state agricultural departments must ultimately join with the various farmers' and agricultural organizations in the effort to secure greater efficiency and attractiveness in country life.

In view of the pressing importance of this subject I should be glad to have you report before the end of next December. For that reason the commission will doubtless find it impracticable to undertake extensive investigations, but will rather confine itself to a summary of what is already known, a statement of the problem, and the recommendation of measures tending toward its solution. With the single exception of the conservation of our natural resources, which underlies the problem of rural life, there is no other material question of greater importance now before the American people. I shall look forward with the keenest interest to your report.

Sincerely, yours,   THEODORE ROOSEVELT.

Prof. L. H. BAILEY,
New York State College of Agriculture, Ithaca, N.Y.

Subsequently Charles S. Barrett, of Georgia, and William A. Beard, of California, were added to the commission.

The means that may be suggested for amelioration of country life fall under one or more of three general classes: (*a*) Definite recommendations for executive or legislative action by the Federal Government; (*b*) suggestions for legislative enactment on the part of States; (*c*) suggestions or recommendations to the public at large as to what the commission thinks would be the most fruitful lines of action and policy on the part of individuals, communities, or States.

The problem before the commission is to state, with some fullness of detail, the present conditions of country life, to point out the causes that may have led to its present lack of organization, to suggest methods by which it may be redirected, the drift to the city arrested, the natural rights of the farmer maintained, and an organized rural life developed that will promote the prosperity of the whole nation.

We are convinced that the forces that make for rural betterment must themselves be rural. We must arouse the country folk to the necessity for action, and suggest agencies which, when properly employed, will set them to work to develop a distinctly rural civilization.

In making its inquiries, the commission has had constantly in mind the relation of the farmer to his community and to society in general. It has made no inquiry into problems of technical farming except as they may have bearing on general welfare and public questions.

The commission has not assumed that country-life conditions are either good or bad, nor is it within its province to compare country conditions with city conditions; but it has assumed that we have not yet arrived at that state of society in which conditions may not be bettered.

It is our place, therefore, to point out the deficiencies rather than the advantages and the progress. In doing this we must be distinctly understood as speaking only in general terms. The conditions that we describe do not, of course, apply equally in all parts of the country, and we have not been able to make studies of the problems of particular localities.

Before discussing the shortcomings more fully, we may explain how the commission undertook its work.

Methods Pursued by the Commission

The field of inquiry has been the general social, economic, sanitary, educational, and labor conditions of the open country. Within the time at its disposal, the commission has not been able to make scientific investigations into any of these questions, but, following the suggestion of the President, has endeavored to give "a summary of what is already known, a statement of the problem, and the recommendation of measures looking toward its solution." We have been able to make a rather extensive exploration or reconnaissance of the field, to arrive at a judgement as to the main deficiencies of country life in the United States to-day, and to suggest some of the means of supplying these deficiencies.

The commission and its work have met with the fullest cooperation and confidence on the part of the farmers and others, and the interest in the subject has been widespread. The people have been frank in giving information and expressing opinions, and in stating their problems and discouragements. There is every evidence that the people in rural districts have welcomed the commission as an agency that is much needed in the interest of country life, and in many of the hearings they have asked that the commission be continued in order that it may make thorough investigations of the subjects that it has considered. The press has taken great interest in the work, and in many cases has been of special service to the commission in securing direct information from country people.

The activities of the commission have been directed mainly along four lines: The issuing of questions designed to bring out a statement of conditions in all parts of the United States; correspondence and inquiries by different members of the commission, so far as time would permit, each in a particular field; the holding of hearings in many widely separated places; discussions in local meetings held in response to a special suggestion by the President.

The Circular of Questions

As a means of securing the opinions of the people themselves on some of the main aspects of country life, a set of questions was distributed, as follows:

  I. Are the farm homes in your neighborhood as good as they should be under existing conditions?

  II. Are the schools in your neighborhood training boys and girls satisfactorily for life on the farm?

  III. Do the farmers in your neighborhood get the returns they reasonably should from the sale of their products?

  IV. Do the farmers in your neighborhood receive from the railroads, highroads, trolley lines, etc., the services they reasonably should have?

  V. Do the farmers in your neighborhood receive from the United States postal service, rural telephones, etc., the service they reasonably should expect?

  VI. Are the farmers and their wives in your neighborhood satisfactorily organized to promote their mutual buying and selling interest?

  VII. Are the renters of farms in your neighborhood making a satisfactory living?

  VIII. Is the supply of farm labor in your neighborhood satisfactory?

  IX. Are the conditions surrounding hired labor on the farms in your neighborhood satisfactory to the hired man?

  X. Have the farmers in your neighborhood satisfactory facilities for doing their business in banking, credit, insurance, etc.?

  XI. Are the sanitary conditions of farms in your neighborhood satisfactory?

  XII. Do the farmers and their wives and families in your neighborhood get together for mutual improvement, entertainment, and social intercourse as much as they should?

What, in your judgment, is the most single thing to be done for the general betterment of country life?

(NOTE. — Following each question are the subquestions: *(a)* Why? *(b)* What suggestions have you to make?)

About 550,000 copies of the circular questions were sent to names supplied by the United States Department of Agriculture, state experiment stations, farmers' societies, women's clubs, to rural free deliverymen, country physicians and ministers, and others. To these inquiries about 115,000 persons have now replied, mostly with much care and with every evidence of good faith. Nearly 100,000 of these circulars have been arranged and some of the information tabulated in a preliminary way by the Census Bureau. In addition to the replies to the circulars, great numbers of letters and carefully written statements have been received, making altogether an invaluable body of information, opinion, and suggestion.

The Hearings

Hearings were held at 30 places by the whole commission, or part of it, between November 9 and December 22, 1908; and frequently two or more long sessions were held. Very full notes were taken of the proceedings. They were attended by good audiences, in some instances overflowing the hall. At several, especially in the Northwest, delegates were in attendance representing associations and communities in the vicinity, who were anxious to present their views and needs. Speeches were numerous and usually short and pithy, and represented every sort of person concerned with rural life, including many women, who contributed much to the domestic and educational aspects of the subject. The governors and principal officials of the States were often present; and also the presidents and professors of institutions of learning, clergymen, physicians, librarians, and others, but the bulk of the speakers and audiences was country people. No attempt was made to follow a definite programme of questioning, but general discussions proceeded, with an occasional show of hands or outburst of applause to signify general assent to the speaker's words.

The hearings were held as follows:

November 9.—College Park, Md.
        10.—Richmond, Va.
        11.—Raleigh, N.C., and Athens, Ga.
        12.—Spartanburg, S.C.
        13.—Knoxville, Tenn.
        14.—Lexington, Ky.
   16–18.—Washington, D.C.
   19–21.—Dallas, Tex.
   22–23.—El Paso, Tex.
        24.—Tucson, Ariz.
   25–26.—Los Angeles, Cal.
   27–28.—Fresno, Cal.
   28–29.—San Francisco, Cal.
        30.—Sacramento, Cal.
December 1.—Reno, Nev.
        2.—Portland, Oreg.
     2–3.—Salt Lake City, Utah.
     4–5.—Spokane, Wash. (and at Opportunity, near by).
        5.—Cheyenne, Wyo.
        6.—Bozeman, Mont.
     7–8.—Denver, Colo.
    9–10.—Omaha, Nebr.
       10.—Council Bluffs, Iowa.
       11.—Minneapolis, Minn. (St. Anthony Park).
       12.—Madison, Wis.
       14.—Champaign, Ill.
       16.—Ithaca, N.Y.
       17.—Springfield, Mass.
       18.—Boston, Mass.
       22.—Washington, D.C.

The Schoolhouse Meetings

The suggestion of the President that the country people of the United States come together in their district schoolhouses to discuss country-life questions under consideration by the commission was officially transmitted by the commission to the state and county superintendents of schools of every State and Territory. A great part of the press of the country quoted the suggestion in full, often printing with it the original list of questions issued by the commission. School officials, ministers of country churches, and other persons concerned in the advancement of country matters contributed their active efforts for organizing such meetings. Reports of meetings have already come in from almost every State, and we have notice of many meetings still to be held. Separate States have set specific days for simultaneous meetings in all their country schoolhouses, notably Nebraska and Missouri. The States of Washington, Oregon, Montana, and Idaho, by concerted arrangement, held meetings December 5, the date suggested by the President. Suggestion has come from many parts of the country for the regular establishment of such meetings for annual national observance by the country people as an inventory-taking day and for planning community advancement for the ensuing year.

II. The Main Special Deficiencies in Country Life

The numbers of problems and suggestions that have been presented to the commission in the hearings and through the correspondence are very great. We have chosen for special discussion those that are most significant and that seem most to call for immediate action. The main single deficiency is, of course, lack of the proper kind of education, but inasmuch as the redirection of educational methods is also the main remedy for the shortcomings of country life, as also of any other life, the discussion of it may be reserved for Part III.

1. Disregard of the Inherent Rights of Land Workers

Notwithstanding an almost universal recognition of the importance of agriculture to the maintenance of our people there is nevertheless a widespread disregard of the rights of the men who own and work the land. This results directly in social depression, as well as in economic disadvantage.

The organized and corporate interests represented in mining, manufacturing, merchandising, transportation, and the like, seem often to hold the idea that their business may be developed and exploited without regard to the farmers, who should, however, have an equal opportunity for enjoyment of the land, forests, and streams and of the right to buy and sell in the open markets without prejudice.

The question of the moral intention of the consolidated interests is not involved in these statements. The present condition has grown up, and without going into the reasons it is imperative that we recognize these disadvantages to country-life interests and seek to correct them. The way in which discriminating conditions may arise is well illustrated in the inequalities of taxation of farm property. It is natural that visible and stationary property should be taxed freely under our present system; it is equally natural that invisible and changeable property should tend to evade taxation. The inevitable result is that the farmer's property bears an unjust part in taxation schemes.

Nor is this disregard of the inherent rights of the land worker confined to corporations and companies or to the recognized inequalities of taxation. It is often shared by cities. Instead of taking care of their own undesirables, they often turn them off on the country districts. The "fringe" of a city thereby becomes a low-class or even vicious community, and its influence often extends far into the country districts. The commission hears complaints that hoboes are driven from the cities and towns into the country districts, where there is no machinery for controlling them.

The subjects to which we are here inviting attention are, of course, not confined to country life alone. They express an attitude toward public questions in general. We look for the development of a sentiment that will protect and promote the welfare of all the people whenever there is a conflict with the interests of a small or particular class.

The handicaps that we now have specially in mind may be stated under four heads: Speculative holding of lands; monopolistic control of streams; wastage and monopolistic control of forests; restraint of trade.

Speculative Holding of Lands

Certain landowners procure large areas of agricultural land in the most available location, sometimes by questionable methods, and hold it for speculative purposes. This not only withdraws the land itself from settlement, but in many cases prevents the development of an agricultural community. The smaller landowners are isolated and unable to establish their necessary institutions or to attract the attention of the market. The holding of large areas by one party tends to develop a system of tenantry and absentee farming. The whole development may be in the direction of social and economic ineffectiveness. In parts of the West and South this evil is so pronounced that persons have requested the commission to recommend measures of relief by restricting, under law, the size of speculative holdings of agricultural lands.

A similar problem arises in respect to the utilization of the swamp lands of the United States. According to the reports of the United States Geological Survey, there are more than 75,000,000 acres of swamp land in this country, the greater part of which are capable of reclamation at probably a nominal cost as compared to their value. It is important to the development of the best type of country life that the reclamation of the lands in rural regions proceed under conditions insuring their subdivision into small farm units and their settlement by men who would both own them and till them. Some of these lands are near the centers of population. They become a menace to health, and they often prevent the development of good social conditions in very large areas of country. As a rule, they are extremely fertile. They are capable of sustaining an agricultural population numbering many millions, and the conditions under which these millions must live are properly a matter of national concern. In view of these facts, the Federal Government should act to the fullest extent of its constitutional powers in securing the reclamation of these lands under proper safeguards against speculative holding and landlordism. It may be that in the case of those lands ceded to the States for the purpose of reclamation, the greater part of which are unreclaimed, there exists a special authority on the part of the Federal Government by reason of failure to comply with the terms of the grant; and there should be a vigorous legal inquiry into the present rights of the Government with respect to them, followed, if the status warrants it, by legal steps to rescind the grants and to begin the practical work of reclamation.

Monopolistic Control of Streams

The legitimate farming interests of the whole country would be vastly benefited by a systematic conservation and utilization, under the auspices of the State and Federal Governments, of our waterways, both great and small. Important advantages of these waterways are likely to be appropriated in perpetuity and without adequate return to the people by monopolistic interests that deprive the permanent agricultural inhabitants of the use of them.

The rivers are valuable to the farmers as drainage lines, as sources of irrigation supply, as carriers and equalizers of transportation rates, as a readily available power resource, and for the raising of food fish. The wise development of these and other uses is important to both agricultural and other interests; their protection from monopoly is one of the first responsibilities of government. The streams belong to the people; under a proper system of development their resources would remain an estate of all the people, and become available as needed. A broad constructive programme involving coordinate development of the many uses of streams, under conditions insuring their permanent control in the interest of the people themselves, is urgently needed, and none should be more concerned in this than the farmers.

River navigation affords the best and cheapest transportation of farm products of a nonperishable nature. The rivers afford the best means of competition with railroads, because river carriage is cheap, and because the rivers once opened by the Government for navigation are open to all, and monopoly of their use should be an impossibility. Interest in river improvement for the purpose of navigation is very keen among the farmers who actually use river transportation, and to some extent among farmers who enjoy advantages in railway rates due to parallel water lines; but the great mass of farmers, while complaining of what they affirm to be unjust and exorbitant railway rates, have given too little thought to the means of relief with which nature has favored them. This probably due to lack of knowledge of the actual economies of river transportation. For example, one community located 200 miles from a former head of navigation ships wheat by rail to a market that is 1,033 miles distant, at a cost of 21 cents per bushel, yet it showed no interest in the reopening of the channel that would reduce the train haul to less than one-fifth the distance.

This failure to consider the waterways is probably due very largely to the high rates per ton-mile charged by railroads for short hauls. Under the present methods of fixing the railway tariffs, local rates are often almost or quite as great as between points far distant, and there is small inducement to use cheap river freights because of the cost of reaching the river banks. The remedy for this lies in two directions: It must come either from a rearrangement of freight schedules, which may involve a complete change in the present policy of the railway companies with reference thereto, or by means of competition by independent or local companies.

It must be remembered, also, that no interests inimical to the public welfare should be allowed to acquire permanent control of the stream banks. Facilities for ready and economical approach are practically as important as the channels themselves.

River transportation is not usually antagonistic to railway interests. Population and production are increasing rapidly, with corresponding increase in the demands made on transportation facilities. It may be reasonably expected that in the evolution of the transportation business, the rivers will eventually carry a large part of the freight that does not require prompt delivery, while the railways will carry that requiring expeditious handling. This is already foreseen by leading railway men; and its importance to the farmer is such that he should encourage and aid, by every means in his power, the movement for large use of the rivers. The country will produce enough business to tax both streams and railroads to their utmost.

In many regions the streams afford facilities for the development of power, which, since the successful inauguration of electrical transmission, is available for local rail lines and offers the best solution of local transportation problems. In many parts of the country local and interurban lines are providing transportation to farm areas, thereby increasing the facilities for moving crops and adding to the profit and convenience of farm life. Notwithstanding this development, however, there seems to be a very general lack of appreciation on the part of farmers of the possibilities of this water-power resource as a factor in governing transportation costs.

The streams may also be used as a source of small water power on thousands of farms. This is particularly true of the small streams. Much of the manual labor about the house and barn can be performed from transmission of power from small water wheels running on the farms themselves or in the neighborhood. This power could be used for electric lighting and for small manufacture. It is more important that small power be developed on the farms of the United States than that we harness Niagara.

Unfortunately, the tendency of the present laws is to encourage the acquisition of these resources on easy terms, or on their own terms, by the first applicants, and the power of the streams is rapidly being acquired under conditions that lead to the concentration of ownership in the hands of monopolies. This state of things constitutes a real and immediate danger, not to the country-life interests alone, but to the entire nation, and it is time that the whole people become aroused to it.

The laws under which water is appropriated or flowage rights secured for power were enacted prior to the introduction of electrical transmission, and, consequently, before there was any possibility of water power becoming of more than local importance or value. Monopoly of water power was practically impossible while the sources and uses were alike isolated, but the present ability to concentrate the power of streams and to develop transportation, manufacturing, heating, and lighting on a vast scale invites monopolization.

It appears as a result of governmental investigation that practically in the last five years there has been a very significant concentration of water powers; that this concentration has now placed about 33 per cent of the total developed water powers of the country under the control of a group of 13 companies or interests; that there are very strong economic and technical reasons forcing such concentration. The rapid concentration already accomplished, together with the obvious technical reasons for further control and the financial advantages to be gained by a substantial monopoly, justifies the fear that the concentration already accomplished is but the forerunner of a far greater degree of monopoly of water power. Unless the people become aroused to the danger to their interests, there will probably be developed a monopoly greater than any the world has yet seen.

The development of power plants and of industries using this power ought to be encouraged by every legitimate and proper means. It should not be necessary, however, to grant perpetual rights in order to encourage this development. There should be no perpetual grant of water-power privileges. On the contrary, the ownership of the people should be perpetually maintained, and grants should be in the nature of terminable franchises.

The irrigation water should be protected. Farm life in the irrigated regions is usually of an advanced type, due principally to the small size of farms and the resulting social and educational advantages and to intensive agriculture. Because of these facts the development of the arid regions by irrigation may be a distinct contribution to the improvement of the country life of the nation. In the use of streams for irrigation, as in other uses, monopoly should be discouraged. The ownership of water for irrigation is no less important than the ownership of land; "waterlordism" is as much to be feared as landlordism. In the irrigated regions the water is more valuable than the land to which it is applied; the availability of the water supply often gives to the land all the value that it has, and when this is true it must follow that the farmer must own both the water and the land if he is to be master of his own fortunes. One of the very best elements of any population is the independent homeowning farmer, and the tendency of government, so far as may be practicable, should be toward securing the ownership of the land by the man who lives on it and tills it. It should seek to vest in the farmer of the irrigated region the title to his water supply and to protect his tenure of it. The national reclamation act, under which large areas of arid land are now being placed under irrigation, is commended as a contribution to the development of a good country life in the West, not alone because it renders available for settlement large areas of previously worthless land, but still more because it insures to settlers the ownership of both the land and the water.

The need to utilize the streams is to be considered in the East as well as in the West.

The commission suggests that a special inquiry be made of the control and stream resources of the United States, with the object of protecting the people in their ownership and of reserving to agricultural uses such benefits as should be reserved for these purposes.

Wastage and Control of Forests

The forests have been exploited for private gain until not only has the timber been seriously reduced, but until streams have been ruined for navigation, power, irrigation, and common water supplies and whole regions have been exposed to floods and disastrous soil erosion. Probably there has never occurred a more reckless destruction of property that of right should belong to all the people. These devastations are checked on the government lands, but similar devastation in other parts of the country is equally in need of attention. The commission has heard strong demands from farmers for the establishment of forest reservations in the White Mountains and the Southern Appalachian region to save the timber and to control the sources of streams, and no statements in opposition to the proposal. Measures should be enacted creating such reservations. The forests as well as the streams should be saved from monopolistic control.

The conservation of forests and brush on watershed areas is important to the farmer along the full length of streams, regardless of the distance between the farm and these areas. The loss of soil in denuded areas increases the menace of flood, not alone because of the more rapid run-off, but by the filling of channels and the greater erosion of stream banks when soil matter is carried in suspension.

Loss of soil by washing is a serious menace to the fertility of the American farm. A high authority on this subject recently made the statement that soil wash is "the heaviest impost borne by the American farmer."

The wood-lot property of the country needs to be saved and increased. Wood-lot yield is one of the most important crops of the farm, and is of great value to the public in controlling streams, saving the run-off, checking winds, and in adding to the attractiveness of the region. In many regions, where poor and hilly lands prevail, the town or county could well afford to purchase forest land, expecting thereby to add to the value of the property and eventually to make the forests a source of revenue. Such communal forests in Europe yield revenue to the cities and towns by which they are owned and managed.

Restraint of Trade

The commission has heard much complaint, in all parts of the country and by all classes of farmers, of injustice, inequalities, and discrimination on the part of transportation companies and middlemen. These are the most universal direct complaints that have been presented to the commission. If the statements can be trusted, the business of farming as a whole is greatly repressed by lack of mutual understanding and good faith in the transportation and marketing of agricultural produce.

Without expressing an opinion on these questions, we feel that there should be a free understanding between transportation companies and farmers in respect to their mutual business. We find that farmers who have well-informed opinions on tariff, education, and other public questions are yet wholly uninformed in respect to the transportation man's point of view on freight rates and express rates that may be in dispute. A disposition on the part of all parties to discuss the misunderstandings fairly would probably accomplish much.

The whole matter of railway freight rates should be made more understandable. There should be a simplifying or codifying of rates that will enable the farmer or a group of farmers or of other citizens who use the railways to ascertain readily from the published tariffs the actual rate on any given commodity between two points. Railway rate making is fundamentally a matter of public importance. The rates are a large factor in the development of population; in many instances the railway rates determine both the character of the population and the development of industry. The railway companies, by their rates, may decide where the centers of distribution shall be, what areas shall develop manufactures, and other special industries. To the extent that they do this they exercise a purely public function, and for this reason alone, if for no other, the Government should exercise a wise supervision over the making and publication of rates. Favoritism to large shippers has been one of the principal abuses of the transportation business and has contributed to the growth of monopolies of trade. While rebating is largely discontinued, it is very generally believed that this favoritism is still practiced, in various forms, to an extent that works a hardship on the small shipper and the unorganized interests. Complaint is not confined to steam roads alone, but is directed toward the trolley lines as well. There is a feeling that trolley systems should be feeders to the steam roads, and that these systems, which are rapidly being extended through rural districts, should afford to farmers a freight service that is ready, rapid, and cheap. It is charged that this is not done; that steam lines discourage the use of the trolleys for freight, or absorb them and eliminate competition, to the detriment of the farm population which they should most benefit.

The Interstate Commerce Commission exercises a most valuable governmental function. It is a body to which complaint may be made of any rate considered to be unreasonable. It has been of great benefit to the farmers of the country. What is needed now is a careful study of the railway situation with a view to reaching and correcting abuses and practices still in existence that operate against the unorganized and the rural interests.

In this connection attention is invited to the fact that many States have railway commissions charged with the duty of protecting the public from paying exorbitant freight rates, and farmers who feel that they are charged more than is fair should see to it, first, that their state railway commissions are composed of men who will do their duty; and second, that these men are sustained in honest efforts to do their duty with fairness to all concerned. The charge is frequently made that these commissions are not effective; but as they are a part of the machinery of the State, it would seem that the farmers have here an excellent opportunity to serve their interests by active devotion to a plain political duty.

Dissatisfaction with the prevailing systems of marketing is very general. There is a widespread belief that certain middlemen consume a share of agricultural sales out of all proportion to the services they render, either to the consumer or the producer, making a larger profit — often without risk — in the selling of the product than the famer makes in producing it. We have no desire to condemn middlemen as a class. We have no doubt that there are many businesses of this kind that are conducted on a square-deal basis, but we are led to believe that grave abuses are practiced by unscrupulous persons and firms, and we recommend a searching inquiry into the methods employed in the sale of produce on commission.

Remedies for the Disregard of the Inherent Rights of the Farmer

We need, in the first place, as a people, to recognize the necessary rights of the individual farmer to the use of the native resources and agencies that go with the utilization of agricultural lands and to protect him from hindrance and encroachment in the normal development of his business. If the farmer suffers because his business is small, isolated, and unsyndicated, then it is the part of government to see that he has a natural opportunity among his fellows and a square deal.

In the second place, we need such an attitude of government, both state and national, as will safeguard the separate and individual rights of the farmer, in the interest of the public good. As a contribution toward this attitude, we commend the general policy of the present administration to safeguard the streams, forests, coal lands, and phosphate lands, and in endeavoring to develop a home-owning settlement in the irrigated regions.

At the moment, one of the most available and effective single means of giving the farmer the benefit of his natural opportunities is the enlargement of government service to the country people through the post-office. We hold that a parcels post and a postal savings bank system are necessities; and as rapidly as possible the rural free delivery of mails should be extended. Everywhere we have found the farmers demanding the parcels post. It is opposed by many merchants, transportation organizations, and established interests. We do not think that the parcels post will injure the merchant in the small town or elsewhere. Whatever will permanently benefit the farmer will benefit the country as a whole. Both town and country would readjust themselves to the new conditions. We recognize the great value of the small town to the country districts and would not see it displaced or crippled; but the character of the open country largely makes or unmakes the country town.

In order that fundamental correctives may be applied, we recommend that a thoroughgoing study or investigation be made of the relation of business practices and of taxation to the welfare of the farmer, with a view to ascertaining what discriminations and deficiencies may exist, whether legislation is needed, and to give publicity to the entire subject. This investigation should include the entire middleman system, farmers' cooperative organizations, transportation rates and practices, taxation of agricultural property, methods of securing funds on reasonable conditions for agricultural uses, and the entire range of economic questions involved in the relation of the farmer to the accustomed methods of doing business.

We find that there is need of a new general attitude toward legislation, in the way of safeguarding the farmer's natural rights and interests. It is natural that the organized and consolidated interests should be strongly in mind in the making of legislation. We recommend that the welfare of the farmer and countryman be also kept in mind in the construction of laws. We specially recommend that his interests be considered and safeguarded in any new legislation on the tariff, on regulation of railroads, control or regulating of corporations and of speculation, river, swamp, and forest legislation, and public-health regulation. At the present moment it is especially important that the farmer's interests be well considered in the revision of the tariff. One of the particular needs is such an application of the reciprocity principle as to open European markets for our flour, meats, and live cattle. One of the great economic problems of our agriculture is how to feed the corn crop and other grains profitably, for it must be fed if the fertility of the land is to be maintained; to dispose of the crop profitably requires the best markets that can be secured.

Highways

The demand for good highways is general among the farmers of the entire United States. Education and good roads are the two needs most frequently mentioned in the hearings. Highways that are usable at all times of the year are now imperative not only for the marketing of produce, but for the elevation of the social and intellectual status of the open country and the improvement of health by insuring better medical and surgical attendance.

The advantages are so well understood that arguments for better roads are not necessary here. Our respondents are now concerned largely with the methods of organizing and financing the work. With only unimportant exceptions, the farmers who have expressed themselves to us on this question consider that the Federal Government is fairly under obligation to aid in the work.

We hold that the development of a fully serviceable highway system is a matter of national concern, coordinate with the development of waterways and the conservation of our native resources. It is absolutely essential to our internal development. The first thing necessary is to provide expert supervision and direction and to develop a national plan. All the work should be cooperative between the Federal Government and the States. The question of federal appropriation for highway work in the States may well be held in abeyance until a national service is provided and tested. We suggest that the United States Government establish a highway engineering service, or equivalent organization, to be at the call of the States in working out effective and economical highway systems.

Soil Depletion and Its Effects

A condition calling for serious comment is the lessening productiveness of the land. Our farming has been largely exploitational, consisting of mining the virgin fertility. On the better lands this primitive system of land exploitation may last for two generations without results pernicious to society, but on the poorer lands the limit of satisfactory living conditions may be reached in less than one generation.

The social condition of any agricultural community is closely related to the available fertility of the soil. "Poor land, poor people," and "rough land, rough people" have long since passed into proverbs. Rich land well farmed does not necessarily mean high ideals or good society. It may mean land greed and dollar worship; but, on the other hand, high ideals can not be realized without at least a fair degree of prosperity, and this can not be secured without the maintenance of fertility.

When the land begins to yield with difficulty the farmer may move to new land, develop a system of self-sustaining agriculture (becoming thereby a real farmer), or be driven into poverty and degradation. The first of these results has been marked for many years, but it is now greatly checked because most of the available lands have been occupied. The second result — the evolution of a really scientific and self-perpetuating agriculture — is beginning to appear here and there, mostly in the long-settled regions. The drift to poverty and degradation is pronounced in many parts of the country. In every region a certain class of the population is forced to the poor lands, becoming a handicap to the community and constituting a very difficult social problem.

There are two great classes of farmers — those who make farming a real and active constructive business, as much as the successful manufacturer or merchant makes his effort a business; and those who merely passively live on the land, often because they can not do anything else, and by dint of hard work and the strictest economy manage to subsist. Each class has its difficulties. The problems of the former class are largely those arising from the man's relation to the whole at large. The farmer of the latter class is not only powerless as against trade in general, but is also more or less helpless in his own farming problems. In applying corrective measures, we must recognize these two classes of persons.

When no change of system has followed the depletion of the virgin fertility, the saddest results have followed. The former owners have often lost the land, and a system of tenantry farming has gradually developed. This is marked in all regions that are dominated by a one-crop system of agriculture. In parts of the Southern States this loss of available fertility is specially noticeable, particularly where cotton is the main if not the only crop. In some parts of the country this condition and the social results are pathetic, and particularly where the farmers, whether white or black, by reason of poverty and lack of credit and want of experience in other kinds of farming, are compelled to continue to grow cotton. Large numbers of southern farmers are still obliged to mortgage their unplanted crop to secure the means of living while it is growing; and, as a matter of course, they pay exorbitant prices for the barest necessities of life. The only security that the man can give, either to the banker or the merchant, is cotton, and this forces the continued cultivation of a crop that decreases the soil fertility in a country of open winters where the waste by erosion is necessarily at the maximum. The tenants have little interest in the land, and move from year to year in the vain hope of better luck. The average income of the tenant-farmer family growing cotton is about $150 a year; and the family usually does not raise its poultry, meat, fruit, vegetables, or breadstuffs. The landlords in large sections are little better off than the tenants. The price of the product is manipulated by speculators. The tenant farmer, and even the landlord, is preyed upon by other interests, and is practically powerless. The effect of the social stratification into landlord, tenant, and money-lending merchant still further complicates a situation that in some regions is desperate and that demands vigorous treatment.

The recent years of good prices for cotton have enabled many farmers to get out of debt and to be able to handle their own business. These farmers are then free to begin a new system of husbandry. The problems still remain, however, of how to help the man who is still in bondage.

While these conditions are specially marked in the cotton-growing States, they are arising in all regions of a single-crop system, except, perhaps, in the case of fruit regions and vegetable regions. They are beginning to appear in the exclusive wheat regions, where the yields are constantly growing less and where the social life is usually monotonous and barren. The hay-selling system of many parts of the Northeastern States presents similar results, as does also the exclusive corn growing for the general market when stock raising is not a part of the business.

The loss of fertility in the Northern States is less rapid because of the climatic conditions that arrest the winter waste; fewer landlords, and these for the most part retired farmers who live near their farms and largely control the methods of cultivating the land; and a different kind of agriculture and a different social structure. It is, however, serious enough even in the Northern States, and especially in the Mississippi Valley, particularly when lands are held as an investment by capitalists who know nothing about farming and care only for annual returns, and also when held by speculators in the hope of harvesting the unearned increment, which has been large of late years, due probably to some world-wide cause which it is beyond our province to discuss. In any case, whether North or South, it has become a matter of very serious concern, whether farmers are to continue to dominate and direct the policy of the people as they do now in large part in the more prosperous agricultural sections, or whether because of soil deterioration they shall become a dependent class or shall be tenants in name but laborers in fact and working for an uncertain wage.

Fortunately, there is abundant evidence on every hand, both North and South, that the fertility of the soil can be maintained, or where it has been greatly decreased can be restored at least approximately to its virgin fertility. The hope of the future lies in the work of the public institutions that are devoted to the new agriculture. The United States Department of Agriculture, experiment stations, colleges of agriculture, and other agencies are making great progress in correcting these and other deficiencies, and these institutions deserve the sympathetic support of all the people. The demonstration work of the Department of Agriculture in the Southern States is a marked example of the good that can be done by teaching the people how to diversify their farming and to redeem themselves from the bondage of an hereditary system. Similar work is needed in many parts of the United States, and it is already under way, in various forms, under the leadership of the land-grant institutions.

The great agricultural need of the open country is a system of diversified and rotation farming, carefully adapted in every case to the particular region. Such systems conserve the resources of the land and develop diversified and active institutions. Nor is this wastage of soil resources peculiar to one-crop systems, although it is more marked in such cases. It is a general feature of our agriculture, due to a lack of appreciation of our responsibility to society to protect and save the land. Although we have reason to be proud of our agricultural achievements, we must not close our eyes to the fact that our soil resources are still being lost through poor farming.

This lessening of soil fertility is marked in every part of the United States, even in the richest lands of the prairies. It marks the pioneer stage of land usage. It has now become an acute national danger, and the economic, social, and political problems arising out of it must at once receive the best attention of statesmen. The attention that has been given to these questions is wholly inadequate to the urgency of the dangers involved.

Agricultural Labor

There is a general, but not a universal, complaint of scarcity of farm labor. This scarcity is not an agricultural difficulty alone, but one phase for expression of the general labor-supply problem.

So long as the United States continues to be a true democracy it will have a serious labor problem. As a democracy, we honor labor, and the higher the efficiency of the labor the greater the honor. The laborer, if he has the ambition to be an efficient agent in the development of the country, will be anxious to advance from the lower to the higher forms of effort, and from being a laborer himself he becomes a director of labor. If he has nothing but his hands and brains, he aims to accumulate sufficient capital to become a tenant, and eventually to become the owner, of a farm home. A large number of our immigrants share with the native-born citizen this laudable ambition. Therefore there is a constant decrease of efficient farm labor by these upward movements.

At the same time, there is a receding column of farm owners who, through bad management, have become farm tenants, and who from farm tenants may become farm laborers. While the percentage of this class is small, there are, nevertheless, some who fail to make good, and if they are tenants farm for a living rather than as a business, and if laborers become watchers of the sun rather than efficient workers.

Statement of the General Farm Problem

The farm labor problem, however, is complicated by several special conditions, such as the fact that the need for labor is not continuous, the lack of conveniences of living for the laborer, long hours, the want of companionship, and in some places the apparently low wages. Because of these conditions the necessary drift of workmen is from the open country to the town. On the part of the employer the problem is complicated by the difficulty of securing labor, even at the relatively high prices now prevailing, that is competent to handle modern farm machinery and to care for live stock and to handle the special work of the improved dairy. It is further complicated in all parts of the country by the competition of railroads, mines, and factories, which, by reason of shorter hours, apparently higher pay, and the opportunities for social diversion and often of dissipation, attract the native farm hand to the towns and cities.

The difficulty of securing good labor is so great in many parts of the country that farmers are driven to dispose of their farms, leaving their land to be worked on shares by more or less irresponsible tenants, or selling them outright, often to foreigners. All absentee and proxy farming (which seems to be increasing) creates serious social problems in the regions thus affected. There is not sufficient good labor available in the country to enable us to farm our lands under present systems of agriculture and to develop our institutions effectively. Our native labor supply could be much increased by such hygienic measures as would lessen the unnecessary death rate among country children and insure better health to workmen.

So long as the labor supply is not equal to the demand the country can not compete with the town in securing labor. The country must meet the essential conditions offered by the town or change the kind of farming.

The most marked reaction to the labor difficulty is the change in modes of farm management, whereby farming is slowly adapting itself to the situation. In some cases this change is in the nature of more intensive and businesslike methods whereby the farmer becomes able to secure a better class of labor and to employ it more continuously. More frequently, however, the change is in the nature of a simplification of the business and a less full and active farm life. In the sod regions of the Northeast the tendency is toward a simple or even a primitive nature farming, with the maximum of grazing and meadow and the minimum of hand labor. In many States the more difficult lands are being given up and machinery farming is extending. This results in an unequal development of the country as a whole, with a marked shift in the social equilibrium. The only real solution of the present labor problem must lie in improved methods of farming. These improvements will be forced by the inevitable depletion of soil fertility under any and all one-crop systems in every part of the country, and realized by the adoption on the part of intelligent, progressive farmers of a rotation of crops and a system of husbandry that will enable them to employ their labor by the year and thereby secure a higher type of workman by providing him a home with all its appurtenances. The development of local industries will also contribute to the solution of the problem.

The excessive hours of labor on farms must be shortened. This will come through the working out of the better farm scheme just mentioned and substituting planning for some of the muscular work. Already in certain regions of well-systematized diversified farming the average hours of labor are less than ten.

There is a growing tendency to rely on foreigners for the farm labor supply, although the sentiment is very strong in some regions against immigration. It is the general testimony that the native American labor is less efficient and less reliable than much of the foreign labor. This is due to the fact that the American is less pressed by the dire necessity to labor and to save, and because the better class of laborers is constantly passing on to land ownership on their own account. Because of their great industry and thrift certain foreigners are gradually taking possession of the land in some regions, and it seems to be only a question of time until they will drive out the native stock in those regions.

The most difficult rural labor problem is that of securing household help on the average farm. The larger the farm the more serious the problem becomes. The necessity of giving a suitable education to her children deprives the farm woman largely of home help; while the lure of the city, with its social diversions, more regular hours of labor, and its supposed higher respectability, deprives her of help bred and born in the country. Under these circumstances she is compelled to provide the food that requires the least labor. This simple fact explains much of the lack of variety, in the midst of the greatest possible abundance, so often complained of on the farmer's table. The development of the creamery system over large sections of the country has relieved the farmer's wife of a heavy burden. This gives the hint for further improvement. The community laundering and other work could be done in an establishment connected with the creamery. Labor-saving appliances in the future will greatly lighten the burdens of those who are willing to use them. With the teaching of home subjects in the schools, household labor will again become respectable as well as easier and more interesting.

There is widespread conviction that the farmer must give greater attention to providing good quarters to laborers and to protect them from discouragement and from the saloon. The shortage of labor seems to be the least marked where the laborer is best cared for. It is certain that farming itself must be so modified and organized as to meet the labor problem at least halfway. While all farmers feel the shortage of help, the commission has found that the best farmers usually complain least about the labor difficulty.

The Question of Intemperance

The liquor question has been emphasized to the commission in all parts of the country as complicating the labor question. It seems to be regarded as a burning country life problem. Intemperance is largely the result of the barrenness of farm life, particularly of the lot of the hired man. The commission has made no inquiry into intemperance as such, but it is impressed, from the testimony that has accumulated, that drunkenness is often a very serious menace to country life, and that the saloon is an institution that must be banished from at least all country districts and rural towns if our agricultural interests are to develop to the extent to which they are capable. The evil is specially damning in the South, because it seriously complicates the race problem. Certain States have recently adopted prohibitory regulations, but liquor is shipped into dry territory from adjoining regions, and the evil is thereby often increased. Dry territories must rouse themselves to self-preservation in the face of this grave danger, and legislation must be enacted that will protect them. When a State goes dry, it should be allowed to keep dry.

There is most urgent need for a quickened public sentiment on this whole question of intoxication in rural communities in order to relieve country life of one of its most threatening handicaps. At the same time it is incumbent on every person to exert his best effort to provide the open country with such intellectual and social interests as will lesson the appeal and attractiveness of the saloon.

Developing the Local Attachments of the Farm Laborer

The best labor, other things being equal, is resident labor. Such reorganization of agriculture must take place as will tend more and more to employ the man the year round and to tie him to the land. The employer bears a distinct responsibility to the laborer, and also to society, to house him well and to help him to contribute his part to the community welfare.

Eventually some kind of school or training facilities must be provided for the farm laborer to cause him to develop skill and to interest him intellectually in his work.

Some kind of simple saving institution should also be developed in order to encourage thrift on the part of the laborer. It would be well, also, to study systems of life insurance in reference to farm workmen. The establishment of postal savings banks should contribute toward greater stability of farm labor.

The development of various kinds of cooperative buying and selling associations might be expected to train workmen in habits of thrift, if the men were encouraged to join them.

Health in the Open Country

Theoretically the farm should be the most healthful place in which to live, and there are numberless farm-houses, especially of the farm-owner class, that possess most excellent modern sanitary conveniences. Still it is a fact that there are also numberless other farm-houses, especially of the tenant class, and even numerous rural schoolhouses, that do not have the rudiments of sanitary arrangement. Health conditions in many parts of the open country, therefore, are in urgent need of betterment. There are many questions of nationwide importance, such as soil, milk, and water pollution; too much visiting in case of contagious diseases; patent medicines, advertising quacks, and intemperance; feeding of offal to animals at local slaughterhouses and general insanitary conditions of those houses not under federal or other rigid sanitary control; in some regions unwholesome and poorly prepared and monotonous diet; lack of recreation; too long hours of work.

Added to these and other conditions, are important regional questions, such as the extensive spread of the hook-worm disease in the large Gulf-Atlantic States, the prevalence of typhoid fever and malaria, and other difficulties due to neglect in the localities.

In general, the rural population is less safeguarded by boards of health than is the urban population. The physicians are farther apart and are called in later in case of sickness, and in some districts medical attendance is relatively more expensive. The necessity for disease prevention is therefore self-evident, and it becomes even more emphatic when we recall that infection may be spread from farms to cities in the streams and also in the milk, meat, and other farm products. Quite aside from the humanitarian point of view, the aggregate annual loss to the nation from insanitary conditions on the farms must, when expressed in money values, reach an enormous sum, and a betterment of these conditions is a nation-wide obligation.

There is great need for the teaching of the simplest and commonest laws of hygiene and sanitation in all the schools. The people need knowledge, and no traditions should prevent them from having it. How and what to eat, the nature of disease, the importance of fresh air, the necessity of physical training even on the farm, the ineffectiveness or even the danger of nostrums, the physical evils of intemperance, all should be known in some useful degree to every boy and girl on leaving school.

Some of the most helpful work in improving rural sanitary conditions and in relieving suffering is now proceeding from women's organizations. This work should be encouraged in every way. We especially commend the suggestion that such organizations, and other interests, provide visiting nurses for rural communities when they are needed.

We find urgent need for better supervision of public health in rural communities on the part of States and localities. The control is now likely to be exercised only when some alarming condition prevails. We think that the Federal Government should be given the right to send its health officers into the various States on request of these States, at any time, for the purpose of investigating and controlling public health; it does not now have this right except at quarantine stations, although it may attend to diseases of domestic animals. It should also engage in publicity work on this subject.

Woman's Work on the Farm

Realizing that the success of country life depends in very large degree on the woman's part, the commission has made special effort to ascertain the condition of women on the farm. Often this condition is all that can be desired, with home duties so organized that the labor is not excessive, with kindly cooperation on the part of husbands and sons, and with household machines and conveniences well provided. Very many farm homes in all parts of the country are provided with books and periodicals, musical instruments, and all the necessary amenities. There are good gardens and attractive premises and a sympathetic love of nature and of farm life on the part of the entire family.

On the other hand, the reverse of these conditions often obtains, sometimes because of pioneer conditions and more frequently because of lack of prosperity and of ideals. Conveniences for outdoor work are likely to have precedence over those for household work.

The routine work of woman on the farm is to prepare three meals a day. This regularity of duty recurs regardless of season, weather, planting, harvesting, social demands, or any other factor. The only differences in different seasons are those of degree rather than of kind. It follows, therefore, that whatever general hardships, such as poverty, isolation, lack of labor-saving devices, may exist on any given farm, the burden of these hardships falls more heavily on the farmer's wife than on the farmer himself. In general, her life is more monotonous and the more isolated, no matter what the wealth or the poverty of the family may be.

The relief to farm women must come through a general elevation of country living. The women must have more help. In particular these matters may be mentioned: Development of a cooperative spirit in the home, simplification of the diet in many cases, the building of convenient and sanitary houses, providing running water in the house and also more mechanical help, good and convenient gardens, a less exclusive ideal of money getting on the part of the farmer, providing better means of communication, as telephones, roads, and reading circles, and developing of women's organizations. These and other agencies should relieve the woman of many of her manual burdens on the one hand and interest her in outside activities on the other. The farm woman should have sufficient free time and strength so that she may serve the community by participating in its vital affairs.

We have found good women's organizations in some country districts, but as a rule such organizations are few or even none, or where they exist they merely radiate from towns. Some of the stronger central organizations are now pushing the country phase of their work with vigor. Mothers' clubs, reading clubs, church societies, home economics organizations, farmers' institutes, and other associations can accomplish much for farm women. Some of the regular farmers' organizations are now giving much attention to domestic subjects, and women participate freely in the meetings. There is much need among country women themselves of a stronger organizing sense for real cooperative betterment. It is important also that all rural organizations that are attended chiefly by men should discuss the home-making subjects, for the whole difficulty often lies with the attitude of the men.

There is the most imperative need that domestic, household, and health questions be taught in all schools. The home may well be made the center of rural school teaching. The school is capable of changing the whole attitude of the home life and the part that women should play in the development of the best country living.

III. The General Corrective Forces That Should be Set in Motion

The ultimate need of the open country is the development of community effort and of social resources. Here and there the commission has found a rural neighborhood in which the farmers and their wives come together frequently and effectively for social intercourse, but these instances seem to be infrequent exceptions. There is a general lack of wholesome societies that are organized on a social basis. In the region in which the Grange is strong this need is best supplied.

There is need of the greatest diversity in country-life affairs, but there is equal need of a social cohesion operating among all these affairs and tying them all together. This life must be developed, as we have said, directly from native or resident forces. It is neither necessary nor desirable that an exclusive hamlet system be brought about in order to secure these ends. The problem before the commission is to suggest means whereby this development may be directed and hastened directly from the land.

The social disorder is usually unrecognized. If only the farms are financially profitable, the rural condition is commonly pronounced good. Country life must be made thoroughly attractive and satisfying, as well as remunerative and able to hold the center of interest throughout one's lifetime. With most persons this can come only with the development of a strong community sense of feeling. The first condition of a good country life, of course, is good and profitable farming. The farmer must be enabled to live comfortably. Much attention has been given to better farming, and the progress of a generation has been marked. Small manufacture and better handicrafts need now to receive attention, for the open country needs new industries and new interests. The schools must help to bring these things about.

The economic and industrial questions are, of course, of prime importance, and we have dealt with them; but they must all be studied in their relations to the kind of life that should ultimately be established in rural communities. The commission will fail of its purpose if it confines itself merely to providing remedies or correctives for the present and apparent troubles of the farmer, however urgent and important these troubles may be. All these matters must be conceived of as incidents or parts in a large constructive programme. We must begin a campaign for rural progress.

To this end local government must be developed to its highest point of efficiency, and all agencies that are capable of furthering a better country life must be federated. It will be necessary to set the resident forces in motion by means of outside agencies, or at least to direct them, if we are to secure the best results. It is specially necessary to develop the cooperative spirit, whereby all people participate and all become partakers.

The cohesion that is so marked among the different classes of farm folk in older countries can not be reasonably expected at this period in American development, nor is it desirable that a stratified society should be developed in this country. We have here no remnants of a feudal system, fortunately no system of entail, and no clearly drawn distinction between agricultural and other classes. We are as yet a new country with undeveloped resources, many far-away pastures which, as is well known, are always green and inviting. Our farmers have been moving, and numbers of them have not yet become so well settled as to speak habitually of their farm as "home." We have farmers from every European nation and with every phase of religious belief often grouped in large communities, naturally drawn together by a common language and a common faith, and yielding but slowly to the dominating and controlling forces of American farm life. Even where there was once social organization, as in the New England town (or township), the competition of the newly settled West and the wonderful development of urban civilization have disintegrated it. The middle-aged farmer of the Central States sells the old homestead without much hesitation or regret and moves westward to find a greater acreage for his sons and daughters. The farmer of the Middle West sells the old home and moves to the Mountain States, to the Pacific coast, to the South, to Mexico, or to Canada.

Even when permanently settled, the farmer does not easily combine with others for financial or social betterment. The training of generations has made him a strong individualist, and he has been obliged to rely mainly on himself. Self-reliance being the essence of his nature, he does not at once feel the need of cooperation for business purposes or of close association for social objects. In the main, he has been prosperous, and has not felt the need of cooperation. If he is a strong man, he prefers to depend on his own ability. If he is ambitious for social recognition, he usually prefers the society of the town to that of the country. If he wishes to educate his children, he avails himself of the schools of the city. He does not as a rule dream of a rural organization that can supply as completely as the city the four great requirements of man — health, education, occupation, society. While his brother in the city is striving by moving out of the business section into the suburbs to get as much as possible of the country in the city, he does not dream that it is possible to have most that is best of the city in the country.

The time has come when we must give as much attention to the constructive development of the open country as we have given to other affairs. This is necessary not only in the interest of the open country itself, but for the safety and progress of the nation.

It is impossible, of course, to suggest remedies for all the shortcomings of country life. The mere statement of the conditions, as we find them, ought of itself to challenge attention to the needs. We hope that this report of the commission will accelerate all the movements that are now in operation for the betterment of country life. Many of these movements are beyond the reach of legislation. The most important thing for the commission to do is to apprehend the problem and to state the conditions.

The philosophy of the situation requires that the disadvantages and handicaps that are not a natural part of the farmer's business shall be removed, and that such forces shall be encouraged and set in motion as will stimulate and direct local initiative and leadership.

The situation calls for concerted action. It must be aroused and energized. The remedies are of many kinds, and they must come slowly. We need a redirection of thought to bring about a new atmosphere, and a new social and intellectual contact with life. This means that the habits of the people must change. The change will come gradually, of course, as a result of new leadership; and the situation must develop its own leaders.

Care must be taken in all the reconstructive work to see that local initiative is relied on to the fullest extent, and that federal and even state agencies do not perform what might be done by the people in the communities. The centralized agencies should be stimulative and directive, rather than mandatory and formal. Every effort must be made to develop native resources, not only of material things, but also of people.

It is necessary to be careful, also, not to copy too closely the reconstructive methods that have been so successful in Europe. Our conditions and problems differ widely from theirs. We have no historical, social peasantry, a much less centralized form of government, unlike systems of land occupancy, wholly different farming schemes, and different economic and social systems. Our country necessities are peculiarly American.

The correctives for the social sterility of the open country are already in existence or under way, but these agencies all need to be strengthened and especially to be coordinated and federated; and the problem needs to be recognized by all the people. The regular agricultural departments and institutions are aiding in making farming profitable and attractive, and they are also giving attention to the social and community questions. There is a widespread awakening, as a result of this work. This awakening is greatly aided by the rural free delivery of mails, telephones, the gradual improvement of highways, farmers' institutes, cooperative creameries and similar organizations, and other agencies.

The good institutions of cities may often be applied or extended to the open country. It appears that the social evils are in many cases no greater in cities in proportion to the number of people than in country districts; and the very concentration of numbers draws attention to the evils in cities and leads to earlier application of remedies. Recently much attention has been directed, for example, to the subject of juvenile crime, and the probation system in place of jail sentences for young offenders is being put into operation in many places. Petty crime and immorality are certainly not lacking in rural districts, and it would seem that there is a place for the extension of the probation system to towns and villages.

Aside from the regular churches, schools, and agricultural societies, there are special organizations that are now extending their work to the open country, and others that could readily be adapted to country work. One of the most promising of these newer agencies is the rural library that is interested in its community. The libraries are increasing, and they are developing a greater sense of responsibility to the community, not only stimulating the reading habit and directing it, but becoming social centers for the neighborhood. A library, if provided with suitable rooms, can afford a convenient meeting place for many kinds of activities and thereby serve as a coordinating influence. Study clubs and traveling libraries may become parts of it. This may mean that the library will need itself to be redirected so that it will become an active rather than a passive agency; it must be much more than a collection of books.

Another new agency is the county work of the Young Men's Christian Association, which, by placing in each county a field secretary, is seeking to promote the solidarity and effectiveness of rural social life, and to extend the larger influence of the country church. The commission has met the representatives of this county work at the hearings, and is impressed with the purpose of the movement to act as a coordinating agency in rural life.

The organizations in cities and towns that are now beginning to agitate the development of better play, recreation, and entertainment offer a suggestion for country districts. It is important that recreation be made a feature of country life, but we consider it to be important that this recreation, games and entertainment, be developed as far as possible from native sources rather than to be transplanted as a kind of theatricals from exotic sources.

Other organizations that are helping the country social life, or that might be made to help it, are women's clubs, musical clubs, reading clubs, athletic and playground associations, historical and literary societies, local business men's organizations and chambers of commerce, all genuinely cooperative business societies, civic and village improvement societies, local political organizations, granges and other fraternal organizations, and all groups that associate with the church and school.

There is every indication, therefore, that the social life of the open country is in process of improvement, although the progress at the present moment has not been great. The leaders need to be encouraged by an awakened public sentiment, and all the forces should be so related to each other as to increase their total effectiveness while not interfering with the autonomy of any of them.

The proper correctives of the underlying structural deficiencies of the open country are knowledge, education, cooperative organizations, and personal leadership. These we may now discuss in more detail.

Need of Agricultural or Country Life Surveys

The time has now come when we should know in detail what our agricultural resources are. We have long been engaged in making geological surveys, largely with a view to locating our mineral wealth. The country has been explored and mapped. The main native resources have been located in a general way. We must now know what are the capabilities of every agricultural locality, for agriculture is the basis of our prosperity and farming is always a local business. We can not make the best and most permanent progress in the developing of a good country life until we have completed a very careful inventory of the entire country.

This inventory or census should take into account the detailed topography and soil conditions of the localities, the local climate, the whole character of streams and forests, the agricultural products, the cropping systems now in practice, the conditions of highways, markets, facilities in the way of transportation and communication, the institutions and organizations, the adaptability of the neighborhood to the establishment of handicrafts and local industries, the general economic and social status of the people and the character of the people themselves, natural attractions and disadvantages, historical data, and a collation of community experience. This would result in the collection of local fact, on which we could proceed to build a scientifically and economically sound country life.

Beginnings have been made in several States in the collection of these geographical facts, mostly in connection with the land-grant colleges. The United States Department of Agriculture is beginning by means of soil surveys, study of farm management, and other investigations, and its demonstration work in the Southern States is in part of this character. These agencies are beginning the study of conditions in the localities themselves. It is a kind of extension work. All these agencies are doing good work; but we have not yet, as a people, come to an appreciation of the fact that we must take account of stock in detail as well as in the large. We are working mostly around the edges of the problem and feeling of it. The larger part of the responsibility of this work must lie with the different States, for they should develop their internal resources. The whole work should be coordinated, however, by federal agencies acting with the States, and some of the larger relations will need to be studied directly by the Federal Government itself. We must come to a thoroughly nationalized movement to understand what property we have and what uses may best be made of it. This in time will call for large appropriations by State and nation.

In estimating our natural resources we must not forget the value of scenery. This is a distinct asset, and it will be more recognized as time goes on. It will be impossible to develop a satisfactory country life without conserving all the beauty of landscape and developing the people to the point of appreciating it. In parts of the East a regular system of parking the open country of the entire State is already begun, constructing the roads, preserving the natural features, and developing the latent beauty in such a way that the whole country becomes part of one continuing landscape treatment. This in no way interferes with the agricultural utilization of the land, but rather increases it. The scenery is, in fact, capitalized, so that it adds to the property values and contributes to local patriotism and to the thrift of the commonwealth.

Need of a Redirected Education

The subject of paramount importance in our correspondence and in the hearings is education. In every part of the United States there seems to be one mind, on the part of those capable of judging, on the necessity of redirecting the rural schools. There is no such unanimity on any other subject. It is remarkable with what similarity of phrase the subject has been discussed in all parts of the country before the commission. Everywhere there is a demand that education have relation to living, that the schools should express the daily life, and that in the rural districts they should educate by means of agriculture and country life subjects. It is recognized that all difficulties resolve themselves in the end into a question of education.

The schools are held to be largely responsible for ineffective farming, lack of ideals, and the drift to town. This is not because the rural schools, as a whole, are declining, but because they are in a state of arrested development and have not yet put themselves in consonance with all the recently changed conditions of life. The very forces that have built up the city and town school have caused the neglect of the country school. It is probable that the farming population will willingly support better schools as soon as it becomes convinced that the schools will really be changed in such a way as to teach persons how to live.

The country communities are in need of social centers — places where persons may naturally meet, and where a real neighborhood interest exists. There is difference of opinion as to where this center should be, some persons thinking it should be in the town or village, others the library, others the church or school or grange hall. It is probable that more than one social center should develop in large and prosperous communities. Inasmuch as the school is supported by public funds, and is therefore an institution connected with the government of the community, it should form a natural organic center. If the school develops such a center, it must concern itself directly with the interests of the people. It is difficult to make people understand what this really means, for school-teaching is burdened with tradition. The school must express the best cooperation of all social and economic forces that make for the welfare of the community. Merely to add new studies will not meet the need, although it may break the ground for new ideas. The school must be fundamentally redirected, until it becomes a new kind of institution. This will require that the teacher himself be a part of the community and not a migratory factor.

The feeling that agriculture must color the work of rural public schools is beginning to express itself in the interest in nature study, in the introduction of classes in agriculture in high schools and elsewhere, and in the establishment of separate or special schools to teach farm and home subjects. These agencies will help to bring about the complete reconstruction of which we have been speaking. It is specially important that we make the most of the existing public-school system, for it is this very system that should serve the real needs of the people. The real needs of the people are not alone the arts by which they make a living, but the whole range of their customary activities. As the home is the center of our civilization, so the home subjects should be the center of every school.

The most necessary thing now to be done for public-school education in terms of country life is to arouse all the people to the necessity of such education, to coordinate the forces that are beginning to operate, and to project the work beyond the schools for youth into continuation schools for adults. The schools must represent and express the community in which they stand, although, of course, they should not be confined to the community. They should teach health and sanitation, even if it is necessary to modify the customary teaching of physiology. The teaching should be visual, direct, and applicable. Of course the whole tendency of the schools will be ethical if they teach the vital subjects truthfully; but particular care should be taken that they stand for the morals of the pupils and of the communities.

We find a general demand for federal encouragement in educational propaganda, to be in some way cooperative with the States. The people realize that the incubus of ignorance and inertia is so heavy and so widespread as to constitute a national danger, and that it should be removed as rapidly as possible. It will be increasingly necessary for the national and state governments to cooperate to bring about the results that are needed in agricultural and other industrial education.

The consideration of the educational problem raises the greatest single question that has come before the commission, and which the commission has to place before the American people. Education has now come to have vastly more significance than the mere establishing and maintaining of schools. The education motive has been taken into all kinds of work with the people, directly in their homes and on their farms, and it reaches mature persons as well as youths. Beyond and behind all educational work there must be an aroused intelligent public sentiment; to make this sentiment is the most important work immediately before us. The whole country is alive with educational activity. While this activity may all be good, it nevertheless needs to be directed and correlated, and all the agencies should be more or less federated.

The arousing of the people must be accomplished in terms of their daily lives or of their welfare. For the country people this means that it must be largely in terms of agriculture. Some of the colleges of agriculture are now doing this kind of work effectively although on a pitiably small scale as compared with the needs. This is extension work, by which is meant all kinds of educational effort directly with the people, both old and young, at their homes and on their farms; it comprises all educational work that is conducted away from the institution and for those who can not go to schools and colleges. The best extension work now proceeding in this country — if measured by the effort to reach the people in their homes and on their own ground — is that coming from some of the colleges of agriculture and the United States Department of Agriculture. Within the last five or ten years the colleges of agriculture have been able to attack the problem of rural life in a new way. This extension work includes such efforts as local agricultural surveys, demonstrations on farms, nature study, and other work in schools, boys' and girls' clubs of many kinds, crop organizations, redirection of rural societies, reading clubs, library extension, lectures, traveling schools, farmers' institutes, inspections of herds, barns, crops, orchards, and farms, publications of many kinds, and similar educational effort directly in the field.

To accomplish these ends, we suggest the establishment of a nation-wide extension work. The first, or original, work of the agricultural branches of the land-grant colleges was academic in the old sense; later there was added the great field of experiment and research; there now should be added the third coordinate branch, comprising extension work, without which no college of agriculture can adequately serve its State. It is to the extension department of these colleges, if properly conducted, that we must now look for the most effective rousing of the people on the land.

In order that all public educational work in the United States may be adequately studied and guided, we also recommend that the United States Bureau of Education be enlarged and supported in such a way that it will really represent the educational activities of the nation, becoming a clearing house, and a collecting, distributing, and investigating organization. It is now wholly inadequate to accomplish these ends. In a country in which education is said to be the national religion, this condition of our one expressly federal educational agency is pathetic. The good use already made of the small appropriations provided for the bureau shows clearly that it can render a most important service if sufficient funds are made available for its use.

Necessity of Working Together

It is of the greatest consequence that the people of the open country should learn to work together, not only for the purpose of forwarding their economic interests and of competing with other men who are organized, but also to develop themselves and to establish an effective community spirit. This effort should be a genuinely cooperative or common effort in which all the associated persons have a voice in the management of the organization and share proportionately in its benefits. Many of the so-called "cooperative" organizations are really not such, for they are likely to be controlled in the interest of a few persons rather than for all and with no thought of the good of the community at large. Some of the societies that are cooperative in name are really strong centralized corporations or stock companies that have no greater interest in the welfare of the patrons than other corporations have.

At present the cooperative spirit works itself out chiefly in business organizations devoted to selling and buying. So far as possible, these business organizations should have more or less social uses; but even if the organizations can not be so used, the growth of the cooperative spirit should of itself have great social value, and it should give the hint for other cooperating groups. There is great need of associations in which persons cooperate directly for social results. The primary cooperation is social and should arise in the home, between all members of the family.

The associations that have an educational purpose are very numerous, such as the common agricultural societies and clubs devoted to stock raising, fruit growing, grain growing, poultry keeping, floriculture, bee culture, and the like, mostly following the lines of occupation. These are scarcely truly cooperative, since they usually do not effect a real organization to accomplish a definite end, and they may meet only once or twice a year; they hold conventions, but usually do not maintain a continuous activity. These societies are of the greatest benefit, however, and they have distinct social value. No doubt a great many of them could be so reorganized or developed as to operate continuously throughout the year and become truly cooperative in effort, thereby greatly increasing their influence and importance.

A few great farmers' organizations have included in their declarations of purposes the whole field of social, educational, and economic work. Of such, of national scope, are Patrons of Husbandry and the Farmers' Union. These and similar large societies are effective in proportion as they maintain local branches that work toward specific ends in their communities.

While there are very many excellent agricultural cooperative organizations of many kinds, the farmers nearly everywhere complain that there is still a great dearth of association that really helps them in buying and selling and developing their communities. Naturally the effective cooperative groups are in the most highly developed communities; the general farmer is yet insufficiently helped by the societies. The need is not so much for a greater number of societies as for a more complete organization within them and for a more continuous active work.

Farmers seem to be increasingly feeling the pressure of the organized interests that sell to them and buy from them. They complain of business understandings or agreements between all dealers, from the wholesaler and jobber to the remote country merchants, that prevent farmers and their organizations from doing an independent business.

The greatest pressure on the farmer is felt in regions of undiversified one-crop farming. Under such conditions he is subject to great risk of crop failure; his land is soon reduced in productiveness; he usually does not raise his home supplies, and is therefore dependent on the store for his living, and his crop, being a staple and produced in enormous quantities, is subject to world prices and to speculation, so that he has no personal market. In the exclusive cotton and wheat regions the hardships of the farmer and the monotony of rural life are usually very marked. Similar conditions are likely to obtain in large-area stock ranging, hay raising, tobacco growing, and the like. In such regions great discontent is likely to prevail and economic heresies to breed. The remedy is diversification in farming on one hand and organization on the other.

The commission has found many organizations that seem to be satisfactorily handling the transporting, distributing, and marketing of farm products. They are often incorporated stock companies, in which the cooperators have the spur of money investment to hold them to their mutual obligations. In nearly all cases the most successful organizations are in regions that are strongly dominated by similar products, as fruit, dairy, grain, or live stock.

Two principles may be applied in these business societies: In one class the organization is in the nature of a combination, and attempts to establish prices and perhaps to control the production; in the other class the organization seeks its results by studying and understanding the natural laws of trade and taking advantage of conditions and regulating such evils as may arise, in the same spirit as a merchant studies them, or as a good farmer understands the natural laws of fertility.

With some crops, notably cotton and the grains, it is advantageous to provide cooperative warehouses in which the grower may hold his products till prices rise, and also in which scientific systems of grading of the products may be introduced. In certain fruit regions community packing houses have proved to be of the greatest benefit. In the meantime the cotton or grain in the warehouse becomes, for business purposes, practically as good as cash (subject to charge for insurance) in the form of negotiable warehouse receipts. This form of handling products is now coming to be well understood, and, combined with good systems of farming, it is capable of producing most satisfactory results.

Organized effort must come as the voluntary expression of the people; but it is essential that every State should enact laws that will stimulate and facilitate the organization of such cooperative associations, care being taken that the working of the laws be not cumbersome. These laws should provide the associations with every legal facility for the transaction of the business in which they are to engage. They are as important to the State as other organizations of capital and should be fostered with as much care, and their members and patrons be adequately safeguarded. It is especially important that these organizations be granted all the powers and advantages given to corporations or other aggregations of capital, to the end that they may meet these corporations on equal legal ground when it is necessary to compete with them. Such laws should not only protect the cooperative societies but should provide means that will allow the societies to regulate themselves, so that they may be safeguarded from becoming merely commercial organizations through the purchase or control of the stock by dealers in the products that they handle. It is not unlikely that federal laws may also be needed to encourage cooperation.

Organized associative effort may take on special forms. It is probable, for example, that cooperation to secure and to employ farm labor would be helpful. It may have for its object the securing of telephone service (which is already contributing much to country life, and is capable of contributing much more), the extension of electric lines, the improvement of highways, and other forms of betterment. Particular temporary needs of the neighborhood may be met by combined effort, and this may be made the beginning of a broader permanent organization.

A method of cooperative credit would undoubtedly prove of great service. In other countries credit associations loan money to their members on easy terms and for long enough time to cover the making of a crop, demanding security not on the property of the borrower but on the moral warranty of his character and industry. The American farmer has needed money less, perhaps, than land workers in some other countries, but he could be greatly benefited by a different system of credit, particularly where the lien system is still in operation. It would be the purpose of such systems, aside from providing loans on the best terms and with the utmost freedom consistent with safety, to keep as much as possible of the money in circulation in the open country where the values originate. The present banking systems tend to take the money out of the open country and to loan it in town or to town-centered interests. We suggest that the national-bank examiners be instructed to determine, for a series of years, what proportion of the loanable funds of rural banks is loaned to the farmers in their localities, in order that data may be secured on this question. All unnecessary drain from the open country should be checked, in order that the country may be allowed and encouraged to develop itself.

It is essential that all rural organizations, both social and economic, should develop into something like a system, or at least that all the efforts be known and studied by central authorities. There should be, in other words, a voluntary union of associative effort, from the localities to the counties, States, and the nation. Manifestly, government in the United States can not manage the work of voluntary rural organization. Personal initiative and a cultivated cooperative spirit are the very core of this kind of work; yet both State and National Government, as suggested, might exert a powerful influence toward the complete organization of rural affairs.

Steps should be taken whereby the United States Department of Agriculture, the State departments of agriculture, the land-grant colleges and experiment stations, the United States Bureau of Education, the normal and other schools, shall cooperate in a broad programme for aiding country life in such a way that each institution may do its appropriate work at the same time that it aids all the others and contributes to the general effort to develop a new rural social life.

The Country Church

This commission has no desire to give advice to the institutions of religion nor to attempt to dictate their policies. Yet any consideration of the problem of rural life that leaves out of account the function and the possibilities of the church, and of related institutions, would be grossly inadequate. This is not only because in the last analysis the country life problem is a moral problem, or that in the best development of the individual the great motives and results are religious and spiritual, but because from the pure sociological point of view the church is fundamentally a necessary institution in country life. In a peculiar way the church is intimately related to the agricultural industry. The work and the life of the farm are closely bound together, and the institutions of the country react on that life and on one another more intimately than they do in the city. This gives the rural church a position of peculiar difficulty and one of unequaled opportunity. The time has arrived when the church must take a larger leadership, both as an institution and through its pastors, in the social reorganization of rural life.

The great spiritual needs of the country community just at present are higher personal and community ideals. Rural people need to have an aspiration for the highest possible development of the community. There must be an ambition on the part of the people themselves constantly to progress in all of those things that make the community life wholesome, satisfying, educative, and complete. There must be a desire to develop a permanent environment for the country boy and girl, of which they will become passionately fond. As a pure matter of education, the countryman must learn to love the country and to have an intellectual appreciation of it. More than this, the spiritual nature of the individual must be kept thoroughly alive. His personal ideals of conduct and ambition must be cultivated.

Of course the church has an indispensable function as a conservator of morals. But from the social point of view, it is to hold aloft the torch of personal and community idealism. It must be a leader in the attempt to idealize country life.

The country church doubtless faces special difficulties. As a rule, it is a small field. The country people are conservative. Ordinarily the financial support is inadequate. Often there are too many churches in a given community. Sectarian ideas divide unduly and unfortunately. While there are many rural churches that are effective agents in the social evolution of their communities, it is true that as a whole the country church needs new direction and to assume new responsibilities. Few of the churches in the open country are provided with resident pastors. They are supplied mostly from the neighboring towns and by a representative of some single denomination. Sometimes the pulpit is supplied by pastors of different denominations in turn. Without a resident minister the church work is likely to be confined chiefly to services once a week. In many regions there is little personal visitation except in cases of sickness, death, marriage, christening, or other special circumstance. The Sunday school is sometimes continued only during the months of settled weather. There are young people's organizations to some extent, but they are often inactive or irregular. The social activity of the real country church is likely to be limited to the short informal meetings before and after services and to suppers that are held for the purpose of raising funds. Most of the gatherings are designed for the church people themselves rather than for the community. The range of social influence is therefore generally restricted to the families particularly related to the special church organization, and there is likely to be no sense of social responsibility for the entire community.

In the rural villages there are generally several or a number of churches of different denominations, one or more of which are likely to be weak. The salaries range from $400 to $1,000. Among Protestants there is considerable denominational competition and consequent jealousy or even conflict. United effort for cooperative activity is likely to be perfunctory rather than sympathetic and vital. The pastor is often overloaded with station work in neighboring communities.

It is not the purpose of the commission to discuss the difficulties of the rural church at this time nor to present a solution for them, but in the interests of rural betterment it seems proper to indicate a few considerations that seem to be fundamental.

1. In New England and in some other parts of the North the tremendous drawback of denominational rivalry is fairly well recognized and active measures for church federation are well under way. This does not mean organic union. It means cooperation for the purpose of trying to reach and influence every individual in the community. It means that "some church is to be responsible for every square mile." When a community is overchurched, it means giving up the superfluous church or churches. When a church is needed, it means a friendly agreement on the particular church to be placed there. This movement for federation is one of the most promising in the whole religious field, because it does not attempt to break down denominational influence or standards of thought. It puts emphasis, not on the church itself, but on the work to be done by the church for all men — churched and unchurched. It is possible that all parts of the country are not quite ready for federation, although a national church federation movement is under way. But it hardly seems necessary to urge that the spirit of cooperation among churches, the diminution of sectarian strife, the attempt to reach the entire community, must become the guiding principles everywhere if the rural church is long to retain its hold.

The rural church must be more completely than now a social center. This means not so much a place for holding social gatherings, although this is legitimate and desirable, but a place whence constantly emanates influences that go to build up the moral and spiritual tone of the whole community. The country church of the future is to be held responsible for the great ideals of community life as well as of personal character.

2. There should be a large extension of the work of the Young Men's Christian Association into the rural communities. There is apparently no other way to grip the hearts and lives of the boys and young men of the average country neighborhood. This association must regard itself as an ally of the church, with a special function and a special field.

3. We must have a complete conception of the country pastorate. The country pastor must be a community leader. He must know the rural problems. He must have sympathy with rural ideals and aspirations. He must love the country. He must know country life, the difficulties that the farmer has to face in his business, some of the great scientific revelations made in behalf of agriculture, the great industrial forces at work for the making or the unmaking of the farmer, the fundamental social problems of the life of the open country.

Consequently, the rural pastor must have special training for his work. Ministerial colleges and theological seminaries should unite with agricultural colleges in this preparation of the country clergyman. There should be better financial support for the clergyman. In many country districts it is pitiably small. There is little incentive for a man to stay in a country parish, and yet this residence is just what must come about. Perhaps it will require an appeal to the heroic young men, but we must have more men going into the country pastorates, not as a means of getting a foothold, but as a permanent work. The clergyman has an excellent chance for leadership in the country. In some sections he is still the dominating personality. But everywhere he may become one of the great community leaders. He is the key to the country church problem.

Personal Ideals and Local Leadership

Everything resolves itself at the end into a question of personality. Society or government can not do much for country life unless there is voluntary response in the personal ideals of those who live in the country. Inquiries by the commission, for example, find that one reason for the shift from the country to town is the lack of ideals in many country homes and even the desire of the countryman and his wife that the children do not remain on the farm. The obligation to keep as many youths on the farms as are needed there rests on the home more than on the school or on society.

It is often said that better rural institutions and more attractive homes and yards will necessarily follow an increase in profitableness of farming; but, as a matter of fact, high ideals may be quite independent of income, although they can not be realized without sufficient income to provide good support. Many of the most thrifty farmers are the least concerned about the character of the home and school and church. One often finds the most attractive and useful farm homes in the difficult farming regions. On the other hand, some of the most prosperous agricultural regions possess most unattractive farm premises and school buildings. Many persons who complain most loudly about their incomes are the last to improve their home conditions when their incomes are increased; they are more likely to purchase additional land and thereby further emphasize the barrenness of home life. Land hunger is naturally strongest in the most prosperous regions.

When an entire region or industry is not financially prosperous, it is impossible, of course, to develop the best personal and community ideals. In the cotton-growing States, for example, the greatest social and mental development has been apparent in the years of high prices for cotton; and the same is true in exclusive wheat regions, hay regions, and other large areas devoted mainly to one industry.

While it is of course necessary that the farmer receive good remuneration for his efforts, it is nevertheless true that the money consideration is frequently too exclusively emphasized in farm homes. This consideration often obscures every other interest, allowing little opportunity for the development of the intellectual, social, and moral qualities. The open country abounds in men and women of the finest ideals; yet it is necessary to say that other ends in life than the making of more money and the getting of more goods are much needed in country districts; and that this, more than anything else, will correct the unsatisfying nature of rural life.

Teachers of agriculture have placed too much relative emphasis on the remuneration and production sides of country life. Money hunger is as strong in the open country as elsewhere, and as there are fewer opportunities and demands for the expenditure of this money for others and for society, there often develops a hoarding and a lack of public spirit that is disastrous to the general good. So completely does the money purpose often control the motive that other purposes in farming often remain dormant. The complacent contentment in many rural neighborhoods is itself the very evidence of social incapacity or decay.

It must not be assumed that these deficiencies are to be charged as a fault against the farmer as a group. They are rather to be looked on as evidence of an uncorrelated and unadjusted society. Society is itself largely to blame. The social structure has been unequally developed. The townsman is likely to assume superiority and to develop the town in disregard of the real interests of the open country or even in opposition to them. The city exploits the country; the country does not exploit the city. The press still delights in archaic cartoons of the farmer. There is as much need of a new attitude on the part of the townsman as on the part of the farmer.

This leads us to say that the country ideals, while derived largely from the country itself, should not be exclusive; and the same applies to city and village ideals. There should be more frequent social intercourse on equal terms between the people of the country and those of the city or village. This community of interests is being accomplished to a degree at present, but there is hardly yet the knowledge and sympathy and actual social life that there should be between those who live on the land and those who do not. The business men's organizations of cities could well take the lead in some of this work. The country town in particular has similar interests with the open country about it; but beyond this, all people are bettered and broadened by association with those of far different environment.

We have now discussed some of the forces and agencies that will aid in bringing about a new rural society. The development of the best country life in the United States is seen, therefore, to be largely a question of guidance. The exercise of a wise advice, stimulus, and direction from some central national agency, extending over a series of years, could accomplish untold good, not only for the open country, but for all the people and for our institutions.

In the communities themselves, the same kind of guidance is needed, operating in good farming, in schools, churches, societies, and all useful public work. The great need everywhere is new and young leadership, and the commission desires to make an appeal to all young men and women who love the open country to consider this field when determining their careers. We need young people of quality, energy, capacity, aspiration, and conviction, who will live in the open country as permanent residents on farms, or as teachers, or in other useful fields, and who, while developing their own business or affairs to the greatest perfection, will still have unselfish interest in the welfare of their communities. The farming country is by no means devoid of leaders, and is not lost or incapable of helping itself, but it has been relatively overlooked by persons who are seeking great fields of usefulness. It will be well for us as a people if we recognize the opportunity for usefulness in the open country and consider that there is a call for service.

L. H. Bailey.
Henry Wallace.
Kenyon L. Butterfield.
Walter H. Page.
Gifford Pinchot.
C. S. Barrett.
W. A. Beard.

Wheat Farming Outlook, 1909

From Mark Alfred Carleton, "The Future Wheat Supply of the United States," U.S. Department of Agriculture, *Yearbook*, 1909, pp. 259–72.

Because of the scarcity of wheat and accompanying high prices in recent years, there has been considerable discussion of the question of future wheat production in this country. Doubts have even been expressed by some that we shall be able much longer to furnish our own people with sufficient wheat for bread. Others, on the contrary, contend that high prices will induce a revival of interest in wheat cultivation, and that a large acreage in the older States, devoted to other crops because of previous low prices of wheat, will be again planted with that cereal. This, together with the possible increase of acreage in the undeveloped lands of western States and the increase in acre yields likely to follow improvements in the crop and in methods of culture, will, it is claimed, enable us to maintain an abundant supply for an indefinite time.

In this article the attempt is made to reach as near as possible the proper viewpoint of the question, after an analysis of recent conditions as to production, export, home consumption, etc., and comparison of these with future probabilities in the same lines. Analogies are also drawn from conditions now existing in other countries.

Recent Conditions

Evidently any calculation of future wheat production and its relation to consumption must be based chiefly upon inferences that may be drawn from present and past conditions, it being a generally accepted proposition that the average trend of things in future will be about the same over a considerable period of time as in the past.

The total land area of the United States is 1,900,947,200 acres. Ten years ago considerably less than half of this area was included in farms, a little more than one-fifth of the area was improved, and less than 3 per cent was devoted to wheat culture.

In the following table are given the total farm acreage, the improved farm acreage, and the wheat acreage of the United States for each census year that they were determined from 1850 to 1900, also the percentage that each of these comprises of the total land area. The facts are taken from the Statistical Abstract of the United States for 1908, pages 119–121, except wheat acreages, which are calculated as 10-year averages from regular reports of the Bureau of Statistics of this Department.

The total farm acreage is the total area in farms, whether in actual cultivation or not, and includes often large stock ranges.

As the wheat acreage is obtained yearly and varies considerably, it is considered that 10-year averages show more accurately its relation to farm acreage than the wheat acreage of the census years themselves. Therefore, for the census years of 1880, 1890, and 1900, averages for the periods 1874–1883, 1884–1893, and

Year.	Farms.		Improved.		Wheat.	
	Acreage.	Percentage.	Acreage.	Percentage.	Acreage.	Percentage
1900.........	838,591,774	44.1	414,498,487	21.8	41,971,000	2.2
1890.........	623,218,619	32.8	537,616,755	18.8	37,275,000	2.0
1880.........	536,081,835	28.2	284,771,042	15.0	31,912,000	1.7
1870.........	407,735,041	21.4	188,921,099	9.9	18,386,000	1.0
1860.........	407,212,538	21.4	163,110,720	8.6	[a] 15,424,496	.8
1850.........	293,590,614	15.4	113,032,614	6.0	......	......

[a] This sum is the acreage for 1886.

1894–1903, respectively, are employed, and for 1870 the average for the period of 1866–1871, as the figures for wheat acreage in this period do not go back farther than 1866.

The figures of the table show a remarkable expansion in both the improved farm area and the wheat acreage. The question now is, to what extent can we expect such increases to continue.

We have no definite statement of farm acreage since 1900. We have, however, a statement for the period 1900–1908 of the yearly "disposal of public lands for cash." These public lands include original homestead entries as much the larger portion, timber-culture claims, lands obtained with agricultural college and other scrip and under military bounty land warrants, and lands (a comparatively small amount) selected by States and railroads. We may therefore assume these lands to make up much the largest portion of the total additions to farm acreage. The total amount of these lands up to 1908 was 164,159,599 acres. These figures, of course, exclude public lands similarly disposed of in Texas, which, according to the reports of the commissioner of the Texas general land office, amounted to 22,470,856 acres from September 1, 1900, to August 31, 1908. If we then consider the further amounts of such lands added after 1908, and the enormous tracts of railroad lands sold to new settlers in recent years, particularly in Kansas, Nebraska, and Colorado, it appears that at least 200,000,000 acres must have been added to the farm area from 1900 to the present time. This would bring the total farm area up almost to 1,050,000,000 acres, making the percentage of the total land area in farms in 1910 approximately 55 per cent.

The area in cultivated crops in 1909, as reported by the Bureau of Statistics of this Department, was about 10 per cent greater than ten years ago. It is therefore reasonable to believe that at the present time nearly 25 per cent of the total land area is improved. The present average wheat acreage is about 46,500,000 acres, or 2.4 per cent of the total land area.

Up to 1910 these different areas have, therefore, all increased greatly, and apparently at the same rate as in the preceding decade.

It is of interest to note also the percentage of the farm area employed for wheat in succeeding census years. In 1870 the average wheat acreage was 4.5 per cent of the farm area, in 1880 it was almost 6 per cent, in 1890 it was practically the same as in 1880, in 1900 it was 5 per cent, and at the present time approximately 4.4 per cent. The percentage remains almost the same as in 1870, but stood much higher from 1880 to 1890, during a period of unusual expansion in wheat acreage, and fell again in 1900 and later years, during a period of proportionally greater expansion in farm area. This percentage is likely to get larger soon, as the farm area, of course, can not increase indefinitely and is likely even, during the next decade, to increase less than heretofore. On the other hand, there has apparently already begun a considerable expansion in wheat area.

Probable Future Wheat Acreage

The trend of all these areas, it is seen, is constantly toward an increase, though, as stated, the rate of increase of farm area will hereafter become much less. The percentage of farm area improved and that devoted to wheat will become correspondingly greater, until the farm area finally reaches its limit. What is this limit likely to be? To be more definite, what will be the probable farm area in 1950?

According to the Report of the General Land Office for 1908 there remained at that time, exclusive of Alaska, 386,873,787 acres of government lands "unappropriated and unreserved." Probably 75,000,000 to 100,000,000 acres of these lands will be included in farms. There will be other additions from present Indian reservations, from western Texas, from the reclamation of swamp lands, etc. Add to these the natural expansion of farm area in the older States, which amount will hereafter be proportionally greater than heretofore, and it seems reasonable to expect nearly 300,000,000 acres additional farm area in the next forty years, making a total amount of over 1,300,000,000 acres, or about 70 per cent of the total land area.

The improved farm area has heretofore been about half of the total farm area, but will hereafter increase more rapidly than the latter. It should therefore reach at least 40 per cent of the total land area, or about 760,000,000 acres.

As before stated, the present wheat acreage appears to be approximately 4.4 per cent of the farm area, a slightly less proportion than in 1870. By 1950 the proportion should easily reach 6 per cent, as that rate was attained before in 1880 to 1890, and the farm area will hereafter increase less rapidly. That percentage will allow a wheat acreage of about 80,000,000 acres.

Analogies From Foreign Countries

Some confirmation of the preceding estimates may be secured, reasoning by analogy from conditions now existing in other countries.

In the accompanying table are given the total land area, the wheat acreage, and the percentage of total land area in wheat in a number of other important countries. The wheat acreage in each case is an average for ten years, 1899–1908.

It is seen that the percentage of the total land area in wheat runs from 1 per cent in case of Denmark to even 16.5 per cent in case of Italy. It would require only about 4.2 per cent of the total land area in the United States to give us 80,000,000 acres of wheat. Yet Spain, which is considerably mountainous, is now employing 7.3 per cent, while even in Germany, where there is much waste land, the present proportion is 3.5 per cent, though rye is the really important crop, comprising 10 per cent of the total area. Some of the countries noted for wheat growing, such as Russia, Hungary, Roumania, Bulgaria, France, and Italy, employ from 3.9 to 16.5

Country.	Total Acres.	In wheat.	Percentage in wheat.
Great Britain	[a]56,787,082	1,745,000	3.1
Austria	74,102,001	2,742,000	3.7
Hungary	80,979,000	9,044,000	11.2
Belgium	7,277,000	[b]390,000	5.1
Bulgaria	23,797,000	1,990,000	8.4
Denmark	[c]9,500,000	90,000	1.0
France	130,374,000	16,100,000	12.3
Germany	133,585,000	4,610,000	3.5
Italy	[a]70,787,000	11,660,000	16.5
Japan	94,499,000	1,100,000	1.2
Netherlands	8,038,000	140,000	1.8
Roumania	32,444,191	4,690,000	14.5
Russia in Europe (exclusive of Poland)	1,244,367,000	48,550,000	3.9
Poland	31,451,000	1,240,000	3.9
Servia	11,931,000	895,000	7.5
Spain	124,616,000	9,100,000	7.3
United States (contintental)	1,900,947,200	46,500,000	2.4
Argentina	714,918,000	14,000,000	1.9
British India	556,599,000	27,000,000	4.9
Manitoba	41,169,000	[d]2,700,000	6.6

[a] Area including water.
[b] 1904, 1905, 1906 averages.
[c] Area exclusive of lakes and rivers.
[d] Approximately.

per cent of their total area for wheat. Even in Great Britain, where there is the most intensive cultivation, wheat is grown on 3.1 per cent of the total area.

In England about 75 per cent of the land area is cultivated. In Germany 48.7 per cent is arable, while in France 85 per cent is productive. In face of these facts it certainly seems very conservative to estimate 70 per cent of our total area as the area in farms and 40 per cent as the improved farm area in 1950.

It may be added that in Hungary, one of the important wheat countries, but much older than our own, the wheat acreage has increased even since 1884 from 6,797,800 acres to 9,474,415 acres in 1908. In Austria proper during the same period the increase was from 2,735,600 acres to 2,959,557 acres. In total European Russia the acreage has increased from 39,711,200 acres in 1894 to 62,766,700 acres in 1908. In three other smaller countries wheat acreage increases have been as follows: Roumania, 2,903,700 acres (1886) to 4,452,000 acres (1908); Bulgaria, 2,167,200 acres (1897) to 2,422,700 acres (1908); Servia, 783,500 acres (1893) to 931,300 acres (1908).

Supply and Demand, or the Factor of Profit

In estimates of this kind, forecasting probable production, it is of course taken for granted that there will be sufficient incentive in the way of demand and therefore profit, to keep up the movement of progressive increases. The most decisive question, after all, is simply one of supply and demand. The farmer, like the man in any other business, will grow what pays best. In 1908 to some a wheat shortage seemed very near. But similar periods have occurred before and have been followed by periods of wheat expansion, the higher prices naturally inducing a larger acreage. Here, again, a review of past conditions will show what is probable in the future.

*　　*　　*

Again, in some instances the acreage and price variations, though apparently interdependent, do not occur the same year. This fact may probably be explained as follows: Several good crops having occurred, the farmer holds his wheat in spite of fair prices, expecting still better, so that an unusual amount is delivered the following year, thus affecting prices of that year instead of the year the crop was grown.

A period of remarkable conditions is that of 1892–1896. For many years a steady high production had been maintained until, in 1892, accumulations beyond the needs of the people assumed tidal-wave proportions and inundated the country with a large surplus of wheat, followed by low prices. This is at least a partial explanation of the great depression in wheat during this period. However, good crops in other countries permitted no relief through export, a matter perhaps of equal importance. Not only were low acreages not accompanied by high prices, but by extremely low prices, the lowest in our history, 49.1 cents being reached in 1894. In the light of recent wheat scarcity and high prices, it is of interest to look back at these conditions. Wheat became a drug on the market, and in Kansas it was estimated that 4,000,000 bushels of the 1893 crop, or almost one-sixth, were fed to farm animals. It was seriously considered whether "with corn and wheat approximating the same price per bushel it is unprofitable or wicked to feed the wheat." It was quite commonly believed in the Great Plains States, where acre yields are usually low, that wheat growing would never again be profitable.

This period closed only thirteen years ago, and during the preceding period the highest ratio of wheat acreage to farm acreage was attained. Now the trend in acreage is again upward and will continue, no doubt, through another period of wheat expansion. Recent high prices in the face of big crops (in this country) have probably excited fully as much comment as the low prices in the face of low acreages in 1892 to 1896.

Increase of Wheat Acreage in Older States

It is a natural inference from the preceding discussion that there must occasionally be a considerable increase in wheat acreage hereafter within the present farm area, and particularly in the older States, to allow sufficient production to satisfy unusual demands that will arise. Even since beginning the preparation of this article, a report from the Bureau of Statistics shows that just such an increase in acreage has occurred. This report states an increase in the winter-wheat acreage alone for the season of 1910 of almost 2,500,000 acres over that of last year, the increase being largely in the States east of the Mississippi River.

From further data, partly furnished by the Bureau of Statistics, it is found that in Maryland the proportion of total land area devoted to wheat has increased from 7.5 per cent for the period 1870–1879 to 12.3 per cent for the period 1900–1909. Here follows a tabulation of all States whose percentage of total area devoted to wheat has increased between the same periods above mentioned, with the percentages for each period:

State.	Proportion of total area in wheat.		State.	Proportion of total area in wheat.	
	1870–1879.	1900–1909.		1870–1879.	1900–1909.
	Per cent.	*Per cent.*		*Per cent.*	*Per cent.*
Maine............	0.1	0.6	Minnesota.......	3.3	10.5
Pennsylvania ...	4.4	5.6	Missouri.........	2.7	4.5
Delaware........	5.0	8.9	Nebraska........	.9	5.4
Maryland........	7.5	12.3	Kansas..........	1.5	10.5
West Virginia ..	1.9	2.5	Kentucky........	2.7	3.1
North Carolina.	1.4	1.9	Texas	.1	.6
South Carolina.	.6	1.5	Arkansas	.4	.7
Ohio	6.4	7.2	Oregon	.4	1.3
Indiana..........	8.0	9.0	California	.2	1.7

While there are large increases in the newer States, as would be natural, it is of more interest to note the considerable increases in some of the older States. It is an indication of what may yet be expected.

Yield Per Acre

We come now to another topic, concerning which an erroneous opinion has prevailed for some time. In recent literature repeated statements have been made leading one to infer that acre yields of wheat are decreasing in this country, and in farm journals even the causes of such a decrease have been discussed. As a matter of fact, acre yields, even in this country, are not decreasing, but, on the other hand, have considerably increased, showing that farmers are already giving some attention to better methods of cultivation and using better varieties.

As yields per acre often vary sharply in succeeding years, it is necessary to compare periods instead of single years to get satisfactory information. Ten-year averages of yield per acre in this country, from 1866 to 1905, are as follows: 1866–1875, 11.9 bushels; 1876–1885, 12.3 bushels; 1886–1895, 12.7 bushels; 1896–1905, 13.5 bushels. There is seen to be an increase in acre yields in the last period over the first period of 1.6 bushels. Arranging a different series of ten-year periods, from 1869 to 1908, results are as follows: 1869–1878, 12.31 bushels; 1879–1888, 12.13 bushels; 1889–1898, 13.21 bushels; 1898–1908, 13.75 bushels. Here also is shown an increase in acre yields of 1.4 bushels in the last period over that of the first period. The increase in the last period over that of the second period, however, is 1.6 bushels, practically the same as the total increase in the other calculation. In other words, since 1866, or about 1870, our wheat yield per acre has really increased 1-3/5 bushels, and, on the basis of our present average of 46,400,000 acres, is already giving us an increase in production of 74,241,000 bushels above what it would be at the rate prevailing forty years ago.

Future Wheat Production

At the same rate of increase the added yield per acre by 1950 would be 4-1/5 bushels. This increase in acre yields, however, goes on much more rapidly each decade, as there is a more rapid diffusion of knowledge of improved methods of culture and seed selection, use of better varieties, etc. All farming will also become more intensive. Six bushels of actual increase in acre yields by 1950, or about 20 bushels per acre, is therefore surely a safe estimate. Twenty bushels per acre on a basis of 80,000,000 acres, before estimated for 1950, will furnish 1,600,000,000 bushels.

What may occur after 1950 will presumably concern ourselves or the coming generation some other time, but it is practically certain that acre yields will go on increasing, and probably also the acreage. In view of the preceding data showing percentages of total land area devoted to wheat in foreign countries 8 or even 10 per cent of the total area does not seem an unreasonable limit for this country, and yet it would mean the planting of 150,000,000 to 190,000,000 acres in wheat at some future time. Also, 20 bushels per acre in yield is still much below what is actually being obtained even now in places in Europe. In Germany, where the yield has increased 6 bushels since 1897, it is now (1907) 28.4 bushels. In Great Britain it is 32.6, and even in that country of extremely intensive farming long practiced the increase has been 2.5 bushels (Winchester) since 1897. At least 25 bushels per acre should, therefore, be attained in this country, which, on a basis of 150,000,000 acres, would furnish 3,750,000,000 bushels, and on a basis of 190,000,000 acres, 4,750,000,000 bushels.

Home Consumption

To calculate probable future home consumption of wheat, it is requisite to determine the probable population, and, if possible, the trend of per capita consumption, whether upward or downward, and at what rate. The population of continental United States, the average home consumption of wheat, including seed, and wheat flour, and the per capita consumption for each census year from 1870 are given below. Wheat flour is reduced to wheat at the rate of 4½ bushels to the barrel. The home consumption is an average in each case for five years, of which the middle year is the year preceding that of the census, except in case of 1908, for which an average for the years 1905–1907 is employed.

Year.	Population.	Home consumption.	Per capita consumption.
		Bushels.	Bushels.
1870...	38,558,371	193,698,324	5.02
1880...	50,189,209	276,864,727	5.52
1890...	62,979,766	345,602,279	5.49
1900...	76,149,386	389,331,530	5.11
1906...	[a]84,024,026	536,706,866	6.39
1907..	[a]87,000,000	551,801,954	6.34

[a] Estimated

It is seen that the yearly consumption per capita increased from about 5 bushels in 1870 to approximately 5½ bushels in 1880, at which point it remained until 1890, through the period of high wheat acreages already discussed, and then fell again to a little over 5 bushels in 1900. This last five-year period, 1897–1901, follows close after the period of low wheat acreages, low prices, and general financial depression of 1892–1896. If the estimates of population for 1906 and 1908 come near the facts, there was a great increase in per capita consumption after 1900, amounting to about 1¼ bushels. The high per capita figures would indicate that if the population estimates are much in error they are underestimates rather than overestimates, though they can hardly be so much too small as to bring the per capita consumption much below 6 bushels. These per capita figures do, however, vary up and down, just as acreage figures, prices, etc., will do, and may settle at somewhere near 6 bushels for 1910. This is about 1 bushel increase since 1870, and it seems quite possible that there will be an increase of another bushel in the equal period ending with 1950. We will suppose the per capita consumption for 1950, therefore, to be 7 bushels, though it may be considerably less.

The census population figures show that, starting with an increase of nearly 12,000,000 from 1870 to 1880, the succeeding increase has been rather constantly about 1,000,000 more for each ten years than for the preceding ten years. At this rate of gain the population in 1910 should be about 90,000,000, in 1920 about 105,000,000, in 1930 about 121,000,000, in 1940 about 138,000,000, and in 1950 about 156,000,000. Allowing for a considerably higher rate of increase, however, for safer calculation, we may assume it to be 160,000,000 in 1950.

At the rate of 7 bushels per capita this population would require 1,120,000,000 bushels of wheat. This amount taken from the preceding estimate of production for that year would leave a surplus of 500,000,000 bushels. Some predictions of our future population have placed it much higher for 1950 than 160,000,000, one putting it as high as 200,000,000. Supposing this last to be correct, at 7 bushels per capita consumption this population would require 1,400,000,000 bushels, leaving still a 200,000,000 bushel surplus.

World Production, Reserves, and Export

With the menace of wheat famine at least far away, and with a large present average production, many will inquire why prices have been high. It is explained largely by low reserves and the amount of world production. The unusual reverse conditions of the period 1892–1896, already discussed, are explained chiefly in the same way. To make clear the further discussion of this topic, some tabulations may well be made. The following table shows the annual world production of wheat since 1890, the stock of wheat of each year on hand March 1 of the following year since 1890, or rather the percentage it is of the entire crop, and our wheat export since 1890. The export set down for each year really begins July 1 of that year and includes both wheat and wheat flour.

It is seen that there is a natural preparation for low prices and low acreages in 1892–1896. There is a considerable surplus of wheat all along, shown by the very large proportion of each crop yet on hand March 1 of the following year, the average percentage being about 28.5 per cent, or almost one-third, up to 1893. During the same time world production was good, allowing little relief through export, though the export was fairly good, particularly that of the large crop of 1891. The 1893 crop was unusually low, and by March 1, 1895, the reserve amounted to less than one-sixth. Probably through a reacting influence of the

Crop year.	Percentage of crop on farms March 1 of following year.	United States export.	World production.	Crop year.	Percentage of crop on farms March 1 of following year.	United States export.	World production.
	Per cent.	Bushels.	Bushels.		Per cent.	Bushels.	Bushels.
1890......	28.2	106,181,316	....	1900......	24.5	215,990,073	2,640,751,000
1891......	27.9	225,665,811	2,369,746,000	1901......	23.2	234,772,516	2,945,275,000
1892......	26.3	191,912,635	2,414,414,000	1902......	24.5	202,905,598	3,148,517,000
1893......	29.6	164,283,129	2,426,731,000	1903......	28.0	120,727,613	3,230,580,000
1894......	16.3	144,812,718	2,590,121,000	1904......	20.0	44,112,910	3,163,542,000
1895......	29.0	126,443,968	2,593,312,000	1905......	22.9	97,609,007	3,330,431,000
1896......	20.6	145,124,972	2,506,320,000	1906......	28.3	146,700,425	3,432,931,000
1897......	22.9	217,306,005	2,233,637,000	1907......	23.8	163,043,669	3,145,101,000
1898......	29.3	222,618,420	2,921,045,000	1908......	21.6	....	3,181,115,000
1899......	29.0	186,096,762	2,725,407,000				

extremely low price of 1894 the reserve increased again temporarily for 1895, then from 1897 permanently decreased, with very few exceptions. The wheat overflow was checked by persistent low acreages, a very small world production occurred in 1897, prices went up, and acreage increased again. A temporary depression for two years followed the very large crop of 1898, the world crop that year also being large, reaching almost 3,000,000,000 bushels. The price fell from 81 cents to 58 cents and March 1 reserves increased. This depression continued to be felt until 1902, with the largest crop of our history occurring in 1901 and world crops increasing. Another temporary depression occurred in 1906, when we had our second largest crop and the largest world crop in history, the exports of the two preceding years having been very small. The price fell from 75 cents to 67 cents; then renewed activity began. The crops of 1907 and 1908 were only moderate, the export rose to 163,000,000 bushels in 1907, world crops of 1907 and 1908 fell considerably, and accordingly prices advanced again to 87 cents in 1907 and then to 93 cents in 1908.

Production in Other Countries

The necessity of considering world production in calculating the trend of acreage and prices has been shown. It acts as a balance in finally bringing local extreme conditions approximately to the same level. While it does not affect our potential wheat area, a large world production puts a check upon export, and a small world production stimulates an increase in our acreage through better prices. The possible future wheat acreage of the world, also, will indicate whether we may continue to expect very much longer an occasional surplus in the world's crop.

The three principal regions upon which the world depends at present to supply the needs of other countries are (1) the plains of North America; (2) the "Black Earth" of east and south Russia, Roumania, and Hungary, and including a large indefinite area in Siberia, and (3) Argentina.

Space does not permit a detailed discussion of the probable increase in production to be expected from the countries comprised in these regions. The two provinces of Canada of any considerable importance in producing a surplus are Saskatchewan and Alberta. From a rough calculation based upon the available farm area as reported by the provincial governments we may estimate the increase in wheat production of these provinces, together with Manitoba, to be at least 400,000,000 bushels by 1950. Similar calculations will show that Russia (in Europe) should increase her production at least 600,000,000 bushels and Argentina at least 300,000,000 bushels. Outside the United States, therefore, the chief exporting countries of the world should furnish a total increase in production by 1950 of 1,300,000,000 bushels. Add to this the probable increase of about 900,000,000 bushels in our own production, and the total increase for the chief exporting countries becomes 2,200,000,000 bushels.

On the basis of increase of production heretofore compared with increase in population, and considering the increase in substitute foods that is sure to occur, the world is likely to require, we may suppose, about 5,500,000,000 bushels of wheat by 1950, an increase of 2,000,000,000 over present production. The above estimated total icrease more than satisfies this requirement. This increase also leaves out the numerous smaller increases that will surely occur in other countries, such as Hungary, Austria, South Africa, etc., and the possible resources of the vast agriculturally unknown regions in Siberia, Brazil, and the central plateau of Africa.

The Drought of 1910

From Lewis A. Merrill, "The Drouth of 1910," *Desert Farmer*, August 13, 1910, VII, pp. 1, 4, 5, 12.

The year 1910 will probably pass into history as the year of drouth, not only in Utah and the inter-mountain country but throughout a large portion of the Middle West.

These years of light precipitation and continued long dry spells have occurred at more or less irregular intervals since the history of this section has been known. They do not occur in regular series and no one is able to foretell their arrival. The writer is in possession of data giving the precipitation for thirty-six years; during all of this time there have been a few occasions when the annual precipitation has been less than 12 inches at Salt Lake City, though there have been but six of such years. These dry years do not occur in cycles; to prove this compare the year 1880 when the total precipitation at Salt Lake City was 10.94 inches with the following year (1881) when the precipitation was 16.88 inches, again in 1890 the precipitation was 10.33 inches and this was followed the next year with a precipitation of 15.92 inches. Another year when the precipitation was 11.53 inches the total precipitation during the following year reached 16.08 inches; and still another year when the precipitation was 11.41 inches the total for the following year reached 14.62 inches. As has been said, the particular year of drouth does not occur at regular intervals yet it may be more of a coincidence that the precipitation in 1880 was 10.94, — 1890 but 10.33 and in 1900 but 11.53 inches. It may be that we should have been prepared to expect another dry season in ten years or during 1910.

Dry Farming

Because of the limited rain-fall in the early spring and summer, there has been considerable uneasiness on the part of the dry farmers throughout the whole western country. When it is recalled that the precipitation during the first seven months of 1909 was 12.03 inches and that during this year (1910) the total precipitation for the corresponding season was but 5.39 inches it is apparent that this uneasiness was justifiable.

Even the most conservative and safe farmer felt, that under these conditions this was to be the crucial year; the year when a severe test would be given the system. The harvest season on the dry farms is now over and the returns from all sections of the State and of the inter-mountain country are at hand and confirm the doctrine of scientific soil-culture promulgated in the last few years by the officers of the Experiment Station.

The principle of fall plowing, of thin seeding, of summer fallowing, and of spring harrowing have been shown to be essential and attention to these details of management have insured success even during this the driest of years.

Dr. Widtsoe, some years ago, proclaimed the doctrine of moisture conservation and by experiments proved that it was possible to store two years precipitation away in the soil for the use of one crop and the farmers who have rigidly practiced this doctrine have this year reaped an ample harvest.

History of Dry Farming

It would be folly to say that the doctrine of moisture conservation is new; these same principles were applied by the growers of grapes and olives in Northern Africa in the days of old Carthage. The Navajos grew beans and corn by dry farming methods hundreds of years ago. The Mexicans and Indians of Old Mexico were practicing dry farming when the American Nation was still in its infancy.

In Utah, too, dry farming has been successfully practiced for some forty years now, though the early efforts were confined very largely to isolated sections and a few of the choice locations in the northern counties of the State.

Some six years ago now, the State established and has since maintained a number of experimental farms for the purpose of testing the possibilities of Utah deserts in producing a crop without the use of irrigation. During these years a great many valuable results have been obtained and a wonderful impetus given to the industry.

During all of this time, however, the precipitation has been normal, and above normal, up until this year. This year of drouth has been the opportune time for a real test of dry farming methods. That these methods have succeeded is proven by the returns from all of the experimental farms as well as from the results secured from a large number of dry farmers in every section of the state.

In Cache Valley the yeilds have been more than satisfactory, partly because this is one of the oldest dry farm sections in the State and partly because of the influence of the Agricultural College. . . .

In Salt Lake County Mr. Marcus Bennion and Mr. N. F. Rasmussen, both of whom follow the advice of the dry farming experts, have obtained excellent crops and it is said by their neighbors, that their yields will be in the neighborhood of forty bushels per acre.

In Tooele County the results have been fairly satisfactory. The methods however, of the dry farmers in Tooele County are not in the main of the approved kind. Too many of them fail to practice the fallow; little care is taken in seed selection and it is conceded that the failure to secure maximum crops in that county this year is due more to improper methods than to drouth. . . .

In Utah County results have been surprisingly good. Mr. Stephen L. Chipman, who operates in Cedar Valley, in a recent letter says, "Our grain is remarkable to see this year; we have not had any rains since March but we will harvest in the neighborhood of twenty bushels per acre, from about two hundred acres. It is simply standing the drouth fine and especially is this the case with the Turkey Red wheat. This has been the best year for converting the people to dry farming that we have ever had."

Mr. James Meldrum of Provo Bench has a hundred acres for which he paid twenty-five dollars per acre only four years ago. Last year he obtained 44 bushels of good marketable grain per acre and his neighbors estimate that his yield this year will be even better. When the writer visited this field a few weeks ago, just at the time it was being harvested, it appeared that the yield would not be less than fifty bushels per acre. . . .

The Methods

The methods by which these results are obtained are very simple, and can be briefly summarized. It has been shown in Bulletin No. 91 of the Utah Experiment Station that fall plowing is essential in conserving moisture. The experimenters found in Cache Valley a difference amounting to more than 506 tons of water to the acre in the first five feet of soil in favor of land plowed in the fall.

They advise that plowing land in the fall and leaving it in a rough lumpy condition through the winter benefits the soil by weathering agencies and this reacts favorably upon the crop. It must be conceded, however, that fall plowed land is more likely to be infested with weeds during the fallow period than spring plowed land. The factor of weediness is met by the Grace Brothers of Nephi. They plow their land in the ordinary way and in the early June of the following year when the weeds and volunteer wheat are well started, give the ground a thorough plowing. They have very little trouble after that in keeping their fallow in good condition. Their yields are exceptionally good.

It is generally conceded that the most successful practice is to plow to a depth of from seven to ten inches. In some instances plowing deeper than ten inches and sub-soiling to a depth of from fifteen to eighteen inches have given profitable results, but this of course, involves considerable more expense and unless considerable difference in yield can be obtained would not be found profitable.

The Fallow

The "fallow" as interpreted by dry farmers means permitting the soil to lie idle and it is recommended that this be followed every other year; thus the dry farmer has only half of his land under cultivation each year. It was for this reason that Senator Smoot secured the passage of the Dry Farm Home-stead Act which allows the farmer to secure 320 acres instead of 160 as originally.

The objects sought by the fallow are: First — Conservation of soil moisture, so that two years precipitation may be available for one year's crop. Second — The eradication of weeds and volunteer wheat; the securing of a satisfactory seed bed and, Fourth — increasing the available fertility of the soil.

In a recent bulletin from the Utah Experiment Station (Bulletin No. 105) Dr. Widtsoe points out as the most important result of his experiments the conclusive evidence that the amount of water actually required for the soil is increased. Fallowing sets free plant food which enables the plant to reach maturity with the smallest amount of water.

Pure Seed

The profits of dry land grain production are much increased by using only pure seed, and a great many failures are due to the use of inferior seed. If the seed planted is of more than one variety losses are likely to follow on account of the irregularity in the time of ripening which results in the shattering of large quantities of the early-maturing grain. Furthermore mixed grain never is as likely to command top prices as grain of one variety. The inadvisability of planting grain containing weeds is too well known to require extensive discussion. In selecting grain the farmer should obtain the best variety grown in his section or in a locality of similar conditions. He should see that the seed is as nearly as possible of one variety and that all weeds seeds and light shrunken kernels of grain are removed from the seed before the time of planting. The cleaning is quickly and easily done by the use of a common fanning mill, which can be purchased for about $40. This simple machine should be included in the equipment of every grain farm.

Treatment of Smut

The Mountain States are fortunate in having few grain diseases. Bunt (stinking smut) is the only disease that causes serious damage to the dry land wheat crop. This disease can usually be avoided by soaking the seed from five to ten minutes in a solution of formaldehyde in forty gallons of water. If possible the farmer should use seed that contains little or no smut. If there are smut balls present in the seed, they should be removed by pouring the grain in a tank of water and skimming off the smut balls as they rise to the surface.

If this is done, the seed carefully treated, and the drills thoroughly washed out with the formalin solution, there is very little danger that the resultant crop will be smutted.

Time of Planting

There are several important points to consider in connection with time of planting. The behavior of the crop is determined largely by the amount of moisture in the soil, particularly in the surface foot, at the time of planting is done by the temperature. When the grain is planted early — August 15 to September 15 — there are two possible dangers. The first is that the moisture may be sufficient to start the growth of the plants but insufficient to maintain the growth during the long dry periods which commonly occur during September and October. In this case a large number of plants die from lack of moisture and a thin and irregular stand is the result. . .

When the wheat is planted late — November 1st or there about — there is a strong liklihood that it will not come up until the following spring. Frequently this is not a disadvantage, but it is usually found best to have the plants up in the autumn, especially if the soil contains seeds of weeds that germinate early in the spring. Where this is the case the plants are in danger of being crowded out in the struggle for growing space that invariably takes place when plants of different kinds occur on the same soil.

No particular time can be positively designed as the best time to plant. There are cases where very early planting has produced better results than medium or late planting; occasionally late planting produces maximum yields.

In Utah where the rainfall is never very high, a variation of an inch or two one way or the other may produce striking results, and such variations frequently occur. The records covering a number of years show, however, that on the average the summers are very dry and there are usually long dry periods in September and October. With these facts in mind it is plain that the grain should be planted at such a time as to insure the crop against the possible ill effects of the dry spells which can reasonably be expected. The undesirable influences or low and varying temperatures common in the month of November should also be guarded against. There will undoubtedly be occasional cases in favor of the late planting, but for a practice to be followed through a series of years the medium dates will likely prove the most dependable.

Rate of Seeding Wheat

The test to determine the best rate of seeding has not progressed far enough to warrant the use of results. All the varieties grown at the substation in the variety tests are seeded at the rate of approximately three pecks per acre. This rate has produced satisfactory results not only at the substation but also on the farms all over the mountain area. In deciding on the rate or seed, the farmer should consider two points, (1) the moisture demands of the crop during the dry season and (2) the danger of weeds. If the stand is too thick, the moisture in the soil will be exhausted before the crop is matured; if it is too thin weeds are likely to come up and crowd the plants.

The seeding rate that will be best to meet both of these conditions depends on the condition of the soil and the quality of the seed. If the seed bed is properly prepared and the seed is well cleaned and pure, from 35 to 45 pounds per acre is sufficient. Whether to sow 35 or 45 pounds should be determined by the average size of the kernels to be planted, seed consisting of large kernels requiring the larger rate.

The results in testing the best depth of planting have been rather variable. Plats are planted at the depth of 1½ inches, 3 inches and 6 inches respectively. Until the test is continued considerable longer positive conclusions are unwarranted, but the indications favor three inches as the most desirable depth of the three. In 1909 the plat planted 1½ inches deep produced somewhat better than the one planted 6 inches deep. It is believed that three inches is sufficiently deep, if the seed bed is well prepared and a good drill is used.

Broadcasting Compared with Drilling

It would naturally be thought that a test of the two methods of planting wheat, broadcasting and drilling, would be unnecessary. There are still a few advocates of the old method of planting by hand however, and this test is conducted mainly as a demonstration of the inferiority of this method. The plat planted with a drill has invariably so far, outyielded the other as to put the advisability of broadcasting beyond all question. The broadcasted plat has averaged from two bushels to less than nine bushels to the acre, while the drilled plat has yielded between twenty and twenty-five bushels per acre. There is no good reason why any dry farmer should not use a drill. No matter how small the field is, broadcasting should never be practiced.

Farm Labor, 1910

From George K. Holmes, "Supply and Wages of Farm Labor," U.S. Department of Agriculture, *Yearbook*, 1910, pp. 189–200.

Number of Persons Engaged in Agriculture

Movement From the Farm

Industrialism and city expansion have advanced in this country in greater degree than agriculture. The lure of the city and the city's illusion of higher wages are robbing the farm of its laborer and of the farmers' children who would otherwise be the potential farm owners of the future.

The more or less imperfect census record is the only information possessed in regard to the number of persons engaged gainfully in agriculture in this country. It is very considerably an imperfect record previous to the census of 1900, for the reason, principally, that enumerators often reported agricultural laborers as laborers without any designation of kind of work done by them, and for this reason the agricultural element in the population is represented as being less than the fact. It may be that in some small degree this observation applies to the census of 1900.

In 1820 the number of persons of both sexes reported as being engaged in agriculture was 2,068,958, including slaves, and with the same inclusions the number for 1840 was 3,719,951; by 1880 the number had increased to 7,663,043; by 1890 to 8,466,363; and by 1900 to 10,249,651 (census report on occupations). In the later censuses the persons are described as having been employed gainfully, a distinction not made in the earlier ones. The statements are for the contiguous States and Territories of the Union.

The agricultural element was 83.1 per cent of persons having occupations in 1820; 77.5 per cent in 1840; for gainful occupations, 44.1 per cent in 1880; 37.2 per cent in 1890; 35.3 per cent in 1900. For 1910 the inference is that one-third or less of the persons having gainful occupations are embraced in the agricultural class.

Agricultural laborers constitute one of the primary classes of occupations, and their number, as before stated, has been reported by all censuses as below the fact because the enumerators have reported many of them as general laborers. Another element of error has been the reporting of negro ''croppers'' in the South in the census of 1870 and subsequent ones as farmers, whereas they would have been more properly designated as farm laborers, since they worked for wages, although the wages were contingent. Taking the record as it stands, the number of agricultural laborers in 1880 was 3,323,876; in 1890 it was 3,004,061; in 1900, 4,410,877. The erroneous character of the census enumeration with regard to agricultural laborers appears when it is observed that they were represented as being 43.4 per cent of all persons engaged gainfully in agriculture in 1880; only 35.5 per cent in 1890; and 43 per cent in 1900.

Analysis of the occupation figures of the census of 1900 discovers that 12.3 per cent of all persons having gainful occupations in the North Atlantic division of the States was engaged in agriculture; 26.1 per cent in the Western division; 36.3 per cent in the North Central division; 49.9 per cent in the South Atlantic division; and 62.8 per cent in the South Central division, the average for the United States being 35.3 per cent. Agriculture as an occupation is of least account, relatively, in New England, New York, New Jersey, and Pennsylvania, the group of States constituting the North Atlantic division, and is of greatest account in the lower section of the Mississippi Valley, constituting the South Central division.

Subject to the imperfections of the record, the agricultural laborers in 1900 were 35.2 per cent of all persons gainfully engaged in agriculture in the North Central States, 36 per cent in the Western States, 39.3 per cent in the North Atlantic States, 47.8 per cent in the South Central States, and 52.5 per cent in the South Atlantic States — the lowest percentage being found in the North Central States and the highest in the South Atlantic.

The agricultural element in the population, as indicated by the occupation statistics of the census, is relatively a diminishing one, and it is generally believed that the agricultural laborers, or those who work for hire, are a diminishing relative element in the agricultural population, although this does not appear in the imperfect census record.

Machines Increase the Productiveness of Labor

The reason why agricultural labor could decline relative to National consumption of agricultural products and still leave an enormous National surplus for export is forcibly expressed in the report of the United States Bureau of Labor concerning hand and machine labor, issued some years ago. The facts established in that report warrant the conclusions that follow.

From 1855 to 1894 the time of human labor required to produce 1 bushel of corn on an average declined from four hours and thirty-four minutes to forty-one minutes. This was because inventors had given to the farmers of 1894 the gang plow, the disk harrow, the corn planter drawn by horses, and the four-section harrow for pulverizing the top soil; because they had given to the farmer the self-binder drawn by horses to cut the stalks and bind them; a machine for removing the husks from the ears and in the same operation for cutting the husks, stalks, and blades for feeding, the power being supplied by a steam engine; because they had given to the farmer a marvelous corn sheller, operated by steam and shelling 1 bushel of corn per minute instead of the old way of corn shelling in which the labor of one man was required for one hundred minutes to do the same work.

In the matter of wheat production, 1894 being compared with 1830, the required human labor declined from three hours and three minutes to ten minutes. The heavy, clumsy plow of 1830 had given way to the disk plow that both plowed and pulverized the soil in the same operation; hand sowing had been displaced by the mechanical seeder drawn by horses; the cradling and thrashing with flails and hand winnowing had given way to reaping, thrashing, and sacking with the combined reaper and thrasher drawn by horses.

Herein lies the strength of the horse as an economic animal. He has been assailed by the bicycle, the electric street and suburban car, and by the automobile, but all combined have not prevented horses from increasing in numbers and in value. As a source of farm power and as a substitute for human labor in combination with machines, the horse's economic place on the farm is more strongly established than ever before.

Immigration Not Contributing Much to Farm Labor

Immigration contributed much to the agricultural population until the supply of cheap and otherwise desirable public land was nearly exhausted. At the present time, when land that immigrants can readily utilize for agriculture is high priced, they are not contributing appreciably to the agricultural population. During the year ending June 30, 1908, the immigrant aliens admitted to this country numbered 782,870, of whom, or their equivalent, 50 per cent returned to their native countries on account of the industrial depression they found here; the number arriving in the fiscal year 1909 was 751,786, of whom 30 per cent returned; and in 1910 the arrivals were 1,041,570, of whom 17 per cent did not remain.

By means of census publications, the white foreign-born agricultural laborers, as an element of the total white agricultural laborers, may be determined. In 1890 the white foreign-born element was 13.1 per cent of all white agricultural laborers, and the percentage declined to 8.5 in 1900. In the latter year only 258,479 agricultural laborers were foreign-born whites in a total of 3,038,884 white agricultural laborers. The white foreign born as an element of the total white agricultural laborers was 0.6 per cent in the South Atlantic States in 1900; 2.6 per cent in the South Central; 11.8 per cent in the North Central; 15.6 per cent in the North Atlantic; 20.9 per cent in the Western.

If the number of agricultural laborers of foreign parentage be taken for 1900, and this number includes many laborers who were American born, it appears that they are 17.4 per cent of all agricultural laborers; but the percentages vary widely among the geographic divisions — in the South Atlantic division, 0.8 per cent; South Central, 3.6 per cent; North Atlantic, 30.4 per cent; North Central, 40.7 per cent; and Western, 48 per cent.

Labor of Women Declining

Women, as contributing to agricultural labor, are taking a smaller and smaller part, both relatively and absolutely. The census record gives 534,900 women as performing agricultural labor for hire in 1880; 447,104 in 1890; and 663,209 in 1900. The apparent tendency expressed by these numbers is unbelievable and is directly contrary to a Nation-wide acquaintance with the conditions of agricultural labor in this country. The deficiencies of the earlier censuses can not be estimated, and it may be assumed that the number of female laborers reported in 1900 is near the fact.

The female element of agricultural laborers for hire in 1900 in the total number of women engaged in agriculture is largest in the South Atlantic States, for which the percentage is 79.9; for the South Central States the percentage is 76.5; North Central, 13.5; Western, 12.8; North Atlantic, 11; the United States, 67.9.

In 1900 women were 10.9 per cent of all persons gainfully engaged in agriculture. Among the geographic divisions, the South Central States were highest with 35.6 per cent, and the South Atlantic follows with 25.8 per cent. The North Central percentage is 0.07; Western, 0.02; North Atlantic, 0.01.

As an element of negro agricultural laborers for hire, the female laborers are represented by 37.9 per cent in the United States for 1900; 40.6 per cent for the South Central States; 36.4 per cent for the South Atlantic; 1.3 per cent for the North Central; 1.2 per cent for the Western; and 0.6 per cent for the North Atlantic.

Dependence must be placed upon the general knowledge of conditions with regard to female labor on the farm. The outdoor work of white women on farms of medium or better sorts has greatly declined from early days, and the decline has been rapid during the last generation. Farmers' wives and daughters no longer milk the cows and work in the field and care for the live stock as of yore; they do not work in the kitchen and garden as before; nor assist in the fruit and berry harvest. They are making less butter, and cheese making on the farm has become a lost art. They may care for the poultry and the bees, do housework and gather vegetables for the table, and cook and keep the dwelling in order. This is substantially the limit. Of course negro women do much labor in the cotton field, but this diminishes year by year.

The Negro Element

It is not advisable to base any fine distinctions upon the censuses of 1890 and 1900 with regard to negroes employed in agriculture. But the comparison may indicate numerically the drift of negroes in their relation to agriculture. In 1890 the negroes who were gainfully engaged in agriculture numbered 1,704,904, and in 1900 they numbered 2,108,980, an increase of one-half of 1 per cent in their ratio to the entire number of persons gainfully employed in agriculture. The negro agricultural laborers of 1890 numbered 1,006,728, and in 1900 they numbered 1,344,116, or a decline from 64.9 to 63.7 per cent in their ratio to negroes of all agricultural occupations.

Negro farm labor in the South presents special problems which southern farmers fully understand. The census of 1900 disclosed the fact that negro labor was leaving the farm and migrating to town and city, to the railroad, to the logging and lumbering camp. The negro is still a necessity to southern agriculture, but he is gradually yielding his place to white labor. One of the old arguments in favor of slavery was that a white man could not work in a field under the southern sun, and it is still a common belief in the North that southern farm labor is performed almost exclusively by negroes. This, however, is not the fact. More than half the cotton crop is raised by white labor; in Texas three-fourths or more. In the sugar and rice fields white labor is common and in some places all but exclusive. Negroes are often disposed to migrate in pursuit of chimeras, so that they are easily induced to go to other parts of the country when employment is promised to them, and agents to promote their migration are found where States have not taxed them out of occupation or made it a criminal offense.

If negroes and whites be combined, the negroes will be found to represent 13.7 per cent of all persons in all gainful occupations in 1900, 20.6 per cent of all persons engaged gainfully in agricultural occupations, and 30.5 per cent of all agricultural laborers. The percentages are almost exactly the same for 1890, except that the negro agricultural laborers were 36.8 per cent of the white and negro total, so that there was apparent decline in the negro element of agricultural laborers from 1890 to 1900.

Investigations by the Bureau of Statistics

The First of Nineteen Began in 1866

The subject of the wage rates of farm labor was first systematically investigated in this country by the Bureau of Statistics of the Department of Agriculture in 1866. The investigation was repeated with variations every few years until the latest one in 1909. The results of nineteen investigations are of record, covering the period of forty-four years, beginning with the abnormal conditions at the close of the civil war and passing through the two severe industrial depressions of 1873–1877 and 1893–1897, and the less severe depressions of 1884–86, 1903–4, and 1907–8.

From the beginning of this period to about 1897 agricultural over-production was frequent. Immense areas of new public land came into cultivation, and farmers were painfully in debt, and often the prices of products were unprofitable, if not positively below the cost of production. Since 1897, and more especially since 1902, the financial condition of farmers has much improved. All of the conditions mentioned may be related to the wages of farm labor, and, in fact, apparently have been.

In the statement of wage rates, contained in this article, all original rates during the currency period 1866–1878 have been converted to gold. Some of the investigations were made in the spring with no explanation whether the published rates represented the current year or the preceding year; indeed, some of the wage rates, as, for instance, the rates of day labor in harvest, must necessarily have belonged to the preceding year. In another case two investigations were made, but the published results were combined. These statements account for the use of a double year in several instances.

Wage Rates of Men per Month

The average wage rate of $15.50 was paid for the labor of men on farms per month, in hiring by the year without board, in the United States in 1866. This average rate was maintained in 1869, after which there was an increase to $17.10 in 1875; to $18.52 in 1880 or 1881; to $19.22 in 1885; and in 1909 to $25.46. During the entire period the wage rate increased about two-thirds. From 1866 to 1909 the increase in the North Atlantic States was from $22.04 to $30.89; in the South Atlantic States, from $10.67 to $18.76; in the North Central States, from $20.39 to $30.55; in the South Central States, from $12.57 to $20.27; and in the Western States, from $40.28 to $44.35, a rate of increase in the last-mentioned group far below that of the other divisions.

The foregoing are money rates of wages, and do not include supplemental wages not expressed in money which are more or less customary in all parts of the country. Among the items of supplemental wages are use of dwelling, often with garden and accommodations for cow and swine; wood for fuel; pasture for cow, horse, or swine; and other items.

For only two years, 1866 and 1909, was the wage rate ascertained for the outdoor labor of men per month in hiring by the season without board, and the rates are higher than they are for hiring by the year. In 1866 the average rate was $18.08; in 1909, $28.22.

The highest monthly rate, in hiring by the season, paid in any geographic division in 1909 was $48.04 in the Western; after which follow in order, $35.11 in the North Atlantic; $33.64 in the North Central; $22.48 in the South Central; and $20.86 in the South Atlantic.

During the period 1890–1906 wage rates were not ascertained for hiring by the year and season separately, but for the two combined, and the hirings were combined for 1909. During this period monthly wage rates in hiring for the season and year combined, without board, increased from $19.45 to $27.43. The increase in the North Atlantic division was from $24.72 to $33.68; in the South Atlantic from $13.94 to $20.13; in the North Central from $22.25 to $32.90; in the South Central from $16.10 to $21.85; and in the Western from $33.96 to $47.24.

Rates Per Day

Every one of the nineteen investigations of the wage rates of farm labor included the rate per day in harvest work with board. At the beginning of the period, in 1866, the rate was $1.04 and the increase was to $1.18 in 1875, followed by a decline to $1.04 at the end of the industrial depression of that time, after which there was an advance continuously to $1.20 in 1882; but the depression of 1884–1886 and a period of overproduction and low prices for farm products reduced the rate below that of 1882 until, in the depression of 1893–1897, the rate was as low as 96 cents, after which three was a marked advance to $1.45 in 1906 and a rate of $1.43 in 1909.

Among the geographic divisions in 1909 the highest wage rate for harvest work with board was $2.02 in the Western States, after which follow in order, $1.87 in the North Central States; $1.62 in the North Atlantic; $1.10 in the South Central; and $1.03 in the South Atlantic.

In the North Atlantic division the rate increased throughout this period, 1866–1909, from $1.32 to $1.62; in the South Atlantic division from 79 cents to $1.03; in the North Central States from $1.31 to $1.87; in the South Central States from 92 cents to $1.10; and in the Western States from $1.93 to $2.02.

Lower rates than the foregoing were paid for day labor in other than harvest work with board. The average for the United States begins with 64 cents in 1866, followed by fluctuations similar to those of harvest wages, and ends the period in 1909 with $1.03.

The gain during the forty-four years was from 86 cents to $1.16 in the North Atlantic division; from 43 cents to 73 cents in the South Atlantic; from 83 cents to $1.32 in the North Central; and from 55 cents to 82 cents in the South Central; while on the contrary there was a decline from $1.49 in 1866 and $1.50 in 1869 to $1.48 in 1909 in the Western States.

Industrialism, Trade, and Transportation

Several causes affecting farm wages were investigated in 1909. In the matter that follows dependence was placed on the census of 1900, except for the rates of wages. Farm wages are high in States in which there has been large development of manufacturing, mining, mechanical pursuits, trade, and transportation in comparison with States poorly or less developed in these directions, and conversely wages are lower in those States in which agriculture is predominant than in States where it is a subordinate industry. States in which the urban population is a large percentage of the entire population are those States in which the wages of farm labor are higher than in those in which urban population is of minor account.

Relation Between Production and Wage Rates

Necessarily in the long course of time the employing farmer must depend upon the value of his products for the wages that he pays to his laborers. He can not go on indefinitely paying wages out of capital, but he must in the general experience pay them out of farm products. Hence it follows as a matter of inference that farm wages may be higher in those States in which the value of the products per worker is higher than in those States in which the value of products per worker is lower.

This conclusion is amply substantiated in the investigation of farm wages in 1909. The highest wages are paid in the Western division of States, and in this division the average value of farm products per agricultural worker in 1899 was $759. Next below this division in both rate of wages and average value of farm products per worker, $678, is the North Central division; and third in order in both respects is the North Atlantic division. The South Central division is fourth in order in both rate of wages and value of products per worker, which is $271; and last of all is the South Atlantic division in both respects, the average value of products per worker being $233. These values stand for gross amount of products, and not for net wealth produced.

Wages Supplementary to Money Rates

The nominal money rate of wages paid for farm labor by no means fully represents the real wages received by the laborer. There are two important additions to the nominal money rate of wages which enter little if at all into the thoughts and plans of agricultural laborers. A farm laborer receiving, say, $30 per month, as he did in the North Atlantic and North Central States in 1909, often receives supplemental wages in the form of use of dwelling and garden, accommodations for cow, pigs, and poultry.

The value of the supplemental wage allowances was investigated in all parts of the United States, with the result that their estimated value per month is relatively a large addition to the nominal rate.

In the case of the man receiving $30 in money wages, the rental value of dwelling and appurtenances would probably be about $3.25 to $4.50. If the farm laborer gets firewood as an item of supplemental wages, its reported value per month ranges from about $1.06 to $2.39, the latter figure being applicable to the $30 laborer in the North.

It often happens that the laborer receives supplementary to his money rate of wages the privilege of pasturing his cow, horse, or swine, and the estimated monthly cost of this as an average for the United States is from 65 cents to $1.61. Or, there may be an allowance for feed outside of pasturage for cow, or horse, or swine, or poultry, and the cost of this as established by this investigation ranges from $1.11 to $3.11.

A very common supplementary wage allowance in some parts of the country, especially in the North Central States, is the frequent use of a horse and buggy by the farm laborer. The monthly value of this has been estimated by the correspondents of the Bureau of Statistics in all parts of the United States, with the result that it ranges from 87 cents to $2.37. Or, the laborer may own a horse, and stabling and feed are provided by his employer in addition to the money rate of wages. For this service it is estimated that the cost ranges from 45 cents to $2 per month throughout the entire country.

Perhaps the laborer's family also receives without specific charge a considerable quantity of fruit. The value of this fruit is estimated on a monthly basis, although it may have been received within one season, and ranges from 62 cents to $1.64 monthly throughout the year. If the laborer is a single man, his employer hires a woman to do his laundry work as a part of the family wash, and the value of this service is estimated to range from 75 cents to $2 per month.

No laborer receives all of these supplemental wages, but it often happens that he receives more than one item of them. If he is a man of family, an increase of his monthly money rate of wages by $5 to $10 worth of supplemental allowances and even more is not uncommon in many States.

Advantage of Farm Wages in Purchasing Power

If the farm laborer is comparing his nominal rate of money wages with the similar rate of the motorman or conductor of the electric railway who lives in the city, he must take into consideration the less costly living that he gets on the farm. In some respects it is a better living, against which of course there must be made a set-off of features that are in some respects worse.

The farm laborer gets many things at prices which are as low as wholesale prices in the motorman's city, and sometimes lower. He can get his supply of poultry at low prices, if he does not produce it himself; and so with eggs, milk, and butter; sometimes flour and meal; very likely potatoes and other vegetables and fruit. At low prices he may also get fresh and salt pork, his fuel and, in many parts of the country, his tobacco. If he pays rent for his dwelling, he will pay, say, $40 per year, whereas the motorman with a family pays $150.

All things considered — the allowances received by the farm laborer supplemental to the money rate of wages and the lower cost of many things that he buys as compared with the cost in the city — the farm laborer receiving nominally $30 per month really gets, in comparison with his situation as it would be if he lived in the city, perhaps more than the motorman or street-car conductor gets, and very likely in most cases a larger amount than he would be likely to earn in any occupation open to him in the city.

The money wage rates of farm laborers have increased in a marked degree within the last few years, and in this respect a comparison may be made with the wages of workingmen. A still further comparison may be made between the purchasing power of the wages of the farm laborer in terms of food and the purchasing power of the wages of workingmen. The investigations of the United States Bureau of Labor make possible this comparison.

If the mean wage rates of agricultural laborers for the years 1890–1898 be regarded as 100, the rate per month of the outdoor labor of men on farms in hiring by the year and season in 1890 is represented by 100.9. The relative number increased to 103.6 in 1893, and there was a sudden decline to 96.3 in 1894, after which there was an unbroken increase in this relative number until in 1907 it was 141.1.

The purchasing power of the wages of the farm laborer in 1907 in terms of actual food consumption in comparison with the mean of 1890–1898 is represented by the comparative number 117.1. In 1907 the corresponding relative number standing for the wages of the workingman was 122.5 and the purchasing power of his wages in terms of actual food consumption in 1907 is represented by the relative number 101.7 as compared with the mean of 1890–1898 which, as before stated, is represented by 100.

As time advanced after 1890 the farm laborer, setting out with wages having a relative purchasing power in terms of food about equal to that of the workingman, passed him in this respect in 1899, and rapidly gained upon him in subsequent years.

Qualifications of Laborers to Become Tenants

In the investigation of farm wages in 1909 inquiries were made to ascertain to what extent male outdoor farm laborers were qualified to become farm tenants. In the opinion of the correspondents who supplied answers, 48 per cent of the laborers of the South Central States are so qualified; 46 per cent in the North Central States; 37 per cent in the Western; 35 per cent in the South Atlantic; and, lowest of all, 33 per cent in the North Atlantic States.

Ability of Laborers and Tenants to Become Owners

Correspondents were asked whether it was reasonably possible for farm laborers and tenants to save enough to buy a farm that would support a family even with the help of a mortgage, and their replies indicated that 72 per cent of farm laborers and tenants find it reasonably possible to acquire farm ownership. The percentages for the geographic divisions are all over 70 and under 80 — a remarkably uniform condition of affairs with regard to this matter throughout the United States.

Small Movement from City to Farm

The movement from city to farm for the purpose of permanent farm life and labor, either for hire or under ownership, has hardly become general enough in this country to present recognizable proportions. There is a little of this movement here and a little there, but nearly all cases are sporadic.

But there is one sort of labor that goes from city to farm which has become large enough to be perceptible, and that is seasonal labor for employment, not in general farming operations, but for special purposes. The migration of men from cities to follow the wheat harvest from Oklahoma to North Dakota is the best known feature of this sort of farm labor. It is not so generally known that women and children and some men, too, go from the city to the farm at certain seasons to harvest cucumbers to be sold to the pickle factory; to pick, grade, pack, and dry fruits; to harvest hops and berries, and dig potatoes, and so on with other crops that need a rush of labor at time of harvest. Some labor of this sort is applied also to the cultivation of crops, as in pulling weeds from beets and onions, but this labor does not seem to be used much for cultivating crops and not at all for planting.

Holding the Country Population to the Soil

There are no indications that the town and city population will supply any considerable part of the agricultural labor of the future. At any rate, the farmer would not need to get his labor from the cities if he could hold the country population to the soil, and the recognition of the importance of retaining the children on the farm and of keeping country labor from migrating to cities is governing most of the work by Nation and States in behalf of agriculture.

The old practice was to trust to the printed page for the instruction of the farmer, but in the course of time it was found that this was poorly productive of results. Then followed the farmers' institute movement, which consisted of lectures; sometimes later with practical demonstrations.

In the meantime the United States Department of Agriculture and the experiment stations got into more practical lines of work by means of special advice in particular cases, formerly by mail and now also by personal visits; so that it has been discovered that the most successful promotion of agricultural knowledge and practice is caused by practical demonstration under the observation of the farmers to be instructed.

The largest exponent of this latter plan of instruction is the farmers' cooperative demonstration work, maintained in the South by the Department of Agriculture with outside financial assistance and with the effective help of farmers and planters, without whose aid it would be a failure.

Along with the foregoing is the very recent movement to instruct country children in agriculture at the beginning of their school life and to continue this instruction in the high school and the college. In this way the foundation will be laid for successful farming, and such farming implies the retention of children upon the farm.

Still further and to the same end, many agencies are at work upon the country people to improve their dwellings, their modes of living, their home life and their social life, which are already beginning to count against the unpleasantness of country life and in favor of making such life attractive. Influences of this sort, joined to the agricultural education of the young and to the practical teaching of the farmer how to do by doing, at the time when farming is prosperous and profitable, may be depended upon to save to our agriculture all the labor it will need for the maintenance of our National self-sufficiency.

Act Regulating Sale of Insecticides and Fungicides, 1910

From 36 U.S. Statutes at Large 331.

For preventing the manufacture, sale, or transportation of adulterated or misbranded Paris greens, lead arsenates, and other insecticides, and also fungicides, and for regulating traffic therein, and for other purposes.

Be it enacted by the Senate and House of Representatives of the United States of America in Congress assembled, That it shall be unlawful for any person to manufacture within any Territory or the District of Columbia any insecticide, Paris green, lead arsenate, or fungicide which is adulterated or misbranded within the meaning of this Act; and any person who shall violate any of the provisions of this section shall be guilty of a misdemeanor, and shall, upon conviction thereof, be fined not to exceed two hundred dollars for the first offense, and upon conviction for each subsequent offense be fined not to exceed three hundred dollars, or sentenced to imprisonment for not to exceed one year, or both such fine and imprisonment, in the discretion of the court.

SEC. 2. That the introduction into any State or Territory or the District of Columbia from any other State or Territory or the District of Columbia, or from any foreign country, or shipment to any foreign country, of any insecticide, or Paris green, or lead arsenate, or fungicide which is adulterated or misbranded within the meaning of this Act is hereby prohibited; and any person who shall ship or deliver for shipment from any State or Territory or the District of Columbia to any other State or Territory or the District of Columbia, or to a foreign country, or who shall receive in any State or Territory or the District of Columbia from any other State or Territory or the District of Columbia, or foreign country, and having so received, shall deliver, in original unbroken packages, for pay or otherwise, or offer to deliver, to any other person, any such article so adulterated or misbranded within the meaning of this Act, or any person who shall sell or offer for sale in the District of Columbia or any Territory of the United States any such adulterated or misbranded insecticide, or Paris green, or lead arsenate, or fungicide, or export or offer to export the same to any foreign country, shall be guilty of a misdemeanor, and for such offense be fined not exceeding two hundred dollars for the first offense, and upon conviction for each subsequent offense not exceeding three hundred dollars, or be imprisoned not exceeding one year, or both, in the discretion of the court: *Provided,* That no article shall be deemed misbranded or adulterated within the provisions of this Act when intended for export to any foreign country and prepared or packed according to the specifications or directions of the foreign purchaser; but if said articles shall be in fact sold or offered for sale for domestic use or consumption, then this proviso shall not exempt said article from the operation of any of the other provisions of this Act.

SEC. 3. That the Secretary of the Treasury, the Secretary of Agriculture, and the Secretary of Commerce and Labor shall make uniform rules and regulations for carrying out the provisions of this Act, including the collection and examination of specimens of insecticides, Paris greens, lead arsenates, and fungicides manufactured or offered for sale in the District of Columbia or in any Territory of the United States, or which shall be offered for sale in unbroken packages in any State other than that in which they shall have been respectively manufactured or produced, or which shall be received from any foreign country or intended for shipment to any foreign country, or which may be submitted for examination by the director of the experiment station of any State, Territory, or the District of Columbia (acting under the direction of the Secretary of Agriculture), or at any domestic or foreign port through which such product is offered for interstate commerce, or for export or import between the United States and any foreign port or country.

SEC. 4. That the examination of specimens of insecticides, Paris greens, lead arsenates, and fungicides shall be made in the Department of Agriculture, by such existing bureau or bureaus as may be directed by the Secretary, for the purpose of determining from such examination whether such articles are adulterated or misbranded within the meaning of this Act; and if it shall appear from any such examination that any of such specimens are adulterated or misbranded within the meaning of this Act, the Secretary of Agriculture shall cause notice thereof to be given to the party from whom such sample was obtained. Any party so notified shall be given an opportunity to be heard, under such rules and regulations as may be prescribed as aforesaid, and if it appears that any of the provisions of this Act have been violated by such party, then the Secretary of Agriculture shall at once certify the facts to the proper United States district attorney, with a copy of the results of the analysis or the examination of such article duly authenticated by the analyst or officer making such examination, under the oath of such officer. After judgment of the court, notice shall be given by publication in such manner as may be prescribed by the rules and regulations aforesaid.

SEC. 5. That it shall be the duty of each district attorney to whom the Secretary of Agriculture shall report any violation of this Act, or to whom any director of experiment station or agent of any State, Territory, or the District of Columbia, under authority of the Secretary of Agriculture, shall present satisfactory evidences of any such violation, to cause appropriate proceedings to be commenced and prosecuted in the proper courts of the United States, without delay, for the enforcement of the penalties as in such case herein provided.

SEC. 6. That the term "insecticide" as used in this Act shall include any substance or mixture of substances intended to be used for preventing, destroying, repelling, or mitigating any insects which may infest vegetation, man or other animals, or households, or be present in any environment whatsoever. The term "Paris green" as used in this Act shall include the product sold in commerce as Paris green and chemically known as the aceto-arsenite of copper. The term "lead arsenate" as used in this Act shall include the product or products sold in commerce as lead arsenate and consisting chemically of products derived from arsenic acid (H_3AsO_4) by replacing one or more hydrogen atoms by lead. That the term "fungicide" as used in this Act shall include any substance or mixture of substances intended to be used for preventing, destroying, repelling, or mitigating any and all fungi that may infest vegetation or be present in any environment whatsoever.

SEC. 7. That for the purpose of this Act an article shall be deemed to be adulterated —

In the case of Paris green: First, if it does not contain at least fifty per centum of arsenious oxide; second, if it contains arsenic in water-soluble forms equivalent to more than three and one-half per centum of arsenious oxide; third, if any substance has been mixed and packed with it so as to reduce or lower or injuriously affect its quality or strength.

In the case of lead arsenate: First, if it contains more than fifty per centum of water; second, if it contains total arsenic equivalent to less than twelve and one-half per centum of arsenic oxid (As_2O_5); third, if it contains arsenic in water-soluble forms equivalent to more than seventy-five one-hundredths per centum of arsenic oxid (As_2O_5); fourth, if any substances have been mixed and packed with it so as to reduce, lower, or injuriously affect its quality or strength: *Provided, however,* That extra water may be added to lead arsenate (as described in this paragraph) if the resulting mixture is labeled lead arsenate and water, the percentage of extra water being plainly and correctly stated on the label.

In the case of insecticides or fungicides, other than Paris green and lead arsenate: First, if its strength or purity fall below the professed standard or quality under which it is sold; second, if any substance has been substituted wholly or in part for the article; third, if any valuable constituent of the article has been wholly or in part abstracted; fourth, if it is intended for use on vegetation and shall contain any substance or substances which, although preventing, destroying, repelling, or mitigating insects, shall be injurious to such vegetation when used.

SEC. 8. That the term "misbranded" as used herein shall apply to all insecticides, Paris greens, lead arsenates, or fungicides, or articles which enter into the composition of insecticides or fungicides, the package or label of which shall bear any statement, design, or device regarding such article or the ingredients or substances contained therein which shall be false or misleading in any particular, and to all insecticides, Paris greens, lead arsenates, or fungicides which are falsely branded as to the State, Territory, or country in which they are manufactured or produced.

That for the purpose of this Act an article shall be deemed to be misbranded —

In the case of insecticides, Paris greens, lead arsenates, and fungicides: First, if it be an imitation or offered for sale under the name of another article; second, if it be labeled or branded so as to deceive or mislead the purchaser, or if the contents of the package as originally put up shall have been removed in whole or in part and other contents shall have been placed in such package; third, if in package form, and the contents are stated in terms of weight or measure, they are not plainly and correctly stated on the outside of the package.

In the case of insecticides (other than Paris greens and lead arsenates) and fungicides: First, if it contains arsenic in any of its combinations or in the elemental form and the total amount of arsenic present (expressed as per centum of metallic arsenic) is not stated on the label; second, if it contains arsenic in any of its combinations or in the elemental form and the amount of arsenic in water-soluble forms (expressed as per centum of metallic arsenic) is not stated on the label; third, if it consists partially or completely of an inert substance or substances which do not prevent, destroy, repel, or mitigate insects or fungi and does not have the names and percentage amounts of each and every one of such inert ingredients plainly and correctly stated on the label: *Provided, however*, That in lieu of naming and stating the percentage amount of each and every inert ingredient the producer may at his discretion state plainly upon the label the correct names and percentage amounts of each and every ingredient of the insecticide or fungicide having insecticidal or fungicidal properties, and make no mention of the inert ingredients, except in so far as to state the total percentage of inert ingredients present.

SEC. 9. That no dealer shall be prosecuted under the provisions of this Act when he can establish a guaranty signed by the wholesaler, jobber, manufacturer, or other party residing in the United States, from whom he purchased such articles, to the effect that the same is not adulterated or misbranded within the meaning of this Act, designating it. Said guaranty, to afford protection, shall contain the name and address of the party or parties making the sale of such articles to such dealer, and in such case said party or parties shall be amenable to the prosecutions, fines, and other penalties which would attach in due course to the dealer under the provisions of this Act.

SEC. 10. That any insecticide, Paris green, lead arsenate, or fungicide that is adulterated or misbranded within the meaning of this Act and is being transported from one State, Territory, or District, to another for sale, or, having been transported, remains unloaded, unsold, or in original unbroken packages, or if it be sold or offered for sale in the District of Columbia or any Territory of the United States, or if it be imported from a foreign country for sale, shall be liable to be proceeded against in any district court of the United States within the district wherein the same is found and seized for confiscation by a process of libel for condemnation.

And if such article is condemned as being adulterated or misbranded, within the meaning of this Act, the same shall be disposed of by destruction or sale as the said court may direct, and the proceeds thereof, if sold, less the legal costs and charges, shall be paid into the Treasury of the United States, but such goods shall not be sold in any jurisdiction contrary to the provisions of this Act or the laws of that jurisdiction: *Provided, however*, That upon the payment of the costs of such libel proceedings and the execution and delivery of a good and sufficient bond to the effect that such articles shall not be sold or otherwise disposed of contrary to the provisions of this Act or the laws of any State, Territory, or District, the court may by order direct that such articles be delivered to the owner thereof. The proceedings of such libel cases shall conform, as near as may be, to the proceedings in admiralty, except that either party may demand trial by jury of any issue of fact joined in any such case, and all such proceedings shall be at the suit of and in the name of the United States.

SEC. 11. That the Secretary of the Treasury shall deliver to the Secretary of Agriculture, upon his request, from time to time, samples of insecticides, Paris greens, lead arsenates, and fungicides which are being imported into the United States or offered for import, giving notice thereof to the owner or consignee, who may appear before the Secretary of Agriculture and have the right to introduce testimony; and if it appear from the examination of such samples that any insecticide, or Paris green, or lead arsenate, or fungicide offered to be imported into the United States is adulterated or misbranded within the meaning of this Act, or is otherwise dangerous to the health of the people of the United States, or is of a kind forbidden entry into or forbidden to be sold or restricted in sale in the country in which it is made or from which it is exported, or is otherwise falsely labeled in any respect, the said article shall be refused admission, and the Secretary of the Treasury shall refuse delivery to the consignee and shall cause the destruction of any goods refused delivery which shall not be exported by the consignee within three months from the date of notice of such refusal under such regulations as the Secretary of the Treasury may prescribe: *Provided,* That the Secretary of the Treasury may deliver to the consignee such goods pending examination and decision in the matter on execution of a penal bond for the amount of the full invoice value of such goods, together with the duty thereon, and on refusal to return such goods for any cause to the custody of the Secretary of the Treasury, when demanded, for the purpose of excluding them from the country, or for any other purpose, said consignee shall forfeit the full amount of the bond: *And provided further,* That all charges for storage, cartage, and labor on goods which are refused admission or delivery shall be paid by the owner or consignee, and in default of such payment shall constitute a lien against any future importation made by such owner or consignee.

SEC. 12. That the term "Territory," as used in this Act, shall include the District of Alaska and the insular possessions of the United States. The word "person," as used in this Act, shall be construed to import both the plural and the singular, as the case demands, and shall include corporations, companies, societies, and associations. When construing and enforcing the provisions of this Act, the act, omission, or failure of any officer, agent, or other person acting for or employed by any corporation, company, society, or association, within the scope of his employment or office, shall in every case be also deemed to be the act, omission, or failure of such corporation, company, society, or association, as well as that of the other person.

SEC. 13. That this Act shall be known and referred to as "The Insecticide Act of 1910."

SEC. 14. That this Act shall be in force and effect from and after the first day of January, nineteen hundred and eleven.

Approved, April 26, 1910.

Farmers Conference of North Carolina Negroes

From *Pittsburgh Courier,* **March 25, 1911.**

Greensboro, N.C. — (Special.) — The largest number of Negro farmers that has ever assembled at one place in North Carolina, for their peculiar interest met in the second annual Farmer's conference at the North Carolina Agricultural and Mechanical college for the colored race in this city. Dr. James B. Dudley, the president of this excellent institution, is a potent factor in the farmers' activities in his state and this enthusiastic meeting, which was highly beneficial, is due largely to the great work of Doctor Dudley.

Every section of the state was represented. Lectures the first day were by Professor Conover, of the state department of agriculture and Doctor Flower, assistant state veterinarian. Among the farmers who spoke during the afternoon of the first day were: J. K. Lytle and S. W. Slade. Their talks were practical and evinced much good.

The sessions on the second day were given over to lectures and practical demonstrations. In the forenoon lectures were given by Professor Conover and Doctor Flowe. the farmers were deeply interested in a clinic of sick animals which was held by Doctor Flowe. Following an address by C. R. Hudson, state agent for the farmers' co-operative demonstration work, Bureau of Plant Industry, Washington, D.C., the farmers' expressed themselves on various phases of farm activities. W. R. Richardson of Anson County, said that during the past year he had made on 20 acres of land 16 bales of cotton; 300 bushels of corn; 170 bushels of wheat; 190 bushels of oats, and sold $100.00 worth of hogs. S. W. White of Cararrus county, proved himself to be witty and yet philosophical. He, in part, said: "My motto is never let your wagon break down going away from town, but let it break down going to town with things to sell." The third day was "Seed Corn Day." The following prominent men gave practical and comprehensive lectures that absorbed the attention of every farmer to the extent that made many queries: C. R. Hudson, state agent; Professor Burgess from the state department of agriculture; Professor Sherman, state entomologist; Professor C. K. Graham of Hampton Normal and Industrial Institute, and Mr. Long, a farmer trustee of the institution, but now connected with the department of agriculture, in charge of the farmers' co-operative demonstration work.

The last day the cardinal features were the lectures of Doctor Stedman of the National department of agriculture; two lectures on spraying and spraying mixtures by Professor Sherman.

— George F. King

Development of Grain Sorghums, 1914

From Carleton R. Ball, "The Grain Sorghums: Immigrant Crops that Have Made Good," U.S. Department of Agriculture, *Yearbook*, 1913, pp. 221–38.

Introduction

The world is being searched for new plants for the American farm and garden. Some of those introduced in comparatively recent years have become staple and valuable crops. Among these are durum wheats, Swedish Select and Kherson Sixty-Day oats, and others. We call them no longer foreigners but Americans. Other introductions which now seem strange and new will become familiar in the next decade or two. Many others will never become known because they are not adapted to our environmental or economic conditions.

The grain sorghums are rather stout and mostly tall plants of the grass family, distantly related to corn. The grain is not found in ears, for they have none, but in heads which they bear where corn carries its tassel. There are several groups of these grain makers, known by different names. Among them are the durras, including feterita, and the milos, which have mostly short, fat heads and large flat seeds; the stout, broad-leaved kafirs, which have longer heads, full of small, egg-shaped seeds, and the slender, dry-stemmed kaoliangs with mostly small, oval seeds borne in heads of various shapes.

While not of wide adaptation under present conditions, the grain sorghums are so perfectly adapted and so evidently supreme in their particular domain that they achieve an importance in excess of their statistical rank as farm crops. To those who wonder why their use has not developed more rapidly, in view of their proven value, it can only be said that changes in crops or cropping methods must necessarily be slow. Progress must be measured not by years but by decades if stability of production is to be assured. Farmers are confessedly conservative. It is well. Were it not so the world might face famine as often as business faces panic.

In The Ancestral Home — Users and Uses

Wherever the white man's love of adventure and discovery has led him, he has always found primitive peoples using strange new plants for food. The early explorers and colonists of America found the Amerinds cultivating maize and the native Indians of the Titicaca plateau in Peru, at elevations of 11,000 to 14,000 feet, making use of quinoa, a kind of lamb's-quarter (*Chenopodium quinoa*). The traders and adventurers who first touched India and China gained their principal impressions from the port cities and recorded that the people of those countries lived chiefly on rice, a fiction that still persists. Later travelers, who reached the interior, found wheat, sorghums, and millets to be staple articles of diet. The sorghums were used mainly by the poorer classes or in times of scarcity.

In India the two large southern presidencies, Bombay and Madras, nearly 1,500 miles long and half as wide, are the best-known areas of sorghum production. The crop is important, however, in the States lying farther to the north. It was estimated a few years ago that the area annually devoted to sorghums in India was 25,000,000 acres. More than 300 varieties have been imported from there and grown by the United States Department of Agriculture. A great diversity of forms was found, the plants varying from dwarf and stocky to tall and slender and the heads having as wide a range of variation. Some curious varieties were found, having two seeds in each spikelet instead of the customary one, a phenomenon occurring regularly in occasional spikelets of cultivated sorgos in this country. Other forms had long and pointed glumes, like the hulls of oats, projecting far beyond the apex of the seed.

In China, Manchuria, and Chosen (Korea) a distinct group of grain-producing sorghums, the kaoliangs, have been developed. They range from Yunnan, on the mountainous frontier of Tibet, to far Manchuria, a stretch of more than 2,000 miles. Dwarfs less than a yard in height and slender sapling stems 20 feet or more tall are found. Between these are all the intermediates one might well expect. In head forms and seed colors the gamut is equally complete.

It is among the frugal and industrious Chinese and Manchus that the grain sorghums are put to the most varied uses. Besides the meal and porridge made from the seeds and the fodder derived from the whole plant, the thrashed heads are used for fuel and certain sorts for brooms; the leaves are used for fodder and for mats; the stalks for baskets, light bridges, fences, fuel, hedges, house-building material, kite frames, laths, matting, playthings, posts, thatching, trellises, windbreaks, withes, and window shades, while even the roots and attached stubble are carefully dug and saved for fuel. The seed is also commonly used to make a fermented drink, or beer.

When we survey Africa, however, the real abundance and diversity of the cultivated members of the sorghum family are seen. They are found in every nook and corner of the great peninsular continent. Five thousand miles from northern sea to southern cape she lies, and 4,000 from ocean to ocean. From Morocco to Egypt, from Egypt to the Cape; again from the Cape northward to the old Slave Coast; and throughout the length of the Sudan, from Senegal on the west to Abyssinia on the east, this crop occurs. On the dry plains, in the oases of the Sahara, on high plateaus, and in mountain valleys, in tropical jungles and temperate veldts, throughout the length and breadth of Africa, sorghum is the one ever-present crop, though the forms are as diverse as the conditions under which they grow. The plants vary in height from 3 or 4 to probably 20 feet. The heads vary in shape and structure from ovate and densely compact to loosely cylindrical, to fan-shaped forms, and to long and flowing feathery plumes. In length they vary from 5 to 25 inches. The seeds vary in color from white to pink, red, brown, and yellow, with an occasional tinge of blue. Everywhere they are used by the native tribes for human food, for the making of fermented drinks, and as fodder for live stock where such is owned.

Immigrants in a New Country

The Durras

In 1874, two durras, Brown and White, arrived at the port of San Francisco, though whether by first cabin, second cabin, or steerage is not recorded. Their passage had been booked from Egypt, but it is now known that their African home was in the old Barbary States of Algeria and Tunis and in the oases of the Sahara. Out to the ranches in the two great inland valleys of the State they went and proved their entire ability to withstand the far-famed California climate. During the next few years they were allowed to occupy the wide space between rows of young grapes, almonds, and plums until it was needed by the growing fruits. In return, they fed the rancher's work stock, cows, and chickens.

The Kafirs

While this little foreign colony was being planted in California, something was doing on the Atlantic coast, 2,500 miles away. In the year 1876 a great international exposition was held in Philadelphia to commemorate the hundredth anniversary of American independence. Among the many foreign exhibits at the Centennial Exposition was that of the Orange River Colony, later known as the Orange Free State, and now a part of the great Union of South Africa. In this exhibit were two samples of small, hard, egg-shaped seeds, one white, the other a red-brown, two varieties of the so-called "Kafir corn" of South Africa.

How slender is the chain which connects these two samples of seed lying in a Philadelphia exhibit with the thriving industry of the dry-land West! Probably hundreds and thousands of visitors looked at the strange new seeds and thought no more of them, or noted only that they were sorghums from South Africa, whence had come, some 20 years before, the sorgos or sweet sorghums which America still hoped would one day fill her sugar bowl. Of all these sightseers, only two, so far as we have any record, were interested enough to ask for samples. Perhaps these two had come in touch at Philadelphia; who knows? One was a Georgia planter, Mr. J. A. Meeker, of Marietta, who took the seeds home and grew the plants for a few years, but finally lost his stock of seed by mice and rats. The second was an English officer from Egypt, said to have been a Gen. Graves, who traveled through the South after visiting the exposition. He left a very small quantity of the white seed at the Georgia State Department of Agriculture, during his stop in Atlanta.

On February 14, 1877, a thimbleful of the seed was sent by Dr. T. P. Janes, then State commissioner of agriculture, to Dr. J. H. Watkins, of Palmetto, Ga. For eight years, from 1877 to 1884, he grew it, selected it, and increased his stock of seed. In 1885 and 1886 he began to distribute it personally and through the Georgia State Department of Agriculture, and in 1886 through Hon. Norman J. Colman, United States Commissioner of Agriculture.

The Milos

Just at the time the White kafir was being sent out on its first missionary journeys to the dry-land West, there appeared a new sorghum immigrant in the South. It was first brought to notice in South Carolina, but no one knows just when or whence it came. Almost certainly, however, it arrived from Africa, and perhaps as a stowaway. Relatives have since been found in irrigated Egypt, but the same plant has not again appeared. In this country it was first known as "yellow millo maize." The crop most commonly known at that time as "millo maize," however, was a white-seeded variety from the West Indies, called there "Guinea corn" by the English and "petit millet" by the French. The yellow-seeded immigrant never became well known in the South, but was carried westward early by emigrating planters and soon became established in Texas.

Fighting Drought on the Plains

While the immigrant crops already described were finding place in the older settled States, the thin skirmish line of pioneer farmers had been thrown far out into the Great American Desert. These were followed closely by the larger army of settlers seeking homes on the newer, cheaper lands of the West.

Kansas bore the brunt of the battle against the desert. Oklahoma was largely closed to settlement until 1890, and much of western Texas was occupied and dominated by immense cattle ranches. Within the borders of Kansas, however, the influx of settlers was very rapid. The population increased more in the three years 1871–1873, inclusive, than in the entire decade previous. This was due partly to the early history of the State, partly to encouragement given to settlers by State agencies, and partly because of the early building of two transcontinental railways across the Commonwealth.

Settlers from the older and more humid States, good farmers under the conditions with which they were familiar, poured out into the Plains area during the decade beginning with 1871. The crop varieties used were those adapted to more humid conditions. The principles of dry farming were then unknown, and experiments to determine them were not yet begun.

Disappointment and discouragement awaited many of the new settlers, especially those in the farthest West. Climatic conditions were much more severe than they had experienced or expected. Years of deficient rainfall and drought occurred. Sometimes gales of wind in spring destroyed young crops and moved vast quantities of soil from the fields to fence rows, farmyards, and other drift-making shelters. Hot and scorching winds in midsummer sometimes blasted crops in a single day. Immense swarms of hungry grasshoppers moved to and fro during 1874, devouring growing crops almost in a night. They appeared again in some sections for periods of two and three years thereafter. These conditions, especially the destructive winds and recurring drought, were wholly new and strange to most of the farmers.

Successive periods of drought rolled back the advancing wave of settlement time after time, now here, now there, leaving deserted farms and ruined villages in their wake. Settlers surveying the grass-covered and flower-tinted prairies in the warmth and beauty of spring could not realize the pitiless sky and parched earth of many a midsummer. It seemed to them incredible that so fair a prospect could be utterly mocked by the lack of a few inches of rain. Nor was the advice given them always of the best. As late as the end of 1880, a year of great drought, Kansas settlers were assured by the then professor of meteorology at their State University that increased rainfall with increased settlement was practically a certainty. Doubtless he was misled by the unsuspected incompleteness of early rainfall records from frontier army posts and by a certain apparent periodicity of precipitation in that area. At any rate, most who heard believed, because it was what they wanted to believe. Bad as 1880 had been, 1881 was far worse. Corn was a complete failure in the western counties, and the average acre yield for the entire State was less than 20 bushels. The native vegetation of the Plains consists of types which can withstand such adverse conditions, through one adaptation or another. Manifestly farm crops and farm practices also must have special adaptations in order to be successful in such an environment.

New Crops and a New Hope

Under the conditions described, one may well believe that earnest search was made for adapted crops. Sorghums were quickly in the minds of many. Sorgos or sweet sorghums had been grown by the earliest settlers and their drought resistance proved. Were all sorghums drought resistant? No one knew, but plenty were willing to try. Out in California, the two durras, there called "Egyptian corn," had been found to grow well on dry farms. They were brought to Kansas in 1879 and in the years 1880–1882 over 30,000 acres were grown annually, after which their production declined. In spite of their ability to withstand drought, they were not profitable. Of low stature and scanty foliage, they yielded little fodder where fodder was greatly in demand. The heads were pendent and troublesome to gather. The grain also shattered badly in the field in windy weather and during harvest. So sorgos were grown for forage and the search for an adapted grain crop continued.

In 1885 Dr. Watkins and the Georgia State Department of Agriculture first began to distribute the White kafir, and in 1886 the United States Department of Agriculture took part in the propaganda. As soon as it reached the dry lands it was seen to be adapted to the conditions. By 1888 it was appearing on the farms of Kansas. It was as drought resistant as any sorghum in the peculiar ability to suspend growth through considerable periods of drought and to resume growth when favorable conditions were restored. The stalks were erect and leafy and remained green until the seed was ripe, thus making good fodder as well as grain. The seed remained firmly held in the glumes while the crop cured in the field, thus preventing any waste. Here was the ideal crop for the dry country. Farm settlement took a fresh start, and the new crop and the new farm developed together.

Data on the acreage of kafir were first available for 1893, when there were 47,000 acres in Kansas. The acreage increased 100 per cent annually for the next three years and continued to increase to the end of the first decade covered by statistics, reaching high-water mark at three-quarters of a million acres in 1902. This maximum followed the seriously unfavorable season of 1901, when corn was a total failure in the western sections and yielded little more than 6 bushels to the acre for the entire State. Two or three years more favorable to corn and the lack of a profitable market for surplus kafir then checked the increase for the next eight years. From 1903 to 1910 the Kansas grain-sorghum acreage varied between 530,000 and 740,000 acres annually. In Oklahoma from 1904 to 1910 the area varied between 390,000 and 685,000 acres, the maximum occurring in 1909.

Meantime chemical analysis had shown the grain sorghums to be very similar to corn in composition. Digestion trials and feeding tests had proved them to have 90 per cent of the value of corn for feeding purposes. A 10 per cent advantage in drought resistance and consequent average yield would make the grain sorghums equal to corn as farm crops. This advantage they had, and more. At the same time field experiments with these crops were showing the need of new theories to account for the behavior of different varieties under similar conditions.

Resisting or Escaping Drought

That sorghums of all kinds were drought resistant was very early apparent. That some sorts escaped from as well as resisted drought was slower to be realized. Such varieties as did best in dry seasons were thought to be more drought resistant in some way than other varieties. Gradually came a better knowledge of the movement and storage of soil moisture and of its transpiration by dry-land crops. It was seen that earliness aided a crop to escape drought by shortening the period during which water was required. Dwarf stature and small leaf area also helped to reduce the quantity of water needed in any given period.

Thus was recognized the existence and value of characters which enable drought-resistant crops further to escape and evade drought. Dwarf plants with small leaf area may escape drought when it occurs because they use the stored soil water more slowly than larger plants with larger leaf areas. Thus the stored supply may last until they are mature or until the drought is broken. Earliness aids the plant to evade drought by bringing it to maturity before the drought occurs or becomes severe. When these principles became fully recognized, the quest for dwarf and early strains was given a great impetus. The need of such strains for use farther north and at higher elevations had been felt before. To this need was now added the equally pressing need for drought escapers.

Breeding Drought Escapers

The search for dwarf and early strains to meet these needs and conditions was begun promptly by the United States Department of Agriculture. While explorers ransacked the corners of the earth for desirable forms, breeding was commenced with the most promising material in hand.

A dwarf strain of milo, its origin unknown, was already here, needing little improvement except in the matter of pendent heads. The White kafir as originally introduced in the Plains was fairly dwarf and early, but it had one serious defect, namely, the tendency of the heads to remain partly included in the boot. This must be overcome if it was to be of value. Dwarf strains and early strains of Blackhull kafir, the favorite crop, were yet to be created.

From the many strains of Blackhull kafir under test a large number of head selections were made from stalks having low stature and other desirable characters. In the summer of 1908 an extra dwarf row appeared in the series of dwarf selections. From this row was bred the Dwarf kafir, now becoming so popular. It reaches a height of only 3 to 4 feet and matures 7 to 10 days earlier than ordinary acclimated strains of Blackhull kafir. It can thus be grown in a shorter season than other strains and is also more drought escaping. At the same time and from the same source was produced an early-maturing strain which retains the height of the ordinary kafir.

In 1907 another immigrant came to us out of Africa. This time it was from the wild and turbulent region of the British Egyptian Sudan — from historic Khartum, where "Chinese" Gordon wrought and ruled and where he finally perished in the fanatical uprising that closed the Sudan for long and bitter years. This durra variety, known as feterita, or Sudan durra, is marked by erect heads, white seed, fairly dwarf stature, and early maturity. These are all desirable characters, and it gives promise of some value as a dry-land crop. Just now enormously inflated values are being ascribed to it because in many cases it produced grain in 1913 when kafir and even milo failed. However, its larger, softer seed and somewhat weaker germination cause rather thinner stands than are obtained from kafir and milo. In the dry season of 1913 these thin stands were its salvation, as has been noted also in other seasons. What its permanent place and value shall be it is yet too early to predict.

It was soon found that the milos and durras could not be depended upon to furnish grain as far north as Nebraska and South Dakota. The heat units available, especially at night, seemed insufficient. Could sorghums be found which had acquired, through the centuries, that acclimation and adaptation to northern climates needed in this case? The southern boundary of South Dakota is in latitude 43° and the north line about 46°. The only region in the world which grows sorghums abundantly as far as 40° from the equator is Manchuria. Many varieties of the kaoliang from northern China, Manchuria, and Korea were obtained, tested, and classified. The earliest of all proved to be a plant of medium size from Manchuria, which was described and named Manchu Brown (C.I. Nos. 171, 261, and 328). While not a heavy yielder, it has consistently outyielded corn in the central part of

South Dakota and is now being distributed to South Dakota farmers by the State experiment station and the United States Department of Agriculture.

Making Good

During those years when the grain-sorghum acreage was increasing most rapidly, as also in the later 8-year period when it remained stationary, the area devoted to corn was steadily enlarged. Corn was king, his supremacy as yet unchallenged. To deny his royalty was treason. But the appreciation of kafir and milo as comparatively safe crops in dry seasons was increasing. So was the knowledge that corn was a doomed crop in a year of drought. Land sellers still said corn was the crop to grow; ergo, corn must be grown. But facts are stubborn things. The theory of increasing rainfall had long since been dried out of the most credulous minds. Empty pockets and empty stomachs speak louder than tongues and are far more efficient in opening eyes and disarming prejudice. Promoters and growers alike began to see a great light. Reduction of the corn acreage was openly advocated. Farmers, farm papers, scientists, merchants, bankers, land men, and railroads all joined in an aggressive campaign to promote the growing of kafir and milo instead of corn in the drier Plains. In Oklahoma it was even seriously proposed that credit and loans be denied to any farmer not planting at least a certain acreage of kafir. Doubtless some foolish talk was indulged in and much foolish advice given during the campaign, but of the results there can be no doubt. There was a decided decrease in the acreage of corn and a comparatively enormous increase in the area devoted to grain sorghums.

The coincidence of the declining corn area and the increasing acreage of kafir and milo in Kansas can be seen at a glance in figures 5 and 9. Figure 5 tells the story for Kansas as a whole and figure 9 for the 46 counties comprising the western half. In this State the grain-sorghum area jumped to 1,093,000 acres in 1911, 1,605,000 acres in 1912, and 1,633,000 acres in 1913. The maximum area devoted to corn in Kansas was 8,590,000 acres grown in 1910. In 1911 and 1912 the area decreased nearly 1,000,000 acres a year.

What caused the rapid change in comparative acreage? A growing knowledge of comparative acre values! Mere acres count for little unless they produce

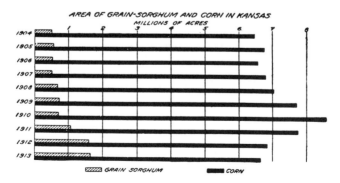

F IG. 5. — Graphic presentation of the comparative area in millions of acres of grain sorghum and corn in Kansas for the ten years 1904–1913, inclusive.

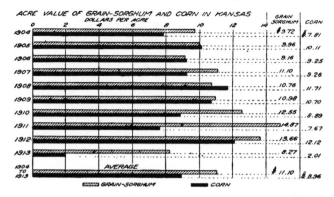

FIG. 6. — Graphic presentation of the annual acre value in dollars per acre of grain sorghum and corn in Kansas for the ten years 1904–1913, inclusive, and average acre value for the 10-year period.

profits. . . . Figure 6 shows the acre value of both crops in Kansas during the last 10 years. For the entire State the average acre value of kafir and milo was $2.14 greater than that of corn. The production of these crops is also more regular and evenly distributed. These statistics, taken from the reports of the Kansas State Board of Agriculture, are not wholly fair to corn, however. They include the value of both grain and stover in grain sorghums, but only the grain value of the corn. If the stover value of corn were included the average values would be more nearly equal.

How nature helped to swing the pendulum is seen when corn yields are considered. For 1907 to 1909 the average yield in Kansas was only about 20 bushels per acre; in 1910 less than 18 bushels; in 1911 less than 13 bushels; in 1912 it increased to nearly 23 bushels, but in 1913 was only 2.75 bushels. It would be very interesting to compare the yields of grain sorghum and corn, but unfortunately statistics of the former are given in tons of crop and of the latter in bushels of grain.

While this was being done in Kansas, Oklahoma also was making history. She produced 625,000 acres of grain sorghums in 1910 and 873,000 acres in 1911, an increase of a quarter million acres. No data for 1912 and 1913 are available, but there is every reason to believe, from the vigorous campaign waged, that the increase was proportional to that in Kansas. Oklahoma reached her maximum corn

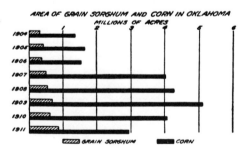

FIG. 7. — Graphic presentation of the comparative area in millions of acres of grain sorghum and corn in Oklahoma for the eight years 1904–1911, inclusive.

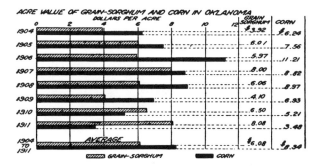

FIG. 8. — Graphic presentation of the annual acre value in dollars per acre of grain sorghum and corn in Oklahoma for the eight years 1904–1911, inclusive and average acre value for the eight-year period.

area in 1909 with 5,135,000 acres. In 1910 and 1911 the decline was at the rate of more than a million acres a year, as shown in figure 7.

Figure 8 shows the acre value of both crops in Oklahoma for eight years, beginning in 1904. Corn has an average advantage of $2.26 per acre for the period. This reversal of the Kansas figures is due to three or four things which profit corn. Oklahoma lies in a more southerly latitude than Kansas. The Oklahoma statistics include the stover value of only a small part of the grain sorghum. The grain sorghums are largely restricted to the drier western third of Oklahoma. (See fig. 11.) The very unfavorable season of 1913 is not included, for lack of data.

In Oklahoma the average yield of corn in 1907 and 1908 was less than 19 bushels; in 1909 less than 14 bushels; in 1910 less than 12 bushels; and in 1911 little more than 6 bushels. Statistics of production for 1912 and 1913 are not available, but it is certain that the average yield in 1913 was very small. Such yields for the entire State usually mean almost complete failure of corn in the western portions. The actual annual yields of the grain sorghums would be very desirable here, also, but a portion of the crop is reported in bushels of grain and the remainder in tons of crop and the acreage is not separated.

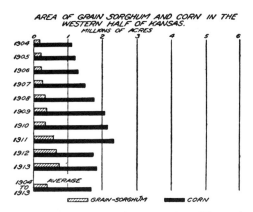

FIG. 9. — Graphic presentation of the area in millions of acres of grain sorghum and corn in the 46 counties comprising the western half of Kansas and lying wholly west of the ninety-eighth meridian, for the 10 years 1904–1913, inclusive, and average area for the 10-year period.

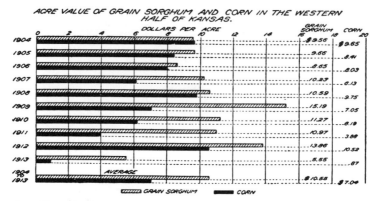

FIG. 10 — Graphic presentation of the annual acre value in dollars per acre of grain sorghum and corn in the 46 counties comprising the western half of Kansas and lying wholly west of the ninety-eighth meridian, for the 10 years 1904–1913, inclusive, and average acre value for the 10- year period.

Where then should kafir and milo be grown in preference to corn? Figures 9, 10, 11, and 12 assist in answering this question. Half of Kansas, containing 46 counties, lies west of the ninety-eighth meridian. Figure 9 shows the area of grain sorghum and corn in those counties. Nineteen of them already grow more kafir and milo than corn. The average acre value for this area, as shown in figure 10, proves the grain sorghum to be the more profitable crop. We have already seen that for the whole State of Kansas the average acre value of the grain sorghums was $2.14 higher than that of corn during the 10-year period, while in the western half of the State it was $3.51 higher. These figures include the value of the grain-sorghum stover, but not that of corn. However, corn stover is scanty and worth but little in dry areas. After allowing a fair price for it, the grain sorghums are still worth considerably more per acre than corn in the drier portion of the State. This fact, together with their more uniformly certain production, ought to cause further increase in the acreage of kafir and milo in western Kansas.

A comparison of figure 9 with figure 5 shows that fully half of the Kansas grain sorghum is grown in the eastern half of the State. The acre value for the entire

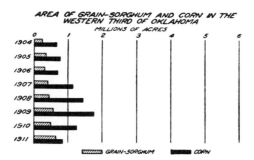

FIG. 11 — Graphic presentation of the annual area in millions of acres of grain sorghum and corn in the 21 counties comprising the western third of Oklahoma and lying wholly west of the ninety-eighth meridian, for the 8 years 1904–1911, inclusive.

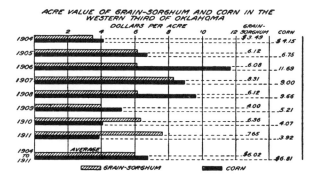

ACRE VALUE OF GRAIN-SORGHUM AND CORN IN THE
WESTERN THIRD OF OKLAHOMA

FIG. 12 — Graphic presentation of the annual acre value in dollars per acre
of grain sorghum and corn in the 21 counties comprising the western third
of Oklahoma and lying wholly west of the ninety-eighth meridian, for the
8 years 1904–1911, inclusive, and average acre value for the 8-year
period.

State indicates, moreover, that it pays to grow it in eastern Kansas, at least on the
uplands.

Similarly, one-third of Oklahoma, containing 21 counties, lies west of the
ninety-eighth meridian. Figure 11 shows the acreage in this area of the two crops
under discussion. Nine of these counties in 1911 grew more kafir and milo than
corn. Figure 12 tells why they did it and why more of them probably were doing it
in 1913. In sharp contrast to Kansas, a comparison of figure 11 and figure 7 shows
only about one-fifth of the grain-sorghum crop grown in the eastern two-thirds of
the State. When we consider the acre values given in figure 8 for all Oklahoma and
in figure 12 for the western third, there is developed a deep suspicion that it would
be very profitable to grow kafir and milo farther east in Oklahoma.

Meanwhile what of Texas, the great dry-farming empire of the South? We
know that during the years when the kafir industry was developing in Kansas, milo
had been carried into Texas by westward-faring emigrants. Gradually it became
established on the farms and ranches of the drier western portions of the State. No
statistical data are to be had, but we know it increased steadily and also that the
kafirs were soon introduced and became popular. There is every reason to believe
that the area devoted to these two crops in Texas has more than equaled the area
grown in Kansas, at least until the recent enormous increase.

It is to be regretted that no complete and separate statistics of the acreage and
production of grain sorghums are obtained by the Federal Census Bureau. Separate
data are now gathered and reported on that portion of the crop from which the grain
is thrashed. The portion, however, which is not thrashed, but fed either in the head
or bundle, or used for silage, is lumped with fodder and silage corn, sorgos (saccharine sorghums), pearl millet, teosinte, etc., as coarse forage. The acreage represented by each crop is not shown separately. Much of the kafir and milo crop
grown in western Oklahoma and western Texas is not thrashed because of the
scarcity of grain separators, this section not producing very large quantities of other
cereals. The acreage and importance of grain sorghums would now seem fully to
warrant the obtaining and publication of complete statistics of acreage and production wholly apart from those of any other crop.

Feeding the Farm Stock and the Farm Family

From the beginning the kafirs and milos have fed the farm horses that worked to raise the settler's crop and the faithful cow that gave his children drink. They have fed the hogs that fit so handily into the economy of every farm. They have fed the chickens that, more often than is known, have stood between the new settler and privation or failure.

With the testimony of the chemical analysis and feeding experiment, kafir and milo grain began to enter the feeding ration of beef cattle on the Plains. Kafir chops and milo chops became staple articles of bovine diet and kafir-fed cattle were commended at the great stock markets. Meantime the manufacturers of poultry feeds found in kafir the most desirable form of feeding grain. In the thousands of tons of such feeds made annually in the United States about 25 per cent of the material is kafir grain.

These grains have also a place in the human diet. Ground in the coffee mill on the wall of the farm kitchen, the meal has made many a stack of batter cakes on winter mornings. Mixed with varying proportions of wheat flour it is susceptible of every use to which corn meal may be put. As flour it will always be a failure. Like corn meal, it contains no gluten and so will not rise as dough, no matter how much it be coaxed. But as meal it has a flavor of its own and a wide range of usefulness in plain and tasty cooking. Muffins, brown bread, corn cakes, and pancakes par excellence are for him who uses it. In puddings and in pastries it will do all that corn meal may.

At last the grain sorghums had come into their own. No longer were they to be regarded as servants, faithful indeed, but inferior; no longer as poor relations of corn, honest, perhaps, but ragged. Now they were friends and equals, with a standing in the community won strictly on their merits.

In Society at Last — A Kafir Carnival

It was left to Butler County, Kans., to honor herself by arranging the first public reception ever given to kafir and milo in this country. Butler County is not in the drier western part of the State, but in the more humid southeastern section. Part of her soil, however, as that of some adjacent counties, is underlain at slight depths by rock, and the crops grown thereon are likely to suffer at times from lack of soil moisture. Kafir was first grown in Butler County in 1892, and it did not take her farmers long to realize that to such soils kafir was better adapted than corn. So the acreage of kafir increased year by year, until 100,000 acres were planted in 1911.

In the autumn of that year it occurred to the boosters of Butler County to celebrate their popular crop. A three-day kafir carnival was planned to take place on October 18–20 at El Dorado, the county seat. The carnival was an overwhelming success. For three days El Dorado was a kaleidoscope of color, a mecca of merriment. Fully 30,000 people are said to be have been present during the celebration. Kafir was in evidence everywhere. The booths were constructed of it, the buildings were decorated with it, the prizes were given for it. People came from all over Kansas to question and to ponder, and went away to praise.

In Conclusion

The grain sorghums have made good on the farm; they have been honored in the city. Their names are written in the social register and in the Who's Who of agronomy. They mingle with wheat and corn, the elect, on the boards of trade; they are rated high in the directories of commerce and finance. Hats off, and a hearty cheer as they go forward in the full strength of youth to quietly continue what they have thus far so splendidly done.

Rural Disorganization, 1913

From T. N. Carver, "The Organization of Rural Interests," U.S. Department of Agriculture, *Yearbook*, 1913, pp. 239–58.

The Causes of the Present Disorganization

The application of steam to the driving of machinery and the hauling of loads is commonly regarded as the cause, on the one hand, of the marvelous industrial expansion of the nineteenth century, and, on the other, of the general economic disorganization which accompanied that expansion. The breaking up of household and domestic industries and the substitution therefor of the factory system, with, in its early stages at least, its hordes of unorganized workers, has usually been referred to as the industrial revolution. This transformation was by no means so sudden as it is sometimes pictured, and it brought much less disaster and much more benefit than pessimistic and reactionary reformers are willing to admit. Nevertheless, there is no doubt that many of the acute problems of the urban economy of the present day grow out of the efforts of the laboring classes to find a new basis of organization to take the place of the old organization whose foundations were swept away by the creation of a world market and the rise of the factory system. This is the philosophy of that which is known as the labor movement.

A change no less profound, though perhaps less spectacular, has taken place in the rural economy of the civilized world, that is to say, of those countries where mechanical inventions have played such a powerful role as they have in America and western Europe. Steam and electricity applied to transportation and communication have created a world market for most agricultural products instead of the series of local, restricted markets which existed formerly. Not only were the markets local and restricted, but around such markets there were little communities which were self-sufficing or nearly so. Most of the manufacturing was done either on the farms or in small shops whose goods were exchanged for the products of the farms. The farms were organized at one time in village communities, which were really groups of small farms, where the crops, their rotation, the time of plowing, planting, and harvesting, were determined by the customs of the village or the authority of the villagers as a whole, where, in fact, everything connected with farming was organized — overorganized, as we should now say. At another time they were under what is known as the manorial system, in which the villagers, known as villeins, were under the supervision and leadership of the lord of the manor, and compelled by his authority to perform certain common work, such as road building, diking, draining, etc., besides working the lands reserved for the support of the manor house. Inasmuch as the lord of the manor was the local ruler and responsible to the King for the safety and order of the community, these services on his land may be regarded as substitutes for taxes in an age when there was very little commerce and practically no money in circulation. Whatever we may think of the village community with its tyranny of inflexible custom, or of the manor with its practical serfdom, still we must admit that both these systems furnished a kind of organization which made it possible to think in terms of the whole community, and to direct the affairs of the community as a unit. In short, the community rather than the individual farm was the economic unit.

The weakness of both these systems was that the cooperation, if that is the right word to use, was compulsory and not voluntary. In the village community the individual was controlled by the tyranny of the mass, and it was impossible for the individual farmer, however wise or skillful he might be, to improve his methods more rapidly than the average intelligence would permit. The manorial system was somewhat more flexible, and, especially under a wise landlord, permitted improvements which were impossible in the village community; nevertheless every villager was subject to the will of the lord of the manor and was permitted to exercise little or no initiative. The mill for the grinding of grain usually belonged to the lord, as did the bull and other expensive articles connected with agricultural enterprise. Thus there were certain important economies effected by this system of compulsory cooperation, but, like all systems of compulsion, it left little room for individual development. It was therefore a distinct step in advance when the manorial system gave way to a more individualistic type of farming.

Long after the decay of the manorial system, many of the advantages of an organized country life remained. On the large English estates, for example, with their numerous tenants and their resident landlords, the latter remained the leaders in agricultural enterprise. The fact that the owners lived on their estates and took a deep interest and pride in their ancestral acres helped to soften the evils of the tenant system. An intelligent landlord who advised his tenants, directed all large enterprises, experimented with different crops and methods, and improved the breeds of live stock performed most of the functions now performed by a county agent or demonstrator, and many more besides. Again, certain communal rights remained to the villagers and the small farmers, such as the right of gathering fire wood, cutting turf, and pasturing cattle on the common. These common interests compelled a certain amount of united action and gave a certain organic character to rural life. Every member of a rural community realized that he had a definite status in the community, that the community could command his services in a considerable number of details, and that he in turn possessed certain rights to the common utilities of the place.

In the New World, particularly in New England, the methods of founding settlements generally promoted an organized rural life. Sometimes the minister of a church gathered a congregation about him, led them out into the wilderness, and planted them on the soil with the church as the center of the community life. Even where this particular type of "swarming" was not followed, the grant of land was commonly made, not directly to an individual, but to a town or township, and the individual in turn got his grant from the township. The management of the common lands was a perennial problem calling for the effective organization of all the citizens of the township. The townships became, therefore, the units of local government. Being a small and effective unit, and having certain definite problems of an economic nature forced upon it, the township easily undertook other tasks of a voluntary nature, such as drainage operations, the branding of live stock, the appointment of herdsmen to guard all the cattle of the town, the public ownership of bulls, the fencing of the common lands, the construction of roads, etc.

Not only in New England, but everywhere on the frontier, there were common overwhelming needs, such as common defense, the clearing of the forest, the erection of buildings, and other tasks demanding the united strength of the whole community, which forced the people into a kind of cooperation. After the passing of the frontier days there remained such common local interests as the local school, the care of the roads, and the maintenance of the cemetery, to bring the people together around a common interest and give the neighborhood at least the germ of an organization.

Under the public-land policy of the Federal Government, however, particularly under the preemption and homestead laws, an extremely individualistic method of settlement was promoted. This doubtless served important public purposes, but it tended to promote disorganization rather than organization. Lately the tendency has been to take the roads and schools out of the hands of local units and put them directly under county and State administration. Doubtless a higher administrative efficiency is secured by this change, but it tends to remove the last vestiges of the old basis of rural organization. It is doubtless to be desired that this centralizing process should go on until the entire school system of a State is administered as a unit and every country child is provided with as good a school as any city child. At the same time it will be necessary to find a new basis of organization to take the place of the old bases which have been swept away.

Efforts at Reorganization

Efforts have not been wanting in this direction. Beginning with the granger movement of the late sixties and the early seventies of the last century, the country has witnessed a series of movements, some ephemeral and some lasting, until at the present time we have the National Grange, which is the dominant agricultural organization in the northeastern section of the country; the Farmers' Educational and Cooperative Union, which is very strong in the South; the Gleaners, who are particularly strong in Michigan and parts of adjoining States; and the American Society of Equity, which is strong in the entire Northwest, besides many smaller organizations. These various movements toward an effective organization of rural interests have been very uneven in their results, with many conspicuous failures as well as successes. It is doubtful if any one of them has yet demonstrated that it has found the key to universal success in this direction. There is need, in the interest both of these existing organizations and of the multitudes of farmers not yet affiliated with any organization, that a permanent body of some kind should begin a comprehensive study of the whole problem of organizing rural life for economic, sanitary, educational, and social purposes. Even if such a body should do no more than keep a permanent record of the successes and failures among farmers' organizations, it would eventually become of incalculable value as a guide for future organizers. But if, in addition to such a record, this body could formulate principles of organization, and give permanency and consistency to the efforts of active field organizers, its work would be of much greater value.

Aside from these fraternal and social organizations among farmers, there

FIG. 13. — Cooperative creameries in the United States. Small dot = 1 creamery; large dot = 10 creameries.

Arkansas	1	Illinois	62	Michigan	105
Arizona	1	Indiana	67	Minnesota	632
California	36	Iowa	308	Mississippi	1
Colorado	14	Kansas	7	Missouri	16
Connecticut	15	Kentucky	14	Montana	9
Delaware	2	Maine	7	Nebraska	14
Georgia	2	Maryland	3	Nevada	3
Idaho	3	Massachusetts	8	New Hampshire	6

have been vast numbers of organizations to promote special agricultural interests. The States of the upper Mississippi Valley are honeycombed with farmers' mutual insurance companies. These have had a longer history of uniform success than any other type of business organization among our farmers. The accompanying table shows the number of such companies in States which publish official lists. There are farmers' mutual insurance companies in other States which report that they publish no official lists, and these States are necessarily omitted from the table. (See fig. 16 and 16 A.)

FIG. 13A. — Cooperative creameries in the United States. Small dot = 1 creamery; large dot = 10 creameries.

New York	120	South Carolina	1	Washington	17
North Carolina	2	South Dakota	46	West Virginia	2
North Dakota	43	Tennessee	3	Wisconsin	355
Ohio	32	Texas	19	Wyoming	1
Oklahoma	10	Utah	6		
Oregon	8	Vermont	59	Total	2,165
Pennsylvania	99	Virginia	6		

Farmers' mutual insurance companies.

Arkansas	7	Maine	54	Oregon	3
California	18	Maryland	17	Pennsylvania	237
Colorado	5	Michigan	77	Rhode Island	1
Connecticut	14	Minnesota	150	South Carolina	19-
Delaware	8	Montana	7	South Dakota	33
Georgia	7	Nebraska	66	Tennessee	17
Idaho	5	New Hampshire	19	Texas	25
Illinois	230	New Jersey	23	Washington	6
Indiana	76	New York	163	West Virginia	11
Iowa	176	North Dakota	33	Wisconsin	203
Kansas	29	Ohio	102		
Kentucky	25	Oklahoma	1	Total	1,867

FIG. 14. — Cooperative cheese factories in the United States. Small dot = 1
cheese factory; large dot = 10 cheese factories.

California	3	Michigan	4	Missouri	2
Illinois	2	Minnesota	15	New York	34
Indiana	1				

The organization of farmers' mutual telephone companies has had a phenomenal development in the last two decades. As an agency for bringing farms into closer contact with one another and creating thus a basis for further organization, the importance of a rural telephone system can scarcely be overstated, especially when it is established and managed by the farmers themselves.

Cooperative creameries, cheese factories, and elevators, according to our latest reports, are distributed through the middle Northwest as indicated in figures 13, 13 A, 14, 14A, 15, and 15A. The question is often raised as to whether these are all strictly cooperative. Undoubtedly many of them are, in form at least, merely joint stock companies, and it may be claimed that such companies are not cooperative in the strict technical sense. Such a claim, however, is based upon the letter than the spirit of the enterprise. Any organization of this kind may be said to be

Fig. 14A. — Cooperative cheese factories in the United States. Small dot = 1 cheese factory; large dot = 10 cheese factories.

Ohio	2	South Dakota	1	Washington	3
Oregon	2	Utah	6	Wisconsin	247
Pennslyvania	13	Vermont	1		
				Total	336

cooperative in spirit when it is managed exclusively with a view to giving the farmer a better price for his butterfat or his grain, and not at all for the purpose of securing dividends on the stock. If the stock is owned by farmers and if each share of stock is in practice limited to a normal rate of interest and all surplus earnings go to the farmers in the form of better prices, the enterprise is cooperative in spirit, even though its form be that of the ordinary profit-making corporation.

However, it must in frankness be admitted that there is always danger, under the joint stock form of organization, that the cooperative spirit will be destroyed and the organization shifted to the profit-making purpose. In a creamery, for example, if one man owns a large number of shares and very few cows, or none at all, he will naturally be more interested in dividends than in the price of butterfat. If a majority of the shares are owned by such men, the company is almost certain to be managed

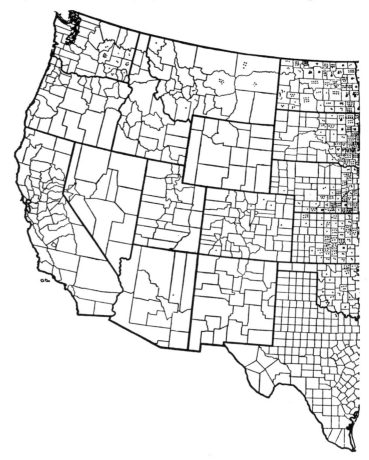

FIG. 15. — Farmers' cooperative elevators in the United States. Small dot = 1 elevator; large dot = 10 elevators.

Arkansas	2	Indiana	28	Michigan	22
Colorado	4	Iowa	332	Minnesota	286
Idaho	4	Kansas	149	Missouri	8
Illinois	260	Kentucky	1	Montana	25

in the interest of dividends rather than in the interest of the price of butterfat. It is therefore highly desirable that the form of organization be such as to prevent this result and insure that the management shall always be in the interest of the producers. Nevertheless, so long as the management is in the interest of the producer, it is reasonable to list such an organization as cooperative.

A multitude of cow-testing associations, breeders' associations of various kinds, purchasing associations for securing better prices on fertilizers, seed, and feed stuffs, and cooperative stores dealing in general merchandise dot the entire country.

The large farmers' organizations, such as the Grange, the Farmers' Union, the American Society of Equity, and the Gleaners, are also, in many localities, transacting business for the individual farmer. Cooperative warehouses, under the Farmers' Union, are doing business aggregating tens of millions of dollars annually.

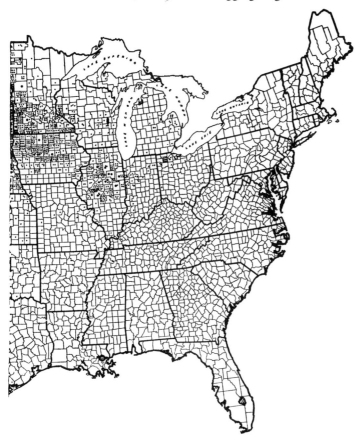

FIG. 15A. — Farmers' cooperative elevators in the United States. Small dot = 1 elevator; large dot = 10 elevators.

Nebraska	224	Oregon	3	Wisconsin	51
North Dakota	320	South Dakota	220		———
Ohio	23	Texas	4		2,020
Oklahoma	36	Washington	18		

Need of a Permanent Body to Give Consistency to the Movement

It is not too much to suggest again that it is of the utmost importance that all these scattered movements should be brought together and the work systematized in order that the number of failures may be diminished and the number of successes be increased. It is doubtful if any single agency can do this satisfactorily, but the Rural Organization Service of the Department of Agriculture may easily become one of the most effective agencies for bringing about this result.

Fɪɢ. 16. — Farmers' mutual insurance companies in the United States. Small dot = 1 company; large dot = 10 companies.

Arkansas	7	Idaho	5	Maine	54
California	18	Illinois	230	Maryland	17
Colorado	5	Indiana	76	Michigan	77
Connecticut	14	Iowa	176	Minnesota	150
Delaware	8	Kansas	29	Montana	7
Georgia	7	Kentucky	25	Nebraska	66

New Bases of Rural Organization

Markets

One of the first tasks of such an agency must be to formulate the general principles which must control all successful organizations, and also to find a satisfactory basis upon which to build a comprehensive organization of rural life to take the place of the old basis that has been swept away by general reorganization of the economic world. During this age of mechanical inventions it will never again be possible to build a rural community on the self-sufficing basis on which the farmers

Fig. 16A. — Farmers' mutual insurance companies in the United States. Small dot = 1 company; large dot = 10 companies.

New Hampshire	19	Oregon	3	Texas	25
New Jersey	23	Pennsylvania	237	Washington	6
New York	163	Rhode Island	1	West Virginia	11
North Dakota.......	33	South Carolina	19	Wisconsin	203
Ohio	102	South Dakota.......	33		
Oklahoma	1	Tennessee	17	Total 1,867	

produce for their own local market and get the most of their supplies from the local handicrafts. Each farming community is a part of a world market and the bulk of its produce must be shipped out and the bulk of its articles of consumption shipped in. This must be taken as a fundamental fact in all schemes for a new rural organization. Therefore it would seem that the reason for the existence of a rural organization must be found, in part at least, in the necessity for the successful marketing of products on the one hand and the successful purchasing of supplies on the other.

Capital

Another large and fundamental fact in the modern economic world, also growing out of the mechanical inventions which characterize it, is the demand for increased capital in all successful agricultural enterprises. In an age when farming was done with a few simple tools, the most of which could be made by the farmer himself during his spare time, the demand for capital could be ignored. But at the present time one of the paramount needs of agriculture is an adequate supply of expensive tools or capital. In order that the average farmer may properly equip himself, it is necessary that he be put in possession of purchasing power. This can only be secured through his own savings or through the savings of others from whom he can borrow. This means the development of credit facilities.

Sanitation

In an age when sickness was regarded as a visitation of Providence from which there was no reasonable means of escape, the problem of sanitation was unknown. Such a thing as an organization for rural sanitation would have been unthinkable, for the reason that, knowing little or nothing about the sources of disease, such an organization would not have known what to do with itself. But now that medical science has put us into possession of certain large and definite facts regarding the prevention of some of the more common diseases, the problem of protecting the health of rural communities is becoming practical. We are in a position to combat certain diseases if we are ready to go about it in the right way. Our great lack now is not so much the lack of knowledge as the lack of organization for applying our knowledge. It is quite as possible for us to exterminate certain disease germs as it was for our ancestors to exterminate the wolves and bears which preyed upon them and their flocks. When we awaken to the situation we shall find here an overwhelming need as great as that which existed on the frontier to force us into an organization for the protection of country life.

Thus the organization of the community so as to function more effectively in the world market may furnish a substitute for the local self-sufficing market of an earlier period; the organization of the community may supply the need for capital, which was an unknown need before the age of machinery, and organization for the purpose of fighting the invisible enemies known as disease germs may take the place of the older organizations to fight the visible enemies of the frontier.

Method of Procedure

It will occur at once to any thoughtful student that the first task in the general reorganization of country life must be to learn the facts as they exist at the present time. This necessitates a better survey of the entire field of American country life for the purpose of finding out what types of organization are now succeeding, and why; and what types have failed and are failing, and why; what special needs exist for which there are no effective organizations, and where these needs are greatest. A preliminary study of credit conditions has already shown that the farmers of different sections of the country are very unevenly provided with credit facilities, some sections having excellent, others very poor ones. The reasons for this variation need to be carefully studied before any satisfactory solution can be suggested. Until such a survey can be completed, not only with respect to rural credits, but also with respect to farmers' organizations of all kinds, very little advice can be given except in the most general terms.

Principles to be Observed

The following suggestions are made as a general guide for organizers in different fields of endeavor:

In Cooperation

There is no magic about cooperation. If, as the result of cooperation, farmers are led to improve their business methods, it will succeed; otherwise it will fail. These improvements in their business methods should include the following points:

(1) Accounting and bookkeeping. No cooperative organization of any kind can hope to succeed, nor would it deserve to succeed, unless it kept its books accurately and completely. Correct accounting is the key to all successful administration, public or private, cooperative or individualistic.

(2) Auditing. No one with any feeling of responsibility will undertake to advise a cooperative society or stand in any way responsible for its affairs, unless that society will submit its books annually for a thorough auditing by a competent and reliable auditing company.

(3) Motive. It must be prompted by a constructive desire for well-understood economies and not by rancor, or jealousy, or covetousness, or any other destructive sentiment. One of the most frequent causes of failure in cooperative enterprises is the fact that the whole enterprise was started out of something very closely resembling spite, or the fear that somebody might be making something in the way of profit. If a storekeeper or anyone else is making a profit by reason of the efficiency with which he runs his business or serves his customers, he is entitled to it, and any cooperative society which is started merely for the purpose of keeping him from making that profit is doomed to fail. If, however, there are clearly perceived wastes occurring, due to inefficiency, bad management, or the taking of excessive profits, and a cooperative society is formed for the constructive purpose of eliminating those wastes through better management, the society will have the first requisite of success, namely, the fact that it deserves to succeed.

In Marketing

The general subject of marketing is provided for under the capable management of the Office of Markets of the Department of Agriculture. Inasmuch, however, as the subject of organization is very closely associated with the subject of markets, and the Rural Organization Service and the Office of Markets are working in the closest cooperation, it is not out of place to suggest here a few of the main conditions of successful marketing. They are:

(1) The improvement of the product. This ought to be one of the first results of cooperation. A group of farmers, all interested in growing the same product, by meeting frequently and discussing the problems connected with the growing of that product, will normally educate one another and thus improve their methods of production.

(2) The standardization of the product through organized production. Standardization follows naturally and easily if the cooperators are wise enough to see its importance. Not only must the product be a good product, but it must be graded according to the tastes or desires of the consumers or ultimate purchasers. If the producers insist on throwing an unstandardized, nondescript product upon the market, the consumers, each one of whom wants a small and simple parcel, and wants that to be of a certain kind and quality, will never buy of the producers. Some one, then, must intervene to do the grading and standardizing. But if the producers will grade their products and pack them the way the consumers want them, they will be able either to sell directly to the consumer or so to reduce the toll charged by the middleman as to enlarge their own profits.

(3) Branding. An excellent product, graded and standardized, must then be so branded or trade-marked as to enable the consumer to identify it or to recognize it when he sees it. That is really all there is to the stamp on a coin. It adds nothing to the intrinsic value of the metal, but it makes it circulate. Without such a stamp, each individual would have to weigh and test a piece of metal which was offered him, and the circulation or salability of the metal would be greatly restricted; but a stamp upon it, which the average receiver recognizes at once and in which he has confidence, makes him instantly willing to accept it. This may be an extreme case, but it does not differ in principle from the stamping of any other salable piece of material. A private stamp is quite as good as a Government stamp *if* people have as much confidence in it as they have in a Government stamp and if it is as reliable and as uniform. Private coins have circulated many times in the past. However, without taking such an extreme case as the coinage of metal except by way of illustration, it will not take much argument to convince the average person that if a box of apples bearing a certain stamp or trade-mark gets to be known as reliable and good all the way through, the producer or the producing association whose stamp has thus gained confidence will be able to sell where unstamped products equally good will fail altogether.

(4) Education of the consumer. The consumer must be educated as to the meaning of a stamp or trade-mark on goods which are excellent in themselves and uniform in quality.

Let these four things be done and the problem of marketing will become fairly simple. But it must be remembered that these four things can be done only by organization.

In Purchasing Supplies

Much complaint is heard from farmers and farmers' associations regarding the unwillingness of manufacturers to sell directly to them and eliminate agents' profits. There is doubtless some ground for this complaint, in many cases at least. Where this unwillingness is arbitrary and without reason, the farmers, through their organizations, must try by every legitimate means, both legislative and nonlegislative, to overcome it. But he is no friend to the farmer who does not tell him the disagreeable truth that he is himself sometimes to blame for this situation. Not being trained in commercial practices, the farmer, or the farmers' organization, is sometimes unprepared to handle the business of buying in a businesslike way. The manufacturer will then prefer to sell through an agent or a regular dealer who is accustomed to handling business promptly and who does not need to be shown how. Again, farmers' organizations are not always prompt in paying bills. Where this is the case the manufacturer can not be blamed for preferring to sell through a regular dealer in whom he has confidence. Another and more serious complaint on the part of the manufacturer is that farmers' organizations frequently lack a keen sense of business obligation. They will order a carload of goods, for example, at a given price. Before the goods can be delivered, someone else offers to supply the farmer at a slightly lower price. In spite of the fact that their previous order is a virtual contract, they take the lower bid and refuse to take the goods delivered on the previous order when they arrive. Naturally this does not please the manufacturer who filled the order in good faith. He can not be blamed for being unwilling to fill similar orders thereafter. Possibly he ought to discriminate between such irresponsible farmers' organizations as this and others which have a true sense of business responsibility; but all men are prone to generalize. The way to cure this situation is for farmers who have business training and a sense of business responsibility to lend their aid in eliminating irresponsible organizations from the field. Otherwise they will suffer from the company they keep.

In Securing Credit

There is no mystery about credit. It is simply a means by which the possessor of purchasing power, which he does not care to use at once, is enabled to transfer that purchasing power to some one who does not possess it but who needs it at once in his business. Again, the possession of credit on the part of the farmer does not insure his success. When wisely used, credit is a powerful agency for good; so is dynamite. When unwisely used, or handled by one who does not understand it, it is dangerous; so is dynamite. Speaking by and large of facts as they actually are at the present moment, it is probable that as many farmers are suffering because they have too much credit as because their credit opportunities are too limited. To be able to borrow a thousand dollars even at the lowest possible rate of interest, say 2 per cent, is a loss to a man who invests it in a way to only bring back $1,001. The only possible advantage of having credit is to have an investment which is reasonably certain to return not only the principal but the interest and a little more besides.

Much has been said about the cooperative credit organizations of other countries. One fact which has never been sufficiently emphasized, and which can not be too much emphasized, is that these cooperative credit societies refuse credit quite as often as they give it, and they refuse credit not simply on the ground that the would-be borrower has no security to give, but equally on the ground that they do not think it would pay him to borrow. That is, he has no investment which, in the opinion of the directors, will be profitable to him. If his investment is unprofitable, the chances are that he will be unable to pay back a loan, and thus it would be unsafe. And, what is more important, even if he were able to pay it back, he would be poorer instead of richer by reason of the loan. The fact that the directors of one of these cooperative banks have to discuss the purpose for which the borrower wishes to borrow, and to decide whether or not it will probably turn out to be a good investment for the borrower, not only protects the borrower against himself but educates all the members of the society. That is to say, it compels them to discuss very carefully the probable results of all the classes of small investments, and this discussion itself is one of the most valuable kinds of business education.

Development of Hard Wheats, 1914

From Mark Alfred Carleton, "Hard Wheats Winning Their Way," U.S. Department of Agriculture, *Yearbook*, 1914, pp. 391–420.

Introduction

During the year 1870 a man named La Croix came to Minneapolis and constructed a wheat-flour purifier in one of the mills of that city. Such machines had been in use for several years in France, but until this time they were unknown in this country. By means of the purifier, which rapidly came into use, a complete separation of the milled products became possible, enabling the miller to produce from the strongly colored but nutritious middlings of hard wheat a flour suited in texture and color to the popular demand.

Eight years later, in 1878, Gov. C. C. Washburn, founder of the Washburn-Crosby series of flour mills, installed a small roller mill, claimed to be the first complete roller mill in the United States, and thus initiated, for this country, the most radical advance ever made in the history of milling. This mill was at first to be purely experimental. In fact, the new process was considered so uncertain for practical use that even during the same year, the Washburn A mill having been destroyed by an explosion of flour dust (May 2), the new mill erected in its place was fitted with stone burrs, as usual. At the close of 1877 the total runs of stone in the 21 Minneapolis mills were 197, and all the mills had water power but one, which was run by steam.

However, the use of rolls soon passed the experimental stage, and in a few years all plants in Minneapolis and all the principal mills elsewhere in the United States were roller mills. Rolls cause a crushing and flaking of the kernel instead of pulverization, as with stone burrs, and thus allow a more perfect separation of particles afterwards. They were at first made of various materials, chiefly porcelain, but finally the present perfectly formed steel rolls were adopted.

Upon these two innovations — the roll and the purifier — was based a new and complicated system of "high grinding," which worked a complete revolution in the milling business. A tremendous increase in the business itself followed, because of greater efficiency in production, accompanied by cheapness of flour and increased consumption. The special significance of the new system in this connection is that the miller was enabled by its employment to operate successfully with hard wheats, which were destined to be the prevailing wheats in the prairie region.

Adaptation

What are the conditions which made the cultivation of hard wheats inevitable in this country? Briefly these: They are the kinds of wheat best adapted to dry prairie regions, having come from such a region, the Chernozëm (black earth) in Russia, where they have long been established. They are therefore best suited to our own very similar prairie region, the Great Plains, where they are now grown, and will give better yields there than other wheats. With greater yield and the same price the farmer will naturally grow what pays him best — an axiomatic principle in any business. Although all hard wheats originally sold at a lower price than other wheats, the yield per acre of the former has almost always been sufficiently greater to more than offset the price discrimination. Later prices have become equal to or greater than those of other wheats. Add to these conditions the higher protein content of hard wheats, greater percentage of certain other nutritious constituents, and greater absorption of water by the flour, and we have ample reasons why these wheats must naturally prevail.

Classes

Three classes of hard wheats have so far been introduced into this country. These, in the order of their introduction, are (1) hard spring wheat, (2) hard winter wheat, and (3) durum wheat. Each has had an interesting history and has become established under difficulties. While each class has been a little more difficult than the preceding for the miller and baker to handle to their satisfaction, on the other hand these men have been better prepared each time to overcome the difficulties by improvements in machinery such as those already described.

Hard Spring Wheat

Hard spring wheat, although introduced into the northern Great Plains of this country and Canada about the middle of the last century, did not become firmly established as a profitable crop until after 1870, coincident with the introduction of the purifier and roller mill. There are two chief varieties, Fife and Bluestem. The Fife was the first to be established. It is a little more hardy than the Bluestem and has a slightly harder kernel. The kernel is particularly distinguished by its greater breadth in proportion to length and by its very broad groove. The Fife has white bare chaff and the Bluestem white velvet chaff. Both varieties have red kernels and no beards.

Origin of Hard Spring Wheat

It is pretty generally agreed that Fife wheat came from the northern Volga River Valley district of Russia, but details of the introduction are lacking. Much credence is given to the following statement from the Canadian Agriculturist of 1861:

About the year 1842, Mr. David Fife, of the township of Otonabee, Canada West, now Ontario, procured, through a friend in Glasgow, Scotland, a quantity of wheat which had been obtained from a cargo direct from Danzig. As it came to hand just before spring seed time, and not knowing whether it was a fall or spring variety, Mr. Fife concluded to sow a part of it that spring and wait for the result. It proved to be a fall wheat, as it never ripened, except three ears, which grew apparently from a single grain. These were preserved, and although sown the next year under unfavorable circumstances, being quite late and in a shady place, it proved at harvest to be entirely free from rust, when all wheat in the neighborhood was badly rusted. The produce of this was carefully preserved and from it sprung the variety of wheat known over Canada and the Northern States by the different names of Fife, Scotch, and Glasgow.

This traces the introduction no farther than Danzig, but it is very probable that the shipment was made from Russia.

Opposition to the Wheat

Up to the year 1870 hard spring wheat was very unpopular, probably fully as much so as any other hard wheat has been, including the durum. Hard spring wheat sold at 10 to 15 cents less than soft spring and 20 to 25 cents less than soft winter wheat. As some writers put it, it was a "despised" wheat and considered quite unfit for making bread, particularly because of its strong color. Millers and bakers declined to receive it except at a considerable discount in price.

Change in Sentiment

With the advent of the roll and the purifier there was an immediate change of sentiment. It was then possible to so handle the wheat as to produce a flour satisfactory in appearance to the consumer in comparison with soft winter-wheat flour. This was not accomplished at once, however. The new product persisted still in being a "creamy" flour, not white, and required considerable time to establish a reputation. It was seen, finally, that creaminess is really an indication of good quality. Others besides Washburn were pioneers in pushing spring-wheat flour to the front in these early days. Among these were George H. Christian; C. A. Pillsbury, founder of the present series of Pillsbury mills, including Pillsbury A, the largest mill in the world; and W. H. Dunwoody, an associate of Washburn.

Grading and Prices at Chicago

For a long time there was no definite recognition of hard spring wheat. Spring wheat was any wheat spring sown, regardless of color or hardness.

At the Chicago Board of Trade, the prices of different grades of certain dates were as shown in the table on the following page.

The grade of amber Iowa was adopted in 1862, said to be a spring wheat from Minnesota, northern Iowa, and northern Wisconsin, which sold at 3 to 4 cents higher than No. 1 spring. The grades of Nos. 1 and 2 northwestern spring began in 1873 and sold at 1 cent higher than Nos. 1 and 2 spring, and in 1876 at 3 to 5 cents higher. On September 1, 1877, these grades were changed to Nos. 1 and 2 hard spring. Later on, the grade No. 1 northern was adopted as the standard milling and contract grade of hard spring the same as in Minneapolis. December 30, 1911, No.

Prices per bushel of No. 1 spring, No. 1 red winter, and No. 1 white winter wheat on the Chicago Board of Trade on dates mentioned.

Date.	Price per bushel.		
	No. 1 spring.	No. 1 red winter.	No. 1 white winter.
	Cents.	*Cents.*	*Cents.*
Dec. 25, 1858[1]	83 to 85	108 to 110	124 to 125
Dec. 21, 1861[1]	68 to 70	74 to 76	85 to 86
Mar. 26, 1864	115½ to 116	140 to 145	....
Dec. 31, 1869..	84 to 86	103 to 105	....

[1] Average prices for week ending on date given.

1 northern sold at $1.05 to $1.10 per bushel, while No. 2 red winter (contract soft winter grade) sold at 91½ to 98½ cents, showing a complete reversal of attitude toward hard spring wheat.

On March 27, 1869, prices of flour per barrel were as follows:

White winter..	$7.00 to $10.00
Red winter	6.50 to 7.75
Fancy brands spring extras..	6.25 to 6.75
Fair to choice spring extras	5.00 to 5.75
Spring superfine..	3.75 to 4.50

Seven years later, in 1876, spring patent flour first sold at a price above that of white winter.

Grading and Prices at Minneapolis

The grades Nos. 1 and 2 hard spring were adopted by the Minneapolis Chamber of Commerce August 16, 1882, and sold at 5 cents above corresponding grades of ordinary spring called "regular." In 1885, the grades Nos. 1 and 2 northern were established, and No. 1 northern became thereafter the standard milling and contract grade. No. 1 hard, however, was retained as a grade for the best Fife wheat, though in recent years there is very little wheat to which this grade may properly be applied. About 7 years ago two more grades, Nos. 3 and 4 northern, were added.

Growth of the Hard Spring-Wheat Industry

From 1878 onward hard spring-wheat cultivation and northwestern milling progressed with rapidity. New lands in the Dakotas and western Canada were occupied by the wheat farmer, and new mills were constantly being erected in new settlements. The center of milling moved westward from New York to Minnesota, and Minneapolis succeeded Rochester as the "Flour City." Hard spring wheat had won its way (figs. 22 and 23). In 1878, when the first roller mill was built, the total output of flour of Minneapolis mills was 940,000 barrels. A large flour-export market was developed in Great Britain, and the first export was made in 1878, amounting to 109,183 barrels. In 1902 the export alone from Minneapolis was over 3,000,000 barrels, while the total output was over 16,000,000 barrels. In 1909 the total flour production in Minnesota was 22,737,404 barrels, and the same year the production of the three spring-wheat States, Minnesota, North Dakota, and South Dakota, was 25,531,610 barrels.

Production and Geographic Limits

The area of hard spring-wheat cultivation at present includes the three States just mentioned, portions of Iowa, Nebraska, Illinois, and Wisconsin, and eastern Montana. Hard winter wheat has steadily encroached upon this area from the south, and in the Dakotas, especially, there is an extensive substitution of durum for hard spring wheat. The yearly production of hard spring wheat for the three States, Minnesota, North Dakota, and South Dakota, from 1909 to 1914, inclusive, is shown in the following table:

Annual production of spring wheat in Minnesota, North Dakota, and South Dakota, in thousands of bushels, for the six years from 1909 to 1914.

State.	Production, in thousands of bushels.					
	1909	1910	1911	1912	1913	1914
Minnesota..........................	54,284	61,376	42,441	64,704	66,348	41,010
North Dakota......................	97,606	32,224	62,074	125,936	68,553	71,133
South Dakota......................	31,215	31,489	11,396	37,842	24,440	23,876
Total	183,105	125,089	115,911	228,482	159,341	136,019

The average production of these three chief spring-wheat States for the past six years was 157,993,000 bushels, exclusive of durum but including Preston (the so-called Velvet Chaff).

Hard Winter Wheat

In this country the term "hard winter wheat" is applied chiefly to two closely related varieties or strains called Turkey and Kharkof. Other names, such as Crimean and Malakof, are often used for the same kind of wheat. The characters are a medium-sized head, bearded, with white smooth chaff, and a hard red kernel, a little smaller than the usual winter-wheat kernel. There is little or no difference in visible characters between the Turkey and the Kharkof, but the kernel of the latter appears to be, as a rule, slightly larger and a little darker colored than that of the former. The gluten content of hard winter wheat is large, about equal to that of hard spring, but differs somewhat in quality. The expansive power or "strength" is slightly less in hard winter. There is also perhaps a trifle more color in hard winter-wheat bread.

Original Home

The original home of hard winter wheat is in the area of Russia just north and east of the Black Sea and north of the Caucasus Mountains. The area includes chiefly the governments of Taurida (including the Crimea), Ekaterinoslav, Kharkof, and Stavropol, and the Don and Kuban territories. In that region the wheat is generally called simply winter wheat, but is known locally by various names as Krimka (Crimean), Kharkof, Beloglina, Ulta, Torgova, etc. Our introductions from Russia are chiefly of the Crimean (the original Turkey) and Kharkof strains. In this country the area producing hard winter wheat, corresponding to the Russian area described above, is chiefly that portion of the Great Plains including Kansas, Oklahoma, small portions of Texas and Colorado, nearly all of Nebraska, and a small part of South Dakota. The original home is strikingly similar in conditions of soil and climate to that portion of our Great Plains just mentioned (figs. 24 and 25).

Kansas and the Crimea

A traveler on the plains of Kansas, if suddenly transported while asleep to southern Russia and deposited in the Crimea, would discover very little difference in his surroundings, except as to the people and the character of farm improvements and live stock. Even these last would be of the same kind if he were transported from certain localities in Kansas, where Russian immigrants now live. It is therefore natural that the center of hard winter-wheat production in this country should be in Kansas, since in Russia it is in the Crimea. The climate of the Russian district is a little more severe, which fact makes Crimean wheat all the more satisfactory for Kansas.

The Russian Mennonite People

The history of hard winter wheat is closely associated with the movement of Russian Mennonite immigrants to the middle Great Plains. These people originally went from west Prussia to southern Russia about 1770 because of certain land grants and civil privileges offered by the Government under Empress Catherine. One hundred years later their descendants, desiring further advantages to be obtained in America, emigrated to the middle Great Plains and settled principally in Kansas. The greater number were from the Molochna colonies in northern Taurida, but some were from the Crimea proper and others from Ekaterinoslav. The first settlements in Kansas were made in 1873 near Newton, Halstead, and Moundridge. Each family brought over a bushel or more of Crimean wheat for seed, and from this seed was grown the first crop of Kansas hard winter wheat. Bernard Warkentin, a miller, who erected mills at Newton and Halstead, was chiefly instrumental in introducing the Turkey wheat, but in this pioneer movement of the Mennonites two other men were associated — Christian Krehbiel, first a farmer, but who later, in 1886, erected a mill at Moundridge, and C. B. Schmidt, acting as immigration agent for the Santa Fe railroad.

Human Immigrants and Cereal Immigrants

There is an interesting feature of this introduction of a great crop in the fact that the crop and the people who knew best how to grow it migrated together. The Mennonites had been growing the wheat in its original home many years, although in the Molochna district spring wheat was grown up to 1860, when Turkey wheat was introduced there from the Crimea, and entirely replaced the spring wheat. On account of the small rainfall in Taurida, an important feature of cultivation there is the "chernui par," or black fallow, called black simply from the very dark color of the rich turned-over soil. It is really a summer tillage, and there are four cultivations: First, a deep plowing, and then three lighter operations at intervals of a month afterwards, made by very small gang plows or cultivators. Therefore, these people, on coming to the Great Plains, were already acquainted with the practices of early deep plowing and thorough surface cultivation, which not until a quarter of a century later were widely advocated in this country in connection with "dry farming."

Making Headway Slowly

The good qualities of Turkey wheat were not generally appreciated much before the close of the last century, 25 years after its introduction into Kansas by the Mennonites. At the Kansas experiment station its superiority came to light about 1897, though it had been under experiment for some time. Previously, Currell, or Zimmerman, had been the favorite wheat. In northwestern Kansas, Turkey was scarcely known even as late as 1890, though it had been grown already in scattering localities in that territory.

Opposition

The difficulties in milling and baking seemed to be a little greater than those met with in the hard spring wheat. Even Kansas millers for some time either declined to receive hard winter wheat or paid a lower price for it than for softer wheats. At Minneapolis, millers who had already had similar difficulties in milling hard spring wheat and would therefore know better than others how to handle it, nevertheless rejected it.

Grading and Prices at Kansas City

In 1875–76 the following grades were recognized at Kansas City: Nos. 1, 2, and 3 red winter, Nos. 2 and 3 white winter, and Nos. 1, 2, and 3 spring. December 1, 1879, No. 2 red winter sold for cash at $1.17, and No. 2 spring at $1. In 1880 winter and hard winter sold on the dates mentioned at the prices shown in the table on the following page.

During this year the grades Nos. 1, 2, 3, and 4 hard winter were first mentioned. In August, 1886, soft winter wheat still sold higher than red winter. June 30, 1891, the grades of hard winter were first included in the inspection report. Prices on September 3, 1892, were as follows: No. 2 soft winter, 70 to 71 cents; No. 2 hard winter, 65¾ to 66¾ cents; and No. 2 spring, 65 cents, showing hard winter still selling lower than soft winter, though there was now a large quantity of

Prices per bushel of Nos. 1 and 2 winter and Nos. 1 and 2 hard winter wheat at Kansas City, Mo., on three dates in 1880.

Date	Price per bushel.			
	No. 2 winter.	No. 3 winter.	No. 2 hard winter.	No. 3 hard winter.
	Cents.	*Cents.*	*Cents.*	*Cents.*
August 3	83½	74⅝ to 75	76	72
September 1	80	72¼	73	71
October 7	86	78¾	76½	76

Turkey wheat grown. Out of a total of 70,218 cars received that year, 54,108 were hard winter wheat. Even 16 years later, in 1908, hard winter still sold at a discount, the price difference being from 3 to 7 cents on September 1 and from 1½ to 2 cents on December 1. In May, June, and July, 1910, it sold a little higher than red winter for the first time, but quickly fell again until April, 1911, and then again exceeded red winter to July 1, 1912. For December 15 to 21, inclusive, 1914, No. 2 hard winter ranged from $1.12 to $1.17¾, as against $1.11¾ to $1.17½ for No. 2 red winter.

Conditions at Minneapolis

In 1891, 1,386,185 bushels of winter wheat were inspected at Minneapolis, the first considerable quantity mentioned, but how much, if any, of this was hard winter was not reported. After this no further very large quantities of winter wheat were reported at that place until 1901, when 5,353,340 bushels were inspected. About 1905 hard winter wheat was received in Minneapolis with hesitation, and then in small lots. Separate grades of Nos. 1, 2, 3, and 4 for the hard winter wheat were first made in Minneapolis in 1907. On December 1, 1914, the price of No. 2 hard Montana (the same class of wheat) ranged from 2 cents above the same grade of northern spring to 1½ cents under, and 2 cents to 3½ cents under No. 1 northern. On December 22, the difference was 1 cent less or 1 to 1½ cents under No. 1 northern.

Conditions at New York City

As early as 1901, hard winter wheat at New York was quoted at a fairly good price compared with No. 1 northern, and in 1902 the average price was only one-half cent below that of No. 1 northern. Afterwards it ran constantly several cents under in average yearly price, and under No. 2 red winter up to 1913, when it exceeded No. 1 northern by 1-9/16 cents, but was still 4⅛ cents under No. 2 red winter. On December 19,1914, No. 2 hard winter to arrive was quoted at $1.31½, 2 cents higher than No. 2 northern to arrive.

Hard Winter Wheat at St. Louis

As St. Louis is situated in a soft or semihard wheat area, hard winter would not be expected to be popular there. Nevertheless it sold a little higher than red winter in 1911, then became lower again in 1912 and 1913. After long contention, No. 2 hard winter was admitted to contract grade in June, 1914. In 1913, the receipts of hard winter at St. Louis were almost equal to those of red winter for the first time. Recently (December, 1914) prices of the two grades have kept near together.

Final Success

All recent prices at the important markets show a decided but gradual change in attitude toward hard winter wheat, so that it is now ranked, where it should be, among the first-class wheats. It has "won its way" through difficulties, in accordance with the motto of the State where its production is greatest.

In recent years hard winter wheat has been used in considerable quantity by Minnesota mills, while Kansas millers, who originally paid a lower price for it, long ago turned about and now will use no other wheat. In the meantime hard winter patent flour has gained a large export trade, is accepted everywhere, and has made Kansas the second flour-producing State of the Union. Kansas flour production in 1909 was 10,887,744 barrels.

Hard winter wheat is now more generally in favor in this country than any other winter wheat. In California, where it is not adapted, a third to a half of all wheat annually used by the mills is imported from the middle Great Plains. It has encroached upon the hard spring-wheat area to the northward in Iowa and Nebraska and upon the area of softer wheats to the westward in the Rocky Mountain States, and has made Montana a wheat State.

Turkey Wheat in Iowa

Turkey wheat has for a long time been grown in Iowa, and it has been claimed that it was introduced there from Illinois even before its introduction into Kansas. Whether this is true or not, it could well have happened, as the earliest Mennonite immigrants settled first in Illinois before 1870, and no doubt, as was their custom, brought seed of Turkey wheat to that State. There is a published statement that Turkey wheat was introduced from Mason County, Ill., into Iowa in 1870. It is also reported that George W. Franklin, of Atlantic, Iowa, first distributed this wheat in that State in 1886.

Introduction of Kharkof Wheat

The Kharkof strain of hard winter wheat was obtained by the writer, acting for the United States Department of Agriculture, in 1900, in Starobelsk district, eastern Kharkof government. This district is characterized climatically by great drought and piercing cold winter winds. It is much farther north than Taurida. Kharkof wheat has been able, therefore, to withstand the weather a little farther west and north than Turkey. It is particularly better for a combination of cold and drought. At about two-thirds of the points where Kharkof has been accurately compared with Turkey for several years, it has given a little better average yield. At present about half the entire wheat crop of Kansas is of the Kharkof variety. For 1914, therefore, the Kansas production of Kharkof wheat alone should be about 80,000,000 bushels.

Later Importations of Turkey Wheat

At the time of the introduction of Kharkof wheat several lots of Turkey or Crimean wheat were imported by the Department of Agriculture from the Molochna district of Taurida. A year later the Kansas Millers' Association, through Mr. Warkentin, imported 15,000 bushels of Turkey from central Taurida, which was sold as seed to farmers in Kansas and adjoining States, the source of seed being recommended to Mr. Warkentin by the writer. For a time this strain really appeared to give slightly better results than the usual Kansas seed, but in a few years its influence disappeared.

Durum Wheat

Near the close of the last century the hard spring and hard winter wheats had become established in a large portion of the Great Plains region, from Canada southward to and including Oklahoma. In the continued progress of settlement westward, however, extremes of drought and combinations of cold and drought were encountered, which even these wheats, hardy as they were, could not always overcome. So much new land had been taken that settlements were being made up to and beyond the one hundredth meridian. There was, therefore, great demand for more drought-resistant crops for the newer semiarid districts, but especially for such crops as wheat, which would give cash returns to the new settler.

Shall the Northwestern Plains Grow Wheat?

Briefly, out of the situation grew the question: Can wheat be grown profitably in the extreme western or semiarid portion of the Great Plains? As the hard winter wheat is a little more drought resistant than the hard spring, and as winter wheat always yields better than spring wheat, other things being equal, the need appeared more urgent in the northern Plains States, making it desirable to secure a spring wheat able to resist more extreme conditions. It should be added that there was considerable commercial demand for more wheat. So many mills had been erected in response to previous extension of the wheat area, as described under "Hard spring wheat," and such deterioration in quantity and quality of the wheat crop had been reported, that there appeared to be a real lack of good wheat.

Introduction of Durum Wheat

It was therefore in response to a growing demand of both millers and farmers that the Department of Agriculture, in 1898 to 1900, attempted to increase and improve the wheat crop by the introduction of hardier varieties of still better quality from east and south Russia. From results of experiments previously conducted and after a careful comparative study of soil and climatic conditions, it was already suspected that new varieties from these districts would be of benefit in this country. While several good new strains of winter wheat were obtained, including the Kharkof already mentioned, the chief result of this work was the introduction of Kubanka durum wheat from the Kirghiz Steppe district of western Siberia, in the vicinity of Uralsk and Orenburg.

Characteristics of Kubanka Wheat

The Kubanka variety, which represents practically all the durum wheat of this country, is a bearded wheat with compact, flattened heads, yellowish-white chaff, and large light-amber colored kernels, which are extremely hard and vitreous in fracture when of good quality. The gluten content is very large, and there is also a large percentage of ash, oil, and sugar. Pererodka and perhaps Arnautka are other names for the same wheat. Beloturka also usually means the same thing, though in Russia it is claimed that this variety, when pure, is distinct from Kubanka, having longer and narrower heads. The varieties Gharnovka, Velvet Don (Chernouska), and Black Don (Chernokoloska) were also obtained from south Russia, but were soon found to be not so well adapted to our northern Plains.

Original Home

The original home of Kubanka durum wheat is approximately Samara, Saratof, and Orenburg governments, Uralsk territory, and adjacent portions of the Kirghiz Steppe. The best quality comes from the Kirghiz Steppe district, where the annual rainfall averages little more than 12 inches. The center of production is about in southern Samara and Uralsk territory.

Adaptation in This Country

On the basis of similarity in climatic conditions, the center of production in this country would be logically in western North and South Dakota. Other conditions than climate, however, have had such influence that the trend of production has not always been in the logical direction. The greatest production, as a matter of fact, has been near the Red River, a long distance eastward from where it should be. There are probably two chief reasons for this fact, out of several that are possible: (1) Durum wheat is resistant to rust as well as drought, and rust occurs in greatest abundance eastward toward the Red River; (2) millers of the smaller western towns are either not able or not willing to adapt their mills to a new wheat, unless forced to do so by lack of other wheats. At present the center of durum-wheat production appears to be in Ransome and Sargent Counties, in south-eastern North Dakota. No doubt, since durum-wheat prices have greatly increased, a greater extension of the crop westward will occur and the center of production will move westward.

Rust Resistance

A quality of durum wheat of no little importance is its rust resistance. This fact was clearly brought out in the spring-wheat crop of 1904. There was a loss that year of 25,000,000 to 40,000,000 bushels in the crop of the three States of Minnesota, North Dakota, and South Dakota, practically all of which would have been avoided if the total crop had been durum. In many instances durum wheat made 15 to 20 bushels per acre, while Fife or Bluestem on the same farm was a total failure. One effect of this rust epidemic upon the farmer was a very great increase in durum-wheat acreage the following year. Again in 1914 fields of Bluestem wheat were abandoned as not worth cutting in many localities in North Dakota because of rust. The new Marquis wheat fared little better; Preston wheat was still better, while Kubanka was apparently unaffected.

Establishing a New Crop

Though durum wheat had been grown in small quantities at scattering points many years before its introduction by the Department of Agriculture, commercially it did not exist. The trifling quantity grown was sold for stock and poultry food at a price absurdly low for wheat. There was no financial incentive for growing it, and its good qualities were unknown. The task before the department, therefore, was far more than the mere introduction of Kubanka wheat seed. It was the long, tedious process of establishing a new crop, with all its attendant difficulties, a process of sheer persistence and education of the people.

Difficulties of Milling and Baking

Changes of some kind in milling operations have accompanied the introductions of each group of hard wheat. Durum wheat has the hardest kernels of all. Even the modern roller mill would not handle it satisfactorily without some modifications, among which is a larger area of corrugated surface. The kernels must be softened much more by steam or water before being ground. After grinding, additional grades of bolting cloth are desirable for proper separation of the products. The closest grinding of durum gives a patent flour very sharp and gritty, with no pastiness.

In baking the flour absorbs more water, an advantage to the baker, and the loaf expands less and is heavier than in bakings of other flours. The excess of oil and ash imparts a stronger yellow color to the flour, and the excess of sugar causes a slightly sweet flavor (again to the advantage of the baker, as little or no sugar need be added) and a darker brown crust on the loaf. All these qualities are desirable to most people. However, yellow color and lack of expansion have been the stumbling blocks to the baker and the housewife. It is still a matter of education of the eye and taste together and of dogged persistence on the part of certain enterprising millers and bakers, who will undoubtedly win their way in the end.

Opposition to Durum Wheat

Naturally, durum, the hardest of hard wheats, met at once with the most violent opposition, chiefly from millers, but also from all grain men. Various epithets, such as "bastard" and "goose," were applied to the wheat without restriction. At first the tendency was to ridicule it, as it was not thought possible that such a wheat could prevail. However, a crop of somewhere near 10,000,000 bushels in 1903 and receipts of over 1,000,000 bushels at Duluth alone made it apparent that durum wheat was something to be reckoned with. The following is quoted from the report of the Duluth Board of Trade for the year ending December 31, 1903:

> This variety of wheat, new, yet not new, made this year its first appearance in this market in any considerable quantity — the receipts being 1,149,263 bushels. Prices range from 60 to 70 cents per bushel for No. 1. Opinions differ as to its future position in the grain market. . . . Millers do not seem to be very profuse in its praise.

For a time opposition seemed to increase, and the difference in price became greater. For 1903 the average price of durum at Duluth was 13½ cents under No. 1

northern; in 1904, 15 cents; in 1905, 16⅝ cents; and in 1906, 10 cents. Later the price difference became as much as 20 cents and more.

Increase in Production

The production of durum wheat nevertheless increased greatly each year. In 1907 the farm value of the crop was about $30,000,000, or more than 3,000 times the original cost of introduction, and three times the entire appropriation for the Department of Agriculture for that fiscal year. The yield per acre became constantly 30 to 50 per cent greater than that of other wheat, on the same farm, and often 100 per cent greater in very dry localities. In the annual report of the Duluth Board of Trade for 1905 it was stated that durum wheat ''has evidently come to stay, as evidenced by the fact that 25 per cent of the wheat received at Duluth in 1905 was of this variety.'' The following more lengthy quotation from the 1906 report of the same board of trade gives a fair statement of the remarkable change in conditions respecting this wheat by the end of the year 1906:

The movement of durum wheat and the easy manner in which the large and sudden increase in its production has been absorbed have attracted the attention of the entire grain trade of the country. It was in the year 1903 that this variety of wheat made its appearance in the Northwest in any amount worthy of notice. It was not received with open arms. The American miller did not take to it, and to this day, the fourth year of its appearance in any volume, he still maintains his attitude of disfavor. With the American millers disposed against it, grain men naturally discouraged its production. The farmer, however, found that it grew easily and that it produced in more generous quantity than spring wheat, and its production increased. The year 1904 saw a somewhat larger amount grown, but it was in 1905 that the great increase came. So much greater was the volume of durum wheat that poured to market that grain merchants at the beginning of the movement of the crop despaired of ever finding a market for the yield. Good fortune was with the American grower, however, for the countries of Europe and in the Mediterranean district of Africa, which had always been large producers of this variety of grain, had reverses and were unable to supply those who had always looked to them for their hard macaroni wheat. The American exporter was quick to see the opportunity, and soon the foreigners were heavy buyers of durum wheat from America. Prices were advanced steadily, and the demand grew until there were times when durum wheat could actually be placed in some markets at better prices than No. 1 northern spring wheat. The entire crop was easily absorbed and at good prices.

But one result could be expected from this — another great increase in the crop of durum — and the year 1906 brought this. Again there was considerable uneasiness among grain merchants as to whether markets could be found for all of it. There was some fear that the buying of the 1905 crop by the Europeans had only been a temporary movement that would die out with the resumption of normal production by the macaroni-wheat raising countries of the other side. Nothing to justify this belief has as yet developed. The durum wheat crop of 1906 is being steadily absorbed, and the short sellers who looked for durum wheat to go to very low prices have been badly mistaken. Europe seems to have been well pleased with the wheat supplied by America from the 1905 crop and is again buying it heavily this year. Even Russia, one of the foremost wheat exporting countries of the world, has been a good buyer of this wheat in the Duluth market.

A further statement from the same source in the report for 1907 shows no abatement in the durum demand:

In the year 1907 durum wheat again made up a large percentage of the receipts of grain at Duluth, and it was in good demand. Foreign markets continue to absorb the larger part of the shipments from here, but its use shows some sign of growing with American millers. Millers of the United Kingdom also use it to some extent when the price level is attractive. The crop of 1907 was much larger than that of the year previous, but the increased yield was absorbed without trouble.

A Decided Change of Attitude

As an interesting illustration of the great change in attitude toward durum wheat, the following two letters, quite opposite in sentiment, from a prominent grain-exporting firm to commercial journals, are here reproduced. The first was written to Bradstreet's in September, 1903, and from it the following is quoted:

There are arid portions of the Northwest where this wheat will grow and where ordinary wheat fails. It is not surprising that the farmers in these regions eagerly accepted the statement of Mr. Carleton that "goose" wheat (now under the name of macaroni) contained valuable qualities for breadmaking — in fact, equal to that of our Scotch Fife. This theory exploited by Mr. Carleton has resulted in the raising of an enormous crop of this class of wheat, estimated at 10,000,000 bushels.

As indicated in the extracts from our Minneapolis letter, the millers view the situation with alarm. They are confronted with a large decrease in merchantable wheat, and also the danger of mixture of macaroni and other wheat, such mixture being useful only as food for stock.

From a shipper's standpoint this macaroni wheat must meet the competition in Liverpool of similar wheats from Russia, the Danube, and India. These at present are very low, and about 67 cents at Duluth is the best the exporter can pay for it. Last year's experience for the exporters of macaroni wheat was discouraging. They were encouraged to keep in the market through the fall, and were obliged to carry through the winter a block of macaroni wheat which failed to find a market. Its value as an export article is entirely independent of the price of other wheats. In view of this situation I think it is in good order to suggest that the Government exercise some caution in launching this variety of wheat and insisting that the millers and grain men meet the situation.

I heartily commend the Government for the establishment of its experimental stations and for the aid given the farmer in the development of proper seed grain, but I think Mr. Carleton's enthusiasm has warped his judgment. He has been instrumental in producing a condition of things in the Northwest that, to say the least, is unhealthy. The question of supply and demand, which Mr. Carleton has apparently ignored, must settle the question in value. I think the farmer should be advised to go slow in raising macaroni wheat until a safe market is found for it.

The second very different letter from the same firm was published in a Minneapolis journal in October, 1907 after having been refused the columns of another well-known journal in the same city. It is quoted here as follows:

Just as a matter of interest, No. 1 durum wheat in Duluth sold to-day at $1 per bushel in store, and one durum wheat on track by sample is selling at $1.01 to $1.02. At the same time cash No. 2 red in Chicago can be bought at $1.03 in store at Chicago. Some of our export offers last night offered both the No. 1 durum and the No. 2 red Chicago at less than 3 cents per bushel difference, and the No. 1 durum is accepted and the Chicago No. 2 red not taken. Now, in view of this, and the fact that the buying is being done by English millers and German millers, and not by the Mediterranean macaroni trade, why not come out frankly and state that you have been unintentionally misrepresenting this wheat for some time, or that you have misjudged its milling qualities altogether. With the situation now, and the relative price between durum and red wheat for a milling mixture by a United Kingdom miller who can draw both, or draw any cheap wheat in the world, the plea that it is used because of its cheapness will not bear scrutiny. The fact is this durum wheat is a good yielder in the milling process. The percentage of off-grade is smaller than in a great many varieties of wheat. It makes a satisfactory body for a flour mixture, and it has a real value as a milling wheat, notwithstanding all that yourselves and other northwestern milling journals have said of it. In a large section of the Northwest it is the most profitable wheat to grow, and if the journals in the milling centers had treated this question from the start on a plain common-sense business basis, they would stand to-day in a better light in view of recent developments in the durum trade. We should like to see you frankly retrace your recent course regarding durum wheat.

Durum as a Milling Wheat

In the Minneapolis letter referred to but not quoted in the above letter to Bradstreet's it is stated that durum wheat flour yields less bread per barrel. Quite the opposite result has been obtained in all bakings known to this department, and for a very simple reason — the greater water absorption of the durum flour. Note also the very different statement as to this question in the second letter: "The fact is this durum wheat is a good yielder in the milling process," etc.

As a matter of fact not one objection to durum wheat flour for bread making has been made good, except possibly the one of greater cost of production. This disadvantage is becoming constantly less, and will no doubt soon disappear as the miller becomes better acquainted with proper methods of operation. Even the yellow color, claimed to be so serious an objection, can be and has been eliminated by sufficient aeration of the dough, which is made possible by the use of several mixers recently invented. However, this is only a suggestion to those desiring it. As a fact, the color should not be eliminated. It is the stamp of quality. The fact that northwestern spring patents, which are not white, have been established in the face of great opposition to their color is ample evidence that durum patents will also succeed.

Semolina and Macaroni

That durum-wheat semolina makes the best macaroni is a fact that probably needs no argument. We import chiefly from Italy, and the Italians use only durum wheat. Nevertheless, only a rather small percentage of macaroni is made from durum wheat in this country. Few Americans know what constitutes good macaroni. There is the ever-present idea again of whiteness, and when the color is good it is often spoiled by bleaching. It is then cooked into a pasty mass, wholly unlike the proper article, which should permanently hold its form, like rubber, although well cooked, and should be yellow or yellowish-white in color.

Durum Wheat at Duluth

Durum wheat was first recognized commercially at Duluth. The grades of Nos. 1 and 2 durum were established there, at the board of trade, in 1902. Later, Nos. 3 and 4 were added. Much aid was given to the exploitation of durum, in the early days of its history, by exporters at this place. It also soon became a speculative wheat, equally so with spring. Durum sold readily as an export grain, as its qualities have long been known in Europe.

The first great increase in production was in 1905, following the rust epidemic of 1904, which brought out clearly the rust-resistant quality of durum. There was a good foreign demand ready for this surplus. In recent years Minneapolis and local mills have so far taken the crop that there is a constant scarcity for export. The receipts of durum, its percentage of the total wheat receipts, and comparative prices at Duluth for the first five years of its commercial history are shown in the table following.

Annual receipts of durum wheat, percentage of total wheat receipts, and prices of No. 1 durum and No. 1 northern wheat at Duluth, Minn., 1903–1907.

Year.	Durum wheat receipts.	Durum wheat in total receipts.	Price per bushel.	
			No. 1 durum.	No. 1 northern.
	Bushels.	Per cent.	Cents.	Cents.
1903	1,149,000	4.38	67½	81
1904	1,707,000	7.19	87½	102
1905	7,824,000	12.55	83⅜	100
1906	15,026,000	37.47	70⅝	80⅝
1907	26,721,000	48.07	80	97

The receipts of durum wheat, total wheat receipts, durum percentage of the total receipts, and average end-of-the-month prices for No. 1 durum and No. 1 northern at Duluth for 1908 to 1911 are shown in the following table:

Annual receipts of durum and of all wheat, percentage of durum wheat in total wheat receipts, and average prices of No. 1 durum and No. 1 spring at Duluth, Minn., 1908–1911.

Year.	Receipts.		Durum wheat in total receipts.	Price per bushel.	
	Durum.	All wheat.		No. 1 durum.	No. 1 northern.
	Bushels.	Bushels.	Per cent.	Cents.	Cents.
1908	22,631,000	46,873,000	53.90	90	107
1909	17,863,000	48,529,000	36.81	100	114
1910	8,831,000	27,841,000	31.72	90	110
1911	3,517,000	28,503,000	12.34	92	101

By 1907 almost half the total wheat received at Duluth was durum. Soon the low prices, as shown above, caused a decrease in acreage and also caused a larger quantity to be used by the mills. In 1911 even the durum that reached Duluth was reported to be practically all absorbed afterwards by Minnesota and other mills.

In 1910 it was evident that European millers were using our durum, as so much of it went to markets outside of France and Italy. Even British millers bought it. Antwerp offered one-half cent more for durum than for Manitoba No. 3.

On September 5, 1911, durum wheat at Duluth sold at a premium over No. 1 northern for the first time, the price being $1.04½ and for No. 1 northern $1.04⅛.

Since then it has continued to be sold at a premium, at intervals, during three more crop years. Recently, for over two months (November and December, 1914, and onward) it has sold constantly above hard spring, often more than 20 cents above.

Durum Wheat at Minneapolis

Durum wheat for some time met with very conservative treatment by Minneapolis millers, as was expected, although its objectionable qualities were of the same nature as those met with in first handling spring wheat, but present to a greater degree, and therefore should have been considered evidence at once of its superiority.

After the first large durum crop, in 1905, following the rust epidemic, Minneapolis appeared to give more attention to the wheat, seeing that it had evidently come to stay. Also the great discrimination in price against durum, at that time increasing, and no doubt furthered by the very opposition to the wheat, now made it possible to use it in an experimental way, and it was soon admitted to be a very excellent milling wheat, if for no other purpose than blending with other softer wheats.

The grades of Nos. 1 and 2 macaroni appear to have been first recognized on the Minneapolis Exchange in 1902. In 1904, the term "durum (macaroni)" was adopted and grade No. 3 added. In 1905 the grades Nos. 1, 2, 3, and 4 durum were established. The first considerable quantity of durum wheat inspected into Minneapolis, nearly 7,000,000 bushels, was in 1906, and very little seems to have been inspected out. In that year a full report of inspection and prices of durum was first given by the board of trade. From that time onward the receipts steadily increased, up to 1910, when the quantity of durum received was over one-seventh of the total wheat receipts. By this time, also, the period of great price discrimination, which, however, had already lessened the production, was about ended. This fact, together with a stronger foreign demand, caused a sharp decrease in Minneapolis consumption. The receipts of hard spring wheat and durum wheat at Minneapolis and the prices of each on December 1, for the years 1906 to 1913, inclusive, are given in the table following:

Receipts of hard spring and of durum wheat at Minneapolis, Minn., 1906–1913, with the price per bushel for each on December 1.

Year.	Receipts.		Price per bushel.	
	Hard spring.	Durum.	Hard spring.	Durum.
	Bushels.	*Bushels.*	*Cents.*	*Cents.*
1906	66,789,110	6,950,950	78¼	63¼
1907	66,382,470	8,656,410	106	84½
1908	62,847,180	8,094,060	110¼	89¾
1909	63,211,410	8,996,950	106	87¾
1910	71,619,960	12,929,790	106	88
1911	76,879,960	4,818,590	102¾	99
1912	101,213,460	5,140,010	82⅜	79¼
1913	98,903,080	5,284,480	85⅛	80⅞

Note that the price of durum jumped from a discount of 18 cents in 1910 to one of less than 4 cents in 1911, and, what is more important, has since been steadily maintained at an average of only 3 to 5 cents below that of spring wheat. At present (December, 1914) durum is selling as much above No. 1 hard as it was below it in 1909–10.

The two following items are from the Northwestern Miller:

November 18, 1914: Durum wheat on track at Minneapolis is commanding a premium of 6¾ to 8¾ cents per bushel over No. 1 northern.

December 2, 1914: Durum wheat sharply advanced in the last week on export inquiry from France to Italy. No. 1 durum on track at Minneapolis is held at 7⅝ to 10⅛ cents over No. 1 northern compared with ½ cent under to 2⅛ cents over a week ago.

On December 22, 1914, durum-wheat patent flour sold at 30 to 50 cents per barrel higher than hard spring patent, while durum semolina was still higher.

Durum Wheat at New York

New York early became an important durum-wheat point because of the European export demand. At first the shipments were almost wholly to France and Italy for use in making macaroni, but in recent years large quantities have gone to Belgium, Holland, Germany, Switzerland, and some even to Great Britain, where the softest wheats are usually employed. There is sufficient evidence accompanying the reports of these facts to show that usually the wheat was ground for bread.

The following table shows comparative wheat prices at New York from 1901 to 1913, inclusive. Note that even the average yearly price of durum finally exceeded that of all other wheats except No. 2 red winter (the popular eastern wheat) in 1913.

Recent Prices of Durum Wheat

For a long time the discouraging feature of durum-wheat production was the steadily decreasing comparative price. This continued, with variations, up to 1910. So long as the difference was not more than 3 to 5 cents, the greater yield of durum made it possible still to grow that wheat at a greater profit, where it was adapted, than other wheat. With a price difference of 15 to 20 cents in 1908 to 1910, it was inevitable that the acreage should decrease. From 1911 conditions in this respect have entirely changed. Durum is now often the premium wheat and always sells near to No. 1 hard. At the time of this writing durum wheat has already sold at a premium as high as was ever reached by No. 1 hard over durum. A steadily increasing premium has been maintained for two months. Durum first reached the $1.50 mark at Philadelphia on December 17, 1914. On December 1, 1914, No. 1 durum sold at New York at $1.61 per bushel.

A Prediction Fulfilled

During the week of September 19–25, 1898, the prices of Kubanka durum wheat at Samara, Russia, ranged from 17 to 23 cents per bushel above those of Russian, the latter a grade of spring wheat very similar to our No. 1 hard, and corresponding to it. This fact was personally observed by the writer of this article, who was in Samara during the time mentioned in search of good seed of durum

Average yearly prices of various grades of wheat at New York, 1901–1913.

Year.	Price per bushel.				
	No. 2 red.	No. 1 northern.	No. 2 hard winter.	No. 1 hard Nanitoba.	No. 1 durum.
Cents.	*Cents.*	*Cents.*	*Cents.*	*Cents.*	
1901	80¼	81⅜	79⅝	....	....
1902	83⁹/₁₆	82⅞	82⅜	....	....
1903	85³/₁₆	90⁷/₁₆	[1]85⁷/₁₂	[2]91¹/₄₈	....
1904	110¹¹/₁₆	112¼	102¹⁵/₁₆	....	....
1905	102¹³/₁₆	108⅞	[3]92⁹/₄₀	[4]94⁵/₃₂	[1]90³/₁₆
1906	86½	89⅝	85⅞	88¹¹/₁₆	83³/₁₆
1907	96⁵/₁₆	106⁷/₁₆	99³/₁₆	[5]101¹³/₁₆	90¹⁵/₁₆
1908	104⅞	116⅝	109¹³/₁₆	113²⁷/₁₆	101¾
1909	124⅝	125⅛	123³/₁₆	120¹⁵/₁₆	107⁹/₁₆
1910	111¹³/₁₆	121⁵/₁₆	[7]110⁵/₉	118⅛	103⁹/₁₆
1911	97³/₁₆	111¹⁵/₁₆	103⁵/₁₆	106⅝	[3]109¾
1912	109⅛	112⅞	108⅞	110¼	[8]105⁵/₁₆
1913	104⁹/₁₆	98⅞	100⁷/₁₆	101¼	101⅝

[1] Average for 3 months, October to December, inclusive.
[2] Average for 9 months, January to September, inclusive.
[3] Average for 5 months, August to December, inclusive.
[4] Average for 2 months, October to November, inclusive.
[5] Average for 10 months, January to July, September to November, inclusive.
[6] Average for 2 months, November to December, inclusive.
[7] Average for 9 months, January and February, June to December, inclusive.
[8] Average for 5 months, January, September to December, inclusive.

wheat. In referring to this matter in another publication, the writer made the following statement:

> It is interesting to note that just five years later almost an exact reverse of the relations in price of these two classes of wheat existed in this country at Minneapolis, and yet we have the same system of milling and largely the same export outlet for our wheat and flour as Russia. The explanation is that the American trade is only now becoming acquainted with durum wheat.

Later, in the years 1907 to 1910, when durum sold at 20 cents or more under No. 1 northern at Minneapolis, the writer, in discussing the conditions with grain men in that city at different times, made the prediction that in the future such conditions would be reversed and become similar to those at Samara, with durum wheat selling at a premium over No. 1 hard, and that the dealer who was first prepared and on the right side would reap the first profits. The idea was scouted as being hardly worth consideration. Several times in December, 1914, the prediction has been amply fulfilled, and the prices of durum and hard spring have finally stood in their proper relations, and as they were at Samara in September, 16 years ago.

Cooperative Efforts

A number of business firms have aided greatly in establishing the durum wheat crop, while at the same time profiting by their operations. Perhaps the greatest aid was given by the actual opposition of its enemies, thereby cheapening the wheat so that tests of it on a large scale were financially possible. These tests were all that was necessary to bring it into favor.

The Fixity of Durum Wheat

In earlier years there was much doubt as to the permanency of the market for durum wheat until three large crops in succession were readily absorbed. So in 1911, when it first sold at a premium over hard spring, it was not believed by some that this could be anything more than a sporadic occurrence and that the former relation of prices between the two wheats, with its great margin against durum, would soon be resumed. But there was a second surprise, and the former relation was not again resumed, even in four years. On the contrary, the higher price of durum has become more and more frequent and finally the regular thing. Hence, even taking into full consideration the present disturbing conditions of foreign war, the chances are that durum will continue to be in great demand and will ever be in future a preferred wheat. This most triumphant career of a once rejected wheat is simply a good illustration of results that are bound to follow persistent efforts based upon facts of science.

Average Total Production of the Hard Wheats

It is impossible to determine accurately the total production of hard wheat, but it can be roughly estimated. The three Northwestern States produce about 180,000,000 bushels, including durum, each year. Other spring-wheat States produce about 15,000,000 bushels more of hard wheat, making 205,000,000 bushels of hard spring and durum. Kansas, Nebraska, and Oklahoma grow about 136,000,000 bushels, of which probably 120,000,000 are hard winter. This added gives 325,000,000 bushels. Other winter-wheat States, such as Iowa, Montana, etc., will furnish about 25,000,000 more, making in all 350,000,000 bushels as the approximate average annual hard-wheat production in this country. This is about half of the average total wheat production.

Extension of the Hard Wheat Area

As may be inferred from the preceding discussion, there are only two regions in the world where the strictly hard wheats may be successfully grown, these being the eastern and southern portions of Russia and the Great Plains and western intermountain districts of the United States and Canada. At the same time, only these wheats can be depended upon to give any profitable returns where the climate is extremely dry. Therefore, because of their excellent quality and the fact that they must be used in the extension of wheat growing into localities where the summers are drier and the winters colder than where wheat is at present grown, it is of vital importance for the future wheat supply to endeavor to improve them so that they will become adapted to localities at present still more unfavorable for wheat growing. For example, the hard winter wheat may be so improved in both winter hardiness and drought resistance that it can be grown farther north and west than the present Kharkof and Turkey varieties, while, on the other hand, the durum wheat may be so improved in drought resistance that it will be more successful in localities west of the one hundredth meridian.

Cotton Act of 1914

From 38 U.S. Statutes at Large 693.

An Act To tax the privilege of dealing on exchanges, boards of trade, and similar places in contracts of sale of cotton for future delivery, and for other purposes.

Be it enacted by the Senate and House of Representatives of the United States of America in Congress assembled, That this Act shall be known by the short title of the "United States cotton futures Act."

SEC. 2. That, for the purposes of this Act, the term "contract of sale" shall be held to include sales, agreements of sale, and agreements to sell. That the word "person," wherever used in this Act, shall be construed to import the plural or singular, as the case demands, and shall include individuals, associations, partnerships, and corporations. When construing and enforcing the provisions of this Act, the act, omission, or failure of any official, agent, or other person acting for or employed by any association, partnership, or corporation within the scope of his employment or office, shall, in every case, also be deemed the act, omission, or failure of such association, partnership, or corporation as well as that of the person.

SEC. 3. That upon each contract of sale of any cotton for future delivery made at, on, or in any exchange, board of trade, or similar institution or place of business, there is hereby levied a tax in the nature of an excise of 2 cents for each pound of the cotton involved in any such contract.

SEC. 4. That each contract of sale of cotton for future delivery mentioned in section three of this Act shall be in writing plainly stating, or evidenced by written memorandum showing, the terms of such contract, including the quantity of the cotton involved and the names and addresses of the seller and buyer in such contract, and shall be signed by the party to be charged, or by his agent in his behalf. If the contract or memorandum specify in bales the quantity of the cotton involved, without giving the weight, each bale shall, for the purposes of this Act, be deemed to weigh five hundred pounds.

SEC. 5. That no tax shall be levied under this Act on any contract of sale mentioned in section three hereof, if the contract comply with each of the following conditions:

First. Conform to the requirements of section four of, and the rules and regulations made pursuant to, this Act.

Second. Specify the basis grade for the cotton involved in the contract, which shall be one of the grades for which standards are established by the Secretary of Agriculture except grades prohibited from being delivered on a contract made under this section by the fifth subdivision of this section, the price per pound at which the cotton of such basis grade is contracted to be bought or sold, the date when the purchase or sale was made, and the month or months in which the contract is to be fulfilled or settled: *Provided*, That middling shall be deemed the basis grade incorporated into the contract if no other basis grade be specified either in the contract or in the memorandum evidencing the same.

Third. Provide that the cotton dealt with therein or delivered thereunder shall be of or within the grades for which standards are established by the Secretary of Agriculture except grades prohibited from being delivered on a contract made under this section by the fifth subdivision of this section and no other grade or grades.

Fourth. Provide that in case cotton of grade other than the basis grade be tendered or delivered in settlement of such contract, the differences above or below the contract price which the receiver shall pay for such grades other than the basis grade shall be the actual commercial differences, determined as hereinafter provided.

Fifth. Provide that cotton that, because of the presence of extraneous matter of any character or irregularities or defects, is reduced in value below that of Good Ordinary, or cotton that is below the grade of Good Ordinary, or, if tinged, cotton that is below the grade of Low Middling, or, if stained, cotton that is below the grade of Middling, the grades mentioned being of the official cotton standards of the United States, or cotton that is less than seven-eighths of an inch in length of staple, or cotton of perished staple or of immature staple, or cotton that is "gin cut" or reginned, or cotton that is "repacked" or "false packed" or "mixed packed" or "water packed," shall not be delivered on, under, or in settlement of such contract.

Sixth. Provide that all tenders of cotton under such contract shall be the full number of bales involved therein, except that such variations of the number of bales may be permitted as is necessary to bring the total weight of the cotton tendered within the provisions of the contract as to weight; that, on the fifth business day prior to delivery, the person making the tender shall give to the person receiving the same written notice of the date of delivery, and that, on or prior to the date so fixed for delivery, and in advance of final settlement of the contract, the person making the tender shall furnish to the person receiving the same a written notice or certificate stating the grade of each individual bale to be delivered and, by means of marks or numbers, identifying each bale with its grade.

Seventh. Provide that, in case a dispute arises between the person making the tender and the person receiving the same, as to the quality, or the grade, or the length of staple, of any cotton tendered under the contract, either party may refer the question to the Secretary of Agriculture for determination, and that such dispute shall be referred and determined, and the costs thereof, fixed, assessed, collected and paid, in such manner and in accordance with such rules and regulations as may be prescribed by the Secretary of Agriculture.

The provisions of the third, fourth, fifth, sixth, and seventh subdivisions of this section shall be deemed fully incorporated into any such contract if there be written or printed thereon, or on the memorandum evidencing the same, at or prior to the time the same is signed, the phrase, "Subject to United States cotton futures Act, section five."

The Secretary of Agriculture is authorized to prescribe rules and regulations for carrying out the purposes of the seventh subdivision of this section, and his findings, upon any dispute referred to him under said seventh subdivision, made after the parties in interest have had an opportunity to be heard by him or such officer, officers, agent, or agents of the Department of Agriculture as he may designate, shall be accepted in the courts of the United States in all suits between such parties, or their privies, as prima facie evidence of the true quality, or grade, or length of staple, of the cotton involved.

SEC. 6. That for the purposes of section five of this Act the differences above or below the contract price which the receiver shall pay for cotton of grades above or below the basis grade in the settlement of a contract of sale for the future delivery of cotton shall be determined by the actual commercial differences in value thereof upon the sixth business day prior to the day fixed, in accordance with the sixth subdivision of section five, for the delivery of cotton on the contract, established by the sale of spot cotton in the market where the future transaction involved occurs and is consummated if such market be a bona fide spot market; and in the event there be no bona fide spot market at or in the place in which such future transaction occurs, then, and in that case, the said differences above or below the contract price which the receiver shall pay for cotton above or below the basis grade shall be determined by the average actual commercial differences in value thereof, upon the sixth business day prior to the day fixed, in accordance with the sixth subdivision of section five, for the delivery of cotton on the contract, in the spot markets of not less than five places designated for the purpose from time to time by the Secretary of Agriculture, as such values were established by the sales of spot cotton, in such designated five or more markets: *Provided*, That for the purposes of this section such values in the said spot markets be based upon the standards for grades of cotton established by the Secretary of Agriculture: *And provided further,* That whenever the value of one grade is to be determined from the sale or sales of spot cotton of another grade or grades, such value shall be fixed in accordance with rules and regulations which shall be prescribed for the purpose by the Secretary of Agriculture.

SEC. 7. That for the purposes of this Act the only markets which shall be considered bona fide spot markets shall be those which the Secretary of Agriculture shall, from time to time, after investigation, determine and designate to be such, and of which he shall give public notice.

SEC. 8. That in determining, pursuant to the provisions of this Act, what markets are bona fide spot markets, the Secretary of Agriculture is directed to consider only markets in which spot cotton is sold in such volume and under such conditions as customarily to reflect accurately the value of middling cotton and the differences between the prices or values of middling cotton and of other grades of cotton for which standards shall have been established by the Secretary of Agriculture: *Provided*, That if there be not sufficient places, in the markets of which are made bona fide sales of spot cotton of grades for which standards are established by the Secretary of Agriculture, to enable him to designate at least five spot markets in accordance with section six of this Act, he shall, from data as to spot sales collected by him, make rules and regulations for determining the actual commercial differences in the value of spot cotton of the grades established by him as reflected by bona fide sales of spot cotton, of the same or different grades, in the markets selected and designated by him, from time to time, for that purpose, and in that event, differences in value of cotton of various grades involved in contracts made pursuant to section five of this Act shall be determined in compliance with such rules and regulations.

SEC. 9. That the Secretary of Agriculture is authorized, from time to time, to establish and promulgate standards of cotton by which its quality or value may be judged or determined, including its grade, length of staple, strength of staple, color, and such other qualities, properties, and conditions as may be standardized in practical form, which, for the purposes of this Act, shall be known as the "Official cotton standards of the United States," and to adopt, change, or replace the standard for any grade of cotton established under the Act making appropriations for the Department of Agriculture for the fiscal year ending June thirtieth, nineteen hundred and nine (Thirty-fifth Statutes at Large, page two hundred and fifty-one), and Acts supplementary thereto: *Provided,* That any standard of any cotton established and promulgated under this Act by the Secretary of Agriculture shall not be changed or replaced within a period less than one year from and after the date of the promulgation thereof by the Secretary of Agriculture: *Provided further*, That, subsequent to six months after the date section three of this Act becomes effective, no change or replacement of any standard of any cotton established and promulgated under this Act by the Secretary of Agriculture shall become effective until after one year's public notice thereof, which notice shall specify the date when the same is to become effective. The Secretary of Agriculture is authorized and directed to prepare practical forms of the official cotton standards which shall be established by him, and to furnish such practical forms from time to time, upon request, to any person, the cost thereof, as determined by the Secretary of Agriculture, to be paid by the person requesting the same, and to certify such practical forms under the seal of the Department of Agriculture and under the signature of the said Secretary, thereto affixed by himself or by some official or employee of the Department of Agriculture thereunto duly authorized by the said Secretary.

SEC. 10. That no tax shall be levied under this Act on any contract of sale mentioned in section three hereof, if the contract comply with each of the following conditions:

First. Conform to the rules and regulations made pursuant to this Act.

Second. Specify the grade, type, sample, or description of the cotton involved in the contract, the price per pound at which such cotton is contracted to be bought or sold, the date of the purchase or sale, and the time when shipment or delivery of such cotton is to be made.

Third. Provide that cotton of or within the grade or of the type, or according to the sample or description, specified in the contract shall be delivered thereunder, and that no cotton which does not conform to the type, sample, or description, or which is not of or within the grade, specified in the contract shall be tendered or delivered thereunder.

Fourth. Provide that the delivery of cotton under the contract shall not be effected by means of "set-off" or "ring" settlement, but only by the actual transfer of the specified cotton mentioned in the contract.

The provisions of the first, third, and fourth subdivisions of this section shall be deemed fully incorporated into any such contract if there be written or printed thereon, or on the document or memorandum evidencing the same, at or prior to the time the same is entered into, the words "Subject to United States cotton futures Act, section ten."

This Act shall not be construed to impose a tax on any sale of spot cotton.

This section shall not be construed to apply to any contract of sale made in compliance with section five of this Act.

SEC. 11. That upon each order transmitted, or directed or authorized to be transmitted, by any person within the United States for the making of any contract of sale of cotton grown in the United States for future delivery in cases in which the contract of sale is or is to be made at, on, or in any exchange, board of trade, or similar institution or place of business in any foreign country, there is hereby levied an excise tax at the rate of 2 cents for each pound of the cotton so ordered to be bought or sold under such contract: *Provided*, That no tax shall be levied under this Act on any such order if the contract made in pursuance thereof comply either with the conditions specified in the first, second, third, fourth, fifth, and sixth subdivisions of section five, or with all the conditions specified in section ten of this Act, except that the quantity of the cotton involved in the contract may be expressed therein in terms of kilograms instead of pounds.

SEC. 12. That the tax imposed by section three of this Act shall be paid by the seller of the cotton involved in the contract of sale, by means of stamps which shall be affixed to such contracts, or to the memoranda evidencing the same, and canceled in compliance with rules and regulations which shall be prescribed by the Secretary of the Treasury. The tax imposed by section eleven of this Act shall be paid by the sender of the order and collected in accordance with rules and regulations which shall be prescribed by the Secretary of the Treasury.

SEC. 13. That no contract of sale of cotton for future delivery mentioned in section three of this Act which does not conform to the requirements of section four hereof and has not the necessary stamps affixed thereto as required by section twelve hereof shall be enforceable in any court of the United States by, or on behalf of, any party to such contract or his privies. That no contract of sale of cotton for future delivery, made in pursuance of any order mentioned in section eleven of this Act, shall be enforceable in any court of the United States by or on behalf of any party to such contract or his privies unless it conforms to the requirements of section four hereof and the tax imposed by section eleven upon the order for such contract shall have been paid in compliance with section twelve of this Act.

SEC. 14. That the Secretary of the Treasury is authorized to make and promulgate such rules and regulations as he may deem necessary to collect the tax imposed by this Act and otherwise to enforce its provisions. Further to effect this purpose, he shall require all persons coming within its provisions to keep such records and statements of account as will fully and correctly disclose all transactions mentioned in sections three and eleven of this Act; and he may appoint agents to conduct the inspection necessary to collect said tax and otherwise to enforce this Act and all rules and regulations made by him in pursuance hereof, and may fix the compensation of such agents.

SEC. 15. That any person liable to the payment of any tax imposed by this Act who fails to pay, or evades or attempts to evade the payment of such tax, and any person who otherwise violates any provision of this Act, or any rule or regulation made in pursuance hereof, shall be deemed guilty of a misdemeanor, and, upon conviction thereof, shall be fined not less than $100 nor more than $20,000, in the discretion of the court; and, in case of natural persons, may, in addition, be punished by imprisonment for not less than sixty days nor more than three years, in the discretion of the court.

SEC. 16. That in addition to the foregoing punishment there is hereby imposed, on account of each violation of this Act, a penalty of $2,000, to be recovered in an action founded on this Act in the name of the United States as plaintiff, and when so recovered one-half of said amount shall be paid over to the person giving the information upon which such recovery was based. It shall be the duty of United States attorneys, to whom satisfactory evidence of violations of this Act is furnished, to institute and prosecute actions for the recovery of the penalties prescribed by this section.

SEC. 17. That no person whose evidence is deemed material by the officer prosecuting on behalf of the United States in any case brought under any provision of this Act shall withhold his testimony because of complicity by him in any violation of this Act or of any regulation made pursuant to this Act, but any such person called by such officer who testifies in such case shall be exempt from prosecution for any offense to which his testimony relates.

SEC. 18. That the payment of any tax levied by this Act shall not exempt any person from any penalty or punishment now or hereafter provided by the laws of any State for entering into contracts of sale of cotton for future delivery, nor shall the payment of any tax imposed by this Act be held to prohibit any State or municipality from imposing a tax on the same transaction.

SEC. 19. That there is hereby appropriated, out of any moneys in the Treasury not otherwise appropriated, for the fiscal year ending June thirtieth, nineteen hundred and fifteen, the sum of $50,000 or so much thereof as may be necessary to enable the Secretary of the Treasury to carry out the provisions of this Act.

SEC. 20. That there is hereby appropriated, out of any moneys in the Treasury not otherwise appropriated, available until expended, the sum of $150,000 or so much thereof as may be necessary to enable the Secretary of Agriculture to make such investigations, to collect such data, and to use such methods and means as he may deem necessary to determine and designate what are bona fide spot markets within the meaning of this Act, to prescribe rules and regulations pursuant to sections five, six, and eight hereof, to establish and promulgate standards for cotton and to furnish practical forms thereof as authorized by section nine hereof, to publish the results of his investigations, to pay rent and to employ such persons as he may deem necessary, in the city of Washington and elsewhere. The Secretary of Agriculture is hereby directed to publish from time to time the results of investigations made in pursuance of this Act. All sums collected by the Secretary of Agriculture as costs under section five, or for furnishing practical forms under section nine of this Act, shall be deposited and covered into the Treasury as miscellaneous receipts.

Sec. 21. That sections nine, nineteen, and twenty of this Act and all provisions of this Act authorizing rules and regulations to be prescribed shall be effective immediately. All other sections of this Act shall become and be effective on and after six months from the date of the passage of this Act: *Provided*, That nothing in this Act shall be construed to apply to any contract of sale of any cotton for future delivery mentioned in section three of this Act which shall have been made prior to the date when section three becomes effective.

Approved, August 18, 1914.